Chapter Title	Chapter Focus Company	Company Logo	Type of Company	Contrast Companies	Key Ratios
8 Reporting and Interpreting Receivables, Bad Debt Expense, and Interest Revenue	**Skechers Shoes**		Shoe company	Crocs Boeing Rocky Mountain Chocolate Factory, Inc. Reitmans (Canada) Limited	Receivables Turnover Ratio
9 Reporting and Interpreting Long-Lived Tangible and Intangible Assets	**Cedar Fair**	Cedar fair. L.P.	Entertainment company	Hasbro Inc. FedEx Corporation Apple Inc.	Fixed Asset Turnover Ratio
10 Reporting and Interpreting Liabilities	**General Mills**	GENERAL MILLS	Food company	Hudson's Bay Company Kraft Foods, Inc. Readers' Digest Inc.	Quick Ratio, Times Interest Earned Ratios
11 Reporting and Interpreting Shareholders' Equity	**Sun-Rype Products Ltd.**	SUN-RYPE	Food and beverage manufacturer	Winnebago Dell Corporation	Earnings per Share (EPS), Return on Equity (ROE), Price/Earnings (P/E) Ratios
12 Reporting and Interpreting the Statement of Cash Flows	**Under Armour**		Sports clothing and accessories company	Brunswick Corporation Cybex International Walt Disney Company	Quality of Income, Capital Acquisitions Ratios
13 Measuring and Evaluating Financial Performance	**The Home Depot Inc.**	THE HOME DEPOT	Retailer of home improvement, construction products and services	Rona Inc. SportChek Mattel Inc.	Comprehensive Summary (Exhibit 13.5)

fundamentals of
Financial
Accounting

third Canadian edition

FRED PHILLIPS
University of Saskatchewan

ROBERT LIBBY
Cornell University

PATRICIA A. LIBBY
Ithaca College

BRANDY MACKINTOSH
University of Saskatchewan

McGraw-Hill Ryerson
Connect. Learn. Succeed.

McGraw-Hill Ryerson
Connect. Learn. Succeed.

FUNDAMENTALS OF FINANCIAL ACCOUNTING
Third Canadian Edition

The Internet addresses listed in the text were accurate at the time of publication. The inclusion of a website does not indicate an endorsement by the authors or McGraw-Hill Ryerson, and McGraw-Hill Ryerson does not guarantee the accuracy of information presented at these sites.

ISBN-13: 978-0-07-040195-2
ISBN-10: 0-07-040195-0

4 5 6 7 8 9 CTPS 1 9 8 7 6 5 4

Printed and bound in China

Care has been taken to trace ownership of copyright material contained in this text; however, the publisher will welcome any information that enables it to rectify any reference or credit for subsequent editions.

Executive Editor: *Rhondda McNabb*
Executive Marketing Manager: *Joy Armitage-Taylor*
Developmental Editor: *My Editor, Inc.*
Supervising Editor: *Cathy Biribauer*
Senior Editorial Associate: *Christine Lomas*
Photo/Permissions Researcher: *Indu Arora*
Copy Editor: *June Trusty*
Production Coordinator: *Emily Hickey*
Cover and Inside Design: *David Montle/Pixel Hive Studio*
Composition: *Laserwords Private Limited*
Cover Photo: *Whistle: Feng Yu/Shutterstock; Tablet: Created by Chandra Ganegoda*
Printer: *CTPS*

Library and Archives Canada Cataloguing in Publication Data
    Fundamentals of financial accounting / Fred Phillips . . . [et al.].
    3rd Canadian ed.
    Includes index.
    ISBN 978-0-07-040195-2
    1. Accounting—Textbooks. 2. Accounting—Canada. I. Phillips, Fred, 1964-
HF5636.F85 2012   657   C2011-905788-3

Dedication

I dedicate this book to the best teachers I've ever had:
my Mom and Dad, Barb, Harrison, and Daniel

FRED PHILLIPS

Jenni, John, and Emma Rose Drago, Herman and Doris Hargenrater,
Laura Libby, Oscar and Selma Libby

PATRICIA AND ROBERT LIBBY

I dedicate this book to my two daughters,
who teach me something new every day

BRANDY MACKINTOSH

Meet the Authors

Fred Phillips

Fred Phillips is a professor of accounting and the Baxter Scholar at the Edwards School of Business at the University of Saskatchewan, where he has taught courses in financial accounting and assurance. He holds a Ph.D. from the University of Texas at Austin, a bachelor's degree in accounting from the University of Manitoba, and the chartered accountancy designation from the Institute of Chartered Accountants of Saskatchewan.

Fred has published four textbooks and more than 30 articles and cases in peer-reviewed journals, including *Issues in Accounting Education*, *Journal of Accounting Research*, and *Organizational Behavior and Human Decision Processes*. He is an active member of the editorial boards of *Contemporary Accounting Research* and *Accounting Perspectives*. Fred has received many awards for his writing, research, and teaching, including the Canadian Academic Accounting Association Case Writing Award (four times), the American Accounting Association Award for Outstanding Research in Accounting Education (twice), the Edwards School of Business Most Effective Professor award (three times), the University of Saskatchewan Students' Union Teaching Excellence Award (twice), the University of Saskatchewan's Master Teacher Award, the University of Saskatchewan Provost's Award for Outstanding Innovation in Learning, and the 3M National Teaching Fellowship (the highest award for undergraduate teaching in Canada).

Robert Libby

Robert Libby is the David A. Thomas Professor of Accounting at Cornell University, where he teaches the introductory financial accounting course. He previously taught at the University of Illinois, Pennsylvania State University, the University of Texas at Austin, the University of Chicago, and the University of Michigan. He received his B.S. from Pennsylvania State University and his M.A.S. and Ph.D. from the University of Illinois; he also is a CPA.

Bob is a widely published author specializing in behavioural accounting. He was selected as the AAA Outstanding Educator in 2000 and received the AAA Outstanding Service Award in 2006. His prior text, *Accounting and Human Information Processing* (Prentice Hall, 1981), was awarded the AICPA/AAA Notable Contributions to the Accounting Literature Award. He received this award again in 1996 for a paper. He has published numerous articles in *The Accounting Review*; *Journal of Accounting Research*; *Accounting, Organizations and Society*; and other accounting journals. He has held a variety of offices in the American Accounting Association and is a member of the American Institute of CPAs and the editorial boards of *The Accounting Review*; *Accounting, Organizations and Society*; *Journal of Accounting Literature*; and *Journal of Behavioral Decision Making*.

Patricia A. Libby

Patricia Libby is associate professor of accounting and coordinator of the financial accounting course at Ithaca College, as well as faculty adviser to Beta Alpha Psi, Ithaca College Accounting Association, and Ithaca College National Association of Black Accountants. She previously taught graduate and undergraduate financial accounting at Eastern Michigan University and the University of Texas at Austin. Before entering academe, she was an auditor with Price Waterhouse (now PricewaterhouseCoopers) and a financial administrator at the University of Chicago. She received her B.S. from Pennsylvania State University, her M.B.A. from DePaul University, and her Ph.D. from the University of Michigan; she also is a CPA.

Pat conducts research on using cases in the introductory course and other parts of the accounting curriculum. She has published articles in *The Accounting Review, Issues in Accounting Education,* and *The Michigan CPA.* She has also conducted seminars nationwide on active learning strategies, including cooperative learning methods.

Brandy Mackintosh

Brandy Mackintosh is an assistant professor at the Edwards School of Business at the University of Saskatchewan, where she teaches introductory and intermediate financial accounting. She has also taught advanced financial accounting, external auditing, and advanced financial reporting at the graduate level. Brandy is a past recipient of the University of Saskatchewan's Teaching Excellence Award and a finalist for the Edwards School of Business Most Effective Professor Award. Her scholarly interests relate to accounting education and case writing. She won the 2011 Canadian Academic Accounting Association case-writing competition (with Fred Phillips) and has published this work in *Issues in Accounting Education.*

Prior to joining the University of Saskatchewan, Brandy worked as an audit manager at Deloitte. She has an undergraduate accounting degree from the University of Saskatchewan and is a CA.

BRIEF CONTENTS

CONTENTS

CHAPTER 7

Reporting and Interpreting Inventories and Cost of Goods Sold 285

AMERICAN EAGLE OUTFITTERS, INC. 285

CHAPTER 8

Reporting and Interpreting Receivables, Bad Debt Expense, and Interest Revenue 328

SKECHERS 328

CHAPTER 9

Reporting and Interpreting Long-Lived Tangible and Intangible Assets 367

CEDAR FAIR 367

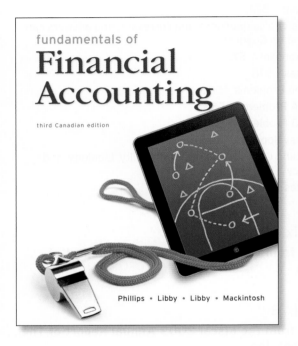

FUNDAMENTALS OF FINANCIAL ACCOUNTING, THIRD CANADIAN EDITION

Phillips, Libby, Libby, and Mackintosh's *Fundamentals of Financial Accounting*, third Canadian edition, arms students with a secret weapon for success in financial accounting—the best personal coach on the market. The cover of this text contains the quintessential representation of a coach—a whistle. Simple, maybe, but this whistle captures the essence of this text as your coach. The following are highlights of Phillips' innovative student-centred approach:

WRITING THAT STUDENTS CAN READ. What does it mean to say that a book is "readable"? In the case of *Fundamentals of Financial Accounting*, third Canadian edition, it simply means that it's the most enjoyable accounting textbook your students have ever read. Through a mix of conversational wording, humour, and everyday examples, *Fundamentals of Financial Accounting* achieves a style that maintains rigour without sacrificing student engagement. Open this textbook to any page and read for yourself; *Fundamentals of Financial Accounting* offers **the most engaging read** of any financial text.

STUDENT-FRIENDLY COVERAGE OF DIFFICULT TOPICS. Written with students in mind, *Fundamentals of Financial Accounting* handles difficult concepts in a way that reflects the balance of preparer and user concepts and keeps students from being overwhelmed.

- **The accounting process** is covered in three chapters (2, 3, and 4) rather than two.
- The purpose of a **statement of cash flows** is introduced at the beginning of the text, but the mechanics of preparing one are studied at the end.
- **Financial statement analysis** is covered in two chapters (5 and 13) rather than one.
- **Ratios** are introduced throughout the chapters and then pulled together at the end.
- **Individual concepts** are introduced throughout the text as needed to explain specific accounting practices, and then pulled together at the end.

. . . in Financial Accounting

CURRENT. Phillips reflects current accounting standards in Canada. Covering both International Financial Reporting Standards (IFRS) and Accounting Standards for Private Enterprise (ASPE), Phillips discusses key differences between IFRS and ASPE in a boxed feature at the end of each chapter.

BALANCED. Phillips delivers a balanced approach. Throughout, understanding the preparation of financial statements is balanced with the importance of using the financial statements to guide decision making.

EXTENSIVE END-OF-CHAPTER EXERCISES AND PROBLEMS. Students build confidence and success with a wealth of end-of-chapter discussion questions, exercises, coached and comprehensive problems, and skills development cases.

INNOVATIVE TECHNOLOGY. New to the third Canadian edition, every copy of Phillips includes access to Connect—McGraw-Hill's innovative online study and testing program. In addition to an easy-to-use eBook and study resources, Connect also includes algorithmic problems within the homework assessment tool that are directly from the end-of-chapter material. This fully integrated tool helps students master the concepts, practise solving problems, and ultimately achieve success in financial accounting.

Stay Focused . . .

The best way to learn to prepare and use financial statements is to study accounting in real business contexts.

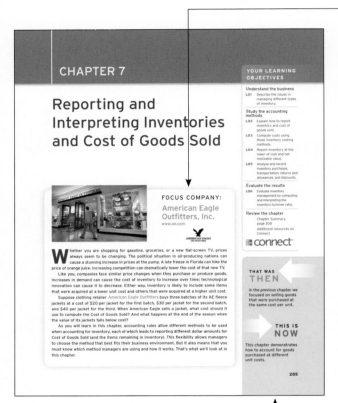

FOCUS COMPANY APPROACH. The **focus company** approach integrates each chapter's material around a real-world company, its decisions, its financial statements.

In choosing focus companies to use in *Fundamentals of Financial Accounting* third Canadian edition, we took care that our companies' products and services are used by students and will appeal to their curiosity. We further heighten student engagement by injecting our discussions with issues and questions that actually matter in the real world. *What decisions does Activision Blizzard make that keeps it running as the interactive entertainment software industry's leading publisher? How did Walmart go from yearly sales of $1 billion to making the same amount within a week 14 years later?* These are but a couple of the companies and issues discussed over the course of this book.

Students often feel that they lack the real-world experience needed to understand accounting, a subject they believe has little impact on their daily lives. *Fundamentals of Financial Accounting*'s chapter openers provide real-world situations and examples that illustrate how accounting principles are part of day-to-day activities that students might not have thought about from an accounting perspective—such as what's involved when Cedar Fair purchases a new roller coaster or how American Eagle manages its inventory. There's no better way to help students feel comfortable with accounting topics and to trigger an interest that invites them into the chapter.

THAT WAS THEN/THIS IS NOW. To provide connectivity in students' minds, each chapter opens by briefly putting into perspective the information learned in the previous chapter and what will be learned in the present chapter.

YOU SHOULD KNOW. All key terms are defined in You Should Know boxes in the margin beside the text in which the terms are first introduced, reinforcing student understanding and recapping important text points.

YOU SHOULD KNOW

Conservatism: Using the least optimistic measures when uncertainty exists about the value of an asset or liability.

...on the Real World

SPOTLIGHT FEATURES

SPOTLIGHT ON Financial Reporting

Surviving a Financial Crunch

In difficult economic times, it is imperative for companies to have adequate financing in place. Prior to the economic downturn in 2008, General Mills had established a line of credit that provides up to $3 billion cash on an as-needed basis. Rather than hold extra cash, General Mills uses its line of credit to borrow only when money is needed. Not all companies are able to establish lines of credit, but those that do are able to survive with a quick ratio less than 1.0. To determine whether a company has a line of credit available, be sure to read the company's notes to the financial statements. General Mills reports its line of credit in its long-term debt note.

Spotlight on Financial Reporting These features connect chapter topics with real-world disclosures provided in the financial statements of our focus companies and other contrasting companies.

Spotlight on IFRS and ASPE Specific discussions on International Financial Reporting Standards (IFRS) and how they differ from Accounting Standards for Private Enterprises (ASPE) are grouped together in the Spotlight on IFRS and ASPE box at the end of each chapter.

SPOTLIGHT ON IFRS and ASPE

What Is a Strong Balance Sheet?

During the fall of 2008, companies experienced a crisis unlike anything since the Great Depression of the 1930s. Financial institutions, such as Lehman Brothers, had collapsed or were on the verge of collapse. Consequently, banks became ultra-conservative and stopped lending to one another, which severely limited the amount of cash available to lend to businesses. The best way for a company to survive this credit crisis was to have a strong balance sheet, which meant having lots of cash and other current assets relative to the amount of liabilities owed.

SPOTLIGHT ON Ethics

What Is a Strong Balance Sheet?

During the fall of 2008, companies experienced a crisis unlike anything since the Great Depression of the 1930s. Financial institutions, such as Lehman Brothers, had collapsed or were on the verge of collapse. Consequently, banks became ultra-conservative and stopped lending to one another, which severely limited the amount of cash available to lend to businesses. The best way for a company to survive this credit crisis was to have a strong balance sheet, which meant having lots of cash and other current assets relative to the amount of liabilities owed.

Spotlight on Ethics The text ensures that students start off with a solid grounding in ethics. Shining the spotlight on ethical issues in each chapter prompts the student to think about tough ethical decisions and to practise making these decisions in the end-of-chapter cases.

Spotlight on the World Students are kept apprised of the ongoing changes in the accounting profession around the world through these features.

SPOTLIGHT ON THE WORLD

Violated Loan Covenants

Most lending agreements allow the lender to revise loan terms (e.g., interest rates, due dates) if a borrower's financial condition deteriorates significantly. These escape hatches, called **loan covenants**, are often based on financial statement ratios such as those you have learned about in earlier chapters. Under ASPE, if a company violates loan covenants on long-term debt but renegotiates the loan prior to releasing its financial statements, the debt remains classified as long term. Under IFRS, the company must reclassify that long-term debt as a current liability.

SPOTLIGHT ON Business Decisions

Dividend Cuts in Difficult Times

Under pressure to save cash during the global economic crisis, many big-name companies reversed or cut their policy to pay cash dividends in 2009. Although dividends are discretionary, companies are reluctant to cut them because doing so suggests the company is facing significant financial challenges. Huge percentage declines in 2009 dividends, as compared to prior years, were announced by

General Electric	67%	CBS Corp.	81%
Motorola, Inc.	75%	Black & Decker	71%

Spotlight on Business Decisions Found throughout the text, these features help students to develop strong decision-making skills by illustrating the relevance of accounting in real-world decision making and the lessons learned from global economic crises.

SPOTLIGHT ON Controls

Segregating Collections and Write-Offs

One way to control accounts receivable is to ensure that the same person does not both receive collections from customers and write off account balances. This segregation of duties helps to prevent errors and fraud. Without adequate segregation between these duties, a single dishonest employee could divert customer payments to his or her own bank account and then cover up the theft by writing off the customer's balance.

Spotlight on Controls These features highlight applications of internal control principles in the workplace.

A Book with Its Own . . .

Fundamentals of Financial Accounting, third Canadian edition, is loaded with so many innovative pedagogical features that you'll think we sent a teaching assistant along with the book. From quick review to head-scratching ethical dilemmas, this text's pedagogy gives students every opportunity to reinforce and expand on what they're learning.

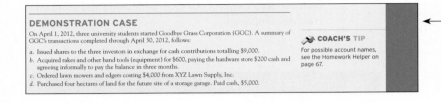

DEMONSTRATION CASE

On April 1, 2012, three university students started Goodbye Grass Corporation (GGC). A summary of GGC's transactions completed through April 30, 2012, follows:

a. Issued shares to the three investors in exchange for cash contributions totalling $9,000.
b. Acquired rakes and other hand tools (equipment) for $600, paying the hardware store $200 cash and agreeing informally to pay the balance in three months.
c. Ordered lawn mowers and edgers costing $4,000 from XYZ Lawn Supply, Inc.
d. Purchased four hectares of land for the future site of a storage garage. Paid cash, $5,000.

🏃 **COACH'S TIP**

For possible account names, see the Homework Helper on page 67.

COACH'S TIP. Virtually every student has been inspired by a great coach at some time or another. Throughout the chapters, Coach's Tips provide students with advice and guidance on learning the material. Coach's Tips appear again in the problem material to offer encouragement as students work to reinforce what they've learned.

COACHED PROBLEMS. Every chapter includes three problem sets: Coached Problems, Group A Problems, and Group B Problems. The Coached Problems go beyond the traditional check figures to advise students on the process of solving a problem rather than just its outcome.

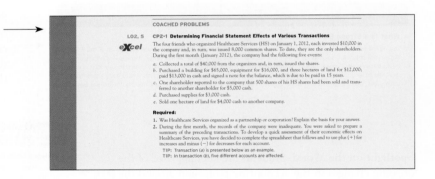

COACHED PROBLEMS

LO2, 5 **CP2-1 Determining Financial Statement Effects of Various Transactions**

e**X**cel The four friends who organized Healthcare Services (HS) on January 1, 2012, each invested $10,000 in the company and, in turn, was issued 8,000 common shares. To date, they are the only shareholders. During the first month (January 2012), the company had the following five events:

a. Collected a total of $40,000 from the organizers and, in turn, issued the shares.
b. Purchased a building for $65,000, equipment for $16,000, and three hectares of land for $12,000; paid $13,000 in cash and signed a note for the balance, which is due to be paid in 15 years.
c. One shareholder reported to the company that 500 shares of his HS shares had been sold and transferred to another shareholder for $5,000 cash.
d. Purchased supplies for $3,000 cash.
e. Sold one hectare of land for $4,000 cash to another company.

Required:

1. Was Healthcare Services organized as a partnership or corporation? Explain the basis for your answer.
2. During the first month, the records of the company were inadequate. You were asked to prepare a summary of the preceding transactions. To develop a quick assessment of their economic effects on Healthcare Services, you have decided to complete the spreadsheet that follows and to use plus (+) for increases and minus (−) for decreases for each account.

   TIP: Transaction (a) is presented below as an example.
   TIP: In transaction (b), five different accounts are affected.

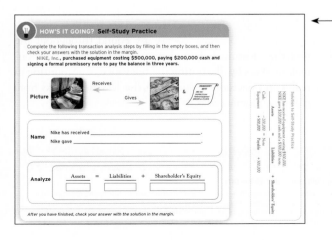

HOW'S IT GOING? Self-Study Practice

Complete the following transaction analysis steps by filling in the empty boxes, and then check your answers with the solution in the margin.

NIKE, Inc., purchased equipment costing $500,000, paying $200,000 cash and signing a formal promissory note to pay the balance in three years.

Picture Receives / Gives

Name Nike has received _____
Nike gave _____

Analyze Assets = Liabilities + Shareholder's Equity

After you have finished, check your answer with the solution in the margin.

HOW'S IT GOING? Nothing helps like a quiz for mastering tricky subjects, so *Fundamentals of Financial Accounting* provides plenty of these innovative review boxes throughout each chapter. "How's It Going" features pose a review question about the recent material and provide the answer right there on the page, printed sideways so that students don't accidentally read it before answering the question.

. . . Teaching Assistant Included

THE USER FRAMEWORK. The USER Framework provides a "road map" to each chapter, delineating how accounting functions work at all levels of the firm. Students learn to

Understand the business decisions that managers make,
Study the accounting methods used,
Evaluate the reported results from the viewpoint of financial statement users, and
Reconsider how the accounting methods affect the managers' decisions.

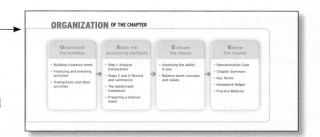

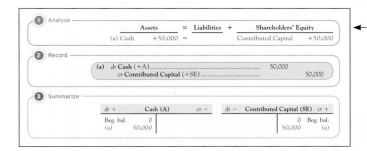

ANALYZE, RECORD, SUMMARIZE. A systematic accounting process is used to capture and report the financial effects of a company's activities. This process includes three basic steps:

Step 1: Analyze Transactions
Transaction analysis involves determining whether a transaction exists and, if it does, analyzing its impact on the accounting equation.

Steps 2 and 3: Record and Summarize
One way to record and summarize the financial effects of transactions would be to enter your understanding of their effects into a spreadsheet. By summing each spreadsheet column, you could compute new balances at the end of each month and report them on a balance sheet.

These helpful steps appear throughout various chapters to support learning.

Review and Practice Materials . . .

REVIEW OF THE CHAPTER

To effectively evaluate and guide student success with the appropriate feedback, you need homework and test materials that are easy to use and tied to the chapter discussions.

Each chapter of *Fundamentals of Financial Accounting* is followed by an extensive variety of end-of-chapter material that applies and integrates topics presented in the chapter. We have retained many of the popular items from prior editions and added new types of end-of-chapter materials, including a Homework Helper, multi-perspective discussion questions, comprehensive problems, and a continuing case.

DEMONSTRATION CASE. Each chapter provides demonstration cases of activities in real-life situations. These exercises have students analyzing, preparing, and summarizing actual information.

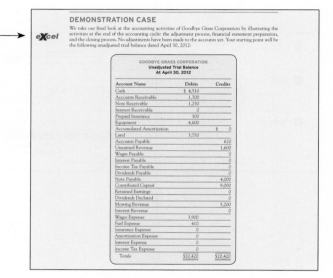

CHAPTER SUMMARY. Each chapter concludes with an end-of-chapter summary, organized by chapter learning objectives, that revisits the learning objectives from the beginning of the chapter.

KEY TERMS. The Key Terms list includes key terms and page references. Full definitions of all key terms are found in the Glossary near the back of the text.

HOMEWORK HELPER. The Homework Helper immediately precedes each chapter's homework materials, highlighting subtleties discussed in the chapter and providing practice advice so that students can avoid common pitfalls when completing homework.

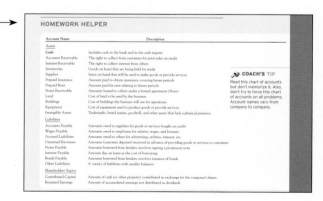

. . . Build Confidence and Success

PRACTICE MATERIAL

QUESTIONS. Each chapter includes 10 to 20 multi-perspective discussion questions that ask students to explain and discuss terms and concepts presented in the chapter. Selected questions, denoted with an icon, are designed to help students begin developing critical thinking skills. These questions are ideal for sparking debate at the beginning of class or when transitioning between or reviewing topics.

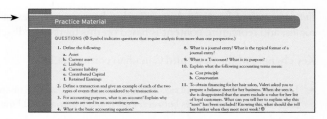

MINI-EXERCISES. These assignments illustrate and apply a single learning objective from the chapter.

EXERCISES. These additional assignments illustrate and apply single and multiple learning objectives from the chapter.

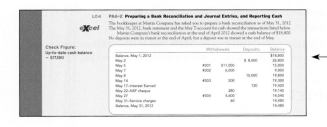

PROBLEMS (COACHED, GROUP A, AND GROUP B). Each chapter includes three problem sets to help students develop decision-making skills. Coached problems include question-specific tips to assist students who need a little help getting started. Groups A and B are similar problems, but without the coaching. Excel templates are tied to selected end-of-chapter assignments designated with this icon.

COMPREHENSIVE PROBLEMS. Selected chapters include prob-lems that cover topics from earlier chapters to refresh, reinforce, and build an integrative understanding of the course material. These are a great resource for helping students stay up to date throughout the course.

SKILLS DEVELOPMENT CASES. Each chapter offers cases designed to help students develop analytical, critical thinking and technological skills. These cases are ideal for individual assignments, class discussions, and group projects.

CONTINUING CASE. In Chapter 1, students are introduced to Nicole's Getaway Spa (NGS). In each chapter, the Continuing Case feature extends this case and requires students to apply topics from the current chapter.

What's New in the Third Edition?

Fundamentals of Financial Accounting has been reviewed extensively in the market. The authors' efforts to clarify discussions, present new topics, and reorganize content is based on this market feedback.

Key changes in the new third Canadian edition include

- Updates to reflect current accounting standards in Canada, giving prominence to the Accounting Standards for Private Enterprise (ASPE) but also discussing key differences between ASPE and International Financial Reporting Standards (IFRS) in a boxed feature at the end of each chapter.
- New focus companies for all chapters, and their financial statements have been updated to the most recent annual reports available, typically with year-ends of December 2009 or later.
- A new approach to transaction analysis: Analyze (Picture, Name, Analyze), Record, and Summarize.
- Updated and refreshed end-of-chapter material.
- Check figures for some Exercises and some Group A and Group B Problems; allows students to see if they are on the right track before they get too far along in answering the question.
- New Canadian text author, Brandy Mackintosh, brings both teaching excellence and industry experience to the third Canadian edition. Brandy is an assistant professor at the University of Saskatchewan, where she has taught introductory, intermediate, and advanced financial accounting and auditing courses.

DETAILED CHANGES BY CHAPTER:

CHAPTER 1
- New focus company story.
- More discussion of organization forms and business decision makers has been provided.

CHAPTER 2
- New focus company story continued.
- Summary of accounting cycle and the introduction of the current ratio have been updated.

CHAPTER 3
- New focus company story continued.
- Misconceptions about the income statement are discussed.
- New visuals have been provided to demonstrate operating cycle transactions.

CHAPTER 4
- New focus company story continued.
- New visuals have been provided to illustrate the analyses required in making adjustments.

CHAPTER 5
- New focus company story.
- The discussion of law-making and standard-setting in Canada and how the financial reporting environment has changed in Canada has been revised.

- More material has been provided on comparative balance sheets and multiple-step income statements.
- A new section explaining how transactions affect ratios has been provided.
- In addition to comparisons of ASPE and IFRS, explanations of the reasons for, and the effects of, using IFRS have been added.

CHAPTER 6
- New focus company story.
- A new section on analyzing a merchandiser's multi-step income statement has been added.
- The discussion about the different types of operations (service, merchandising, and manufacturing) has been expanded.
- Discussion of the application of internal control principles to cash receipts and payments has been extended.

CHAPTER 7
- Chapters 7 and 8 have been switched in the text, as it was felt that the flow of information was better presented this way. Chapter 7 now deals with inventories and cost of goods sold, while Chapter 8 covers receivables.
- New focus company story.
- A discussion of balance sheet and income statement reporting of inventory has been added.
- Explanation of changed lower of cost and market (LCM) rule to lower of cost and net realizable value (LC&NRV) rule has been provided.

- The fact that LIFO is no longer an acceptable method of inventory costing is discussed. All LIFO information has been moved from the main body of the chapter to a supplement at the end of the chapter. LIFO questions are no longer included in the end-of-chapter material.
- Examples have been added to compare perpetual vs. periodic inventory systems.

CHAPTER 8
As mentioned before, Chapters 7 and 8 have been switched and Chapter 8 now covers receivables.
- New focus company story.
- New visuals have been provided to help illustrate the recording and reporting of estimated bad debts.
- Updated visuals help to illustrate the calculation of interest earned on a note receivable.

CHAPTER 9
- New focus company story.
- A discussion of the changes in amortization estimates has been added.
- Partial year amortization is now integrated into the chapter.

CHAPTER 10
- New focus company story.
- New visuals and discussion of payroll have been provided.
- Bond amortization is demonstrated with the assistance of new visuals.

- A new section on the quick ratio has been added.
- Updated visuals assist in the calculation of interest on a note payable.

CHAPTER 11
- New focus company story.
- A new Spotlight on Business Decisions feature provides information on choosing between stock dividends and stock splits.
- A discussion of the price/earnings ratio and analysis of what this ratio means has been added.
- Since treasury shares are rarely used in Canada, all treasury share instruction, examples, and exhibits have been removed from the textbook and made available on Connect.

CHAPTER 12
- New focus company story.
- New illustrations contrast indirect and direct methods of preparing a cash flow statement.
- A discussion of the treatment of gains and losses when preparing a cash flow statement under the indirect method has been provided.

CHAPTER 13
- New focus company story.
- New visuals on horizontal and vertical analyses have been added.
- Expanded discussion of the going-concern assumption and the full disclosure principle has been provided.

Digital Learning Solutions

CONNECT

McGraw-Hill Connect™ is a Web-based assignment and assessment platform that gives students the means to better connect with their coursework, with their instructors, and with the important concepts that they will need to know for success now and in the future.

With Connect, instructors can deliver assignments, quizzes, and tests online. Nearly all the questions from the text are presented in an auto-gradable format and tied to the text's learning objectives. Instructors can edit existing questions and author entirely new problems, track individual student performance—by question, assignment, or in relation to the class overall—with detailed grade reports, and integrate grade reports easily with Learning Management Systems (LMS) such as WebCT and Blackboard. And much more.

By choosing Connect, instructors are providing their students with a powerful tool for improving academic performance and truly mastering course material. Connect allows students to practise important skills at their own pace and on their own schedule. Importantly, students' assessment results and instructors' feedback are all saved online—so students can continually review their progress and plot their course to success.

Connect also provides 24/7 online access to an eBook—an online edition of the text—to aid them in successfully completing their work, wherever and whenever they choose.

KEY FEATURES

SIMPLE ASSIGNMENT MANAGEMENT. With Connect, creating assignments is easier than ever, so you can spend more time teaching and less time managing.

- Create and deliver assignments easily with selectable end-of-chapter questions and test bank material to assign online
- Streamline lesson planning, student progress reporting, and assignment grading to make classroom management more efficient than ever
- Go paperless with the eBook and online submission and grading of student assignments

SMART GRADING. When it comes to studying, time is precious. Connect helps students learn more efficiently by providing feedback and practice material when they need it, where they need it.

- Automatically score assignments, giving students immediate feedback on their work and side-by-side comparisons with correct answers
- Access and review each response; manually change grades or leave comments for students to review
- Reinforce classroom concepts with practice tests and instant quizzes

INSTRUCTOR LIBRARY. The Connect Instructor Library is your course creation hub. It provides all the critical resources you'll need to build your course, just how you want to teach it.

- Assign eBook readings and draw from a rich collection of textbook-specific assignments
- Access instructor resources, including ready-made PowerPoint presentations and media to use in your lectures
- View assignments and resources created for past sections
- Post your own resources for students to use

eBOOK. Connect reinvents the textbook learning experience for the modern student. Every Connect subject area is seamlessly integrated with Connect eBooks, which are designed to keep students focused on the concepts key to their success.

- Provide students with a Connect eBook, allowing for anytime, anywhere access to the textbook
- Merge media, animation, and assessments with the text's narrative to engage students and improve learning and retention
- Pinpoint and connect key concepts in a snap using the powerful eBook search engine
- Manage notes, highlights, and bookmarks in one place for simple, comprehensive review

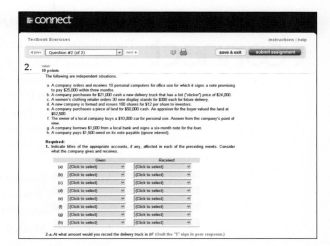

INSTRUCTOR SUPPORT

The following resources are available on Connect to support instructors:

- **Solutions Manual:** Prepared by Brandy Mackintosh, University of Saskatchewan, and technically checked by Susan Cohlmeyer, Memorial University of Newfoundland, the Solutions Manual provides solutions for all end-of-chapter material.

- **Computerized Test Bank:** The computerized test bank includes thousands of true/false, multiple-choice, and short-answer questions; producing quizzes and tests is as easy as clicking the mouse. All questions have been revised by Bashir Ahmed, University of Guelph-Humber, to reflect this new edition.

- **Microsoft® PowerPoint® Presentations:** These presentations are a great visual complement to your lectures. Revised by Meredith Delaney, Seneca College, a complete set of slides covers the key concepts presented in each chapter.

- **Instructor's Manual:** This robust supplement is a definite asset to your own course. Revised by Seth Brouwers, University of Waterloo, it follows the text but provides additional teaching tips as well as further information about the subject.

- **Solutions to Excel Template Assignments:** Some problems include spreadsheet templates, revised by Ian Feltmate, Acadia University, for students to work with. The solutions for all of these are included in on Connect.

- **Image Library:** Instructors will find images from the text to personalize their lecture slides.

OTHER SERVICES AND SUPPORT

Service takes on a whole new meaning with McGraw-Hill Ryerson and *Fundamentals of Financial Accounting,* third Canadian edition. More than just bringing you a textbook, we have raised the bar for innovation and educational research. These investments in learning and the academic community have helped us understand the needs of students and educators across the country, and allowed us to foster the growth of integrated learning.

Course Management

McGraw-Hill Ryerson offers a range of flexible integration solutions for Blackboard, WebCT, Desire-2Learn, Moodle and other leading learning management platforms. Please contact your local McGraw-Hill Ryerson *i*Learning Sales Specialist for details.

Tegrity

Tegrity is a service that makes class time available all the time by automatically capturing every lecture in a searchable format for students to review when they study and complete assignments. With a simple one-click start-and-stop process, you capture all computer screens and corresponding audio. Students replay any part of any class with easy-to-use browser-based viewing on a PC or Mac. Educators know that the more students can see, hear, and experience class resources, the better they learn. With Tegrity, students quickly recall key moments by using Tegrity's unique search feature. This search helps students efficiently find what they need, when they need it across an entire semester of class recordings. Help turn all your students' study time into learning moments immediately supported by your lecture. To learn more about Tegrity watch a two-minute Flash demo at http://tegritycampus.mhhe.com.

CourseSmart

CourseSmart brings together thousands of textbooks across hundreds of courses in an eTextbook format, providing unique benefits to students and faculty. By purchasing an eTextbook, students can save up to 50 percent of the cost of a print textbook, reduce their impact on the environment, and gain access to powerful Web tools for learning, including full-text search, notes and highlighting, and e-mail tools for sharing notes between classmates. For faculty, CourseSmart provides instant access for reviewing and comparing textbooks and course materials in their discipline area without the time, cost, and environmental impact of mailing print examination copies. For further details, contact your *i*Learning Sales Specialist or go to www.coursesmart.com.

Create

McGraw-Hill's Create Online gives you access to the most abundant resource at your fingertips—literally. With a few mouse clicks, you can create customized learning tools simply and affordably. McGraw-Hill Ryerson has included many of our market-leading textbooks within Create Online for eBook and print customization as well as many licensed readings and cases. For more information, go to www.mcgrawhillcreate.com.

*i*Learning Services

At McGraw-Hill Ryerson, we take great pride in developing high-quality learning resources while working hard to provide you with the tools necessary to utilize them. We want to bring your teaching to life, and we do this by integrating technology, events, conferences, training, and other services. We call it *i*Services. For more information, contact your *i*Learning Sales Specialist.

Acknowledgements

I am extremely grateful to have had this opportunity to work on such an exciting project. The entire process has been an incredible journey that you can truly appreciate only when you have been directly involved. The process has been rewarding and enjoyable thanks to the contributions made by everyone.

The committed team at McGraw-Hill Ryerson was outstanding. A huge thank you goes out to Rhondda McNabb, the executive editor, and Katherine Goodes, the senior developmental editor, for their talent, commitment, and support throughout this process. Their patience and insights were invaluable to me. Thanks to Katie Litt at My Editor, Inc., for assisting in the manuscript preparation process.

I am exceptionally grateful to have worked with such a great copy editor as June Trusty. Her significant input and careful attention to details and deadlines were vital to me throughout this process. Thank you to the entire production staff, Cathy Biribauer, supervising editor, and Emily Hickey, production coordinator. Thanks also to our technical checkers; your attention to detail has been greatly appreciated. Thank you to Doug Tuomi for working with me on this project by assisting in the development of the end-of-chapter material.

I am extremely appreciative for the dedication and professionalism that was shown by everyone involved, as this made my job more manageable, including all the reviewers who provided such valuable comments and suggestions for improvements.

I am also genuinely grateful to Fred Phillips for his valuable resources and expertise. His guidance and wealth of knowledge are greatly appreciated and his commitment to be of assistance was unwavering.

I would also like to recognize the invaluable advice and suggestions provided by the many people who participated in the manuscript development reviews. For this assistance, I thank the following colleagues:

Reviewers for the Third Canadian Edition
Ann Clarke-Okah, *Carleton University*
Robert Collier, *University of Ottawa*
Han Donker, *University of Northern British Columbia*
Cynthia Duncan, *Seneca College*
Else Grech, *Ryerson University*
Colin Haime, *Vancouver Island University*
Glen Kobussen, *University of Saskatchewan*
Howard Leaman, *University of Guelph-Humber*
Jennifer Li, *Brock University*
Ken Macaulay, *St Francis Xavier University*
Amy MacFarlane, *University of Prince Edward Island*
Kelsie McKay, *Georgian College*
Vanessa Oltmann, *Vancouver Island University*
Michel Paquet, *SAIT Polytechnic*
Jay Perry, *Niagara College*
Glenys Sylvestre, *University of Regina*
Rod Tilley, *Mount Saint Vincent University*

Barrie Tober, *Niagara College*
Gilles Valade, *Thompson Rivers University*
Shu-Lun Wong, *Memorial University of Newfoundland*

Reviewers for previous editions
Ron Baker, *University of Regina*
Hilary Becker, *Carleton University*
Paul Berry, *Mount Allison University*
Catherine Byers, *Seneca College of Applied Arts*
Andrea Chance, *George Brown College, University of Guelph*
Sandra Daga, *University of Toronto at Scarborough*
Angela Davis, *University of Winnipeg*
Han Donker, *University of Northern British Columbia*
Gerry Dupont, *Carleton University*
Ian Feltmate, *Acadia University*
George Gekas, *Ryerson University*
Elizabeth Grasby, *University of Western Ontario*
Colin Haime, *Malapina University College*

Mahlon Harvey, *University of Winnipeg*
Gordon Holyer, *Maraspina University College*
Melissa Jean, *University of Western Ontario*
Glen Kobussen, *University of Saskatchewan*
Walter Krystia, *Ryerson University*
Rafik Kurji, *Mount Royal University*
Marie Madil-Payne, *George Brown College*
Muriel McKenna, *Seneca College of Applied Arts & Technology*
Carol Meissner, *Georgian College*
Robert C. Nichols, *Capilano University*
John Siambanopoulos, *University of Western Ontario*
Glenys Sylvestre, *University of Regina*
Shu-Lin Wong, *Memorial University of Newfoundland*

Richard Wright, *Fanshawe College*
Eliza Zuliani, *University of Toronto*

Most especially I want to thank my husband, our two daughters, and the other members of my family. Words alone cannot express the gratitude I feel for their encouragement, support, and patience throughout this process. Thank you for being just as excited about this textbook as I am!

Brandy Mackintosh
Edwards School of Business
University of Saskatchewan

Business Decisions and Financial Accounting

YOUR LEARNING OBJECTIVES

Understand the business

LO1 Describe various organizational forms and types of business decision makers.

Study the accounting methods

LO2 Describe the purpose, structure, and content of the four basic financial statements.

Evaluate the results

LO3 Explain how financial statements are used by decision makers.

LO4 Describe factors that contribute to useful financial information.

Review the chapter

Chapter Summary, page 21

Additional resources on Connect

 connect™

FOCUS COMPANY:
Pizza Palace

 PIZZA PALACE

Welcome to the world of business and financial accounting. One of our goals for this book is to help you see the role that accounting plays in helping people turn their good ideas into successful businesses. The founder of FedEx first introduced his ideas about a nationwide transportation business in a college essay. With the help of accounting, FedEx has become a multibillion dollar business. Perhaps the only thing stopping you from aspiring to have your own business is that you don't know everything that's involved in starting and running a business. We're here to help with that.

Another important goal for us is to explain topics in ways that you can relate to. We want you to see that your personal life experiences help you to learn accounting. Often, we will explain topics in the context of a real business. By reading about these experiences, you'll gain a realistic understanding of how accounting is a key part of all businesses. So, let's get started.

Pizza Palace is a fictional company owned by Emilio Santos. For ten years, Emilio had worked in several pizza restaurants in downtown Vancouver. During this time, he perfected a gourmet pizza concept that he believed would be a great addition to the local restaurant scene, so Emilio decided to start his own pizza business. Although eager to get started, Emilio had several questions to consider and decisions to make. He contacted Ally Paddison, a local chartered accountant (CA), to ask her advice. As you will read in this chapter, Ally met with Emilio in June to help him understand what's involved in starting a business and monitoring its success. In the first four chapters, you will learn the steps that Emilio took to start his own business and turn his dream into reality.

THAT WAS
THEN

If you think accounting is far removed from your personal life, you might be in for a surprise. Your ordinary life experiences, especially as a student, actually prepare you well to learn accounting.

THIS IS
NOW

This chapter focuses on the key financial reports that businesspeople rely on when evaluating a company's performance.

ORGANIZATION OF THE CHAPTER

Understand the business	Study the accounting methods	Evaluate the results	Review the chapter
• Organizational forms • Accounting for business decisions	• The basic accounting equation • Financial statements	• Using financial statements • Useful financial information	• Demonstration Case • Chapter Summary • Key Terms • Homework Helper • Practice Material

Understand the Business

 "Emilio, we should start by talking about how you want to organize your business."

"Well, I'm opening a gourmet pizza restaurant. What else do I need to know?"

ORGANIZATIONAL FORMS

Learning Objective 1

Describe various organizational forms and types of business decision makers.

Ally outlined three primary ways in which businesses can be organized. While other business forms exist, such as limited liability companies, the following three are the most common: sole proprietorship, partnership, and corporation.

Sole Proprietorship

This is a form of business owned (and usually operated) by one individual. It is the easiest form of business to start because it doesn't require any special legal manoeuvres. Just get a business licence and you're good to go. A sole proprietorship is considered a part of the owner's life, with all profits (or losses) becoming part of the taxable income of the owner, and the owner being personally liable for all debts of the business.

Partnership

A partnership is similar to a sole proprietorship, except that profits, taxes, and legal liability are the responsibility of two or more owners instead of just one. It is slightly more expensive to form than a sole proprietorship because a lawyer typically is needed to draw up a partnership agreement. The partnership agreement describes how profits are shared between partners and how that would change if new partners are added or existing partners leave. The key advantage of a partnership over a sole proprietorship is that it typically has more resources available to it, which can fuel the business's growth.

Corporation

Unlike sole proprietorships and partnerships, a corporation is a separate entity from both a legal and accounting perspective. This means that a corporation, not its owners, is legally responsible for its own taxes and debts. Thus, owners cannot lose more than their investment in the corporation, which is a major advantage to the owners. Two disadvantages of incorporation are that the legal fees for creating a corporation can be high and income tax returns must be filed for both the corporation and its owners.

Corporations can raise large amounts of money for growth because they divide ownership of the corporation into shares that can be sold to new owners. A share of the corporation's ownership is indicated in a legal document called a *share certificate*. The owners of a company's shares (shareholders) can buy and sell shares privately or publicly on a stock exchange if the company has legally registered to do so. Most corporations start out as private companies and will apply to become public companies ("go public") if they need a lot of financing, which they obtain from selling new share certificates to investors. Some big-name corporations, like London Drugs and Kal Tire, haven't gone public because they get enough financing from private sources, but many that you are familiar with such as Rogers Communications Inc. and Boston Pizza International Inc. are public companies.

> "I'm interested in limiting my legal liability and getting some financing by selling ownership shares to investors, so I will create a private corporation called Pizza Palace, Inc. What's next?"

ACCOUNTING FOR BUSINESS DECISIONS

Most companies exist to earn profits for their shareholders. They earn profits by selling goods or services to customers for more than they cost to produce. Emilio's company will be successful if it is able to make pizzas at a cost of $2 and sell them for $9. To know just how successful his company is, Emilio will need to establish and maintain a good system of financial record-keeping—an accounting system. **Accounting** is an information system designed by an organization to capture (analyze, record, and summarize) the activities affecting its financial condition and performance and then report the results to decision makers, both inside and outside the organization. It's such a key part of business that businesspeople typically talk about their companies using accounting terms, which is why accounting terminology is often called the "language of business."

Every organization needs accountants to assist in reporting financial information for decision making and to help its owners understand the financial effects of those business decisions. Emilio can get this help in one of two ways. He can hire an accountant to work as an employee of his business (a private accountant) or he can contract with someone like Ally, who provides advice to a variety of businesses (a public accountant). Accounting graduates often start their careers in public accounting firms and then at some point move into private accounting within business, governmental organizations such as Canada Revenue Agency (CRA), or not-for-profit organizations (NPOs). Many become top managers of large companies. Some even enter academia to teach and conduct research.

Accountants may pursue a variety of certifications, including CA (chartered accountant), CFE (certified fraud examiner), CGA (certified general accountant), CMA (certified management accountant), and CIA (certified internal auditor), among others. For additional information on accounting careers, certifications, salaries, and opportunities, visit the Web sites of the Canadian Institute of Chartered Accountants (www.cica.ca), Certified Management Accountants (www.cma-canada.org), and the Certified General Accountants Association of Canada (www.cga-canada.org).

YOU SHOULD KNOW

Accounting: A system of analyzing, recording, and summarizing the results of a business's activities and then reporting the results to decision makers.

Because Emilio's business is small, he doesn't yet need a full-time accountant. Instead, he agrees that Pizza Palace will pay fees to Ally for basic services. She'll help him to set up an accounting system and advise him on key business decisions.

"How will an accounting system help me run my business?"

The main goal of an accounting system is to capture information about the business and financing activities of a company so that it can be reported to decision makers, both inside and outside the business. Exhibit 1.1 illustrates this role and shows that this information can be presented in two kinds of reports. Managerial accounting reports include detailed financial plans and continually updated reports about the operating performance of the company. These reports are made available only to the company's employees (internal users) so that they can make business decisions related to production, marketing, human resources, and finance. For example, managerial accounting reports are needed when determining whether to build, buy, or rent a building; whether to continue or discontinue making particular products; how much to pay employees; and how much to borrow. As manager of a restaurant, Emilio will regularly need managerial accounting reports to monitor the quantity of supplies on hand, evaluate the various costs associated with making and selling his gourmet pizza, and assess the productivity of his employees.

 "Others outside your business will need financial information about your restaurant. For example, where will the money come from to start your business?"

"My wife and I will probably contribute $30,000 from personal savings. But I'll still need to ask the bank for a $20,000 loan to buy equipment. What will the bank want to know?"

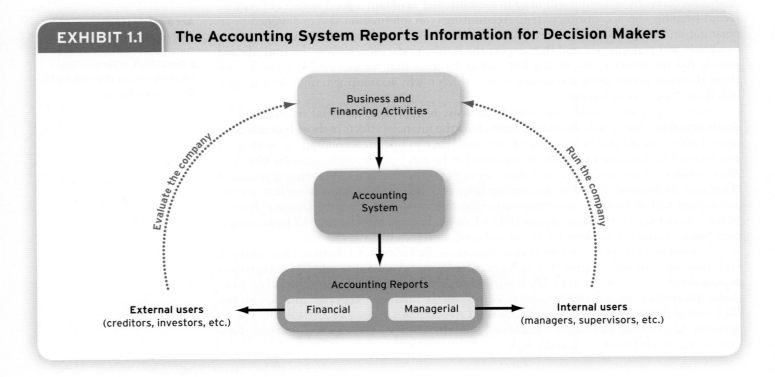

EXHIBIT 1.1   **The Accounting System Reports Information for Decision Makers**

Business and Financing Activities

↓ Accounting System

↓ Accounting Reports

Evaluate the company

Run the company

External users (creditors, investors, etc.) ← Financial | Managerial → Internal users (managers, supervisors, etc.)

Ally described **financial accounting reports**, called **financial statements,** which are prepared periodically to provide information to people not employed by the business. These external financial statement users aren't given access to detailed internal records of the company, so they rely extensively on the financial statements. Creditors and investors are the two primary external user groups, but other external users also find the information helpful.

- **Creditors**—anyone to whom money is owed.
  - **Banks** use financial statements to evaluate the risk that they will not be repaid the money they've loaned to a company. Because banks are taking a risk when they loan money to a company, they want periodic financial reports from the company so they can keep an eye on how it is doing and intervene if it looks like the company will have trouble repaying the loan.
  - **Suppliers** also want to be sure a business can pay them for the goods or services they deliver. They usually check the business's credit standing and may also ask for its financial statements before entering into significant business relationships.
- **Investors**
  - **Shareholders** are a major external user group. Both existing and future shareholders rely on financial statements to evaluate whether the company is financially secure and likely to be a profitable investment.
- **Other external users**
  - Certain **customers** use financial statements to judge the company's ability to provide service on its products and honour warranties.
  - Various local, provincial, territorial, and federal **governments** also collect taxes based on information used to prepare the financial statements.

In Pizza Palace's case, the bank will be the main external user. Emilio will be expected to prepare financial statements to obtain the loan and then regularly provide updated financial reports until the loan is repaid. If the company's shares are ever sold to other investors, these shareholders will rely on financial statements to estimate the value of their shares and determine whether to buy, sell, or hold Pizza Palace shares.

While Emilio understood everything Ally had told him up to this point, he had another major concern.

"I want to sound intelligent when I talk to my banker, but I don't know much about accounting."

 "This is a common concern for new business owners, so let's start with the most basic thing you need to know about accounting."

Study the Accounting Methods

THE BASIC ACCOUNTING EQUATION

One of the central concepts to understanding financial reports is that what a company owns must equal what a company owes to its creditors and shareholders. In accounting, there are special names for what a company owns and what a company owes to creditors and shareholders, as shown below.

Resources Owned . . .	=	Resources Owed . . .		
by the **company**		to **creditors**		to **shareholders**
Assets	**=**	**Liabilities**	**+**	**Shareholders' Equity**

The relationship between assets (A), liabilities (L), and shareholders' equity (SE) is known as the **basic accounting equation** (also called the *balance sheet equation*). The business itself, not the shareholders who own the business, is viewed as owning the assets and owing the liabilities. This is called the **separate entity assumption,** which requires that a business's financial reports include only the activities of the business and not those of its shareholders.

The elements of the basic accounting equation are fundamental to reading and understanding financial statements, so let's look at each in detail.

Assets

An asset is an economic resource presently controlled by the company; it has measurable value and is expected to benefit the company by producing cash inflows or reducing cash outflows in the future. For Pizza Palace, assets include things like cash, supplies, and cookware, and equipment such as tables, chairs, and pizza ovens.

Liabilities

Liabilities are measurable amounts that the company owes to creditors. If Pizza Palace borrows from a bank, it would owe a liability called a *Note Payable*. This particular name is used because banks require borrowers to sign a legal document called a *note*, which describes details about the company's promise to repay the bank. Pizza Palace is likely to also owe suppliers for ingredients and other supplies delivered to Pizza Palace. When a company buys goods from another company, it usually does so on credit by promising to pay for the goods at a later date. The amount owed is called an *Account Payable* because purchases made using credit are said to be "on account." Pizza Palace could also owe wages to employees (Wages Payable) and taxes to governments (Taxes Payable). From a legal perspective, creditors have priority over shareholders. Thus, if a company goes out of business, liabilities must be paid before any amounts are paid to shareholders.

Shareholders' Equity

Shareholders' equity represents the owners' claims on the business. As illustrated below, these claims arise for two reasons:

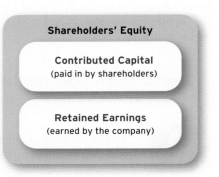

1. First, the owners have a claim on amounts they contributed directly to the company in exchange for its shares (Contributed Capital).
2. Second, the owners have a claim on amounts the company has earned through profitable business operations (Retained Earnings).

Retained Earnings is particularly important because a business can survive only if it is profitable. It will be profitable if the total amount earned from selling goods and services is greater than the costs incurred to generate those sales. Theoretically, these profits belong to the company's owners, so they increase shareholders' equity. Through these profits, owners can get back more money from the company than they paid in (a return on their investment).

Given the importance of a company's profits, accounting systems separately track the two components of profit: revenues and expenses.

Revenues   Revenues are earned by selling goods or services to customers. For Pizza Palace, revenues are measured at the amount the company charges its customers for pizza.

Expenses   Expenses are all costs of doing business that are necessary to earn revenues. For Pizza Palace, these include advertising, utilities, rent, wages, insurance, repairs, and supplies used in making pizza. Expenses are said to be incurred to generate revenues. The word *incurred* means that the activities giving rise to a cost (e.g., running an ad, using electricity) have occurred in the period in which the related revenues have been generated.

Net Income   Although *profit* is used in casual conversation, the preferred term in accounting is *net income*. Net income is calculated as revenues minus expenses. For Pizza Palace to be profitable, its revenues must be greater than its expenses. (If revenues are less than expenses, the company would have a net loss, but for now we'll be optimistic and assume that Pizza Palace is going to earn a profit.) By generating net income, a company increases its shareholders' equity, as illustrated below. This net income can be left in the company to accumulate (with earnings that have been retained from prior years) or it can be paid out to the company's shareholders for their own personal use (called *dividends*).

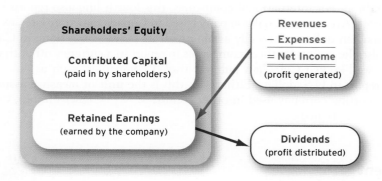

Dividends   A company's profits are accumulated in Retained Earnings until a decision is made to distribute them to shareholders in what is called a *dividend*. The simplest type of dividend, and the most common for a small business like Pizza Palace, is a dividend paid in cash. Dividends are not an expense incurred to generate earnings. Rather, dividends are a distribution of earnings. They are determined at the discretion of the company's board of directors. If Emilio wanted, he could choose to leave all the profits in Pizza Palace by never declaring a dividend.

"Okay, I think I get it, but can you tell me how all those items relate to each other and where they are reported in the financial statements?"

FINANCIAL STATEMENTS

Assets, liabilities, shareholders' equity, revenues, expenses, and dividends appear in different reports that collectively are called *financial statements*. The term *financial statements* refers to four accounting reports, typically prepared in the following order:

1. **Income Statement**
2. **Statement of Retained Earnings**
3. **Balance Sheet**
4. **Statement of Cash Flows**

Financial statements can be prepared at any time during the year, although they are most commonly prepared monthly, every three months (quarterly reports), and at the end of the year (annual reports). Companies are allowed to choose their fiscal year-end date. The fiscal year can be a 12-month period ending on a day other than December 31, or the fiscal year can be what is called a calendar year-end, which is a 12-month period ending on December 31. The toy maker Mattel, Inc., uses a calendar year-end because this is the start of its slow business period. Fewer toys are sold in January through May than in the first three weeks of December. The Saskatchewan Roughriders Football Club Inc. has chosen a fiscal year-end of March 31, which is during the off-season of the football schedule and is a slower time of year for the organization.

The Income Statement

YOU SHOULD KNOW

Income statement: Reports the amount of revenues less expenses for a period of time.

Unit of measure assumption: Results of business activities should be reported in an appropriate monetary unit, which in Canada is the Canadian dollar.

The first financial statement prepared is the **income statement** (also called the *statement of operations*). Ally gives Emilio Exhibit 1.2 to show what Pizza Palace's income statement might look like for the month ended September 30, assuming he is able to open his restaurant on September 1. The heading of the income statement identifies who, what, and when: the name of the business, the title of the report, and the time period covered by the financial statement. Larger businesses with thousands or millions of dollars in revenues and expenses add a fourth line under the date to indicate if the numbers reported are rounded to the nearest thousand or million. For international companies, this fourth line also reports the currency used in the report. An international company based in Canada may translate any foreign currency into Canadian dollars—basically assuming all its business was done in Canadian dollars. There is also the option for these companies to report in a currency other than Canadian dollars. Many well-known Canadian publicly traded companies, such as Nortel Networks Corporation, report in U.S. dollars. Either way, this is the **unit of measure assumption.** We see it in the reporting currency used in other countries: Nestlé (Swiss franc), Lego (Danish kronen), and Adidas (euro).

EXHIBIT 1.2	Income Statement

PIZZA PALACE, INC. Income Statement For the Month Ended September 30, 2012		Explanation
		Who: Name of the business **What:** Title of the statement **When:** Accounting period
Revenues		
Pizza Revenue	$11,000	Revenue earned from the sale and delivery of pizza to customers
Total Revenues	11,000	**Total amount earned during September**
Expenses		
Supplies Expense	4,000	Cost of pizza ingredients used up in September
Wages Expense	2,000	Cost of employee wages for work done in September
Rent Expense	1,500	Cost of rent for the month of September
Utilities Expense	600	Cost of utilities used in September
Insurance Expense	300	Cost of insurance coverage for September
Advertising Expense	100	Cost of advertising done in September
Income Tax Expense	500	Cost of taxes on September's income
Total Expenses	9,000	**Total expenses incurred in September to generate revenues**
Net Income	$ 2,000	**Difference between total revenues and total expenses**

YOU SHOULD KNOW

Accounts: Accumulate and report the effects of each different business activity.

Notice that an income statement for Pizza Palace would have three major captions—revenues, expenses, and net income—corresponding to the equation for the income statement (Revenues − Expenses = Net Income). Individual types of revenues and expenses would be reported under the revenue and expense headings. These **accounts,** as they are called, are typical for most businesses, whether small or big. Notice that each major caption has a subtotal, and the bottom line amount for net income has a double underline to highlight it. Finally, a dollar sign appears at the top and bottom of the column of numbers.

When listing the accounts on the income statement, revenues are on top, usually with the largest, most relevant revenue listed first. Then expenses are subtracted, again from largest to smallest, except that Income Tax Expense is the last expense listed. Net Income is the difference between total revenues and total expenses.

"So, does the $2,000 of Net Income mean I'll have that much more cash?"

"No. Net income is a measure of how much better off your business is, not how much cash you made."

Ally's point is one of the key ideas of the income statement. It's quite common for a business to provide goods or services to customers in one month but not collect cash from them until a later month. Similarly, expenses for the current month's activities may actually be paid in a different month. You'll have a chance to learn this in more detail later, but it's worth trying to understand from the beginning that revenues don't necessarily equal cash coming in during the month, and expenses don't always equal cash going out during the month.

Emilio seemed disappointed to see only $2,000 of projected net income for the first month. Ally reassured him that it's typical for new businesses like Pizza Palace to initially struggle to generate a profit because they have lots of expenses related to advertising and employee training but relatively small revenues because they haven't yet built a loyal customer base.[1] Pizza Palace's net income will likely increase in the future after the business becomes well known. By selling more pizza, revenues will increase without a major increase in expenses, except for the cost of ingredients and supplies that will be used in making the additional pizzas. Expenses like employee wages and rent will likely not increase all that much.

"I guess that's not so bad. It does make me want to watch my expenses and try to boost my pizza sales quickly. What about the amount Pizza Palace owes to the bank? Should we talk about the balance sheet?"

"Before we look at that, I want to show you the next statement that connects the income statement to the balance sheet, so you'll understand the relationships between the reports."

The Statement of Retained Earnings

Pizza Palace will report a **statement of retained earnings,** as shown in Exhibit 1.3. A more comprehensive statement of shareholders' equity that explains changes in all shareholders' equity accounts is provided by large corporations. But for Pizza Palace, most changes in shareholders' equity relate to generating and distributing earnings, so a statement of retained earnings is just as good as a full-blown statement of shareholders' equity. The heading in Exhibit 1.3 identifies the name of the company, the title of the report, and the accounting period. The statement starts with the Retained Earnings balance at the beginning of the period. Remember that retained earnings are the profits that have accumulated in the company over time. Because this is a new business, there aren't any accumulated profits yet so the beginning balance is $0. Next, the statement adds Net Income and subtracts any Dividends for the current period, to arrive at Retained Earnings at the end of the period.[2] Again, a dollar sign is used at the top and bottom of the column of numbers and a double underline appears at the bottom.

The Balance Sheet

The next financial report is the **balance sheet.** It is also known as the *statement of financial position*. The balance sheet's purpose is to report the amount of a business's assets, liabilities, and shareholders' equity at a specific point in time. Exhibit 1.4 presents Pizza Palace's

EXHIBIT 1.3   **Statement of Retained Earnings**

		Explanation
PIZZA PALACE, INC.		Who: Name of the business
Statement of Retained Earnings		What: Title of the statement
For the Month Ended September 30, 2012		When: Accounting period
Retained Earnings, September 1, 2012	$ 0	Last period's ending Retained Earnings balance
Add: Net Income	2,000	Reported on the income statement (Exhibit 1.2)
Subtract: Dividends	(1,000)	Distributions to shareholders in the current period
Retained Earnings, September 30, 2012	$1,000	This period's ending Retained Earnings balance

EXHIBIT 1.4   **Balance Sheet**

		Explanation
PIZZA PALACE, INC.		Who: Name of the business
Balance Sheet		What: Title of the statement
At September 30, 2012		When: Point in time
Assets		**Resources controlled by the company**
Cash	$14,000	Amount of cash on hand and in the business's bank account
Accounts Receivable	1,000	Pizza Palace's right to collect from customers for prior credit sales
Supplies	3,000	Amount of food and paper supplies on hand
Equipment	40,000	Cost of ovens, tables, etc.
Total Assets	**$58,000**	**Total amount of the company's resources**
Liabilities and Shareholders' Equity		**Claims on the company's resources**
Liabilities		Creditors' claims on the company's resources
Accounts Payable	$ 7,000	Amount owed to suppliers for prior credit purchases (on account)
Note Payable	20,000	Amount of loan owed to the bank (for promissory note)
Total Liabilities	27,000	Total claims on the resources by creditors
Shareholders' Equity		Shareholders' claims on the company's resources
Contributed Capital	30,000	Amount shareholders contributed for company shares
Retained Earnings	1,000	Total earnings retained in the business (Exhibit 1.3)
Total Shareholders' Equity	31,000	Total claims on the company's resources by shareholders
Total Liabilities and Shareholders' Equity	**$58,000**	**Total claims on the company's resources**

projected balance sheet. Think of the balance sheet as a picture or screen capture of Pizza Palace's resources and claims to resources at the end of the day on September 30, 2012.

Notice again that the heading specifically identifies the name of the company and title of the statement. Unlike the other financial reports, the balance sheet is presented for a point in time (at September 30, 2012). The assets are listed in order of how soon they are to be used or turned into cash. Likewise, liabilities are listed in order of how soon each is to be paid or settled.

The balance sheet first lists the assets of the business, which for Pizza Palace total $58,000. The second section lists the business's liabilities and shareholders' equity balances, also totalling $58,000. The balance sheet "balances" because the resources equal the claims to the resources. The basic accounting equation (also called the *balance sheet equation*) reflects the business's financial position at September 30, 2012:

Assets	=	Liabilities	+	Shareholders' Equity
$58,000	=	$27,000	+	$31,000

Cash is the first asset reported on the balance sheet. The $14,000 would represent the total amount of cash on hand and in Pizza Palace's bank account. The $1,000 reported as Accounts Receivable would represent Pizza Palace's right to collect from customers for sales made on credit. Pizza Palace intends to allow local colleges and universities to buy pizza for fundraising events on account by running a tab that Pizza Palace sends as a bill when the deliveries are made. The $3,000 reported for Supplies indicates the cost of pizza supplies that are expected to remain on hand at September 30, 2012. The same is true for the $40,000 of Equipment. According to the cost principle of accounting, assets are initially reported on the balance sheet based on their original cost to the company.

Under liabilities, the $7,000 of Accounts Payable is the amount that Ally expects Pizza Palace will owe suppliers for food and paper supplies purchased on account. The Note Payable is the written promise to repay the loan from the bank. As with all liabilities, these are financial obligations of the business arising from past business activities.

Finally, within shareholders' equity, Contributed Capital reflects the dollar amount of the company's shares that will be given when Emilio and his wife contribute $30,000 to the company. Retained Earnings reports the earnings expected to be retained in the company as of September 30, 2012. It matches the ending amount of Retained Earnings on the statement of retained earnings (Exhibit 1.3).

"Besides monitoring my revenues and expenses, it looks like I need to make sure I have enough assets to pay my liabilities."

"Sharp observation! Your creditors are most interested in your ability to pay cash to them in the future. However, not all assets can be easily turned into cash and not all revenues and expenses are received or paid in cash. So, there is one more important financial statement."

The Statement of Cash Flows

Pizza Palace's projected income statement (back in Exhibit 1.2) shows a positive net income of $2,000. However, net income is not necessarily equal to cash because revenues are reported when earned and expenses when incurred regardless of when cash is received or paid. The fourth financial report of interest to external users, then, is the **statement of cash flows.** It includes only those activities that result in cash changing hands. Exhibit 1.5 shows Pizza Palace's projected statement of cash flows for the month ended September 30, 2012.

The statement of cash flows is divided into three types of activities:

1. **Operating:** These activities are directly related to running the business to earn profit. They include buying supplies, making pizza, serving food to customers, cleaning the store, buying advertising, renting a building, repairing ovens, and obtaining insurance coverage.

2. **Investing:** These activities involve buying and selling productive resources with long lives (such as buildings, land, equipment, and tools), purchasing investments, and lending to others. As Exhibit 1.5 shows, Pizza Palace expects to purchase equipment for $40,000 cash.

3. **Financing:** Any borrowing from banks, repaying bank loans, receiving contributions from shareholders, or paying dividends to shareholders are considered financing activities.

YOU SHOULD KNOW

Statement of cash flows: Reports the operating, investing, and financing activities that caused increases and decreases in cash during the period.

EXHIBIT 1.5 **Statement of Cash Flows**

		Explanation
PIZZA PALACE, INC. **Statement of Cash Flows** **For the Month Ended September 30, 2012**		Who: Name of the entity What: Title of the statement When: Accounting period
Cash Flows from Operating Activities		**Activities directly related to earning income**
Cash received from customers	$10,000	Amount of cash received from customers
Cash paid to suppliers and employees	(5,000)	Amount of cash paid to suppliers and employees
Cash Provided by Operating Activities	5,000	Cash inflows minus outflows ($10,000 − $5,000)
Cash Flows from Investing Activities		**Activities related to the sale/purchase of productive assets**
Cash used to buy equipment	(40,000)	Amount of cash spent on equipment
Cash Used in Investing Activities	(40,000)	
Cash Flows from Financing Activities		**Activities involving investors and banks**
Capital contributed by shareholders	30,000	Amount of cash received from owners
Cash dividends paid to shareholders	(1,000)	Amount of cash paid to owners
Cash borrowed from the bank	20,000	Amount of cash received from the bank
Cash Provided by Financing Activities	49,000	Cash inflows minus outflows ($30,000 − $1,000 + $20,000)
Change in Cash	14,000	Sum of three categories of cash flows ($5,000 − $40,000 + $49,000)
Beginning Cash, September 1, 2012	0	Cash balance at the beginning of the accounting period
Ending Cash, September 30, 2012	$14,000	Cash balance reported on the balance sheet (Exhibit 1.4)

Pizza Palace's statement of cash flows is typical of a new start-up business or a business in expansion. The negative number for investing cash flows occurs because the company needs to buy a significant amount of equipment. The bank will be interested in watching how the cash flows reported on this statement change in the future to assess Pizza Palace's ability to make cash payments on the loan.

Notes to the Financial Statements

The four basic financial statements are not complete without notes to help financial statement users understand how the amounts were derived and what other information may affect their decisions. We'll talk about notes in more detail in later chapters.

"How does the whole picture fit together?"

Relationships among the Financial Statements

Exhibit 1.6 shows how the four basic financial statements connect to one another. The arrows show that

1 Net Income, from the income statement, is a component in determining ending Retained Earnings on the statement of retained earnings.

2 Ending Retained Earnings from the statement of retained earnings is then reported on the balance sheet.

3 The Cash on the balance sheet is equal to the ending Cash reported on the statement of cash flows.

EXHIBIT 1.6 | **Relationships among the Financial Statements**

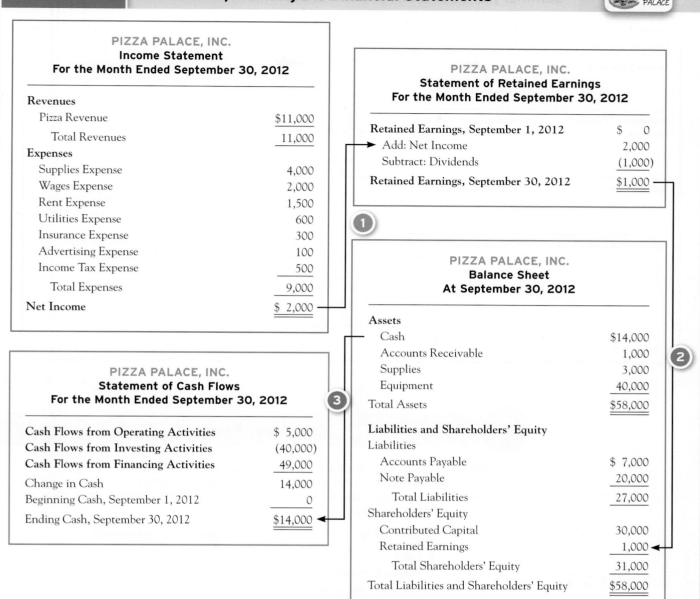

PIZZA PALACE, INC.
Income Statement
For the Month Ended September 30, 2012

Revenues	
Pizza Revenue	$11,000
Total Revenues	11,000
Expenses	
Supplies Expense	4,000
Wages Expense	2,000
Rent Expense	1,500
Utilities Expense	600
Insurance Expense	300
Advertising Expense	100
Income Tax Expense	500
Total Expenses	9,000
Net Income	**$ 2,000**

PIZZA PALACE, INC.
Statement of Retained Earnings
For the Month Ended September 30, 2012

Retained Earnings, September 1, 2012	$ 0
Add: Net Income	2,000
Subtract: Dividends	(1,000)
Retained Earnings, September 30, 2012	**$1,000**

PIZZA PALACE, INC.
Balance Sheet
At September 30, 2012

Assets	
Cash	$14,000
Accounts Receivable	1,000
Supplies	3,000
Equipment	40,000
Total Assets	$58,000
Liabilities and Shareholders' Equity	
Liabilities	
Accounts Payable	$ 7,000
Note Payable	20,000
Total Liabilities	27,000
Shareholders' Equity	
Contributed Capital	30,000
Retained Earnings	1,000
Total Shareholders' Equity	31,000
Total Liabilities and Shareholders' Equity	$58,000

PIZZA PALACE, INC.
Statement of Cash Flows
For the Month Ended September 30, 2012

Cash Flows from Operating Activities	$ 5,000
Cash Flows from Investing Activities	(40,000)
Cash Flows from Financing Activities	49,000
Change in Cash	14,000
Beginning Cash, September 1, 2012	0
Ending Cash, September 30, 2012	$14,000

A summary of the four basic financial statements is presented in Exhibit 1.7.

You have seen lots of new and important material in this section. Before moving on, take a moment to practise what you've read by completing the "How's It Going" exercise on the next page. This is the best way to make sure you've paid enough attention when reading about how business activities are reported in financial statements.

 "So, you've just seen how your financial statements should look in one month and how they relate. Are you feeling okay with all this?"

"It actually makes me anxious to get started. What will my external users look for?"

Financial Statement	Purpose: To report . . .	Structure	Examples of Content
Income Statement	The financial performance of the business *during the current accounting period*.	Revenues − Expenses = Net Income	Sales revenue, wages expense, supplies expense, rent expense
Statement of Retained Earnings	The accumulation of earnings retained in the business *during the current accounting period* with that of prior periods.	Beginning Retained Earnings + Net Income (this period) − Dividends (this period) = Ending Retained Earnings	Net income is from the income statement. Dividends are amounts distributed this period.
Balance Sheet	The financial position of a business *at a point in time*.	Liabilities Assets = + Shareholders' Equity	Cash, receivables, supplies, equipment, accounts payable, notes payable, contributed capital, retained earnings
Statement of Cash Flows	Activities that caused increases and decreases in cash *during the current accounting period*.	+/− Cash Flows from Operating Activities +/− Cash Flows from Investing Activities +/− Cash Flows from Financing Activities = Change in Cash + Beginning Cash = Ending Cash	Cash collected from customers, cash paid to suppliers, cash paid for equipment, cash borrowed from banks, cash received from selling shares

HOW'S IT GOING? Self-Study Practice

In the space provided, indicate (1) the type of account (A = asset, L = liability, SE = shareholders' equity, R = revenue, E = expense), and (2) whether it is reported on the income statement (I/S), statement of retained earnings (SRE), balance sheet (B/S), or statement of cash flows (SCF).

Account Title	Type	Statement
1. Land	_____	_____
2. Wages Expense	_____	_____
3. Accounts Receivable	_____	_____
4. Rent Revenue	_____	_____
5. Contributed Capital	_____	_____
6. Note Payable	_____	_____

After you have finished, check your answers with the solution in the margin.

Solution to Self-Study Practice

	Type	Statement
1.	A	B/S
2.	E	I/S
3.	A	B/S
4.	R	I/S
5.	SE	B/S
6.	L	B/S

Evaluate the Results

Learning Objective 3

Explain how financial statements are used by decision makers.

USING FINANCIAL STATEMENTS

The financial statements are a key source of information when external users, like creditors and investors, make decisions concerning a company. As you will see throughout this course, the amounts reported in the financial statements can be used to calculate percentages and ratios that reveal important insights about a company's performance. For now, however, let's consider how creditors and investors might gain valuable information simply by reading the dollar amounts reported in each financial statement.

- Creditors are mainly interested in assessing:
  1. **Is the company generating enough cash to make payments on its loan?** Answers to this question will come from the statement of cash flows. In particular, creditors would be interested in seeing whether operating activities are producing positive cash flows. Pizza Palace's expected net inflow of $5,000 cash from operating activities is very good for a new business.
  2. **Does the company have enough assets to cover its liabilities?** Answers to this question will come from comparing assets and liabilities reported on the balance sheet. Pizza Palace is expected to own slightly more than twice what it owes to creditors at September 30 (total assets of $58,000 versus total liabilities of $27,000). With $14,000 in Cash, Pizza Palace would be able to immediately pay all of its Accounts Payable and part of its Note Payable if needed.

- Investors expect a return on their contributions to a company. The return may be immediate (through dividends) or long-term (through selling share certificates at a price higher than their original cost). Dividends and higher share prices are more likely if a company is profitable. As a result, investors look closely at the income statement (and statement of retained earnings) for information about the company's ability to generate profits (and distribute dividends).

> "I've heard a lot about 'cooking the books.' How do users know that the information they're getting is useful and can be trusted?"

USEFUL FINANCIAL INFORMATION

Ally indicated that businesses must apply accounting principles in an ethical business environment.

Generally Accepted Accounting Principles

As it turns out, the system of financial statement reporting in use today has a long history—all the way back to a publication in 1494 by an Italian monk and mathematician, Luca Pacioli. Currently, the Canadian Institute of Chartered Accountants (CICA) has the primary responsibility for setting the underlying rules of accounting in Canada. As a group, these rules are called **generally accepted accounting principles,** or **GAAP** for short (pronounced like the name of the clothing store).

The Accounting Standards Board (AcSB) is an independent body supported by the CICA to develop and establish standards and guidance that govern financial accounting and reporting in Canada. After much deliberation, the AcSB determined that one of two different sets of accounting rules would be appropriate for use in Canada. Publicly accountable profit-oriented enterprises, such as Lululemon and Shoppers Drug Mart, must follow the principles and rules set out in the **International Financial Reporting Standards (IFRS).** In contrast, private enterprises whose shares are not traded on a public stock exchange can choose to follow either IFRS or Canadian Accounting Standards for Private Enterprises (ASPE). Each of these sets of standards is discussed below.

What does **"publicly accountable profit-oriented enterprise"** mean? According to the *CICA Handbook,* a publicly accountable enterprise is an entity, other than a not-for-profit organization, that

- has issued, or is in the process of issuing, debt or equity instruments that are, or will be, outstanding and traded in a public market (a domestic or foreign stock exchange or an over-the-counter market); or
- holds assets in a fiduciary capacity for a broad group of outsiders as one of its primary businesses.

A fiduciary is an individual, corporation, or association that is holding assets for another party, often with the legal authority and duty to make decisions regarding financial matters on behalf of the other party. Banks, credit unions, and insurance companies are all examples of fiduciaries.

So what does this mean for companies that do not meet these criteria? A **private enterprise** is a profit-oriented entity that is not a publicly accountable enterprise and therefore is not required to use IFRS. A private enterprise may still choose to use IFRS if, for example, it is expecting to become publicly accountable in the near future. IFRS deal with many complex accounting issues and disclosures that may not be applicable to private enterprises. Given this and the fact that many private enterprises have a limited number of users of their financial statements, it does not make financial sense for these types of companies to incur the additional time and costs of reporting their financial statements under IFRS. So, an alternative for private enterprises is to use Canadian **Accounting Standards for Private Enterprises (ASPE).** These standards address accounting issues that are more typical in a private enterprise environment that may not require the complexities and detailed disclosures that a publicly accountable enterprise would need.

Exhibit 1.8 illustrates the financial reporting options available to Canadian companies. Both IFRS and ASPE are considered to be GAAP. The focus of the material in this textbook is on private enterprises; however, at the end of each chapter, we'll use a feature called *Spotlight on IFRS and ASPE* to alert you to the important differences between ASPE and IFRS.

Private enterprises: Do not have publicly traded shares in an open market nor do they hold assets in a fiduciary capacity for someone else. Have the option to use IFRS or ASPE.

Accounting Standards for Private Enterprises (ASPE): Rules of accounting that address issues that are more relevant in a private enterprise environment and therefore can be used by private enterprises only.

EXHIBIT 1.8	Financial Reporting Standards in Canada

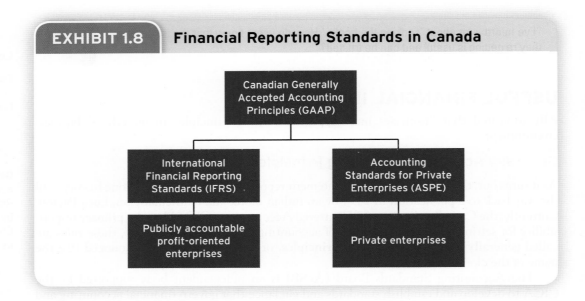

The main goal of ASPE and IFRS is to ensure that companies produce financial information that is useful to present and potential investors, lenders, and other creditors in making decisions in their capacity as capital providers. For financial information to be judged useful, it must possess two fundamental characteristics: relevance and faithful representation. Information is relevant if it makes a difference in decision making, and it is a faithful representation if it fully depicts the economic substance of business activities. The usefulness of financial information is enhanced when it is (1) comparable (to prior periods and other companies), (2) verifiable, (3) timely, and (4) understandable. To achieve these broad objectives, the AcSB and IASB have developed a framework that outlines the financial elements to be measured and reported, as well as various concepts for measuring and reporting financial information (see the Conceptual Framework for Financial Accounting and Reporting on the inside back cover of this book).

Ally summarized these elements and concepts for Emilio, highlighting in colour the concepts briefly introduced already (see Exhibit 1.9). (The remaining concepts will be introduced in later chapters and all will be reviewed in the final chapter.)

EXHIBIT 1.9 Key Concepts for External Financial Reporting

Objective of External Financial Reporting

To provide useful financial information to external users for decision making
- It must be relevant and a faithful representation of the business
- It is more useful if it is comparable, verifiable, timely, and understandable

Elements to Be Measured and Reported
- Assets, Liabilities, Shareholders' Equity, Revenues, Expenses, Dividends

Concepts for Measuring and Reporting Information
- **Assumptions:** Unit of Measure, Separate Entity, Going Concern, Time Period
- **Principles:** Cost, Revenue Recognition, Matching, Full Disclosure
- **Exceptions:** Cost–Benefit, Materiality, Industry Practices

"Who is responsible for ensuring that businesses follow GAAP?"

Ally told Emilio that a company's managers have primary responsibility for following GAAP. To provide additional assurance, some private companies and all public companies hire independent auditors to scrutinize their financial records. Auditors must follow **Canadian Auditing Standards (CAS)** while planning and performing financial statement audits. Canadian Auditing Standards provide auditors with the required tools, procedures, and guidance they need to carry out high-quality audits. These auditors must then report whether, beyond reasonable doubt, the financial statements represent what they claim to represent and whether they comply with GAAP. In a sense, GAAP are to auditors and accountants what Canada's Criminal Code is to lawyers and the public.

 "Overall, users expect information that is truthful, and this assumes that the company is following strong ethical business and accounting practices."

Ethical Conduct

Ethics refers to the standards of conduct for judging right from wrong, honest from dishonest, and fair from unfair. Intentional financial misreporting is both unethical and illegal. As you will see throughout this course, some accounting and business issues have clear answers that are either right or wrong. However, many situations require accountants, auditors, and managers to weigh the pros and cons of alternatives before making final decisions. To help ensure these decisions are made in a professional and ethical manner, the CICA requires that all its members adhere to a Code of Professional Conduct.

Emilio's concern about "cooking the books" likely stems from hearing about several high-profile accounting frauds that occurred a few years ago in North America involving Enron, WorldCom (now owned by Verizon), Nortel, and Livent Inc. In response to these frauds, the U.S. Congress stepped into the crisis in 2002 to create the **Sarbanes-Oxley Act (SOX).** The Act requires top managers of public companies to sign a report certifying their responsibilities for the financial statements, maintain an audited system of internal controls to ensure accuracy in the accounting reports, and maintain an independent committee to oversee top management and ensure that they cooperate with auditors. As a result of the Act, corporate executives now face severe consequences—20 years in prison and $5 million in fines—if they are found guilty of committing accounting fraud.

Following closely what the United States had done in response to these scandals, the Government of Ontario passed Bill 198, also known as the Budget Measures Act or **C-SOX** (pronounced see-sox). Bill 198 replicates many of the SOX requirements that resulted in the Canadian Securities Administrators (CSA) introducing a series of new rules that accommodated the unique nature of the Canadian financial market. Similar to the U.S. Act, these rules also include the requirement of CEO/CFO certification, adopting a system of internal controls that will ensure the accuracy of the company's financial reporting and, in addition, an expanded role for the audit committee. Major Canadian public companies are required to have fully independent and financially literate audit committees. There are however some differences between C-SOX and SOX. One major difference is the auditor involvement around the internal controls assessment made by management. SOX requires auditors to assess and report on the effectiveness of the internal controls that management has reported on. There is no requirement under C-SOX for the same auditor involvement around the management's report on internal controls. Also in this time of change, the Canadian Public Accountability Board was established. One of its main objectives is to conduct inspections of audit firms who audit reporting issuers of the provincial and territorial securities commissions. This in turn monitors the independence that auditors must have with their clients.

Ethical conduct is just as important for small private businesses as it is for large public companies. Ally's advice to Emilio and to all managers is to strive to create an ethical environment and establish a strong system of checks and controls inside the company. Do not tolerate blatant acts of fraud, such as employees making up false expenses for reimbursement, punching in a time card belonging to a co-worker who will be late for work, or copying someone's ideas and claiming them as his or her own. Also, be aware that not all ethical dilemmas are clear-cut. Some situations will require you to weigh one moral principle (e.g., honesty) against another (e.g., loyalty). Advise your employees that, when faced with an ethical dilemma, they should follow a three-step process:

1. **Identify who will benefit from the situation** (often the manager or employee) and the harm it could cause others (other employees, the company's reputation, owners, creditors, and the public in general).

2. **Identify the alternative courses of action.**

3. **Choose the alternative that is the most ethical**—and that you would be proud to have reported in the news.

Often, there is no one right answer to ethical dilemmas and hard choices will need to be made. In the end, however, following strong ethical practices is a key factor in business success and in ensuring good financial reporting.

Epilogue for Pizza Palace

Emilio got going quickly and, in August, created a corporation called Pizza Palace, Inc. The next three chapters will take you step by step through the financing, investing, and operating decisions that occurred at Pizza Palace during its first month of business. We will look at the way accountants collect data about business activities and process this data to construct the financial statements. The key to success in this course is to practise the skills that are presented in this text. It is very difficult to learn accounting without doing the assignments and keeping up with the reading.

As mentioned earlier, the focus of this textbook is on the Accounting Standards for Private Enterprises (ASPE) and the Spotlight on IFRS and ASPE segment of every chapter will alert you to the significant differences between ASPE and IFRS (International Financial Reporting Standards).

Topic	ASPE	IFRS
Four basic financial reports that comprise the financial statements	Under ASPE, the four basic financial reports are labelled as	Under IFRS, these reports can also be referred to as

ASPE

1. Income Statement
The income statement presents net income resulting from revenue, expense, gain, and loss transactions for the period. ASPE does not use other comprehensive income.

2. Statement of Retained Earnings
The statement of retained earnings reconciles the opening retained earnings balance at the beginning of an accounting period to the ending retained earnings balance at the end of the accounting period. This would include items affecting retained earnings such as net income and dividends.

3. Balance Sheet

4. Statement of Cash Flows

IFRS

1. Statement of Comprehensive Income
The statement of comprehensive income includes all revenues and gains and expenses and losses reported in net income, as well as other comprehensive income.

Other comprehensive income consists of other gains or losses that are not required by primary sources of GAAP to be included in net income. An example would be unrealized gains and losses on revaluation of property, plant, and equipment under the revaluation model discussed in greater detail in Chapter 9.

2. Statement of Changes in Equity
The statement of changes in equity reports the changes in each individual shareholder's equity account, as well as the overall change in total shareholders' equity during the year. This will include comprehensive income. This statement is usually presented in a columnar format with a column for each shareholder's equity account and total shareholders' equity.

3. Statement of Financial Position

4. Statement of Cash Flows

Review the Chapter

This section provides a chance to solidify your understanding of key points. It's worth your time to work through the following demonstration case, scan the chapter summary, test your understanding of key terms, and then practise, practise, practise.

DEMONSTRATION CASE

The introductory case presented here reviews the items reported on the income statement, statement of retained earnings, and balance sheet, using the financial statements of a fictional company, Over Armour, Inc., that develops, markets, and distributes athletic apparel and gear. Following is a list of items and amounts (in thousands of Canadian dollars) in Over Armour's financial statements for the quarter ended September 30, 2012.

Accounts Payable	$129,724	Other Expenses	$ 1,736
Accounts Receivable	151,086	Other Liabilities	10,425
Cash	40,152	Property and Equipment	70,645
Contributed Capital	176,330	Retained Earnings, September 30, 2012	143,445
Dividends	0	Retained Earnings, July 1, 2012	117,782
General and Administrative Expenses	71,788	Sales Revenues	231,946
Income Tax Expense	19,080	Total Assets	474,886
Inventories	163,612	Total Expenses	206,283
Net Income	25,663	Total Liabilities	155,111
Notes Payable	14,962	Total Liabilities and Shareholders' Equity	474,886
Operating Expenses	113,679	Total Revenues	231,946
Other Assets	49,391	Total Shareholders' Equity	319,775

Required:

1. Prepare an income statement, statement of retained earnings, and a balance sheet for the quarter, following the formats in Exhibits 1.2, 1.3, and 1.4.
2. Describe the content of these three statements.
3. Name the other statement that Over Armour would include in its financial statements.
4. Did financing for Over Armour's assets come primarily from liabilities or from shareholders' equity?
5. Explain why Over Armour would subject its statements to an independent audit.

Suggested Solution

1. The first step to reach a solution is to distinguish accounts as belonging to the income statement (revenues and expenses), the statement of retained earnings (retained earnings and dividends), or the balance sheet (assets, liabilities, and shareholders' equity). Organize the accounts in proper format and follow the flow from one to another (as shown by the arrows in the following statements).

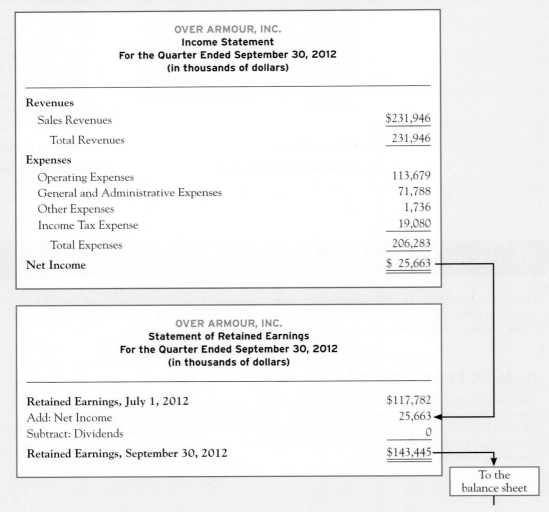

OVER ARMOUR, INC.
Income Statement
For the Quarter Ended September 30, 2012
(in thousands of dollars)

Revenues	
Sales Revenues	$231,946
Total Revenues	231,946
Expenses	
Operating Expenses	113,679
General and Administrative Expenses	71,788
Other Expenses	1,736
Income Tax Expense	19,080
Total Expenses	206,283
Net Income	$ 25,663

OVER ARMOUR, INC.
Statement of Retained Earnings
For the Quarter Ended September 30, 2012
(in thousands of dollars)

Retained Earnings, July 1, 2012	$117,782
Add: Net Income	25,663
Subtract: Dividends	0
Retained Earnings, September 30, 2012	$143,445

To the balance sheet

OVER ARMOUR, INC.
Balance Sheet
At September 30, 2012
(in thousands of dollars)

	From the statement of retained earnings

Assets

Cash	$ 40,152
Accounts Receivable	151,086
Inventories	163,612
Property and Equipment	70,645
Other Assets	49,391
Total Assets	**$474,886**

Liabilities

Accounts Payable	$129,724
Notes Payable	14,962
Other Liabilities	10,425
Total Liabilities	155,111

Shareholders' Equity

Contributed Capital	176,330
Retained Earnings	143,445
Total Shareholders' Equity	319,775
Total Liabilities and Shareholders' Equity	**$474,886**

2. The income statement reports the most common measure of financial performance for a business: net income (revenues minus expenses during the accounting period). The statement of retained earnings links the net income number from the income statement to the end-of-period retained earnings balance on the balance sheet. The balance sheet reports the amount of assets, liabilities, and shareholders' equity of a business at a point in time.

3. Over Armour would also present a statement of cash flows.

4. The balance sheet indicates that financing for Over Armour's assets is provided primarily from shareholders' equity ($319,775) rather than liabilities ($155,111).

5. Like all public companies, Over Armour will subject its financial statements to an audit because the Canadian Securities Administrators require an independent audit. Also, an audit will give users greater confidence in the accuracy of financial statement information because the people who audit the statements are required to meet professional standards of ethics and competence.

CHAPTER SUMMARY

Describe various organizational forms and types of business decision makers. p. 2　　　　**LO1**

- Sole proprietorships are owned by one individual, are relatively inexpensive to form, and are not treated legally as separate from their owners. Thus, all profits or losses become part of the taxable income of the owner, who is also responsible personally for all debts of the business.

- Partnerships are businesses legally similar to sole proprietorships, but with two or more owners.

- Corporations are separate legal entities (thus, corporations pay taxes) that issue shares to investors (shareholders) and are more costly to establish. Shareholders cannot be held liable for more than their investment in the corporation. Private corporations issue shares to a few individuals while public corporations issue shares in the stock market.

- Business decision makers include creditors (banks, suppliers), investors (shareholders), customers, governments, and other external users.

LO2 Describe the purpose, structure, and content of the four basic financial statements. p. 5

- The *income statement* reports the net amount that a business earned (net income) over a period of time by subtracting the costs of running the business (expenses) from the total amount earned (revenues).
- The *statement of retained earnings* explains changes in the retained earnings account over a period of time by considering increases (from net income) and decreases (from dividends to shareholders).
- The *balance sheet* reports what the business owns (reported as assets) at a particular point in time and how much of the financing for these assets came from creditors (reported as liabilities) and shareholders (reported as shareholders' equity).
- The *statement of cash flows* explains changes in the cash account over a period of time by reporting inflows and outflows of cash from the business's operating, investing, and financing activities.

LO3 Explain how financial statements are used by decision makers. p. 14

- Creditors are mainly interested in assessing whether the company (1) is generating enough cash to make payments on its loan, and (2) has enough assets to cover its liabilities. Answers to these questions are indicated by the statement of cash flows and the balance sheet.
- Investors look closely at the income statement for information about a company's ability to generate profits, and at the statement of retained earnings for information about a company's dividend distributions.

LO4 Describe factors that contribute to useful financial information. p. 15

- Companies generate useful financial information by applying generally accepted accounting principles in an ethical business environment. Companies can use either IFRS or ASPE, depending on the type of enterprise involved.
- To be useful, information must be relevant and a faithful representation of reality. Information is more useful when it is comparable, verifiable, timely, and understandable.

KEY TERMS

Accounting p. 3

Accounting Standards for Private Enterprises (ASPE) p. 16

Accounts p. 8

Balance Sheet p. 9

Basic Accounting Equation p. 6

Canadian Auditing Standards p. 17

Financial Statements p. 5

Generally Accepted Accounting Principles (GAAP) p. 15

Income Statement p. 8

International Financial Reporting Standards (IFRS) p. 15

Private Enterprises p. 16

Publicly Accountable Profit-Oriented Enterprises p. 15

Sarbanes-Oxley Act (SOX) p. 18

Separate Entity Assumption p. 6

Statement of Cash Flows p. 11

Statement of Retained Earnings p. 9

Unit of Measure Assumption p. 8

See complete definitions in the glossary in the back of this text.

HOMEWORK HELPER

Alternative terms

- The balance sheet also can be called the *statement of financial position*.
- The income statement also can be called the *statement of operations*.
- Net Income can also be called *Net Earnings*.

Helpful reminders

- The balance in each account is reported once and only once in one of the following: the balance sheet, income statement, or statement of retained earnings.

Frequent mistakes

- Dividends are not expenses. Dividends relate to distributing (not generating) earnings. Consequently, a company's dividends are reported on its statement of retained earnings (not its income statement).

QUESTIONS (⑤ Symbol indicates questions that require analysis from more than one perspective.)

1. Define *accounting*.

2. Valeri is opening a hair salon but she does not know what business form she should select. What can you tell her about the advantages and disadvantages of operating as a sole proprietorship versus a corporation? ⑤

3. Briefly explain the difference between financial accounting and managerial accounting.

4. The accounting process generates financial reports for both internal and external users. Describe some of the specific groups of internal and external users.

5. Explain what the separate entity assumption means when it says that a business is treated as separate from its owners for accounting purposes.

6. List the three main types of business activities on the statement of cash flows and give an example of each.

7. What information should be included in the heading of each of the four primary financial statements?

8. What are the purposes of (*a*) the balance sheet, (*b*) the income statement, (*c*) the statement of retained earnings, and (*d*) the statement of cash flows?

9. Explain why the income statement, statement of retained earnings, and statement of cash flows would be dated "For the Year Ended December 31, 2012," whereas the balance sheet would be dated "At December 31, 2012."

10. Briefly explain the difference between *net income* and *net loss*.

11. Describe the basic accounting equation that provides the structure for the balance sheet. Define the three major components reported on the balance sheet.

12. Describe the equation that provides the structure for the income statement. Explain the three major items reported on the income statement.

13. Describe the equation that provides the structure for the statement of retained earnings. Explain the four major items reported on the statement of retained earnings.

14. Describe the equation that provides the structure for the statement of cash flows. Explain the three major types of activities reported on the statement.

15. Briefly describe the organization that is responsible for developing accounting measurement rules (generally accepted accounting principles) in Canada.

16. What is the main goal for accounting rules in Canada and around the world? What characteristics must financial information possess to reach that goal?

17. Briefly define what an ethical dilemma is and describe the steps to consider when evaluating ethical dilemmas.

18. In what ways might accounting frauds be similar to cases of academic dishonesty?

Multiple-choice questions and corresponding answers can be found on Connect.

MINI-EXERCISES

M1-1 Matching Definitions with Terms or Abbreviations

LO1, 2, 4

Match each definition with its related term or abbreviation by entering the appropriate letter in the space provided.

Term or Abbreviation	Definition
_____ 1. Investing activities	A. A system that collects and processes financial information about an organization and reports that information to decision makers.
_____ 2. Private company	
_____ 3. Corporation	
_____ 4. Accounting	B. Measurement of information about a business in the monetary unit (dollars or other national currency).
_____ 5. Partnership	
_____ 6. AcSB	C. An unincorporated business owned by two or more persons.
_____ 7. Financing activities	
_____ 8. Unit of measure	D. A company that sells its shares privately and is not required to release its financial statements to the public.
_____ 9. GAAP	
_____ 10. Public company	E. An incorporated business that issues shares as evidence of ownership.
_____ 11. Operating activities	
	F. Buying and selling productive resources with long lives.

G. Transactions with lenders (borrowing and repaying cash) and shareholders (selling company shares and paying dividends).

H. Activities directly related to running the business to earn profit.

I. Accounting Standards Board.

J. A company that has its shares bought and sold by investors on established stock exchanges.

K. Generally accepted accounting principles.

LO2, 4 **M1-2 Matching Definitions with Terms**

Match each definition with its related term by entering the appropriate letter in the space provided.

Term	Definition
____ 1. Relevance	A. The financial reports of a business are assumed to include the results of only that business's activities.
____ 2. Faithful representation	
____ 3. Comparability	B. The resources owned by a business.
____ 4. Separate entity	C. Financial information that can be compared across businesses because similar accounting methods have been applied.
____ 5. Assets	
____ 6. Liabilities	D. The total amounts invested and reinvested in the business by its owners.
____ 7. Shareholders' equity	
____ 8. Revenues	E. The costs of business necessary to earn revenues.
____ 9. Expenses	F. A feature of financial information that allows it to influence a decision.
____ 10. Unit of measure	
	G. Earned by selling goods or services to customers.
	H. The amounts owed by the business.
	I. Financial information that depicts the economic substance of business activities.
	J. The assumption that states that results of business activities should be reported in an appropriate monetary unit.

LO2 **M1-3 Matching Financial Statement Items to Balance Sheet and Income Statement Categories**

 According to its annual report, Procter & Gamble brands "are some of the world's most well-known household names—including innovative new products that comprised five of the top ten most successful new introductions in 2009." Leading brands include Tide, Downy, Crest, Pringles, Duracell, and Pampers. The following are items taken from its recent balance sheet and income statement. Mark each item in the following list with a letter or letters to indicate whether it would be reported as an Asset, Liability, or Shareholders' Equity account on the balance sheet or a Revenue or Expense account on the income statement.

____ 1. Accounts Payable   ____ 5. General, Selling, and Administrative Expenses

____ 2. Accounts Receivable   ____ 6. Sales Revenue

____ 3. Cash   ____ 7. Long-Term Debt

____ 4. Income Tax Expense   ____ 8. Retained Earnings

LO2 **M1-4 Matching Financial Statement Items to Balance Sheet and Income Statement Categories**

 Tootsie Roll Industries manufactures and sells more than 60 million Tootsie Rolls and 20 million Tootsie Roll Pops each day. The following items were listed on a Tootsie Roll income statement and balance sheet. Mark each item from the balance sheet as an Asset, Liability, or Shareholders' Equity and each item from the income statement as a Revenue or Expense.

_____ 1. Accounts Receivable
_____ 2. Rental and Royalty Revenue
_____ 3. Cash
_____ 4. Machinery and Equipment
_____ 5. Selling, Marketing, and Administrative Expenses

_____ 6. Sales Revenue
_____ 7. Accrued Liabilities
_____ 8. Retained Earnings
_____ 9. Accounts Payable

M1-5 Matching Financial Statement Items to Balance Sheet and Income Statement Categories

LO2

General Mills is a manufacturer of food products, such as Lucky Charms cereal, Pillsbury crescent rolls, and Green Giant vegetables. The following items were presented in the company's financial statements. Mark each item from the balance sheet as an Asset, Liability, or Shareholders' Equity and each item from the income statement as a Revenue or Expense.

GENERAL MILLS

_____ 1. Accounts Payable
_____ 2. Contributed Capital
_____ 3. Land, Building, and Equipment
_____ 4. Accounts Receivable
_____ 5. Notes Payable

_____ 6. Cash
_____ 7. Retained Earnings
_____ 8. General, Selling, and Administrative Expenses
_____ 9. Sales Revenue
_____ 10. Inventories

M1-6 Matching Financial Statement Items to the Four Basic Financial Statements

LO2

Match each element with its financial statement by entering the appropriate letters in the space provided (balance sheet, B/S; income statement, I/S; statement of retained earnings, SRE; or statement of cash flows, SCF).

Element	Financial Statement
_____ 1. Cash Flows from Financing Activities	A. Balance Sheet
_____ 2. Expenses	B. Income Statement
_____ 3. Cash Flows from Investing Activities	C. Statement of Retained Earnings
_____ 4. Assets	D. Statement of Cash Flows
_____ 5. Dividends	
_____ 6. Revenues	
_____ 7. Cash Flows from Operating Activities	
_____ 8. Liabilities	

M1-7 Matching Financial Statement Items to the Four Basic Financial Statements

LO2

Luxottica Group

Prior to being acquired in November 2007 by Luxottica Group—an Italian eyeware company—Oakley, Inc., reported the following items in its financial statements. Indicate whether these items would have appeared on the balance sheet (B/S), income statement (I/S), statement of retained earnings (SRE), or statement of cash flows (SCF).

OAKLEY

_____ 1. Dividends
_____ 2. Total Shareholders' Equity
_____ 3. Sales Revenue
_____ 4. Total Assets

_____ 5. Cash Flows from Operating Activities
_____ 6. Total Liabilities
_____ 7. Net Income
_____ 8. Cash Flows from Financing Activities

M1-8 Reporting Amounts on the Statement of Cash Flows

LO2

Learning which items belong in each category of the statement of cash flows is an important first step in understanding their meaning. Use a letter to mark each item in the following list as a cash flow from Operating, Investing, or Financing activities. **Put parentheses around the letter if it is a cash *outflow* and use no parentheses if it's an *inflow*.**

_____ 1. Cash paid to purchase equipment
_____ 2. Cash collected from customers
_____ 3. Cash received from selling equipment

_____ 4. Cash paid for dividends
_____ 5. Cash paid to suppliers and employees
_____ 6. Cash received from issuing shares

LO2 **M1-9 Preparing a Statement of Retained Earnings**

Stone Culture Corporation was organized on January 1, 2011. For its first two years of operations, it reported the following:

Net Income for 2011	$36,000	Dividends for 2012	$ 20,000
Net Income for 2012	45,000	Total assets at the end of 2011	125,000
Dividends for 2011	15,000	Total assets at the end of 2012	242,000

On the basis of the data given, prepare a statement of retained earnings for 2011 (its first year of operations) and 2012.

LO2, 3 **M1-10 Preparing an Income Statement, Statement of Retained Earnings, and Balance Sheet**

WestJet

Assume the following information was reported in the December 31, 2012, financial statements of WestJet (listed alphabetically, amounts in millions).

Accounts Payable	$1,731	Other Assets	$ 2,581
Accounts Receivable	845	Other Liabilities	3,107
Aircraft Fuel Expense	2,536	Other Operating Expenses	2,145
Cash	2,213	Other Revenue	336
Contributed Capital	2,153	Property and Equipment	10,874
Dividends	14	Repairs and Maintenance Expense	616
Income Tax Expense	413	Retained Earnings (as of December 31, 2012)	4,788
Interest Expense	69	Salaries Expense	3,213
Landing Fees Expense	560	Supplies on Hand	259
Notes Payable	4,993	Ticket Revenues	9,861

1. Prepare an income statement for the year ended December 31, 2012.
2. Prepare a statement of retained earnings for the year ended December 31, 2012.
   TIP: Assume the balance in retained earnings was $4,157 (million) at January 1, 2012.
3. Prepare a balance sheet at December 31, 2012.
4. Using the balance sheet, indicate whether the total assets of WestJet at the end of the year were financed primarily by liabilities or shareholders' equity.

EXERCISES

LO2 **E1-1 Reporting Amounts on the Four Basic Financial Statements**

Using the following table and the equations underlying each of the four basic financial statements, show (*a*) that the balance sheet is in balance, (*b*) that net income is properly calculated, (*c*) what caused changes in the retained earnings account, and (*d*) what caused changes in the cash account.

Assets	$18,200	Beginning Retained Earnings	$3,500
Liabilities	13,750	Ending Retained Earnings	4,300
Shareholders' Equity	4,450	Cash Flows from Operating Activities	1,600
Revenue	10,500	Cash Flows from Investing Activities	(1,000)
Expenses	9,200	Cash Flows from Financing Activities	(900)
Net Income	1,300	Beginning Cash	1,000
Dividends	500	Ending Cash	700

LO2 **E1-2 Reporting Amounts on the Four Basic Financial Statements**

Using the following table and the equations underlying each of the four basic financial statements, show (*a*) that the balance sheet is in balance, (*b*) that net income is properly calculated,

(c) what caused changes in the retained earnings account, and (d) what caused changes in the cash account.

Assets	$79,500	Beginning Retained Earnings	$20,500
Liabilities	18,500	Ending Retained Earnings	28,750
Shareholders' Equity	61,000	Cash Flows from Operating Activities	15,700
Revenue	32,100	Cash Flows from Investing Activities	(7,200)
Expenses	18,950	Cash Flows from Financing Activities	(5,300)
Net Income	13,150	Beginning Cash	3,200
Dividends	4,900	Ending Cash	6,400

E1-3 Preparing a Balance Sheet

LO2, 3

Designer Footwear Inc. is a designer shoe warehouse that sells luxurious and fashionable shoes at prices that people can actually afford. Its balance sheet, at November 1, 2012, contained the following (listed alphabetically, amounts in thousands).

Accounts Payable	$136,405	Other Liabilities	$ 79,148
Accounts Receivable	11,888	Property, Plant, and Equipment	233,631
Cash	45,570	Retained Earnings	179,538
Contributed Capital	291,248	Total Assets	785,383
Notes Payable	99,044	Total Liabilities and Shareholders' Equity	?
Other Assets	494,294		

Required:

1. Prepare the balance sheet as of November 1, solving for the missing amount.
2. As of November 1, did most of the financing for assets come from creditors or shareholders?

E1-4 Completing a Balance Sheet and Inferring Net Income

LO2, 3

Ken Young and Kim Sherwood organized Reader Direct as a corporation; each contributed $49,000 cash to start the business and received 4,000 shares. The store completed its first year of operations on December 31, 2011. On that date, the following financial items for the year were determined: cash on hand and in the bank, $47,500; amounts due from customers from sales of books, $26,900; property and equipment, $48,000; amounts owed to publishers for books purchased, $8,000; one-year note payable to a local bank for $2,850. No dividends were declared or paid to the shareholders during the year.

Check Figure:
Total Assets = $122,400

Required:

1. Complete the following balance sheet at December 31, 2011.

Assets		Liabilities and Shareholders' Equity	
Cash	$_____	**Liabilities**	
Accounts Receivable	_____	Accounts Payable	$_____
Property and Equipment	_____	Note Payable	_____
		Total Liabilities	_____
		Shareholders' Equity	
		Contributed Capital	_____
		Retained Earnings	13,550
		Total Shareholders' Equity	_____
Total Assets	$_____	Total Liabilities and Shareholders' Equity	$_____

2. Using the retained earnings equation and an opening balance of $0, work backward to compute the amount of net income for the year ended December 31, 2011.

3. As of December 31, 2011, did most of the financing for assets come from creditors or shareholders?

4. Assuming that Reader Direct generates net income of $3,000 and pays dividends of $2,000 in 2012, what would be the ending Retained Earnings balance at December 31, 2012?

LO2

E1-5 Labelling and Classifying Business Transactions

Collectibles Canada
(Coins, Bullion, Currency)

The following items relate to business transactions involving Collectibles Canada.

a. Coins, bullion, and currency
b. Amounts that Collectibles Canada owes to suppliers of coins, bullion, and currency
c. Amounts that Collectibles Canada can collect from customers
d. Amounts owed to bank for loan to buy building
e. Property on which buildings will be built
f. Amounts distributed from profits to shareholders
g. Amounts earned by Collectibles Canada by selling coin-collecting supplies
h. Unused paper in Collectibles Canada head office
i. Cost of paper used up during month
j. Amounts contributed to Collectibles Canada by shareholders

Required:

1. Identify an appropriate label (account name) for each item as it would be reported in the company's financial statements.

2. Classify each item as an asset (A), liability (L), shareholders' equity (SE), revenue (R), or expense (E).

LO2, 3

E1-6 Preparing an Income Statement and Inferring Missing Values

Cineplex Entertainment

Cineplex Entertainment operates movie theatres and food concession counters throughout Canada. Assume its income statement for the quarter ended June 26, 2012, reported the following (listed alphabetically, amounts in thousands):

Admissions Revenues	$455,700	Net Income	?
Concessions Expenses	25,500	Other Expenses	$233,800
Concessions Revenues	188,900	Other Revenues	31,200
Film Rental Expenses	247,000	Rent Expense	90,000
General, Selling, and Administrative Expenses	65,700	Total Expenses	?

Required:

1. Solve for the missing amounts and prepare an income statement for the quarter ended June 26, 2012.

   TIP: First put the items in the order they would appear on the income statement and then solve for the missing values.

2. What is Cineplex's main source of revenue? Biggest expense?

LO2

E1-7 Preparing an Income Statement

Check Figure:
Total Expenses = $130,825

Home Realty, Incorporated, has been operating for three years and is owned by three investors. J. Doe owns 60 percent of the total outstanding shares of 9,000 shares and is the managing executive in charge. On December 31, 2012, the following financial items for the entire year were determined: sales revenue, $166,000; selling expenses, $97,000; interest expense, $6,300; promotion and advertising expenses, $9,025; and income tax expense, $18,500. Also during the year, the company declared and paid the owners dividends amounting to $12,000. Prepare the company's income statement.

LO2

E1-8 Inferring Values Using the Income Statement and Balance Sheet Equations

Review the chapter explanations of the income statement and the balance sheet equations. Apply these equations in each of the following independent cases to compute the two missing amounts for each case. Assume that it is the end of the first full year of operations for the company.

   TIP: First identify the numerical relationships among the columns using the balance sheet and income statement equations. Then compute the missing amounts.

Independent Cases	Total Revenues	Total Expenses	Net Income (Loss)	Total Assets	Total Liabilities	Shareholders' Equity
A	$100,000	$82,000	$	$150,000	$70,000	$
B		80,000	12,000	112,000		60,000
C	80,000	86,000		104,000	26,000	
D	50,000		13,000		22,000	77,000
E		81,000	(6,000)		73,000	28,000

E1-9 Preparing an Income Statement and Balance Sheet

LO2, 3

Five individuals organized Moncton Clay Corporation on January 1, 2012. At January 31, 2012, the following monthly financial data are available:

Total Revenues	$131,000
Operating Expenses	90,500
Cash	30,800
Accounts Receivable	25,300
Supplies	40,700
Accounts Payable	25,700
Contributed Capital	30,600

No dividends were declared or paid during January.

Required:

1. Complete the following income statement and balance sheet for the month of January.

MONCTON CLAY CORPORATION
Income Statement
For the Month Ended January 31, 2012

Total Revenues	$_____
Operating Expenses	_____
Net Income	$_____

MONCTON CLAY CORPORATION
Balance Sheet
At January 31, 2012

Assets
Cash $_____
Accounts Receivable   _____
Supplies   _____
Total Assets $_____

Liabilities
Accounts Payable $_____
Total Liabilities   _____
Shareholders' Equity
Contributed Capital   _____
Retained Earnings   _____
Total Shareholders' Equity   _____
Total Liabilities and Shareholders' Equity $_____

2. Discuss whether Moncton Clay Corporation will be able to pay its liabilities. Consider the relationship between total assets and total liabilities.

E1-10 Analyzing and Interpreting an Income Statement

Three individuals organized Pest B-Gone Professionals on January 1, 2012, to provide insect extermination services. The company paid dividends of $10,000 during the year. At the end of 2012, the following income statement was prepared:

PEST B-GONE PROFESSIONALS
Income Statement
For the Year Ended December 31, 2012

Revenues		
Service Revenue	$192,000	
Sales Revenue	24,000	
Total Revenues		$216,000
Expenses		
Supplies Expense	$ 76,000	
Salaries and Wages Expense	33,000	
Advertising Expense	22,000	
Other Expenses	46,000	
Total Expenses		177,000
Net Income		$ 39,000

Required:

1. What was the amount of average monthly revenue?
2. What was the average amount of monthly salaries and wages expense?
3. Explain why advertising is reported as an expense.
4. Explain why the dividends are not reported as an expense.
5. Can you determine how much cash the company had on December 31, 2012? Answer yes or no, and explain your reasoning.

E1-11 Matching Cash Flow Statement Items to Business Activity Categories

Tech Data Corporation

Tech Data Corporation is a leading distributor of computer peripherals and network solutions and was ranked by *Fortune* as the second most admired company in its industry category. The following items were taken from one of its cash flow statements. Mark each item in the following list with a letter to indicate whether it is a cash flow from Operating, Investing, or Financing activities. **Put parentheses around the letter if it is a cash *outflow* and use no parentheses if it's an *inflow*.**

____ 1. Cash paid to suppliers and employees

____ 2. Cash received from customers

____ 3. Cash received from borrowing long-term debt

____ 4. Cash received from issuing shares

____ 5. Cash paid to purchase equipment

E1-12 Matching Cash Flow Statement Items to Business Activity Categories

Coca-Cola Company

The Coca-Cola Company is one of the world's leading manufacturers, marketers, and distributors of nonalcoholic beverage concentrates and syrups, producing more than 300 beverage brands. Mark each item in the following list with a letter to indicate whether it is a cash flow from Operating, Investing, or Financing activities. **Put parentheses around the letter if it is a cash *outflow* and use no parentheses if it's an *inflow*.**

____ 1. Purchases of equipment

____ 2. Cash received from customers

____ 3. Cash received from issuing shares

____ 4. Cash paid to suppliers and employees

____ 5. Cash paid on notes payable

____ 6. Cash received from selling equipment

CP1-1 Preparing an Income Statement, Statement of Retained Earnings, and Balance Sheet

LO2

Assume that you are the president of Nuclear Company. At the end of the first year of operations (December 31, 2012), the following financial data for the company are available:

Cash	$12,000
Accounts Receivable	59,500
Supplies on Hand	8,000
Equipment	36,000
Accounts Payable	30,297
Notes Payable	1,470
Sales Revenue	88,000
Operating Expenses	57,200
Other Expenses	8,850
Contributed Capital	61,983
Dividends	200

Required:

1. Prepare an income statement for the year ended December 31, 2012.

   TIP: Begin by classifying each account as asset, liability, shareholders' equity, revenue, or expense. Each account is reported on only one financial statement.
   TIP: Net Income = $21,950
2. Prepare a statement of retained earnings for the year ended December 31, 2012.

   TIP: Because this is the first year of operations, the beginning balance in Retained Earnings will be zero.
3. Prepare a balance sheet at December 31, 2012.

   TIP: The balance sheet includes the ending balance from the statement of retained earnings.
   TIP: Total Assets = $115,500.

CP1-2 Interpreting the Financial Statements

LO3

Refer to CP1-1.

Required:

1. Evaluate whether the company was profitable.
2. Evaluate whether the company could have paid a greater amount for dividends.
3. Evaluate whether the company is financed mainly by creditors or shareholders.
4. Determine the amount of cash increase or decrease that would be shown in the statement of cash flows.

CP1-3 Reporting Amounts on the Four Basic Financial Statements (Challenging Problem)

LO2

Assume that Fitness and Fun, Inc., reported the following information for the nine-month period ended September 30, 2012. Items are listed alphabetically, and are in thousands of dollars.

Accounts Payable	$ 102,665	Other Liabilities	$ 86,234
Accounts Receivable	5,318	Retained Earnings (January 1, 2012)	199,890
Cash (December 31, 2011)	5,354	Gym Revenues	575,667
Cash (September 30, 2012)	7,119	Gym Operating Expenses	350,835
Contributed Capital	381,728	Advertising and Marketing Expense	23,608
Supplies on Hand	14,739	General, Selling, and Administrative	
Notes Payable	647,120	Expense	83,207
Rent and Other Expenses Payable	119,482	Interest and Other Expenses	20,316
Property and Equipment	1,451,641	Income Tax Expense	38,895
Other Assets	117,108		

Other cash flow information:

Cash received from issuing common shares	$ 9,061
Cash paid to purchase equipment	354,255
Cash paid to suppliers and employees	472,265
Repayments of borrowings	13,043
Cash received from customers	574,824
Cash received from borrowings	95,558
Cash received from sale of long-term assets	161,885
Dividends paid to shareholders	0

Required:

Prepare the four basic financial statements for the nine months ended September 30, 2012.

    TIP: Prepare the four statements in the following order:

a. Income statement
    TIP: Net Income = $58,806
b. Statement of retained earnings
    TIP: Closing Retained Earnings = $258,696
c. Balance sheet
    TIP: Total Assets = $1,595,925
d. Statement of cash flows
    TIP: Cash Provided by Operating Activities = $102,559.
    TIP: Cash Used in Investing Activities = $192,370.
    TIP: Cash Provided by Financing Activities = $91,576.

GROUP A PROBLEMS

Practise and learn online with Connect.

LO2   **PA1-1 Preparing an Income Statement, Statement of Retained Earnings, and Balance Sheet**

*e*X*cel*

Assume that you are the president of High Power Corporation. At the end of the first year of operations (December 31, 2012), the following financial data for the company are available:

Check Figures:
Net Income = $23,450
Total Liabilities = $33,247

Cash	$13,300
Accounts Receivable	9,550
Supplies	5,000
Equipment	86,000
Accounts Payable	32,087
Notes Payable	1,160
Sales Revenue	91,000
Operating Expenses	58,700
Other Expenses	8,850
Contributed Capital	59,103
Dividends	1,950

Required:

1. Prepare an income statement for the year ended December 31, 2012.
2. Prepare a statement of retained earnings for the year ended December 31, 2012.
3. Prepare a balance sheet at December 31, 2012.

LO3   **PA1-2 Interpreting the Financial Statements**

Refer to PA1-1.

Required:

1. Evaluate whether the company was profitable.
2. Evaluate whether the company could have paid a greater amount for dividends.

3. Evaluate whether the company is financed mainly by creditors or shareholders.

4. Determine the amount of cash increase or decrease that would be shown in the statement of cash flows.

PA1-3 Preparing an Income Statement, Statement of Retained Earnings, and Balance Sheet

LO2

Assume that you are the owner/operator of College Park Veterinary Clinic. At the end of the second year of operations (June 30, 2012), the following financial data for the company are available:

Cash	$ 5,000
Accounts Receivable	125,600
Supplies	25,000
Property and Equipment	242,500
Other Assets	13,500
Accounts Payable	87,000
Notes Payable	150,000
Other Liabilities	37,000
Sales Revenue	250,000
Operating Expenses	185,700
General, Selling, and Administrative Expenses	53,400
Advertising and Marketing Expenses	27,800
Interest Expense	5,000
Retained Earnings, July 1, 2011	50,000
Contributed Capital	137,000
Dividends	27,500

Check Figures:
Retained Earnings,
June 30, 2012 = $600
Total Assets = $411,600

Required:

1. Prepare an income statement for the year ended June 30, 2012.
2. Prepare a statement of retained earnings for the year ended June 30, 2012.
3. Prepare a balance sheet at June 30, 2012.

PA1-4 Interpreting the Financial Statements

LO3

Refer to PA1-3.

Required:

1. Evaluate whether the company was profitable.
2. Evaluate whether the company could have paid a greater amount for dividends.
3. Evaluate whether the company is financed mainly by creditors or shareholders.
4. Is it possible to determine the amount of cash increase or decrease that would be shown in the statement of cash flows from the information presented? If not, why not.

PA1-5 Reporting Amounts on the Four Basic Financial Statements

LO2

Assume that the following information for the year ended December 31, 2012, was reported by OSI Restaurant Partners, Inc., the company that owns and operates Outback Steakhouse and Carrabba's Italian Grill restaurants. Amounts are in millions of dollars.

OSI Restaurant Partners, Inc.

Accounts Payable	$ 166	Dividends	$ 39
Wages and Taxes Payable	120	Other Liabilities	517
Cash (balance on January 1, 2012)	84	Other Revenues	21
Cash (balance on December 31, 2012)	94	Property, Fixtures, and Equipment	1,549
Food and Supplies Expense	1,415	Restaurant Sales Revenue	3,920
General, Selling, and Administrative Expenses	235	Utilities and Other Expenses	1,104
		Wages Expense	1,087
Food and Supply Inventories	87	Retained Earnings, January 1, 2012	1,074
Notes Payable	235	Contributed Capital	86
Other Assets	529		

Other cash flow information:

Cash paid to purchase equipment	$ 384
Cash paid to suppliers and employees	2,578
Cash received from customers	2,946
Cash received from bank borrowings	375
Repayments of bank borrowings	294
Cash received from sale of fixtures and equipment	32
Other cash outflows used for financing activities	62
Other cash outflows used for investing activities	2
Common shares issued to owners	16
Dividends paid in cash	39

Required:

Prepare the four basic financial statements for 2012.

GROUP B PROBLEMS

LO2   **PB1-1 Preparing an Income Statement and Balance Sheet**

Assume that you are the president of Aerospace Explorations. At the end of the first year of operations (December 31, 2012), the following financial data for the company are available:

Cash	$13,900
Accounts Receivable	9,500
Supplies	9,000
Equipment	86,000
Accounts Payable	30,277
Notes Payable	1,220
Sales Revenue	94,000
Operating Expenses	60,000
Other Expenses	8,850
Contributed Capital	62,853
Dividends	1,100

Required:

1. Prepare an income statement for the year ended December 31, 2012.
2. Prepare a statement of retained earnings for the year ended December 31, 2012.
3. Prepare a balance sheet at December 31, 2012.

LO3   **PB1-2 Interpreting the Financial Statements**

Refer to PB1-1.

Required:

1. Evaluate whether the company was profitable.
2. Evaluate whether the company could have paid a greater amount for dividends.
3. Evaluate whether the company is financed mainly by creditors or shareholders.
4. Determine the amount of cash increase or decrease that would be shown in the statement of cash flows.

LO2   **PB1-3 Preparing an Income Statement and Balance Sheet**

Assume that you are the president of Rock Point Adventures Inc. At the end of the second year of operations (June 30, 2012), the following financial data for the company are available:

Bank Overdraft	$ 2,058
Accounts Receivable	124,579
Supplies	14,356
Property and Equipment	136,897
Other Assets	3,857
Accounts Payable	58,973
Notes Payable	74,985
Other Liabilities	3,765
Sales Revenue	143,098
Rental Revenue	34,986
Concessions Revenue	25,873
Operating Expenses	74,390
Rent Expense	25,198
Concessions Expenses	21,985
Other Expenses	4,278
Contributed Capital	58,346
Retained Earnings, July 1, 2011	53,456
Dividends	50,000

Required:

1. Prepare an income statement for the year ended June 30, 2012.
2. Prepare a statement of retained earnings for the year ended June 30, 2012.
3. Prepare a balance sheet at June 30, 2012.

PB1-4 Interpreting the Financial Statements

LO2

Refer to PB1-3.

Required:

1. Evaluate whether the company was profitable.
2. Evaluate whether the company could have paid a greater amount for dividends.
3. Evaluate whether the company is financed mainly by creditors or shareholders.
4. Is it possible to determine the amount of cash increase or decrease that would be shown in the statement of cash flows from the information presented? If not, why not.

PB1-5 Reporting Amounts on the Four Basic Financial Statements

LO2

Assume that the Cheesecake Factory reported the following information for the fiscal year ended January 2, 2012. Amounts are in thousands of dollars.

Accounts Payable	$ 45,570	Other Assets	$ 186,453
Accounts Receivable	11,639	Other Liabilities	126,012
Wages and Other Expenses Payable	117,226	Other Revenues	8,171
Cash (balance on January 3, 2011)	31,052	Retained Earnings (beginning)	440,510
Cash (balance on January 2, 2012)	44,790	Prepaid Rent	43,870
Food and Supplies Expense	333,528	Property and Equipment	732,204
General, Selling, and Administrative		Restaurant Sales Revenue	1,315,325
Expenses	72,751	Utilities and Other Expenses	414,978
Food and Supply Inventories	20,775	Wages Expense	420,957
Notes Payable	39,381	Dividends	49,994
Contributed Capital	239,744		

Check Figures:
Net Income = $81,282
Cash Provided by Operating
Activities = $152,655

Other cash flow information:	
Additional investments by shareholders	$ 33,555
Cash paid to purchase equipment	243,211
Cash paid to suppliers and employees	1,123,353
Repayments of borrowings	170,242
Cash received from customers	1,276,008
Cash received from borrowings	175,000
Cash received from sale of long-term assets	115,975
Dividends paid in cash	49,994

Required:

Prepare the four basic financial statements for the fiscal year ended January 2, 2012.

SKILLS DEVELOPMENT CASES

LO1, 2, 3

Rona Inc.

S1-1 Finding Financial Information

Refer to the financial statements of Rona Inc. in Appendix A at the back of this book, or download the annual report from the *Cases* section of Connect.

Required:

1. What is the amount of net income for the year ended December 27, 2009?
2. What amount of sales revenue was earned for the year ended December 27, 2009?
3. How much inventory does the company have on December 27, 2009?
4. How much does Rona Inc. have in cash on December 27, 2009?
5. Rona Inc.'s shares are traded on the Toronto Stock Exchange under the symbol RON. What kind of company does this make Rona Inc.?

LO1, 2, 3

Rona Inc.

S1-2 Comparing Financial Information

Refer to the financial statements of Rona Inc. in Appendix A and those of The Home Depot in Appendix B at the back of this book, or download the annual reports from the *Cases* section of Connect.

Required:

1. Was The Home Depot's net income for the year ended January 31, 2010, greater (or less) than Rona's?
2. Was The Home Depot's sales revenue for the year ended January 31, 2010, greater (or less) than Rona's?
3. Did The Home Depot have more (or less) inventories than Rona at the end of the 2009 fiscal year?
4. Did The Home Depot have more (or less) cash than Rona at the end of the 2009 fiscal year?
5. Is The Home Depot the same type of business organization as Rona Inc.?
6. On an overall basis, was The Home Depot or Rona more successful in the 2009 fiscal year?

LO1, 2, 3

Reuters

S1-3 Internet-Based Team Research: Examining an Annual Report

As a team, select an industry to analyze. Reuters provides lists of industries and their makeup at www.reuters.com. Each group member should access the annual report for one publicly traded company in the industry, with each member selecting a different company. (In addition to the company's own Web site, a great source is the Canadian Securities Administrators' System for Electronic Document Analysis and Retrieval (SEDAR) service. This free source is available by going to the "Search Database" section of www.sedar.com and clicking on "Search for Public Company Documents" and then filling in the required information.

Required:

1. On an individual basis, each team member should write a short report that lists the following information:
    a. What type of business organization is it?
    b. What types of products or services does it sell?

c. On what day of the year does its fiscal year end?

d. For how many years does it present complete balance sheets? Income statements? Cash flow statements?

e. Are its financial statements audited by independent CAs? If so, by whom?

f. Did its total assets increase or decrease over the last year?

g. Did its net income increase or decrease over the last year?

2. Then, as a team, write a short report comparing and contrasting your companies using these attributes. Discuss any patterns across the companies that you as a team observe. Provide potential explanations for any differences discovered.

S1-4 Ethical Decision Making: A Real-Life Example

LO2, 3, 4

Adelphia Communications

In June 2005, John Rigas, the 80-year-old founder and former chief executive officer (CEO) of Adelphia Communications was sentenced to 15 years in jail for defrauding investors and lenders of over a billion dollars. His son, the former chief financial officer (CFO), was sentenced to 20 years in jail. To understand the charges, you need to first understand a bit about Adelphia's history. Adelphia started as a one-town cable company in 1952 and, at the time the fraud accusations were made public, had grown into the sixth-largest cable television provider in the United States. With the company starting as a family-owned business, Adelphia's operations were always a central part of the personal lives of the Rigas family members. However, the extent to which their personal lives were mixed in with the business activities was never clear to shareholders—at least, not nearly as clear as when they were reported in an article in the August 12, 2002, issue of *Fortune*. Under the following questions, we present a table from that article that summarizes how the Rigas family allegedly used over $1.2 billion of Adelphia's money—money that ultimately belonged to Adelphia's shareholders.

1. What is the accounting concept that the Rigas family is accused of violating?

2. Based on the information provided in the following table, can you determine which of the family's dealings are clearly inappropriate and which are clearly appropriate?

3. As a shareholder, how might you attempt to ensure that this kind of behaviour does not occur or, at least, does not occur without you knowing about it?

4. Aside from Adelphia's shareholders, who else might be harmed by these actions committed by the Rigas family?

Family Assets—Sort Of

Some of the notable ways the Rigas family used Adelphia shareholder dollars.

On the Receiving End	Who's Behind the Entity	How Much?
Dobaire Designs	Adelphia paid this company, owned by Doris Rigas (John's wife), for design services.	$371,000
Wending Creek Farms	Adelphia paid John Rigas's farm for lawn care and snowplowing.	$2 million
SongCatcher Films	Adelphia financed the production of a movie by Ellen Rigas (John's daughter).	$3 million
Eleni Interiors	The company made payments to a furniture store run by Doris Rigas and owned by John.	$12 million
The Golf Club at Wending Creek Farms	Adelphia began developing a ritzy golf club.	$13 million
Wending Creek 3656	The company bought timber rights that would eventually revert to a Rigas family partnership.	$26 million
Praxis Capital Ventures	Adelphia funded a venture capital firm run by Ellen Rigas's husband.	$65 million
Niagara Frontier Hockey LP	Adelphia underwrote the Rigas's purchase of the Buffalo Sabres hockey team.	$150 million
Highland 2000	Adelphia guaranteed loans to a Rigas family partnership, which used the funds to buy shares.	$1 billion
Total		$1,271,371,000

S1-5 Ethical Decision Making: A Mini-Case

LO4

You are one of three partners who own and operate Mary's Maid Service. The company has been operating for seven years. One of the other partners has always prepared the company's annual financial statements. Recently, you proposed that the statements be audited each year because it would benefit the partners and prevent possible disagreements about the division of profits. The partner who prepares the statements proposed that his uncle, who has a lot of financial experience, can do the job at little cost. Your other partner remained silent.

Required:

1. What position would you take on the proposal? Justify your response in writing.
2. What would you strongly recommend? Give the basis for your recommendation.

LO2, 3, 4　**S1-6 Critical Thinking: Developing a Balance Sheet and Income Statement**

On September 30, Ashley and Jason started arguing about who is better off. Jason said he was better off because he owned a PlayStation console that he bought last year for $350. He figures that, if needed, he could sell it to a friend for $280. Ashley argued that she was better off because she had $1,000 cash in her bank account and a vintage car that she bought two years ago for $800 but could now sell for $1,400. Jason countered that Ashley still owed $250 on her car loan and that Jason's dad promised to buy him a Porsche if he does really well in his accounting class. Jason said he had $6,000 cash in his bank account right now because he just received a $4,800 student loan. Ashley knows that Jason also owes a tuition instalment of $800 for this term.

　　Ashley and Jason met again in early November. They asked how each other was doing. Ashley claimed that she'd become much more successful than Jason. She had a part-time job, where she earned $1,500 per month. Jason laughed at Ashley because he had won $1,950 on a lottery ticket he bought in October, and that was merely for the "work" of standing in line for a minute. It was just what he needed because his apartment costs $800 each month. Ashley, on the other hand, pays $470 for her share of the rent. Both Ashley and Jason have other normal living costs that total $950 each month.

1. Prepare a financial report that compares what Ashley and Jason each own and owe on September 30. Make a list of any decisions you had to make when preparing your report.
2. In a written report, identify and justify which of the two characters is better off. If you were a creditor, to whom would you rather lend money?
3. Prepare a report that compares what Ashley and Jason each earned during October. Make a list of any decisions you had to make when preparing your report.
4. In a written report, identify and justify which of the two characters is more successful. If you were a creditor considering a three-year loan to one of these characters, to whom would you rather lend money?

LO2　**S1-7 Preparing an Income Statement and Balance Sheet**

Electronic Arts
Sony
Nintendo
Microsoft

Electronic Arts is the world's leading developer and publisher of interactive entertainment software for personal computers and advanced entertainment systems made by Sony, Nintendo, and Microsoft. Assume that the company is revising its methods for displaying its financial statements, and the controller in the accounting department has asked you to create electronic worksheets that the department can use as its standard format for financial statement reporting. The controller has provided you with an alphabetical list of statement categories and account names (below), with corresponding balances (in millions) as of September 30. She has asked you to use a spreadsheet program to create two worksheets that organize the accounts into a properly formatted balance sheet and income statement, and that use formulas to compute amounts represented by question marks below.

Accounts Payable	$ 171	Liabilities		Revenue		
Accounts Receivable	328	Net Income	?	Sales Revenue		$675
Assets		Notes Payable	$ 12	Selling Expense		223
Cash	2,412	Other Assets	283	Shareholders' Equity		
Contributed Capital	986	Other Expenses	1	Total Assets		?
Cost of Goods Sold Expense	284	Other Liabilities	587	Total Expenses		?
Expenses		Promotion Expense	107	Total Liabilities		?
Income Tax Expense	9	Property and Equipment	364	Total Liabilities and		
Inventories	367	Retained Earnings	1,998	Shareholders' Equity		?
				Total Shareholders' Equity		?

Not knowing where to start, you e-mailed your friend Owen for advice on using a spreadsheet. Owen's detailed reply follows.

Required:

Follow Owen's advice to create a balance sheet and income statement, with each statement saved on a separate worksheet in a file called *me*EA.xls where the *me* part of the file name uniquely identifies you.

From:	Owentheaccountant@yahoo.com
To:	Helpme@hotmail.com
Cc:	
Subject:	Excel Help

Hey, pal. Long time, no chat. Here's the scoop on creating those worksheets, with a screenshot too. If you need more help, let me know and I'll submit an application for your position there. ☺

1. Start up Excel to open a new spreadsheet file. You'll need only two worksheets for this assignment, so delete the third worksheet by right-clicking on the *Sheet3* tab at the bottom of the worksheet and selecting Delete. While you're at it, rename *Sheet1* and *Sheet2* to *Balance Sheet* and *Income Statement* by double-clicking on the worksheet tabs and typing in the new names.

2. Plan the layout for your reports. Use the first column as a blank margin, the second column for account names and their headings, and the third column for the numbers corresponding to each account name or total. If you want to apply the same format to all worksheets, begin by right-clicking on the tab at the bottom of a worksheet and choosing Select All Sheets. Next, resize the first column by clicking on the A at the top of that column, then from the Home tab, in the Cells group, click on Format then Column Width . . . , and enter a width of 2. Using this same procedure, resize columns B and C to 50 and 15, respectively.

3. Starting with cell B1, enter the company's name. Enter the report name and date in cells B2 and B3. To merge cells so these headings span more than one column, select the cells to be merged and then click on Format in the Cells group, select Format Cells . . . and click the Merge Cells box in the Text Control section of the Alignment tab. Continue with the body of the report in cell B5, entering any necessary amounts in column C.

4. To use formulas to compute subtotals and totals, the equals sign = is entered first into the cell and is followed immediately by the formula. So, to add a series of amounts, say C7 through C11, use a formula like = SUM(C7:C11), as shown in the screenshot below.

5. After you enter all the data and calculate totals, be sure to save the file. To do this, just click on the Office button in the top left and choose Save As. . . .

6. If you need to print the worksheets, it might be best to highlight what you want printed, then click on the Office button, choose Print. . . , and choose Selection in the Print What box.

7. Go to it, you accounting guru!

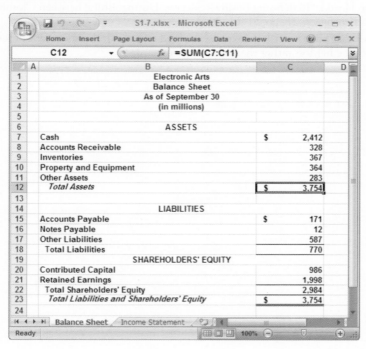

LO2, 3 **CC1 Financial Statements for a Business Plan**

Nicole Mackisey is thinking of forming her own spa business, Nicole's Getaway Spa (NGS). Nicole expects that she and two family members will each contribute $10,000 to the business and receive 1,000 shares each. Nicole forecasts the following amounts for the first year of operations, ending December 31, 2012: cash on hand and in the bank, $2,150; amounts due from customers from spa treatments, $1,780; building and equipment, $70,000; amounts owed to beauty supply outlets for spa equipment, $4,660; notes payable to a local bank for $38,870. Cash dividends of $2,000 will be paid to the shareholders during the year. Nicole also forecasts that first-year sales revenues will be $40,000; wages will be $24,000; the cost of supplies used up will be $7,000; general, selling, and administrative expenses will be $5,000; and income taxes will be $1,600.

Required:

1. Based on Nicole's estimates, prepare a (forecasted) income statement for Nicole's Getaway Spa for the year ended December 31, 2012.
2. Prepare a (forecasted) statement of retained earnings for Nicole's Getaway Spa for the year ended December 31, 2012.
3. Prepare a (forecasted) balance sheet for Nicole's Getaway Spa at December 31, 2012.
4. As of December 31, 2012, would most of the financing for assets come from creditors or shareholders?

Endnotes

1. In fact, 50 percent of all new businesses fail or close within the first six years of opening. Not many start out with a positive net income in the first month. For more information on small business failures, see Brian Headd, "Redefining Business Success: Distinguishing between Closure and Failures," *Small Business Economics, 21*, pp. 51–61, 2003.
2. For companies that have a net loss (expenses exceed revenues), the statement of retained earnings would subtract the net loss rather than add net income.

Practise and learn online with Connect.

CHAPTER 2

Reporting Investing and Financing Results on the Balance Sheet

FOCUS COMPANY:
Pizza Palace, Inc.

PIZZA PALACE

YOUR LEARNING OBJECTIVES

Understand the business

LO1   Identify financial effects of common financing and investing activities.

Study the accounting methods

LO2   Apply transaction analysis to financing and investing transactions.

LO3   Use journal entries and T-accounts to show how transactions affect the balance sheet.

LO4   Prepare a classified balance sheet.

Evaluate the results

LO5   Interpret the balance sheet using the current ratio and an understanding of related concepts.

Review the chapter

Chapter Summary, page 66

Additional resources on Connect

McGraw Hill **connect**™

I n Chapter 1, you read about Emilio Santos' plans for starting a pizza company in Vancouver. Emilio's local CA, Ally, advised him that all businesses, big and small, need systems for gathering and organizing financial information. Just as FedEx must have a way to monitor and evaluate its use of $14.8 billion in delivery equipment,[1] smaller companies like Pizza Palace, Inc., must track the financial results of their activities. With Ally's help, Emilio will implement an accounting system to do this for Pizza Palace. This system will provide the financial information that he needs to manage the company and to report its results to others interested in his business.

The focus in this chapter is on the financing and investing activities that occurred during August when Emilio was establishing Pizza Palace, long before it could open its doors to customers. You will learn how these activities are captured in an accounting system, leading to the assets, liabilities, and shareholders' equity that are reported in a balance sheet. Later, in Chapter 3, you will learn about the operating activities that occur after a business opens its doors to customers and begins generating the revenues and expenses that are reported in an income statement. Your introduction to the accounting system will conclude in Chapter 4, where you will learn about the steps needed to adjust the accounting records before finalizing and evaluating a company's financial results.

THAT WAS
THEN

In the previous chapter, you were introduced to the four main financial statements: the balance sheet, income statement, statement of retained earnings, and statement of cash flows.

THIS IS
NOW

This chapter focuses on just the balance sheet and the accounting system used to produce it.

ORGANIZATION OF THE CHAPTER

Understand the business	Study the accounting methods	Evaluate the results	Review the chapter
• Building a balance sheet • Financing and investing activities • Transactions and other activities	• Step 1: Analyze transactions • Steps 2 and 3: Record and summarize • The debit/credit framework • Preparing a balance sheet	• Assessing the ability to pay • Balance sheet concepts and values	• Demonstration Case • Chapter Summary • Key Terms • Homework Helper • Practice Material

Understand the Business

Learning Objective 1

Identify financial effects of common financing and investing activities.

YOU SHOULD KNOW

Assets: Resources presently owned by a business that generate future economic benefits.

Liabilities: Amounts presently owed by a business.

Shareholders' equity: The amount invested and reinvested in a company by its shareholders.

BUILDING A BALANCE SHEET

After meeting with Ally, Emilio understood that before he could open his restaurant, he would first have to establish the business. This would involve acquiring **assets** that Pizza Palace would use for many months or years to come. The assets would be owned by Pizza Palace, but creditors would have a claim to those assets equal to the amount of **liabilities** that the company owed. As owners of Pizza Palace, Emilio and his wife also would have a claim on the company's assets (**shareholders' equity**), but their claim would be secondary to creditors' claims. Emilio remembered that the balance sheet was structured like the basic accounting equation (A = L + SE), but it was only by accounting for Pizza Palace's actual activities that he truly learned how a balance sheet was built.

FINANCING AND INVESTING ACTIVITIES

A key activity for any start-up company, such as Pizza Palace, is to obtain financing. Two sources of financing are available to businesses: equity and debt. *Equity* refers to financing that a business obtains through owners' contributions and reinvestments of profit. *Debt* refers to financing that the business obtains through loans. A business is obligated to repay debt financing, but it is not obligated to repay its equity financing.

Like most small business owners, Emilio and his wife used their personal savings to make an initial cash contribution to the company. They decided to contribute $50,000, which is more than they had originally planned, but by relying more on equity financing, the company wouldn't require quite as much debt financing. When a business receives cash contributions from its owners like this, it gives documents called *share certificates* to the owners as evidence of their ownership.

Emilio had determined that Pizza Palace would need additional money to become established so, on behalf of the company, he applied for a loan from a bank. Soon after the loan was approved, Pizza Palace received $20,000 cash in exchange for its promise to repay the loan in two years. The terms for repaying the loan were described in detail on a legal document called a *promissory note*. Pizza Palace's initial financing activities are pictured in Exhibit 2.1.

EXHIBIT 2.1 **Financing Activities**

Issue shares
The business receives $50,000 cash.
The business gives share certificates.

Obtain loan
The business receives $20,000 cash.
The business gives a promissory note.

After obtaining initial financing, a company will start **investing** in assets that will be used later when the business opens. In the case of Pizza Palace, Emilio first spent $42,000 cash by writing company cheques to buy and install restaurant booths, cash registers, and other equipment. The company also needed to buy cookware and related items like pizza pans, pizza cutters, serving plates, cutlery, drink glasses, napkin holders, and cheese and spice shakers. These items could be purchased with cash, but that would be inconvenient and inefficient. Instead, businesses typically buy goods or services from others on credit, by promising to pay within 30 days of the purchase. Pizza Palace bought $630 of these items on credit, as indicated by the supplier's bill (or *invoice*). These examples, pictured in Exhibit 2.2, are just a few of Pizza Palace's investing activities.

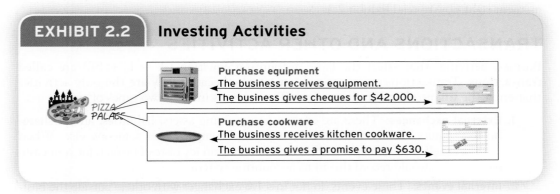

EXHIBIT 2.2 **Investing Activities**

Purchase equipment
The business receives equipment.
The business gives cheques for $42,000.

Purchase cookware
The business receives kitchen cookware.
The business gives a promise to pay $630.

By carefully reading Exhibits 2.1 and 2.2, you will see three features that will be important for understanding how accounting works:

1. The company always **documents** its activities. Share certificates, promissory notes, cheques, and invoices indicate the nature of the underlying business activity.

2. The company always **receives** something and **gives** something. This is a basic feature of all business activities. A business enters into an exchange either to earn a profit immediately or to obtain resources that will allow it to earn a profit later. This is the fundamental idea of business: to create value through exchange. Any exchange that affects the company's assets, liabilities, or shareholders' equity must be captured in and reported by the accounting system. Because the accounting system captures both what is received and what is given, it is often referred to as a *double-entry* system.

3. Each exchange is analyzed to determine a dollar amount that represents the value of items given and received. This value is called the **cost** and is used to measure the financial effects of the exchange, as required by the **cost principle**.

As illustrated in Exhibit 2.3, these three features are key inputs into the process used when accounting for business activities. After each activity is documented, accountants assign

YOU SHOULD KNOW

Cost principle: Assets and liabilities should be initially recorded at their original cost to the company.

EXHIBIT 2.3 **Accounting for Business Activities**

Picture the documented activity
Picture what is described in words. This step is easily overlooked but is vital to succeeding in the next step.

Name what's exchanged
Building on the previous step, assign names to what your business has received and given.

Analyze the financial effects
Building on the last step, show how the costs cause elements of the accounting equation to increase and/or decrease.

names to the items exchanged and then analyze their financial effects on the accounting equation. The ultimate goal is to capture these financial effects so that they can be reported in the financial statements for use by decision makers inside and outside the company. Take a moment right now to read Exhibit 2.3.

TRANSACTIONS AND OTHER ACTIVITIES

YOU SHOULD KNOW

Transaction: An event or activity that has a direct and measurable financial effect on the assets, liabilities, or shareholders' equity of a business.

Business activities that affect the basic accounting equation (A = L + SE) are called **transactions**. Transactions are of special importance because they are the only activities that enter the financial accounting system. Transactions include two types of events:

1. **External exchanges:** These are exchanges involving assets, liabilities, and/or shareholders' equity that you can see between the company and someone else. When Starbucks sells you a Frappucino®, it is exchanging an icy taste of heaven for your cash, so Starbucks would record this in its accounting system.
2. **Internal events:** These events do not involve exchanges with others outside the business, but rather occur within the company itself. For example, when the company Red Bull combines sugar, water, taurine, and caffeine, something magical happens: these ingredients turn into Red Bull Energy Drink. This internal event is a transaction because it has a direct financial effect whereby some assets (supplies of sugar, etc.) are used up to create a different asset (an inventory of Red Bull drinks).

During the first month of business, some important activities that occur will not be captured by the accounting system because they are not transactions. For example, Emilio signed a contract on behalf of Pizza Palace to rent restaurant space in a building. This activity was not a transaction because no assets or services were exchanged at that time. The landlord exchanged a promise to rent the building for Pizza Palace's promise to pay rent, but **an exchange of only promises is not an accounting transaction**. For this same reason, Pizza Palace's accounting system did not capture other activities such as placing orders with suppliers or promising to hire employees. Documents were created to indicate that these activities occurred, but they were appropriately excluded from the accounting records because these were not transactions. Later, when these promises result in actually receiving or giving an asset or service, they will become transactions to be captured by the accounting system.

A systematic accounting process is used to capture and report the financial effects of a company's activities. This process includes three basic steps:

① Analyze ⟶ ② Record ⟶ ③ Summarize

Learning Objective 2

Apply transaction analysis to financing and investing transactions.

STEP 1: ANALYZE TRANSACTIONS

The process in Exhibit 2.3 is commonly referred to as *transaction analysis,* which involves determining whether a transaction exists and, if it does, analyzing its impact on the accounting equation. Two simple ideas are used when analyzing transactions:

1. **Duality of effects.** It's a fancy name, but the idea is simple. Every transaction has at least two effects on the basic accounting equation. To remember this, just think of expressions like "give and receive" or "push and pull" or, if you're a closet scientist, Newton's Third Law of Motion.

2. **A = L + SE.** You know this already, right? Well, just remember that the dollar amount for assets must always equal the total of liabilities plus shareholders' equity for every accounting transaction. If it doesn't, then you are missing something and you should go back to the first idea (duality of effects).

As part of transaction analysis, a name is given to each item exchanged. Accountants refer to these names as *account titles.* To ensure account titles are used consistently, every company establishes a **chart of accounts**—a list that designates a name and reference number that the company will use when accounting for each item that it exchanges. A partial chart of accounts for Pizza Palace is shown in Exhibit 2.4. (The chart of accounts shown in this chapter includes only balance sheet accounts. Chapter 3 will expand this to include additional assets and liabilities as well as revenue and expense accounts.) A more comprehensive chart of accounts to use when completing homework assignments is presented in the Homework Helper on page 67.

YOU SHOULD KNOW

Chart of accounts: A summary of all account names (and corresponding account numbers) used to record financial results in the accounting system.

EXHIBIT 2.4	Pizza Palace's (Partial) Chart of Accounts

Account Number	Account Name	Description
101	Cash	– Dollar amount of coins, paper money, funds in bank
113	Cookware	– Cost of cutlery, pizza pans, dishes, etc.
135	Equipment	– Cost of pizza ovens, restaurant booths, dishwashers, etc.
201	Accounts Payable	– Owed to suppliers for goods or services bought on credit
222	Note Payable	– Owed to lenders, as per terms of promissory note
301	Contributed Capital	– Shares issued for contributions made to the company
310	Retained Earnings	– Accumulated earnings (not yet distributed as dividends)

The chart of accounts is tailored to each company's business, so although some account titles are common across all companies (Cash, Accounts Payable), others may be used only by a particular company (Cookware). Depending on the company, you may see a liability for a bank loan called a *Note Payable* or a *Loan Payable*.[2]

The best way to learn how to account for business activities is to work through examples. So skim the names and descriptions in Exhibit 2.4 one more time and then let's look more closely at Pizza Palace's financing and investing activities.

(a) Issue Shares to Owners Emilio Santos incorporates Pizza Palace, Inc., on August 1. The company issues shares to Emilio and his wife as evidence of their contribution of $50,000 cash, which is deposited in the company's bank account.

 **COACH'S TIP**

Analyze transactions from the standpoint of the business, not of its owners.

Picture   Receives   Gives

Name
- Pizza Palace has received **$50,000 in cash.**
- Pizza Palace gave **$50,000** of **shares (contributed capital).**

Analyze

	Assets		=	Liabilities	+	Shareholders' Equity	
(a)	Cash	+50,000	=			Contributed Capital	+50,000

Notice that in the accounting equation table above, we included a reference (a) so that we can refer back to the original transaction description if needed. You too should use transaction letters (or numbers or dates) as references in your homework problems. The goal of transaction analysis is to identify the specific accounts affected, the dollar amount of the change in the accounts, and the direction of this change (+ or −) on the accounting equation category. In example (a), an asset (Cash) increases by $50,000, which equals the increase in the shareholders' equity account (Contributed Capital).

(b) Invest in Equipment Pizza Palace pays $42,000 cash to buy restaurant booths and other equipment.

Picture   Receives   Gives

Name
- Pizza Palace has received **$42,000** of **equipment.**
- Pizza Palace gave **$42,000 cash.**

Analyze

	Assets		=	Liabilities	+	Shareholders' Equity
(b)	Cash	−42,000	=			No Change
	Equipment	+42,000				

Notice that even though transaction (b) did not affect liabilities or shareholders' equity, the accounting equation remained in balance because the decrease in one asset (Cash) was offset by the increase in another asset (Equipment). The accounting equation must always "balance" (be equal) for each transaction.

(c) Obtain Loan from Bank Pizza Palace borrows $20,000 from a bank, depositing those funds in its bank account and signing a formal agreement to repay the loan in two years.

Picture   Receives   Gives

Name
- Pizza Palace has received $20,000 cash.
- Pizza Palace gave a **note payable** to the bank for $20,000.

COACH'S TIP

Notes payable are like accounts payable except that they (a) charge interest, (b) can be outstanding for long periods (more than one year), and (c) are documented using formal documents called *notes*.

Analyze

	Assets	=	Liabilities	+	Shareholders' Equity
(c)	Cash + 20,000	=	Note Payable +20,000		

(d) Invest in Equipment Pizza Palace purchases $18,000 in pizza ovens and other restaurant equipment, paying $16,000 in cash and giving an informal promise to pay $2,000 at the end of the month.

Picture   Receives   Gives   &

Name
- Pizza Palace has received $18,000 of equipment.
- Pizza Palace gave $16,000 cash and a promise to **pay $2,000** on **account**.

COACH'S TIP

Although we use the same format for all of our examples, the content in each differs. Don't skip this section with the plan of coming back to it later, because the next part of this chapter builds on this part. Most students say that, of all the topics in this course, transaction analysis is the one they wished they had spent more time on when first learning it.

Analyze

	Assets	=	Liabilities	+	Shareholders' Equity
(d)	Cash −16,000	=	Accounts Payable +2,000		
	Equipment +18,000				

If you ever run into a transaction that you have no idea how to analyze, try to break it down. Rather than trying to solve it all at once, begin by looking just for what is received.

Another strategy is to look for any cash exchanged because by getting a handle on that part of the transaction, the other parts often become easier to see. Always be sure to summarize the effects in terms of the accounting equation, because it must balance if you've detected all the accounts affected by the transaction.

(e) Order Cookware Pizza Palace orders $630 of pans, dishes, and other cookware. None have been received yet.

COACH'S TIP

Not all business activities are considered accounting transactions.

| **Picture** | Promise of Future Delivery | ← Receives | Gives → | Promise to Pay for Purchase |

| **Name** | • An exchange of only promises is not a transaction.
• This does not affect the accounting equation. |

| **Analyze** | Assets = Liabilities + Shareholders' Equity
(e) No Change = No Change |

Not all documented business activities are considered accounting transactions. As shown in (e), Pizza Palace and the supplier have documented the order, but it involves an exchange of only promises, so it is not an accounting transaction.

(f) Pay Supplier Pizza Palace pays $2,000 to the equipment supplier in (d).

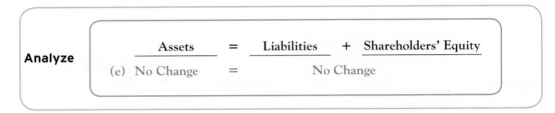

| **Picture** | [PAID invoice 664251] | ← Receives | Gives → | [cash] |

| **Name** | • Pizza Palace has received a release from its **$2,000** promise to pay **on account.**
• Pizza Palace gave **$2,000 cash.** |

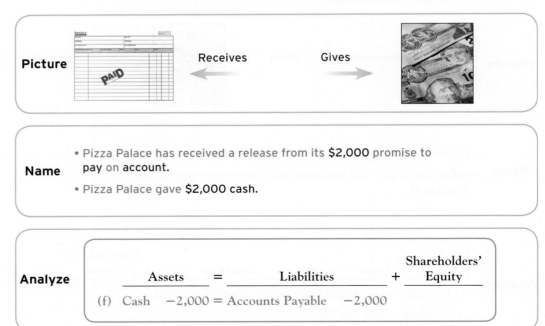

| **Analyze** | Assets = Liabilities + Shareholders' Equity
(f) Cash −2,000 = Accounts Payable −2,000 |

In (f), Pizza Palace fulfills its liability by paying the amount owed to a supplier. Thus, the Accounts Payable is decreased because, in exchange for its payment to the supplier, Pizza Palace receives a release from its original promise to pay the supplier.

(g) Receive Cookware Pizza Palace receives $630 of the cookware ordered in (e) and promises to pay for it next month.

Picture	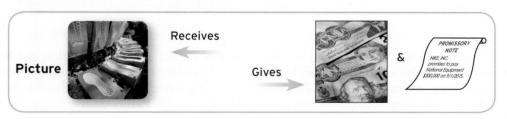

Name
- Pizza Palace has received **cookware** costing **$630.**
- Pizza Palace gave a promise to **pay $630** on **account.**

Analyze

	Assets	=	Liabilities	+	Shareholders' Equity
(g)	Cookware +630	=	Accounts Payable +630		

As we said before, the best way to learn accounting is to do examples, so try the following practice question. (Cover the answers in the margin until you're finished.)

💡 HOW'S IT GOING? Self-Study Practice

Complete the following transaction analysis steps by filling in the empty boxes, and then check your answers with the solution in the margin.

NIKE, Inc., purchased equipment costing $500,000, paying $200,000 cash and signing a formal promissory note to pay the balance in three years.

Picture	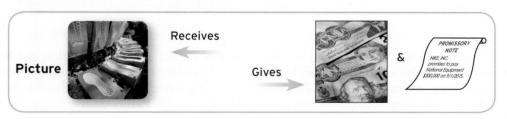

Name

Nike has received _____.

Nike gave _____.

Analyze

	Assets	=	Liabilities	+	Shareholder's Equity
	☐	=	☐	+	☐

After you have finished, check your answer with the solution in the margin.

Solution to Self-Study Practice

NIKE has received equipment costing $500,000.
NIKE gave $200,000 cash and a $300,000 note.

Assets	=	Liabilities	+	Shareholders' Equity
Cash −200,000	=	Note Payable +300,000		
Equipment +500,000				

STEPS 2 AND 3: RECORD AND SUMMARIZE

In the previous section, you learned how to analyze transactions, which ended with an understanding of the financial effects of each transaction on a company's asset, liability, and shareholders' equity accounts. In an academic setting, we have encouraged you to write down these accounting equation effects. In the workplace, an accountant would not actually capture the effects in this way. Instead, after determining the financial effects of a transaction, an accountant would capture the effects through two additional steps: recording and summarizing.

One way to record and summarize the financial effects of transactions would be to enter your understanding of their effects into a spreadsheet like the one shown in Exhibit 2.5. By summing each spreadsheet column, you could compute new balances at the end of each month and report them on a balance sheet.

EXHIBIT 2.5	Using a Spreadsheet to Record and Summarize Transactions

Exhibit 2.5.xlsx - Microsoft Excel

	A	B	C	D	E	F	G	H	I	J
1				Assets		=	Liabilities		+	Shareholders' Equity
2			Cash	Cookware	Equipment		Accounts Payable	Notes Payable		Contributed Capital
3		Beginning	0	0	0	=	0	0		0
4		(a)	+50,000			=				+50,000
5		(b)	-42,000		+42,000	=				
6		(c)	+20,000			=		+20,000		
7		(d)	-16,000		+18,000	=	+2,000			
8		(e)		no change		=		no change		
9		(f)	-2,000			=	-2,000			
10		(g)		+630		=	+630			
11		Ending	10,000	630	60,000	=	630	20,000	+	50,000

A spreadsheet makes it easy to see the individual impact of each transaction and how transactions combine with beginning balances to yield ending balances, but it is impractical for most large organizations to use. Just imagine how big a spreadsheet would have to be to handle millions of transactions affecting hundreds of accounts. Rather than create a spreadsheet the size of three football fields, a more manageable system is used.

Most companies record and summarize the financial effects of transactions with computerized accounting systems, which can handle a large number of transactions. These systems follow a cycle, called the accounting cycle, which is repeated day after day, month after month, and year after year. As shown in Exhibit 2.6, a three-step analyze–record–summarize process is applied to daily transactions and is then followed by adjustments and closing processes at the end of the accounting period. Our focus in Chapter 2 is on applying the three-step process during the period to activities that affect only balance sheet accounts. After you have become comfortable with this process, you will learn (in Chapter 3) to apply this process to operating activities that affect both balance sheet and income statement accounts. In Chapter 4, you will learn how the process is applied at the end of the accounting period, when the accounting records are adjusted and closed.

The three-step process of analyzing, recording, and summarizing is a lot like what you do as a student when attending class, taking notes, and preparing for exams. Day after day, you analyze what is said in class and you record important points in a notebook, which is kind of like an academic diary or journal. Later, when preparing for exams, you copy your notes to summary sheets to study from. The same ideas are used in the accounting cycle. Transactions

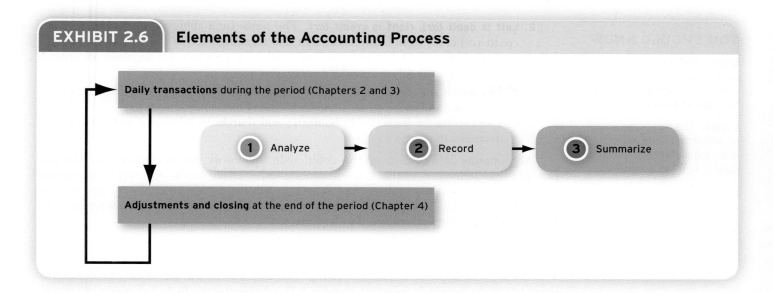

EXHIBIT 2.6 | **Elements of the Accounting Process**

Daily transactions during the period (Chapters 2 and 3)

1 Analyze → **2** Record → **3** Summarize

Adjustments and closing at the end of the period (Chapter 4)

are analyzed, and their financial effects are entered into **journals** each day they occur. Later, these journal entries are summarized in **ledger** accounts that keep track of the financial effects on each account. To make this process as efficient as possible, journals and ledger accounts share the same underlying framework discussed in the following section.

THE DEBIT/CREDIT FRAMEWORK

The framework used for journals and ledger accounts was created more than 500 years ago, yet it continues to exist in accounting systems today. Although computers now perform many routine accounting tasks involving journals and ledger accounts, most computerized systems still require you to know how these accounting records work. To understand this framework, think of the accounting equation (A = L + SE) as an old-fashioned weight scale that tips at the equals sign. Assets—like Cash and Equipment—are put on the left side of the scale and liabilities and shareholders' equity accounts are put on the right. Likewise, each individual account has two sides, with one side used for increases and the other for decreases, similar to what is shown in Exhibit 2.7.

Learning Objective 3

Use journal entries and T-accounts to show how transactions affect the balance sheet

EXHIBIT 2.7 | **The Debit/Credit Framework**

	Assets	=		Liabilities	+		Shareholders' Equity	
+	Assets	**−**	**−**	Liabilities	**+**	**−**	Shareholders' Equity	**+**
Increase using Debit		Decrease using Credit	Decrease using Debit		Increase using Credit	Decrease using Debit		Increase using Credit

Take special note of two important rules illustrated in Exhibit 2.7:

1. **Accounts increase on the same side as they appear in A = L + SE.** Accounts on the left side of the accounting equation increase on the left side of the account and accounts on the right side of the equation increase on the right. So
   • Assets increase on the left side of the account.
   • Liabilities increase on the right side of the account.
   • Shareholders' equity accounts increase on the right side of the account.
   • Decreases are the opposite, as shown in Exhibit 2.7.

YOU SHOULD KNOW

Debit: The left side of an account, or the act of entering an amount into the left side of an account.

Credit: The right side of an account, or the act of entering an amount into the right side of an account.

2. **Left is debit (*dr*), right is credit (*cr*).** The terms (and abbreviations) **debit** (*dr*) and **credit** (*cr*) come from Latin words that had meaning back in the day, but today they just mean *left* and *right*. When combined with how increases and decreases are entered into accounts, the following rules emerge:

- Use debits for increases in assets (and for decreases in liabilities and shareholders' equity accounts).
- Use credits for increases in liabilities and shareholders' equity accounts (and for decreases in assets).

Accountants didn't dream up this debit/credit framework just to confuse you. The purpose of this double-entry system is to introduce another check on the accuracy of accounting numbers. In addition to requiring that A = L + SE, the double-entry system also requires that debits = credits. If either of these relationships is not equal, then you know for sure that you've made an error that will need to be corrected.

Step 1: Analyzing Transactions

The debit/credit framework does not change this first step of the accounting process. Continue to use the approach shown in Exhibit 2.3 to determine the financial effects of transactions, which you will learn to enter into the accounting system in step 2.

Step 2: Recording Journal Entries

YOU SHOULD KNOW

Journal entries: Indicate the effects of each day's transactions in a debits-equal-credits format.

The financial effects of transactions are entered into a journal using a debits-equal-credits format, as shown in Exhibit 2.8. When looking at these **journal entries**, as they are called, notice the following:

- A date is included for each transaction.
- Debits appear first (on top). Credits are written below the debits and are indented to the right (both the words and the amounts). The order of the debited accounts or credited accounts doesn't matter, as long as for each journal entry debits are on top and credits are on the bottom and indented.
- Total debits equal total credits for each transaction (for example, see the entry on August 5 where $18,000 = $16,000 + $2,000).
- Dollar signs are not used because the journal is understood to be a record of financial effects.

EXHIBIT 2.8 **Formal Journal Page**

General Journal				Page G1
Date	Account Titles and Explanation	Ref.	Debit	Credit
2012				
Aug. 1	Cash		50,000	
	Contributed Capital			50,000
	(Financing from shareholders.)			
Aug. 2	Equipment		42,000	
	Cash			42,000
	(Bought equipment using cash.)			
Aug. 5	Equipment		18,000	
	Cash			16,000
	Accounts Payable			2,000
	(Bought equipment using cash and			
	credit.)			

- The reference column (Ref.) will be used later (in step 3) to indicate when the journal entry has been summarized in the ledger accounts.
- A brief explanation of the transaction is written below the debits and credits.
- The line after the explanation is left blank before writing the next journal entry.

When writing journal entries in this course, we'll make a few minor changes to the formal entries, which should make it easier for you to learn the most important aspects of recording journal entries. The way we would show the journal entry for August 5 is

(d)   *dr* **Equipment** (+A).. 18,000
      cr **Cash** (−A)   16,000
      cr **Accounts Payable** (+L)   2,000

The main differences between our simplified format and a formal journal entry are

- When a date is not given, use some form of reference for each transaction, such as (d), to identify the event.
- Omit the reference column and transaction explanation to simplify the entry.
- Indicate whether you are debiting (*dr*) or crediting (*cr*) each account. This will help to reinforce the debit/credit framework shown in Exhibit 2.7. Plus, it will make it easier to interpret journal entries when indents are not clear (sometimes an issue in handwritten homework).
- Include the appropriate account type (A, L, or SE) along with the direction of the effect (+ or −) next to each account title to clarify the effects of the transaction on each account. Again, this will reinforce the debit/credit framework and help you to determine whether the accounting equation has remained in balance.

Step 3: Summarizing in Ledger Accounts

By themselves, journal entries show the effects of each individual transaction but they do not provide account balances. That's why ledger accounts are needed. After journal entries have been recorded (in step 2), their dollar amounts are copied (**posted**) to each ledger account affected by the transaction so that account balances can be computed. In most computerized accounting systems, this happens automatically. In homework assignments, you'll have to do it yourself, so Exhibit 2.9 shows you how this is done using the journal entry for August 5. If account numbers are provided, keep track of the posting of journal entries to general ledger accounts by writing the account number in the Ref. column of the journal and the journal page number in the Ref. column of the ledger.

As we did earlier for journal entries, we will use a simplified format for ledger accounts to make it easier to focus on their main features. The simplified version of a ledger account is called a **T-account**. Each T-account represents the debit and credit columns of a ledger account. Exhibit 2.10 shows the T-accounts for Pizza Palace's Equipment, Cash, and Accounts Payable based on transactions (a) through (d) on pages 46–48. It also shows how an individual journal entry's effects would be summarized in these T-accounts. The debit to Equipment in the journal entry is copied into the debit (left) side of its T-account. The credits to Cash and Accounts Payable are copied into the credit (right) side of those T-accounts. (If you've forgotten why the transaction is recorded this way, take a quick look back at Exhibit 2.7 on page 51 or at the graphic to the right.)

In Exhibit 2.10, notice the following:

- Every account starts with a beginning balance, usually on the side where increases are summarized. For balance sheet accounts, the ending balance from the prior period is the beginning balance for the current period. Because Pizza Palace is in its first month of business, the beginning balance in each account is zero in this example.

YOU SHOULD KNOW

Posting: The process of transferring details of journal entries into the corresponding ledger accounts.

T-account: A simplified version of a ledger account used for summarizing the effects of journal entries.

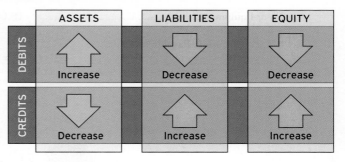

	ASSETS	LIABILITIES	EQUITY
DEBITS	⬆ Increase	⬇ Decrease	⬇ Decrease
CREDITS	⬇ Decrease	⬆ Increase	⬆ Increase

EXHIBIT 2.9   Posting from the Journal to the Ledger

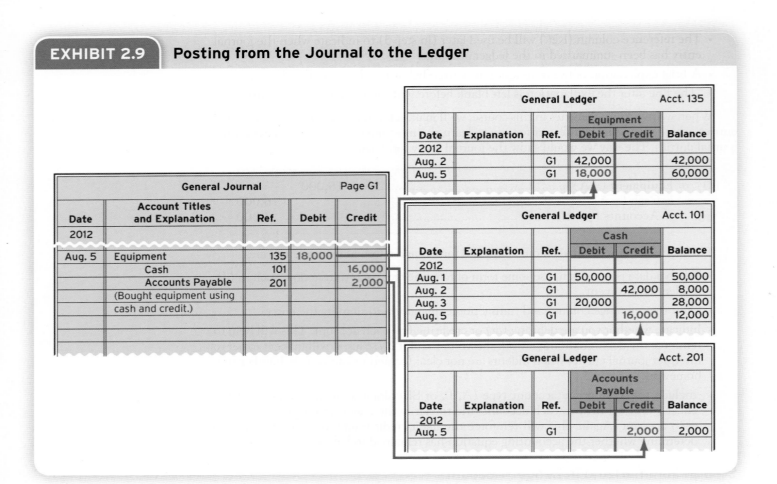

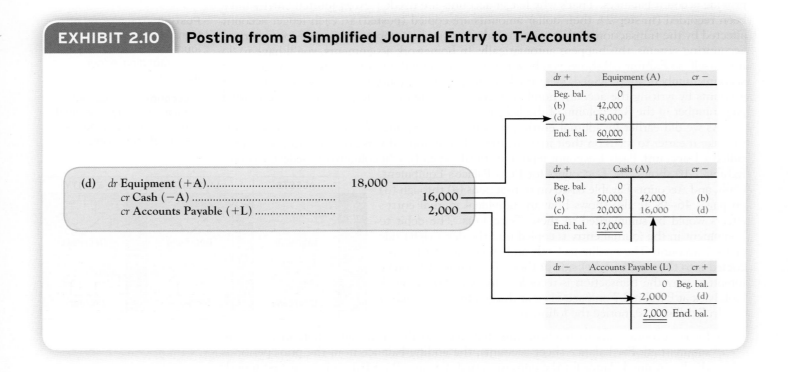

- Dollar signs are not needed.
- Each amount is accompanied by a reference to the related journal entry, which makes it easy to trace back to the original transaction should errors occur.
- To find ending account balances, express the T-accounts as equations:

	Equipment	Cash	Accounts Payable
Beginning balance	0	0	0
Add: "+" side	42,000	+50,000	+2,000
	18,000	+20,000	
Subtract: "−" side		−42,000	
		−16,000	
Ending balance	60,000	12,000	2,000

COACH'S TIP

Assets normally end with a debit balance (because debits to assets normally exceed credits) and liabilities and shareholders' equity accounts normally end with credit balances (credits exceed debits).

Knowing how to use T-accounts in this way will help you answer homework questions that involve solving for missing values in accounts.

- The ending balance is double underlined to distinguish it from transactions and symbolize the final result of a computation. The ending balance is shown on the side that has the greater total dollar amount.

Pizza Palace's Accounting Records

In this section, we will work with you to account for the transactions that were presented earlier in this chapter for Pizza Palace. Because we show the analyze step in detail on pages 45–49, we do not show it in detail here. Instead, we pick up where step 1 left off—with the effects of each transaction on the accounting equation. By reviewing steps 2 and 3 of the accounting cycle in detail, you will be able to practise using the new concepts of debits, credits, journal entries, and T-accounts. Study the following examples carefully. The biggest mistake people make when first learning accounting is that they think they understand how it all works without actually going through enough examples. To understand accounting, you have to practise, practise, practise, as if you're learning to play a new sport or a musical instrument.

(a) Issue Shares to Owners Emilio Santos incorporates Pizza Palace, Inc., on August 1. The company issues shares to Emilio and his wife as evidence of their contribution of $50,000 cash, which is deposited in the company's bank account.

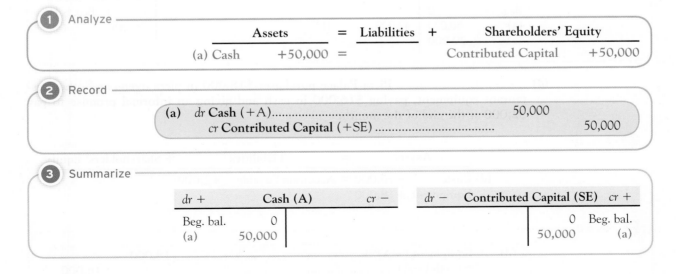

1 Analyze

	Assets	=	Liabilities	+	Shareholders' Equity
(a) Cash	+50,000	=			Contributed Capital +50,000

2 Record

(a)	dr **Cash** (+A)...	50,000	
	cr **Contributed Capital** (+SE)		50,000

3 Summarize

dr +	Cash (A)	cr −		dr −	Contributed Capital (SE)	cr +
Beg. bal.	0				0	Beg. bal.
(a)	50,000				50,000	(a)

(b) Invest in Equipment Pizza Palace pays $42,000 cash to buy restaurant booths and other equipment.

1 Analyze

	Assets		=	Liabilities	+	Shareholders' Equity
(b) Cash		−42,000				
Equipment		+42,000				

2 Record

(b)	*dr* **Equipment** (+A)..	42,000	
	cr **Cash** (−A)..		42,000

3 Summarize

dr +	Cash (A)		*cr* −		*dr* +	Equipment (A)		*cr* −
Beg. bal.	0				Beg. bal.	0		
(a)	50,000	42,000	(b)		(b)	42,000		

(c) Obtain Loan from Bank Pizza Palace borrows $20,000 from a bank, depositing those funds in its bank account and signing a formal agreement to repay the loan in two years.

1 Analyze

	Assets		=	Liabilities		+ Shareholders' Equity
(c) Cash	+20,000		=	Note Payable	+20,000	

2 Record

(c)	*dr* **Cash** (+A)..	20,000	
	cr **Note Payable** (+L)..		20,000

3 Summarize

dr +	Cash (A)		*cr* −		*dr* −	Note Payable (L)		*cr* +
Beg. bal.	0						0	Beg. bal.
(a)	50,000	42,000	(b)				20,000	(c)
(c)	20,000							

(d) Invest in Equipment Pizza Palace purchases $18,000 in pizza ovens and other restaurant equipment, paying $16,000 in cash and giving an informal promise to pay $2,000 at the end of the month.

1 Analyze

	Assets		=	Liabilities		+ Shareholders' Equity
(d) Cash	−16,000		=	Accounts Payable	+2,000	
Equipment	+18,000					

2 Record

(d)	*dr* **Equipment** (+A)..	18,000	
	cr **Cash** (−A)..		16,000
	cr **Accounts Payable** (+L)		2,000

dr +	Cash (A)		cr −
Beg. bal.	0		
(a)	50,000	42,000	(b)
(c)	20,000	16,000	(d)

dr +	Equipment (A)	cr −
Beg. bal.	0	
(b)	42,000	
(d)	18,000	

dr −	Accounts Payable (L)	cr +
	0	Beg. bal.
	2,000	(d)

(e) Order Cookware Pizza Palace orders $630 of pans, dishes, and other cookware. None have been received yet. Because this event involves the exchange of only promises, it is not considered a transaction. No journal entry is needed.

(f) Pay Supplier Pizza Palace pays $2,000 to the equipment supplier in (d).

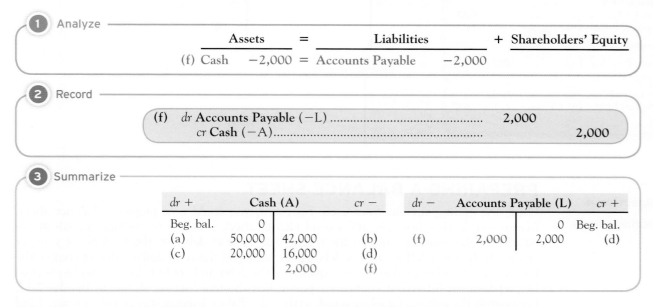

① Analyze

Assets	=	Liabilities	+	Shareholders' Equity
(f) Cash −2,000	=	Accounts Payable −2,000		

② Record

(f) dr Accounts Payable (−L) 2,000
       cr Cash (−A)... 2,000

③ Summarize

dr +	Cash (A)		cr −
Beg. bal.	0		
(a)	50,000	42,000	(b)
(c)	20,000	16,000	(d)
		2,000	(f)

dr −	Accounts Payable (L)	cr +
(f)	2,000	0 Beg. bal.
		2,000 (d)

(g) Receive Cookware Pizza Palace receives $630 of the cookware ordered in (e) and promises to pay for it next month.

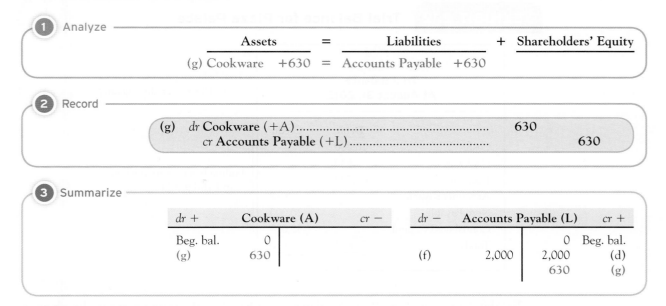

① Analyze

Assets	=	Liabilities	+	Shareholders' Equity
(g) Cookware +630	=	Accounts Payable +630		

② Record

(g) dr Cookware (+A)... 630
       cr Accounts Payable (+L)... 630

③ Summarize

dr +	Cookware (A)	cr −
Beg. bal.	0	
(g)	630	

dr −	Accounts Payable (L)	cr +
(f)	2,000	0 Beg. bal.
		2,000 (d)
		630 (g)

Exhibit 2.11 summarizes the journal entries and T-accounts affected by events (a) through (g) for Pizza Palace. It also reports the ending balances for each account.

EXHIBIT 2.11 **Journal Entries and T-Accounts for Pizza Palace**

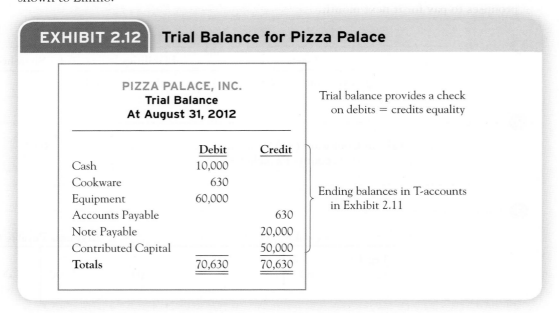

| Assets | = | Liabilities | + | Shareholders' Equity |

Cash (A)

Beg. bal.	0		
(a)	50,000	42,000	(b)
(c)	20,000	16,000	(d)
		2,000	(f)
End. bal.	10,000		

Cookware (A)

Beg. bal.	0		
(g)	630		
End. bal.	630		

Equipment (A)

Beg. bal.	0		
(b)	42,000		
(d)	18,000		
End. bal.	60,000		

Accounts Payable (L)

		0	Beg. bal.
(f)	2,000	2,000	(d)
		630	(g)
		630	End. bal.

Note Payable (L)

		0	Beg. bal.
		20,000	(c)
		20,000	End. bal.

Contributed Capital (SE)

		0	Beg. bal.
		50,000	(a)
		50,000	End. bal.

Journal Entries

(a) *dr* Cash (+A)..................................... 50,000
    cr Contributed Capital (+SE)...... 50,000

(b) *dr* Equipment (+A)......................... 42,000
    cr Cash (−A)................................. 42,000

(c) *dr* Cash (+A)..................................... 20,000
    cr Note Payable (+L).................. 20,000

(d) *dr* Equipment (+A)......................... 18,000
    cr Cash (−A)................................. 16,000
    cr Accounts Payable (+L)........... 2,000

(e) Not a transaction.

(f) *dr* Accounts Payable (−L)................ 2,000
    cr Cash (−A)................................. 2,000

(g) *dr* Cookware (+A)........................... 630
    cr Accounts Payable (+L)........... 630

PREPARING A BALANCE SHEET

Learning Objective 4

Prepare a classified balance sheet.

Using the ending amount from each T-account, you could now prepare a balance sheet. Before you do this, however, it's a good idea to check that the accounting records are in balance by determining whether the total dollar value of debits = the total dollar value of credits. If the total dollar value of debits does not equal the total dollar value of credits, the balance sheet will not balance. The equality of the debit and credit balances can be checked by preparing an internal accounting report called the *trial balance*, shown in Exhibit 2.12. Fortunately the column totals are equal, so the Pizza Palace balance sheet can be prepared and shown to Emilio.

EXHIBIT 2.12 **Trial Balance for Pizza Palace**

PIZZA PALACE, INC.
Trial Balance
At August 31, 2012

	Debit	Credit
Cash	10,000	
Cookware	630	
Equipment	60,000	
Accounts Payable		630
Note Payable		20,000
Contributed Capital		50,000
Totals	**70,630**	**70,630**

Trial balance provides a check on debits = credits equality

Ending balances in T-accounts in Exhibit 2.11

Exhibit 2.13 shows Pizza Palace's balance sheet based on the transactions in this chapter. The balance sheet is prepared by taking the ending balances for each account and grouping them as assets, liabilities, and shareholders' equity in balance sheet format. We've used a

EXHIBIT 2.13 | **Classified Balance Sheet**

PIZZA PALACE, INC. Balance Sheet At August 31, 2012		**Explanation of Classification**
Assets		
Current Assets		Current assets will be used up or turned into cash within 12 months.
Cash	$10,000	Cash in the company's bank account to be used up.
Cookware	630	Pizza pans and dishes will likely be used up or replaced before August
Total Current Assets	10,630	31, 2013.
Equipment	60,000	Ovens and restaurant booths will be used for many years.
Total Assets	$70,630	
Liabilities and Shareholders' Equity		
Current Liabilities		Current liabilities will be paid or fulfilled within 12 months.
Accounts Payable	$ 630	Amounts owed to suppliers are usually paid within one or two months.
Total Current Liabilities	630	
Note Payable	20,000	The promissory note is not to be repaid until September 1, 2014.
Total Liabilities	20,630	
Shareholders' Equity		
Contributed Capital	50,000	
Retained Earnings	0	Shareholders' equity accounts are classified as current or noncurrent.
Total Shareholders' Equity	50,000	
Total Liabilities and Shareholders' Equity	$ 70,630	

balance sheet format in Exhibit 2.13 called the **classified balance sheet**. A classified balance sheet contains subcategories for assets and liabilities labelled *current*. **Current assets** are assets the business will use up or turn into cash within 12 months of the balance sheet date. **Current liabilities** are debts and other obligations that will be paid or fulfilled within 12 months of the balance sheet date. In our example, Accounts Payable is the only current liability. The other liability—Note Payable—is expected to be paid in two years, so it is considered **noncurrent**. Most companies list assets in order of liquidity (how soon they will be used up or turned into cash) and liabilities in order of maturity (how soon they will be paid in cash or fulfilled by providing a service). Refer to Spotlight on IFRS and ASPE on page 63, which discusses the presentation differences between ASPE and IFRS.

Like Pizza Palace's Equipment and Note Payable accounts, its shareholders' equity accounts are understood to be long term in nature, although they are not labelled as such. Exhibit 2.13 includes the Retained Earnings account in shareholders' equity despite its zero balance because we don't want you to forget about this account. It will become a key link to the income statement, when this is introduced in Chapter 3.

YOU SHOULD KNOW

Classified balance sheet: A balance sheet that shows a subtotal for current assets and current liabilities.

Current assets: To be used up or converted into cash within 12 months of the balance sheet date.

Current liabilities: Debts and obligations that will be paid, settled, or fulfilled within 12 months of the balance sheet date.

Noncurrent (or long-term): Assets and liabilities that do not meet the definition of *current*.

Evaluate the Results

ASSESSING THE ABILITY TO PAY

The classified balance sheet format makes it easy to see whether current assets are sufficient to pay current liabilities. In Pizza Palace's case, $10,630 of current assets is greater than the $630 of current liabilities, making it obvious that the company's current assets are sufficient to cover its current liabilities.

Learning Objective 5

Interpret the balance sheet using the current ratio and an understanding of related concepts.

The only problem with looking at total dollar amounts is the difficulty in comparing across companies. It is far easier to express the relationship as a ratio, by dividing current assets by current liabilities. This calculation is known as the *current ratio*. It is used to evaluate liquidity, which is the ability to pay liabilities as they come due in the short run. Generally speaking, a high current ratio suggests good liquidity. Pizza Palace's current ratio ($10,630 ÷ $630 = 16.9) is unusually high. Current ratios typically vary from 1.0 to 2.0. Recently, Yum! Brands, Inc.'s current ratio was 0.94, as shown below.

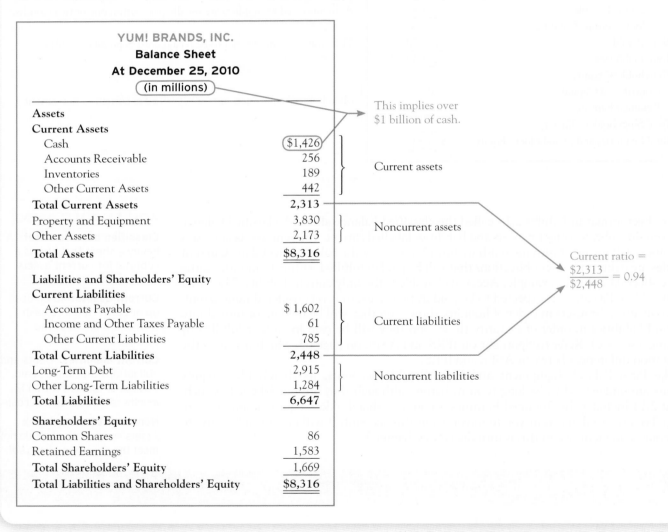

SPOTLIGHT ON **Financial Reporting** *Yum!*

Balance Sheet and Current Ratio Example

Yum! Brands, Inc., is the world's largest restaurant company, well known for its brands such as KFC, Taco Bell, and Pizza Hut. Yum! Brands is significantly larger than Pizza Palace, but the structure of its balance sheet and its account titles are quite similar. Its current ratio is typical of many large companies.

YUM! BRANDS, INC.
Balance Sheet
At December 25, 2010
(in millions)

Assets	
Current Assets	
Cash	$1,426
Accounts Receivable	256
Inventories	189
Other Current Assets	442
Total Current Assets	2,313
Property and Equipment	3,830
Other Assets	2,173
Total Assets	$8,316
Liabilities and Shareholders' Equity	
Current Liabilities	
Accounts Payable	$ 1,602
Income and Other Taxes Payable	61
Other Current Liabilities	785
Total Current Liabilities	2,448
Long-Term Debt	2,915
Other Long-Term Liabilities	1,284
Total Liabilities	6,647
Shareholders' Equity	
Common Shares	86
Retained Earnings	1,583
Total Shareholders' Equity	1,669
Total Liabilities and Shareholders' Equity	$8,316

This implies over $1 billion of cash.

Current assets

Noncurrent assets

Current liabilities

Noncurrent liabilities

Current ratio = $\dfrac{\$2,313}{\$2,448} = 0.94$

Name of Measure	Formula	What It Tells You
Current ratio	$$\frac{\text{Current Assets}}{\text{Current Liabilities}}$$	• Whether current assets are sufficient to pay current liabilities • A higher ratio means better ability to pay

BALANCE SHEET CONCEPTS AND VALUES

The purpose of a balance sheet is to report what a company owns and owes, but not necessarily what the company is worth. Some people mistakenly believe that the balance sheet reports a company's current value. To them, this is not a crazy idea because the balance sheet lists a company's assets and liabilities, so the net difference between the two must be the company's worth. In fact, *net worth* is a term that many accountants and analysts use when referring to shareholders' equity. So why is it wrong to think that the balance sheet reports a company's current value?

The answer comes from knowing that accounting is based on recording and reporting transactions, as you have seen over and over in this chapter. This focus on transactions does two things to the balance sheet: (1) it affects what is (and is not) recorded, and (2) it affects the amounts assigned to recorded items.

1. **What is (and is not) recorded?**
   - Measurable exchanges, such as a purchase of ovens, are recorded. Pizza Palace's gourmet pizza recipes, on the other hand, were not acquired in an exchange, so they are not listed on the balance sheet.

2. **What amounts are assigned to recorded items?**
   - Following the cost principle, assets and liabilities are first recorded at the amounts that were measurable at the time that transactions occurred. Later, if an asset's value increases, the increase is generally not recorded under ASPE. However, if an asset's value falls, it is generally reported at that lower value. This can cause a difference between the book value and the market value. **Conservatism** is followed when doubt exists about the amount at which to report assets and liabilities (and revenues and expenses).

SPOTLIGHT ON Financial Reporting

The Motivation to Be Conservative

Why are accountants conservative? It's primarily because they know that the financial statements are going to be used by outsiders such as bankers and investors to make decisions, and accountants don't want to mislead them. This is a very important issue for accountants. If they paint too rosy a picture and lead someone to buy shares in a questionable company, investors may lose their money when things go wrong. So, when faced with uncertainty about the numbers, accountants tend to take a conservative approach. Those who do not are said to be *aggressive*.

Summary of the Accounting Cycle

To show that the accounting process explained in this chapter can apply to any business, Exhibit 2.14 illustrates it for a fictitious construction company.

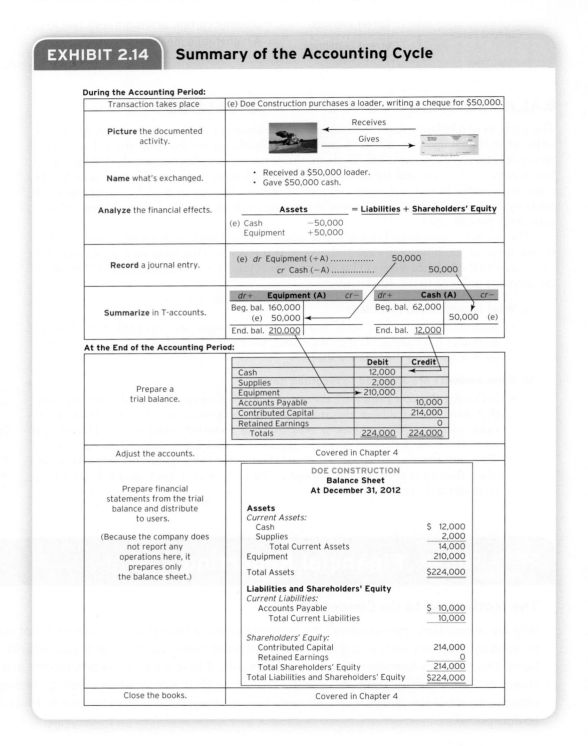

EXHIBIT 2.14 | **Summary of the Accounting Cycle**

During the Accounting Period:

Transaction takes place	(e) Doe Construction purchases a loader, writing a cheque for $50,000.
Picture the documented activity.	Receives ← / Gives →
Name what's exchanged.	• Received a $50,000 loader. • Gave $50,000 cash.
Analyze the financial effects.	**Assets** = **Liabilities** + **Shareholders' Equity** (e) Cash −50,000 Equipment +50,000
Record a journal entry.	(e) *dr* Equipment (+A) .... 50,000 *cr* Cash (−A) 50,000
Summarize in T-accounts.	*dr+* **Equipment (A)** *cr−* *dr+* **Cash (A)** *cr−* Beg. bal. 160,000 Beg. bal. 62,000 (e) 50,000 50,000 (e) End. bal. 210,000 End. bal. 12,000

At the End of the Accounting Period:

		Debit	Credit
Prepare a trial balance.	Cash	12,000	
	Supplies	2,000	
	Equipment	210,000	
	Accounts Payable		10,000
	Contributed Capital		214,000
	Retained Earnings		0
	Totals	224,000	224,000

Adjust the accounts.	Covered in Chapter 4

Prepare financial statements from the trial balance and distribute to users.
 	
(Because the company does not report any operations here, it prepares only the balance sheet.)
	DOE CONSTRUCTION
	Balance Sheet
	At December 31, 2012
	
	Assets
	Current Assets:
	  Cash .... $ 12,000
	  Supplies 2,000
	   Total Current Assets 14,000
	Equipment 210,000
	
	Total Assets $224,000
	
	Liabilities and Shareholders' Equity
	Current Liabilities:
	  Accounts Payable .... $ 10,000
	   Total Current Liabilities ... 10,000
	
	Shareholders' Equity:
	  Contributed Capital 214,000
	  Retained Earnings 0
	   Total Shareholders' Equity . 214,000
	Total Liabilities and Shareholders' Equity $224,000

Close the books.	Covered in Chapter 4

As International Financial Reporting Standards (IFRS) are adopted around the world, the three-step transaction analysis process in this chapter becomes even more important. In contrast to U.S. GAAP, which explain accounting rules in detail, ASPE and IFRS are less detailed and require more judgment when analyzing transactions. This difference in emphasis exists because IFRS are used across many different countries, where business practices and legal environments vary. By placing slightly more emphasis on general principles than on detailed rules, IFRS are more easily and broadly applied around the world.

Differences between ASPE and IFRS

As discussed earlier in this chapter, a private entity will distinguish between current and noncurrent assets and liabilities on the entity's balance sheet. Under IFRS, a public company has a choice as to how the company's balance sheet is presented. A public company can present its assets and liabilities in the order of current and then noncurrent on the balance sheet, except when the presentation based on liquidity would provide more reliable and relevant information. In the latter case, the company would then present all assets and liabilities in the order of liquidity.

Also discussed in this chapter was the cost principle, where assets and liabilities should be originally recorded at the initial cost to the company. If the asset's value increases, ASPE does not allow companies to record this increase. Under IFRS, a public company has the option of recording an asset at cost using the cost model, or it can choose to use the revaluation model. The revaluation model under IFRS, allows a company to report property, plant, and equipment assets at their fair value at the date of the revaluation, as long as the fair value can be measured reliably. Fair value of an asset is considered to be the price that could be received upon selling that asset. So in other words, the company can record the asset's increases and decreases in value from one revaluation date to the next. See Spotlight on IFRS and ASPE in Chapter 9 for more details.

Review the Chapter

This section provides a chance to solidify your understanding of key points. It's worth your time to work through the following demonstration case, scan the chapter summary, test your understanding of key terms, and then practise, practise, practise.

DEMONSTRATION CASE

On April 1, 2012, three university students started Goodbye Grass Corporation (GGC). A summary of GGC's transactions completed through April 30, 2012, follows:

a. Issued shares to the three investors in exchange for cash contributions totalling $9,000.
b. Acquired rakes and other hand tools (equipment) for $600, paying the hardware store $200 cash and agreeing informally to pay the balance in three months.
c. Ordered lawn mowers and edgers costing $4,000 from XYZ Lawn Supply, Inc.
d. Purchased four hectares of land for the future site of a storage garage. Paid cash, $5,000.

 **COACH'S TIP**

For possible account names, see the Homework Helper on page 67.

e. Received the mowers and edgers that had been ordered and signed a promissory note to pay XYZ Lawn Supply in full in 60 days.

f. Sold for $1,250 one hectare of land to the city for a park and accepted a note from the city indicating payment will be received by GGC in six months.

g. One of the owners borrowed $3,000 from a local bank for personal use.

Required:

1. Analyze each event to determine its effects on the accounting equation.

2. Prepare journal entries to record transactions listed above (omit explanations).

3. Set up T-accounts for Cash, Note Receivable (from the city), Equipment (hand tools and mowing equipment), Land, Accounts Payable (to hardware store), Note Payable (to equipment supply company), and Contributed Capital. Indicate the beginning balances of $0 in each T-account, and then summarize the effects of each journal entry in the appropriate T-accounts. Determine the ending balance in each account.

4. Use the T-accounts developed in requirement 3 to prepare a trial balance in order to ensure that the total dollar value of debits equals the total dollar value of credits for the ending balances of these T-accounts.

5. Use the trial balance developed in requirement 4 to prepare a classified balance sheet for Goodbye Grass Corporation at April 30, 2012. Show the balances for all assets, liabilities, and shareholders' equity accounts.

6. As of April 30, 2012, has financing for GGC's assets come primarily from liabilities or shareholders' equity?

7. Use the necessary information from the classified balance sheet developed in requirement 5 to calculate the current ratio for GGC as of April 30, 2012. Evaluate GGC's liquidity and explain how this could potentially impact GGC's suppliers and creditors.

Suggested Solution

1. Analyze transactions:

	Assets				=	Liabilities		+	Shareholders' Equity
	Cash	Note Receivable	Equipment	Land	=	Accounts Payable	Note Payable		Contributed Capital
(a)	+9,000				=				+9,000
(b)	−200		+600		=	+400			
(c)		No change*			=		No change		
(d)	−5,000			+5,000	=		No change		
(e)			+4,000		=		+4,000		
(f)		+1,250		−1,250	=		No change		
(g)		No change*			=		No change		

*Event (c) is not considered a transaction because it involves only the exchange of promises. Event (g) is not considered a transaction of the company because the separate entity assumption (from Chapter 1) states that transactions of the owners are separate from transactions of the business.

2. Record journal entries:

a. dr Cash (+A) 9,000
   cr Contributed Capital (+SE) 9,000

b. dr Equipment (+A) 600
   cr Cash (−A) 200
   cr Accounts Payable (+L) 400

c. This is not an accounting transaction, so a journal entry is not needed.

d. dr Land (+A) 5,000
   cr Cash (−A) 5,000

e. dr Equipment (+A) 4,000
   cr Note Payable (+L) 4,000

f. dr Note Receivable (+A) 1,250
   cr Land (−A) 1,250

g. This is not a transaction of the business, so a journal entry is not needed.

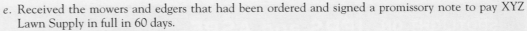

3. Summarize journal entries in T-accounts:

| Assets | = | Liabilities | + | Shareholders' Equity |

Cash (A)

Beg. bal.	0			
(a)	9,000	200	(b)	
		5,000	(d)	
End. bal.	3,800			

Equipment (A)

Beg. bal.	0	
(b)	600	
(e)	4,000	
End. bal.	4,600	

Accounts Payable (L)

	0	Beg. bal.
	400	(b)
	400	End. bal.

Contributed Capital (SE)

	0	Beg. bal.
	9,000	(a)
	9,000	End. bal.

Note Receivable (A)

Beg. bal.	0	
(f)	1,250	
End. bal.	1,250	

Land (A)

Beg. bal.	0			
(d)	5,000	1,250	(f)	
End. bal.	3,750			

Note Payable (L)

	0	Beg. bal.
	4,000	(e)
	4,000	End. bal.

4. Prepare a trial balance from the ending balances in the T-accounts:

GOODBYE GRASS CORPORATION
Trial Balance
At April 30, 2012

	Debit	Credit
Cash	3,800	
Note Receivable	1,250	
Equipment	4,600	
Land	3,750	
Accounts Payable		400
Note Payable		4,000
Contributed Capital		9,000
Totals	13,400	13,400

5. Prepare a classified balance sheet from the trial balance:

GOODBYE GRASS CORPORATION
Balance Sheet
At April 30, 2012

Assets		Liabilities	
Current Assets		Current Liabilities	
Cash	$ 3,800	Accounts Payable	$ 400
Note Receivable	1,250	Note Payable	4,000
Total Current Assets	5,050	Total Current Liabilities	4,400
Equipment	4,600		
Land	3,750	**Shareholders' Equity**	
		Contributed Capital	9,000
		Retained Earnings	0
		Total Shareholders' Equity	9,000
Total Assets	$13,400	Total Liabilities and Shareholders' Equity	$13,400

6. The primary source of financing for GGC's assets (totalling $13,400) has come from shareholders' equity ($9,000) rather than from liabilities ($4,400).

7. $\text{Current Ratio} = \dfrac{\text{Current Assets}}{\text{Current Liabilities}}$

$$= \dfrac{5,050}{4,400}$$

$$= 1.15$$

GGC's current ratio is 1.15 and greater than 1, which indicates that the company's assets are greater than its liabilities. This suggests good liquidity and would convey to existing and potential suppliers and creditors that GGC is able to pay its liabilities as they become due. This in turn represents lower risk involved for suppliers and creditors with respect to lending money to GGC. This is attractive for any new suppliers or creditors that GGC would like to do business with in the future.

CHAPTER SUMMARY

LO1 **Identify financial effects of common financing and investing activities.** p. 42

- Financing activities involve debt transactions with lenders (e.g., Notes Payable) and equity transactions with investors (e.g., Contributed Capital).
- Investing activities involve buying and selling long-term assets (e.g., Buildings, Equipment).

LO2 **Apply transaction analysis to financing and investing transactions.** p. 45

- Transactions include external exchanges and internal events.
- Transaction analysis is based on the duality of effects and the basic accounting equation. *Duality of effects* means that every transaction affects at least two accounts.
- Transaction analysis follows a systematic approach of picturing the documented business activity; naming the assets, liabilities, or shareholders' equity that are exchanged; and analyzing the financial effects on the basic accounting equation.

LO3 **Use journal entries and T-accounts to show how transactions affect the balance sheet.** p. 51

- *Debit* means left and *credit* means right.
- Debits increase assets and decrease liabilities and shareholders' equity.
- Credits decrease assets and increase liabilities and shareholders' equity.
- Journal entries express, in debits-equal-credits form, the effects of a transaction on various asset, liability, and shareholders' equity accounts. Journal entries are used to record financial information in the accounting system, which is later summarized by accounts in the ledger (T-accounts).
- T-accounts are a simplified version of the ledger, which summarizes transaction effects for each account. T-accounts show increases on the left (debit) side for assets, which are on the left side of the accounting equation. T-accounts show increases on the right (credit) side for liabilities and shareholders' equity, which are on the right side of the accounting equation.

LO4 **Prepare a classified balance sheet.** p. 58

- A *classified balance sheet* separately classifies assets as current if they will be used up or turned into cash within one year. Liabilities are classified as current if they will be paid, settled, or fulfilled within one year.

LO5 **Interpret the balance sheet using the current ratio and an understanding of related concepts.** p. 59

- The current ratio divides current assets by current liabilities to determine the extent to which current assets are likely to be sufficient for paying current liabilities.
- Because accounting is transaction-based, the balance sheet does not necessarily represent the current value of a business.
- Some assets are not recorded because they do not arise from transactions.
- The amounts recorded for assets and liabilities may not represent current values because under the cost principle they generally are recorded at cost, using the exchange amounts established at the time of the initial transaction.
- The concept of conservatism states that when uncertainty exists about the value of an asset or liability, care should be taken to not overstate the reported value of assets or understate the reported value of liabilities.

ACCOUNTING DECISION TOOLS

Name of Measure	Formula	What It Tells You
Current ratio	$\dfrac{\text{Current Assets}}{\text{Current Liabilities}}$	• Whether current assets are sufficient to pay current liabilities • A higher ratio means better ability to pay

KEY TERMS

Assets p. 42
Chart of Accounts p. 45
Classified Balance Sheet p. 59
Conservatism p. 61
Cost Principle p. 43
Credits p. 52

Current Assets p. 59
Current Liabilities p. 59
Debits p. 52
Journals p. 51
Journal Entries p. 52
Ledger p. 51

Liabilities p. 42
Noncurrent p. 59
Posting p. 53
Shareholders' Equity p. 42
T-account p. 53
Transaction p. 44

See complete definitions in the glossary in the back of this text.

HOMEWORK HELPER

Account Name	Description
Assets	
Cash	Includes cash in the bank and in the cash register
Accounts Receivable	The right to collect from customers for prior sales on credit
Interest Receivable	The right to collect interest from others
Inventories	Goods on hand that are being held for resale
Supplies	Items on hand that will be used to make goods or provide services
Prepaid Insurance	Amount paid to obtain insurance covering future periods
Prepaid Rent	Amount paid for rent relating to future periods
Notes Receivable	Amounts loaned to others under a formal agreement (Note)
Land	Cost of land to be used by the business
Buildings	Cost of buildings the business will use for operations
Equipment	Cost of equipment used to produce goods or provide services
Intangible Assets	Trademarks, brand names, goodwill, and other assets that lack a physical presence
Liabilities	
Accounts Payable	Amounts owed to suppliers for goods or services bought on credit
Wages Payable	Amounts owed to employees for salaries, wages, and bonuses
Accrued Liabilities	Amounts owed to others for advertising, utilities, interest, etc.
Unearned Revenues	Amounts (customer deposits) received in advance of providing goods or services to customers
Notes Payable	Amounts borrowed from lenders; involves signing a promissory note
Interest Payable	Amount due on loans as the cost of borrowing
Bonds Payable	Amounts borrowed from lenders; involves issuance of bonds
Other Liabilities	A variety of liabilities with smaller balances
Shareholders' Equity	
Contributed Capital	Amount of cash (or other property) contributed in exchange for the company's shares
Retained Earnings	Amount of accumulated earnings not distributed as dividends

> **COACH'S TIP**
>
> Read this chart of accounts but don't memorize it. Also, don't try to force this chart of accounts on all problems. Account names vary from company to company.

Alternative terms

• Shareholders' equity also can be called *stockholders' equity*.

Helpful reminders

- It's easier to account for a transaction if you can accurately determine how it might affect Cash before determining its impact on other account(s).
- The word *pay* and the expression *purchase with cash* both imply a reduction in Cash.

Frequent mistakes

- When accounting for transactions, avoid thinking of yourself as the customer, investor, or creditor. Instead, put yourself in the position of the company you're accounting for.
- *Shareholders'* is plural; *shareholder's* is singular.

Practice Material

QUESTIONS (**S** Symbol indicates questions that require analysis from more than one perspective.)

1. Define the following:
   a. Asset
   b. Current asset
   c. Liability
   d. Current liability
   e. Contributed Capital
   f. Retained Earnings

2. Define a transaction and give an example of each of the two types of events that are considered to be transactions.

3. For accounting purposes, what is an account? Explain why accounts are used in an accounting system.

4. What is the basic accounting equation?

5. Explain what *debit* and *credit* mean.

6. Briefly explain what is meant by *transaction analysis*. What are the two principles underlying transaction analysis?

7. What two different accounting equalities must be maintained in transaction analysis?

8. What is a journal entry? What is the typical format of a journal entry?

9. What is a T-account? What is its purpose?

10. Explain what the following accounting terms mean:
    a. *Cost principle*
    b. *Conservatism*

11. To obtain financing for her hair salon, Valeri asked you to prepare a balance sheet for her business. When she sees it, she is disappointed that the assets exclude a value for her list of loyal customers. What can you tell her to explain why this "asset" has been excluded? Knowing this, what should she tell her banker when they meet next week? **S**

12. Is transaction analysis as important under IFRS as it is under ASPE? Why or why not?

Multiple-choice questions and corresponding answers can be found on Connect.

MINI-EXERCISES

LO1, 3, 4 **M2-1 Identifying Accounts on a Classified Balance Sheet and Their Normal Debit or Credit Balances**

Netflix, Inc.

With more than 23 million members in Canada and the United States, Netflix, Inc. (Nasdaq: NFLX) is the world's leading Internet subscription service for enjoying movies and TV shows. Assume that the following are several of the accounts included in a Netflix balance sheet:

1. Income Taxes Payable
2. Accounts Receivable
3. Cash
4. Contributed Capital
5. Long-Term Debt
6. Property and Equipment
7. Retained Earnings
8. Accounts Payable

Required:

1. Indicate how each account normally should be categorized on a classified balance sheet. Use the acronym CA for current asset, NCA for noncurrent asset, CL for current liability, NCL for noncurrent liability, and SE for shareholders' equity.

2. Indicate whether the account normally has a debit or credit balance.

M2-2 Identifying Events as Accounting Transactions

LO2

With 40 locations in eight provinces, Discount Books is the country's favourite new and used book-store chain. Do the following events result in a recordable transaction for Discount Books? Answer yes or no for each.

_____ 1. Discount Books bought an old laundromat in Toronto.

_____ 2. The privately held company issued shares to new investors.

_____ 3. The company signed an agreement to rent store space in Columbia Plaza near Vancouver.

_____ 4. The company paid for renovations to prepare its Calgary store for operations.

_____ 5. The vice-president of the company spoke at a literacy luncheon in Saskatchewan, which contributed to building the company's reputation as a responsible company.

M2-3 Determining Financial Statement Effects of Several Transactions

LO2

For each of the following transactions of Spotlighter Inc. for the month of January 2012, indicate the accounts, amounts, and direction of the effects on the accounting equation. A sample is provided.

a. (Sample) Borrowed $3,940 from a local bank on a note due in six months.
b. Received $4,630 cash from investors and issued shares to them.
c. Purchased $920 in equipment, paying $190 cash and promising the rest on a note due in one year.
d. Paid $372 cash for supplies.
e. Bought $700 of supplies on account.

	Assets	=	Liabilities	+	Shareholders' Equity
a. Sample:	Cash +3,940		Notes Payable +3,940		

M2-4 Preparing Journal Entries

LO3

For each of the transactions in M2-3 (including the sample), write the journal entry using the format shown in this chapter (omit explanations).

M2-5 Posting to T-Accounts

LO3

For each of the transactions in M2-3 (including the sample), post the effects to the appropriate T-accounts and determine ending account balances.

+ Cash (A) −	+ Supplies (A) −	+ Equipment (A) −

− Accounts Payable (L) +	− Notes Payable (L) +	− Contributed Capital (SE) +

M2-6 Reporting a Classified Balance Sheet

LO4

Given the transactions in M2-3 (including the sample), prepare a classified balance sheet for Spotlighter Inc. as of January 31, 2012.

M2-7 Ordering Current Assets and Current Liabilities within a Classified Balance Sheet

LO4

Charlie's Crispy Chicken (CCC) operates a fast-food restaurant. When accounting for its first year of business, CCC created several accounts. Using the following descriptions, prepare a classified balance sheet at September 30, 2012.

Account Name	Balance	Description
Accounts Payable	$ 2,000	Payment is due in 30 days
Bank Loan Payable	10,000	Payment is due in 2016
Cash	1,800	Includes cash in register and in bank account
Contributed Capital	20,000	Shares issued in exchange for owners' contributions
Food Ingredients	400	Includes frozen chicken, French fries, beverages, etc.
Kitchen Equipment	13,000	Includes deep fryers, microwaves, dishwasher, etc.
Kitchen Supplies	1,400	Includes serving trays, condiment dispensers, etc.
Land	8,900	Held for future site of new restaurant
Note Payable	15,000	Payment is due in 2018
Restaurant Booths	25,000	Likely to be used through 2022
Retained Earnings	3,000	Total earnings through September 30, 2012
Utilities Payable	300	Payment is due in 30–45 days
Wages Payable	200	Payment is due in 7 days

L04   **M2-8 Preparing a Classified Balance Sheet**

The following accounts are taken from the financial statements of Knight Entertainments Resorts, Inc., at its September 30, 2012, year-end. (Amounts are in thousands.)

General Expenses	$ 48,735
Salaries Payable	22,082
Interest Expense	32,066
Accounts Payable	58,462
Other Current Liabilities	115,663
Food and Beverage Revenue	12,065
Cash	88,761
Accounts Receivable	56,777
Other Current Assets	283,692
Property and Equipment	1,647,050
Long-Term Note Payable	1,835,192
Contributed Capital	32
Retained Earnings	44,849

Required:

1. Prepare a classified balance sheet at September 30, 2012.

   TIP: This exercise requires you to remember material from Chapter 1. (Some of the above accounts are not reported on the balance sheet.)

2. Using the balance sheet, indicate whether the total assets of Knight Entertainments Resorts, Inc., at the end of the year were financed primarily by liabilities or by shareholders' equity.

L05   **M2-9 Calculating and Interpreting the Current Ratio**

The balance sheet of Robust Ribs Restaurant reports current assets of $30,000 and current liabilities of $15,000. Calculate and interpret the current ratio. Does it appear likely that Robust Ribs will be able to pay its current liabilities as they come due in the next year?

L05   **M2-10 Evaluating the Impact of Transactions on the Current Ratio**

Refer to M2-9. Evaluate whether the current ratio of Robust Ribs Restaurant will increase or decrease as a result of the following transactions.

a. Paid $2,000 cash for a new oven.

b. Borrowed $5,000 cash from a bank, issuing a note that must be repaid in three years.

c. Received a $2,000 cash contribution from the company's main shareholder.

d. Purchased $500 of napkins, paper cups, and other disposable supplies on account.

E2-1 Matching Terms with Definitions

LO2, 3, 5

Match each term with its related definition by entering the appropriate letter in the space provided. There should be only one definition per term. (That is, there are more definitions than terms.)

Term	Definition
___ 1. Journal entry	A. An exchange or event that has a direct and measurable financial effect.
___ 2. Assets = Liabilities + Shareholders' Equity; Debits = Credits	B. Four periodic financial statements.
___ 3. Transaction	C. The two equalities in accounting that aid in providing accuracy.
___ 4. Liabilities	D. The results of transaction analysis in debits-equal-credits format.
___ 5. Assets	E. The account that is debited when money is borrowed from a bank.
___ 6. Income statement, balance sheet, statement of retained earnings, and statement of cash flows	F. A resource owned by a business, with measurable value and expected future benefits.
	G. Cumulative earnings of a company that are not distributed to the owners.
	H. Every transaction has a least two effects.
	I. Amounts presently owed by a business.
	J. Assigning dollar amounts to transactions.

E2-2 Matching Terms with Definitions

LO1, 2, 3, 5

Match each term with its related definition by entering the appropriate letter in the space provided. There should be only one definition per term (that is, there are more definitions than terms).

Term	Definition
___ 1. Separate Entity Assumption	A. Economic resources to be used or turned into cash within one year.
___ 2. Balance Sheet	B. Reports assets, liabilities, and shareholders' equity.
___ 3. Current Assets	C. Decrease assets; increase liabilities and shareholders' equity.
___ 4. Notes Payable	D. Increase assets; decrease liabilities and shareholders' equity.
___ 5. Duality of Effects	E. Accounts for a business separate from its owners.
___ 6. Retained Earnings	F. The principle that assets should be recorded at their original cost to the company.
___ 7. Debit	G. A standardized format used to accumulate data about each item reported on financial statements.
	H. The two equalities in accounting that aid in providing accuracy.
	I. The account credited when money is borrowed from a bank using a promissory note.
	J. Cumulative earnings of a company that are not distributed to the owners.
	K. Every transaction has at least two effects.

LO1, 2, 5   **E2-3 Identifying Account Titles**

The following are independent situations.

a. A company orders and receives 10 personal computers for office use for which it signs a note promising to pay $25,000 within three months.

b. A company purchases for $21,000 cash a new delivery truck that has a list ("sticker") price of $24,000.

c. A women's clothing retailer orders 30 new display stands for $300 each for future delivery.

d. A new company is formed and issues 100 shares for $12 per share to investors.

e. A company purchases a piece of land for $50,000 cash. An appraiser for the buyer valued the land at $52,500.

f. The owner of a local company buys a $10,000 car for personal use. Answer from the company's point of view.

g. A company borrows $1,000 from a local bank and signs a six-month note for the loan.

h. A company pays $1,500 owed on its note payable (ignore interest).

Required:

1. Indicate titles of the appropriate accounts, if any, affected in each of the preceding events. Consider what the company gives and receives.

2. At what amount would you record the delivery truck in b? The piece of land in e? What measurement principle are you applying?

3. What reasoning did you apply in c? For f, what accounting concept did you apply?

LO1, 3, 4   **E2-4 Classifying Accounts and Their Usual Balances**

Digital Design Diversions, Inc. (DDDI) designs, develops, and distributes videogames for computers and advanced game systems such as Playnation, Y-Box, and Yeee. DDDI has been operating for only one full year.

Required:

For each of the following accounts from DDDI's recent balance sheet, complete the following table. Indicate whether the account is classified as a current asset (CA), noncurrent asset (NCA), current liability (CL), noncurrent liability (NCL), or shareholders' equity (SE), and whether the account usually has a debit (*dr*) or credit (*cr*) balance.

Account	Balance Sheet Classification	Debit or Credit Balance
1. Land		
2. Retained Earnings		
3. Notes Payable (due in three years)		
4. Accounts Receivable		
5. Supplies		
6. Contributed Capital		
7. Equipment		
8. Accounts Payable		
9. Cash		
10. Taxes Payable		

LO1, 2   **E2-5 Determining Financial Statement Effects of Several Transactions**

The following events occurred for Favanta Company:

a. Received $10,000 cash from owners and issued shares to them.

b. Borrowed $7,000 cash from a bank and signed a note.

c. Purchased land for $12,000; paid $1,000 in cash and signed a note for the balance.

d. Bought $800 of equipment on account.

e. Purchased $3,000 of equipment, paying $1,000 in cash and signing a note for the rest.

Required:

For each of the events (*a*) through (*e*), perform transaction analysis and indicate the account, amount, and direction of the effect (+ for increase and − for decrease) on the accounting equation. Check that the accounting equation remains in balance after each transaction. Use the following headings:

Event	Assets	=	Liabilities	+	Shareholders' Equity

E2-6 Determining Financial Statement Effects of Several Transactions

LO1, 2, 5

NIKE, Inc., with its Canadian headquarters in Thornhill, Ontario, is one of the world's leading manufacturers of athletic shoes and sports apparel. The following activities occurred during a recent year. The amounts are presented in millions of dollars.

NIKE, Inc.

a. Purchased $216.3 in equipment; paid by signing a $5 long-term note and fulfilling the rest with cash.

b. Issued $21.1 in additional shares for cash contributions made by shareholders.

c. Several Nike investors sold their own shares to other investors on the stock exchange for $21 per share.

Required:

1. For each of these events, perform transaction analysis and indicate the account, amount (in millions), and direction of the effect on the accounting equation. Check that the accounting equation remains in balance after each transaction. Use the following headings:

Event	Assets	=	Liabilities	+	Shareholders' Equity

2. Explain your response to transaction (*c*).

E2-7 Recording Investing and Financing Activities

LO3

Refer to E2-5.

Required:

For each of the events in E2-5, prepare journal entries, checking that debits equal credits.

E2-8 Recording Investing and Financing Activities

LO3, 5

Refer to E2-6.

Required:

For each of the events in E2-6, prepare journal entries, checking that debits equal credits.

E2-9 Analyzing the Effects of Transactions in T-Accounts

LO2, 3, 5

Harrigan Service Company, Inc., was incorporated by Ian Harrigan and five other managers. The following activities occurred during the year:

a. Received $60,000 cash from the managers; each was issued 1,000 shares.

b. Purchased equipment for use in the business at a cost of $12,000; one-fourth was paid in cash and the company signed a note for the balance (due in six months).

c. Signed an agreement with a cleaning service to pay it $120 per week for cleaning the corporate offices, beginning next week.

d. Ian Harrigan borrowed $10,000 for personal use from a local bank, signing a one-year note.

Check Figure:
Ending Cash balance =
$57,000 debit

Required:

1. Create T-accounts for the following accounts: Cash, Equipment, Note Payable, and Contributed Capital. Beginning balances are zero. For each of the above transactions, record its effects in the appropriate T-accounts. Include referencing and totals for each T-account.

2. Using the balances in the T-accounts, fill in the following amounts for the accounting equation:

Assets $_____ = Liabilities $_____ + Shareholders' Equity $_____

3. Explain your response to events (*c*) and (*d*).

E2-10 Inferring Investing and Financing Transactions and Preparing a Balance Sheet

During its first week of operations, January 1–7, 2012, Cosy Comfort Furniture Company completed six transactions with the dollar effects indicated in the following schedule:

Check Figure:

Ending Notes Payable
balance = $65,000 credit

	Assets			=	Liabilities	+	Shareholders' Equity
	Cash	Equipment	Land		Notes Payable		Contributed Capital
Beginning	$ 0	$ 0	$ 0	=	$ 0		$ 0
(1)	+12,000			=			+12,000
(2)	+50,000			=	+50,000		
(3)	−4,000		+12,000	=	+8,000		
(4)	+4,000			=	+4,000		
(5)	−7,000	+7,000		=			
(6)			+3,000	=	+3,000		
Ending	$_____	$_____	$_____	=	$_____		$_____

Required:

1. Write a brief explanation of transactions 1 through 6. Explain any assumptions that you made.
2. Compute the ending balance in each account and prepare a classified balance sheet for Cosy Comfort Furniture Company on January 7, 2012.
3. As of January 7, 2012, has most of the financing for Cosy Comfort's investments in assets come from liabilities or shareholders' equity?

E2-11 Inferring Investing and Financing Transactions and Preparing a Balance Sheet

During its first month of operations, March 2012, Falla Fashions, Inc., completed four transactions with the dollar effects indicated in the following schedule:

DOLLAR EFFECT OF EACH OF THE FOUR TRANSACTIONS					
Accounts	1	2	3	4	Ending Balance
Cash	$50,000	$(4,000)	$5,000	$(4,000)	
Computer Equipment				4,000	
Delivery Truck		25,000			
Short-Term Bank Loan			5,000		
Long-Term Notes Payable		21,000			
Contributed Capital	50,000				

Required:

1. Write a brief explanation of transactions 1 through 4. Explain any assumptions that you made.
2. Compute the ending balance in each account and prepare a classified balance sheet for Falla Fashions, Inc., at the end of March 2012.
3. As of March 31, 2012, has most of the financing for Falla's investment in assets come from liabilities or shareholders' equity?

E2-12 Recording Journal Entries

Assume that Down.com was organized on May 1, 2012, to compete with Despair, Inc.®—a company that sells demotivational posters and office products. The following events occurred during the first month of Down.com's operations.

a. Received $60,000 cash from the investors who organized Down.com Corporation.
b. Borrowed $20,000 cash and signed a note due in two years.
c. Ordered computer equipment costing $16,000.
d. Purchased $10,000 in equipment, paying $1,000 in cash and signing a six-month note for the balance.
e. Received and paid for the computer equipment ordered in (*c*).

Required:

Prepare journal entries for each transaction. (Remember that debits go on top and credits go on the bottom, indented.) Be sure to use referencing and categorize each account as an asset (A), liability (L), or shareholders' equity (SE). If a transaction does not require a journal entry, explain the reason.

E2-13 Analyzing the Effects of Transactions Using T-Accounts; Preparing and Interpreting a Balance Sheet

LO2, 3, 4

Lee Delivery Company Inc. (LDC) was incorporated in 2012. The following transactions occurred during the year:

a. Received $40,000 cash from organizers in exchange for shares in the new company.

b. Purchased land for $12,000, signing a two-year note (ignore interest).

c. Bought two used delivery trucks at the start of the year at a cost of $10,000 each; paid $2,000 cash and signed a note due in three years for the rest (ignore interest).

d. Paid $2,000 cash to a truck repair shop for a new motor, which increased the cost of one of the trucks.

e. Shareholder Jonah Lee paid $122,000 cash for a house for his personal use.

Check Figure:
Ending Equipment
balance = $22,000

Required:

1. Analyze each item for its effects on the accounting equation of LDC, for the year ended December 31, 2012.

   TIP: Transaction (a) is presented below as an example.

Assets	=	Liabilities	+	Shareholders' Equity
(a) Cash +40,000	=	Notes		Contributed Capital +40,000

   TIP: The new motor in transaction (d) is treated as an increase to the cost of the truck.

2. Record the effects of each item using a journal entry.

   TIP: Use the simplified journal entry format shown in the demonstration case on page 64.

3. Summarize the effects of the journal entries by account, using the T-account format shown in the chapter.

4. Prepare a classified balance sheet for LDC at the end of 2012.

5. Using the balance sheet, indicate whether LDC's assets at the end of the year were financed primarily by liabilities or shareholders' equity.

E2-14 Explaining the Effects of Transactions on Balance Sheet Accounts Using T-Accounts

LO1, 2, 3

Heavey and Lovas Furniture Repair Service, a company with two shareholders, began operations on June 1, 2012. The following T-accounts indicate the activities for the month of June.

Cash (A)			
(a)	17,000	10,000	(b)
		1,500	(c)

Supplies (A)		
(c)	1,500	

Building (A)		
(b)	50,000	

Notes Payable (L)		
		40,000	(b)

Contributed Capital (SE)		
		17,000	(a)

Required:

Explain events (a) through (c) that resulted in the entries in the T-accounts. That is, for each account, what transactions made it increase and/or decrease?

E2-15 Calculating and Evaluating the Current Ratio

LO1, 5

Delamy Design Ltd. is a clothing designer, marketer, and distributor. The company reported the following in recent balance sheets (amounts in thousands):

	September 30, 2012	December 31, 2011
Assets		
Current Assets:		
Cash	$ 73,324	$ 92,962
Accounts Receivable	81,336	58,270
Inventories	25,816	20,440
Other Current Assets	5,512	5,002
Total Current Assets	185,988	176,674
Property, Equipment, and Other Long-Term Assets	54,128	25,820
Total Assets	$240,116	$202,494
Liabilities and Shareholders' Equity		
Current Liabilities:		
Accounts Payable	$ 19,207	$ 18,694
Other Current Liabilities	12,880	10,633
Income Taxes Payable	3,512	—
Total Current Liabilities	35,599	29,327
Long-Term Liabilities	1,709	312
Shareholders' Equity	202,808	172,855
Total Liabilities and Shareholders' Equity	$240,116	$202,494

Required:

1. Calculate the current ratio at September 30, 2012, and December 31, 2011.

2. Did the company's current ratio increase or decrease? What does this imply about the company's ability to pay its current liabilities as they come due?

3. What would Delamy's current ratio have been if, on September 30, 2012, the company was to have paid down $10,000 of its Accounts Payable?

4. Are the company's total assets financed primarily by liabilities or shareholders' equity at September 30, 2012?

COACHED PROBLEMS

LO2, 5

CP2-1 Determining Financial Statement Effects of Various Transactions

The four friends who organized Healthcare Services (HS) on January 1, 2012, each invested $10,000 in the company and, in turn, was issued 8,000 common shares. To date, they are the only shareholders. During the first month (January 2012), the company had the following five events:

a. Collected a total of $40,000 from the organizers and, in turn, issued the shares.

b. Purchased a building for $65,000, equipment for $16,000, and three hectares of land for $12,000; paid $13,000 in cash and signed a note for the balance, which is due to be paid in 15 years.

c. One shareholder reported to the company that 500 shares of his HS shares had been sold and transferred to another shareholder for $5,000 cash.

d. Purchased supplies for $3,000 cash.

e. Sold one hectare of land for $4,000 cash to another company.

Required:

1. Was Healthcare Services organized as a partnership or corporation? Explain the basis for your answer.

2. During the first month, the records of the company were inadequate. You were asked to prepare a summary of the preceding transactions. To develop a quick assessment of their economic effects on Healthcare Services, you have decided to complete the spreadsheet that follows and to use plus (+) for increases and minus (−) for decreases for each account.

    TIP: Transaction (a) is presented below as an example.

    TIP: In transaction (b), five different accounts are affected.

Assets					=	Liabilities +		Shareholders' Equity	
						Notes		Contributed	Retained
Cash	Supplies	Land	Building	Equipment =		Payable		Capital	Earnings
(a) +40,000								+40,000	

3. Did you include the transaction between the two shareholders—event (c)—in the spreadsheet? Why?

   TIP: Think about whether this event caused HS to receive or give up anything.

4. Based only on the completed spreadsheet, provide the following amounts (show computations):
   a. Total assets at the end of the month.
   b. Total liabilities at the end of the month.
   c. Total shareholders' equity at the end of the month.
   d. Cash balance at the end of the month.
   e. Total current assets at the end of the month.

5. As of January 31, 2012, has the financing for HS's investment in assets primarily come from liabilities or from shareholders' equity?

CP2-2 Recording Transactions (in a Journal and T-Accounts); Preparing and Interpreting the Balance Sheet

LO2, 3, 4, 5

Athletic Professional Training Company (APTC) was incorporated as a private company on June 1, 2012. The company's accounts included the following at July 1, 2012:

Accounts Payable	$ 4,000	Land	$100,000
Building	200,000	Notes Payable	17,000
Cash	16,000	Retained Earnings	0
Contributed Capital	318,000	Supplies	5,000
Equipment	18,000		

During the month of July, the company had the following activities:

a. Issued 2,000 shares for $200,000 cash.

b. Borrowed $30,000 cash from a local bank, payable June 30, 2014.

c. Bought a building for $141,000; paid $41,000 in cash and signed a three-year note for the balance.

d. Paid cash for equipment that cost $100,000.

e. Purchased supplies for $10,000 on account.

Required:

1. Analyze transactions (a)–(e) to determine their effects on the accounting equation. Using a spreadsheet format with a column for each account, enter the July 1, 2012, amounts in the first line under the account headings, and calculate ending balances.

   TIP: You won't need new accounts to record the transactions described above, so have a quick look at the ones listed before you begin.

   TIP: In transaction (c), three different accounts are affected.

2. Record the transaction effects determined in requirement 1 using journal entries.

3. Summarize the journal entry effects from requirement 2 using T-accounts.

   TIP: Create a T-account for each account listed above. Enter the July 1, 2012, balances as the month's beginning balances.

4. Prepare a classified balance sheet at July 31, 2012.

   TIP: Total Assets equals $679,000.

5. As of July 31, 2012, has the financing for APTC's investment in assets come primarily from liabilities or shareholders' equity?

CP2-3 Recording Transactions (in a Journal and T-Accounts); Preparing and Interpreting the Balance Sheet

LO2, 3, 4, 5

Plaudere Plastics Company (PPC) has been operating for three years. The December 31, 2011, account balances are:

Cash	$ 35,000	Land	$ 30,000
Accounts Receivable	5,000	Supplies	5,000
Inventory	40,000	Accounts Payable	37,000
Notes Receivable (due 2014)	2,000	Notes Payable (due 2014)	80,000
Equipment	80,000	Contributed Capital	150,000
Factory Building	120,000	Retained Earnings	50,000

During the year 2012, the company had the following summarized activities:

a. Purchased equipment that cost $21,000; paid $5,000 cash and signed a two-year note for the balance.

b. Issued an additional 2,000 shares for $20,000 cash.

c. Borrowed $30,000 cash from a local bank, payable June 30, 2014.

d. Purchased supplies for $4,000 cash.

e. Built an addition to the factory for $41,000; paid $12,000 in cash and signed a three-year note for the balance.

f. Hired a new president to start January 1, 2013. The contract was for $95,000 for each full year worked.

Required:

1. Analyze transactions (a)–(f) to determine their effects on the accounting equation.

   TIP: You won't need new accounts to record the transactions described above, so have a quick look at the ones listed in the beginning of this question before you begin.

   TIP: In transaction (e), three different accounts are affected.

   TIP: In transaction (f), consider whether PPC owes anything to its new president for the year ended December 31, 2012.

2. Record the transaction effects determined in requirement 1 using journal entries.

3. Summarize the journal entry effects from requirement 2 using T-accounts.

   TIP: Create a T-account for each account listed above. Enter the December 31, 2011, balances as the 2012 beginning balances.

4. Explain your response to event (f).

5. Prepare a classified balance sheet at December 31, 2012.

   TIP: Total Assets equals $412,000.

6. As of December 31, 2012, has the financing for PPC's investment in assets primarily come from liabilities or shareholders' equity?

GROUP A PROBLEMS

Practise and learn online with Connect.

LO2, 5   **PA2-1 Determining Financial Statement Effects of Various Transactions**

Model trains for sale to toy stores are produced by Whistle Stop Incorporated, a small manufacturing company. Whistle Stop also has a small service department that repairs customers' model trains for a fee. The company has been in business for five years. At the end of the most recent year, 2011, the accounting records reflected total assets of $500,000 and total liabilities of $200,000. During the current year, 2012, the following summarized events occurred:

a. Issued additional shares for $100,000 cash.

b. Borrowed $120,000 cash from the bank and signed a 10-year note.

c. Built an addition on the factory for $200,000 and paid cash to the contractor.

d. Purchased equipment for the new addition for $30,000, paying $3,000 in cash and signing a note due in six months for the balance.

e. Returned a $3,000 piece of equipment, from (d), because it proved to be defective; received a reduction of the note payable.

f. Purchased a delivery truck (equipment) for $10,000; paid $5,000 cash and signed a nine-month note for the remainder.

g. A shareholder sold $5,000 worth of his shares in Whistle Stop Incorporated to his neighbour.

Required:

1. Complete the spreadsheet that follows, using plus (+) for increases and minus (−) for decreases for each account. The first transaction is used as an example.

	Assets		=	Liabilities	+	Shareholders' Equity	
Cash	Equipment	Building	=	Notes Payable		Contributed Capital	Retained Earnings
(a) +100,000						+100,000	

2. Did you include event (g) in the spreadsheet? Why or why not?

3. Based on beginning balances plus the completed spreadsheet, provide the following amounts (show computations):

   a. Total assets at the end of the year.
   b. Total liabilities at the end of the year.
   c. Total shareholders' equity at the end of the year.

4. As of December 31, 2012, has the financing for Whistle Stop's investment in assets primarily come from liabilities or shareholders' equity?

PA2-2 Determining Financial Statement Effects of Various Transactions

LO2, 5

Lex Systems Inc.

eXcel

Lex Systems Inc. is a computer software company that makes online public access cataloguing systems for library, business, or home use. It also has a small service department that provides initial data inputting for a fee. The company has been in business for ten years. At the end of the most recent year, 2011, the accounting records reflected total assets of $100,000 and total liabilities of $25,000. During the current year, 2012, the following summarized events occurred:

a. Repaid $5,000 cash on a bank note borrowed in a previous year.

b. Bought a computer from a shareholder for $2,000; signed a one-year note for the liability.

c. Disposed of a printer that was obsolete (net book value of zero) by turning it in to a salvage centre. No proceeds from the disposal.

d. Purchased office equipment for $1,000; paid cash.

e. Paid a $500 cash dividend to the shareholders.

f. Made a $10,000 down payment on a $50,000 building; signed a four-year note for the remainder.

g. A shareholder sold $5,000 worth of his shares in Lex Systems Inc. to the company at cost.

Required:

1. Complete the spreadsheet that follows, using plus (+) for increases and minus (−) for decreases for each account. The first transaction is used as an example.

	Assets		=	Liabilities	+	Shareholders' Equity	
Cash	Equipment	Building	=	Notes Payable		Contributed Capital	Retained Earnings
(a) −5,000						−5,000	

2. Did you include event (c) in the spreadsheet? Why or why not?

3. Based on beginning balances plus the completed spreadsheet, provide the following amounts (show computations):

   a. Total assets at the end of the year.
   b. Total liabilities at the end of the year.
   c. Total shareholders' equity at the end of the year.

4. As of December 31, 2012, has the financing for Lex Systems Inc.'s investment in assets primarily come from liabilities or from shareholders' equity?

PA2-3 Recording Transactions (in a Journal and T-Accounts); Preparing and Interpreting the Balance Sheet

LO2, 3, 4, 5

Deliberate Speed Corporation (DSC) was incorporated as a private company on June 1, 2012. The company's accounts included the following at June 30, 2012:

Accounts Payable	$ 10,000	Land	$200,000
Factory Building	100,000	Notes Payable	2,000
Cash	26,000	Retained Earnings	259,000
Contributed Capital	180,000	Supplies	7,000
Equipment	118,000		

Check Figure:
Ending Contributed Capital balance = $580,000

During the month of July, the company had the following activities:

a. Issued 4,000 shares for $400,000 cash.
b. Borrowed $90,000 cash from a local bank, payable June 30, 2015.
c. Bought a factory building for $182,000; paid $82,000 in cash and signed a three-year note for the balance.
d. Paid cash for equipment that cost $200,000.
e. Purchased supplies for $30,000 on account.

Required:

1. Analyze transactions (a)–(e) to determine their effects on the accounting equation.
2. Record the transaction effects determined in requirement 1 using a journal entry format.
3. Summarize the journal entry effects from requirement 2 using T-accounts.
4. Prepare a classified balance sheet at July 31, 2012.
5. As of July 31, 2012, has the financing for DSC's investment in assets primarily come from liabilities or from shareholders' equity?

LO2, 3, 4, 5   **PA2-4 Recording Transactions (in a Journal and T-Accounts); Preparing and Interpreting the Balance Sheet**

Fruitopia Farms was incorporated as a private company on January 1, 2012. The company's accounts included the following at January 31, 2012:

Check Figure:
Ending Retained Earnings
balance = $59,000

Accounts Payable	$ 20,000	Land	$100,000
Buildings	50,000	Notes Payable	22,000
Bank Overdraft	9,000	Retained Earnings	74,000
Contributed Capital	75,000	Supplies	3,000
Equipment	47,000		

During the month of February, the company had the following activities:

a. Paid a dividend to shareholders of $15,000.
b. Repaid $10,000 cash to a local bank.
c. Issued 500 shares for $50,000 cash.
d. Purchased equipment for $30,000, paying $3,000 in cash and signing a note due in six months for the balance.
e. Purchased supplies for $3,000 on account.

Required:

1. Analyze transactions (a)–(e) to determine their effects on the accounting equation.
2. Record the transaction effects determined in requirement 1 using a journal entry format.
3. Summarize the journal entry effects from requirement 2 using T-accounts.
4. Prepare a classified balance sheet at February 29, 2012.
5. As of February 29, 2012, has the financing for Fruitopia's investment in assets primarily come from liabilities or from shareholders' equity?

LO2, 3, 4, 5   **PA2-5 Recording Transactions (in a Journal and T-Accounts); Preparing and Interpreting the Balance Sheet**

Alexander's Interiors, Inc., is a leading international manufacturer and retailer of home furnishings. The following is adapted from Alexander's balance sheet as of September 30, 2012. Dollars are in millions.

Cash	$ 80	Accounts Payable	$ 26
Accounts Receivable	12	Wages and Other Expenses Payable	111
Inventories	188	Long-Term Debt	203
Other Current Assets	26	Other Long-Term Liabilities	44
Property, Plant, and Equipment	355	Contributed Capital	356
Other Assets	99	Retained Earnings	20

Assume that the following events occurred in the quarter ended December 31. Dollars are in millions.

a. Paid $2 cash for an additional "other asset."

b. Issued additional shares for $2 in cash.

c. Purchased property, plant, and equipment; paid $2 in cash and signed a note to pay the remaining $9 in two years.

d. Sold, at cost, other assets for $1 cash.

e. Conducted negotiations to purchase a sawmill, which is expected to cost $36.

Required:

1. Analyze transactions (a)–(e) to determine their effects on the accounting equation. Use the format shown in the demonstration case on page 64.

2. Record the transaction effects determined in requirement 1 using journal entries.

3. Summarize the journal entry effects from requirement 2 using T-accounts. Use the September 2012 ending balances as the beginning balances for the October–December 2012 quarter.

4. Explain your response to event (e).

5. Prepare a classified balance sheet at December 31, 2012.

6. As of December 31, 2012, has the financing for Alexander's investment in assets primarily come from liabilities or from shareholders' equity?

GROUP B PROBLEMS

PB2-1 Determining Financial Statement Effects of Various Transactions

LO2, 5

Swish Watch Corporation manufactures, sells, and services expensive watches. The company has been in business for three years. At the end of the most recent year, 2011, the accounting records reported total assets of $2,255,000 and total liabilities of $1,780,000. During the current year, 2012, the following summarized events occurred:

a. Issued additional shares for $109,000 cash.

b. Borrowed $186,000 cash from the bank and signed a ten-year note.

c. A shareholder sold $5,000 of his shares in Swish Watch Corporation to another investor.

d. Built an addition onto the factory for $200,000 and paid cash to the construction company.

e. Purchased equipment for the new addition for $44,000, paying $12,000 in cash and signing a six-month note for the balance.

f. Returned a $4,000 piece of equipment, from (e), because it proved to be defective; received a cash refund.

Required:

1. Complete the spreadsheet that follows, using plus (+) for increases and minus (−) for decreases for each account. The first transaction is used as an example.

	Assets			=	Liabilities	+	Shareholders' Equity	
	Cash	Equipment	Building	=	Notes Payable		Contributed Capital	Retained Earnings
(a)	+109,000						+109,000	

2. Did you include event (c) in the spreadsheet? Why?

3. Based on beginning balances plus the completed spreadsheet, provide the following amounts (show computations):
   a. Total assets at the end of the year.
   b. Total liabilities at the end of the year.
   c. Total shareholders' equity at the end of the year.

4. As of December 31, 2012, has the financing for Swish Watch Corporation's investment in assets primarily come from liabilities or from shareholders' equity?

PB2-2 Determining Financial Statement Effects of Various Transactions

Blockhead and Sons is a motor vehicle repair centre specializing in engine repair. At the end of the most recent year, 2011, the accounting records reported total assets of $746,000 and total liabilities of $534,000. During the current year, 2012, the following summarized events occurred:

a. Repaid $50,000 cash on a bank note borrowed in a previous year.
b. Bought a tow truck (equipment) from a supplier for $25,000; signed a one-year note for the liability.
c. Disposed of a computer that was obsolete (net book value of zero) by turning it in to a salvage centre. No proceeds from the disposal.
d. Purchased shop equipment for $100,000; paid cash.
e. Paid a $50,000 cash dividend to the shareholders.
f. Made a $100,000 down payment on a $500,000 building; signed a 40-year note for the remainder.
g. Borrowed $100,000 cash from the bank and signed a ten-year note

Required:

1. Complete the spreadsheet that follows, using plus (+) for increases and minus (−) for decreases for each account. The first transaction is used as an example.

	Assets			=	Liabilities	+	Shareholders' Equity	
							Contributed Capital	Retained Earnings
	Cash	Equipment	Building	=	Notes Payable			
(a)	−50,000				−50,000			

2. Did you include event (c) in the spreadsheet? Why?

3. Based on beginning balances plus the completed spreadsheet, provide the following amounts (show computations):
   a. Total assets at the end of the year.
   b. Total liabilities at the end of the year.
   c. Total shareholders' equity at the end of the year.

4. As of December 31, 2012, has the financing for Blockhead and Sons' investment in assets primarily come from liabilities or from shareholders' equity?

PB2-3 Recording Transactions (in a Journal and T-Accounts); Preparing and Interpreting the Balance Sheet

Bearings & Brakes Corporation (B&B) was incorporated as a private company on June 1, 2012. The company's accounts included the following at June 30, 2012:

Accounts Payable	$ 50,000	Land	$444,000
Factory Building	500,000	Notes Payable, due 2014	5,000
Cash	90,000	Retained Earnings	966,000
Contributed Capital	170,000	Supplies	9,000
Equipment	148,000		

During the month of July, the company had the following activities:

a. Issued 6,000 shares for $600,000 cash.
b. Borrowed $60,000 cash from a local bank, payable June 30, 2015.
c. Bought a factory building for $166,000; paid $66,000 in cash and signed a three-year note for the balance.
d. Paid cash for equipment that cost $90,000.
e. Purchased supplies for $90,000 on account.

Required:

1. Analyze transactions (a)–(e) to determine their effects on the accounting equation. Use the format shown in the demonstration case on page 64.
2. Record the transaction effects determined in requirement 1 using a journal entry format.
3. Summarize the journal entry effects from requirement 2 using T-accounts.
4. Prepare a classified balance sheet at July 31, 2012.
5. As of July 31, 2012, has the financing for B&B's investment in assets primarily come from liabilities or from shareholders' equity?

PB2-4 Recording Transactions (in a Journal and T-Accounts); Preparing and Interpreting the Balance Sheet

Lakeshore Cottages was incorporated as a private company on January 1, 2012. The company's accounts included the following at January 31, 2012:

Accounts Payable	$156,000	Land	$144,000
Buildings	500,000	Notes Payable	583,000
Cash	24,000	Retained Earnings	66,000
Contributed Capital	170,000	Supplies	99,000
Equipment	208,000		

During the month of February, the company had the following activities:

a. Borrowed $150,000 cash from a local bank, payable June 30, 2015.

b. Repaid $250,000 cash to a local bank.

c. Issued 1,500 shares for $150,000 cash.

d. Purchased equipment for $30,000, paying $3,000 in cash and signing a note due in six months for the balance.

e. Purchased supplies for $30,000 on account.

Required:

1. Analyze transactions (a)–(e) to determine their effects on the accounting equation. Use the format shown in the demonstration case on page 64.
2. Record the transaction effects determined in requirement 1 using a journal entry format.
3. Summarize the journal entry effects from requirement 2 using T-accounts.
4. Prepare a classified balance sheet at February 29, 2012.
5. As of February 29, 2012, has the financing for Lakeshore Cottages' investment in assets primarily come from liabilities or from shareholders' equity?

PB2-5 Recording Transactions (in a Journal and T-Accounts); Preparing and Interpreting the Balance Sheet

Starbucks is a coffee company—a *big* coffee company, with more than 15,000 stores in 50 countries. Let's assume that the following is adapted from Starbucks' annual report for the year ended September 30, 2012, and dollars are reported in thousands.

Cash	$ 269,800	Accounts Payable	$ 324,900
Accounts Receivable	329,500	Short-Term Bank Loans	1,864,800
Inventories	692,800	Long-Term Debt	549,600
Other Current Assets	455,900	Other Long-Term Liabilities	442,400
Property, Plant, and Equipment	2,956,400	Contributed Capital	40,100
Other Long-Term Assets	968,200	Retained Earnings	2,450,800

Check Figure:
Total Current Liabilities = $2,189,700

Assume that the following events occurred in the following quarter, which ended December 31, 2012. Dollars are in thousands.

a. Paid $10,000 cash for additional other long-term assets.

b. Issued additional shares for $5,100 in cash.

c. Purchased property, plant, and equipment; paid $11,200 in cash and signed additional long-term loans for $9,500.

d. Sold, at cost, other long-term assets for $6,000 cash.

e. Conducted negotiations to purchase a coffee farm, which is expected to cost $8,400.

Required:

1. Analyze transactions (a)–(e) to determine their effects on the accounting equation. Use the format shown in the demonstration case on page 64.
2. Record the transaction effects determined in requirement 1 using journal entries.

3. Summarize the journal entry effects from requirement 2 using T-accounts. Use the September 2012 ending balances (reported above) as the beginning balances for the October–December 2012 quarter.
4. Explain your response to event (e).
5. Prepare a classified balance sheet at December 31, 2012.
6. As of December 31, 2012, has the financing for the investment in assets made by Starbucks primarily come from liabilities or from shareholders' equity?

SKILLS DEVELOPMENT CASES

LO1, 4, 5

Rona Inc.

S2-1 Finding and Analyzing Financial Information

Refer to the financial statements of Rona Inc. in Appendix A at the back of this book, or download the annual report from the *Cases* section on Connect.

Required:

1. What is the company's fiscal year-end? Where did you find the exact date?
2. Use the company's balance sheet to determine the amounts in the accounting equation (A = L + SE).
3. What is the amount of the company's current liabilities on December 27, 2009? Are current assets sufficient to cover current liabilities?
4. Has financing for the company's investment in assets primarily come from liabilities or from shareholders' equity?

LO1, 4, 5

Rona Inc.

S2-2 Finding and Analyzing Financial Information

Refer to the financial statements of Rona Inc. in Appendix A and The Home Depot in Appendix B at the back of this book, or download the annual reports from the *Cases* section on Connect.

Required:

1. Use each company's balance sheet to determine the amounts in the accounting equation (A = L + SE). Is Rona or The Home Depot larger in terms of total assets?
2. Does Rona have more or less current liabilities than The Home Depot at the end of the 2009 fiscal year? Which company has a larger current ratio?
3. On the balance sheet, The Home Depot reports inventories of $10,188,000,000. Does this amount represent the expected selling price? Why or why not?
4. Has financing for The Home Depot's investment in assets primarily come from liabilities or from shareholders' equity at January 31, 2010? Thinking back to Chapter 1, what does this imply about the risk assumed by The Home Depot's investors, relative to those investing in Rona?

LO1, 4, 5

S2-3 Team Research, Financial Analysis, Technology, and Communication: Examining the Balance Sheet

As a team, select an industry to analyze. Using your Web browser, each team member should access the annual report for one publicly traded company in the industry, with each member selecting a different company. (See S1-3 in Chapter 1 for a description of possible resources for these tasks.)

Required:

1. On an individual basis, each team member should write a short report that lists the following information:
    a. The date of the balance sheet.
    b. The major noncurrent asset accounts and any significant changes in them.
    c. The major noncurrent liability accounts and any significant changes in them.
    d. Any significant changes in total shareholders' equity.
    e. Whether financing for the investment in assets primarily comes from liabilities or from shareholders' equity.
2. Then, as a team, write a short report comparing and contrasting your companies using the above dimensions. Discuss any similarities across the companies that you as a team observe, and provide potential explanations for any differences discovered.

S2-4 Ethical Reasoning, Critical Thinking, and Communication: A Real-Life Fraud

LO1, 2, 5

In the world of financial fraud, the "Ponzi scheme" is famous. Here is the story behind how the scam got its name. Charles Ponzi started the Security Exchange Company on December 26, 1919. He thought he had discovered a way to purchase American stamps in a foreign country at significantly lower amounts than they were worth in the United States. He claimed his idea was so successful that anyone who gave money to his company would be repaid their original loan plus 50 percent interest within 90 days. Friends and family quickly offered their money to Ponzi and they were handsomely rewarded, being repaid their original loan and the 50 percent interest within just 45 days. Thanks to an article in *The New York Times*, word spread quickly about Ponzi's business, attracting thousands of people seeking a similar payback. He might have had a successful business had his idea actually worked. The problem, however, was that it didn't. The 50 percent interest paid to early investors did not come from the profits of a successful underlying business idea (which didn't even exist) but instead was obtained fraudulently from funds contributed by later lenders. Eventually, the Ponzi scheme collapsed on August 10, 1920, after an auditor examined Ponzi's accounting records.

*Charles Ponzi
Security Exchange Company*

Required:

1. Assume that on December 27, 1919, Ponzi's first three lenders provided his company with $5,000 each. Use the basic accounting equation to show the effects of these transactions on December 27, 1919.
2. If the first two lenders are repaid their original loan amounts plus the 50 percent interest promised to them, how much cash is left in Ponzi's business to repay the third lender? Given what you discovered, how was it possible for Ponzi's company to remain in "business" for over eight months?
3. Who was harmed by Ponzi's scheme?

Epilogue: After taking in nearly $15 million from 40,000 people, Ponzi's company failed with just $1.5 million in total assets. Ponzi spent four years in prison before jumping bail—and then became involved in fraudulently selling swampland in Florida.

In December 2008, Bernard Madoff was arrested for using a modern-day Ponzi scheme to defraud investors of $65,000,000,000. On June 29, 2009, he was sentenced to 150 years in prison.

S2-5 Ethical Reasoning, Critical Thinking, and Communication: A Mini-Case

LO1, 5

You work as an accountant for a small land development company that desperately needs additional financing to continue in business. The president of your company is meeting with the manager of a local bank at the end of the month to try to obtain this financing. The president has approached you with two ideas to improve the company's reported financial position. First, he claims that because a big part of the company's value comes from its knowledgeable and dedicated employees, you should report their "Intellectual Abilities" as an asset on the balance sheet. Second, he claims that although the local economy is doing poorly and almost no one is buying land or new houses, he is optimistic that eventually things will turn around. For this reason, he asks you to continue reporting the company's land on the balance sheet at its cost, rather than the much lower amount that real estate appraisers say it's really worth.

Required:

1. Thinking back to Chapter 1, why do you think the president is so concerned with the amount of assets reported on the balance sheet?
2. What accounting concept introduced in Chapter 2 relates to the president's first suggestion to report "Intellectual Abilities" as an asset?
3. What accounting concept introduced in Chapter 2 relates to the president's second suggestion to continue reporting land at its cost?
4. Who might be hurt by the president's suggestions, if you were to do as he asks? What should you do?

S2-6 Financial Analysis and Critical Thinking: Evaluating the Reliability of a Balance Sheet

LO1, 4, 5

Betsey Jordan asked a local bank for a $50,000 loan to expand her small company. The bank asked Betsey to submit a financial statement of the business to supplement the loan application. Betsey prepared the following balance sheet.

Balance Sheet
June 30, 2012

Assets

Cash	$ 9,000
Inventory	30,000
Equipment	46,000
Personal Residence (monthly payments, $2,800)	300,000
Remaining Assets	20,000
Total Assets	$405,000

Liabilities

Short-Term Debt to Suppliers	$ 62,000
Long-Term Debt on Equipment	38,000
Total Debt	100,000
Shareholders' Equity	305,000
Total Liabilities and Shareholders' Equity	$405,000

Required:

The balance sheet has several flaws. However, there is at least one major deficiency. Identify it and explain its significance.

LO2 **S2-7 Using Technology to Analyze Transactions and Prepare a Balance Sheet**

Elizabeth Arden, Inc.

Assume you recently obtained a part-time accounting position at the corporate headquarters of Elizabeth Arden, Inc., in Miami Lakes, Florida. Elizabeth Arden is a leading manufacturer and marketer of prestige beauty products, prominently led by the Red Door line of fragrances. Assume that the following table summarizes accounts and their balances (in thousands) reported by Elizabeth Arden, Inc., in a September 30 balance sheet.

Cash	$ 14,300	Short-Term Notes Payable	$ 125,000
Accounts Receivable	285,400	Accounts Payable	111,800
Inventories	199,700	Other Current Liabilities	75,700
Other Current Assets	31,600	Long-Term Debt	323,600
Property and Equipment	35,800	Other Long-Term Liabilities	10,100
Other Noncurrent Assets	224,100	Contributed Capital	101,800
		Retained Earnings	42,900

Assume the company entered into the following transactions during October (amounts in thousands):

(*a*) Purchased an additional manufacturing facility at a cost of $15,000 by issuing a promissory note that becomes payable in three years.

(*b*) Used $7,000 cash to repay one of the short-term loans.

(*c*) Issued additional shares for $20,000 cash contributed by shareholders.

(*d*) Used cash to buy land for $8,000.

Required:

The controller at Elizabeth Arden has asked you to create a spreadsheet in which to display:

a. The account balances at September 30.

b. The effects of the four October transactions.

c. Totals that combine the September 30 balances with the October transactions. You feel like you might be ready to tackle this assignment, but just to be sure, you e-mail your friend Owen for advice. Here's his reply.

From:	Owentheaccountant@yahoo.com
To:	Helpme@hotmail.com
Cc:	
Subject:	Excel Help

1. My thinking is that you'll really impress your boss if you set up the spreadsheet to look like a bunch of T-accounts, one beside another. Use two columns for each balance sheet account (with the account name spanning the two columns) to make it look just like a T-account. You do remember how to use the cell merge command to make a header span two columns, right? If not, check the last e-mail I sent you (S1-7, Chapter 1). Here's a screenshot of how your worksheet might look just before you enter the October transactions.

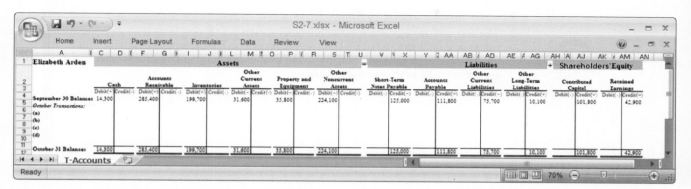

2. For spreadsheet skills in addition to cell merging, you might try creating a balance sheet with cells that are linked to the corresponding cells in the T-accounts. To do this, open a worksheet in the same file as the T-accounts. Then click on a cell in the balance sheet worksheet where you want to import a number from the T-accounts, then type =, then click on the tab for the T-account worksheet, click on the cell with the total to be transferred, and then press Enter. This links the cells so that any changes to the T-accounts automatically update the balance sheet. Also, Excel will let you hide row and column gridlines if you want. Just search Excel's help index for "hide gridlines."

3. I guess the only thing that's left is to remind you that to compute the ending balances in each T-account, you have to add the increases to the beginning balance and subtract the decreases. So, to compute the totals for a particular account, your formula might look like =(SUM(C4:C9)-SUM(D5:D9)).

4. Oh yeah, when you're all done, don't forget to save the file using a name that uniquely identifies you.

CONTINUING CASE

CC2 Accounting for the Establishment of a Business

Practise and learn online with Connect.

LO1, 2, 3, 4, 5

Nicole has decided that she is going to start her business, Nicole's Getaway Spa (NGS). A lot has to be done when starting a new business. Here are some transactions that have occurred prior to April 30, 2012.

a. Received $80,000 cash when issuing 8,000 new shares.

b. Purchased some land by paying $2,000 cash and signing a note payable for $7,000 due in 2015.

c. Hired a new esthetician for a salary of $1,000 a month, starting next month.

d. Bought $1,000 in soaps and aromatherapy supplies for the spa on credit.

e. NGS purchased a company car for $18,000 cash (list price of $21,000) to assist in running errands for the business.

f. Nicole sold 100 of her own personal shares to Raea Gooding for $300.

g. Paid $350 of the amount owed in (d).

Required:

1. For each of the events, prepare journal entries if a transaction exists, checking that debits equal credits. If a transaction does not exist explain why there is no transaction.

2. Assuming that the beginning balances in each of the accounts are zero, complete T-accounts to summarize the transactions (a)–(g).

3. Prepare a classified balance sheet at April 30, 2012, using the information given in the transactions.

4. Calculate the current ratio at April 30, 2012. What does this ratio indicate about the ability of NGS to pay its current liabilities?

Endnotes

FedEx

1. FedEx Investor Relations, Annual Reports: http://ir.fedex.com/annuals.cfm.

2. The account names you see in the financial statements of most large businesses are actually aggregations (or combinations) of several specific accounts. For example, Papa John's International keeps separate accounts for land, buildings, and equipment but combines them into one title on its balance sheet called *Property and Equipment*.

Practise and learn online with Connect.

CHAPTER 3

Reporting Operating Results on the Income Statement

YOUR LEARNING OBJECTIVES

Understand the business

LO1 Describe common operating transactions and select appropriate income statement account titles.

Study the accounting methods

LO2 Explain and apply the revenue and matching principles.

LO3 Analyze, record, and summarize the effects of operating transactions, using the accounting equation, journal entries, and T-accounts.

LO4 Prepare an unadjusted trial balance.

Evaluate the results

LO5 Describe limitations of the income statement.

Review the chapter

Chapter Summary, page 113

Additional resources on Connect

FOCUS COMPANY:
Pizza Palace, Inc.

PIZZA PALACE

In Chapter 2, Emilio Santos, owner-manager of Pizza Palace, established his new gourmet pizza business. Using money he and his wife had contributed, plus a loan from the bank, he purchased the ovens, restaurant booths, and other equipment he needed to run the business. His next step is to draw customers into the restaurant and provide them with the product and service that will keep them coming back. These day-to-day operating activities will determine whether Pizza Palace makes a profit.

The first goal of this chapter is to help you understand common operating activities and see how an income statement indicates whether a business generated a profit (or loss). Then, we'll show how the transaction analysis approach from Chapter 2 can be used to analyze and record transactions affecting the income statement. Finally, at the end of the chapter, we will highlight some limitations of the income statement.

**THAT WAS
THEN**

In the previous chapter, you learned how to analyze, record, and summarize the effects of transactions on balance sheet accounts.

**THIS IS
NOW**

This chapter focuses on analyzing, recording, and summarizing the effects of operating transactions on balance sheet and income statement accounts.

ORGANIZATION OF THE CHAPTER

Understand the business	Study the accounting methods	Evaluate the results	Review the chapter
• Operating activities • Income statement accounts	• Cash basis accounting • Accrual basis accounting • The expanded accounting equation • Unadjusted trial balance • Review of revenues and expenses	• Income statement limitations	• Demonstration Cases • Chapter Summary • Key Terms • Homework Helper • Practice Material

Understand the Business

OPERATING ACTIVITIES

Learning Objective 1

Describe common operating transactions and select appropriate income statement account titles.

Operating activities are the day-to-day functions involved in running a business. Unlike the investing and financing activities in Chapter 2 that occur infrequently and typically produce long-lasting effects, operating activities occur regularly and often have a shorter duration of effect. Operating activities include buying goods and services from suppliers and employees and selling goods and services to customers and then collecting cash from them. The period from buying goods and services through to collecting cash from customers is known as the *operating cycle*. Exhibit 3.1 illustrates the operating cycle for Pizza Palace.

EXHIBIT 3.1   Typical Operating Cycle Activities

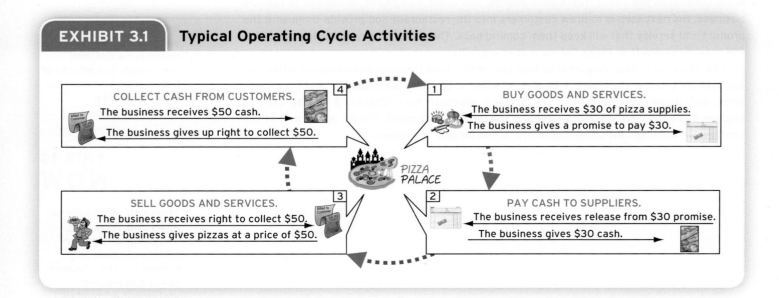

Although most businesses have the same steps in their operating cycles, the length of time for each step varies from company to company. For example, Pizza Palace usually collects cash from restaurant customers within minutes of making a sale, whereas the breakfast cereal company Kellogg Canada Inc. might wait several weeks to collect on sales it makes to grocery stores.

To be successful, Emilio must closely monitor Pizza Palace's operating activities. Operating activities are the primary source of revenues and expenses and, thus, can determine whether a company earns a profit (or incurs a loss). Although Emilio may intuitively sense how his business is doing, a more reliable management approach is to evaluate the revenues and expenses reported on the income statement. Emilio takes a quick look at the projected income statement Ally had prepared (Exhibit 3.2) based on the operating activities that were expected for Pizza Palace (in Chapter 1). This projected income statement will provide a benchmark for him to evaluate actual results.

EXHIBIT 3.2 | **Projected Income Statement**

PIZZA PALACE, INC.
Income Statement
For the Month Ended September 30, 2012

Explanation
Who: Name of the business
What: Title of the statement
When: Accounting period

Revenues		
Pizza Revenue	$11,000	Revenue earned from the sale of pizza to customers in September
Total Revenues	11,000	**Total amount earned during September**
Expenses		
Supplies Expense	4,000	Cost of pizza ingredients used up in September
Wages Expense	2,000	Cost of employee wages for work done in September
Rent Expense	1,500	Cost of rent for the month of September
Utilities Expense	600	Cost of utilities used in September
Insurance Expense	300	Cost of insurance coverage for September
Advertising Expense	100	Cost of advertising done in September
Income Tax Expense	500	Cost of taxes on September's income
Total Expenses	9,000	**Total expenses incurred in September to generate revenues**
Net Income	$ 2,000	**Difference between total revenues and total expenses**

INCOME STATEMENT ACCOUNTS

The income statement summarizes the financial impact of operating activities undertaken by the company during the accounting period. It includes three main sections: revenues, expenses, and net income.

Revenues

Revenues are the amounts a business charges its customers when it provides goods or services. If Pizza Palace sells 1,100 pizzas in September and charges $10 per pizza, Pizza Revenue would total $11,000. The amount of revenues earned during the period is the first thing reported in the body of the income statement.

Expenses

Expenses are costs of operating the business, incurred to generate revenues in the period covered by the income statement. When a business uses up its resources to generate revenues during the period, it reports an expense, regardless of when the resources were or will be paid for.

Expenses are reported in the body of the income statement after revenues. Some of Pizza Palace's typical expenses are listed in the income statement shown in Exhibit 3.2.

Net Income

Net income is a total that is calculated by subtracting expenses from revenues; it is not an account like Pizza Revenue or Wages Expense. Because it is a total, net income summarizes the overall impact of revenues and expenses in a single number. It is called a *net loss* if expenses are greater than revenues, and a *net income* if revenues are greater than expenses. Net income indicates the amount by which shareholders' equity increases as a result of a company's profitable operations. For this reason, net income (or loss) is a closely watched measure of a company's success.

Exhibit 3.2 shows how revenues, expenses, and net income would be reported in Pizza Palace's income statement. Each account title describes the specific type of revenue or expense arising from the business's particular operations. This is true for all companies. Pizza Palace reports "Pizza Revenues," but Rogers Plus reports "Movie Rental Revenues." Google reports "Traffic Acquisition Expenses," and Air Canada reports "Airport and Navigation Fees." You'll become more comfortable with various account titles as this course progresses but to keep things simple right now we'll stick to common types of revenues and expenses.

The income statement in Exhibit 3.2 is for the month ended September 30, 2012. As it turns out, September 30, 2012, is a Sunday. You might wonder what's so special about this date. The answer is that there is nothing particularly special about this date—it's just the last day of the month. By dividing the company's long life into meaningful and shorter chunks of time, Emilio can measure and evaluate Pizza Palace's financial performance on a timely basis. This is known in accounting as the **time period assumption**. If net income is low in the current month, Emilio will find out about it quickly and be able to take steps to become more profitable in the following month.

Notice that the income statement reports the financial effects of business activities that occurred during just the current period. They relate only to the current period. They do not have a lingering financial impact beyond the end of the current period. This is a key distinction between the income statement and the balance sheet. The revenues and expenses on an income statement report the financial impact of activities in just the current period, whereas items on a balance sheet will continue to have a financial impact beyond the end of the current period. Balance sheet accounts are considered permanent, whereas income statement accounts are considered temporary. Another way people describe this difference is that the balance sheet takes stock of what exists at a point in time, whereas the income statement depicts a flow of what happened over a period of time.

HOW'S IT GOING? Self-Study Practice

For each item listed below, indicate whether the company should report it on the income statement this period (yes/no). If yes, indicate an appropriate account title for the item described.

Description	Yes/No	Account Title
1. The Royal Bank of Canada charges customers a monthly service fee.	_____	_____
2. Canadian Tire buys a new building to use as a retail store.	_____	_____
3. Dell pays to deliver computers to customers.	_____	_____
4. Tim Hortons buys supplies to be used next month.	_____	_____
5. Shoppers Drug Mart pays this week's wages to employees.	_____	_____

After you have finished, check your answers with the solution in the margin.

Solution to Self-Study Practice

	Yes/No	Account Title
1.	Yes	Service Fee Revenue
2.	No	(a building is an asset not an expense)
3.	Yes	Delivery Expense
4.	No	(supplies are assets until used up)
5.	Yes	Salaries and Wages Expense

35 Days Hath September?

It seems some managers—specifically those at Computer Associates (CA)—haven't learned the **time period assumption**. CA was charged with financial statement fraud for improperly recording 35 days of sales in September—a month that has only 30 days. To make it look like managers had met their September sales targets, CA included the first five days of sales from October in its September income statement. This accounting fraud led managers to be paid bonuses they hadn't earned and tricked investors into thinking CA was a successful company.

When the truth was revealed later, CA's shareholders quickly abandoned the company, causing its share price to fall 43 percent in a single day. CA ultimately paid shareholders $225 million to make up for its bad accounting and agreed to ensure all inappropriate management bonuses were paid back to the company. In addition, several marketing and accounting personnel were sent to jail.

Proper revenue reporting is obviously a very serious matter.

Study the Accounting Methods

CASH BASIS ACCOUNTING

What's a good way to determine whether you're doing well financially? Many people simply look at the balance in their bank accounts to gauge their financial performance. If the overall balance increased this month, they take that as a sign that they've done a good job of managing their finances. If it has gone down, that's a clue they need to tame their spending next month. The reason that the change in your bank balance tends to give a decent measure of financial performance is that your cash flows (in and out) occur closely in time to the activities that cause those cash flows. Reporting your income on this basis, called **cash basis accounting**, is fine for managing personal finances, but not for running a business.

Cash basis accounting doesn't measure financial performance very well when transactions are conducted using credit rather than cash. Credit often introduces a significant delay between the time an activity occurs and the time it impacts a bank account balance. If you are paid for work once a month, for example, the results of your hard work don't show up until the end of the month. Similarly, if you go crazy with your credit card at the mall, these transactions won't affect your bank balance until you pay the bill the following month.

Because most companies use credit for their transactions, cash basis accounting is not likely to correspond to the business activities that actually occur during a given period. UPS, for example, often pays its employees to deliver packages in one month but doesn't get paid by its customers until the following month. Under cash basis accounting, UPS would report expenses in Month 1 but wouldn't report revenues until it received payments from its customers in Month 2. This leads to a rather distorted view of the company's financial performance, as shown in Exhibit 3.3.

YOU SHOULD KNOW

Cash basis accounting:
Reports revenues when cash is received and expenses when cash is paid; not allowed under GAAP.

EXHIBIT 3.3	Cash Basis Can Distort Reported Profits

	MONTH 1 (Delivery occurs, and **cash is paid**)		MONTH 2 (No delivery, but **cash is received**)	
Revenues	$ 0	Revenues	$15,000
Expenses	10,000	Expenses	0
Net Income (Loss)	$(10,000)	Net Income	$15,000

Under cash basis accounting, the company would report a net loss in Month 1 and a huge net income in Month 2, when the truth is that the business activities generate revenue of $15,000, expenses of $10,000, and net income of $5,000, all of which relate to the activities that occurred in Month 1 when the packages were delivered. A better method of accounting is needed—one that reports the revenues and related expenses during the same period.

ACCRUAL BASIS ACCOUNTING

Learning Objective 2

Explain and apply the revenue and matching principles.

An alternative method of accounting would be for UPS to report revenues and expenses when packages are delivered, regardless of when cash is received or paid. This approach, called **accrual basis accounting**, produces a better measure of the profits arising from the company's activities. As shown in Exhibit 3.4, accrual accounting would require that UPS report all its revenues, expenses, and net income in the period the delivery occurs (Month 1). In the following month, UPS does not deliver packages, so it does not report revenues and expenses. According to ASPE and IFRS, the accrual basis is the only acceptable method for external reporting of income. The cash basis can be used internally by some small companies, but ASPE and IFRS do not allow it for external reporting. The "rule of accrual" is that the financial effects of business activities are measured and reported when the activities actually occur, not when the cash related to them is received or paid. The two basic accounting principles that determine when revenues and expenses are recognized under accrual basis accounting are called the *revenue principle* and the *matching principle*.

YOU SHOULD KNOW

Accrual basis accounting: Reports revenues when they are earned and expenses when they are incurred, regardless of the timing of cash receipts or payments; required under GAAP.

EXHIBIT 3.4	Accrual Basis Relates Profit to Underlying Activities

	MONTH 1 (**Delivery occurs**, and cash is paid)	MONTH 2 (**No delivery**, but cash is received)
Revenues	$15,000	Revenues $ 0
Expenses	10,000	Expenses 0
Net Income	$ 5,000	Net Income $ 0

YOU SHOULD KNOW

Revenue principle: The requirement under accrual basis accounting to record revenues when they are earned, not necessarily when cash is received for them.

Revenue Principle–Revenue Recognition

According to the **revenue principle**, revenues should be recognized when they are earned. The word *recognized* means revenues are measured and recorded in the accounting system. The word *earned* means the company has performed the acts promised to the customer. For example, when Pizza Palace delivers a pizza to a customer, one would agree that the acts promised to the customer have been performed. Therefore revenue has been earned and can therefore be recognized. You may not have realized it, but there were actually two more conditions that were met, allowing revenue to be recognized. The three conditions that must be met for revenue to be recognized are

1. Risks and rewards have passed or the earnings process is substantially complete.
2. Measurability is reasonably certain.
3. Collectability is reasonably assured.

For most businesses, these conditions are met at the point of delivery of goods or services.

All companies expect to receive cash in exchange for providing goods and services, but the timing of cash receipts does not dictate when revenues are recognized. Instead, the key factor in determining when to recognize revenue is whether the company has met the three conditions listed above during the accounting period. Regardless of the length of the period (month, quarter, or year), cash can be received (1) in the same period as the goods or services are provided, (2) in a period before they are provided, or (3) in a period after they are provided, as shown on the timeline in Exhibit 3.5. Let's see how to handle each of these cases.

EXHIBIT 3.5 — Timing of Reporting Revenue versus Cash Receipts

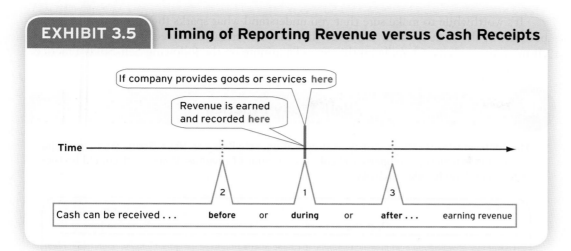

 Cash is received in the same period as the goods or services are provided. This is a common occurrence for Pizza Palace. Pizza Palace earns revenue by delivering pizza to the customer as ordered. Within minutes, Pizza Palace receives cash from the customer.

 Cash is received in a period before goods or services are provided. This situation can occur when Pizza Palace receives cash for gift cards that customers can use to pay for pizza in the future. Pizza Palace will record the cash received, but since it hasn't delivered pizza for these customers, no revenue is recorded yet. Instead, Pizza Palace has an obligation to accept the gift card as payment for the supply of pizza in the future. This obligation to supply pizza in the future is recorded as an increase in a liability account called **Unearned Revenue**. Unearned revenue is recorded on the balance sheet equal to the amount of cash received for the gift card. There is no impact to the income statement at this time because Pizza Palace has only exchanged a promise for the customer's cash. When Pizza Palace provides the pizza to the customer, revenue will be reported on the income statement and the Unearned Revenue account on the balance sheet will be reduced. Businesses that routinely receive cash before delivering goods or services include airlines, magazine publishers, and insurance companies.

 Cash is to be received in a period after goods or services are provided. This situation typically arises when a company sells to a customer on account. Selling on account means that the company provides goods or services to a customer not for cash, but instead for the right to collect cash in the future. This right is an asset called *Accounts Receivable*. Thus, if Pizza Palace delivers pizza sold on account to a college organization in September, it will report Pizza Revenue on the September income statement. Accounts Receivable will be reported on the balance sheet until Pizza Palace receives the customer's payment, at which time Pizza Palace will increase its Cash account and decrease its Accounts Receivable. No additional revenue is reported when the customer's payment is received because the revenue was already recorded when the pizza was delivered.

YOU SHOULD KNOW

Unearned Revenue: A liability representing a company's obligation to provide goods or services to customers in the future.

SPOTLIGHT ON Financial Reporting

Revenue Recognition Policy

Every company is required (under ASPE and IFRS) to report its revenue recognition policy in its notes to the financial statements. Pizza Palace follows the same revenue recognition policy as Papa John's, which explains its policy as follows.

> Papa John's International Inc.
>
> Restaurant sales are recognized as revenues when the products are delivered to or carried out by customers.

PIZZA
PAPA JOHNS
Better Ingredients.
Better Pizza.

It's worthwhile to make sure that you understand what sparks the recording of revenues because, in the next section, you'll see that this also triggers the recording of expenses. To ensure that you have a handle on this, spend a minute on the following Self-Study Practice.

💡 HOW'S IT GOING? Self-Study Practice

The following transactions are typical operating activities for Nova Scotia Seas, a scuba diving and instruction company. Indicate the amount of revenue, if any, that should be recognized in June for each activity.

Operating Activity	Amount of Revenue Earned in June
1. In June, Nova Scotia Seas provided $32,000 in diving instruction to customers for cash.	
2. In June, new customers paid $8,200 cash for diving trips to be provided by Nova Scotia Seas; $5,200 in trips were made in June and the rest will be provided in July.	
3. In June, customers paid $3,900 cash for instruction they received in May.	

After you have finished, check your answers with the solution in the margin.

Solution to Self-Study Practice

1. $32,000.
2. $5,200 in June (the remaining $3,000 will be recognized as revenue in July; until then, it is reported as a liability called Unearned Revenue).
3. No revenue in June for this activity; revenue was earned and recognized in May (along with Accounts Receivable). The cash received in June reduces Accounts Receivable.

Matching Principle—Expense Recognition

The business activities that generate revenues also create expenses. Under accrual basis accounting, expenses are recognized in the same period as the revenues to which they relate, not necessarily the period in which cash is paid for them. For example, for Pizza Palace to deliver pizza in September, it must rent space in a building and have its employees work that month. Under accrual basis accounting, Pizza Palace would report rent expense and wages expense in September, even if the rent was paid in August and the wages were paid in October. This is what accountants call the **matching principle**: record expenses in the same period as the revenues with which they can reasonably be associated. If an expense cannot be directly associated with revenues, it is recorded in the period that the underlying business activity occurs. For example, because it's not clear how or when advertising affects revenue, advertising expense is simply reported in the period that ads are run. Notice that it is the timing of the underlying business activities, not the cash payments, that dictates when expenses are recognized. Cash payments may occur (1) at the same time as, (2) before, or (3) after the related expenses are incurred to generate revenue, as shown in Exhibit 3.6.

YOU SHOULD KNOW

Matching principle: The requirement under accrual basis accounting to record expenses in the same period as the revenues they generate, not necessarily the period in which cash is paid for them.

 Cash is paid at the same time as the cost is incurred to generate revenue. Although this isn't as common in business as in your personal life, expenses are sometimes paid for in the period in which they arise. For example, Pizza Palace could spend $50 cash for balloons to celebrate its grand opening this month. It would report this cost on this month's income statement because the balloons were used for an activity occurring this month. In other words, the benefits of incurring the cost are entirely used up in the current accounting period.

 Cash is paid before the expense is incurred to generate revenue. It is common for businesses to pay for something that provides benefits only in future periods. For example, Pizza Palace might buy paper napkins now but does not use them until next month. Given the matching principle, the expense from using these supplies is reported next month when the supplies are used to earn revenue, not in the current month when purchased. This month, the supplies represent an asset because they will

EXHIBIT 3.6 Timing of Reporting Expenses versus Cash Payments

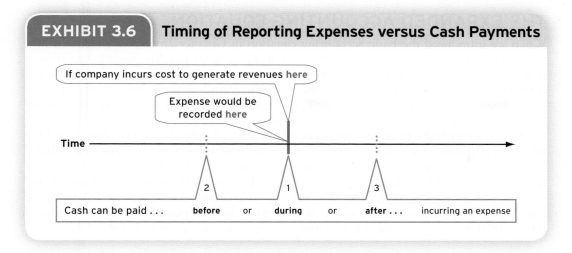

benefit a future period. When they are used later, Supplies Expense will be reported on next month's income statement and the asset Supplies will decrease. Similar situations arise when a company prepays rent or insurance.

 3 ▷ **Cash is paid after the cost is incurred to generate revenue.** Although rent is paid and supplies are purchased before they are used, many costs are paid after receiving and using goods or services. For example, Pizza Palace uses electricity to heat the ovens and light the restaurant this month but does not pay for its electricity usage until next month. Because the cost of the electricity relates to revenues earned now, it represents an expense that will be reported on this month's income statement. Because the cost has not yet been paid at the end of the month, the balance sheet reports a corresponding liability called *Accounts Payable*. Similar situations arise when employees work in the current period but are not paid their wages until the following period. This period's wages are reported as Wages Expense on the income statement and any unpaid wages are reported as Wages Payable on the balance sheet.

It's time for you to practise determining which costs should be reported as expenses on an income statement prepared using accrual basis accounting. As you work through the next Self-Study Practice, feel free to glance at Exhibit 3.6 for help.

 COACH'S TIP

Promises exchanged for promises are not considered transactions, as you learned in Chapter 2. Here, a service has been received in exchange for a promise (of future payment), so it is considered a transaction.

HOW'S IT GOING? Self-Study Practice

The following transactions are typical operating activities for Nova Scotia Seas, a scuba diving and instruction company. Indicate the amount of expense, if any, that should be recognized in June for each activity.

Operating Activity	Amount of Expense Incurred in June
1. In June, Nova Scotia Seas paid $6,000 cash for insurance for July–December.	
2. In June, Nova Scotia Seas paid $4,000 in wages to employees for work performed in June.	
3. In June, Nova Scotia Seas used $2,400 of electricity, to be paid in July.	

After you have finished, check your answers with the solution in the margin.

Solution to Self-Study Practice

1. No expense in June for the $6,000 payment; the $6,000 will be reported as an asset called Prepaid Insurance until used up in July–December.
2. $4,000.
3. $2,400; this cost relates to business activities in June, so the $2,400 is reported as an expense in June (a corresponding liability is reported on the balance sheet).

Learning Objective 3

Analyze, record, and summarize the effects of operating transactions, using the accounting equation, journal entries, and T-accounts.

THE EXPANDED ACCOUNTING EQUATION

When we introduced the basic accounting equation in Chapter 2, we didn't mention how to account for the income statement effects of operating activities. You already had enough to learn, relating to the effects of investing and financing activities on assets, liabilities, and contributed capital. The time has now come for you to learn how to analyze, record, and summarize the effects of operating activities. To do this, you first need to know how the debit/credit framework works with revenues and expenses.

Let's start with the basic accounting equation from Chapter 2. That is, assets equal liabilities plus shareholders' equity, or A = L + SE. For now, we're going to focus on the shareholders' equity category. As you already know from Chapters 1 and 2, shareholders' equity represents shareholders' claims on the company, which come from either (1) Contributed Capital, given to the company by shareholders in exchange for shares, or (2) Retained Earnings, generated by the company itself through profitable operations. Retained earnings is the part that expands to include revenues and expenses, as shown in Exhibit 3.7.

EXHIBIT 3.7	The Expanded Debit/Credit Framework

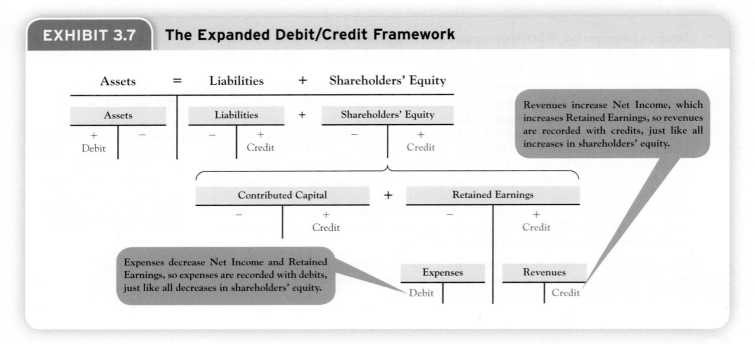

Take a moment to look at how Exhibit 3.7 encourages you to think of revenues and expenses as subcategories within retained earnings. They are shown this way because revenues and expenses eventually flow into Retained Earnings, but they aren't initially recorded there. Instead, each revenue and expense is accumulated in a separate account, making it easier to identify the amount to report for each item on the income statement. At the end of each accounting year, these separate revenue and expense accounts are transferred to (or "closed") into Retained Earnings through a process that we'll demonstrate in Chapter 4. For now, just focus on learning how revenues and expenses are recorded to indicate increases and decreases in the company's earnings, with corresponding effects recorded in the company's asset and/or liability accounts.

Because revenue and expense accounts are subcategories of Retained Earnings, they are affected by debits and credits in the same way as all shareholders' equity accounts. You already know that increases in shareholders' equity are recorded on the right side. You also know that revenues increase net income, which increases the shareholders' equity account Retained Earnings. So putting these ideas together should lead to the conclusion that revenues are recorded on the right (credit). Here's the logic again: Increases in shareholders' equity are on the right, revenues increase shareholders' equity, so revenues are recorded on the right (credit). Decreases in shareholders' equity are recorded on the left side, so to show that expenses decrease net income and retained earnings, expenses are recorded on the left (debit). Exhibit 3.7 summarizes these effects.

Transaction Analysis, Recording, and Summarizing

To learn how to use your new knowledge of the revenue and matching principles, the expanded accounting equation, and the debit/credit framework, you'll need lots of practice. The best place to start is by reading our analysis of the following examples, which involve Pizza Palace's operating activities during September.

(a) Provide Services for Cash In September, Pizza Palace delivered pizza to customers for $15,000 cash. These activities qualify as accounting transactions because Pizza Palace received cash and delivered pizza, which generates revenues. The increase in Cash (an asset) must be recorded (with a debit) along with the revenue (which, as a subcategory of shareholders' equity, is recorded with a credit). To indicate that the pizza deliveries increase revenue, which ultimately increases shareholders' equity, we use the notation (+R, +SE) in the journal entry. The increase in Cash is summarized in the Cash T-account, which carried a debit balance of $10,000 forward from the end of August (Chapter 2). The revenues earned are recorded in a new account called *Pizza Revenue*, which has a beginning balance of zero because the company began operating only this month.

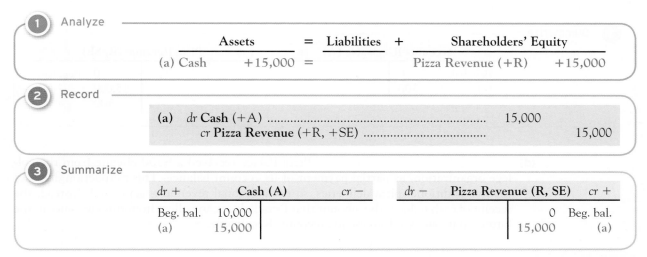

① Analyze

	Assets	=	Liabilities	+	Shareholders' Equity	
(a) Cash	+15,000	=			Pizza Revenue (+R)	+15,000

② Record

(a) dr Cash (+A) 15,000
         cr Pizza Revenue (+R, +SE)   15,000

③ Summarize

dr +	Cash (A)	cr −		dr −	Pizza Revenue (R, SE)	cr +
Beg. bal.	10,000				0	Beg. bal.
(a)	15,000				15,000	(a)

(b) Receive Cash for Future Services Pizza Palace sold three $100 gift cards at the beginning of September. Pizza Palace receives cash but gives only gift cards, which creates an obligation to accept the gift cards as payment for pizzas in the future. This obligation is recorded as a liability called *Unearned Revenue*.

COACH'S TIP

The word *unearned* in the Unearned Revenue account means the company hasn't done everything it was paid to do. It has a liability to do the work or return the cash.

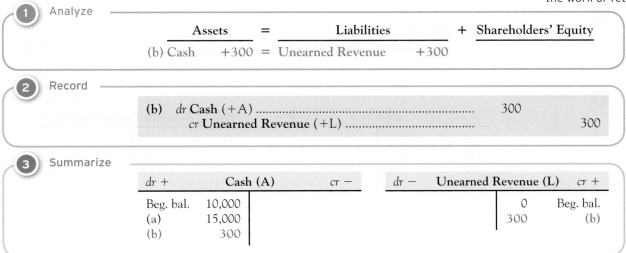

① Analyze

	Assets	=	Liabilities		+	Shareholders' Equity
(b) Cash	+300	=	Unearned Revenue	+300		

② Record

(b) dr Cash (+A) 300
         cr Unearned Revenue (+L)   300

③ Summarize

dr +	Cash (A)	cr −		dr −	Unearned Revenue (L)	cr +
Beg. bal.	10,000				0	Beg. bal.
(a)	15,000				300	(b)
(b)	300					

(c) Provide Services on Credit Pizza Palace delivers $500 of pizza to a college organization, billing this customer on account. Once again, this is another instance where revenues are recorded based on whether the work has been done, not whether cash has been received. Because the pizza has been delivered, Pizza Palace has earned revenue and now has the right to collect $500 from the college organization. The right to collect money is an asset called *Accounts Receivable*.

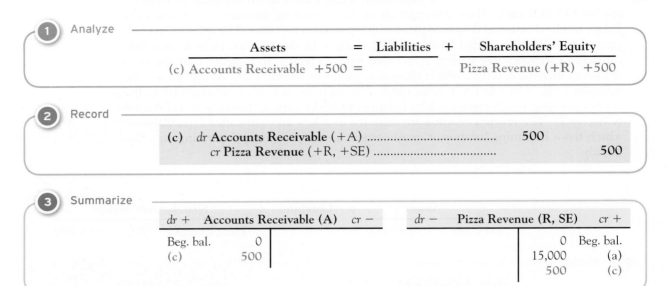

1 Analyze

Assets	=	Liabilities	+	Shareholders' Equity
(c) Accounts Receivable +500 =				Pizza Revenue (+R) +500

2 Record

(c)	dr Accounts Receivable (+A)	500	
	cr Pizza Revenue (+R, +SE)		500

3 Summarize

dr +	Accounts Receivable (A)	cr −		dr −	Pizza Revenue (R, SE)	cr +
Beg. bal.	0				0	Beg. bal.
(c)	500				15,000	(a)
					500	(c)

(d) Receive Payment on Account Pizza Palace received a $300 cheque from the college organization, as partial payment of its account balance. This transaction does not involve additional pizza deliveries, so no additional revenue is generated. Instead, the receipt of cash reduces the amount that Pizza Palace can collect from this customer in the future, so it causes a decrease in Accounts Receivable.

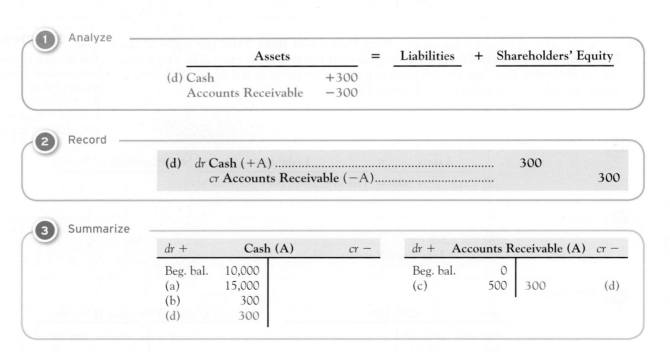

1 Analyze

Assets		=	Liabilities	+	Shareholders' Equity
(d) Cash	+300				
Accounts Receivable	−300				

2 Record

(d)	dr Cash (+A)	300	
	cr Accounts Receivable (−A).................................		300

3 Summarize

dr +	Cash (A)	cr −		dr +	Accounts Receivable (A)	cr −
Beg. bal.	10,000			Beg. bal.	0	
(a)	15,000			(c)	500	300	(d)
(b)	300					
(d)	300					

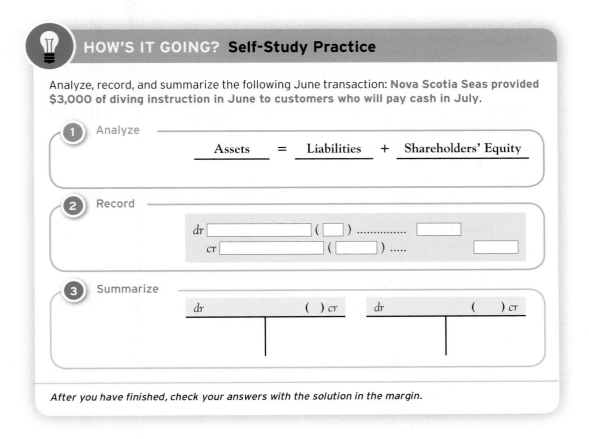

HOW'S IT GOING? Self-Study Practice

Analyze, record, and summarize the following June transaction: **Nova Scotia Seas provided $3,000 of diving instruction in June to customers who will pay cash in July.**

1 Analyze

Assets	=	Liabilities	+	Shareholders' Equity

2 Record

dr ☐ (☐) .... ☐
cr ☐ (☐) .....

3 Summarize

dr ☐ ( ) cr ☐ dr ☐ ( ) cr

After you have finished, check your answers with the solution in the margin.

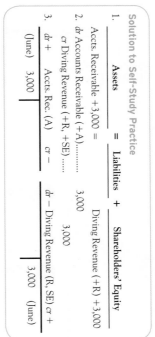

Solution to Self-Study Practice

1.

Assets	=	Liabilities	+	Shareholders' Equity
Accts. Receivable +3,000	=			Diving Revenue (+R) +3,000

2. dr Accounts Receivable (+A).......... 3,000
   cr Diving Revenue (+R, +SE) 3,000

3.

dr + Accts. Rec. (A) cr − dr − Diving Revenue (R, SE) cr +
(June) 3,000 | 3,000 | 3,000 (June)

(e) Pay Cash to Employees Pizza Palace wrote cheques to employees, totalling **$8,700 for wages related to hours worked in September**. The matching principle requires that all expenses that relate to revenues earned in the current period be recorded in the current period. Thus, this transaction involves an expense. We show (+E, −SE) because as expenses increase, net income decreases, which causes shareholders' equity to decrease.

 **COACH'S TIP**

To review why expenses are recorded using a debit, see Exhibit 3.7 (page 98).

1 Analyze

Assets	=	Liabilities	+	Shareholders' Equity
(e) Cash −8,700	=			Wages Expense (+E) −8,700

2 Record

(e) dr Wages Expense (+E, −SE) 8,700
    cr Cash (−A) 8,700

3 Summarize

dr +	Cash (A)		cr −		dr +	Wages Expense (E, SE)	cr −
Beg. bal.	10,000				Beg. bal.	0	
(a)	15,000	8,700	(e)		(e)	8,700	
(b)	300						
(d)	300						

(f) Pay Cash in Advance On September 1, Pizza Palace paid $7,200 in advance for September, October, and November rent. This transaction involves paying for the right to use the rented building for three months following the payment. This payment provides an economic resource to Pizza Palace (building space for three months), so it will initially be reported as an asset called *Prepaid Rent*. Each month, when the rented space has been used, Pizza Palace will reduce Prepaid Rent and show the amount used up as Rent Expense. The adjustment needed to report September's share of the total rent expense ($1/3 \times \$7,200 = \$2,400$) will be covered in Chapter 4. For now, we will record just the $7,200 rent prepayment.

Pay rent now

| Rent benefits consumed later → |
| Rent Expense recorded later |

Record asset now
(Prepaid Rent)

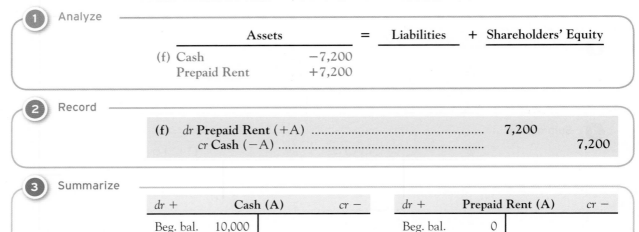

① Analyze

	Assets		=	Liabilities	+	Shareholders' Equity
(f) Cash		−7,200				
Prepaid Rent		+7,200				

② Record

(f)   dr **Prepaid Rent** (+A) 7,200
       cr **Cash** (−A)   7,200

③ Summarize

dr +	Cash (A)		cr −		dr +	Prepaid Rent (A)	cr −
Beg. bal.	10,000				Beg. bal.	0	
(a)	15,000	8,700	(e)		(f)	7,200	
(b)	300	7,200	(f)				
(d)	300						

Prepayments for insurance and other time-based services would be analyzed and recorded in a similar manner.

(g) Pay Cash in Advance On September 2, Pizza Palace wrote a cheque for $1,600 for pizza sauce, dough, cheese, and paper products. This transaction provides another example of a prepayment that is initially recorded as an asset. The supplies are an asset because they can be used to make and sell pizza in the future. Later, when that happens and the supplies have been used up, Pizza Palace will reduce the Supplies account balance and report the amount used up as Supplies Expense. The adjustment to be made at the end of September will be covered in Chapter 4.

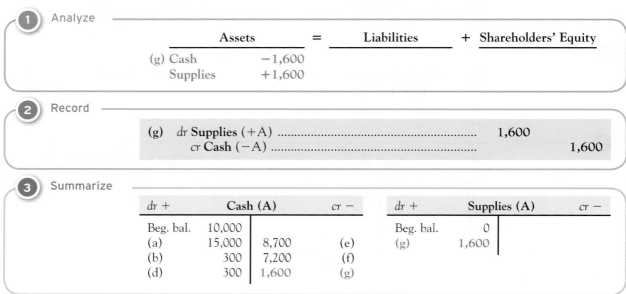

① Analyze

	Assets		=	Liabilities	+	Shareholders' Equity
(g) Cash		−1,600				
Supplies		+1,600				

② Record

(g)   dr **Supplies** (+A) 1,600
       cr **Cash** (−A)   1,600

③ Summarize

dr +	Cash (A)		cr −		dr +	Supplies (A)	cr −
Beg. bal.	10,000				Beg. bal.	0	
(a)	15,000	8,700	(e)		(g)	1,600	
(b)	300	7,200	(f)				
(d)	300	1,600	(g)				

(h) Incur Cost to Be Paid Later Pizza Palace received a bill for $400 for running a newspaper ad in September. The bill will be paid in October. This cost was incurred for September advertising services, so according to the matching principle, it should be recorded as an expense in September. Rather than pay cash for this expense, Pizza Palace gave a promise to pay, which increases the liability called *Accounts Payable*.

 **COACH'S TIP**

The beginning balance in Accounts Payable is carried forward from the previous month's activities discussed in Chapter 2.

1 Analyze

	Assets	=	Liabilities	+	Shareholders' Equity
(h)			Accounts Payable +400		Advertising Expense (+E) −400

2 Record

(h)   *dr* Advertising Expense (+E, −SE) 400
        cr Accounts Payable (+L)..   400

3 Summarize

dr −	Accounts Payable (L)	*cr* +		*dr* +	Advertising Exp. (E, SE)	*cr* −
		630 Beg. bal.		Beg. bal. 0		
		400 (h)		(h) 400		

(i) Pay Cash for Expenses Pizza Palace received and paid bills totalling $600 for September utilities services. Just like transaction (e), the cash payment and expense occurred during the same period.

1 Analyze

	Assets	=	Liabilities	+	Shareholders' Equity
(i) Cash	−600	=			Utilities Expense (+E) −600

2 Record

(i)   *dr* Utilities Expense (+E, −SE) 600
        cr Cash (−A)   600

3 Summarize

dr +	Cash (A)		*cr* −		*dr* +	Utilities Expense (E, SE)	*cr* −
Beg. bal.	10,000				Beg. bal.	0	
(a)	15,000	8,700	(e)		(i)	600	
(b)	300	7,200	(f)				
(d)	300	1,600	(g)				
		600	(i)				

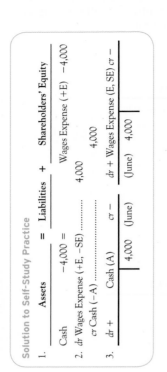
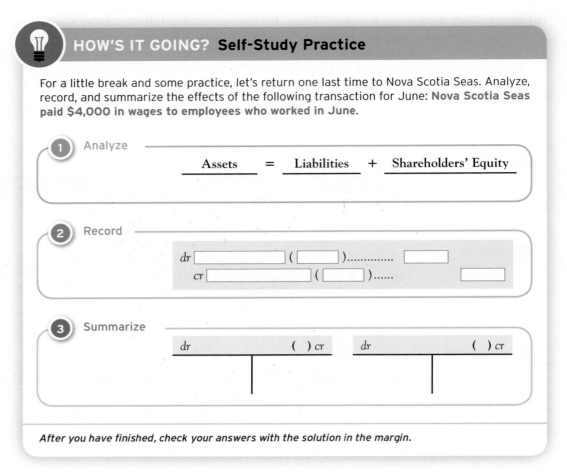

HOW'S IT GOING? Self-Study Practice

For a little break and some practice, let's return one last time to Nova Scotia Seas. Analyze, record, and summarize the effects of the following transaction for June: **Nova Scotia Seas paid $4,000 in wages to employees who worked in June.**

1 Analyze

Assets   =   Liabilities   +   Shareholders' Equity

2 Record

dr [   ] ([   ])............. [   ]
cr [   ] ([   ])...... [   ]

3 Summarize

dr   ( ) cr   dr   ( ) cr

After you have finished, check your answers with the solution in the margin.

Calculating Account Balances   Having entered ("posted") the effects of each journal entry into the T-accounts, we can now calculate the ending balances. In Exhibit 3.8, we have included all the T-accounts for Pizza Palace (from this chapter as well as Chapter 2). You've heard it before, but we'll just remind you that the ending balance in each account is the amount by which the total of the increase (+) side exceeds the total of the decrease (−) side.

UNADJUSTED TRIAL BALANCE

After summarizing journal entries in the various accounts and then calculating ending balances for each account, you should check that the total recorded debits equal the total recorded credits. It's easy to make mistakes when you're doing the recording and summarizing steps by hand. Typical mistakes involve (a) forgetting to post both sides of a journal entry, (b) posting a debit in the credit column (or vice versa), (c) recording the wrong amount, or (d) miscalculating the ending account balance. The best way to ensure your accounts are "in balance" is to prepare a **trial balance**, like the one in Exhibit 3.9. A trial balance is an internal report used to determine whether the dollar value of the total debits equals the dollar value of the total credits. Also, as you will see in Chapter 4, it's a great tool to use when preparing the financial statements. Typically, a trial balance lists every account name in one column (usually in the order of assets, liabilities, shareholders' equity, revenues, and expenses). The ending balances obtained from the ledgers (T-accounts) are listed in the appropriate debit or credit column.

If your trial balance indicates that total debits don't equal total credits, you will experience a sick feeling because this means you've made an error somewhere in preparing or posting the journal entries to the T-accounts. Don't panic or start randomly changing numbers. The first thing to do when you find yourself in a hole is stop digging. Calmly look at the

EXHIBIT 3.8 | T-Accounts for Pizza Palace

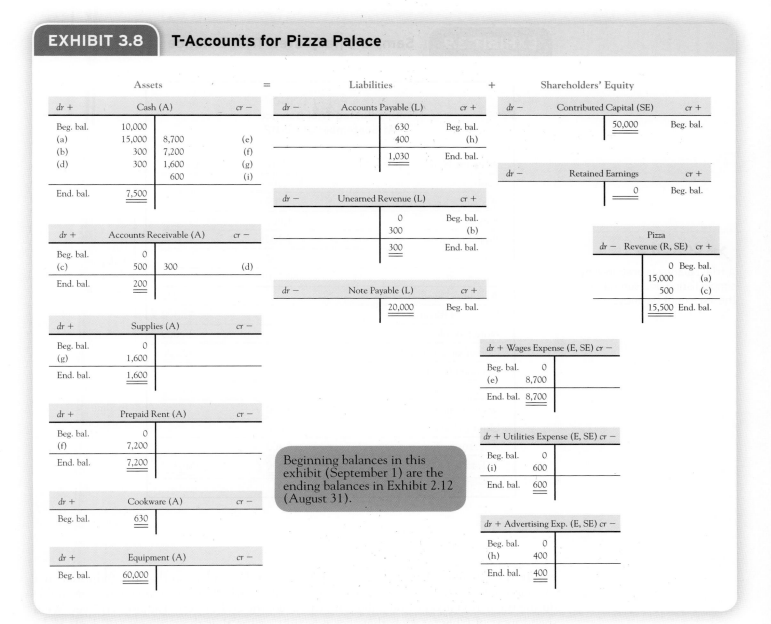

Assets = Liabilities + Shareholders' Equity

Cash (A) dr + / cr −

Beg. bal.	10,000		
(a)	15,000	8,700	(e)
(b)	300	7,200	(f)
(d)	300	1,600	(g)
		600	(i)
End. bal.	7,500		

Accounts Receivable (A) dr + / cr −

Beg. bal.	0		
(c)	500	300	(d)
End. bal.	200		

Supplies (A) dr + / cr −

Beg. bal.	0	
(g)	1,600	
End. bal.	1,600	

Prepaid Rent (A) dr + / cr −

Beg. bal.	0	
(f)	7,200	
End. bal.	7,200	

Cookware (A) dr + / cr −

Beg. bal.	630

Equipment (A) dr + / cr −

Beg. bal.	60,000

Accounts Payable (L) dr − / cr +

		630	Beg. bal.
		400	(h)
		1,030	End. bal.

Unearned Revenue (L) dr − / cr +

		0	Beg. bal.
		300	(b)
		300	End. bal.

Note Payable (L) dr − / cr +

		20,000	Beg. bal.

Contributed Capital (SE) dr − / cr +

	50,000	Beg. bal.

Retained Earnings dr − / cr +

	0	Beg. bal.

Pizza Revenue (R, SE) dr − / cr +

		0	Beg. bal.
		15,000	(a)
		500	(c)
		15,500	End. bal.

Wages Expense (E, SE) dr + / cr −

Beg. bal.	0	
(e)	8,700	
End. bal.	8,700	

Utilities Expense (E, SE) dr + / cr −

Beg. bal.	0	
(i)	600	
End. bal.	600	

Advertising Exp. (E, SE) dr + / cr −

Beg. bal.	0	
(h)	400	
End. bal.	400	

> Beginning balances in this exhibit (September 1) are the ending balances in Exhibit 2.12 (August 31).

difference between total debits and credits and consult the Homework Helper section on page 114 for tips on how to find the error causing that difference.

We don't want to depress you, but even if total debits equal total credits, it's still possible that you've made an error. For example, if you accidentally debit an asset rather than an expense, or credit Accounts Payable instead of Unearned Revenue, total debits would still equal total credits. So if the trial balance doesn't balance, you know you've made an error for sure. If the trial balance does balance, it's still possible that you've made a mistake.

If you haven't already scanned the trial balance in Exhibit 3.9, take a moment to do it now. Notice that the title says unadjusted trial balance. It is called this because several adjustments will have to be made at the end of the accounting period to update the accounts. For example, some of the benefits of Prepaid Rent were used up in September, but this wasn't recorded yet. If you're really sharp, you'll also have noticed that income taxes haven't been calculated and recorded yet. Although it's possible to prepare preliminary financial statements using the numbers on the unadjusted trial balance, most companies don't. They wait until after the final adjustments are made. These adjustments will

EXHIBIT 3.9   Sample Unadjusted Trial Balance

PIZZA PALACE, INC.
Unadjusted Trial Balance
At September 30, 2012

Account Name	Debits	Credits	
Cash	$ 7,500		
Accounts Receivable	200		
Supplies	1,600		
Prepaid Rent	7,200		Balance
Cookware	630		sheet
Equipment	60,000		accounts
Accounts Payable		$ 1,030	
Unearned Revenue		300	
Note Payable		20,000	
Contributed Capital		50,000	
Retained Earnings		0	
Pizza Revenue		15,500	
Wages Expense	8,700		Income
Utilities Expense	600		statement
Advertising Expense	400		accounts
Totals	$86,830	$86,830	

ensure the revenues and expenses are up to date and complete so that the (adjusted) net income number will provide a good indication about whether the company was profitable during the period. Don't worry about how to make the end-of-period adjustments yet. We'll spend most of Chapter 4 on that. For now, just realize that the accounts still have to be adjusted before we can prepare financial statements that follow generally accepted accounting principles.

REVIEW OF REVENUES AND EXPENSES

Up to this point in the chapter, you've analyzed some transactions—nine, actually—that involve operating activities. While this is a good introduction, it doesn't quite prepare you for the variety of operating activities that most companies engage in. What you really need is a general summary of everything you've learned about revenues, expenses, and journal entries, and then lots of practice applying it to a broad range of activities. Let's start with revenues.

Remember that revenues are recorded when the business fulfills its promise to provide goods or services to customers, which is not necessarily the same time that cash is received. Because of this, we look at three cases, where cash is received (1) before the revenue is earned by delivering goods or services, (2) in the same period the revenue is earned, and (3) after the revenue is earned. The journal entries for these situations are shown in the following panels.

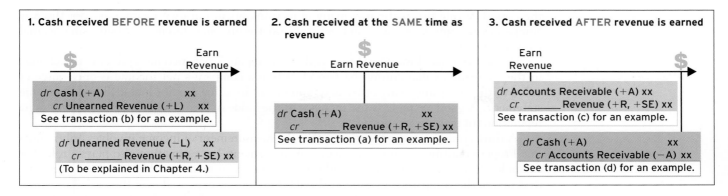

Although these three panels correspond to the revenue transactions for Pizza Palace analyzed earlier in this chapter, they can be applied to any business. We use a generic label "_____ Revenue" with the expectation that you will fill in the blank with whatever type of revenue you are recording. That is, when accounting for revenue from delivering pizza, you should use an account name like Pizza Revenue. A more complete list of account names is provided in the Homework Helper section on page 114.

Let's look at a similar summary for expenses now. Under accrual accounting, expenses are recorded when incurred (by using up the economic benefits of acquired items). Expenses are not necessarily incurred at the same time that cash is paid. Because of this, we look at three cases, where cash is paid (1) before the expense is incurred, (2) in the same period the expense is incurred, and (3) after the expense is incurred. The corresponding journal entries are summarized in the following panels.

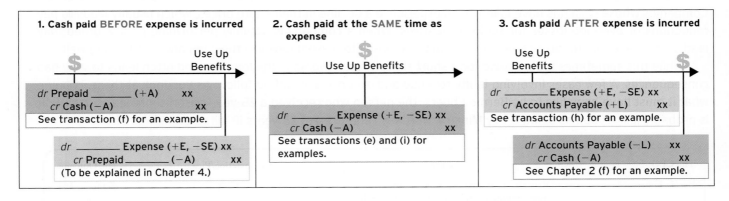

Again, we use generic labels like "Prepaid _____" and "_____ Expense" with the expectation that you will fill in the blank with whatever type of item you are recording (e.g., Prepaid Rent, Rent Expense).

Evaluate the Results

The income statement provides the main measure of a company's operating performance. The key thing to look for is whether net income is positive (revenues exceed expenses). Beyond that, it's useful to consider whether revenues are growing faster than expenses. If so, the company's net income will be increasing. To be successful, a company's net income should be stable or growing from period to period.

INCOME STATEMENT LIMITATIONS

Although an income statement is useful for assessing a company's performance, it does have some limitations that lead to common misconceptions. One of the most common is that some people think net income equals the amount of cash generated by the business during

Learning Objective 5

Describe limitations of the income statement.

the period. While this is the way many of us think about our own income, it's not the way companies recognize revenues and expenses on the income statement when using accrual basis accounting.

A second, related misconception is that a company's net income represents the change in the company's value during the period. While a company's net income is one source of value to the company, many other determinants of its value are not included in the income statement. A good example is the increase in the value of Pizza Palace's name as it grows its reputation for making great pizza.

A third common misconception is that the measurement of income involves only counting. Proper counting is critical to income measurement, but estimation also plays a role. For example, Pizza Palace's equipment will not last forever. Instead, it will be "used up" over time to generate the company's revenue. It should therefore be expensed over the period in which it is used. Doing so requires an estimate of the period over which each category of equipment will be used. We will discuss this particular example in Chapter 4; many other examples of the role of estimates in income measurement will arise in later chapters.

SPOTLIGHT ON Ethics

Why All the Scandals?

You may have heard about accounting scandals, such as those at Enron and WorldCom (now owned by Verizon), in which managers have been accused of "cooking the books." Why did they do it? The simple answer is greed. Companies whose earnings have fallen often experience a decline in their share prices, which usually leads to pay reductions or even job losses for senior executives. When a company is actually performing poorly, greed may lead some managers to falsify revenues and hide expenses to make it look like the company is still doing well.

While this sometimes fools people for a short time, it rarely works in the long run and often leads to very bad consequences. A few cases involving faulty revenue and expense accounting follow. As you look at these, imagine what it must have been like to be Bernie Ebbers—the person who received a 25-year prison sentence at age 65. It is probably just as bad as being Barry Minkow, who was sentenced to 25 years in jail when he was 21.

The CEO	The Fraud	Conviction/Plea	The Outcome
Bernie Ebbers, 65 WorldCom	Recorded operating expenses as if they were assets; resulted in the largest fraud in U.S. history	Convicted July 2005	Sentenced to 25 years
Garth Drabinsky, 61 Livent Inc.	Moved operating expenses from one period to another; recorded operating expenses as if they were assets	Convicted August 2009	Sentenced to 7 years
Sanjay Kumar, 44 Computer Associates	Recorded sales in the wrong accounting period	Pleaded guilty April 2006	Sentenced to 12 years
Martin Grass, 49 Rite Aid Corporation	Recorded rebates from drug companies before they were earned	Pleaded guilty June 2003	Sentenced to 8 years
Barry Minkow, 21 ZZZZ Best	Made up customers and sales to show profits when, in reality, the company was a sham	Convicted December 1988	Sentenced to 25 years

In this chapter, you learned how to measure and report revenues and expenses for the accounting period as a starting point for determining net income. The next step is to adjust the financial statements so that they will be complete and up to date at the end of the accounting period. Currently, Pizza Palace's accounting records report revenues of $15,500 and expenses of $8,700, $600, and $400, suggesting a net income of $5,800. But Ally cautions Emilio that this measure of net income is preliminary and will change when the accounting records are adjusted at the end of September. The adjustment process is the main topic of Chapter 4.

Due to the nature of the material in Chapter 3, there are no differences between ASPE and IFRS. Both require the same basis of accounting for external reporting of financial statements and both follow the same revenue and matching principles.

Topic	ASPE	IFRS
Basis of Accounting	Accrual basis of accounting is the only acceptable method for external reporting of financial statements.	Accrual basis of accounting is the only acceptable method for external reporting of financial statements.
Revenue Principle	Revenues should be recognized when they are earned.	Revenues should be recognized when they are earned.
Matching Principle	Expenses are recognized in the same period as the revenues to which they relate.	Expenses are recognized in the same period as the revenues to which they relate.

Review the Chapter

This section provides a chance to solidify your understanding of key points. It's worth your time to work through the following demonstration cases, scan the chapter summary, test your understanding of key terms, and then practise, practise, practise.

DEMONSTRATION CASE A

1. From the following list of balance sheet and income statement account balances for Castle Cruises Corporation, prepare an income statement for the year ended November 30, 2012. (Amounts are reported in millions of Canadian dollars.)

2. Explain what the results suggest about the cruise ship company's operating performance. Net income for the same period last year was $2,408 (in millions of Canadian dollars).

Transportation Expenses	$ 2,232	Wages Expense	$1,470	Selling Expenses	$1,629
Passenger Ticket Revenue	11,210	Fuel Expenses	1,774	Prepaid Expenses	267
Onboard Revenue	3,436	Accounts Payable	512	Ship Expenses	4,308
Food Expenses	856	Income Tax Expense	47	Unearned Revenue	2,519

Suggested Solution

1. Income Statement

CASTLE CRUISES CORPORATION
Income Statement
For the Year Ended November 30, 2012
(amounts in millions of Canadian dollars)

Revenues	
Passenger Ticket Revenue	$11,210
Onboard Revenue	3,436
Total Revenues	14,646
Expenses	
Ship Expenses	4,308
Transportation Expenses	2,232
Selling Expenses	1,629
Fuel Expenses	1,774
Wages Expense	1,470
Food Expenses	856
Income Tax Expense	47
Total Expenses	12,316
Net Income	$ 2,330

> **COACH'S TIP**
>
> Prepaid Expenses of $267 is excluded from the income statement because it is an asset on the balance sheet. Accounts Payable of $512 and Unearned Revenue of $2,519 are excluded from the income statement because they are liabilities on the balance sheet.

2. The net income of $2,330 (million) indicates that Castle Cruises Corporation was profitable, meaning that the revenues it earned were greater than the expenses it incurred. Generally, this is a positive sign. However, the decline from the net income of $2,408 (million) reported in the prior year suggests the company is not doing as well as it once did.

DEMONSTRATION CASE B

This case is a continuation of the Goodbye Grass Corporation case introduced in Chapter 2. The company was established and property and equipment were purchased. The balance sheet at April 30, 2012, based on only the investing and financing activities (from Chapter 2) is as follows:

GOODBYE GRASS CORPORATION
Balance Sheet
At April 30, 2012

Assets			Liabilities		
Current Assets			**Current Liabilities**		
Cash	$ 3,800		Accounts Payable	$ 400	
Note Receivable	1,250		Note Payable	4,000	
Total Current Assets	5,050		Total Current Liabilities	4,400	
Equipment	4,600		**Shareholders' Equity**		
Land	3,750		Contributed Capital	9,000	
			Retained Earnings	0	
			Total Shareholders' Equity	9,000	
Total Assets	$13,400		Total Liabilities and Shareholders' Equity	$13,400	

The following activities also occurred during April 2012:

a. Purchased and used gasoline for mowers and edgers, paying $90 in cash at a local gas station.

b. In early April, received $1,600 cash from the city in advance for lawn maintenance service for April through July ($400 each month). The entire amount is to be recorded as Unearned Revenue.

c. In early April, purchased $300 of insurance covering six months, April through September. The entire payment is to be recorded as Prepaid Insurance.

d. Mowed lawns for residential customers who are billed every two weeks. A total of $5,200 of service was billed and is to be recorded in April.

e. Residential customers paid $3,500 on their accounts.

f. Paid wages every two weeks. Total cash paid in April was $3,900.

g. Received a bill for $320 from the local gas station for additional gasoline purchased on account and used in April.

h. Paid $100 on accounts payable.

Required:

1. Analyze activities (a)–(h) with the goal of indicating their effects on the basic accounting equation (Assets = Liabilities + Shareholders' Equity), using the format shown in the chapter.

2. Prepare journal entries to record the transactions identified among activities (a)–(h).

   TIP: Treat insurance (in c) in the same manner as Pizza Palace's rent in transaction (f) on page 102.

3. Summarize the effects of each transaction in the appropriate T-accounts. Before entering these effects, set up T-accounts for Cash, Accounts Receivable, Note Receivable, Prepaid Insurance, Equipment, Land, Accounts Payable, Unearned Revenue, Note Payable, Contributed Capital, Retained Earnings, Mowing Revenue, Wages Expense, and Fuel Expense. The beginning balance in

each T-account should be the amount shown on the balance sheet above or $0 if the account does not appear on the above balance sheet. After posting the journal entries to the T-accounts, compute ending balances for each of the T-accounts.

4. Use the amounts in the T-accounts to prepare an unadjusted trial balance for Goodbye Grass Corporation at April 30, 2012.

After completing the above requirements, check your answers with the following solution.

Suggested Solution

1. Transaction analysis:

	Assets		=	Liabilities		+	Shareholders' Equity	
a.	Cash	−90	=				Fuel Expense (+E)	−90
b.	Cash	+1,600	=	Unearned Revenue	+1,600			
c.	Cash	−300	=			No change		
	Prepaid Insurance	+300						
d.	Accounts Receivable	+5,200	=				Mowing Revenue (+R)	+5,200
e.	Cash	+3,500	=			No change		
	Accounts Receivable	−3,500						
f.	Cash	−3,900	=				Wages Expense (+E)	−3,900
g.	No change		=	Accounts Payable	+320		Fuel Expense (+E)	−320
h.	Cash	−100	=	Accounts Payable	−100			

2. Journal entries:

a.	dr Fuel Expense (+E, −SE)	90	
	cr Cash (−A)		90
b.	dr Cash (+A)..	1,600	
	cr Unearned Revenue (+L).......................................		1,600
c.	dr Prepaid Insurance (+A)	300	
	cr Cash (−A)		300
d.	dr Accounts Receivable (+A)......................................	5,200	
	cr Mowing Revenue (+R, +SE)		5,200
e.	dr Cash (+A)	3,500	
	cr Accounts Receivable (−A).....................................		3,500
f.	dr Wages Expense (+E, −SE)	3,900	
	cr Cash (−A)		3,900
g.	dr Fuel Expense (+E, −SE)	320	
	cr Accounts Payable (+L)		320
h.	dr Accounts Payable (−L)	100	
	cr Cash (−A)		100

3. T-Accounts:

Assets	=	Liabilities	+	Shareholders' Equity

dr + Cash (A) cr −

Beg. bal.	3,800	90	(a)
(b)	1,600	300	(c)
(e)	3,500	3,900	(f)
		100	(h)
End. bal.	4,510		

dr − Accounts Payable (L) cr +

		400 Beg. bal.	
(h)	100	320	(g)
		620 End. bal.	

dr − Contributed Capital (SE) cr +

	9,000 Beg. bal.
	9,000 End. bal.

dr + Accounts Receivable (A) cr −

Beg. bal.	0		
(d)	5,200	3,500	(e)
End. bal.	1,700		

dr − Unearned Revenue (L) cr +

	0 Beg. bal.
	1,600 (b)
	1,600 End. bal.

dr − Retained Earnings (SE) cr +

	0 Beg. bal.
	0 End. bal.

dr + Note Receivable (A) cr −

Beg. bal.	1,250
End. bal.	1,250

dr − Note Payable (L) cr +

	4,000 Beg. bal.
	4,000 End. bal.

dr + Wages Expense (E) cr −

Beg. bal.	0
(f)	3,900
End. bal.	3,900

dr − Mowing Revenue (R) cr +

	0 Beg. bal.
	5,200 (d)
	5,200 End. bal.

dr + Prepaid Insurance (A) cr −

Beg. bal.	0
(c)	300
End. Bal.	300

dr + Fuel Expense (E) cr −

Beg. bal.	0
(a)	90
(g)	320
End. bal.	410

dr + Equipment (A) cr −

Beg. bal.	4,600
End. bal.	4,600

dr + Land (A) cr −

Beg. bal.	3,750
End. bal.	3,750

4. Unadjusted trial balance:

GOODBYE GRASS CORPORATION
Unadjusted Trial Balance
At April 30, 2012

Account Name	Debits	Credits
Cash	$ 4,510	
Accounts Receivable	1,700	
Note Receivable	1,250	
Prepaid Insurance	300	
Equipment	4,600	
Land	3,750	
Accounts Payable		$ 620
Unearned Revenue		1,600
Note Payable		4,000
Contributed Capital		9,000
Retained Earnings		0
Mowing Revenue		5,200
Wages Expense	3,900	
Fuel Expense	410	
Totals	$20,420	$20,420

CHAPTER SUMMARY

Describe common operating transactions and select appropriate income statement account titles. p. 90   **LO1**

- The income statement reports the results of transactions that affect net income, which includes

  Revenues—amounts charged to customers for sales of goods or services provided.

  Expenses—costs of business activities undertaken to earn revenues.

- See Exhibit 3.2 on page 91 for basic income statement format.

Explain and apply the revenue and matching principles. p. 94   **LO2**

- The two key concepts underlying accrual basis accounting and the income statement are

  Revenue principle—recognize revenues when they are earned by providing goods or services.

  Matching principle—recognize expenses when they are incurred in generating revenue.

Analyze, record, and summarize the effects of operating transactions, using the accounting equation, journal entries, and T-accounts. p. 98   **LO3**

- The expanded transaction analysis model includes revenues and expenses as subcategories of Retained Earnings. Increases, decreases, and normal account balances (*dr* or *cr*) are shown below.

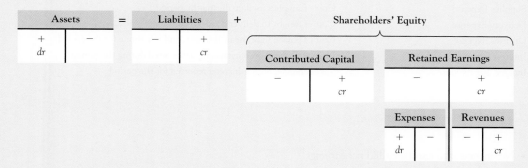

Prepare an unadjusted trial balance. p. 104   **LO4**

- The unadjusted trial balance is a list of all accounts and their unadjusted balances, and is used to check on the equality of recorded debits and credits.

Describe limitations of the income statement. p. 107   **LO5**

- The income statement indicates whether the company is profitable, but this might not explain whether cash increased or decreased.
- The income statement does not directly measure the change in value of a company during the period.
- Estimation plays a key role when measuring income.

KEY TERMS

See complete definitions in the glossary in the back of this text.

HOMEWORK HELPER

Account Name	Description
Revenues	
Sales	Arise from delivering products in the ordinary course of business
Service Revenues	Arise from providing services in the ordinary course of business
Rental Revenues	Amounts earned by renting out company property
Interest Revenues	Amounts earned on savings and loans to others
Dividend Revenues	Dividends earned from investing in other companies
Fees Earned	Fees that the company charges its customers
Expenses	
Cost of Goods Sold	Cost of products sold in the ordinary course of business
Repairs & Maintenance Expense	Cost of routine maintenance and upkeep of buildings/equipment
Advertising Expense	Cost of advertising services obtained during the period
Amortization Expense	Cost of plant, equipment, and intangible assets used up during the period
Insurance Expense	Cost of insurance coverage for the current period
Salaries and Wages Expense	Cost of employees' salaries and wages for the period
Rent Expense	Cost of rent for the period
Supplies Expense	Cost of supplies used up during the period
Delivery Expense	Cost of freight to deliver goods to customers
Utilities Expense	Cost of power, light, heat, Internet, and telephone for the period
Interest Expense	Interest charged on outstanding debts owed during the period
Income Tax Expense	Taxes charged on net income reported for the period

Alternative terms

- *Net income* also can be called *net earnings*.
- *Prepaid Rent* and *Prepaid Insurance* can be called *Prepaid Expenses*, which is reported as a current asset on the balance sheet.

Helpful reminders

- To properly understand why Prepaid Expenses is an asset and Unearned Revenue is a liability, emphasize the first word (prepaid and unearned).
- If the trial balance doesn't balance, look at the difference between total debits and total credits. If it is
  - The same as one of your T-account balances, you probably forgot to include the account in your trial balance.
  - Twice the amount of an account balance, you may have included it in the wrong column of the trial balance.
  - Twice the amount of a transaction, you may have posted a debit as a credit or a credit as a debit in your T-accounts.
  - Evenly divisible by 9, you may have reversed the order of two digits in a number (a transposition error) or left a zero off the end of a number.
  - Evenly divisible by 3, you may have hit the key above or below the one you intended to hit (like a 9 instead of a 6) on your numeric keypad.

Frequent mistakes

- *Accrual* is *not* spelled *accural*.

Practice Material

QUESTIONS (✪ Symbol indicates questions that require analysis from more than one perspective.)

1. Show the income statement equation and define each element.

2. When accounting was developed in the 14th and 15th centuries, some businesses had very short lives. For instance, a business might have been created for a ship to sail from Europe to North America and return with furs and other goods. After the goods were delivered and profits were distributed among those who financed the shipment, the business ceased to exist. In more recent centuries, businesses began to experience longer lives. Identify the accounting concept that is needed when accounting for businesses with long lives. Explain what this concept means and why it is necessary for modern-day accounting. ✪

3. Define *accrual basis accounting* and contrast it with *cash basis accounting*.

4. Why is it appropriate to use cash basis accounting in your personal life but not in the business world? ✪

5. What does it mean to *recognize* an accounting transaction?

6. When is revenue typically recognized under accrual basis accounting?

7. Explain the matching principle.

8. Explain why shareholders' equity is increased by revenues and decreased by expenses.

9. Explain why revenues are recorded as credits and expenses as debits.

10. Complete the following table by entering either *debit* or *credit* in each cell:

Item	Increase	Decrease
Revenues		
Expenses		

11. Complete the following table by entering either *increase* or *decrease* in each cell:

Item	Debit	Credit
Revenues		
Expenses		

12. What basic characteristic distinguishes items reported on the income statement from items reported on the balance sheet?

13. Which of the four basic accounting reports indicates that it is appropriate to consider revenues and expenses as subcategories of retained earnings? Explain.

14. What is the difference between Accounts Receivable and Revenue?

15. What is the difference between Accounts Payable for advertising and Advertising Expense?

16. For each of the following situations, indicate whether it represents an accounting error and explain why it is or is not an error. Also state whether a trial balance would indicate that an error exists for each situation. ✪

   a. Cash received from a customer was debited to Accounts Receivable and credited to Cash.

   b. Revenue was recognized when a customer purchased a gift card for future use.

   c. An expense was recorded as an asset.

   d. The debit side of a journal entry was recorded in the accounts, but the credit side was not.

   e. A company shareholder purchased a new car, but this was not recorded by the company.

17. What are three limitations of the income statement that often lead to misconceptions?

Multiple-choice questions and corresponding answers can be found on Connect.

MINI-EXERCISES

M3-1 Reporting Cash Basis versus Accrual Basis Income   LO2

Bachman Music Company had the following transactions in March:

a. Sold music lessons to customers for $10,000; received $6,000 in cash and the rest on account.

b. Paid $600 in wages for the month.

c. Received a $200 bill for utilities that will be paid in April.

d. Received $1,000 from customers as deposits on music lessons to be given in April.

Complete the following statements for March:

Cash Basis Income Statement		Accrual Basis Income Statement	
Revenues		Revenues	
Cash Sales	$	Sales to Customers	$
Customer Deposits			
Expenses		Expenses	
Wages Paid		Wages Expense	
		Utilities Expense	
Cash Income	$	Net Income	$

LO2, 3   **M3-2 Identifying Accrual Basis Revenues**

The following transactions are July 2012 activities of Bill's Extreme Bowling, Inc., which operates several bowling centres. If revenue is to be recognized in July, indicate the amount. If revenue is not to be recognized in July, explain why.

Activity	Amount or Explanation
a. Bill collected $12,000 from customers for games played in July.	
b. Bill invoiced a customer for $250 for a party held at the centre on the last day of July. The bill is to be paid in August.	
c. Bill received $1,000 from credit sales made to customers last month (in June).	
d. The men's and women's bowling leagues gave Bill advance payments totalling $1,500 for the fall season that starts in September.	

For each of the transactions, write the journal entry using the format shown in the chapter.

LO2, 3   **M3-3 Identifying Accrual Basis Expenses**

Again, the following transactions are July 2012 activities of Bill's Extreme Bowling, Inc. If an expense is to be recognized in July, indicate the amount. If an expense is not to be recognized in July, explain why.

Activity	Amount or Explanation
e. Bill paid $1,500 to plumbers for repairing a broken pipe in the restrooms.	
f. Bill paid $2,000 for the June electricity bill and received the July bill for $2,500, which will be paid in August.	
g. Bill paid $5,475 to employees for work in July.	

For each of the transactions in M3-3, write the journal entry using the format shown in the chapter.

LO2, 3   **M3-4 Determining the Accounting Equation Effects of Operating Activities Involving Revenues and Expenses**

For each of the following July 2012 transactions of Bill's Extreme Bowling, Inc., complete the spreadsheet, indicating the amount and effect (+ for increase and − for decrease) of each transaction under the accrual basis. Write NE if there is no effect. Include revenues as a subcategory of shareholders' equity, as shown for the first transaction, which is provided as an example.

Transaction	Assets	Liabilities	Shareholders' Equity
a. Bill collected $12,000 from customers for games played in July.	+12,000	NE	Games Fee Revenue (+R) + 12,000
b. Bill invoiced a customer for $250 for a party held at the centre on the last day of July. The bill is to be paid in August.			
c. Bill received $1,000 from credit sales made to customers last month (in June).			
d. The men's and women's bowling leagues gave Bill advance payments totalling $1,500 for the fall season that starts in September.			
e. Bill paid $1,500 to plumbers for repairing a broken pipe in the restrooms.			
f. Bill paid $2,000 for the June electricity bill and received the July bill for $2,500, which will be paid in August.			
g. Bill paid $5,475 to employees for work in July.			

M3-5 Preparing an Income Statement

LO1

Given the transactions in M3-4 (including the examples), prepare an income statement for Bill's Extreme Bowling, Inc., for the month ended July 31, 2012. (This income statement would be considered "preliminary" because it uses unadjusted balances.)

M3-6 Preparing Accrual Basis Journal Entries for Business Activities

LO3

Quick Cleaners Inc. (QCI) has been in business for several years. It specializes in cleaning houses but has some small-business clients as well. Prepare journal entries for the following transactions, which occurred during a recent month:

a. Incurred $600 of heating and electrical costs this month and will pay them next month.
b. Issued $25,000 of QCI shares for cash.
c. Paid wages for the current month, totalling $2,000.
d. Performed cleaning services on account worth $2,800.
e. Some of Quick Cleaners' equipment was repaired at a total cost of $150. The company paid the full amount immediately.

M3-7 Determining the Accounting Equation Effects of Operating Activities Involving Revenues and Expenses

LO2, 3

The following transactions are February 2012 activities of Swing Right Incorporated, which offers golfing lessons in eastern Canada. For each of the following transactions, complete the spreadsheet, indicating the amount and effect (+ for increase and − for decrease) of each transaction under the accrual basis. Write NE if there is no effect. Include revenues as a subcategory of shareholders' equity, as shown for the first transaction, which is provided as an example.

Transaction	Assets	Liabilities	Shareholders' Equity
a. Swing Right collected $15,000 from customers for lessons given in February.	+15,000	NE	Lesson Revenue (+R) + 15,000
b. Swing Right sold a gift card for golf lessons for $150 cash in February.			
c. Swing Right received $4,000 from credit sales made to customers in January.			
d. Swing Right collected $2,250 in advance payments for golf lessons to start in June.			
e. Swing Right billed a customer $125 for golf lessons given from February 25 through February 29. The bill is to be paid in March.			
f. Swing Right paid $4,750 for wages to its golf instructors for the month of February.			
g. Swing Right paid $1,750 for electricity used in the month of January.			
h. Swing Right received an electricity bill for $800 for the month of February, to be paid in March.			

M3-8 Preparing an Income Statement

Given the transactions in M3-7 (including the examples), prepare an income statement for Swing Right Incorporated for the month ended February 29, 2012. (This income statement would be considered "preliminary" because it uses unadjusted balances.)

LO1, 4

M3-9 Preparing Financial Statements from a Trial Balance (Dividends Included)

The following accounts are taken from Buck Up! Inc., a company that specializes in horse-breaking services and rodeo lessons, as of December 31, 2012.

	BUCK UP! INC.	
	Unadjusted Trial Balance	
	At December 31, 2012	
Account Name	Debits	Credits
Cash	$ 59,750	
Accounts Receivable	3,300	
Prepaid Insurance	1,200	
Equipment	64,600	
Land	23,000	
Accounts Payable		$ 29,230
Unearned Revenue		1,500
Long-Term Notes Payable		74,000
Contributed Capital		5,000
Retained Earnings		14,500
Dividends	3,500	
Horse-Breaking Revenue		25,200
Rodeo Lesson Revenue		10,500
Wages Expense	3,900	
Maintenance Expense	410	
Other Expenses	270	
Totals	$159,930	$159,930

Required:

Using the unadjusted trial balance provided, create a classified balance sheet, statement of retained earnings, and income statement for Buck Up! Inc., for the year ended December 31, 2012. (These financial statements would be considered "preliminary" because they use unadjusted balances.)

> **TIP:** Create the income statement first, followed by the statement of retained earnings, and finally the classified balance sheet. Follow the formats presented in Exhibits 1.2, 1.3, and 2.13.

LO1, 4

Rogers Communications Inc.

M3-10 Preparing an Income Statement

Assume that the following accounts are taken from the December 31, 2012, financial statements of Rogers Communications Inc. (Amounts are in millions.)

Subscription Revenue	$24,904
Other Revenues	12,779
Salaries Expense	9,653
Cash	1,516
Accounts Receivable	7,296
Interest Expense	2,299
Accounts Payable	1,470
Advertising Revenue	8,799
Long-Term Debt	37,004
Other Expenses	381
Unearned Revenue	1,178
Equipment	18,048
Income Tax Expense	2,336
Operating Expense	27,426

Required:

Prepare an income statement for the year ended December 31, 2012.

> **TIP:** Some of the above accounts are not reported on the income statement.

EXERCISES

E3-1 Matching Definitions with Terms

LO1

Match each definition with its related term by entering the appropriate letter in the space provided.

Term	Definition
____ 1. Expenses	A. Record expenses when incurred in earning revenue.
____ 2. Matching principle	B. A liability account used to record the obligation to provide future services or return cash that has been received before revenues have been earned.
____ 3. Revenue principle	
____ 4. Cash basis accounting	
____ 5. Unearned Revenue	C. Costs that result when a company sacrifices resources to generate revenues.
____ 6. Accrual basis accounting	D. Record revenues when earned, not necessarily when cash is received.
____ 7. Prepaid Expenses	E. Record revenues when received and expenses when paid.
	F. A type of asset account used to record the benefits obtained when cash is paid before expenses are incurred.
	G. Record revenues when earned and expenses when incurred.

E3-2 Identifying Accrual Basis Revenues

LO1, 2

Apple

Shaw Communications

WestJet

Check Figure [Part (b)]:
Revenue earned = $2,000

According to the revenue principle, revenues should be recognized when they are earned, which happens when the company performs acts promised to the customer. For most businesses, this condition is met at the point of delivery of goods or services. Assume that the following transactions occurred in September 2012:

a. A customer pays $10 cash for 10 song files from Apple's iTunes store. Answer from Apple's standpoint.

b. The Home Depot provides a carpet installation for $2,000 cash. A comparable installation by other companies costs $3,000.

c. Shaw Communications is scheduled to install digital cable at 1,000 homes during the month of September. The installation charge is $100 per home. The terms require payment within 30 days of installation. Answer from Shaw's standpoint.

d. Shaw completes the installations described in (c). Answer from Shaw's standpoint.

e. Shaw receives payment from customers for the installations described in (c). Answer from Shaw's standpoint.

f. A customer purchases a ticket from WestJet in September for $500 cash to travel in December. Answer from WestJet's standpoint.

Required:

For each of the transactions, if revenue is to be recognized in September, indicate the amount. If revenue is not to be recognized in September, explain why.

E3-3 Identifying Accrual Basis Revenues

LO1, 2

Fido

According to the revenue principle, revenues should be recognized when they are earned, which happens when the company performs acts promised to the customer. For most businesses, this condition is met at the point of delivery of goods or services. The following transactions occurred in September 2012:

a. Gilligan Enterprises Inc. issues $26 million in new common shares.

b. Western University receives $20,000,000 cash for 80,000 five-game season football tickets. None of the games have been played.

c. Western University plays the first football game referred to in (b).

d. Harld Construction Company signs a contract with a customer for the construction of a new $500,000 warehouse to be started in October. At the signing, Harld receives a cheque for $50,000 as a deposit to be applied against amounts earned during the first phase of construction. Answer from Harld's standpoint.

e. A popular snowboarding magazine company today receives a total of $1,800 from subscribers. The subscriptions begin in the next fiscal year, which is after September 30. Answer from the magazine company's standpoint.

f. Fido sells a $100 cellphone plan for service in September to a customer who charges the sale on his credit card. Answer from the standpoint of Fido.

Required:

For each of the transactions, if revenue is to be recognized in September, indicate the amount. If revenue is not to be recognized in September, explain why.

LO1, 2

Gateway

Mc Graw Hill

E3-4 Identifying Accrual Basis Expenses

Under accrual basis accounting, expenses are recognized when incurred, which means the activity giving rise to the expense has occurred. Assume the following transactions occurred in January 2012:

a. Gateway pays its computer service technicians $90,000 in salary for work done in January 2012. Answer from Gateway's standpoint.

b. At the beginning of January, Turnboldt Construction Company pays $4,500 in rent for February–April 2012.

c. Assume that McGraw-Hill Companies—publisher of this textbook and *BusinessWeek*—use $1,000 worth of electricity and natural gas in January for which it has not yet been billed.

d. Pooler Company receives and pays in January a $1,500 invoice from a consulting firm for services received in January.

e. The campus bookstore receives consulting services at a cost of $5,000. The terms indicate that payment is due within 30 days of the consultation.

f. Schergevitch Incorporated has its delivery van repaired in January for $280 and charges the amount on account.

Required:

For each of the transactions, if an expense is to be recognized in January, indicate the amount. If an expense is not to be recognized in January, indicate why.

LO1, 2

American Express
Waste Management, Inc.

E3-5 Identifying Accrual Basis Expenses

Under accrual basis accounting, expenses are recognized when incurred. Assume that the following transactions occurred in January 2012:

a. American Express pays its salespeople $3,500 in commissions related to December financial advisory services sales. Answer from American Express's standpoint.

b. On January 31, American Express determines that it will pay its salespeople $4,200 in commissions related to January sales. The payment will be made in early February. Answer from American Express's standpoint.

Check Figure [Part (c)]:
Expenses incurred
$600,000

c. The City of Ottawa hires Waste Management, Inc., to provide trash collection services beginning in January. The city pays $7.2 million for the entire year. Answer from the City's standpoint.

d. The University of Saskatchewan pays $10,000 in advance for refundable airline tickets to fly the basketball team to a tournament in Toronto. The first game will be played in March. Answer from the university's standpoint.

e. A Business College employee works eight hours, at $15 per hour, on January 31; payday is not until February 3. Answer from the college's point of view.

f. Wang Company paid $3,600 for a fire insurance policy on January 1. The policy covers 12 months beginning on January 1. Answer from Wang's point of view.

g. Ziegler Company, a farm equipment company, receives a phone bill for $230 of January calls. The bill has not been paid to date.

Required:

For each of the transactions, if an expense is to be recognized in January, indicate the amount. If an expense is not to be recognized in January, indicate why.

E3-6 Determining Accounting Equation Effects of Various Transactions

LO2, 3

The following transactions occurred during a recent year:

a. Paid wages of $1,000 for the current period (example).
b. Borrowed $5,000 cash from local bank.
c. Purchased $2,000 of equipment on credit.
d. Earned $400 of sales revenue, collected cash.
e. Received $800 of utilities services, on credit.
f. Earned $700 of service revenue, on credit.
g. Paid $300 cash on account to a supplier.
h. Incurred $70 of delivery expenses, paid cash.
i. Earned $400 of service revenue, collected half in cash, balance on credit.
j. Collected $100 cash from customers on account.
k. Incurred $300 of advertising costs, paid half in cash, balance on credit.

Required:

For each of the transactions, complete the table below, indicating the account, amount, and direction of the effect (+ for increase and − for decrease) of each transaction under the accrual basis. Write NE if there is no effect. Include revenues and expenses as subcategories of shareholders' equity, as shown for the first transaction, which is provided as an example.

Transaction	Assets	=	Liabilities	+	Shareholders' Equity
(a) (Example)	Cash −1,000		NE		Wages Expense (+E) −1,000

E3-7 Determining Accounting Equation Effects of Various Transactions

LO2, 3

Wolverine World Wide, Inc., manufactures military, work, sport, and casual footwear and leather accessories under a variety of brand names, such as Cat Footwear, Hush Puppies, Wolverine, and Harley-Davidson Footwear. Assume that the following transactions occurred during a recent year. Dollars are in thousands.

a. Made cash sales of $49,000 (example).
b. Purchased $3,000 of additional supplies on account.
c. Borrowed $58,000 on long-term notes.
d. Purchased $18,600 in additional equipment, paying in cash.
e. Incurred $87,000 in selling expenses, paying two-thirds in cash and owing the rest on account.
f. Paid $4,700 in rent for this period.

Required:

For each of the transactions, complete the table below, indicating the account, amount, and direction of the effect (+ for increase and − for decrease) and amount of each transaction under the accrual basis. Write NE if there is no effect. Include revenues and expenses as subcategories of shareholders' equity, as shown for the first transaction, which is provided as an example.

Transaction	Assets	Liabilities	Shareholders' Equity
(a) (Example)	Cash +49,000	NE	Sales Revenue (+R) +49,000

E3-8 Recording Accrual Basis Journal Entries

LO2, 3

Sysco is a global leader in marketing and distributing food products to restaurants, health-care and educational facilities, lodging establishments, and other customers who prepare meals away from home. The following transactions are typical of those that occurred in a recent year. (All amounts are rounded to the nearest thousand.)

Sysco

a. Borrowed $80,000 from a bank, signing a short-term note payable.
b. Provided $10,000 in service to customers, with $9,500 on account and the rest received in cash.
c. Purchased plant and equipment for $130,000 in cash.

d. Paid employee wages of $1,000.

e. Received $410 on account from a customer.

f. Purchased and used fuel of $400 in delivery vehicles during the year (paid for in cash).

g. Paid $8,200 cash on accounts payable.

h. Incurred $20,000 in utility expenses during the year, of which $15,000 was paid in cash and the rest owed on account.

Required:

For each of the transactions, prepare journal entries. Determine whether the accounting equation remains in balance and debits equal credits after each entry.

LO2, 3

Silver Star Mountain Resort

E3-9 Recording Accrual Basis Journal Entries

Silver Star Mountain Resort is a ski resort northeast of Vernon in British Columbia. Besides maintaining well-groomed ski runs, the company sells lift tickets, ski lessons, and ski equipment. It operates several restaurants and rents townhouses to vacationing skiers. The following hypothetical December 2012 transactions are typical of those that occur at the resort.

a. Borrowed $500,000 from the bank on December 1, signing a note payable due in six months.

b. Purchased a new snowplow for $20,000 cash on December 31.

c. Purchased ski supplies for $10,000 on account.

d. Incurred $22,000 in routine maintenance expenses for the chairlifts; paid cash.

e. Received $72,000 for season passes (beginning in the new year).

f. Daily lift passes were sold this month for a total of $76,000 cash.

g. Received a $320 deposit on a townhouse to be rented for five days in January 2013.

h. Paid half the charges incurred on account in (c).

i. Paid $18,000 in wages to employees for the month of December.

Required:

Prepare journal entries for each transaction. Be sure to categorize each account as an asset (A), liability (L), shareholders' equity (SE), revenue (R), or expense (E), and check that debits equal credits for each journal entry.

LO2, 3

E3-10 Recording Accrual Basis Journal Entries

Rowland & Sons Air Transport Service Ltd. has been in operation for three years. The following transactions occurred in February 2012:

Feb. 1	Paid $200 for rent of hangar space in February.
Feb. 2	Purchased fuel costing $450 on account for the next flight to Yellowknife.
Feb. 4	Received customer payment of $800 to ship several items to Victoria next month.
Feb. 7	Flew cargo from Winnipeg to Regina; the customer paid in full ($900 cash).
Feb. 10	Paid pilot $1,200 in wages for flying in February.
Feb. 14	Paid $60 for an advertisement run in the local paper on February 14.
Feb. 18	Flew cargo for two customers from Edmonton to Lake Louise for $1,700; one customer paid $500 cash and the other asked to be billed $1,200.
Feb. 25	Purchased on account $1,350 in spare parts for the planes.

Required:

Prepare journal entries for each transaction. Be sure to categorize each account as an asset (A), liability (L), shareholders' equity (SE), revenue (R), or expense (E).

LO2, 3

E3-11 Recording and Posting Accrual Basis Journal Entries

Ricky's Piano Rebuilding Company has been operating for one year (2011). At the start of 2012, its income statement accounts had zero balances and its balance sheet account balances were as follows:

Cash	$ 6,000	Accounts Payable	$ 8,000
Accounts Receivable	25,000	Unearned Revenue (deposits)	3,200
Supplies	1,200	Notes Payable	40,000
Equipment	8,000	Contributed Capital	8,000
Land	6,000	Retained Earnings	9,000
Building	22,000		

Required:

1. Create T-accounts for the balance sheet accounts and for these additional accounts: Piano Rebuilding Revenue, Rent Revenue, Wages Expense, and Utilities Expense. Enter the beginning balances.
2. Prepare journal entries for the following January 2012 transactions, using the letter of each transaction as a reference:

   a. Received a $500 deposit from a customer who wanted her piano rebuilt in February.
   b. Rented a part of the building to a bicycle repair shop; $300 rent received for January.
   c. Delivered five rebuilt pianos to customers who paid $14,500 in cash.
   d. Delivered two rebuilt pianos to customers for $7,000 charged on account.
   e. Received $6,000 from customers as payment on their accounts.
   f. Received an electric and gas utility bill for $350 for January services to be paid in February.
   g. Ordered $800 in supplies.
   h. Paid $1,700 on account in January.
   i. Paid $10,000 in wages to employees in January for work done this month.
   j. Received and paid cash for the supplies in (g).

3. Post the journal entries to the T-accounts. Show the unadjusted ending balances in the T-accounts.

E3-12 Preparing an Unadjusted Trial Balance   LO4

Refer to E3-11.

Required:

Use the balances in the completed T-accounts in E3-11 to prepare an unadjusted trial balance at the end of January 2012.

E3-13 Inferring Operating Transactions and Preparing an Unadjusted Trial Balance   LO2, 3, 4

Virtual Golf Corporation operates indoor golf simulators that allow individual customers and golf club members to experience courses like Pebble Beach and Augusta without leaving their own neighbourhood. Its stores are located in rented space in malls and shopping centres. During its first month of business ended April 30, 2012, Virtual Golf Corporation completed seven transactions with the dollar effects indicated in the following schedule:

Accounts	Cash	Assets — Accounts Receivable	Supplies	Equipment	= Liabilities — Accounts Payable	Unearned Revenue	+ Shareholders' Equity — Contributed Capital	Retained Earnings
Beginning balance	$ 0	$ 0	$ 0	$ 0	$ 0	$ 0	$ 0	$ 0
a	+100,000						+100,000	
b	−30,000			+30,000				
c	−200		+1,000		+800			
d	+9,000	+1,000						Sales Revenue +10,000
e	−1,000							Wages Expense −1,000
f					+1,200			Utilities Expense −1,200
g	+2,000					+2,000		
Ending balance	$ 79,800	$ 1,000	$ 1,000	$ 30,000	$ 2,000	$ 2,000	$ 100,000	

Required:

1. Write a brief explanation of transactions (a) through (g). Include any assumptions that you made.
2. Using the ending balance in each account, prepare an unadjusted trial balance for Virtual Golf Corporation on April 30, 2012.

E3-14 Inferring Transactions and Computing Effects Using T-Accounts   LO1, 2, 3

Assume a recent annual report of Dow Jones & Company, the world leader in business and financial news and information (and publisher of *The Wall Street Journal*), included the following accounts. Dollars are in millions.

Dow Jones & Company

dr + Accounts Receivable (A) cr −			dr + Prepaid Expenses (A) cr −			dr − Unearned Revenue (L) cr +		
1/1	313		1/1	25			240	1/1
	2,573	[a]		43	[b]	[c]	328	
12/31	295		12/31	26			253	12/31

Required:

1. For each T-account, describe the typical transactions that cause it to increase and decrease.
2. Express each T-account in equation format (Beginning + Increase Side − Decrease Side = Ending) and then solve for the missing amounts (in millions). For example, the Accounts Receivable T-account can be expressed as 313 + 2,573 − a = 295. By rearranging the equation, you can solve for 313 + 2,573 − 295 = a.

E3-15 Determining Accounting Equation Effects of Several Transactions

In January 2012, Tongo Inc., a branding consultant, had the following transactions. Indicate the accounts, amounts, and direction of the effects on the accounting equation under the accrual basis. A sample is provided.

a. (Sample) Received $9,500 cash for consulting services rendered in January.
b. Issued shares to investors for $10,000 cash.
c. Purchased $12,000 of equipment, paying 25 percent in cash and owing the rest on a note due in 2 years.
d. Received $7,500 cash for consulting services to be performed in February.
e. Bought $1,000 of supplies on account.
f. Received utility bill for January for $1,250, due February 15.
g. Consulted for customers in January for fees totalling $15,900, due in February.
h. Received $12,000 cash for consulting services rendered in December.
i. Paid $500 toward supplies purchased in (e).

	Assets	=	Liabilities	+	Shareholders' Equity	
a.	Cash +9,500 =				Service Revenue (+R)	+9,500

LO3

E3-16 Preparing Journal Entries

For each of the transactions in E3-15 (including the sample), write the journal entry using the format shown in this chapter.

LO3

E3-17 Posting to T-Accounts

For each of the transactions in E3-15 (including the sample), post the effects to the appropriate T-accounts and determine ending account balances. Beginning account balances have been given. The sample transaction has been posted as an example.

dr + Cash (A) cr −			dr − Accounts Payable (L) cr +			dr − Contributed Capital (SE) cr +		
1/1/11	10,000			5,000	1/1/11		12,000	1/1/11
a.	9,500							

dr + Accounts Receivable (A) cr −		dr − Unearned Revenue (L) cr +		dr − Retained Earnings (SE) cr +	
1/1/11	12,500		2,500 1/1/11		8,800 1/1/11

dr + Supplies (A) cr −		dr − Note Payable (L) cr +		dr − Service Revenues (R) cr +	
1/1/11	800		0 1/1/11		0 1/1/11
					9,500 a.

dr + Equipment (A) cr −		dr + Utilities Expense (E) cr −	
1/1/11	5,000	1/1/11 0	

124 **CHAPTER 3** Reporting Operating Results on the Income Statement

E3-18 Creating an Unadjusted Trial Balance

LO4

Based on the transactions posted to T-accounts in E3-17, create an unadjusted trial balance for Tongo Inc. for the month ended January 31, 2012. Distinguish the balance sheet and income statement accounts as shown in Exhibit 3.9.

E3-19 Inferring Transactions and Creating Financial Statements

LO2, 3

An analysis of transactions made during July 2012 by NepCo, an Internet service provider, during its first month of operations is shown below. Increases and decreases affecting revenues and expenses are explained.

		Assets			=	Liabilities	+		Shareholders' Equity	
	Cash	Accounts Receivable	Supplies	Equipment		Accounts Payable		Contributed Capital	Retained Earnings	
(a)	+11,000							+11,000		
(b)						+710			−710 Utilities Expense
(c)		+5,000							+5,000 Service Revenue
(d)	−6,000			+10,000		+4,000			
(e)	+1,000								+1,000 Service Revenue
(f)			+550			+550			
(g)	−3,000					−3,000			
(h)	−2,000								−2,000 Wages Expense
(i)	−750								−750 Rent Expense
(j)	+1,500	−1,500							
	1,750	3,500	550	10,000		2,260		11,000	2,540

Required:

1. Describe the business activities that led to the accounting equation effects for each transaction shown above.
2. Prepare an income statement and a statement of retained earnings for July, and a classified balance sheet as of July 31, 2012. (These financial statements would be considered "preliminary" because they use unadjusted balances.)

E3-20 Determining the Effects of Various Transactions

LO1, 2, 3

E&Z Reader was founded in January 2012 to provide text reading and recording services. Selected transactions for E&Z Reader's first month of business are as follows:

a. Issued shares to investors for $50,000 cash.
b. Billed customers $10,500 for services performed in January.
c. Purchased car for $24,500 for use in the business. Paid in cash.
d. Purchased $2,400 of supplies on account.
e. Received $7,500 cash from customers billed in transaction (b).
f. Used $1,500 in utilities, which will be paid in February.
g. Paid employees $3,500 cash for work done in January.
h. Paid $1,200 cash toward supplies purchased in transaction (d).

Required:

For each transaction, give (a) the name of the account being debited or credited, (b) the basic account type (A, L, SE, R, E), (c) whether the account is increased (+) or decreased (−) due to the transaction, and (d) whether the account normally holds a debit or credit balance. Transaction (a) has been given as an example.

	Debit Side of Journal Entry					Credit Side of Journal Entry			
	Account Name	Account Type	Direction of Change	Normal Balance		Account Name	Account Type	Direction of Change	Normal Balance
(a)	Cash	A	+	Debit		Contributed Capital	SE	+	Credit

E3-21 Comprehensive Exercise

Vanishing Games Corporation (VGC) operates a massively multiplayer online game, charging players a monthly subscription of $15. At the start of 2012, VGC's income statement accounts had zero balances and its balance sheet account balances were as follows:

Cash	$1,500,000	Accounts Payable	$ 108,000
Accounts Receivable	150,000	Unearned Revenue	73,500
Supplies	14,700	Notes Payable (due 2015)	60,000
Equipment	874,500	Contributed Capital	2,500,000
Land	1,200,000	Retained Earnings	1,419,700
Building	422,000		

In addition to the above accounts, VGC's chart of accounts includes the following: Subscription Revenue, Licensing Revenue, Wages Expense, Advertising Expense, and Utilities Expense.

Required:

1. Analyze the effect of the following January 2012 transactions on the accounting equation, using the format shown in this chapter's Demonstration Case B:

   a. Received $50,000 cash from customers for subscriptions that had already been earned in 2011.
   b. Received $25,000 cash from Electronic Artists, Inc., for licensing revenue earned in the month of January 2012.
   c. Purchased 10 new computer servers for $33,500; paid $10,000 cash and signed a three-year note for the remainder owed.
   d. Paid $10,000 for an Internet advertisement run on Yahoo! in January 2012.
   e. Sold 15,000 monthly subscriptions at $15 each for services provided during the month of January 2012. Half of the amount due was collected in cash and half was sold on account.
   f. Received an electric and gas utility bill for $5,350 for January 2012 utility services. The bill will be paid in February.
   g. Paid $378,000 in wages to employees for work done in January 2012.
   h. Purchased $3,000 of supplies on account.
   i. Paid $3,000 cash to the supplier in (h).

2. Prepare journal entries for the January 2012 transactions listed in requirement 1, using the letter of each transaction as a reference.

3. Create T-accounts, enter the beginning balances shown above, post the journal entries to the T-accounts, and show the unadjusted ending balances in the T-accounts.

4. Prepare an unadjusted trial balance as of January 31, 2012.

5. Prepare an income statement for the month ended January 31, 2012, using unadjusted balances from requirement 4.

6. Prepare a statement of retained earnings for the month ended January 31, 2012, using the beginning balance given above and the net income from requirement 5. Assume VGC has no dividends.

7. Prepare a classified balance sheet at January 31, 2012, using your response to requirement 6.

8. Why does the income statement total not equal the change in cash?

COACHED PROBLEMS

CP3-1 Recording Nonquantitative Journal Entries

The following list includes a series of accounts for B-Ball Corporation, which has been operating for three years. These accounts are listed alphabetically and numbered for identification. Following the accounts is a series of transactions. For each transaction, indicate the account(s) that should be debited and credited by entering the appropriate account number(s) to the right of each transaction. If no journal entry is needed, write *none* after the transaction. The first transaction is used as an example.

   TIP: In transaction (h), remember what the matching principle says.
   TIP: Think of transaction (j) as two transactions: (1) incur expenses and liability and (2) pay part of the liability.

Account No.	Account Title	Account No.	Account Title
1	Accounts Payable	8	Note Payable
2	Accounts Receivable	9	Prepaid Insurance
3	Cash	10	Rent Expense
4	Contributed Capital	11	Service Revenue
5	Equipment	12	Supplies Expense
6	Income Tax Expense	13	Supplies
7	Income Tax Payable		

Transactions	Debit	Credit
a. Example: Purchased equipment for use in the business; paid one-third cash and signed a note payable for the balance.	5	3, 8
b. Received cash for issuing shares to new investors.	_____	_____
c. Paid cash for rent this period.	_____	_____
d. Collected cash for services performed this period.	_____	_____
e. Collected cash on accounts receivable for services performed last period.	_____	_____
f. Performed services this period on credit.	_____	_____
g. Paid cash on accounts payable for expenses incurred last period.	_____	_____
h. Purchased supplies to be used later; paid cash.	_____	_____
i. Used some of the supplies for operations.	_____	_____
j. Paid three-fourths of the income tax expense for the year; the balance will be paid next year.	_____	_____
k. On the last day of the current period, paid cash for an insurance policy covering the next two years.	_____	_____

CP3-2 Recording Journal Entries

LO2, 3

Ryan Olson organized a new company, MeToo, Inc. The company provides networking management services on social network sites. You have been hired to record the transactions occurring in the first two weeks of operations, beginning May 1, 2012.

a. May 1: Issued 1,000 shares to investors for $30 per share.

b. May 1: Borrowed $50,000 from the bank to provide additional funding to begin operations; the note is due in two years.

c. May 1: Paid $2,400 for a one-year fire insurance policy.

> **TIP:** For convenience, simply record the full amount of the payment as an asset (Prepaid Insurance). At the end of the month, this account will be adjusted to its proper balance. We will study this adjustment process in Chapter 4, so just leave it as Prepaid Insurance for now.

d. May 3: Purchased furniture and fixtures for the store for $15,000 on account. The amount is due within 30 days.

e. May 5: Placed advertisements in local newspapers for a total of $250 cash.

f. May 9: Sold services for $400 cash.

g. May 14: Made full payment for the furniture and fixtures purchased on account on May 3.

Required:

For each of the transactions, prepare journal entries. Be sure to categorize each account as an asset (A), liability (L), shareholders' equity (SE), revenue (R), or expense (E).

CP3-3 Analyzing the Effects of Transactions Using T-Accounts and Preparing an Unadjusted Trial Balance

LO1, 2, 3, 4

Barbara Jones opened Barb's Book Business on February 1, 2012. The company specializes in editing accounting textbooks. You have been hired as manager. Your duties include maintaining the company's financial records. The following transactions occurred in February 2012, the first month of operations:

a. Received shareholders' cash contributions totalling $16,000 to form the corporation; issued shares.

b. Paid $2,400 cash for three months' rent for office space.

> **TIP:** For convenience, simply record the full amount of the payment as an asset (Prepaid Rent). At the end of the month, this account will be adjusted to its proper balance. We will study this adjustment process in Chapter 4, so just leave it as Prepaid Rent for now.

c. Purchased supplies for $300 cash.

d. Signed a promissory note, payable in two years; deposited $10,000 in the company's bank account.

e. Used the money from (*d*) to purchase equipment for $2,500 and furniture and fixtures for $7,500.

f. Placed an advertisement in the local paper for $425 cash.

g. Made sales totalling $1,800; $1,525 was in cash and the rest on accounts receivable.

h. Incurred and paid employee wages of $420.

i. Collected accounts receivable of $50 from customers.

j. Repaired one of the computers for $120 cash.

> **TIP:** Most repairs involve costs that do *not* provide additional future economic benefits.

Required:

1. Set up appropriate T-accounts for Cash, Accounts Receivable, Supplies, Prepaid Rent, Equipment, Furniture and Fixtures, Notes Payable, Contributed Capital, Service Revenue, Advertising Expense, Wages Expense, and Repair Expense. All accounts begin with zero balances.

> **TIP:** When preparing the T-accounts, you might find it useful to group them by type: assets, liabilities, shareholders' equity, revenues, and expenses.

2. Record in the T-accounts the effects of each transaction for Barb's Book Business in February, referencing each transaction in the accounts with the transaction letter. Show the unadjusted ending balances in the T-accounts.

3. Prepare an unadjusted trial balance at the end of February.

> **TIP:** Total Debits equals $27,800.

4. Refer to the revenues and expenses shown on the unadjusted trial balance. Based on this information, write a short memo to Barbara offering your opinion on the results of operations during the first month of business.

GROUP A PROBLEMS

Practise and learn online with Connect.

LO1, 2, 3 **PA3-1 Recording Nonquantitative Journal Entries**

The following is a series of accounts for Dewan & Allard Incorporated, which has been operating for two years. The accounts are listed alphabetically and numbered for identification. Following the accounts is a series of transactions. For each transaction, indicate the account(s) that should be debited and credited by entering the appropriate account number(s) to the right of each transaction. If no journal entry is needed, write *none* after the transaction. The first transaction is given as an example.

Account No.	Account Title	Account No.	Account Title
1	Accounts Payable	9	Land
2	Accounts Receivable	10	Note Payable
3	Advertising Expense	11	Prepaid Insurance
4	Buildings	12	Service Revenue
5	Cash	13	Supplies Expense
6	Contributed Capital	14	Supplies
7	Income Tax Expense	15	Wages Expense
8	Income Tax Payable		

Transactions	Debit	Credit
a. Example: Issued shares to new investors.	5	6
b. Performed services for customers this period on credit.	___	___
c. Purchased on credit but did not use supplies this period.	___	___
d. Prepaid a fire insurance policy this period to cover the next 12 months.	___	___
e. Purchased a building this period by making a 20 percent cash down payment and signing a note payable for the balance.	___	___
f. Collected cash for services that had been provided and recorded in the prior year.	___	___
g. Paid cash for wages that had been incurred this period.	___	___
h. Paid cash for supplies that had been purchased on accounts payable in the prior period.	___	___
i. Paid cash for advertising expense incurred in the current period.	___	___
j. Incurred advertising expenses this period to be paid next period.	___	___
k. Collected cash for services rendered this period.	___	___
l. Used supplies on hand to clean the offices.	___	___
m. Recorded income taxes for this period to be paid at the beginning of the next period.	___	___
n. This period, a shareholder sold some of her shares to another person for an amount above the original issuance price.	___	___

Check Figures [Part (l)]:
Debit 13 and Credit 14

PA3-2 Recording Journal Entries

LO2, 3

Diana Mark is the president of TempEmp, Inc., a company that provides temporary employees for not-for-profit companies. TempEmp has been operating for five years; its revenues have increased each year. You have been hired to help Diana in analyzing the following transactions for the first two weeks of April 2012:

April 2	Purchased office supplies for $500 on account.
April 5	Billed the local United Way office $1,950 for temporary services provided.
April 8	Paid $250 for supplies purchased and recorded on account last period.
April 8	Placed an advertisement in the local paper for $400 cash.
April 9	Purchased new equipment for the office costing $2,300 cash.
April 10	Paid employee wages of $1,200, which were incurred in April.
April 11	Received $1,000 on account from the local United Way office billed on April 5.
April 12	Purchased land as the site of a future office for $10,000. Paid $2,000 down and signed a note payable for the balance.
April 13	Issued 2,000 additional shares for $40 per share in anticipation of building a new office.
April 14	Billed Family & Children's Services $2,000 for services rendered this month.
April 15	Received the April telephone bill for $245 to be paid next month.

Required:

For each of the transactions, prepare journal entries. Be sure to categorize each account as an asset (A), liability (L), shareholders' equity (SE), revenue (R), or expense (E).

PA3-3 Recording Journal Entries

LO2, 3

The following transactions are February 2012 activities of GameHelp, which offers indoor golfing lessons. You have been hired to analyze the following transactions for a week in February 2012:

February 15	GameHelp collected $15,000 from customers for lessons given in February.
February 15	GameHelp sold a gift card for golf lessons for $150 cash in February.
February 18	GameHelp received $4,000 from credit sales made to customers in January.
February 18	GameHelp collects $2,250 in advance payments for golf lessons to start in June.
February 19	GameHelp bills a customer $125 for golf lessons given between February 15 and February 18. The bill is to be paid in March.
February 20	GameHelp paid $4,750 to its golf instructors for the month of February.
February 21	GameHelp paid $1,750 for electricity used in the month of January.
February 22	GameHelp received an electricity bill for $800 for the month of February, to be paid in March.

Required:

For each of the transactions, prepare journal entries. Be sure to categorize each account as an asset (A), liability (L), shareholders' equity (SE), revenue (R), or expense (E).

LO1, 2, 3, 4

PA3-4 Analyzing the Effects of Transactions Using T-Accounts and Preparing an Unadjusted Trial Balance

Sunny Valley Stables Inc. was established on April 1, 2012. The company provides stables, care for animals, and grounds for riding and showing horses. You have been hired as the new assistant controller. The following transactions for April 2012 are provided for your review.

Check Figure:
Ending cash balance = $134,560 *dr*

a. Received contributions from five investors of $200,000 in cash ($40,000 each).

b. Built a barn for $142,000. The company paid half the amount in cash on April 1 and signed a three-year note payable for the balance.

c. Provided $15,260 in animal care services for customers, all on credit.

d. Rented stables to customers who cared for their own animals; received cash of $13,200.

e. Received from a customer $1,500 to board her horse in May, June, and July (record as Unearned Revenue).

f. Purchased hay and feed supplies on account for $3,210.

g. Paid $840 in cash for water utilities incurred in the month.

h. Paid $1,700 on accounts payable for previous purchases.

i. Received $1,000 from customers on accounts receivable.

j. Paid $4,000 in wages to employees who worked during the month.

k. At the end of the month, prepaid a two-year insurance policy for $3,600.

l. Received an electric utility bill for $1,200 for usage in April; the bill will be paid next month.

Required:

1. Set up appropriate T-accounts. All accounts begin with zero balances.
2. Record in the T-accounts the effects of each transaction for Sunny Valley Stables in April, referencing each transaction in the accounts with the transaction letter. Show the unadjusted ending balances in the T-accounts.
3. Prepare an unadjusted trial balance as of April 30, 2012.
4. Refer to the revenues and expenses shown on the unadjusted trial balance. Based on this information, write a short memo to the five owners offering your opinion on the results of operations during the first month of business.

LO1, 2, 3, 4

PA3-5 Analyzing the Effects of Transactions Using T-Accounts and Preparing an Unadjusted Trial Balance

You have been hired as the new assistant controller for Autobody Corp., an auto body repair shop. Prepare journal entries for the following transactions, which occurred during August 2012.

a. At the end of the month, prepaid a two-year insurance policy for $5,000.

b. Received contributions from three investors of $90,000 in cash ($30,000 each).

c. Purchased a building for $250,000. The company paid a deposit of $25,000 in cash on August 15 and signed a nine-year note payable for the balance.

d. Paid $8,000 in wages to employees who worked during the month.

e. Rented an unused service bay to an oil change franchise; received cash of $26,000.

f. Provided $30,000 in repair services for customers, all on credit.

g. Received from a customer $5,000 to store some vehicles on the property for the winter (record as Unearned Revenue).

h. Paid $750 in cash for water utilities used during the month.

i. Received an electric utility bill for $1,800 for usage in August; the bill will be paid next month.

j. Purchased cleaning supplies on account for $6,000.

k. Paid $3,500 on accounts payable for previous purchases.

l. Received $3,000 from customers on accounts receivable.

Required:

1. Set up appropriate T-accounts. All accounts begin with zero balances.

2. Record in the T-accounts the effects of each transaction for Autobody Corp. in April, referencing each transaction in the accounts with the transaction letter. Show the unadjusted ending balances in the T-accounts.

3. Prepare an unadjusted trial balance as of August 31, 2012.

4. Refer to the revenues and expenses shown on the unadjusted trial balance. Based on this information, write a short memo to the five owners offering your opinion on the results of operations during the first month of business.

GROUP B PROBLEMS

PB3-1 Recording Nonquantitative Journal Entries

LO1, 2, 3

Abercrombie & Fitch

The Limited

Abercrombie & Fitch Co. is a specialty retailer of casual apparel. The company's brand was established in 1892. It was first publicly traded in 1996 and was spun off from The Limited in 1998. Assume that the following is a series of accounts for Abercrombie. The accounts are listed alphabetically and numbered for identification. Following the accounts is a series of hypothetical transactions. For each transaction, indicate the account(s) that should be debited and credited by entering the appropriate account number(s) to the right of each transaction. If no journal entry is needed, write *none* after the transaction. The first transaction is given as an example.

Account No.	Account Title	Account No.	Account Title
1	Accounts Payable	7	Prepaid Rent
2	Accounts Receivable	8	Rent Expense
3	Cash	9	Supplies Expense
4	Contributed Capital	10	Supplies
5	Equipment	11	Unearned Revenue
6	Interest Revenue	12	Wages Expense

Transactions	Debit	Credit
a. Example: Incurred wages expense; paid cash.	12	3
b. Collected cash on account.	——	——
c. Used up supplies (washroom paper towels, etc.) this period.	——	——
d. Sold gift certificates to customers; none redeemed this period.	——	——
e. Purchased equipment, paying part in cash and charging the balance on account.	——	——
f. Paid cash to suppliers on account.	——	——
g. Issued additional shares for cash.	——	——
h. Paid rent to landlords for next month's use of mall space.	——	——
i. Earned and received cash for interest on investments.	——	——

Check Figures [Part (*i*)]:
Debit 3 and Credit 6

PB3-2 Recording Journal Entries

Robin Harrington established Timely Delivery on January 1, 2012. The following transactions occurred during the company's most recent quarter.

a. Issued shares for $80,000.

b. Provided delivery service to customers, receiving $72,000 in accounts receivable and $16,000 in cash.

c. Purchased equipment costing $82,000 and signed a long-term note for the full amount.

d. Incurred repair costs of $3,000 on account.

e. Collected $65,000 from customers on account.

f. Borrowed $90,000 by signing a long-term note.

g. Prepaid $74,400 cash to rent equipment and aircraft next quarter.

h. Paid employees $38,000 for work done during the quarter.

i. Purchased (with cash) and used $49,000 in fuel for delivery equipment.

j. Paid $2,000 on accounts payable.

k. Ordered, but haven't yet received, $700 in supplies.

Required:

For each of the transactions, prepare journal entries. Be sure to categorize each account as an asset (A), liability (L), shareholders' equity (SE), revenue (R), or expense (E).

PB3-3 Preparing Accrual Basis Journal Entries for Business Activities

SmartTrader is an online company that specializes in matching buyers and sellers of used items. Buyers and sellers can purchase a membership with SmartTrader, which provides them with advance notice of potentially attractive offers. The following transactions occurred during the company's most recent quarter:

a. SmartTrader provided online advertising services for another company for $200 on account.

b. On the last day of the month, SmartTrader paid $50 cash to run an ad promoting the company's services. The ad ran that day in the local newspaper.

c. Received $200 cash in membership fees for the month from new members.

d. Received an electricity bill for $85, for usage this month. The bill will be paid next month.

e. Billed a customer $180 for expediting the sale of some items. SmartTrader expects to receive the customer's payment by the end of next month.

f. Received $4,000 in cash and cheques from membership sales.

g. Paid $2,000 cash for employee wages this month.

h. Paid $1,000 cash on a loan from the bank (ignore interest).

i. Bought $3,000 worth of supplies from a large manufacturer, paying $1,000 cash and signing a short-term note for $2,000.

j. Signed a long-term note and received a $150,000 loan from a local bank.

k. Billed a customer $2,000 for services provided. Payment is expected in 45 days.

l. Wrote a cheque for $600 for rent.

m. Received $450 cash from a customer for work done the same day.

n. The company incurred $400 in advertising costs for the current month and is planning to pay these costs next month.

Required:

For each of the transactions, prepare journal entries. Be sure to categorize each account as an asset (A), liability (L), shareholders' equity (SE), revenue (R), or expense (E).

PB3-4 Analyzing the Effects of Transactions Using T-Accounts and Preparing an Unadjusted Trial Balance

Since June 1, 2012, FantasyFlatables has been renting out fun items like moon walks and inflatable slides for parties and corporate events. The company has obtained the use of an abandoned ice rink located in a local shopping mall, where its rental products are displayed and available for casual hourly rental by mall patrons. The following transactions occurred during the first month of operations.

a. Jessica Carnoble contributed $50,000 cash to the company in exchange for company shares.

b. Purchased inflatable rides and inflation equipment, paying $20,000 cash.

c. Received $5,000 cash from casual hourly rentals at the mall.

d. Rented rides and equipment to customers for $10,000. Received cash of $2,000 and the rest is due from customers.

e. Received $2,500 from a large corporate customer as a deposit on a party booking for July 4.

f. Began to prepare for the July 4 party by purchasing various party supplies on account for $600.

g. Paid $6,000 in cash for renting the mall space this month.

h. Prepaid next month's mall space rental charge of $6,000.

i. Received $1,000 from customers on accounts receivable.

j. Paid $4,000 in wages to employees for work done during the month.

k. Paid $1,000 for running a television ad this month.

Required:

1. Set up appropriate T-accounts. All accounts begin with zero balances.
2. Record in the T-accounts the effects of each transaction for FantasyFlatables in June, referencing each transaction in the accounts with the transaction letter. Show the unadjusted ending balances in the T-accounts.
3. Prepare an unadjusted trial balance for the end of June 2012.
4. Refer to the revenues and expenses shown on the unadjusted trial balance and write a short memo to Jessica offering your opinion on the results of operations during the first month of business.

PB3-5 Analyzing the Effects of Transactions Using T-Accounts and Preparing an Unadjusted Trial Balance

LO1, 2, 3, 4

Assume you are the owner of The College Shop, which specializes in items of special interest to college students. You opened your doors for business on September 1, 2012. The following transactions occurred during the first month of operations.

a. You contributed $5,000 cash to the company in exchange for its shares.

b. Paid $1,000 for running a television ad this month.

c. Received $5,000 cash from photocopier rentals.

d. Received $2,500 from a college student council as a deposit for a large order of items to be delivered for Christmas.

e. Purchased sales equipment, paying $10,000 cash.

f. Paid $5,000 in cash for renting the space on campus this month.

g. Paid yourself $5,000 in wages for work done during the month.

h. Sales to customers totalled $10,000 for the month. Received cash of $5,000 and the rest is due from customers (friends).

i. Began to prepare for the large Christmas order by purchasing inventory on account for $6,000.

j. Prepaid next month's rental charge of $5,000.

k. Received $1,000 from customers on accounts receivable.

Required:

Check Figure:
Ending Accounts Receivable balance $4,000 *dr*

1. Set up appropriate T-accounts. All accounts begin with zero balances.
2. Record in the T-accounts the effects of each transaction for The College Shop in September, referencing each transaction in the accounts with the transaction letter. Show the unadjusted ending balances in the T-accounts.
3. Prepare an unadjusted trial balance for the end of September 2012.
4. Refer to the revenues and expenses shown on the unadjusted trial balance and write a short memo to your parents, who loaned you the money to start the company, offering your opinion on the results of operations during the first month of business.

SKILLS DEVELOPMENT CASES

S3-1 Finding Financial Information

LO1

Rona Inc.

Refer to the financial statements of Rona Inc. in Appendix A at the back of this book or download the annual report from the *Cases* section of Connect.

Required:

1. Did Rona Inc.'s sales revenues increase or decrease in the year ended December 27, 2009, as compared to the previous year? By how much? Calculate this change as a percentage of the previous year's sales revenues by dividing the amount of the change by the previous year's sales revenues and multiplying by 100.
2. Rona's largest expense for its 2009 fiscal year was Cost of Sales, but Cost of Sales does not appear as a line item in the annual report's income statement. However, the Management Discussion and Analysis that accompanies the financial statements mentions that Rona's gross margin for fiscal 2009 was 27.36 percent. Calculate the actual dollar amount of Cost of Sales for Rona using this information.

LO1

Rona Inc.

S3-2 Comparing Financial Information

Refer to the financial statements of Rona Inc. in Appendix A and those of The Home Depot in Appendix B at the back of this book or download the annual reports from the *Cases* section of Connect.

Required:

1. Did The Home Depot's sales revenues increase or decrease in the year ended January 31, 2010, as compared to the previous year? By how much? Calculate this change as a percentage of the previous year's sales revenues. Is the trend in The Home Depot's sales revenues more or less favourable than Rona's?

2. State the amount of the largest expense on the income statement of The Home Depot for the year ended January 31, 2010, and describe the transaction represented by the expense. Did this expense increase or decrease and by what percentage, as compared to the previous year?

LO1, 5

S3-3 Internet-Based Team Research: Examining the Income Statement

As a team, select an industry to analyze. Using your Web browser, each team member should access the annual report for one publicly traded company in the industry, with each member selecting a different company. (See S1-3 in Chapter 1 for a description of possible resources for these tasks.)

Required:

1. On an individual basis, each team member should write a short report that lists the following information:
   a. The major revenue and expense accounts on the most recent income statement.
   b. Description of how the company has followed the conditions of the revenue principle.
   c. The percentage of revenues that go to covering expenses, and that are in excess of expenses (in other words, the percentage that remains as net income).

2. Then, as a team, write a short report comparing and contrasting your companies using these attributes. Discuss any patterns across the companies that you as a team observe. Provide potential explanations for any differences discovered.

LO1, 2, 3, 5

WorldCom

S3-4 Ethical Decision Making: A Real-Life Example

Read the following excerpt from a September 2, 2002, article in *Fortune* magazine and answer the questions that appear below.

> Forget about fraud. Companies don't need to lie, cheat, and steal to fool investors. Clever managers have always had, and continue to have, access to perfectly legal tricks to help make their balance sheets and income statements look better than they really are—tricks that *even today* won't jeopardize their ability to swear to the SEC that their books are on the up and up. . . . One of the most controversial of all number games—the one that got WorldCom in trouble—is to capitalize expenses. That can have a tremendous impact on the bottom line.

1. When a company incurs a cost, its accountants have to decide whether to record the cost as an asset or expense. When costs are recorded as an asset, they are said to be *capitalized*. This builds on ideas first presented in Chapter 2, where you learned that it was appropriate to record costs as assets, provided that they possess certain characteristics. What are those characteristics?

2. The author of the article argues that even with clear rules like those referenced in question 1 above, accounting still allows managers to use "tricks" like capitalizing expenses. What do you suppose the author means by the expression *to capitalize expenses*?

3. Suppose that, in the current year, a company inappropriately records a cost as an asset when it should be recorded as an expense. What is the effect of this accounting decision on the current year's net income? What is the effect of this accounting decision on the following year's net income?

4. Later in the article (not shown) the author says that the video game industry is one where companies frequently capitalize software development costs as assets. These costs include wages paid to programmers, fees paid to graphic designers, and amounts paid to game testers. Evaluate whether software development costs are likely to possess the main characteristics possessed by all assets. Can you think of a situation where software development costs might not possess these main characteristics?

5. Do you think it is always easy and straightforward to determine whether costs should be capitalized or expensed? Do you think it is always easy and straightforward to determine whether a manager is acting ethically or unethically? Give examples to illustrate your views.

S3-5 Ethical Decision Making: A Mini-Case

Mike Lynch is the manager of a Toronto office for an insurance company. As the regional manager, his pay package includes a base salary, commissions, and a bonus when the region sells new policies in excess of its quota. Mike has been under enormous pressure lately, stemming largely from two factors. First, he is experiencing mounting personal debt due to some unfortunate circumstances. Second, compounding his worries, the region's sales of new insurance policies have dipped below the normal quota for the first time in years.

You have been working for Mike for two years, and like everyone else in the office, you consider yourself lucky to work for such a supportive boss. You also feel great sympathy for his personal problems over the last few months. In your position as accountant for the regional office, you are only too aware of the drop in new policy sales and the impact this will have on the manager's bonus. While you are working on the year-end financial statements, Mike stops by your office.

Mike asks you to change the manner in which you have accounted for a new property insurance policy for a large local business. A cheque for the premium, substantial in amount, came in the mail on December 31, the last day of the reporting year. The premium covers a period beginning on January 5. You deposited the cheque and correctly debited Cash and credited Unearned Revenue. Mike says, "Hey, we have the money this year, so why not count the revenue this year? I never did understand why you accountants are so picky about these things anyway. I'd like you to change the way you've recorded the transaction. I want you to credit a revenue account. And anyway, I've done favours for you in the past, and I am asking for such a small thing in return." With that, he leaves your office.

Required:

How should you handle this situation? What are the ethical implications of Mike's request? Who are the parties who would be helped or harmed if you went along with the request? If you fail to comply with his request, how will you explain your position to him? Justify your answers in writing.

S3-6 Critical Thinking: Analyzing Changes in Accounts and Preparing a Trial Balance

Hordichuk Painting Service Company was organized on January 20, 2012, by three individuals, each receiving 5,000 shares from the new company. The following is a schedule of the cumulative account balances immediately after each of the first nine transactions, ending on January 31, 2012.

Accounts	Cumulative Balances								
	a	b	c	d	e	f	g	h	i
Cash	$75,000	$70,000	$85,000	$71,000	$61,000	$61,000	$46,000	$44,000	$60,000
Accounts Receivable			12,000	12,000	12,000	26,000	26,000	26,000	10,000
Supplies					5,000	5,000	4,000	4,000	4,000
Equipment		20,000	20,000	20,000	20,000	20,000	20,000	20,000	20,000
Land				18,000	18,000	18,000	18,000	18,000	18,000
Accounts Payable					3,000	3,000	3,000	1,000	1,000
Notes Payable		15,000	15,000	19,000	19,000	19,000	19,000	19,000	19,000
Contributed Capital	75,000	75,000	75,000	75,000	75,000	75,000	75,000	75,000	75,000
Paint Revenue			27,000	27,000	27,000	41,000	41,000	41,000	41,000
Supplies Expense							1,000	1,000	1,000
Wages Expense					8,000	8,000	23,000	23,000	23,000

Required:

1. Analyze the changes in this schedule for each transaction; then explain the transaction. Transactions (a) and (b) are examples:
   a. Cash increased $75,000, and Contributed Capital (shareholders' equity) increased $75,000. Therefore, transaction (a) was an issuance of the capital shares of the corporation for $75,000 cash.
   b. Cash decreased $5,000, Equipment (an asset) increased $20,000, and Notes Payable (a liability) increased $15,000. Therefore, transaction (b) was a purchase of equipment for $20,000. Payment was made as follows: cash, $5,000; notes payable, $15,000.
2. Based only on the preceding schedule, prepare an unadjusted trial balance.

S3-7 Analyzing Transactions and Preparing an Unadjusted Trial Balance

Assume you recently started up a new company that rents machines for making frozen drinks like smoothies, frozen juices, tea slush, and iced cappuccinos. For $100, your business will deliver a machine, provide supplies (straws, paper cups), set up the machine, and pick up the machine the next morning. Drink mix and other supplies are sold by other businesses in your city. Being a one-person operation, you are responsible for everything from purchasing to marketing to operations to accounting.

You've decided that you'll just write notes about what happens during the month and then do the accounting at the end of the month. You figure this will be more efficient. Plus, by waiting until the end of the month to do the accounting, you'll be less likely to make a mistake because by that time you'll better understand the accounting cycle. Your notes said the following about your first month of operations:

Oct. 2	Incorporated Slusher Gusher Inc. and contributed $10,000 for shares in the company.
Oct. 12	Paid cash to buy three frozen drink machines on eBay at a total cost of $1,500. What a deal!
Oct. 13	Paid cash to buy $70 of supplies. Walmart was packed.
Oct. 16	Received $500 cash for this past week's rentals. I'm rich!
Oct. 17	Determined that $45 of supplies had been used up. Hmm, looks like I'll need some more.
Oct. 20	Bought $100 of supplies on account. I can't believe the party store gave me credit like that.
Oct. 23	Feeling tired after a busy week (6 rentals this time). Received $400 cash and expect to receive $200 more sometime this week.
Oct. 25	Received $100 cash from one of the customers who hadn't paid up yet. Called the other customer to remind him I'm waiting.
Oct. 26	Ran an ad in the local paper today. Paid $25 cash.
Oct. 27	Received $150 cash for a two-machine All Saints' Day party to be held on November 1. It's a good thing I got this money because no other bookings are in sight for the rest of the month.

Required:

Create a spreadsheet in which to record the effects of the October transactions and calculate end-of-month totals. Using the spreadsheet, prepare a trial balance that checks whether debits = credits. Because you want to be sure that you do this right, you e-mail your friend Owen for advice. Here's his reply:

From: Owentheaccountant@yahoo.com
To: Helpme@hotmail.com
Cc:
Subject: Excel Help

Wow, you're a CEO already? I always thought you were a mover and a shaker! So you want my advice on how to set up your spreadsheet? My advice is *read the last e-mail I sent*. The main thing that's new here is you'll need to include some columns for revenue and expenses under the shareholders' equity heading. Here's a screenshot of how your worksheet might look just before you enter the October transactions. Notice that because shareholders' equity is decreased by expenses, the debit side is used to record expenses.

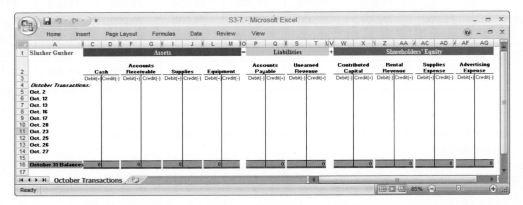

To prepare the trial balance, create three columns. In the first, enter the account names (one per row). In the second column, link in each debit balance by entering = in a cell and then clicking on the debit total from the T-account. Repeat this with all the accounts. Then do the same with the credit balances. At the bottom of the trial balance, use the SUM function to compute total debits and credits.

Don't forget to save the file using a name that uniquely identifies you (as my true hero).

CC3 Accounting for Business Operations

LO2, 3

Starting in May 2012, Nicole has decided that she has everything that she needs to open her doors to customers. To keep up with competition, Nicole has added items such as gift certificates and has started to advertise her company more and put things into place to keep her business going in the long term. Here is a sample of some transactions that occurred in the month of May at Nicole's Getaway Spa.

May 1	Paid $3,000 cash for an insurance policy that covers the period from June 1 until May 31 next year.
May 4	Ordered five new massage tables from Spa Supplies Unlimited for $250 each for future delivery.
May 7	Provided $860 of spa services to customers on account.
May 10	Purchased spa supplies for $800 on account to use at Nicole's Getaway Spa.
May 13	Received a bill for $45 for running an advertisement in the newspaper in May. The bill was paid in cash.
May 16	Paid one-quarter of the amount owed from May 10.
May 19	Sold $1,900 of gift certificates to customers for cash.
May 20	Obtained financing from the bank by signing a $5,000 note payable.
May 22	Received two of the massage tables ordered on May 4 and paid the full amount in cash.
May 25	Paid $500 cash for utility bills for services received and billed in May.

Required:

For each of the transactions prepare journal entries, using the date of the transaction as the reference.

YOUR LEARNING OBJECTIVES

Understand the business

LO1 Explain why adjustments are needed.

Study the accounting methods

LO2 Prepare adjustments needed at the end of the period.

LO3 Prepare an adjusted trial balance.

LO4 Prepare financial statements.

LO5 Explain the closing process.

Evaluate the results

LO6 Explain how adjustments affect financial results.

Review the chapter

Chapter Summary, page 167

Additional resources on Connect

CHAPTER 4

Adjustments, Financial Statements, and Financial Results

FOCUS COMPANY:
Pizza Palace, Inc.

I n Chapter 3, you saw that Pizza Palace sold a lot of pizza during its first month of operations—more than owner-manager Emilio Santos had expected. Emilio was very curious to know how the business performed, so he computed net income based on the company's unadjusted balances. When he saw that $15,500 of revenues had led to net income of $5,800, Emilio was very excited.

Emilio's CA, Ally, cautioned him that because he had been using unadjusted amounts in his computations, his results were not meaningful. She emphasized that at the end of an accounting period, adjustments need to be made to (1) update amounts already recorded in the accounting records and (2) include events that had occurred but had not yet been recorded. These adjustments ensure that the recognition of revenues and expenses occurs in the proper period, and that assets and liabilities are reported at appropriate amounts.

In the first section of this chapter, we'll help you to understand why adjustments are a necessary part of accrual basis accounting. In the second part of the chapter, we'll show you how to determine what adjustments are needed and how they are recorded and summarized in the accounting system. This second section concludes with the final steps involved in the accounting cycle. In the third part of this chapter, you will learn the importance of adjustments for external financial statement users and, as always, the final section provides lots of opportunities for you to review and work with the material presented in this chapter.

THAT WAS
THEN

In the previous chapter, you learned how to analyze, record, and summarize the effects of operating transactions on balance sheet and income statement accounts.

THIS IS
NOW

This chapter concludes the accounting cycle by focusing on adjustments, financial statement preparation, and the closing process.

ORGANIZATION OF THE CHAPTER

Understand the business	**S**tudy the accounting methods	**E**valuate the results	**R**eview the chapter
• Why adjustments are needed	• Making required adjustments • Preparing an adjusted trial balance and the financial statements • Closing temporary accounts	• Adjusted financial results	• Demonstration Case • Chapter Summary • Key Terms • Homework Helper • Practice Material

Understand the Business

WHY ADJUSTMENTS ARE NEEDED

Accounting systems are designed to record most recurring daily transactions, particularly any involving cash. As cash is received or paid, it is recorded in the accounting system. This focus on cash works well, especially when cash receipts and payments occur in the same period as the activities that lead to revenues and expenses. However, as you learned in Chapter 3, cash is not always received in the period in which the company earns the related revenue; likewise, cash is not always paid in the period in which the company incurs the related expense. In these situations, **adjustments** are made to the accounting records at the end of the period to ensure that assets and liabilities are reported at appropriate amounts. These adjustments also ensure that the related revenues and expenses are reported in the proper period, as required by the revenue and matching principles.

Adjustments involve both income statement and balance sheet accounts. They are needed to ensure

- Revenues are recorded when earned (the revenue principle).
- Expenses are recorded in the same period as the revenues to which they relate (the matching principle).
- Assets are reported at amounts representing the economic benefits that remain at the end of the current period.
- Liabilities are reported at amounts owed at the end of the current period that will require a future sacrifice of resources.

Companies wait until the end of the accounting period to adjust their accounts because adjusting the records daily would be costly and time-consuming. In practice, almost every financial statement account could require adjustment. Rather than try to memorize an endless list of examples, you should instead focus on learning what types of adjustments are needed in general. Later, we'll apply these general concepts to specific examples and give you lots of material to practise working with. In general, adjustments can be grouped into two categories: (1) deferrals, and (2) accruals.

Learning Objective 1

Explain why adjustments are needed.

YOU SHOULD KNOW

Adjustments: Entries made at the end of every accounting period to report revenues and expenses in the proper period and assets and liabilities at appropriate amounts.

1. Deferral Adjustments

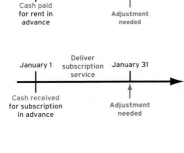

The word *defer* means to postpone until later. In accounting, we say an expense or revenue has been deferred if we have postponed reporting it on the income statement until a later period. As you saw in Chapter 3, when Pizza Palace pays its rent in advance, the expense is initially deferred as an asset on the balance sheet (in an account called *Prepaid Rent*). The adjustment part comes later, at the end of the month, when one month of the prepaid rent benefits have been used up. The deferral adjustment involves reducing Prepaid Rent and increasing Rent Expense on the income statement.

Deferral adjustments also can involve revenues. For example, when *Maclean's* receives cash for subscriptions before it has delivered magazines to subscribers, this revenue is initially deferred as a liability on the balance sheet (in an account called *Unearned Subscriptions Revenue*). The liability indicates the company's obligation to deliver magazines in the future. Later, when the company delivers the magazines, thereby meeting its obligation and earning the revenue, a deferral adjustment is made to reduce Unearned Subscriptions Revenue on the balance sheet and increase Subscriptions Revenue on the income statement.

You should note two key ideas here.

1. **Deferral adjustments are used to decrease balance sheet accounts and increase corresponding income statement accounts.** Previously deferred amounts exist on the balance sheet because the company paid cash before incurring the expense or received cash before earning revenue. When revenues are earned (as defined by the revenue principle) or expenses incurred (as defined by the matching principle), the previously deferred amounts are adjusted and amounts are transferred to the income statement using a deferral adjustment.

2. **Each deferral adjustment involves one asset and one expense account, or one liability and one revenue account.** The left side of Exhibit 4.1 shows a partial list of accounts that require deferral adjustments.

EXHIBIT 4.1	**Examples of Accounts Affected by Adjustments**

	Deferral Adjustments				Accrual Adjustments		
	Balance Sheet	Income Statement			Balance Sheet	Income Statement	
Assets	Supplies	Supplies Expense	**Expenses**	**Assets**	Interest Receivable	Interest Revenue	**Revenues**
	Prepaid Rent	Rent Expense			Rent Receivable	Rent Revenue	
	Prepaid Insurance	Insurance Expense					
Liabilities	Unearned Ticket Revenue	Ticket Sales Revenue	**Revenues**	**Liabilities**	Income Tax Payable	Income Tax Expense	**Expenses**
	Unearned Subscriptions Revenue	Subscriptions Revenue			Wages Payable	Wages Expense	
					Interest Payable	Interest Expense	

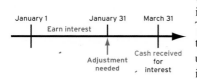

2. Accrual Adjustments

Accrual adjustments are needed when a company has earned revenue or incurred an expense in the current period but has not yet recorded it because the related cash will not be received or paid until a later period. For example, Pizza Palace will eventually pay taxes on the income it earns this period, so an accrual adjustment will be needed at the end of the month to record increases in its Income Tax Expense and Income Tax Payable accounts. This adjustment matches Income Tax Expense to the period in which the company earned the income that caused the income taxes. Likewise, if interest revenue is earned on investments this month but not received in cash until a later month, an accrual adjustment is needed at the end of the current month to record increases in the company's Interest Revenue and Interest Receivable accounts.

You should note two key ideas here.

1. **Accrual adjustments are used to record revenue or expenses when they occur prior to receiving or paying cash, and to adjust corresponding balance sheet accounts.**

2. **Each accrual adjustment involves one asset and one revenue account, or one liability and one expense account.** Notice that this differs from deferral adjustments, which pair assets with expenses and liabilities with revenues. The right side of Exhibit 4.1 shows a partial list of accounts that require accrual adjustments.

 HOW'S IT GOING? Self-Study Practice

For each of the following, indicate whether a deferral (D) or accrual (A) adjustment is required on October 31, and what two accounts will be affected by it.

| | | ACCOUNTS AFFECTED | |
	Type of Adjustment	Balance Sheet	Income Statement
1. In October, Air Canada provided flight services to customers who had paid for their tickets in August.			
2. The Trump Organization earned office rent from tenants in October, but is not expecting payment until November.			
3. In October, *Fortune* magazine incurred interest on a bank loan that must be paid at the end of the year.			
4. In October, Apple Inc. used up one month of insurance coverage that it had prepaid in July.			

After you have finished, check your answers with the solution in the margin.

Study the Accounting Methods

MAKING REQUIRED ADJUSTMENTS

The process of making adjustments is similar to the process you learned in Chapters 2 and 3 when accounting for daily transactions. As shown in Exhibit 4.2, the main difference is that adjustments are made at the end of each accounting period immediately prior to preparing financial statements. Adjustments are not made on a daily basis because it's more efficient to do them all at once at the end of each period. After determining the necessary adjustments (in Step 1), they are recorded using **adjusting journal entries** (in Step 2) and then summarized in the accounts (in Step 3). An adjusted trial balance is prepared to ensure total debits still equal total credits after having posted the adjusting journal entries to the accounts. If the trial balance is in balance, the financial statements can be prepared and then distributed to interested users.

Adjustment Analysis, Recording, and Summarizing

The first step, Analyze, involves determining the necessary adjustments to make to the accounting records. To complete this step, you need to know the balance currently reported

Learning Objective 2

Prepare adjustments needed at the end of the period.

YOU SHOULD KNOW

Adjusting journal entries (AJEs): Record the effects of each period's adjustments in a debits-equal-credits format.

EXHIBIT 4.2 Month-End Adjustments as Part of the Accounting Cycle

Timing	**1** Analyze	**2** Record	**3** Summarize
Daily	Transactions	Journal entries (JEs)	• Ledgers (T-accounts) • Unadjusted trial balance
Month-end	Adjustments	Adjusting journal entries (AJEs)	• Ledgers (T-accounts) • Adjusted trial balance • Financial statements

in each account, then determine what should be reported as the balance, and finally figure out the adjustment that will take you from the current (unadjusted) balance to the desired (adjusted) balance. Exhibit 4.3 illustrates this thinking process.

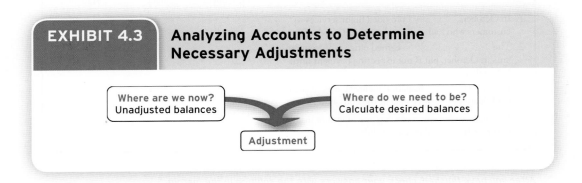

EXHIBIT 4.3 Analyzing Accounts to Determine Necessary Adjustments

The unadjusted trial balance is a key starting point for the adjustment process because it presents the unadjusted balances for every account, which will help you identify accounts that require adjustment. Exhibit 4.4 shows Pizza Palace's unadjusted trial balance at the end of September. This trial balance is identical to Exhibit 3.9 on page 106, except we've included balances for all accounts in Pizza Palace's chart of accounts, including those that currently have zero balances. Alongside the unadjusted trial balance, we've identified accounts requiring adjustment at the end of September.

In the remainder of this section, we show how to analyze, record, and summarize the required adjustments. Read these pages carefully. They contain the topics that people typically find the most challenging in this chapter.

Deferral Adjustments   Let's begin by looking at deferral adjustments, which are used to update amounts that have been previously deferred on the balance sheet.

(a) Supplies Used during the Period Of the $1,600 in supplies received in early September, $400 remains on hand at September 30.

The supplies were initially recorded as an asset on September 2 (in Chapter 3), but some of them have now been used up as of September 30. The matching principle requires an adjustment be made to report the cost of supplies used up this month as an expense (to match against revenues). To determine the cost of supplies used up, you have to do a little calculating. If you had $1,600 of supplies available for use and only $400 of supplies are left at the end of the month, then the $1,200 difference must be the cost of supplies used this month.

EXHIBIT 4.4 **Unadjusted Trial Balance**

PIZZA PALACE, INC.
Unadjusted Trial Balance
At September 30, 2012

Explanation of Adjustments Needed

Account Name	Debit	Credit
Cash	$ 7,500	
Accounts Receivable	200	
Supplies	1,600	
Prepaid Rent	7,200	
Cookware	630	
Equipment	60,000	
Accumulated Amortization		$ 0
Accounts Payable		1,030
Unearned Revenue		300
Wages Payable		0
Income Tax Payable		0
Interest Payable		0
Note Payable		20,000
Contributed Capital		50,000
Retained Earnings		0
Dividends Declared	0	
Pizza Revenue		15,500
Wages Expense	8,700	
Rent Expense	0	
Supplies Expense	0	
Amortization Expense	0	
Utilities Expense	600	
Advertising Expense	400	
Interest Expense	0	
Income Tax Expense	0	
Totals	**$86,830**	**$86,830**

Increase for right to collect cash from Emilio's friend for pizza delivery.
Decrease for supplies used up during September.
Decrease for prepaid September rent benefits now used up.

Adjust for equipment benefits used up in September.

Decrease for gift card obligations met in September.
Increase for September wages incurred but not yet paid.
Increase for tax owed on income generated in September.
Increase for interest owed on unpaid note in September.

Increase for revenues earned by delivering pizza to Emilio's friend.
Increase for wages incurred, but not yet recorded, for employees' work in September.
Increase for expense incurred for September rent.
Increase for supplies used up in September.
Increase for expense incurred by using equipment in September.

Increase for September interest incurred on unpaid note.
Increase for taxes on income generated in September.

In accounting terms, you should reduce the asset (Supplies) by $1,200 and show this amount as an expense (Supplies Expense).

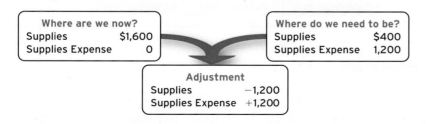

The effects of this adjustment on the accounting equation are shown on the next page, along with the required adjusting journal entry (AJE) and the accounts affected by it.

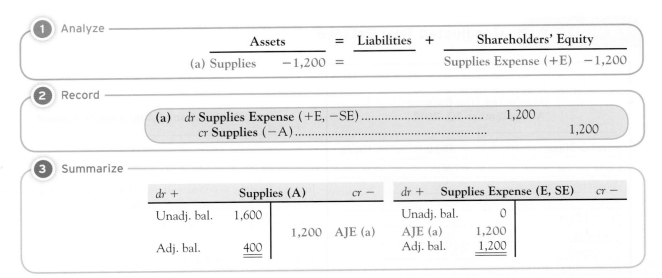

① Analyze

	Assets	=	Liabilities	+	Shareholders' Equity
(a) Supplies	−1,200	=			Supplies Expense (+E) −1,200

② Record

(a) *dr* Supplies Expense (+E, −SE) 1,200
        cr Supplies (−A) 1,200

③ Summarize

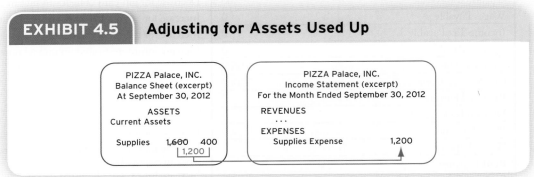

dr +	Supplies (A)		*cr* −
Unadj. bal.	1,600		
		1,200	AJE (a)
Adj. bal.	400		

dr +	Supplies Expense (E, SE)	*cr* −
Unadj. bal.	0	
AJE (a)	1,200	
Adj. bal.	1,200	

COACH'S TIP

The notation "Supplies Expense (+E, −SE) − 1,200" implies that the increase in an expense causes a decrease in shareholders' equity (through its negative impact on net income and retained earnings). To review this point see Exhibit 3.7 on page 98.

The financial statement effects of this adjustment are pictured in Exhibit 4.5.

EXHIBIT 4.5   Adjusting for Assets Used Up

PIZZA Palace, INC.
Balance Sheet (excerpt)
At September 30, 2012

ASSETS
Current Assets

Supplies   ~~1,600~~   400
            | 1,200 |

PIZZA Palace, INC.
Income Statement (excerpt)
For the Month Ended September 30, 2012

REVENUES
. . .
EXPENSES
    Supplies Expense   1,200

(b) Rent Benefits Expired during the Period Three months of rent were prepaid on September 1 for $7,200, but one month has now expired, leaving only two months prepaid at September 30.

To picture how costs relate to various time periods, it's useful to draw a timeline like the one shown in Exhibit 4.6.

EXHIBIT 4.6   Using a Timeline to Calculate Adjustments

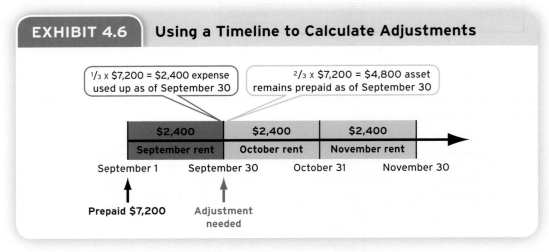

¹/₃ x $7,200 = $2,400 expense used up as of September 30

²/₃ x $7,200 = $4,800 asset remains prepaid as of September 30

$2,400	$2,400	$2,400
September rent	October rent	November rent

September 1   September 30   October 31   November 30

↑ Prepaid $7,200   ↑ Adjustment needed

The timeline in Exhibit 4.6 shows that the September prepayment of $7,200 represented three equal pieces of $2,400. The benefits of the first piece (pictured in red) have now expired, so they should be reported as an expense on the September income statement. Only two of the three months (2/3) remain prepaid on September 30. Thus, the $7,200 that was prepaid on September 1 needs to be adjusted on September 30 to $4,800 (2/3 × $7,200), which is the cost of the two remaining months of Prepaid Rent to be reported on the September 30 balance sheet (pictured in blue).

The preceding analysis has determined that an adjustment is needed to reduce Prepaid Rent by $2,400, from $7,200 to $4,800. Likewise, the adjustment needs to increase Rent Expense by $2,400. These effects are accounted for as follows:

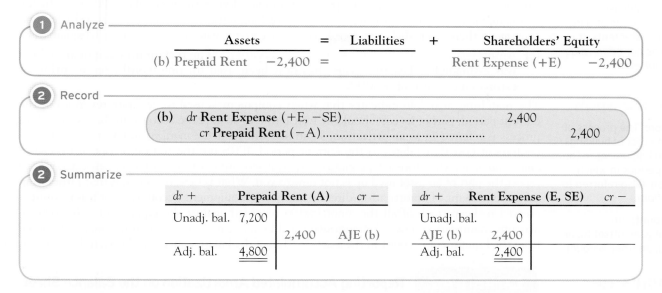

1 Analyze

	Assets		=	Liabilities	+	Shareholders' Equity	
(b) Prepaid Rent	−2,400	=				Rent Expense (+E)	−2,400

2 Record

(b) dr **Rent Expense** (+E, −SE)... 2,400
    cr **Prepaid Rent** (−A)... 2,400

2 Summarize

dr +	Prepaid Rent (A)	cr −		dr +	Rent Expense (E, SE)	cr −
Unadj. bal. 7,200				Unadj. bal. 0		
	2,400	AJE (b)		AJE (b) 2,400		
Adj. bal. 4,800				Adj. bal. 2,400		

Similar adjustments are made for other prepayments such as Prepaid Insurance. If the company pays the cost of services in advance of receiving them, the company initially defers that cost as an asset on the balance sheet. At the end of each accounting period in which the services are used up, a deferral adjustment is made to decrease the asset and increase the related expense on the income statement. Practise doing this one more time in the following Self-Study Practice.

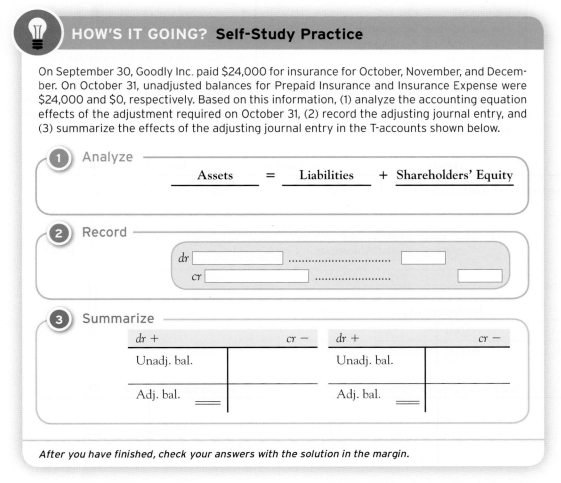

HOW'S IT GOING? Self-Study Practice

On September 30, Goodly Inc. paid $24,000 for insurance for October, November, and December. On October 31, unadjusted balances for Prepaid Insurance and Insurance Expense were $24,000 and $0, respectively. Based on this information, (1) analyze the accounting equation effects of the adjustment required on October 31, (2) record the adjusting journal entry, and (3) summarize the effects of the adjusting journal entry in the T-accounts shown below.

1 Analyze

	Assets	=	Liabilities	+	Shareholders' Equity

2 Record

dr [   ] .... [   ]
cr [   ] .... [   ]

3 Summarize

dr +		cr −		dr +		cr −
Unadj. bal.				Unadj. bal.		
Adj. bal.				Adj. bal.		

After you have finished, check your answers with the solution in the margin.

Solution to Self-Study Practice

1.
	Assets	=	Liabilities	+	Shareholders' Equity
	Prepaid Insurance −8,000	=			Insurance Expense (+E) −8,000

2. dr Insurance Expense (+E, −SE) 8,000
   cr Prepaid Insurance (−A) 8,000

3.
dr +	Prepaid Insurance (A)	cr −		dr +	Insurance Expense (E, SE)	cr −
Unadj. bal. 24,000				Unadj. bal. 0		
	8,000	AJE		AJE 8,000		
Adj. bal. 16,000				Adj. bal. 8,000		

Notice that for events in (a), (b), and the Self-Study Practice, the deferral adjustments have two effects: (1) they reduce the **carrying value** of assets on the balance sheet, and (2) they transfer the amount of the reductions to related expense accounts on the income statement. This happens whether we're adjusting supplies, prepaid rent, or even long-term assets like buildings, vehicles, and equipment. When accounting for the use of long-term assets like buildings, vehicles, and equipment, there is one slight difference in how the carrying value is reduced, as we'll explain next.

(c) Amortization Is Recorded for Use of Equipment The restaurant equipment, which was estimated to last five years, has now been used for one month, representing an estimated expense of $1,000.

The matching principle indicates that when equipment is used to generate revenues in the current period, part of its cost should be transferred to an expense account in that period. This process is referred to as **amortization,** so an account named *Amortization Expense* reports the equipment cost that relates to the current period. IFRS use the term *depreciation* instead of *amortization* and therefore a depreciation expense account exists. Use of an expense account to report the part of an asset used up is not new to you. What is new, however, is that rather than take the amount of amortization directly out of the Equipment account, a **contra-account** is created to keep track of all the amortization recorded against the equipment. This contra-account, named *Accumulated Amortization,* is like a negative asset account that is subtracted from the Equipment account in the assets section of the balance sheet, as shown in Exhibit 4.7.

EXHIBIT 4.7	Reporting Accumulated Amortization on the Balance Sheet

PIZZA PALACE, INC.
Balance Sheet (excerpt)
At September 30, 2012

Assets		
Equipment	$60,000	← Original cost of equipment
Less: Accumulated Amortization	(1,000)	← Running total of amortization recorded
Equipment, Net of Accumulated Amortization	59,000	← Carrying value (or book value)

In our analyses below, we use a small "x" to indicate a contra-account, so the notation for a contra-account for an asset is "xA." An increase in a contra-asset account (+xA) decreases the carrying value of the underlying asset (−A).

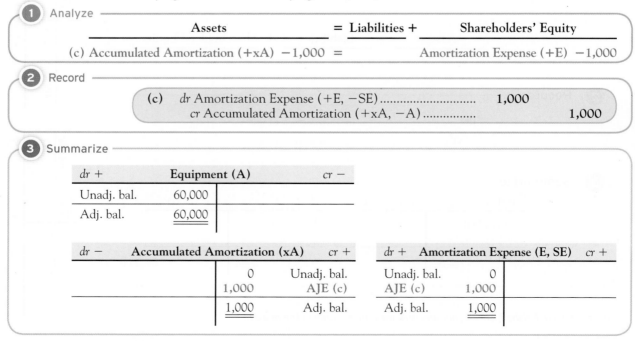

1 Analyze

Assets	= Liabilities +	Shareholders' Equity
(c) Accumulated Amortization (+xA) −1,000 =		Amortization Expense (+E) −1,000

2 Record

(c)   *dr* Amortization Expense (+E, −SE) 1,000
       cr Accumulated Amortization (+xA, −A)   1,000

3 Summarize

dr +	Equipment (A)	*cr* −
Unadj. bal.	60,000	
Adj. bal.	60,000	

dr −	Accumulated Amortization (xA)	*cr* +
	0	Unadj. bal.
	1,000	AJE (c)
	1,000	Adj. bal.

dr +	Amortization Expense (E, SE)	*cr* +
Unadj. bal.	0	
AJE (c)	1,000	
Adj. bal.	1,000	

There are four aspects of this example that you should note:

1. **Accumulated Amortization is a balance sheet account and Amortization Expense is an income statement account.** As a balance sheet account, Accumulated Amortization will increase over time as it accumulates the amortization of each period until the asset is fully amortized. As an income statement account, Amortization Expense will include only the amortization of the current accounting year.

2. **By recording amortization in Accumulated Amortization separate from the Equipment account, you can report both the original cost of equipment and a running total of the amount that has been amortized.** This gives financial statement users a rough idea of how much of the asset's original cost (representing its original usefulness) has been used up as of the balance sheet date. In our example, approximately 1/60 ($1,000/$60,000) of the equipment's total usefulness has been used up as of September 30, 2012.

3. **The normal balance in a contra-account is always the opposite of the account it off-sets.** For example, the increase in Accumulated Amortization is recorded with a credit because the account that it offsets, Equipment, is recorded with a debit.

4. **The amount of amortization depends on the method used for determining it.** Amortization methods (and their formulas) will be discussed in Chapter 9.

Just as deferral adjustments are used to record expenses incurred when assets are used up, they also are used to record the revenues earned when a company meets its obligation to provide goods or services to customers. For example, when Air Canada, *The Globe and Mail*, and Rogers Communications Inc. receive cash in advance of providing flights, newspapers, and cellphone service, they initially increase (debit) Cash and increase (credit) a liability account called *Unearned Revenue*. Later, when they meet their obligations, a deferral adjustment is recorded, reducing the liability (with a debit) and reporting the revenue earned from these services (with a credit). Let's see how this idea applies to Pizza Palace.

(d) Gift Cards Redeemed for Service Pizza Palace redeemed $160 of gift cards that customers used to pay for pizza.

The unadjusted trial balance reports $300 of Unearned Revenue, which represents Pizza Palace's obligation to honour gift cards previously issued to customers. By accepting $160 of gift cards in exchange for pizza this month, Pizza Palace has fulfilled a portion of its obligation and has earned additional revenue. Thus, a deferral adjustment is needed to reduce Unearned Revenue and increase Pizza Revenue.

 **COACH'S TIP**

The word "unearned" in the Unearned Revenue account title means that the company hasn't done what it was paid to do. In other words, the company has an obligation (liability) to do the work or return the cash.

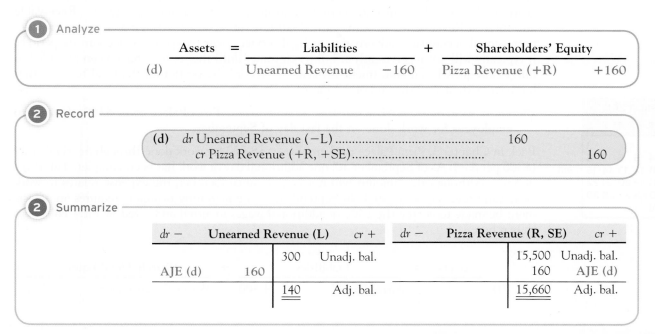

1 Analyze

	Assets	=	Liabilities		+	Shareholders' Equity	
(d)			Unearned Revenue	−160		Pizza Revenue (+R)	+160

2 Record

(d)	dr Unearned Revenue (−L)	160	
	cr Pizza Revenue (+R, +SE)		160

2 Summarize

dr −	Unearned Revenue (L)	cr +		dr −	Pizza Revenue (R, SE)	cr +
		300 Unadj. bal.				15,500 Unadj. bal.
AJE (d)	160					160 AJE (d)
		140 Adj. bal.				15,660 Adj. bal.

Accrual Adjustments Let's now look at common examples of accrual adjustments, which are adjustments that make the accounting records complete by including transactions that have occurred but have not been recorded.

(e) Revenues Earned but Not Yet Recorded Pizza Palace provided $40 of pizza to Emilio's close friend on the last day of September, with payment to be received in October.

Companies that regularly provide services on credit will design their accounting systems to record transactions like this on a daily basis. However, for a business like Pizza Palace that does not typically extend credit to its customers, these kinds of events may require an accrual adjustment at month-end. Because these revenues and the right to collect them (Accounts Receivable) are earned in September, the revenue principle indicates they should be recorded in September. The accrual adjustment will increase Accounts Receivable on the balance sheet and increase Pizza Revenue on the income statement.

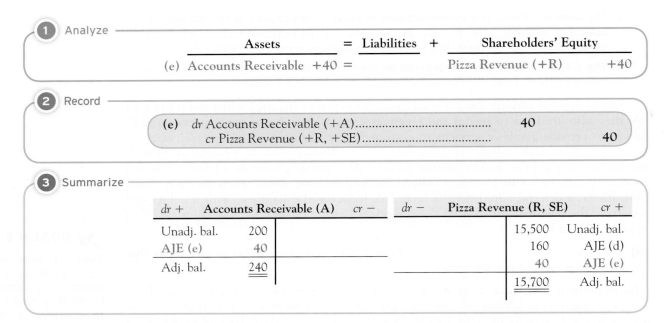

1 Analyze

	Assets	= Liabilities +	Shareholders' Equity	
(e)	Accounts Receivable +40 =		Pizza Revenue (+R)	+40

2 Record

(e)	dr Accounts Receivable (+A)...	40	
	cr Pizza Revenue (+R, +SE)..		40

3 Summarize

dr +	Accounts Receivable (A)	cr −	dr −	Pizza Revenue (R, SE)	cr +
Unadj. bal.	200			15,500	Unadj. bal.
AJE (e)	40			160	AJE (d)
Adj. bal.	240			40	AJE (e)
				15,700	Adj. bal.

Other situations require accrual adjustments for revenue earned but not yet recorded. For example, interest on investments is earned daily but typically is received in cash on a yearly basis, so each month an accrual adjustment is made to increase Interest Receivable and Interest Revenue for amounts earned but not yet recorded. Also, if a company provides professional accounting, advertising, or legal services over two or more accounting periods, it typically will not receive cash or bill its customer until the services have been provided in full. Consequently, an adjustment is needed to record the portion of the total revenue that has been earned as of the end of the month.

(f) Wage Expense Incurred but Not Yet Recorded Pizza Palace owes $300 of wages to employees for work done on the last day of September.

Back in Chapter 3, Pizza Palace paid employees $8,700 for work done through September 29 ($300 per day). As of September 30, one additional day of work has been completed at a cost of $300. Although this amount will not be paid until October, the expense relates to work done (and revenues generated) in September, so the matching principle requires an adjustment be made to accrue the $300 of additional wages incurred and owed by Pizza Palace, as shown here.

September 2012

S	M	T	W	T	F	S	
						1	
2	3	4	5	6	7	8	
9	10	11	12	13	14	15	Paid
16	17	18	19	20	21	22	
23	24	25	26	27	28	29	
30	Owed						

1 Analyze

	Assets	=	Liabilities	+	Shareholders' Equity	
(f)			Wages Payable	+300	Wages Expense (+E)	−300

(f) dr Wages Expense (+E, −SE) 300
    cr Wages Payable (+L) 300

③ Summarize

dr −	Wages Payable (L)	cr +		dr +	Wages Expense (E, SE)	cr −
	0	Unadj. bal.		Unadj. bal.	8,700	
	300	AJE (f)		AJE (f)	300	
	300	Adj. bal.		Adj. bal.	9,000	

When the $300 of wages is paid in cash the following month, Pizza Palace will decrease Wages Payable (with a debit) and decrease Cash (with a credit).

(g) **Interest Expense Incurred but Not Yet Recorded** Pizza Palace has not paid or recorded the $100 interest that it owes for this month on its note payable to the bank.

As we saw in Exhibit 4.4, Pizza Palace incurs interest on its unpaid note each month. An adjustment is needed to record the Interest Expense relating to September and, because this interest has not yet been paid, the adjustment also must record a liability called *Interest Payable*. Currently, the unadjusted trial balance shows $0 of Interest Payable and $0 of Interest Expense.

① Analyze

	Assets	=	Liabilities	+	Shareholders' Equity	
(g)			Interest Payable +100		Interest Expense (+E) −100	

② Record

(g) dr Interest Expense (+E, −SE) 100
    cr Interest Payable (+L) 100

③ Summarize

dr −	Interest Payable (L)	cr +		dr +	Interest Expense (E, SE)	cr −
	0	Unadj. bal.		Unadj. bal.	0	
	100	AJE (g)		AJE (g)	100	
	100	Adj. bal.		Adj. bal.	100	

Accrual adjustments also may be required for other expenses, like property taxes and utilities, if incurred and owed during the current period (but not yet recorded). The adjusting journal entry required for each of these items would be identical to the one shown in (g), except that the word *interest* would be replaced with the particular type of cost incurred and the applicable amounts would be used. For the purpose of our Pizza Palace example, we'll assume that the only remaining expense to record is the accrual of income taxes that are incurred this month but won't be paid until a later period.

(h) **Income Taxes Incurred but Not Yet Recorded** Pizza Palace pays income tax at an average rate equal to 40 percent of the company's income before taxes.

Just like you, a corporation is responsible for income tax when it generates more revenue than expenses in the current period. Income tax is calculated by multiplying (1) the company's adjusted income (before income taxes) by (2) the company's tax rate. To calculate adjusted income (before income tax), the following table starts with the unadjusted revenue and expense numbers from the unadjusted trial balance (Exhibit 4.4) and then includes the effects of adjustments to revenues and expenses. Multiply the adjusted income before income tax ($1,000) by the tax rate (40 percent) to get the amount of income tax ($400).

COACH'S TIP

Always calculate income tax expense **after** taking into account all revenue and expense adjustments.

	Revenues	Expenses	
Unadjusted totals	$15,500	$ 9,700	← Calculated from Exhibit 4.4 ($9,700 = $8,700 + $600 + $400)
Adjustments: (a)		+1,200	
(b)		+2,400	
(c)		+1,000	
(d)	+ 160		
(e)	+ 40		
(f)		+ 300	
(g)		+ 100	
Adjusted totals	$ 15,700 −	$14,700	= $1,000 ← Adjusted income before income tax expense

The unadjusted trial balance shows that no income tax has been recorded (both Income Tax Payable and Income Tax Expense are $0). Because income was reported in September, the matching principle requires that we record the $400 tax expense in September. Because the tax hasn't been paid yet, a liability also must be recorded.

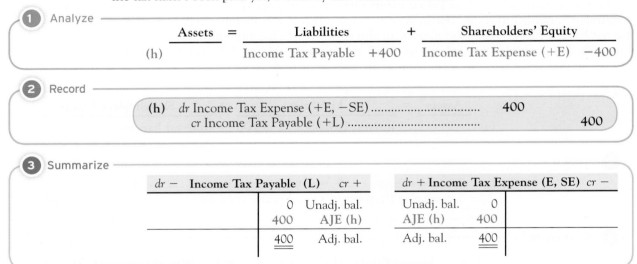

1 Analyze

Assets	=	Liabilities	+	Shareholders' Equity
(h)		Income Tax Payable +400		Income Tax Expense (+E) −400

2 Record

(h) dr Income Tax Expense (+E, −SE) 400
      cr Income Tax Payable (+L) 400

3 Summarize

dr − Income Tax Payable (L) cr +		dr + Income Tax Expense (E, SE) cr −	
	0 Unadj. bal.	Unadj. bal. 0	
	400 AJE (h)	AJE (h) 400	
	400 Adj. bal.	Adj. bal. 400	

HOW'S IT GOING? Self-Study Practice

Assume that, prior to accruing marketing expenses of $5 million, Pixar's adjusted income before income taxes was $245 million. Assuming the company's average tax rate was 40 percent, (1) analyze the effect of the required income tax adjustment on the accounting equation, and (2) prepare the adjusting journal entry, assuming that no amounts have been recorded yet for income taxes.

1 Analyze

Assets	=	Liabilities	+	Shareholders' Equity

2 Record

dr [   ] .... [   ]
cr [   ] .... [   ]

After you have finished, check your answers with the solution in the margin.

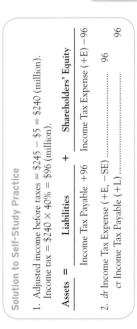

Solution to Self-Study Practice

1. Adjusted income before taxes = $245 − $5 = $240 (million).
   Income tax = $240 × 40% = $96 (million).

Assets	=	Liabilities	+	Shareholders' Equity
		Income Tax Payable +96		Income Tax Expense (+E) −96

2. dr Income Tax Expense (+E, −SE) 96
   cr Income Tax Payable (+L) 96

Additional Comments

There are three final points to learn before finishing this section. First, notice that none of the adjusting journal entries affected the Cash account. Adjusting journal entries never involve cash. Second, adjusting entries always include one balance sheet and one income statement account.

The third point doesn't relate to adjusting entries. Instead, it relates to dividends, which a corporation uses to distribute profits to shareholders as a return on their investment in the corporation. The decision to pay a dividend is made by the company's board of directors after profits have been generated, so dividends are not expenses of the business. Instead, they are a reduction of the retained earnings. Consequently, dividends are not reported on the income statement, but instead are subtracted on the Statement of Retained Earnings (as shown in Chapter 1). Dividends are recorded in their own special account called *Dividends Declared*. Because dividends reduce shareholders' equity, they are recorded with a debit just like all reductions in shareholders' equity. Now that we know Pizza Palace has generated a profit for the month, we'll assume that the company pays a dividend to shareholders. (Technically speaking, a dividend can occur any time during the year so it is typically recorded as a daily transaction when declared, rather than at the end of the period as an adjusting journal entry. But we'll show it here for convenience.)

(i) Dividend Declared and Paid Pizza Palace declares and pays a $500 cash dividend.

The dividend is recorded as a reduction in shareholders' equity in a special account called *Dividends Declared*. Because it reduces shareholders' equity, it is recorded as a debit. The corresponding reduction in Cash is recorded as a credit.

1 Analyze

	Assets	=	Liabilities	+	Shareholders' Equity	
(i) Cash	−500 =				Dividends Declared (+D)	−500

2 Record

(i)	*dr* Dividends Declared (+D, −SE)	500	
	cr Cash (−A)		500

3 Summarize

dr +	Cash (A)	*cr* −		*dr* +	Dividends Declared (D, SE) *cr* −	
Unadj. bal. 7,500				Unadj. bal.	0	
	500	(i)		(i)	500	
Adj. bal. 7,000				Adj. bal.	500	

It is important to note that companies have key financial requirements or restrictions that the board of directors must consider when declaring a cash dividend. These are further discussed in Chapter 11 on page 469.

Exhibit 4.8 summarizes the work we've done to this point. Starting with the unadjusted trial balance prepared at the end of Chapter 3 (see the left side of Exhibit 4.8), we determined the journal entries that needed to be recorded at the end of this month (see the right side of Exhibit 4.8). Next, we posted journal entries (a) through (i) to the T-accounts, as summarized in Exhibit 4.9. Next we need to check that the accounting records are still in balance by using the adjusted T-account balances to prepare an adjusted trial balance. Assuming the trial balance shows that debits equal credits, we will finally be able to prepare the financial statements.

EXHIBIT 4.8   Summary of Unadjusted Balances and Adjusting Journal Entries

PIZZA PALACE, INC.
Unadjusted Trial Balance
At September 30, 2012

Account Name	Debit	Credit
Cash	$ 7,500	
Accounts Receivable	200	
Supplies	1,600	
Prepaid Rent	7,200	
Cookware	630	
Equipment	60,000	
Accumulated Amortization		$ 0
Accounts Payable		1,030
Unearned Revenue		300
Wages Payable		0
Income Tax Payable		0
Interest Payable		0
Note Payable		20,000
Contributed Capital		50,000
Retained Earnings		0
Dividends Declared	0	
Pizza Revenue		15,500
Wages Expense	8,700	
Rent Expense	0	
Supplies Expense	0	
Amortization Expense	0	
Utilities Expense	600	
Advertising Expense	400	
Interest Expense	0	
Income Tax Expense	0	
Totals	**$86,830**	**$86,830**

PIZZA PALACE, INC.
General Journal

(a)	dr Supplies Expense (+E, −SE)	1,200	
	cr Supplies (−A)		1,200
(b)	dr Rent Expense (+E, −SE)	2,400	
	cr Prepaid Rent (−A)		2,400
(c)	dr Amortization Expense (+E, −SE)	1,000	
	cr Accumulated Amortization (+xA, −A)		1,000
(d)	dr Unearned Revenue (−L)	160	
	cr Pizza Revenue (+R, +SE)		160
(e)	dr Accounts Receivable (+A)	40	
	cr Pizza Revenue (+R, +SE)		40
(f)	dr Wages Expense (+E, −SE)	300	
	cr Wages Payable (+L)		300
(g)	dr Interest Expense (+E, −SE)	100	
	cr Interest Payable (+L)		100
(h)	dr Income Tax Expense (+E, −SE)	400	
	cr Income Tax Payable (+L)		400
(i)	dr Dividends Declared (+D, −SE)	500	
	cr Cash (−A)		500

PREPARING AN ADJUSTED TRIAL BALANCE AND THE FINANCIAL STATEMENTS

Adjusted Trial Balance

Learning Objective 3

Prepare an adjusted trial balance.

An **adjusted trial balance** is prepared to check that the accounting records are still in balance after having posted all adjusting entries to the T-accounts. To prepare an adjusted trial balance, just copy the adjusted T-account balances (Exhibit 4.9) into the debit or credit columns of the adjusted trial balance (left side of Exhibit 4.10).

List the accounts in the order they will appear in the balance sheet, statement of retained earnings, and income statement. As you can see in Exhibit 4.10 on page 154, the trial balance proves that Pizza Palace's accounting records are in balance (total debits = $88,670 = total credits), so the financial statements can be prepared. The balance for each account in the trial balance is reported only once on either the income statement, statement of retained earnings, or balance sheet. Typically, the income statement is prepared first because the net income number from it flows into the statement of retained earnings, and then the retained earnings number from the statement of retained earnings flows into the balance sheet. As you will see in later chapters of this book, the statement of cash flows and notes to the financial

YOU SHOULD KNOW

Adjusted trial balance: A list of all accounts and their adjusted balances to check on the equality of recorded debits and credits.

EXHIBIT 4.9 | **Pizza Palace's Adjusted Accounts**

dr +	Cash (A)		cr −
Unadj. bal.	7,500		
		500	(i)
Adj. bal.	7,000		

dr +	Accounts Receivable (A)		cr −
Unadj. bal.	200		
AJE (e)	40		
Adj. bal.	240		

dr +	Supplies (A)		cr −
Unadj. bal.	1,600		
		1,200	AJE (a)
Adj. bal.	400		

dr −	Prepaid Rent (A)		cr −
Unadj. bal.	7,200		
		2,400	AJE (b)
Adj. bal.	4,800		

dr +	Cookware (A)		cr −
Adj. bal.	630		

dr +	Equipment (A)		cr −
Adj. bal.	60,000		

dr −	Accumulated Amortization (xA)		cr +
		0	Unadj. bal.
		1,000	AJE (c)
		1,000	Adj. bal.

dr −	Accounts Payable (L)		cr +
		1,030	Adj. bal.

dr −	Unearned Revenue (L)		cr +
		300	Unadj. bal.
AJE (d)	160		
		140	Adj. bal.

dr −	Wages Payable (L)		cr +
		0	Unadj. bal.
		300	AJE (f)
		300	Adj. bal.

dr −	Income Tax Payable (L)		cr +
		0	Unadj. bal.
		400	AJE (h)
		400	Adj. bal.

dr −	Interest Payable (L)		cr +
		0	Unadj. bal.
		100	AJE (g)
		100	Adj. bal.

dr −	Note Payable (L)		cr +
		20,000	Adj. bal.

dr −	Contributed Capital (SE)		cr +
		50,000	Adj. bal.

dr −	Retained Earnings (SE)		cr +
		0	Adj. bal.

dr +	Dividends Declared (D, SE)		cr −
Unadj. bal.	0		
(i)	500		
Adj. bal.	500		

dr −	Pizza Revenue (R, SE)		cr +
		15,500	Unadj. bal.
		160	AJE (d)
		40	AJE (e)
		15,700	Adj. bal.

dr +	Wages Expense (E, SE)		cr −
Unadj. bal.	8,700		
AJE (f)	300		
Adj. bal.	9,000		

dr +	Rent Expense (E, SE)		cr −
Unadj. bal.	0		
AJE (b)	2,400		
Adj. bal.	2,400		

dr +	Supplies Expense (E, SE)		cr −
Unadj. bal.	0		
AJE (a)	1,200		
Adj. bal.	1,200		

dr +	Amortization Expense (E, SE)		cr −
Unadj. bal.	0		
AJE (c)	1,000		
Adj. bal.	1,000		

dr +	Utilities Expense (E, SE)		cr −
Adj. bal.	600		

dr +	Advertising Expense (E, SE)		cr −
Adj. bal.	400		

dr +	Interest Expense (E, SE)		cr −
Unadj. bal.	0		
AJE (g)	100		
Adj. bal.	100		

dr +	Income Tax Expense (E, SE)		cr −
Unadj. bal.	0		
AJE (h)	400		
Adj. bal.	400		

statements are prepared last because they include information obtained from the income statement, statement of retained earnings, and balance sheet (plus other sources).

Income Statement and Statement of Retained Earnings

Prepare the income statement by creating the usual heading (who, what, when) and listing the names and amounts for each revenue and expense account from the adjusted trial balance, as shown in Exhibit 4.10. Notice that each major category of items on the income statement is subtotalled prior to computing net income for the period.

Learning Objective 4

Prepare financial statements.

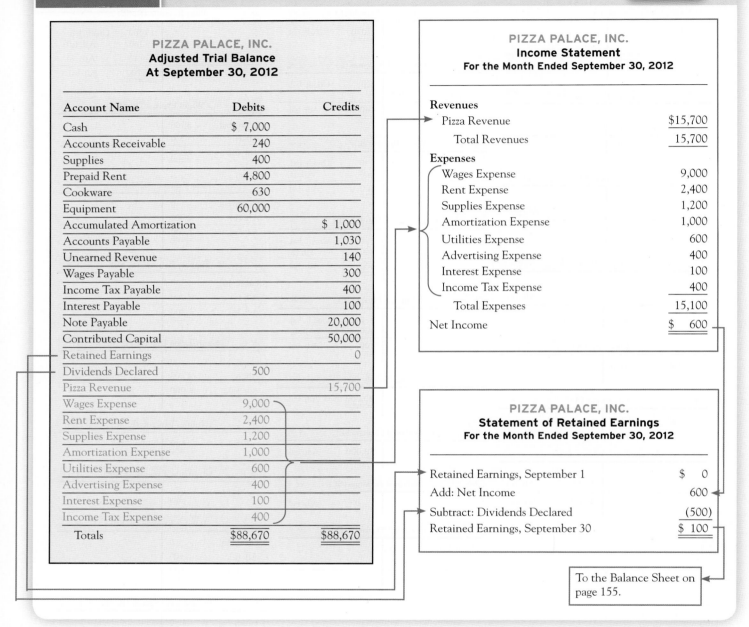

PIZZA PALACE, INC.
Adjusted Trial Balance
At September 30, 2012

Account Name	Debits	Credits
Cash	$ 7,000	
Accounts Receivable	240	
Supplies	400	
Prepaid Rent	4,800	
Cookware	630	
Equipment	60,000	
Accumulated Amortization		$ 1,000
Accounts Payable		1,030
Unearned Revenue		140
Wages Payable		300
Income Tax Payable		400
Interest Payable		100
Note Payable		20,000
Contributed Capital		50,000
Retained Earnings		0
Dividends Declared	500	
Pizza Revenue		15,700
Wages Expense	9,000	
Rent Expense	2,400	
Supplies Expense	1,200	
Amortization Expense	1,000	
Utilities Expense	600	
Advertising Expense	400	
Interest Expense	100	
Income Tax Expense	400	
Totals	$88,670	$88,670

PIZZA PALACE, INC.
Income Statement
For the Month Ended September 30, 2012

Revenues	
Pizza Revenue	$15,700
Total Revenues	15,700
Expenses	
Wages Expense	9,000
Rent Expense	2,400
Supplies Expense	1,200
Amortization Expense	1,000
Utilities Expense	600
Advertising Expense	400
Interest Expense	100
Income Tax Expense	400
Total Expenses	15,100
Net Income	$ 600

PIZZA PALACE, INC.
Statement of Retained Earnings
For the Month Ended September 30, 2012

Retained Earnings, September 1	$ 0
Add: Net Income	600
Subtract: Dividends Declared	(500)
Retained Earnings, September 30	$ 100

To the Balance Sheet on page 155.

To the Balance Sheet on page 155.

COACH'S TIP

Dividends Declared is reported only on the statement of retained earnings.

Account balances from the adjusted trial balance are also used in the statement of retained earnings, as shown in Exhibit 4.10. Notice that the amount coming from the adjusted trial balance is the beginning-of-year balance for Retained Earnings. This account balance doesn't yet include revenues, expenses, and dividends for the current period because they've been recorded in their own separate accounts. Eventually we will transfer ("close") those accounts into Retained Earnings, but that's done only at the end of the year. For now, the Retained Earnings account on the adjusted trial balance provides the opening amount on the statement of retained earnings. The amount for Net Income on the next line of the statement of retained earnings comes from the income statement, and the Dividends Declared number comes from the adjusted trial balance.

Balance Sheet

Like the other statements, the balance sheet is prepared from the adjusted trial balance, as shown in Exhibit 4.11. When preparing the balance sheet, watch out for three things. First, remember to classify assets and liabilities as current if they will be turned into cash or used

EXHIBIT 4.11 **Preparing the Balance Sheet**

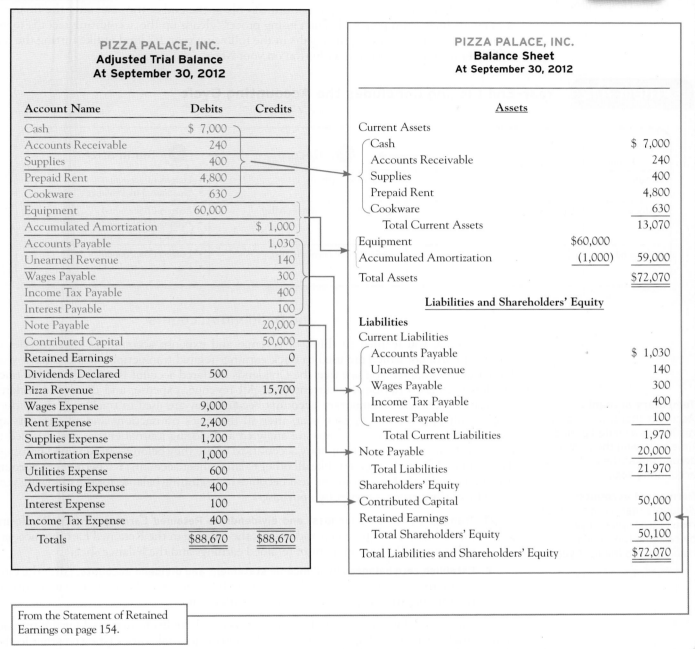

PIZZA PALACE, INC.
Adjusted Trial Balance
At September 30, 2012

Account Name	Debits	Credits
Cash	$ 7,000	
Accounts Receivable	240	
Supplies	400	
Prepaid Rent	4,800	
Cookware	630	
Equipment	60,000	
Accumulated Amortization		$ 1,000
Accounts Payable		1,030
Unearned Revenue		140
Wages Payable		300
Income Tax Payable		400
Interest Payable		100
Note Payable		20,000
Contributed Capital		50,000
Retained Earnings		0
Dividends Declared	500	
Pizza Revenue		15,700
Wages Expense	9,000	
Rent Expense	2,400	
Supplies Expense	1,200	
Amortization Expense	1,000	
Utilities Expense	600	
Advertising Expense	400	
Interest Expense	100	
Income Tax Expense	400	
Totals	$88,670	$88,670

PIZZA PALACE, INC.
Balance Sheet
At September 30, 2012

Assets

Current Assets		
Cash		$ 7,000
Accounts Receivable		240
Supplies		400
Prepaid Rent		4,800
Cookware		630
Total Current Assets		13,070
Equipment	$60,000	
Accumulated Amortization	(1,000)	59,000
Total Assets		$72,070

Liabilities and Shareholders' Equity

Liabilities		
Current Liabilities		
Accounts Payable		$ 1,030
Unearned Revenue		140
Wages Payable		300
Income Tax Payable		400
Interest Payable		100
Total Current Liabilities		1,970
Note Payable		20,000
Total Liabilities		21,970
Shareholders' Equity		
Contributed Capital		50,000
Retained Earnings		100
Total Shareholders' Equity		50,100
Total Liabilities and Shareholders' Equity		$72,070

From the Statement of Retained Earnings on page 154.

up within 12 months. Liabilities should be classified as current if they will be fulfilled (paid) within 12 months. Second, note that Accumulated Amortization is subtracted from Equipment in the assets section. Third, get the Retained Earnings balance from the statement of retained earnings, not from the adjusted trial balance. (The adjusted trial balance still reports only the period's opening Retained Earnings balance.)

Statement of Cash Flows and Notes

We don't want you to forget that the statement of cash flows (SCF) and notes to the financial statements must also be prepared as part of the financial statements. But you look a little tired, so we'll leave the SCF for Chapter 12 and we'll slide information about financial statement notes into each of the remaining chapters.

CLOSING TEMPORARY ACCOUNTS

Learning Objective 5

Explain the closing process.

The last step of the accounting cycle is referred to as the *closing process*. As shown in the first column in Exhibit 4.12, this step is performed only at the end of the year, after the financial statements have been prepared. The closing process cleans up the accounting records to get them ready to begin tracking the results in the following year. It's kind of like hitting the trip odometer on your car or the reset button on your Xbox.

EXHIBIT 4.12	Year-End Closing Concludes the Accounting Cycle

Timing	① Analyze	② Record	③ Summarize
Daily	Transactions	Journal entries (JEs)	• Ledgers (T-accounts) • Unadjusted trial balance
Month-end	Adjustments	Adjusting journal entries (AJEs)	• Ledgers (T-accounts) • Adjusted trial balance • Financial statements
Year-end	Closing	Closing journal entries (CJEs)	• Ledgers (T-accounts) • Post-closing trial balance

Closing Income Statement and Dividend Accounts

YOU SHOULD KNOW

Temporary accounts:
Accounts that track financial results for a limited period of time by having their balances zeroed out at the end of each accounting year.

Permanent accounts:
Accounts that track financial results from year to year by carrying their ending balances into the next year.

In Chapter 3, you learned to think of revenue and expense accounts as subcategories of Retained Earnings, which are used to track earnings-related transactions of the current year. Earlier in this chapter, you saw that the Dividends Declared account is similarly used to track dividends declared during the current year. All revenue, expense, and dividends declared accounts are known as **temporary accounts** because they are used to track only the current year's results. At the end of each year, after all the year's transactions and adjustments are recorded, these temporary accounts are analyzed and closing journal entries are recorded to move the balances from the temporary accounts to where they belong—in Retained Earnings. The Retained Earnings account, like all other balance sheet accounts, is a **permanent account** because its ending balance from one year becomes its beginning balance for the following year.

The closing process serves two purposes:

1. **Transfer net income (or loss) and dividends to Retained Earnings.** After the closing journal entries are prepared and posted, the balance in the Retained Earnings account will agree with the statement of retained earnings and the balance sheet.

2. **Establish zero balances in all income statement and dividend accounts.** After the closing journal entries are prepared and posted, the balances in the temporary accounts are reset to zero to start accumulating next year's results.

Closing journal entries follow the usual debits-equal-credits format used for the transaction journal entries (in Chapters 2 and 3) and adjusting journal entries (shown earlier in this chapter). Because they're the last thing done during the year, they're posted immediately to the accounts. (Some computerized systems record and post closing journal entries automatically.) Two closing journal entries are needed:

1. Debit each revenue account for the amount of its credit balance, credit each expense account for the amount of its debit balance, and record the difference in Retained Earnings. If you've done it right, the amount credited to Retained Earnings should equal Net Income on the Income Statement. (If the company has a net loss, Retained Earnings will be debited.)

2. Credit the Dividends Declared account for the amount of its debit balance and debit Retained Earnings for the same amount.

Exhibit 4.13 shows the closing process for Pizza Palace (assuming, for the sake of illustration, that it closes its books on the last day of September).

EXHIBIT 4.13 Analyzing, Preparing, and Summarizing the Closing Journal Entries

1 Analyze

The analysis step for closing the temporary accounts requires only that you identify, from the adjusted trial balance, the temporary accounts with debit balances (to be credited below) and credit balances (to be debited below).

2 Record

CJE 1. Close revenue and expense accounts:

dr Pizza Revenue (−R)	15,700	
cr Wages Expense (−E)		9,000
cr Rent Expense (−E)		2,400
cr Supplies Expense (−E)		1,200
cr Amortization Expense (−E)		1,000
cr Utilities Expense (−E)		600
cr Advertising Expense (−E)		400
cr Interest Expense (−E)		100
cr Income Tax Expense (−E)		400
cr Retained Earnings (+SE)		600

CJE 2. Close the dividends declared account:

dr Retained Earnings (−SE)	500	
cr Dividends Declared (−D)		500

3 Summarize

dr −	**Pizza Revenue** (R, SE)		cr +
		15,700	Adj. bal.
CJE (1)	15,700		
		0	Closed bal.

dr +	**Advertising Expense** (E, SE)		cr −
Adj. bal.	400		
		400	CJE (1)
Closed bal.	0		

dr +	**Wages Expense** (E, SE)		cr −
Adj. bal.	9,000		
		9,000	CJE (1)
Closed bal.	0		

dr +	**Interest Expense** (E, SE)		cr −
Adj. bal.	100		
		100	CJE (1)
Closed bal.	0		

dr +	**Rent Expense** (E, SE)		cr −
Adj. bal.	2,400		
		2,400	CJE (1)
Closed bal.	0		

dr +	**Income Tax Expense** (E, SE)		cr −
Adj. bal.	400		
		400	CJE (1)
Closed bal.	0		

dr +	**Supplies Expense** (E, SE)		cr −
Adj. bal.	1,200		
		1,200	CJE (1)
Closed bal.	0		

dr +	**Dividends Declared** (D, SE)		cr −
Adj. bal.	500		
		500	CJE (2)
Closed bal.	0		

dr +	**Amortization Expense** (E, SE)		cr −
Adj. bal.	1,000		
		1,000	. CJE (1)
Closed bal.	0		

dr −	**Retained Earnings** (SE)		cr +
		0	Adj. bal.
CJE (2)	500	600	CJE (1)
		100	Closed bal.

dr +	**Utilities Expense** (E, SE)		cr −
Adj. bal.	600		
		600	CJE (1)
Closed bal.	0		

Post-closing trial balance:
An internal report prepared
as the last step in the
accounting cycle to check
that debits equal credits and
all temporary accounts have
been closed.

It is important to note that some companies use a four-step process by closing (1) revenue and (2) expense accounts to a special summary account, called (3) Income Summary, which then is closed to (4) Retained Earnings, along with Dividends Declared. The end result is exactly the same, but the process of how you get there is slightly different.

Post-Closing Trial Balance

After the closing journal entries are posted, all temporary accounts should have zero balances. These accounts will be ready for summarizing transactions recorded next year. The ending balance in Retained Earnings is now up to date (it matches the year-end amount on the statement of retained earnings and balance sheet) and is carried forward as the beginning balance for the next year. As the last step of the accounting cycle, you should prepare a **post-closing trial balance** (as shown in Exhibit 4.14). In this context, *post* means "after,"

EXHIBIT 4.14 — **Pizza Palace's Post-Closing Trial Balance**

PIZZA PALACE, INC.
Post-Closing Trial Balance
At September 30, 2012

Account Name	Debits	Credits
Cash	$ 7,000	
Accounts Receivable	240	
Supplies	400	
Prepaid Rent	4,800	
Cookware	630	
Equipment	60,000	
Accumulated Amortization		$ 1,000
Accounts Payable		1,030
Unearned Revenue		140
Wages Payable		300
Income Tax Payable		400
Interest Payable		100
Note Payable		20,000
Contributed Capital		50,000
Retained Earnings		100
Dividends Declared	0	
Pizza Revenue		0
Wages Expense	0	
Rent Expense	0	
Supplies Expense	0	
Amortization Expense	0	
Utilities Expense	0	
Advertising Expense	0	
Interest Expense	0	
Income Tax Expense	0	
Totals	$73,070	$73,070

COACH'S TIP

Total debits on the post-closing trial balance don't equal the total assets on the balance sheet because Accumulated Amortization (a credit balance on the trial balance) is subtracted from assets on the balance sheet.

so a post-closing trial balance is an "after-closing" trial balance that is prepared as a final check that total debits still equal total credits and that all temporary accounts have been closed.

Now that we've completed the accounting cycle, it seems appropriate to summarize it one more time. Exhibit 4.12 (on page 156) showed one way to organize the various steps of the accounting cycle. Exhibit 4.15 presents the same ideas in a slightly different format. The steps in the coral, blue, and gold boxes are done daily, monthly, and yearly, respectively.

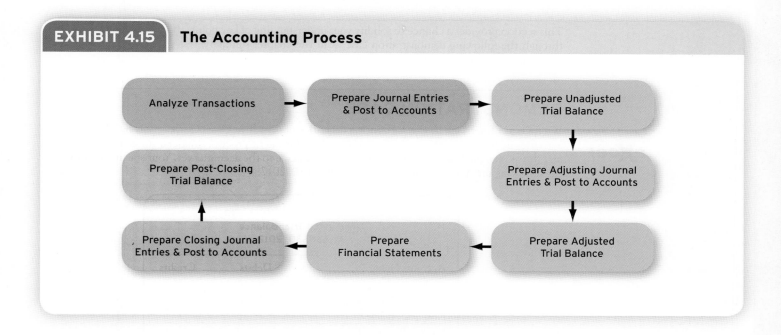

EXHIBIT 4.15   **The Accounting Process**

Analyze Transactions → Prepare Journal Entries & Post to Accounts → Prepare Unadjusted Trial Balance ↓

Prepare Adjusting Journal Entries & Post to Accounts ↓

Prepare Post-Closing Trial Balance ← Prepare Closing Journal Entries & Post to Accounts ← Prepare Financial Statements ← Prepare Adjusted Trial Balance

Evaluate the Results

ADJUSTED FINANCIAL RESULTS

Throughout this chapter, you learned various adjustments that must be made to the accounting records when finalizing and preparing the financial statements. These adjustments help to ensure that all revenues and expenses are reported in the period in which they are earned and incurred. As a result of these adjustments, the financial statements present the best picture of whether the company's business activities were profitable that period and what economic resources the company owns and owes at the end of that period. Without these adjustments, the financial statements present an incomplete and misleading picture of the company's financial performance.

Pizza Palace provides a good example of the extent to which unadjusted balances may change during the adjustment process. In contrast to Emilio's initial impression that Pizza Palace had earned a sizable profit (net income of $5,800 from revenue of $15,500), the company's adjusted results indicated a much different picture (net income of $600 from revenue of $15,700). Consequently, Emilio learned that he had much to improve upon in the upcoming months. He set a goal of attempting to increase the company's revenue by expanding his customer base, while at the same time trying to control expenses. He was well aware that even large companies go out of business if they fail to maintain revenues and control their expenses.

Learning Objective 6

Explain how adjustments affect financial results.

Given the nature of the material in this chapter, there are no significant differences between ASPE and IFRS.

Review the Chapter

This section provides a chance to solidify your understanding of key points. It's worth your time to work through the following demonstration case, scan the chapter summary, test your understanding of key terms, and then practise, practise, practise.

DEMONSTRATION CASE

We take our final look at the accounting activities of Goodbye Grass Corporation by illustrating the activities at the end of the accounting cycle: the adjustment process, financial statement preparation, and the closing process. No adjustments have been made to the accounts yet. Your starting point will be the following unadjusted trial balance dated April 30, 2012:

GOODBYE GRASS CORPORATION
Unadjusted Trial Balance
At April 30, 2012

Account Name	Debits	Credits
Cash	$ 4,510	
Accounts Receivable	1,700	
Note Receivable	1,250	
Interest Receivable	0	
Prepaid Insurance	300	
Equipment	4,600	
Accumulated Amortization		$ 0
Land	3,750	
Accounts Payable		620
Unearned Revenue		1,600
Wages Payable		0
Interest Payable		0
Income Tax Payable		0
Dividends Payable		0
Note Payable		4,000
Contributed Capital		9,000
Retained Earnings		0
Dividends Declared		0
Mowing Revenue		5,200
Interest Revenue		0
Wages Expense	3,900	
Fuel Expense	410	
Insurance Expense	0	
Amortization Expense	0	
Interest Expense	0	
Income Tax Expense	0	
Totals	$20,420	$20,420

By reviewing the unadjusted trial balance, you identify three deferral accounts (Prepaid Insurance, Equipment, and Unearned Revenue) that may need to be adjusted in addition to accruals that may be necessary relating to wages, income taxes, and interest on the Note Receivable and Note Payable. The following information is determined at the end of the accounting cycle:

Deferral Adjustments

a. One-fourth of the $1,600 cash received from the city at the beginning of April for future mowing service has been earned in April. The $1,600 in Unearned Revenue represents four months of service (April through July).

b. Insurance purchased at the beginning of April for $300 provides coverage for six months (April through September). The insurance coverage for April has now been used.

> **TIP:** Account for the expiry of prepaid insurance just like the expiry of prepaid rent.

c. Mowers, edgers, rakes, and hand tools (equipment) have been used in April to generate revenues. The company estimates $300 in amortization each year.

Accrual Adjustments

d. Wages have been paid through April 28. Employees worked the last two days of April and will be paid in May. Wages amount to $200 per day.

e. Interest incurred and payable on the note payable is $45 for the month of April.

f. Interest earned and receivable on the note receivable is $10 for the month of April.

g. The estimated income tax rate for Goodbye Grass Corporation is 35 percent.

h. Dividends were declared on April 30 for $200.

Required:

1. Analyze items (a)–(h) with the goal of identifying the effects of required adjustments on the basic accounting equation (Assets = Liabilities + Shareholders' Equity), using the format shown in the chapter.

2. Record the adjusting journal entries required at the end of April.

3. Summarize the effects of each adjusting journal entry in T-accounts for each account affected. Obtain beginning balances from the unadjusted trial balance, then post the adjusting journal entries from requirement 2, and calculate adjusted April 30 balances.

4. Prepare an adjusted trial balance to ensure debit and credit balances are equal, remembering to include all accounts in the trial balance (and not just the ones affected by the adjusting journal entries).

5. Prepare an income statement, statement of retained earnings, and classified balance sheet from the amounts in the adjusted trial balance.

6. Prepare the closing journal entries that would be required if Goodbye Grass Corporation's fiscal year ended April 30, 2012.

7. Prepare the post-closing trial balance as a final check that all debits still equal credits and that all temporary accounts have been closed.

After completing requirements 1–7, check your answers with the following solution.

Suggested Solution

1. Adjustment analysis:

a. The unadjusted balances are $1,600 for Unearned Revenue and $5,200 for Mowing Revenue. One-fourth of the $1,600 has been earned in April ($400 = ¼ × $1,600), bringing total mowing revenues for the month to $5,600 ($5,200 + $400). Three-fourths of the $1,600 remain unearned at the end of April ($1,200 = ¾ × $1,600). To reach these desired balances, we need an adjustment that decreases Unearned Revenue by $400 and increases Mowing Revenue by $400.

$1,600 × ¼ = $400 | $1,600 × ¾ = $1,200
Revenue | Still unearned
Apr. 1 — Apr. 30 — July 31
$1,600 — Adjustment
Unearned

Assets	=	Liabilities	+	Shareholders' Equity
		Unearned Revenue −400		Mowing Revenue (+R) +400

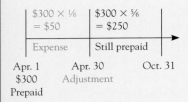

$300 × ⅙ = $50 | $300 × ⅚ = $250

Expense | Still prepaid

Apr. 1 — Apr. 30 — Oct. 31
$300 — Adjustment
Prepaid

b. The unadjusted balances are $300 for Prepaid Insurance and $0 for Insurance Expense. One-sixth of the $300 has expired in April resulting in an insurance expense for the month of $50 (= ⅙ × $300). Five of the six months of insurance coverage remain unused at the end of April ($250 = ⅚ × $300). To reach these desired balances, we need an adjustment that decreases Prepaid Insurance by $50 and increases Insurance Expense by $50.

Assets	=	Liabilities	+	Shareholders' Equity
Prepaid Insurance −50				Insurance Expense (+E) −50

c. The unadjusted balances are $0 for Accumulated Amortization and $0 for Amortization Expense. Yearly amortization of $300 equals $25 for just one month ($300 × 1/12). To go from the unadjusted balances of $0 to the desired adjusted balances of $25, we increase the expense and contra-account balances by $25.

Assets	=	Liabilities +	Shareholders' Equity
Accumulated Amortization (+xA) −25			Amortization Expense (+E) −25

d. The unadjusted balances are $0 for Wages Payable and $3,900 for Wages Expense. Because the final two days of work done in April are unpaid, we need to record a liability for $400 (2 × $200). Total wages expense for the month should include the $3,900 paid for work from April 1–28 plus the $400 not yet paid for work on April 29 and 30. To reach these desired balances, we need an adjustment increasing Wages Payable by $400 and increasing Wages Expense by $400.

Assets	=	Liabilities	+	Shareholders' Equity
		Wages Payable +400		Wages Expense (+E) −400

e. The unadjusted balances are $0 for Interest Payable and $0 for Interest Expense. Interest of $45 was incurred in April, so the adjustment needs to increase both accounts by $45.

Assets	=	Liabilities	+	Shareholders' Equity
		Interest Payable +45		Interest Expense (+E) −45

f. The unadjusted balances are $0 for Interest Receivable and $0 for Interest Revenue. Interest of $10 was earned in April, so the adjustment needs to increase both accounts by $10.

Assets	=	Liabilities	+	Shareholders' Equity
Interest Receivable +10				Interest Revenue (+R) +10

g. The unadjusted balances are $0 for Income Tax Payable and $0 for Income Tax Expense. The amount of calculated income taxes will increase both of these accounts. Income taxes are calculated as 35 percent of adjusted income before tax for the month, as follows:

		Revenues	Expenses	
Unadjusted totals		$5,200	$4,310	← Calculated from unadjusted trial balance
Adjustments:	(a)	+400		($4,310 = $3,900 + $410)
	(b)		+ 50	
	(c)		+ 25	
	(d)		+ 400	
	(e)		+ 45	
	(f)	+ 10		
Adjusted totals		$5,610	$4,830	= $780 Adjusted income before income tax
				× 35% Tax rate
				$273 **Income tax**

Assets	=	Liabilities	+	Shareholders' Equity
		Income Tax Payable +273		Income Tax Expense (+E) −273

h. The unadjusted balances are \$0 for Dividends Payable and \$0 for Dividends Declared. Dividends of \$200 were declared in April, so the adjustment needs to increase both accounts by \$200.

Assets	=	Liabilities	+	Shareholders' Equity
		Dividends Payable +200		Dividends Declared (+D) −200

2. Adjusting journal entries:

a. dr Unearned Revenue (−L).. 400
　　cr Mowing Revenue (+R, +SE).. 　　400

b. dr Insurance Expense (+E, −SE) 50
　　cr Prepaid Insurance (−A)... 　　50

c. dr Amortization Expense (+E, −SE) 25
　　cr Accumulated Amortization (+xA, −A)........................... 　　25

d. dr Wages Expense (+E, −SE)... 400
　　cr Wages Payable (+L).. 　　400

e. dr Interest Expense (+E, −SE)... 45
　　cr Interest Payable (+L).. 　　45

f. dr Interest Receivable (+A)... 10
　　cr Interest Revenue (+R, +SE)... 　　10

g. dr Income Tax Expense (+E, −SE) 273
　　cr Income Tax Payable (+L)... 　　273

h. dr Dividends Declared (+D, −SE)....................................... 200
　　cr Dividends Payable (+L).. 　　200

3. T-accounts affected by adjusting journal entries:*

dr +	Interest Receivable (A)	cr −
Beg. bal.	0	
(f)	10	
End. bal.	10	

dr −	Interest Payable (L)	cr +
	0	Beg. bal.
	45	(e)
	45	End. bal.

dr +	Insurance Expense (E)	cr −
Beg. bal.	0	
(b)	50	
End. bal.	50	

dr +	Prepaid Insurance (A)	cr −
Beg. bal.	300	
	50	(b)
End. bal.	250	

dr −	Income Tax Payable (L)	cr +
	0	Beg. bal.
	273	(g)
	273	End. bal.

dr +	Amortization Expense (E)	cr −
Beg. bal.	0	
(c)	25	
End. bal.	25	

dr −	Accumulated Amortization (xA)	cr +
	0	Beg. bal.
	25	(c)
	25	End. bal.

dr −	Mowing Revenue (R, SE)	cr +
	5,200	Beg. bal.
	400	(a)
	5,600	End. bal.

dr +	Interest Expense (E, SE)	cr −
Beg. bal.	0	
(e)	45	
End. bal.	45	

dr −	Unearned Revenue (L)	cr +
	1,600	Beg. bal.
(a)	400	
	1,200	End. bal.

dr −	Interest Revenue (R, SE)	cr +
	0	Beg. bal.
	10	(f)
	10	End. bal.

dr +	Income Tax Expense (E, SE)	cr −
Beg. bal.	0	
(g)	273	
End. bal.	273	

* See page 109 (Chapter 3) for balances of T-accounts not affected by adjusting journal entries.

dr −	Wages Payable (L)	cr +
	0	Beg. bal.
	400	(d)
	400	End. bal.

dr +	Wages Expense (E, SE)	cr −
Beg. bal.	3,900	
(d)	400	
End. bal.	4,300	

dr −	Dividends Payable (L)	cr +
	0	Beg. bal.
	200	(h)
	200	End. bal.

dr +	Dividends Declared (D, SE)	cr −
Beg. bal.	0	
(h)	200	
End. bal.	200	

4. Adjusted trial balance:

GOODBYE GRASS CORPORATION
Adjusted Trial Balance
At April 30, 2012

Account Name	Debits	Credits	
Cash	$ 4,510		
Accounts Receivable	1,700		
Note Receivable	1,250		
Interest Receivable	10		
Prepaid Insurance	250		
Equipment	4,600		
Accumulated Amortization		$ 25	
Land	3,750		
Accounts Payable		620	To Balance Sheet
Unearned Revenue		1,200	
Wages Payable		400	
Interest Payable		45	
Income Tax Payable		273	
Dividends Payable		200	
Note Payable		4,000	
Contributed Capital		9,000	
Retained Earnings		0	To Statement of Retained Earnings
Dividends Declared	200		
Mowing Revenue		5,600	
Interest Revenue		10	
Wages Expense	4,300		
Fuel Expense	410		To Income Statement
Insurance Expense	50		
Amortization Expense	25		
Interest Expense	45		
Income Tax Expense	273		
Totals	$21,373	$21,373	

5. Income statement, statement of retained earnings, and balance sheet:

GOODBYE GRASS CORPORATION
Income Statement
For the Month Ended April 30, 2012

Revenues:	
Mowing Revenue	$ 5,600
Interest Revenue	10
Total Revenues	5,610
Expenses:	
Wages Expense	4,300
Fuel Expense	410
Insurance Expense	50
Amortization Expense	25
Interest Expense	45
Income Tax Expense	273
Total Expenses	5,103
Net Income	**$ 507**

GOODBYE GRASS CORPORATION
Statement of Retained Earnings
For the Month Ended April 30, 2012

Balance, April 1, 2012	$ 0
Add: Net Income	507
Subtract: Dividends Declared	200
Balance, April 30, 2012	$307

GOODBYE GRASS CORPORATION
Balance Sheet
At April 30, 2012

Assets			Liabilities and Shareholders' Equity		
Current Assets:			Liabilities		
Cash		$ 4,510	Current Liabilities:		
Accounts Receivable		1,700	Accounts Payable		$ 620
Note Receivable		1,250	Unearned Revenue		1,200
Interest Receivable		10	Wages Payable		400
Prepaid Insurance		250	Interest Payable		45
Total Current Assets		7,720	Income Tax Payable		273
Equipment	$ 4,600		Dividends Payable		200
Less: Accumulated Amortization	(25)		Note Payable		4,000
			Total Current Liabilities		6,738
Equipment, Net		4,575	Shareholders' Equity		
Land		3,750	Contributed Capital		9,000
Total Assets		$16,045	Retained Earnings		307
			Total Liabilities and Shareholders' Equity		$16,045

---

6. Closing journal entry:

If Goodbye Grass Corporation had adopted an April 30 year-end, the company would require a journal entry to close its revenue and expense accounts into Retained Earnings. It would also need a second journal entry to close the Dividends Declared account into Retained Earnings. The closing journal entry needed to close revenues and expenses into Retained Earnings is

dr Mowing Revenue (−R) 5,600
dr Interest Revenue (−R) 10
    cr Wages Expense (−E)... 4,300
    cr Fuel Expense (−E) 410
    cr Insurance Expense (−E) 50
    cr Amortization Expense (−E) 25
    cr Interest Expense (−E) 45
    cr Income Tax Expense (−E)....................................... 273
    cr Retained Earnings (+SE) 507

The second closing journal entry needed to close Dividends Declared into Retained Earnings is

dr Retained Earnings (+SE)..... 200
    cr Dividends Declared (−D)...................................... 200

7. Post-closing trial balance:

GOODBYE GRASS CORPORATION
Post-Closing Trial Balance
At April 30, 2012

Account Name	Debits	Credits
Cash	$ 4,510	
Accounts Receivable	1,700	
Note Receivable	1,250	
Interest Receivable	10	
Prepaid Insurance	250	
Equipment	4,600	
Accumulated Amortization		$ 25
Land	3,750	
Accounts Payable		620
Unearned Revenue		1,200
Wages Payable		400
Interest Payable		45
Income Tax Payable		273
Dividends Payable		200
Note Payable		4,000
Contributed Capital		9,000
Retained Earnings		307
Dividends Declared	0	
Mowing Revenue		0
Interest Revenue		0
Wages Expense	0	
Fuel Expense	0	
Insurance Expense	0	
Amortization Expense	0	
Interest Expense	0	
Income Tax Expense	0	
Totals	$16,070	$16,070

CHAPTER SUMMARY

Explain why adjustments are needed. p. 139
LO1

Adjustments are needed to ensure

- Revenues are recorded when earned (the revenue principle)
- Expenses are recorded when incurred to generate revenues (the matching principle)
- Assets are reported at amounts representing the economic benefits that remain at the end of the current period
- Liabilities are reported at amounts owed at the end of the current period that will require a future sacrifice of resources

Prepare adjustments needed at the end of the period. p. 141
LO2

- The process for preparing adjustments includes

  1. Analyzing the unadjusted balances in balance sheet and income statement accounts, and calculating the amount of the adjustment needed, using a timeline where appropriate
  2. Preparing an adjusting journal entry to make the adjustment
  3. Summarizing the adjusting journal entry in the applicable ledger (T-accounts)

- Each adjusting journal entry affects one balance sheet and one income statement account

Prepare an adjusted trial balance. p. 152
LO3

An adjusted trial balance is a list of all accounts with their adjusted debit or credit balances indicated in the appropriate column to provide a check on the equality of the debits and credits.

Prepare financial statements. p. 153
LO4

Adjusted account balances are used in preparing the following financial statements:

- Income Statement: Revenues − Expenses = Net Income
- Statement of Retained Earnings: Beginning Retained Earnings + Net Income − Dividends Declared = Ending Retained Earnings
- Balance Sheet: Assets = Liabilities + Shareholders' Equity
- The statement of cash flows and notes to the financial statements are important components of adjusted financial statements, but they will be studied in later chapters.

Explain the closing process. p. 156
LO5

- Closing journal entries are required to (*a*) transfer net income (or loss) and dividends declared into retained earnings, and (*b*) prepare all temporary accounts (revenues, expenses, dividends declared) for the following year by establishing zero balances in these accounts.
- Two closing journal entries are needed:

  1. Debit each revenue account, credit each expense account, and record the difference (equal to net income) in Retained Earnings
  2. Credit the Dividends Declared account for the amount of its balance and debit Retained Earnings for the same amount

Explain how adjustments affect financial results. p. 159
LO6

Adjustments help ensure that all revenues and expenses are reported in the period in which they are earned and incurred as a result of a company's activities. Without these adjustments, the financial statements present an incomplete and potentially misleading picture of the company's financial performance.

KEY TERMS

Adjusted Trial Balance p. 152
Adjusting Journal Entries (AJEs) p. 141
Adjustments p. 139
Amortization p. 146

Carrying Value (Net Book Value, Book Value) p. 146
Contra-Account p. 146

Permanent Accounts p. 156
Post-Closing Trial Balance p. 158
Temporary Accounts p. 156

See complete definitions in the glossary in the back of this text.

HOMEWORK HELPER

Alternative terms

- *Accrued Liabilities* is a generic account name that can include liabilities recorded using accrual adjustments for salaries, utilities, income taxes, and many other items.

Helpful reminders

- When determining each adjustment, draw timelines to picture where we are now, where we need to be, and the adjustment to get us there.
- Cash is never part of an accrual or deferral adjustment.
- The income statement is the temporary home for revenue and expense accounts, and Retained Earnings in the shareholders' equity section of the balance sheet is their permanent home.

Frequent mistakes

- Accumulated Amortization and Amortization Expense are not the same accounts. Accumulated Amortization is a permanent balance sheet account that accumulates each period of amortization. Amortization Expense is a temporary income statement account that reports only the current period's amortization.
- Dividends are not expenses, but rather are distributions to shareholders of the company's prior profits that have accumulated in Retained Earnings.
- The amount in Retained Earnings on an adjusted trial balance is not reported on the balance sheet; it is the beginning balance on the statement of retained earnings. The ending balance from the statement of retained earnings is reported on the balance sheet.

Practice Material

QUESTIONS (⑤ Symbol indicates questions that require analysis from more than one perspective.)

1. Briefly explain the purposes of adjusting journal entries.

2. Explain the relationships between adjustments and the following Chapter 3 concepts: (*a*) the time period assumption, (*b*) the revenue principle, and (*c*) the matching principle.

3. List the two types of adjusting journal entries and give an example of an adjustment affecting revenues and expenses for each type.

4. Explain the effect of adjusting journal entries on cash.

5. What is a contra-asset? Give an example of one.

6. Explain the differences between amortization expense and accumulated amortization.

7. What is an adjusted trial balance? What is its purpose?

8. On December 31, a company makes a $9,000 payment for renting a warehouse in January, February, and March of the following year. Show the accounting equation effects of the transaction on December 31, as well as the adjustments required on January 31, February 28, and March 31.

9. Using the information in question 8, determine the amounts and accounts that will be reported on the January 31 balance sheet and the income statement for the month ended January 31.

10. Using the information in question 8, prepare the journal entry and adjusting journal entries to be made on December 31, January 31, February 28, and March 31.

11. What is the equation for each of the following statements: (*a*) income statement, (*b*) balance sheet, and (*c*) statement of retained earnings?

12. Explain how the financial statements in question 11 relate to each other.

13. What is the purpose of closing journal entries?

14. How do permanent accounts differ from temporary accounts?

15. Why are the income statement accounts closed but the balance sheet accounts are not?

16. Is Dividends Declared considered an asset, liability, or shareholders' equity account? Is it a permanent or temporary account? Does it normally have a debit or credit balance?

17. What is a post-closing trial balance? Is it a useful part of the accounting cycle? Explain.

18. The owner of a local business complains that the adjustments process consumes a lot of time and delays reporting month-end financial results. How would you convince her of the importance of this process? ⑤

Multiple-choice questions and corresponding answers can be found on Connect.

M4-1 Understanding Concepts Related to Adjustments

Match each situation below to two applicable reasons that require an adjustment to be made.

_____ 1. WestJet Airlines provided flights this month for customers who paid cash last month for tickets.

_____ 2. Shoppers Drug Mart received a telephone bill for services this month, which must be paid next month.

_____ 3. The Jim Pattison Group completed work on an advertising campaign that will be collected next month.

_____ 4. The Lyton Foundation used up some of the benefits of its 3,250-m² building (when teaching students about forensic science, aerospace, and video production).

A. Revenue has been earned.

B. Expense has been incurred.

C. Liability has been incurred.

D. Liability has been fulfilled.

E. Asset has been acquired.

F. Asset has been used up.

LO1

WestJet
Shoppers Drug Mart
Jim Pattison Group

M4-2 Matching Transactions with Type of Adjustment

LO1, 2

Match each transaction with the type of adjustment that will be required, by entering the appropriate letter in the space provided.

Transaction	Type of Adjustment

_____ 1. Supplies for office use were purchased during the year for $500, of which $100 remained on hand (unused) at year-end.

_____ 2. Interest of $250 on a note receivable was earned at year-end, although collection of the interest is not due until the following year.

_____ 3. At year-end, wages payable of $3,600 had not been recorded or paid.

_____ 4. At year-end, one-half of a $2,000 advertising project had been completed for a client, but nothing had been billed or collected.

A. Accrual adjustment

B. Deferral adjustment

Using the information, prepare the adjusting journal entries required.

M4-3 Determining Accounting Equation Effects of Adjustments

LO2

For each of the following transactions for the Sky Blue Corporation, give the accounting equation effects of the adjustments required at the end of the month on December 31, 2012:

a. Received a $600 utility bill for electricity usage in December to be paid in January 2013.

b. Owed wages to 10 employees who worked three days at $100 each per day at the end of December. The company will pay employees at the end of the first week of January 2013.

c. On December 1, 2012, loaned money to an employee who agreed to repay the loan in one year along with $1,200 for one full year of interest. No interest has been recorded yet.

Using the information, prepare the adjusting journal entries required on December 31, 2012.

M4-4 **Preparing Journal Entries for Deferral Transactions and Adjustments**

For each of the following independent situations, prepare journal entries to record the initial transaction on December 31 and the adjustment required on January 31.

a. Magnificent Magazines received $12,000 on December 31, 2011, for subscriptions to magazines that will be published and distributed in January through December 2012.

b. Walker Window Washing paid $1,200 cash for supplies on December 31, 2011. As of January 31, 2012, $200 of these supplies had been used up.

c. Indoor Raceway received $3,000 on December 31, 2011, from race participants for three races. One race was held January 31, 2012, and the other two in March 2012.

M4-5 **Preparing an Adjusted Trial Balance**

Macro Company had the following adjusted accounts and balances at year-end (June 30, 2012):

Accounts Payable	$ 300	Cash	$1,020	Prepaid Expenses	$ 40
Accounts Receivable	550	Contributed Capital	300	Salaries Expense	660
Accrued Liabilities	150	Amortization Expense	110	Sales Revenue	3,600
Accumulated		Income Tax Expense	110	Supplies	710
Amortization	250	Income Tax Payable	30	Rent Expense	400
Administrative		Interest Expense	180	Retained Earnings	120
Expense	820	Interest Revenue	50	Unearned Revenue	100
Buildings and		Land	200		
Equipment	1,400	Long-Term Debt	1,300		

Required:

Prepare an adjusted trial balance for Macro Company at June 30, 2012.

M4-6 **Reporting an Income Statement**

The Sky Blue Corporation has the following adjusted trial balance at December 31, 2012.

	Debit	Credit
Cash	$ 1,230	
Accounts Receivable	2,000	
Prepaid Insurance	2,300	
Notes Receivable	3,000	
Equipment	12,000	
Accumulated Amortization		$ 2,600
Accounts Payable		1,600
Accrued Liabilities Payable		3,820
Wages Payable		1,000
Income Taxes Payable		2,900
Unearned Rent Revenue		600
Contributed Capital		2,400
Retained Earnings		1,000
Dividends Declared	300	
Sales Revenue		42,030
Rent Revenue		300
Wages Expense	21,600	
Amortization Expense	1,300	
Utilities Expense	1,220	
Insurance Expense	1,400	
Rent Expense	9,000	
Income Tax Expense	2,900	
Total	$58,250	$58,250

Prepare an income statement for the year ended December 31, 2012. How much net income did the Sky Blue Corporation generate during 2012?

M4-7 Reporting a Statement of Retained Earnings

LO4

Refer to M4-6. Prepare a statement of retained earnings for 2012.

M4-8 Reporting a Balance Sheet

LO4

Refer to M4-6. Prepare a classified balance sheet at December 31, 2012. Are the Sky Blue Corporation's assets financed primarily by debt or equity?

M4-9 Recording Closing Journal Entries

LO5

Refer to the adjusted trial balance in M4-6. Prepare closing journal entries on December 31, 2012.

M4-10 Preparing and Posting Journal Entries for Dividends

LO2

At December 31, the unadjusted trial balance of H&R Tacks reports Dividends Declared of $0 and Dividends Payable of $0. A $200 dividend was declared on December 27, with payment in cash to occur three weeks later. Prepare the required journal entry. In separate T-accounts for each account, enter the unadjusted balances, post the journal entry, and report the adjusted balance.

M4-11 Progression of Prepaid Expenses over Several Periods

LO2, 4, 5

Midcounty Manufacturing purchased a three-year insurance policy for $30,000 on January 2, 2011. Prepare any journal entries, adjusting journal entries, and closing journal entries required on January 2, 2011, December 31, 2011, and December 31, 2012. Summarize these entries in T-accounts for Prepaid Insurance, Insurance Expense, Cash, and Retained Earnings. Assume the January 2, 2011, balances in these accounts were $0, $0, $90,000, and $80,000, respectively. Given only the entries for insurance, indicate what amounts would be reported for each of these accounts on the balance sheet and income statement prepared on December 31, 2011, and December 31, 2012.

EXERCISES

Practise and learn online with Connect.

E4-1 Preparing an Adjusted Trial Balance from Adjusted Account Balances

LO3

Glidden Consulting provides marketing research for clients in the retail industry. The company had the following adjusted balances at December 31, 2012 (listed alphabetically):

Accounts Payable		Accumulated Amortization		Consulting Fees Earned		General and Administrative Expense	
	86,830		18,100		2,564,200	320,050	

Accounts Receivable		Building and Equipment		Contributed Capital		Income Taxes Payable	
225,400		323,040			233,370		2,030

Accrued Liabilities		Cash		Dividends Declared		Interest Expense	
	25,650	173,000		5,000		17,200	

Land		Other Revenue		Supplies		Utilities Expense	
60,000			20,800	12,200		25,230	

Notes Payable		Prepaid Expenses		Training Expenses		Wages and Benefits Expense	
	160,000	10,200		18,600		1,590,000	

Other Assets		Rent Expense		Travel Expense	
145,000		152,080		23,990	

Other Operating Expenses		Retained Earnings		Unearned Consulting Fees	
188,000			?		32,500

Required:

1. Prepare an adjusted trial balance listing the accounts in proper order at December 31, 2012. Solve for the "?" in Retained Earnings.
2. Does the Retained Earnings balance determined in requirement 1 represent the balance at December 31, 2012, or December 31, 2011? Explain.

LO1 **E4-2 Identifying Adjustments by Scanning a Trial Balance**

Sara Lee Corporation

Coach, Inc.—the maker of handbags and other women's and men's accessories—was owned by Sara Lee Corporation until April 2001, when Coach was spun off as a separate company. Assume the following were reported in Coach's adjusted trial balance and were used to prepare its June 28, 2011, year-end financial statements.

COACH, INC.
Adjusted Trial Balance
At June 28, 2011
(millions of dollars)

	Debit	Credit
Cash	$ 698	
Accounts Receivable	107	
Inventories	345	
Prepaid Expenses	234	
Property and Equipment	755	
Accumulated Amortization		$ 291
Other Assets	426	
Accounts Payable		134
Wages Payable		304
Income Taxes Payable		12
Other Current Liabilities		308
Contributed Capital		24
Retained Earnings		709
Sales Revenue		3,181
Cost of Sales	774	
Selling, General, and Administrative Expenses	1,260	
Interest Revenue		48
Income Tax Expense	412	
	$5,011	$5,011

Required:

1. Based on the information in the trial balance, list two pairs of balance sheet and income statement accounts that likely required *deferral adjustments* as of June 30 (no computations are necessary).
2. Based on the information in the trial balance, list two pairs of balance sheet and income statement accounts that likely required *accrual adjustments* as of June 30 (no computations are necessary).

LO1, 2 **E4-3 Recording Initial Transactions and Subsequent Adjustments**

During the month of September, the Bridge City Go-Kart Company had the following business activities:

a. On September 1, paid rent on the track facility for six months at a total cost of $12,000.
b. On September 1, received $60,000 for season tickets for 12-month admission to the race track.
c. On September 1, booked the race track for a private organization that will use the track one day per month for $2,000 each time, to be paid in the following month. The organization uses the track on September 30.
d. On September 1, hired a new manager at a monthly salary of $3,000, to be paid the first Monday following the end of the month.

Required:

First prepare the journal entry, if any, required to record each of the initial business activities on September 1. Then, prepare the adjusting journal entries, if any, required on September 30.

E4-4 Recording Adjusting Journal Entries

LO2

Mobol, a wireless phone carrier, completed its first year of operations on December 31, 2011. All of the 2011 entries have been recorded, except for the following:

a. At year-end, employees earned wages of $6,000, which will be paid on the next payroll date, January 13, 2012.

b. At year-end, the company had earned interest revenue of $3,000. It will be collected March 1, 2012.

Required:

1. What is the annual reporting period for this company?
2. Identify whether each required adjustment is a deferral or an accrual.
3. Show the accounting equation effects of each required adjustment, using the format shown in the demonstration case.
4. Why are these adjustments needed?

E4-5 Recording Adjusting Journal Entries

LO1, 2

Refer to E4-4.

Required:

Record the required adjusting journal entry for transactions (a) and (b).

Check Figure [Part (a)]:
Wages Payable
is credited $6,000.

E4-6 Determining Adjustments and Accounting Equation Effects

LO1, 2

Fesel Company is making adjusting journal entries for the year ended December 31, 2012. In developing information for the adjusting journal entries, you learned the following:

a. A two-year insurance premium of $7,200 was paid on January 1, 2012, for coverage beginning on that date. As of December 31, 2012, the unadjusted balances were $7,200 for Prepaid Insurance and $0 for Insurance Expense.

b. At December 31, 2012, you obtained the following data relating to shipping supplies.

Unadjusted balance in Shipping Supplies on December 31, 2012	$15,000
Unadjusted balance in Shipping Supplies Expense on December 31, 2012	72,000
Shipping supplies on hand, counted on December 31, 2012	10,000

Required:

1. Of the $7,200 paid for insurance, what amount should be reported on the 2012 income statement as Insurance Expense? What amount should be reported on the December 31, 2012, balance sheet as Prepaid Insurance?
2. What amount should be reported on the 2012 income statement as Shipping Supplies Expense? What amount should be reported on the December 31, 2012, balance sheet as Shipping Supplies?
3. Using the format shown in the demonstration case, indicate the accounting equation effects of the adjustment required for (a) insurance and (b) shipping supplies.

Check Figure [Req. 2]:
Shipping Supplies
Expense = $77,000

E4-7 Recording Adjusting Journal Entries

LO2

Refer to E4-6.

Required:

Prepare adjusting journal entries at December 31, 2012, for (a) insurance, and (b) shipping supplies.

E4-8 Recording Typical Adjusting Journal Entries

Nickleby's Ski Store is completing the accounting process for its first year ended December 31, 2012. The transactions during 2012 have been journalized and posted. The following data are available to determine adjusting journal entries:

a. The unadjusted balance in Office Supplies was $850 at December 31, 2012. The unadjusted balance in Supplies Expense was $0 at December 31, 2012. A year-end count showed $100 of supplies on hand.

b. Wages earned by employees during December 2012, unpaid and unrecorded at December 31, 2012, amounted to $3,700. The last paycheques were issued December 28; the next payments will be made on January 6, 2013. The unadjusted balance in Wages Expense was $40,000 at December 31, 2012.

c. A portion of the store's basement is now being rented for $1,100 per month to K. Frey. On November 1, 2012, the store collected six months' rent in advance from Frey in the amount of $6,600. It was credited in full to Unearned Rent Revenue when collected. The unadjusted balance in Rent Revenue was $0 at December 31, 2012.

d. The store purchased delivery equipment at the beginning of the year. The estimated amortization for 2012 is $3,000, although none has been recorded yet.

e. On December 31, 2012, the unadjusted balance in Prepaid Insurance was $4,800. This was the amount paid in the middle of the year for a two-year insurance policy, with coverage beginning on July 1, 2012. The unadjusted balance in Insurance Expense was $800, which was the cost of insurance from January 1 to June 30, 2012.

f. Nickleby's store did some ski repair work for Frey. At the end of December 31, 2012, Frey had not paid for work completed, amounting to $750. This amount has not yet been recorded as Repair Shop Revenue. Collection is expected during January 2013.

Required:

Earlier in 2012, Nickleby's store had already provided, recorded, and collected cash for $5,000 of repair services for other customers.

1. For each of the items listed above, indicate the account names and adjusted balances that should be reported on Nickleby's year-end balance sheet and income statement.

2. For each situation, prepare the adjusting journal entry that should be recorded for Nickleby's at December 31, 2012.

E4-9 Determining Accounting Equation Effects of Typical Adjusting Journal Entries

Refer to E4-8.

Required:

For each of the transactions in E4-8, indicate the amount and direction of effects of the adjusting journal entry on the elements of the accounting equation. Using the following format, indicate + for increase, − for decrease, and NE for no effect. Include account names using the format shown for the following sample.

Transaction	Assets	Liabilities	Shareholders' Equity
a	Office Supplies −750		Supplies Expense (+E) −750
Etc.			

E4-10 Recording Transactions Including Adjusting and Closing Journal Entries

The following accounts are used by Mouse Potato, Inc., a computer game maker.

Code	Account	Code	Account
A	Accounts Receivable	K	Note Payable
B	Accumulated Amortization	L	Office Equipment
C	Cash	M	Office Supplies
D	Contributed Capital	N	Retained Earnings
E	Amortization Expense	O	Service Revenue
F	Dividends Declared	P	Supplies Expense
G	Dividends Payable	Q	Unearned Service Revenue
H	Interest Expense	R	Wage Expense
I	Interest Payable	S	Wages Payable
J	Interest Revenue	T	None of the above

Required:

For each of the following independent situations, give the journal entry by entering the appropriate code(s) and amount(s). We've done the first one for you as an example.

	Independent Situation	Debit Code	Debit Amount	Credit Code	Credit Amount
a.	Accrued wages, unrecorded and unpaid at year-end, $400 (example).	R	400	S	400
b.	Service revenue collected in advance, $600.				
c.	Dividends declared and paid during year, $900.				
d.	Amortization expense for year, $1,000.				
e.	Service revenue earned but not yet collected at year-end, $1,000.				
f.	Balance in Office Supplies account, $400; supplies on hand at year-end, $150.				
g.	At year-end, interest on note payable not yet recorded or paid, $220.				
h.	Adjusted balance at year-end in Service Revenue account, $75,000. Give the journal entry to close this one account at year-end.				
i.	Adjusted balance at year-end in Interest Expense account, $420. Give the journal entry to close this one account at year-end.				

Check Figure [Part (f)]:
Debit "P" for $250; credit "M" for $250

E4-11 Inferring Transactions from Accrual and Deferral Accounts

LO1, 2

Deere & Company

Deere & Company was founded in 1837 and today is the world's leading producer of agricultural equipment. Assume the following information is taken from its annual report for the year ended October 31, 2011 (in millions of dollars):

Income Tax Payable		
	135	Beg. bal.
712	?	(a)
	79	End. bal.

Wages Payable		
	1,060	Beg. bal.
(b) ?	19,575	
	1,175	End. bal.

Interest Payable		
	140	Beg. bal.
1,127	?	(c)
	150	End. bal.

Required:

1. For each accrued liability account, describe the typical transactions that cause it to increase and decrease.
2. Express each T-account in equation format and then solve for the missing amounts for (a), (b), and (c) (in millions). For example, the Interest Payable T-account can be expressed as: Beg. bal. (140) + increases (?) − decreases (1,127) = End. bal. (150). By rearranging the equation, you can solve for ? = 150 + 1,127 − 140.

E4-12 Analyzing the Effects of Adjusting Journal Entries on the Income Statement and Balance Sheet

LO2, 6

On December 31, 2012, J. Alan and Company prepared an income statement and balance sheet but failed to take into account four adjusting journal entries. The income statement, prepared on this incorrect basis, reported income before income tax of $30,000. The balance sheet (before the effect of income taxes) reflected total assets, $90,000; total liabilities, $40,000; and shareholders' equity, $50,000. The data for the four adjusting journal entries follow:

a. Amortization of $8,000 for the year on equipment was not recorded.
b. Wages amounting to $17,000 for the last three days of December 2012 were not paid and not recorded (the next payroll will be on January 10, 2013).

c. Rent revenue of $4,800 was collected on December 1, 2012, for office space for the three-month period December 1, 2012, to February 28, 2013. The $4,800 was credited in full to Unearned Rent Revenue when collected.

d. Income taxes were not recorded. The income tax rate for the company is 30 percent.

Required:

Complete the following table to show the effects of the four adjusting journal entries (indicate deductions with parentheses):

Items	Net Income	Total Assets	Total Liabilities	Shareholders' Equity
Amounts reported	$30,000	$90,000	$40,000	$50,000
Effect of Amortization				
Effect of wages				
Effect of rent revenue				
Adjusted balances	6,600	82,000	55,400	26,600
Effect of income tax				
Correct amounts				

LO2, 4, 6 | **E4-13 Reporting an Adjusted Income Statement**

Dyer Inc. completed its first year of operations on December 31, 2012. Because this is the end of the annual accounting period, the company bookkeeper prepared the following preliminary income statement:

Income Statement, 2012

Rental Revenue		$114,000
Expenses:		
Salaries and Wages Expense	$28,500	
Maintenance Expense	12,000	
Rent Expense	9,000	
Utilities Expense	4,000	
Gas and Oil Expense	3,000	
Other Expenses	1,000	
Total Expenses		57,500
Income		$ 56,500

You are an independent CA hired by the company to audit the firm's accounting systems and financial statements. In your audit, you developed additional data as follows:

a. Wages for the last three days of December amounting to $310 were not recorded or paid.

b. The $400 telephone bill for December 2012 has not been recorded or paid.

c. Amortization on rental autos, amounting to $23,000 for 2012, was not recorded.

d. Interest of $500 was not recorded on the note payable by Dyer Inc.

e. The Rental Revenue account includes $4,000 of revenue to be earned in January 2013.

f. Maintenance supplies costing $600 were used during 2012, but this has not yet been recorded.

g. The income tax expense for 2012 is $7,000, but it won't actually be paid until 2013.

Required:

Check Figure [Req. 2]:
Net income from
the adjusted income
statement = $20,690

1. What adjusting journal entry for each item (a) through (g) should be recorded at December 31, 2012? If none is required, explain why.

2. Prepare, in proper form, an adjusted income statement for 2012.

3. Did the adjustments have a significant overall effect on the company's net income?

E4-14 Recording Adjusting Entries and Preparing an Adjusted Trial Balance

Ninja Sockeye Star prepared the following unadjusted trial balance at the end of its second year of operations, ending December 31, 2012.

Account Titles	Debit	Credit
Cash	$12,000	
Accounts Receivable	6,000	
Prepaid Rent	2,400	
Machinery	21,000	
Accumulated Amortization		$ 1,000
Accounts Payable		1,000
Utilities Payable		0
Income Tax Payable		0
Contributed Capital		29,800
Retained Earnings		2,100
Sales Revenue		45,000
Wages Expense	25,000	
Utilities Expense	12,500	
Rent Expense	0	
Amortization Expense	0	
Income Tax Expense	0	
Totals	$78,900	$78,900

Other data not yet recorded at December 31, 2012:

a. Rent expired during 2012, $1,200.
b. Amortization expense for 2012, $1,000.
c. Utilities payable, $9,000.
d. Income tax expense, $800.

Required:

1. Using the format shown in the demonstration case, indicate the accounting equation effects of each required adjustment.
2. Prepare the adjusting journal entries required at December 31, 2012.
3. Summarize the adjusting journal entries in T-accounts. After entering the beginning balances and computing the adjusted ending balances, prepare an adjusted trial balance as of December 31, 2012.

E4-15 Recording Four Adjusting Journal Entries and Preparing an Adjusted Trial Balance

Mint Cleaning Inc. prepared the following unadjusted trial balance at the end of its second year of operations, ending December 31, 2012. To simplify this exercise, the amounts given are in thousands of dollars.

Account Titles	Debit	Credit
Cash	$ 38	
Accounts Receivable	9	
Prepaid Insurance	6	
Machinery	80	
Accumulated Amortization		$ 0
Accounts Payable		9
Contributed Capital		76
Retained Earnings		4
Sales Revenue		80
Administrative Expenses	26	
Wages Expense	10	
Totals	$169	$169

Other data not yet recorded at December 31, 2012:

a. Insurance expired during 2012, $5.
b. Amortization expense for 2012, $4.
c. Wages payable, $7.
d. Income tax expense, $9.

Required:

1. Prepare the adjusting journal entries for 2012.
2. Using T-accounts, determine the adjusted balances in each account and prepare an adjusted trial balance as of December 31, 2012.

LO4

E4-16 Reporting an Income Statement, Statement of Retained Earnings, and Balance Sheet

Refer to E4-15.

Check Figure:
Total assets = $124

Required:

Using the adjusted balances in E4-15, prepare an income statement, statement of retained earnings, and balance sheet for 2012.

LO5

E4-17 Recording Closing Entries

Refer to E4-15.

Required:

Using the adjusted balances in E4-15, give the closing journal entry for 2012. What is the purpose of "closing the books" at the end of the accounting period?

LO1, 2, 6

E4-18 Analyzing, Recording, and Summarizing Business Activities and Adjustments

The following relates to a magazine company called My Style Mag (MSM). You will use your understanding of the relationships among (1) business activities, (2) accounting equation effects, (3) journal entries, and (4) T-accounts to complete a four-part table similar to the following. Prepare a separate table for each item (a)–(f) listed at the top of the next page.

(1)	(Description of the business activity.)

(2)	Assets	=	Liabilities	+	Shareholders' Equity

(3)	Account Names		Debit	Credit

(4)		

Required:

For each item (a)–(f) listed below, use the information provided to prepare and complete a four-part table similar to that shown above.

a. | (1) | On January 22, 2012, MSM received $24,000 cash from customers for one-year subscriptions to the magazine for February 2012–January 2013. |

b. (3)

	Account Names	Debit	Credit
Jan. 31	Utilities Expense (+E, −SE)	3,000	
	Accounts Payable (+L)		3,000

c. (2)

Assets	=	Liabilities	+	Shareholders' Equity
Feb. 28		Unearned Subscription Revenue −2,000		Subscription Revenue (+R) +2,000

d. | (1) | On March 31, 2012, MSM recorded an adjusting entry for the month's amortization of $10,000. |

e. (4)

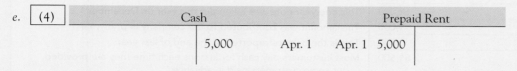

Cash

5,000   Apr. 1

Prepaid Rent

Apr. 1   5,000

f. (4)

Accounts Receivable

Apr. 30   10,000

Advertising Revenue

10,000 Apr. 30

COACHED PROBLEMS

CP4-1 Preparing an Adjusted Trial Balance, Closing Journal Entry, and Post-Closing Trial Balance

LO3, 5

Building on its brand's success in boardsports, Empire Inc. has become a premium designer, marketer, and distributor of clothing and accessories for young men and women. The following is a list of accounts and amounts reported for the fiscal year ended December 31, 2011. The accounts have normal debit or credit balances and the dollars are rounded to the nearest thousand.

Accounts Payable	$ 15,291	Long-Term Debt	$ 531
Accounts Receivable	60,914	Other Assets	27,294
Accrued Liabilities	12,098	Other Revenue	1,288
Accumulated Amortization	7,315	Product Cost Expense	171,208
Cash	79,613	Property and Equipment	34,031
Contributed Capital	91,768	Retained Earnings	80,226
Income Tax Expense	11,787	Sales Revenue	332,110
Inventories	27,086	Selling, General, and	
		Administrative Expenses	128,694

Required:

1. Prepare an adjusted trial balance at December 31, 2011. Is the Retained Earnings balance of $80,226 the amount that would be reported on the balance sheet as of December 31, 2011?

   TIP: Empire Inc. did not declare a dividend during 2011, but it did earn net income.
   TIP: Total Debits equals $540,627.

2. Prepare the closing entry required at December 31, 2011.

3. Prepare a post-closing trial balance at December 31, 2011.

   TIP: Total Debits equals $228,938.

LO1, 2, 3, 6 **CP4-2 Identifying and Preparing Adjusting Journal Entries**

Golf Academy Limited provides private golf lessons. Its unadjusted trial balance at December 31, 2012, follows, along with information about selected accounts.

Account Names	Debit	Credit	Further Information
Cash	$ 31,900		As reported on December 31 bank statement.
Supplies	600		Based on count, only $200 of supplies still exist.
Unearned Revenue		$ 3,500	Of this amount, $3,000 was received for December lessons and $500 for January lessons.
Wages Payable		0	Employees were paid $1,000 for 10 days of work through December 28 but have not yet been paid for work on December 29 and 30.
Income Tax Payable		0	The company has paid last year's income taxes but not this year's taxes.
Interest Payable		0	The company has not paid the $100 of interest owed on its note payable for the current period.
Note Payable		12,000	This one-year note was taken out this year on December 1.
Contributed Capital		1,000	This amount was contributed to the company in prior years.
Retained Earnings		3,000	This is the balance reported at the end of last year.
Lesson Revenue		51,500	Most customers pay cash for lessons each time they are provided, but some customers paid in advance.
Wages Expense	36,100		An employee worked through December 30, but did not work on December 31.
Supplies Expense	2,400		This is the cost of supplies used through November 30.
Interest Expense	0		The company has not paid the $100 of interest owed on its note payable for the current period.
Income Tax Expense	0		The company has an average tax rate of 30 percent.
Totals	$71,000	$71,000	

Required:

1. Calculate the (preliminary) unadjusted net income for the year ended December 31, 2012.
   TIP: Net Income equals $13,000.
2. Name the five pairs of balance sheet and income statement accounts that require adjustment.
3. Calculate the desired balances for each account listed in the unadjusted trial balance.
   TIP: Total Debits equals $75,890.
4. Prepare the adjusting journal entries that are required at December 31, 2012.
5. Calculate the adjusted net income that the company should report for the year ended December 31, 2012. By how much did the adjustments in requirement (4) cause net income to increase or decrease?
   TIP: Net Income equals $10,710.

LO1, 2, 3, 4, 5, 6 **CP4-3 Comprehensive Review Problem: From Recording Transactions (Including Adjusting Journal Entries) to Preparing Financial Statements and Closing Journal Entries (Chapters 2, 3, and 4)**

Brothers Harry and Herman Hausyerday began operations of their machine shop (H & H Tool Co.) on January 1, 2010. The annual reporting period ends December 31. The trial balance on January 1, 2012, appears at the top of the next page (the amounts are rounded to thousands of dollars to simplify).

Transactions during 2012 (summarized in thousands of dollars) follow:

a. Borrowed $12 cash on a six-month note payable dated March 1, 2012.
b. Purchased land for future building site, paid cash, $9.
c. Earned revenues for 2012, $160, including $40 on credit and $120 collected in cash.
d. Issued additional shares for $3.
e. Recognized operating expenses for 2012, $85, including $15 on credit and $70 paid in cash.
f. Collected accounts receivable, $24.
g. Purchased other assets, $10 cash.

Account Titles	Debit	Credit
Cash	$ 3	
Accounts Receivable	5	
Supplies	12	
Land	0	
Equipment	60	
Accumulated Amortization (on Equipment)		$ 6
Other Assets	4	
Accounts Payable		5
Notes Payable		0
Wages Payable		0
Interest Payable		0
Income Tax Payable		0
Contributed Capital		65
Retained Earnings		8
Dividends Declared	0	
Service Revenue	0	
Amortization Expense	0	
Income Tax Expense	0	
Interest Expense	0	
Supplies and Operating Expenses	0	
Totals	$84	$84

h. Paid accounts payable, $13.

i. Purchased supplies on account for future use, $18.

j. Signed a $25 service contract to start February 1, 2013.

k. Declared and paid a cash dividend, $17.

Data for adjusting journal entries:

l. Supplies counted on December 31, 2012, $10.

m. Amortization for the year on the equipment, $6.

n. Accrued interest on notes payable of $1.

o. Wages earned since the December 24 payroll not yet paid, $12.

p. Income tax for the year was $8. It will be paid in 2013.

Required:

1. Set up T-accounts for the accounts on the trial balance and enter beginning balances.
2. Record journal entries for transactions (*a*) through (*k*), and post them to the T-accounts.

   TIP: In transaction (*e*), when operating costs are incurred on credit, Accounts Payable typically is used rather than Accrued Liabilities. The account Accrued Liabilities typically is used only for accrual adjustments made at the end of the period.
3. Prepare an unadjusted trial balance.

   TIP: Total Debits equals $279.
4. Record and post the adjusting journal entries (*l*) through (*p*).

   TIP: To determine the adjustment in (*l*), consider the beginning account balance shown in the trial balance and the information in (*i*) and (*l*).

   TIP: For the adjustment in (*o*), include Wages Expense in the Supplies and Operating Expense account.
5. Prepare an adjusted trial balance.

   TIP: Total Debits equals $306.
6. Prepare an income statement, statement of retained earnings, and balance sheet.

   TIP: Net Income equals $28.

TIP: Closing Retained Earnings equals $19.

TIP: Total Assets equals $145.

7. Prepare and post the closing journal entries.

8. Prepare a post-closing trial balance.

TIP: Total Debits equals $157.

9. How much net income did H & H Tool Co. generate during 2012? Is the company financed primarily by liabilities or shareholders' equity?

GROUP A PROBLEMS

Practise and learn online with Connect.

LO3, 5

PA4-1 Preparing a Trial Balance, Closing Journal Entry, and Post-Closing Trial Balance

ElecBooks Corporation provides an online bookstore for electronic books. The following is a simplified list of accounts and amounts reported in its accounting records. The accounts have normal debit or credit balances and the dollars are rounded to the nearest thousand. Assume the year ended on September 30, 2012.

Accounts Payable	$ 221	Other Current Assets	$ 71
Accounts Receivable	191	Other Long-Lived Assets	461
Accrued Liabilities	354	Other Operating Expenses	197
Accumulated Amortization	300	Prepaid Expenses	94
Amortization Expense	340	Property and Equipment	2,142
Cash	307	Retained Earnings	1,445
Contributed Capital	151	Selling Expenses	2,605
General and Administrative Expenses	357	Service Revenues	6,369
Income Tax Expense	302	Short-Term Bank Loan	476
Interest Revenue	92	Store Operating Expenses	2,166
Long-Term Debt	196	Supplies	546
		Unearned Revenue	175

Required:

Check Figure [Req. 3]:
Total debits and total credits = $3,812

1. Prepare an adjusted trial balance at September 30, 2012. Is the Retained Earnings balance of $1,445 the amount that would be reported on the balance sheet as of September 30, 2012?

2. Prepare the closing entry required at September 30, 2012.

3. Prepare a post-closing trial balance at September 30, 2012.

LO1, 2

PA4-2 Analyzing and Recording Adjusting Journal Entries

Brokeback Towing Company is at the end of its accounting year, December 31, 2012. The following data that must be considered were developed from the company's records and related documents:

a. On July 1, 2012, a three-year insurance premium on equipment in the amount of $600 was paid and debited in full to Prepaid Insurance on that date. Coverage began on July 1.

b. At the end of 2012, the unadjusted balance in the Office Supplies account was $1,000. A physical count of supplies on December 31, 2012, indicated supplies costing $300 were still on hand.

c. On December 31, 2012, YY's Garage completed repairs on one of Brokeback's trucks at a cost of $800. The amount is not yet recorded. It will be paid during January 2013.

d. In December, the 2012 property tax bill for $1,600 was received from the city. The taxes, which have not been recorded, will be paid on February 15, 2013.

e. On December 31, 2012, the company completed the work on a contract for an out-of-province company for $7,900 payable by the customer within 30 days. No cash has been collected and no journal entry has been made for this transaction.

f. On July 1, 2012, the company purchased a new hauling van. Amortization for July–December 2012, estimated to total $2,750, has not been recorded.

g. As of December 31, the company owes interest of $500 on a bank loan taken out on October 1, 2012. The interest will be paid when the loan is repaid on September 30, 2013. No interest has been recorded yet.

h. The income before any of the adjustments or income taxes was $30,000. The company's federal income tax rate is 30 percent. Compute adjusted income based on all of the preceding information, and then determine and record income tax expense.

Required:

1. Determine the accounting equation effects of each required adjustment.
2. Give the adjusting journal entry required for each transaction at December 31, 2012.

PA4-3 Determining Accounting Equation Effects of Adjusting Journal Entries   LO2, 6

Refer to PA4-2.

eXcel

Required:

Indicate the accounting equation effects (amount and direction) of each adjusting journal entry. Use + for increase, − for decrease, and NE for no effect. Provide an appropriate account name for any revenue and expense effects.

Transaction	Assets	Liabilities	Shareholders' Equity
a			
b			
Etc.			

PA4-4 Identifying and Preparing Adjusting Journal Entries   LO1, 2, 3, 6

Val's Hair Emporium is a hair salon. Its unadjusted trial balance as of December 31, 2012, follows, along with information about selected accounts.

Account Name	Debit	Credit	Further Information
Cash	$ 3,800		As reported on December 31 bank statement.
Supplies	4,300		Based on count, only $3,200 of supplies still exist.
Prepaid Rent	6,000		This amount was paid November 1 for rent through the end of January.
Accounts Payable		$ 1,500	This represents the total amount of bills received for supplies and utilities through December 15. Val estimates that the company has received $450 of utility services through December 31 for which it has not yet been billed.
Wages Payable		0	Stylists have not yet been paid $150 for their work on December 31.
Income Tax Payable		0	The company has paid last year's income taxes but not this year's taxes.
Contributed Capital		2,000	This amount was contributed to the company in prior years.
Retained Earnings		900	This is the balance reported at the end of last year.
Hair Styling Revenue		75,800	Customers pay cash when they receive services.
Wages Expense	29,100		This is the cost of stylist wages through December 30.
Utilities Expense	12,200		This is the cost of utilities through December 15.
Rent Expense	20,000		This year's rent was $2,000 per month.
Supplies Expense	4,800		This is the cost of supplies used through November 30.
Income Tax Expense	0		The company has an average tax rate of 30 percent.
Totals	$80,200	$80,200	

Required:

1. Calculate the (preliminary) unadjusted net income for the year ended December 31, 2012.
2. Name the five pairs of balance sheet and income statement accounts that require adjustment.

3. Calculate the desired balances for each account listed in the unadjusted trial balance.

4. Prepare the adjusting journal entries that are required at December 31, 2012.

5. Calculate the adjusted net income that the company should report for the year ended December 31, 2012. By how much did the adjustments in requirement (4) cause net income to increase or decrease?

LO1, 2, 3, 4, 5, 6

eXcel

PA4-5 Comprehensive Review Problem: From Recording Transactions (Including Adjusting Journal Entries) to Preparing Financial Statements and Closing Journal Entries (Chapters 2, 3, and 4)

Drs. Elaine Newton and Alicia Donland began operation of their physical therapy clinic, called North-land Physical Therapy, on January 1, 2011. The annual reporting period ends December 31. The trial balance on January 1, 2012, was as follows (the amounts are rounded to thousands of dollars to simplify):

Account Title	Debit	Credit
Cash	$ 7	
Accounts Receivable	3	
Supplies	3	
Equipment	6	
Accumulated Amortization (equipment)		$ 1
Other Assets	6	
Accounts Payable		5
Notes Payable		0
Wages Payable		0
Interest Payable		0
Income Taxes Payable		0
Unearned Revenue		0
Contributed Capital		15
Retained Earnings		4
Dividends Declared	0	
Service Revenue		0
Amortization Expense	0	
Income Tax Expense	0	
Interest Expense	0	
Operating Expenses	0	
Totals	$25	$25

Transactions during 2012 (summarized in thousands of dollars) follow:

a. Borrowed $22 cash on July 1, 2012, signing a six-month note payable.

b. Purchased equipment for $25 cash on July 1, 2012.

c. Issued additional shares for $5.

d. Earned revenues for 2012 of $55, including $8 on credit and $47 received in cash.

e. Recognized operating expenses for 2012 of $30, including $5 on credit and $25 in cash.

f. Purchased other assets, $3 cash.

g. Collected accounts receivable, $9.

h. Paid accounts payable, $10.

i. Purchased supplies on account for future use, $7.

j. Received a $3 deposit from a hospital for a contract to start January 5, 2013.

k. Declared and paid a cash dividend, $4.

   Data for adjusting journal entries:

l. Supplies of $3 were counted on December 31, 2012.

m. Amortization for 2012, $4.

n. Accrued interest on notes payable of $1.

o. Wages incurred since the December 27 payroll not yet paid, $3.

p. Income tax expense for 2012 was $4, and will be paid in 2013.

Required:

1. Set up T-accounts for the accounts on the trial balance and enter beginning balances.
2. Record journal entries for transactions (*a*) through (*k*), and post them to the T-accounts.
3. Prepare an unadjusted trial balance.
4. Record and post the adjusting journal entries (*l*) through (*p*).
5. Prepare an adjusted trial balance.
6. Prepare an income statement, statement of retained earnings, and balance sheet.
7. Prepare and post the closing journal entries.
8. Prepare a post-closing trial balance.
9. How much net income did the physical therapy clinic generate during 2012? Is the business financed primarily by liabilities or shareholders' equity?

Check Figures [Req. 6]:
Net income = $6
Retained Earnings
Dec. 31/12 = $6

GROUP B PROBLEMS

PB4-1 Preparing a Trial Balance, Closing Journal Entry, and Post-Closing Trial Balance

LO3, 5

Regis Corporation operates hair salons under various brand names including Supercuts, Mia & Maxx, and Style America. Assume the following is a simplified list of accounts and amounts (in millions) reported in the company's accounts for the year ended June 30, 2011.

Regis Corporation

Accounts Payable	$ 70	Income Tax Expense	$ 54
Accounts Receivable	38	Interest Expense	36
Accrued Liabilities	208	Inventories	212
Accumulated Amortization	586	Long-Term Liabilities	982
Cash	128	Other Current Assets	67
Contributed Capital	247	Other Long-Lived Assets	1,309
Cost of Operations	1,690	Property, Plant, and Equipment	1,068
Amortization Expense	131	Retained Earnings	644
General and		Rent Expense	406
Administrative Expenses	337	Salon Revenue	2,739

Required:

1. Prepare an adjusted trial balance at June 30, 2011. Is the Retained Earnings balance of $644 the amount that would be reported on the balance sheet as of June 30, 2011?
2. Prepare the closing entry required at June 30, 2011.
3. Prepare a post-closing trial balance at June 30, 2011.

PB4-2 Recording Adjusting Journal Entries

LO1, 2

Cactus Company's annual accounting year ends on June 30. It is June 30, 2012, and all of the 2012 entries except the following adjusting journal entries have been made:

a. The company earned service revenue of $2,000 on a special job that was completed June 29, 2012. Collection will be made during July 2012; no entry has been recorded.

b. On March 31, 2012, Cactus paid a six-month premium for property insurance in the amount of $3,200 for coverage starting on that date. Cash was credited and Prepaid Insurance was debited for this amount.

c. At June 30, 2012, wages of $900 were earned by employees but not yet paid. The employees will be paid on the next payroll date, which is July 13, 2012.

d. On June 1, 2012, Cactus collected two months' maintenance revenue of $450. At that date, Cactus debited Cash and credited Unearned Maintenance Revenue for $450. One-half of it has now been earned but not yet recorded.

e. Amortization of $1,500 must be recognized on a service truck purchased on July 1, 2011.

f. Cash of $4,200 was collected on May 1, 2012, for services to be rendered evenly over the next year, beginning on May 1. Unearned Service Revenue was credited when the cash was received. Some of it has now been earned but not yet recorded.

g. The company owes interest of $600 on a bank loan taken out on February 1, 2012. The interest will be paid when the loan is repaid on January 31, 2013.

h. The income before any of the adjustments or income taxes was $31,675. The company's federal income tax rate is 30 percent. Compute adjusted income based on all of the preceding information, and then determine and record income tax expense.

Check Figure [Part (h)]:
Income Tax Expense
= $9,000

Required:

1. Determine the accounting equation effects of each required adjustment.
2. Give the adjusting journal entry required for each transaction at June 30, 2012.

LO2, 6   **PB4-3 Determining Accounting Equation Effects of Adjusting Journal Entries**

Refer to PB4-2.

Required:

Indicate the accounting equation effects (amount and direction) of each adjusting journal entry. Use + for increase, − for decrease, and NE for no effect. Provide an appropriate account name for any revenue and expense effects.

Transaction	Assets	Liabilities	Shareholders' Equity
a			
b			
c			
Etc.			

LO1, 2, 3, 6   **PB4-4 Identifying and Preparing Adjusting Journal Entries**

Learn to Play, Inc., is a one-person company that provides private piano lessons. Its unadjusted trial balance at December 31, 2012, follows along with information about selected accounts.

Account Name	Debit	Credit	Further Information
Cash	$ 23,800		As reported on December 31 bank statement.
Supplies	300		Based on count, only $200 of supplies still exist.
Unearned Revenue		$ 1,500	Of this amount, $500 was received for December lessons and $1,000 for January lessons.
Wages Payable		0	Employees were paid $500 for 10 days of work through December 28. They have not yet been paid for work on December 29 and 30.
Income Tax Payable		0	The company has paid last year's income tax but not this year's tax.
Interest Payable		0	The company has not paid the $100 of interest owed on its note payable for the current period.
Note Payable		12,000	This one-year note was taken out this year on December 1.
Contributed Capital		1,000	This amount was contributed to the company in prior years.
Retained Earnings		3,000	This is the balance reported at the end of last year.
Lesson Revenue		25,500	Most customers pay cash for lessons each time they are provided, but some customers pay in advance.
Wages Expense	18,100		Employees worked through December 30, but did not work on December 31.
Supplies Expense	800		This is the cost of supplies used through November 30.
Interest Expense	0		The company has not paid the $100 of interest owed on its note payable for the current period.
Income Tax Expense	0		The company has an average tax rate of 30 percent.
Totals	$43,000	$43,000	

Required:

1. Calculate the (preliminary) unadjusted net income for the year ended December 31, 2012.

2. Name the five pairs of balance sheet and income statement accounts that require adjustment.

3. Calculate the desired balances for each account listed in the unadjusted trial balance.

4. Prepare the adjusting journal entries that are required at December 31, 2012.

5. Calculate the adjusted net income that the company should report for the year ended December 31, 2012. By how much did the adjustments in requirement (4) cause net income to increase or decrease?

PB4-5 Comprehensive Review Problem: From Recording Transactions (Including Adjusting Journal Entries) to Preparing Financial Statements and Closing Journal Entries (Chapters 2, 3, and 4)   LO1, 2, 3, 4, 5, 6

Alison and Chuck Renny began operations of their furniture repair shop (Lazy Sofa Furniture, Inc.) on January 1, 2011. The annual reporting period ends December 31. The trial balance on January 1, 2012, was as follows (the amounts are rounded to thousands of dollars to simplify):

Account Title	Debit	Credit
Cash	$ 5	
Accounts Receivable	4	
Supplies	2	
Small Tools	6	
Equipment	0	
Accumulated Amortization		$ 0
Other Assets	9	
Accounts Payable		7
Notes Payable		0
Wages Payable		0
Interest Payable		0
Income Tax Payable		0
Unearned Revenue		0
Contributed Capital		15
Retained Earnings		4
Dividends Declared	0	
Service Revenue		0
Amortization Expense	0	
Income Tax Expense	0	
Interest Expense	0	
Operating Expenses	0	
Totals	$26	$26

Transactions during 2012 (summarized in thousands of dollars) follow:

a. Borrowed $21 cash on July 1, 2012, signing a six-month note payable.

b. Purchased equipment for $18 cash on July 1, 2012.

c. Issued additional shares for $5.

d. Earned revenues for 2012 in the amount of $65, including $9 on credit and $56 received in cash.

e. Recognized operating expenses for 2012, $35, including $7 on credit and $28 in cash.

f. Purchased additional small tools, $3 cash.

g. Collected accounts receivable, $8.

h. Paid accounts payable, $11.

i. Purchased on account supplies for future use, $10.

j. Received a $3 deposit on work to start January 15, 2013.

k. Declared and paid a cash dividend, $10.

Data for adjusting journal entries:

l. Supplies of $4 were counted on December 31, 2012.

m. Amortization for 2012, $2.

n. Accrued interest on notes payable of $1.

o. Wages earned since the December 24 payroll not yet paid, $3.

p. Income tax for 2012 was $4, and will be paid in 2013.

Required:

1. Set up T-accounts for the accounts on the trial balance and enter beginning balances.
2. Record journal entries for transactions (*a*) through (*k*), and post them to the T-accounts.
3. Prepare an unadjusted trial balance.
4. Record and post the adjusting journal entries (*l*) through (*p*).
5. Prepare an adjusted trial balance.
6. Prepare an income statement, statement of retained earnings, and balance sheet.
7. Prepare and post the closing journal entries.
8. Prepare a post-closing trial balance.
9. How much net income did Lazy Sofa Furniture, Inc., generate during 2012? Is the company financed primarily by liabilities or shareholders' equity?

Check Figure [Req. 6]:
Total liabilities and shareholders' equity for Dec. 31/12 = $71

SKILLS DEVELOPMENT CASES

LO1, 6

Rona Inc.

S4-1 Finding Financial Information

Refer to the financial statements of Rona Inc. in Appendix A at the back of this book or download the annual report from the *Cases* section of Connect.

Required:

1. How much does Rona have recorded as prepaid expenses on the balance sheet as of December 27, 2009? Give a couple of examples of items that could make up this prepaid expense amount.
2. How much did Rona owe for accounts payable and accrued liabilities at December 27, 2009? Was this an increase or decrease from the previous year?

LO1, 6

Rona Inc.

S4-2 Comparing Financial Information

Refer to the financial statements of Rona Inc. in Appendix A and The Home Depot's in Appendix B at the back of this book or download the annual reports from the *Cases* section of Connect.

Required:

1. How much did The Home Depot owe for salaries and wages at January 31, 2010? Was this an increase or decrease from the previous year? What factors could cause these two numbers to be different?
2. Refer to the Revenues note in the Summary of Significant Accounting Policies that follows The Home Depot's statements of cash flows. How does the company account for customer payments received in advance of providing services? What adjusting journal entry must The Home Depot make when it provides these services?

LO1, 4

S4-3 Internet-Based Team Research: Examining Deferrals and Accruals

As a team, select an industry to analyze. Using your Web browser, each team member should access the annual report for one publicly traded company in the industry, with each member selecting a different company. (See S1-3 in Chapter 1 for a description of possible resources for these tasks.)

Required:

1. On an individual basis, each team member should write a short report listing the following:
   a. The company's total assets and total liabilities at the end of each year.
   b. The company's prepaid expenses and accrued liabilities at the end of each year.
   c. The percentage of prepaid expenses to total assets and the percentage of accrued liabilities to total liabilities.

d. Describe and explain the types of accrued liabilities reported in the notes to the financial statements.

2. Discuss any patterns that you as a team observe. Then, as a team, write a short report comparing and contrasting your companies according to the preceding attributes. Provide potential explanations for any differences discovered.

S4-4 Ethical Decision Making: A Real-Life Example

LO1, 2, 6

Safety-Kleen Corp.

On December 12, 2002, the U.S. Securities and Exchange Commission (SEC) filed a lawsuit against four executives of Safety-Kleen Corp., a leading provider of industrial waste collection and disposal services. The primary issue was that the executives had directed others in the company to record improper adjustments in 1999 and 2000, which had the effect of overstating net income during those periods. The following table was included in the SEC's court documents to demonstrate the (combined) effect of proper and improper adjustments on net income. (All amounts are in millions.)

	Year (Quarter)				
	1999 (Q1)	1999 (Q2)	1999 (Q3)	1999 (Q4)	2000 (Q1)
Net income before adjustments	$ 90.9	$ 76.7	$ 47.9	$ 57.3	$ 47.0
Effect of adjustments	36.6	30.9	75.5	53.1	69.8
Net income after adjustments	$127.5	$107.6	$123.4	$110.4	$116.8

The following excerpts from the SEC's complaint describe two of the allegedly improper adjustments:

Improper Capitalization of Operating Expenses

26. As part of the fraudulent accounting scheme, [three top executives] improperly recorded several adjusting entries to capitalize certain operating expenses. These adjustments caused the company to materially overstate both its assets and its earnings. For example, at the end of the third quarter of fiscal 1999, they improperly capitalized approximately $4.6 million of payroll expenses relating to certain marketing and start-up activities.

Improper Treatment of Accruals

33. During the fourth quarter of fiscal 1999, Humphreys [the CFO] created additional fictitious income by directing [other accounting executives] to eliminate a $7.6 million accrual that had been established to provide for management bonuses that had been earned in fiscal 1999, but were to be paid the following quarter. Humphreys' action suggested that no bonuses were going to be paid for that year. In fact, the bonuses for 1999 were paid as scheduled.

Required:

1. Discuss whether large adjustments, such as those included by Safety-Kleen in 1999 and 2000, necessarily indicate improper accounting procedures.

2. What does the SEC's document mean in paragraph 26 when it says three top executives "improperly recorded several adjusting entries to *capitalize* certain operating expenses"? Drawing on concepts presented in Chapters 2 and 3, explain why it is improper to record payroll expenses for marketing personnel as assets.

3. Assume the $7.6 million in bonuses referred to in paragraph 33 were recorded in the third quarter of 1999. What journal entry would have been used to record this accrual? Assume this accrual was eliminated in the fourth quarter of 1999. What adjusting journal entry would have been recorded to eliminate (remove) the previous accrual? What journal entry would have been used to record the $7.6 million in bonuses paid in the first quarter of 2000 (assuming the accrual had been removed in the fourth quarter of 1999)? What accounting concept is violated by recording an expense for management bonuses when they are paid rather than when they are earned by managers?

Epilogue:

In April 2005, a federal judge found the company's former CEO and CFO liable for $200 million for their role in the fraud.

S4-5 Ethical Decision Making: A Mini-Case

Assume you work as an assistant accountant in the head office of a national movie rental business, Movie Madness. With the increasing popularity of online movie rental operations, your company has struggled to meet its earnings targets for the year. It is important for the company to meet its earnings targets this year because the company is renegotiating a bank loan next month, and the terms of that loan are likely to depend on the company's reported financial success. Also, the company plans to issue more shares to the public in the upcoming year, to obtain funds for establishing its own presence in the online movie rental business. The chief financial officer has approached you with a solution to the earnings dilemma. She proposes that the amortization period for the inventory of reusable DVDs be extended from 3 months to 15 months. She explains that by lengthening the amortization period, a smaller amount of amortization expense will be recorded in the current year, resulting in a higher net income. She claims that generally accepted accounting principles require estimates like this, so it wouldn't involve doing anything wrong.

Required:

Discuss the CFO's proposed solution. In your discussion, consider the following questions. Will the change in amortization affect net income in the current year in the way that the CFO described? How will it affect net income in the following year? Is the CFO correct when she claims that the change in estimated amortization is allowed by GAAP? Who relies on the video company's financial statements when making decisions? Why might their decisions be affected by the CFO's proposed solution? Is it possible that their decisions would not be affected? What should you do?

S4-6 Critical Thinking: Adjusting an Income Statement and Balance Sheet for Deferrals and Accruals

Pirate Pete Moving Corporation has been in operation since January 1, 2012. It is now December 31, 2012, the end of the annual accounting period. The company has not done well financially during its first year, although revenue has been fairly good. Three shareholders manage the company, but they have not given much attention to record-keeping. In view of a serious cash shortage, they have applied to your bank for a $20,000 loan. As a loan officer, you requested a complete set of financial statements. The following 2012 annual financial statements were prepared by the company's office staff.

PIRATE PETE MOVING CORPORATION	
Income Statement	
For the Period Ended December 31, 2012	
Transportation Revenue	$85,000
Expenses:	
Salaries Expense	17,000
Supplies Expense	12,000
Other Expenses	18,000
Total Expenses	47,000
Net Income	$38,000

PIRATE PETE MOVING CORPORATION	
Balance Sheet	
At December 31, 2012	
Assets	
Cash	$ 2,000
Accounts Receivable	3,000
Supplies	6,000
Equipment	40,000
Prepaid Insurance	4,000
Remaining Assets	27,000
Total Assets	$82,000
Liabilities	
Accounts Payable	$ 9,000
Shareholders' Equity	
Contributed Capital	35,000
Retained Earnings	38,000
Total Liabilities and Shareholders' Equity	$82,000

After briefly reviewing the statements and "looking into the situation," you requested that the statements be redone (with some expert help) to "incorporate amortization, accruals, supply counts, income taxes, and so on." As a result of a review of the records and supporting documents, the following additional information was developed:

a. The Supplies amount of $6,000 shown on the balance sheet has not been adjusted for supplies used during 2012. A count of the supplies on hand on December 31, 2012, showed $1,800.

b. The insurance premium paid in 2012 was for years 2012 and 2013. The total insurance premium was debited in full to Prepaid Insurance when paid in 2012 and no adjustment has been made.

c. The equipment cost $40,000 when purchased January 1, 2012. It had an estimated annual amortization of $8,000. No amortization has been recorded for 2012.

d. Unpaid (and unrecorded) salaries at December 31, 2012, amounted to $2,200.

e. At December 31, 2012, transportation revenue collected in advance amounted to $7,000. This amount was credited in full to Transportation Revenue when the cash was collected earlier during 2012.

f. Income taxes for the year are calculated as 25 percent of income before tax.

Required:

1. Prepare the adjusting journal entries required on December 31, 2012, based on the preceding additional information. You may need to create new accounts not yet included in the income statement or balance sheet.

2. Redo the preceding statements after taking into account the adjusting journal entries. One way to organize your response follows:

		Changes		
	Amounts			Corrected
Items	Reported	Plus	Minus	Amounts
(List here each item from the two statements)				

3. The effects of recording the adjusting journal entries were to
   a. *Increase* or *decrease* (select one) net income by $____.
   b. *Increase* or *decrease* (select one) total assets by $____.

4. Write a letter to the company explaining the results of the adjustments and your preliminary analysis.

S4-7 Aggregating Accounts on an Adjusted Trial Balance to Prepare an Income Statement, Statement of Retained Earnings, and Balance Sheet

LO3, 4, 6

Escalade, Inc.

Assume you recently were hired for a job in Evansville, Indiana, at the head office of Escalade, Inc.—the company that makes Goalrilla™ and Goaliath® basketball systems, and is the exclusive supplier of Ping Pong® and Stiga® equipment for table tennis. Your first assignment is to review the company's lengthy adjusted trial balance to determine the accounts that can be combined ("aggregated") into single line-items that will be reported on the financial statements. By querying the accounting system, you were able to obtain the following alphabetical list of accounts and their adjusted balances (in thousands) for the year ended December 31.

Accounts Payable	$ 2,792	Inventory of Finished Goods	$ 10,263	Prepaid Insurance	$ 108
Accounts Receivable	34,141	Inventory of Goods being Made	4,536	Prepaid Rent	434
Accrued Interest Payable	42	Inventory of Supplies and Materials	5,750	Rent Expense	7,350
Accrued Wages Payable	5,856	Long-Term Bank Loan	14,000	Retained Earnings	27,571
Accrued Warranties Payable	1,324	Long-Term Contract Payable	1,837	Salaries Expense	3,582
Accumulated Amortization	26,198	Long-Term Note Payable	2,700	Sales Commissions Expense	3,349
Cash	3,370	Manufacturing Equipment	12,962	Sales of Basketball Systems	98,998
Contributed Capital	7,165	Notes Payable (current)	11,390	Sales of Other Products	28,710
Cost of Goods Sold	111,164	Notes Receivable	400	Sales of Ping Pong Tables	27,747
Amortization Expense	862	Office Building	2,301	Shipping Expenses	1,448
Factory Buildings	7,070	Office Equipment	2,363	Transport Equipment	7,560
Income Tax Expense	5,804	Office Supplies Expense	69	Unearned Revenue	8,144
Income Tax Payable	1,189	Other Accrued Liabilities	1,638	Utilities Expense	2,111
Insurance Expense	2,368	Other Long-Term Assets	28,310	Wages Expense	3,024
Interest Expense	950	Packaging Expenses	1,010	Warranties Expense	1,226
Interest Receivable	415			Warehouse Buildings	3,001

Required:

With the above account names and balances, prepare an adjusted trial balance using a spreadsheet. Also prepare an income statement, statement of retained earnings, and balance sheet that import their numbers from the adjusted trial balance or from the other statements where appropriate. If similar accounts can be aggregated into a single line-item for each financial statement, use a formula to compute the aggregated amount. To be sure that you understand how to import numbers from other parts of a spreadsheet, you e-mail your friend Owen for advice. His reply is as follows.

From:	Owentheaccountant@yahoo.com
To:	Helpme@hotmail.com
Cc:	
Subject:	Excel Help

Hey, pal. You're bouncing from job to job like one of those ping-pong balls that your company sells. OK, to import a number from another spreadsheet, you first click on the cell where you want the number to appear. For example, if you want to enter the Cash balance in the balance sheet, click on the cell in the balance sheet where the cash number is supposed to appear. Enter the equals sign (=) and then click on the tab that takes you to the worksheet containing the adjusted trial balance. In that worksheet, click on the cell that contains the amount you want to import into the balance sheet and then press Enter. This will create a link from the adjusted trial balance cell to the balance sheet cell. At the end of this message, I've pasted a screen shot showing the formula I would enter on the balance sheet to import the total of three related inventory accounts from the adjusted trial balance. Don't forget to save the file using a name that indicates who you are.

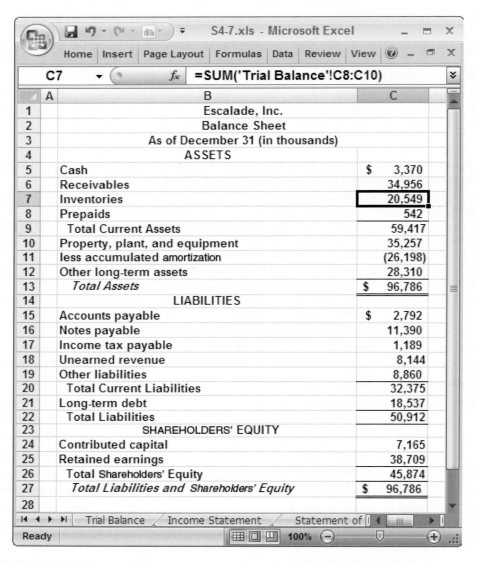

CC4 Adjusting the Accounting Records

Assume it is now December 31, 2012, and Nicole has just completed her first year of operations at Nicole's Getaway Spa. Looking through her trial balance, she notices that there are some items that have either not been recorded or are no longer up to date.

a. Nicole's Getaway Spa is renting its space at a cost of $600 per month. On September 1, 2012, Nicole paid eight months rent in advance using cash. This prepayment was recorded in the account Prepaid Rent back in September.

b. The building purchased at the beginning of the year for $47,000 cash has estimated amortization of $2,000 for 2012, but none has been recorded yet.

c. Wages to the support staff at Nicole's Getaway Spa have been paid up to December 26, 2012. The support staff worked both December 27 and 28 and will be paid on January 5, 2013. Wages amount to $1,000 per day.

d. The insurance policy, purchased on June 1 for $3,000 cash, provides coverage for 12 months. The insurance coverage since June has now been used up.

e. The unadjusted amount in the Spa Supplies account was $2,000 at December 31, 2012, for supplies purchased on account. A year-end count showed $700 of supplies remain on hand.

f. On the last day of December, a customer obtained spa services by using a $90 gift certificate that was purchased earlier in the month. Use of the gift certificate to pay for these services had not yet been recorded.

Required:

1. For each of the items listed above, identify whether an accrual adjustment, a deferral adjustment, or no adjustment is required.
2. For each of the deferral adjustments, prepare the initial journal entry that would have been recorded.
3. Prepare the adjusting journal entries that should be recorded for Nicole's Getaway Spa at December 31, 2012, assuming that the items have not been adjusted prior to December 31, 2012.

CHAPTER 5

YOUR LEARNING OBJECTIVES

Understand the business

LO1 Explain the needs of financial statement users.

LO2 Describe the environment for financial reporting, including the recent changes to corporate governance.

Study the accounting methods

LO3 Prepare a comparative balance sheet, multiple-step income statement, and statement of shareholders' equity.

LO4 Describe other significant aspects of the financial reporting process, including external audits and the distribution of financial information.

LO5 Explain the reasons for, and financial statement presentation effects of, using IFRS.

Evaluate the results

LO6 Compare results to common benchmarks.

LO7 Calculate and interpret the debt-to-assets, asset turnover, and net profit margin ratios.

Review the chapter

Chapter Summary, page 217
Additional resources on Connect

Financial Reporting and Analysis

FOCUS COMPANY:

Activision Blizzard, Inc.
www.activisionblizzard.com

ACTIVISION®

THAT WAS
THEN

In the previous chapters, you learned about the accounting system that produces the basic financial statements.

THIS IS
NOW

This chapter describes the environment in which financial statements are used, and introduces common ratio analyses.

As you have seen in Chapters 1 through 4, accounting plays a vital role when establishing and operating a small business like Pizza Palace. This chapter will continue to broaden your understanding by looking at the role accounting plays in large public companies that carry out their business activities in many cities and countries throughout the world. As you will learn in this chapter, accounting is actually one of the most pressure-filled, fast-paced elements of business. In the past ten years alone, the accounting world has tackled frauds and scandals, increasing regulation, globalization, and economic turmoil. The purposes of this chapter are to explain these four major topics and begin to equip you with tools that will help you to use financial statement information.

In keeping with the theme that accounting can be useful and fun, we focus on an exciting company that is bringing smiles to people of all ages, whether they live in Canada, India, China, Europe, or the home of its headquarters in Santa Monica, California. Activision started as a private company in 1979, went public in 1983, survived economic troubles in the late 1980s, and became known as Activision Blizzard in late 2008 when it merged with a European video game company (Vivendi Games) to create the world's largest video game company. Famous for its Tony Hawk® video games and World of Warcraft® online role-playing game, Activision Blizzard provides an ideal background for learning about the role of accounting in business and the ways in which accounting rules are changing to become more comparable with those used in Europe and other countries throughout the world.

ORGANIZATION OF THE CHAPTER

Understand the business	Study the accounting methods	Evaluate the results	Review the chapter
• The needs of financial statement users • The financial reporting environment	• Financial reporting in Canada • Globalization and International Financial Reporting Standards (IFRS)	• Economic crisis • Comparison to common benchmarks • Financial statement ratio analysis	• Demonstration Case • Chapter Summary • Key Terms • Homework Helper • Practice Material

Understand the Business

THE NEEDS OF FINANCIAL STATEMENT USERS

Chapter 1 provided an overview of the many people who use financial statements to make decisions. A more detailed look at the main user groups is presented in Exhibit 5.1 and explained below.

Managers

Managers at all levels within a company use accounting information to run the business. To make good decisions at Activision Blizzard, managers need to know detailed information such as sales by game (e.g., DJ Hero, Tony Hawk) and game platform (PlayStation, Xbox, Wii, PC), profits by genre (e.g., action, role-playing), and costs by game developer. When accounting information is used to manage the business, it is being used to fulfill a *management* function.

Directors

Directors is the short title used to describe members of the board of directors, who are elected by the company's shareholders to serve as their representatives. Directors oversee the managers of the company, with the primary goal of ensuring that management and financial decisions aim to benefit shareholders. Directors will use the financial statements to evaluate

Learning Objective 1

Explain the needs of financial statement users.

Directors

oversee

Officers and Top Managers

EXHIBIT 5.1   Users and Uses of Accounting Information

Users	Uses
Managers	Management (Run the business)
Directors	Governance (Oversee the business)
Creditors	Contracting (Administer business contracts)
Investors	Valuation (Value the business)
Government	Regulation (Ensure compliance, calculate taxes)

whether the chief executive officer (CEO), chief financial officer (CFO), and other top managers have made wise decisions about the amount to invest in assets and have managed to generate sufficient sales and net income from those assets. When accounting information is used to oversee the business, it is being used in a *governance* role.

Creditors

All creditors use accounting information. Suppliers, for example, use it to decide whether to enter into contracts to supply other companies, based in part on whether those companies have sufficient assets to pay their liabilities. Bankers use financial statement information to evaluate (and sometimes limit) a company's activities by measuring the company's ability to satisfy certain financial targets, such as maintaining specific levels of assets or shareholders' equity. These **loan covenants** help to ensure the company will be able to repay loans owed to the bank. When accounting information is used to administer contract terms such as these, it is being used in a *contracting* role.

Investors

Investors (and their advisers) look to accounting information to help assess the financial strength of a business and, ultimately, to estimate its value. Part of this analysis involves forecasting the company's future revenues, expenses, and net income. Ultimately, the goal is to determine whether to buy, hold, or sell the shares of the company. When accounting information is used to assess share prices, it is being used in a *valuation* role.

Government

Several government agencies look closely at the financial statements prepared by companies. The Canadian Securities Administrators (CSA), which has regulators from every province and territory in Canada, closely monitors the information that is reported in financial statements prepared by public companies. This is to ensure that the financial statements present fair results and that no improper or fraudulent practices were used. This helps to protect the investors and promotes efficient capital markets. The Canada Revenue Agency (CRA) also is interested in financial statements because the income statement provides a starting point for determining the amount of taxes that should be paid by private and public corporations.

As Exhibit 5.1 indicates, many different groups use accounting information to make decisions. These decisions can be wide-ranging, affecting employee bonuses, share prices, and the interest paid on loans. All this attention to a company's financial results creates a high-pressure and potentially explosive environment, as discussed in the next section.

THE FINANCIAL REPORTING ENVIRONMENT

The key organizations that play an important role in developing financial reporting standards in Canada are

1. *Canadian Accounting Standards Board (AcSB)*

   The Canadian Accounting Standards Board (AcSB) has the primary responsibility of setting GAAP in Canada and produces the *CICA Handbook*. This handbook contains several volumes of accounting and assurance guidance. Prior to the Canadian AcSB taking on this responsibility, this role was filled by the Canadian Institute of Chartered Accountants. The foundation for establishing financial accounting standards in Canada is designed to ensure that the needs of the entire economic society are being responded to. It is also designed to ensure that the process gives everyone an opportunity to have input.

2. *International Accounting Standards Board (IASB)*

   The International Accounting Standards Board (*IASB*) was formed to make more uniform standards and harmonize regulations in regards to the presentation of financial statements throughout the world, otherwise known as International Financial Reporting Standards (IFRS). As discussed in an earlier chapter, Canada adopted these international standards in 2011.

YOU SHOULD KNOW

Loan covenants: Terms of a loan agreement that, if broken, entitle the lender to renegotiate loan terms or to force repayment.

Learning Objective 2

Describe the environment for financial reporting, including the recent changes in corporate governance.

3. Provincial and territorial securities commissions

The provincial and territorial securities commissions observe and monitor the capital marketplace to ensure that it is fair. This is done by making sure that all members of the marketplace are following securities legislation, which requires public companies to produce GAAP financial statements. This in turn allows users to access company financial information and make informed decisions.

The accounting world was rocked in the last decade with scandal and fraud, leading to significant changes in the financial reporting environment. In this section, we describe what appears to have fuelled the fraud and how accounting regulators have responded with changes that are likely to affect your future career.

Accounting Fraud

Three things have to exist for accounting fraud to occur. First, there must be an incentive for someone to commit the fraud. Second, an opportunity must exist to commit the fraud. Third, the person committing the fraud must possess a personality that leads to rationalizing and concealing the fraud. Fraud investigators refer to these three elements as the *fraud triangle*, which is shown in Exhibit 5.2.

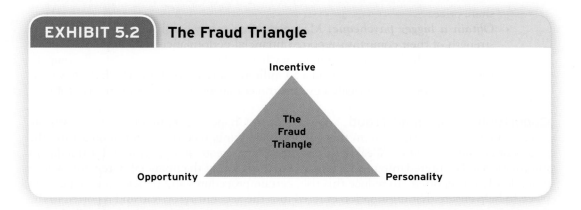

EXHIBIT 5.2   The Fraud Triangle

Incentive to Commit Fraud   Financial misreporting is both unethical and illegal, so there must be enormous incentives driving some accountants and business managers to commit fraud. As shown in Exhibit 5.3, incentives can be divided into two categories: (1) creating business opportunities and (2) satisfying personal greed.

1. **Creating business opportunities.** Management is under constant pressure to produce pleasing financial results for at least three business reasons:
    - *Satisfy loan covenants.* As you learned earlier in this chapter, lenders rely on financial statements to determine whether a company has violated its loan covenants by failing to meet specific financial targets. By overstating their company's financial

EXHIBIT 5.3   Possible Incentives for Committing Accounting Fraud

Creating Business Opportunities	Satisfying Personal Greed
• Satisfy loan covenants	• Enhance job security
• Increase equity financing	• Increase personal wealth
• Attract business partners	• Obtain bigger paycheque

condition, managers can avoid violating loan covenants, which otherwise could require the company to pay a higher interest rate, repay its loan balance right away, or be forced to put up extra collateral to secure its loan.

- *Increase equity financing.* The amount of money obtained from issuing shares depends, in part, on the price of the shares when they are issued. An issuance of 100,000 shares will yield double the money if the share price is $20 per share rather than $10 per share. Managers can lead investors to pay more for the company's shares if they overstate the company's financial performance.
- *Attract business partners.* By making the business appear more stable than it actually is, management can mislead suppliers and other companies into wanting to pursue a business relationship with the company.

2. **Satisfying personal greed.** By producing pleasing financial results, members of top management can benefit personally in three ways:
- *Enhance job security.* The financial statements are a report card on both the company and the company's management. If top management reports strong financial results, they'll likely get to keep their high-paying jobs.
- *Increase personal wealth.* Members of top management often own shares of their company, so their personal shareholdings will be worth more (and their personal wealth will increase) if their company reports financial results that increase its share price.
- *Obtain a bigger paycheque.* Managers often receive cash bonuses based on the strength of their company's reported financial performance. The more net income they report, the bigger the bonuses they'll get. One of Activision Blizzard's competitors (Take-Two Interactive) paid a $3 million bonus to its (former) CEO a few years ago, but was soon investigated by government agencies for overstating its profits.

Opportunity to Commit Fraud   As you saw in Chapters 2–4, financial statements are produced by an accounting system that involves analyzing, recording, and summarizing the results of business activities. Weaknesses in this system create an opportunity for fraudulent information to be entered into it, which increases the risk that the financial statements will be fraudulently misreported. To reduce this risk, certain procedures and policies can be put into place to help ensure that information entered into the accounting system and reported in the financial statements is accurate and complete. These *internal controls*, as they are called, can't completely eliminate the opportunity for fraud, but they can limit it if they operate effectively. You will learn about internal controls in detail in Chapter 6.

Personality to Rationalize and Conceal Fraud   For people to commit fraud and keep it secret, they have to feel "okay" with their actions. Most fraudsters achieve this through a sense of personal entitlement, which outweighs other moral principles, such as fairness, honesty, and concern for others. Many are said to be egotistical and possess an ability to lie or pressure others to look the other way.[1] It's not easy to counteract these undesirable traits, but recent changes in the financial reporting environment begin to do so, as we discuss in the next section.

Recent Changes to Corporate Governance in Canada

As mentioned in Chapter 1, the Canadian financial reporting environment has significantly changed over the past few years due to the occurrence of several high-profile accounting frauds and scandals occurring in the late 1990s and early 2000s. Confidence in the stock markets was shaken by frauds involving Enron (now bankrupt) and WorldCom (now owned by Verizon). Investors, of course, had serious reservations about the reliability of reported financial information and the credibility of external auditors. So, in an attempt to improve the financial reporting environment and restore investor confidence, the Canadian Securities Administrators introduced a series of rules that accommodated the uniqueness of the Canadian financial market. All Canadian publicly accountable enterprises must comply with these rules and regulations. Some of the key changes are summarized in Exhibit 5.4.

EXHIBIT 5.4 **Significant Changes Made to the Canadian Financial Reporting Environment**

Counteract Incentives
- Stiffer fines and prison terms

Reduce Opportunities
- Internal control report from management
- Stronger oversight by directors
- Internal control audit by external auditors

Encourage Honesty
- Anonymous tip lines
- Whistle-blower protection
- Code of ethics

Counteract Incentives for Committing Fraud Those who willfully misrepresent financial results face stiff penalties, including fines of up to $5 million. Also, maximum jail sentences are now 20 years.

Reduce Opportunities for Fraud Of the three parts of the fraud triangle, reducing opportunities for fraud is the area that business owners, managers, and accountants can do the most about. Not surprisingly, then, it's also the area affected most by the financial reporting changes. The main thrust of the resulting rules put in place here in Canada is to improve internal control over companies' financial reporting. These rules aim to achieve this in three ways:

1. Managers must review how well their company's internal controls worked during the year and issue a report that indicates whether the controls over financial reporting operated effectively. This requirement means that most marketing managers, for example, now have some accounting responsibilities, such as determining whether their staff submits accurate sales and expense reports.

2. The company's board of directors is required to establish an audit committee of independent directors to oversee financial matters of the company. One of the primary functions of this committee is to communicate with external auditors and ensure they are able to effectively perform the work described below in (3).

3. The company's external auditors must review and test the effectiveness of the company's internal controls. As was the case before, the external auditors also must examine the company's financial statements and report whether they were presented fairly (no material misstatements) in accordance with GAAP.

Encourage Honesty in Employees Admittedly, it's difficult for any law to achieve honesty in all employees, but some of the changes should help honest employees confront those whose actions are questionable. For example, audit committees are now encouraged to create tip lines that allow employees to secretly submit concerns about questionable accounting or auditing practices being committed by others. Further, these changes provide legal protection for whistle-blowers so that they aren't retaliated against by those charged with fraud. If you tattle on your boss for submitting a fraudulent expense claim, you can't be fired for it. Finally, to reinforce the importance of good character, companies are required to adopt a code of ethics for their senior financial officers. Google begins its code with "Don't be evil" and then explains what this means in plain English (see investor .google.com/conduct.html).

Solution to Self-Study Practice

1. +I (greater pressure to report stronger financial results)
2. −P (less likely that unethical behaviour will go unreported)
3. −O (strong oversight by directors)

HOW'S IT GOING? Self-Study Practice

Identify whether each of the following increases (+) or decreases (−) the risk of fraud, arising from incentives (I), opportunities (O), or personality (P).

	+/−	I/O/P
1. Enron was notorious for its "rank and yank" practice that involved ranking the financial performance of each business unit and then firing managers in the lowest 20 percent.		
2. Microsoft Corporation invites anonymous or confidential submission of questionable accounting or auditing matters to www.microsoftintegrity.com.		
3. The H. J. Heinz Company board of directors is one of the strongest boards in North America, according to Institutional Shareholder Services Inc.		

After you have finished, check your answers with the solution in the margin.

SPOTLIGHT ON ETHICS

You Can't Count That!

Most of the big accounting frauds involve uncertain judgments or complex accounting decisions that later are found to be inappropriate, such as the early revenue recognition practices used at Nortel. However, some frauds have involved blatantly unethical acts. In one famous case, managers at Bausch & Lomb shipped as much as two years' worth of contact lenses to opticians who hadn't even ordered them. These shipments were counted as sales revenue, which led to overstated financial results and unwarranted bonuses. An investigation later found: (1) an environment of extreme pressure created incentives, (2) weak internal controls provided opportunities, and (3) unscrupulous managers possessed the personalities to commit the fraud.

Study the Accounting Methods

Learning Objective 3

Prepare a comparative balance sheet, multiple-step income statement, and statement of shareholders' equity.

In the previous section, we discussed some of the *regulatory* changes made to improve the quality of publicly reported financial statements. In this section, we describe some of the *financial reporting* changes that publicly traded companies make to improve the quality and usefulness of their financial statements. We also describe how increasing globalization has created a need for common accounting rules worldwide, which led Canadian standard setters to adopt International Financial Reporting Standards (IFRS) in 2011.

FINANCIAL REPORTING IN CANADA

The good news is that the accounting and financial statement preparation processes that you learned in Chapters 1–4 for small private companies continue to apply for even the largest publicly accountable corporations. To further improve the usefulness of financial statements for their external users, though, all public companies and some private companies take three additional steps: (1) enhance the financial statement format, (2) obtain an independent external audit, and (3) release additional financial information. Exhibit 5.5 presents

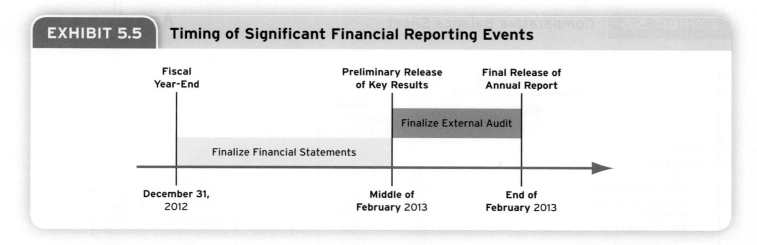

EXHIBIT 5.5 | **Timing of Significant Financial Reporting Events**

Fiscal Year-End — December 31, 2012

Preliminary Release of Key Results — Middle of February 2013

Final Release of Annual Report — End of February 2013

Finalize External Audit

Finalize Financial Statements

a timeline showing how this financial reporting process typically occurs for a company that ends its year on December 31, 2012.

Financial Statement Formatting

The financial statements shown in previous chapters provided a good introduction to their basic structure and content. However, in comparison to what you'll see in the corporate world, they were somewhat simplified. In this section, we show three enhancements that are intended to provide additional information for financial statement users: comparative financial statements, multiple-step income statements, and the statement of shareholders' equity.

Comparative Financial Statements   To make it easy for financial statement users to compare account balances from one period to the next, most companies report **comparative financial statements.** Comparative financial statements contain two or more columns of numbers, with each column representing the financial results for different time periods. For example, Exhibit 5.6 shows a slightly modified version of Activision Blizzard's comparative balance sheets. It shows one column with account balances at the end of the most recent year (December 31, 2009) and another column with balances at the end of the previous year (December 31, 2008). This allows you to quickly see that Short-Term Investments increased dramatically (from $44 million to $477 million), while Accounts Receivable decreased by $235 million. Note that the balance sheet is still classified, as introduced in Chapter 2. The only difference in a comparative balance sheet is that it uses separate columns to report different points in time.

Income statements also can be presented in a comparative format, often reporting three periods of results as shown in Exhibit 5.7. By including three columns, managers and accountants help reveal trends that persist over longer periods of time. For example, Exhibit 5.7 indicates that Activision Blizzard has grown its revenues each year since 2007, with a huge jump in 2008 when the company had two of the best-selling video games in the world (Guitar Hero and Call of Duty).

Multiple-Step Income Statements   If you look carefully at Exhibit 5.7, you'll notice the income statement format differs in another way from that used in earlier chapters. Earlier chapters used a format that contained a single grouping of revenues and a single grouping of expenses in what is typically called a **single-step income statement** format. Exhibit 5.7 presents a variation on the single-step income statement by displaying subtotals that indicate multiple steps before reaching Net Income at the bottom. The purpose of these multiple steps is to display important measures of profit in addition to net income. Exhibit 5.7 shows two new subtotals:

1. **Income from Operations**—As an investor or creditor interested in Activision Blizzard's long-term success, you probably care most about the company's ability to generate income from its core business activities like developing, making, and

EXHIBIT 5.6 — Comparative Balance Sheet

ACTIVISION BLIZZARD, INC.
Balance Sheet
(in millions of U.S. dollars)

	December 31, 2009	December 31, 2008
Assets		
Current Assets:		
Cash	$ 2,768	$ 2,958
Short-Term Investments	477	44
Accounts Receivable	739	974
Inventories	241	262
Other Current Assets	1,104	1,021
Total Current Assets	5,329	5,259
Property and Equipment, net	138	149
Other Noncurrent Assets	1,121	1,830
Goodwill	7,154	7,227
Total Assets	$13,742	$14,465
Liabilities and Shareholders' Equity		
Current Liabilities:		
Accounts Payable	$ 302	$ 319
Accrued and Other Liabilities	2,205	1,765
Total Current Liabilities	2,507	2,084
Other Noncurrent Liabilities	479	854
Total Liabilities	2,986	2,938
Shareholders' Equity:		
Contributed Capital	11,117	12,001
Accumulated Deficit	(361)	(474)
Total Shareholders' Equity	10,756	11,527
Total Liabilities and Shareholders' Equity	$13,742	$14,465

A comparative format reveals changes over time, such as Activision Blizzard's huge increase in Short-Term Investments and a decline in Accounts Receivable.

Changes in shareholders' equity accounts are shown in the Statement of Shareholders' Equity, as shown in Exhibit 5.8.

EXHIBIT 5.7 — Income Statement with Multiple Steps

ACTIVISION BLIZZARD, INC.
Income Statement
(in millions of U.S. dollars)

	Year Ended December 31,		
	2009	2008	2007
Sales and Service Revenues	$ 4,279	$ 3,026	$ 1,349
Expenses:			
Production	2,307	1,839	436
Research and Development	627	592	397
Marketing and Sales	544	464	172
General and Administrative	395	271	166
Other	432	93	(1)
Total Operating Expenses	4,305	3,259	1,170
Income (loss) from Operations	(26)	(233)	179
Income (loss) from Investments	18	46	(4)
Income (loss) before Income Tax Expense	(8)	(187)	175
Income Tax Benefit	(121)	(80)	(52)
Net Income (loss)	$ 113	$ (107)	$ 227

Core results—include revenues and expenses from the company's main business activities.

Peripheral results—include any revenues and expenses from activities other than the company's main business.

selling video games. Peripheral activities, like earning revenue from investments, aren't as important in the long run because they're not the key reason Activision Blizzard is in business (and they're not as likely to recur in the future). To make it easy for you to distinguish core and peripheral results, the top portion of the income statement reports revenues and expenses relating only to core activities, as shown in Exhibit 5.7. After the core revenues and expenses, a multiple-step income statement presents a subtotal called *Income from Operations*. Revenue from Investments did contribute to net income so it is included in the income statement, but since it's not a core business activity for Activision Blizzard, it is shown after Income from Operations. Other companies, particularly financial institutions like Bank of Montreal and Bank of Canada, would consider Revenue from Investments a core business activity. But Activision Blizzard is in business to generate profit from video game sales, not from interest on investments.

2. **Income before Income Tax Expense**—This other new subtotal in Exhibit 5.7 indicates how much profit the company would have reported had there been no income taxes. This subtotal is useful because not all companies pay the same rate of tax. Net Income, which is obtained by subtracting Income Tax Expense from Income before Income Tax Expense, is the same whether a single-step or multiple-step income statement is presented.

Statement of Shareholders' Equity   Previous chapters indicated that companies report a statement of retained earnings to show how net income increased and dividends decreased the retained earnings balance during the period. While this information is useful, it doesn't tell the full story because Retained Earnings is only one of the shareholders' equity accounts. Contributed Capital is another important shareholders' equity account whose balance increases and decreases during the accounting period. To show all the changes, public companies report a more comprehensive version of the statement of retained earnings called the *statement of shareholders' equity*. The statement of shareholders' equity has a column for each shareholder's equity account and shows the factors that increased and decreased these account balances during the period. Exhibit 5.8 shows a modified version of Activision Blizzard's statement. Notice how the beginning and ending balances for each account correspond to the balance sheet (in Exhibit 5.6). From this statement, we can see that Activision Blizzard issued additional shares in 2009, while an increase in shareholders' equity ($113 million) came from the company's own generation (and retention) of net income.

| EXHIBIT 5.8 | Statement of Shareholders' Equity | ACTIVISION. |

ACTIVISION BLIZZARD, INC.
Statement of Shareholders' Equity
For the Year Ended December 31, 2009
(in millions of U.S. dollars)

	Contributed Capital	Retained Earnings
Balances at December 31, 2008	$12,001	$ (474)
Net Income		113
Dividends Declared		(0)
Shares Issued	332	
Repurchased Shares	(1,216)	
Balances at December 31, 2009	$11,117	$ (361)

Complete the blanks in the following comparative income statements, statement of shareholders' equity, and balance sheets.

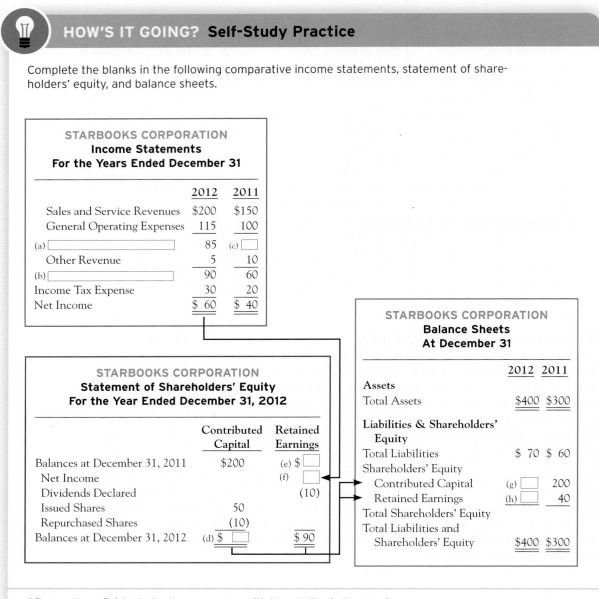

STARBOOKS CORPORATION
Income Statements
For the Years Ended December 31

	2012	2011
Sales and Service Revenues	$200	$150
General Operating Expenses	115	100
(a)	85	(c)
Other Revenue	5	10
(b)	90	60
Income Tax Expense	30	20
Net Income	$ 60	$ 40

STARBOOKS CORPORATION
Statement of Shareholders' Equity
For the Year Ended December 31, 2012

	Contributed Capital	Retained Earnings
Balances at December 31, 2011	$200	(e) $
Net Income		(f)
Dividends Declared		(10)
Issued Shares	50	
Repurchased Shares	(10)	
Balances at December 31, 2012	(d) $	$ 90

STARBOOKS CORPORATION
Balance Sheets
At December 31

	2012	2011
Assets		
Total Assets	$400	$300
Liabilities & Shareholders' Equity		
Total Liabilities	$ 70	$ 60
Shareholders' Equity		
Contributed Capital	(g)	200
Retained Earnings	(h)	40
Total Shareholders' Equity		
Total Liabilities and Shareholders' Equity	$400	$300

After you have finished, check your answers with the solution in the margin.

Independent External Audit

To ensure that financial statements are prepared properly, all publicly traded companies are required to have their financial statements audited by external auditors. Many privately owned companies have their financial statements audited, too, often at the request of lenders or private investors. External audits are conducted by professionally designated accountants who are independent of the company. These trained professionals examine the company's financial statements (and its accounting system) with the concept of **materiality** in mind, with the goal of detecting material misstatements. It is not practical for auditors to check every single business transaction to ensure that it was accurately reported, so they can't be 100 percent sure they have caught *every* error. Instead, their audits provide *reasonable* assurance to financial statement users. After completing the audit, external auditors will attach a report to the financial statements that gives a pass/fail type of opinion. An **unqualified audit opinion** represents a passing grade. If the financial statements fail to follow GAAP or if the auditors were not able to complete the tests needed to determine whether GAAP was followed, the auditors will issue a **qualified audit opinion**.

Releasing Financial Information

Preliminary Releases   To provide timely information for all external users, public companies announce annual (and quarterly) results through a press release sent to news agencies. This press release is issued three to five weeks after the accounting period ends. The press release typically includes key figures, management's discussion of the results, and attachments containing a condensed income statement and balance sheet. Exhibit 5.9 shows an excerpt from a typical press release for Activision (the company's name had not yet been changed to Activision Blizzard). Notice that five weeks elapsed between the end of the company's year (March 31) and the date of the press release (May 8). During this time, Activision's accountants were busy making adjusting journal entries and finalizing the financial statements, and its managers were preparing an analysis and discussion of the results.

EXHIBIT 5.9	Preliminary Release of Key Results

ACTIVISION REPORTS RECORD Q4 AND FISCAL YEAR 2008 RESULTS

SANTA MONICA, CA—May 8, 2008—Activision, Inc. (Nasdaq: ATVI) today announced record fiscal year 2008 and fourth quarter results.

Net revenues for the fiscal year ended March 31, 2008, were $2.90 billion, as compared to $1.51 billion for the fiscal year ended March 31, 2007. Net income for the fiscal year was $344.9 million, or $1.10 in earnings per share, as compared to net income of $85.8 million for the last fiscal year.

Robert Kotick, chairman and CEO of Activision, Inc. commented, "Fiscal 2008 was the best year in our history and Q4 was the largest and most profitable nonholiday quarter, even though we did not release any new titles. During the fiscal year, we were the #1 U.S. console and handheld publisher in dollars for the first time ever."

Today at 4:30 p.m. EDT, Activision's management will host a conference call and Webcast to discuss its fiscal 2008 year-end results and outlook for fiscal 2009.

Many companies, including Activision Blizzard, follow up the press release with a conference call broadcast on the Internet that allows analysts to grill the company's senior executives with questions about the financial results. By listening to these calls, you can learn a lot about a company's business strategy, its expectations for the future, and the key factors that analysts consider when they evaluate a company. You can check out this useful source of information by visiting each company's own Web site or the archive of conference calls at biz.yahoo.com/cc.

Financial Statement Release   Several weeks after the preliminary press release, public companies release their complete financial statements as part of an annual (or quarterly) report. The annual report is organized into two main sections. The first part of the report usually begins with a friendly letter to investors from the company's CEO. This is followed by glossy pictures of the company's products and commentaries about the company's positioning in its industry. The annual report then presents the financial section. The typical elements of an annual report's financial section are listed and explained in Exhibit 5.10.

A company's **quarterly** report is like a supercondensed version of its annual report. Following a short letter to shareholders and abbreviated discussion of the financial results, a quarterly report presents a condensed income statement for the quarter, a condensed balance sheet dated at the end of the quarter, and a condensed statement of cash flows. These condensed financial statements typically show less detail than the annual statements, often omitting items 4, 7, 8, and 9 in Exhibit 5.10. Quarterly financial statements are not audited, so they are labelled as *unaudited*. Obviously, with all these limitations, the quarterly reports aren't quite as informative as the annual reports, but they have the benefit of being released on a timelier basis (every three months rather than every year).

Canadian Securities Administrators (CSA) Filings   To ensure that sufficient, relevant information is available to investors, all Canadian public companies are required to electronically

EXHIBIT 5.10 — Typical Elements of an Annual Report's Financial Section

EXHIBIT 5.10 — **Typical Elements of an Annual Report's Financial Section**

Name of Financial Section	Information Presented
1. Summarized financial data	• key figures covering a period of 5 or 10 years.
2. Management's discussion and analysis (MD&A)	• an honest and detailed analysis of the company's financial condition and operating results; a must-read for any serious financial statement user.
3. Management's report on internal control	• statements that describe management's responsibility for ensuring adequate internal control over financial reporting and that report on the effectiveness of these controls during the year.
4. Auditor's report	• the auditor's conclusion about whether GAAP was followed (and, for public companies, whether internal controls were effective).
5. Comparative financial statements	• a multi-year presentation of the four basic statements.
6. Financial statement notes	• further information about the financial statements; crucial to understanding the financial statement data.
7. Recent share price data	• brief summary of highs and lows during the year.
8. Unaudited quarterly data	• condensed summary of each quarter's results.
9. Directors and officers	• a list of who's overseeing and running the company.

file certain reports, including the annual report. Several of these reports require release of additional information beyond that reported in quarterly or annual reports. In fact, many companies use these reports as substitutes for their glossy annual and quarterly reports. The additional information in these filings can provide great insight about a company. For example, various reports for Activision's 2008 fiscal year-end describe 30 significant business risks that the company faces and outlines the business strategies for addressing those risks. These reports also show significant business events that occur between financial statement dates, such as the acquisition of another company (e.g., Activision's 2008 merger with European video game company Vivendi), a change in its year-end (from March 31 to December 31), or a change in auditor.

These filings are available to the public as soon as they are received by the System for Electronic Document Analysis and Retrieval service (SEDAR), found at www.sedar.com. As a result, most users can get all the details about a company's financial results in the CSA filings several weeks before the company's glossy reports reach them in the mail or are posted on the company's Web site.

GLOBALIZATION AND INTERNATIONAL FINANCIAL REPORTING STANDARDS (IFRS)

Learning Objective 5

Explain the reasons for, and financial statement presentation effects of, using IFRS.

It's become a cliché, but business really has gone global. Lululemon is opening stores in Australia and Hong Kong, and Swedish companies like IKEA and H&M are opening stores throughout Canada. Similar trends are occurring in the investing world, where shares of foreign companies like Allied Gold Limited (a mining company in Australia) are traded on the Toronto Stock Exchange (TSX). Until recently, investors struggled to compare the financial statements of companies like these because different countries used different accounting rules. All this is changing now with the increasing acceptance of International Financial Reporting Standards (IFRS).

As you learned in Chapter 1, IFRS are developed by the International Accounting Standards Board (IASB). Over 100 different countries including Canada, Australia, Brazil, China, the European Union, South Africa, and New Zealand currently require or permit the use of IFRS or a local version of IFRS.

Although IFRS differ from Accounting Standards for Private Enterprises (ASPE), they do not dramatically alter what you have learned to this point in this course. IFRS use the same system of analyzing, recording, and summarizing the results of business activities that you learned in Chapters 1–4. The most significant differences between IFRS and ASPE relate to technical issues that are typically taught in intermediate and advanced accounting courses. For the topics discussed in this introductory course, differences between IFRS and ASPE are limited. One place where IFRS differ from ASPE is in the formatting of financial statements.

IFRS Formatting of Financial Statements

Although financial statements prepared using ASPE and IFRS include the same items (assets, liabilities, revenues, expenses, etc.), a single, consistent format has not been mandated. Consequently, various formats have evolved over time. You can gain a good understanding of the most common differences by reading Exhibit 5.11.

EXHIBIT 5.11	Financial Statement Presentation under ASPE and IFRS

	ASPE	IFRS
Financial Statement Titles • The financial statements report similar items but under different titles.	Balance sheet Income statement Statement of shareholders' equity Statement of cash flows	Statement of financial position Statement of comprehensive income Statement of changes in equity Statement of cash flows
Presentation of Expenses • Similar expenses are reported, but may be grouped in different ways.	Companies categorize expenses by business **function**, which focuses on the nature of the activity to which the expense relates (e.g., production, research, marketing, general operations).	Companies can categorize expenses by either function **or nature**, which focuses on the type of expense itself (e.g., salaries, rent, supplies, electricity).

Balance Sheet Order
• Similar accounts are shown, but differ in order of liquidity (for assets) and order of maturity (for liabilities).
	Assets
	  Current
	  Noncurrent
	Liabilities
	  Current
	  Noncurrent
	Shareholders' Equity
		Assets
		  Noncurrent
		  Current
		Shareholders' Equity
		Liabilities
		  Noncurrent
		  Current

Of the differences listed in Exhibit 5.11, balance sheet order is the most striking. Most companies that follow ASPE begin with current items whereas those that follow IFRS tend to begin with noncurrent items. Consistent with this, assets are listed in decreasing order of liquidity under ASPE, but internationally they are usually listed in increasing order of liquidity. IFRS similarly emphasize longer-term financing sources by listing equity before liabilities and, within liabilities, by listing noncurrent liabilities before current liabilities (decreasing time to maturity).

Activision provides an ideal case for illustrating these differences. If we compare the balance sheet for Activision prior to its merger with Vivendi to the statement of financial position based on IFRS for Vivendi, you can see some of the main differences. A side-by-side comparison is shown in Exhibit 5.12. As you can see, Vivendi was a larger company than Activision (one euro was equal to about $1.34 in U.S. dollars in mid-2008) and it reports its assets, liabilities, and shareholders' equity accounts in the typical IFRS order. But, despite these differences in appearance, the two companies are involved in the same sort of business activities, so the specific items on the financial statements are similar. It may take you a moment or two, but you should be able to find Cash, Short-Term Investments, and so on, on both companies' financial statements. Locating this kind of information is the first step to evaluating the companies' financial results, as you will see in the next section.

ACTIVISION, INC.
Balance Sheet
(in millions of U.S. dollars)

	March 31, 2008	March 31, 2007
Assets		
Current Assets:		
Cash	$ 1,396	$ 384
Short-Term Investments	53	570
Accounts Receivable	203	149
Inventories	147	91
Other Current Assets	180	207
Total Current Assets	1,979	1,401
Property and Equipment, net	55	47
Other Noncurrent Assets	217	151
Goodwill	279	195
Total Assets	$ 2,530	$ 1,794
Liabilities and Shareholders' Equity		
Current Liabilities:		
Accounts Payable	$ 130	$ 136
Accrued and Other Liabilities	426	205
Total Current Liabilities	556	341
Other Noncurrent Liabilities	26	41
Total Liabilities	582	382
Shareholders' Equity:		
Contributed Capital	1,175	984
Retained Earnings	773	428
Total Shareholders' Equity	1,948	1,412
Total Liabilities and Shareholders' Equity	$ 2,530	$ 1,794

Differences

← Title →

← Order of Liquidity (Decreasing vs. Increasing) →

← Time to Maturity (Increasing vs. Decreasing) →

VIVENDI
Statement of Financial Position
(in millions of euros)

	December 31, 2008	December 31, 2007
Assets		
Goodwill	€22,612	€15,427
Other Noncurrent Assets	15,229	15,361
Property and Equipment, net	6,317	4,675
Total Noncurrent Assets	44,158	35,463
Current Assets:		
Inventories	763	429
Other Current Assets	1,529	1,743
Accounts Receivable	6,777	5,208
Short-Term Investments	287	187
Cash	3,152	2,049
Total Current Assets	12,508	9,616
Total Assets	€56,666	€45,079
Equity and Liabilities		
Shareholders' Equity:		
Contributed Capital	€13,840	€13,736
Retained Earnings and Other	12,786	8,506
Total Shareholders' Equity	26,626	22,242
Long-Term Borrowings	9,975	5,610
Other Noncurrent Liabilities	4,370	3,768
Total Noncurrent Liabilities	14,345	9,378
Current Liabilities:		
Accrued and Other Current Liabilities	822	909
Short-Term Borrowings	1,655	1,766
Accounts Payable	13,218	10,784
Total Current Liabilities	15,695	13,459
Total Liabilities	30,040	22,837
Total Shareholders' Equity and Liabilities	€56,666	€45,079

ECONOMIC CRISIS

The end of 2008 and throughout 2009 was a difficult time for most businesses, whether they were based in Canada, the United States, China, India, or Europe. Companies were unable to find financing and they struggled to generate sales. In an effort to control expenses, they cut back on workers through massive layoffs (e.g., 1,000 at Hudson's Bay Company, 2,200 at Office Depot, 66,000 at General Motors). Whether they will withstand this economic turmoil is still being determined, but by understanding how to read financial statements, you're in a better position to identify the companies that are likely to survive.

COMPARISON TO COMMON BENCHMARKS

If you're like most people, you probably find it hard to know whether Activision Blizzard's $113 million in net income in 2009 was a decent level of performance (Exhibit 5.7). It seems like a good number, but to interpret financial statement amounts, it's useful to have points of comparison, or benchmarks. Two commonly used benchmarks are

1. **Prior periods.** By comparing a company's current period results to its own results in prior periods, we can gain a sense of how the company's performance is changing over time. The trend is your friend. In Bay Street language, this comparison of the same company over a series of prior time periods is called **time-series analysis.**

2. **Competitors.** Although an analysis focused on one company is useful, it doesn't show what's happening in the industry. It's possible that the company is improving (good), but still hasn't caught up to others in the same industry (not so good). Or it could be that the company's performance is declining (bad), but it has avoided the severe financial problems that others experienced (not so bad). To get this industrywide perspective, most analysts will compare competitors within a particular industry. The name for comparing across companies that compete in the same section of an industry is **cross-sectional analysis.**

In Exhibit 5.13, we present a time-series chart that compares Activision Blizzard to itself on several key totals from the balance sheet and income statement. From the chart, we can see that Activision Blizzard grew in all dimensions, between 2008 and 2009. To gain an understanding of whether this growth enhances Activision Blizzard's standing in the video game industry, analysts also would compare Activision Blizzard to competitors, such as Electronic Arts (maker of Rock Band and Madden NFL).

Learning Objective 6

Compare results to common benchmarks.

YOU SHOULD KNOW

Time-series analysis: Compares a company's results for one period to its own results over a series of time periods.

YOU SHOULD KNOW

Cross-sectional analysis: Compares the results of one company with those of others in the same section of the industry.

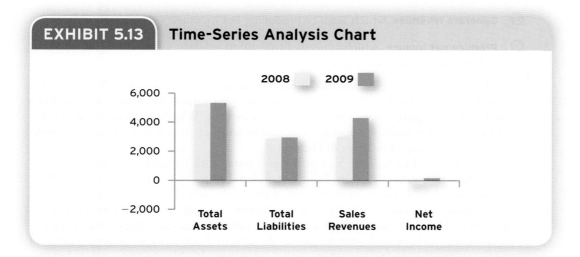

EXHIBIT 5.13 Time-Series Analysis Chart

In Exhibit 5.14, we present a cross-sectional chart that compares Activision Blizzard to Electronic Arts (stock ticker symbol ERTS) based on financial statement data for the fiscal year 2009. The bar chart in this exhibit shows that Activision Blizzard is surpassing Electronic Arts in every category. Given these differences, do analysts simply conclude that Activision Blizzard is the winner and give it a pocketful of investment tokens? In a word, no. This means only that Activision Blizzard is a slightly bigger company. It says nothing about whether it's best at using its resources. To fully understand the differences, analysts rely on financial statement ratio analysis.

> ### COACH'S TIP
>
> Average measures for each industry also can be used in cross-sectional analysis. Obtain these measures from the *Annual Statement Studies* published by the Risk Management Association or by clicking on the ratios link in the stock section of reuters.com/finance.

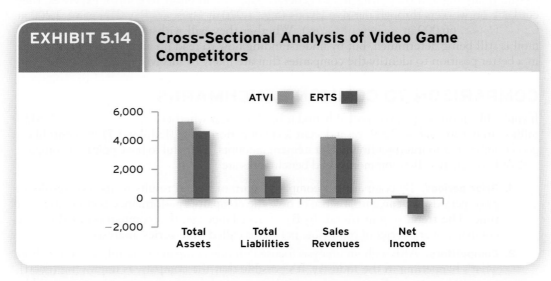

EXHIBIT 5.14 Cross-Sectional Analysis of Video Game Competitors

FINANCIAL STATEMENT RATIO ANALYSIS

> ### Learning Objective 7
>
> Calculate and interpret the debt-to-assets, asset turnover, and net profit margin ratios.

The goal of ratio analysis is to get to the heart of how well a company performed given the resources it had available. By using ratios, you can take into account differences in company size and uncover results that aren't easily detected by looking at total dollar amounts.

A Basic Business Model

Before evaluating Activision Blizzard's financial performance, it is useful to first consider what's involved in running a business. Most businesses can be broken down into four elements:

1. **Obtain financing** from lenders and investors, which is used to invest in assets.

2. **Invest in assets**, which are used to generate revenues.

3. **Generate revenues**, which leads to producing net income.

4. **Produce net income**, which is needed to comfort lenders, satisfy investors, and provide resources for future expansion.

From this description, a business model can be created, as shown in Exhibit 5.15. This business model includes the key financial measures analyzed earlier, including total liabilities (debt), shareholders' equity, assets, revenues, and net income. What's really useful about this business model is that it links one business element to another, so you aren't limited to looking at just total dollar amounts, as we did before.

The business model in Exhibit 5.15 provides a framework for understanding the ratios that we introduce in the next section. Ratios provide measures of key business results, often examining relationships between one element of the business and the next. This is a useful way to think about ratios because it's the same way businesses operate—as a series of interconnected decisions. The last thing we want is for you to view ratios as just a list of individual formulas to memorize without understanding what they mean. Rather, we want you to think of ratios as ways to measure key relationships within a business. It's like using your speedometer

EXHIBIT 5.15   **A Basic Business Model**

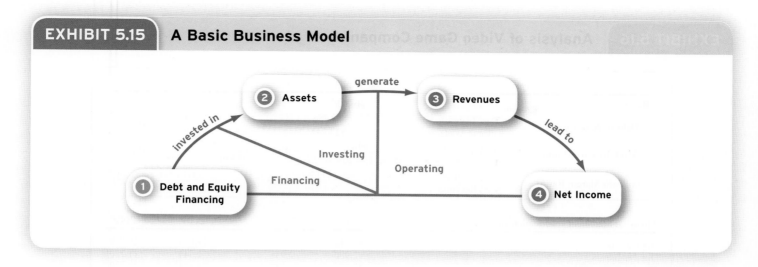

to gauge how fast you're going in the car, and then using kilometres per litre to understand how it's affecting your fuel efficiency.

Financial Statement Ratios

The business model in Exhibit 5.15 contains three links: (1) debt and equity financing is invested in assets, (2) assets are used to generate revenues, and (3) revenues lead to net income. Using these links, three key financial ratios can be created, as shown below.

ACCOUNTING DECISION TOOLS

Name of Measure	Formula	What It Tells You
1. Debt-to-assets ratio	$\dfrac{\text{Total Liabilities}}{\text{Total Assets}}$	• The percentage of assets financed by debt • A higher ratio means greater financing risk
2. Asset turnover ratio	$\dfrac{\text{Sales Revenue}}{\text{Average Total Assets}}$	• How well assets are used to generate revenues • A higher ratio means greater efficiency
3. Net profit margin ratio	$\dfrac{\text{Net Income}}{\text{Sales Revenue}}$	• How well expenses are controlled • A higher ratio means better performance

These three ratios are calculated in the top panel of Exhibit 5.16, using relevant amounts (in the bottom panel) from the financial statements of Activision Blizzard and Electronic Arts. In addition to making it possible to compare companies of different sizes, a benefit of ratio analysis is that it enables comparisons between companies reporting in different currencies, for example, dollars vs. euros.[2]

Note that, to calculate average total assets in the bottom of the asset turnover ratio, you need amounts from two balance sheets. An average is needed in the asset turnover ratio so that the bottom part spans the entire year, just like the top part. In the following discussion, we explain the significance of each of the three ratios and provide examples of how you could conduct similar analyses with other companies.

1. Debt-to-Assets Ratio   The **debt-to-assets ratio** compares total liabilities to total assets. It is usually calculated to three decimal places, and can be expressed as a percentage

YOU SHOULD KNOW

Debt-to-assets ratio:
Indicates financing risk by computing the proportion of total assets financed by debt.

EXHIBIT 5.16 | Analysis of Video Game Companies

		Activision Blizzard Inc.	Electronic Arts Inc.
Ratios			
Debt-to-Assets Ratio	$\dfrac{\text{Total Liabilities}}{\text{Total Assets}}$	$\dfrac{\$2{,}986}{\$13{,}742} = 0.217$	$\dfrac{\$1{,}544}{\$4{,}678} = 0.330$
Asset Turnover Ratio	$\dfrac{\text{Sales Revenue}}{\text{Average Total Assets}}$	$\dfrac{\$4{,}279}{(\$13{,}742 + \$14{,}465)/2} = 0.30$	$\dfrac{\$4{,}212}{(\$4{,}678 + \$6{,}059)/2} = 0.78$
Net Profit Margin Ratio	$\dfrac{\text{Net Income}}{\text{Sales Revenue}}$	$\dfrac{\$113}{\$\,4{,}279} = 0.026$	$\dfrac{\$(1{,}088)}{\$\,4{,}212} = (0.258)$

Financial Statement Information (millions)	2009	2008	2009	2008
Total assets	$13,742	$14,465	$4,678	$6,059
Total liabilities	2,986	2,938	1,544	1,720
Total shareholders' equity	10,756	11,527	3,134	4,339
Total sales revenue	4,279	3,026	4,212	3,665
Net income (loss)	113	(107)	(1,088)	(454)

by multiplying by 100. This ratio indicates the proportion of total assets that are financed by debt. It's important to know how much debt is used to finance assets because debt has to be repaid whether or not a company is doing well financially. If assets are financed mainly by debt, rather than equity, then this ratio will be high, which would suggest the company has adopted a risky financing strategy. Ultimately, a company could be forced into bankruptcy if it took on more debt than it could ever repay. Exhibit 5.16 shows that, for both companies, debt plays a fairly small role in financing the companies' assets. Activision Blizzard is the lowest with a debt-to-assets ratio of 0.217 or 21.7 percent, in comparison to Electronic Arts at 0.330 or 33 percent. This means that the likelihood of Activision Blizzard being able to repay its existing liabilities is very high, so the company has little financing risk.

2. Asset Turnover Ratio

The **asset turnover ratio** compares total sales revenue to average total assets. It is usually calculated to two decimal places and not expressed as a percentage. This ratio indicates the sales revenue per dollar invested in the assets of the business. The higher the ratio, the more efficiently the company is utilizing its assets. Inefficiently run businesses will have lower ratios because their assets will be more likely to sit around idle and not generate revenue. Exhibit 5.16 shows that neither company is generating more than one dollar in sales revenue per dollar invested in assets (as indicated with ratios below 1.0). Electronic Arts asset turnover ratio is 0.78 in comparison to Activision Blizzard's sluggish ratio of 0.30. This indicates that Activision Blizzard generated $0.30 dollars of sales revenue (30 cents) per dollar of assets. By reading the notes to the financial statements of Activision Blizzard, we found that part of the reason for this lower ratio is that Activision Blizzard merged with Vivendi in late 2008, and it has taken a while for Activision Blizzard to be able to use these new assets to generate significant sales.

3. Net Profit Margin Ratio

The **net profit margin ratio** measures the amount of net income (profit) generated from each dollar of sales revenue. It is usually calculated to three decimal places and can be expressed as a percentage by multiplying by 100. Net profit margin is a key ratio because it indicates how well a company has controlled its expenses. Although it's important for companies to generate lots of revenue, it's equally important to control expenses. A company generating tons of revenue will go bankrupt if its expenses are out of control. Exhibit 5.16 shows that Activision Blizzard was able to generate net profit margin of 0.026 (or 2.6 percent). In other words, each dollar in sales revenue produced $0.03 in profit. Electronic Arts stumbled, as indicated by its loss of almost $0.26 on each dollar of sales. As world economies struggle, these kinds of financial results become more typical. **A small negative net profit margin (NPM) does not usually cause a company to go out of business; however, large or repeating negative NPMs are definitely cause for concern.**

Many other financial statement ratios exist to assess profitability (the ability to generate income in the current period), liquidity (the ability to use current assets to pay liabilities), and solvency (the ability to repay lenders when debt matures). Rather than load you up with them all at once, we will introduce them gradually in Chapters 6–12, and then we'll summarize and apply them in a comprehensive analysis in Chapter 13.

HOW'S IT GOING? Self-Study Practice

Vivendi owns a significant part of Activision Blizzard). In the year ended December 31, 2008, Vivendi reported (in millions of euros) total sales revenues of €25,392 and net income of €3,699. Using this information and Exhibit 5.12, calculate ratios to indicate whether, relative to Activision Blizzard, Vivendi has higher or lower levels of (a) financing risk, (b) asset efficiency, and (c) profitability.

After you have finished, check your answers with the solution in the margin.

How Transactions Affect Ratios

To properly interpret financial statement ratios, you will find it useful to understand how they are affected by transactions. Apply the following three-step process to determine the impact of each transaction on a particular ratio:

1. **Analyze the transaction to determine its effects on the accounting equation**, just as you have learned to do in Chapters 2–4.

2. **Relate the effects in step 1 to the ratio's components**, to determine whether each component increases, decreases, or stays the same.

3. **Evaluate the combined impact of the effects in step 2 on the overall ratio**.

A ratio will increase if (a) its top number increases and the bottom number does not change, (b) its bottom number decreases and its top number does not change, or (c) the top number increases while the bottom number decreases. Changes in the opposite direction have the opposite effect. A ratio will decrease if (a) its top number decreases and the bottom number does not change, (b) its bottom number increases and its top number does not change, or (c) the top number decreases while the bottom number increases.

When a transaction causes both the top and bottom numbers to change in the same direction, the overall impact on a ratio depends on whether the ratio is greater or less than 1.0 before the transaction. A useful approach for determining the impact of a transaction on a ratio in these cases is to assume some simple numbers for the ratio's starting point and then recalculate the ratio after taking into account the effects of the transaction. Exhibit 5.17 illustrates this approach for two situations.

In the first situation, the $5 increases in the top and bottom of the ratio cause the overall ratio to increase from 0.50 to 0.67. In the second situation, the $5 increases cause the overall ratio to decrease from 2.0 to 1.5. These different outcomes occur because in situation (1), the increase has a greater proportionate effect on the top number than on the bottom, whereas in situation (2), the change has a greater proportionate effect on the bottom number than on the top.

For many situations, you will know whether a ratio is greater or less than one, as a result of understanding the relationship between the ratio's components. For example,

EXHIBIT 5.17 | Changes in Ratios Given Changes in Its Components

Situation	Before	Change	After
1. Ratio < 1	$\frac{5}{10}$ = 0.50	$\frac{+5}{+5}$	$\frac{10}{15}$ = 0.67
2. Ratio > 1	$\frac{10}{5}$ = 2.0	$\frac{+5}{+5}$	$\frac{15}{10}$ = 1.5

the debt-to-assets ratio is likely to be less than 1.0 because the balance sheet equation ($A = L + SE$) indicates that liabilities are less than assets. Similarly, the net profit margin ratio is less than 1.0 because the income statement equation (Revenues − Expenses = Net Income) implies that revenues are greater than net income. Only in a few cases (e.g., asset turnover ratio) will you need to know whether the ratio is greater or less than 1.0 to determine the impact of a transaction that causes both the top and bottom numbers of a ratio to change in the same direction.

SPOTLIGHT ON ETHICS

Livent: The Final Act

The Live Entertainment Corporation of Canada, Inc., also known as Livent, was a theatre production company in Toronto. It was founded in 1990 by Garth Drabinsky and Myron Gottlieb, former Cineplex Odeon Corp. executives, and went public in 1993.

Livent appeared to be a very successful company, winning three Tony Awards, including Best Musical. It opened a refurbished theatre on Broadway in New York City at a cost of (US)$22.5 million and had plans to build a second theatre in Toronto for $30 million.

All was not as it seemed, however. In April 1998, former Hollywood agent and Disney executive Michael Ovitz made a deal to invest (US)$20 million in Livent for control of the company. It was then that the Livent facade started to crumble. Ovitz's new management team reported "massive, systematic, accounting irregularities that permeated the company." By November, Livent had filed for bankruptcy and civil lawsuits were filed against Drabinsky and Gottlieb, alleging that they overstated earnings and assets and hid losses to make Livent's financial situation appear better than it was. It is claimed that investors lost approximately $500 million.

After an 11-month trial, on March 25, 2009, Drabinsky and Gottlieb were convicted of two counts of fraud and one count of uttering forged documents. Drabinsky was sentenced to serve seven years in jail and Gottlieb received a sentence of six years.

Several features of the Livent scandal make it similar to other major financial frauds. These similarities are consistent with the fraud triangle referred to earlier in this chapter. The incentive in this situation was that Livent had a constant and growing need for additional capital. The opportunity was created from the weaknesses in the control system, which allowed the accountants to develop computer software for senior management to track both the "real" numbers and the manipulated numbers at the same time. The management team was very aggressive and growth-oriented and felt that their actions were justified, as evidenced by the matter-of-fact manner in which they organized and carried out the fraud.

Topic	ASPE	IFRS
Financial Statement Title • The financial statements report similar items but under different titles.	Balance sheet Income statement Statement of shareholders' equity Statement of cash flows	Statement of financial position Statement of comprehensive income Statement of changes in equity Statement of cash flows
Presentation of Expenses • Similar expenses are reported but may be grouped in different ways.	Companies categorize expenses by business **function** (e.g., production, research, marketing, general operations).	Companies can categorize expenses by either function or **nature** (e.g., salaries, rent, supplies, electricity).
Balance Sheet Order • Similar accounts are shown, but differ in order of liquidity (for assets) and order of maturity (for liabilities).	**Assets** 　Current 　Noncurrent **Liabilities** 　Current 　Noncurrent **Shareholders' Equity**	**Assets** 　Noncurrent 　Current **Shareholders' Equity** **Liabilities** 　Noncurrent 　Current

Review the Chapter

DEMONSTRATION CASE

Some analysts claim that the video game business is similar to the book business. In this demonstration case, we'll take a look at just how similar they are in terms of financial results. Books 'R' Us, Inc., is a company that operates only in the book business. Shortened versions of that company's financial statements are shown below.

BOOKS 'R' US, INC.
Income Statement (modified)
(millions of dollars)
For the Years Ended April 30

	2012	2011
Total Sales Revenue	$1,674	$1,235
Cost of Sales	537	394
Operating and Administrative Expenses	875	659
Other Expenses	39	21
Income from Operations	223	161
Interest Expense	61	21
Income before Income Tax Expense	162	140
Income Tax Expense	14	40
Net Income	$ 148	$ 100

BOOKS 'R' US, INC.
Balance Sheet (modified)
(millions of dollars)
April 30

	2012	2011
Assets		
Current Assets	$ 448	$ 421
Other Assets	2,141	2,132
Total Assets	$2,589	$2,553
Liabilities and Shareholders' Equity		
Current Liabilities	$ 691	$ 620
Other Liabilities	1,209	1,403
Total Liabilities	1,900	2,023
Shareholders' Equity	689	530
Total Liabilities and Shareholders' Equity	$2,589	$2,553

Required:

1. Compute Books 'R' Us's debt-to-assets ratio at the end of the 2012 and 2011 fiscal years. How has Books 'R' Us changed its financing strategy from 2011 to 2012? Is this likely to be considered a riskier or safer strategy? How similar is the proportion of debt financing used by the book publisher to that used by the video game companies analyzed in Exhibit 5.16?

2. Compute Books 'R' Us's asset turnover ratio for 2012 and 2011. (In millions, Books 'R' Us's total assets at April 30, 2010, were $1,026.) Between 2011 and 2012, was there a change in Books 'R' Us's efficiency in using its assets to generate revenues? Does the book publisher generate more or less sales from each dollar invested in assets than the video game companies analyzed in Exhibit 5.16?

3. Compute Books 'R' Us's net profit margin ratio for the 2012 and 2011 fiscal years. How has this aspect of Books 'R' Us's financial performance changed? Does the book publisher make more or less profit from each dollar of sales than the video game companies analyzed in Exhibit 5.16?

After completing requirements 1–3, check your answers with the following solution.

Suggested Solution

1. Debt-to-Assets Ratio = Total Liabilities ÷ Total Assets

	2012	2011
$\dfrac{\text{Total Liabilities}}{\text{Total Assets}}$	$\dfrac{\$1,900}{\$2,589} = 0.734$ or 73.4%	$\dfrac{\$2,023}{\$2,553} = 0.792$ or 79.2%

Books 'R' Us has moved toward a safer financing strategy in 2012 by relying less on debt (down from 79.2 percent in 2011 to 73.4 percent in 2012). Despite this change, Books 'R' Us still relies much more on debt than the video game companies in Exhibit 5.16, which financed less than 35 percent of their total assets using debt.

2. Asset Turnover Ratio = Sales Revenue ÷ Average Total Assets

	2012	2011
$\dfrac{\text{Total Sales Revenue}}{\text{Average Total Assets}}$	$\dfrac{\$1,674}{(\$2,589 + \$2,553)/2} = 0.65$	$\dfrac{\$1,235}{(\$2,553 + \$1,026)/2} = 0.69$

Books 'R' Us generated weaker sales per dollar invested in assets in 2012 (0.65) than in 2011 (0.69). In comparison to the video game companies in Exhibit 5.16, it appears that Books 'R' Us's assets are generating sales with less efficiency than Electronic Arts' but with more efficiency than Activision Blizzard's.

3. Net Profit Margin Ratio = Net Income ÷ Sales Revenue

	2012		2011	
Net Income / Total Sales Revenue	$\dfrac{\$148}{\$1,674}$	= 0.088 or 8.8%	$\dfrac{\$100}{\$1,235}$	= 0.081 or 8.1%

Books 'R' Us improved its net profit margin from 8.1 percent in 2011 to 8.8 percent in 2012. This means that, in 2012, Books 'R' Us made about 8.8 cents of profit for each dollar of sales, which is higher than those for Activision Blizzard and Electronic Arts.

CHAPTER SUMMARY

Explain the needs of financial statement users. p. 195 **LO1**

- The main financial statement users are

  Managers, who use accounting information to run the business.

  Directors, who use accounting information to oversee the business.

  Creditors, who use accounting information to administer business contracts.

  Investors, who use accounting information to value the business.

  Government, which uses accounting information to ensure compliance with regulations.

Describe the environment for financial reporting, including the recent changes to corporate governance. p. 196 **LO2**

- For someone to commit fraud, three things must exist: incentive, opportunity, and the personality to rationalize and conceal.

- Incentives that motivate managers to misreport financial results include creating business opportunities (by satisfying loan covenants, increasing equity financing, and attracting business partners) and satisfying personal greed (enhancing job security, increasing personal wealth, and obtaining a bigger paycheque).

- The Canadian Securities Administrators reduced the incentive to commit fraud by introducing stiffer penalties. It also limits opportunities by improving internal controls through management reporting, audit committee functioning, and external audit reporting. Finally, it attempts to support honest employees confronting those with questionable personalities.

Prepare a comparative balance sheet, multiple-step income statement, and statement of shareholders' equity. p. 200 **LO3**

- Comparative financial statements include separate columns for each period's results. See Exhibit 5.6 (p. 202) for an example.

- A multiple-step income statement displays subtotals that indicate multiple steps before reaching Net Income at the bottom. See Exhibit 5.7 (p. 202) for an example.

- The statement of shareholders' equity, which replaces the statement of retained earnings, has columns for each shareholder's equity account and shows the factors that increased and decreased these account balances during the period. See Exhibit 5.8 (p. 203) for an example.

Describe other significant aspects of the financial reporting process, including external audits and the distribution of financial information. p. 204 **LO4**

- Financial information can be distributed through press releases, SEC filings, investor information Web sites, and quarterly and annual reports.

- Press releases typically include key figures (sales revenues, net income), management's discussion of the results, and attachments containing a condensed income statement and balance sheet.

- The annual report includes the annual financial statements, auditor's report, management's discussion and analysis, share price data, and other financial schedules. A quarterly report includes the quarterly financial statements and management's discussion and analysis. Other reports are used for companies to report significant current events, such as changes in auditors, press releases issued, and acquisitions of other companies.

LO5 **Explain the reasons for, and financial statement presentation effects of, using IFRS. p. 206**

- IFRS are intended to reduce or eliminate differences in accounting rules that have developed previously on a country-by-country basis.
- These improvements in comparability are needed as a result of increasing globalization in corporate operations and investing.
- IFRS introduce new financial statement titles, order of balance sheet accounts, and groupings of expenses, as summarized in Exhibit 5.11 (p. 207).

LO6 **Compare results to common benchmarks. p. 209**

- Common benchmarks include prior periods (used in time-series analysis) and competitors (used in cross-sectional analysis).

LO7 **Calculate and interpret the debt-to-assets, asset turnover, and net profit margin ratios. p. 210**

- The debt-to-assets ratio is calculated by dividing total liabilities by total assets. It indicates the percentage of assets financed by debt, with a higher ratio indicating a riskier financing strategy.
- The asset turnover ratio is calculated by dividing total sales revenue for the period by average total assets held during the period. Average total assets usually are calculated by adding the beginning and ending total assets together and dividing by 2. The asset turnover ratio indicates how well assets are used to generate sales, with a higher ratio indicating greater efficiency.
- The net profit margin ratio is calculated by dividing net income by total sales revenue. It indicates the ability to control expenses, with a higher ratio indicating better performance.

ACCOUNTING DECISION TOOLS

Name of Measure	Formula	What It Tells You
1. Debt-to-assets ratio	$\dfrac{\text{Total Liabilities}}{\text{Total Assets}}$	• The percentage of assets financed by debt • A higher ratio means greater financing risk
2. Asset turnover ratio	$\dfrac{\text{Sales Revenue}}{\text{Average Total Assets}}$	• How well assets are used to generate sales • A higher ratio means greater efficiency
3. Net profit margin ratio	$\dfrac{\text{Net Income}}{\text{Sales Revenue}}$	• How well expenses are controlled • A higher ratio means better performance

KEY TERMS

Asset Turnover Ratio p. 212

Comparative Financial Statements p. 201

Cross-Sectional Analysis p. 209

Debt-to-Assets Ratio p. 211

Loan Covenants p. 196

Materiality p. 204

Net Profit Margin Ratio p. 212

Qualified Audit Opinion p. 204

Single-Step Income Statement p. 201

Time-Series Analysis p. 209

Unqualified Audit Opinion p. 204

See complete definitions in the glossary in the back of this text.

HOMEWORK HELPER

Alternative terms

- Under IFRS, the balance sheet is called the *statement of financial position*, and the income statement is called the *statement of comprehensive income*.

Helpful reminders

- If you're not sure how a transaction affects a particular ratio, assume simple numbers for the ratio's starting point (before the transaction) and then recalculate the ratio after taking into account the effects of the transaction.

Frequent mistakes

- Some students assume that a ratio does not change when its numerator and denominator change by the same amount. A ratio is likely to change even if both its top and bottom parts increase (or decrease) by an equal dollar amount.

Practice Material

QUESTIONS (⊖ Symbol indicates questions that require analysis from more than one perspective.)

1. Describe one way that each of the main financial statement user groups uses financial statement information.

2. What are the three points of the fraud triangle? Is fraud more or less likely to occur if one of these elements is missing?

3. Why would managers misrepresent the financial results of their companies? What are the incentives for doing this?

4. What aspect(s) of the changes made to corporate governance in Canada might counteract the incentive to commit fraud?

5. What aspect(s) of the changes made to corporate governance in Canada might reduce the opportunities for fraud?

6. What aspect(s) of the changes made to corporate governance in Canada might allow honest employees to prevail?

7. What roles do auditors play in the financial reporting process?

8. In what ways are fraudulent financial reporting and academic dishonesty (e.g., cheating on exams) similar? Consider the three points of the fraud triangle.

9. In what three ways might corporate financial statements of a company using IFRS differ from the examples shown in Chapters 1–4?

10. Switching to International Financial Reporting Standards (IFRS) will require companies to incur significant costs. What are the benefits of countries adopting IFRS? ⊖

11. In what three general ways might financial statements prepared using IFRS differ from those prepared using GAAP?

12. What two benchmarks are commonly used to interpret and evaluate amounts reported for specific financial statement items?

13. What is the goal of ratio analysis?

14. Explain the simple business model that starts with obtaining financing and then proceeds through other investing and operating decisions.

15. Why do some ratios use just the ending balance sheet amounts, whereas others use averages of the beginning and ending balances?

16. What are the key business activities that the debt-to-assets, asset turnover, and net profit margin ratios assess?

Multiple-choice questions and corresponding answers can be found on Connect.

MINI-EXERCISES

M5-1 Matching Players in the Financial Reporting Process with Their Definitions

LO1

Match each player with the related definition by entering the appropriate letter in the space provided.

Players	Definitions
____ 1. Independent auditors	A. Investors and creditors (among others).
____ 2. External users	B. People who are elected by shareholders to oversee a company's management.
____ 3. Directors	C. Professional accountants who examine financial statements and attest to their fairness.

LO3, 7 **M5-2 Preparing and Interpreting a Multiple-Step Income Statement**

Nutboy Theatre Company reported the following single-step income statement. Prepare a multiple-step income statement that distinguishes the financial results of the local theatre company's core and peripheral activities. Also, calculate the net profit margin and compare it to the 8 percent earned in 2012. In which year did the company generate more profit from each dollar of sales?

NUTBOY THEATRE COMPANY
Income Statement
For the year ended December 31, 2012

Revenues	
Ticket Sales	$50,000
Concession Sales	2,500
Interest Revenue	200
Other Revenue	50
Total revenues	52,750
Expenses	
Salaries and Wage Expense	30,000
Advertising Expense	8,000
Utilities Expense	7,000
Income Tax Expense	2,500
Total Expenses	47,500
Net Income	$ 5,250

LO3 **M5-3 Preparing a Statement of Shareholders' Equity**

On December 31, 2011, WOR Productions reported $100,000 of contributed capital and $20,000 of retained earnings. During 2012, the company had the following transactions. Prepare a statement of shareholders' equity for the year ended December 31, 2012.

a. Issued shares for $50,000.

b. Declared and paid a cash dividend of $5,000.

c. Reported total revenue of $120,000 and total expenses of $87,000.

LO3 **M5-4 Determining the Accounting Equation Effects of Transactions**

Complete the following table, indicating the sign and amount of the effect (+ for increase, − for decrease, and NE for no effect) of each transaction. Provide an account name for any revenue or expense transactions included in shareholders' equity. Consider each item independently.

a. Recorded services provided to a customer on account for $500.

b. Recorded $50 of supplies purchased from a supplier on account.

c. Recorded advertising services of $1,000 received but not yet paid for.

Transaction	Assets	Liabilities	Shareholders' Equity
a			
b			
c			

LO7 **M5-5 Determining the Effects of Transactions on Debt-to-Assets, Asset Turnover, and Net Profit Margin Ratios**

Using the transactions in M5-4, complete the following table by indicating the sign of the effect (+ for increase, − for decrease, NE for no effect, and CD for cannot determine) of each transaction. Consider each item independently.

Transaction	Debt-to-Assets	Asset Turnover	Net Profit Margin
a			
b			
c			

M5-6 Preparing Comparative Financial Statements

LO3

Complete the blanks in the following comparative income statements, statement of shareholders' equity, and balance sheets.

ELECBOOKS CORPORATION
Income Statements
For the Years Ended December 31

	2012	2011
Sales and Service Revenues	$400	$300
General Operating Expenses	230	200
(a) [ ]	170	(c) [ ]
Other Revenue	10	20
(b) [ ]	180	120
Income Tax Expense	60	40
Net Income	$120	$ 80

ELECBOOKS CORPORATION
Statement of Shareholders' Equity
For the Year Ended December 31, 2012

	Contributed Capital	Retained Earnings
Balances at December 31, 2011	$400	(e) $ [ ]
Net Income		(f) [ ]
Dividends Declared		(20)
Issued Shares	100	
Repurchased Shares	(20)	
Balances at December 31, 2012	(d) $ [ ]	$180

ELECBOOKS CORPORATION
Balance Sheets
December 31

	2012	2011
Assets		
Total Assets	$800	$600
Liabilities & Shareholders' Equity		
Total Liabilities	$140	$120
Shareholders' Equity		
Contributed Capital	(g) [ ]	400
Retained Earnings	(h) [ ]	80
Total Shareholders' Equity		
Total Liabilities & Shareholders' Equity	$800	$600

M5-7 Preparing a Financial Statement under IFRS

LO5

Show how the balance sheet in M5-6 would be presented under International Financial Reporting Standards.

M5-8 Computing and Interpreting the Net Profit Margin Ratio

LO7

Happy's Golf Corporation recently reported the following December 31 amounts in its financial statements (in thousands):

	Prior Year	Current Year
Income from Operations	$ 1,700	$1,400
Net Income	850	700
Total Assets	10,000	9,000
Total Shareholders' Equity	8,000	7,500
Sales Revenue	9,000	7,000

Compute the net profit margin ratio for the current and prior years. What do these analyses indicate?

LO7 M5-9 Computing and Interpreting the Debt-to-Assets Ratio

Using the data in M5-8, compute the debt-to-assets ratio for the current and prior years. What do these analyses indicate?

LO7 M5-10 Computing and Interpreting the Asset Turnover Ratio

Using the data in M5-8, compute the asset turnover ratio for the current year. Assuming the asset turnover ratio in the prior year was 85.2 percent (0.852), what does your analysis indicate?

EXERCISES

Practise and learn online with Connect.

LO1, 4 E5-1 Matching Components of the Financial Reporting Process with Their Definitions

Match each component with the related definition by entering the appropriate letter in the space provided.

Components	Definitions
___ 1. Investor information Web site	A. Individual who purchases shares in companies for personal ownership or for pension funds or mutual funds.
___ 2. External auditor	B. Financial institution or supplier that lends money to a company.
___ 3. Investor	C. Independent professional accountant who examines financial statements and attests to their fairness.
___ 4. Creditor	D. Gathers, combines, and transmits financial and related information from various sources.

LO1 E5-2 Matching Events with Concepts

Following are accounting concepts covered in Chapters 1 through 5. Match each event (A–J) with its related concept (1–10) by entering the appropriate letter in the space provided. Use one letter for each blank.

Concepts	Events
___ 1. Users of financial statements	A. Counted unused supplies at the end of the period and valued them in Canadian dollars.
___ 2. Objective of financial statements	B. Valued an asset at the amount paid to acquire it, even though its market value has increased considerably.
___ 3. Faithful representation	C. Analyzed the financial statements to assess the company's performance.
___ 4. Comparability	D. Established an accounting policy that sales revenue will be recognized only when services have been provided to the customer.
___ 5. Separate entity	E. Prepared and distributed financial statements that provide useful financial information for creditors and investors.
___ 6. Unit of measure	
___ 7. Cost principle	F. Established a policy not to include in the financial statements the personal financial affairs of the owners of the business.
___ 8. Revenue principle	G. Used the same accounting policies over several years to facilitate analysis.
___ 9. Matching principle	
___ 10. Conservatism	H. Established policies to report the company's business activities in a way that depicts the economic substance of these activities.
	I. Adjusted the rent accounts to show the cost of rent used up in the current period.
	J. Acquired a vehicle for use in the business, reporting it at the agreed-upon purchase price rather than its higher sticker price.

Check Figure [Item 10]:
Conservatism = B

E5-3 Understanding the Characteristics of Useful Financial Information and the Financial Reporting Process

LO1, 4, 7

Atari Incorporated
Time-Warner
Hasbro
Infogrames

Atari Incorporated began with $250 and an idea for a video game named Pong, eventually becoming a $28 million enterprise. Over the years, Atari has been owned by a variety of companies, including Time-Warner, Hasbro, and, most recently, Infogrames (a public company in France). Assume that Infogrames made the following announcement:

> On March 28, 2012, Infogrames announced that it has changed its fiscal year-end from June 30 to March 31. As a result of this change, Infogrames' fiscal year 2012 was a nine-month period. Infogrames believes that the March 31 year-end is consistent with more of its peers in the video game industry, allowing for more meaningful analysis and comparisons within the sector.

Required:

1. To which of the four factors that enhance the usefulness of information, introduced in Chapter 1, is the company referring?

   TIP: Rather than look for key words in the announcement, read it for meaning.
2. Since the 2012 fiscal period includes only nine months, will the debt-to-assets, asset turnover, and net profit margin ratios be meaningful in 2012? Explain your reasoning.

E5-4 Understanding the Characteristics of Useful Financial Information and the Financial Reporting Process

LO1, 4, 7

THQ Inc.

THQ Inc. is among the biggest video game makers in the world. Assume that THQ made the following announcement:

> On February 13, 2012, we announced a fiscal year-end change from December 31 of each year to March 31 of each year, effective March 31, 2012. We believe that the change in fiscal year will better reflect our natural business year and allow us to provide financial guidance after the holiday selling season.

Required:

1. Does the reason given for the change in year-end indicate that this change will make THQ's financial statements more useful to users? Can you think of a reason that the change in year-end ultimately will result in more useful information for users?
2. Since the March 31, 2012, fiscal period includes only three months, will the debt-to-assets, asset turnover, and net profit margin ratios be meaningful in this period? Explain your reasoning.

E5-5 Computing and Interpreting the Net Profit Margin Ratio

LO7

Cendant Corporation
Super 8 Motels
Ramada
Howard Johnson
Century 21
Orbitz.com
Avis
Budget

Before spinning off its businesses in 2006, Cendant Corporation owned and operated Super 8 Motels, Ramada, Howard Johnson, Century 21, Orbitz.com, Avis, and Budget. Cendant also was notorious for committing a $3.3 billion accounting fraud in the late 1990s, which sent its former vice-chairman to prison for ten years. Assume that on February 13, 2012, the company issued a press release that reported the following amounts (in millions) for the year just ended on December 31, 2011:

	2011	2010
Total Fee Revenue	$18,236	$16,689
Income from Operations	869	1,365
Net Income	1,341	2,082

Check Figure:
2011 Net profit
margin = 7.4%

Required:

Compute the net profit margin ratio for the current and prior years. What do these analyses indicate?

E5-6 Understanding the Financial Reporting Process

LO4

The information in E5-5 indicated that the Cendant Corporation press release was issued on February 13, yet the company's year-end was six weeks earlier on December 31. Why did the company wait so long to issue the press release? Why weren't the financial results announced on January 1?

Better Ingredients.
Better Pizza.

LO1, 7

E5-7 Analyzing and Interpreting Asset Turnover and Net Profit Margin Ratios

Papa John's International is one of the fastest-growing pizza delivery and carry-out restaurant chains. Presented here are selected hypothetical income statement and balance sheet amounts (in millions).

	2012	2011
Total Revenues	$1,132	$1,064
Net Income	37	33
Total Assets, beginning of year	402	380
Total Assets, end of year	386	402

Required:

1. Compute the asset turnover and net profit margin ratios for 2012 and 2011.
2. Would analysts more likely increase or decrease their estimates of share value on the basis of these changes? Explain by interpreting what the changes in these two ratios mean.

LO1, 7

E5-8 Analyzing and Interpreting Asset Turnover and Net Profit Margin Ratios

The following amounts (in millions) were reported in the SnarkShark income statement and balance sheet.

	2012	2011	2010
Sales Revenue	$4,225	$4,252	$4,778
Net Income	192	237	73
Total Assets	2,284	1,990	2,070
Total Liabilities	1,466	1,220	1,416

Required:

1. Compute the asset turnover and net profit margin ratios for 2012 and 2011.
2. Would analysts be more likely to increase or decrease their estimates of share value on the basis of these changes? Explain what the changes in these two ratios mean.
3. Compute the debt-to-assets ratio for 2012 and 2011.
4. Would analysts be more likely to increase or decrease their estimates of SnarkShark's ability to repay lenders on the basis of this change? Explain by interpreting what the change in this ratio means.

LO3

La-Z-Boy Incorporated

E5-9 Determining the Accounting Equation Effects of Transactions

La-Z-Boy Incorporated is a furniture manufacturer. Listed here are typical aggregate transactions from the first quarter of a recent year (in millions). Complete the following table, indicating the sign (+ for increase, − for decrease, and NE for no effect) and amount of the effect of each transaction. Provide an account name for any revenue or expense transactions included in shareholders' equity. Consider each item independently.

a. Repaid $10 on a note payable to a bank. (Interest was paid separately.)
b. Recorded collections of cash from customers who owed $32.

Transaction	Assets	Liabilities	Shareholders' Equity
a			
b			

LO7

E5-10 Determining the Effects of Transactions on Debt-to-Assets, Asset Turnover, and Net Profit Margin Ratios

Using the transactions in E5-9, complete the following table by indicating the sign of the effect (+ for increase, − for decrease, NE for no effect, and CD for cannot determine) of each transaction. Consider each item independently.

Transaction	Debt-to-Assets	Asset Turnover	Net Profit Margin
a			
b			

Check Figure [Part (a)]:
Net Profit Margin—no effect

E5-11 Preparing and Interpreting Financial Statements

LO3, 6, 7

The December 31, 2012 and 2011, adjusted trial balances for Sportlife Gym Corporation are shown below.

	2012 Debit	2012 Credit	2011 Debit	2011 Credit
Cash	$ 31,500		$ 30,000	
Accounts Receivable	2,500		2,000	
Supplies	13,000		13,000	
Prepaid Rent	3,000		3,000	
Equipment	350,000		350,000	
Accumulated Amortization		$ 20,000		$ 10,000
Other Long-Term Assets	20,000		12,000	
Accounts Payable		5,000		6,000
Unearned Revenue		72,000		80,000
Income Taxes Payable		13,000		14,000
Long-Term Debt		10,000		200,000
Contributed Capital		214,000		50,000
Retained Earnings		50,000		19,400
Dividends Declared	5,000		0	
Membership Revenue		399,000		398,000
Coaching Revenue		11,000		10,000
Coaching and Assistants' Wages	221,000		219,400	
Management Salaries	100,000		100,000	
Facilities Rent Expense	12,000		12,000	
Amortization Expense	10,000		10,000	
General Operating Expenses	6,150		7,700	
Interest Revenue		750		700
Interest Expense	600		15,000	
Income Tax Expense	20,000		14,000	
	$794,750	$794,750	$788,100	$788,100

Required:

1. Prepare a comparative income statement for 2012 and 2011, a statement of shareholders' equity for 2012, and a comparative classified balance sheet for 2012 and 2011. The income statement should distinguish the gym's core and peripheral results, and group expenses by function (coaching, facilities, and general management). The change in Contributed Capital was caused by the issuance of new shares in 2012.

2. Identify two balance sheet and two income statement accounts that changed significantly in 2012. What might be the cause of these changes?

3. Calculate and interpret the debt-to-assets, asset turnover and net profit margin ratios in 2012 and 2011. Total assets were $400,000 on December 31, 2010.

Check Figure [Req. 3]:
2011 Asset Turnover = 1.02

E5-12 Preparing Financial Statements using IFRS

LO5

Refer to E5-11.

Required:

1. Prepare a comparative classified statement of financial position, as typically presented using IFRS.

2. Prepare a comparative income statement, which IFRS calls a *statement of comprehensive income*.

   TIP: Use Exhibit 5.7 as a guide, except group expenses by nature (e.g., salaries and wages, rent, etc.) as outlined in Exhibit 5.11.

LO3 **E5-13 Finding Financial Statement Information**

Indicate whether each of the following would be reported on the balance sheet (B/S), income statement (I/S), or statement of shareholders' equity (SSE).

1. Insurance costs paid this year, to expire next year.
2. Insurance costs expired this year.
3. Insurance costs still owed.
4. Cost of equipment used up this accounting year.
5. Equipment book value (carrying value).
6. Amounts contributed by shareholders during the year.
7. Cost of supplies unused at the end of the year.
8. Cost of supplies used during the accounting year.
9. Amount of unpaid loans at end of year.
10. Dividends declared and paid during this year.

COACHED PROBLEMS

LO3 **CP5-1 Determining the Accounting Equation Effects of Transactions**

YAHOO!

eXcel

Yahoo! Inc. is a leading provider of Internet products and services. Listed here are selected hypothetical aggregate transactions from 2011 (in millions). Complete the following table, indicating the sign (+ for increase, − for decrease, and NE for no effect) and the amount of the effect of each transaction. Provide an account name for any revenue or expense transactions included in shareholders' equity. Consider each item independently.

a. Recorded marketing revenues on account of $7,208.
b. Obtained $363 cash by issuing shares.
c. Incurred product development expense of $1,222, which was paid in cash.

Transaction	Assets	Liabilities	Shareholders' Equity
a			
b			
c			

LO7 **CP5-2 Interpreting Debt-to-Assets, Asset Turnover, and Net Profit Margin Ratios**

Compare two companies—Best Boys Company and its competitor, GameStar Corporation—based on the following ratios:

Ratio	Best Boys	GameStar
Debt-to-assets	0.42	0.21
Asset turnover ratio	2.42	2.10
Net profit margin	2.69%	4.35%

Required:

1. Which company appears to rely more on debt financing? Describe the ratio that you used to reach this decision, and explain what the ratio means.
2. Which company appears to use its assets more efficiently? Describe the ratio that you used to reach this decision, and explain what the ratio means.
3. Which company appears to better control its expenses? Describe the ratio that you used to reach this decision, and explain what the ratio means.

LO3, 6, 7 **CP5-3 Preparing and Interpreting IFRS Financial Statements**

M&H, an international retail clothing company headquartered in Sweden, began its 2011 fiscal year with assets totalling 41,734 (in millions of Swedish krona) but ended the year (on November 30, 2011) with 51,243 in total assets. Account balances on November 30, 2011, are listed below (in millions of Swedish krona).

Accounts Payable	3,658	Long-Term Liabilities	2,414
Accounts Receivable	3,197	Other Current Liabilities	4,534
Accrued Liabilities	3,687	Other Noncurrent Assets	1,775
Accumulated Depreciation	9,243	Prepaid Expenses	948
Buildings and Equipment	21,616	Profit for the Year (Net Income)	15,294
Contributed Capital	1,617	Retained Earnings, Dec. 1, 2010	20,039
Goodwill and Intangible Assets	1,656	Sales Revenues	192,573
Land	68	Shares-in-Trade (Inventory)	8,500
Liquid Funds (Cash)	22,726		

Required:

1. Prepare a statement of financial position at November 30, 2011, using Exhibit 5.12 as a guide.
   TIP: Not all of the accounts listed are reported on the statement of financial position.
   TIP: Total Assets equals $51,243.
2. Use an appropriate ratio to compute M&H's financing risk. Compare M&H's ratio to the 0.126 reported for Vulcan (a clothing company headquartered in Canada) on December 31, 2011. Which company appears more likely to pay its liabilities?
3. Use an appropriate ratio to compute the amount of profit M&H earns from each dollar of sales. Compare M&H's ratio to that of Vulcan, which earned 6.5 cents of profit for each dollar of sales in the year ended December 31, 2011.
4. Use an appropriate ratio to compute M&H's efficiency at using assets to generate sales. Compare M&H's ratio to the 1.58 reported for Vulcan for the year ended December 31, 2011.

GROUP A PROBLEMS

Practise and learn online with Connect.

PA5-1 Determining the Accounting Equation Effects of Transactions

LO3

Papa John's International began in the back of a tavern in Jeffersonville, Indiana, and has since become the third-largest pizza company in the United States. Listed here are transactions that typically occur each year (in millions). Complete the following table, indicating the sign (+ for increase, − for decrease, and NE for no effect) and amount of the effect of each transaction. Provide an account name for any revenue or expense transactions included in shareholders' equity. Consider each item independently.

a. Repaid bank loan payable of $7. (Interest was paid separately.)
b. Paid cash to purchase property and equipment costing $6.
c. Purchased additional property and equipment costing $2 by issuing a note payable.
d. Recorded franchise royalty revenues on account of $20.

Transaction	Assets	Liabilities	Shareholders' Equity
a			
Etc.			

PA5-2 Determining the Effects of Transactions on Debt-to-Assets, Asset Turnover, and Net Profit Margin Ratios

LO7

Using the transactions in PA5-1, complete the following table by indicating the sign of the effect (+ for increase, − for decrease, NE for no effect, and CD for cannot determine) of each transaction. Consider each item independently.

Transaction	Debt-to-Assets	Asset Turnover	Net Profit Margin
a			
Etc.			

Check Figure [Part (d)]: Asset Turnover—cannot determine

L07 **PA5-3 Interpreting Debt-to-Assets, Asset Turnover, and Net Profit Margin Ratios**

The following ratios for Kool's Corporation and its competitor Willant's, Inc., were obtained from independent sources. Compare the two companies based on the following ratios:

Ratio	Kool's	Willant's
Debt-to-assets	0.24	0.35
Asset turnover ratio	1.50	1.39
Net profit margin	5.4%	−3.4%

Required:

1. Which company appears to rely more on debt for financing? Describe the ratio that you used to reach this decision, and explain what the ratio means.
2. Which company appears to use its assets more efficiently? Describe the ratio that you used to reach this decision, and explain what the ratio means.
3. Which company appears to better control its expenses? Describe the ratio that you used to reach this decision, and explain what the ratio means.

L06, 7 **PA5-4 Computing and Interpreting Financial Ratios**

Key financial data for Columbia Company and Strauss Ltd. follow (amounts in millions).

	Columbia Company	Strauss Ltd.
Sales	$1,318	$4,303
Net Income	95	229
Total Assets, 2012	1,148	2,777
Total Assets, 2011	1,166	2,851

Required:

1. Using two ratios included in this chapter, compare their relative abilities to generate (a) sales from assets and (b) net income from sales.
2. Which company appears more successful on each of the measures?

L05, 6, 7 **PA5-5 Preparing and Interpreting IFRS Financial Statements**

Glücklich Golfspieler (GG) is a golf club company headquartered in Germany. The company began its 2011 fiscal year with assets totalling 10 million euro but ended the year (on December 31, 2012) with total assets of 13 million euro. Account balances on December 31, 2012, appear below (in thousands of euro).

Accounts Payable	1,000	Contributed Capital	400	Other Noncurrent Assets	400
Accounts Receivable	500	Goodwill and Intangible Assets	450	Prepaid Expenses	250
Accrued Liabilities	900	Inventory	2,500	Profit for the Year (Net Income)	4,000
Accumulated Depreciation	2,500	Land	100	Retained Earnings, Jan. 1, 2012	5,000
Buildings and Equipment	5,500	Notes Payable, due 2014	600	Sales Revenues	44,000
Cash	5,800	Other Long-Term Liabilities	1,100		

Required:

1. Prepare a statement of financial position at December 31, 2012, using Exhibit 5.12 as a guide.
2. Use an appropriate ratio to compute GG's financing risk. Compare GG's ratio to the 0.20 reported for one of its close competitors. Which company appears more likely to pay its liabilities?

Check Figure [Req. 3]:
2012 Net Profit
Margin = 9.1%

3. Use an appropriate ratio to compute the amount of profit GG earns from each euro of sales. Compare GG's ratio to that of its competitor, which had a ratio of 0.05. Which company is better able to control its expenses?
4. Use an appropriate ratio to compute GG's efficiency at using assets to generate sales. Compare GG's ratio to the 2.60 reported for its competitor. Which company is more efficient at using its assets to generate sales?

GROUP B PROBLEMS

PB5-1 Determining the Accounting Equation Effects of Transactions

LO3

Cineplex Entertainment

Cineplex Entertainment is the largest motion picture exhibitor in Canada. Complete the following table, indicating the sign (+ for increase, − for decrease, and NE for no effect) and amount of the effect of each hypothetical transaction (in millions). Provide an account name for any revenue or expense transactions included in shareholders' equity. Consider each item independently.

a. Paid cash to purchase property and equipment costing $30.
b. Declared and paid a cash dividend totalling $40.
c. Recorded amortization on property and equipment totalling $78.
d. Recorded cash admissions revenues of $450.

Check Figure [Part (a)]:
Liabilities and Shareholders' Equity−no effect

Transaction	Assets	Liabilities	Shareholders' Equity
a			
Etc.			

PB5-2 Determining the Effects of Transactions on Debt-to-Assets, Asset Turnover, and Net Profit Margin Ratios

LO7

Using the transactions in PB5-1, complete the following table by indicating the sign of the effect (+ for increase, − for decrease, NE for no effect, and CD for cannot determine) of each transaction. Consider each item independently.

Transaction	Debt-to-Assets	Asset Turnover	Net Profit Margin
a			
Etc.			

PB5-3 Interpreting Debt-to-Assets, Asset Turnover, and Net Profit Margin Ratios

LO7

YUM! Brands, Inc.

The following ratios for McDonald's Corporation and its competitor YUM! Brands, Inc., (the owner of KFC, Pizza Hut, and Taco Bell) were obtained from **reuters.com/finance**. Compare the two companies based on the following ratios:

Ratio	McDonald's	YUM!
Debt-to-Assets	0.43	0.99
Asset Turnover Ratio	0.81	1.64
Net Profit Margin	18.34%	8.6%

Required:

1. Which company appears to rely more on debt than shareholders' equity for financing? Describe the ratio that you used to reach this decision, and explain what the ratio means.
2. Which company appears to use its assets more efficiently? Describe the ratio that you used to reach this decision, and explain what the ratio means.
3. Which company appears to better control its expenses? Describe the ratio that you used to reach this decision, and explain what the ratio means.

PB5-4 Preparing and Interpreting IFRS Financial Statements

LO5, 6, 7

Latteria Limited (LL) is a dairy company headquartered in Italy. The company began its 2012 fiscal year with assets totalling 9 million euros but ended the year (on December 31, 2012) with 13 million euros of total assets. Account balances on December 31, 2012, appear below (in thousands of euros).

Accounts Payable	1,300	Cash	1,200	Prepaid Expenses	250
Accounts Receivable	500	Contributed Capital	400	Profit for the Year (Net Income)	2,200
Accrued Liabilities	600	Inventory	2,500	Retained Earnings, Jan. 1, 2012	6,800
Accumulated Depreciation	3,600	Land	5,550	Sales Revenues	22,000
Buildings and Equipment	6,600	Notes Payable, due 2014	1,700		

Required:

1. Prepare a statement of financial position at December 31, 2012, using Exhibit 5.12 as a guide.
2. Use an appropriate ratio to compute LL's financing risk. Compare LL's ratio to the 0.40 reported in a recent year for Sargossy (a dairy company in Canada). Which company appears more likely to pay its liabilities?
3. Use an appropriate ratio to compute the amount of profit LL earns from each euro of sales. Compare LL's ratio to Sargossy, which had a ratio of 0.06. Which company is better able to control its expenses?
4. Use an appropriate ratio to compute LL's efficiency at using assets to generate sales. Compare LL's ratio to the 1.94 reported for Sargossy. Which company is more efficient at using its assets to generate sales?

LO5, 6, 7

Carnival Cruise Lines

PB5-5 Preparing and Interpreting IFRS Financial Statements

Carnival Cruise Lines prides itself on delivering memorable vacations to its guests by offering a wide array of quality cruises. Assume the company began its 2012 fiscal year with assets totalling 33.4 million U.S. dollars but ended the year (on December 31, 2012) with 36.8 million U.S. dollars of total assets. Account balances on December 31, 2012, appear below (in thousands of U.S. dollars).

Accounts Payable	568	Cash	538	Prepaid Expenses	298
Accounts Receivable	362	Contributed Capital	5,803	Profit for the Year (Net Income)	2,252
Accrued Liabilities	3,449	Inventory	320	Retained Earnings, Jan. 1, 2012	13,980
Accumulated Depreciation	7,864	Other Noncurrent Assets	5,447	Sales Revenues	13,157
Property and Equipment	37,734	Notes Payable, due 2015	9,097	Other Long-Term Liabilities	736
Short-Term debt	950				

Required:

1. Prepare a statement of financial position at December 31, 2012, using Exhibit 5.12 as a guide.

Check Figure [Req. 2]:
2012 Debt-to-Assets
= 40.2%

2. Use an appropriate ratio to compute Carnival's financing risk. Compare Carnival's ratio to the hypothetical 0.60 industry standard. Would Carnival be more likely to pay its liabilities than the industry standard?
3. Use an appropriate ratio to compute the amount of profit Carnival earns from each U.S. dollar of sales. Compare Carnival's ratio to the industry standard, which had a hypothetical ratio of 0.10. Would Carnival be able to control its expenses better than others in its industry?
4. Use an appropriate ratio to compute Carnival's efficiency at using assets to generate sales. Compare Carnival's ratio to the hypothetical 0.34 reported for the industry standard. Is Carnival more efficient at using its assets to generate sales than others in its industry?

SKILLS DEVELOPMENT CASES

LO7

Rona Inc.

S5-1 Finding Financial Information

Refer to the financial statements of Rona Inc. in Appendix A at the back of this book or download the annual report from the *Cases* section of Connect.

Required:

1. Calculate the debt-to-assets ratio at December 27, 2009, and December 28, 2008. Based on these calculations, has Rona's financing become more or less risky over these two years?
2. Calculate the asset turnover ratio for the December 2009 and 2008 year-ends. Rona's total assets at the end of fiscal 2007 were $2,482,446 (thousand). Based on these calculations, has Rona used its assets more or less efficiently in the 2009 year-end than in the 2008 year-end?
3. Calculate the net profit margin ratio for 2008–2009 and 2007–2008. Based on these calculations, has Rona generated more or less profit per dollar of sales in 2008–2009 than in 2007–2008?

Comparing Financial Information

Refer to the financial statements of Rona Inc. in Appendix A and The Home Depot in Appendix B at the back of this book or download the annual reports from the *Cases* section of Connect.

Required:

1. Calculate the debt-to-assets ratio for The Home Depot at January 31, 2010. Based on this calculation, was The Home Depot's financing more or less risky than Rona's at fiscal year-end 2009?
2. Calculate the asset turnover ratio for The Home Depot for the year ended January 31, 2010. Based on this calculation, did The Home Depot use its assets more or less efficiently than Rona for fiscal year-end 2009?
3. Calculate the net profit margin ratio for The Home Depot for the year ended January 31, 2010. Based on this calculation, did The Home Depot generate more or less profit per dollar of sales than Rona for fiscal year-end 2009?

S5-3 Internet-Based Team Research: Examining an Annual Report

As a team, select an industry to analyze. Using your Web browser, each team member should access the annual report for one publicly traded company in the industry, with each member selecting a different company (see S1-3 in Chapter 1 for a description of possible resources for these tasks).

Required:

1. On an individual basis, each team member should write a short report that incorporates the following:
    a. Calculate the debt-to-assets ratio at the end of the current and prior years, and explain any change between the two years.
    b. Calculate the asset turnover ratio at the end of the current and prior years and explain any change between the two years. (To calculate average assets for the prior year, you will need the total assets number for the beginning of the prior year. If this isn't reported in the summarized financial data section in the current annual report, you will need to get it from the prior year's annual report.)
    c. Calculate the net profit margin ratio at the end of the current and prior years and explain any change between the two years.
2. Then, as a team, write a short report comparing and contrasting your companies using these attributes. Discuss any patterns across the companies that you observe as a team. Provide potential explanations for any differences discovered.

S5-4 Ethical Decision Making: A Real-Life Example

On February 18, 2000, the board of directors of Aurora Foods Inc.—the maker of Duncan Hines® and Mrs. Butterworth's® products—issued a press release announcing that a special committee had been formed to conduct an investigation into the company's accounting practices. During the financial statement audit for the year ended December 31, 1999, Aurora's auditors had discovered documents that raised questions about how the company accounted for marketing costs incurred to entice grocery stores to promote Aurora's products. The company's share price fell by 50 percent in the week following this announcement.

After nearly a year of investigation, Aurora filed revised quarterly reports with the SEC, showing that the company had not accrued adequately for liabilities and expenses that had been incurred during the third and fourth quarters of 1998 and during the first three quarters of 1999. Key financial figures for these quarters as initially reported and as later restated are shown below.

(in millions of U.S. dollars)	1998 Q3 (September 30)		1998 Q4 (December 31)		1999 Q1 (March 31)		1999 Q2 (June 30)		1999 Q3 (September 30)	
	Initial Report	Restated Report	Initial Report	Restated Report	Initial Report	Restated Report	Initial Report	Restated Report	Initial Report	Restated Report
Assets	$1,457	$1,455	$1,434	$1,448	$1,474	$1,463	$1,558	$1,521	$1,614	$1,553
Liabilities	869	879	830	868	862	882	937	944	983	972
Revenues	220	219	280	277	261	254	222	214	238	231
Net income (loss)	1	(12)	16	5	8	0	8	(4)	11	4

The SEC also investigated and filed a legal claim alleging that Aurora's 36-year-old chief financial officer (CFO) had violated federal securities laws by instructing accounting staff to make false journal entries and prepare two sets of records—one for the company's internal use and another to be provided to the auditors. The SEC alleged that her actions allowed Aurora to meet the net income targets set by Wall Street analysts and the expectations of Aurora investors and to obtain loans from Chase Manhattan Bank and other lenders. The CFO pled guilty to the charges, was sentenced to 57 months in prison, was barred for life from ever serving as an executive of a public company, and had to return to the company the shares and bonuses that had been awarded to her on the basis of Aurora's false and substantially inflated financial results.

Epilogue: On December 8, 2003, Aurora Foods filed for bankruptcy protection after violating several of its lenders' loan covenants. On March 19, 2004, Aurora emerged from bankruptcy and has since merged with Pinnacle Foods, the maker of Vlasic pickles and Hungry-Man frozen dinners.

Required:

1. Using the initially reported numbers, calculate the debt-to-assets, asset turnover, and net profit margin ratios at the end of each quarter. (Note that the asset turnover ratio will be substantially less than the examples shown earlier in this chapter because only three months of revenues are used. Do not attempt to convert them to annual amounts.)

2. Using the restated numbers, calculate the debt-to-assets, asset turnover, and net profit margin ratios at the end of each quarter.

3. On an overall basis, did the initially reported numbers suggest more or less financing risk than the restated numbers? Of the financial statement users mentioned earlier in this chapter in Exhibit 5.1, which would be most influenced by this impact on the debt-to-assets ratio?

4. On an overall basis, did the initially reported numbers or the restated numbers present Aurora's efficiency in using assets to generate sales in a better light? Of the financial statement users mentioned earlier in this chapter in Exhibit 5.1, which would be most influenced by this impact on the asset turnover ratio?

5. On an overall basis, did the initially reported numbers or the restated numbers present Aurora's profitability in a better light? Of the financial statement users mentioned earlier in this chapter in Exhibit 5.1, which would be most influenced by this impact on the net profit margin ratio?

6. What important role(s) did Aurora's auditors play in this case?

7. Based on specific information in the case, identify the incentives or goals that might have led the CFO to misreport Aurora's financial results. Looking back at the consequences of her dishonest actions, did she fulfill those goals in the short run and long run?

LO1, 2, 7   S5-5 Ethical Decision Making: A Mini-Case

Assume you've been hired to replace an accounting clerk for a small public company. After your second month on the job, the chief financial officer approached you directly with a "special project." The company had just finished installing a new production line earlier in the year, and the CFO wanted you to go through all of the company's expense accounts with the goal of finding any costs that might be related to the machinery's installation or to "tinkering with it" to get the line working just right. He said that the previous accounting clerk, whom you had replaced, didn't understand that these costs should have been recorded as part of the production line (an asset) rather than as expenses of the period. The CFO indicated that there was some urgency, as the company had to finalize its quarterly financial statements so that they could be filed with the SEC. Also, the company was close to violating its loan covenants and it needed a few extra dollars of profit this quarter to ensure that the bank didn't demand immediate repayment of the loan. As you thought about this situation, you tried to remember what Chapter 2 in your accounting textbook said regarding the key characteristics of assets.

Required:

1. Which of the three ratios discussed in this chapter (debt-to-assets, asset turnover, and net profit margin) are affected by the decision to record costs as an asset rather than an expense? Indicate whether each ratio will be higher or lower if costs are recorded as an asset rather than an expense.

2. Is there anything in the case that makes you uncomfortable with the work that you've been asked to do?

3. What should you do?

S5-6 Critical Thinking: Analyzing Income Statement-Based Executive Bonuses

LO2, 7

Callaway Golf believes in tying executives' compensation to the company's performance as measured by accounting numbers. Suppose, in a recent year, Callaway had agreed to pay its executive officers bonuses if (a) asset turnover meets or exceeds 0.8, and (b) net profit margin meets or exceeds 5.0 percent. Their bonuses will be even larger if asset turnover meets (or exceeds) 1.6 and net profit margin meets (or exceeds) 7.0 percent. Total assets were $855 (million) and $838 (million) at December 31, 2012 and 2011, respectively. For the year ended December 31, 2012, total sales revenue was $1,117 (million) and net income was $66 (million).

Required:

1. Use the preceding information to determine whether Callaway executives met the two bonus targets in 2012.
2. Explain why the bonus arrangement might be based on both asset turnover and net profit margin ratios, rather than just one of these two ratios.

S5-7 Computing, Charting, and Interpreting Time-Series and Cross-Sectional Analyses

LO6, 7

Hershey Foods Corporation

Assume that *Candy Industry* magazine has contracted you to write an article discussing the financial status of Hershey Foods Corporation over the last few years. The editor suggests that your article should also compare Hershey's recent financial performance to competitors like Tootsie Roll Industries and Rocky Mountain Chocolate Factory. Assume that the following information was in the 2012 annual reports of the three companies.

(in millions of U.S. dollars)	Hershey Foods Corporation			Tootsie Roll Industries	Rocky Mountain Chocolate Factory
	2010	2011	2012	2012	2012
Total Liabilities	$3,474	$3,626	$3,285	$177	$ 4
Total Assets	4,157	4,247	3,634	812	16
Sales Revenues	4,944	4,947	5,133	496	32
Net Income	559	214	311	39	5

Required:

Enter the above information into a spreadsheet and perform the following analyses:
1. *Time-series analysis:* Demonstrate the changes in Hershey's size over the three years by charting its total liabilities, total assets, sales revenues, and net income.
2. *Cross-sectional analysis:* Demonstrate the size of Hershey relative to Tootsie Roll and Rocky Mountain Chocolate Factory by charting the three companies' total liabilities, total assets, sales revenues, and net income for 2012.
3. *Ratio analysis:* Compare the performance of Hershey relative to Tootsie Roll and Rocky Mountain Chocolate Factory by computing the debt-to-assets and net profit margin ratios for 2012.

CONTINUING CASE

Practise and learn online with Connect.

CC5 Evaluating the Impact of Typical Transactions

LO7

After finishing her first year of operations, Nicole used the debt-to-assets, asset turnover, and net profit margin ratios to determine how effective she was in running the business. Listed here are a few company transactions from the past quarter that may have influenced these ratios.
a. Acquired, but haven't yet paid for, equipment costing $320.
b. Recorded spa treatment revenues of $1,500 on account.
c. Incurred advertising expense of $40, paid in cash.

d. Accrued $750 for utility bills.

e. Received $50,000 cash from an investor in exchange for company shares.

f. Received $2,500 cash by signing a note payable.

g. Recorded $1,800 in amortization expense.

h. Customers used $200 of gift certificates to pay for spa services.

Required:

1. Complete the following table, indicating the effects (account, amount, and direction) of each transaction. Use + for increase, − for decrease, and NE for no effect.

Transaction	Assets	Liabilities	Shareholders' Equity
a			
Etc.			

2. Complete the following table, indicating the sign (+ for increase, − for decrease, and NE for no effect) for each transaction. Assume that, prior to recording items (a)–(h), Nicole's Getaway Spa had more assets than liabilities, more revenues than net income, and more revenues than average assets.

Transaction	Debt-to-Assets	Asset Turnover	Net Profit Margin
a			
Etc.			

Endnotes

1. David T. Wolfe and Dana R. Hermanson, "The Fraud Diamond: Considering the Four Elements of Fraud," *The CPA Journal*, December 2004, pp. 38–41.

2. Any differences in accounting methods, which are discussed in later chapters, can limit the ability to draw conclusions from ratio analysis. One of the goals in moving to IFRS is to eliminate cross-country differences and thereby improve comparability.

Practise and learn online with Connect.

Internal Control and Financial Reporting for Cash and Merchandise Sales

YOUR LEARNING OBJECTIVES

Understand the business

LO1 Distinguish among service, merchandising, and manufacturing operations.

LO2 Explain common principles and limitations of internal control.

Study the accounting methods

LO3 Apply internal control principles to cash receipts and payments.

LO4 Perform the key control of reconciling cash to bank statements.

LO5 Explain the use of a perpetual inventory system as a control.

LO6 Analyze sales transactions under a perpetual inventory system.

Evaluate the results

LO7 Analyze a merchandiser's multistep income statement.

Review the chapter

Chapter Summary, page 260
Additional resources on Connect

FOCUS COMPANY:
Walmart
www.walmart.com

Seventeen years after the company was founded, Walmart rang up yearly sales of $1 billion. Fourteen years later, it sold that much in a week. Thanks to the millions of Canadians who shop at Walmart, its sales now average over $1 billion a day. And that's not all. Walmart has been able to earn sizable profits, even during difficult economic times.

One secret to its success is the state-of-the-art accounting system that controls Walmart's merchandise sales and cash collections. In this chapter, you will learn about this kind of system and the other aspects of merchandising companies that make them unique and interesting. You'll also learn how to analyze a merchandiser's financial statements to figure out the amount of markup that it includes in the prices you pay. You might be surprised by how much you're contributing to Walmart's profits.

THAT WAS
THEN

Earlier chapters have focused on companies whose operating activities relate to providing services to customers, rather than selling goods.

THIS IS
NOW

This chapter focuses on companies that sell merchandise to customers, and the way they control and report their operating results.

ORGANIZATION OF THE CHAPTER

Understand the business	**S**tudy the accounting methods	**E**valuate the results	**R**eview the chapter
• Operating cycles • Internal control	• Controlling and reporting cash • Controlling and reporting merchandise sales	• Gross profit analysis	• Demonstration Cases • Chapter Summary • Key Terms • Homework Helper • Practice Material

Understand the Business

OPERATING CYCLES

For any company to be successful, it must be able to efficiently circle through its operating cycle. The operating cycle is a series of activities that a company undertakes to generate sales and, ultimately, cash. Exhibit 6.1 contrasts the operating cycles of three types of businesses: (1) service companies, (2) merchandising companies, and (3) manufacturing companies.

Service companies such as WorldGym follow a simple operating cycle: sell services to customers, collect cash from them, and use that money to pay for operating expenses. Merchandising companies differ in that their cycle begins with buying products. These products, called *inventory*, are sold to customers, which leads to collecting cash that can be used to pay for operating expenses and buy more inventory. Merchandising companies such as Walmart and Costco are called retailers when they sell directly to individual consumers and wholesalers when they sell their inventory to retail businesses for resale to consumers. This chapter applies equally to both retail and wholesale merchandisers. This chapter does not include manufacturing companies such as Mattel and Goodyear because they make their own products from raw materials rather than acquire them in a ready-to-sell format. The manufacturing process involves complexities that require much more discussion than is possible in this introductory course. Consequently, accounting for manufacturing companies is discussed in detail in managerial and cost accounting courses.

A goal of most merchandising companies is to generate more and more cash by reducing the time they take to circle through their operating cycles. To promote this efficiency, companies establish and follow specific procedures and policies that describe how the business is to be run. These procedures and policies are called internal controls. In your personal life, internal controls include basic precautions such as locking your car door and checking the accuracy of your bank statement. As you will learn in the following section, similar controls apply to all government, not-for-profit, and business organizations, both large and small. When internal controls operate effectively, they contribute not only to improving operating efficiency, but also to reducing waste, minimizing unintentional errors, and deterring fraud. It's little wonder, then, that Walmart has established strong internal controls at each of its 8,600 store locations worldwide, to ensure the company's transactions are processed with efficiency, consistency, accuracy, and honesty.

Service Companies

Merchandising Companies

Manufacturing Companies

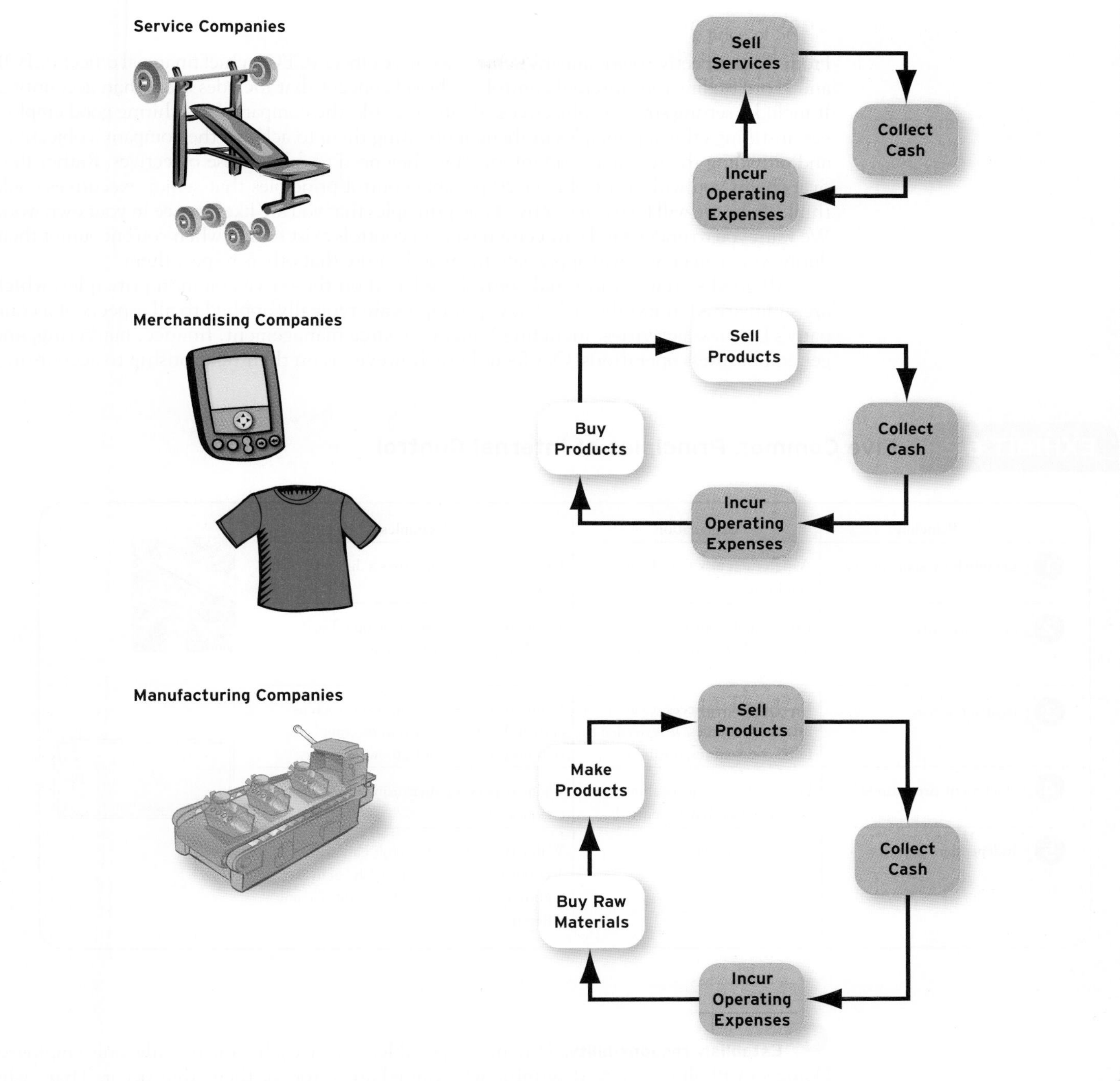

INTERNAL CONTROL

Internal control has always been important to all types and sizes of organizations. However, with the business failures and accounting scandals involving Enron and other companies in the early 2000s, internal control has gained a lot more attention. As you may recall from Chapter 1, C-SOX, or Bill 198, requires management of public companies to report on the effectiveness of internal controls over the financial reporting within their company. These rules have led companies to strengthen their internal controls and better inform financial

Learning Objective 2

Explain common principles and limitations of internal control.

statement users about how effective their accounting systems are in producing accurate financial statements. **Effective internal controls play an essential role in creating an ethical business environment and in improving financial performance.**[1]

Common Control Principles

From the perspective of a company's chief executive officer (CEO), chief financial officer (CFO), and board of directors, internal control is a broad concept that includes more than accounting. It includes setting strategic objectives, identifying risks the company faces, hiring good employees, instilling ethical principles in them, motivating them to achieve the company's objectives, and providing the resources and information they need to fulfill those objectives. Rather than overwhelm you with a list of over 20 possible control principles that senior executives could think about, we will focus on just five basic principles that you are likely to see in your own work. We want you to understand why certain types of controls exist so that when you encounter them during your career, you will appreciate them and ensure that others respect them.

All good systems of internal control are based on these five common principles, which are summarized in Exhibit 6.2. These principles are typically applied to all aspects of a company's business activities, including human resource management, finance, marketing, and general business operations. Our focus here, however, is on their relationship to accounting.

EXHIBIT 6.2	Five Common Principles of Internal Control

Principle	Explanation	Examples	
1 Establish raesponsibility	Assign each task to only one employee.	Each Walmart cashier uses a different cash drawer.	
2 Segregate duties	Do not make one employee responsible for all parts of a process.	Walmart cashiers, who ring up sales, do not also approve price changes.	
3 Restrict access	Do not provide access to assets or information unless it is needed to fulfill assigned responsibilities.	Walmart secures valuable assets such as cash and restricts access to its computer systems (via passwords, firewalls).	
4 Document procedures	Prepare documents to show activities that have occurred.	Walmart pays suppliers using prenumbered cheques.	
5 Independently verify	Check others' work.	Walmart compares the cash balances in its accounting records to the cash balances reported by its bank, and accounts for any differences.	

1 **Establish responsibility.** Whenever possible, assign each task to only one employee. Doing so will allow you to determine who caused any errors or thefts that occur. That's why Walmart assigns a separate cash register drawer to each employee at the beginning of a shift. If two cashiers were to use the same drawer, it would be impossible to know which cashier caused the drawer to be short on cash. With only one person responsible for adding and removing money from the drawer, there's no doubt about who is responsible for a cash shortage.

2 **Segregate duties.** **Segregation of duties** involves assigning responsibilities so that one employee can't make a mistake or commit a dishonest act without someone else knowing it. That's why cashiers at Walmart need a manager to approve price changes at the checkout. Without this control, cashiers could lower the sales price for a friend. Segregation of duties is most effective when a company assigns responsibilities for related activities to two or more people and assigns responsibilities for record-keeping to people who do not handle the assets

YOU SHOULD KNOW

Segregation of duties: An internal control designed into the accounting system to prevent an employee from making a mistake or committing a dishonest act as part of one assigned duty, and then also covering it up through another assigned duty.

that they are accounting for. One employee should not initiate, approve, record, and have access to the items involved in the same transaction.

③ Restrict access. Some controls involve rather obvious steps such as physically locking up valuable assets and electronically securing access to other assets and information. Walmart restricts access to cheque-signing equipment, requires a password to open cash registers, and protects computer systems with firewalls. The company provides access to important assets and valuable information on an as-needed basis. If employees do not need assets or information to fulfill their assigned responsibilities, they are denied access.

④ Document procedures. Digital and paper documents are such common features of business that you may not realize they represent an internal control. By documenting each business activity, a company creates a record of whether goods were shipped, customers were billed, cash was received, and so on. Without these documents, a company wouldn't know what transactions have been or need to be entered into the accounting system. To enhance this control, most companies assign sequential numbers to their documents and then check at the end of every accounting period that each document number corresponds to one and only one accounting entry. Walmart's computer system automatically assigns sequential numbers to cash sales so that the accounting staff can ensure that every sale has been recorded.

⑤ Independently verify. A business can perform independent verification in various ways. The most obvious is to hire someone (an auditor) to check that the work done by others within the company is appropriate and supported by documentation. Independent verification also can be made part of a person's job. For example, before Walmart issues a cheque to pay the bill for a truckload of merchandise, a clerk first verifies that the bill relates to goods actually received and is calculated correctly. A third form of independent verification involves comparing the company's accounting information to information kept by an independent third party. For example, the company may compare internal cash records to a statement of account issued by the bank. The next section of this chapter demonstrates this procedure, called a *bank reconciliation*.

Control Limitations

Internal controls can never completely prevent and detect errors and fraud for two reasons. First, an organization will implement internal controls only to the extent that the benefits of the controls exceed their costs. Walmart could nearly eliminate shoplifting by body searching every customer who leaves the store, but such an irritating policy would soon drive customers away. The cost of the lost sales would far exceed the benefits of reduced shoplifting. For smaller companies, the cost of hiring additional employees to fully segregate duties exceeds the benefits. In these cases, other controls such as independent verification by top management must compensate for the lack of segregation of duties. A second limitation is that internal controls can fail as a result of human error or fraud. People do make simple mistakes in performing control procedures, especially if they are tired, careless, or confused. Criminally minded employees have been known to override (disarm) internal controls or collude (work together) to get around them.

SPOTLIGHT ON Controls

Is That a Control, Too?

The five principles covered in this section do not represent all possible forms of internal control. Many other policies and procedures exist, some of which contribute in subtle ways to internal control. For example, most businesses establish a **mandatory vacation** policy for employees who handle cash because it is difficult for them to cover prior thefts while they are away from the business. Another simple control is an **anonymous hotline** that allows anyone to tip off independent auditors about suspected fraud. The Association of Certified Fraud Examiners claims that more than 46 percent of workplace fraud cases are identified in this way. A final example of a control that can limit losses from theft is **bonding** employees, which involves obtaining an insurance policy that partially reimburses the organization for losses caused by employee fraud.

CONTROLLING AND REPORTING CASH

Learning Objective 3

Apply internal control principles to cash receipts and payments.

Internal control of cash is important to any organization for two main reasons. First, because the volume of transactions affecting cash is enormous, any errors that are made in handling cash can quickly add up. By our estimates, Walmart received about $405 billion from customers in 2010 and paid $382 billion for inventory, wages, and other operating expenses. Second, because cash is valuable, portable, and "owned" by the person who possesses it, thieves often target it. The Association of Certified Fraud Examiners reports that 86 percent of all known asset thefts involve cash. The following discussion describes common applications of internal control principles to cash receipts and cash payments.

Cash Receipts

Businesses can receive cash in two different ways. They can receive it in person at the time of a sale, or they can receive it from a remote source as payment on an account. Most businesses, including Walmart, receive cash either physically, in the form of dollars, coins, and cheques payable to the business, or through electronic transactions involving credit cards, debit cards, and electronic funds transfers. Generally speaking, Walmart applies similar controls to cash received in both these forms, so in the following discussion, we do not distinguish between them. Regardless of the way or form in which a business receives cash, the primary internal control goal for cash receipts is to ensure that the business receives the appropriate amount of cash and safely deposits it in the bank.

Cash Received in Person   To properly segregate duties involving cash receipts, specific responsibilities are established and usually assigned to three different employee groups, as shown in the left side of Exhibit 6.3. First, cashiers are responsible for collecting cash and issuing a receipt at the point of sale. Second, a supervisor is responsible for taking custody of the cash at the end of each cashier's shift and depositing it in the bank. Third, members of the accounting staff are responsible for ensuring that the receipts from cash sales are properly recorded in the accounting system. If this segregation of duties did not exist, employees could steal the cash and cover up the theft by changing the accounting records. Segregating the duties ensures that those who handle the cash (the cashiers and supervisor) do not have access to those who record it (the accounting staff).

The cash register shown in Exhibit 6.3 performs three important functions: (1) it restricts access to cash, (2) it documents the amount charged for each item sold, and (3) it summarizes the total cash sales. By restricting access, the cash register reduces the risk of cash being lost or stolen. In documenting each item sold (both on screen and on a paper receipt), the cash register reduces errors by allowing customers to dispute overcharges should they occur. By summarizing the total cash sales, the cash register provides an independent record of the amount of cash the cashier should have collected and passed on for deposit at the bank. This record is securely forwarded to the accounting department (see the black arrow in Exhibit 6.3). The cashier also uses it to complete a cash count sheet at the end of each shift (see the red arrow in Exhibit 6.3).

The cash count sheet is used to determine the amount of cash available for deposit at the bank. The cash count sheet documents the amount of cash the cashier received and determines any cash shortage or overage that occurred during the shift. The supervisor independently verifies each cashier's count sheet and prepares a daily cash receipts summary that summarizes all cashiers' count sheets and sends one copy to the accounting department (see the blue arrow in Exhibit 6.3). The supervisor is also responsible for placing the cash in a locked safe until the end of the day, at which time it is taken to the bank for deposit. At that time, a deposit slip listing the amounts included in the deposit is prepared and presented to the bank for a teller to verify. After verifying and receiving the funds, the bank teller stamps the deposit slip, which is then forwarded to the company's accounting department. The green arrows in Exhibit 6.3 indicate this process.

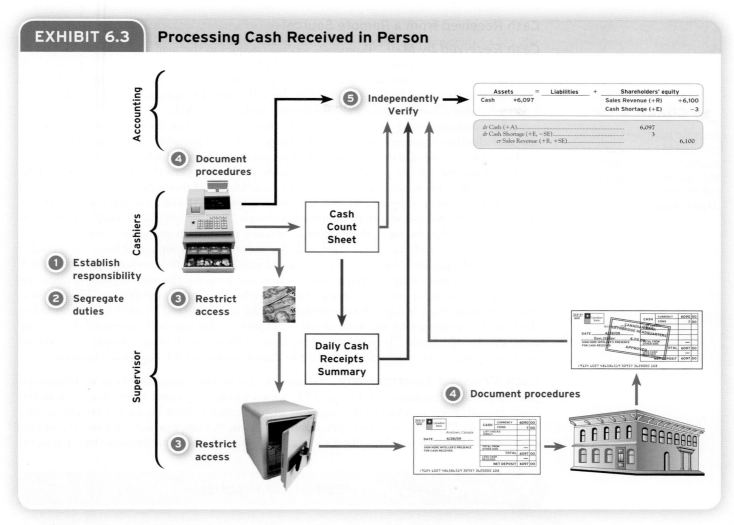

EXHIBIT 6.3 Processing Cash Received in Person

The accounting department compares the record of cash sales maintained by the cash register with the count sheet prepared by the cashier, the daily cash receipts summary prepared by the supervisor, and the stamped bank deposit slip returned by the bank (see Exhibit 6.3). This comparison provides independent verification that the amount of cash rung up at the time of sale was deposited into the bank account. Based on this information, a journal entry is prepared to record Sales Revenue at the amount rung up by the cash register and Cash at the amount deposited in the bank. Any difference between the two amounts is recorded in a Cash Shortage (or Overage) account, which is reported on the income statement as a miscellaneous expense (or revenue). For example, if cashiers rang up sales totalling $6,100 but had only $6,097 to deposit, the following financial statement effects would be recorded with the journal entry that follows.

① Analyze

Assets		=	Liabilities	+	Shareholders' Equity	
Cash	+ 6,097				Sales Revenue (+R)	+6,100
					Cash Shortage (+E)	−3

② Record

dr Cash (+A)	6,097	
dr Cash Shortage (+E, −SE)	3	
cr Sales Revenue (+R, +SE)		6,100

Cash Received from a Remote Source

Cash Received by Mail   Businesses receive cheques in the mail when customers pay on account. Because this cash is not received in the form of currency and coins, a cashier is not needed to enter these amounts into a cash register. Instead, the clerk who opens the mail performs this function. In fact, to visualize the following description, you need only glance back at Exhibit 6.3 and replace the cash register with a mail clerk.

Like a cash register, the mail clerk lists all amounts received on the cash receipt list, which also includes the customers' names and the purpose of each payment. The customer typically explains the purpose of the payment using a remittance advice, which the customer includes with the payment. Ideally, someone supervises the clerk who opens the mail to ensure that he or she takes no cash receipts for personal use. As evidence of this supervision, both the mail clerk and the supervisor sign the completed cash receipts list. To ensure that no one diverts the cheques for personal use, the clerk stamps each cheque "For Deposit Only," which instructs the bank to deposit the cheque in the company's account rather than exchange it for cash.

After these steps have been completed, the cash received is separated from the record of cash received, and each follows a separate route similar to the routes shown in Exhibit 6.3. Cheques and money orders are given to the person who prepares the bank deposit, whereas the cash receipts list and remittance advices are sent to the accounting department. The accounting department then independently verifies that all cash received by mail was deposited in the bank by ensuring that the total on the cash receipts list equals the stamped deposit slip received from the bank. The accounting department then uses the cash receipts list to record the journal entries that debit Cash and credit Accounts Receivable from each customer.

Cash Received Electronically   Businesses also receive payments from customers via electronic funds transfer (EFT). An EFT occurs when a customer electronically transfers funds from its bank account to the company's bank account. Most businesses encourage customers to use EFTs because they speed up collections. A company may not receive mailed payments for five to seven days, but it receives EFTs immediately. And because these payments

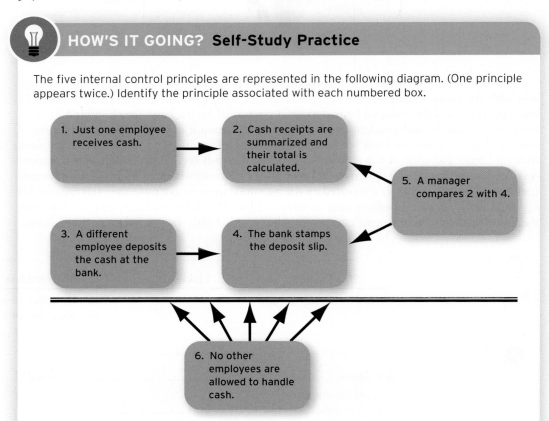

HOW'S IT GOING? Self-Study Practice

The five internal control principles are represented in the following diagram. (One principle appears twice.) Identify the principle associated with each numbered box.

1. Just one employee receives cash.

2. Cash receipts are summarized and their total is calculated.

3. A different employee deposits the cash at the bank.

4. The bank stamps the deposit slip.

5. A manager compares 2 with 4.

6. No other employees are allowed to handle cash.

After you have finished, check your answers with the solution in the margin.

Solution to Self-Study Practice
1. Establish responsibility
2. Document procedures
3. Segregate duties
4. Document procedures
5. Independently verify
6. Restrict access

are deposited directly into the company's bank account, EFTs eliminate the need for some internal controls. To process an EFT, the accounting department merely records journal entries to debit Cash and credit each customer's account receivable.

Cash Payments

Companies rarely use paper money and coins to pay for purchases. Instead, most cash payments involve (1) writing a cheque to a supplier or (2) paying employees via EFT. The primary goal of internal controls for cash payments is to ensure that the business pays only for properly authorized transactions.

Cash Paid by Cheque for Purchases on Account

Most businesses purchase goods and services on account and pay for them later by cheque. Purchases and payments cause increases and decreases in Accounts Payable, so they are closely controlled for financial reporting reasons. Control over purchases and payments is also important to avoid inefficiency and fraud. Because companies incur substantial internal costs to process each transaction with a supplier, controls that promote efficiency can significantly improve a company's profits. Companies can also avoid or reduce losses due to fraud by having strong internal controls. A 2008 report by the Association of Certified Fraud Examiners estimated that most fraud losses involved falsified purchases (24 percent of cases) or illegitimate payments (15 percent of cases).

Most companies rely on a voucher system to control these transactions. A **voucher system** is a process for approving and documenting all purchases and payments made on account. The voucher includes the documents prepared at each step in the system. See Exhibit 6.4 for the typical steps involved in obtaining goods or services from a supplier and the documentation prepared at each step. Exhibit 6.4 also gives some examples of the related cash controls and applicable control principles. Study this exhibit in detail, noticing how at each step, employee responsibilities are limited to specific tasks that occur only after obtaining and documenting proper authorization in the prior step. The purchasing, receiving, and bill payment duties are segregated to ensure that the company obtains and pays only for the goods or services that have been properly authorized.

EXHIBIT 6.4	Steps, Documentation, and Controls in a Voucher System		

Steps	Documentation	Sample Control(s)	Control Principle
1. Request that goods or services be ordered.	Purchase requisition	Ensure that the request is made by someone who is approved to order goods or services of the type and amount requested.	**1** Establish responsibility.
2. Order goods or services.	Purchase order	Place the order only with approved suppliers at approved prices.	**3** Restrict access.
3. Receive goods or services.	Receiving report	Record goods received.	**4** Document procedures.
		Notify the accounting department so that the purchase and liability can be recorded.	**2** Segregate duties.
4. Obtain bill for goods or services.	Supplier invoice	Ensure that the supplier charges only for items received at approved prices.	**5** Independently verify.
5. Write cheque to pay the bill.	Company cheque	Use prenumbered cheque and account for its sequence. Missing cheques may signal theft.	**4** Document procedures.
		Make payments only when a purchase is supported by complete voucher documentation.	**5** Independently verify.
		Mark the voucher "paid" after each cheque is written to avoid duplicating the payment.	**4** Document procedures.
		Notify the accounting department of the payment so that it can be recorded.	**2** Segregate duties.

Cash Paid to Employees via Electronic Funds Transfer   Most companies pay cash to their employees through EFTs, which are known by employees as **direct deposits**. The company initiates the EFT when it instructs its bank to transfer the net pay due to each employee directly from the company's bank account to each employee's chequing account. This system is convenient and efficient for the employer because it eliminates the tasks of physically writing and distributing the cheques and for the employee who has access to the funds without having to deposit a cheque. One risk, however, is that the bank might accidentally overpay or underpay an employee by transfering the wrong amount of money out of the company's bank account.

To avoid this risk, many companies use an imprest system for paying employees. An **imprest system** restricts the total amount paid to others by limiting the amount of money available to be transferred. Using an imprest payroll system, the company instructs the bank to transfer the total net pay of all employees for the pay period out of the company's general bank account and into a special payroll account established for that purpose. Then the bank transfers the individual amounts from the payroll account to the employees' chequing accounts. If the transfers occur without error, the special payroll account equals zero after all employees have been paid. If the account is overdrawn or a balance remains, the company knows that an error has occurred.

An imprest payroll system is one example of how banking procedures can help a company control its cash. Other basic banking procedures contribute to a company's internal control, as discussed in the next section.

Bank Procedures and Reconciliation

Banks provide important services to individuals and businesses. They accept deposits, process payments to others, and provide statements that account for these and other transactions. Their services help businesses to control cash in several ways:

1. **Restricting access.** Because banks provide a secure place to deposit cash, businesses need to keep only a limited amount of cash on hand, which reduces the risk that it will be stolen or misplaced.

2. **Documenting procedures.** By processing payments made by cheque or EFT, banks facilitate and document business transactions.

3. **Independently verifying.** Company accountants can use the statement of account prepared by the bank to double-check the accuracy of the cash records. By comparing these two sets of records and investigating any differences, they can verify that the company's records are accurate or identify necessary adjustments.

The process of comparing two sets of records is called *reconciling*. Thus, the internal accounting report that compares the company's cash records with the bank's is a **bank reconciliation**. A bank reconciliation is a key internal control because it provides independent verification of all cash transactions that the bank has processed for the company. This procedure is done monthly, ideally by a company employee whose duties are segregated from recording and handling cash. You should prepare a bank reconciliation for your personal accounts, too, every month. To prepare a bank reconciliation, you must first understand the items on a bank statement.

Bank Statement   Large businesses such as Walmart can have many bank accounts. For each account that a business opens, the bank generates a monthly statement that it either mails to the business or makes available online. The format varies from bank to bank, but the statement in Exhibit 6.5 is typical. This statement, prepared by Anysavings Bank for one of the accounts opened by Wonderful Merchandise and Things (WMT), provides an overall summary of the activity in the account (labelled ① in Exhibit 6.5). The summary is followed by a list of specific transactions posted to the account (labelled ② through ④) and a running balance in the account (labelled ⑤). In the following section, we explain the transactions that caused changes in the account's balance.

Cheques Cleared   After a cheque is written, the payee (to whom the cheque is written) usually presents the cheque to a financial institution for deposit or cash. That financial

YOU SHOULD KNOW

Imprest system: A process that controls the amount paid to others by limiting the total amount of money available for making payments to others.

Learning Objective 4

Perform the key control of reconciling cash to bank statements.

YOU SHOULD KNOW

Bank reconciliation: An internal report prepared to verify the accuracy of both the bank statement and the cash accounts of a business or individual.

institution contacts the cheque writer's bank, which in turn withdraws the amount of the cheque from the cheque writer's account and reports it as a deduction on the bank statement. The cheque is then said to have cleared the bank.

Cheques are listed on the bank statement in the order in which they clear the bank. Look closely at the "Description" column in Exhibit 6.5 and you will see that four cheques cleared the bank in June. Because WMT's cheques are used in their prenumbered order, the bank statement provides a hint that Cheque 103 did not clear the bank this month. (This fact will be important later when we prepare the bank reconciliation.)

Deposits Made Deposits are listed on the bank statement in the order in which the bank processes them. If you make a deposit after the bank closes (using an ATM or a night deposit chute), it will not appear on the bank statement until the bank processes it the following business day. Knowing this detail will help you to prepare the bank reconciliation.

Other Transactions The balance in a bank account can change for a variety of reasons other than cheques and deposits. For example, the account balance increases when the account earns interest and when funds are transferred into the account electronically. The account balance decreases when the bank charges a service fee or transfers funds out of the account electronically.

To understand how these items are reported on a bank statement, it is important to realize that the bank statement is presented from the bank's point of view. The amounts in a company's bank account are liabilities to the bank because they will eventually be used by or returned to the company. As with all liabilities, increases are reported as credits on the bank statement. Amounts that are removed from a bank account reduce the bank's liability, so they are reported as debits on the bank statement. Banks typically explain the reasons for these increases (credits) and decreases (debits) with symbols or in a short memo, appropriately called a *credit memo* or *debit memo*.

Need for Reconciliation A bank reconciliation involves comparing the company's records to the bank's statement of account to determine whether they agree. The company's records can differ from the bank's records for two basic reasons: (1) the company has recorded some items

COACH'S TIP

Bank statements often refer to cheques as *debits* and deposits as *credits*. This apparent reversal of debit and credit rules occurs because the bank reports from its perspective, not yours. To the bank, your account is a liability that decreases when you take money out (debit the liability) and increases when you deposit money (credit the liability).

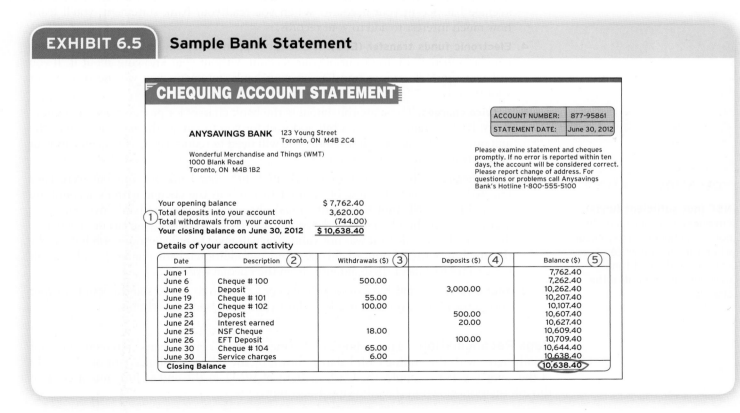

| EXHIBIT 6.5 | **Sample Bank Statement** |

CHEQUING ACCOUNT STATEMENT

| ACCOUNT NUMBER: | 877-95861 |
| STATEMENT DATE: | June 30, 2012 |

ANYSAVINGS BANK 123 Young Street
Toronto, ON M4B 2C4

Wonderful Merchandise and Things (WMT)
1000 Blank Road
Toronto, ON M4B 1B2

Please examine statement and cheques promptly. If no error is reported within ten days, the account will be considered correct. Please report change of address. For questions or problems call Anysavings Bank's Hotline 1-800-555-5100

Your opening balance	$ 7,762.40
Total deposits into your account	3,620.00
Total withdrawals from your account	(744.00)
Your closing balance on June 30, 2012	**$ 10,638.40**

(1)

Details of your account activity

Date	Description (2)	Withdrawals ($) (3)	Deposits ($) (4)	Balance ($) (5)
June 1				7,762.40
June 6	Cheque # 100	500.00		7,262.40
June 6	Deposit		3,000.00	10,262.40
June 19	Cheque # 101	55.00		10,207.40
June 23	Cheque # 102	100.00		10,107.40
June 23	Deposit		500.00	10,607.40
June 24	Interest earned		20.00	10,627.40
June 25	NSF Cheque	18.00		10,609.40
June 26	EFT Deposit		100.00	10,709.40
June 30	Cheque # 104	65.00		10,644.40
June 30	Service charges	6.00		10,638.40
Closing Balance				**10,638.40**

that the bank doesn't know about at the time it prepares the statement of account or (2) the bank has recorded some items that the company doesn't know about until the bank statement arrives. Exhibit 6.6 lists specific causes of these differences, which we discuss below.

COACH'S TIP

You'll need to adjust your cash records only for items that appear on the right-hand side of this table.

| EXHIBIT 6.6 | Reconciling Differences |

Your Bank May Not Know About	You May Not Know About

1. Errors made by the bank
2. Time lags
   a. Deposits that you made recently
   b. Cheques that you wrote recently
	3. Interest the bank has put into your account
	4. Electronic funds transfers (EFTs)
	5. Service charges taken out of your account
	6. Cheques you deposited but that bounced
	7. Errors made by you

1. **Bank errors.** Bank errors happen in real life, just as they do in Monopoly. If you discover a bank error, you should ask the bank to correct its records, but you should not change yours.

2. **Time lags.** Time lags are common. A time lag occurs, for example, when you make a deposit after the bank's normal business hours. *You* know you made the deposit, but your bank does not know until it processes the deposit the next day. Time lags involving deposits are called **deposits in transit.** Another common time lag is an **outstanding cheque.** This lag occurs when you write and mail a cheque to a company, but your bank doesn't find out about it until that company deposits the cheque in its own bank, which then notifies your bank. As you will see later, although deposits in transit and outstanding cheques may be a significant part of a bank reconciliation, they do not require any further action on your part because you have already recorded them.

3. **Interest deposited.** You may know that your bank pays interest, but you probably do not know exactly how much interest you'll get because it varies depending on the average balance in your account. When you read your bank statement, you'll learn how much interest to add to your records.

4. **Electronic funds transfer (EFT).** It doesn't happen every day, but occasionally funds may be transferred into or out of your account without your knowing about it. If you discover these electronic transfers on your bank statement, you will need to adjust your records.

5. **Service charges.** These are the amounts the bank charges for processing your transactions. Rather than send you a bill and wait for you to pay it, the bank just takes the amount directly out of your account. You will need to reduce the Cash balance in your accounting records for these charges.

6. **NSF cheques.** Cheques that were deposited into your bank account but were later rejected ("bounced") because of insufficient funds in the cheque writer's account are referred to as **NSF (not sufficient funds) cheques.** Because the bank increased your account when the cheque was deposited, the bank decreases your account when it discovers that the deposit was not valid. You will need to reduce your Cash balance by the amount of these bounced cheques (and any additional bank charges), and you will have to try to collect these amounts from the cheque writer.

7. **Your errors.** You may have made mistakes or forgotten to record some amounts in your chequebook. If so, you will need to adjust your records for these items.

YOU SHOULD KNOW

NSF (not sufficient funds) cheques: Another name for bounced cheques. They occur when the cheque writer does not have sufficient funds to cover the amount of the cheque.

Bank Reconciliation   The ending cash balance as shown on the bank statement does not usually agree with the ending cash balance shown by the related Cash account on the books of the company. For example, the Cash account of WMT at the end of June might contain the information shown in the following T-account.

dr +	Cash (A)			cr −
June 1 balance	7,762.40			
June 6 deposit	3,000.00	500.00		Cheque 100 written June 4
June 23 deposit	500.00	55.00		Cheque 101 written June 17
June 30 deposit	1,800.00	100.00		Cheque 102 written June 20
		145.00		Cheque 103 written June 24
		56.00		Cheque 104 written June 30
		815.00		Cheque 105 written June 30
Ending balance	11,391.40			

Notice that WMT's ending cash balance of $11,391.40 differs from the $10,638.40 ending cash balance shown on the bank statement in Exhibit 6.5. To determine the appropriate cash balance, these balances need to be reconciled.

Exhibit 6.7 shows the bank reconciliation prepared by WMT for the month of June. The completed reconciliation finds that the up-to-date cash balance is $11,478.40, an amount that differs from both the bank's statement and WMT's accounting records. This balance is the amount that WMT will report as Cash on its balance sheet after adjusting its records with the journal entries that we present later.

To prepare the bank reconciliation in Exhibit 6.7, WMT compared the entries in its Cash account to the bank statement (Exhibit 6.5) with the following goals:

1. **Identify the deposits in transit.** A comparison of WMT's recorded deposits with those listed on the bank statement revealed that WMT made a deposit of $1,800 on June 30 that was not listed on the bank statement. More than likely, the bank will process this deposit the next business day (July 1). WMT doesn't have to change its records for this item because it already was in WMT's books on June 30. It is simply a timing difference so WMT entered the amount on the bank reconciliation as an addition to update the bank's records.

2. **Identify the outstanding cheques.** A comparison of the cheques listed on the bank statement with the company's record of written cheques showed that Cheques 103 and 105 were still outstanding at the end of June (that is, they had not cleared the bank). They

EXHIBIT 6.7	Sample Bank Reconciliation

WMT BANK RECONCILIATION
At June 30, 2012

UPDATES TO BANK STATEMENT			UPDATES TO COMPANY'S BOOKS	
Ending cash balance per bank statement		$10,638.40	Ending cash balance per books	$11,391.40
Additions			Additions	
(1) Deposit in transit		1,800.00	(3a) Interest received from the bank	20.00
		12,438.40	(3b) EFT received from customer	100.00
				11,511.40
Deductions			Deductions	
(2) Outstanding cheques:			(3c) NSF check of R. Smith	18.00
# 103	145.00		(3d) Bank service charges	6.00
# 105	815.00	960.00	(4) Error in recording cheque 104	9.00
Up-to-date ending cash balance		$11,478.40	Up-to-date ending cash balance	$11,478.40

were entered on the reconciliation (in Exhibit 6.7) as a deduction from the bank account because the bank will eventually reduce the account balance when these cheques clear the bank. (WMT had already deducted Cheques 103 and 105 from its cash records.)

3. **Record other transactions on the bank statement.**
   a. Interest received from the bank, $20—entered on the bank reconciliation in Exhibit 6.7 as an addition to the book balance because it's included in the bank balance but not yet in the company's books.
   b. Electronic funds transfer received from customer, $100—entered on the bank reconciliation as an addition to the book balance because it's included in the bank balance but not yet in the company's books.
   c. NSF cheque rejected, $18—entered on the bank reconciliation as a deduction from the book balance because it was deducted from the bank statement balance but has not yet been deducted from the company's cash records.
   d. Service charges, $6—entered on the bank reconciliation as a deduction from the book balance because it has been deducted from the bank balance but not yet removed from the Cash account in the company's books.

4. **Determine the impact of errors.** After performing the three steps listed above, WMT found that the reconciliation was out of balance by $9. On checking the journal entries made during the month, WMT found that Cheque 104 was recorded in the company's accounts as $56 when, in fact, the cheque had been filled out for $65 (in payment of Accounts Payable). As Exhibit 6.5 shows on page 245, the bank correctly processed the cheque (on June 30) as $65. To correct its own error, WMT must deduct $9 ($65 − $56) from the company's books side of the bank reconciliation.

Now that we know the up-to-date cash balance is $11,478.40, we need to prepare and record journal entries that will bring the Cash account to that balance. Remember that the entries on the bank statement side of the bank reconciliation do not need to be adjusted by WMT because they will work out automatically when the bank processes them next month. Only the items on the company's books side of the bank reconciliation need to be recorded in the company's records, using the following journal entries:

Interest Received:
(a) dr Cash (+A).. 20
        cr Interest Revenue (+R, +SE).. 20
     To record interest received from the bank.

EFT Received from Customer:
(b) dr Cash (+A).. 100
        cr Accounts Receivable (−A).. 100
     To record electronic funds transfer received from customer.

Customer's Cheque Rejected as NSF:
(c) dr Accounts Receivable (+A)... 18
        cr Cash (−A)... 18
     To record amount rejected by bank and still owed by customer.

Service Charges:
(d) dr Office Expenses (+E, −SE).. 6
        cr Cash (−A)... 6
     To record service charge deducted by bank.

Company Error (Understated Payment to Supplier):
(e) dr Accounts Payable (−L)... 9
        cr Cash (−A)... 9
     To correct error made in recording a cheque paid to a creditor.

HOW'S IT GOING? Self-Study Practice

Indicate which of the following items discovered when preparing a bank reconciliation for HBC will need to be recorded in the Cash account on the company's books.

1. Outstanding cheques.
2. Deposits in transit.
3. Bank service charges.
4. NSF cheques that were deposited.

After you have finished, check your answers with the solution in the margin.

Solution to Self-Study Practice

Only 3 and 4 need to be recorded.

3. Bank service charges are deducted from the company's bank account, so Cash must be reduced and Office Expense must be recorded.

4. All cheques are recorded on the books as increases in the Cash account when they are deposited. When the bank later rejects an NSF cheque, Cash must be decreased and the related Accounts Receivable increased.

Reporting Cash and Cash Equivalents   The account called *Cash* on the balance sheet includes **cash** deposited with banks as well as cash on hand (also called *petty cash*) and cash equivalents. **Cash equivalents** are short-term, highly liquid investments purchased within three months of maturity. They are considered equivalent to cash because they are both readily convertible to known amounts of cash and so near to maturity that there is little risk their value will change. In your personal life, cash equivalents could include guaranteed investment certificates (GICs), treasury bills or money market funds that you've purchased within three months of maturity.

YOU SHOULD KNOW

Cash: Money or any instrument that banks will accept for deposit and immediate credit to a company's account.

Cash equivalents: Short-term, highly liquid investments purchased within three months of maturity.

SPOTLIGHT ON Controls

Granny Does Time

Grandmothers seem so trustworthy, but in one well-known case, a granny stole nearly half a million dollars from the small company where she worked as a bookkeeper. How did she do it? It was easy because the owner knew little about accounting, so he gave her responsibility for all of the company's accounting work but never independently verified her work. Granny realized this lack of internal control gave her unlimited opportunity, so she wrote cheques to herself and recorded them as inventory purchases. Then, when she did the bank reconciliation, she destroyed the cheques to cover her tracks. Granny kept this fraud going for eight years, but then confessed after becoming overwhelmed with guilt. If you're wondering why no one ever became suspicious about the recorded inventory purchases that didn't actually occur, keep reading. The next section will tell you why.

CONTROLLING AND REPORTING MERCHANDISE SALES

The success of all merchandisers depends on their ability to sell large quantities of merchandise at prices that exceed their cost. Knowing this, merchandisers spend a great deal of time and money tracking their inventory transactions. A strong accounting system plays three roles in this process:

1. It provides information on inventory quantities so that managers can control inventory levels.
2. It provides information on inventory costs so that managers can set appropriate selling prices.

Learning Objective 5

Explain the use of a perpetual inventory system as a control.

3. It provides information for preparing financial statements, which can be used to evaluate the amount of profit generated from merchandise sales in the current period. Until inventory is sold, it is an asset reported at its cost on the balance sheet. After inventory is sold, its cost is removed from the balance sheet and reported on the income statement as an expense, called *Cost of Goods Sold.* The difference between the selling price (reported as Sales Revenue) and the Cost of Goods Sold is the gross profit earned by the merchandiser.

To perform these functions, companies can use either type of inventory accounting system: perpetual or periodic.

Perpetual Inventory System

A **perpetual inventory system** updates inventory records every time an item is bought, sold, or returned. You may not realize it, but the bar-code readers at Walmart's checkouts serve two purposes: (1) they calculate and record the sales revenue for each product you're buying and (2) they remove the product and its cost from Walmart's inventory records. Similar scanners are used back in the "employees only" part of the store, where products are unloaded from the trucks or returned to suppliers. As a result of this continuous, or "perpetual," updating, the balances in Walmart's Inventory and Cost of Goods Sold accounts are always up to date.

Periodic Inventory System

Unlike a perpetual system, which updates the inventory records immediately after each purchase, sale, and return of merchandise, a **periodic inventory system** updates the inventory records only at the end of the accounting period. Although simple to maintain, a major drawback of a periodic system is that accurate records of the inventory on hand and the inventory that has been sold are unavailable. To determine these amounts, employees must physically count the inventory, which they do at the end of the period, when the store is "closed for inventory." This inventory count is then used to adjust the balances for Inventory and Cost of Goods Sold.

Inventory Control

A perpetual inventory system provides the best inventory control because its continuous tracking of transactions allows companies to instantly determine the quantity of products on the shelves and to evaluate the amount of time they have spent there. Using this information, companies can better manage their inventory and save a great deal of money in financing and storage charges. This also benefits consumers, who pay less for the products they buy. When companies use less money or labour to produce a product or service, the productivity of our entire economy goes up.

Another benefit of a perpetual inventory system is that it allows managers to estimate **shrinkage,** the term for loss of inventory from theft, fraud, and error. You might wonder how companies can estimate how much of their inventory is missing because isn't it, by definition, *missing?* They use the information in the perpetual inventory system and their understanding of the following inventory equation. Assume Walmart reports the following for one of its lines of cellphones.

Equation		Information in the company's perpetual records					Physical inventory count
		Quantity		Cost per Unit		Total Cost	
Beginning Inventory		3	×	$100	=	$300	
+ Purchases		3	×	$100	=	300	
− Goods Sold		(2)	×	$100	=	(200)	vs.
= Ending Inventory		4	×	$100	=	$400	

Because a perpetual inventory system records all goods purchased and sold, the ending inventory in the company's perpetual records indicates how many units should be on hand. In our example, four units should be on hand at a unit cost of $100, for a total cost of $400. By physically counting the inventory that is actually on hand, the company can determine whether items have been physically removed without being recorded as an approved transaction. In our example, a physical inventory count showed that just three units were on hand, so the shrinkage was one unit, with a cost of $100.

Notice that you can't do this kind of detective work with a periodic inventory system because it doesn't provide an up-to-date record of the inventory that should be on hand when you count it. Also note that, even if you're using a perpetual inventory system, you still need to count the inventory occasionally (at least yearly) to ensure the accounting records are accurate and that any shrinkage is detected. If you don't do this physical count, you could end up like the company in the Spotlight on Controls on page 249. The grandmother was able to falsely record payments to herself as if they were inventory purchases because no one checked to see whether the recorded inventory actually existed.

Until recently, perpetual inventory systems were too costly for most merchandisers to implement. Today, however, computerized inventory systems have become so cheap that most merchandisers use a perpetual system. Accordingly, this chapter focuses on the accounting process that perpetual systems use. Because you may still encounter a periodic system, particularly in small companies or large ones that have been slow to switch, we discuss the accounting process for periodic systems in Chapter 7.

SPOTLIGHT ON **Ethics**

Sources of Inventory Shrinkage

Independent verification of inventory quantities is important. Although shoplifting is a major cause of shrinkage (accounting for 33 percent of lost units), an even larger portion (47 percent) results from employee theft. To avoid hiring dishonest employees, companies screen job applicants using employment and criminal background checks. To deter and detect employee theft, they use security tags, closed-circuit TV, and complex computer programs that monitor cash registers.

Sales Transactions

As required by the revenue principle, merchandisers record revenue when it is earned. Merchandisers earn revenues by making a "sale," which means transferring ownership of merchandise to a customer, either for cash or on credit. For a retail merchandiser like Walmart, this transfer of ownership occurs when a customer buys and takes possession of the goods at checkout. For a wholesale merchandiser who is shipping goods to a customer, the transfer of ownership occurs at a time stated in the written sales agreement. The sales agreement will specify one of two possible times:

1. **FOB shipping point**—the sale is recorded when the goods leave the seller's shipping department.
2. **FOB destination**—the sale is recorded when the goods reach their destination (the customer).

Unless otherwise indicated, the examples in this book assume that ownership transfers when goods are shipped (FOB shipping point), which usually means that the buyer pays for all transportation costs.[2]

Every merchandise sale has two components, each of which requires an entry in a perpetual inventory system:

Learning Objective 6

Analyze sales transactions under a perpetual inventory system.

YOU SHOULD KNOW

FOB shipping point: A term of sale indicating that goods are owned by the customer the moment they leave the seller's premises.

FOB destination: A term of sale indicating that goods are owned by the seller until they are delivered to the customer.

1. **Selling price.** Walmart's *sales price* is recorded as an increase in Sales Revenue and a corresponding increase in either Cash (for a cash sale) or Accounts Receivable (for a credit sale).

2. **Cost.** The *cost* that Walmart incurred to initially buy the merchandise is removed from Inventory and reported as an expense called *Cost of Goods Sold* (CGS).

For example, assume Walmart sells two Schwinn mountain bikes at a selling price of $200 per bike, for a total of $400 cash. The bikes had previously been recorded in Walmart's Inventory at a total cost of $350. This transaction is illustrated, analyzed, and recorded in Exhibit 6.8.

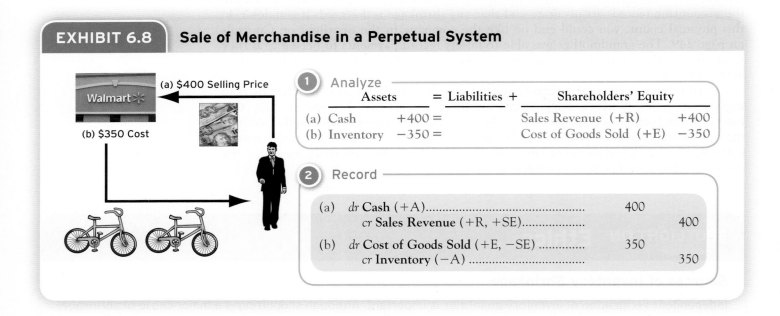

EXHIBIT 6.8   **Sale of Merchandise in a Perpetual System**

Notice in Exhibit 6.8 that the first part of Walmart's journal entry involving Cash and Sales Revenue is recorded at the total selling price ($400). The second part involving Cost of Goods Sold and Inventory uses Walmart's total cost ($350). The $50 difference between selling price and cost ($400 − $350) is called the *gross profit*. **Gross profit is not directly recorded in an account by itself**, but instead is a subtotal produced by subtracting Cost of Goods Sold from Sales Revenue on the income statement.

To keep things simple, we use only one Sales Revenue account and one Cost of Goods Sold account for our examples. In the workplace, however, merchandising companies use different Sales and Cost of Goods Sold accounts for different product lines. This allows managers at Walmart to separately evaluate sales of different products. When reporting to external financial statement users, Walmart combines these individual accounts into a single number for Sales and a single number for Cost of Goods Sold, which avoids cluttering its income statement with numerous accounts and also prevents its competitors from discovering details about its sales of specific products.

Sales Returns and Allowances

When goods sold to a customer arrive in damaged condition or are otherwise unsatisfactory, the customer can (1) return them for a full refund or (2) keep them and ask for a reduction in the selling price, called an *allowance*. These **sales returns and allowances** require Walmart to revise the previously recorded sale and, in the case of returns, to revise the previously recorded inventory reduction and cost of goods sold. To illustrate this, suppose that after Walmart sold the two Schwinn mountain bikes, the customer returned one to Walmart. Assuming that the bike is still like new, Walmart would refund the $200 selling price to the customer and take the bike back into inventory.

To account for this transaction, Walmart would make two entries to basically reverse the entries recorded when the bike was sold. We say "basically" because there is one catch: Walmart does not directly reduce its Sales Revenue account. Instead, Walmart tracks sales returns and allowances in a contra-revenue account that is deducted from total sales revenue.

Just as a contra-asset account such as Accumulated Amortization reduces the total in an asset account such as Equipment, a contra-revenue account such as Sales Returns and Allowances reduces the total in a revenue account such as Sales Revenues. Using a contra-revenue account instead of directly reducing the Sales account allows Walmart to track the value of goods returned, providing clues about whether customers are happy with the quality and price of Walmart's products.[3] Sales returns are recorded as follows:

1 Analyze

Assets		=	Liabilities	+	Shareholders' Equity		
Cash	−200	=			Sales Returns & Allowances (+xR)	−200
Inventory	+175	=			Cost of Goods Sold (−E)	+175

2 Record

dr Sales Returns & Allowances (+xR, −SE)	200	
cr Cash (−A)		200
dr Inventory (+A)	175	
cr Cost of Goods Sold (−E, +SE)		175

Sales on Account and Sales Discounts

When a merchandiser makes a sale on account, it gives up its inventory but receives only a promise of being paid cash later. To encourage customers to make these payments promptly, a merchandiser often specifies payment terms such as "2/10, n/30." The "2/10" means that if the customer pays within 10 days of the sale date, a 2 percent **sales discount** will be deducted from the selling price. The "n/30" part implies that if payment is not made within the 10-day discount period, the full amount will be due 30 days after the date of sale. See Exhibit 6.9 for an illustration of a 2/10, n/30 sale that occurred on November 1.

When a sales discount is offered to and later taken by the customer, the seller accounts for two transactions: (1) the initial sale and (2) the sales discount taken by the customer.

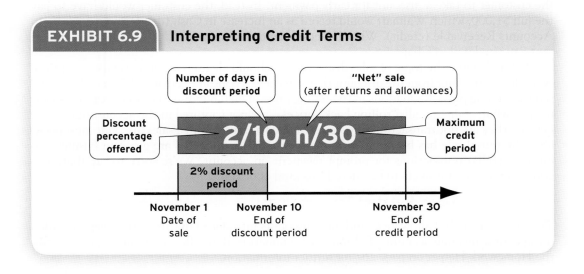

EXHIBIT 6.9 **Interpreting Credit Terms**

Suppose that Walmart's warehouse store (Sam's Club) sells printer paper on account to a local business for $1,000 with payment terms of 2/10, n/30. The paper cost Sam's Club $700. Walmart accounts for this initial sale as follows:

1 Analyze

Assets		= Liabilities +	Shareholders' Equity	
Accounts Receivable	+1,000		Sales Revenue (+R)	+1,000
Inventory	−700		Cost of Goods Sold (+E)	−700

2 Record

dr Accounts Receivable (+A)..	1,000	
cr Sales Revenue (+R, +SE)		1,000
dr Cost of Goods Sold (+E, −SE).......................................	700	
cr Inventory (−A)...		700

To take advantage of this 2 percent discount, the customer must pay Walmart within 10 days. If the customer does so, it will deduct the $20 discount (2% × $1,000) from the total owed ($1,000), and then pay $980 to Walmart. Walmart accounts for the $20 sales discount using a contra-revenue account, as follows:

1 Analyze

Assets		= Liabilities +	Shareholders' Equity	
Cash	+980		Sales Discounts (+xR)	−20
Accounts Receivable	−1,000			

2 Record

dr Cash (+A)..	980	
dr Sales Discounts (+xR, −SE)	20	
cr Accounts Receivable (−A)...		1,000

COACH'S TIP

Sales discounts are calculated after taking into account any sales returns and allowances. Customers that pay a portion of what they owe are entitled to a discount on that portion if they pay within the discount period.

If the customer doesn't pay by the end of the discount period, Walmart would not allow the customer to take a discount for early payment. Instead, the customer would have to pay the full $1,000, which Walmart would record as an increase in Cash (debit) and a decrease in Accounts Receivable (credit). What if a customer doesn't pay at all? We discuss that important issue in detail in Chapter 8.

Before leaving the topic of sales discounts, we should clear up a common misconception. Sales discounts differ from the discount that you get as a consumer buying clearance items at a reduced selling price. Reductions in the selling price of merchandise that occur before a sale is made—what Walmart calls "rolling back" prices—are not captured in the accounting system because they are not transactions. To be considered a transaction, a sales discount must occur after the initial sale has been made. These types of sales discounts are given in business-to-business (B2B) transactions for prompt payment on account. We're sorry to say that, as a consumer, you're not likely to be offered this kind of discount.

Summary of Sales-Related Transactions

The sales returns and allowances and sales discounts introduced in this section were recorded using contra-revenue accounts. Exhibit 6.10 summarizes their effects on sales reporting. See the Homework Helper on page 262 for further information.

Sales Revenue	$1,400*
Less: Sales Returns and Allowances	(200)
Sales Discounts	(20)
Net Sales	$1,180

* $1,400 = $400 (bikes) + $1,000 (printer paper)

SPOTLIGHT ON Financial Reporting

The Makeup of Net Sales

As you have seen, the documentation procedure involving contra-revenue accounts allows managers to monitor and control how sales discounts, returns, and allowances affect the company's revenues. For example, frequent returns of defective products would show up as an increase in the Sales Returns and Allowances account. In response to such an increase, Walmart's managers might decide to discontinue the product or find a new supplier.

Detailed information relating to sales discounts and returns is a key part of a merchandiser's business operations. To avoid revealing these secrets to competitors, most companies report these contra-accounts only on their internal financial statements, as in Exhibit 6.10. Externally reported income statements almost never include contra-revenue accounts. Instead, externally reported income statements begin with **Net Sales**. Despite this secrecy, external financial statement users can still conduct useful financial statement analyses, as we'll see in the next section.

Evaluate the Results

GROSS PROFIT ANALYSIS

One of the basic facts of merchandising is that to survive, a merchandiser must sell goods for more than their cost. Sure, cash has to be controlled, but the fact remains that there won't be much cash to control unless goods are sold at a profit. That's the only way companies like Walmart can generate enough money to cover their operating expenses. To make it easy for financial statement users to see how much is earned from product sales, without being clouded by other operating costs, merchandise companies often present their income statement using a multistep format.

A **multistep income statement** is similar to what you saw in the first few chapters, with expenses being subtracted from revenues to arrive at net income. The difference is that a multistep format separates the revenues and expenses that relate to core operations from all the other (peripheral) items that affect net income. For merchandisers, a key measure is the amount of profit earned over the cost of goods sold, so their multistep income statements separate Cost of Goods Sold from other expenses. As shown in Exhibit 6.11, this extra step produces a subtotal called **gross profit,** which is the amount the company earned from selling goods, over and above the cost of the goods. If you buy something for $70 and sell it for $100, you'll have a gross profit of $30.

Notice in Exhibit 6.11 that after the gross profit line, the multistep income statement presents other items in a format similar to what you saw for a service company in Chapter 3 (Exhibit 3.2). The category called *Selling, General, and Administrative Expenses* includes a variety of operating expenses including wages, utilities, advertising, rent, and the costs of

Learning Objective 7

Analyze a merchandiser's multistep income statement.

YOU SHOULD KNOW

Multistep income statement: Presents important subtotals, such as gross profit, to help distinguish core operating results from other, less significant items that affect net income. **Gross profit** (also called *gross margin* or *simply margin*): Net sales minus cost of goods sold. It is a subtotal, not an account.

EXHIBIT 6.11 | **Sample Multistep Income Statement**

WALMART STORES, INC. Income Statements For the Years Ended January 31 (amounts in millions)			
	2010	2009	2008
Net Sales	$408,214	$404,374	$377,023
Cost of Goods Sold	304,657	304,056	284,137
Gross Profit	103,557	100,318	92,886
Selling, General, and Administrative Expenses	79,607	77,520	70,934
Income from Operations	23,950	22,798	21,952
Other Expenses	1,884	1,900	1,794
Income before Income Taxes	22,066	20,898	20,158
Income Tax Expense	7,139	7,145	6,889
Net Income	$ 14,927	$ 13,753	$ 13,269

delivering merchandise to customers. These expenses are subtracted from gross profit to yield Income from Operations, which is a measure of the company's income from regular operating activities, before considering the effects of interest, income taxes, and any nonrecurring items.

Gross Profit Percentage

Let's focus again on the gross profit line in the income statement in Exhibit 6.11. Although the dollar amount of gross profit can be impressive—yes, Walmart really did generate over $103 billion of gross profit in 2010—this number is difficult to interpret by itself. In Exhibit 6.11, we see that Walmart's gross profit increased from 2008 to 2009 to 2010. The difficulty in interpreting this is that Walmart also increased its sales over these three years, so we don't know whether the increase in gross profit dollars arises because Walmart increased its sales volume or whether it is generating more profit per sale. To determine the amount of gross profit included in each dollar of sales, analysts typically evaluate the gross profit percentage.

ACCOUNTING DECISION TOOLS

Name of Measure	Formula	What It Tells You
Gross profit percentage	$\dfrac{\text{Net Sales} - \text{CGS}}{\text{Net Sales}} \times 100$	• The percentage of profit earned on each dollar of sales, after considering the cost of products sold • A higher ratio means that greater profit is available to cover operating and other expenses

YOU SHOULD KNOW

Gross profit percentage: A ratio indicating the percentage of profit earned on each dollar of sales, after considering the cost of products sold.

The **gross profit percentage** measures the percentage of profit earned on each dollar of sales. As discussed below, this ratio is used (1) to analyze changes in the company's operations over time, (2) to compare one company to another, and (3) to determine whether a company is earning enough on each sale to cover its operating expenses. A higher gross profit percentage means that the company is selling products for a greater markup over its cost.

As we can see in the graphic in the margin, Walmart's gross profit percentage increased slightly from 2008 through 2010. Each dollar of sales in 2010 included 25.4 cents of gross profit whereas in the prior two years, an average dollar of sales included 24.8 or 24.6 cents of gross profit. So not only did Walmart sell more in 2010 than in the prior years, it also generated more profit per sale. How was this possible? To find out, you could read the Management's Discussion and Analysis section of Walmart's annual report. You'd find out that Walmart has reduced inventory shrinkage and markdowns, which means more profit from each dollar of sales. You might wonder whether it's even worth talking about a gross profit percentage increase of less than half a percent. Just remember that a small change in the gross profit percentage can lead to a big change in net income. In Walmart's case, because the company has such a huge sales volume ($408 billion), even just one-tenth of a percentage point increase in gross profit translates into almost half a billion dollars. Yes, that's billion with a **b** ($408 billion × 0.001 = $0.4 billion).

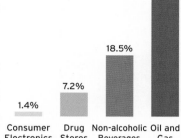

WALMART'S GROSS PROFIT PERCENTAGE			
	2010	2009	2008
$\dfrac{\text{Gross Profit}}{\text{Net Sales}}$	$\dfrac{\$103,557}{\$408,214}$	$\dfrac{\$100,318}{\$404,374}$	$\dfrac{\$92,886}{\$377,023}$
=	0.254	0.248	0.246
	× 100	× 100	× 100
=	25.4%	24.8%	24.6%

Comparing Operating Results across Companies and Industries   Be aware that gross profit percentages can vary greatly between companies. Walmart's gross profit percentage of 25.4 percent is characteristic of its slogan of "Saving people money so they can live better." Walmart's strategy is to earn a relatively small amount of profit on each dollar of sales, but to compensate by generating a huge volume of sales. In contrast, high-end department stores carry fashions with high-end prices, resulting in fewer sales but more profit on each sale. In 2009, Sak's reported a 31.9 percent gross profit percentage.

Gross profit percentages can vary across industries too. Oil and gas companies recently reported an average gross profit percentage of 37.2 percent, which they need to cover their research and exploration expenses.[4]

Gross Profit Percentage by Industry

SPOTLIGHT ON IFRS and ASPE

The majority of the differences between ASPE and IFRS for cash and merchandise sales are in the accounting for the inventory costs themselves and the valuation of this inventory. These differences will be outlined in Chapter 7.

Review the Chapter

This section provides a chance to solidify your understanding of key points. It's worth your time to work through the following demonstration cases, scan the chapter summary, test your understanding of key terms, and then practise, practise, practise.

DEMONSTRATION CASE A: BANK RECONCILIATION

Kat Bardash, a student at a small college, has just received her first chequing account statement for the month ended September 30. This was her first chance to attempt a bank reconciliation. The bank's statement of account showed the following:

Bank balance, September 1	$1,150.00
Deposits during September	650.00
Cheques cleared during September	900.00
Bank service charge	25.00
Interest earned	5.00
Bank balance, September 30	880.00

Kat was surprised that her bank had not yet reported the deposit of $50 she made on September 29 and was pleased that a cheque she wrote for $200 had not cleared her account. Her September 30 chequebook balance was $750.

Required:

1. Complete Kat's bank reconciliation. What adjustments, if any, does she need to make in her chequebook?
2. Why is it important for individuals and businesses to do a bank reconciliation each month?

Suggested Solution

1. Kat's bank reconciliation:

Updates to Bank Statement		Updates to Kat's Books	
September 30 cash balance	$ 880.00	September 30 cash balance	$750.00
Additions		Additions	
Deposit in transit	50.00	Interest earned	5.00
Deductions		Deductions	
Outstanding cheque	(200.00)	Bank service charge	(25.00)
Up-to-date cash balance	$ 730.00	Up-to-date cash balance	$730.00

Kat should increase her chequebook balance by $5 for the cash given by the bank for interest and reduce her chequebook balance by $25 for the cash given to the bank for service charges. In journal entry format, this would involve the following:

dr Cash (+A)	5.00	
cr Interest Revenue (+R, +SE)		5.00
dr Office Expenses (+E, −SE)	25.00	
cr Cash (−A)		25.00

2. Bank statements, whether personal or business, should be reconciled each month to help ensure that a correct balance is reflected in the depositor's books. Failure to reconcile a bank statement increases the chance that an error will not be discovered and may result in NSF cheques being written. Businesses reconcile their bank statements for an additional reason: The up-to-date balance that is calculated during reconciliation is reported on the balance sheet.

DEMONSTRATION CASE B: MERCHANDISE SALES

OAKLEY

Sunglass Hut

Assume Oakley, Inc.—the maker of sunglasses, goggles, and other products—made merchandise costing $137,200 and sold it on credit to Sunglass Hut for $405,000 with terms 2/10, n/30. Some of the merchandise differed from what Sunglass Hut had ordered, so Oakley agreed to give an allowance of $5,000. Sunglass Hut satisfied the remaining balance (of $400,000) by paying within the discount period.

Required:

1. Assuming that Oakley uses a perpetual inventory system, analyze the accounting equation effects and record the journal entries that Oakley would use for the following transactions:
   a. Sale from Oakley to Sunglass Hut.
   b. Allowance granted by Oakley.
   c. Payment made by Sunglass Hut to Oakley.

2. Compute Oakley's net sales, assuming that sales returns and allowances and sales discounts are treated as contra-revenues.

3. Compute Oakley's gross profit and gross profit percentage on the sale. Compare this ratio to the 66.5 percent gross profit percentage earned by the Luxottica Group—the Italian company that makes Killer Loop® and Ray-Ban® sunglasses, which are sold through its Sunglass Hut stores. What does it imply about the two companies?

Suggested Solution

1. **a.** Sale from Oakley to Sunglass Hut

① Analyze

Assets		=	Liabilities	+	Shareholders' Equity	
Accounts Receivable	+405,000				Sales Revenue (+R)	+405,000
Inventory	−137,200				Cost of Goods Sold (+E)	−137,200

② Record

dr Accounts Receivable (+A)...	405,000	
cr Sales Revenue (+R, +SE)		405,000
dr Cost of Goods Sold (+E, −SE)..	137,200	
cr Inventory (−A)		137,200

b. Allowance granted by Oakley

① Analyze

Assets		=	Liabilities	+	Shareholders' Equity	
Accounts Receivable	−5,000				Sales Returns and Allowances (+xR)	−5,000

② Record

dr Sales Returns and Allowances (+xR, −SE)........................	5,000	
cr Accounts Receivable (−A).....................................		5,000

c. Payment made by Sunglass Hut to Oakley

① Analyze

Assets		=	Liabilities	+	Shareholders' Equity	
Cash	+392,000				Sales Discounts (+xR)	−8,000
Accounts Receivable	−400,000					

② Record

dr Cash (+A)...	392,000	
dr Sales Discounts (+xR, −SE)	8,000	
cr Accounts Receivable (−A).....................................		400,000

COACH'S TIP

Transaction (b) depicts an allowance but no return of goods. Had goods been returned, Oakley also would increase its Inventory and decrease its Cost of Goods Sold.

2. Sales returns and allowances and sales discounts should be subtracted from sales revenue to compute net sales:

Sales Revenue	$405,000
Less: Sales Returns and Allowances	5,000
Sales Discounts	8,000*
Net Sales	392,000

*$8,000 = 2% × ($405,000 − $5,000)

3. Gross profit and gross profit percentage are calculated as follows:

	In Dollars	% of Net Sales
Net Sales (calculated in 2 above)	$392,000	100.0%
Less: Cost of Goods Sold	137,200	35.0
Gross Profit	$254,800	65.0%

The 65 percent gross profit percentage indicates that Oakley generates 65 cents of gross profit on each dollar of sales. This is 1.5 cents less gross profit on each dollar of sales than Luxottica (1.5 = 66.5 − 65.0). This difference implies that Luxottica is including a higher markup in its selling prices than Oakley.

CHAPTER SUMMARY

LO1   **Distinguish among service, merchandising, and manufacturing operations.** p. 236

- Service companies sell services rather than physical goods; consequently, their income statements show costs of services rather than cost of goods sold.
- Merchandising companies sell goods that have been obtained from a supplier. Retail merchandising companies sell directly to consumers, whereas wholesale merchandising companies sell to retail companies.
- Manufacturing companies sell goods that they have made themselves.

LO2   **Explain common principles and limitations of internal control.** p. 237

- The concept of internal control is broad. Most employees working within a company will encounter five basic principles: (1) establish responsibility for each task; (2) segregate duties so that one employee cannot initiate, record, approve, and handle a single transaction; (3) restrict access to those employees who have been assigned responsibility; (4) document procedures performed; and (5) independently verify work done by others inside and outside the business.
- Internal controls may be limited by cost, human error, and fraud.

LO3   **Apply internal control principles to cash receipts and payments.** p. 240

- When applied to cash receipts, internal control principles require that (1) cashiers be held individually responsible for the cash they receive, (2) different individuals be assigned to receive, maintain custody of, and record cash, (3) cash be stored in a locked safe until it has been securely deposited in a bank, (4) cash register receipts, cash count sheets, daily cash summary reports, and bank deposit slips be prepared to document the cash received and deposited, and (5) cash register receipts be matched to cash counts and deposit slips, to independently verify that all cash was received and deposited.
- When applied to cash payments, internal control principles require that (1) only certain individuals or departments initiate purchase requests, (2) different individuals be assigned to order, receive, and pay for purchases, (3) access to cheques and valuable property be restricted, (4) purchase requisitions, purchase orders, receiving reports, and prenumbered cheques be used to document the work done,

and (5) each step in the payment process occurs only after the preceding step has been independently verified using the documents listed in (4).

Perform the key control of reconciling cash to bank statements. p. 244   **LO4**

- The bank reconciliation requires determining two categories of items: (1) those that have been recorded in the company's books but not in the bank's statement of account, and (2) those that have been reported in the bank's statement of account but not in the company's books. The second category of items provides the data needed to adjust the Cash account to the balance that will be reported on the balance sheet.

Explain the use of a perpetual inventory system as a control. p. 249   **LO5**

- Perpetual inventory systems protect against undetected theft because they provide an up-to-date record of inventory that should be on hand at any given time, which can be compared to a count of the physical quantity that actually is on hand.
- Perpetual inventory systems serve to promote efficient and effective operations because they are updated every time inventory is purchased, sold, or returned.

Analyze sales transactions under a perpetual inventory system. p. 251   **LO6**

- In a perpetual inventory system, two entries are made every time inventory is sold: one entry records the sale (and corresponding debit to Cash or Accounts Receivable) and the other entry records the Cost of Goods Sold (and corresponding credit to Inventory).
- Sales discounts and sales returns and allowances are reported as contra-revenues, reducing net sales.

Analyze a merchandiser's multistep income statement. p. 255   **LO7**

- One of the key items in a merchandiser's multistep income statement is gross profit, which is a subtotal calculated by subtracting cost of goods sold from net sales. The gross profit percentage is calculated and interpreted as follows.

ACCOUNTING DECISION TOOLS

Name of Measure	Formula	What It Tells You
Gross profit percentage	$\dfrac{\text{Net Sales} - \text{CGS}}{\text{Net Sales}} \times 100$	• The percentage of profit earned on each dollar of sales, after considering the cost of products sold • A higher ratio means that greater profit is available to cover operating and other expenses

KEY TERMS

See complete definitions in the glossary in the back of this text.

HOMEWORK HELPER

Multistep Income Statement Format

Sales Revenue	$100,000
Less: Sales Returns and Allowances	(2,500)
Sales Discounts	(1,500)
Net Sales	96,000
Cost of Goods Sold	55,000
Gross Profit	41,000
Selling, General, and Administrative Expenses	21,000
Income from Operations	20,000
Other Revenue (Expenses)	5,000
Income before Income Tax Expense	25,000
Income Tax Expense	10,000
Net Income	$ 15,000

Reported Internally
Reported Externally

Alternative terms

- *Gross profit* is also called *gross margin* or *margin*.

Helpful reminders

- When preparing a bank reconciliation, your goals are to determine which transactions the bank has not yet processed and which transactions your company has not yet processed. You will record transactions correctly processed by the bank but not yet processed by your company.
- Sales Returns have two components: (1) an adjustment to the selling price (record a contra-revenue and a decrease in Cash or Accounts Receivable) and (2) return of goods previously recorded as sold (record an increase in Inventory and a decrease in Cost of Goods Sold). Sales Allowances involve only the first component, because no goods are returned to the seller.

Frequent mistakes

- Discounts (or "markdowns") in the selling price of merchandise occur prior to making a sale, so they are not recorded. Sales Discounts, given to customers after making a sale, are recorded in a contra-revenue account, to offset the Sales Revenue recorded on the initial sales transaction.
- Gross profit percentage is calculated as a percentage of Net Sales, not Cost of Goods Sold.

Practice Material

QUESTIONS (S Symbol indicates questions that require analysis from more than one perspective.)

1. What is the distinction between service and merchandising companies? What is the distinction between merchandising and manufacturing companies? What is the distinction between retail and wholesale merchandising companies?

2. From the perspective of a CEO or CFO, what does *internal control* mean?

3. What are five common internal control principles?

4. Why is it a good idea to assign each task to only one employee?

5. Why should responsibilities for certain duties, like cash handling and cash recording, be separated? What types of responsibilities should be separated?

6. What are some of the methods for restricting access?

7. In what ways does documentation act as a control?

8. In what ways can independent verification occur?

9. In what way does a mandatory vacation policy act as a control?

10. What are two limitations of internal control?

11. What is the primary internal control goal for cash receipts?

12. What internal control functions are performed by a cash register? How are these functions performed when cash is received by mail? S

13. How is cash that is received in person independently verified if a cash register is being used?

14. What is the primary internal control goal for cash payments?

15. What are the purposes of a bank reconciliation? What balances are reconciled?

16. Define *Cash* and *Cash Equivalents*, and indicate the types of items that should be reported as cash and cash equivalents.

17. What is the main distinction between perpetual and periodic inventory systems? Which type of system provides better internal control over inventory? Explain why.

18. Why is a physical count of inventory necessary in a periodic inventory system? Why is it still necessary in a perpetual inventory system?

19. What is the difference between FOB shipping point and FOB destination? How do these terms relate to the revenue principle?

20. Describe in words the journal entries that are made in a perpetual inventory system when inventory is sold on credit.

21. What is the distinction between Sales Returns and Sales Allowances?

22. What is a Sales Discount? Use 1/10, n/30 in your explanation.

23. In response to the weak economy, your company's sales force is urging you, the sales manager, to change sales terms from 1/10, n/30 to 2/10, n/45. Explain what these terms mean and how this switch could increase or decrease your company's profits. 🔵

24. Explain the difference between Sales Revenue and Net Sales.

25. Why are contra-revenue accounts used rather than directly deducting from the Sales Revenue account?

26. What is gross profit? How is the gross profit percentage computed? Illustrate its calculation and interpretation assuming Net Sales is $100,000 and Cost of Goods Sold is $60,000.

Multiple-choice questions and corresponding answers can be found on Connect.

MINI-EXERCISES

M6-1 Matching Cash Receipt Processes to Internal Control Principles

LO3

Match each of the following cash receipt activities to the internal control principle to which it best relates. Enter the appropriate letter in the space provided.

_____ 1. A list of cheques received in the mail is prepared.

_____ 2. Total cash receipts are compared to the amount on the bank deposit slip.

_____ 3. A password is required to open the cash register.

_____ 4. Price changes at the checkout require a manager's approval.

_____ 5. Cashiers are required to count the cash in their register at the beginning and end of each shift.

A. Establish responsibility
B. Segregate duties
C. Restrict access
D. Document procedures
E. Independently verify

M6-2 Identifying Internal Control Weaknesses in Descriptions of the Cash Receipts Process

LO3

Each situation below describes an internal control weakness in the cash receipts process. Identify which of the five internal control principles is violated, explain the weakness, and then suggest a change that would improve internal control.

a. Cashiers prepare a cash count summary, attach tapes from the cash register showing total receipts, and then prepare a bank deposit slip, which they take to the bank for deposit. After the deposit is made, all documents are forwarded to the accounting department for review and recording.

b. The receptionist opens the mail each morning, sorts it into piles, and then gives cheques received from customers to the mail clerk for delivery to the accounting department, where a cash receipts list is prepared.

c. The accounting department receives cash register totals each day and promptly files them by cash register number. The accounting department also receives cash count sheets from cashiers each day and files them by employee number. The accounting department receives stamped bank deposit slips the morning after the bank deposit is made, prepares the journal entry, and files the deposit slips by date.

d. To avoid boredom, the employee who works the cash register at the movie theatre trades off with either the employee who collects the tickets or an employee who works at the concessions stand.

e. To enhance efficiency, cashiers are assigned the responsibility of authorizing price changes at the cash register.

LO3

M6-3 Matching Cash Payment Processes to Internal Control Principles

Match each of the following cash payment activities to the internal control principle to which it best relates. Enter the appropriate letter in the space provided.

_____ 1. The business manager has the only key to the cheque-signing equipment.

_____ 2. The purchasing manager orders all goods and services for the business.

_____ 3. A bank reconciliation is prepared monthly.

_____ 4. Prenumbered cheques are used for all payments.

_____ 5. The company asks suppliers to deliver their merchandise to the warehouse but mail their invoices to the accounting department.

A. Establish responsibility
B. Segregate duties
C. Restrict access
D. Document procedures
E. Independently verify

LO4

M6-4 Organizing Items on the Bank Reconciliation

Indicate whether the following items would be added (+) or subtracted (−) from the company's books or the bank statement side of a bank reconciliation.

Reconciling Item	Bank Statement	Company's Books
a. Outstanding cheques of $12,000		
b. Bank service charge of $15		
c. Deposit in transit of $2,300		
d. Interest earned of $5		

Using the information, prepare any journal entries needed to adjust the company's books.

LO5

Nordstrom, Inc.

M6-5 Choosing between a Perpetual and Periodic Inventory System

Nordstrom, Inc., started in business in 1901. It took only 100 years, but eventually the company changed from a periodic inventory system to a perpetual inventory system (in 2002). Write a brief report describing how this change would improve the company's inventory control.

LO6

AMERICAN EAGLE
OUTFITTERS

M6-6 Choosing between FOB Shipping Point and FOB Destination

In its 2009 annual report, American Eagle Outfitters states that its "e-commerce operation records revenue upon the estimated customer receipt date of the merchandise." Is this FOB shipping point or FOB destination? If American Eagle was to change to the other terms of shipment, would it report its Sales Revenues earlier, or later?

LO6

M6-7 Reporting Net Sales and Gross Profit with Sales Discounts

Merchandise costing $1,500 is sold for $2,000 on terms 2/10, n/30. If the buyer pays within the discount period, what amount will be reported on the income statement as net sales and as gross profit?

Using this information, prepare the journal entries needed at the time of sale and collection, assuming the company uses a perpetual inventory system.

LO6

M6-8 Journal Entries to Record Sales Discounts

Inventory that cost $500 is sold for $700, with terms of 2/10, n/30. Give the journal entries to record (*a*) the sale of merchandise and (*b*) collection of the accounts receivable assuming that it occurs during the discount period.

M6-9 Preparing a Multistep Income Statement

LO7

Sellall Department Stores reported the following amounts in its adjusted trial balance prepared as of its December 31, 2012, year-end: Administrative Expenses, $2,400; Cost of Goods Sold, $22,728; Income Tax Expense, $3,000; Interest Expense, $1,600; Interest Revenue, $200; General Expenses, $2,600; Sales Revenue, $42,000; Sales Discounts, $2,200; Sales Returns and Allowances, $1,920; and Delivery (freight-out) Expense, $300. Prepare a multistep income statement for distribution to external financial statement users, using a format similar to Exhibit 6.11.

M6-10 Determining the Cause of Decreasing Gross Profit

LO7

Progolf Corp. sells a variety of products, including golf balls and golf shoes. Assume that, like many other companies, Progolf reported a drop in net sales from $8.6 million in 2011 to $7.6 million in 2012, and a drop in gross profit from $4.0 million in 2011 to $3.6 million in 2012. Based on these numbers, determine whether the drop in gross profit was caused by a decline in gross profit per sale, a decline in sales volume, or a combination of the two.

EXERCISES

Practise and learn online with Connect.

E6-1 Identifying the Internal Control Principle and Financial Reporting Control Objective

LO2, 3

At most movie theatres, one employee sells tickets and another employee collects them. One night, when you're at the movies, your friend comments that this is a waste of the theatre's money.

Required:

1. Identify the name of the control principle to which this situation relates.
2. Explain to your friend what could happen if the same person did both jobs.

E6-2 Identifying Financial Reporting Control Objectives

LO2

Your student club recently volunteered to go door to door collecting cash donations on behalf of a local charity. The charity's accountant went berserk when you said you wrote receipts only for donors who asked for one.

Required:

Identify the control principle that you violated, and explain why the accountant reacted so strongly. What controls might be appropriate to use in the future?

E6-3 Identifying Internal Control Principles in Cash Receipt Processes

LO3

Locker Rentals Corp. (LRC) operates locker rental services at several locations throughout the city, including the airport, bus depot, shopping malls, and athletics facilities. Unlike some of the old mechanical lockers that charge a fixed amount per use, LRC's lockers operate electronically and are able to charge based on hours of use. The locker system transmits a daily message to LRC's office indicating the number of hours that lockers have been used, which the office manager uses to determine when cash should be picked up at each location. LRC's cash receipts system is described below.

a. Two employees ("cash collection clerks") are responsible for collecting cash from the lockers. Based on instructions from the office manager, one clerk collects cash from specific locations on the west side of the city and the other collects from specific locations on the east side.
b. When each cash collection clerk returns the cash, a supervisor counts the cash and prepares a cash count sheet.
c. The supervisor summarizes the cash count sheets in a prenumbered daily cash summary, and files the prenumbered cash count sheets by date.
d. The supervisor places the cash in a locked cashbox until it is taken to the bank for deposit.
e. The supervisor, not the cash collection clerks, takes the cash to the bank for deposit.
f. The supervisor prepares a duplicate deposit slip, which the bank stamps after the deposit is made, to indicate the date and amount of the deposit.
g. The supervisor sends the stamped bank deposit slip and daily cash summary to the accountant, who compares them before preparing a journal entry debiting Cash and crediting Locker Rental Revenue.

Required:

1. For each statement (a)–(g), identify the internal control principle being applied.
2. Prepare a diagram similar to Exhibit 6.3 showing the flow of information and materials. In what ways does LRC's system differ from Exhibit 6.3?
3. After several months, LRC's supervisor is arrested for stealing nearly $10,000 from the company. Identify the internal control weakness that allowed this theft to occur.

LO3

E6-4 Identifying Internal Control Principles in Cash Payment Processes

Home Repair Corp. (HRC) operates a building maintenance and repair business. The business has three office employees—a sales manager, a materials/crew manager, and an accountant. HRC's cash payments system is described below.

Check Figure:
[Part (b)]
Segregate duties/Document procedures

a. After a contract is signed with a customer, the sales manager prepares a prenumbered purchase requisition form that indicates the materials needed for the work at the repair site.
b. Based on the purchase requisition form, the materials/crew manager prepares and sends a prenumbered purchase order to suppliers of materials, advising them of the specific materials needed and the repair site to which they should be delivered.
c. The materials/crew manager is the only employee authorized to order goods.
d. Upon receiving a supplier's invoice, the accountant compares it to terms indicated on the purchase order, noting in particular the prices charged and quantity ordered.
e. If these documents are in agreement, the accountant prepares a prenumbered cheque, stamps the invoice "Paid," and prepares a journal entry to record the payment. The journal entry explanation references the sequential number on the purchase order.
f. HRC's owner prepares a monthly bank reconciliation and reviews cheques returned with the bank statement to ensure they have been issued to valid suppliers.

Required:

1. For each statement (a)–(f), identify the internal control principle being applied.
2. Using the above description, prepare a list of steps and documentation similar to Exhibit 6.4. Which document in Exhibit 6.4 is excluded from the above description?
3. After several months, HRC's materials/crew manager is arrested for having $20,000 of materials delivered to his home but charged to the company. Identify the internal control weakness that allowed this theft to occur.

LO4

E6-5 Preparing a Bank Reconciliation and Journal Entries, and Reporting Cash

Hills Company's June 30, 2012, bank statement and the June ledger account for cash are summarized here:

Check Figure:
Up-to-date cash balance
= $6,370

	Withdrawals	Deposits	Balance
Balance, June 1, 2012			$ 7,200
Deposits during June		$18,000	25,200
Cheques cleared during June	$19,100		6,100
Bank service charges	30		6,070
Balance, June 30, 2012			6,070

		+	Cash (A)		–	
June 1	Balance	6,800				
June	Deposits	19,000	19,400	Cheques written	June
June 30	Balance	6,400				

Required:

1. Prepare a bank reconciliation. A comparison of the cheques written with the cheques that have cleared the bank shows outstanding cheques of $700. Some of the cheques that cleared in June were

written prior to June. No deposits in transit were noted in May, but a deposit is in transit at the end of June.

2. Give any journal entries that should be made as a result of the bank reconciliation.

3. What is the balance in the Cash account after the reconciliation entries?

4. In addition to the balance in its bank account, Hills Company also has $300 cash on hand. This amount is recorded in a separate T-account called *Cash on Hand*. What is the total amount of cash that should be reported on the balance sheet at June 30?

E6-6 Preparing a Bank Reconciliation and Journal Entries, and Reporting Cash

LO4

The September 30, 2012, bank statement for Cadieux Company and the September ledger account for cash are summarized here:

	Withdrawals		Deposits	Balance
Balance, September 1, 2012				$ 2,000
September 7–NSF Cheque		$100		1,900
September 11			$3,000	4,900
September 12	#101	800		4,100
September 17	#102	1,700		2,400
September 26	#103	2,300		100
September 29–EFT deposit			150	250
September 30–Service Charge		20		230

+	Cash (A)	−			
Sept 1	Balance	2,000			
Sept 10		3,000	800	Sept 10	#101
Sept 30		2,500	1,700	Sept 15	#102
			2,300	Sept 22	#103
			50	Sept 28	#104
Sept 30	Balance	2,650			

No outstanding cheques and no deposits in transit were noted in August. However, there are deposits in transit and cheques outstanding at the end of September. The NSF cheque and electronic funds transfer (EFT) involved transactions with Cadieux Company's customers.

Required:

1. Prepare a bank reconciliation.

2. Give any journal entries that should be made as the result of the bank reconciliation.

3. What should the balance in the Cash account be after recording the journal entries in requirement 2?

4. If the company also has $400 of cash on hand (recorded in a separate account), what total amount of cash should the company report on the September 30 balance sheet?

E6-7 Identifying Shrinkage and Other Missing Inventory Information

LO5

Calculate the missing information for each of the following independent cases:

Cases	Beginning Inventory	Purchases	Cost of Goods Sold	Ending Inventory (perpetual system)	Ending Inventory (as counted)	Shrinkage
A	$100	$700	$300	?	$420	$?
B	200	800	?	150	150	?
C	150	500	200	450	?	10
D	260	?	650	210	200	?

E6-8 Inferring Shrinkage Using a Perpetual Inventory System

Hudson's Bay Company (HBC) is Canada's largest diversified general merchandise retailer, with over 600 retail locations and nearly 60,000 associates located in every province in Canada. HBC's four banners are The Bay, Zellers, Home Outfitters, and Fields. In 2012, assume that HBC reported Cost of Goods sold of $11,571 million, Ending Inventory for the current year of $3,259 million, and Ending Inventory for the previous year (2011) of $3,641 million.

Required:

If you knew that the cost of inventory purchases was $11,289 million, could you estimate the cost of shrinkage during the year? If so, prepare the estimate and, if not, explain why not.

E6-9 Reporting Net Sales with Credit Sales and Sales Discounts

Check Figure:
Net Sales = $228

During the months of January and February, Solitare Corporation sold goods to three customers. The sequence of events was as follows:

Jan. 6	Sold goods for $100 to Wizard Inc. with terms 2/10, n/30. The goods cost Solitare $70.
6	Sold goods to SpyderCorp. for $80 with terms 2/10, n/30. The goods cost Solitare $60.
14	Collected cash due from Wizard Inc.
Feb. 2	Collected cash due from SpyderCorp.
28	Sold goods for $50 to Bridges with terms 2/10, n/45. The goods cost Solitare $30.

Required:

Assuming that Sales Discounts are reported as contra-revenue, compute Net Sales for the two months ended February 28.

E6-10 Recording Journal Entries for Net Sales with Credit Sales and Sales Discounts

Using the information in E6-9, prepare journal entries to record the transactions, assuming Solitare uses a perpetual inventory system.

E6-11 Reporting Net Sales with Credit Sales and Sales Discounts

The following transactions were selected from the records of Evergreen Company:

July 12	Sold merchandise to Wally Butler, who paid for the $1,000 purchase with cash. The goods cost Evergreen Company $600.
15	Sold merchandise to Claudio's Chair Company at a selling price of $5,000 on terms 3/10, n/30. The goods cost Evergreen Company $3,500.
20	Sold merchandise to Otto's Ottomans at a selling price of $3,000 on terms 3/10, n/30. The goods cost Evergreen Company $1,900.
23	Collected payment from Claudio's Chair Company from the July 15 sale.
Aug. 25	Collected payment from Otto's Ottomans from the July 20 sale.

Required:

Assuming that Sales Discounts are reported as contra-revenue, compute Net Sales for the two months ended August 31.

E6-12 Recording Journal Entries for Net Sales with Credit Sales and Sales Discounts

Using the information in E6-11, prepare journal entries to record the transactions, assuming Evergreen Company uses a perpetual inventory system.

E6-13 Reporting Net Sales with Credit Sales, Sales Discounts, and Sales Returns

The following transactions were selected from among those completed by Bear's Retail Store in 2012:

Nov. 20	Sold two items of merchandise to Cheryl Jahn, who paid the $400 sales price in cash. The goods cost Bear's $300.
25	Sold 20 items of merchandise to Vasko Athletics at a selling price of $4,000 (total); terms 3/10, n/30. The goods cost Bear's $2,500.
28	Sold 10 identical items of merchandise to Nancy's Gym at a selling price of $6,000 (total); terms 3/10, n/30. The goods cost Bear's $4,000.
29	Nancy's Gym returned one of the items purchased on the 28th. The item was in perfect condition, and credit was given to the customer.
Dec. 6	Nancy's Gym paid the account balance in full.
30	Vasko Athletics paid in full for the invoice of November 25, 2012.

Check Figure:
Sales Returns and
Allowances = $600

Required:

Assuming that Sales Returns and Sales Discounts are reported as contra-revenues, compute Net Sales for the two months ended December 31, 2012.

E6-14 Recording Journal Entries for Net Sales with Credit Sales, Sales Discounts, and Sales Returns

LO6

Using the information in E6-13, prepare journal entries to record the transactions, assuming Bear's Retail Store uses a perpetual inventory system.

E6-15 Determining the Effects of Credit Sales, Sales Discounts, and Sales Returns and Allowances on Income Statement Categories

LO6, 7

Rockland Shoe Company records Sales Returns and Allowances and Sales Discounts as contra-revenues. Complete the following table, indicating the amount and direction of effect (+ for increase, − for decrease, and NE for no effect) of each transaction on each item reported in Rockland's income statement prepared for internal use. Be sure to total the effects.

July 12	Rockland sold merchandise to Kristina Zee at its factory store. Kristina paid for the $300 purchase in cash. The goods cost Rockland $160.
15	Sold merchandise to Shoe Express at a selling price of $5,000, with terms 3/10, n/30. Rockland's cost was $3,000.
20	Collected cash due from Shoe Express.
21	Sold merchandise to Fleet Foot Co. at a selling price of $2,000, with terms 2/10, n/30. Rockland's cost was $1,200.
23	Fleet Foot Co. returned $1,000 of shoes and promised to pay for the remaining goods in August. The returned shoes were in perfect condition and had cost Rockland $600.

Transaction Date:	July 12	July 15	July 20	July 21	July 23	Totals
Sales Revenues						
Sales Returns and Allowances						
Sales Discounts						
Net Sales						
Cost of Goods Sold						
Gross Profit						

E6-16 Analyzing and Recording Sales and Gross Profit with and without Sales Discounts

LO6, 7

Cycle Wholesaling sells merchandise on credit terms of 2/10, n/30. A sale for $800 (cost of goods sold of $500) was made to Sarah's Cycles on February 1, 2012. Assume Cycle Wholesaling uses a perpetual inventory system.

Required:

1. Give the journal entry Cycle Wholesaling would make to record the sale to Sarah's Cycles.
2. Give the journal entry to record the collection of the account, assuming it was collected in full on February 9, 2012.
3. Give the journal entry, assuming, instead, that the account was collected in full on March 2, 2012.
4. Calculate the gross profit percentage for the sale to Sarah's Cycles, assuming the account was collected in full on February 9, 2012.

L07 **E6-17 Inferring Missing Amounts Based on Income Statement Relationships**

Supply the missing dollar amounts for the income statement of Williamson Company for each of the following independent cases:

Check Figure:
[Case A]
Gross Profit = $2,100

	Case A	Case B	Case C
Sales Revenues	$8,000	$6,000	$?
Sales Returns and Allowances	150	?	275
Net Sales	?	?	5,920
Cost of Goods Sold	5,750	4,050	5,400
Gross Profit	?	1,450	?

L07 **E6-18 Analyzing Gross Profit Percentage on the Basis of a Multistep Income Statement**

The following summarized data were provided by the records of Mystery Incorporated for the year ended December 31, 2012:

Administrative Expense	$ 19,000
Cost of Goods Sold	165,000
Income Tax Expense	17,600
Sales Returns and Allowances	7,000
Selling Expense	40,200
Sales of merchandise for cash	240,000
Sales of merchandise on credit	42,000

Required:

1. Based on these data, prepare a multistep income statement for internal reporting purposes (showing all appropriate subtotals and totals).
2. What was the amount of gross profit? What was the gross profit percentage (calculated using the formula shown in this chapter)? Explain what these two amounts mean.
3. Evaluate the 2012 results in light of the company's 38 percent gross profit percentage in 2011.

L07 **E6-19 Analyzing Gross Profit Percentage on the Basis of an Income Statement**

Grizzly World Wide Inc. prides itself as being the world's leading marketer of Canadian branded non-athletic footwear. The following data (in millions) were taken from its annual report for the fiscal year ended January 3, 2012:

Sales of Merchandise	$1,220
Income Tax Expense	45
Cash Dividends Paid	21
Selling and Administrative Expense	345
Cost of Products Sold	735
Interest Expense	3
Other Revenues	3

Required:

1. Based on these data, prepare a multistep income statement.
2. How much was the gross profit? What was the gross profit percentage? (Round to the nearest tenth of a percentage point.) Explain what these two amounts mean.
3. Evaluate the results in light of the company's 39.2 percent gross profit percentage in the prior year.
4. Compare Grizzly's gross profit percentage to Walmart's average gross profit percentage of 24.5 percent. From this information, can you determine which company is more successful? Why or why not?

E6-20 Evaluating the Effect of Discounts and Returns on Gross Profit

LO7

One of the few companies to ever report the extent of sales discounts and returns was sunglass maker Oakley, Inc. Assume that in the Management Discussion and Analysis section of its 2012 annual report, Oakley reported the following information about its Sales Discounts and Returns.

(in thousands)	Year Ended December 31, 2012	Year Ended December 31, 2011
Gross Sales	$693,342	$621,652
Sales Discounts and Returns	(45,211)	(36,184)
Net Sales	648,131	585,468
Cost of Goods Sold	277,230	262,483
Gross Profit	$370,901	$322,985

Required:

1. For each year, calculate the percentage of sales discounts and returns by dividing Sales Discounts and Returns by Gross Sales and multiplying by 100. Based on these percentages, explain whether Sales Discounts and Returns had a greater impact in 2012 or 2011.
2. For each year, calculate the gross profit percentage using the formula shown in this chapter (i.e., using net sales). Did Oakley's gross profit improve or worsen in 2012, as compared to 2011?

COACHED PROBLEMS

CP6-1 Identifying Outstanding Cheques and Deposits in Transit and Preparing a Bank Reconciliation and Journal Entries

LO4

The August 2012 bank statement and cash T-account for Martha Company follow:

Date	Withdrawals	Deposits	Balance
Aug. 1			$17,470
2–Cheque	$300		17,170
3		$12,000	29,170
4–Cheque	400		28,770
5–Cheque	250		28,520
9–Cheque	890		27,630
10–Cheque	310		27,320
15		4,000	31,320
21–Cheque	400		30,920
24–Cheque	21,000		9,920
25		7,000	16,920
30–Cheque	800		16,120
30–Interest earned		20	16,140
31–Service charge	10		16,130

	+	Cash (A)		−	
Aug. 1	Balance	17,470	Cheques written		
Deposits					
Aug. 2		12,000	300		Aug. 1
12		4,000	400		2
24		7,000	250		3
31		5,000	310		4
			890		5
			290		15
			550		17
			800		18
			400		19
			21,000		23
Aug. 31	Balance	20,280			

No deposits were in transit and no cheques were outstanding at the end of July.

Required:

1. Identify and list the deposits in transit at the end of August.

   TIP: Put a check mark beside each item that appears on both the bank statement and what's already been recorded in the accounting records (shown in the T-account).
2. Identify and list the outstanding cheques at the end of August.
3. Prepare a bank reconciliation for August.

   TIP: Any items in the accounting records without check marks should appear on the bank state-ment side of the bank reconciliation. Any items in the bank statement without check marks should appear on the company's books side of the bank reconciliation.

   TIP: Up-to-date cash balance equals $20,290.
4. Give any journal entries that the company should make as a result of the bank reconciliation. Why are they necessary?
5. After the reconciliation journal entries are posted, what balance will be reflected in the Cash account in the ledger?
6. If the company also has $100 on hand, which is recorded in a different account called Cash on Hand, what total amount of Cash and Cash Equivalents should be reported on the August 31, 2012, balance sheet?

L06, 7 **CP6-2 Recording Cash Sales, Credit Sales, Sales Discounts, Sales Returns, and Sales Allowances, and Analyzing Gross Profit Percentage**

Campus Co-Op, which is operated by students, uses a perpetual inventory system. The following trans-actions (summarized) have been selected from 2012:

a.	Sold merchandise for cash (cost of merchandise, $152,070).	$275,000
b.	Received merchandise returned by customers as unsatisfactory (but in perfect condition), for cash refund (original cost of merchandise, $800).	1,600
c.	Sold merchandise (costing $9,000) to a customer, on account with terms 2/10, n/30.	20,000
d.	Collected half of the balance owed by the customer in (c) within the discount period.	9,800
e.	Granted an allowance to the customer in (c).	1,800

Required:

1. Compute Sales Revenue, Net Sales, and Gross Profit for Campus Co-Op.
2. Compute the gross profit percentage (using the formula shown in this chapter).

3. Prepare journal entries to record transactions (*a*)–(*e*).

4. Campus Co-Op is considering a contract to sell merchandise to a campus organization for $15,000. This merchandise will cost Campus Co-Op $12,000. Would this contract increase (or decrease) Campus Co-Op's gross profit and gross profit percentage? How should Campus Co-Op decide whether to accept the contract?

> TIP: The impact on gross profit (a dollar amount) may differ from the impact on gross profit percentage.

CP6-3 Sales Transactions between Wholesale and Retail Merchandisers, with Sales Allowances and Sales Discounts Using a Perpetual Inventory System

LO6, 7

The transactions listed below are typical of those involving Amalgam Textiles and Fine Fashions. Amalgam is a wholesale merchandiser and Fine Fashions is a retail merchandiser. Assume all sales of merchandise from Amalgam to Fine Fashions are made with terms 2/10, n/30, and that the two companies use perpetual inventory systems. Assume the following transactions between the two companies occurred in the order listed during the year ended December 31, 2012.

a. Amalgam sold merchandise to Fine Fashions at a selling price of $230,000. The merchandise had cost Amalgam $175,000.

b. Two days later, Fine Fashions complained to Amalgam that some of the merchandise differed from what Fine Fashions had ordered. Amalgam agreed to give an allowance of $5,000 to Fine Fashions.

c. Just three days later, Fine Fashions paid Amalgam, which settled all amounts owed.

Required:

1. For each of the events (*a*) through (*c*), indicate the amount and direction of the effect (+ for increase, − for decrease, and NE for no effect) on Amalgam Textiles in terms of the following items.

Sales Revenues	Sales Returns and Allowances	Sales Discounts	Net Sales	Cost of Goods Sold	Gross Profit

2. Which of the above items are likely to be reported on Amalgam's external financial statements, and which items will be combined "behind the scenes"?

3. Prepare the journal entries that Amalgam Textiles would record, and show any computations.

> TIP: When using a perpetual inventory system, the seller always makes two journal entries when goods are sold.

GROUP A PROBLEMS

Practise and learn online with Connect.

PA6-1 Evaluating Internal Control Strengths and Weaknesses in Cash Receipts and Disbursements

LO3

The following procedures are used by Tico Taco Shop.

a. Customers pay cash for all food orders. Cash is placed in a cash register and a receipt is issued when requested by the customer.

b. At the end of each day, the cashier counts the cash, prepares a cash count sheet, and has the manager review and sign the cash count sheet.

c. At three times during the day, excess cash is removed from the cash register and placed in a vault until it is taken for night deposit at the local bank.

d. Orders for drink cups, straws, condiments, and other supplies are written on prenumbered purchase order forms and are approved by the manager before being sent to an authorized supplier.

e. When supplies are received, they are stacked just inside the back door to the kitchen, which is left unlocked because part-time employees frequently arrive and leave at various times during the day.

Required:

1. Indicate whether each procedure represents a strength or weakness. Explain your reasons.

2. For each weakness, describe a change in procedures that would address the weakness.

PA6-2 Preparing a Bank Reconciliation and Journal Entries, and Reporting Cash

The bookkeeper at Martin Company has asked you to prepare a bank reconciliation as of May 31, 2012. The May 31, 2012, bank statement and the May T-account for cash showed the transactions listed below.

Martin Company's bank reconciliation at the end of April 2012 showed a cash balance of $18,800. No deposits were in transit at the end of April, but a deposit was in transit at the end of May.

Check Figure:
Up-to-date cash balance
= $17,180

		Withdrawals	Deposits	Balance
Balance, May 1, 2012				$18,800
May 2			$ 8,000	26,800
May 5	#301	$11,000		15,800
May 7	#302	6,000		9,800
May 8			10,000	19,800
May 14	#303	500		19,300
May 17–Interest Earned			120	19,420
May 22–NSF cheque			280	19,140
May 27	#304	4,600		14,540
May 31–Service charges			60	14,480
Balance, May 31, 2012				14,480

		+	Cash (A)	−	
May 1	Balance	18,800			
May 1		8,000	11,000	# 301	May 2
May 7		10,000	6,000	# 302	May 4
May 29		4,000	500	#303	May 11
			4,600	#304	May 23
			1,300	#305	May 29
May 31	Balance	17,400			

Required:

1. Prepare a bank reconciliation for May.
2. Prepare any journal entries required as a result of the bank reconciliation. Why are they necessary?
3. After the reconciliation journal entries are posted, what balance will be reflected in the Cash account in the ledger?
4. If the company also has $50 on hand, which is recorded in a different account called Cash on Hand, what total amount of Cash and Cash Equivalents should be reported on the balance sheet at the end of May?

PA6-3 Identifying Outstanding Cheques and Deposits in Transit and Preparing a Bank Reconciliation and Journal Entries

The December 2012 bank statement and cash T-account for Stewart Company follow:

Date	Withdrawals	Deposits	Balance
Dec. 1			$48,000
2–Cheque	$500		47,500
4–Cheque	7,000		40,500
6–Cheque	120		40,380
11–Cheque	550	$28,000	67,830
13–Cheque	1,900		65,930
17–Cheque	12,000		53,930
23–Cheque	60	36,000	89,870
26–Cheque	900		88,970
28–Cheque	2,200		86,770
30–Cheque	17,000	19,000	88,770
30–NSF*	300		88,470
31–Cheque	1,650		86,820
31–Interest earned		50	86,870
31–Service charge	150		86,720

* NSF cheque from J. Left, a customer.

		+	Cash (A)	–	
Dec. 1	Balance	48,000	Cheques written during December:		
Deposits					
Dec. 11		28,000	500		60
23		36,000	7,000		900
30		19,000	120		150
31		13,000	550		17,000
			1,900		3,500
			12,000		1,650
			2,200		
Dec. 31	Balance	96,470			

There were no deposits in transit or outstanding cheques at November 30.

Required:

1. Identify and list the deposits in transit at the end of December.
2. Identify and list the outstanding cheques at the end of December.
3. Prepare a bank reconciliation for December.
4. Give any journal entries that the company should make as a result of the bank reconciliation. Why are they necessary?
5. After the reconciliation journal entries are posted, what balance will be reflected in the Cash account in the ledger?
6. If the company also has $300 on hand, which is recorded in a different account called *Cash on Hand*, what total amount of Cash and Cash Equivalents should be reported on the December 31, 2012, balance sheet?

PA6-4 Preparing a Multistep Income Statement with Sales Discounts and Sales Returns and Allowances and Computing the Gross Profit Percentage LO7

Big Billy Corporation is a local grocery store organized seven years ago as a corporation. The store is in an excellent location, and sales have increased each year. At the end of 2012, the bookkeeper prepared the following statement (assume that all amounts are correct, but note the incorrect terminology and format):

BIG BILLY CORPORATION
Profit and Loss
December 31, 2012

	Debit	Credit
Sales		$420,000
Cost of Goods Sold	$279,000	
Sales Returns and Allowances	10,000	
Sales Discounts	6,000	
Selling Expense	58,000	
Administrative Expense	16,000	
General Expenses	1,000	
Income Tax Expense	15,000	
Net Profit	35,000	
Totals	$420,000	$420,000

Required:

1. Prepare a multistep income statement that would be used for internal reporting purposes. Treat Sales Returns and Allowances and Sales Discounts as contra-revenue accounts.

2. Prepare a multistep income statement that would be used for external reporting purposes, beginning with the amount for Net Sales.

3. Compute and interpret the gross profit percentage (using the formula shown in this chapter).

LO6, 7 **PA6-5** **Recording Sales with Discounts and Returns and Analyzing Gross Profit Percentage**

Hair Care Inc. is a wholesaler of hair supplies. Hair Care uses a perpetual inventory system. The following transactions (summarized) have been selected from 2012:

Check Figure:
Net Sales = $60,340

a.	Sold merchandise for cash (cost of merchandise $28,797).	$51,200
b.	Received merchandise returned by customers as unsatisfactory (but in perfect condition), for cash refund (original cost of merchandise $360).	600
c.	Sold merchandise (costing $4,750) to a customer, on account with terms 2/10, n/30.	10,000
d.	Collected half of the balance owed by the customer in (*c*) within the discount period.	4,900
e.	Granted an allowance to the customer in (*c*).	160

Required:

1. Compute Sales Revenue, Net Sales, and Gross Profit for Hair World.
2. Compute the gross profit percentage (using the formula shown in this chapter).
3. Prepare journal entries to record transactions (*a*)–(*e*).
4. Hair Care is considering a contract to sell merchandise to a hair salon chain for $15,000. This merchandise will cost Hair Care $10,000. Would this contract increase (or decrease) Hair Care's gross profit and gross profit percentage? How should Hair Care decide whether to accept the contract?

LO6, 7 **PA6-6** **Reporting Sales Transactions between Wholesale and Retail Merchandisers, with Sales Allowances and Sales Discounts Using a Perpetual Inventory System**

The transactions listed below are typical of those involving New Books Inc. and Readers' Choice. New Books is a wholesale merchandiser and Readers' Choice is a retail merchandiser. Assume all sales of merchandise from New Books to Readers' Choice are made with terms 2/10, n/30, and that the two companies use perpetual inventory systems. Assume the following transactions between the two companies occurred in the order listed during the year ended August 31, 2012.

a. New Books sold merchandise to Readers' Choice at a selling price of $550,000. The merchandise had cost New Books $415,000.
b. Two days later, Readers' Choice complained to New Books that some of the merchandise differed from what Readers' Choice had ordered. New Books agreed to give an allowance of $10,000 to Readers' Choice.
c. Just three days later, Readers' Choice paid New Books, which settled all amounts owed.

Required:

1. For each of the events (*a*) through (*c*), indicate the amount and direction of the effect (+ for increase, − for decrease, and NE for no effect) on New Books in terms of the following items.

Sales Revenues	Sales Returns and Allowances	Sales Discounts	Net Sales	Cost of Goods Sold	Gross Profit

2. Which of the above items are likely to be reported on New Books' external financial statements, and which items will be combined "behind the scenes"?
3. Prepare the journal entries that New Books would record, and show any computations.

GROUP B PROBLEMS

LO3 **PB6-1** **Evaluating Internal Control Strengths and Weaknesses in Cash Receipts and Disbursements**

The following procedures are used by Principal Wholesale Incorporated:

a. All sales are made on account, with each sale being indicated on a sequentially numbered sales invoice.

b. Customer payments are received in the mail by the office receptionist, who sends the cheques to a cashier for deposit and the remittance advices to the accounting department for recording against the customer's account balance.

c. The office receptionist is assigned the job of handling all customer complaints.

d. When a customer has a legitimate complaint about goods sold to the customer on account, the receptionist will phone the accounting department to request that the customer's account be credited for the sales allowance.

e. The company's inventory is stored in a locked warehouse that is monitored by surveillance cameras.

f. Payments to the company's suppliers are made only after the supplier's invoice is received and compared to the receiving report.

Required:

1. Indicate whether each procedure represents a strength or weakness. Explain your reasons.

2. For each weakness, describe a change in procedures that would address the weakness.

PB6-2 Preparing a Bank Reconciliation and Journal Entries and Reporting Cash   LO4

The bookkeeper at Tony Company has asked you to prepare a bank reconciliation as of February 28, 2012. The February 28, 2012, bank statement and the February T-account for cash showed the following (summarized):

		Withdrawals	Deposits	Balance
Balance, February 1, 2012				$49,400
February 2	#101	$15,000		34,400
February 4			$ 7,000	41,400
February 5–NSF Cheque		320		41,080
February 9	#102	11,000		30,080
February 12	#103	7,500		22,580
February 14			9,500	32,080
February 19	#104	9,000		23,080
February 23			14,150	37,230
February 26	#105	6,700		30,530
February 27–Interest earned			150	30,680
February 28–Service charges		40		30,640

		+	Cash (A)	−	
Feb 1	Balance	49,400			
Feb 2		7,000	15,000		Feb 1 #101
Feb 13		9,500	11,000		Feb 7 #102
Feb 21		14,150	7,500		Feb 11 #103
Feb 28		7,800	9,000		Feb 17 #104
			6,700		Feb 25 #105
			1,200		Feb 29 #106
Feb 28	Balance	37,450			

Tony Company's bank reconciliation at the end of January 2012 showed no outstanding cheques. No deposits were in transit at the end of January, but a deposit was in transit at the end of February.

Required:

1. Prepare a bank reconciliation for February.

2. Prepare any journal entries required as a result of the bank reconciliation. Why are they necessary?

3. After the reconciliation journal entries are posted, what balance will be reflected in the Cash account in the ledger?

4. If the company also has $50 on hand, which is recorded in a different account called *Cash on Hand*, what total amount of Cash and Cash Equivalents should be reported on the balance sheet at the end of February?

PB6-3 Identifying Outstanding Cheques and Deposits in Transit and Preparing a Bank Reconciliation and Journal Entries

The September 2012 bank statement and cash T-account for Terrick Company follow:

Check Figure:
Total deposits in transit at Sept. 30: $21,000

Date	Withdrawals	Deposits	Balance
Sept. 1			$ 75,900
2–Cheque	$620		75,280
4–Cheque	2,000		73,280
6–Cheque	1,500		71,780
11–Cheque	300	$14,000	85,480
13–Cheque	650		84,830
17–Cheque	10,000		74,830
23–Cheque	90	27,000	101,740
26–Cheque	700		101,040
28–Cheque	8,000		93,040
29–Cheque	730	17,000	109,310
29–NSF cheque*	500		108,810
30–Cheque	400		108,410
30–Interest earned		60	108,470
30–Service charges	40		108,430

* NSF cheque from B. Frank, a customer.

			+ Cash (A) −		
Sept. 1	Balance	75,900	Cheques written during September:		
Deposits			620		8,000
Sept. 11		14,000	2,000		730
23		27,000	1,500		400
29		17,000	300		500
30		21,000	650		6,000
			10,000		90
			700		
Sept. 30	Balance	123,410			

There were no deposits in transit or outstanding cheques at August 31.

Required:

1. Identify and list the deposits in transit at the end of September.
2. Identify and list the outstanding cheques at the end of September.
3. Prepare a bank reconciliation for September.
4. Give any journal entries that the company should make as a result of the bank reconciliation. Why are they necessary?
5. After the reconciliation journal entries are posted, what balance will be reflected in the Cash account in the ledger?
6. If the company also has $200 on hand, which is recorded in a different account called *Cash on Hand*, what total amount of Cash and Cash Equivalents should be reported on the September 30, 2012, balance sheet?

PB6-4 Preparing a Multistep Income Statement with Sales Discounts and Sales Returns and Allowances and Computing the Gross Profit Percentage

Jacquie's Greenhouse Corporation is a local greenhouse organized ten years ago as a corporation. The greenhouse is in an excellent location, and sales have increased each year. At the end of 2012, the bookkeeper prepared the following statement (assume that all amounts are correct, but note the incorrect terminology and format):

JACQUIE'S GREENHOUSE CORPORATION
Profit and Loss
December 31, 2012

	Debit	Credit
Sales		$504,000
Cost of Goods Sold	$311,000	
Sales Returns and Allowances	11,000	
Sales Discounts	8,000	
Selling Expense	61,000	
Administrative Expense	13,000	
General Expenses	3,000	
Income Tax Expense	18,000	
Net Profit	79,000	
Totals	$504,000	$504,000

Required:

1. Prepare a multistep income statement that would be used for internal reporting purposes. Treat Sales Returns and Allowances and Sales Discounts as contra-revenue accounts.
2. Prepare a multistep income statement that would be used for external reporting purposes, beginning with the amount for Net Sales.
3. Compute and interpret the gross profit percentage (using the formula shown in this chapter).

PB6-5 Recording Sales and Purchases with Discounts and Returns and Analyzing Gross Profit Percentage

LO6, 7

Lonny's Building Supplies (LBS) is a locally owned and operated hardware store. LBS uses a perpetual inventory system. The following transactions (summarized) have been selected from 2012:

a.	Sold merchandise for cash (cost of merchandise $224,350).	$500,000
b.	Received merchandise returned by customers as unsatisfactory (but in perfect condition), for cash refund (original cost of merchandise $1,900).	3,000
c.	Sold merchandise (costing $3,000) to a customer, on account with terms 2/10, n/30.	5,000
d.	Collected half of the balance owed by the customer in (c) within the discount period.	2,450
e.	Granted an allowance to the customer in (c).	950

Check Figure:
Net sales = $501,000

Required:

1. Compute Sales Revenue, Net Sales, and Gross Profit for LBS.
2. Compute the gross profit percentage (using the formula shown in this chapter).
3. Prepare journal entries to record transactions (a)–(e).
4. LBS is considering a contract to sell building supplies to a local home builder for $20,000. These materials will cost LBS $16,000. Would this contract increase (or decrease) LBS's gross profit and gross profit percentage? How should LBS decide whether to accept the contract?

PB6-6 Reporting Sales Transactions between Wholesale and Retail Merchandisers, with Sales Allowances and Sales Discounts Using a Perpetual Inventory System

LO5, 6, 7

The transactions listed below are typical of those involving Sassy's Sporting Goods and Sports 4 All. Sassy's Sporting Goods is a wholesale merchandiser and Sports 4 All is a retail merchandiser. Assume all sales of merchandise from Sassy's Sporting Goods to Sports 4 All are made with terms 2/10, n/30, and that the two companies use perpetual inventory systems. Assume the following transactions between the two companies occurred in the order listed during the year ended December 31, 2012.

a. Sassy's Sporting Goods sold merchandise to Sports 4 All at a selling price of $125,000. The merchandise had cost Sassy's Sporting Goods $94,000.
b. Two days later, Sports 4 All complained to Sassy's Sporting Goods that some of the merchandise differed from what Sports 4 All had ordered. Sassy's Sporting Goods agreed to give an allowance of $3,000 to Sports 4 All.
c. Just three days later Sports 4 All paid Sassy's Sporting Goods, which settled all amounts owed.

Required:

1. For each of the events (*a*) through (*c*), indicate the amount and direction of the effect (+ for increase, − for decrease, and NE for no effect) on Sassy's Sporting Goods in terms of the following items.

Sales Revenues	Sales Returns and Allowances	Sales Discounts	Net Sales	Cost of Goods Sold	Gross Profit

2. Which of the above items are likely to be reported on Sassy's Sporting Goods' external financial statements, and which items will be combined "behind the scenes"?
3. Prepare the journal entries that Sassy's Sporting Goods would record and show any computations.

SKILLS DEVELOPMENT CASES

LO2, 7

Rona Inc.

S6-1 Finding Financial Information

Refer to the financial statements of Rona Inc. in Appendix A at the back of this book or download the annual report from the *Cases* section of Connect.

Required:

1. What amount of Net Sales does the company report during the year ended December 27, 2009?
2. The company's Cost of Goods Sold for this year end was $3,397,634,000. Compute the company's gross profit percentage for the year ended December 27, 2009, and explain what this means.
3. Assume that Rona experienced no shrinkage in the most current year. Using the balance sheet and income statement, estimate the amount of purchases in the year ended December 27, 2009.

LO2, 7

Rona Inc.

S6-2 Comparing Financial Information

Refer to the financial statements of Rona Inc. in Appendix A and The Home Depot's in Appendix B at the back of this book or download the annual reports from the *Cases* section of Connect.

1. Does The Home Depot report higher or lower Net Sales than Rona during the year ending January 31, 2010?
2. Assuming that Cost of Sales is the same thing as Cost of Goods Sold, compute The Home Depot's gross profit percentage for the most recent year. Is it greater or less than Rona's? Based on this, where are consumers likely to find lower markups?
3. Assume that The Home Depot experienced no shrinkage in the most recent year. Using the balance sheet and income statement, estimate the amount of purchases in the 2009–2010 year. How much greater (or less) were The Home Depot's purchases than Rona's in that year?

LO1, 7

S6-3 Internet-Based Team Research: Examining an Annual Report

As a team, select an industry to analyze. Using your Web browser, each team member should access the annual report for one publicly traded company in the industry, with each member selecting a different company. (See S1-3 in Chapter 1 for a description of possible resources for these tasks.)

Required:

1. On an individual basis, each team member should write a short report that incorporates the following:
   a. Describe the company's business in sufficient detail to be able to classify it as a service, merchandising, or manufacturing company. What products or services does the company provide?
   b. Calculate the gross profit percentage at the end of the current and prior years, and explain any change between the two years.
2. Then, as a team, write a short report comparing and contrasting your companies using these attributes. Discuss any patterns across the companies that you as a team observe. Provide potential explanations for any differences discovered.

LO2, 5

S6-4 Ethical Decision Making: A Real-Life Example

When some people think about inventory theft, they imagine a shoplifter running out of a store with goods stuffed inside a jacket or bag. But that's not what the managers thought at the Famous Footwear store on Chicago's Madison Street. No, they suspected their own employees were the main cause of their unusually high shrinkage. One scam involved dishonest cashiers who would let their friends take a pair of Skechers without paying for them. To make it look like the shoes had been bought, cashiers would ring up a sale, but instead of charging $50 for shoes, they would charge only $2 for a bottle of shoe polish. That's when the company's managers decided to put its accounting system to work. In just two years, the company cut its Madison Street inventory losses in half. Here's how a newspaper described the store's improvements:

> ### Retailers Crack Down on Employee Theft
> *SouthCoast Today,* September 10, 2000, Chicago
> By Calmetta Coleman, *The Wall Street Journal* Staff Writer
>
> . . . Famous Footwear installed a chainwide register-monitoring system to sniff out suspicious transactions, such as unusually large numbers of refunds or voids, or repeated sales of cheap goods.
>
> . . . [B]efore an employee can issue a cash refund, a second worker must be present to see the customer and inspect the merchandise.
>
> . . . [T]he chain has set up a toll-free hotline for employees to use to report suspicions about co-workers.

These improvements in inventory control came as welcome news for investors and creditors of Brown Shoe Company, the company that owns Famous Footwear. Despite these improvements at the Chicago store, Brown Shoe has been forced to shut down operations in other cities.

Required:

1. Explain how the register-monitoring system would allow Famous Footwear to cut down on employee theft.
2. What is the name of the control principle that is addressed by Famous Footwear's new cash refund procedure?
3. If Famous Footwear used a periodic inventory system, rather than a perpetual inventory system, how would the company detect shrinkage?
4. Think of and describe at least four different parties that are harmed by the type of inventory theft described in this case.

S6-5 Ethical Decision Making: A Mini-Case   LO6, 7

Assume you work as an accountant in the merchandising division of a large public company that makes and sells athletic clothing. To encourage the merchandising division to earn as much profit on each individual sale as possible, the division manager's pay is based, in part, on the division's gross profit percentage. To encourage control over the division's operating expenses, the manager's pay also is based on the division's net income.

You are currently preparing the division's financial statements. The division had a good year, with sales of $100,000, cost of goods sold of $50,000, sales returns and allowances of $6,000, sales discounts of $4,000, and other selling expenses of $30,000. (Assume the division does not report income taxes.) The division manager stresses that "*it would be in your personal interest*" to classify sales returns and allowances and sales discounts as selling expenses rather than as contra-revenues on the division's income statement. He justifies this "friendly advice" by saying that he's not asking you to fake the numbers—he just believes that those items are more accurately reported as expenses. Plus, he claims, being a division of a larger company, you don't have to follow GAAP.

Required:

1. Prepare an income statement for the division using the classifications shown in this chapter. Using this income statement, calculate the division's gross profit percentage.
2. Prepare an income statement for the division using the classifications advised by the manager. Using this income statement, calculate the division's gross profit percentage.
3. What reason (other than reporting "more accurately") do you think is motivating the manager's advice to you?
4. Do you agree with the manager's statement that he's "not asking you to fake the numbers"?
5. Do you agree with the manager's statement about not having to follow GAAP?
6. How should you respond to the division manager's "friendly advice"?

S6-6 Critical Thinking: Analyzing Internal Control Weaknesses

Snake Creek Company has a trusted employee who, as the owner said, "handles all of the bookkeeping and paperwork for the company." This employee is responsible for counting, verifying, and recording cash receipts and payments, making the weekly bank deposit, preparing cheques for major expenditures (signed by the owner), making small expenditures from the cash register for daily expenses, and collecting accounts receivable. The owner asked the local bank for a $20,000 loan. The bank asked that an audit be performed covering the year just ended. The independent auditor (a local CA), in a private conference with the owner, presented some evidence of the following activities of the trusted employee during the past year:

a. Cash sales sometimes were not entered in the cash register, and the trusted employee pocketed approximately $50 per month.

b. Cash taken from the cash register (and pocketed by the trusted employee) was replaced with expense memos with fictitious signatures (approximately $12 per day).

c. $300 collected on an account receivable from a valued out-of-town customer was pocketed by the trusted employee and was covered by making a $300 entry as a debit to Sales Returns and a credit to Accounts Receivable.

d. $800 collected on an account receivable from a local customer was pocketed by the trusted employee and was covered by making an $800 entry as a debit to Sales Discounts and a credit to Accounts Receivable.

Required:

1. What was the approximate amount stolen during the past year?

   TIP: Assume employees work 5 days a week, 52 weeks a year.

2. What would be your recommendations to the owner?

S6-7 Preparing Multistep Income Statements and Calculating Gross Profit Percentage

Assume that you have been hired by Big Sky Corporation as a summer intern. The company is in the process of preparing its annual financial statements. To help in the process, you are asked to prepare an income statement for internal reporting purposes and an income statement for external reporting purposes. Your boss has also requested that you determine the company's gross profit percentage based on the statements that you are to prepare. The following adjusted trial balance was created from the general ledger accounts on May 31, 2012.

Account Titles	Debits	Credits
Cash	$ 57,000	
Accounts Receivable	67,000	
Inventory	103,000	
Property and Equipment	252,000	
Accumulated Amortization		$103,000
Liabilities		75,000
Contributed Capital		120,000
Retained Earnings, June 1, 2011		145,900
Sales Revenue		369,000
Sales Returns and Allowances	9,500	
Sales Discounts	14,000	
Cost of Goods Sold	248,000	
Selling Expense	19,000	
Administrative Expense	23,000	
General Expenses	5,000	
Income Tax Expense	15,400	
Totals	$812,900	$812,900

Your boss wants you to create the spreadsheet in a way that automatically recalculates net sales and any other related amounts whenever changes are made to the contra-revenue accounts. To do this, you know that you'll have to use formulas throughout the worksheets and even import or link cells from one worksheet to another. Once again, your friend Owen is willing to help.

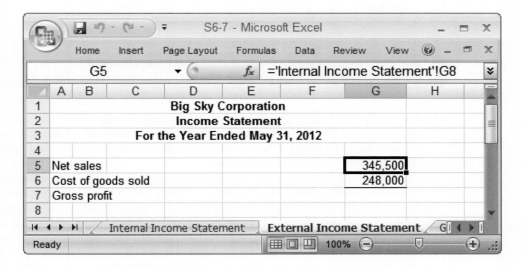

Sounds like you are going to get some great experience this summer. Okay, to import a number from another spreadsheet, you first click on the cell where you want the number to appear. For example, if you want to enter the Net Sales balance in the external income statement, click on the cell in the external income statement where the Net Sales number is supposed to appear. Enter the equals sign (=) and then click on the tab that takes you to the worksheet containing the internal income statement. In that worksheet, click on the cell that contains the amount you want to import into the external income statement and then press Enter. This will create a link from the internal income statement cell to the external income statement cell. Here's a screen shot showing the formula that will appear after you import the number.

Don't forget to save the file using a name that indicates who you are.

Required:

Enter the trial balance information into a spreadsheet and complete the following:

1. Prepare a multistep income statement that would be used for internal reporting purposes. Classify sales returns and allowances and sales discounts as contra-revenue accounts.

2. Prepare a multistep income statement that would be used for external reporting purposes, beginning with the amount for Net Sales.

3. Compute the gross profit percentage.

CONTINUING CASE

Practise and learn online with Connect.

CC6 Accounting for Merchandising Operations   LO6, 7

Nicole's Getaway Spa (NGS) has been so successful that Nicole has decided to expand her spa by selling merchandise. She sells things such as nail polish, at-home spa kits, cosmetics, and Palacetherapy items. Nicole uses a perpetual inventory system and is starting to realize all of the work that is created when inventory is involved in a business. The following transactions were selected from among those completed by NGS in August.

Aug. 2   Sold 10 items of merchandise to Salon World on account at a selling price of $1,000 (total); terms 2/10, n/30. The goods cost NGS $650.

Aug. 3   Sold 5 identical items of merchandise to Cosmetics 4 You on account at a selling price of $825 (total); terms 2/10, n/30. The goods cost NGS $400.

Aug. 6   Cosmetics 4 You returned one of the items purchased on August 3. The item could still be sold by NGS in the future, and credit was given to the customer.

Aug. 10	Collected payment from Salon World, fully paying off the account balance.
Aug. 20	Sold two at-home spa kits to Meghan Witzel for $300 cash. The goods cost NGS $96.
Aug. 22	Cosmetics 4 You paid its remaining account balance in full.

Required:

1. Prepare journal entries for each transaction.

2. Calculate the amount of Net Sales and Cost of Goods Sold for the transactions listed above. What is Nicole's Getaway Spa's gross profit percentage? Explain to Nicole what this gross profit percentage means.

3. At the end of August, Nicole noticed that the bank account balance did not equal the company's Cash account balance. Explain to her why these balances do not equal and what related internal control she needs to establish.

Endnotes

1. One study found that companies emphasizing strong internal control and an ethical culture grew their revenues four times faster and increased their share prices 12 times as much as companies without these practices. J. P. Kotter and J. L. Heskett, *Corporate Culture and Performance*, 1992. New York: Maxwell MacMillan International.

2. Any transportation costs paid by the seller (called *freight-out*) are reported as Delivery Expenses on the seller's income statement. Chapter 7 discusses buyers' accounting for transportation costs.

3. We have assumed that the return occurs in the same period as the sale. When significant returns are likely to occur after the period of sale, the seller records an estimate of those expected returns, using methods described in Chapter 8. We also have assumed that the returned bike was as good as new. Chapter 7 describes how to account for damaged inventory.

4. Industry statistics were retrieved on April 13, 2009, from Reuters: www.reuters.com/finance/industries.

Practise and learn online with Connect.

CHAPTER 7

Reporting and Interpreting Inventories and Cost of Goods Sold

YOUR LEARNING OBJECTIVES

Understand the business

LO1 Describe the issues in managing different types of inventory.

Study the accounting methods

LO2 Explain how to report inventory and cost of goods sold.

LO3 Compute costs using three inventory costing methods.

LO4 Report inventory at the lower of cost and net realizable value.

LO5 Analyze and record inventory purchases, transportation, returns and allowances, and discounts.

Evaluate the results

LO6 Evaluate inventory management by computing and interpreting the inventory turnover ratio.

Review the chapter

Chapter Summary, page 308

Additional resources on Connect

FOCUS COMPANY:

American Eagle Outfitters, Inc.

www.ae.com

AMERICAN EAGLE
OUTFITTERS

Whether you are shopping for gasoline, groceries, or a new flat-screen TV, prices always seem to be changing. The political situation in oil-producing nations can cause a stunning increase in prices at the pump. A late freeze in Florida can hike the price of orange juice. Increasing competition can dramatically lower the cost of that new TV.

Like you, companies face similar price changes when they purchase or produce goods. Increases in demand can cause the cost of inventory to increase over time; technological innovation can cause it to decrease. Either way, inventory is likely to include some items that were acquired at a lower unit cost and others that were acquired at a higher unit cost.

Suppose clothing retailer American Eagle Outfitters buys three batches of its AE fleece jackets at a cost of $20 per jacket for the first batch, $30 per jacket for the second batch, and $40 per jacket for the third. When American Eagle sells a jacket, what cost should it use to compute the Cost of Goods Sold? And what happens at the end of the season when the value of its jackets falls below cost?

As you will learn in this chapter, accounting rules allow different methods to be used when accounting for inventory, each of which leads to reporting different dollar amounts for Cost of Goods Sold (and the items remaining in inventory). This flexibility allows managers to choose the method that best fits their business environment. But it also means that you must know which method managers are using and how it works. That's what we'll look at in this chapter.

THAT WAS THEN

In the previous chapter, we focused on selling goods that were purchased at the same cost per unit.

THIS IS NOW

This chapter demonstrates how to account for goods purchased at different unit costs.

ORGANIZATION OF THE CHAPTER

Understand the business	**S**tudy the accounting methods	**E**valuate the results	**R**eview the chapter
• Inventory management decisions • Types of inventory	• Balance sheet and income statement reporting • Inventory costing methods • Lower of cost and net realizable value • Recording inventory transactions	• Inventory turnover analysis	• Demonstration Case • Chapter Summary • Key Terms • Homework Helper • Practice Material

Understand the Business

INVENTORY MANAGEMENT DECISIONS

Learning Objective 1

Describe the issues in managing different types of inventory.

You may not make or sell inventory, but you buy it all the time. The things that concern you as a consumer also concern managers who make inventory decisions. The primary goals of inventory managers are to (1) maintain a sufficient quantity of inventory to meet customers' needs and (2) ensure inventory quality meets customers' expectations and company standards. At the same time, they try to (3) minimize the cost of acquiring and carrying inventory (including costs related to purchasing, production, storage, spoilage, theft, obsolescence, and financing). These factors are tricky to manage because as one of them changes (e.g., quality) so, too, do the others (e.g., cost). Ultimately, inventory management often comes down to purchasing goods that can be sold soon after they are acquired.

TYPES OF INVENTORY

The generic term *inventory* means goods that are held for sale in the normal course of business or are used to produce other goods for sale. Merchandisers hold merchandise inventory, which consists of products acquired in a finished condition, ready for sale without further processing. Manufacturers often hold three types of inventory, with each representing a different stage in the manufacturing process. They start with raw materials inventory such as plastic, steel, or fabrics. When these raw materials enter the production process, they become part of work in process inventory, which includes goods that are in the process of being manufactured. When completed, work in process inventory becomes finished goods inventory, which is ready for sale just like merchandise inventory. For the purposes of this chapter, we'll focus on merchandise inventory, but be aware that the concepts we cover apply equally to manufacturers' inventory.

Two other accounting terms may be used to describe inventory. *Consignment inventory* refers to goods a company is holding on behalf of the goods' owner. Typically, this arises when a company is willing to sell the goods for the owner (for a fee) but does not want to take ownership of the goods in the event the goods are difficult to sell. Consignment inventory is reported on the balance sheet of the owner, not the company holding the inventory. *Goods in transit* are inventory items being transported. This type of inventory is reported on the balance sheet of the owner, not the company transporting it. As you may remember from

Chapter 6, ownership of inventory is determined by the terms of the inventory sales agreement. If a sale is made FOB destination, the goods belong to the seller until they reach their destination (the customer). If a sale is made FOB shipping point, inventory belongs to the customer at the point of shipping (from the seller's premises).

Study the Accounting Methods

BALANCE SHEET AND INCOME STATEMENT REPORTING

Because inventory will be used or converted into cash within one year, it is reported on the balance sheet as a current asset. Goods placed in inventory are initially recorded at cost, which is the amount paid to acquire the asset and prepare it for sale. See Exhibit 7.1 for the way American Eagle reports inventory.

Learning Objective 2

Explain how to report inventory and cost of goods sold.

EXHIBIT 7.1	Reporting Inventory on the Balance Sheet (Partial)

AMERICAN EAGLE
OUTFITTERS

AMERICAN EAGLE OUTFITTERS, INC.
Balance Sheets (Partial)
At January 31, 2010 and 2009

(in millions)	2010	2009
Assets		
Current Assets		
Cash and Cash Equivalents	$694	$473
Short-Term Investments	5	11
Inventory	326	295
Accounts and Note Receivable	35	41
Prepaid Expenses and Other	107	105

When a company sells goods, it removes their cost from the Inventory account and reports the cost on the income statement as the expense Cost of Goods Sold. See Exhibit 7.2 for how American Eagle reports the Cost of Goods Sold (CGS) on its partial income statement. Notice that it follows directly after Net Sales. The difference between these two line items is a subtotal called *Gross Profit*.

EXHIBIT 7.2	Reporting Cost of Goods Sold on the Income Statement (Partial)

AMERICAN EAGLE
OUTFITTERS

AMERICAN EAGLE OUTFITTERS, INC.
Income Statements (Partial)
For the Years Ended January 31, 2010, 2009, and 2008

(in millions)	2010	2009	2008
Net Sales	$2,991	$2,989	$3,055
Cost of Goods Sold	1,832	1,815	1,632
Gross Profit	1,159	1,174	1,423

Cost of Goods Sold Equation

YOU SHOULD KNOW

Goods available for sale:
The sum of beginning inventory and purchases for the period.

Although the cost of inventory and the cost of goods sold are reported on different financial statements, they are related. A company starts each accounting period with a stock of inventory called *beginning inventory* (**BI**). During the accounting period, new **purchases** (**P**) are added to the beginning inventory. As in Exhibit 7.3, the sum of these two amounts (BI + P) becomes the cost of **goods available for sale** during the period.

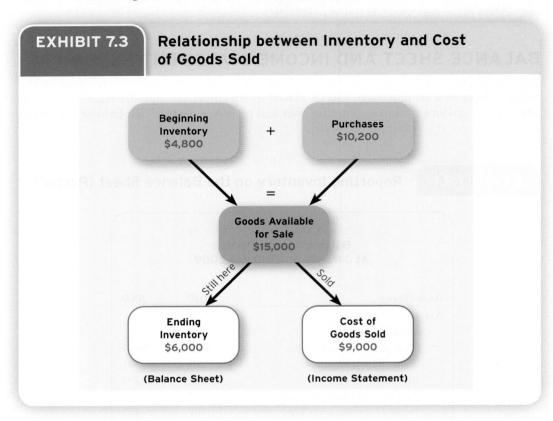

EXHIBIT 7.3 | **Relationship between Inventory and Cost of Goods Sold**

Goods available for sale either will be sold during the period (reported as the cost of goods sold on the income statement) or not (reported as **ending inventory** (**EI**) on the balance sheet). The ending inventory for one accounting period then becomes the beginning inventory for the next period. The **Cost of Goods Sold** (**CGS**) **equation** summarizes the relationships between these inventory amounts:

YOU SHOULD KNOW

Cost of Goods Sold (CGS) equation: BI + P − EI = CGS.

$$BI + P - CGS = EI$$

To illustrate the CGS equation, assume that, as in Exhibit 7.3, American Eagle Outfitters began the period with $4,800 of vintage jeans in beginning inventory. During the period, the company purchased more of these jeans for $10,200. This meant that American Eagle had goods costing $15,000 that were available for sale. If the cost of goods sold for the period was $9,000, $6,000 of jeans was left in inventory at the end of the period. These amounts can be represented in the following CGS calculation or Inventory T-account:

Cost of Goods Sold Calculation

Beginning Inventory	$ 4,800
+ Purchases	+10,200
Goods Available for Sale	15,000
− Cost of Goods Sold	− 9,000
Ending Inventory	$ 6,000

+	Inventory (A)		−
Beginning Inventory	4,800		
Purchases of Inventory	10,200	9,000	Cost of Goods Sold
Ending Inventory	6,000		

If one of these values is unknown, you can use either the CGS equation or the inventory T-account to solve for the missing value. See for yourself in the following Self-Study Practice.

HOW'S IT GOING? Self-Study Practice

Use the Cost of Goods Sold equation to solve for the missing information for Cases 1 and 2. Then enter the information for either Case 1 or Case 2 into the T-account on the right.

		Case 1	Case 2
Beginning Inventory	5 units × $10	$ 50	$ 50
+ Purchases	20 units × $10	200	200
Goods Available for Sale			250
− Ending Inventory		100	
Cost of Goods Sold			$150

dr +	Inventory		cr −
Beginning	50		
Purchases	200		
Goods Available			
			Goods Sold
Ending Inventory			

After you have finished, check your answers with the solution in the margin.

INVENTORY COSTING METHODS

In the example presented in the Self-Study Practice, the cost of all units of the item was the same—$10. If inventory costs normally remained constant, we'd be finished right now. But just as you notice every time you fill up your car with gas, the cost of goods does not always stay the same. In recent years, the costs of many items have risen moderately. In other cases, such as LCD TVs, costs have dropped dramatically.

When the costs of inventory change over time, it is not obvious how to determine the cost of goods sold (and the cost of ending inventory). To see why, think about the following simple example:

May 3	Purchased 1 unit for **$70.**
May 5	Purchased 1 more unit for **$75.**
May 6	Purchased 1 more unit for **$95.**
May 8	Sold 2 units for $125 each.

The sale on May 8 of two units, at a selling price of $125 each, would generate sales revenue of $250 ($125 × 2), but what amount would be considered the cost of goods sold? The answer depends on which goods are assumed to have been sold.

Three inventory costing methods are available under ASPE and IFRS for determining the cost of goods sold and the cost of goods remaining in ending inventory. Keep in mind that the method chosen does not have to correspond to the physical flow of goods, so any one of these three acceptable methods can be used in Canada.

The **specific identification** method individually identifies and records the cost of each item sold as Cost of Goods Sold. This method requires accountants to keep track of the purchase cost of each item. In the example just given, if the items sold were identified as the ones received on May 3 and May 6, which cost $70 and $95, the total cost of those items ($70 + $95 = $165) would be reported as Cost of Goods Sold. The cost of the remaining item ($75) would be reported as Inventory on the balance sheet at the end of the period. Companies tend to use the specific identification method when accounting for individually expensive and unique items. Bridal shops and art galleries are two examples of companies that would most likely use the specific identification method due to the uniqueness of their inventories.

The units within each American Eagle product line are identical, so the company does not use the specific identification method. Like most companies, American Eagle uses one of the two other cost flow methods to account for inventory items. These two other inventory costing methods are **not based on the physical flow** of goods on and off the shelves. Instead, these methods are based on **assumptions** that accountants make about the flow of inventory costs. These two cost flow assumptions are applied to our simple three-unit example in Exhibit 7.4 as follows:

1. **First-in, first-out (FIFO)** assumes that the inventory costs flow out in the order the goods are received. As in Exhibit 7.4, the earliest items received, the $70 and $75 units received on May 3 and 5, become the $145 Cost of Goods Sold on the income statement and the remaining $95 unit received on May 6 becomes Ending Inventory on the balance sheet.

2. **Weighted average cost** uses the weighted average of the costs of goods available for sale for both the cost of each item sold and those remaining in inventory. As in Exhibit 7.4, the average of the costs [($70 + $75 + $95) ÷ 3 = $80] is assigned to the two items sold, resulting in $160 as Cost of Goods Sold on the income statement. The same $80 average cost is assigned to the one item in Ending Inventory reported on the balance sheet.

As Exhibit 7.4 illustrates, the choice of cost flow assumption can have a major effect on Gross Profit on the income statement and Inventory on the balance sheet.

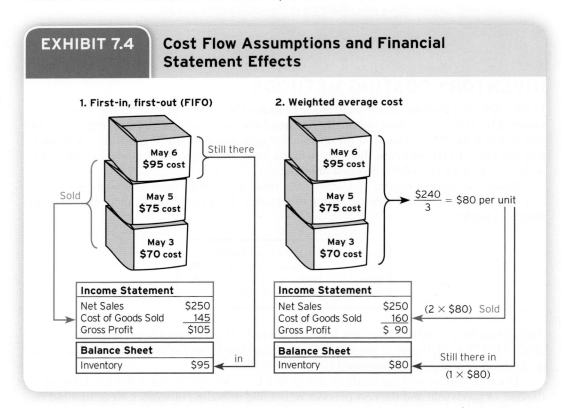

EXHIBIT 7.4 **Cost Flow Assumptions and Financial Statement Effects**

Notice that although they're called "inventory" costing methods, their names actually describe how to calculate the cost of goods sold. That is, the "first-out" part of FIFO refers to the goods that are sold (i.e., first out) not the goods that are still in ending inventory. Here's a summary of whether the oldest, newest, or average unit costs are used to calculate amounts on the balance sheet or income statement.

	FIFO	Weighted Average
Cost of Goods Sold (Income Statement)	Oldest cost	Average cost
Inventory (Balance Sheet)	Newest cost	Average cost

Inventory Cost Flow Computations

Now that you've seen how these cost flow assumptions work and that they actually make a difference in a company's balance sheet and income statement, you're ready for a more realistic example. So, let's assume that during the first week of October, American Eagle entered into the following transactions for its Henley T-shirt product line. All sales were made at a selling price of $15 per unit. These sales occurred after American Eagle made two batches of T-shirt purchases, which were added to inventory purchased the previous month.

Date	Description	No. of Units	Cost per Unit	Total Cost
Oct. 1	Beginning Inventory	10	$ 7	$ 70
Oct. 3	Purchase	30	8	240
Oct. 5	Purchase	10	10	100
Oct. 6	Sales	(35)	To calculate	To calculate
	Ending Inventory	15	To calculate	To calculate

FIFO (First-In, First-Out)   The first-in, first-out (FIFO) method assumes that the oldest goods (the first into inventory) are the first ones sold (the first out of inventory). So to calculate the cost of the 35 units sold, use the costs of the first-in (oldest) goods (10 units at $7 plus 25 of the 30 units at $8 = a total of $270). The costs of the newer goods are included in the cost of the ending inventory (10 units at $10 plus 5 units remaining from the 30 units at $8 = a total of $140). These calculations are summarized in the table below.

FIFO		
Beginning Inventory	10 units × $7	$ 70
+ Purchases	30 units × $8	240
	10 units × $10	100
Goods Available for Sale		410
− Ending Inventory (10 × $10) + (5 × $8)		140
Cost of Goods Sold (10 × $7) + (25 × $8)		$270

COACH'S TIP

Notice that the name of the method (first-in, first-out) describes how to calculate the cost of goods sold. The cost of ending inventory using FIFO is based on costs last-in.

Notice in the table that the Cost of Goods Sold can be calculated directly (10 times $7 plus 25 times $8 = a total of $270) or it can be "backed into" by subtracting the cost of ending inventory from the cost of goods available for sale ($410 − $140 = $270). This latter approach is helpful if the number of units sold is not known, which can occur when a company uses a periodic inventory system.[1]

Weighted Average Cost   The weighted average cost method is calculated in two steps. The first step is to calculate the total cost of the goods available for sale. You multiply the number of units at each cost by the cost per unit and then add to get the total cost:

Beginning Inventory	10 units × $7	$ 70
+ Purchases	30 units × $8	240
	10 units × $10	100
Goods Available for Sale	**50 units**	**$410**

Then you calculate the weighted average cost per unit using the following formula:

$$\frac{\text{Weighted}}{\text{Average Cost}} = \frac{\text{Cost of Goods Available for Sale}}{\text{Number of Units Available for Sale}} = \frac{\$410}{50 \text{ Units}} = \frac{\$8.20}{\text{per unit}}$$

Cost of goods sold and ending inventory are both calculated using the same weighted average cost per unit, as in the following table.

Weighted Average		
Beginning Inventory	10 units × $7	$ 70
+ Purchases	30 units × $8	240
	10 units × $10	100
Goods Available for Sale	**50 units**	410
− Ending Inventory (15 × $8.20)		123
Cost of Goods Sold (35 × $8.20)		$287

Financial Statement Effects   Exhibit 7.5 summarizes the financial statement effects of the FIFO and weighted average cost methods. Remember that these methods differ only in the way they split the cost of goods available for sale between ending inventory and cost of goods sold. If a cost goes into Inventory, it doesn't go into Cost of Goods Sold. Thus, the method that assigns the highest cost to ending inventory will assign the lowest cost to cost of goods sold (and vice versa). As you can see in Exhibit 7.5, the effect on Cost of Goods Sold affects many other items on the income statement including Gross Profit, Income from Operations, Income before Income Tax Expense, Income Tax Expense, and Net Income.

EXHIBIT 7.5	Financial Statement Effects of Inventory Costing Methods

Effects on the Income Statement	FIFO	Weighted Average
Sales	$525	$525
Cost of Goods Sold	270	287
Gross Profit	255	238
Operating Expenses	125	125
Income from Operations	130	113
Other Revenue (Expenses)	20	20
Income before Income Tax Expense	150	133
Income Tax Expense (assume 30%)	45	40
Net Income	$105	$ 93
Effects on the Balance Sheet		
Inventory	$140	$123

Depending on whether costs are rising or falling, different methods have different effects on the financial statements. When costs are rising, as they are in our example, FIFO produces a higher inventory value (making the balance sheet appear to be stronger) and a lower cost of goods sold (resulting in a higher gross profit, which makes the company look more profitable). When costs are falling, these effects are reversed; FIFO produces a lower ending inventory value and a higher cost of goods sold—a double whammy. These are not "real" economic effects, however, because the same number of units is sold or held in ending inventory under either method. The following table summarizes the effects:

Effects of Increasing Costs on the Financial Statements	
	FIFO
Inventory (Balance Sheet)	Higher
Cost of Goods Sold (Income Statement)	Lower
Effects of Decreasing Costs on the Financial Statements	
	FIFO
Inventory (Balance Sheet)	Lower
Cost of Goods Sold (Income Statement)	Higher

Tax Implications and Cash Flow Effects

Given the financial statement effects, you might wonder why a company would ever use a method that produces a lower inventory amount and a higher cost of goods sold. The answer is suggested in Exhibit 7.5, in the line called *Income Tax Expense*. When faced with increasing costs per unit, as in our example, a company that uses FIFO will have a higher income tax expense. This income tax effect is a real cost, in the sense that the company will actually have to pay more income taxes in the current year, thereby reducing the company's cash.

HOW'S IT GOING? Self-Study Practice

Ultima Modia, Inc., purchased one designer suit at a cost of $200 and then purchased three more for $400 each. Three of the suits are then sold at a price of $1,000 each. Compute the Sales Revenue, Cost of Goods Sold, Gross Profit, and the cost of Ending Inventory using (*a*) FIFO and (*b*) weighted average. Which inventory costing method will minimize Ultima's income taxes?

After you have finished, check your answers with the solution in the margin.

Consistency in Reporting

A common question people ask is whether managers are free to choose one inventory costing method one period, and then switch to another inventory costing method the next period, depending on whether unit costs are rising or declining during the period. Because this constant switching would make it difficult to compare financial results across periods, accounting rules discourage it. A change in method is allowed only if it will improve the relevance of the company's financial results and financial position. A company can, however, use different methods for inventories that differ in nature or use, provided that the methods are used consistently over time.

Solution to Self-Study Practice

	(a) FIFO	(b) Weighted Average
Sales Revenue (3 × $1,000)	$3,000	$3,000
Cost of Goods Sold*	1,000	1,050
Gross Profit	2,000	1,950
Ending Inventory	$ 400	$ 350

*(a) $1,000 = (1 × $200) + (2 × $400); (b) $1,050 = 3 × [(1 × $200) + (3 × $400)]/4; Weighted average minimizes Ultima's gross profit and, therefore, minimizes its income taxes.

SPOTLIGHT ON THE WORLD

Last-In, First-Out (LIFO)

The last-in, first-out (LIFO) inventory costing method, which is no longer permitted under ASPE or IFRS, assumes that the newest goods (the last into inventory) are the first ones sold (the first out of inventory). The cost of Ending Inventory using LIFO is based on costs first-in. (Think of this as "first-in, still there" or FIST.)

LIFO is no longer permitted because

1. In most situations, LIFO does not fairly represent the actual flow of costs.

2. The cost of Ending Inventory that is reported on the balance sheet is not a fair representation of the most recent costs of inventories on hand.

3. The use of LIFO can result in large distortions of reported income when older inventory costs, which are typically lower, are expensed to cost of goods sold.

The Canada Revenue Agency has never allowed companies to use LIFO in calculating their income for tax purposes, so this inventory costing method was not widely used in Canada. However, it is permitted under U.S. GAAP, since the United States is one country that has not yet adopted IFRS. As a result, approximately 36 percent of companies in the United States currently use LIFO.*

Public companies in Canada that are listed on a U.S. stock exchange and also on a Canadian exchange are allowed to prepare their financial statements using U.S. GAAP, and therefore can use the LIFO inventory costing method. We have therefore added Supplement 7A, starting on page 300 of this chapter, where we examine LIFO more closely, using the same examples that we've used in this early part of the chapter.

*American Institute of Certified Public Accountants, *Accounting Trends and Techniques*, 62nd ed., 2008, p. 159.

LOWER OF COST AND NET REALIZABLE VALUE

Learning Objective 4

Report inventory at the lower of cost and net realizable value.

The value of inventory can fall below its recorded cost for two reasons: (1) it's easily replaced by identical goods at a lower cost or (2) it's become outdated or damaged. The first case typically involves high-tech goods such as cellphones. As companies become more efficient at making these cutting-edge products, the products become cheaper to make. The second case commonly occurs with fad items or seasonal goods such as American Eagle's winter coats, which tend to drop in value at the end of the season.

In either instance, when the value of inventory falls below its recorded cost, GAAP require that the amount that was originally recorded for inventory be written down to its lower net realizable value. This rule is known as reporting inventories at the **lower of cost and net realizable value (LC&NRV).** It results in reporting inventory conservatively, at an amount that does not exceed its actual value. Also, by recording the write-down in the period in which a loss in value occurs, companies better match their revenues and expenses of that period.

YOU SHOULD KNOW

Lower of cost and net realizable value (LC&NRV): A valuation rule that requires Inventory to be written down when its net realizable value or current replacement cost falls below its original historical cost.

Let's look at how the inventory write-down is determined and recorded. Assume that American Eagle's ending inventory includes two items whose replacement costs have recently changed: leather coats and vintage jeans.[2] The replacement costs of these items can be used as estimates of the net realizable value and compared to the original recorded cost per unit. You then take the lower of those two amounts (the lower of cost and net realizable value) and multiply it by the number of units on hand. The result is the amount at which the inventory should be reported after all adjustments have been made:

Item	Cost per Item	Net Realizable Value per Item	LC&NRV per Item	Quantity	Total Lower of Cost and Net Realizable Value	Total Cost	Write-Down
Leather coats	$165	$150	$150	1,000	1,000 × $150 = $150,000	$165,000	$15,000
Vintage jeans	20	25	20	400	400 × $ 20 = 8,000	8,000	0

Because the net realizable value of the 1,000 leather coats ($150) is lower than the recorded cost ($165), the recorded amount for ending inventory should be written down by $15 per unit ($165 − $150). If American Eagle has 1,000 units in inventory, the total write-down should be $15,000 ($15 × 1,000). The effect of this write-down on the accounting equation and the journal entry to record it would be

1 Analyze

Assets	=	Liabilities	+	Shareholders' Equity	
Inventory −15,000	=			Cost of Goods Sold (+E)	−15,000

2 Record

(a)	dr Cost of Goods Sold (+E, −SE).................................	15,000	
	cr Inventory (−A)		15,000

Because the net realizable value of the vintage jeans ($25) is higher than the original cost ($20), no write-down is necessary. The vintage jeans remain on the books at their cost of $20 per unit ($8,000 in total). Their value should not be increased based on the higher replacement cost because GAAP require that they be reported at the lower of cost and net realizable value.

Most companies report their inventory write-down expense as Cost of Goods Sold, even though the written-down goods may not have been sold. This reporting is appropriate because writing down goods that haven't yet sold is a necessary cost of carrying the goods that did sell.

COACH'S TIP

Companies generally report their accounting policy for inventory in the first note to the financial statements.

By recording the write-down in the period in which a loss in value occurs, companies better match their revenues and expenses of that period.

Most analysts view an inventory write-down to the LC&NRV as a sign of inventory management problems. Knowing this, some executives have gone out of their way to avoid inventory write-downs, as the following Spotlight on Ethics explains. The failure to follow inventory LC&NRV rules is one of the most common types of financial statement misstatements. To learn more about how this misstatement and other inventory errors can affect the financial statements, see Supplement 7C later in this chapter.

SPOTLIGHT ON ETHICS

Dodging Bullets

David H. Brooks, the founder and former chief executive officer of DHB Industries Inc. was charged in October 2007 for his involvement in fraudulently misstating DHB's financial statements. His company produced 50,000 bulletproof vests using a material (Zylon) that allegedly was known to degrade rapidly. The fraud charge claimed that DHB knew that these quality problems led to a decline in the inventory's net realizable value but failed to write down the inventory to the LC&NRV on a timely basis. The company eventually did record inventory write-downs totalling $18 million, causing a reduction in assets and net income. But this information came too late for some DHB shareholders who had unsuspectingly invested in a failing company. To learn more about this fraud, see Exercise E7-11 near the end of this chapter.

RECORDING INVENTORY TRANSACTIONS

To this point in the chapter, we have described the requirement that inventory must be reported at the lower of cost and net realizable value, and we have shown how those values are determined. But we haven't discussed the details about how to record inventory transactions. Until now, we have considered only inventory purchases but not other related transactions including transportation, purchase returns and allowances, and purchase discounts. In this section, we demonstrate the accounting for these other transactions. For purposes of this demonstration, we record all inventory-related transactions in the Inventory account. This approach is generally associated with a perpetual inventory system because it maintains an up-to-date balance in the Inventory account at all times. An alternative approach, which maintains separate accounts for purchases, transportation, and so on, is generally used in a periodic inventory system and is demonstrated in Supplement 7D near the end of this chapter.

Learning Objective 5

Analyze and record inventory purchases, transportation, returns and allowances, and discounts.

Inventory Purchases

To enhance efficiency and internal control, most companies buy inventory on credit rather than with cash. If American Eagle Outfitters purchases $10,500 of vintage jeans on credit, the transaction would affect the accounting equation and would be recorded as follows:

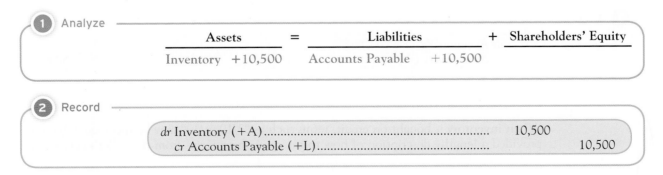

1 Analyze

Assets	=	Liabilities	+	Shareholders' Equity
Inventory +10,500		Accounts Payable +10,500		

2 Record

dr Inventory (+A)	10,500	
cr Accounts Payable (+L)		10,500

The $10,500 owed to the supplier remains in Accounts Payable until it is paid, at which time Accounts Payable is decreased (with a debit) and Cash is decreased (with a credit). The Inventory account remains at $10,500, unless the inventory is sold or any of the following transactions occur.

Transportation Cost

The inventory that American Eagle purchases does not magically appear in its stores. It must be shipped from the supplier to American Eagle. If the terms are FOB shipping point, the purchaser pays for the shipping. If the terms are FOB destination, the seller pays for the shipping. When the purchaser pays for the shipping, the additional cost of transporting the goods (called *freight-in*) is added to the Inventory account.

Assume that American Eagle pays $400 cash to a trucker who delivers the $10,500 of vintage jeans to one of its stores. American Eagle would account for this transportation cost as follows:

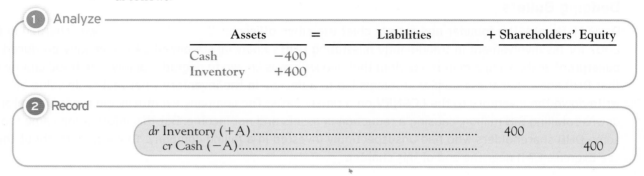

1 Analyze

	Assets	=	Liabilities	+ Shareholders' Equity
Cash	−400			
Inventory	+400			

2 Record

dr Inventory (+A)..	400	
cr Cash (−A)..		400

In general, a purchaser should include in the Inventory account any costs needed to get the inventory into a condition and location ready for sale. Costs that are incurred after the inventory has been made ready for sale, such as freight-out to deliver goods to customers, should be treated as selling expenses.

Purchase Returns and Allowances

When goods purchased from a supplier arrive in damaged condition or fail to meet specifications, the buyer can (1) return them for a full refund or (2) keep them and ask for a cost reduction, called an *allowance*. Either way, these **purchase returns and allowances** are accounted for by reducing the cost of the inventory and either recording a cash refund or by reducing the liability owed to the supplier.

Assume, for example, that American Eagle returned some of the vintage jeans to the supplier and received a $500 reduction in the balance owed. This purchase return would be analyzed and recorded as follows:

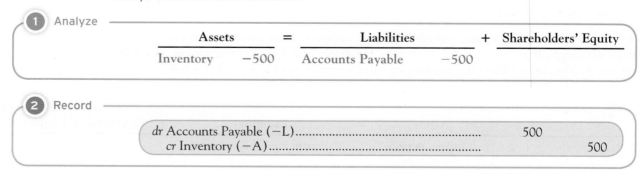

1 Analyze

	Assets	=	Liabilities		+ Shareholders' Equity
Inventory	−500		Accounts Payable	−500	

2 Record

dr Accounts Payable (−L).......................................	500	
cr Inventory (−A)..		500

Purchase Discounts

When inventory is bought on credit, terms such as "2/10, n/30" may be specified. Chapter 6 provided a lengthy description of how to interpret these terms from the seller's perspective.

From the purchaser's perspective, these terms mean that the purchaser is allowed to deduct a 2 percent **purchase discount** if payment is made within 10 days of the date of purchase; otherwise the purchase cost (net of any returns or allowances) is due within 30 days of the purchase date.

When offered a purchase discount at the time of purchase, the purchaser accounts for it in two stages. Initially, the purchase is accounted for at full cost because it is not clear whether the company will take advantage of the discount. Later, if payment is made within the discount period, the purchaser reduces the Inventory account by the amount of the discount because it effectively reduces the cost of the inventory. The purchase discount is calculated using the net amount owing to the supplier, after considering purchase returns and allowances.

Assume, for example, that American Eagle's purchase of vintage jeans for $10,500 occurred with terms 2/10, n/30. The initial purchase would be accounted for as shown earlier, by recording a $10,500 increase in Inventory (with a debit) and a $10,500 increase in Accounts Payable (with a credit). In our example, American Eagle returned inventory costing $500 and received a $500 reduction in its Accounts Payable. Consequently, American Eagle owed the supplier $10,000 for the purchase. Multiplying this balance by the 2 percent discount, we find that American Eagle's purchase discount is $200 (2% × $10,000 = $200). This discount means that American Eagle has to pay only $9,800 ($10,000 − $200 = $9,800) to fully satisfy its $10,000 of Accounts Payable. The $200 discount also reduces the cost of inventory as follows:

1 Analyze

	Assets	=	Liabilities		+ Shareholders' Equity
Cash	−9,800	=	Accounts Payable	−10,000	
Inventory	−200				

2 Record

dr Accounts Payable (−L)	10,000	
cr Cash (−A)		9,800
cr Inventory (−A)		200

Summary of Inventory Transactions

You have now seen how several types of inventory transactions affect the Inventory account on the balance sheet. Exhibit 7.6 summarizes, in table and T-account forms, how these transactions affect inventory, assuming beginning inventory was $4,800. Take a moment to flip back to Exhibit 7.3 on page 288 so that you can see that these are the values that will either become assigned to Cost of Goods Sold (when the goods are sold) or remain in Inventory.

EXHIBIT 7.6	**Effects of Inventory Transactions Related to Purchases**

Beginning Inventory		$ 4,800
+ Purchases	$10,500	
+ Freight-in	400	
− Purchase Returns and Allowances	(500)	
− Purchase Discounts	(200)	
Net Purchases		10,200
Cost of Goods Available for Sale		$15,000

dr +	Inventory			*cr* −
Beginning	4,800			
Purchases	10,500	500	Purchase Returns	
Freight-in	400	200	Purchase Discounts	
Goods Available	15,000			

INVENTORY TURNOVER ANALYSIS

Learning Objective 6

Evaluate inventory management by computing and interpreting the inventory turnover ratio.

YOU SHOULD KNOW

Inventory turnover:
The process of buying and selling inventory.

If a company's inventory balance increases from $100,000 in one period to $130,000 in the next, is that good news or bad news? If the increase occurs because management is building up stock in anticipation of higher sales, it could be good news. But if it results from an accumulation of old inventory items that nobody wants, it is probably bad news. Those who work inside the company can easily determine whether the change is good or bad news by talking with the sales managers. But if you are looking at the company's financial statements from the outside, how can you tell?

The method most analysts use to evaluate such changes is called *inventory turnover analysis*. Exhibit 7.7 illustrates the idea behind inventory turnover analysis. As a company buys goods, its inventory balance goes up; as it sells goods, its inventory balance goes down. This process of buying and selling, which is called **inventory turnover**, is repeated over and over during each accounting period for each line of products.

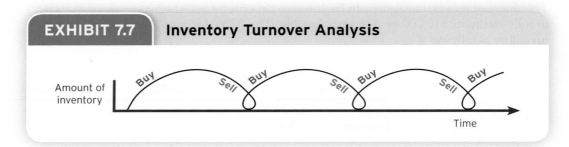

EXHIBIT 7.7 — Inventory Turnover Analysis

Analysts can assess how many times, on average, inventory has been bought and sold during the period by calculating the inventory turnover ratio. A higher ratio indicates that inventory moves more quickly from purchase to sale, reducing storage and obsolescence costs. Because less money is tied up in inventory, the excess can be invested to earn interest or reduce borrowing, which reduces interest expense. More efficient purchasing and production techniques as well as high product demand will boost this ratio. A sudden decline in the inventory turnover ratio may signal an unexpected drop in demand for the company's products or sloppy inventory management.

Rather than evaluate the number of times inventory turns over during the year, some analysts prefer to think in terms of the length of time (in days) required to sell inventory. Converting the inventory turnover ratio to the number of days needed to sell the inventory is easy. You simply divide 365 days by the year's inventory turnover ratio to get the **days to sell.** This measure provides the same basic information, but it is a little easier to interpret than the inventory turnover ratio. In terms of Exhibit 7.7, the inventory turnover ratio indicates the number of loops in a given period; days to sell indicates the average number of days between loops.

YOU SHOULD KNOW

Days to sell: A measure of the average number of days from the time inventory is bought to the time it is sold.

ACCOUNTING DECISION TOOLS

Name of Measure	Formula	What It Tells You
Inventory turnover ratio	$\dfrac{\text{Cost of Goods Sold}}{\text{Average Inventory}}$	• The number of times inventory turns over during the period • A higher ratio means faster turnover
Days to sell	$\dfrac{365}{\text{Inventory Turnover Ratio}}$	• Average number of days from purchase to sale • A higher number means a longer time to sell

Comparison to Benchmarks

Inventory turnover ratios and the number of days to sell can be helpful in comparing different companies' inventory management practices. But use them cautiously because these measures can vary significantly between industries. For merchandisers, inventory turnover refers to buying and selling goods, whereas for manufacturers, it refers to producing inventory and delivering it to customers. These differences are reflected in Exhibit 7.8, which shows that McDonald's has a turnover ratio of 47.5, which means that it takes about 7–8 days to sell its entire food inventory (including the stuff in its freezers). The motorcycles at Harley-Davidson hog more time, as indicated by the company's inventory turnover ratio of 8.0, which equates to about 46 days to produce and sell. American Eagle's inventory turned over only 5.9 times during the year, which is just once every 61.9 days.

EXHIBIT 7.8 **Summary of Inventory Turnover Ratio Analyses**

Company	Relevant Information (in millions)			2009–10 Inventory Turnover Calculation	2009–10 Days to Sell Calculation
HARLEY-DAVIDSON MOTORCYCLES		2009–10	2008–09	$\dfrac{\$2{,}901}{(\$323 + \$401)/2} = 8.0$ times	$\dfrac{365 \text{ days}}{8.0 \text{ times}} = 45.6$ days
	CGS	$2,901	$3,663		
	Inventory	$323	$401		
M i'm lovin' it		2009–10	2008–09	$\dfrac{\$5{,}178}{(\$106 + \$112)/2} = 47.5$ times	$\dfrac{365 \text{ days}}{47.5 \text{ times}} = 7.7$ days
	CGS	$5,178	$5,586		
	Inventory	$106	$112		
AMERICAN EAGLE OUTFITTERS		2009–10	2008–09	$\dfrac{\$1{,}832}{(\$326 + \$295)/2} = 5.9$ times	$\dfrac{365 \text{ days}}{5.9 \text{ times}} = 61.9$ days
	CGS	$1,832	$1,815		
	Inventory	$326	$295		

Inventory turnover also can vary significantly between companies within the same industry, particularly if they take different approaches to pricing their inventories. In Chapter 6, we saw that Walmart follows a low-cost pricing policy, which means setting its sales prices only slightly above cost. This policy led Walmart to earn about 25.4 cents of gross profit on each dollar of sales whereas Sears Canada Inc. earned 38.9 cents of gross profit. But when you consider the inventory turnover measures, you can see the full implications of this pricing policy. Walmart turns over its inventory about 9 times a year (41 days), whereas Sears turns over its inventory 3.5 times a year (104 days). Often, the company with a lower gross profit percentage has a faster inventory turnover.

With inventory turnover ratios varying between industries and companies, it's most useful to compare a company's turnover with its own results from prior periods. For practice at computing and comparing to prior periods, try the following Self-Study Practice.

 HOW'S IT GOING? Self-Study Practice

American Eagle's balance sheet and income statement information for prior years are presented in Exhibits 7.1 and 7.2 (page 287).

(a) Calculate American Eagle's inventory turnover and days to sell for the year ended January 31, 2009. The inventory balance on January 31, 2008, was $286 (million).

(b) Did American Eagle's inventory turnover improve or decline from 2008-09 (calculated in (a) to 2009-10 (shown in Exhibit 7.8)?

After you have finished, check your answers with the solution in the margin.

Solution to Self-Study Practice

a. $\dfrac{\$1{,}815}{(\$295 + \$286)/2} = 6.2$ times

$\dfrac{365 \text{ days}}{6.2 \text{ times}} = 58.9$ days

b. American Eagle's inventory turnover slowed down in 2009–2010 (3 days longer to sell).

Like ASPE, IFRS require that inventory be reported at the lower of cost and net realizable value (LC&NRV). However, inventory LC&NRV rules under IFRS differ from ASPE in an important way. With IFRS, if a decline in the net realizable value reverses, perhaps because of an economic recovery, the value of inventory is written back up to its original cost and the recovery is credited to Cost of Goods Sold. With ASPE, reversals of inventory write-downs are not allowed.

Topic	ASPE	IFRS
Inventory valuation	• Inventory is required to be reported at the lower of cost and net realizable value.	• Inventory is required to be reported at the lower of cost and net realizable value.
	• If a write-down of inventory is necessary because of the LC&NRV rule, this write-down cannot be reversed even if a decline in the net realizable value reverses.	• If a write-down of inventory is necessary because of the LC&NRV rule, this write-down can be reversed and the value of inventory can be written back up only to its original cost.

SUPPLEMENT 7A: Recording Inventory Transactions Using Last-In, First-Out (LIFO)

Inventory Costing Methods

YOU SHOULD KNOW

Last-in, first-out (LIFO):
Assumes that the most recently purchased units (the last in) are sold first.

As discussed earlier in this chapter, ASPE and IFRS do not permit companies to use the **last-in, first-out (LIFO)** inventory costing method. However, if a Canadian public company is listed on a U.S. stock exchange, it is permitted to use U.S. GAAP and therefore can apply the LIFO inventory costing method. For this reason, we felt it was appropriate to include in this supplement the examples from the chapter material but using LIFO as the inventory costing method. First, our simple example where the following transactions took place:

> May 3   Purchased 1 unit for **$70.**
> May 5   Purchased 1 more unit for **$75.**
> May 6   Purchased 1 more unit for **$95.**
> May 8   Sold 2 units for $125 each.

The sale on May 8 of two units, at a selling price of $125 each, would generate sales revenue of $250 ($125 × 2), and the amount of Cost of Goods Sold would depend on which goods are assumed to have been sold. LIFO assumes that the inventory costs flow out in the opposite order to which the goods are received. In other words, the costs of the last goods purchased (last in) are the costs of the first goods sold (first out). As in our example, the latest items received, the $95 and $75 units received on May 6 and 5, become the $170 Cost of Goods Sold on the income statement, and the remaining $70 unit received on May 3 becomes Ending Inventory on the balance sheet. This is shown in Exhibit 7A.1.

The following summary shows whether the oldest, newest, or average unit costs are used to calculate the amounts on the balance sheet or income statement.

	FIFO	LIFO	Weighted Average
Cost of Goods Sold (Income Statement)	Oldest cost	Newest cost	Average cost
Inventory (Balance Sheet)	Newest cost	Oldest cost	Average cost

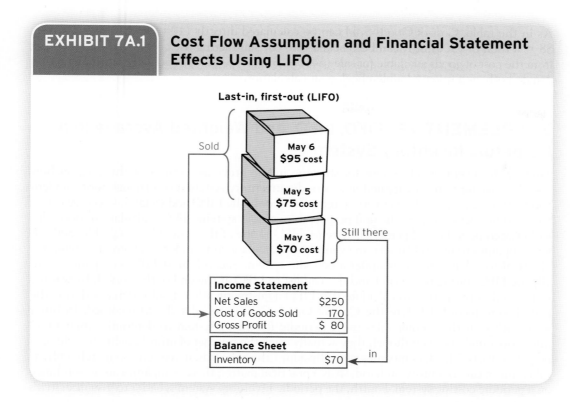

EXHIBIT 7A.1 **Cost Flow Assumption and Financial Statement Effects Using LIFO**

Last-in, first-out (LIFO)

Sold

May 6 $95 cost

May 5 $75 cost

May 3 $70 cost — Still there

Income Statement	
Net Sales	$250
Cost of Goods Sold	170
Gross Profit	$ 80

Balance Sheet	
Inventory	$70

in

Inventory Cost Flow Computations

Now that you've seen how the LIFO cost flow assumption works, let's go back to our more real-istic example of American Eagle. Let's assume that during the first week of October, American Eagle entered into the following transactions for its Henley T-shirt product line. All sales were made at a selling price of $15 per unit. These sales occurred after American Eagle made two batches of T-shirt purchases, which were added to inventory purchased the previous month.

Date	Description	No. of Units	Cost per Unit	Total Cost
Oct. 1	Beginning Inventory	10	$ 7	$ 70
Oct. 3	Purchase	30	8	240
Oct. 5	Purchase	10	10	100
Oct. 6	Sales	(35)	To calculate	To calculate
	Ending Inventory	15	To calculate	To calculate

The last-in, first-out (LIFO) method assumes that the newest goods (the last into inventory) are the first ones sold (the first out of inventory). So to calculate the cost of the 35 units sold, use the costs of the last-in (newest) goods (10 units at $10 plus 25 of the 30 units at $8 = total of $300). The costs of the older goods are included in the cost of the ending inventory (10 units at $7 plus 5 units remaining from the 30 units at $8 = a total of $110). These calculations are summarized in the table below.

LIFO		
Beginning Inventory	10 units × $7	$ 70
+ Purchases	30 units × $8	240
	10 units × $10	100
Goods Available for Sale		410
− Ending Inventory (10 × $7) + (5 × $8)		110
Cost of Goods Sold (10 × $10) + (25 × $8)		$300

As in the table, Cost of Goods Sold can be calculated directly (10 times $10 plus 25 times $8 = a total of $300) or it can be "backed into" by subtracting the cost of ending inventory from the cost of goods available for sale ($410 − $110 = $300). We actually recommend that you do both, as a way to double-check your calculations.

SUPPLEMENT 7B: FIFO, LIFO, and Weighted Average in a Perpetual Inventory System

There were several good reasons for showing in the previous sections of this chapter how cost flow assumptions are applied in a periodic inventory system, even though most modern companies use perpetual inventory systems. First, only the LIFO and weighted average calculations differ between periodic and perpetual inventory systems. FIFO calculations don't differ between periodic and perpetual systems. FIFO is one of the generally acceptable methods for companies to use in Canada, so even if they calculate costs under a perpetual system, it is identical to calculating costs under a periodic system. Second, most LIFO companies actually use FIFO during the period and then adjust to LIFO at the end of the period. By waiting to the end of the period to calculate this LIFO adjustment, it's *as if* all purchases during the period were recorded before the Cost of Goods Sold is calculated and recorded. In other words, it's as if these companies use a periodic inventory system to determine their LIFO inventory numbers, even though they actually track the number of units bought and sold on a perpetual basis. Third, companies typically adjust their records at year-end to match a physical count of the inventory on hand, so as a practical matter, these companies are in substance on a periodic costing system. Fourth, the periodic inventory system is easier to visualize, so it's easier for you to learn.

Despite these reasons, it can be useful to know how to apply cost flow assumptions in a perpetual inventory system. In this supplement, we show how to calculate the Cost of Goods Sold and cost of Ending Inventory on a perpetual basis using the same basic cost flow information used in the body of the chapter (on pages 291–293). The only difference in the following table is that we have assumed the sales occurred on October 4, prior to the final inventory purchase.

Date	Description	# of Units	Cost per Unit	Total Cost
Oct. 1	Beginning Inventory	10	$ 7	$ 70
Oct. 3	Purchase	30	$ 8	240
Oct. 4	Sales	(35)	To calculate	To calculate
Oct. 5	Purchase	10	$10	100
	Ending Inventory	15	To calculate	To calculate

FIFO (First-In, First-Out)

The first-in, first-out (FIFO) method assumes that the oldest goods (the first into inventory) are the first ones sold (the first out of inventory). So to calculate the cost of the 35 units sold, use the costs of the first-in (oldest) goods (10 units at $7 plus 25 of the 30 units at $8 = a total of $270). The costs of the newer goods are included in the cost of the ending inventory (5 units remaining from the 30 units at $8 plus 10 units at $10 = a total of $140). These calculations are summarized in the left-hand side of the following table (the right-hand side summarizes periodic calculations, which were explained in the body of the chapter). As you can see, FIFO yields identical amounts under perpetual and periodic. The only difference is that perpetual does not allow you to "back into" the Cost of Goods Sold; you must calculate it directly.

<table>
<tr><td colspan="3">FIFO – Perpetual</td></tr>
<tr><td>Beginning Inventory</td><td>10 units × $7</td><td>$ 70</td></tr>
<tr><td>+ Purchases</td><td>30 units × $8</td><td>240</td></tr>
<tr><td></td><td>10 units × $10</td><td>100</td></tr>
<tr><td>Goods Available for Sale</td><td></td><td>410</td></tr>
<tr><td>− Cost of Goods Sold (10 × $7) + (25 × $8)</td><td></td><td>270</td></tr>
<tr><td>Ending Inventory (10 × $10) + (5 × $8)</td><td></td><td>$140</td></tr>
</table>

<table>
<tr><td colspan="3">FIFO – Periodic</td></tr>
<tr><td>Beginning Inventory</td><td>10 units × $7</td><td>$ 70</td></tr>
<tr><td>+ Purchases</td><td>30 units × $8</td><td>240</td></tr>
<tr><td></td><td>10 units × $10</td><td>100</td></tr>
<tr><td>Goods Available for Sale</td><td></td><td>410</td></tr>
<tr><td>− Ending Inventory (10 × $10) + (5 × $8)</td><td></td><td>140</td></tr>
<tr><td>Cost of Goods Sold (10 × $7) + (25 × $8)</td><td></td><td>$270</td></tr>
</table>

LIFO (Last-In, First-Out)

The last-in, first-out (LIFO) method assumes that the newest goods (the last into inventory) as of the date of the sale are the first ones sold (the first out of inventory). So to calculate the cost of the 35 units sold, use the costs of the last-in (newest) goods as of the date of the sale (30 units at $8 plus 5 of the 10 units at $7 = a total of $275). The costs of the older goods (5 units remaining from the 10 units at $7 = $35) plus any later purchases (10 units at $10 = $100) are included in the cost of the ending inventory ($35 + $100 = $135). These calculations appear in the following table on the left.

<table>
<tr><td colspan="3">LIFO – Perpetual</td></tr>
<tr><td>Beginning Inventory</td><td>10 units × $7</td><td>$ 70</td></tr>
<tr><td>+ Purchase</td><td>30 units × $8</td><td>240</td></tr>
<tr><td>Goods Available for Sale</td><td></td><td>310</td></tr>
<tr><td>− Cost of Goods Sold (30 × $8) + (5 × $7)</td><td></td><td>275</td></tr>
<tr><td>Goods Available for Sale</td><td>5 units × $7</td><td>35</td></tr>
<tr><td>+ Purchase</td><td>10 units × $10</td><td>100</td></tr>
<tr><td>Ending Inventory (5 × $7) + (10 × $10)</td><td></td><td>$135</td></tr>
</table>

<table>
<tr><td colspan="3">LIFO – Periodic</td></tr>
<tr><td>Beginning Inventory</td><td>10 units × $7</td><td>$ 70</td></tr>
<tr><td>+ Purchases</td><td>30 units × $8</td><td>240</td></tr>
<tr><td></td><td>10 units × $10</td><td>100</td></tr>
<tr><td>Goods Available for Sale</td><td></td><td>410</td></tr>
<tr><td>− Ending Inventory (10 × $7) + (5 × $8)</td><td></td><td>110</td></tr>
<tr><td>Cost of Goods Sold (10 × $10) + (25 × $8)</td><td></td><td>$300</td></tr>
</table>

Notice that LIFO–Perpetual calculates Cost of Goods Sold using the cost of goods last-in at the time of the sale, whereas LIFO–Periodic uses the cost of goods last-in at the end of the period.

Weighted Average Cost

In a perpetual inventory system, the weighted average cost must be calculated each time a sale is recorded. Use the same two steps shown in the body of the chapter: (1) calculate the total cost of the goods available for sale and (2) divide by the number of units available for sale. For example, in the following table on the left, the weighted average cost at the time of sale is calculated by dividing $310 by the 40 units available for sale ($310 ÷ 40 = $7.75 per unit). This cost is then multiplied by the number of units sold to calculate Cost of Goods Sold (35 × $7.75 = $271.25). The remaining 5 units are also valued at the same weighted average cost (5 × $7.75 = $38.75). Additional inventory purchases ($100) are added to these inventory costs to calculate the cost of ending inventory ($38.75 + $100 = $138.75).[3]

<table>
<tr><td colspan="3">WA – Perpetual</td></tr>
<tr><td>Beginning Inventory</td><td>10 units × $7</td><td>$ 70.00</td></tr>
<tr><td>+ Purchase</td><td>30 units × $8</td><td>240.00</td></tr>
<tr><td>Goods Available for Sale</td><td>40 units</td><td>310.00</td></tr>
<tr><td>− Cost of Goods Sold (35 × $7.75)</td><td></td><td>271.25</td></tr>
<tr><td>Goods Available for Sale</td><td>5 units</td><td>38.75</td></tr>
<tr><td>+ Purchase</td><td>10 units × $10</td><td>100.00</td></tr>
<tr><td>Ending Inventory</td><td>15 units</td><td>$138.75</td></tr>
</table>

<table>
<tr><td colspan="3">WA – Periodic</td></tr>
<tr><td>Beginning Inventory</td><td>10 units × $7</td><td>$ 70</td></tr>
<tr><td>+ Purchases</td><td>30 units × $8</td><td>240</td></tr>
<tr><td></td><td>10 units × $10</td><td>100</td></tr>
<tr><td>Goods Available for Sale</td><td>50 units</td><td>410</td></tr>
<tr><td>− Ending Inventory (15 × $8.20)</td><td></td><td>123</td></tr>
<tr><td>Cost of Goods Sold (35 × $8.20)</td><td></td><td>$287</td></tr>
</table>

EXHIBIT 7B.1 | Financial Statement Effects of Inventory Costing Methods (Perpetual)

Effects on the Income Statement	FIFO	LIFO	Weighted Average
Sales	$525	$525	$ 525.00
Cost of Goods Sold	270	275	271.25
Gross Profit	255	250	253.75

Effects on the Balance Sheet	FIFO	LIFO	Weighted Average
Inventory	$140	$135	$138.75

Financial Statement Effects

Exhibit 7B.1 summarizes the financial statement effects of using a perpetual inventory system with FIFO, LIFO, or weighted average cost methods. These methods differ only in the way they split the cost of goods available for sale between Ending Inventory and Cost of Goods Sold. If a cost goes into Cost of Goods Sold, it must be taken out of Inventory. Thus, the method that assigns the highest cost to Cost of Goods Sold assigns the lowest cost to Ending Inventory (and vice versa).

SUPPLEMENT 7C: The Effects of Errors in Ending Inventory

As mentioned earlier in the chapter, the failure to correctly apply the LC&NRV rule to Ending Inventory is considered an error. Other errors can occur when inappropriate quantities or unit costs are used in calculating inventory cost. Regardless of the reason, errors in inventory can significantly affect both the balance sheet and the income statement. As the Cost of Goods Sold equation indicates, a direct relationship exists between Ending Inventory and Cost of Goods Sold because items not in the ending inventory are assumed to have been sold. Thus, any errors in ending inventory will affect the balance sheet (current assets) and the income statement (Cost of Goods Sold, Gross Profit, and Net Income). The effects of inventory errors are felt in more than one year because the ending inventory for one year becomes the beginning inventory for the next year.

To determine the effects of inventory errors on the financial statements in both the current year and the following year, use the Cost of Goods-Sold equation. For example, let's assume that ending inventory was overstated in 2011 by $10,000 due to an error that was not discovered until 2012. This would have the following effects in 2011:

2011	
Beginning Inventory	Accurate
+ Purchases	Accurate
− Ending Inventory	Overstated $10,000
= Cost of Goods Sold	Understated $10,000

Because Cost of Goods Sold was understated, Gross Profit and Income before Income Tax Expense would be overstated by $10,000 in 2011, as shown in Exhibit 7C.1. (Net Income would be overstated as well, although the effects would be offset somewhat by overstated Income Tax Expense.)

The 2011 ending inventory becomes the 2012 beginning inventory, so even if 2012 ending inventory is calculated correctly, the error in 2011 creates an error in 2012, as shown in the following table:

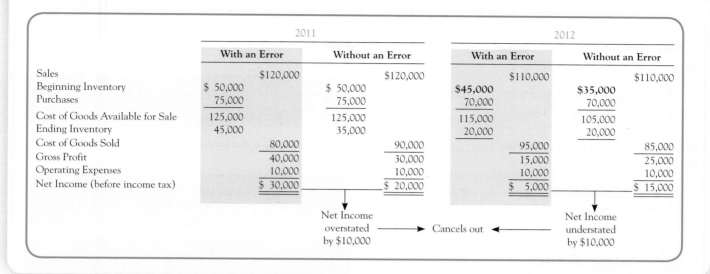

	2011			2012		
	With an Error		Without an Error	With an Error		Without an Error
Sales		$120,000	$120,000		$110,000	$110,000
Beginning Inventory	$ 50,000		$ 50,000	$45,000		$35,000
Purchases	75,000		75,000	70,000		70,000
Cost of Goods Available for Sale	125,000		125,000	115,000		105,000
Ending Inventory	45,000		35,000	20,000		20,000
Cost of Goods Sold		80,000	90,000		95,000	85,000
Gross Profit		40,000	30,000		15,000	25,000
Operating Expenses		10,000	10,000		10,000	10,000
Net Income (before income tax)		$ 30,000	$ 20,000		$ 5,000	$ 15,000

Net Income overstated by $10,000 ——→ Cancels out ←—— Net Income understated by $10,000

2012	
Beginning Inventory	Overstated $10,000
+ Purchases	Accurate
− Ending Inventory	Accurate
= Cost of Goods Sold	Overstated $10,000

Because Cost of Goods Sold is overstated in 2012, that year's Gross Profit and Income before Income Tax Expense would be understated by the same amount in 2012. (Net Income would be understated as well, although the effects would be offset somewhat by understated Income Tax Expense.)

Ignoring income taxes, the effects of these errors on Net Income in each of the two years is shown in Exhibit 7C.1. Notice that the Cost of Goods Sold is understated in the first year and overstated in the second year. Over the two years, these errors offset one another. Inventory errors will "self-correct" like this only if ending inventory is accurately calculated at the end of the following year and adjusted to that correct balance. (The fact that these errors are self-correcting does not make them "okay.")

SUPPLEMENT 7D: Recording Inventory Transactions in a Periodic System

As you have learned, businesses using a periodic inventory system update inventory records only at the end of the accounting period. Unlike a perpetual inventory system, a periodic system does not track the cost of goods sold during the accounting period.

This supplement illustrates typical journal entries made when using a periodic inventory system. Exhibit 7D.1 contrasts those entries with the entries that would be recorded using a perpetual inventory system. A summary of the effects of the journal entries on the accounting equation follows them. Note that the total effects and the resulting financial statements are identical. Only the timing and nature of the entries differ.

Assume for the purposes of this illustration that a local cellphone dealer stocks and sells just one item, the MOTORAZR phone, and that only the following events occurred in 2012:

Jan. 1	Beginning inventory: 80 units at a unit cost of $60.
Apr. 14	Purchased 170 additional units on account at a unit cost of $60.
Nov. 30	Sold 150 units on account at a unit sales price of $80.
Dec. 31	Counted 100 units at a unit cost of $60.

PERIODIC RECORDS | PERPETUAL RECORDS

A. Record purchases:

April 14, 2012:

| Purchases (+A) (170 units at $60) | 10,200 | |
| Accounts Payable (+L) | | 10,200 |

A. Record purchases:

April 14, 2012:

| Inventory (+A) (170 units at $60) | 10,200 | |
| Accounts Payable (+L) | | 10,200 |

B. Record sales (but not cost of goods sold):

November 30, 2012:

| Accounts Receivable (+A) | 12,000 | |
| Sales Revenue (+R, +SE) (150 units at $80) | | 12,000 |

No cost of goods sold entry

B. Record sales and cost of goods sold:

November 30, 2012:

| Accounts Receivable (+A) | 12,000 | |
| Sales Revenue (+R, +SE) (150 units at $80) | | 12,000 |

| Cost of Goods Sold (+E, −SE) | 9,000 | |
| Inventory (−A) (150 units at $60) | | 9,000 |

C. Record end-of-period adjustments:

  a. Count the number of units on hand.
  b. Compute the dollar valuation of the ending inventory.
  c. Compute and record the cost of goods sold.

Beginning Inventory (last period's ending) (80 units at $60)	$ 4,800
Add: Net Purchases	10,200
Cost of Goods Available for Sale	15,000
Deduct: Ending Inventory (physical count—100 units at $60)	6,000
Cost of Goods Sold	$ 9,000

December 31, 2012:

Transfer beginning inventory and net purchases to cost of goods sold (act as if all goods were sold):

Cost of Goods Sold (+E, −SE)	15,000	
Inventory (−A) (beginning)		4,800
Purchases (−A)		10,200

Adjust the cost of goods sold by subtracting the amount of ending inventory still on hand (recognize that not all goods were sold):

| Inventory (+A) (ending) | 6,000 | |
| Cost of Goods Sold (−E, +SE) | | 6,000 |

C. Record end-of-period adjustments:

At the end of the accounting period, the balance in the Cost of Goods Sold account is reported on the income statement. Computing the cost of goods sold is not necessary because the **Cost of Goods Sold** account is up to date. Also, the **Inventory** account shows the ending inventory amount reported on the balance sheet. A physical inventory count is still necessary to assess the accuracy of the perpetual records and identify theft and other forms of shrinkage. Any shrinkage would be recorded by reducing the **Inventory** account and increasing an expense account (such as **Inventory Shrinkage** or **Cost of Goods Sold**). This illustration assumes that no shrinkage has been detected.

No entries

PERIODIC

Assets	=	Liabilities	+	Shareholders' Equity	
Purchases +10,200		Accounts Payable +10,200			
Accts. Rec. +12,000				Sales Revenue (+R)	+12,000
Inventory −4,800				Cost of Goods Sold (+E)	−15,000
Purchases −10,200					
Inventory +6,000				Cost of Goods Sold (−E)	+6,000
Totals +13,200 =		+10,200			+3,000

PERPETUAL

Assets	=	Liabilities	+	Shareholders' Equity	
Inventory +10,200		Accounts Payable +10,200			
Accts. Rec. +12,000				Sales Revenue (+R)	+12,000
Inventory −9,000				Cost of Goods Sold (+E)	−9,000
Totals +13,200 =		+10,200			+3,000

This section provides a chance to solidify your understanding of key points. It's worth your time to work through the following demonstration case, scan the chapter summary, test your understanding of key terms, and then practise, practise, practise.

DEMONSTRATION CASE

Bondel Electronics sells one type of consumer electronics product. Assume that the following summarized transactions were completed during the month ended January 31, 2012, in the order given.

	Units	Unit Cost
Beginning inventory (January 1)	11	$200
New inventory purchases (January 3)	5	209
New inventory purchases (January 4)	9	220
Sale (January 5 at a price of $420 per item)	(12)	
	13	

Required:

1. Using the formats shown in the chapter, compute the Cost of Goods Available for Sale, Ending Inventory, and Cost of Goods Sold under (a) FIFO and (b) weighted average.
2. Which method would minimize income taxes? Explain your answer.
3. Assuming that operating expenses were $500 and the income tax rate is 25 percent, prepare the income statement for the month using the method selected in requirement 2.
4. If the replacement cost fell to $205 in February, compute the adjustment that would be made to the Inventory account assuming the company uses (a) FIFO and (b) weighted average.
5. Describe the impact of an adjustment in requirement 4 on the inventory turnover ratio. Computations are not required.

Suggested Solution

1.

(a) FIFO

Beginning Inventory	11 units × $200	$ 2,200
+ Purchases	5 units × $209	1,045
	9 units × $220	1,980
Goods Available for Sale		5,225
− Ending Inventory (9 × $220) + (4 × $209)		2,816
Cost of Goods Sold (11 × $200) + (1 × $209)		$2,409

(b) Weighted Average

Beginning Inventory	11 units × $200	$ 2,200
+ Purchases	5 units × $209	1,045
	9 units × $220	1,980
Goods Available for Sale		5,225
− Ending Inventory (13 × $209)		2,717
Cost of Goods Sold (12 × $209)		$2,508

$$\frac{\text{Weighted}}{\text{Average Cost}} = \frac{\text{Cost of Goods Available for Sale}}{\text{Number of Units Available for Sale}} = \frac{\$5,225}{25\ \text{Units}} = \frac{\$209}{\text{per unit}}$$

2. Weighted average would minimize income taxes. Because costs are rising, weighted average produces higher Cost of Goods Sold, lower Income before Income Tax Expense, and lower Income Tax Expense.

3.

BONDEL ELECTRONICS	
Income Statement	
For the Month Ended January 31, 2012	
Sales (12 × $420)	$5,040
Cost of Goods Sold	2,508
Gross Profit	2,532
Operating Expenses	500
Income before Income Tax Expense	2,032
Income Tax Expense (25%)	508
Net Income	$1,524

4. The total net realizable value of the 13 units in ending inventory, with a per unit replacement cost of $205, is $2,665 (13 × $205 = $2,665). The LC&NRV analysis follows:

	Cost	Net Realizable Value	LC&NRV	Adjustment Needed
(a) FIFO	$2,816	$2,665	$2,665	$(151) = $2,816 − $2,665
(b) Weighted Average	$2,717	$2,665	$2,665	(52) = $2,717 − $2,665

5. An adjustment for LC&NRV decreases the Inventory balance and increases the Cost of Goods Sold. Both of these changes (individually or together) increase the inventory turnover ratio.

CHAPTER SUMMARY

LO1 **Describe the issues in managing different types of inventory.** p. 286

- Make or buy a sufficient *quantity* of *quality* products, at the lowest possible *cost*, so that they can be sold as quickly as possible to earn the desired amount of gross profit.
- *Merchandise inventory* is bought by merchandisers in a ready-to-sell format. When *raw materials* enter a manufacturer's production process, they become *work in process* inventory, which is further transformed into *finished goods* that are ultimately sold to customers.

LO2 **Explain how to report inventory and cost of goods sold.** p. 287

- The costs of goods purchased are added to Inventory (on the balance sheet).
- The costs of goods sold are removed from Inventory and reported as an expense called Cost of Goods Sold (on the income statement).
- The costs remaining in Inventory at the end of a period become the cost of Inventory at the beginning of the next period.
- The relationships among beginning inventory (BI), purchases (P), ending inventory (EI), and cost of goods sold (CGS) are BI + P − EI = CGS or BI + P − CGS = EI.

LO3 **Compute costs using three inventory costing methods.** p. 289

- Four methods can be used to allocate the cost of inventory, but in Canada, only three of these methods are generally accepted, whether a company uses ASPE or IFRS. LIFO is the one method that is not acceptable in Canada. Any of the remaining three methods—specific identification, FIFO, and weighted average—can be used to allocate the cost of inventory available for sale between goods that are sold and goods that remain on hand at the end of the accounting period.
- Specific identification assigns costs to Ending Inventory and Cost of Goods Sold by tracking and identifying each specific item of inventory.
- Under FIFO, the costs first in are assigned to Cost of Goods Sold, and the costs last in (most recent) are assigned to the inventory that is still on hand in Ending Inventory.
- Under weighted average cost, the weighted average cost per unit of inventory is assigned equally to goods sold and those still on hand in Ending Inventory.

Report inventory at the lower of cost and net realizable value. p. 294　　　　**LO4**

- The lower of cost and net realizable value rule ensures inventory assets are not reported at more than they are worth.

Analyze and record inventory purchases, transportation, returns and allowances, and discounts. p. 295　　　　**LO5**

- The Inventory account should include costs incurred to get inventory into a condition and location ready for sale.
- The cost of inventory includes its purchase price and transportation (freight-in) minus cost reductions for purchase returns and allowances and purchase discounts. Costs to deliver inventory to customers (freight-out) are a selling expense and are not included in inventory.

Evaluate inventory management by computing and interpreting the inventory turnover ratio. p. 298　　　　**LO6**

- The inventory turnover ratio measures the efficiency of inventory management. It reflects how many times average inventory was acquired and sold during the period. The inventory turnover ratio is calculated by dividing Cost of Goods Sold by Average Inventory.

ACCOUNTING DECISION TOOLS

Name of Measure	Formula	What It Tells You
Inventory turnover ratio	$\dfrac{\text{Cost of Goods Sold}}{\text{Average Inventory}}$	• The number of times inventory turns over during the period • A higher ratio means faster turnover
Days to sell	$\dfrac{365}{\text{Inventory Turnover Ratio}}$	• Average number of days from purchase to sale • A higher number means a longer time to sell

KEY TERMS

Cost of Goods Sold (CGS) Equation p. 288
Days to Sell p. 298
First-In, First-Out (FIFO) p. 290
Goods Available for Sale p. 288

Inventory Turnover p. 298
Last-In, First-Out (LIFO) p. 300
Lower of Cost and Net Realizable Value (LC&NRV) p. 294
Purchase Discount p. 297

Purchase Returns and Allowances p. 296
Specific Identification p. 289
Weighted Average Cost p. 290

See complete definitions in the glossary in the back of this text.

HOMEWORK HELPER

Alternative terms

- Cost of Goods Sold is also called *Cost of Sales*.
- Days to Sell is also called *days in inventory* and *days' sales in inventory*.

Helpful reminders

- The "first-out" part of FIFO and LIFO describes the costs going out of inventory into Cost of Goods Sold. To calculate ending inventory cost using LIFO, think FIST (first-in, still there). For FIFO inventory, think LIST (last-in, still there).
- Purchase discounts are calculated after taking into account any purchase returns and allowances. A partial payment within the discount period (such as one-half of the total cost) usually entitles the purchaser to a partial discount (apply the discount to one-half of the total cost).

Frequent mistakes

- Do not calculate purchase discounts on transportation costs unless the shipping company offers a purchase discount for early payment. Do not apply purchase discounts to returned merchandise.
- Do not simply average the costs per unit when calculating weighted average cost. Instead, divide the total cost of goods available for sale by the number of goods available for sale.
- Do not use Sales Revenue when calculating inventory turnover (use Cost of Goods Sold). Also, use the average inventory, not the Ending Inventory balance.

Practice Material

QUESTIONS (⑤ Symbol indicates questions that require analysis from more than one perspective.)

1. What are three goals of inventory management?

2. Describe the specific types of inventory reported by merchandisers and manufacturers.

3. If a Toronto-based company ships goods on September 30 to a customer in Hawaii with sales terms FOB destination, does the Toronto-based company include the inventory or the sale in its September financial statements?

4. Define *goods available for sale*. How does it differ from cost of goods sold?

5. Define *beginning inventory* and *ending inventory*.

6. The chapter discussed three inventory costing methods that are acceptable in Canada. List the three methods and briefly explain each.

7. Which inventory cost flow method is most similar to the flow of products involving (a) a gumball machine, (b) bricks off a stack, and (c) gasoline out of a tank?

8. "Where possible, the inventory costing method should mimic actual product flows." Do you agree? Explain.

9. Several managers in your company are experiencing personal financial problems and have asked that your company switch from weighted average to FIFO so that they can receive bigger bonuses, which are tied to the company's net income. How would you respond to this request if you were the company's chief financial officer? Would such a switch help the managers? Who could it hurt? ⑤

10. Explain briefly the application of the LC&NRV rule to ending inventory. Describe its effect on the balance sheet and income statement when the net realizable value is lower than cost.

11. Describe how transportation costs to obtain inventory (freight-in) are accounted for by a merchandising company using a perpetual inventory system. Explain the reasoning behind this accounting treatment.

12. As a sales representative for a publicly traded pharmaceutical company, you become aware of new evidence that one of your company's main drugs has significant life-threatening side effects that were not previously reported. Your company has a large inventory of this drug. What income statement accounts other than Net Sales will be affected by the news? A friend asks you whether he should invest in your company. What should you say? ⑤

13. You work for a made-to-order clothing company whose reputation is based on its fast turnaround from order to delivery. The owner of your company is considering outsourcing much of the clothing production because she thinks this will improve inventory turnover and customer satisfaction. In what way is she correct? In what way might she be wrong? ⑤

14. (Supplement B) Distinguish perpetual inventory systems from periodic inventory systems by describing when and how Cost of Goods Sold is calculated when using LIFO.

15. (Supplement C) Explain why an error in Ending Inventory in one period affects the following period.

16. (Supplement D) The summary in Supplement D shows two entries recorded in a periodic system that are not recorded in a perpetual system and only one entry in the perpetual system that is not recorded in a periodic system. Why then is a periodic system considered less onerous than a perpetual system?

Multiple-choice questions and corresponding answers can be found on Connect.

MINI-EXERCISES

LO2   **M7-1 Inferring Purchases Using the Cost of Goods Sold Equation**

Willard's, Inc., operates 31 department stores. In its annual report for the year ended January 31, 2012, the company reported Cost of Goods Sold of $4,827 million, ending inventory for the current year of $1,374 million, and ending inventory for the previous year of $1,779 million. Is it possible to develop a reasonable estimate of the merchandise purchases for the year? If so, prepare the estimate. If not, explain why.

M7-2 Calculating Cost of Goods Available for Sale, Ending Inventory, Sales, Cost of Goods Sold, and Gross Profit under Periodic FIFO and Weighted Average Cost

LO3

Given the following information, calculate cost of goods available for sale and ending inventory, then sales, cost of goods sold, and gross profit, under (a) FIFO and (b) weighted average. Assume that a periodic inventory system is used.

		Units	Unit Cost	Unit Selling Price
July 1	Beginning Inventory	100	$10	
July 13	Purchase	500	13	
July 25	Sold	(200)		$15
July 31	Ending Inventory	400		

M7-3 Calculating Cost of Goods Available for Sale, Cost of Goods Sold, and Ending Inventory under FIFO and Weighted Average Cost (Periodic Inventory)

LO3

Aircard Corporation tracks the number of units purchased and sold throughout each accounting period, but applies its inventory costing method at the end of each period as if it uses a periodic inventory system. Given the following information, calculate the cost of goods available for sale, ending inventory, and cost of goods sold, if Aircard uses (a) FIFO or (b) weighted average cost.

		Units	Unit Cost
July 1	Beginning Inventory	2,000	$20
July 5	Sold	1,000	
July 13	Purchased	6,000	22
July 17	Sold	3,000	
July 25	Purchased	8,000	25
July 27	Sold	5,000	

M7-4 Reporting Inventory under Lower of Cost and Net Realizable Value (LC&NRV)

LO4

The Jewel Fool had the following inventory items on hand at the end of the year:

	Quantity	Cost per Item	Replacement Cost per Item
Necklaces	50	$75	$70
Bracelets	25	60	50

Determine the lower of cost and net realizable value per unit and the total amount that should be reported on the balance sheet for each item of inventory.

M7-5 Preparing the Journal Entry to Record Lower of Cost and Net Realizable Value Adjustments

LO4

General Motors

Assume in its annual report filed with the SEC for the year ended December 31, 2011, General Motors reported that it wrote down inventory by $336 million because its cost exceeded its net realizable value. Show the effects of this adjustment on the accounting equation as well as the journal entry that the company would have made to record it.

M7-6 Evaluating Inventory Cost Components

LO5

Assume Anderson's General Store bought, on credit, a truckload of merchandise from American Wholesaling costing $23,000. If the company was charged $650 in transportation cost by National Trucking, immediately returned goods to American Wholesaling costing $1,200, and then took advantage of American Wholesaling's 2/10, n/30 purchase discount, how much did this inventory cost Anderson's?

LO5   **M7-7 Preparing Journal Entries for Purchases, Purchase Discounts, and Purchase Returns Using a Perpetual System**

Using the information in M7-6, prepare journal entries to record the inventory transactions, assuming Anderson's uses a perpetual inventory system.

LO2, 5   **M7-8 Recording Journal Entries for Purchases and Sales Using a Perpetual Inventory System**

Inventory at the beginning of the year cost $13,400. During the year, the company purchased (on account) inventory costing $54,000. Inventory that had cost $60,000 was sold on account for $75,000. At the end of the year, inventory was counted and its cost was determined to be $7,400. (*a*) Show the Cost of Goods Sold equation using these numbers. (*b*) What was the Gross Profit? (*c*) Prepare journal entries to record these transactions, assuming a perpetual inventory system is used.

LO6   **M7-9 Calculating the Inventory Turnover Ratio and Days to Sell**

★macy's   Using the data in M7-1, calculate to one decimal place the inventory turnover ratio and days to sell for Willard's. In a recent year, Macy's reported an inventory turnover ratio of 3.1. Which company's inventory turnover is faster?

LO6   **M7-10 (Supplement 7C) Determining the Financial Statement Effects of Inventory Errors**

Assume the 2012 ending inventory of Shea's Shrimp Shack was understated by $10,000. Explain how this error would affect the amounts reported for cost of goods sold and gross profit for 2012 and 2013.

EXERCISES

Practise and learn online with Connect.

LO1, 2   **E7-1 Items Included in Inventory**

PC Club, Inc   PC Club, Inc., is a direct marketer of computer hardware, software, peripherals, and electronics. In its 2011 annual report, the company reported that its revenue is recognized upon receipt of the product by the customer and that its inventories include goods in transit to customers at December 31, 2011.

Required:

1. Indicate whether PC Club's sales terms are FOB shipping point or FOB destination.
2. Assume PC Club sold inventory on account to eCOST.com on December 28, 2011, which was to be delivered January 3, 2012. The inventory cost PC Club $25,000 and the selling price was $30,000. What amounts, if any, related to this transaction would be reported on PC Club's balance sheet and income statement in 2011? In 2012?
3. PC Club placed inventory on consignment with one of its customers. Would this inventory have been reported on the balance sheet of PC Club or of its customer?
4. Assume PC Club purchased electronics on December 29, 2011, that were received on January 2, 2012. Would these goods be included in PC Club's inventory on December 31, 2011, under FOB destination or FOB shipping point?

LO2   **E7-2 Inferring Missing Amounts Based on Income Statement Relationships**

Check Figure:
[Case E]
Cost of Goods Sold = $500

Supply the missing dollar amounts for Lewis Retailers' income statement for each of the following independent cases:

Cases	Sales Revenue	Beginning Inventory	Purchases	Cost of Goods Available for Sale	Cost of Goods Sold	Cost of Ending Inventory	Gross Profit
A	$ 650	$100	$700	$?	$300	$?	$?
B	900	200	800	?	?	150	?
C	?	150	?	?	200	300	400
D	800	?	600	?	650	250	?
E	1,000	50	900	?	?	?	500

E7-3 Inferring Missing Amounts Based on Income Statement Relationships

LO2

Supply the missing dollar amounts for Lewis Retailers' income statement for each of the following independent cases:

Cases	Sales Revenue	Beginning Inventory	Purchases	Total Available	Ending Inventory	Cost of Goods Sold	Gross Profit	Selling and General Expenses	Income from Operations
A	$800	$100	$700	$?	$500	$?	$?	$200	$?
B	900	200	700	?	?	?	?	150	0
C	?	150	?	?	250	200	400	100	?
D	800	?	600	?	250	?	?	250	100

E7-4 Inferring Merchandise Purchases

LO2

Gap Inc.

Gap Inc. is a specialty retailer that operates stores selling clothes under the trade names Gap, Banana Republic, and Old Navy. Assume that you are employed as a stock analyst and your boss has just completed a review of Gap's annual report for the year ended January 31, 2012. She provided you with her notes, but they are missing some information that you need. Her notes show that the ending inventory for Gap in the current year was $1,506 million and in the previous year it was $1,575 million. Net Sales for the current year were $14,526 million. Gross Profit was $5,447 million and Net Income was $967 million. For your analysis, you determine that you need to know the amount of Cost of Goods Sold and Purchases for the year.

Required:

Do you need to ask your boss for her copy of the annual report, or can you develop the information from her notes? Explain and show calculations.

E7-5 Calculating Cost of Ending Inventory and Cost of Goods Sold under Periodic FIFO and Weighted Average Cost

LO3

Oahu Kiki tracks the number of units purchased and sold throughout each accounting period but applies its inventory costing method at the end of each month as if it uses a periodic inventory system. Assume Oahu Kiki's records show the following for the month of January. Sales totalled 240 units.

	Date	Units	Unit Cost	Total Cost
Beginning Inventory	January 1	120	$ 8	$ 960
Purchase	January 15	380	9	3,420
Purchase	January 24	200	11	2,200

Required:

1. Calculate the number and cost of goods available for sale.
2. Calculate the number of units in ending inventory.
3. Calculate the cost of ending inventory and cost of goods sold using the (a) FIFO and (b) weighted average cost methods.

E7-6 Analyzing and Interpreting the Financial Statement Effects of Periodic FIFO and Weighted Average Cost

LO3

Orion Iron Corp. tracks the number of units purchased and sold throughout each year but applies its inventory costing method at the end of the year as if it uses a periodic inventory system. Assume its accounting records provided the following information at the end of the annual accounting period, December 31, 2012.

Transactions	Units	Unit Cost
a. Inventory, December 31, 2011	3,000	$12
For the year 2012:		
b. Purchase, April 11	9,000	10
c. Purchase, June 1	8,000	13
d. Sale, May 1 (sold for $40 per unit)	3,000	
e. Sale, July 3 (sold for $40 per unit)	6,000	
f. Operating expenses (excluding income tax expense), $195,000		

Required:

Check Figure:

[Req. 1]

Cost of Goods Sold − FIFO
= $96,000

1. Calculate the number and cost of goods available for sale.
2. Calculate the number of units in ending inventory.
3. Compute the cost of ending inventory and cost of goods sold under (a) FIFO and (b) weighted average cost.
4. Prepare an income statement that shows 2012 amounts for the FIFO method in one column and for the weighted average method in another column. Include the following line items in the income statement: Sales, Cost of Goods Sold, Gross Profit, Operating Expenses, and Income from Operations.
5. Compare the Income from Operations and the Ending Inventory amounts that would be reported under the two methods. Explain the similarities and differences.
6. Which inventory costing method may be preferred by Orion Iron Corp. for income tax purposes? Explain.

LO3   **E7-7 Analyzing and Interpreting the Financial Statement Effects of FIFO and Weighted Average Cost**

Scoresby Inc. tracks the number of units purchased and sold throughout each year but applies its inventory costing method at the end of the year as if it uses a periodic inventory system. Assume its accounting records provided the following information at the end of the annual accounting period, December 31, 2012.

Transactions	Units	Unit Cost
a. Inventory, December 31, 2011	3,000	$ 8
For the year 2012:		
b. Purchase, March 5	9,500	9
c. Purchase, September 19	5,000	11
d. Sale, April 15 (sold for $29 per unit)	4,000	
e. Sale, October 31 (sold for $31 per unit)	8,000	
f. Operating expenses (excluding income tax expense), $250,000		

Required:

1. Calculate the number and cost of goods available for sale.
2. Calculate the number of units in ending inventory.
3. Compute the cost of ending inventory and cost of goods sold under (a) FIFO and (b) weighted average cost.
4. Prepare an income statement that shows 2012 amounts for the FIFO method in one column and the weighted average method in another column. Include the following line items in the income statement: Sales, Cost of Goods Sold, Gross Profit, Operating Expenses, and Income from Operations.
5. Compare the Income from Operations and the Ending Inventory amounts that would be reported under the two methods. Explain the similarities and differences.
6. Which inventory costing method may be preferred by Scoresby for income tax purposes? Explain.

LO3   **E7-8 Evaluating the Effects of Inventory Methods on Income from Operations, Income Taxes, and Net Income (Periodic)**

Courtney Company uses a periodic inventory system. Data for 2012: beginning merchandise inventory (December 31, 2011), 1,000 units at $35; purchases, 4,000 units at $38; operating expenses (excluding income taxes), $91,500; ending inventory per physical count at December 31, 2012, 900 units; sales price per unit, $75; and average income tax rate, 30 percent.

Required:

Prepare income statements under the FIFO and weighted average costing methods. Use a format similar to the following:

Income Statement	Units	FIFO	Weighted Average
Sales Revenue	_____	$ _____	$ _____
Cost of Goods Sold*	_____	_____	_____
Gross Profit		_____	_____
Operating Expenses		_____	_____
Income from Operations		_____	_____
Income Tax Expense		_____	_____
Net Income		_____	_____

*Cost of Goods Sold equation:			
Beginning Inventory	_____	$ _____	$ _____
Purchases	_____	_____	_____
Goods Available for Sale	_____	_____	_____
Ending Inventory	_____	_____	_____
Cost of Goods Sold	_____	_____	_____

E7-9 Reporting Inventory at Lower of Cost and Net Realizable Value

LO4

Peterson Furniture Designs is preparing its annual financial statements dated December 31, 2012. Ending inventory information about the five major items stocked for regular sale follows:

	Ending Inventory, 2012				
Item	Quantity on Hand	Unit Cost When Acquired (FIFO)	Net Realizable Value at Year-End	LC&NRV per Item	Total LC&NRV
Alligator Armoires	50	$15	$12		
Bear Bureaus	75	40	40		
Cougar Beds	10	50	52		
Dingo Cribs	30	30	30		
Elephant Dressers	400	10	6		

Required:

1. Complete the final two columns of the table and then compute the amount that should be reported for the 2012 ending inventory using the LC&NRV rule applied to each item.
2. Prepare the journal entry that Peterson Furniture Designs would record on December 31, 2012.
3. If the net realizable value recovered by June 30, 2013, to greater than original cost, would the journal entry in requirement 2 be reversed under ASPE? Under IFRS?

E7-10 Reporting Inventory at Lower of Cost and Net Realizable Value

LO4

Sublime Sandals Company was formed on January 1, 2012, and is preparing its annual financial statements dated December 31, 2012. Ending inventory information about the four major items stocked for regular sale follows:

	Ending Inventory, 2012		
Product Line	Quantity on Hand	Unit Cost When Acquired (FIFO)	Net Realizable Value at Year-End
Air Flow	20	$12	$14
Blister Buster	75	40	38
Coolonite	35	55	50
Dudesly	10	30	35

Check Figure:
Ending Inventory = $5,140

Required:

1. Compute the amount that should be reported for the 2012 ending inventory, using the LC&NRV rule applied to each item.

2. How will the write-down of inventory to lower of cost and net realizable value affect the company's expenses reported for the year ended December 31, 2012?

3. How would the methods used by Sublime Sandals Company to account for its inventory be affected by a switch from ASPE to IFRS?

LO4   **E7-11 Failing to Report Inventory at the Lower of Cost and Net Realizable Value**

David H. Brooks, a university graduate with an accounting degree and the former CEO of DHB Industries, Inc., was charged in October 2007 with accounting and securities fraud for failing to report the company's inventory at the lower of cost and net realizable value. From 2001 to 2005, DHB purchased large quantities of a material called Zylon and used it in making bulletproof vests that were sold to the U.S. military and local law enforcement agencies. During this same period, DHB learned that Zylon deteriorated rapidly when exposed to light, heat, and body perspiration. DHB knew that one of its competitors, Second Chance Body Armor, had stopped using Zylon in its vests and, eventually, discontinued its business because customer demand for its Zylon-based vests had evaporated. DHB did not write down its own inventory of Zylon and Zylon-based vests because it had a large contract to supply the U.S. military with bulletproof vests. In its financial statements for the year ended December 31, 2004, DHB reported inventories of $86 million, sales of $90 million, net income of $8.3 million, but no inventory write-down. Yet, only eight months later, DHB admitted it should have written down its inventory by $18 million.

Required:

1. Show the impact of the inventory write-down on the accounting equation, and also show the journal entry that should have been recorded on December 31, 2004.

2. Calculate (*a*) the Inventory balance that should have been reported on December 31, 2004, and (*b*) the amount of Net Income that should have been reported for the year ended December 31, 2004. (Assume the inventory write-down does not affect income tax.)

3. DHB's share price reached an all-time high ($20–$22 per share) in November and December 2004, but then the company's CEO, CFO, and other executives began selling their shares in the company. Within a few weeks, they had cashed in over $200 million of shares. In August 2005, after DHB announced its inventory would have to be written down, the share price fell to less than $5 per share. If you were a lawyer representing DHB's investors, what evidence would you present to assert that a fraud had occurred? If you were a lawyer defending DHB, what counterarguments would you make?

LO5   **E7-12 Reporting Purchases and Purchase Discounts Using a Perpetual Inventory System**

During the months of January and February, Axen Corporation purchased goods from three suppliers. The sequence of events was as follows:

Jan. 6	Purchased goods for $1,200 from Green with terms 2/10, n/30.
6	Purchased goods from Munoz for $900 with terms 2/10, n/30.
14	Paid Green in full.
Feb. 2	Paid Munoz in full.
28	Purchased goods for $350 from Reynolds with terms 2/10, n/45.

Required:

Assume that Axen uses a perpetual inventory system, the company had no inventory on hand at the beginning of January, and no sales were made during January and February. Calculate the cost of inventory as of February 28.

LO5   **E7-13 Recording Journal Entries for Purchases and Purchase Discounts Using a Perpetual Inventory System**

Using the information in E7-12, prepare journal entries to record the transactions, assuming Axen uses a perpetual inventory system.

LO5   **E7-14 Reporting Purchases, Purchase Discounts, and Purchase Returns Using a Perpetual Inventory System**

During the month of June, Ace Incorporated purchased goods from two suppliers. The sequence of events was as follows:

June 3	Purchased goods for $3,200 from Diamond Inc. with terms 2/10, n/30.	
5	Returned goods costing $1,100 to Diamond Inc. for full credit.	
6	Purchased goods from Club Corp. for $1,000 with terms 2/10, n/30.	
11	Paid the balance owed to Diamond Inc.	
22	Paid Club Corp. in full.	

Check Figure:
Cost of Inventory = $3,058

Required:

Assume that Ace uses a perpetual inventory system and that the company had no inventory on hand at the beginning of the month. Calculate the cost of inventory as of June 30.

E7-15 Recording Journal Entries for Purchases, Purchase Discounts, and Purchase Returns Using a Perpetual Inventory System

LO5

Using the information in E7-14, prepare journal entries to record the transactions, assuming Ace uses a perpetual inventory system.

E7-16 Analyzing and Interpreting the Inventory Turnover Ratio

LO6

Polaris Industries Inc. is the biggest snowmobile manufacturer in the world. Assume that it reported the following amounts in its financial statements (in millions):

Polaris Industries Inc.

	2011	2010	2009	2008
Net Sales Revenue	$1,948	$1,780	$1,657	$1,870
Cost of Goods Sold	1,502	1,387	1,297	1,452
Average Inventory	220	224	216	188

Required:

1. Calculate to one decimal place the inventory turnover ratio and average days to sell inventory for 2011, 2010, and 2009.
2. Comment on any trends, and compare the effectiveness of inventory managers at Polaris to inventory managers at a competitor, where inventory turns over 4.5 times per year (81.1 days to sell). Both companies use the same inventory costing method (FIFO).

E7-17 (Supplement 7B) Calculating Cost of Ending Inventory and Cost of Goods Sold under Perpetual FIFO

Refer to the information in E7-5. Assume Oahu Kiki applies its inventory costing method perpetually at the time of each sale. The company sold 240 units between January 16 and 23. Calculate the cost of ending inventory and the cost of goods sold using the FIFO method.

E7-18 (Supplement 7B) Calculating Cost of Ending Inventory and Cost of Goods Sold under Perpetual FIFO

Refer to the information in E7-6. Assume Orion Iron applies its inventory costing method perpetually at the time of each sale. Calculate the cost of ending inventory and the cost of goods sold using the FIFO method.

E7-19 (Supplement 7C) Analyzing and Interpreting the Impact of an Inventory Error

G. Douglas Corporation prepared the following two income statements:

	First Quarter 2012		Second Quarter 2012	
Sales Revenue		$15,000		$18,000
Cost of Goods Sold				
Beginning Inventory	$ 3,000		$ 4,000	
Purchases	7,000		12,000	
Goods Available for Sale	10,000		16,000	
Ending Inventory	4,000		9,000	
Cost of Goods Sold		6,000		7,000
Gross Profit		9,000		11,000
Operating Expenses		5,000		6,000
Income from Operations		$ 4,000		$ 5,000

During the third quarter, the company's internal auditors discovered that the ending inventory for the first quarter should have been $4,400. The ending inventory for the second quarter was correct.

Check Figure:
[Req. 3]
First quarter Income from
Operations = $4,400

Required:

1. What effect would the error have on total Income from Operations for the two quarters combined? Explain.
2. What effect would the error have on Income from Operations for each of the two quarters? Explain.
3. Prepare corrected income statements for each quarter. Ignore income taxes.

E7-20 (Supplement 7D) Recording Purchases and Sales Using Perpetual and Periodic Inventory Systems

Kangaroo Jim Company reported beginning inventory of 100 units at a per unit cost of $25. It had the following purchase and sales transactions during 2012:

Jan. 14	Sold 25 units at unit sales price of $45 on account.
Apr. 9	Purchased 15 additional units at a per unit cost of $25 on account.
Sep. 2	Sold 50 units at a sales price of $50 on account.
Dec. 31	Counted inventory and determined 40 units were still on hand.

Required:

Record each transaction, assuming that Kangaroo Jim Company uses (a) a perpetual inventory system and (b) a periodic inventory system.

COACHED PROBLEMS

LO3

CP7-1 Analyzing the Effects of Four Alternative Inventory Costing Methods

Scrappers Supplies tracks the number of units purchased and sold throughout each accounting period but applies its inventory costing method at the end of each period, as if it uses a periodic inventory system. Assume its accounting records provided the following information at the end of the annual accounting period, December 31, 2012.

Transactions	Units	Unit Cost
Beginning inventory, January 1, 2012	200	$30
Transactions during 2012:		
a. Purchase on account, March 2	300	32
b. Cash sale, April 1 ($46 each)	(350)	
c. Purchase on account, June 30	250	36
d. Cash sale, August 1 ($46 each)	(50)	

TIP: Although the purchases and sales are listed in chronological order, Scrappers determines the cost of goods sold *after* all of the purchases have occurred.

Required:

1. Compute the cost of goods available for sale, cost of ending inventory, and cost of goods sold at December 31, 2012, under each of the following inventory costing methods:
   a. Weighted average cost.
   b. First-in, first-out.
   c. Specific identification, assuming that the April 1, 2012, sale was selected one-fifth from the beginning inventory and four-fifths from the purchase of March 2, 2012. Assume that the sale of August 1, 2012, was selected from the purchase of June 30, 2012.
   TIP: Cost of goods available for sale is the same for all methods.
2. Of the three methods, which will result in the highest gross profit? Which will result in the lowest income taxes?

CP7-2 Evaluating the Income Statement and Income Tax Effects of Lower of Cost and Net Realizable Value   LO4

L. Smart Company prepared its annual financial statements dated December 31, 2012. The company used the FIFO inventory costing method, but it failed to apply the LC&NRV to the ending inventory. The preliminary 2012 income statement follows:

Sales Revenue		$280,000
Cost of Goods Sold		
Beginning Inventory	$ 30,000	
Purchases	182,000	
Goods Available for Sale	212,000	
Ending Inventory (FIFO cost)	44,000	
Cost of Goods Sold		168,000
Gross Profit		112,000
Operating Expenses		61,000
Income from Operations		51,000
Income Tax Expense (30%)		15,300
Net Income		$ 35,700

TIP: Inventory write-downs do not affect the cost of goods available for sale. Instead, the effect of the write-down is to reduce ending inventory, which increases Cost of Goods Sold and then affects other amounts reported lower in the income statement.

Assume that you have been asked to restate the 2012 financial statements to incorporate the LC&NRV. You have developed the following data relating to the 2012 ending inventory:

		Purchase Cost		Current Replacement Cost per Unit (Net Realizable Value)
Item	Quantity	Per Unit	Total	
A	3,000	$3	$ 9,000	$4
B	1,500	4	6,000	2
C	7,000	2	14,000	4
D	3,000	5	15,000	2
			$44,000	

Required:

1. Restate the income statement to reflect the LC&NRV rule of the 2012 ending inventory. Apply the lower of cost and net realizable value on an item-by-item basis and show computations.

   TIP: Net Income equals $27,300.

2. Compare and explain the lower of cost and net realizable value effect on each amount that was changed in requirement 1.

   TIP: Net Income decreases by $8,400.

3. What is the conceptual basis for applying the lower of cost and net realizable value to merchandise inventories?

GROUP A PROBLEMS

Practise and learn online with Connect.

PA7-1 Analyzing the Effects of Three Alternative Inventory Methods in a Periodic Inventory System   LO3

Gladstone Limited tracks the number of units purchased and sold throughout each accounting period but applies its inventory costing method at the end of each period, as if it uses a periodic inventory system. Assume its accounting records provided the following information at the end of the annual accounting period, December 31, 2012.

Transactions	Units	Unit Cost
Beginning inventory, January 1, 2012	1,800	$5.00
Transactions during 2012:		
a. Purchase, January 30	2,500	6.20
b. Sale, March 14 ($10 each)	(1,450)	
c. Purchase, May 1	1,200	8.00
d. Sale, August 31 ($10 each)	(1,900)	

Check Figure:
[Req. 1(a)]
Ending inventory using
weighted average cost
= $13,330

Required:

1. Compute the amount of goods available for sale, ending inventory, and cost of goods sold at December 31, 2012, under each of the following inventory costing methods:

   a. Weighted average cost.
   b. First-in, first-out.
   c. Specific identification, assuming that the March 14, 2012, sale was selected two-fifths from the beginning inventory and three-fifths from the purchase of January 30, 2012. Assume that the sale of August 31, 2012, was selected from the remainder of the beginning inventory, with the balance from the purchase of May 1, 2012.

2. Of the three methods, which will result in the highest gross profit? Which will result in the lowest income taxes?

LO4   **PA7-2 Evaluating the Income Statement and Income Tax Effects of Lower of Cost and Net Realizable Value**

Springer Anderson Gymnastics prepared its annual financial statements dated December 31, 2012. The company used the FIFO inventory costing method, but it failed to apply the LC&NRV to the ending inventory. The preliminary 2012 income statement follows:

Sales Revenue		$140,000
Cost of Goods Sold		
Beginning Inventory	$ 15,000	
Purchases	91,000	
Goods Available for Sale	106,000	
Ending Inventory (FIFO cost)	22,000	
Cost of Goods Sold		84,000
Gross Profit		56,000
Operating Expenses		31,000
Income from Operations		25,000
Income Tax Expense (30%)		7,500
Net Income		$ 17,500

Assume that you have been asked to restate the 2012 financial statements to incorporate the LC&NRV. You have developed the following data relating to the 2012 ending inventory:

		Purchase Cost		Current Replacement Cost per Unit (Net Realizable Value)
Item	Quantity	Per Unit	Total	
A	1,500	$3	$ 4,500	$4
B	750	4	3,000	2
C	3,500	2	7,000	1
D	1,500	5	7,500	3
			$22,000	

Required:

1. Restate the income statement to reflect the LC&NRV rule of the 2012 ending inventory. Apply the lower of cost and net realizable value on an item-by-item basis and show computations.

2. Compare and explain the lower of cost and net realizable value effect on each amount that was changed in requirement 1.

3. What is the conceptual basis for applying the lower of cost and net realizable value to merchandise inventories?

PA7-3 Accounting for Inventory Purchase Transactions Including Allowances and Discounts Using a Perpetual Inventory System

LO5

Use the information in PA6-6 (page 276 in Chapter 6) to complete the following requirements.

Required:

1. Indicate the effect (direction and amount) of each transaction on the Inventory balance of Readers' Choice.

2. Prepare the journal entries that Readers' Choice would record and show any computations.

PA7-4 (Supplement 7C) Analyzing and Interpreting the Effects of Inventory Errors

Partial income statements for Sherwood Company summarized for a four-year period show the following:

	2009	2010	2011	2012
Net Sales	$2,000,000	$2,400,000	$2,500,000	$3,000,000
Cost of Goods Sold	1,400,000	1,660,000	1,770,000	2,100,000
Gross Profit	600,000	740,000	730,000	900,000

An audit revealed that in determining these amounts, the ending inventory for 2010 was overstated by $20,000. The inventory balance on December 31, 2011, was accurately stated. The company uses a periodic inventory system.

Required:

1. Restate the partial income statements to reflect the correct amounts, after fixing the inventory error.

2. Compute the gross profit percentage for each year (*a*) before the correction and (*b*) after the correction, rounding to the nearest percentage. Do the results lend confidence to your corrected amounts? Explain.

Check Figure:
[Req. 1]
2010 Gross Profit
= $720,000

GROUP B PROBLEMS

PB7-1 Analyzing the Effects of Three Alternative Inventory Methods in a Periodic Inventory System

LO3

Mojohava Industries tracks the number of units purchased and sold throughout each accounting period but applies its inventory costing method at the end of each period, as if it uses a periodic inventory system. Assume its accounting records provided the following information at the end of the accounting period, January 31, 2012. The inventory's selling price is $9 per unit.

Transactions	Unit Cost	Units	Total Cost
Inventory, January 1, 2012	$2.50	250	$625
Sale, January 10		(200)	
Purchase, January 12	3.00	300	900
Sale, January 17		(150)	
Purchase, January 26	4.00	80	320

Required:

1. Compute the amount of goods available for sale, ending inventory, and cost of goods sold at January 31, 2012, under each of the following inventory costing methods:
   a. Weighted average cost.
   b. First-in, first-out.
   c. Specific identification, assuming that the January 10 sale was from the beginning inventory and the January 17 sale was from the January 12 purchase.

2. Of the three methods, which will result in the highest gross profit? Which will result in the lowest income taxes?

PB7-2 Evaluating the Income Statement and Income Tax Effects of Lower of Cost and Net Realizable Value

Mondeara Clothing prepared its annual financial statements dated December 31, 2012. The company used the FIFO inventory costing method, but it failed to apply LC&NRV to the ending inventory. The preliminary 2012 income statement follows:

Net Sales		$420,000
Cost of Goods Sold		
Beginning Inventory	$ 45,000	
Purchases	273,000	
Goods Available for Sale	318,000	
Ending Inventory (FIFO cost)	66,000	
Cost of Goods Sold		252,000
Gross Profit		168,000
Operating Expenses		93,000
Income from Operations		75,000
Income Tax Expense (30%)		22,500
Net Income		$ 52,500

Assume that you have been asked to restate the 2012 financial statements to incorporate LC&NRV. You have developed the following data relating to the 2012 ending inventory:

Item	Quantity	Acquisition Cost Per Unit	Total	Current Replacement Cost per Unit (Net Realizable Value)
A	3,000	$4.50	$13,500	$6.00
B	1,500	6.00	9,000	3.00
C	7,000	3.00	21,000	6.00
D	3,000	7.50	22,500	4.50
			$66,000	

Required

Check Figure:
[Req. 1]
2012 Net Income = $43,050

1. Restate the income statement to reflect LC&NRV valuation of the 2012 ending inventory. Apply LC&NRV on an item-by-item basis and show computations.
2. Compare and explain the LC&NRV effect on each amount that was changed in requirement 1.
3. What is the conceptual basis for applying LC&NRV to merchandise inventories?

LO5 **PB7-3 Accounting for Inventory Purchase Transactions Including Allowances and Discounts Using a Perpetual Inventory System**

Use the information in PB6-6 (page 279 in Chapter 6) to complete the following requirements.

Required:

1. Indicate the effect (direction and amount) of each transaction on the Inventory balance of Sports 4 All.
2. Prepare the journal entries that Sports 4 All would record and show any computations.

LO5 **PB7-4 (Supplement 7C) Analyzing and Interpreting the Effects of Inventory Errors**

Spears & Cantrell announced inventory had been overstated by $30 (million) at the end of its 2012 second quarter. The error wasn't discovered and corrected in the company's periodic inventory system until after the end of the third quarter. The following table shows the amounts (in millions) that were originally reported by the company.

	Q1	Q2	Q3
Net Sales	$3,000	$3,600	$3,750
Cost of Goods Sold	2,100	2,490	2,655
Gross Profit	900	1,110	1,095

Required:

1. Restate the income statements to reflect the correct amounts, after fixing the inventory error.
2. Compute the gross profit percentage for each quarter (*a*) before the correction and (*b*) after the correction, rounding to the nearest percentage. Do the results lend confidence to your corrected amounts? Explain.

Check Figure:
[Req. 1]
Second Quarter Gross Profit
= $1,080

COMPREHENSIVE PROBLEM

C7-1 Comprehensive Problem (Chapters 4, 6, and 7)

LO3, 5

Custom College Coasters specializes in logo-imprinted drink coasters. The company reported the following balances in its unadjusted trial balance at December 1, 2012.

Cash	$10,005	Accounts Payable	$ 1,500	Cost of Goods Sold	$8,900
Accounts Receivable	2,000	Wages Payable	300	Rent Expense	1,100
Inventory	500	Taxes Payable	0	Wages Expense	2,000
Prepaid Rent	600	Contributed Capital	6,500	Amortization Expense	110
Equipment	810	Retained Earnings	3,030	Income Tax Expense	0
Accumulated Amortization	110	Sales Revenue	15,985	Selling Expenses	1,400

The company buys coasters from one supplier. All amounts in Accounts Payable on December 1 are owed to that supplier. The inventory on December 1, 2012, consisted of 1,000 coasters, all of which were purchased in a batch on July 10 at a unit cost of $0.50. Custom College Coasters uses the FIFO cost flow method.

During December 2012, the company entered into the following transactions. Some of these transactions are explained in greater detail below.

Dec. 1	Purchased 500 coasters on account from the regular supplier at a unit cost of $0.52, with terms of 2/10, n/30.
Dec. 2	Purchased 1,000 coasters on account from the regular supplier at a unit cost of $0.55, with terms of 2/10, n/30.
Dec. 15	Paid the supplier $1,600 cash on account.
Dec. 17	Sold 2,000 coasters on account at a unit price of $0.90.
Dec. 23	Paid employees $500, $300 of which related to work done in November and $200 for wages up to December 22.
Dec. 24	Collected $1,000 from customers on account.
Dec. 31	Loaded 1,000 coasters on a cargo ship to be delivered to a customer in Hawaii. The sale was made FOB destination with terms of 2/10, n/30.

Other relevant information includes the following:

a. Custom College Coasters has not yet recorded $200 of selling expenses incurred in December on account.
b. The company estimates that the equipment depreciates at a rate of $10 per month. One month of amortization needs to be recorded.
c. Wages for the period from December 23–31 are $100 and will be paid on January 15, 2013.
d. The $600 of Prepaid Rent relates to a six-month period ending on May 31, 2013.
e. No shrinkage or damage was discovered when the inventory was counted on December 31, 2012.
f. The company did not declare dividends and there were no transactions involving contributed capital.
g. The company has a 30 percent tax rate and has made no tax payments this year.

Required:

1. Analyze the accounting equation effects of each transaction and any adjustments required at month-end.
2. Prepare journal entries to record each transaction and any adjustments required at month-end.

3. Summarize the journal entries in T-accounts. Be sure to include the balances on December 1, 2012, as beginning account balances.

4. Prepare an income statement, statement of shareholders' equity, and classified balance sheet, using the formats presented in Exhibits 5.6 and 5.8 in Chapter 5 and Exhibit 6.11 in Chapter 6.

5. Calculate to one decimal place the inventory turnover ratio and days to sell in 2012, assuming that inventory was $500 on January 1, 2012. Evaluate these measures in comparison to an inventory turnover ratio of 12.0 during the year ended December 31, 2011.

SKILLS DEVELOPMENT CASES

LO2, 4, 6

Rona Inc.

S7-1 Finding Financial Information

Refer to the financial statements of Rona Inc. in Appendix A at the back of this book or download the annual report from the *Cases* section of Connect.
1. How much inventory does the company hold on December 27, 2009? Does this represent an increase or decrease in comparison to the prior year?
2. Does the company follow the lower of cost and net realizable value rule? What method(s) does the company use to determine the cost of its inventory? Describe where you found this information.
3. Compute to one decimal place the company's inventory turnover ratio and days to sell for the most recent year, given that the cost of goods sold is $3,397,634 (thousand).

LO2, 4, 6

Rona Inc.

S7-2 Comparing Financial Information

Refer to the financial statements of Rona Inc. in Appendix A and The Home Depot's in Appendix B at the back of this book or download the annual reports from the *Cases* section of Connect.
1. Does The Home Depot hold more or less inventory than Rona at the end of January 2010?
2. Does The Home Depot follow the lower of cost and net realizable value rule? What method does The Home Depot use to determine the cost of its inventory?
3. Compute to one decimal place The Home Depot's inventory turnover ratio and days to sell for the 2009–10 fiscal year and compare these to Rona's. What does this analysis suggest to you?

LO1, 2, 3, 4, 6

S7-3 Internet-Based Team Research: Examining an Annual Report

As a team, select an industry to analyze. Using your Web browser, each team member should access the annual report for one publicly traded company in the industry, with each member selecting a different company. (See S1-3 in Chapter 1 for a description of possible resources for these tasks.)

Required:
1. On an individual basis, each team member should write a short report that incorporates the following:
   a. Describe the types of inventory held by the company. Does the company indicate its inventory management goals anywhere in its annual report?
   b. Describe the inventory costing method that is used. Why do you think the company chose this method rather than the other acceptable methods? Do you think its inventory costs are rising or falling?
   c. Calculate the inventory turnover ratio for the current and prior year, and explain any change between the two years. (To obtain the beginning inventory number for the prior year, you will need the prior year's annual report.)
   d. Search the annual report for information about the company's approach for applying the LC&NRV rule to inventory. Did the company report the amount of inventory written down during the year?
2. Then, as a team, write a short report comparing and contrasting your companies using these attributes. Discuss any patterns across the companies that you as a team observe. Provide potential explanations for any differences discovered.

LO2, 4

S7-4 Ethical Decision Making: A Real-Life Example

Assume you are on a jury hearing a trial involving a large national drugstore company. Your immediate task is to identify suspicious events in the following evidence that suggest financial fraud may have occurred.

In just seven years, the company grew from 15 to 310 stores, reporting sales of more than $3 billion. Some retail experts believed the company was going to be the next Walmart. The apparent secret of the company's success was its ability to attract customers to its stores by selling items below cost. Then the company would make it easy for customers to buy other items, particularly pharmaceuticals, which earned a high gross profit. This strategy appeared to be working, so the company's top executives built up massive pharmaceutical inventories at its stores, causing total inventory to increase from $11 million to $36 million to $153 million in the past three years. The company hadn't installed a perpetual inventory system, so inventory had to be physically counted at each store to determine the cost of goods sold. To help its auditors verify the accuracy of these inventory counts, top management agreed to close selected stores on the day inventory was counted. All they asked was that they be given advance notice of which stores' inventory counts the auditors were planning to attend, so that the temporary closures could be conveyed to employees and customers at those stores. The external auditors selected four stores to test each year and informed the company several weeks in advance. To further assist the auditors with counting the inventory, top management reduced the inventory levels at the selected stores by shipping some of their goods to other stores that the auditors weren't attending.

After the inventory was counted and its cost was calculated, the company applied the LC&NRV test. On a store-by-store basis, top management compared the unit cost and net realizable value of inventory items and then prepared journal entries to write down the inventory. Some of the journal entries were large in amount and involved debiting an account called "Cookies" and crediting the inventory account. Management reported that the Cookies account was used to accumulate the required write-downs for all the company's stores. Just before the financial statements were finalized, the Cookies account was emptied by allocating it back to each of the stores. In one instance, $9,999,999.99 was allocated from Cookies to a store's account called "Accrued Inventory."

Required:

Prepare a list that summarizes the pieces of evidence that indicate that fraud might have occurred and, for each item on the list, explain why it contributes to your suspicion.

Epilogue: This case is based on a fraud involving Phar Mor, as described by David Cottrell and Steven Glover in the July 1997 issue of the *CPA Journal*. Phar Mor's management was collectively fined over $1 million and two top managers received prison sentences ranging from 33 months to five years. The company's auditors paid over $300 million in civil judgments for failing to uncover the fraud.

Phar Mor

S7-5 Ethical Decision Making: A Mini-Case

L03

David Eltner is the CEO of Aquatic Gear Enterprises, a seven-year-old manufacturer of boats. After many long months of debate with the company's board of directors, David obtained the board's approval to expand into water ski sales. David firmly believed that Aquatic Gear could generate significant profits in this market, despite recent increases in the cost of skis. A board meeting will be held later this month for David to present the financial results for the first quarter of ski sales. As Aquatic Gear's corporate controller, you reported to David that the results weren't great. Although sales were better than expected at $165,000 (3,000 units at $55 per unit), the cost of goods sold was $147,500. This left a gross profit of $17,500. David knew this amount wouldn't please the board. Desperate to save the ski division, David asks you to "take another look at the cost calculations to see if there's any way to reduce the cost of goods sold. I know you accountants have different methods for figuring things out, so maybe you can do your magic now when I need it most." You dig out your summary of inventory purchases for the quarter to recheck your calculations, using the LIFO method that has always been used for the company's inventory of boats.

	Date	Units	Unit Cost	Total Cost
Beginning inventory of water skis	January 1	0	—	—
Purchases	January 15	1,500	$30	$45,000
Purchases	February 18	2,000	45	90,000
Purchases	March 29	2,500	50	125,000

Required:

1. Calculate Cost of Goods Sold using the LIFO method. Does this confirm the statement you made to David about the Gross Profit earned on water ski sales in the first quarter?
2. Without doing any calculations, is it likely that any alternative inventory costing method will produce a lower Cost of Goods Sold? Explain.

3. Calculate Cost of Goods Sold using the FIFO method. Would use of this method solve David's current dilemma?

4. Is it acceptable within GAAP to report the water skis using one inventory costing method and the boats using a different method?

5. Do you see any problems with using the FIFO numbers for purposes of David's meeting with the board?

S7-6 Calculating and Recording the Effects of Lower of Cost and Net Realizable Value on Ending Inventory

Perfumania

Assume you recently obtained a job with Perfumania, the largest specialty retailer of discounted fragrances in the United States. Your job is to estimate the amount of write-down required to value inventory at the lower of cost and net realizable value. The cost of inventory is calculated using the weighted average cost method and, at $368 million, it represents the company's biggest and most important asset. Assume the corporate controller asked you to prepare a spreadsheet that can be used to determine the amount of the LC&NRV write-down for the current year. The controller provides the following hypothetical numbers for you to use in the spreadsheet.

Product Line	Weighted Average Unit Cost	Replacement Cost (Net Realizable Value) at Year-End	Quantity on Hand
Alfred Sung Shi	$22	$20	80
Animale	15	16	75
Azzaro	10	10	50
Mambo	16	17	30
OP Juice	8	7	400

You realize that you'll need to multiply the quantity of each item by the lower of cost and net realizable value per unit. You e-mailed your friend Owen for Excel help.

From:	Owentheaccountant@yahoo.com
To:	Helpme@hotmail.com
Cc:	
Subject:	Excel Help

So you don't have any idea how to pick the lower of cost and net realizable value? You can do this several different ways, but the easiest is to use the MIN command. Set up your spreadsheet similar to the table you sent me, and then add two new columns. In the first new column, enter the command "= MIN(costcell, net realizable valuecell)" where costcell is the cell containing the cost per unit and net realizable value cell is the cell containing the net realizable value per unit. Next, in the second new column, multiply the quantity by the lower of cost or net realizable value per unit, and then SUM the column.

Required:

1. Prepare a spreadsheet that calculates total lower of cost and net realizable value for inventory, applied on an item-by-item basis.

2. Prepare a journal entry to record the inventory lower of cost and net realizable value write-down.

CONTINUING CASE

Practise and learn online with Connect.

CC7 Accounting for Changing Inventory Costs

In October 2011, Nicole of Nicole's Getaway Spa (NGS) eliminated all existing inventory of cosmetic items. The trouble of ordering and tracking each product line had exceeded the profits earned. In December, a supplier asked her to sell a prepackaged spa kit. Feeling she could manage a single product line, Nicole agreed. NGS would make monthly purchases from the supplier at a cost that included production costs and a transportation charge. The spa would use a perpetual inventory system to keep track of its new inventory.

On December 30, 2011, NGS purchased 10 units at a total cost of $6 per unit. NGS purchased 30 more units at $8 in February 2012, but returned 5 defective units to the supplier. In March, NGS purchased 15 units at $10 per unit. In May, 50 units were purchased at $10 per unit; however, NGS took advantage of a 2/10, n/30 discount from the supplier. In June, NGS sold 50 units at a selling price of $12 per unit and 35 units at $10 per unit.

Required:

1. Explain whether the transportation cost included in each purchase should be recorded as a cost of the inventory or immediately expensed.
2. Compute the Cost of Goods Available for Sale, Cost of Goods Sold, and Cost of Ending Inventory using the first-in, first-out (FIFO) method.
3. Calculate the inventory turnover ratio (round to one decimal place), using the inventory on hand at December 31, 2011, as the beginning inventory. The supplier reported that the typical inventory turnover ratio was 7.9. How does NGS's ratio compare?

Endnotes

1. By showing all purchases taking place before any Sales and Cost of Goods Sold are computed, we are demonstrating a periodic inventory system. You might think it's odd that we use a periodic system when we said in Chapter 6 that most modern companies use perpetual inventory systems. We actually have several good reasons for doing this, which we explain in Supplement 7B in this chapter, where we also explain how cost flow assumptions are applied in more complex situations involving perpetual inventory systems. For purposes of examples shown in the chapter and for problem materials at the end of this chapter, we assume no shrinkage (a topic discussed in Chapter 6).
2. We apply lower of cost or net realizable value on an item basis. It also may be applied on a product line basis.
3. If inventory is sold immediately after the $100 purchase, the weighted average cost will need to be calculated again ($138.75 ÷ 15 = $9.25 per unit). Notice the change in weighted average cost from $7.75 to $9.25 per unit. Because the weighted average unit cost changes, weighted average perpetual is also called the *moving average method*.

Practise and learn online with Connect.

CHAPTER 8

Reporting and Interpreting Receivables, Bad Debt Expense, and Interest Revenue

FOCUS COMPANY:
Skechers
www.skechers.com

THAT WAS
THEN

In previous chapters, we quietly assumed that all sales on account ultimately are collected as cash.

THIS IS
NOW

In this chapter, you'll learn how companies handle the situation where customers don't pay all that they owe.

O ne of the most challenging parts of your academic and professional career will be managing events that you can't completely control. Think, for example, about a group project that you must complete this term. You may believe that, in theory, the work should take only six days from start to finish. You know from experience, however, that someone in your group is likely to be late with the assigned work or may fail to complete it at all. The problem is you don't know who it will be or how long the delay will be—these matters are largely beyond your control. To allow for the possibility that someone may be late, you might set a shorter time period (say, four days) to complete the work. Establishing a two-day allowance will give you a realistic basis for planning and successfully completing the project.

This situation is similar to a problem faced by many companies, including Skechers, a shoe company that sells on credit to retailers such as Foot Locker. Skechers managers know from experience that some customers won't pay their bills, especially in difficult economic times. The problem is that at the time sales are made, Skechers can't identify which particular customers will be "bad customers." In this chapter, you'll learn about a method of accounting for such uncertainties—one that is similar to the allowance approach you took with your group project. This method allows Skechers managers to report in a timely manner how much money the company is likely to collect from customers. Also in this chapter, you will learn about notes receivable, which arise from selling or lending to others under contract.

ORGANIZATION OF THE CHAPTER

Understand the business	**S**tudy the accounting methods	**E**valuate the results	**R**eview the chapter
• Advantages and Disadvantages of extending credit	• Accounts receivable and bad debts • Methods for estimating bad debts • Notes receivable and interest revenue • Recording notes receivable and interest revenue	• Receivables turnover analysis	• Demonstration Cases • Chapter Summary • Key Terms • Homework Helper • Practice Material

Understand the Business

At December 31, 2010, accounts receivable and notes receivable accounted for over 21 percent of Skechers' total assets. If the company is to be successful, these assets have to be effectively managed. But what factors do managers consider when extending credit on account (accounts receivable) or under contract (notes receivable)?

ADVANTAGES AND DISADVANTAGES OF EXTENDING CREDIT

Learning Objective 1

Describe the trade-offs of extending credit.

Skechers allows business customers like Foot Locker to open an account and buy shoes on credit, yet its retail outlets do not extend this option to you—the individual consumer. Even though extending credit helps customers to buy products and services and therefore increases the seller's revenues, the following additional costs make offering consumer credit a losing deal for Skechers:

1. **Increased wage costs.** If credit is extended, Skechers will have to hire people to (a) evaluate whether each customer is creditworthy, (b) track how much each customer owes, and (c) follow up to collect the receivable from each customer.

2. **Bad debt costs.** Inevitably, some customers dispute what they owe or they run into financial difficulties and pay only a fraction of their account balances. These "bad debts," as they are called, can be a significant additional cost of extending credit. (At December 31, 2010, Skechers estimated that nearly 8 percent of its receivables from other businesses would not be collected.)

3. **Delayed receipt of cash.** Even if Skechers were to collect in full from customers, it would likely have to wait 30–60 days before receiving the cash. During this period, Skechers may have to take out a short-term bank loan to pay for other business activities. The interest on such a loan would be another cost of extending credit to customers.

Most managers find that the additional revenue (or, more accurately, the gross profit) to be gained from selling on account to business customers is greater than the additional costs mentioned above. However, when it comes to individual consumers, the additional gross profit doesn't cover all the additional costs that Skechers would incur.

Similar advantages and disadvantages are considered when deciding whether to create notes receivable. A **note receivable** is created when a formal written contract ("note") is established outlining the terms by which a company will receive amounts it is owed. Notes receivable differ from accounts receivable in that notes generally charge interest from the day they are signed to the day they are collected. Notes receivable are viewed as a stronger legal claim than accounts receivable, but a new note needs to be created for every transaction, so they are used less frequently—typically when a company sells large dollar-value items (e.g., cars), offers extended payment periods, or lends money to individuals or businesses.

Study the Accounting Methods

ACCOUNTS RECEIVABLE AND BAD DEBTS

You already know from earlier chapters that **accounts receivable** arise from the sale of goods or services on credit. What you may not know is that some accounts receivable are never collected. Like that "friend" of yours who *says* he'll pay you later but for one reason or another never gets around to it, some customers just do not pay their bills.

Two objectives when accounting for accounts receivable and bad debts are (1) report Accounts Receivable at the amount the company expects to collect ("net realizable value") and (2) match the cost of bad debts to the accounting period in which the related credit sales are made. These two objectives point to the same solution: reduce both Accounts Receivable and Net Income by the amount of credit sales that are unlikely to be collected as cash.

The only problem with this solution is that, just as it takes you a while to find out which friends you can't trust, some time will pass before Skechers discovers which particular credit sales and customer balances aren't going to be collected. More than likely, these bad debts will be discovered in an accounting period following the sale, rather than in the same period as the sale. As Exhibit 8.1 shows, if you record sales in one period when they occur and bad debts in a different period when they are discovered, you will violate the **matching principle**. This failure to match Bad Debt Expense with Sales Revenue in the same period will lead to distorted views of Net Income in the period of the sale as well as in the period the bad debt is discovered. To see how this could be a problem, take a moment to read Exhibit 8.1 right now.

EXHIBIT 8.1	Distortion Occurs If Bad Debts Are Not Matched to Sales

	PERIOD 1 (Credit Sale Occurs)		PERIOD 2 (Bad Debt Discovered)	
Sales Revenues		$10,000	Sales Revenues	$ 0
Cost of Goods Sold		8,000	Cost of Goods Sold	0
Bad Debt Expense		0	Bad Debt Expense	1,000
Net Income		$ 2,000	Net Income (Loss)	$(1,000)

This example shows why we need to **record bad debts in the same period as the sale.** The only way to do this is to estimate the amount of bad debts when the sale is recorded. Later, the accounting records can be adjusted when uncollectable amounts become known with certainty. This approach is called the **allowance method** and it follows a two-step process, which we'll walk you through below:

1. Make an end-of-period adjustment to **record the estimated bad debts in the period credit sales occur.**

2. Remove ("write off") specific customer balances when they are known to be uncollectable.

1. Adjust for Estimated Bad Debts

Credit sales, when first recorded, affect both the balance sheet (an increase in Accounts Receivable) and the income statement (an increase in Sales Revenue). On occasion, a company will fail to collect receivables that arise from credit sales. To account for these bad sales on account that have been recorded in Sales Revenue and Accounts Receivable, we record offsetting amounts in both the balance sheet and income statement. This adjustment is made at the end of each accounting period to reduce Accounts Receivable (using a contra-asset account called *Allowance for Doubtful Accounts*) and reduce Net Income (using an expense account called **Bad Debt Expense**). If Skechers were to estimate $900 of bad debts this period, the effects on the accounting equation and adjusting journal entry to record them would be as follows.

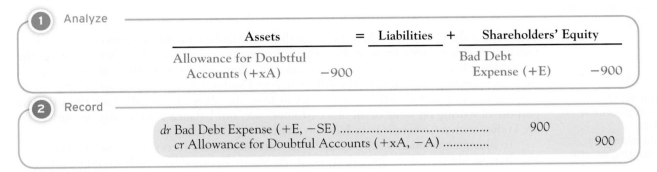

1 Analyze

Assets		= Liabilities +	Shareholders' Equity	
Allowance for Doubtful Accounts (+xA)	−900		Bad Debt Expense (+E)	−900

2 Record

dr Bad Debt Expense (+E, −SE) 900
    cr Allowance for Doubtful Accounts (+xA, −A) 900

Exhibit 8.2 uses blue and red text to show how the accounts in the end-of-period adjusting entry partially offset the original sales on account. The exhibit also shows where the accounts appear in the balance sheet and income statement.

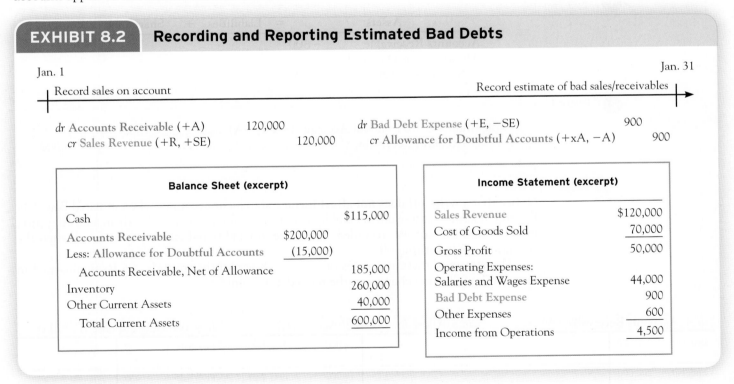

EXHIBIT 8.2	**Recording and Reporting Estimated Bad Debts**

Jan. 1   Jan. 31

Record sales on account   Record estimate of bad sales/receivables

dr Accounts Receivable (+A)   120,000   dr Bad Debt Expense (+E, −SE)   900
    cr Sales Revenue (+R, +SE)   120,000   cr Allowance for Doubtful Accounts (+xA, −A)   900

Balance Sheet (excerpt)		
Cash		$115,000
Accounts Receivable	$200,000	
Less: Allowance for Doubtful Accounts	(15,000)	
Accounts Receivable, Net of Allowance		185,000
Inventory		260,000
Other Current Assets		40,000
Total Current Assets		600,000

Income Statement (excerpt)	
Sales Revenue	$120,000
Cost of Goods Sold	70,000
Gross Profit	50,000
Operating Expenses:	
Salaries and Wages Expense	44,000
Bad Debt Expense	900
Other Expenses	600
Income from Operations	4,500

Like all contra-asset accounts, such as Accumulated Amortization, the Allowance for Doubtful Accounts is a permanent account, so its balance carries forward from one accounting period to the next. Bad Debt Expense, which is a temporary account, will have its balance closed (zeroed out) at the end of each accounting period. Consequently, the balance in the Allowance for Doubtful Accounts will differ from the balance in Bad Debt Expense, except during the first year that the Allowance for Doubtful Accounts is used. This explains why the

Accounts Receivable,
Net of Allowance (shown
in Exhibit 8.2) is not a
separate account. It is a
subtotal that is computed
by subtracting the contra-
asset account *Allowance
for Doubtful Accounts* from
the asset account *Accounts
Receivable.* This subtotal can
also be referred to as the *Net
Realizable Value.*

YOU SHOULD KNOW

Write-off: The act of
removing an uncollectable
account and its
corresponding allowance
from the accounting records.

Allowance for Doubtful Accounts in the balance sheet in Exhibit 8.2 does not equal the Bad Debt Expense in the income statement.

For billing and collection purposes, Skechers internally keeps a separate accounts receivable account (called a **subsidiary account**) for each customer. The total of these accounts is reported as Accounts Receivable on the balance sheet. Given this, you might wonder why the estimated uncollectable accounts aren't taken directly out of these individual accounts. The reason is that, at the time the Allowance for Doubtful Accounts is estimated, no one knows which particular customers' accounts receivable are uncollectable. If Skechers were to remove the specific customer accounts believed to be uncollectable, it would lose track of which customers still owed money. If this were to happen, Skechers would no longer know which customers it should continue pursuing for payment.

2. Remove (Write Off) Specific Customer Balances

Throughout the year, when it becomes clear that a particular customer will never pay, Skechers removes the customer's account from the accounts receivable records. After removing the receivable, Skechers no longer needs to make an allowance for it, so the company removes the corresponding amount from the Allowance for Doubtful Accounts. Removing the uncollectable account and a corresponding amount from the allowance is called a **write-off.** The purpose of writing off some or all of a customer's account balance is to remove amounts that are known with near certainty to have no chance of collection.

To illustrate, assume Skechers decides to write off an $800 receivable from Fast Footwear. Skechers would record an $800 decrease in Accounts Receivable, which would be offset by an $800 decrease in the contra-account Allowance for Doubtful Accounts. These accounting equation effects and the journal entry to record them follow.

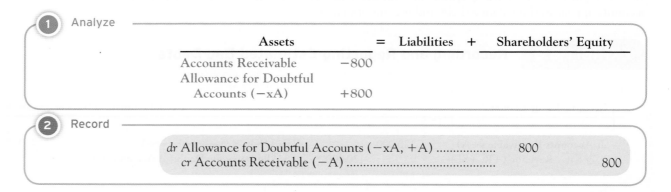

① Analyze

	Assets	=	Liabilities	+	Shareholders' Equity
Accounts Receivable	−800				
Allowance for Doubtful Accounts (−xA)	+800				

② Record

dr Allowance for Doubtful Accounts (−xA, +A)	800	
cr Accounts Receivable (−A)		800

Notice that **a write-off does not affect income statement accounts.** The estimated Bad Debt Expense relating to these uncollectable accounts was already recorded with an adjusting entry in the period the sale was recorded. Therefore, no additional expense is incurred when the account is finally written off.

The effects of these two steps on Skechers's accounting records can be summarized in terms of the following changes in the related T-accounts:

dr + Accounts Receivable (A) *cr* −			
Beg. bal.	200,800		
		800	(2) Write-offs
End. bal.	200,000		

dr − Allow. for Doubtful Accts (xA) *cr* −			
		14,900	Beg. bal.
(2) Write-offs	800	900	(1) Estimate
		15,000	End. bal.

dr + Bad Debt Expense (E, SE) *cr* −			
Beg. bal.	0		
(1) Estimate	900		
End. bal.	900		

Summary of the Allowance Method

A summary of the two main steps in the allowance method follows:

Step	Timing	Journal Entry	FINANCIAL STATEMENT EFFECTS		

1. Adjust for estimated bad debts — Timing: End of each period — Journal Entry: dr Bad Debt Expense (+E, −SE) / cr Allowance for Doubtful Accounts (+xA, −A)

Balance Sheet

Accounts Receivable	no effect
Less: Allowance	increase
Accounts Receivable, Net	decrease

Income Statement

Revenues	no effect
Expenses	
Bad Debt Expense	increase
Net Income	decrease

2. Write off specific customer balances — Timing: When known to be uncollectable — Journal Entry: dr Allowance for Doubtful Accounts (−xA, +A) / cr Accounts Receivable (−A)

Balance Sheet

Accounts Receivable	decrease
Less: Allowance	decrease
Accounts Receivable, Net	no effect

Income Statement

Revenues	no effect
Expenses	
Bad Debt Expense	no effect
Net Income	no effect

 HOW'S IT GOING? Self-Study Practice

Indicate the effect (+ / − / No Effect) of each of the following hypothetical situations on net income and total assets.

	Net Income	Total Assets
1. Polaris Industries recorded an increase in estimated bad debts on December 31, 2012.		
2. Kellogg's wrote off 12 customer account balances during 2012.		

After you have finished, check your answers with the solution in the margin.

METHODS FOR ESTIMATING BAD DEBTS

In the examples given so far, we simply stated the estimated amount of uncollectables to record. In the workplace, these bad debts must be estimated. Such estimates may be based on either (1) a percentage of credit sales for the period or (2) an aging of accounts receivable. Both methods are acceptable under GAAP and IFRS. The percentage of credit sales method is simpler to apply, but the aging method is generally more accurate. Some companies use the simpler method on a weekly or monthly basis and the more accurate method on a monthly or quarterly basis to check the accuracy of earlier estimates.

Percentage of Credit Sales Method

The **percentage of credit sales method** estimates bad debt expense by multiplying the historical percentage of bad debt losses by the current period's credit sales. Assume, for example, that Skechers has experienced bad debt losses of ¾ of 1 percent of credit sales in prior periods. If credit sales in January total $120,000, Skechers could estimate the month's bad debt expense as follows.

YOU SHOULD KNOW

Percentage of credit sales method (also called the *income statement approach*): Estimates bad debts based on the historical percentage of sales that lead to bad debt losses.

Credit sales this month	$120,000
× Bad debt loss rate (0.75%)	× 0.0075
Bad debt expense this month	$ 900

This estimate would be recorded using the journal entry previously shown on page 331.

Aging of Accounts Receivable Method

While the percentage of credit sales method focuses on estimating Bad Debt Expense for the period, the **aging of accounts receivable method** focuses on estimating the ending balance in the Allowance for Doubtful Accounts. The aging method gets its name because it is based on the "age" of each amount in Accounts Receivable. The older and more overdue an account receivable becomes, the less likely it is to be collectable. Based on this idea, credit managers and accountants use their experience to estimate what portion of receivables of a specific age will not be paid.

To illustrate the aging of accounts receivable method, we assume Skechers applies this method to its accounts receivable balances when its quarter ends on March 31. The method includes three steps as shown in Exhibit 8.3:

1. **Prepare an aged listing of accounts receivable** with totals for each age category. Most accounting software will produce this report automatically by counting back the number of days to when each receivable was first recorded.

2. **Estimate bad debt loss percentages for each category.** The percentage each company uses varies according to its circumstances and past experience. Generally, higher percentages are applied to increasingly older receivables.

3. **Compute the total estimate by multiplying the totals in Step 1 by the percentages in Step 2 and then summing across all categories.** The total across all aging categories ($2,040 + $5,200 + $7,600 + $2,400 = **$17,240**) equals the adjusted ending balance in the Allowance for Doubtful Accounts at the end of the period. Therefore an adjustment may need to be made to this account in order to reflect this estimate total.

EXHIBIT 8.3 Estimating Uncollectable Amounts with an Aging of Accounts Receivable

Customer	Total	Number of Days Unpaid				
		0–30	31–60	61–90	Over 90	
Adam's Sports	$ 700	$ 400	$ 200	$ 100		
Backyard Shoe	2,300				$ 2,300	← Step ① — Age
Others (not shown to save space)	189,000	97,600	49,800	37,900	3,700	
Zoom Athletics	6,000	4,000	2,000			
Total Accounts Receivable	**$198,000**	**$102,000**	**$52,000**	**$38,000**	**$6,000**	
Estimated Uncollectable (%)		× 2%	× 10%	× 20%	× 40%	← Step ② — Estimate
Estimated Uncollectable ($)	**$ 17,240**	**$ 2,040**	**$ 5,200**	**$ 7,600**	**$2,400**	← Step ③ — Compute

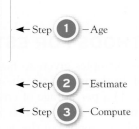

Allowance for	
dr − Doubtful Accounts cr +	
	15,000 Unadj. bal.
	? AJE
	17,240 Desired bal.

The amount computed in Step 3 is the desired balance in the Allowance for Doubtful Accounts, **not** the amount of the adjustment. To compute the amount of the adjustment, you must determine how much to increase (credit) or decrease (debit) the Allowance for Doubtful Accounts to reach the desired adjusted balance computed in Step 3. Assume, for example, that Skechers had an unadjusted credit balance in the Allowance for Doubtful Accounts of $15,000 on March 31 and computed a desired credit balance of $17,240 as shown in Exhibit 8.3. An adjustment of $2,240 ($17,240 − $15,000) needs to be recorded as a credit to the account. A corresponding amount is debited to Bad Debt Expense, as follows.

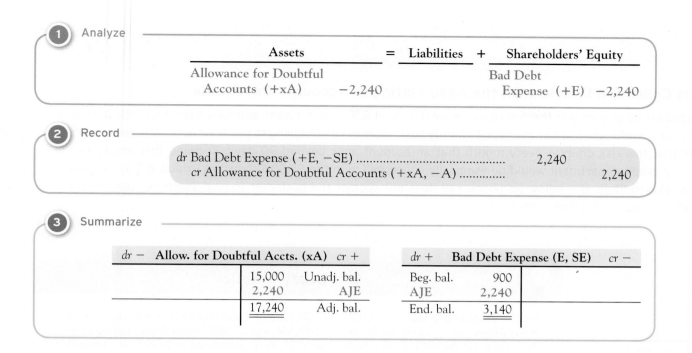

1 Analyze

	Assets	=	Liabilities	+	Shareholders' Equity
Allowance for Doubtful Accounts (+xA)	−2,240				Bad Debt Expense (+E) −2,240

2 Record

dr Bad Debt Expense (+E, −SE) 2,240
  cr Allowance for Doubtful Accounts (+xA, −A) 2,240

3 Summarize

dr −	Allow. for Doubtful Accts. (xA)	cr +
	15,000	Unadj. bal.
	2,240	AJE
	17,240	Adj. bal.

dr +	Bad Debt Expense (E, SE)	cr −
Beg. bal.	900	
AJE	2,240	
End. bal.	3,140	

Although the Allowance for Doubtful Accounts normally has a credit balance, it may in some situations have a **debit balance** before it is adjusted. This happens when a company has recorded write-offs that exceed previous estimates of uncollectable accounts. If this happens, you can still calculate the amount of the adjustment needed to reach the desired balance under the aging of accounts receivable method. The only difference is that to reach the desired balance, you need to record an amount equal to the desired balance **plus** the existing debit balance. After the adjustment is recorded, the Allowance for Doubtful Accounts will once again return to a credit balance. Assume, for example, that Skechers had an unadjusted debit balance in the Allowance for Doubtful Accounts of $7,000 on March 31 and computed a desired credit balance of $17,240 as shown in Exhibit 8.3. An adjustment of **$24,240** ($17,240 + $7,000) needs to be recorded as a credit to the account. A corresponding amount is debited to Bad Debt Expense, as follows.

	Allowance for	
dr −	Doubtful Accounts	cr +
7,000		Unadj. bal.
	?	AJE
	17,240	Desired bal.

1 Analyze

	Assets	=	Liabilities	+	Shareholders' Equity
Allowance for Doubtful Accounts (+xA)	−24,240				Bad Debt Expense (+E) −24,240

2 Record

dr Bad Debt Expense (+E, −SE) 24,240
  cr Allowance for Doubtful Accounts (+xA, −A) 24,240

3 Summarize

dr −	Allow. for Doubtful Accts. (xA)	cr +
Unadj. bal.	7,000	
	24,240	AJE
	17,240	Adj. bal.

dr +	Bad Debt Expense (E, SE)	cr −
Beg. bal.	900	
AJE	24,240	
End. bal.	25,140	

Focus Collection Efforts with the Aged Listing of Accounts Receivable

The aged listing of accounts receivable, as shown in Exhibit 8.3, is useful when estimating uncollectable accounts. But it also is useful when credit managers identify customers at risk of failing to pay their accounts. Some sources report that this risk doubles every month that an account ages beyond 90 days. Knowing this, employees in Skechers' credit department would be especially concerned with the $2,300 shown in Exhibit 8.3 as receivable from Backyard Shoe. If a follow-up phone call does not prompt the customer to pay, Skechers could turn the account over to a collection agency.

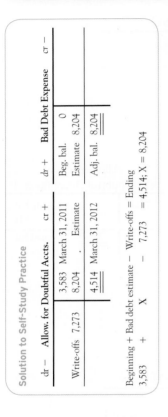

Solution to Self-Study Practice

dr −	Allow. for Doubtful Accts.	cr +
	3,583	March 31, 2011
Write-offs 7,273	8,204	Estimate
	4,514	March 31, 2012

Beginning + Bad debt estimate − Write-offs = Ending
3,583 + X − 7,273 = 4,514; X = 8,204

dr +	Bad Debt Expense	cr −
Beg. bal.	0	
Estimate	8,204	
Adj. bal.	8,204	

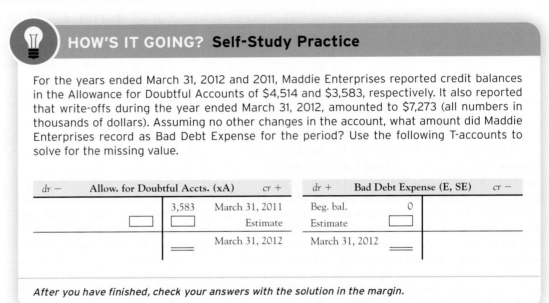

HOW'S IT GOING? Self-Study Practice

For the years ended March 31, 2012 and 2011, Maddie Enterprises reported credit balances in the Allowance for Doubtful Accounts of $4,514 and $3,583, respectively. It also reported that write-offs during the year ended March 31, 2012, amounted to $7,273 (all numbers in thousands of dollars). Assuming no other changes in the account, what amount did Maddie Enterprises record as Bad Debt Expense for the period? Use the following T-accounts to solve for the missing value.

dr −	Allow. for Doubtful Accts. (xA)	cr +
	3,583	March 31, 2011
		Estimate
		March 31, 2012

dr +	Bad Debt Expense (E, SE)	cr −
Beg. bal.	0	
Estimate		
March 31, 2012		

After you have finished, check your answers with the solution in the margin.

Other Issues

Revising Estimates Bad debt estimates always differ from the amounts that are later written off. If these differences are material, companies are required to revise their bad debt estimates for the current period. That is, they correct overestimates of prior periods by lowering estimates in the current period, or they raise estimates in the current period to correct underestimates of prior periods.

Account Recoveries In the same way that someone you've written off as a friend might do something to win you back, a customer might pay an account balance that was previously written off. Collection of a previously written-off account is called a **recovery** and it is accounted for in two parts. First, put the receivable back on the books by recording the opposite of the write-off. Second, record the collection of the account. To illustrate, let's assume that Skechers collects the $800 from Fast Footwear that was previously written off. This recovery would be recorded with the following journal entries:

COACH'S TIP

Like the initial write-off, a recovery does not affect Net Income.

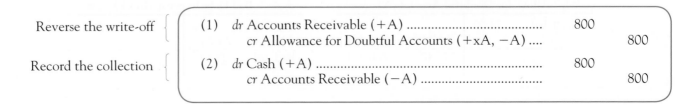

Reverse the write-off
(1) dr Accounts Receivable (+A) 800
     cr Allowance for Doubtful Accounts (+xA, −A) 800

Record the collection
(2) dr Cash (+A) 800
     cr Accounts Receivable (−A) 800

Look closely at the journal entries for recording a recovery and you'll see that Accounts Receivable is debited and then credited for $800. It's tempting to cancel these two out, but don't do this because it would create an inaccurate credit history for the customer. After all is said and done, the customer's balance was removed because it was actually collected, not written off, so the accounting records should reflect that.

Alternative Methods   You should be aware that some small companies don't use the allowance method. Instead, they use an alternative approach called the **direct write-off method**, which we demonstrate in Supplement 8A near the end of this chapter. This alternative method records Bad Debt Expense only when a company writes off specific accounts. Although this alternative method is easier to use, it overstates the value of Accounts Receivable and it violates the matching principle, as explained in Supplement 8A. Thus, it is not considered a generally accepted accounting method.

NOTES RECEIVABLE AND INTEREST REVENUE

Learning Objective 3

Compute and report interest on notes receivable.

A company reports Notes Receivable if it uses a promissory note to document its right to collect money from another party. This usually happens in the following three situations: (1) the company loans money to employees or businesses, (2) the company sells expensive items for which customers require an extended payment period, or (3) the company converts an existing account receivable to a note receivable to allow an extended payment period.

The accounting issues for notes receivable are similar to those for accounts receivable, with one exception. Unlike accounts receivable, which are interest-free until they become overdue, notes receivable charge interest from the day they are created to the day they are due (their **maturity date**). Although interest on a note receivable is earned each day, interest payments typically are received only once or twice a year. This means that a company with a note receivable needs to accrue Interest Revenue and Interest Receivable. Let's look at how to calculate interest.

 COACH'S TIP

The "time" variable refers to the portion of a year for which interest is calculated, not the portion of the note's entire life. A 2-month interest calculation on a 3-year note has a time variable of 2/12 not 2/36.

Calculating Interest

To calculate interest, you need to consider three variables: (1) the **principal**, which is the amount of the note receivable, (2) the annual **interest rate** charged on the note, and (3) the **time** period covered in the interest calculation. Because **interest rates are always stated as an annual percentage even if the note is for less than a year**, the time period is the portion of a year for which interest is calculated. Ask yourself how many months out of 12 or how many days out of 365 the interest period covers. Then use the following **interest formula** to calculate the interest:

$$\text{Interest (I)} = \text{Principal (P)} \times \text{Interest Rate (R)} \times \text{Time (T)}$$

YOU SHOULD KNOW

Interest formula:
$I = P \times R \times T$, where I = interest calculated, P = principal, R = annual interest rate, and T = time period covered in the interest calculation (number of months out of 12).

Many financial institutions use the number of days out of 365 to compute interest. In doing homework assignments, assume that the time is measured in terms of number of months out of 12. See Exhibit 8.4 for the computation of interest for three notes with different terms and different lengths of interest periods. Notice how the time variable depends on the interest period, not the due date for the note.

RECORDING NOTES RECEIVABLE AND INTEREST REVENUE

The four key events that occur with any note receivable are (1) establishing the note, (2) accruing interest earned but not received, (3) recording interest payments received, and (4) recording principal payments received. Assume that on November 1, 2011, Skechers lent $100,000 to a company by creating a note that required the company to pay Skechers 6 percent interest and the $100,000 principal on October 31, 2012. Skechers prepared year-end financial statements as of December 31, 2011, but made no other adjustments for interest during the year.

EXHIBIT 8.4 Sample Interest Computations

GIVEN INFORMATION		INTEREST CALCULATION					
Terms of Note	Interest Period	Principal		Rate		Time	Interest
$200,000, 6%, due in two years	November 1–October 31	$200,000	×	6%	×	12/12 =	$12,000
$200,000, 6%, due in one year	January 1–October 31	200,000	×	6	×	10/12 =	10,000
$200,000, 6%, due in 100 days	November 1–December 31	200,000	×	6	×	2/12 =	2,000

Establishing a Note Receivable

The $100,000 loan that created the note receivable has the following accounting equation effects, which Skechers would record using the following journal entry:

1 Analyze

	Assets	= Liabilities +	Shareholders' Equity
Note Receivable	+100,000		
Cash	−100,000		

2 Record

dr Note Receivable (+A).. 100,000
    cr Cash (−A) 100,000

Notice that no interest is recorded on the day the note is established. Interest is earned over time.

Accruing Interest Earned

Under accrual basis accounting, interest revenue is recorded when it is earned. Rather than record the interest earned as each day passes, Skechers waits until it either receives an interest payment or reaches the end of its accounting period.

The timeline in Exhibit 8.5 shows how Skechers should account for the interest revenue earned from the note over its one-year term. Note that between the date of the note's creation (November 1, 2011) and the year-end (December 31, 2011), Skechers earned two months of interest revenue (the red portion of the time line) because the note was outstanding for all of November and December 2011. As you learned in Chapter 4, when a company has earned interest in the current period but has not yet recorded the interest, the company must make an adjusting entry at the end of the current period to accrue the interest earned. The amount of interest to record for the **two** months of 2011 is computed as follows:

Interest (I) = Principal (P) × Interest Rate (R) × Time (T)
$1,000 = $100,000 × 6% × 2/12

> **COACH'S TIP**
>
> Except for banks and other financial institutions, interest is considered a peripheral source of revenue, so it is reported on the income statement immediately following the Income from Operations subtotal.

EXHIBIT 8.5 Use of a Timeline to Keep Track of Interest Periods

The effect of this adjustment, along with the adjusting journal entry to record the $1,000 of interest revenue that is receivable on December 31, 2011, is as follows.

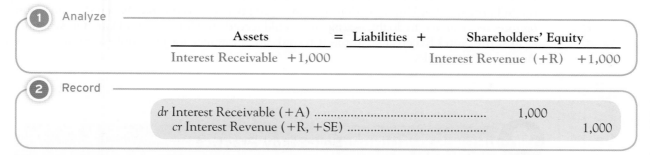

① Analyze

Assets	= Liabilities +	Shareholders' Equity
Interest Receivable +1,000		Interest Revenue (+R) +1,000

② Record

dr Interest Receivable (+A)	1,000	
cr Interest Revenue (+R, +SE)		1,000

Recording Interest Received

On October 31, 2012, Skechers receives a cash interest payment of $6,000 (= $100,000 × 6% × 12/12). As shown on the following timeline, this $6,000 of interest includes the $1,000 that was accrued as Interest Receivable at December 31, 2011, plus $5,000 earned during the 10-month period from January 1 to October 31, 2012, which had yet to be recorded.

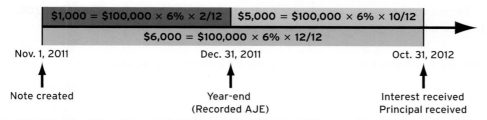

When Skechers receives the interest payment, it will record the $6,000 increase in cash, and it will reduce the $1,000 Interest Receivable that was previously recorded and record the remaining $5,000 as interest revenue in 2012. These effects and the journal entry to record them follow:

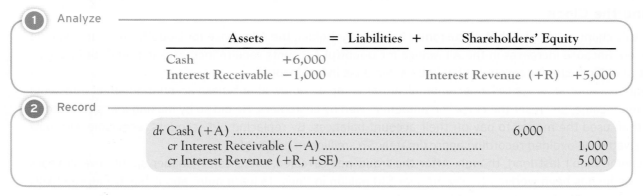

① Analyze

Assets	= Liabilities +	Shareholders' Equity
Cash +6,000		
Interest Receivable −1,000		Interest Revenue (+R) +5,000

② Record

dr Cash (+A)	6,000	
cr Interest Receivable (−A)		1,000
cr Interest Revenue (+R, +SE)		5,000

Recording Principal Received

The collection of a note receivable is accounted for just like the collection of an account receivable. Assuming that Skechers receives the $100,000 principal that is due, the accounting equation effects and journal entry for this transaction would be

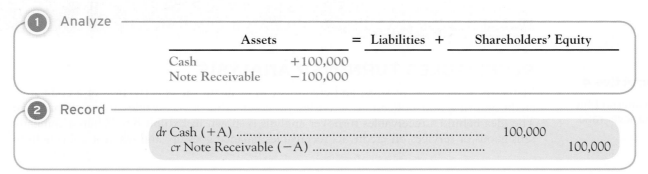

① Analyze

Assets	= Liabilities +	Shareholders' Equity
Cash +100,000		
Note Receivable −100,000		

② Record

dr Cash (+A)	100,000	
cr Note Receivable (−A)		100,000

Accounting for Uncollectable Notes

Just as companies may not collect their accounts receivable in full, they also might not collect the full principal (and interest) that they are owed on a note receivable. When the collection of notes receivable is in doubt, a company should record an Allowance for Doubtful Accounts against the Notes Receivable, just as it records an Allowance for Doubtful Accounts against Accounts Receivable.

HOW'S IT GOING? Self-Study Practice

Assume that Maddie Enterprises loaned $12,000 to an employee on October 1, 2011, by creating a note that required the employee to pay the principal and 8 percent interest on September 30, 2012. Assume that the company makes adjusting entries only at year-end on December 31.

1. Record the creation of the note.
2. Record any necessary end-of-period adjusting entry to be made at the end of 2011.
3. Record the receipt of interest and principal on September 30, 2012.

After you have finished, check your answers with the solution in the margin.

Solution to Self-Study Practice

1. *dr* Note Receivable (+A)		12,000
cr Cash (−A)		12,000
2. *dr* Interest Receivable (+A) ($12,000 × 8% × 3/12)		240
cr Interest Revenue (+R, +SE)		240
3. *dr* Cash (+A) ($12,000 × 8% × 12/12)		960
cr Interest Receivable (−A) ($12,000 × 8% × 3/12)		240
cr Interest Revenue (+R, +SE) ($12,000 × 8% × 9/12)		720
dr Cash (+A)		12,000
cr Note Receivable (−A)		12,000

SPOTLIGHT ON Ethics

Resetting the Clock

Earlier in this chapter, you saw that as customer balances get older, the Allowance for Doubtful Accounts should be increased. Because increases in the Allowance for Doubtful Accounts require increases in Bad Debt Expense, the result of older customer accounts should be a decrease in Net Income.

A credit manager at MCI, a U.S. telecommunications company, knew about these accounting effects. To avoid reducing net income, he "reset the clock" on amounts owed by customers. He did so by making loans to customers, who then used the money to pay off their account balances. By replacing old accounts receivable with new notes receivable, he avoided recording approximately $70 million in bad debts.

His scheme didn't last long, though. After the fraud was revealed, the credit manager spent several years in prison and he has been working to pay off over $10 million in fines. To learn more about this fraud, see Skills Development Case S8-4 near the end of this chapter.

Evaluate the Results

RECEIVABLES TURNOVER ANALYSIS

Learning Objective 4

Compute and interpret the receivables turnover ratio.

Managers, directors, investors, and creditors can evaluate the effectiveness of a company's credit-granting and collection activities by conducting a receivables turnover analysis. The idea behind a receivables turnover analysis is shown in Exhibit 8.6. When a company sells goods or services on credit, its receivables balance goes up, and when it collects from customers, the receivables balance goes down. This process of selling and collecting is called **receivables turnover** and it is repeated over and over for each customer during each accounting period.

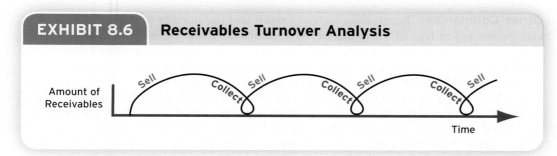

EXHIBIT 8.6 | **Receivables Turnover Analysis**

Amount of Receivables — Sell, Collect, Sell, Collect, Sell, Collect, Sell — Time

The receivables turnover ratio indicates how many times, on average, this process of selling and collecting is repeated during the period. The higher the ratio, the faster the collection of receivables. And, the faster the collection of receivables, the shorter your company's operating cycle, which means more cash available for running the business. A low turnover ratio can be a warning sign, suggesting that the company is allowing too much time for customers to pay. As you learned earlier in this chapter (on page 334), the longer an account goes without being collected, the bigger the risk that it will never be collected. Analysts watch for changes in the receivables turnover ratio because a sudden decline may mean that a company is recording sales of merchandise that customers are likely to return later. It also may mean that the company is selling to less financially secure customers or is allowing customers more time to pay their accounts to entice them to buy as much as possible—a practice known as **channel stuffing**.

Rather than evaluate the **number of times** accounts receivable turn over during a year, some people find it easier to think in terms of the **length of time** (in days) it takes to collect accounts receivable (called **days to collect**). Converting the year's receivables turnover ratio into the average days to collect is easy: Simply divide 365 by the year's receivables turnover ratio. This alternative measure provides the same basic information about the company's ability to collect receivables, but it's a little easier to interpret. In terms of Exhibit 8.6, the receivables turnover ratio counts the number of loops in a given period of time, whereas days to collect tells you the average number of days between loops.

COACH'S TIP

The bottom of the receivables turnover ratio uses the average beginning and ending Net Receivables, so that it spans the same period as the numerator. Ideally, the ratio would use only credit sales, but it is not reported separately, so use Net Sales instead.

YOU SHOULD KNOW

Days to collect: A measure of the average number of days from the time a sale is made on account to the time it is collected.

ACCOUNTING DECISION TOOLS

Name of Measure	Formula	What It Tells You
Receivables turnover ratio	$\dfrac{\text{Net Sales Revenue}}{\text{Average Net Receivables}}$	• The number of times receivables turn over during the period • A higher ratio means faster (better) turnover
Days to collect	$\dfrac{365}{\text{Receivables Turnover Ratio}}$	• Average number of days from sale on account to collection • A higher number means a longer (worse) time to collect

Comparison to Benchmarks

Credit Terms By calculating days to collect, you can compare a company's collection performance to its stated collections policy. You might remember from Chapter 6 that when companies sell on account, they specify the length of credit period (as well as any discounts for prompt payment). By comparing the number of days to collect to the length of credit period, you can gain a sense of whether customers are complying with the stated policy. Managers inside a company watch this closely, and so do investors and creditors on the outside. Why? If customers appear to be disregarding the stated credit period, they may be dissatisfied with the product or service they bought or have cash flow problems and therefore represent a bad credit risk.

Other Companies Receivables turnover ratios and the number of days to collect often vary across industries. To illustrate, we have estimated these measures in Exhibit 8.7 for Skechers, Crocs (another footwear company), and Boeing (an airplane manufacturer). As Exhibit 8.7 shows, Skechers was estimated to have turned over its receivables 7.3 times, which is once every 50 days. Crocs has an estimated receivables turnover ratio of 7.7, which is about 47 days to collect. Boeing had an estimated turnover ratio of 12 times, which means a jet-fast collection period of about 30 days. Because these measures typically vary between industries, you should compare a company's turnover only with other companies in the same industry or with its figures from prior periods. For practice at computing and comparing to prior periods, try the Self-Study Practice that follows Exhibit 8.7.

EXHIBIT 8.7	**Summary of Receivables Turnover Ratio Analyses**

Company	Relevant Information (in millions)			2012 Accounts Receivable Turnover Calculation	2012 Days to Collect Calculation
		2012	**2011**		
Skechers	Net Sales	$1,436	$1,440	$\dfrac{\$1,436}{(\$220 + \$175)/2} = 7.3$ times	$\dfrac{365 \text{ days}}{7.3 \text{ times}} = 50$ days
	Net Accounts Receivable	220	175		
		2012	**2011**		
Crocs	Net Sales	$722	$847	$\dfrac{\$722}{(\$35 + \$153)/2} = 7.7$ times	$\dfrac{365 \text{ days}}{7.7 \text{ times}} = 47.4$ days
	Net Accounts Receivable	35	153		
		2012	**2011**		
Boeing	Net Sales	$68,281	$60,909	$\dfrac{\$68,281}{(\$5,785 + \$5,602)/2} = 12$ times	$\dfrac{365 \text{ days}}{12 \text{ times}} = 30.4$ days
	Net Accounts Receivable	5,785	5,602		

HOW'S IT GOING? **Self-Study Practice**

Assume that Skechers reported net accounts receivable of $167 (million) at December 31, 2010.

a. Use this information, along with that in Exhibit 8.7, to calculate Skechers's receivables turnover and days to collect in 2011.

2011 Receivables Turnover:

$$\frac{\boxed{}}{(\boxed{}+\boxed{})/2} = \boxed{} \text{ times}$$

2011 Days to Collect:

$$\frac{365 \text{ days}}{\boxed{} \text{ times}} = \boxed{} \text{ days}$$

b. Did Skechers's receivables turnover improve or decline from 2011 (calculated in *a*) to 2012 (shown in Exhibit 8.7)?

After you have finished, check your answers with the solution in the margin.

Solution to Self-Study Practice

a. $\dfrac{\$1,440}{(\$175 + \$167)/2} = 8.4$ times

  $365 \div 8.4 = 43.5$ days

b. Skechers' receivables turnover was worse in 2011 (6.5 days slower).

Factoring Receivables   To generate the cash needed to pay for a company's business activities, managers must ensure that receivables are collected on a timely basis. You might wonder what managers can do to speed up sluggish receivables collections. One obvious tactic is to start hounding customers for payment. This forceful approach has at least two drawbacks: (1) it is time-consuming and costly and (2) it can annoy customers and cause them to take their business elsewhere. An alternative approach is to sell outstanding accounts receivable to another company (called a **factor**). The way this **factoring** arrangement works is that your company receives cash for the receivables it sells to the factor (minus a factoring fee) and the factor then has the right to collect the outstanding amounts owed by your customers. Factoring is a fast and easy way for your company to get cash for its receivables but with costs. First, factoring could send a potentially negative message to the users of the financial statements because it might be seen as a last resort for collecting accounts. Second, the factoring fee can be as much as 3 percent of the receivables sold or even higher. If Skechers sold $100,000 of receivables to a factor under such an arrangement of 3 percent, Skechers would receive only $97,000 cash but would give up the potential to collect the full $100,000, resulting in an expense of $3,000. For a company that regularly sells its receivables, this cost of factoring is reported on the income statement as a selling expense. If a company factors infrequently, the fee is considered a peripheral "other" expense.

Credit Card Sales   Another way to avoid lengthy collection periods is to allow customers to pay for goods using national credit cards like Visa, MasterCard, and American Express. Unlike private credit card programs that require the seller to pursue collection from customers, national credit card companies pay the seller within one to three days of the sale. Some banks accept credit card receipts as overnight deposits into the company's bank account as if they're cash. This not only speeds up the seller's cash collection, but also reduces losses from customers writing bad cheques. But, just like factoring, these benefits come at a cost. Credit card companies charge a fee for their services, often around 3 percent of the total sales price. If credit card sales amounted to $100,000, a credit card fee of $3,000 would be deducted, leaving the equivalent of $97,000 cash. These credit card fees are included with selling expenses on the income statement.

> **YOU SHOULD KNOW**
>
> **Factoring:** An arrangement where receivables are sold to another company (called a *factor*) for immediate cash (minus a factoring fee).

SPOTLIGHT ON **Controls**

Segregating Collections and Write-Offs

One way to control accounts receivable is to ensure that the same person does not both receive collections from customers and write off account balances. This segregation of duties helps to prevent errors and fraud. Without adequate segregation between these duties, a single dishonest employee could divert customer payments to his or her own bank account and then cover up the theft by writing off the customer's balance.

SUPPLEMENT 8A: Direct Write-Off Method

As described earlier in this chapter, an alternative method exists to account for uncollectable accounts. This alternative approach, called the **direct write-off method**, does not estimate bad debts and does not use an Allowance for Doubtful Accounts. Instead, it reports Sales when they occur and Bad Debt Expense when it is discovered. This method is not acceptable under ASPE or IFRS. Consequently, it isn't used very often for external financial reporting.

The direct write-off method is not acceptable under GAAP because it reports Accounts Receivable at the total amount owed by customers (an overly optimistic point of view) rather than what is estimated to be collectable (a more realistic viewpoint). The direct write-off

> **YOU SHOULD KNOW**
>
> **Direct write-off method:** A non-GAAP alternative to the allowance method of accounting for uncollectable accounts.

method also breaks the matching principle by recording Bad Debt Expense in the period that customer accounts are determined to be bad rather than matching the expense to the revenues reported in the period when the credit sales are actually made. As illustrated in Exhibit 8.1 on page 330, the failure to match Bad Debt Expense to Sales has a distorting effect on Net Income in the period of the sale as well as in later periods when bad debts are discovered. The only advantage of this method is that it doesn't require estimation of uncollectable amounts.

Under the direct write-off method, no journal entries are made until a bad debt is discovered. The journal entry used by the direct write-off method to record $1,000 of Bad Debt Expense when a customer account is determined to be uncollectable is

dr Bad Debt Expense (+E, −SE)	1,000
cr Accounts Receivable (−A)	1,000

SPOTLIGHT ON IFRS and ASPE

TOPIC	ASPE	IFRS
Methods for Estimating Bad Debts	• Both the percentage of credit sales method and the aging of accounts receivable method are acceptable under ASPE.	• Both the percentage of credit sales method and the aging of accounts receivable method are acceptable under IFRS.
Direct Write-off Method	• The direct write-off method is not acceptable under ASPE.	• The direct write-off method is not acceptable under IFRS.
Matching Principle	• The matching principle, which was introduced in Chapter 3, is the process of recording expenses (such as bad debt expense) on the basis that there is a direct association between the costs incurred and the earning of income.	• Expenses are recognized in the income statement on the basis that there is a direct association between the costs incurred and the earning of income, even though the term *matching principle* has been removed from the conceptual framework for IFRS. Some even refer to it as the "expense recognition principle."

Review the Chapter

This section provides a chance to solidify your understanding of key points. It's worth your time to work through the following demonstration cases, scan the chapter summary, test your understanding of key terms, and then practise, practise, practise.

DEMONSTRATION CASE A: BAD DEBTS

Shooby Dooby Shoe (SDS) reported credit sales of $95,000 during January 2012. Later in 2012, SDS determined that it would not be able to collect a $500 account balance that was owed by a deceased customer (Captain Cutler). SDS uses the percentage of credit sales method for estimating monthly Bad Debt Expense, and the aging of accounts receivable method at its December 31 year-end.

Required:

1. If SDS estimates that 1 percent of credit sales will result in bad debts, what will be the effect on the accounting equation of recording the January 2012 estimate? Prepare the journal entry to record this estimate.

2. Show how the write-off of the account receivable from Captain Cutler would affect the accounting equation, and prepare the journal entry to record the write-off.

3. Assume that SDS estimates that $11,000 of its year-end Accounts Receivable is uncollectable as shown below. As of December 31, 2012, the Allowance for Doubtful Accounts had an unadjusted credit balance of $3,000. Show the accounting equation effects of recording the bad debt estimate, and prepare a journal entry to record this estimate.

		Number of Days Unpaid			
	Total	0–30	31–60	61–90	>90
Total Accounts Receivable	$171,000	$50,000	$80,000	$40,000	$1,000
Estimated uncollectable (%)		× 1%	× 5%	× 15%	× 50%
Estimated uncollectable ($)	$ 11,000	$ 500	$ 4,000	$ 6,000	$ 500

4. Assume the same facts as in (3) above, except that as of December 31, 2012, the Allowance for Doubtful Accounts had an unadjusted *debit* balance of $3,000. Show the accounting equation effects of recording the bad debt estimate, and prepare a journal entry to record this estimate.

5. Assume that SDS reported total sales of $950,000 in 2012, Net Accounts Receivable of $160,000 at December 31, 2012, and $167,586 at December 31, 2011. Calculate the receivables turnover ratio for 2012.

6. If the receivables turnover ratio was 6.4 in 2011, what was the number of days to collect in 2011? Given your calculations in (4) above, conclude whether SDS collections were faster or slower in 2012 than in 2011.

Suggested Solution

1. The percentage of credit sales method multiplies historical bad debt losses (1%) by this period's credit sales ($95,000) to directly estimate the amount of Bad Debt Expense to record ($950 = 1% × $95,000).

Assets	= Liabilities +	Shareholders' Equity
Allowance for Doubtful		Bad Debt Expense (+E) −950
Accounts (+xA) −950		

dr Bad Debt Expense (+E, −SE)(0.01 × $95,000) 950
    cr Allowance for Doubtful Accounts (+xA, −A) 950

2.

Assets	= Liabilities + Shareholders' Equity
Accounts Receivable −500	
Allowance for Doubtful Accounts (−xA) +500	

dr Allowance for Doubtful Accounts (−xA, +A) 500
    cr Accounts Receivable (−A) 500

3. Under the aging of accounts receivable method, we determine the estimated balance for the Allowance for Doubtful Accounts ($11,000) and then subtract its unadjusted balance ($3,000) to determine the amount of the adjustment ($8,000 = $11,000 − $3,000).

Assets	= Liabilities +	Shareholders' Equity
Allowance for Doubtful		Bad Debt Expense (+E) −8,000
Accounts (+xA) −8,000		

dr Bad Debt Expense (+E, −SE) 8,000
    cr Allowance for Doubtful Accounts (+xA, −A) 8,000

4. Under the aging of accounts receivable method, we determine the estimated balance for the Allowance for Doubtful Accounts ($11,000) and then add its unadjusted debit balance ($3,000) to determine the amount of the adjustment ($14,000 = $11,000 + $3,000).

Assets	= Liabilities +	Shareholders' Equity
Allowance for Doubtful		Bad Debt Expense (+E) −14,000
Accounts (+xA) −14,000		

                    dr Bad Debt Expense (+E, −SE) 14,000
                         cr Allowance for Doubtful Accounts (+xA, −A).................. 14,000

5. Receivables turnover ratio is calculated as Net Sales ÷ Average Accounts Receivable. The average accounts receivable in 2012 was $163,793 (= ($160,000 + $167,586)/2), so the receivables turnover ratio for 2012 was 5.8 (= $950,000 ÷ $163,793).

6. Days to collect is calculated as 365 ÷ receivables turnover ratio. The 6.4 turnover in 2011 equates to 57 days (and the 5.8 turnover in 2012 equates to 63 days). Collections are slower in 2012 than in 2011.

DEMONSTRATION CASE B: NOTES RECEIVABLE

Let's assume that, as of February 28, 2011, Rocky Mountain Chocolate Factory, Inc. (RMCF) reported it had approximately $240,000 of Notes Receivable, with an annual interest rate of 8 percent. As a public company, RMCF prepares financial statements for external reporting every quarter, ending on May 31, August 31, November 30, and February 28. Assume that the notes were created on March 1, 2010, when money was loaned to another company, and that RMCF receives interest payments semi-annually, on July 31 and January 31.

Required:

1. Using the interest formula, calculate the amount of interest that RMCF earns each month on the notes.
2. Using the interest formula, calculate the amount of interest payment that RMCF received on July 31, 2011, and on January 31, 2012.
3. Prepare a timeline showing the amount of interest earned each quarter and received on each payment date.
4. Prepare journal entries to record the note's issuance, interest earned, and interest payments received for each quarter and on each payment date.

Suggested Solution

1. Interest earned = Principal × Interest Rate × Time
   = $240,000 × 8% × 1/12 = $1,600 per month.

2. The period from March 1 to July 31 is five months, whereas the period from August 1 to January 31 is six months.
   Interest Payment = Principal × Interest Rate × Time
   = $240,000 × 8% × 5/12 = $8,000 on July 31.
   Interest Payment = Principal × Interest Rate × Time
   = $240,000 × 8% × 6/12 = $9,600 on January 31.

3. Timeline

March 1	May 31	July 31	Aug. 31	Nov. 30	Jan. 31	Feb. 28
$4,800	$3,200	$1,600	$4,800	$3,200	$1,600	
$8,000		$9,600		

4. Journal Entries

March 1, 2011 (Notes Issued)

dr Notes Receivable (+A) 240,000
    cr Cash (−A) 240,000

May 31, 2011 (Interest Accrued)

dr Interest Receivable (+A) 4,800
    cr Interest Revenue (+R, +SE) 4,800

July 31, 2011 (Interest Payment Received)

dr Cash (+A) 8,000
    cr Interest Receivable (2A) 4,800
    cr Interest Revenue (+R, +SE) 3,200

August 31, 2011 (Interest Accrued)

dr Interest Receivable (+A) 1,600
    cr Interest Revenue (+R, +SE) 1,600

November 30, 2011 (Interest Accrued)

dr Interest Receivable (+A)	4,800	
cr Interest Revenue (+R, +SE)		4,800

January 31, 2012 (Interest Payment Received)

dr Cash (+A)	9,600	
cr Interest Receivable (−A)		6,400
cr Interest Revenue (+R, +SE)		3,200

February 28, 2012 (Interest Accrued)

dr Interest Receivable (+A)	1,600	
cr Interest Revenue (+R, +SE)		1,600

CHAPTER SUMMARY

Describe the trade-offs of extending credit. p. 329   LO1

- By extending credit to customers, a company is likely to attract a greater number of customers willing to buy from it.
- The additional costs of extending credit include increased wage costs, bad debt costs, and delayed receipt of cash.

Estimate and report the effects of uncollectable accounts. p. 330   LO2

- Under generally accepted accounting principles, companies must use the allowance method to account for uncollectables. This method involves the following steps:
  1. Estimate and record uncollectables with an end-of-period adjusting journal entry that increases Bad Debt Expense (debit) and increases the Allowance for Doubtful Accounts (credit).
  2. Identify and write off specific customer balances in the period that they are determined to be uncollectable.
- The adjusting entry (in 1 above) reduces Net Income as well as Net Accounts Receivable. The write-off (in 2) has offsetting effects on Accounts Receivable and the Allowance for Doubtful Accounts, ultimately yielding no net effect on Net Accounts Receivable or on Net Income.

Compute and report interest on notes receivable. p. 337   LO3

- Interest is calculated by multiplying the principal, interest rate, and time period (number of months out of 12). As time passes and interest is earned on the note, accountants must record an adjusting journal entry that accrues the interest revenue that is receivable on the note.

Compute and interpret the receivables turnover ratio. p. 340   LO4

- The receivables turnover ratio measures the effectiveness of credit-granting and collection activities. It reflects how many times average trade receivables were recorded and collected during the period.
- Analysts and creditors watch this ratio because a sudden decline may mean that a company is extending payment deadlines in an attempt to prop up lagging sales. Or it may mean that a company is recording sales of merchandise that customers are likely to return later.

ACCOUNTING DECISION TOOLS

Name of Measure	Formula	What It Tells You
Receivables turnover ratio	$\dfrac{\text{Net Sales Revenue}}{\text{Average Net Receivables}}$	• The number of times receivables turn over during the period • A higher ratio means faster (better) turnover
Days to collect	$\dfrac{365}{\text{Receivables Turnover Ratio}}$	• Average number of days from sale on account to collection • A higher number means a longer (worse) time to collect

KEY TERMS

See complete definitions in the glossary in the back of this text.

HOMEWORK HELPER

Alternative terms

- Days to Collect is also called *days' sales outstanding*.

Helpful reminders

- The percentage of credit sales method calculates the amount to record as Bad Debt Expense. The aging of accounts receivable method calculates the desired balance in the Allowance for Doubtful Accounts. This desired balance is compared to the existing balance to determine the amount to record as Bad Debt Expense.
- Interest rates are always for a full year. To calculate interest for a shorter period, multiply the interest rate by the fraction of the year for which you are calculating interest.

Frequent mistakes

- Some students mistakenly think a write-off is an expense. It isn't. It is merely a way to clean up the accounts receivable records. Under the allowance method, no Bad Debt Expense is recorded when removing (writing off) specific customer accounts.

Practice Material

QUESTIONS (⑤ Symbol indicates questions that require analysis from more than one perspective.)

1. What are the advantages and disadvantages of extending credit to customers?

2. In April 2006, Kohl's Corporation decided to discontinue its Kohl's credit card operations. What factors would this department store company have considered prior to making this decision? ⑤

3. Which basic accounting principles does the allowance method of accounting for bad debts satisfy?

4. Using the allowance method, is Bad Debt Expense recognized in the period in which (*a*) sales related to the uncollectable account were made or (*b*) the seller learns that the customer is unable to pay?

5. What is the effect of the write-off of uncollectable accounts (using the allowance method) on (*a*) net income and (*b*) net accounts receivable?

6. How does the use of calculated estimates differ between the aging of accounts receivable method and the percentage of credit sales method?

7. A local phone company had a customer who rang up $300 in charges during September 2011, but did not pay. Despite reminding the customer of this balance, the company was unable to collect in October, November, or December. In March 2012, the company finally gave up and wrote off the account balance. What amount of Sales, Bad Debt Expense, and Net Income would the phone company report from these events in 2011 and 2012 if it used the allowance method of accounting for uncollectable accounts? Assume that the company estimates 5 percent of credit sales will go bad.

8. What is the primary difference between accounts receivable and notes receivable?

9. What are the three components of the interest formula? Explain how this formula adjusts for interest periods that are less than a full year.

10. Assume that, as of February 1, 2012, Tim Hortons had $100,000 of Notes Receivable due before January 31, 2013,

$1,268,000 of Accounts Receivable, and $249,000 in its Allowance for Doubtful Accounts (all related to accounts receivable). How should these accounts be reported on a balance sheet prepared following ASPE? What if the balance sheet follows IFRS, as described in Chapter 5?

11. Does an increase in the receivables turnover ratio generally indicate faster or slower collection of receivables? Explain.

12. What two approaches can managers take to speed up sluggish collections of receivables? List one advantage and disadvantage for each approach.

13. When customers experience economic difficulties, companies consider extending longer credit periods. What are the possible consequences of longer credit periods on Sales, Accounts Receivable, Allowance for Doubtful Accounts, Net Income, and the receivables turnover ratio? **S**

14. (Supplement 8A) Describe how (and when) the direct write-off method accounts for uncollectable accounts. What are the disadvantages of this method?

15. (Supplement 8A) Refer to question 7. What amounts would be reported if the direct write-off method was used? Which method (allowance or direct write-off) more accurately reports the financial results?

Multiple-choice questions and corresponding answers can be found on Connect.

MINI-EXERCISES

M8-1 Evaluating the Decision to Extend Credit

LO1

a. Nutware Productions Inc. generated sales of $30,000 and gross profit of $10,000 last year. The company estimates that it would have generated sales of $60,000 if it had extended credit, but this would involve additional costs for associated wages and bad debts totalling $25,000. Should the company extend credit?

b. Assume Reitmans (Canada) Limited currently allows customers to purchase merchandise using national credit cards like Visa and MasterCard, yet discontinued its own private credit card program. What pros and cons would lead Reitmans to continue with national credit cards but not its own private credit card program? Assume in its annual report for the year ended January 31, 2012, Reitmans removed $56 million of credit card transactions awaiting settlement from Accounts Receivable and instead reported them as Cash and Cash Equivalents. What characteristic of national credit cards makes this reclassification appropriate?

Reitmans (Canada) Limited

M8-2 Reporting Accounts Receivable and Recording Write-Offs Using the Allowance Method

LO2

At the end of 2011, Donnelly Fitness Centre has adjusted balances of $800,000 in Accounts Receivable and $55,000 in Allowance for Doubtful Accounts. On January 2, 2012, the company learns that certain customer accounts are not collectable, so management authorizes a write-off of these accounts totalling $5,000.

a. Show how the company would have reported its receivable accounts on December 31, 2011. As of that date, what amount did Donnelly expect to collect?

b. Prepare the journal entry to write off the accounts on January 2, 2012.

c. Assuming no other transactions occurred between December 31, 2011, and January 3, 2012, show how Donnelly would have reported its receivable accounts on January 3, 2012. As of that date, what amount did Donnelly expect to collect? Has this changed from December 31, 2011? Explain why or why not.

d. Let's go a bit further with this example. Assume that on February 2, 2012, Donnelly received a payment of $500 from one of the customers whose balance had been written off. Prepare the journal entries to record this transaction.

M8-3 Recording Write-Offs and Bad Debt Expense Using the Allowance Method

LO2

Prepare journal entries for each transaction listed.

a. During the period, customer balances are written off in the amount of $17,000.

b. At the end of the period, bad debt expense is estimated to be $14,000.

M8-4 Estimating Bad Debts Using the Percentage of Credit Sales Method

LO2

Assume Simple Co. had credit sales of $250,000 and cost of goods sold of $150,000 for the period. Simple uses the percentage of credit sales method and estimates that ½ percent of credit sales would result in uncollectable accounts. Before the end-of-period adjustment is made, the Allowance for Doubtful Accounts has a credit balance of $250.

a. What amount of Bad Debt Expense would the company record as an end-of-period adjustment?

b. Prepare the journal entry to record the end-of-period adjustment for bad debts.

LO2 **M8-5 Estimating Bad Debts Using the Aging Method**

Assume that Simple Co. had credit sales of $250,000 and cost of goods sold of $150,000 for the period. Simple uses the aging method and estimates that the appropriate ending balance in the Allowance for Doubtful Accounts is $1,600. Before the end-of-period adjustment is made, the Allowance for Doubtful Accounts has a credit balance of $250.

a. What amount of Bad Debt Expense would the company record as an end-of-period adjustment?

b. Prepare the journal entry to record the end-of-period adjustment for bad debts.

LO3 **M8-6 Using the Interest Formula to Compute Interest**

Complete the following table by computing the missing amounts (?) for the following independent cases.

Principal Amount on Note Receivable	Annual Interest Rate	Time Period	Interest Earned
a. $100,000	10%	6 months	?
b. ?	10%	12 months	$4,000
c. $50,000	?	9 months	$3,000

LO3 **M8-7 Recording Note Receivable Transactions**

RecRoom Equipment Company received an $8,000, six-month, 6 percent note to settle an $8,000 unpaid balance owed by a customer. Prepare journal entries to record the following transactions for RecRoom. Rather than use letters to reference each transaction, use the date of the transaction.

a. The note is accepted by RecRoom on November 1, 2012, causing the company to increase its Notes Receivable and decrease its Accounts Receivable.

b. RecRoom adjusts its records for interest earned to December 31, 2012.

c. RecRoom receives the principal and interest on the note's maturity date.

LO2 **M8-8 Reporting Accounts and Notes Receivable in a Classified Balance Sheet**

Caterpillar, Inc.

Assume that Caterpillar, Inc., reported the following accounts and amounts (in millions) in its December 31, 2011, year-end financial statements. Prepare the current assets section of a classified balance sheet. Assume that the Allowance for Doubtful Accounts relates to Accounts Receivable rather than Notes Receivable.

Accounts Payable	$ 4,827	Long-Term Debt	$22,834
Accounts Receivable	9,788	Long-Term Notes Receivable	15,743
Accumulated Amortization	10,963	Notes Receivable—Current	8,731
Allowance for Doubtful Accounts	391	Other Current Assets	1,988
Cash and Cash Equivalents	2,736	Other Current Liabilities	14,033
Inventories	8,781	Other Noncurrent Assets	9,105
Loans Payable—Current	7,209	Property, Plant, and Equipment	23,487

LO4 **M8-9 Determining the Effects of Credit Policy Changes on Receivables Turnover Ratio and Days to Collect**

Indicate the most likely effect of the following changes in credit policy on the receivables turnover ratio and days to collect (+ for increase, − for decrease, and NE for no effect).

a. Granted credit to less creditworthy customers.

b. Granted credit with shorter payment deadlines.

c. Increased effectiveness of collection methods.

M8-10 Evaluating the Effect of Factoring on the Receivables Turnover Ratio and Computing the Cost of Factoring

LO4

After noting that its receivables turnover ratio had declined, Imperative Company decided for the first time in the company's history to sell $500,000 of receivables to a factoring company. The factor charges a factoring fee of 3 percent of the receivables sold. How much cash does Imperative receive on the sale? Calculate the factoring fee and describe how it is reported by Imperative Company. All else equal, how will this affect Imperative's receivables turnover ratio in the future?

EXERCISES

 Practise and learn online with Connect.

E8-1 Recording Bad Debt Expense Estimates and Write-Offs Using the Aging of Receivables Method

LO2

At the end of 2011, Blackberry Hill Productions, Inc., used the aging of accounts receivable method to estimate that its Allowance for Doubtful Accounts should be $19,750. The account had an unadjusted credit balance of $10,000 at December 31, 2011.

Required:

Prepare journal entries for each transaction.

a. The appropriate bad debt adjustment was recorded for the year 2011.

b. On January 31, 2012, an account receivable for $1,000 from March 2011 was determined to be uncollectable and was written off.

E8-2 Determining Financial Statement Effects of Bad Debt Expense Estimates and Write-Offs

LO2

For each transaction listed in E8-1, indicate the amount and direction (+ or −) of effects on the financial statement accounts and on the overall accounting equation.

Assets	=	Liabilities	+	Shareholders' Equity

E8-3 Recording, Reporting, and Evaluating a Bad Debt Estimate Using the Percentage of Credit Sales Method

LO2

During the year ended December 31, 2012, Kelly's Camera Equipment had sales revenue of $170,000, of which $85,000 was on credit. At the start of 2012, Accounts Receivable showed a $10,000 debit balance, and the Allowance for Doubtful Accounts showed an $800 credit balance. Collections of accounts receivable during 2012 amounted to $68,000.

Data during 2012 follow:

a. On December 10, 2012, a customer balance of $1,500 from a prior year was determined to be uncollectable, so it was written off.

b. On December 31, 2012, a decision was made to continue the accounting policy of basing estimated bad debt losses on 2 percent of credit sales for the year.

Required:

1. Give the required journal entries for the two events in December 2012.

2. Show how the amounts related to Accounts Receivable and Bad Debt Expense would be reported on the balance sheet and income statement for 2012.

3. On the basis of the data available, does the 2 percent rate appear to be reasonable? Explain.

E8-4 Recording Write-Offs and Recoveries

LO2

Prior to recording the following, E. Perry Electronics, Incorporated, had a credit balance of $2,000 in its Allowance for Doubtful Accounts.

Required:

Prepare journal entries for each transaction.

a. On August 31, 2012, a customer balance for $300 from a prior year was determined to be uncollectable and was written off.

b. On December 15, 2012, the customer balance for $300 written off on August 31, 2012, was collected in full.

E8-5 Determining Financial Statement Effects of Write-Offs and Recoveries

For each transaction listed in E8-4, indicate the amount and direction (+ or −) of effects on the financial statement accounts and on the overall accounting equation.

Assets	=	Liabilities	+	Shareholders' Equity

E8-6 Computing Bad Debt Expense Using Aging of Accounts Receivable Method

Young and Old Corporation (YOC) uses two aging categories to estimate uncollectable accounts. Accounts less than 60 days are considered young and have a 5% uncollectable rate. Accounts more than 60 days are considered old and have a 35% uncollectable rate.

Required:

1. If YOC has $100,000 of young accounts and $400,000 of old accounts, how much should be reported in the Allowance for Doubtful Accounts?
2. If YOC's Allowance for Doubtful Accounts currently has an unadjusted credit balance of $40,000, how much should be credited to the account?
3. If YOC's Allowance for Doubtful Accounts has an unadjusted debit balance of $5,000, how much should be credited to the account?
4. Explain how YOC's Allowance for Doubtful Accounts could have a debit balance.

Check Figure:
[Req. 3]
Credit to Allowance for
Doubtful Accounts
= $150,000

E8-7 Computing Bad Debt Expense Using Aging of Accounts Receivable Method

Brown Cow Dairy uses the aging approach to estimate Bad Debt Expense. The balance of each account receivable is aged on the basis of three time periods as follows: (1) 1–30 days old, $12,000; (2) 31–90 days old, $5,000; and (3) more than 90 days old, $3,000. Experience has shown that for each age group, the average loss rate on the amount of the receivable due to uncollectability is (1) 3 percent, (2) 15 percent, and (3) 30 percent, respectively. At December 31, 2012 (end of the current year), the Allowance for Doubtful Accounts balance was $800 (credit) before the end-of-period adjusting entry is made.

Required:

1. Prepare a schedule to estimate an appropriate year-end balance for the Allowance for Doubtful Accounts.
2. What amount should be recorded as Bad Debt Expense for the current year?
3. If the unadjusted balance in the Allowance for Doubtful Accounts was a $600 debit balance, what would be the amount of Bad Debt Expense in 2012?

E8-8 Recording and Reporting Allowance for Doubtful Accounts Using the Percentage of Credit Sales and Aging of Accounts Receivable Methods

Innovations Corp (IC) uses the percentage of credit sales method to estimate bad debts each month and then uses the aging method at year-end. During November 2012, IC sold services on account for $100,000 and estimated that ½ of one percent of those sales would be uncollectable. At its December 31 year-end, total Accounts Receivable is $89,000, aged as follows: (1) 1–30 days old, $75,000; (2) 31–90 days old, $10,000; and (3) more than 90 days old, $4,000. Experience has shown that for each age group, the average rate of uncollectability is (1) 1 percent, (2) 15 percent, and (3) 40 percent, respectively. Before the end-of-year adjusting entry is made, the Allowance for Doubtful Accounts has a $1,600 credit balance at December 31, 2012.

Required:

1. Prepare the November 2012 adjusting entry for bad debts.
2. Prepare a schedule to estimate an appropriate year-end balance for the Allowance for Doubtful Accounts.
3. Prepare the December 31, 2012, adjusting entry.
4. Show how the various accounts related to accounts receivable should be shown on the December 31, 2012, balance sheet.

Check Figure:
[Req. 3]
Bad Debt Expense = $2,250

E8-9 Recording and Determining the Effects of Write-Offs, Recoveries, and Bad Debt Expense Estimates on the Balance Sheet and Income Statement

Academic Dishonesty Investigations Ltd. operates a plagiarism detection service for universities and colleges.

Required:

1. Prepare journal entries for each transaction below.

   a. On March 31, 2012 customers were billed for detection services totalling $25,000.

   b. On October 31, a customer balance of $1,500 from a prior year was determined to be uncollectable and was written off.

   c. On December 15, a customer paid an old balance of $900, which had been written off in a prior year.

   d. On December 31, $500 of bad debts were estimated and recorded for the year.

2. Complete the following table, indicating the amount and effect (+ for increase, − for decrease, and NE for no effect) of each transaction. Ignore income taxes.

Transaction	Net Receivables	Net Sales	Income from Operations
a			
b			
c			
d			

E8-10 Recording Note Receivable Transactions, Including Accrual Adjustment for Interest

LO3

The following transactions took place for Christoff Solutions Ltd.

2011

| July 1 | Loaned $70,000 to an employee of the company and received back a one-year, 10 percent note. |
| Dec. 31 | Accrued interest on the note. |

2012

| July 1 | Received interest and principal on the note. (No interest has been recorded since December 31.) |

Required:

Prepare the journal entries that Christoff Solutions Ltd. would record for the above transactions.

E8-11 Recording Note Receivable Transactions, Including Accrual Adjustment for Interest

LO3

The following transactions took place for Parkell's Grocery.

Jan. 1	Loaned $50,000 to a company cashier and received back a one-year, 7 percent note.
June 30	Accrued interest on the note.
Dec. 31	Received interest and principal on the note. (No interest has been recorded since June 30.)

Required:

Prepare the journal entries that Parkell's Grocery would record for the above transactions.

E8-12 Recording Note Receivable Transactions, Including Accrual Adjustment for Interest

LO3

To attract retailers to its shopping centre, the Makepiece Mall will lend money to tenants under formal contracts, provided that they use it to renovate their store space. On November 1, 2012, the company loaned $100,000 to a new tenant on a one-year note with a stated annual interest rate of 6 percent. Interest is to be received by Makepiece Mall on April 30, 2013, and at maturity on October 31, 2013.

Required:

Prepare journal entries that Makepiece Mall would record related to this note on the following dates: (a) November 1, 2012; (b) December 31, 2012 (Makepiece Mall's fiscal year-end); (c) April 30, 2013; and (d) October 31, 2013.

LO2, 4 **E8-13 Using Financial Statement Disclosures to Infer Write-Offs and Bad Debt Expense and to Calculate the Receivables Turnover Ratio**

Microsoft Corporation

Microsoft Corporation develops, produces, and markets a wide range of computer software including the Windows operating system. Assume Microsoft reported the following information about Net Sales Revenue and Accounts Receivable (all amounts in millions).

	June 30, 2012	June 30, 2011
Accounts Receivable, Net of Allowances of $153 and $117	$13,589	$11,338
Net Revenues	60,420	51,122

Assume that, according to its annual report, Microsoft recorded Bad Debt Expense of $88 and did not recover any previously written off accounts during the year ended June 30, 2012.

Required:

1. What amount of accounts receivable was written off during the year ended June 30, 2012?
2. What was Microsoft's receivables turnover ratio (to one decimal place) in the current year?

LO2 **E8-14 Using Financial Statement Disclosures to Infer Bad Debt Expense**

Assume the 2012 annual report for Sears Holding Corporation contained the following information (in millions):

	2012	2011
Accounts Receivable	$881	$781
Allowance for Doubtful Accounts	42	37
Accounts Receivable, Net	$839	$744

A footnote to the financial statements disclosed that accounts receivable write-offs amounted to $13 during 2012 and $3 during 2011. Assume that Sears did not record any recoveries.

Required:

Determine the Bad Debt Expense for 2012 based on the above facts.

LO2, 4 **E8-15 Determining the Effects of Uncollectable Accounts on the Receivables Turnover Ratio**

Refer to the information about Sears given in E8-14.

Required:

Complete the following table indicating the direction of the effect (+ for increase, − for decrease, and NE for no effect) of each transaction during 2012:

Transaction	Net Credit Sales	Average Net Accounts Receivable	Receivables Turnover Ratio
a. Writing off $13,000,000 in uncollectable accounts.			
b. Recording bad debt expense.			

LO4 **E8-16 Analyzing and Interpreting Receivables Turnover Ratio and Days to Collect**

FedEx Corporation

Assume that a recent annual report for FedEx Corporation contained the following data (in millions):

	May 31	
	2012	2011
Accounts Receivable	$ 4,517	$ 4,078
Less: Allowance for Doubtful Accounts	158	136
Accounts Receivable, Net of Allowance	$ 4,359	$ 3,942
Net Sales (assume all on credit)	$37,953	$35,214

Required:

1. Determine the receivables turnover ratio and days to collect for 2012. Round your answers to one decimal place.
2. Explain the meaning of each number.

Check Figure:
[Req. 1]
Receivables Turnover Ratio
= 9.1 times

E8-17 Determining the Effects of Bad Debt Write-Offs on the Receivables Turnover Ratio

LO2, 4

During 2012, Jesse Jericho Enterprises Corporation recorded credit sales of $650,000. At the beginning of the year, Accounts Receivable, Net of Allowance was $50,000. At the end of the year, *after* the Bad Debt Expense adjustment was recorded but *before* any bad debts had been written off, Accounts Receivable, Net of Allowance was $49,000.

Required:

1. Assume that on December 31, 2012, accounts receivable totalling $6,000 for the year were determined to be uncollectable and written off. What was the receivables turnover ratio for 2012? Round to one decimal place.
2. Assume instead that on December 31, 2012, $7,000 of accounts receivable was determined to be uncollectable and written off. What was the receivables turnover ratio for 2012? Round to one decimal place.
3. Explain why the answers to requirements 1 and 2 differ or do not differ.

E8-18 (Supplement 8A) Recording Write-Offs and Reporting Accounts Receivable Using the Direct Write-Off Method

Trevorson Electronics is a small company privately owned by Jon Trevorson, an electrician who installs wiring in new homes. Because the company's financial statements are prepared for internal purposes only, Jon uses the direct write-off method. During 2011, its first year of operations, Trevorson Electronics sold $30,000 of services on account. The company collected $26,000 of these receivables during the year, and Jon believed that the remaining $4,000 was fully collectable. In 2012, Jon discovered that none of the $4,000 would be collected, so he wrote off the entire amount. To make matters worse, Jon sold only $5,000 of services during the year.

Required:

1. Prepare journal entries to record the transactions in 2011 and 2012.
2. Using only the information provided (ignore other operating expenses), prepare comparative income statements for 2011 and 2012. Was 2011 really as profitable as indicated by its income statement? Was 2012 quite as bad as indicated by its income statement? What should Jon do if he wants better information for assessing his company's ability to generate profit?

Check Figure:
[Req. 2]
2012 Net Income = $1,000

COACHED PROBLEMS

CP8-1 Interpreting Disclosure of Allowance for Doubtful Accounts

LO2

McDonald's Corporation

McDonald's Corporation is the world's largest chain of hamburger fast-food restaurants. It has an Allowance for Doubtful Accounts that relates to its accounts and notes receivable. Assume that in its 2011 financial statements, McDonald's reported the following changes in the Allowance for Doubtful Accounts (in thousands):

Balance at Beginning of Period	Charged to Bad Debt Expense	Amounts Written Off	Balance at End of Period
$711	$341	$335	$717

Required:

1. Create a T-account for the Allowance for Doubtful Accounts and enter into it the amounts from the above schedule. Then write the T-account in equation format to prove that the above items account for the changes in the account.

    TIP: The allowance increases when estimates are charged to Bad Debt Expense and when recoveries are reported. The allowance decreases when accounts are written off.

2. Record summary journal entries related to (*a*) estimating bad debt expense, and (*b*) write-offs of specific balances during the year.

    TIP: Use the generic account name "Receivables" to refer to the combined accounts receivable and notes receivable.

3. If McDonald's had written off an additional $20,000 of accounts receivable during the period and the ending allowance balance was estimated to be $717, how would Net Receivables have been affected? How would Net Income have been affected? Explain why.

LO3 **CP8-2 Recording Notes Receivable Transactions**

Jung & Newbicalm Advertising (JNA) recently hired a new creative director, Howard Rachell, for its Bay Street office in Toronto. To persuade Howard to move from Vancouver, JNA agreed to advance him $100,000 on April 30, 2012, on a one-year, 10 percent note, with interest payments required on October 31, 2012, and April 30, 2013. JNA issues quarterly financial statements on March 31, June 30, September 30, and December 31.

Required:

1. Prepare the journal entry that JNA will make to record the promissory note created on April 30, 2012.

    TIP: See Demonstration Case B for a similar problem.

2. Prepare the journal entries that JNA will make to record the interest accruals at each quarter end and interest payments at each payment date.

    TIP: Interest receivable will be accrued at the end of each quarter, and then will be reduced when the interest payment is received.

3. Prepare the journal entry that JNA will make to record the principal payment at the maturity date.

LO2, 3 **CP8-3 Accounting for Accounts and Notes Receivable Transactions**

P & K Consultants has provided business consulting services for several years. The company uses the percentage of credit sales method to estimate bad debts for internal monthly reporting purposes. At the end of each quarter, the company adjusts its records using the aging of accounts receivable method. The company entered into the following selected transactions during the first quarter of 2012.

a. During January, the company provided services for $200,000 on credit.

b. On January 31, the company estimated bad debts using 1 percent of credit sales.

c. On February 4, the company collected $100,000 of accounts receivable.

d. On February 15, the company wrote off a $500 account receivable.

e. During February, the company provided services for $150,000 on credit.

f. On February 28, the company estimated bad debts using 1 percent of credit sales.

g. On March 1, the company loaned $12,000 to an employee who signed a 10% note, due in 3 months.

h. On March 15, the company collected $500 on the account written off one month earlier.

i. On March 31, the company accrued interest earned on the note.

j. On March 31, the company adjusted for uncollectable accounts, based on the following aging analysis. Allowance for Doubtful Accounts has an unadjusted credit balance of $6,000.

Customer	Total	Number of Days Unpaid			
		0–30	31–60	61–90	Over 90
Arrow Ergonomics	$ 1,000	$ 500	$ 400	$ 100	
Asymmetry Architecture	2,000				$2,000
Others (not shown to save space)	85,000	34,000	42,000	5,000	4,000
Weight Whittlers	2,000	2,000			
Total Accounts Receivable	$90,000	$36,500	$42,400	$5,100	$6,000
Estimated Uncollectable (%)		2%	10%	20%	40%

Required:

1. For items *a–j*, analyze the amount and direction (+ or −) of effects on specific financial statement accounts and the overall accounting equation, and prepare journal entries.

2. Show how the receivables related to these transactions would be reported in the current assets section of a classified balance sheet.

3. Name the accounts related to Accounts Receivable and Note Receivable that would be reported on the income statement and indicate whether they would appear before, or after, Income from Operations.

GROUP A PROBLEMS

Practise and learn online with Connect.

PA8-1 Recording Accounts Receivable Transactions Using the Aging Method

LO2

Kraft Foods Inc.

Kraft Foods Inc. is the second-largest food company in the world. Assume the company recently reported the following amounts in its unadjusted trial balance as of December 31, 2011 (all amounts in millions):

	Debits	Credits
Accounts Receivable	$4,833	
Allowance for Doubtful Accounts		$ 129
Sales (assume all on credit)		42,201

Required:

1. Assume Kraft uses ½ of 1 percent of sales to estimate its Bad Debt Expense for the year. Prepare the adjusting journal entry required for the year, assuming no Bad Debt Expense has been recorded yet.

2. Assume instead that Kraft uses the aging of accounts receivable method and estimates that $233 of its Accounts Receivable will be uncollectable. Prepare the adjusting journal entry required at December 31, 2011, for recording Bad Debt Expense.

3. Repeat requirement 3, except this time assume the unadjusted balance in Kraft's Allowance for Doubtful Accounts at December 31, 2011, was a debit balance of $20.

4. If one of Kraft's main customers declared bankruptcy in 2012, what journal entry would be used to write off its $15 balance?

Check Figure:
[Req. 1]
Bad Debt Expense = $211

PA8-2 Interpreting Disclosure of Allowance for Doubtful Accounts

LO2

Wheelys, Inc., designs and sells footwear with a wheel in the heel, worn by sometimes annoying kids at shopping malls. It recently disclosed the following information concerning the Allowance for Doubtful Accounts in its annual report.

		SCHEDULE II			
		Valuation and Qualifying Accounts			
		(dollars in thousands)			
Allowance for Doubtful Accounts	Balance at Beginning of Year	Additions Charged to Bad Debt Expense	Write-Offs	Balance at End of Year
---	---	---	---	---
2011	$189	$ 0	$ 69	$120
2010	410	333	554	189
2009	130	435	?	410

Required:

1. Create a T-account for the Allowance for Doubtful Accounts and enter into it the 2011 amounts from the above schedule. Then write the T-account in equation format to prove that the above items account for the changes in the account.
2. Wheelys reported sales of $70 million in 2011. Why might its Bad Debt Expense equal zero that year?
3. Record summary journal entries for 2010 related to (a) estimating Bad Debt Expense and (b) writing off specific balances.
4. Supply the missing dollar amount noted by ? for 2009.
5. If Wheelys had written off an additional $20 of Accounts Receivable during 2011 and the ending allowance balance was estimated to be $120, how would Net Receivables have been affected? How would Net Income have been affected? Explain why.

LO3 **PA8-3 Recording Notes Receivable Transactions**

C&Q Marketing (CQM) recently hired a new marketing director, Jeff Otos, for its main office. As part of the arrangement, CQM agreed on February 28, 2012, to advance Jeff $50,000 on a one-year, 8 percent note, with interest to be paid at maturity on February 28, 2013. CQM prepares financial statements on June 30 and December 31.

Required:

1. Prepare the journal entry that CSM will make when the note is established.
2. Prepare the journal entries that CSM will make to accrue interest on June 30 and December 31.
3. Prepare the journal entry that CSM will make to record the interest and principal payments on February 28, 2013.

LO2, 3 **PA8-4 Accounting for Accounts and Notes Receivable Transactions**

Web Wizard, Inc., has provided information technology services for several years. The company uses the percentage of credit sales method to estimate bad debts for internal monthly reporting purposes. At the end of each quarter, the company adjusts its records using the aging of accounts receivable method. The company entered into the following selected transactions during the first quarter of 2012.

a. During January, the company provided services for $40,000 on credit.
b. On January 31, the company estimated bad debts using 1 percent of credit sales.
c. On February 4, the company collected $20,000 of accounts receivable.
d. On February 15, the company wrote off a $100 account receivable.
e. During February, the company provided services for $30,000 on credit.
f. On February 28, the company estimated bad debts using 1 percent of credit sales.
g. On March 1, the company loaned $2;400 to an employee who signed a 6% note, due in 6 months.
h. On March 15, the company collected $100 on the account written off one month earlier.
i. On March 31, the company adjusted for uncollectable accounts, based on an aging analysis (below). Allowance for Doubtful Accounts has an unadjusted credit balance of $1,200.
j. On March 31, the company accrued interest earned on the note.

| Customer | Total | Number of Days Unpaid | | | |
		0–30	31–60	61–90	Over 90
Altavista Tourism	$ 200	$ 100	$ 80	$ 20	
Bayling Bungalows	400				$ 400
Others (not shown to save space)	17,000	6,800	8,400	1,000	800
Xciting Xcursions	400	400			
Total Accounts Receivable	**$18,000**	**$7,300**	**$8,480**	**$1,020**	**$1,200**
Estimated uncollectable (%)		**2%**	**10%**	**20%**	**40%**

Required:

1. For items a–j, analyze the amount and direction (+ or −) of effects on specific financial statement accounts and the overall accounting equation and prepare journal entries.

2. Show how the receivables related to these transactions would be reported in the current assets section of a classified balance sheet.

3. Name the accounts related to Accounts Receivable and Note Receivable that would be reported on the income statement and indicate whether they would appear before, or after, Income from Operations.

PA8-5 Analyzing Allowance for Doubtful Accounts, Receivables Turnover Ratio, and Days to Collect

LO4

PepsiCo
Coca-Cola

Coca-Cola and PepsiCo are two of the largest and most successful beverage companies in the world in terms of the products that they sell and their receivables management practices. To evaluate their ability to collect on credit sales, consider the following information assumed to have been reported in their 2011, 2010, and 2009 annual reports (amounts in millions).

	Coca-Cola			PepsiCo		
Fiscal Year Ended:	2011	2010	2009	2011	2010	2009
Net Sales	$31,944	$28,857	$24,088	$43,251	$39,474	$35,137
Accounts Receivable	3,141	3,373	2,650	3,784	3,670	3,147
Allowance for Doubtful Accounts	51	56	63	70	69	64
Accounts Receivable, Net of Allowance	3,090	3,317	2,587	3,714	3,601	3,083

Required:

1. Calculate the receivables turnover ratios and days to collect for Coca-Cola and PepsiCo for 2011 and 2010. (Round to one decimal place.)
2. Which of the companies is quicker to convert its receivables into cash?

Check Figure:
Coca-Cola's 2010 Days to Collect = 37.2 days

GROUP B PROBLEMS

PB8-1 Recording Accounts Receivable Transactions Using the Allowance Method

LO2

Intel Corporation

Intel Corporation is a well-known supplier of computer chips, boards, systems, and software building blocks. Assume the company recently reported the following amounts in its unadjusted trial balance at its year-end of December 27, 2011 (all amounts in millions):

	Debits	Credits
Accounts Receivable	$1,729	
Allowance for Doubtful Accounts		$ 17
Sales (assume all on credit)		37,586

Required:

1. Assume Intel uses ¼ of 1 percent of sales to estimate its Bad Debt Expense for the year. Prepare the adjusting journal entry required for the year, assuming no Bad Debt Expense has been recorded yet.
2. Assume instead that Intel uses the aging of accounts receivable method and estimates that $40 of its Accounts Receivable will be uncollectable. Prepare the adjusting journal entry required at December 27, 2011, for recording Bad Debt Expense.
3. Repeat requirement 2, except this time assume the unadjusted balance in Intel's Allowance for Doubtful Accounts at December 27, 2011, was a debit balance of $20.
4. If one of Intel's main customers declared bankruptcy in 2012, what journal entry would be used to write off its $15 balance?

PB8-2 Interpreting Disclosure of Allowance for Doubtful Accounts

LO2

Xerox Corporation

Xerox Corporation is the company that made the photocopier popular, although it now describes itself as a technology and services enterprise that helps businesses deploy document management strategies and improve productivity. Assume it recently disclosed the following information concerning the allowance for doubtful accounts in its annual report.

		SCHEDULE II Valuation and Qualifying Accounts (dollars in millions)		
Allowance for Doubtful Accounts	Balance at Beginning of Year	Additions Charged to Bad Debt Expense	Write-Offs	Balance at End of Year
2011	$128	$72	$69	$131
2010	116	?	42	128
2009	136	27	?	116

Required:

1. Create a T-account for the Allowance for Doubtful Accounts and enter into it the 2011 amounts from the above schedule. Then, write the T-account in equation format to prove that the above items account for the changes in the account.
2. Record summary journal entries for 2011 related to (a) estimating bad debt expense and (b) writing off specific balances.

Check Figure:
[Req. 3]
2010 Additions Charged to
Bad Debt Expense = $54

3. Supply the missing dollar amounts noted by ? for 2010 and 2009.
4. If Xerox had written off an additional $20 of accounts receivable during 2011 and the ending allowance balance was estimated to be $131, how would it have affected Net Accounts Receivable? How would the write-off have affected Net Income? Explain.

LO3   **PB8-3 Recording Notes Receivable Transactions**

Stintson Company recently agreed to loan an employee $100,000 for the purchase of a new house. The loan was executed on May 31, 2012, and is a one-year, 6 percent note, with interest payments required on November 30, 2012, and May 31, 2013. Stinson issues quarterly financial statements on March 31, June 30, September 30, and December 31.

Required:

1. Prepare the journal entry that Stinson will make when the note is established.
2. Prepare the journal entries that Stinson will make to record the interest accruals at each quarter end and interest payments at each payment date.
3. Prepare the journal entry that Stinson will make to record the principal payment at the maturity date.

LO2, 3   **PB8-4 Accounting for Accounts and Notes Receivable Transactions**

Fleet Events Corporation has provided event planning services for several years. The company uses the percentage of credit sales method to estimate bad debts for internal monthly reporting purposes. At the end of each quarter, the company adjusts its records using the aging of accounts receivable method. The company entered into the following selected transactions during the first quarter of 2012.

a. During January, the company provided services for $300,000 on credit.
b. On January 31, the company estimated bad debts using 1 percent of credit sales.
c. On February 4, the company collected $250,000 of accounts receivable.
d. On February 15, the company wrote off a $3,000 account receivable.
e. During February, the company provided services for $250,000 on credit.
f. On February 28, the company estimated bad debts using 1 percent of credit sales.
g. On March 1, the company loaned $15,000 to an employee who signed a 4% note, due in 9 months.
h. On March 15, the company collected $3,000 on the account written off one month earlier.
i. On March 31, the company accrued interest earned on the note.
j. On March 31, the company adjusted for uncollectable accounts, based on the following aging analysis. Allowance for Doubtful Accounts has an unadjusted credit balance of $9,000.

Customer	Total	Number of Days Unpaid			
		0–30	31–60	61–90	Over 90
Aerosmit	$ 2,000	$ 1,000	$ 1,000		
Biggie Small	2,000			$ 1,000	$ 1,000
Others (not shown to save space)	99,000	39,000	42,000	9,000	9,000
ZZ Top	7,000	7,000			
Total Accounts Receivable	$110,000	$47,000	$43,000	$10,000	$10,000
Estimated uncollectable (%)		2%	10%	20%	40%

Required:

1. For items *a–j*, analyze the amount and direction (+ or −) of effects on specific financial statement accounts and the overall accounting equation, and prepare journal entries.
2. Show how the receivables related to these transactions would be reported in the current assets section of a classified balance sheet.
3. Name the accounts related to Accounts Receivable and Note Receivable that would be reported on the income statement and indicate whether they would appear before, or after, Income from Operations.

PB8-5 Analyzing Allowance for Doubtful Accounts, Receivables Turnover Ratio, and Days to Collect

LO4

Walmart and Target are two of the largest and most successful retail chains in the world. To evaluate their ability to collect on credit sales, consider the following fictional information reported in their annual reports (amounts in millions).

Walmart

Target

	Walmart			Target		
Fiscal Year Ended January 31:	2012	2011	2010	2012	2011	2010
Net Sales	$401,244	$374,307	$344,992	$62,894	$61,471	$57,878
Accounts Receivable, Net of Allowance	3,905	3,642	2,840	8,084	8,054	6,194

Required:

1. Calculate the receivables turnover ratios and days to collect for Walmart and Target for the years ended January 31, 2012 and 2011. (Round to one decimal place.)
2. Which of the companies is quicker to convert its receivables into cash?
3. How did the economic difficulties in 2011–12 affect the accounts receivable collections?

Check Figure:
Walmart's 2012 Receivables
Turnover Ratio = 106.3

COMPREHENSIVE PROBLEM

C8-1 Recording and Reporting Credit Sales and Bad Debts Using the Aging of Accounts Receivable Method (Chapters 6 and 8)

LO2

Okay Optical, Inc., (OOI) began operations in January 2012, selling inexpensive sunglasses to large retailers like Walmart and other smaller stores. Assume the following transactions occurred during its first six months of operations.

Walmart

January	1	Sold merchandise to Walmart for $20,000; the cost of these goods to OOI was $12,000.
February	12	Received payment in full from Walmart.
March	1	Sold merchandise to Tony's Pharmacy on account for $3,000; the cost of these goods to OOI was $1,400.
April	1	Sold merchandise to Travis Pharmaco on account for $8,000. The cost to OOI was $4,400.
May	1	Sold merchandise to Anjuli Stores on account for $2,000; the cost to OOI was $1,200.
June	17	Received $6,500 on account from Travis Pharmaco.

Required:

1. Complete the following aged listing of customer accounts at June 30.

		Unpaid Since			
Customer	Total Balance	June (one month)	May (two months)	April (three months)	March (greater than three months)
Anjuli Stores	$2,000		$2,000		
Tony's Pharmacy	3,000				$3,000
Travis Pharmaco					
Walmart					

2. Estimate the Allowance for Doubtful Accounts required at June 30, 2012, assuming the following uncollectable rates: one month, 1 percent; two months, 5 percent; three months, 20 percent; more than three months, 40 percent.

3. Show how OOI would report its accounts receivable on its June 30 balance sheet. What amounts would be reported on an income statement prepared for the six-month period ended June 30, 2012?

4. Bonus Question: In July 2012, OOI collected the balance due from Tony's Pharmacy but discovered that the balance due from Travis Pharmaco needed to be written off. Using this information, determine how accurate OOI was in estimating the Allowance for Doubtful Accounts needed for each of these two customers and in total.

SKILLS DEVELOPMENT CASES

LO2, 4

Rona Inc.

S8-1 Finding Financial Information

Refer to the financial statements of Rona Inc. in Appendix A at the back of this book or download the annual report from the *Cases* section of Connect.

1. Does the company report an Allowance for Doubtful Accounts on the balance sheet or in the notes? Explain why it does or does not.

2. Compute the company's receivables turnover ratio and days to collect for the year ended December 27, 2009.

LO2, 4

The Home Depot

S8-2 Comparing Financial Information

Refer to the financial statements of The Home Depot in Appendix B at the back of this book or download the annual report from the *Cases* section of Connect.

1. Does the company report Accounts Receivable or an Allowance for Doubtful Accounts in its financial statements? Explain why it does or does not. (*Hint:* The company refers to its Allowance for Doubtful Accounts as a "Valuation Reserve" related to Accounts Receivable.)

2. Based on your observations for requirement 1, describe the usefulness of the receivables turnover ratio and days to collect analyses for companies that are involved in home improvement retail sales.

LO2, 4

S8-3 Internet-Based Team Research: Examining an Annual Report

As a team, select an industry to analyze. Using your Web browser, each team member should access the annual report for one publicly traded company in the industry, with each member selecting a different company. (See S1-3 in Chapter 1 for a description of possible resources for these tasks.)

Required:

1. On an individual basis, each team member should write a short report that incorporates the following:

   a. Calculate the receivables turnover ratio for the current and prior years, and explain any change between the two years. (To obtain the beginning accounts receivable number for the prior year, you will need the prior year's annual report.)

2. Then, as a team, write a short report comparing and contrasting your companies using these attributes. Discuss any patterns across the companies that you as a team observe. Provide potential explanations for any differences discovered.

S8-4 Ethical Decision Making: A Real-Life Example

LO2, 3

MCI

You work for a company named MCI and you have been assigned the job of adjusting the company's Allowance for Doubtful Accounts balance. You obtained the following fictional aged listing of customer account balances for December.

		Accounts Receivable Aged Listing—December 31				
Customer	Total	0–30 days	31–60 days	61–90 days	91–120 days	> 120 days
AfriTel	40,000	20,000	10,000	5,000	5,000	0
CT&T	0	0	0	0	0	0
GlobeCom	28,000	0	18,000	8,000	1,000	1,000
Hi-Rim	35,000	0	0	0	0	35,000
Level 8	162,000	63,000	44,000	29,000	13,000	13,000
NewTel	0	0	0	0	0	0
Telemedia	0	0	0	0	0	0
Others	485,000	257,000	188,000	28,000	11,000	1,000
TOTAL	750,000	340,000	260,000	70,000	30,000	50,000

Historically, bad debt loss rates for each aging category have been 1% (0–30 days), 5% (31–60 days), 8% (61–90 days), 10% (91–120 days), and 50% (>120 days). Using these rates, you calculate a desired balance for the allowance. No entries have been made to the account since the end of November when the account had a credit balance of $46,820.

To check the reasonableness of the calculated balance, you obtain the aged listings for prior months (shown below). As you scan the listings, you notice an interesting pattern. Several account balances, which had grown quite large by the end of November, had disappeared in the final month of the year. You ask the accounts receivable manager, Walter Pavlo, what happened. He said the customers "obtained some financing . . . I guess out of nowhere" and they must have used it to pay off their account balances.

			Total Accounts Receivable as of . . .			
	Q1	Q2	Q3		Q4	
Customer	(March 31)	(June 30)	(September 30)	(October 31)	(November 30)	(December 31)
AfriTel	19,000	19,000	21,000	16,000	20,000	40,000
CT&T	0	30,000	100,000	100,000	100,000	0
GlobeCom	29,000	28,000	31,000	27,000	28,000	28,000
Hi-Rim	0	0	25,000	35,000	35,000	35,000
Level 8	229,000	229,000	198,000	174,000	190,000	162,000
NewTel	0	0	25,000	25,000	25,000	0
Telemedia	0	0	2,000	2,000	2,000	0
Others	524,000	489,000	375,000	503,000	463,000	485,000
TOTAL	801,000	795,000	777,000	882,000	863,000	750,000

Required:

1. Calculate the balance that should be reported in Allowance for Doubtful Accounts as of December 31.
2. Prepare the adjusting journal entry that is required on December 31.
3. Show how Accounts Receivable would be reported on the balance sheet at December 31.
4. If the balances for CT&T, NewTel, and Telemedia at the end of November continued to exist at the end of December (in the over 120 days category), what balance would you have estimated for the Allowance for Doubtful Accounts on December 31? Would this have changed MCI's net income in the current year? Explain.
5. A few days later, you overhear Pavlo talking about the account receivable from Hi-Rim. Apparently, MCI will soon loan Hi-Rim some money, creating a note receivable. Hi-Rim will use the money to pay off the Accounts Receivable balance it owes to MCI. You are aware that Pavlo receives a bonus based on MCI's net income. Should you investigate this matter further? Explain why or why not.

Epilogue: The events described above are based on an article in the June 10, 2002, issue of *Forbes* magazine that describes how, in the mid-1990s, Walter Pavlo was pressured to commit accounting fraud at MCI. Ironically, MCI was later taken over by WorldCom—the company that went on to commit the world's largest accounting fraud at the time.

LO2   **S8-5 Ethical Decision Making: A Mini-Case**

Having just graduated with a business degree, you're excited to begin working as a junior accountant at Sunny Optics, Inc. The company supplies lenses, frames, and sunglasses to opticians and retailers throughout the country. Sunny Optics is currently in the process of finalizing its third quarter (Q3) operating results. All Q3 adjusting entries have been made, except for bad debt expense. The preliminary income statement for Q3 is shown below, along with reported results for Q2 and Q1.

SUNNY OPTICS, INC.
Quarterly Income Statements
(amounts in thousands of dollars)

	Q3 (preliminary)	Q2 (as reported)	Q1 (as reported)
Net Sales	$135,800	$135,460	$130,100
Cost of Goods Sold	58,400	58,250	55,990
Gross Profit	77,400	77,210	74,110
Selling, General, and Administrative Expenses	56,560	53,975	53,690
Bad Debt Expense	—	6,050	4,200
Income before Income Tax Expense	20,840	17,185	16,220
Income Tax Expense	5,620	5,155	5,020
Net Income	$ 15,220	$ 12,030	$ 11,200

The corporate controller has asked you to examine the Allowance for Doubtful Accounts and use the aged listing of accounts receivable to determine the adjustment needed to record estimated bad debts for the quarter. The controller states that "Although our customers are somewhat slower in paying this quarter, we can't afford to increase the Allowance for Doubtful Accounts. If anything, we need to decrease it—an adjusted balance of about $8,000 is what I'd like to see. Play around with our estimated bad debt loss rates until you get it to work."

You were somewhat confused by what the controller had told you, but you chalked it up to your lack of experience and decided to analyze the Allowance for Doubtful Accounts. You summarized the transactions recorded in the Allowance for Doubtful Accounts using the T-account below:

Allowance for Doubtful Accounts (xA)			
		7,900	January 1 bal. fwd.
Q1 Write-offs	4,110	4,200	Q1 Bad debts estimate
		7,990	March 31 adjusted
Q2 Write-offs	4,120	6,050	Q2 Bad debts estimate
		9,920	June 30 adjusted
Q3 Write-offs	4,030	—	
		5,890	September 30 unadjusted

Required:

1. What bad debts estimate for Q3 will produce the $8,000 balance that the controller would like to see?

2. Prepare the adjusting journal entry that would be required to record this estimate.

3. If the entry in requirement 2 is made, what does it do to the Q3 income and the trend in earnings? (Assume that Income Tax Expense does not change.)

4. Reconsider the statement the controller made to you. Is his suggestion a logical way to use the aging method to estimate bad debts?

5. What would be the Q3 net income if the Bad Debt Expense estimate was 4.5 percent of sales, as in Q2? What would this do to the trend in net income across the three quarters? (Assume that Income Tax Expense does not change.)

6. Is there any evidence of unethical behaviour in this case? Explain your answer.

S8-6 Critical Thinking: Analyzing

LO1, 4

Problem Solved Company has been operating for five years as a software consulting firm. During this period, it has experienced rapid growth in Sales Revenue and in Accounts Receivable. To solve its growing receivables problem, the company hired you as its first corporate controller. You have put into place more stringent credit-granting and collection procedures that you expect will reduce receivables by approximately one-third by year-end. You have gathered the following data related to the changes (in thousands):

	(In thousands)	
	Beginning of Year	End of Year (projected)
Accounts Receivable	$1,000,608	$660,495
Less: Allowance for Doubtful Accounts	36,800	10,225
Accounts Receivable, Net	$ 963,808	$650,270
	Prior Year	Current Year (projected)
Net Sales (assume all on credit)	$7,515,444	$7,015,069

Required:

1. Compute, to one decimal place, the accounts receivable turnover ratio based on three different assumptions:
   a. The stringent credit policies reduce Accounts Receivable, Net and decrease Net Sales as projected in the table.
   b. The stringent credit policies reduce Accounts Receivable, Net as projected in the table but do not decrease Net Sales from the prior year.
   c. The stringent credit policies are not implemented, resulting in no change from the beginning of the year Accounts Receivable balance and no change in Net Sales from the prior year.

2. On the basis of your findings in requirement 1, write a brief memo to the chief financial officer explaining the potential benefits and drawbacks of more stringent credit policies and how they are likely to affect the accounts receivable turnover ratio.

S8-7 Using an Aging Schedule to Estimate Bad Debts and Improve Collections from Customers

LO2

Caffe D'Amore

Assume you were recently hired by Caffe D'Amore, the company that formulated the world's first flavoured instant cappuccino and now manufactures several lines of coffee-flavoured cappuccino mixes. Given the company's tremendous sales growth, Caffe D'Amore's receivables also have grown. Your job is to evaluate and improve collections of the company's receivables.

By analyzing collections of accounts receivable over the past five years, you were able to estimate bad debt loss rates for balances of varying ages. To estimate this year's uncollectable accounts, you jotted down the historical loss rates on the last page of a recent aged listing of outstanding customer balances (see below).

Customer	Total	Number of Days Unpaid				
		1–30	31–60	61–90	91–120	Over 120
Subtotal from previous page	$280,000	$150,000	$60,000	$40,000	$20,000	$10,000
Jumpy Jim's Coffee	1,000					1,000
Pasadena Coffee Company	24,500	14,500	8,000	2,000		
Phillips Blender House	17,000	12,000	4,000		1,000	
Pugsly's Trading Post	26,600	19,600	7,000			
Q-Coffee	12,400	8,400	3,000	1,000		
Special Sips	10,000	6,000	4,000			
Uneasy Isaac's	3,500	500				3,000
Total accounts receivable	375,000	211,000	86,000	43,000	21,000	14,000
Bad debt loss rates		1%	5%	10%	15%	30%

Required:

1. Enter the above totals in a spreadsheet and then insert formulas to calculate the total estimated uncollectable balance.

2. Prepare the year-end adjusting journal entry to adjust the Allowance for Doubtful Accounts to the balance you calculated above. Assume the allowance account has an unadjusted credit balance of $8,000.

3. Of the customer account balances shown above on the last page of the aged listing, which should be your highest priority for contacting and pursuing collection?

4. Assume Jumpy Jim's Coffee account is determined to be uncollectable. Prepare the journal entry to write off the entire account balance.

CONTINUING CASE

LO2, 4   **CC8 Accounting for Receivables and Uncollectable Accounts**

Practise and learn online with Connect.

The following transactions occurred over the months of September to December 2012 at Nicole's Getaway Spa (NGS).

September	Sold spa merchandise to Ashley Welch Beauty for $1,800 on account; the cost of these goods to NGS was $900.
October	Sold merchandise to Kelly Fast Nail Gallery for $450 on account; the cost of these goods to NGS was $200.
November	Sold merchandise to Raea Gooding Wellness for $300 on account; the cost of these goods to NGS was $190.
December	Received $1,200 from Ashley Welch Beauty for payment on its account.

Required:

1. Prepare journal entries for each of the transactions. Assume a perpetual inventory system.

2. Estimate the Allowance for Doubtful Accounts required at December 31, 2012, assuming NGS uses the aging of accounts receivable method with the following uncollectable rates: one month, 2%; two months, 6%; three months, 20%; more than three months, 35%.

3. The Allowance for Doubtful Accounts balance was $50 (credit) before the end-of-period adjusting entry is made. Prepare the journal entry to account for the Bad Debt Expense.

4. Assume the end of the previous year showed net accounts receivable of $800, and net sales for the current year is $9,000. Calculate the accounts receivable turnover ratio (round to one decimal place).

5. Audrey's Mineral Spa has an accounts receivable turnover ratio of 9.0 times. How does NGS compare to this competitor?

Practise and learn online with Connect.

CHAPTER 9

Reporting and Interpreting Long-Lived Tangible and Intangible Assets

FOCUS COMPANY:

Cedar Fair
www.cedarfair.com

YOUR LEARNING OBJECTIVES

Understand the business

LO1 Define, classify, and explain the nature of long-lived assets.

Study the accounting methods

LO2 Apply the cost principle to the acquisition of long-lived assets.

LO3 Apply various amortization methods as economic benefits are used up over time.

LO4 Explain the effect of asset impairment on the financial statements.

LO5 Analyze the disposal of long-lived tangible assets.

LO6 Analyze the acquisition, use, and disposal of long-lived intangible assets.

Evaluate the results

LO7 Interpret the fixed asset turnover ratio.

LO8 Describe factors to consider when comparing companies' long-lived assets.

Review the chapter

Chapter Summary, page 391

Additional resources on Connect

Most people agonize over how much money to spend on a house or which car to buy. After all, they will own these expensive items for many years to come. The same concerns exist when companies acquire long-lived assets. One of the major challenges that business managers face is determining the right amount to invest in long-lived assets.

The task is especially challenging for companies such as Disney, Six Flags, and Cedar Fair, which operate amusement parks. Unlike merchandising companies, an amusement park cannot build up an inventory of unused roller-coaster seats to be sold sometime in the future. If managers build more rides than needed to satisfy park-goers, some rides will run with empty seats. Although the company will still incur all the costs of running the rides, it will generate only a fraction of the potential revenue. On the other hand, amusement parks can also run into trouble if they have too few rides to satisfy patrons. Fortunately for managers, accounting reports provide information to evaluate a company's investment in long-lived assets.

In this chapter, by studying specific long-lived asset decisions made by Cedar Fair, you will see the significant effect that long-lived assets can have on a company's financial statements. Although manufacturing companies, retailers, and even airlines must deal with the same issues as Cedar Fair, the impact on this amusement park company is particularly significant because it relies almost exclusively on long-lived assets. As of December 31, 2009, in fact, Cedar Fair's rides, hotels, and other long-lived assets accounted for more than 97 percent of its total assets.

THAT WAS
THEN

In the past few chapters, you learned about the sale of goods and services to customers.

THIS IS
NOW

This chapter focuses on the assets that enable companies to produce and sell goods and services.

ORGANIZATION OF THE CHAPTER

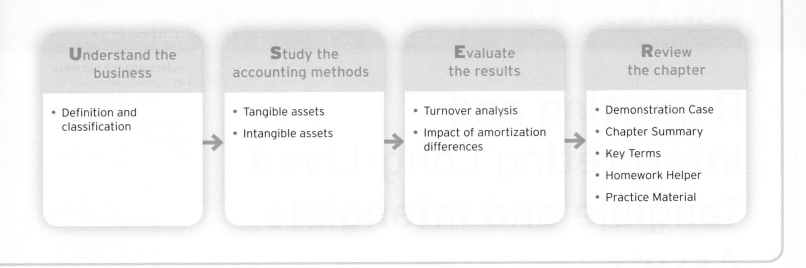

Understand the business	**S**tudy the accounting methods	**E**valuate the results	**R**eview the chapter
• Definition and classification	• Tangible assets • Intangible assets	• Turnover analysis • Impact of amortization differences	• Demonstration Case • Chapter Summary • Key Terms • Homework Helper • Practice Material

Understand the Business

DEFINITION AND CLASSIFICATION

Learning Objective 1

Define, classify, and explain the nature of long-lived assets.

YOU SHOULD KNOW

Long-lived assets:
Resources owned by a business that enable it to produce the goods or services that are sold to customers.

Long-lived assets are business assets acquired for use over one or more years. These assets are not intended for resale. Instead, they are considered "productive" assets in the sense that they enable the business to produce the goods or services that the business then sells to customers. Examples include the ovens in which Pizza Palace bakes pizza, the stores where Walmart sells merchandise, and the legal rights that restrict use of the Skechers logo. So when you hear the term *long-lived assets*, think more broadly than just rusty old equipment. This class of assets includes two major types: tangible and intangible.

1. **Tangible assets.** These are long-lived assets that have physical substance, which simply means that you can see, touch, or kick them. The most prominent examples of tangible assets are land, buildings, machinery, vehicles, office equipment, and furniture and fixtures. These assets are typically grouped into a single line item on the balance sheet called *Property, Plant, and Equipment*. Because many long-lived tangible assets are fixed in place, they are also known as **fixed assets**. Cedar Fair's tangible assets include roller coasters, hotels, and land in Canada and the United States.

2. **Intangible assets.** These long-lived assets have special rights but no physical substance. The existence of most intangible assets is indicated only by legal documents that describe their rights. Compared to the tangible assets that you see in daily life, such as store buildings and cash registers, intangible assets are probably less familiar to you. For this reason, we'll describe the various types of intangibles in detail later in this chapter. For now you can think of this category as including brand names, trademarks, and licensing rights such as the ones that allow Cedar Fair to use PEANUTS® characters throughout its amusement parks.

A third category of long-lived assets that are depleted over time, like an oil well or gold mine, is common in natural resource industries. This chapter's Supplement 9A describes how these natural resource assets are accounted for.

Exhibit 9.1 shows how Cedar Fair reported long-lived assets on its 2010 balance sheet. From this exhibit, you can see how important tangible and intangible assets are to Cedar Fair. Of the nearly $2.1 billion in total assets at December 31, 2010, Cedar Fair owned long-lived assets totalling $1.9 billion ($1,677 + $287 = $1,964, in millions).

EXHIBIT 9.1   Cedar Fair's Assets    Cedar fair. L.P.

| (in millions) | AT DECEMBER 31 | |
	2010	2009
Assets		
Current Assets	$ 70	$ 61
(details omitted to save space)		
Property and Equipment		
Land	310	305
Land Improvements	325	326
Buildings	576	589
Rides and Equipment	1,398	1,352
Construction in Progress	17	35
Property and Equipment, at cost	2,626	2,607
Less: Accumulated Amortization	(949)	(826)
Property and Equipment, Net	1,677	1,781
Goodwill and Other Intangible Assets	287	282
Other Assets	49	21
Total Assets	$2,083	$2,145

COACH'S TIP

Accumulated Amortization is reported here as a total for the entire tangible assets category. Alternatively, it can be reported separately for each type of tangible asset.

Study the Accounting Methods

In this section, you will study the accounting decisions that relate to long-lived assets. We'll start with tangible long-lived assets and consider key accounting decisions related to their (1) acquisition, (2) use, and (3) disposal. Accounting for intangible assets will be the focus of the last part of this section.

TANGIBLE ASSETS

Most companies own a variety of tangible assets. Earlier chapters introduced you to the most common examples: land, buildings, equipment, and vehicles. Other, less common examples include land improvements and construction in progress—both of which Cedar Fair reported on its balance sheet in Exhibit 9.1. Land improvements differ from land in that they deteriorate over time, whereas land is assumed to last forever. Land improvements include the sidewalks, pavement, landscaping, fencing, lighting, and sprinkler systems that are added to improve the usefulness of land. Construction in progress includes the costs of constructing new buildings and equipment. When construction is finished, these costs are moved from this account into the building or equipment account to which they relate.

Acquisition of Tangible Assets

The general rule for tangible assets under the cost principle is that all reasonable and necessary costs to acquire and prepare an asset for use should be recorded as a cost of the asset. Accountants say costs have been **capitalized** when they are recorded as assets (rather than as expenses).

Deciding whether a cost is reasonable and necessary to acquire or prepare tangible assets for use can involve a great deal of judgment. Because capitalizing costs has a significant impact on both the balance sheet (it increases assets) and the income statement (it decreases expenses), some dishonest accountants and managers have exploited the judgment involved in this decision by capitalizing costs that should have been expensed. A well-known example of this tactic is described in the following Spotlight on Ethics feature. As you read the feature and the next couple of pages, focus on distinguishing between what types of costs should be capitalized and what types should be expensed.

Learning Objective 2

Apply the cost principle to the acquisition of long-lived assets.

YOU SHOULD KNOW

Capitalize: To record a cost as an asset, rather than an expense.

The illustration that follows shows the types of costs that should be capitalized when a tangible asset is acquired. All are necessary for acquiring and preparing tangible assets for use. Notice that they are not limited to the amounts paid to purchase or construct the assets. For example, the Land account at Cedar Fair would include legal fees for title searches, fees for land surveys, and commissions paid to brokers. Take a moment right now to read the lists of costs that should be capitalized when buildings (middle) and equipment (right) are acquired.

Land

Purchase cost
Legal fees
Survey fees
Title search fees

Equipment

Purchase/construction cost
Sales taxes
Transportation costs
Installation costs

Buildings

Purchase/construction cost
Legal fees
Appraisal fees
Architect fees

If a company buys land, a building, or a piece of used equipment and incurs demolition, renovation, or repair costs before it can be used, these additional costs would be capitalized as a cost of the land, building, or equipment. These costs are capitalized because they are needed to prepare the asset for use.

In some cases, land, buildings, and equipment are purchased together. On June 30, 2006, Cedar Fair bought five amusement parks, including Canada's Wonderland, from Paramount Parks for $1.2 billion. When this type of "basket purchase" occurs, the total cost is split among the assets in proportion to the market value of the assets as a whole. For example, if Cedar Fair was to pay $10 million for a hotel and the land surrounding it, based on an appraisal that estimates that the land contributes 40 percent of the property's value and the building contributes 60 percent, Cedar Fair would record 40 percent of the total cost as land ($4 million) and the other 60 percent as buildings ($6 million). Splitting the total purchase price among individual assets is necessary because the cost of different asset types may be amortized over different periods. Land is not amortized, so any costs assigned to Land will remain in that account until Cedar Fair sells the land.

To illustrate how the costs of tangible assets are recorded, let's consider the Top Thrill Dragster that Cedar Fair purchased from Intamin, a Swiss roller-coaster manufacturer. When

SPOTLIGHT ON THE WORLD

Component Allocation

IFRS takes the idea of a basket purchase one step further. The cost of an individual asset's components is allocated among each significant component and then amortized separately over that component's useful life. For example, British Airways separates the cost of an aircraft into its body, engines, and interior cabin space, and then depreciates the body, engines, and cabin interior over 25, 18, and 5 years, respectively.

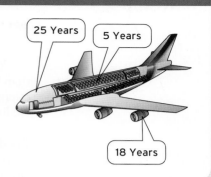

it was purchased, the Top Thrill Dragster was the biggest, fastest roller coaster in the world. Some of its specs are shown in the following graphic.

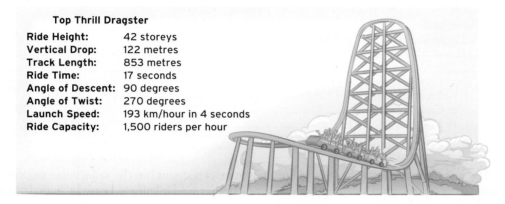

Top Thrill Dragster

Ride Height:	42 storeys
Vertical Drop:	122 metres
Track Length:	853 metres
Ride Time:	17 seconds
Angle of Descent:	90 degrees
Angle of Twist:	270 degrees
Launch Speed:	193 km/hour in 4 seconds
Ride Capacity:	1,500 riders per hour

Assume the list price for the roller coaster (including sales tax) was $26 million but that Cedar Fair received a $1 million discount. In other words, the roller coaster's net purchase price to Cedar Fair was $25 million. Assume too that Cedar Fair paid $125,000 to have the roller coaster delivered and another $625,000 to have it assembled and prepared for use. Cedar Fair would calculate the costs to be capitalized for this asset as follows:

List price	$26,000,000
Less: Discount	1,000,000
Net invoice price	25,000,000
Add: Transportation costs paid by Cedar Fair	125,000
Installation costs paid by Cedar Fair	625,000
Total cost of the roller coaster	$25,750,000

The total $25,750,000 cost would be the amount Cedar Fair recorded in the Rides and Equipment account regardless of how the company paid for or financed the roller coaster. As you will see next, the method of payment or financing affects only whether the purchase reduces cash, increases liabilities, or both.

Cash Purchase   If Cedar Fair paid cash for the roller coaster and related transportation and installation costs, the effects of the transaction and the journal entry to record these effects would be

1 Analyze

	Assets	=	Liabilities	+	Shareholders' Equity
Cash	−25,750,000				
Rides and Equipment	+25,750,000				

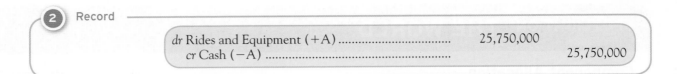

| dr Rides and Equipment (+A) .... | 25,750,000 | |
| cr Cash (−A) .... | | 25,750,000 |

You might find it hard to believe that Cedar Fair would pay cash for assets that cost more than $25 million, but this isn't unusual. Companies often pay with cash generated from operations or with cash that has been borrowed. In addition, it's possible the seller may extend credit to the buyer, a situation we examine next.

Credit Purchase   If we assume that Cedar Fair signed a note payable for the new roller coaster and paid cash for the transportation and installation costs, the accounting equation effects and journal entry would be

1 Analyze

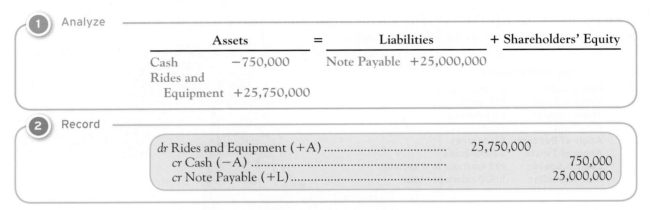

Assets		=	Liabilities	+ Shareholders' Equity
Cash	−750,000		Note Payable +25,000,000	
Rides and				
Equipment	+25,750,000			

2 Record

dr Rides and Equipment (+A)	25,750,000	
cr Cash (−A)		750,000
cr Note Payable (+L)		25,000,000

You will notice that the Rides and Equipment asset account has the same value regardless of how the company paid for the roller coaster. Whether Cedar Fair paid cash or signed a note payable, the asset has the same capitalized amount.

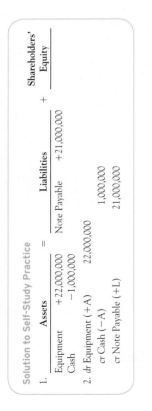

HOW'S IT GOING? Self-Study Practice

In a recent year, the Newton Bakery Company opened a new baking plant that can make 200,000 buns per hour. The equipment cost $21 million. Assume that Newton Bakery financed the equipment purchase using a promissory note and paid in cash $900,000 of sales tax, $60,000 of transportation costs, and $40,000 of installation costs before the equipment could be used. Indicate the effects of the purchase on the accounting equation and give the journal entry to record the purchase.

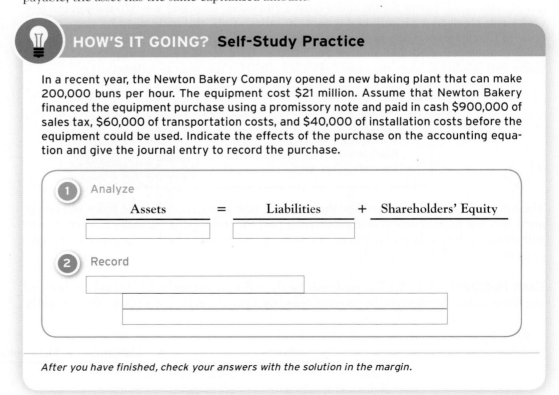

1 Analyze

Assets	=	Liabilities	+	Shareholders' Equity

2 Record

After you have finished, check your answers with the solution in the margin.

Before we leave this section, we should mention that not all fixed asset costs are capitalized. The cost of some fixed assets, like staplers or scissors, is such a small dollar amount that it's not worth the trouble of recording them as fixed assets. Outback Steakhouse, for example, reports in its financial statement notes that it expenses all expenditures less than $1,000. Such policies are acceptable because immaterial (relatively small) amounts will not affect users' analysis of financial statements. Also, when purchases are made in Canada, the applicable Goods and Services Tax (GST) and Provincial Sales Tax (PST), or a Harmonized Sales Tax (HST), increase the purchase price. These taxes are dealt with in more detail in Chapter 10. Other costs that are expensed when incurred include insurance for fixed assets, interest on loans to purchase fixed assets, and ordinary repairs and maintenance, as discussed in the next section.

Use of Tangible Assets

Maintenance Costs Incurred during Use Most tangible assets require substantial expenditures over the course of their lives to maintain or enhance their operation. Maintenance is a big deal in the roller-coaster industry, where safety is vital. Despite the tremendous stress created by frequent use and wicked-fast speeds, surprisingly few accidents occur. According to some estimates, the odds of a serious amusement park injury are 1 in 23 million. Companies achieve this level of safety by spending a lot of money on two types of maintenance: (1) ordinary repairs and maintenance and (2) extraordinary repairs and maintenance.

1. **Ordinary repairs and maintenance. Ordinary repairs and maintenance** are expenditures for the routine maintenance and upkeep of long-lived assets. Just like an oil change for your car, these are recurring, relatively small expenditures that do not directly increase an asset's usefulness. Because these costs occur frequently to maintain the asset's productive capacity for a short time, they are recorded as expenses in the current period. Because these expenses are matched to revenues, ordinary repairs and maintenance are sometimes called **revenue expenditures.**

   In the case of Cedar Fair, ordinary repairs and maintenance would include greasing the tracks on the Behemoth roller coaster at Canada's Wonderland outside of Toronto. It would also include replacing the lights on the century-old Antique Carousel and tightening the seams on the Barracuda Blaster water slide.

2. **Extraordinary repairs, replacements, and additions.** In contrast to ordinary repairs and maintenance, **extraordinary repairs** occur infrequently, involve large expenditures, and increase an asset's economic usefulness through enhanced efficiency, capacity, or life span. Examples include additions, major overhauls, complete reconditioning, and major replacements and improvements, such as the complete replacement of the passenger train on a roller coaster. Because these costs increase the usefulness of tangible assets beyond their original condition, they are added to the appropriate long-lived asset accounts. And because doing so means capitalizing costs, these extraordinary repairs, replacements, and additions are called **capital expenditures.**

HOW'S IT GOING? Self-Study Practice

As you know from living in a house, apartment, or dorm, buildings often require maintenance and repair. For each of the following expenditures, indicate whether it should be expensed in the current period or capitalized.

Expense or Capitalize?

1. Replacing electrical wiring throughout the building.
2. Repairing the hinge on the front door of the building.
3. Yearly cleaning of the building's air-conditioning filters.
4. Making major structural improvements to a clubhouse.

After you have finished, check your answers with the solution in the margin.

Solution to Self-Study Practice
1. Capitalize—Extends life. (Debit the "Buildings" account; credit "Cash.")
2. Expense—Does not increase usefulness. (Debit the "Maintenance Expense" account; credit "Cash.")
3. Expense—Does not increase usefulness. (Debit the "Maintenance Expense" account; credit "Cash.")
4. Capitalize—Extends life. (Debit the "Buildings" account; credit "Cash.")

YOU SHOULD KNOW

Amortization (also called depreciation): The allocation of the cost of long-lived tangible assets over their productive lives using a systematic and rational method.

Amortization Expense In addition to repairs and maintenance expense, a company reports amortization every period that a long-lived asset is used. Amortization doesn't involve new payments for using the asset. Rather, **amortization** (or *depreciation*) is the allocation of existing costs that were already recorded as a long-lived asset. Think of the cost of a long-lived asset as a big prepayment for future benefits. As that asset is used, those prepaid benefits are used up, so the asset needs to be decreased each period. This decrease in the asset creates an expense, which is reported on the income statement to match the revenues generated by the asset.

As you learned in Chapter 4, amortization affects one income statement account and one balance sheet account. The income statement account, Amortization Expense, reports the amortization of the current period. The balance sheet account, Accumulated Amortization, contains the current period's amortization as well as that of prior periods. It is an accumulation over several periods. The effects of $130 of amortization on the accounting equation and the journal entry to record them follow:

1 Analyze

Assets		= Liabilities +	Shareholders' Equity	
Accumulated Amortization (+xA)	−130		Amortization Expense (+E)	−130

2 Record

dr Amortization Expense (+E, −SE)	130	
cr Accumulated Amortization (+xA, −A)		130

YOU SHOULD KNOW

Book (or carrying) value: The acquisition cost of an asset less accumulated amortization.

Exhibit 9.2 shows how Cedar Fair reported its amortization in 2010. The income statement on the right shows the $127 million of Amortization Expense in 2010. The balance sheet on the left shows that this $127 million, when combined with amortization of prior years, brought the total Accumulated Amortization to $949 million at December 31, 2010. The $1,677 difference between the Property and Equipment's $2,626 cost and $949 of Accumulated Amortization is called the **book (or carrying) value.** Most companies report a breakdown of these totals by class of asset (e.g., buildings, equipment) in their financial statement notes.

EXHIBIT 9.2 **Reporting Amortization on the Balance Sheet and Income Statement**

Balance Sheet (in millions)	Dec. 31, 2010
Assets	
Property and Equipment, at cost	$2,626
Less: Accumulated Amortization	(949)
Property and Equipment, net	1,677

Income Statement (in millions)	2010
Net Revenues	$ 978
Operating Expenses:	
Food and Operating Expenses	498
Amortization Expense	127
Selling, General, and Other	134
Impairment Losses	65
Total Operating Expenses	824
Income from Operations	154

One way to interpret the information in Exhibit 9.2 is that the Property and Equipment's $2,626 million cost represents the assets' total economic benefits. Thus, $127 million of Amortization Expense means Cedar Fair used up almost 5 per cent ($127/$2,626 = 0.048) of the assets' benefits in 2010. As of December 31, 2010, 36 per cent ($949/$2,626 = 0.361) of their total benefits had been used up.

To fully understand the amortization numbers in Exhibit 9.2, you need to know how they are calculated. Amortization calculations are based on the following three items:

1. **Asset cost.** This includes all of the asset's capitalized costs, including the purchase cost, sales tax, legal fees, and other costs needed to acquire and prepare the asset for use.

2. **Residual value.** Residual (or salvage) value is an estimate of the amount the company will receive when it disposes of the asset. Cedar Fair will recover some of the initial cost of its roller coasters when it disposes of them by either selling them "as is" to local amusement companies or by dismantling them and selling their parts to other roller-coaster or scrap metal companies.

3. **Useful life.** Useful life is an estimate of the asset's useful economic life to the company (not its economic life to all potential users). It may be expressed in terms of years or units of capacity, such as the number of units it can produce or the number of kilometres it will travel. Land is the only tangible asset that's assumed to have an unlimited (indefinite) useful life. Because of this, land is not amortized.

The basic idea of amortization is to match the economic benefit that will be used up (asset cost minus residual value) to the periods in which the asset will be used to generate revenue (useful life). Residual value is considered when calculating amortization because we want to leave a little of the asset's cost in the accounts after we have finished depreciating it. We do this because, when we dispose of the asset, we're likely to get back some of the money we initially paid for the asset. So the amount to be amortized over the asset's life is the difference between its cost and residual value, an amount called the **amortizable cost.** A company should record amortization each year of an asset's useful life until its total accumulated amortization equals its amortizable cost. After that, the company should report no additional amortization, even if the company continues to use the asset.

If every company used the same techniques for calculating amortization, we'd stop right here. But they don't. Companies own different assets and use them differently, so they are allowed to choose from several alternative amortization methods. These alternative amortization methods produce different patterns of amortization as represented by the amortization amounts recorded each year. The amortization method chosen for each type of property, plant, and equipment should reflect the pattern in which those assets' economic benefits are used up.

Amortization Methods

We discuss the three most common amortization methods:

1. **Straight-line**
2. **Units-of-production**
3. **Declining-balance**

To show how each method works, let's assume that Cedar Fair acquired a new go-cart ride on January 1, 2012. The relevant information is shown in Exhibit 9.3.

EXHIBIT 9.3	Information for Amortization Computations

CEDAR FAIR—Acquisition of a New Go-Cart Ride

Cost, purchased on January 1, 2012	$62,500
Estimated residual value	$2,500
Estimated useful life	3 years; 100,000 km

Straight-Line Method   Managers choose the **straight-line amortization method** if they want to report an equal amount of amortization in each period of the asset's estimated useful life. The straight-line formula for estimating annual amortization expense is

> **Straight-Line Formula**
> $$(\text{Cost} - \text{Residual Value}) \times \frac{1}{\text{Useful Life}} = \textbf{Amortization Expense}$$

In the straight-line formula, Cost − Residual Value is the total amount to be amortized (the amortizable cost). The amortization rate is 1/Useful Life. Using the information in Exhibit 9.3, the amortization expense for Cedar Fair's new ride is $20,000 per year, calculated in the following amortization schedule:

Straight-line (Cost − Residual Value) × (1/Useful Life)		INCOME STATEMENT	BALANCE SHEET		
Year	Yearly Computation	Amortization Expense	Cost	Accumulated Amortization	Book Value
At acquisition			$62,500	$ 0	$62,500
2012	($62,500 − $2,500) × (1/3)	$20,000	62,500	20,000	42,500
2013	($62,500 − $2,500) × (1/3)	20,000	62,500	40,000	22,500
2014	($62,500 − $2,500) × (1/3)	20,000	62,500	60,000	2,500
	Total	$60,000			

Take a moment to study the straight-line amortization schedule. Notice that as the name *straight-line* suggests,

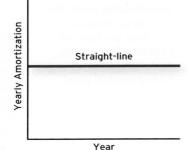

1. Amortization Expense is a constant amount each year.
2. Accumulated Amortization increases by an equal amount each year.
3. Book Value decreases by the same equal amount each year.

Notice too that at the end of the asset's life, accumulated amortization ($60,000) equals the asset's amortizable cost ($62,500 − $2,500), and book value ($2,500) equals residual value.

As you will see with other amortization methods, the amount of amortization depends on estimates of an asset's useful life and residual value at the end of that life. People often ask, **How do accountants estimate useful lives and residual values?** While some of this information can be obtained from the asset's supplier or from other sources such as reseller databases or insurance companies, the simple answer is that professional judgment is required. Because useful lives and residual values are difficult to estimate with precision, accountants are encouraged to update their calculations regularly (see Changes in Amortization Estimates on page 379).

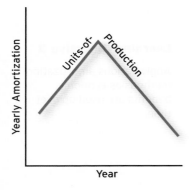

Units-of-Production Method   Choose the **units-of-production amortization method** if the amount of asset production varies significantly from period to period. An asset's production can be defined in terms of kilometres, products, or machine-hours. The units-of-production formula for estimating amortization expense is

> **Units-of-Production Formula**
> $$(\text{Cost} - \text{Residual Value}) \times \frac{\text{Actual Production This Period}}{\text{Estimated Total Production}} = \frac{\text{Amortization}}{\text{Expense}}$$

If the go-cart in Exhibit 9.3 was driven 30,000 km in 2012, 50,000 km in 2013, and 20,000 km in 2014, the units-of-production method would calculate amortization in each year of the asset's life as follows:

Units-of-production (Cost − Residual Value) × (Actual/Estimated Total Production)		INCOME STATEMENT	BALANCE SHEET		
Year	Yearly Computation	Amortization Expense	Cost	Accumulated Amortization	Book Value
At acquisition			$62,500	$ 0	$62,500
2012	($62,500 − $2,500) × (30,000/100,000 km)	$18,000	62,500	18,000	44,500
2013	($62,500 − $2,500) × (50,000/100,000 km)	30,000	62,500	48,000	14,500
2014	($62,500 − $2,500) × (20,000/100,000 km)	12,000	62,500	60,000	2,500
	Total	$60,000			

Under the units-of-production method, the amortization expense, accumulated amortization, and book value vary from period to period, depending on the number of units produced.

Declining-Balance Method

Choose the **declining-balance amortization method** if you want a higher amount of amortization expense in the early years of an asset's life and a lower amount in later years. Because this method speeds up amortization reporting, it is sometimes called an *accelerated amortization method*. Accelerated methods are used more frequently for financial reporting purposes in countries such as Canada and Japan, as well as for tax reporting (a point we discuss in greater detail later). In the United States, however, these accelerated methods are not used as often.

The declining-balance method applies an amortization rate to the book value of the asset at the beginning of each accounting period. Notice that the following formula uses book value (Cost − Accumulated Amortization) rather than amortizable cost (Cost − Residual Value). This slight difference in the formula produces declining amounts of amortization as the asset ages. Because the (2/Useful Life) rate used in the formula is double the straight-line rate, this particular version of the declining-balance method is called the double-declining-balance amortization method.

> **Double-Declining-Balance Formula**
> $$(\text{Cost} - \text{Accumulated Amortization}) \times \frac{2}{\text{Useful Life}} = \text{Amortization Expense}$$

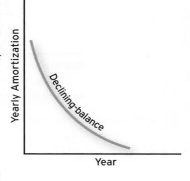

This formula uses the accumulated amortization balance at the beginning of each year. In the first year of an asset's life, the beginning balance in Accumulated Amortization is zero. However, with each passing year as additional amortization is recorded, the Accumulated Amortization balance increases, causing the amount of double-declining amortization expense to decline over time.

Because residual value is not included in the formula for the declining-balance method of computing amortization expense, you must take extra care to ensure that an asset's book value is not amortized beyond its residual value. If the calculated amount of amortization for the year would reduce the book value below the asset's residual value, you must record a lower amount of amortization so that the book value will equal the residual value. The following amortization schedule illustrates this point.

Double-declining-balance (Cost − Accumulated Amortization) × (2/Useful Life)		INCOME STATEMENT	BALANCE SHEET		
Year	Yearly Computation	Amortization Expense	Cost	Accumulated Amortization	Book Value
At acquisition			$62,500	$ 0	$62,500
2012	($62,500 − $0) × (2/3)	$41,667	62,500	41,667	20,833
2013	($62,500 − $41,667) × (2/3)	13,889	62,500	55,556	6,944
2014	($62,500 − $55,556) × (2/3)	4,629	62,500	60,185	2,315
		4,444	62,500	60,000	2,500
	Total	$60,000			

Notice that the calculated amortization expense for 2014 ($4,629) would not be recorded because it would cause the asset's book value to fall below its residual value. Instead, in the final year of the asset's life, just enough amortization ($4,444) is recorded to make the book value of the asset equal its residual value of $2,500.

Summary of Amortization Methods   See Exhibit 9.4 for a summary of the amortization expense that would be reported in each year of our example under the three alternative amortization methods. Notice that the amount of amortization expense recorded in each year of an asset's life depends on the method that is used. That means that the amount of net income that is reported can vary, depending on the amortization method used. At the end of an asset's life, after it has been fully amortized, the total amount of amortization will equal the asset's amortizable cost, regardless of the amortization method used.

EXHIBIT 9.4	**Differences in Amortization Expense by Method**

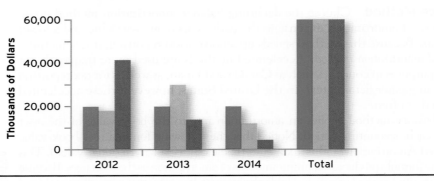

Straight-line	(Cost − Residual Value) × (1/Useful Life)
Units-of-production	(Cost − Residual Value) × (Actual Production/Estimated Total Production)
Double-declining-balance	(Cost − Accumulated Amortization) × (2/Useful Life)

Different amortization methods can be used for different classes of assets provided they are used consistently over time so that financial statement users can compare results across periods. The straight-line method is the preferred choice because it is the easiest to use and understand, and it does a good job of matching amortization expense to revenues when assets are used evenly over their useful lives. The units-of-production method is the typical choice when asset use fluctuates significantly from period to period. Declining-balance methods apply best to assets that are most productive when they are new but quickly lose their usefulness as they get older.

 HOW'S IT GOING? Self-Study Practice

Assume that Cedar Fair has acquired new equipment at a cost of $24,000. The equipment has an estimated life of six years, an estimated operating life of 5,000 hours, and an estimated residual value of $3,000. Determine amortization expense for the **second year** under each of the following methods:

1. Straight-line method.
    $(24,000 − ☐) × ☐/6 = $☐

2. Double-declining-balance method.
    Year: $(24,000 − ☐) × ☐/☐ = $☐

    Year: $(24,000 − ☐) × ☐/☐ = $☐

3. Units-of-production method (assume the equipment ran for 800 hours in Year 2).
    $(☐ − ☐) × ☐/5,000 = $☐

After you have finished, check your answers with the solution in the margin.

Solution to Self-Study Practice

1. $(24,000 − 3,000) × 1/6 = $3,500
2. Year 1: $(24,000 − 0) × 2/6 = $8,000
   Year 2: $(24,000 − 8,000) 2/6 = $5,333
3. $(24,000 − 3,000) × (800/5,000) = $3,360

Partial-Year Amortization Calculations

Purchases of long-lived assets seldom occur on the first day of the accounting period. Consequently, the need arises to calculate amortization for periods shorter than a year. Under the straight-line and declining-balance methods, the annual amortization is multiplied by the fraction of the year for which amortization is being calculated.

For purposes of these calculations, accountants typically assume that assets were purchased at the beginning of the month nearest to the actual purchase date. For example, if Cedar Fair purchased the go-cart ride on October 7, 2012, it would have owned the asset for about three months during the year ended December 31, 2012. Thus, the amortization for the ride in 2012 would be calculated by multiplying the annual straight-line amortization of $20,000 by 3 ÷ 12, representing the 3 months of 12 that Cedar Fair owned it. Similarly, if an asset is disposed of during the year, the annual amortization is multiplied by the fraction of the year during which the asset was owned. These partial-year modifications are not required in the units-of-production method because that method is based on actual production for the period. If the accounting period is shorter than a year, the level of actual production already reflects that shorter period.

Tax Amortization Before we leave the topic of amortization methods, we should note that most companies use one method of amortization for reporting to shareholders and a different method for determining income taxes. Keeping two sets of accounting records like this is both ethical and legal because the primary objective of financial reporting differs from that of income tax reporting.

Financial Reporting	Income Tax Reporting
Objective: Provide economic information about a business that is useful in projecting its future cash flows.	Objective: Raise sufficient tax revenues to pay for the expenditures of the federal government and to encourage certain social and economic behaviours.

One of the behaviours the government wants to encourage is economic renewal and growth. For this reason, Canada Revenue Agency allows companies to deduct larger amounts of tax amortization in the early years of an asset's life than those allowed by ASPE and IFRS. Canada Revenue Agency requires corporations to use the **capital cost allowance (CCA)** method when calculating taxable income and taxes owed to the government. The CCA calculation method is similar, but not identical, to the declining-balance method that was illustrated earlier in this chapter. For example, in order to encourage spending on technology, the government might set the CCA rate at 100 percent for a certain piece of medical equipment. This allows a company to write off or expense the whole cost of this asset in the year it was acquired. This is great for saving taxes, but if that piece of equipment was used for five years, it would violate the matching principle for financial reporting purposes. This is why companies keep two sets of records. The CCA rates will vary depending on the type of asset. For example, some buildings have a CCA rate of 4 percent, while computer hardware has a CCA rate of 45 percent. We will leave further discussion of this topic to more advanced accounting courses.

YOU SHOULD KNOW

Capital cost allowance: The amortization process required by the Canada Revenue Agency for calculating taxable income and income taxes.

Changes in Amortization Estimates

Amortization is based on two estimates, useful life and residual value. These estimates are made at the time an amortizable asset is acquired. As you gain experience with the asset, one or both of these initial estimates may need to be revised. In addition, extraordinary repairs and additions may be added to the original acquisition cost at some time during the asset's use. When it is clear that either estimate should be revised to a significant degree or that the asset's capitalized cost has changed, amortization is revised for the remaining years of the asset's estimated life.

To compute the new amortization expense due to the changes described above, substitute the book value for the original acquisition cost, the new residual value for the original residual value, and the estimated remaining life for the original useful life. As an illustration, the formula using the straight-line method follows:

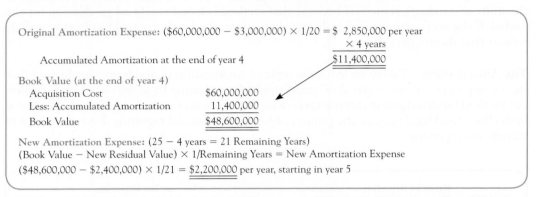

$$(\text{Cost} - \text{Residual Value}) \times \frac{1}{\text{Useful Life}} = \text{Amortization Expense}$$

$$(\text{Book Value} - \text{New Residual Value}) \times \frac{1}{\text{Remaining Life}} = \text{Amortization Expense}$$

Assume Cedar Fair purchased the largest and fastest roller coaster in the world for $60,000,000, with an estimated useful life of 20 years and estimated residual value of $3,000,000. Shortly after the start of year 5, Cedar Fair changed the initial estimated life to 25 years and lowered the estimated residual value to $2,400,000. At the end of year 5, the computation of the new amount for amortization expense is as follows:

Original Amortization Expense: ($60,000,000 − $3,000,000) × 1/20 = $ 2,850,000 per year
                                                                                      × 4 years

    Accumulated Amortization at the end of year 4 $11,400,000

Book Value (at the end of year 4)
   Acquisition Cost $60,000,000
   Less: Accumulated Amortization   11,400,000
   Book Value $48,600,000

New Amortization Expense: (25 − 4 years = 21 Remaining Years)
(Book Value − New Residual Value) × 1/Remaining Years = New Amortization Expense
($48,600,000 − $2,400,000) × 1/21 = $2,200,000 per year, starting in year 5

Companies may also change amortization methods (for example, from declining-balance to straight-line), although such a change requires significantly more disclosure, as described in intermediate accounting textbooks. Under ASPE and IFRS, changes in accounting estimates and amortization methods should be made only when a new estimate or accounting method "better measures" the periodic income of the business.

Asset Impairment Losses

As a result of recording amortization, an asset's book value declines as it ages. However, because amortization is not intended to report an asset at its current value, an asset's book value could exceed its current value, particularly if the asset becomes impaired. **Impairment** occurs when events or changed circumstances cause the estimated future cash flows from a long-lived asset to fall below its book value. If an asset's estimated future cash flows are less than its book value, the book value should be written down to what the asset is worth (called *fair value*), with the amount of the write-down reported as an impairment loss. Impairment losses are classified as an operating expense on the income statement and reported above the Income from Operations subtotal, as shown in Exhibit 9.2 on page 374.

Cedar Fair recorded a write-down in 2002 after a rare engineering phenomenon called *vortex shedding* reportedly caused a steel support tower in one of its VertiGo slingshot rides to snap during the off-season. Even though only one of the rides was affected, Cedar Fair dismantled and removed its two VertiGo rides because few people are willing to go on a ride that snapped apart, even if it is fixable.[1] To see how this event would be accounted for, assume that the book value of Cedar Fair's VertiGo rides was $8 million. If the fair value of the rides was estimated to be $4.8 million—an amount that represents what other amusement park companies and scrap dealers might be expected to pay for the rides' parts—then the impairment loss would be calculated as $8 million minus $4.8 million. The effects of the resulting $3.2 million impairment and the journal entry to record it would be

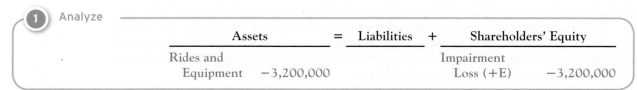

1 Analyze

	Assets	=	Liabilities	+	Shareholders' Equity	
Rides and Equipment	−3,200,000				Impairment Loss (+E)	−3,200,000

$$dr \text{ Impairment Loss } (+E, -SE) \dots\dots\dots\dots\dots\dots\dots\dots\dots \quad 3{,}200{,}000$$
$$cr \text{ Rides and Equipment } (-A) \dots\dots\dots\dots\dots\dots\dots\dots \quad\quad 3{,}200{,}000$$

Disposal of Tangible Assets

Learning Objective 5

Analyze the disposal of long-lived tangible assets.

In some cases, a business may voluntarily decide not to hold a long-term asset for its entire life. For example, your local gym might decide to replace its treadmills with elliptical trainers. Or, if a company discontinues a product, it may sell the equipment that was used to make the product. To get rid of used assets, companies do just what you do. They trade them in on a new asset, sell them, or "retire" them to a junkyard. Sometimes, assets are damaged or destroyed in storms, fires, or accidents, creating what are politely called *involuntary disposals*.

The disposal of an amortizable asset usually requires two accounting adjustments:

1. **Update the Amortization Expense and Accumulated Amortization accounts.** If a long-lived asset is disposed of during the year, it should be amortized to the date of disposal using the partial-year calculations explained on page 379.

2. **Record the disposal.** All disposals of long-lived assets require that you account for (1) the book value of the items given up, (2) the value of the items received on disposal, and (3) any difference between the two amounts, which reflects a gain or loss on the disposal. Any gain or loss on the disposal is included on the income statement when calculating Income from Operations.

Earlier in this chapter, you saw how to compute and record amortization expense on a long-lived asset (step 1 above), so let's look instead at an example where we have to record only the disposal (step 2). Assume that, at the end of year 16, Cedar Fair sold one of its hotels for $3 million cash. The original $20 million cost of the hotel was amortized using the straight-line method over 20 years with no residual value ($1 million amortization expense per year). The gain or loss on disposal is calculated as the difference between the asset's selling price and its book value (BV). Based on the numbers for this example, the book value is

Original cost	$20,000,000
Less: Accumulated Amortization ($1,000,000 × 16 years)	16,000,000
Book value (BV) at date of sale	$ 4,000,000

 **COACH'S TIP**

Be sure to reduce both the asset and accumulated amortization accounts for their full cost and accumulated amortization (updated to the time of disposal).

The selling price ($3,000,000) is less than the book value ($4,000,000), so the difference ($1,000,000) is reported as a loss on sale. The effects of the loss and the hotel sale on Cedar Fair are shown below, along with the journal entry to record them.

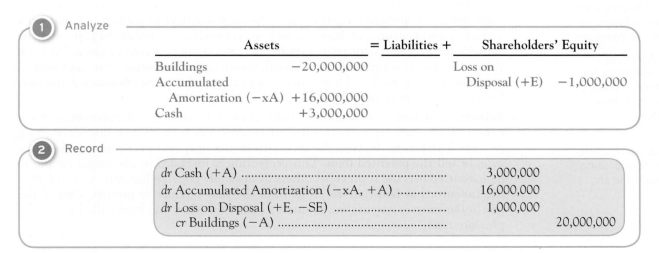

1 Analyze

Assets		= Liabilities +	Shareholders' Equity	
Buildings	−20,000,000		Loss on	
Accumulated			Disposal (+E)	−1,000,000
Amortization (−xA)	+16,000,000			
Cash	+3,000,000			

2 Record

$$dr \text{ Cash } (+A) \dots\dots\dots\dots\dots\dots\dots\dots\dots\dots\dots\dots\dots \quad 3{,}000{,}000$$
$$dr \text{ Accumulated Amortization } (-xA, +A) \dots\dots\dots \quad 16{,}000{,}000$$
$$dr \text{ Loss on Disposal } (+E, -SE) \dots\dots\dots\dots\dots\dots \quad 1{,}000{,}000$$
$$cr \text{ Buildings } (-A) \dots\dots\dots\dots\dots\dots\dots\dots\dots\dots\dots \quad\quad 20{,}000{,}000$$

Loss on Disposal is recorded just like any other expense (with a debit). Had the selling price exceeded the book value, Cedar Fair would have recorded a gain on disposal (with a credit).

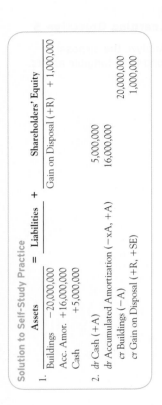

HOW'S IT GOING? **Self-Study Practice**

Assume that Cedar Fair sold the hotel described above at the end of year 16 for $5,000,000 cash. Also assume that amortization had been updated to that point in time, resulting in Accumulated Amortization of $16,000,000 at the time of sale. Complete the accounting equation effects and the journal entry for this disposal below.

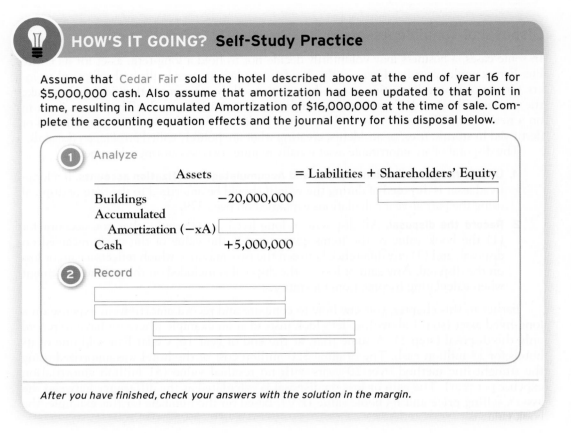

After you have finished, check your answers with the solution in the margin.

INTANGIBLE ASSETS

Intangible assets are long-lived assets that lack physical substance. Their existence is indicated by legal documents of the types described below.

- **Trademarks.** A **trademark** is a special name, image, or slogan identified with a product or company, like the name Kleenex or the image of McDonald's golden arches. The symbol ® signifies a trademark registered with the Canadian Intellectual Property Office and ™ indicates an unregistered trademark. Both types of trademark are considered intangible assets.

- **Copyrights.** A **copyright** gives the owner the exclusive right to publish, use, and sell a literary, musical, artistic, or dramatic work for a period not exceeding 50 years after the author's death. Some countries' copyright laws extend this period to 70 years. The book you are reading is copyrighted. It is illegal, therefore, for an instructor to copy several chapters from this book and hand them out in class without first obtaining permission from the copyright owner.

- **Patents.** A **patent** is an exclusive right granted by the federal government for a period of 20 years, typically to whoever invents a new product or discovers a new process. The patent declares the owner to be the only one who can use, manufacture, or sell the patented item. This protection is intended to encourage people to be inventive because it prevents others from simply copying innovations until after the inventor has had time to profit from the new product or process. One of the first roller-coaster patents was granted in 1884 for what was then called a "gravity pleasure road."

Learning Objective 6

Analyze the acquisition, use, and disposal of long-lived intangible assets.

YOU SHOULD KNOW

Trademark: A special name, image, or slogan identified with a product or company.

Copyright: A form of protection provided to the original authors of literary, musical, artistic, dramatic, and other works of authorship.

Patent: A right to exclude others from making, using, selling, or importing an invention.

- **Licensing rights. Licensing rights** are limited permissions to use something according to specific terms and conditions. Your university or college likely has obtained the licensing right to make computer programs available for use on your campus network. A licensing right also allows Cedar Fair to showcase SNOOPY® at its parks.

- **Franchises. A franchise** is a contractual right to sell certain products or services, use certain trademarks, or perform activities in a geographical region. For example, a business can buy franchise rights that allow it to use the Tim Hortons name, store format, recipes, and ingredients by paying a franchise fee ranging from $430,000 to $480,000 per store.[2]

- **Goodwill. Goodwill** tops the charts as the most frequently reported intangible asset. It encompasses lots of good stuff like a favourable location, an established customer base, a great reputation, and successful business operations. Although many companies have probably built up their own goodwill, GAAP do not allow it to be reported as an intangible asset on the balance sheet unless it has been purchased from another company. To understand the reasons behind this, keep reading. We explain them in the next section.

Acquisition, Use, and Disposal

Acquisition   The costs of intangible assets are recorded as assets only if they have been purchased. If an intangible asset is being self-constructed or internally developed, its costs generally are reported as **research and development expenses**. The primary reason that the cost of self-developed intangibles is reported as an expense rather than an asset is that it's easy for people to claim that they've developed a valuable (but invisible) intangible asset. But to believe what they are saying, you really need to see some evidence that it's actually worth what they say it's worth. And that only happens when someone gives up their hard-earned cash to buy it. At that time, the purchaser records the intangible asset at its acquisition cost. This general rule applies to trademarks, copyrights, patents, licensing rights, franchises, and goodwill.

Goodwill is a particularly interesting type of intangible asset because it represents the value paid for the unidentifiable assets of another business. You might wonder how you can put a value on something you can't identify, but it is possible. When one company buys another business, the purchase price often is greater than the appraised value of all of the **net assets** of the business. Why would a company pay more for a business as a whole than it would pay if it bought the assets individually? The answer is to obtain its goodwill.

SPOTLIGHT ON Business Decisions

Valuing Goodwill in a Business Acquisition

Most business acquisitions involve goodwill. For example, in 2006 Cedar Fair bought five theme parks from Paramount Parks. The total purchase price that Cedar Fair agreed to pay ($1.2 billion) exceeded the fair value of Paramount's net assets ($890 million). As shown below, Cedar Fair paid this extra $310 million to acquire the goodwill associated with the theme parks' businesses.

Cedar Fair Purchase of Five Paramount Parks Theme Parks (in millions)		
Purchase price		$1,200
Assets purchased and liabilities assumed		
Current assets	$ 70	
Property and equipment	1,000	
Intangible assets	80	
Debt and other liabilities	(260)	
Net assets, at fair value		890
Goodwill		$ 310

Use The accounting rules that apply to the use of intangible assets, after they have been purchased, depend on whether the intangible asset has a limited or unlimited life.

- **Limited life.** The cost of intangible assets with a limited life (copyrights, patents, licensing rights, and franchises) is amortized, usually on a straight-line basis, over each period of useful life. Most companies do not estimate a residual value for their intangible assets because, unlike tangible assets that can be sold as scrap, intangibles usually have no value at the end of their useful lives. Amortization is reported as an expense each period on the income statement and also is subtracted directly from the applicable intangible asset accounts on the balance sheet. In contrast to tangible assets, a separate accumulated amortization account is seldom used for intangibles.

  To illustrate, assume Cedar Fair purchased a patent for an uphill water-coaster for $800,000 and intends to use it for 20 years. Each year, the company would record $40,000 in Amortization Expense ($800,000 ÷ 20 years). The effect of this amortization and the journal entry to record it follow:

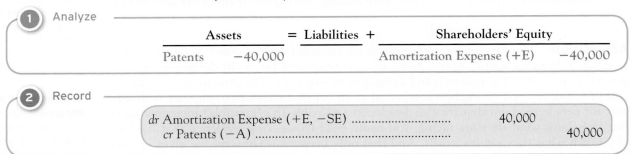

① Analyze

Assets	= Liabilities +	Shareholders' Equity
Patents −40,000		Amortization Expense (+E) −40,000

② Record

dr Amortization Expense (+E, −SE)	40,000	
cr Patents (−A)		40,000

- **Unlimited life.** Intangibles with unlimited or indefinite lives (trademarks and goodwill) are not amortized.

All intangible assets are tested at least annually for possible impairment, just like long-lived tangible assets. If an intangible asset is impaired, its book value is written down (reduced) to its fair value and the amount of the reduction is reported as an expense. For example, in 2010, Cedar Fair determined that declining economic conditions had impaired its Goodwill and Other Intangible Assets by approximately $65 million. These assets were written down on the balance sheet to their remaining fair value of $287 million (shown in Exhibit 9.1 on page 369), with the $65 million reduction reported as an operating expense on the income statement (shown in Exhibit 9.2).

Disposal Just like long-lived tangible assets, disposals of intangible assets result in gains (or losses) if the amounts received on disposal are greater than (less than) their book values.

The accounting rules for long-lived tangible and intangible assets are summarized and compared in the Homework Helper section on page 393.

SPOTLIGHT ON THE WORLD

Differences between ASPE and IFRS

IFRS differ from ASPE in many ways, particularly when accounting for tangible and intangible assets. Two of the most significant differences are

1. ASPE requires tangible and intangible assets to be recorded at cost and not revalued for later increases in asset values. In contrast, IFRS allows companies the option of reporting these assets at fair values (e.g., appraisals), provided they use the fair value method consistently each year.

2. IFRS requires companies to capitalize costs of developing intangible assets, such as prototypes or models for making new products or tools. ASPE generally expenses such development costs because of the uncertainty of their ultimate value.

As countries continue to adopt IFRS, you should carefully read the financial statement notes of companies that you analyze. Cedar Fair chose to use historical costs, but it could have chosen to use fair value instead.

TURNOVER ANALYSIS

A primary goal of financial analysts is to evaluate how well management uses long-lived tangible assets to generate revenues. The fixed asset turnover ratio provides a good measure of this aspect of managerial performance. It is calculated as shown in the table below. The denominator uses the value of average net fixed assets over the same period as the revenues in the numerator. You can calculate the average net fixed assets by summing the beginning and ending balances in fixed assets (net of accumulated amortization) and dividing by 2.

Learning Objective 7

Interpret the fixed asset turnover ratio.

ACCOUNTING DECISION TOOLS

Name of Measure	Formula	What It Tells You
Fixed asset turnover ratio	$\dfrac{\text{Net Sales Revenue}}{\text{Average Net Fixed Assets}}$	• Indicates dollars of sales generated for each dollar invested in fixed assets (long-lived tangible assets) • A higher ratio implies greater efficiency

The fixed asset turnover ratio measures the sales dollars generated by each dollar invested in (tangible) fixed assets. Just as the number of litres per kilometre provides a measure of a car's fuel efficiency, the fixed asset turnover ratio provides a measure of fixed asset operating efficiency. Generally speaking, a high or increasing turnover ratio relative to others in the industry suggests better than average use of fixed assets in the sense that each dollar of fixed assets is generating higher than average sales.

Be aware that fixed asset turnover ratios can vary across industries because capital intensity—the need for tangible assets—varies widely. Compared to Cedar Fair, a company such as Yahoo! needs fewer fixed assets to generate revenues. So Yahoo! is likely to have a high turnover ratio compared to Cedar Fair or Six Flags, which must invest considerable money in fixed assets to attract customers. Exhibit 9.5 shows the fixed asset turnover ratios for the three companies in 2009. Practise computing this ratio and comparing it to prior periods by trying the Self-Study Practice that follows the exhibit.

EXHIBIT 9.5   Summary of Fixed Asset Turnover Ratio Analyses

Company		Relevant Information (in millions)		2009 Fixed Asset Turnover Calculation
		2009	2008	
Cedar fair. L.P.	Net sales	$ 920	$1,000	$\dfrac{\$920}{(\$1,750 + \$1,800)/2} = 0.52$
	Net fixed assets	1,750	1,800	
Six Flags	Net sales	$ 913	$1,020	$\dfrac{\$913}{(\$1,478 + \$1,560)/2} = 0.60$
	Net fixed assets	1,478	1,560	
YAHOO!	Net sales	$6,460	$7,210	$\dfrac{\$6,460}{(\$1,427 + \$1,536)/2} = 4.36$
	Net fixed assets	1,427	1,536	

Solution to Self-Study Practice

a. $\dfrac{\$1,000}{(\$1,800 + \$1,940)/2} = 0.53$

b. Cedar Fair's fixed asset turnover decreased slightly in 2009.

 HOW'S IT GOING? Self-Study Practice

Cedar Fair reported net fixed assets of $1,940 (million) at December 31, 2007.

a. Use this information, along with that in Exhibit 9.5, to calculate Cedar Fair's fixed asset turnover ratio in 2008.

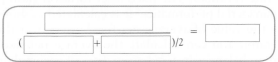

$$\frac{\boxed{}}{(\boxed{} + \boxed{})/2} = \boxed{}$$

b. Did Cedar Fair's fixed asset turnover improve or decline from 2008 (calculated in a) to 2009 (shown in Exhibit 9.5)?

After you have finished, check your answers with the solution in the margin.

Learning Objective 8

Describe factors to consider when comparing companies' long-lived assets.

COACH'S TIP

For tips and practice involving the calculations in Exhibit 9.6, try S9-7 at the end of this chapter.

IMPACT OF AMORTIZATION DIFFERENCES

Just as differences in the nature of business operations affect financial analyses and the conclusions you draw from them, so too do differences in amortization. Amortization varies from one company to the next as a result of differences in amortization methods, estimated useful lives, and estimated residual values. In this section, we present a simple example to show how different amortization methods can affect financial analysis throughout the life of a long-lived asset. Do not be fooled by the simplicity of the example. Differences in amortization can have a significant impact in the real world.

Assume that Cedar Fair and Six Flags each acquired a new roller coaster at the beginning of the year for $15.5 million. The two companies estimate that the roller coasters will have residual values of $1.5 million at the end of their seven-year useful lives. Assume too that everything about the roller coasters is identical. However, Cedar Fair uses the straight-line amortization method and Six Flags uses the double-declining-balance method. Exhibit 9.6 shows the yearly amortization reported by the two companies. Notice that early in the asset's life, before year 4, the straight-line amortization expense reported by Cedar Fair is less than the declining-balance amortization expense reported by Six Flags. Thus, even if the two companies attract exactly the same number of customers and earn exactly the same total revenues, their reported net incomes will differ each year simply because they use two different (but equally acceptable) methods of amortization. This example shows why a user of financial statements needs to understand the accounting methods companies use.

These differences in amortization affect more than just amortization expense, however. Taking this example one step further, assume that the two companies sell the roller coasters at the

---

EXHIBIT 9.6   **Straight-Line versus Double-Declining-Balance Amortization Schedules**

CEDAR FAIR (STRAIGHT-LINE)				SIX FLAGS (DOUBLE-DECLINING-BALANCE)		
Amortization Expense	Accumulated Amortization	Book Value	Year	Amortization Expense	Accumulated Amortization	Book Value
$2,000,000	$ 2,000,000	$13,500,000	1	$4,429,000	$ 4,429,000	$11,071,000
2,000,000	4,000,000	11,500,000	2	3,163,000	7,592,000	7,908,000
2,000,000	6,000,000	9,500,000	3	2,259,000	9,851,000	5,649,000
2,000,000	8,000,000	7,500,000	4	1,614,000	11,465,000	4,035,000
2,000,000	10,000,000	5,500,000	5	1,153,000	12,618,000	2,882,000
2,000,000	12,000,000	3,500,000	6	823,000	13,441,000	2,059,000
2,000,000	14,000,000	1,500,000	7	559,000	14,000,000	1,500,000

end of year 4 for $6,000,000. Because the disposal occurs on the last day of the year, the companies will record a full year of amortization prior to the disposal. Thus, at the time of disposal, Cedar Fair's roller coaster will have a book value of $7,500,000, but Six Flags' roller coaster will have a book value of $4,035,000 (see the highlighted line in Exhibit 9.6). To account for the disposal at the end of year 4, the companies record what they received, remove what they gave up (the book value of the asset), and recognize a gain or loss for the difference between what was received and what was given up. Exhibit 9.7 shows the calculations for the two companies.

EXHIBIT 9.7 **Calculation of Gain/Loss on Disposal**

	Cedar Fair	Six Flags
Selling price	$ 6,000,000	$6,000,000
Book value (see Exhibit 9.6)	(7,500,000)	(4,035,000)
Gain (loss) on disposal	$(1,500,000)	$1,965,000

Based on the information in Exhibit 9.7, which company appears to be better managed? Someone who does not understand accounting is likely to say that Six Flags is better managed because it reported a gain on disposal whereas Cedar Fair reported a loss. You know that cannot be right, however, because both companies experienced exactly the same events. They bought the same asset at the same cost ($15.5 million) and sold it for the same amount of money ($6 million). The only difference between them is that Cedar Fair reported less amortization over the years leading up to the disposal, so its roller coaster had a larger book value at the time of disposal. Six Flags reported more amortization, so its roller coaster had a smaller book value at the time of disposal. As a financial statement user, you should realize that any gain or loss on disposal that is reported on the income statement tells you as much about the method used to amortize the asset as about management's apparent ability to successfully negotiate the sale of long-lived assets.

Although the previous example concerned different amortization methods, the same effects can occur for two companies that use the same amortization method but different estimated useful lives or residual values. Useful lives can vary for several reasons, including differences in (1) the type of equipment each company uses, (2) the frequency of repairs and maintenance, (3) the frequency and duration of use, and (4) the degree of conservatism in management's estimates. How large can these differences be? Even within the same industry, sizable differences can occur. The notes to the financial statements of various companies in the airline industry, for example, reveal the following differences in the estimated useful lives of airplanes and other flight equipment:

Company	Estimated Life (in years)
US Airways	Up to 30
Air Canada	Up to 25
Alaska Airlines	Up to 20
Singapore Airlines	Up to 15

Some analysts try to sidestep such differences in amortization calculations by focusing on financial measures that exclude the effects of amortization. One popular measure is called **EBITDA** (pronounced something like *e bit duh*), which stands for "earnings before interest, taxes, depreciation, and amortization." Analysts calculate EBITDA by starting with net income and then adding back depreciation and amortization expense (as well as nonoperating expenses such as interest and taxes). The idea is that this measure allows analysts to conduct financial analyses without having to deal with possible differences in depreciation and amortization.

SUPPLEMENT 9A: Natural Resources

Industries such as oil and gas, mining, and timber harvesting rely significantly on a third category of long-lived assets called *natural resources*. These natural resources, whether in the form of oil wells, mineral deposits, or timber tracts, provide the raw materials for products that are

YOU SHOULD KNOW

EBITDA: An abbreviation for "earnings before interest, taxes, depreciation, and amortization," which is a measure of operating performance that some managers and analysts use in place of net income.

sold by companies like ExxonMobil and International Paper. When a company first acquires or develops a natural resource, the cost of the natural resource is recorded in conformity with the cost principle. As the natural resource is used up, its acquisition cost must be split among the periods in which revenues are earned in conformity with the matching principle. The term **depletion** describes the process of allocating a natural resource's cost over the period of its extraction or harvesting. The units-of-production method is often used to compute depletion.

YOU SHOULD KNOW

Depletion: The process of allocating a natural resource's cost over the period of its extraction or harvesting.

Depletion is similar to the concepts of amortization discussed earlier in the chapter for tangible and intangible assets, with one important exception. When a natural resource such as timberland is depleted, the company obtains inventory (logs). Because depletion of the natural resource is necessary to obtain the inventory, the depletion computed during a period is added to the cost of the inventory, not expensed in the period. For example, if a timber tract costing $530,000 is depleted over its estimated cutting period based on a "cutting" rate of approximately 20 percent per year, it would be depleted by $106,000 each year. Recording this depletion would have the following effects on the company's accounting equation, which would be recorded with the journal entry shown below:

1 Analyze

Assets		= Liabilities	+ Shareholders' Equity
Timber Inventory	+106,000		
Timber Tract	−106,000		

2 Record

Timber Inventory (+A)	106,000	
Timber Tract (−A) (or Accumulated Depletion +xA, −A)		106,000

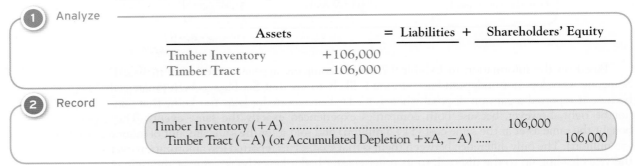

Timber Inventory remains as an asset on the balance sheet until it is sold, at which time its cost is removed from the balance sheet and reported on the income statement as an expense called *Cost of Goods Sold*.

SPOTLIGHT ON IFRS and ASPE

Topic	ASPE	IFRS
Component Allocation	• Significant separable costs of component parts are allocated to those parts when practicable	• Requires that property, plant, and equipment parts with significant costs be amortized separately. There is no mention of practicability, which results in more recognition of components than under ASPE.
Cost versus Fair Value	• Must record at cost • Adjust for amortization and impairment • Do not record increases in value	• Choose between either cost or fair value • Adjust for depreciation and impairment • If using fair value, record increases in value
Research and Development	• Expense all costs of researching and developing intangible assets	• Expense research costs but capitalize measurable costs of developing intangible assets
Goodwill Disclosure		• Under IFRS, an intangible asset is defined as an identifiable nonmonetary asset without physical substance. Goodwill is not considered to be an identifiable asset and therefore does not meet the definition of an intangible asset. Because of this, goodwill needs to be disclosed separately.

This section provides a chance to solidify your understanding of key points. It's worth your time to work through the following demonstration case, scan the chapter summary, test your understanding of key-terms, and then practise, practise, practise.

DEMONSTRATION CASE

Diversified Industries (DI) started as a house construction company. In recent years, it has expanded into heavy construction, ready-mix concrete, sand and gravel, construction supplies, and earth-moving services. The company completed the following transactions during 2012. Amounts have been simplified.

Jan. 1   Management decided to buy a 10-year-old building for $175,000 and the land on which it was situated for $130,000. DI paid $100,000 in cash and signed a note payable for the rest.

Jan. 3   DI paid $38,000 in cash for renovations to the building prior to its use.

July 10   DI paid $1,200 cash for ordinary repairs on the building.

Dec. 31   DI considered the following information to determine year-end adjustments:

a. The building will be amortized on a straight-line basis over an estimated useful life of 30 years. The estimated residual value is $33,000.

b. DI purchased another company two years ago at $100,000 more than the fair values of the net assets acquired. The goodwill has an unlimited life.

c. At the beginning of the year, DI owned equipment with a cost of $650,000 and accumulated amortization of $150,000. The equipment is being amortized using the double-declining-balance method, with a useful life of 20 years and no residual value.

d. At year-end, DI tested its long-lived assets for possible impairment of their value. Included in its equipment was a piece of old excavation equipment with a cost of $156,000 and book value of $120,000, after making the adjustment for (c). Due to its smaller size and lack of safety features, the old equipment has limited use. The future cash flows and fair value are expected to be $35,000. Goodwill was found to be not impaired.

December 31, 2012, is the end of the annual accounting period.

Required:

1. Indicate the accounts affected and the amount and direction (+ for increase and − for decrease) of the effect of each of the preceding events and required adjustments on the financial statement categories at the end of the year. Use the following headings:

Date	Assets	=	Liabilities	+	Shareholders' Equity

2. Prepare the journal entries to record each event that occurred during the year and the adjusting journal entries required at December 31.

3. Which accounts would be reported on the income statement? Where?

4. Show how the December 31, 2012, balance sheet would report these long-lived tangible and intangible assets.

5. Assuming that the company had Net Sales of $1,000,000 for the year and a book value of $500,000 for fixed assets at the beginning of the year, compute the fixed asset turnover ratio. Explain its meaning and evaluate it relative to the prior year's ratio of 1.5.

Suggested Solution

1. Effects of events (with computations in notes below the table):

Date	Assets		=	Liabilities	+	Shareholder's Equity	
Jan. 1	Cash	−100,000		Note Payable	+205,000		
	Land	+130,000					
	Building	+175,000					
Jan. 3 (Note 1)	Cash	−38,000					
	Building	+38,000					
July 10 (Note 2)	Cash	−1,200				Repairs and Maintenance Expense (+E)	−1,200
Dec. 31 (a) (Note 3)	Accumulated Amortization (+xA)	−6,000				Amortization Expense (+E)	−6,000
Dec. 31 (b) (Note 4)	No entry						
Dec. 31 (c) (Note 5)	Accumulated Amortization (+xA)	−50,000				Amortization Expense (+E)	−50,000
Dec. 31 (d) (Note 6)	Equipment	−85,000				Impairment Loss (+E)	−85,000

Notes

(1) Capitalize the $38,000 expenditure because it is necessary to prepare the asset for use.

(2) This is an ordinary repair and should be expensed.

(3)

Cost of building		Straight-line amortization (building)
Initial payment	$175,000	($213,000 cost − $33,000 residual value) ×
Renovations prior to use	38,000	1/30 years = $6,000 annual amortization
Acquisition cost	$213,000	

(4) Goodwill has an indefinite life and is therefore not amortized. Goodwill is tested for impairment but as described later in the case, was found to be not impaired.

(5) Double-declining-balance amortization (equipment)

($650,000 cost − $150,000 accumulated amortization) × 2/20 years = $50,000 amortization for the year.

(6) Asset impairment test

The book value of the old equipment ($120,000) exceeds expected future cash flows ($35,000). The asset has become impaired, so it needs to be written down to its fair value:

Impairment loss:	
Book Value	$120,000
Fair Value	(35,000)
Impairment Loss	$ 85,000

2. Journal entries for events during the year:

Jan. 1, 2012	dr Land (+A	130,000	
	dr Building (+A	175,000	
	cr Cash (−A		100,000
	cr Note Payable (+L		205,000
Jan. 3, 2012	dr Building (+A	38,000	
	cr Cash (−A		38,000
July 10, 2012	dr Repairs and Maintenance Expense (+E, −SE)	1,200	
	cr Cash (−A		1,200

Adjusting journal entries at December 31, 2012:

a.	dr Amortization Expense (+E, −SE)	6,000	
	cr Accumulated Amortization—Building (+xA, −A)		6,000

390 CHAPTER 9 Reporting and Interpreting Long-Lived Tangible and Intangible Assets

b. No adjusting journal entry required because goodwill is assumed to have an unlimited (or indefinite) life.

c. *dr* Amortization Expense (+E, −SE... 50,000
    cr Accumulated Amortization—Equipment (+xA, −A)...... 50,000

d. *dr* Impairment Loss (+E, −SE.. 85,000
    cr Equipment (−A.. 85,000

3. The income statement would report Amortization Expense, Repairs and Maintenance Expense, and Impairment Loss as operating expenses included in the computation of Income from Operations.

4. Partial balance sheet, December 31, 2012:

Assets	
Property, Plant, and Equipment	
Land	$130,000
Building	213,000
Equipment	565,000*
Property, Plant, and Equipment, at cost	908,000
Less: Accumulated Amortization	(206,000)†
Property, Plant, and Equipment, net	702,000
Goodwill	100,000

* $565,000 = $650,000 − $85,000
† $206,000 = $6,000 + $150,000 + $50,000

5. Fixed asset turnover ratio:

$$\frac{\text{Net Sales}}{(\text{Beginning Net Fixed Asset Balance} + \text{Ending Net Fixed Asset Balance})/2} = \frac{\$1,000,000}{(\$500,000 + \$702,000)/2} = 1.66$$

The fixed asset turnover ratio measures the company's efficiency at using its investment in property, plant, and equipment to generate sales. Approximately $1.66 of sales were generated for each dollar of fixed assets, which is an improvement over last year's 1.5.

CHAPTER SUMMARY

Define, classify, and explain the nature of long-lived assets. p. 368   **LO1**

- Long-lived assets are those that a business retains for long periods of time for use in the course of normal operations rather than for sale. They may be divided into tangible assets (land, buildings, equipment) and intangible assets (including goodwill, patents, and franchises).

Apply the cost principle to the acquisition of long-lived assets. p. 369   **LO2**

- The acquisition cost of property, plant, and equipment is the cash-equivalent purchase price plus all reasonable and necessary expenditures made to acquire and prepare the asset for its intended use. Expenditures made after the asset is in use are either expensed or capitalized as a cost of the asset:
  a. Expenditures are expensed if they recur frequently, involve relatively small amounts, and do not directly lengthen the asset's useful life. These are considered ordinary repairs and maintenance expense.
  b. Expenditures are capitalized as a cost of the asset if they provide benefits for one or more accounting periods beyond the current period. This category includes extraordinary repairs, replacements, and additions.

Apply various amortization methods as economic benefits are used up over time. p. 375   **LO3**

- In conformity with the matching principle, the cost of long-lived tangible assets (less any estimated residual value) is allocated to amortization expense over each period benefited by the assets.
- Because of amortization, the book value of an asset declines over time and net income is reduced by the amount of the expense.
- Common amortization methods include straight-line (a constant amount over time), units-of-production (a variable amount over time), and double-declining-balance (a decreasing amount over time).

LO4 **Explain the effect of asset impairment on the financial statements.** p. 380

- When events or changes in circumstances reduce the estimated future cash flows of a long-lived asset below its book value, the book value of the asset should be written down, with the amount of the write-down reported as an impairment loss.

LO5 **Analyze the disposal of long-lived tangible assets.** p. 381

When assets are disposed of through sale or abandonment,

- Record additional amortization arising since the last adjustment was made.
- Remove the cost of the old asset and its related accumulated amortization.
- Recognize the cash proceeds (if any).
- Recognize any gains or losses when the asset's book value is not equal to the cash received.

LO6 **Analyze the acquisition, use, and disposal of long-lived intangible assets.** p. 382

- Intangible assets are recorded at cost, but only when purchased. The costs of most internally developed intangible assets are expensed as research and development when incurred.
- Intangibles are reported at book value on the balance sheet.
- Amortization is calculated for intangibles with limited useful lives, using the straight-line method.
- Intangibles with unlimited useful lives, including goodwill, are not amortized, but are reviewed for impairment.

LO7 **Interpret the fixed asset turnover ratio.** p. 385

- The fixed asset turnover ratio measures the company's efficiency at using its investment in property, plant, and equipment to generate sales. Higher turnover ratios imply greater efficiency.

LO8 **Describe factors to consider when comparing companies' long-lived assets.** p. 386

- Companies in different industries require different levels of investment in long-lived assets. Beyond that, you should consider whether differences exist in amortization methods, estimated useful lives, and estimated residual values, which can affect the book value of long-lived assets as well as ratios calculated using these book values and any gains or losses reported at the time of asset disposal.

ACCOUNTING DECISION TOOLS

Name of Measure	Formula	What It Tells You
Fixed asset turnover ratio	$\dfrac{\text{Net Sales Revenue}}{\text{Average Net Fixed Assets}}$	• Dollars of sales generated for each dollar invested in (tangible) fixed assets • A higher ratio implies greater efficiency

KEY TERMS

Amortizable Cost p. 375

Amortization p. 374

Book (or Carrying) Value p. 374

Capital Cost Allowance p. 379

Capitalize p. 369

Copyright p. 382

Declining-Balance Amortization Method p. 377

Depletion p. 388

Depreciation p. 374

EBITDA p. 387

Extraordinary Repairs p. 373

Franchise p. 383

Goodwill p. 383

Impairment p. 380

Licensing Right p. 383

Long-Lived Assets p. 368

Net Assets p. 383

Ordinary Repairs and Maintenance p. 373

Patent p. 382

Research and Development Expenses p. 383

Residual (or Salvage) Value p. 375

Straight-Line Amortization Method p. 376

Trademark p. 382

Units-of-Production Amortization Method p. 376

Useful Life p. 375

See complete definitions in the glossary in the back of this text.

HOMEWORK HELPER

Stage	Subject	Tangible Assets	Intangible Assets
Acquire	**Purchased asset**	Capitalize all related costs	Capitalize all related costs
Use	**Repairs and maintenance**		
	Ordinary	Expense related costs	Not applicable
	Extraordinary	Capitalize related costs	Not applicable
	Amortization		
	Limited life	One of several methods: • Straight-line • Units-of-production • Declining-balance	Straight-line method
	Unlimited life	Do not amortize (e.g., land)	Do not amortize (e.g., goodwill)
	Impairment test	Write down if necessary	Write down if necessary
Dispose	**Report gain (loss) when . . .**	Receive more (less) on disposal than book value	Receive more (less) on disposal than book value

Alternative terms

- Declining-balance amortization methods are also called *accelerated methods*.

Helpful reminders

- Costs that benefit future periods are capitalized as assets. Costs that benefit the current period are recorded as expenses.
- See Exhibit 9.2 for an income statement showing where to report Amortization Expense, Impairment Losses, and Losses (Gains) on Disposal of Assets.
- Declining-balance amortization methods subtract Accumulated Amortization, not residual value, from the asset's cost. For this reason, take extra care to ensure that you stop depreciating the asset when its book value equals its residual value.

Frequent mistakes

- Amortization does not represent a decline in the current value of an asset; declines in asset values are recorded as impairment losses, not amortization. The purpose of amortization is to allocate the cost of a long-lived asset to each period in which the asset is used to generate revenue.
- When recording an asset disposal, remove its cost and accumulated amortization separately, rather than removing just its book value from the asset's account.

Practice Material

QUESTIONS (Ⓢ Symbol indicates questions that require analysis from more than one perspective.)

1. Define *long-lived assets*. What are the two common categories of long-lived assets? Describe each.

2. Under the cost principle, what amounts should be recorded as a cost of a long-lived asset?

3. What is the term for recording costs as assets rather than as expenses? Describe how the decision to record costs as assets rather than expenses affects the balance sheet and income statement in the period the costs are incurred and in future periods.

4. Waste Management, Inc., regularly incurs costs (e.g., salaries, legal fees, travel) to find new locations for landfill sites. What reasons support capitalizing these costs? What reasons support expensing these costs? Ⓢ

5. Distinguish between ordinary repairs and extraordinary repairs. How is each accounted for?

6. Describe the relationship between the matching principle and accounting for long-lived assets.

7. Why are different amortization methods allowed?

8. In computing amortization, three values must be known or estimated. Identify and describe each.

9. What type of amortization expense pattern is used under each of the following methods and when is its use appropriate?
   a. The straight-line method.
   b. The units-of-production method.
   c. The double-declining-balance method.

10. After merging with Northwest Airlines, Delta Airlines increased the estimated useful life and increased the estimated residual value of its flight equipment. All else equal, how would each of these changes affect Delta's Amortization Expense and Net Income? 🌐

11. What is an *asset impairment*? How is it accounted for?

12. What is *book value*? When equipment is sold for more than book value, how is the transaction recorded? How is it recorded when the selling price is less than book value?

13. Define *goodwill*. When is it appropriate to record goodwill as an intangible asset? When is its value decreased?

14. Blue Sky Flights reports the cost of its aircraft in a single category called *Flight Equipment*. What impact will IFRS have on this aspect of Blue Sky's accounting? 🌐

15. How is the fixed asset turnover ratio computed? Explain its meaning.

16. Johnson & Johnson, the maker of Tylenol, uses U.S. GAAP. Bayer, the maker of Aspirin, uses IFRS. Explain what complications might arise when comparing the Property, Plant, and Equipment category of these two companies. 🌐

17. Over what period should an addition to an existing long-lived asset be amortized? Explain.

18. (Supplement 9A) How does depletion affect the balance sheet and income statement? Why is depletion accounted for in a manner that differs from amortization?

Multiple-choice questions and corresponding answers can be found on Connect.

MINI-EXERCISES

LO3 **M9-1 Computing Book Value (Straight-Line Amortization)**

Calculate the book value of a two-year-old machine that cost $200,000, has an estimated residual value of $40,000, and has an estimated useful life of four years. The company uses straight-line amortization.

LO3 **M9-2 Computing Book Value (Units-of-Production Amortization)**

Calculate the book value of a two-year-old machine that cost $200,000, has an estimated residual value of $40,000, and has an estimated useful life of 20,000 machine hours. The company uses units-of-production amortization and ran the machine 3,000 hours in year 1 and 8,000 hours in year 2.

LO3 **M9-3 Computing Book Value (Double-Declining-Balance Amortization)**

Calculate the book value of a two-year-old machine that cost $200,000, has an estimated residual value of $40,000, and has an estimated useful life of four years. The company uses double-declining-balance amortization. Round to the nearest dollar.

LO3 **M9-4 Calculating Partial-Year Amortization**

Calculate the amount of amortization to report during the year ended December 31, 2010, for equipment that was purchased at a cost of $33,000 on September 1, 2010. The equipment has an estimated residual value of $3,000 and an estimated useful life of five years or 20,000 hours. Assume the equipment was used for 1,000 hours from September 1 to December 31 and the company uses (*a*) straight-line, (*b*) double-declining-balance, or (*c*) units-of-production amortization.

LO4 **M9-5 Understanding the Significance of Asset Impairment Losses**

General Motors Corporation

Assume General Motors Corporation reported a Loss from Operations of $20 billion. The following asset impairment losses were included among its operating expenses:

Goodwill impairment	$ 610 million
HUMMER equipment impairment	290 million
Saab equipment impairment	500 million
Other impairment losses	1,100 million
Total impairment losses	$2,500 million

Do General Motors' asset impairment losses seem significant in terms of total dollar value? What percentage of the company's 2011 operating loss was explained by asset impairments? Why might GM write down its HUMMER and Saab production equipment, but not its Chevrolet production equipment?

M9-6 Recording the Disposal of a Long-Lived Asset

LO5

Prepare journal entries to record these transactions: (*a*) Mortell Limited disposed of two computers at the end of their useful lives. The computers had cost $4,800 and their Accumulated Amortization was $4,800. No residual value was received. (*b*) Assume the same information as (*a*), except that Accumulated Amortization, updated to the date of disposal, was $3,600.

M9-7 Reporting and Recording the Disposal of a Long-Lived Asset (Straight-Line Amortization)

LO5

As part of a major renovation at the beginning of the year, Hunter Pharmaceuticals, Inc., sold shelving units (store fixtures) that were 10 years old for $1,000 cash. The shelves originally cost $6,400 and had been amortized on a straight-line basis over an estimated useful life of 10 years with an estimated residual value of $400. Assuming that amortization has been recorded to the date of sale, show the effect of the disposal on the accounting equation. Prepare the journal entry to record the sale of the shelving units.

M9-8 Capitalizing versus Expensing Intangible Asset Costs

LO6

Most highly visible companies spend significant amounts of money to protect their intellectual property, ensuring that no one uses this property without direct permission. For example, to include logos throughout this book, we had to obtain written permission from each company—a process that stretched over nearly a year and often resulted in requests being denied. Discuss whether companies should capitalize or expense the money paid to employees who evaluate requests for use of their logos and who search for instances where the companies' intellectual property has been used without permission. Draw an analogy to similar costs incurred for employees responsible for the use and upkeep of tangible assets.

M9-9 Computing Goodwill and Patents

LO6

Taste-T Company has been in business for 30 years and has developed a large group of loyal restaurant customers. Downter's Foods made an offer to buy Taste-T Company for $6,000,000. The market value of Taste-T's recorded assets, net of liabilities, on the date of the offer is $5,600,000. Taste-T also holds a patent for a fluting machine that the company invented (the patent with a market value of $200,000 was never recorded by Taste-T because it was developed internally). How much has Downter's Foods included for intangibles in its offer of $6,000,000? Assuming Taste-T accepts this offer, which company will report Goodwill on its balance sheet?

M9-10 Computing and Evaluating the Fixed Asset Turnover Ratio

LO7

The following information was reported by Amuse Yourself Parks (AYP) for 2009:

Net fixed assets (beginning of year)	$8,450,000
Net fixed assets (end of year)	8,250,000
Net sales for the year	4,175,000
Net income for the year	1,700,000

Compute the company's fixed asset turnover ratio for the year. What can you say about AYP's fixed asset turnover ratio when compared to Cedar Fair's 2009 ratio in Exhibit 9.5?

 Cedar fair. L.P.

EXERCISES

Practise and learn online with Connect.

E9-1 Preparing a Classified Balance Sheet

LO1, 7

Assume the following is a list of account titles and amounts (in millions) reported at December 28, 2011, by Hasbro, Inc., a leading manufacturer of games, toys, and interactive entertainment software for children and families:

Buildings and Improvements	$195	Goodwill	$475
Prepaids and Other Current Assets	171	Machinery and Equipment	413
Allowance for Doubtful Accounts	32	Accumulated Amortization	403
Other Noncurrent Assets	200	Inventories	301
Cash and Cash Equivalents	630	Other Intangibles	568
Accounts Receivable	644	Land and Improvements	7

Required:

1. Prepare the asset section of a classified balance sheet for Hasbro, Inc., assuming Hasbro follows ASPE.

2. Assuming that Hasbro's 2011 Net Sales Revenue was $4,022 (million) and its Net Fixed Assets was $188 (million) at December 30, 2010, calculate the fixed asset turnover ratio for 2011. Has the company generated more or less revenue from each dollar of fixed assets than in 2010, when the ratio was 20.75?

LO2, 3 **E9-2 Computing and Recording a Basket Purchase and Straight-Line Amortization**

Bridgadoon Consulting bought a building and the land on which it is located for $182,000 cash. The land is estimated to represent 70 percent of the purchase price. The company paid $22,000 for building renovations before it was ready for use.

Required:

1. Explain how the renovation costs should be accounted for.

2. Give the journal entry to record all expenditures. Assume that all transactions were for cash and they occurred at the start of the year.

3. Compute straight-line amortization on the building at the end of one year, assuming an estimated 12-year useful life and a $4,600 estimated residual value.

4. What should be the book value of the land and building at the end of year 2?

Check Figure:
[Req. 4]
Book value of land at end of year 2 = $192,000

LO2, 3 **E9-3 Determining Financial Statement Effects of an Asset Acquisition and Straight-Line Amortization**

Conover Corp. ordered a machine on January 1, 2012, at a purchase price of $30,000. On the date of delivery, January 2, 2012, the company paid $8,000 on the machine and signed a note payable for the balance. On January 3, 2012, it paid $250 for freight on the machine. On January 5, Conover paid installation costs relating to the machine amounting to $1,500. On December 31, 2012 (the end of the accounting period), Conover recorded amortization on the machine using the straight-line method with an estimated useful life of 10 years and an estimated residual value of $2,750.

Required:

1. Indicate the effects (accounts, amounts, and + or −) of each transaction (on January 1, 2, 3, and 5) on the accounting equation. Use the following schedule:

Date	Assets	=	Liabilities	+	Shareholders' Equity

2. Compute the acquisition cost of the machine.

3. Compute the amortization expense to be reported for 2012.

4. What should be the book value of the machine at the end of 2013?

LO2, 3 **E9-4 Recording Straight-Line Amortization and Repairs**

Wiater Company operates a small manufacturing facility. On January 1, 2012, an asset account for the company showed the following balances:

Manufacturing equipment	$160,000
Accumulated amortization through 2011	110,000

During the first week of January 2012, the following expenditures were incurred for repairs and maintenance:

| Routine maintenance and repairs on the equipment | $ 1,850 |
| Major overhaul of the equipment that improved efficiency | 21,000 |

The equipment is being amortized on a straight-line basis over an estimated life of 15 years with a $10,000 estimated residual value. The annual accounting period ends on December 31.

Required:

Indicate the effects (accounts, amounts, and + or −) of the following two items on the accounting equation, using the headings shown below.

1. The adjustment for amortization made at the end of 2011.
2. The two expenditures for repairs and maintenance during January 2012.

Item	Assets	=	Liabilities	+	Shareholders' Equity

E9-5 Determining Financial Statement Effects of Straight-Line Amortization and Repairs

LO2, 3

Refer to the information in E9-4.

Required:

1. Give the adjusting journal entry that would have been made at the end of 2011 for amortization on the manufacturing equipment.
2. Starting at the beginning of 2012, what is the remaining estimated life?
3. Give the journal entries to record the two expenditures for repairs and maintenance during 2012.

Check Figure:
[Req. 2]
Remaining estimated life
beginning of 2012 = 4 years

E9-6 Computing Amortization under Alternative Methods

LO3

PlasticWorks Corporation bought a machine at the beginning of the year at a cost of $12,000. The estimated useful life was five years, and the residual value was $2,000. Assume that the estimated productive life of the machine is 10,000 units. Expected annual production was: year 1, 3,000 units; year 2, 3,000 units; year 3, 2,000 units; year 4, 1,000 units; and year 5, 1,000 units.

Required:

1. Complete an amortization schedule for each of the alternative methods.
   a. Straight-line.
   b. Units-of-production.
   c. Double-declining-balance.

		Income Statement		Balance Sheet		
Year	Computation	Amortization Expense	Cost	Accumulated Amortization	Book Value
At acquisition						
1						

2. Which method will result in the highest net income in year 2? Does this higher net income mean the machine was used more efficiently under this amortization method?

E9-7 Computing Amortization under Alternative Methods

LO3

Sonin Company purchased and installed electronic payment equipment at its drive-in restaurant at the beginning of the year at a cost of $27,000. The equipment has an estimated residual value of $1,500. The equipment is expected to process 255,000 payments over its three-year useful life. Per year, expected payment transactions are 61,200, year 1; 140,250, year 2; and 53,550, year 3.

Required:

Complete an amortization schedule for each of the alternative methods:
1. Straight-line.
2. Units-of-production.
3. Double-declining-balance.

		Income Statement	Balance Sheet		
Year	Computation	Amortization Expense	Cost	Accumulated Amortization	Book Value
At acquisition					
1					

LO3

E9-8 Interpreting Management's Choice of Different Amortization Methods for Tax and Financial Reporting

FedEx Corporation

The annual report for FedEx Corporation includes the following information: For financial reporting purposes, we record depreciation and amortization of property and equipment on a straight-line basis over the asset's service life or related lease term, if shorter. For income tax purposes, depreciation is computed using accelerated methods when applicable.

Required:

Explain why FedEx uses different methods of amortization for financial reporting and tax purposes.

LO3

E9-9 Inferring Asset Age from Straight-Line Amortization

On January 1, 2012, the records of Great Grass Corp. (GGC) showed the following regarding production equipment:

Equipment (estimated residual value, $4,000)	$14,000
Accumulated Amortization (straight-line, one year)	2,000

Required:

Based on the data given, compute the estimated useful life of the equipment.

LO4

E9-10 Exploring Financial Statement Effects of Asset Impairment

Refer to E9-9.

Required:

If GGC's management estimated that the equipment had future cash flows and a fair value of only $6,800 at December 31, 2012, how would this affect GGC's balance sheet and income statement? Explain.

LO5

E9-11 Demonstrating the Effect of Book Value on Reporting an Asset Disposal

FedEx Corporation

FedEx Corporation is the world's leading express-distribution company. In addition to the world's largest fleet of all-cargo aircraft, the company uses more than 53,700 ground vehicles to pick up and deliver packages. Assume that FedEx sold a delivery truck for $16,000 that it originally purchased for $28,000. The company had recorded amortization for three years.

Required:

Check Figure:
[Req. 1(b)]
Loss on disposal = $2,000

1. Calculate the amount of gain or loss on disposal, assuming that Accumulated Amortization was: (a) $12,000, (b) $10,000, and (c) $15,000.
2. Using the following structure, indicate the effects (accounts, amounts, and + or −) for the disposal of the truck in each of the three preceding situations.

Assets	=	Liabilities	+	Shareholders' Equity

3. Based on the three preceding situations, explain how the amount of amortization recorded up to the time of disposal affects the amount of gain or loss on disposal.
4. Prepare the journal entry to record the disposal of the truck for each situation in requirement 1.

LO6

E9-12 Computing and Reporting the Acquisition and Amortization of Three Different Intangible Assets

Kreiser Company had three intangible assets at the end of 2012 (end of the accounting year):

a. A patent was purchased from J. Miller on January 1, 2012, for a cash cost of $5,640. When purchased, the patent had an estimated life of 15 years.
b. A trademark was registered with the federal government for $10,000. Management estimated that the trademark could be worth as much as $200,000 because it has an indefinite life.

c. Computer licensing rights were purchased on January 1, 2012, for $60,000. The rights are expected to have a four-year useful life to the company.

Required:

1. Compute the acquisition cost of each intangible asset.
2. Compute the amortization of each intangible for the year ended December 31, 2012.
3. Show how these assets and any related expenses should be reported on the balance sheet and income statement for 2012.

E9-13 Recording the Purchase, Amortization, and Impairment of a Patent

LO4, 6

Conrad Inc. purchased a patent for $1,000,000 for "a specialty line of patented switch plate covers and outlet plate covers specifically designed to light up automatically when the power fails." Assume the switch plate patent was purchased January 1, 2012, and it is being amortized over a period of 10 years. Assume that Conrad Inc. does not use an accumulated amortization account but instead charges amortization directly against the intangible asset account.

Required:

1. Describe the effects of the purchase and amortization of the switch plate patent on the 2012 balance sheet and income statement.
2. Give the journal entries to record the purchase and amortization of the switch plate patent in 2012.
3. After many months of unsuccessful attempts to manufacture the switch plate covers, Conrad Inc. determined the patent was significantly impaired and its book value on January 1, 2012, was written off. Describe the financial statement effects of accounting for the asset impairment and give the journal entry to record the impairment.

E9-14 Computing and Interpreting the Fixed Asset Turnover Ratio from a Financial Analyst's Perspective

LO7
Apple Inc.

Assume the following data were included in a recent Apple Inc. annual report (in millions):

	2008	2009	2010	2011
Net sales	$13,931	$19,315	$24,006	$32,479
Net property, plant, and equipment	817	1,281	1,832	2,455

Required:

1. Compute Apple's fixed asset turnover ratio for 2009, 2010, and 2011. Round your answer to one decimal place.
2. Was Apple able to maintain its strong financial performance in recent years when the economy was beginning to falter?

Check Figure:
[Req. 1]
2011 Fixed Asset Turnover
= 15.2

E9-15 Computing Amortization and Book Value for Two Years Using Alternative Amortization Methods and Interpreting the Impact on the Fixed Asset Turnover Ratio

LO3, 7

Torge Company bought a machine for $65,000 cash. The estimated useful life was five years, and the estimated residual value was $5,000. Assume that the estimated useful life in productive units is 150,000. Units actually produced were 40,000 in year 1 and 45,000 in year 2.

Required:

1. Determine the appropriate amounts to complete the following schedule. Show computations.

	Amortization Expense for		Book Value at the End of	
Method of Amortization	Year 1	Year 2	Year 1	Year 2
Straight-line				
Units-of-production				
Double-declining-balance				

2. Which method would result in the lowest net income for year 1? For year 2?
3. Which method would result in the lowest fixed asset turnover ratio for year 1? Why?

E9-16 Determining Financial Statement Effects of a Change in Estimate

Refer to E9-4.

Required:

1. Indicate the effects (accounts, amounts, and + or −) of the 2012 adjustment for amortization of the manufacturing equipment, assuming no change in the estimated life or residual value. Show computations.

Date	Assets	=	Liabilities	+	Shareholders' Equity

2. Give the adjusting entry that should be made at the end of 2012 for amortization.

E9-17 (Supplement 9A) Calculating and Reporting Depletion

Lucky Lake Oil Company (LLOC) paid $3,000,000 for an oil reserve estimated to hold 50,000 barrels of oil. Oil production is expected to be 10,000 barrels in year 1, 30,000 barrels in year 2, and 10,000 barrels in year 3. LLOC expects to begin selling barrels from its oil inventory in year 2.

Required:

Assuming these estimates are accurate, describe the amounts, financial statements, and classifications that would be used for the oil reserves and oil inventory at the end of year 1.

COACHED PROBLEMS

LO2, 3

CP9-1 Computing Acquisition Cost and Recording Amortization under Three Alternative Methods

At the beginning of the year, McCoy Company bought three used machines from Colt, Inc. The machines immediately were overhauled, installed, and started operating. Because the machines were different, each was recorded separately in the accounts.

	Machine A	Machine B	Machine C
Amount paid for asset	$6,600	$25,600	$6,400
Installation costs	300	600	200
Renovation costs prior to use	1,500	400	1,000
Repairs after production began	400	350	325

By the end of the first year, each machine had been operating 8,000 hours.

Required:

1. Compute the cost of each machine. Explain the rationale for capitalizing or expensing the various costs.

   TIP: Total cost for all three machines is $42,600.

2. Give the journal entry to record amortization expense at the end of year 1, assuming the following:

Machine	Estimates		Amortization Method
	Life	Residual Value	
A	5 years	$ 500	Straight-line
B	40,000 hours	1,000	Units-of-production
C	5 years	2,000	Double-declining-balance

TIP: Remember that the formula for double-declining-balance uses cost minus accumulated amortization (not residual value).

CP9-2 Recording and Interpreting the Disposal of Long-Lived Assets

LO5

During 2012, Bhumika Company disposed of two different assets. On January 1, 2012, prior to the assets' disposal, the accounts reflected the following:

Asset	Original Cost	Residual Value	Estimated Life	Accumulated Amortization (straight-line)
Machine A	$76,200	$4,200	15 years	$57,600 (12 years)
Machine B	20,000	3,000	8 years	12,750 (6 years)

The machines were disposed of in the following ways:

a. Machine A: Sold on January 2, 2012, for $8,200 cash.
b. Machine B: On January 2, 2012, this machine suffered irreparable damage from an accident and was removed immediately by a salvage company at no cost.

Required:

1. Give the journal entries related to the disposal of each machine at the beginning of 2012.

   TIP: When no cash is received on disposal, the loss on disposal will equal the book value of the asset at the time of disposal.

   TIP: Loss on disposal for Machine A equals $10,400.

   TIP: Loss on disposal for Machine B equals $7,250.

2. Explain the accounting rationale for the way that you recorded each disposal.

CP9-3 Analyzing and Recording Long-Lived Asset Transactions with Partial-Year Amortization

LO2, 3, 6

Palmer Cook Productions manages and operates two rock bands. The company entered into the following transactions during a recent year.

January 2	Purchased a tour bus for $80,000 by paying $20,000 cash and signing a $60,000 note.
January 8	The bus was painted with the logos of the two bands at a cost of $350, on account.
January 30	Wrote a cheque for the amount owed on account for the work completed on January 8.
February 1	Purchased new speakers and amplifiers and wrote a cheque for the full $12,000 cost.
February 8	Paid $250 cash to tune up the tour bus.
March 1	Paid $20,000 cash and signed a $190,000 note to purchase a small office building and land. An appraisal indicated that the building and land contributed equally to the total price.
March 31	Paid $90,000 cash to acquire the goodwill and certain tangible assets of KrisMyt, Inc. The fair values of the tangible assets acquired were $20,000 for band equipment and $60,000 for recording equipment.

Required:

1. Analyze the accounting equation effects and record journal entries for each of the transactions.

   TIP: Goodwill is recorded as the excess of the purchase price over the fair value of individual assets.

2. For the tangible and intangible assets acquired in the preceding transactions, determine the amount of amortization that Palmer Cook Productions should report for the quarter ended March 31. For convenience, the equipment and vehicle are amortized the same way, using the straight-line method with a useful life of five years and no residual value. The building is amortized using the double-declining-balance method, with a 10-year useful life and residual value of $20,000.

   TIP: Calculate amortization from the acquisition date to the end of the quarter.

3. Prepare a journal entry to record the amortization calculated in requirement 2.

4. What advice would you offer the company in anticipation of switching to IFRS in the future?

   TIP: Consider whether the vehicle and different types of equipment should be grouped together.

LO1, 7 **PA9-1 Preparing a Classified Balance Sheet**

The following is a list of account titles and amounts (in thousands) reported at June 30, 2012, by Darian's Dirt Bikes, Inc., a retail distributor of motorcycles:

Buildings and Improvements	$292	Goodwill	$ 79
Prepaids and Other Current Assets	120	Machinery and Equipment	646
Allowance for Doubtful Accounts	15	Accumulated Amortization	421
Other Noncurrent Assets	30	Inventories	740
Cash and Cash Equivalents	59	Other Intangibles	100
Accounts Receivable	330	Land and Improvements	23

Required:

1. Prepare the asset section of a classified balance sheet for Darian's Dirt Bikes, Inc., assuming ASPE are followed.
2. Using Darian's Dirt Bikes, Inc.'s 2012 Net Sales Revenue of $2,520 (thousand) and its Net Fixed Assets of $471 (thousand) at June 30, 2011, calculate the fixed asset turnover ratio for 2012. Has the company generated more or less revenue from each dollar of fixed assets than in 2011, when the ratio was 5.00?

LO2, 3 **PA9-2 Computing Acquisition Cost and Recording Amortization under Three Alternative Methods**

At the beginning of the year, CCZ Corporation bought three used machines from Pequita Compression Incorporated. The machines immediately were overhauled, installed, and started operating. Because the machines were different from each other, each was recorded separately in the accounts.

	Machine A	Machine B	Machine C
Cost of the asset	$10,000	$31,500	$22,000
Installation costs	1,600	2,100	800
Renovation costs prior to use	600	1,400	1,600
Repairs after production began	500	400	700

By the end of the first year, each machine had been operating 7,000 hours.

Check Figure:
[Req. 1]
Machine C total cost = $24,400

Required:

1. Compute the cost of each machine. Explain the rationale for capitalizing or expensing the various costs.
2. Give the journal entry to record amortization expense at the end of year 1, assuming the following:

Machine	Estimates		Amortization Method
	Life	Residual Value	
A	4 years	$1,000	Straight-line
B	33,000 hours	2,000	Units-of-production
C	5 years	1,400	Double-declining-balance

LO5 **PA9-3 Recording and Interpreting the Disposal of Long-Lived Assets**

During 2012, Ly Company disposed of two different assets. On January 1, 2012, prior to disposal of the assets, the accounts reflected the following:

Asset	Original Cost	Residual Value	Estimated Life	Accumulated Amortization (straight-line)
Machine A	$24,000	$2,000	5 years	$17,600 (4 years)
Machine B	59,200	3,200	14 years	48,000 (12 years)

The machines were disposed of in the following ways:

a. Machine A: Sold on January 1, 2012, for $5,750 cash.
b. Machine B: On January 1, 2012, this machine suffered irreparable damage from an accident and was removed immediately by a salvage company at no cost.

Required:

1. Give the journal entries related to the disposal of each machine at the beginning of 2012.
2. Explain the accounting rationale for the way that you recorded each disposal.

PA9-4 Analyzing and Recording Long-Lived Asset Transactions with Partial-Year Amortization

LO2, 3, 6

Casting Crown Construction entered into the following transactions during a recent year:

January 2	Purchased a bulldozer for $200,000 by paying $20,000 cash and signing a $180,000 note.
January 3	Replaced the steel tracks on the bulldozer at a cost of $20,000, purchased on account.
January 30	Wrote a cheque for the amount owed on account for the work completed on January 3.
February 1	Replaced the seat on the bulldozer and wrote a cheque for the full $600 cost.
March 1	Paid $2,400 cash for the rights to use computer software for a two-year period.

Required:

1. Analyze the accounting equation effects and record journal entries for each of the transactions.
2. For the tangible and intangible assets acquired in the preceding transactions, determine the amount of depreciation and amortization that Casting Crown Construction should report for the quarter ended March 31. The equipment is amortized using the double-declining-balance method with a useful life of five years and $40,000 residual value.
3. Prepare a journal entry to record the amortization calculated in requirement 2.
4. What advice would you offer the company in anticipation of switching to IFRS in the future?

Check Figure:
[Req. 3]
Total amortization expense
= $22,100

PA9-5 Recording Transactions and Adjustments for Tangible and Intangible Assets

LO1, 2, 3, 4, 5, 6

The following transactions and adjusting entries were completed by Gravure Graphics International, a paper-packaging company. The company uses straight-line amortization for trucks and other vehicles, double-declining-balance amortization for buildings, and straight-line amortization for patents.

January 2, 2011	Paid $95,000 cash to purchase storage shed components.
January 3, 2011	Paid $5,000 cash to have the storage shed erected. The storage shed has an estimated life of 10 years and a residual value of $10,000.
April 1, 2011	Paid $38,000 cash to purchase a pickup truck for use in the business. The truck has an estimated useful life of five years and a residual value of $8,000.
May 13, 2011	Paid $250 cash for repairs to the pickup truck.
July 1, 2011	Paid $20,000 cash to purchase patent rights on a new paper bag manufacturing process. The patent is estimated to have a remaining useful life of five years.
December 31, 2011	Recorded amortization on the pickup truck, storage shed, and patent.
June 30, 2012	Sold the pickup truck for $33,000 cash. (Record the amortization on the truck prior to recording its disposal.)
December 31, 2012	Recorded amortization on the storage shed. Determined that the patent was impaired and wrote off its remaining book value (i.e., wrote down the book value to zero).

Required:

Give the journal entries required on each of the above dates.

LO1, 7   **PB9-1 Preparing a Classified Balance Sheet**

The following is a list of account titles and amounts (in thousands) reported at December 31, 2012, by Megan's Veterinary Clinic:

Buildings and Improvements	$95	Goodwill	$45
Prepaids and Other Current Assets	71	Machinery and Equipment	43
Allowance for Doubtful Accounts	3	Accumulated Amortization	43
Other Noncurrent Assets	20	Inventories	31
Cash and Cash Equivalents	63	Other Intangibles	58
Accounts Receivable	64	Land and Improvements	7

Required:

1. Prepare the asset section of a classified balance sheet for Megan's Veterinary Clinic, assuming ASPE are followed.

2. Using Megan's Veterinary Clinic's 2012 Net Sales Revenue of $402 (thousand) and its Net Fixed Assets of $118 (thousand) at December 31, 2011, calculate the fixed asset turnover ratio for 2012. Has the company generated more or less revenue from each dollar of fixed assets than in 2011, when the ratio was 2.75?

Check Figure:
[Req. 2]
2012 Fixed Asset Turnover
= 3.65

LO2, 3   **PB9-2 Computing Acquisition Cost and Recording Amortization under Three Alternative Methods**

At the beginning of the year, Oakmountain Company bought three used machines from Canadian Manufacturing, Inc. The machines immediately were overhauled, installed, and started operating. Because the machines were different from each other, each was recorded separately in the accounts.

	Machine A	Machine B	Machine C
Amount paid for asset	$19,600	$10,100	$9,800
Installation costs	300	500	200
Renovation costs prior to use	100	300	600
Repairs after production began	220	900	480

By the end of the first year, each machine had been operating 4,000 hours.

Required:

1. Compute the cost of each machine. Explain the rationale for capitalizing or expensing the various costs.

2. Give the journal entry to record amortization expense at the end of year 1, assuming the following:

	Estimates		
Machine	Life	Residual Value	Amortization Method
A	7 years	$1,100	Straight-line
B	40,000 hours	900	Units-of-production
C	4 years	2,000	Double-declining-balance

LO5   **PB9-3 Recording and Interpreting the Disposal of Long-Lived Assets**

During 2012, Rayon Corporation disposed of two different assets. On January 1, 2012, prior to disposal of the assets, the accounts reflected the following:

Asset	Original Cost	Residual Value	Estimated Life	Accumulated Amortization (straight-line)
Machine A	$60,000	$11,000	7 years	$28,000 (4 years)
Machine B	14,200	1,925	5 years	7,365 (3 years)

The machines were disposed of in the following ways:

a. Machine A: Sold on January 2, 2012, for $33,500 cash.

b. Machine B: On January 2, 2012, this machine suffered irreparable damage from an accident and was removed immediately by a salvage company at no cost.

Required:

1. Give the journal entries related to the disposal of each machine at the beginning of 2012.

2. Explain the accounting rationale for the way in which you recorded each disposal.

Check Figure:
[Req. 1]
Gain on disposal for
Machine A = $1,500

PB9-4 Analyzing and Recording Long-Lived Asset Transactions with Partial-Year Amortization

LO2, 3, 6

Grondy's Restaurant Company (GRC) entered into the following transactions during a recent year.

April 1	Purchased a new food locker for $5,000 by paying $1,000 cash and signing a $4,000 note.
April 2	Installed an air-conditioning system in the food locker at a cost of $3,000, purchased on account.
April 30	Wrote a cheque for the amount owed on account for the work completed on April 2.
May 1	A local carpentry company repaired the restaurant's front door, for which GRC wrote a cheque for the full $120 cost.
June 1	Paid $9,120 cash for the rights to use the name and store concept created by a different restaurant that has been successful in the region. For the next four years, GRC will operate under the Mullet Restaurant name.

Required:

1. Analyze the accounting equation effects and record journal entries for each of the transactions.

2. For the tangible and intangible assets acquired in the preceding transactions, determine the amount of amortization that Grondy's Restaurant Company should report for the quarter ended June 30. For convenience, the food locker and air-conditioning system are amortized as a group using the straight-line method, with a useful life of five years and no residual value.

3. Prepare a journal entry to record the amortization calculated in requirement 2.

4. What advice would you offer the company in anticipation of switching to IFRS in the future?

PB9-5 Recording Transactions and Adjustments for Tangible and Intangible Assets

LO1, 2, 3, 4, 5, 6

The following transactions and adjusting entries were completed by Super Swift, a local delivery company. The company uses straight-line amortization for delivery vehicles, double-declining-balance amortization for buildings, and straight-line amortization for franchise rights.

January 2, 2011	Paid $75,000 cash to purchase a small warehouse building near the airport. The building has an estimated life of 20 years and a residual value of $15,000.
July 1, 2011	Paid $40,000 cash to purchase a delivery van. The van has an estimated useful life of five years, and a residual value of $8,000.
October 2, 2011	Paid $400 cash to paint a small office in the warehouse building.
October 13, 2011	Paid $150 cash to get the oil changed in the delivery van.
December 1, 2011	Paid $60,000 cash to Clairmont Parcel Service (CPS) to begin operating a Super Swift business as a franchise using the name The CPS Store. This franchise right expires in five years.
December 31, 2011	Recorded amortization on the delivery van, warehouse building, and franchise right.
June 30, 2012	Sold the warehouse building for $64,000 cash. (Record the amortization on the building prior to recording its disposal.)
December 31, 2012	Recorded amortization on the delivery van and amortization on the franchise right. Determined that the franchise right was not impaired in value.

Required:

Give the journal entries required on each of the above dates.

LO2, 3   **C9-1 Accounting for Operating Activities (Including Amortization) and Preparing Financial Statements (Chapters 4, 8, and 9)**

Grid Iron Prep Inc. (GIPI) is a service business incorporated in January 2012 to provide personal training for athletes aspiring to play college or university football. The following transactions occurred during the year ended December 31, 2012.

a. GIPI issued shares in exchange for $90,000 cash.

b. GIPI purchased a gymnasium building and gym equipment at the beginning of the year for $50,000, 80 percent of which related to the gymnasium and 20 percent to the equipment.

c. GIPI paid $250 cash to have the gym equipment refurbished before it could be used.

d. GIPI collected $36,000 cash in training fees during the year, of which $2,000 were customer deposits to be earned in 2012.

e. GIPI paid $23,000 of wages and $7,000 in utilities.

f. GIPI provided $3,000 in training during the final month of the year and expected collection in 2013.

g. GIPI will depreciate the gymnasium building using the double-declining-balance method over 20 years. Gym equipment will be amortized using the straight-line method, with an estimated residual value of $2,250 at the end of its four-year useful life.

h. GIPI received a bill for $350 of advertising done during December. The bill has not been paid or recorded.

i. GIPI will record an estimated 5 percent of its Accounts Receivable as not collectable.

j. GIPI's income tax rate is 30 percent. Assume amortization for tax is the same amount as amortization for financial reporting purposes.

Required:

1. Prepare journal entries to record the transactions and adjustments listed in (a)–(j).

2. Prepare GIPI's annual income statement, statement of retained earnings, and classified balance sheet.

SKILLS DEVELOPMENT CASES

LO2, 3, 6, 7   **S9-1 Finding Financial Information**

Rona Inc.

Refer to the financial statements of Rona Inc. Appendix A at the back of this book or download the annual report from the *Cases* section of Connect.

Required:

1. What method of amortization does the company use?

2. What is the amount of Accumulated Amortization at December 27, 2009? What percentage is this of the total cost of property and equipment?

3. For amortization purposes, what is the range of estimated useful lives for the buildings?

4. What amount of Depreciation and Amortization Expense was reported for the year ended December 27, 2009? What percentage of net sales is it?

5. What is the fixed asset turnover ratio for the current year?

6. For each of the preceding questions, where did you locate the information?

LO2, 3, 6, 7 8   **S9-2 Comparing Financial Information**

Rona Inc.

Refer to the financial statements of Rona Inc. in Appendix A and The Home Depot in Appendix B at the back of this book or download the annual report from the *Cases* section of Connect.

Required:

1. What method of amortization does The Home Depot use?

2. What amount of Accumulated Amortization did The Home Depot report at January 31, 2010? What percentage is this of the total cost of property and equipment? Is this a larger (or smaller) percentage of the total cost of property and equipment than for Rona Inc. (in S9-1)? What does it suggest to you about the length of time the assets have been amortized?

3. The Home Depot's estimated useful life of buildings is between 5 and 45 years. In some cases this could be shorter or longer than that estimated by Rona Inc. How will this affect the fixed asset turnover ratios of the two companies?

4. What amount of Amortization Expense was reported on The Home Depot's income statement for the year ended January 31, 2010? What percentage of net sales is it? Compare this percentage to that of Rona Inc. and describe what this implies about the two companies' operations.

5. What is The Home Depot's fixed asset turnover ratio for the current year? Compare this ratio to that of Rona Inc. and describe what it implies about the operations of the two companies.

S9-3 Internet-Based Team Research: Examining an Annual Report
LO1, 3, 6, 7

As a team, select an industry to analyze. Using your Web browser, each team member should access the annual report for one publicly traded company in the industry, with each member selecting a different company. (See S1-3 in Chapter 1 for a description of possible resources for these tasks.)

Required:

1. On an individual basis, each team member should write a short report that incorporates the following:
   a. Description of the amortization methods used.
   b. Computation of the percentage of fixed asset cost that has been amortized. What does this imply about the length of time the assets have been amortized?
   c. Computation of the fixed asset turnover ratios for the current and prior years. What does this tell you about the efficiency of the company's asset use?
   d. Description of the kinds of intangible assets, if any, that the company reports on the balance sheet.

2. Then, as a team, write a short report comparing and contrasting your companies using these attributes. Discuss any patterns across the companies that you as a team observe. Provide potential explanations for any differences discovered.

S9-4 Ethical Decision Making: A Real-Life Example
LO2, 7

Assume you work as a staff member in a large accounting department for a multinational public company. Your job requires you to review documents relating to the company's equipment purchases. Once you've verified that purchases were properly approved, you prepare journal entries to record the equipment purchases in the accounting system. Typically, you handle equipment purchases costing $100,000 or less.

This morning, you were contacted by the executive assistant to the chief financial officer. She says that the CFO has asked to see you immediately in his office. Although your boss's boss has attended a few meetings where the CFO was present, you have never met the CFO during your three years with the company. Needless to say, you are anxious about the meeting.

When you enter the CFO's office, you are warmly greeted with a smile and friendly handshake. The CFO compliments you on the great work that you've been doing for the company. You soon feel a little more comfortable, particularly when the CFO mentions that he has a special project for you. He states that he and the chief executive officer have negotiated significant new arrangements with the company's equipment suppliers, which require the company to make advance payments for equipment to be purchased in the future. The CFO says that, for various reasons that he didn't want to discuss, he will be processing the payments through the operating division of the company rather than through the equipment accounting group. Given that the payments will be made through the operating division, they will initially be classified as operating expenses of the company. He indicates that clearly these advance payments for property and equipment should be recorded as assets, so he will be contacting you at the end of every quarter to make an adjusting journal entry to capitalize the amounts inappropriately classified as operating expenses. He advises you that a new account, called Prepaid Equipment, has been established for this purpose. He quickly wraps up the meeting by telling you that it is important that you not talk about the special project with anyone. You assume he doesn't want others to become jealous of your new important responsibility.

A few weeks later, at the end of the first quarter, you receive a voice mail from the CFO stating, "The adjustment that we discussed is $771,000,000 for this quarter." Before deleting the message, you replay it to make sure you heard it right. Your company generates over $8 billion in revenues and incurs $6 billion in operating expenses every quarter, but you've never made a journal entry for that much money. So, just to be sure there's not a mistake, you send an e-mail to the CFO confirming the amount. He phones you back immediately to abruptly inform you, "There's no mistake. That's the number." Feeling embarrassed that you may have annoyed the CFO, you quietly make the adjusting journal entry.

For each of the remaining three quarters in that year and for the first quarter in the following year, you continue to make these end-of-quarter adjustments. The "magic number," as the CFO liked to call it, was $560,000,000 for Q2, $742,745,000 for Q3, $941,000,000 for Q4, and $818,204,000 for Q1 of the following year. During this time, you've had several meetings and lunches with the CFO where he provides you with the magic number, sometimes supported with nothing more than a Post-it note with the number written on it. He frequently compliments you on your good work and promises that you'll soon be in line for a big promotion.

Despite the CFO's compliments and promises, you are growing increasingly uncomfortable with the journal entries that you've been making. Typically, whenever an ordinary equipment purchase involves an advance payment, the purchase is completed a few weeks later. At that time, the amount of the advance is removed from an Equipment Deposit account and transferred to the appropriate equipment account. This hasn't been the case with the CFO's special project. Instead, the Prepaid Equipment account has continued to grow, now standing at over $3.8 billion. There's been no discussion about how or when this balance will be reduced, and no amortization has been recorded for it.

Just as you begin to reflect on the effect the adjustments have had on your company's fixed assets, operating expenses, and operating income, you receive a call from the vice-president for internal audit. She needs to talk with you this afternoon about "a peculiar trend in the company's fixed asset turnover ratio and some suspicious journal entries that you've been making."

Required:

1. Complete the following table to determine what the company's accounting records would have looked like had you not made the journal entries as part of the CFO's special project. Comment on how the decision to capitalize amounts, which were initially recorded as operating expenses, has affected the level of income from operations in each quarter.

(Amounts in millions of dollars)	Q1 Year 1 (March 31) With the Entries	Q1 Year 1 (March 31) Without the Entries	Q2 Year 1 (June 30) With the Entries	Q2 Year 1 (June 30) Without the Entries	Q3 Year 1 (September 30) With the Entries	Q3 Year 1 (September 30) Without the Entries	Q4 Year 1 (December 31) With the Entries	Q4 Year 1 (December 31) Without the Entries	Q1 Year 2 (March 31) With the Entries	Q1 Year 2 (March 31) Without the Entries
Property and Equipment, Net	$38,614	$	$35,982	$	$38,151	$	$38,809	$	$39,155	$
Sales Revenues	8,825	8,825	8,910	8,910	8,966	8,966	8,478	8,478	8,120	8,120
Operating Expenses	7,628		8,526		7,786		7,725		7,277	
Income from Operations	1,197		384		1,180		753		843	

2. Using the publicly reported numbers (which include the special journal entries that you recorded), compute the fixed asset turnover ratio (rounded to two decimal places) for the periods ended Q2–Q4 of year 1 and Q1 of year 2. What does the trend in this ratio suggest to you? Is this consistent with the changes in operating income reported by the company?

3. Before your meeting with the vice-president for internal audit, you think about the above computations and the variety of peculiar circumstances surrounding the "special project" for the CFO. What in particular might have raised your suspicion about the real nature of your work?

4. Your meeting with internal audit was short and unpleasant. The vice-president indicated that she had discussed her findings with the CFO before meeting with you. The CFO claimed that he too had noticed the peculiar trend in the fixed assets turnover ratio, but that he hadn't had a chance to investigate it further. He urged internal audit to get to the bottom of things, suggesting that perhaps someone might be making unapproved journal entries. Internal audit had identified you as the source of the journal entries and had been unable to find any documents that approved or substantiated the entries. She ended the meeting by advising you to find a good lawyer. Given your current circumstances, describe how you would have acted earlier had you been able to foresee where it might lead you.

5. In the real case on which this one is based, the internal auditors agonized over the question of whether they had actually uncovered a fraud or whether they were jumping to the wrong conclusion. *The Wall Street Journal* mentioned this on October 30, 2002, by stating, "it was clear . . . that their findings would be devastating for the company. They worried about whether their revelations would result in layoffs. Plus, they feared that they would somehow end up being blamed for the mess." Beyond the personal consequences mentioned in this quote, describe other potential ways in

which the findings of the internal auditors would likely be devastating for the publicly traded company and those associated with it.

Epilogue: This case is based on a fraud committed at WorldCom (now owned by Verizon). The case draws its numbers, the nature of the unsupported journal entries, and the CFO's role in carrying out the fraud from a report issued by WorldCom's bankruptcy examiner. Year 1 in this case was actually 2001 and year 2 was 2002. This case excludes other fraudulent activities that contributed to WorldCom's $11 billion fraud. The 63-year-old CEO was sentenced to 25 years in prison for planning and executing the biggest fraud in the history of American business. The CFO, who cooperated in the investigation of the CEO, was sentenced to five years in prison.

WorldCom

Verizon

S9-5 Ethical Decision Making: A Mini-Case

LO3

Assume you are one of three members of the accounting staff working for a small private company. At the beginning of this year, the company expanded into a new industry by acquiring equipment that will be used to make several new lines of products. The owner and general manager of the company has indicated that, as one of the conditions for providing financing for the new equipment, the company's bank will receive a copy of the company's annual financial statements. Another condition of the loan is that the company's total assets cannot fall below $250,000. Violation of this condition gives the bank the option to demand immediate repayment of the loan. Before making the adjustment for this year's amortization, the company's total assets are reported at $255,000. The owner has asked you to take a look at the facts regarding the new equipment and "work with the numbers to make sure everything stays onside with the bank."

An amortization method has not yet been adopted for the new equipment. Equipment used in other parts of the company is amortized using the double-declining-balance method. The cost of the new equipment was $35,000 and the manager estimates it will be worth "at least $7,000" at the end of its four-year useful life. Because the products made with the new equipment are only beginning to catch on with consumers, the company used the equipment to produce just 4,000 units this year. It is expected that, over all four years of its useful life, the new equipment will make a total of 28,000 units.

Required:

1. Calculate the amortization that would be reported this year under each of the three methods shown in this chapter. Which of the methods would meet the owner's objective?

2. Evaluate whether it is ethical to recommend that the company use the method identified in requirement 1. What two parties are most directly affected by this recommendation? How would each party benefit from or be harmed by the recommendation? Does the recommendation violate any laws or applicable rules? Are there any other factors that you would consider before making a recommendation?

S9-6 Critical Thinking: Analyzing the Effects of Amortization Policies on Income

LO3, 5, 8

As an aspiring financial analyst, you have applied to a major Bay Street firm for a summer job. To screen potential applicants, the firm provides you with a short case study and asks you to evaluate the financial success of two hypothetical companies that started operations on January 1, 2011. Both companies operate in the same industry, use very similar assets, and have very similar customer bases. Among the additional information provided about the companies are the following comparative income statements.

	Fast Corporation		Slow Corporation	
	2012	2011	2012	2011
Net Sales	$60,000	$60,000	$60,000	$60,000
Cost of Goods Sold	20,000	20,000	20,000	20,000
Gross Profit	40,000	40,000	40,000	40,000
Selling, General, and Administrative Expenses	19,000	19,000	19,000	19,000
Amortization Expense	3,555	10,667	5,000	5,000
Gains (Losses) on Disposal	2,222	—	(2,000)	—
Income from Operations	$19,667	$10,333	$14,000	$16,000

Required:

Prepare an analysis of the two companies with the goal of determining which company is better managed. If you could request two additional pieces of information from these companies' financial statements, describe specifically what they would be and explain how they would help you to make a decision.

S9-7 Preparing Amortization Schedules for Straight-Line and Double-Declining-Balance

To make some extra money, you've started preparing templates of business forms and schedules for others to download from the Internet (for a small fee). After relevant information is entered into each template, it automatically performs calculations using formulas you have entered into the template. For the amortization template, you decide to produce two worksheets—one that calculates amortization and book value under the straight-line method and another that calculates these amounts using the double-declining-balance method. The templates perform straightforward calculations of amortization and book value when given the cost of an asset, its estimated useful life, and its estimated residual value. These particular templates won't handle disposals or changes in estimates—you plan to create a deluxe version for those functions. To illustrate that your templates actually work, you enter the information used to produce the amortization schedules shown in Exhibit 9.6, with Cedar Fair and Six Flags as examples.

Although you're confident you can use appropriate formulas in the spreadsheet to create a template for the straight-line method, you're a little uncertain about how to make the double-declining-balance method work. As usual, you e-mail your friend Owen for advice. Here's what he said:

From:	Owentheaccountant@yahoo.com
To:	Helpme@hotmail.com
Cc:	
Subject:	Excel Help

I wish I'd thought of charging money for showing people how to do ordinary accounting activities. You'd have made me rich by now. ☺ Here's how to set up your worksheets. Begin by creating an "input values" section. This section will allow someone to enter the asset cost, residual value, and estimated life in an area removed from the actual amortization schedule. You don't want someone accidentally entering amounts over formulas that you've entered into the schedule.

The cells from the input values section will be referenced by other cells in the amortization schedule. You will want to enter formulas into the cells for the first year row, and then copy and paste them into rows for the other years. When doing this, you will need to use what is called an "absolute reference," which means that the cell reference does not change when one row is copied and pasted into a different row. Unlike an ordinary cell reference that has a format of A1, an absolute reference has the format of A1, which prevents the spreadsheet from changing either the column (A) or row (1) when copying the cell to other cells. You may find this useful when preparing both the straight-line and double-declining-balance schedules.

To create the amortization schedules, use five columns labelled (1) year, (2) beginning of year accumulated amortization, (3) amortization, (4) end of year accumulated amortization, and (5) end of year book value.

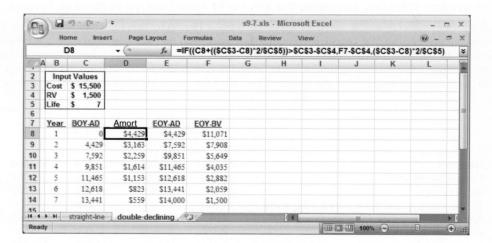

The double-declining-balance template will be the trickiest to create because you need to be concerned that the book value is not amortized below the residual value in the last year of the asset's life. To force the template to automatically watch for this, you will need to use the IF function. I have included a screenshot of a template I created, using the IF function to properly calculate amortization for all years of the asset's life. Notice the formula shown in the formula bar at the top.

Required:

Create the spreadsheet templates to calculate amortization and book value using the straight-line and double-declining-balance methods. Demonstrate that the template works by reproducing the schedules in Exhibit 9.6.

> **TIP:** To switch between displaying cell formulas and their values, press CTRL and ~ (tilde) at the same time. Also, use Excel's help feature to obtain further information about the IF function.

CONTINUING CASE

Practise and learn online with Connect.

CC9 Accounting for the Use and Disposal of Long-Lived Assets

LO3, 5

Nicole's Getaway Spa (NGS) purchased a hydrotherapy tub system to add to the wellness programs at NGS. The machine was purchased at the beginning of 2012 at a cost of $5,000. The estimated useful life was five years, and the residual value was $500. Assume that the estimated productive life of the machine is 15,000 hours. Expected annual production was: year 1, 4,100 hours; year 2, 2,500 hours; year 3, 3,400 hours; year 4, 1,800 hours; and year 5, 3,200 hours.

Required:

1. Complete an amortization schedule for each of the alternative methods.
   a. Straight-line.
   b. Units-of-production.
   c. Double-declining-balance.
2. Assume NGS sold the hydrotherapy tub system for $2,100 at the end of year 3. Prepare the journal entry to account for the disposal of this asset under the three different methods.
3. The following amounts were forecast for the year ended December 31, 2014: Sales Revenues $42,000; Cost of Goods Sold $33,000; Other Operating Expenses $4,000; and Interest Expense $800. Create an income statement for the year ended December 31, 2014 (end of year three) for each of the different amortization methods, ending at Income before Income Tax Expense. (Don't forget to include a loss or gain on disposal for each method.)

Endnotes

1. "Insurer Refuses Damage Payment to Sandusky, Ohio-Based Amusement Park Company," *Knight Ridder/Tribune Business News*, February 11, 2003.
2. Tim Hortons, Franchising Program: www.timhortons.com/ca/en/join/franchise_ca_program.html.

Practise and learn online with Connect.

Understand the business

LO1 Explain the role of liabilities in financing a business.

Study the accounting methods

LO2 Explain how to account for common types of current liabilities.

LO3 Analyze and record bond liability transactions.

LO4 Describe how to account for contingent liabilities.

Evaluate the results

LO5 Calculate and interpret the quick ratio and the times interest earned ratio.

Review the chapter

Chapter Summary, page 444

Additional resources on Connect

CHAPTER 10

Reporting and Interpreting Liabilities

FOCUS COMPANY:
General Mills
www.generalmills.com

GENERAL MILLS

They've turned in the reports, and they're just waiting to hear their letter grade. They're expecting an A and will be devastated if it's a B. Sounds like some high-achieving students, right? It could be. But it's actually the Jolly Green Giant, Lucky the Leprechaun, Poppin' Fresh, and their corporate bosses at General Mills. That's right. This magically delicious company and all its characters receive a letter grade just like you and your friends. Their grading process differs a bit from yours, because their grade is assigned by credit-rating agencies like Standard & Poor's, Fitch, and Moody's, indicating the company's ability to pay its liabilities on a timely basis. Another difference is that their grades can range from AAA to D. The AAA rating is given to companies in rock-solid financial condition, and the D goes to those likely to pay less than half of what they owe. In general, anything above BB is considered a good to high-quality credit rating, which is what General Mills typically earns.

In this chapter, you will learn about the accounting procedures and financial ratios used to report and interpret liabilities, and how they influence credit ratings. Although we focus on corporate reporting and analyses, this chapter also can help you to understand the kind of information others use to evaluate your own personal credit rating.

THAT WAS
THEN

Previous chapters focused on items related to the assets section of the balance sheet.

THIS IS
NOW

This chapter focuses on items related to the liabilities section of the balance sheet.

ORGANIZATION OF THE CHAPTER

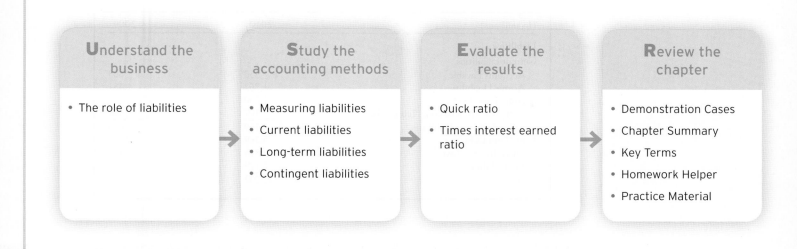

Understand the business	Study the accounting methods	Evaluate the results	Review the chapter
• The role of liabilities	• Measuring liabilities • Current liabilities • Long-term liabilities • Contingent liabilities	• Quick ratio • Times interest earned ratio	• Demonstration Cases • Chapter Summary • Key Terms • Homework Helper • Practice Material

Understand the Business

THE ROLE OF LIABILITIES

Liabilities play a significant role in financing most business activities. Liabilities are created when a company buys goods and services on credit, obtains short-term loans to cover gaps in cash flows, and issues long-term debt to obtain money for expanding into new regions and markets. The importance of liabilities became most apparent during the financial crisis of 2008–2009. Soon after banks restricted their lending activities and suppliers tightened their credit terms, companies began to fail. Circuit City, for example, filed for bankruptcy protection just one week after its suppliers required the company to pay cash on delivery (COD). Less than two months later, when the company discovered it could not obtain alternative sources of financing, Circuit City terminated its 30,000 employees and shut down the business.

General Mills survived the financial crisis because it was able to pay suppliers on time and its BBB+ credit rating helped it obtain short-term financing as needed. Also, just prior to the crisis, the company had arranged long-term debt financing that will not come due until the year 2037. With these critical sources of financing in place, the company was able to ride out the rough economic times.

To help financial statement users know when liabilities must be repaid, companies prepare a classified balance sheet, as shown in Exhibit 10.1. In Chapter 2, you learned that a classified balance sheet reports current liabilities separate from other liabilities. Technically, **current liabilities** are defined as short-term obligations that will be paid with current assets within the company's current operating cycle or within one year of the balance sheet date, whichever is longer. Practically, this definition can be simplified as liabilities that are due within one year (because most companies have operating cycles that are shorter than a year). This means that, as shown in Exhibit 10.1, General Mills will have to pay nearly $3.8 billion in the year following its 2010 fiscal year. An additional $8.3 billion will need to be paid in the longer term. Although these long-term obligations rarely get a separate subheading of their own, people often refer to them as *noncurrent* or *long-term liabilities*.

Learning Objective 1

Explain the role of liabilities in financing a business.

EXHIBIT 10.1	Excerpt from General Mills's Balance Sheet

(In millions)	2010	2009
Liabilities		
Current Liabilities		
Accounts Payable	$ 850	$ 803
Accrued Liabilities	1,762	1,481
Notes Payable	1,050	812
Current Portion of Long-Term Debt	107	509
Total Current Liabilities	3,769	3,605
Long-Term Debt	5,269	5,755
Deferred Income Taxes	875	1,165
Other Liabilities	2,119	1,932
Total Liabilities	12,032	12,457

Study the Accounting Methods

MEASURING LIABILITIES

Learning Objective 2

Explain how to account for common types of current liabilities.

As Exhibit 10.1 illustrates, General Mills owed various types of liabilities at the end of its 2010 fiscal year. In this section, we will describe each of these liabilities and how they are accounted for. In general, the amount reported for each liability is the result of three factors:

1. **The initial amount of the liability.** Initially, the company records each liability at its cash equivalent, which is the amount of cash a creditor would accept to settle the liability immediately after a transaction or event creates the liability.

2. **Additional amounts owed to the creditor.** The company increases liabilities whenever additional obligations arise, by purchasing goods and services or by incurring interest charges over time.

3. **Payments or services provided to the creditor.** The company decreases liabilities whenever the company makes a payment or provides services to the creditor.

Notice that a liability is first recorded at a cash-equivalent amount, which excludes interest charges. Interest arises only when time passes, so no interest is recorded on the day the company purchases an item on account or the day the company receives a loan. This practice makes sense because if you borrowed $10 from a friend and paid it back a split-second later, you wouldn't have to pay interest.

CURRENT LIABILITIES

Let's look more closely at each current liability listed in Exhibit 10.1.

Accounts Payable

You've used this account in previous chapters, so we'll keep this discussion short. Accounts Payable is increased (credited) when a company receives goods or services on credit, and it is decreased (debited) when the company pays on its account. Accounts Payable is interest-free unless it becomes overdue.

Accrued Liabilities

Chapter 4 showed how to use an adjusting journal entry at the end of the accounting period to record increases in both Wages Expense (debit) and Wages Payable (credit) when a company had incurred but not yet paid that period's wages. Similar adjustments were made for interest incurred but not paid, and income taxes incurred but not paid. Because these adjustments are called *accruals*, the liabilities (Wages Payable, Interest Payable, etc.) are generally referred to as *accrued liabilities*. **Accrued liabilities** relate to various unpaid expenses, including advertising, electricity, corporate income tax, interest, payroll tax, and warranties. General Mills itemizes its nearly $1.8 billion of Accrued Liabilities in a note to its financial statements, similar to Exhibit 10.2.

EXHIBIT 10.2 — **Examples of Accrued Liabilities**

GENERAL MILLS

(In millions)	2010
Accrued Advertising	$ 555
Accrued Payroll	331
Accrued Taxes	440
Accrued Interest	137
Other	299
Total Accrued Liabilities	$1,762

Accrued Payroll In addition to Wages Payable, companies record liabilities for other aspects of payroll. Two significant payroll liabilities relate to payroll deductions and employer payroll taxes.

Payroll Deductions Payroll deductions are amounts subtracted from employees' gross earnings to determine their net pay. Gross earnings are computed by multiplying the time worked by the pay rate promised by the employer (40 hours × $15 per hour = $600 gross earnings). From these gross earnings, certain payroll deductions are subtracted, for items such as federal and provincial and territorial income taxes, Canada Pension Plan (CPP), and Employment Insurance (EI). The tear-away portion of the paycheque shown in Exhibit 10.3 illustrates payroll deductions totalling $149.30. Net pay equals gross earnings less payroll deductions ($450.70 = $600.00 − $149.30).

You might think your employer keeps the deductions from your gross earnings, but that's not true. Your employer is obligated to remit those deductions to another organization or government agency on your behalf. As Exhibit 10.3 shows, payroll deductions create liabilities for your employer.

Payroll deductions are either required by law or voluntarily requested by employees. The law requires that employers deduct federal and provincial and territorial income taxes from

---

EXHIBIT 10.3 — **Accounting for Gross Earnings, Payroll Deductions, and Net Pay**

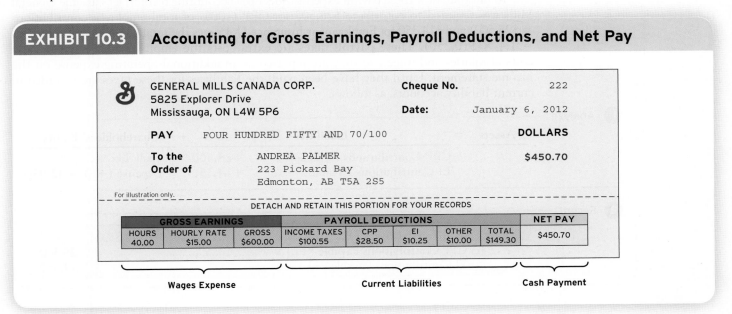

GENERAL MILLS CANADA CORP.
5825 Explorer Drive
Mississauga, ON L4W 5P6

Cheque No.   222

Date: January 6, 2012

PAY   FOUR HUNDRED FIFTY AND 70/100   **DOLLARS**

To the
Order of
ANDREA PALMER
223 Pickard Bay
Edmonton, AB T5A 2S5
$450.70

For illustration only.

DETACH AND RETAIN THIS PORTION FOR YOUR RECORDS

GROSS EARNINGS			PAYROLL DEDUCTIONS					NET PAY
HOURS	HOURLY RATE	GROSS	INCOME TAXES	CPP	EI	OTHER	TOTAL	$450.70
40.00	$15.00	$600.00	$100.55	$28.50	$10.25	$10.00	$149.30	

Wages Expense   Current Liabilities   Cash Payment

each employee's gross earnings. The law also requires that each employee support the Canada Pension Plan and the Employment Insurance Act through employee payroll deductions. Employers use these same methods to account for any other payroll deductions (including voluntary deductions for charitable donations, union dues, retirement savings, parking, etc.). The employer classifies payroll deductions as *current* liabilities because they must be paid within the current year.

To illustrate how to record these items, let's assume (for simplicity) that General Mills has 1,000 employees who receive paycheques like the one in Exhibit 10.3. The accounting equation effects and journal entry would be as follows:

① Analyze

Assets	=	Liabilities		+	Shareholders' Equity
Cash −450,700		Withheld Income Tax Payable	+100,550		Wages Expense (+E) −600,000
		CPP Contributions Payable	+28,500		
		EI Contributions Payable	+10,250		
		United Way Contributions Payable	+10,000		

② Record

dr Wages Expense (+E, −SE)	600,000	
cr Withheld Income Tax Payable (+L)		100,550
cr CPP Contributions Payable (+L)		28,500
cr EI Contributions Payable (+L)		10,250
cr United Way Contributions Payable (+L)		10,000
cr Cash (−A)		450,700

Employer Payroll Taxes Beyond paying employees and remitting payroll deductions, employers have other responsibilities that lead to substantial additional labour costs. In the remainder of this section, we consider two employer payroll taxes: Canada Pension Plan and Employment Insurance contributions.

All employers are required to match the amount paid by employees to the Canada Pension Plan. In addition, employers are required by the Employment Insurance Act to pay 1.4 times the total employee contribution. So what does this all mean? This means that employers pay slightly more to the Employment Insurance program than employees do, whereas for the Canada Pension Plan, the costs are the same for the employer as they are for the employee.

To illustrate how these payroll expenses affect the accounting records, let's assume General Mills was required to contribute $28,500 for CPP (100% of total employee contributions = $28,500) and $14,350 for Employment Insurance (1.4 times the total employee contributions = 1.4 × $10,250). These payroll taxes are extra costs the employer incurs beyond the costs of salaries and wages, so they are reported as an additional operating expense on the income statement. Until they have been paid, the liabilities for these taxes are recorded in current liability accounts, as follows:

① Analyze

Assets	=	Liabilities		+	Shareholders' Equity
		CPP Contributions Payable	+28,500		Payroll Tax
		EI Contributions Payable	+14,350		Expense (+E) −42,850

② Record

dr Payroll Tax Expense (+E, −SE)	42,850	
cr CPP Contributions Payable (+L)		28,500
cr EI Contributions Payable (+L)		14,350

When the employer pays these taxes (and the payroll deductions shown earlier), it decreases the liability accounts (with debits) and decreases its Cash account (with a credit).

Accrued Income Taxes   Corporations pay taxes not only on payroll but also on income they earn, just as you do. A corporation's tax return, which the CRA calls a T2, is similar to a company's income statement, except that it calculates *taxable* income by subtracting tax-allowed expenses from revenues. This taxable income is then multiplied by a tax rate, which for most large corporations is about 35 percent. Corporate income taxes are due three months after year-end, although most corporations are required to pay advance instalments during the year.

COACH'S TIP

The adjusting journal entry to accrue income taxes was presented in Chapter 4 on pages 149–150.

Notes Payable

The next liability reported by General Mills in Exhibit 10.1 is Notes Payable. This liability represents the amount the company owes to others as a result of issuing promissory notes. It is the flip side of the notes receivable transactions that were explained in Chapter 8.

Four key events occur with any note payable: (1) establishing the note, (2) accruing interest incurred but not paid, (3) recording interest paid, and (4) recording principal paid. Financial effects are recorded for each of these four events. As an example, assume that on November 1, 2012, General Mills borrowed $100,000 cash on a one-year note that required General Mills to pay 6 percent interest and $100,000 principal, both on October 31, 2013.

1. **Establish the note payable.** The $100,000 loan that created the note payable has the following accounting equation effects, which General Mills would record using the following journal entry:

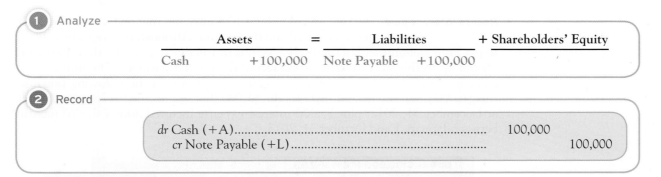

1 Analyze

	Assets	=	Liabilities	+ Shareholders' Equity
Cash	+100,000		Note Payable +100,000	

2 Record

dr Cash (+A)... 100,000
   cr Note Payable (+L)...   100,000

2. **Accrue interest incurred but not paid.** Interest occurs as time passes. It is not owed the day the note is established, but rather it accumulates as each day passes. Under accrual accounting, interest must be recorded as it is incurred over time. The timeline in Exhibit 10.4 shows how General Mills should account for the interest incurred on the note over its one-year term. In reality, General Mills would record an adjustment each month or quarter for interest incurred in that period, but for simplicity, we have assumed it occurs only once, at the end of the year. From the date the note was established (November 1, 2012) to the end of the year (December 31, 2012), General Mills incurred two months of interest expense.

EXHIBIT 10.4   **Timeline for Notes Payable**

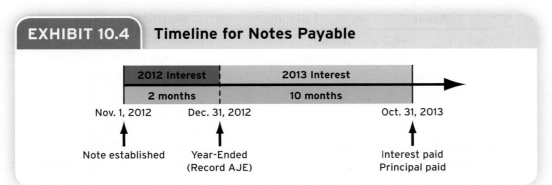

COACH'S TIP

This example shows how to account for the note from the borrower's perspective. The same example is presented on pages 337–340 from the lender's perspective.

The amount of interest to record for two months is computed using the interest formula, as follows:

$$\text{Interest (I)} = \text{Principal (P)} \times \text{Interest Rate (R)} \times \text{Time (T)}$$
$$\$1{,}000 = \$100{,}000 \times 6\% \times \mathbf{2/12}$$

The effect of this adjustment, along with the adjusting journal entry to record the $1,000 of interest expense that is payable on December 31, 2012, is as follows:

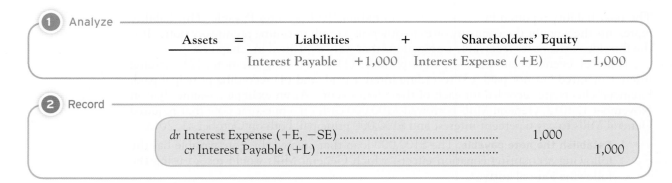

① Analyze

Assets	=	Liabilities	+	Shareholders' Equity	
		Interest Payable +1,000		Interest Expense (+E)	−1,000

② Record

dr Interest Expense (+E, −SE) 1,000
  cr Interest Payable (+L)   1,000

3. **Record interest paid.** The timeline in Exhibit 10.4 indicates that on October 31, 2013, General Mills pays both the principal and the interest. Although the company is likely to pay both amounts with a single cheque, it is instructive to consider these payments separately. In this step, we analyze and record the interest payment. The interest payment is $6,000 (= $100,000 × 6% × 12/12). As shown in the following timeline, this $6,000 interest payment includes the $1,000 that was accrued as Interest Payable at December 31, 2012, plus $5,000 interest expense incurred during the 10 months between January 1 and October 31, 2013.

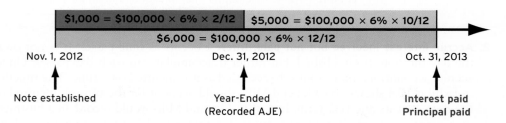

$1,000 = $100,000 × 6% × 2/12	$5,000 = $100,000 × 6% × 10/12
$6,000 = $100,000 × 6% × 12/12	

Nov. 1, 2012	Dec. 31, 2012	Oct. 31, 2013
Note established	**Year-Ended** **(Recorded AJE)**	**Interest paid** **Principal paid**

The $6,000 interest payment is analyzed and recorded as follows:

① Analyze

	Assets	=	Liabilities	+	Shareholders' Equity	
Cash	−6,000		Interest Payable −1,000		Interest Expense (+E)	−5,000

② Record

dr Interest Payable (−L)... 1,000
dr Interest Expense (+E, −SE) 5,000
  cr Cash (−A)   6,000

4. Record principal paid. The accounting equation effects and journal entry to record the $100,000 principal payment on October 31, 2013, are as follows.

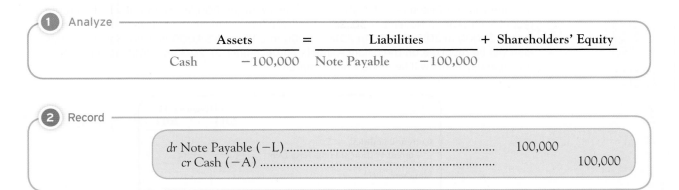

1 Analyze

	Assets	=	Liabilities	+ Shareholders' Equity
Cash	−100,000	Note Payable	−100,000	

2 Record

dr Note Payable (−L) 100,000
   cr Cash (−A)   100,000

HOW'S IT GOING? Self-Study Practice

Assume Starbucks issues a 5 percent, $12,000 note on December 1. How would this transaction and the month-end interest adjustment affect the accounting equation?

1 Analyze

	Assets	=	Liabilities	+	Shareholders' Equity
December 1					
December 31					

After you have finished, check your answers with the solution in the margin.

Solution to Self-Study Practice

	Assets	=	Liabilities	+	Shareholders' Equity
Dec. 1 Cash	+12,000	Note Payable	+12,000		
Dec. 31		Interest Payable	+50	Interest Expense (+E)	−50
				($50 = $12,000 × 5% × 1/12)	

Current Portion of Long-Term Debt

Remember when you were in Grade 9 and it seemed as if it would be forever before you'd graduate from high school? At that time, graduation was something that would happen in the long term. Later, when you became a senior, graduation became a current event—one that was less than a year away. A similar progression occurs with long-term debt.

If a company borrows money with the promise to repay it in two years, the loan is classified as a long-term debt. The company reports only the accrued interest on the loan as a current liability in that year's balance sheet. After a year has passed, however, the loan becomes a current liability (just as your graduation became a current event when you reached your senior year). When that happens, the borrower must report the loan in the Current Liabilities section of the balance sheet. Rather than create a different account for this, accountants simply remove the amount of principal to be repaid in the upcoming year from the total long-term debt and report it as a current liability, Current Portion of Long-Term Debt.

The final line item in the Current Liabilities section of the General Mills balance sheet provides an example (see Exhibit 10.1, page 414). Notice that in 2010, General Mills reported a current liability for the $107 million of long-term debt that was expected to be paid in 2011. This reclassification of long-term debt into current liabilities is needed so that the balance sheet accurately reports the dollar amount of existing liabilities that will be paid in the upcoming year.

Assume that on December 31, 2012, Netflix borrowed $10,000, a portion of which is to be repaid each year on November 30. Specifically, Netflix will make the following principal payments: $1,000 in 2013, $2,000 in 2014, $3,000 in 2015, and $4,000 in 2016. Show how this loan will be reported on the balance sheets on December 31, 2013 and 2012, assuming that principal payments will be made when required.

	At December 31	
	2013	2012
Current Liabilities:		
Current Portion of Long-Term Debt	$	$
Long-term Debt		
Total Liabilities	$9,000	$10,000

After you have finished, check your answers with the solution in the margin.

Solution to Self-Study Practice

	At December 31	
	2013	2012
Current Liabilities		
Current Portion of Long-Term Debt	$2,000	$ 1,000
Long-Term Debt	7,000	9,000
Total Liabilities	$9,000	$10,000

SPOTLIGHT ON THE WORLD

Violated Loan Covenants

Most lending agreements allow the lender to revise loan terms (e.g., interest rates, due dates) if a borrower's financial condition deteriorates significantly. These escape hatches, called **loan covenants**, are often based on financial statement ratios such as those you have learned about in earlier chapters. Under ASPE, if a company violates loan covenants on long-term debt but renegotiates the loan prior to releasing its financial statements, the debt remains classified as long term. Under IFRS, the company must reclassify that long-term debt as a current liability.

Additional Current Liabilities

Because of the nature of General Mills' business, the company does not have some current liabilities that are common to other companies. This section covers two such liabilities.

Sales Tax Payable   Retail companies are required to charge a provincial sales tax (PST) in all provinces but Alberta. In addition to PST, the federal government charges a goods and services tax (GST) of 5 percent. In the provinces of Nova Scotia, New Brunswick, Newfoundland and Labrador, and Ontario, the provincial sales tax is combined with the GST to form a single harmonized sales tax (HST). The provincial sales tax rates vary from province to province, as do the goods and services to which the tax is applied and the way the tax is applied. Retailers collect sales tax from consumers at the time of sale and forward it to the provincial and federal governments. Just like payroll taxes, the tax collected by the company is reported as a current liability until it is forwarded to the government. Sales tax is not an expense to the retailer because it is simply collected and passed on to the government. So if Future Shop sold a television in Saskatchewan (where the PST rate is 5 percent) for $1,000 cash plus taxes, Future Shop would collect $1,100 cash, earn $1,000 in sales revenue, recognize a $50 liability (= 5% × $1,000) for the provincial sales tax collected, and also recognize another $50 liability (= 5% × $1,000) for the GST collected. The financial effects of this sale are analyzed below and would be recorded with the journal entry that follows.

1 Analyze

Assets		=	Liabilities		+	Shareholders' Equity	
Cash	+1,100		GST Payable	+50		Sales Revenue (+R)	+1,000
			PST Payable	+50			

2 Record

dr Cash (+A).. 1,100
   cr GST Payable (+L) ($1,000 × 5%) 50
   cr PST Payable (+L) ($1,000 × 5%) 50
   cr Sales Revenue (+R, +SE)................................. 1,000

When Future Shop pays the provincial sales tax to the provincial government and pays the GST to the federal government, its accountants will reduce both PST Payable and GST Payable (with a debit) and reduce Cash (with a credit). If Future Shop sold this same television in Ontario, where the HST is 13 percent, the accountants would recognize a $130 liability (= 13% × $1,000) in the HST Payable account (with a credit). This would then be reduced (with a debit) when Future Shop paid off this current liability. Future Shop would collect $1,130 cash, and still earn $1,000 in sales revenue. Although the sales tax rate was different in these two examples, Future Shop earns only the sales price of the television, and remits the sales tax collected to the federal and provincial governments.

Unearned Revenue   In Chapter 4, you learned that some companies receive cash before they provide goods or services to customers. Airlines are paid in advance of providing flights, retailers receive cash for gift cards that can be used for future purchases of goods and services, and other companies receive money for subscriptions before the subscriptions begin. IAC, the owner of Match.com, provides a great example of this type of liability. Consider what happens when IAC receives cash for subscription services to Match.com. Because IAC receives cash before providing subscription services, accountants initially record a liability in the account Unearned Revenue. As the subscription services are provided, IAC reduces this liability and reports the earned subscription fees as revenue.

Assume, for example, that on October 1, IAC received cash for a three-month subscription paid in advance at a rate of $10 per month (or $30 in total). The financial effects and related journal entries occur in two stages:

1. **Receive cash and create a liability** (on October 1):

1 Analyze
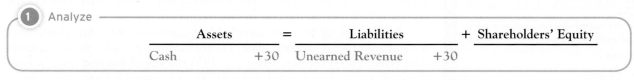

Assets		=	Liabilities		+	Shareholders' Equity
Cash	+30		Unearned Revenue	+30		

2 Record
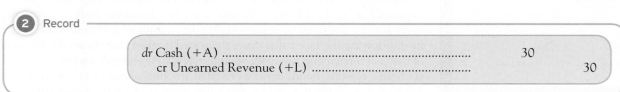

dr Cash (+A) 30
   cr Unearned Revenue (+L) 30

2. Fulfill part of the liability and earn revenue (on October 31):

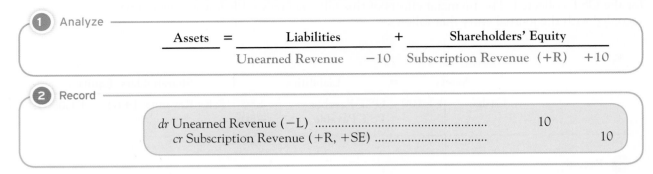

1 Analyze

Assets	=	Liabilities	+	Shareholders' Equity	
		Unearned Revenue −10		Subscription Revenue (+R)	+10

2 Record

dr Unearned Revenue (−L) 10
    cr Subscription Revenue (+R, +SE) 10

As each month passes, IAC would make another adjustment like the one in step 2 to show that it has continued to fulfill its obligation and to earn subscription revenues. Don't let the tiny amounts in our examples fool you. Unearned revenues can be huge. For IAC, they totalled over $57 million at December 31, 2009. That was more than the company's Accounts Payable of $39 million.

LONG-TERM LIABILITIES

Like most companies, General Mills reports several long-term liabilities on its balance sheet (see Exhibit 10.1). Common long-term liabilities include long-term notes payable, deferred income taxes, and bonds payable. Long-term notes payable are accounted for in the same way as the short-term notes payable discussed in the previous section (except, of course, long-term notes are on the books for more than one year). This section focuses on accounting for bonds that a company issues to obtain a significant amount of financing. Later, in Chapter 11, after you become more familiar with this form of long-term debt financing, we will compare it to alternative forms of long-term (equity) financing.

Bonds

Occasionally, governments and very large companies such as General Mills need to borrow more money than any single lender can provide. In 2008, for example, General Mills needed to borrow $750 million. Because issuing a promissory note for such a large amount of money was impractical, the company instead issued bonds. A sample bond certificate is shown here.

Bonds are financial instruments that outline the future payments a company promises to make in exchange for receiving a sum of money now. From the company's perspective, the bond is a long-term liability. From the bondholder's perspective, the bond is an investment. After a company issues the bonds, they can be traded on established exchanges such as the Toronto Stock Exchange. The ability to sell a bond on the bond exchange is attractive to bondholders because it provides them liquidity, or the ability to receive cash for the bond whenever they wish to sell it. In return for this liquidity, bondholders will accept a lower interest rate, which benefits the company by lowering the cost of long-term borrowing.

As you can see from the sample bond certificate, three key elements of a bond are (1) the **maturity date**, (2) the amount payable on the maturity date (often called the **face value**), and (3) the **stated interest rate**. In most cases, the face value of each bond is $1,000. The stated interest rate is always expressed as an annual rate although many bonds require interest payments every six months (that is, semiannually). Each interest payment is computed by multiplying the face value times the stated interest rate (times the fraction of the year if payments are made semiannually). As you will see later, for good economic reasons, bonds may be priced at amounts above or below their face value. A bond's price does not affect the amount of each interest payment,

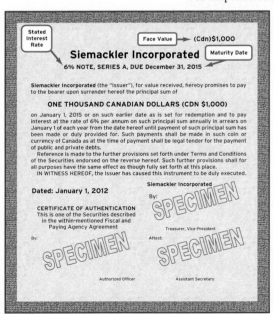

however. For example, a 6 percent bond with a face value of $1,000 will always pay interest of $60 cash each year (= $1,000 × 6% × 12/12).

Bond Pricing

Neither the company nor its financial advisers determine the price at which bonds are issued. Instead, investors in the market establish the issue price. The bond **issue price** represents the amount that investors are willing to pay on the issue date in exchange for the cash payments that the company promises to make over the life of the bond. Theoretically, this amount is based on a mathematical calculation called a **present value**, which is described in Appendix D at the back of this book. (Case C on page D.9 shows the calculations for a $1,000, 6 percent General Mills bond.)

SPOTLIGHT ON **Financial Reporting**

Bond Prices in the Financial Press

The financial press and the Yahoo! Finance Bonds Center report bond prices each day based on transactions that occurred on the bond exchange. The following is typical of the information you will find:

| Company Name | Maturity | INTEREST RATE | | Bond Price |
		Stated	Market	
Costco	2017	5.50	4.73	116.32
General Mills	2013	6.00	4.00	107.26
The Home Depot	2036	5.90	5.60	104.88

GENERAL MILLS

The above listing reports that a General Mills bond will mature in the year 2013. It has a stated interest rate of 6.00 percent. At the present time, 4.00 is the typical interest rate earned by investors in the market when buying similar bonds. Because the 6.00 percent stated interest rate is better than the 4.00 percent market interest rate, investors are attracted to the General Mills bond. Consequently, they are willing to pay a higher bond price. The bond price is quoted as a percentage of face value. In this case, investors were willing to pay 107.26 percent of face value, or $1,072.60 for each $1,000 bond (107.26% × $1,000).

When companies issue bonds, they try to offer competitive interest rates. However, changing economic events can cause the bond's stated interest rate to differ from the market's desired rate, which affects the bond's attractiveness and its price. After a bond has issued, the market's desired rate fluctuates frequently, which affects the bond price in the market. **Daily fluctuations in the market do not directly involve the company, so they are not considered to be transactions of the company**. Except in rare situations, the company continues to account for its bonds using the bond price and interest rates that existed when the bonds were first issued to the market.

Accounting for a Bond Issue

Although it is useful to know how to determine bond prices, it is not a necessary step in accounting for a bond issue. Instead, what we need to know is the amount of cash the company receives from investors when the bonds are first issued. This amount may be equal to the face value, above the face value, or below the face value. A bond issued for more than its face value is said to have been issued at a **premium**, which is the excess of the bond's issue price over its face value. A bond issued for less than its face value is said to have been issued at a **discount**, which is the amount by which the issue price falls short of the bond's face value. The following sections show how to account for bonds issued at face value, at a premium, and at a discount.

Bonds Issued at Face Value If General Mills receives $100,000 cash in exchange for issuing 100 bonds at their $1,000 face value, the transaction will be analyzed and recorded as follows:

1 Analyze

Assets		=	Liabilities		+	Shareholders' Equity
Cash	+100,000		Bonds Payable	+100,000		

2 Record

dr Cash (+A) 100,000
    cr Bonds Payable (+L) 100,000

Bonds Issued at a Premium If General Mills issues 100 of its $1,000 bonds at a price of 107.26, the company will receive $107,260 (= 100 × $1,000 × 1.0726). Thus, the cash-equivalent amount is $107,260, which represents the total liability on that date. The company's accountants will distinguish the $100,000 total face value from the $7,260 premium by recording them in separate liability accounts as follows:

1 Analyze

Assets		=	Liabilities		+	Shareholders' Equity
Cash	+107,260		Bonds Payable	+100,000		
			Premium on			
			Bonds Payable	+7,260		

2 Record

dr Cash (+A) 107,260
    cr Bonds Payable (+L) 100,000
    cr Premium on Bonds Payable (+L) 7,260

COACH'S TIP

Although Discount on Bonds Payable is recorded with a debit, it is not an asset–it is a contra-liability.

Why would bondholders be willing to pay a premium? For the same reason that you might pay a premium to acquire tickets to a great concert or a big game. If a bond offers something attractive, such as a high interest rate, bondholders may be willing to pay a premium to acquire it.

Bonds Issued at a Discount If General Mills receives $93,376 for bonds with a total face value of $100,000, the cash-equivalent amount is $93,376, which represents the liability on that date. As shown in the "Analyze" step below, the discount of $6,624 (= $100,000 − $93,376) offsets the face value, so accountants will record it in a contra-liability account, which we identify using "xL." A contra-liability account is recorded as a debit as in the journal entry that follows:

1 Analyze

Assets		=	Liabilities		+	Shareholders' Equity
Cash	+93,376		Bonds Payable	+100,000		
			Discount on Bonds			
			Payable (+xL)	−6,624		

2 Record

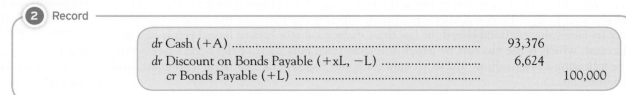

dr Cash (+A) 93,376
dr Discount on Bonds Payable (+xL, −L) 6,624
    cr Bonds Payable (+L) 100,000

Why would companies be willing to discount a bond? The answer is that they must if they want to issue it. If a bond promises to pay interest at a stated rate of 6 percent when other financial instruments offer 8 percent, no one will be willing to buy the bond unless the company discounts it. The discount reduces the initial bond price for investors without changing the interest payments and the face value paid to them. In effect, a discount increases the return that bondholders earn on their initial investment.

To illustrate, suppose you could buy a $1,000 bond that pays a stated interest rate of 6 percent and matures in one year. After one year, you would receive the stated interest of $60 ($1,000 × 6% × 12/12) plus the face value of $1,000. If you had paid $1,000 for the bond, you would receive 1.06 times as much as your initial investment [($60 + $1,000) ÷ $1,000]—a return of 6 percent. If instead the bond price was discounted $19, so that you paid only $981 for it, you would receive 1.08 times as much as your initial investment [($60 + $1,000) ÷ $981 = 1.08]—a return of 8 percent. This percentage represents both the bondholder's rate of return and the company's cost of borrowing. It is commonly referred to as the **market interest rate**.

YOU SHOULD KNOW

Market interest rate: The rate of interest that investors demand from a bond.

Reporting Bond Liabilities   The total face value of a bond plus any related premium or minus any related discount is reported in the liabilities section of the balance sheet as in Exhibit 10.5 for our three examples. The amount of the bond liability, after taking into account any premium or discount, is referred to as the bond's carrying value.

EXHIBIT 10.5	Balance Sheet Reporting of Bond Liabilities

Bonds issued at a premium

Bonds Payable	$100,000
Premium on Bonds Payable	7,260
Carrying Value	107,260

Bonds issued at face value

Bonds Payable	$100,000

Bonds issued at a discount

Bonds Payable	$100,000
Discount on Bonds Payable	(6,624)
Carrying Value	93,376

To determine whether a bond will be issued at a premium, at face value, or at a discount, you need consider only the relationship between the stated interest rate on the bond (what the bond pays in cash) and the market interest rate (the return that bondholders require). Exhibit 10.6 illustrates this relationship.

EXHIBIT 10.6	Relationships between Interest Rates and Bond Pricing

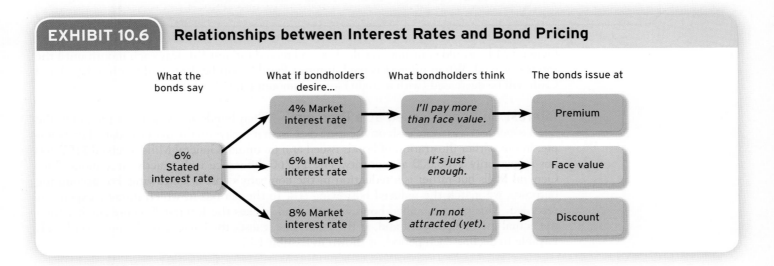

Before you continue, try the following Self-Study Practice.

Interest Expense

As time passes, a bond liability creates interest expense, which is matched to each period in which the liability is owed. Because interest expense arises from a financing decision (not an operating decision), it is reported below the Income from Operations line on the company's income statement.

Interest on Bonds Issued at Face Value   When bonds have been issued at face value, the process of calculating and recording interest on bonds is similar to that for Notes Payable. Assume, for example, that General Mills issues bonds on January 1, 2012, at their total face value of $100,000. If the bonds carry an annual stated interest rate of 6 percent payable in cash on December 31 of each year, General Mills will need to accrue an expense and liability for interest at the end of each accounting period. For the first month ended January 31, 2012, assuming no previous accrual of interest, General Mills would record interest of $500 (= $100,000 × 6% × 1/12) as follows:

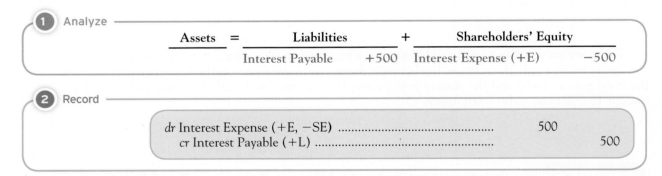

1 Analyze

Assets	=	Liabilities		+	Shareholders' Equity	
		Interest Payable	+500		Interest Expense (+E)	−500

2 Record

dr Interest Expense (+E, −SE)	500	
cr Interest Payable (+L)		500

General Mills would continue to calculate and record interest this way each month until the interest is paid. When interest is paid, Interest Payable will be decreased (with a debit) and Cash will be decreased (with a credit) for the amount paid.

Interest on Bonds Issued at a Premium   When bonds are issued at a premium, the bond issuer receives more cash on the issue date than it repays on the maturity date. For example, in our earlier illustration of bonds issued at a premium, General Mills received $107,260 but repays only $100,000 at maturity. The $7,260 difference isn't exactly "free money" for General Mills but rather is a reduction in the company's cost of borrowing. For accounting purposes, we match the reduced borrowing cost to the periods in which interest expense is recorded. This process, called **bond amortization**, makes the Interest Expense smaller than the actual interest payment and, at the same time, causes the balance in Premium on Bonds Payable to decline each period, as shown in Exhibit 10.7.

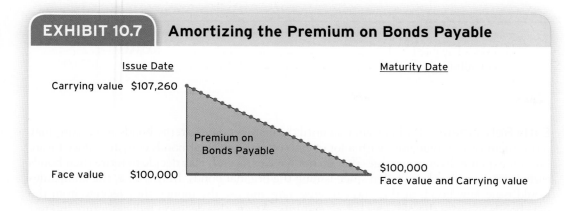

EXHIBIT 10.7 **Amortizing the Premium on Bonds Payable**

Issue Date — Maturity Date

Carrying value $107,260

Premium on Bonds Payable

Face value $100,000

$100,000 Face value and Carrying value

Procedures for amortizing bond premiums are explained in chapter Supplements 10A, 10B, and 10C. If you have been assigned any of these supplements, don't jump to them yet. We'll tell you later when it's best to read them.

Interest on Bonds Issued at a Discount When bonds are issued at a discount, the bond issuer receives less cash on the issue date than it repays on the maturity date. For example, in our earlier illustration of bonds issued at a discount, General Mills receives $93,376 on the issue date but repays $100,000 at maturity. For General Mills, the $6,624 discount represents an extra cost of borrowing, over and above each interest payment. For accounting purposes, we match the extra borrowing cost to the periods in which interest is recorded. This amortization causes the Interest Expense to be more than the interest payment and, at the same time, causes Discount on Bonds Payable to decrease each period. As the Discount on Bonds Payable decreases, the carrying value of the liability increases until it reaches $100,000 on the maturity date, as illustrated in Exhibit 10.8.

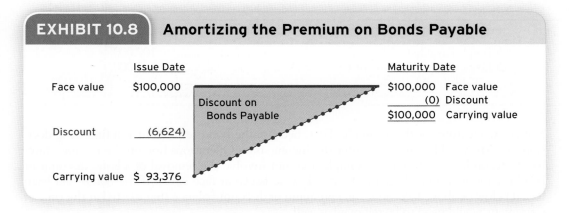

EXHIBIT 10.8 **Amortizing the Premium on Bonds Payable**

Issue Date — Maturity Date

Face value $100,000

Discount on Bonds Payable

Discount (6,624)

Carrying value $ 93,376

$100,000 Face value
(0) Discount
$100,000 Carrying value

At this point, you should read any of the assigned chapter supplements, then come back here and continue with the remainder of this section. The chapter supplements begin on page 431.

Bond Retirements

Retirement at Maturity Most bonds are retired (paid off) at maturity. If interest has been fully paid at the time of maturity, the only remaining account to settle will be Bonds Payable. Assuming the General Mills bonds in our example were retired with a payment equal to their $100,000 face value, the transaction would be analyzed and recorded as follows:

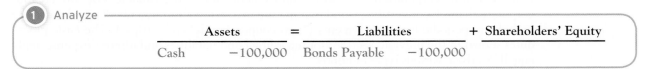

1 Analyze

Assets		=	Liabilities		+ Shareholders' Equity
Cash	−100,000		Bonds Payable	−100,000	

> dr Bonds Payable (−L) 100,000
> cr Cash (−A) 100,000

Early Retirement

Rather than wait until the maturity date to retire bonds, a company may retire them early. Companies with a lot of cash often retire their bonds early to reduce future interest expense. Even companies that do not have extra cash may decide to retire their bonds early if interest rates have fallen since issuing the original bonds. In this case, the companies would issue new bonds at the lower interest rate and use the money they receive from the new bonds to retire the old ones before maturity. Again, this decision reduces future interest expense, which increases future earnings.

The early retirement of bonds has three financial effects. The company (1) pays cash, (2) eliminates the bond liability, and (3) reports either a gain or a loss. A gain arises if the cash paid to retire the bonds is less than the carrying value of the bond liability. A loss is incurred if the company pays more than the carrying value at the time of retirement.

To illustrate these effects, assume that in 2002, General Mills issued $100,000 of bonds at face value. Ten years later, in 2012, the company retired the bonds early. At the time, the bond price was 103, so General Mills made a payment of $103,000 (= $100,000 × 1.03) to retire the bonds. This transaction would be analyzed and recorded as follows:

1 Analyze

Assets	=	Liabilities	+	Shareholders' Equity
Cash −103,000		Bonds Payable −100,000		Loss on Bond Retirement (+E) −3,000

2 Record

> dr Bonds Payable (−L) 100,000
> dr Loss on Bond Retirement (+E, −SE) 3,000
> cr Cash (−A) 103,000

Notice two features of this example. First, because the bond retirement is a financing decision, the loss would be reported after the Income from Operations line on the income statement. Second, this retirement example does not involve the removal of a bond discount or bond premium account because the bonds were issued at face value. If the bonds had been issued below or above face value, any premium or discount balance that existed at the time of retirement would need to be removed as well.

Types of Bonds

When you first start learning about bonds, the number of new terms that describe the bonds might seem to be limitless. These terms can generally be grouped into two categories: (1) those that describe the type of organization that issued the bonds and (2) those that describe specific features of the bond. In the first category are bonds issued by the Government of Canada, municipal organizations such as cities and towns, and corporations. In the second category are bonds that are backed by collateral ("secured") or not ("debentures") that the issuing corporation can call in and exchange for cash ("callable") or convert into corporate shares ("convertible"), and that mature in a series of instalments ("serial bonds") or include no periodic interest payments ("zero-coupon bonds" and "strips"). The basic procedures shown in the previous sections for recording bond liabilities and interest expense apply equally to these various types of bonds.

CONTINGENT LIABILITIES

Learning Objective 4

Describe how to account for contingent liabilities.

Contingent liabilities are potential liabilities that arise as a result of past transactions or events, but their ultimate resolution depends (is contingent) on a future event. Contingent liabilities differ from other liabilities discussed in this chapter because their dependence on a future event introduces a great deal of uncertainty. For example, consider accounting for lawsuits against the company. Some suits may be defended successfully but others may result in huge settlements awarded from the judgment of the case. Given such uncertainties, accounting rules require the company to evaluate whether it is likely to be found liable and, if so, whether the amount of the liability is estimable. As Exhibit 10.9 indicates, if a contingent liability is possible but not probable or its amount cannot be estimated, a liability is not recorded in the accounting records or reported on the balance sheet. Instead, the potential liability and related loss should be described in a note to the financial statements.

YOU SHOULD KNOW

Contingent liabilities: Potential liabilities that have arisen as a result of a past transaction or event; their ultimate outcome will not be known until a future event occurs or fails to occur.

EXHIBIT 10.9 ASPE for Contingent Liabilities

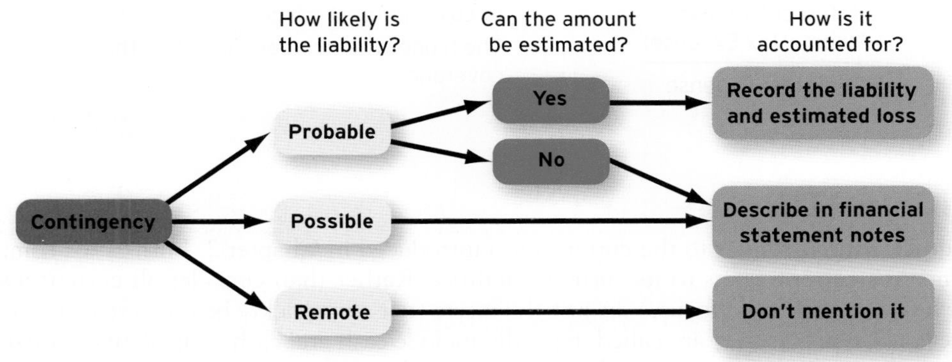

SPOTLIGHT ON THE WORLD

Just How Certain Are You? Differences between ASPE and IFRS

Under ASPE, contingent liabilities (and corresponding losses) are recorded if the estimated loss is probable. Under IFRS, contingent liabilities (and corresponding losses) are recorded if the estimated loss is "more likely than not" to occur. The threshold under IFRS is lower than that under ASPE, which should cause more contingent liabilities to be reported on the balance sheet under IFRS than under ASPE.

Now that you have seen how liabilities are accounted for inside a company, let's consider them again from the outside. How do users judge whether liabilities are likely to be repaid in full?

Evaluate the Results

In evaluating a company's ability to pay its liabilities, a good place to start is with the reports that credit-rating agencies issue. These agencies do not report on all companies, however, particularly not the smaller ones. Even if they did, their reports might not address

Learning Objective 5

Calculate and interpret the quick ratio and the times interest earned ratio.

your specific concerns. So, you need to know how to analyze a set of financial statements in the same way that a credit rater would.

Essentially, you want to assess whether the company has the assets available to pay what it currently owes, and whether the company is likely to generate the resources needed to pay future amounts that will be owed. Two financial ratios are commonly used to make these assessments: the quick ratio and the times interest earned ratio.

ACCOUNTING DECISION TOOLS

Name of Measure	Formula	What It Tells You
Quick ratio	$\dfrac{\text{(Cash + Short-Term Investments + Accounts Receivable, Net)}}{\text{Current Liabilities}}$	• Whether liquid assets are sufficient to pay current liabilities • The higher the number the better able to quickly pay
Times interest earned ratio	$\dfrac{\text{(Net Income + Interest Expense + Income Tax Expense)}}{\text{Interest Expense}}$	• Whether sufficient resources are generated to cover interest costs • The higher the number the better the coverage

---

QUICK RATIO

The **quick ratio** is similar to the current ratio introduced in Chapter 2. Both ratios compare a company's current assets to its current liabilities. Rather than consider all current assets, however, the quick ratio focuses on just the assets that can quickly be converted into cash. These *liquid assets*, as they are called, typically include cash and cash equivalents, short-term investments, and accounts receivable (net of doubtful accounts).

As with all ratios, judgment is required to interpret the quick ratio. Generally speaking, a high quick ratio suggests a high ability to pay current liabilities. For example, a quick ratio greater than 1.0 implies a company could pay all its current liabilities immediately if it was required to. However, lower ratios do not necessarily imply a company will be unable to pay its current liabilities. For example, at the end of its 2010 fiscal year, General Mills reported $673 million of cash and cash equivalents, no short-term investments, and $1,042 million of net accounts receivable. Using these numbers and the $3,769 million in total current liabilities shown in Exhibit 10.1, we can calculate the quick ratio for General Mills as follows:

$$\frac{\text{Cash + Short-Term Investments + Accounts Receivable, Net}}{\text{Current Liabilities}} = \frac{\$673 + \$0 + \$1,042}{\$3,769} = 0.455$$

A quick ratio of 0.455 implies that General Mills would be able to pay only 45.5 percent of its current liabilities, if forced to pay them immediately. However, this interpretation overlooks a few important facts. First, not all current liabilities are to be paid immediately. The $1.1 billion of Notes Payable in Exhibit 10.1, for example, may not be payable until late in the following year and, at that time, could be refinanced over even longer periods. Second, General Mills generates nearly $5 million in cash from its operations each day. These huge future cash inflows aren't included in the existing cash balance. Third, the company has arranged a **line of credit**, as discussed in the following Spotlight feature.

Surviving a Financial Crunch

In difficult economic times, it is imperative for companies to have adequate financing in place. Prior to the economic downturn in 2008, General Mills had established a line of credit that provides up to $3 billion cash on an as-needed basis. Rather than hold extra cash, General Mills uses its line of credit to borrow only when money is needed. Not all companies are able to establish lines of credit, but those that do are able to survive with a quick ratio less than 1.0. To determine whether a company has a line of credit available, be sure to read the company's notes to the financial statements. General Mills reports its line of credit in its long-term debt note.

TIMES INTEREST EARNED RATIO

One way to judge a company's ability to pay interest is to ask whether it has generated enough income to cover its interest expense. The measure that most analysts use for this purpose is the **times interest earned ratio**.

The accounting decision tools feature (on the facing page) showed the formula for the times interest earned ratio. It is reproduced after the following paragraph. Notice that in this ratio, interest and income tax expenses are added back into net income. The reason for this is simple: Analysts want to know whether a company generates enough income to cover its interest expense before the costs of financing and taxes. In general, a high times interest earned ratio is viewed more favourably than a low one. A high ratio indicates an extra margin of protection if the company's profitability declines in the future.

Using information from the fiscal year-end 2010 income statement reported by General Mills, we can compute the times interest earned ratio as follows:

$$\frac{\text{Net Income} + \text{Interest Expense} + \text{Income Tax Expense}}{\text{Interest Expense}} = \frac{\$1,531 + \$402 + \$771}{\$402} = 6.73$$

> **YOU SHOULD KNOW**
>
> **Times interest earned ratio:** Divides net income before interest and taxes by interest expense to determine the extent to which earnings before taxes and financing costs are sufficient to cover interest incurred on debt.

This ratio means that General Mills generates $6.73 of income (before the costs of financing and taxes) for each dollar of interest expense. No doubt this ratio is part of the reason that General Mills has earned a favourable credit rating of BBB+.

Every now and then you will see a times interest earned ratio that is less than 1.0 or even negative. When the times interest earned ratio is less than 1.0, a company is not generating enough income to cover its interest expense. Most companies with a negative times interest earned ratio survive only a couple of years before declaring bankruptcy.

SUPPLEMENT 10A: Straight-Line Method of Amortization

Exhibits 10.7 and 10.8 illustrated how a bond premium or discount decreases each year until it is completely eliminated on the bond's maturity date. This process is called *amortizing the bond premium or discount*. The **straight-line amortization method** reduces the premium or discount by an equal amount each period. Because this method results in an equal amount each period, it is easy to apply. However, it distorts the financial results somewhat because it produces an equal Interest Expense each period, even though the bond's carrying value changes each period. For this reason, ASPE allows the straight-line method to be used only when it does not materially differ from the effective-interest method of amortization (presented in Supplement 10B). This is different however under IFRS, where the effective-interest method of amortization is required.

> **YOU SHOULD KNOW**
>
> **Straight-line amortization method:** For bonds payable, evenly allocates the amount of bond premium or discount over each period of a bond's life to adjust interest expense for differences between its stated interest rate and market interest rate.

Bond Premiums

In our earlier example of bonds issued at a premium, General Mills received $107,260 on the issue date (January 1, 2012) but repays only $100,000 at maturity (December 31, 2015). The $7,260 difference is considered a reduction in the company's borrowing cost over the four-year period the bond is owed. Under the straight-line method, this $7,260 is spread evenly as a reduction in interest expense over the four years ($7,260 ÷ 4 = $1,815 per year). So when General Mills makes its yearly $6,000 cash payment for interest, it will report Interest Expense of only $4,185 ($6,000 − $1,815). The remainder of the $6,000 cash payment is reported as a reduction in the bond liability, as follows:

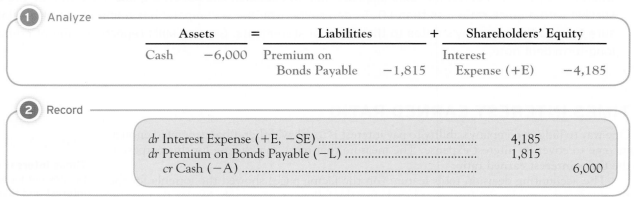

① Analyze

	Assets	=	Liabilities	+	Shareholders' Equity
Cash	−6,000	Premium on Bonds Payable	−1,815	Interest Expense (+E)	−4,185

② Record

dr Interest Expense (+E, −SE) 4,185
dr Premium on Bonds Payable (−L) 1,815
   cr Cash (−A) 6,000

In effect, the $6,000 payment includes both an interest component ($4,185) and a repayment of the bond liability ($1,815). The same accounting equation effects and journal entry will be recorded each year on December 31 until the bonds mature. The following bond amortization schedule summarizes the journal entry effects each period (on the left) and the updated balance sheet account balances (on the right):

Bond Premium Amortization Schedule: Straight-Line Method

	Journal Entry Components			Balance Sheet Accounts		
	(A)	(B) Amortized Premium	(C) (= A − B) Interest Expense	(D) Bonds Payable	(E) Premium on Bonds Payable	(F) (= D + E) Carrying Value
Period Ended	Cash Paid					
01/01/2012				$100,000	$7,260	$107,260
12/31/2012	$6,000	$1,815	$4,185	100,000	5,445	105,445
12/31/2013	6,000	1,815	4,185	100,000	3,630	103,630
12/31/2014	6,000	1,815	4,185	100,000	1,815	101,815
12/31/2015	6,000	1,815	4,185	100,000	0	100,000

Bond Discounts

A discount arises when the bond issuer receives less cash than the issuer repays at maturity. In effect, a discount increases the company's cost of borrowing, so amortization of the discount causes interest expense to be higher than the interest payment each period. To report this effect, accountants record a decrease in Discount on Bonds Payable and an increase in Interest Expense.

In our earlier example, General Mills received $93,376 for four-year bonds with a total face value of $100,000, implying a discount of $6,624. Using the straight-line method, amortization of the discount in each of the four years that the bonds remain unpaid would be $1,656 (= $6,624 ÷ 4). This amount would be added to the interest to be paid ($6,000) to calculate the amount of Interest Expense ($7,656). The effects would be recorded as follows:

① Analyze

	Assets	=	Liabilities	+	Shareholders' Equity
Cash	−6,000	Discount on Bonds Payable (−xL)	+1,656	Interest Expense (+E)	−7,656

dr Interest Expense (+E, −SE) 7,656
dr Discount on Bonds Payable (−xL, +L)...............................   1,656
    cr Cash (−A)   6,000

The same accounting equation effects and journal entry would be recorded each year on December 31 until the bonds mature. The following bond amortization schedule summarizes the effects that must be recorded each period (on the left), producing the end-of-year balance sheet account balances (on the right):

Bond Discount Amortization Schedule: Straight-Line Method

	Journal Entry Components			Balance Sheet Accounts		
Period Ended	(A) Cash Paid	(B) Amortized Discount	(C) (= A + B) Interest Expense	(D) Bonds Payable	(E) Discount on Bonds Payable	(F) (= D − E) Carrying Value
01/01/2012				$100,000	$6,624	$ 93,376
12/31/2012	$6,000	$1,656	$7,656	100,000	4,968	95,032
12/31/2013	6,000	1,656	7,656	100,000	3,312	96,688
12/31/2014	6,000	1,656	7,656	100,000	1,656	98,344
12/31/2015	6,000	1,656	7,656	100,000	0	100,000

SUPPLEMENT 10B: Effective-Interest Method of Amortization

The **effective-interest method of amortization** is considered a conceptually superior method of accounting for bonds because it correctly calculates interest expense by multiplying the true cost of borrowing times the amount of money actually owed to investors. The true cost of borrowing is the market interest rate that investors used to determine the bond issue price. The actual amount owed to investors is the carrying value of the bond, which equals the cash received when the bond was issued plus any interest that has been incurred but not yet paid. It can then be understood why this is the required method under IFRS, where financial statements on a global basis are to be comparative.

To clearly understand the effective-interest method, it helps to see how a bond's issue price depends on the market interest rate. As we mentioned in the chapter, investors in the market decide how much to pay for a bond by using a mathematical calculation called a **present value**. You can read instructions about how to calculate present values in Appendix D at the back of this book, but for now, just focus on understanding what present value is. Present value is the idea that something is worth more if you get it today than if you get it some time in the future. For example, if someone offered to pay you $100,000 today or $100,000 five years from now, you'd be better off taking it today. You could invest the money and earn interest for five years, making it worth more than $100,000. The same idea explains why you could be equally happy with receiving $100,000 in five years or some smaller amount today. To figure out how much this smaller amount is, you just calculate the present value of $100,000. The only pieces of information you need for this calculation are (1) the amounts to be received in the future, (2) the number of months between now and then, and (3) the interest rate you expect to earn during that time.

In the bond context, investors calculate the present value of the amounts received periodically (at the stated interest rate) and at maturity (the face value), using the interest rate that they want to earn. We have summarized this calculation in Exhibit 10B.1 for General Mills' 6 percent, four-year bond. We show three different scenarios, with each one involving different market interest rates but the same 6 percent stated interest rate. The first column calculates the amount of money that investors would be willing to give up if they needed to earn 4 percent on the amount they pay for the bond. The second column calculates the amount investors would pay if they wanted to earn an interest rate of 6 percent. The third column calculates the amount that investors would be willing to pay if they wanted to earn 8 percent on the amount they pay for the bond. (For detailed calculations underlying the amounts in Exhibit 10B.1, see Appendix D at the back of the book.)

EXHIBIT 10B.1 Computing the Present Value of Bond Payments

	MARKET INTEREST RATES		
	4%	6%	8%
Present value of $100,000 face value (principal) paid four years from now	$ 85,480	$ 79,210	$73,503
Present value of $6,000 (6% stated interest rate) paid once a year for four years	21,780	20,790	19,873
Bond price	**$107,260**	**$100,000**	**$93,376**

Notice that when the bond pays interest at a rate that exactly matches the rate required by investors in the market (6 percent), they are willing to pay face value ($100,000) for it. If the 6 percent interest rate stated on the bond is more than investors require (4 percent), they will pay a premium for the bond (as shown in the first column). If the 6 percent interest promised is less than the market interest rate (8 percent), investors pay less than face value for the bond, resulting in a discounted bond price as indicated in the third column. Let's now look at what happens to a bond premium and discount under the effective-interest amortization method.

Bond Premiums

In our earlier example of a bond premium, General Mills promised to make cash interest payments each year at a stated rate of 6 percent. Investors found this stated interest rate attractive, so the bond issued at a $7,260 premium. When General Mills adds this $7,260 premium to the $100,000 face value, it reports a carrying value of $107,260 (= $100,000 + $7,260) on January 1, 2012. Exhibit 10B.1 indicates that the $107,260 total implies the market interest rate was 4 percent. General Mills uses this market interest rate to calculate its Interest Expense on the bond, using a variation of the interest formula. For example, General Mills calculates Interest Expense in the first year ended December 31, 2012, as follows:

2012:

	Interest (I) =	Principal (P)	× Interest Rate (R)	× Time (T)
Interest Expense	=	Carrying Value	× Market Interest Rate	× n/12
$4,290	=	$107,260	× 4%	× 12/12

Use the information *stated* on the *face* of the bond to calculate the **Cash** interest payment:

	Interest (I) =	Principal (P) ×	Interest Rate (R)	× Time (T)
Cash Payment	=	Face Value	× Stated Interest Rate	× n/12
$6,000	=	$100,000	× 6%	× 12/12

Because the $6,000 cash interest payment exceeds the $4,290 Interest Expense by $1,710 ($6,000 − $4,290 = $1,710), General Mills records a $1,710 reduction in its bond liability.

In effect, the $6,000 cash payment includes both an interest component ($4,290) and a partial repayment of the bond liability ($1,710), as analyzed and recorded below:

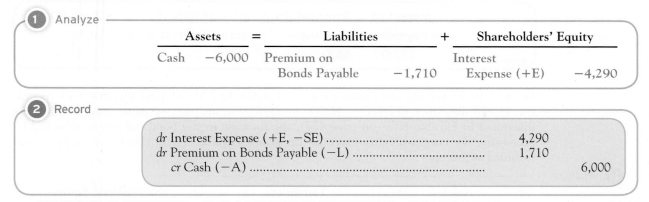

① Analyze

	Assets	=	Liabilities	+	Shareholders' Equity
Cash	−6,000		Premium on Bonds Payable −1,710		Interest Expense (+E) −4,290

② Record

dr Interest Expense (+E, −SE) 4,290
dr Premium on Bonds Payable (−L) 1,710
    cr Cash (−A)   6,000

Similar calculations and accounting effects occur each period until the bonds mature. The only thing to watch out for is that the carrying value of the bond liability decreases each year because the cash payment includes a partial repayment of the bond liability. For example, after the above entry is recorded on December 31, 2012, the Premium on Bonds Payable decreases by $1,710, from $7,260 to $5,550. Thus, the Interest Expense for the second year of the bond (for the year ended December 31, 2013) is

Premium on Bonds Payable (L)

	7,260	1/1/2012
12/31/2012 1,710		
	5,550	12/31/2012

2013:

	Interest (I) =	Principal (P)	× Interest Rate (R)	× Time (T)
Interest Expense =	Carrying Value	× Market Interest Rate	× n/12
$4,222 =	$105,550	× 4%	× 12/12

The following bond amortization schedule summarizes the effects that must be recorded each period (on the left), producing the end-of-year balance sheet account balances (on the right):

	Bond Premium Amortization Schedule: Effective-Interest Method						
	Journal Entry Components				Balance Sheet Accounts		
	(A)	(B) Interest Expense	(C) (= A − B) Amortized Premium		(D) Bonds Payable	(E) Premium on Bonds Payable	(F) (= D + E) Carrying Value
Period Ended	Cash Paid						
01/01/2012					$100,000	$7,260	$107,260
12/31/2012	$6,000	$4,290	$1,710		100,000	5,550	105,550
12/31/2013	6,000	4,222	1,778		100,000	3,772	103,772
12/31/2014	6,000	4,151	1,849		100,000	1,923	101,923
12/31/2015	6,000	4,077	1,923		100,000	0	100,000

Bond Discounts

In our earlier example of a bond discount, General Mills promised to make cash interest payments each year at a stated rate of 6 percent. Investors did not find this stated interest rate attractive, so the bond issued at a $6,624 discount. When General Mills subtracts this $6,624 discount from the $100,000 face value, it reports a carrying value of $93,376 (= $100,000 − $6,624) on January 1, 2012. Exhibit 10B.1 indicates that the $93,376 implies the market interest rate was 8 percent. General Mills uses this market interest rate to calculate its Interest Expense on the bond, as we did in the case of a bond premium. The Interest Expense for the first year ended December 31, 2012, is calculated as

2012:

	Interest (I) =	Principal (P)	× Interest Rate (R)	× Time (T)
Interest Expense =	Carrying Value	× Market Interest Rate	× n/12
$7,470 =	$93,376	× 8%	× 12/12

Use the information *stated* on the *face* of the bond to calculate the cash interest payment:

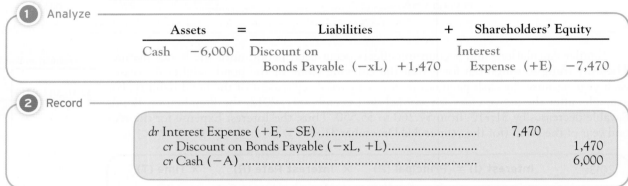

Interest (I) =	Principal (P)	× Interest Rate (R)	× Time (T)
Cash Payment =	Face Value	× Stated Interest Rate	× n/12
$6,000 =	$100,000	× 6%	× 12/12

Because the $7,470 Interest Expense is more than the $6,000 cash paid, General Mills records the $1,470 difference ($7,470 − $6,000 = $1,470) as an increase in its bond liability. As illustrated in Exhibit 10.8 (on page 427), the increase in the bond liability is achieved by decreasing the contra-liability Discount on Bonds Payable. These effects are analyzed and recorded as follows:

1 Analyze

Assets	=	Liabilities	+	Shareholders' Equity
Cash −6,000		Discount on Bonds Payable (−xL) +1,470		Interest Expense (+E) −7,470

2 Record

dr Interest Expense (+E, −SE)	7,470	
cr Discount on Bonds Payable (−xL, +L)..........................		1,470
cr Cash (−A)		6,000

The T-account presented in the margin shows how the above journal entry reduces Discount on Bonds Payable. A reduction of this contra-liability account increases the carrying value of the long-term liability, as you can see by moving from left to right in Exhibit 10B.2.

Discount on Bonds Payable (xL)	
1/1/2012 6,624	
	1,470 12/31/2012
12/31/2012 5,154	

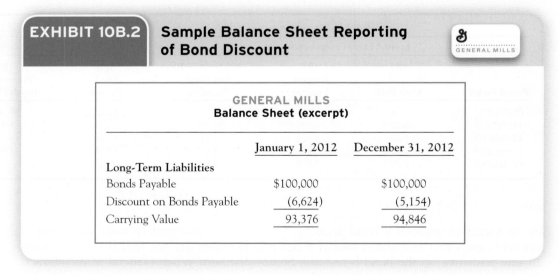

EXHIBIT 10B.2 | **Sample Balance Sheet Reporting of Bond Discount**

GENERAL MILLS

GENERAL MILLS
Balance Sheet (excerpt)

	January 1, 2012	December 31, 2012
Long-Term Liabilities		
Bonds Payable	$100,000	$100,000
Discount on Bonds Payable	(6,624)	(5,154)
Carrying Value	93,376	94,846

> **COACH'S TIP**
>
> The interest expense for 2013 is greater than that for 2012 because the carrying value was greater in 2013 than in 2012.

Let's now consider the interest expense for 2013. As in 2012, the 2013 interest expense is calculated using the market interest rate. However, the carrying value of bonds owed at the end of 2012 increased, as shown in Exhibit 10B.2. Thus, interest expense also will increase in 2013, calculated as follows:

2013:	Interest (I) =	Principal (P)	× Interest Rate (R)	× Time (T)
	Interest Expense =	Carrying Value	× Market Interest Rate	× n/12
	$7,588 =	$94,846	× 8%	× 12/12

Because the Interest Expense ($7,588) is greater than the cash payment ($6,000), the bond liability is increased (by reducing the contra-liability). This is reflected in the accounting equation and recorded with the journal entry on December 31, 2013, as follows:

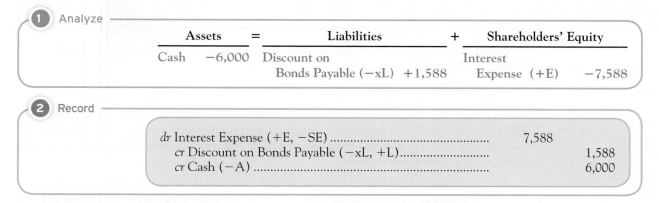

1 Analyze

Assets	=	Liabilities	+	Shareholders' Equity
Cash −6,000		Discount on Bonds Payable (−xL) +1,588		Interest Expense (+E) −7,588

2 Record

dr Interest Expense (+E, −SE)	7,588	
cr Discount on Bonds Payable (−xL, +L)...........................		1,588
cr Cash (−A)		6,000

The following bond amortization schedule summarizes the effects that must be recorded each period (on the left), producing the end-of-year balance sheet account balances (on the right):

Bond Discount Amortization Schedule: Effective-Interest Method						
	Journal Entry Components			Balance Sheet Accounts		
	(A)	(B) Interest Expense	(C) (= B − A) Amortized Discount	(D) Bonds Payable	(E) Discount on Bonds Payable	(F) (= D − E) Carrying Value
Period Ended	Cash Paid					
01/01/2012				$100,000	$6,624	$ 93,376
12/31/2012	$6,000	$7,470	$1,470	100,000	5,154	94,846
12/31/2013	6,000	7,588	1,588	100,000	3,566	96,434
12/31/2014	6,000	7,715	1,715	100,000	1,851	98,149
12/31/2015	6,000	7,851	1,851	100,000	0	100,000

SUPPLEMENT 10C: Simplified Effective-Interest Amortization

This supplement presents a simplified explanation of how to account for bond liabilities and interest expense. Remember that the effective-interest method is required by IFRS and can be used for ASPE. You should be aware that this approach involves taking a shortcut. While the shortcut will help you to focus on the line items that ultimately are reported on the financial statements, it requires that we ignore a few accounts that are typically used behind the scenes in real-world accounting systems. Be sure to check with your instructor (or course outline) to see whether you are expected to read this supplement.

If you're like most people, you probably have to concentrate really hard when reading about how a *reduction* in a contra-liability account causes an *increase* in the carrying value of a bond. You may even whisper this statement quietly to yourself a few times before it starts making sense. In this section, we present a shortcut when accounting for bonds that will allow you to avoid thinking in "double-negatives" like this. Hopefully, it will also help you to stop whispering to yourself when you read.

Accounting for the Bond Issue

The shortcut involves simplifying only one aspect of what you studied earlier in this chapter. Rather than record a discount or premium in a separate account, we combine the discount or premium with the bond's face value in a single account that we will call *Bonds Payable, Net*. This name is used to remind you that we are focusing on what is ultimately reported in the financial statements rather than what is actually used behind the scenes. The following journal entries demonstrate how the shortcut is applied to bonds issued at a premium, at face value, and at a discount.

	Premium	Face Value	Discount
dr Cash (+A)	107,260	100,000	93,376
cr Bonds Payable, Net (+L)	107,260	100,000	93,376

As you can see, the structure of the journal entry does not vary from one case to the next; only the amount varies.

Interest Expense

As time passes, the company incurs Interest Expense on its bond liability. Because the bond liability was recorded in a single account, the interest calculation is the same whether the bond has been issued at a premium or discount. The following version of the interest formula is used to compute Interest Expense.

> **Interest (I) = Principal (P)   × Interest Rate (R)   × Time (T)**
> Interest Expense = Bonds Payable, Net × Market Interest Rate × n/12

The market interest rate is determined by using present value techniques (discussed in Appendix D) that relate the bond's issue price to the payments promised over the life of the bond.

Bond Premiums

Our bond premium example indicated that General Mills received $107,260 on the issue date, which we would record in Bonds Payable, Net, using the journal entry shown above. The $107,260 issue price implies a 4 percent market interest rate. The bonds promise to pay the 6 percent stated interest rate on their total face value of $100,000. This information is used to compute Interest Expense and the annual cash payment as follows:

> 2012:   **Interest (I) = Principal (P)   × Interest Rate (R)   × Time (T)**
> Interest Expense = Bonds Payable, Net × Market Interest Rate × n/12
> $4,290 = $107,260   × 4%   × 12/12

> **Interest (I) = Principal (P) × Interest Rate (R)   × Time (T)**
> Cash Payment = Face Value   × Stated Interest Rate × n/12
> $6,000 = $100,000   × 6%   × 12/12

Because the $6,000 cash interest payment exceeds the $4,290 Interest Expense by $1,710 ($6,000 − $4,290 = $1,710), General Mills records a $1,710 reduction in Bonds Payable, Net. In effect, the $6,000 cash payment includes both an interest component ($4,290) and a partial repayment of the bond liability ($1,710), as analyzed and recorded below:

1 Analyze

Assets	=	Liabilities	+	Shareholders' Equity
Cash −6,000		Bonds Payable, Net −1,710		Interest Expense (+E) −4,290

2 Record

dr Interest Expense (+E, −SE)	4,290	
dr Bonds Payable, Net (−L)	1,710	
cr Cash (−A)		6,000

Similar calculations and accounting effects occur each period until the bonds mature. The only thing to watch out for is that Bonds Payable, Net decreases each year because the cash payment includes a partial repayment of the bond liability. For example, after the above entry is recorded on December 31, 2012, Bonds Payable, Net decreases by $1,710, from $107,260 to $105,550. This new balance is used to compute Interest Expense for the second year of the bond (for the year ended December 31, 2013):

Bonds Payable, Net (L)	
	107,260 1/1/2012
12/31/2012 1,710	
	105,550 12/31/2012

2013:	**Interest (I) =**	**Principal (P)**	× **Interest Rate (R)**	× **Time (T)**
Interest Expense	=	Bonds Payable, Net	× Market Interest Rate	× n/12
$4,222	=	$105,550	× 4%	× 12/12

Because the $6,000 annual cash payment exceeds the $4,222 Interest Expense by $1,778 ($6,000 − $4,222 = $1,778), General Mills records a $1,778 reduction in Bonds Payable, Net in 2013. In effect, the $6,000 cash payment includes both an interest component ($4,222) and a partial repayment of the bond liability ($1,778). As the following amortization schedule shows, the bond liability continues to decrease until, at maturity, it reaches the bonds' face value ($100,000).

Bond Premium Amortization Schedule: Simplified Method

	Beginning of Year	Changes During the Year			End of Year
	(A)	(B)	(C)	(D) = (C − B)	(E) = (A − D)
Period	Bonds Payable, Net	Interest Expense	Cash Paid	Reduction in Bonds Payable, Net	Bonds Payable, Net
1/1/12–12/31/12	$107,260	$4,290	$6,000	$1,710	$105,550
1/1/13–12/31/13	105,550	4,222	6,000	1,778	103,772
1/1/14–12/31/14	103,772	4,151	6,000	1,849	101,923
1/1/15–12/31/15	101,923	4,077	6,000	1,923	100,000

Bond Discounts

Our bond discount example indicated that General Mills received $93,376 on the issue date, which we would record in Bonds Payable, Net, using the journal entry shown on the facing page. This issue price implies an 8 percent market interest rate. The bonds promise to pay the 6 percent stated interest rate on their total face value of $100,000. This information is used to compute Interest Expense and the annual cash payment as follows:

2012:	**Interest (I) =**	**Principal (P)**	× **Interest Rate (R)**	× **Time (T)**
Interest Expense	=	Bonds Payable, Net	× Market Interest Rate	× n/12
$7,470	=	$93,376	× 8%	× 12/12

	Interest (I) =	**Principal (P)**	× **Interest Rate (R)**	× **Time (T)**
Cash Payment	=	Face Value	× Stated Interest Rate	× n/12
$6,000	=	$100,000	× 6%	× 12/12

Because the $7,470 Interest Expense is more than the $6,000 cash paid, General Mills records the $1,470 difference ($7,470 − $6,000 = $1,470) as an increase in its liability Bonds Payable, Net, as follows:

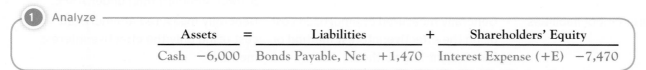

1 Analyze

Assets	=	Liabilities	+	Shareholders' Equity
Cash −6,000		Bonds Payable, Net +1,470		Interest Expense (+E) −7,470

$$dr \text{ Interest Expense } (+E, -SE) \dots\dots\dots\dots\dots\dots\dots\dots\dots\dots\dots \quad 7,470$$
$$cr \text{ Bonds Payable, Net } (+L) \dots\dots\dots\dots\dots\dots\dots\dots\dots\dots\dots \quad\quad 1,470$$
$$cr \text{ Cash } (-A) \dots\dots\dots\dots\dots\dots\dots\dots\dots\dots\dots\dots\dots\dots \quad\quad 6,000$$

Recording the $1,470 as the liability Bonds Payable, Net is appropriate because General Mills will pay this amount at maturity, as part of the face value of the bond.

Similar calculations and accounting effects occur each period until the bonds mature. The only thing to watch out for is that Bonds Payable, Net increases each year because the cash payment is less than the interest expense. For example, after the above entry is recorded on December 31, 2012, Bonds Payable, Net increases by $1,470, from $93,376 to $94,846. This new balance is used to compute Interest Expense for the second year of the bond (for the year ended December 31, 2013):

Bonds Payable, Net (L)	
	93,376 1/1/2012
	1,470 12/31/2012
	94,846 12/31/2012

2013:	**Interest (I)** =	**Principal (P)**	× **Interest Rate (R)**	× **Time (T)**
	Interest Expense =	Bonds Payable, Net	× Market Interest Rate	× n/12
	$7,588 =	$94,846	× 8%	× 12/12

Because the $7,588 Interest Expense exceeds the $6,000 annual cash payment by $1,588 ($7,588 − $6,000 = $1,588), General Mills records a $1,588 increase in Bonds Payable, Net in 2013. In effect, the $1,588 in unpaid interest will be paid at maturity. As the following amortization schedule shows, the bond liability continues to increase until, at maturity, it reaches the bonds' face value ($100,000).

Bond Discount Amortization Schedule: Simplified Method

	Beginning of Year	Changes During the Year			End of Year
Period	(A) Bonds Payable, Net	(B) Interest Expense	(C) Cash Paid	(D) = (B − C) Reduction in Bonds Payable, Net	(E) = (A + D) Bonds Payable, Net
1/1/12–12/31/12	$93,376	$7,470	$6,000	$1,470	$ 94,846
1/1/13–12/31/13	94,846	7,588	6,000	1,588	96,434
1/1/14–12/31/14	96,434	7,715	6,000	1,715	98,149
1/1/15–12/31/15	98,149	7,851	6,000	1,851	100,000

SPOTLIGHT ON IFRS and ASPE

Topic	ASPE	IFRS
Presentation of callable long-term debt (due to a violations of a debt covenant)	The debt can remain as long-term debt if the company renegotiates the loan prior to releasing its financial statements.	The debt must be reported as a current liability.
Recognition of contingent liabilities	Recognize the liability if the occurrence of the future event is "likely," meaning that it is highly probable and also measurable.	Recognize the liability if the occurrence of the future event is "probable," meaning more likely than not and also measurable. This is a lower standard than under ASPE.
Measurement of liabilities	Generally measured at amortized cost using the effective-interest method or the straight-line method.	Generally measured at amortized cost using only the effective-interest method.

This section provides a chance to solidify your understanding of key points. It's worth your time to work through the following demonstration cases, scan the chapter summary, test your understanding of key terms, and then practise, practise, practise.

DEMONSTRATION CASE A: ACCRUED LIABILITIES AND UNEARNED REVENUE

Online Games, Inc., reported the following information in its accounting records on December 31, 2012:

Annual subscription payments received in December 2012 for 2013 services	$12,000
Gross salaries earned by employees (December 26–31, 2012)	3,600
Income taxes withheld from employees (December 26–31, 2012)	610
CPP withheld from employees (December 26–31, 2012)	170
EI withheld from employees (December 26–31, 2012)	60
Net payment to employees (made on December 31, 2012)	2,760

The 2013 subscription payments will be earned equally during each month of 2013. The employees were paid $2,760 on December 31, 2012, but the withholdings have not yet been remitted nor have the employer CPP and EI contributions.

Required:

1. Describe how the 2013 subscription payments should be reported in the balance sheet and income statement on (a) December 31, 2012, and (b) January 31, 2013.
2. Show the accounting equation effects and give the journal entries for (a) the receipt of annual subscription payments in December 2012, and (b) any required adjustments for the subscription payments on January 31, 2013.
3. Compute the total payroll costs relating to the period from December 26–31, 2012.
4. Show the accounting equation effects and give the journal entries on December 31, 2012, to adjust for payroll costs relating to December 26–31, 2012.

Suggested Solution

1. a. On December 31, 2012, the $12,000 of advance subscription payments would be reported on the balance sheet as a current liability called *Unearned Revenue*. No amounts relating to 2013 subscription services would be reported in the 2012 income statement.

    b. On January 31, 2013, one month of subscription services would be earned, so Unearned Revenue on the balance sheet would be reduced by $1,000 (= $12,000 × 1/12) and Subscription Revenue on the income statement would be increased by $1,000.

2. a. December 2012 (receipt of 2013 subscription payments):

Assets	=	Liabilities	+	Shareholders' Equity
Cash +12,000		Unearned Revenue +12,000		

dr Cash (+A) 12,000
  cr Unearned Revenue (+L) 12,000

    b. January 31, 2013 (earned one month of 2013 subscriptions):

Assets =	Liabilities	+	Shareholders' Equity
	Unearned Revenue −1,000		Subscription Revenue (+R) +1,000

dr Unearned Revenue (−L) 1,000
  cr Subscription Revenue (+R, +SE).......... 1,000

3. Computation of total payroll costs:

Salaries and wages:	Net pay to employees	$2,760
	Income taxes withheld from employees	610
	CPP withheld from employees	170
	EI withheld from employees	60
	Total cost of salaries and wages	3,600
Employer payroll taxes:		
	CPP (employer matching contribution)	170
	EI (employer contribution 1.4 times the amount withheld from the employee)	84
Total payroll costs		$3,854

4. Salaries and wage costs:

Assets	=	Liabilities	+	Shareholders' Equity
Cash −2,760		Withheld Income		Salaries and Wages Expense (+E) −3,600
		Taxes Payable +610		
		CPP Payable +170		
		EI Payable +60		

dr Salaries and Wages Expense (+E, −SE) 3,600
 cr Withheld Income Taxes Payable (+L) 610
 cr CPP Payable (+L) 170
 cr EI Payable (+L) 60
 cr Cash (−A) 2,760

Employer-related payroll costs:

Assets	=	Liabilities	+	Shareholders' Equity
		CPP Payable (+L) +170		Payroll Tax Expense (+E) −254
		EI Payable (+L) +84		

dr Payroll Tax Expense (+E, −SE) 254
 cr CPP Payable (+L).. 171
 cr EI Payable (+L) 84

DEMONSTRATION CASE B: NOTES PAYABLE AND ACCRUED INTEREST

Caterpillar Inc.

On December 31, 2012, assume that Caterpillar Inc. had $20.9 billion in Cash, Short-Term Investments, and Accounts Receivable, Net and $26.1 billion in current liabilities. On December 3, 2012, assume that Caterpillar had received $350 million when it issued promissory notes that will mature in 2017. The notes pay interest at the annual rate of 7.00 percent, which was comparable to other interest rates available in the market. Caterpillar's fiscal year ends on December 31.

Required:

1. Describe which sections of Caterpillar's classified balance sheet are affected by its issuance of promissory notes.
2. Give the journal entry on December 3, 2012, to record the issuance of the notes.
3. Give the journal entry on December 31, 2012, to record one month of interest expense, assuming none had been accrued prior to that date.
4. Compute Caterpillar's quick ratio at December 31, 2012. What proportion of its current liabilities could Caterpillar pay quickly if it was required to? What was the likely effect (increase or decrease) of the note issuance on the company's quick ratio?

Suggested Solution

1. The issuance of notes increases Caterpillar's Cash (a current asset) and its Notes Payable (a long-term liability) by $350 million.

2. December 3, 2012 (issuance date):

dr Cash (+A) 350,000,000
    cr Notes Payable (+L) 350,000,000

3. December 31, 2012 (accrual of interest expense for one month):

dr Interest Expense (+E, −SE) ($350,000,000 × 7.00% × 1/12) 2,041,667
    cr Interest Payable (+L) 2,041,667

4. December 31, 2012, Quick Ratio = (Cash + Short-Term Investments
                     + Accounts Receivable, Net) ÷ Current Liabilities
                = $20.9 ÷ $26.1 = 0.80

The quick ratio of 0.80 implies that Caterpillar could quickly pay 80 percent of its current liabilities if it was required to.

    The issuance of the notes increases the quick ratio, because Cash increased by $350 million, but the only increase in current liabilities was a relatively small amount of Interest Payable. The $350 million in Notes Payable increased long-term liabilities.

DEMONSTRATION CASE C: BONDS PAYABLE

To raise funds to build a new plant, Reed Company issued bonds with the following terms:

> Face value of the bonds: $100,000.
> Dates: Issued January 1, 2012; due in 5 years on January 1, 2017.
> Interest rate: 6 percent per year, payable on December 31 each year.

The bonds were issued on January 1, 2012, at 104.3, implying a 5 percent market rate of interest. The annual accounting period for Reed Company ends on December 31.

Required:

1. How much cash did Reed Company receive from the issuance of the bonds? Show computations.
2. What was the amount of premium on the bonds payable? Over how many months should the premium be amortized?
3. Show the accounting equation effects and give the journal entry on January 1, 2012, for recording the issuance of the bonds.
4. (Supplement 10A) Show the accounting equation effects and give the journal entry required on December 31, 2012, relating to interest on the bond. Use the straight-line amortization method.
5. (Supplement 10B) Show the accounting equation effects and give the journal entry required on December 31, 2012, relating to interest on the bond. Use the effective-interest amortization method.
6. (Supplement 10C) Show the accounting equation effects and give the journal entries required on January 1, 2012, relating to the bond issuance and on December 31, 2012, relating to interest on the bond. Use the simplified effective-interest amortization method.

Suggested Solution

1. Issue price of the bonds: $100,000 × 104.3% = $104,300.
2. Premium on the bonds payable: $104,300 − $100,000 = $4,300.

    Months amortized: From date of issue, January 1, 2012, to maturity date, January 1, 2017
                = 5 years × 12 months per year = 60 months.

3. January 1, 2012 (issuance date):

Assets	=	Liabilities	+	Shareholders' Equity
Cash +104,300		Bonds Payable +100,000		
		Premium on		
		Bonds Payable +4,300		

dr Cash (+A) 104,300
    cr Premium on Bonds Payable (+L) 4,300
    cr Bonds Payable (+L) 100,000

4. December 31, 2012:

Assets	=	Liabilities	+	Shareholders' Equity	
Cash	−6,000	Premium on Bonds Payable	−860	Interest Expense (+E)	−5,140

dr Premium on Bonds Payable (−L) ($4,300 × 12/60 months)	860	
dr Interest Expense (+E, −SE) ($6,000 − $860)	5,140	
cr Cash (−A) ($100,000 × 6% × 12/12)		6,000

5. December 31, 2012:

Assets	=	Liabilities	+	Shareholders' Equity	
Cash	−6,000	Premium on Bonds Payable	−785	Interest Expense (+E)	−5,215

dr Interest Expense (+E, −SE) ($104,300 × 5% × 12/12)	5,215	
dr Premium on Bonds Payable (−L) ($6,000 − $5,215)	785	
cr Cash (−A) ($100,000 × 6% × 12/12)		6,000

6. January 1, 2012 (issuance date):

Assets	=	Liabilities	+	Shareholders' Equity
Cash	+104,300	Bonds Payable, Net	+104,300	

dr Cash (+A)	104,300	
cr Bonds Payable, Net (+L)		104,300

December 31, 2012 (interest accrual):

Assets	=	Liabilities	+	Shareholders' Equity	
Cash	−6,000	Bonds Payable, Net	−785	Interest Expense (+E)	−5,215

dr Interest Expense (+E, −SE) ($104,300 × 5% × 12/12)	5,215	
dr Bonds Payable, Net (−L) ($6,000 − $5,215)	785	
cr Cash (−A) ($100,000 × 6% × 12/12)		6,000

CHAPTER SUMMARY

LO1   **Explain the role of liabilities in financing a business.** p. 413

- Liabilities play a vital role in allowing a business to buy goods and services on credit, cover gaps in cash flows, and expand into new regions and markets.
- Liabilities are classified as current if due to be paid with current assets within the current operating cycle of the business or within one year of the balance sheet date (whichever is longer). All other liabilities are considered long term.

LO2   **Explain how to account for common types of current liabilities.** p. 414

- Liabilities are initially reported at their cash-equivalent value, which is the amount of cash that a creditor would accept to settle the liability immediately after the transaction or event occurred.
- Liabilities are increased whenever additional obligations arise (including interest) and are reduced whenever the company makes payments or provides services to the creditor.

LO3   **Analyze and record bond liability transactions.** p. 422

- For most public issuances of debt (bonds), the amount borrowed by the company does not equal the amount repaid at maturity. The effect of a bond discount is to provide the borrower less money than the value stated on the face of the bond, which increases the cost of borrowing above the interest rate stated on the bond. The effect of a bond premium is to provide the borrower with more money than the face value repaid at maturity, which decreases the cost of borrowing below the stated interest rate.
- Interest Expense reports the cost of borrowing, which equals the periodic interest payments plus (or minus) the amount of the bond discount (or premium) amortized in that interest period.

Describe how to account for contingent liabilities p. 429   **LO4**

- A contingent liability is a potential liability (and loss) that has arisen as a result of a past transaction or event. Its ultimate outcome will not be known until a future event occurs or fails to occur. Under ASPE, it is recorded when likely and estimable.

Calculate and interpret the quick ratio and the times interest earned ratio. p. 430   **LO5**

- The quick ratio measures the company's ability to pay its current liabilities using current assets that are quickly converted into cash.
- The times interest earned ratio measures a company's ability to meet its interest obligations with resources generated from its profit-making activities.

ACCOUNTING DECISION TOOLS

Name of Measure	Formula	What It Tells You
Quick ratio	$$\frac{\text{(Cash + Short-Term Investments + Accounts Receivable, Net)}}{\text{Current Liabilities}}$$	• Whether current assets are sufficient to pay current liabilities • The higher the number the better able to quickly pay
Times interest earned ratio	$$\frac{\text{(Net Income + Interest Expense + Income Tax Expense)}}{\text{Interest Expense}}$$	• Whether sufficient resources are generated to cover interest costs • The higher the number the better the coverage

KEY TERMS

Accrued Liabilities p. 415

Contingent Liabilities p. 429

Discount p. 423

Effective-Interest Method of Amortization p. 433

Face Value p. 422

Issue Price p. 423

Line of Credit p. 430

Market Interest Rate p. 425

Maturity Date p. 422

Premium p. 423

Present Value p. 423

Quick Ratio p. 430

Stated Interest Rate p. 422

Straight-Line Amortization Method p. 431

Times Interest Earned Ratio p. 431

See complete definitions in the glossary in the back of this book.

HOMEWORK HELPER

Alternative terms

- The stated interest rate on a bond is also called the *coupon rate* or *contract rate*. The market interest rate is also called the *effective-interest rate* or *yield rate*.
- The word *amortize* comes from the Latin root word *mort*, which means to kill or eliminate; as bond discounts and premiums are amortized, they are gradually eliminated.
- The quick ratio is also called the *acid test ratio*.

Helpful reminders

- From the employer's perspective, payroll deductions create liabilities, not expenses. They are not expenses because they do not increase the employer's wages and salaries cost; they simply redirect part of the wages and salaries payments to a government agency or other organization rather than to employees.

- Bonds issue above face value (at a premium) if their stated interest rate is attractive (more than the market interest rate). If bonds have issued at a premium, their periodic cash payments will be greater than the interest expense, causing a reduction in the bond liability's carrying value.
- Bonds issue below face value (at a discount) if their stated interest is unattractive (less than the market interest rate). If bonds have issued at a discount, their periodic cash payments will be less than the interest expense, causing an increase in the bond liability's carrying value.

Frequent mistakes

- Use the stated interest rate, not the market interest rate, to calculate the cash paid periodically on a bond. (The market interest rate is used to calculate Interest Expense when using the effective-interest method.)

Practice Material

QUESTIONS (⊖ Symbol indicates questions that require analysis from more than one perspective.)

1. Describe three ways in which liabilities are used to finance business activities.

2. Define *liability*. What is the difference between a current liability and a long-term liability?

3. What three factors influence the dollar amount reported for liabilities?

4. Define *accrued liability*. Give an example of a typical accrued liability.

5. Why is Unearned Revenue considered a liability?

6. Why are payroll taxes and sales taxes considered liabilities?

7. Your company plans to hire an employee at a yearly salary of $70,000. Someone in your company says the actual cost will be lower because of payroll deductions. Someone else says it will be higher. Who is right? What is likely to be the total cost to the company? Explain.⊖

8. If a company has a long-term loan that has only two years remaining until it matures, how is it reported on the balance sheet (a) this year, and (b) next year?

9. What are the reasons that some bonds are issued at a discount and others are issued at a premium?

10. What is the difference between the stated interest rate and the market interest rate on a bond?

11. Will the stated interest rate be higher than the market interest rate or will the market interest rate be higher than the stated interest rate when a bond is issued at (a) face value, (b) a discount, and (c) a premium?

12. What is the carrying value of a bond payable?

13. What is the quick ratio? How is it related to the classification of liabilities?

14. What is the difference between a secured bond and a debenture? Which type carries more risk for the lender?

15. What is a contingent liability? How is a contingent liability reported under ASPE? How does this differ under IFRS?

16. (Supplement 10A) How is interest expense calculated using the straight-line method of amortization for a bond issued at (a) a discount and (b) a premium?

17. (Supplement 10B) How is interest expense calculated using the effective-interest method of amortization for a bond issued at (a) a discount and (b) a premium?

18. (Supplement 10C) How is interest expense calculated using the simplified approach to the effective-interest method for a bond issued at (a) a discount and (b) a premium?

Multiple-choice questions and corresponding answers can be found on Connect.

MINI-EXERCISES

LO2 **M10-1 Recording Unearned Revenues**

A local theatre company sells 1,500 season ticket packages at a price of $250 per package. The first show in the five-show season starts this week. Show the accounting equation effects and prepare the journal entries related to (a) the sale of the season tickets before the first show and (b) the revenue earned after putting on the first show.

LO2 **M10-2 Calculating Payroll Tax Liabilities**

Lightning Electronics is a mid-size manufacturer of lithium batteries. The company's payroll records for the November 1–14 pay period show that employees earned wages totalling $100,000 but that employee income taxes totalling $14,000, Canada Pension Plan (CPP) totalling $2,250, and Employment Insurance (EI) totalling $3,000 were withheld from this amount. The net pay was directly deposited into the employees' bank accounts.

a. What was the amount of net pay?

b. Prepare the journal entry or entries that Lightning would use to record the payroll. Include both employee and employer taxes.

>   **TIP:** Employer CPP equals employee CPP. Employer EI equals 1.4 times employee EI.

M10-3 Reporting Current and Noncurrent Portions of Long-Term Debt

LO2

Assume that on December 1, 2012, your company borrowed $14,000, a portion of which is to be repaid each year on November 30. Specifically, your company will make the following principal payments: 2013, $2,000; 2014, $3,000; 2015, $4,000; and 2016, $5,000. Show how this loan will be reported in the December 31, 2013 and 2012 balance sheets, assuming that principal payments will be made when required.

M10-4 Recording a Note Payable

LO2

Greener Pastures Corporation borrowed $1,000,000 on November 1, 2012. The note carried a 6 percent interest rate with the principal and interest payable on June 1, 2013. Show the accounting equation effects and prepare the journal entries for (*a*) the note issued on November 1 and (*b*) the interest accrual on December 31.

M10-5 Reporting Interest and Long-Term Debt, Including Current Portion

LO2

Barton Chocolates used a promissory note to borrow $1,000,000 on July 1, 2012, at an annual interest rate of 6 percent. The note is to be repaid in yearly instalments of $200,000, plus accrued interest, on June 30 of every year until the note is paid in full (on June 30, 2017). Show how the results of this transaction would be reported in a classified balance sheet prepared as of December 31, 2012.

M10-6 Computing and Reporting a Bond Liability

LO3

E-Tech Initiatives Limited plans to issue $500,000, 10-year, 4 percent bonds. Interest is payable annually on December 31. All of the bonds will be issued on January 1, 2013.

a. Show how the bonds would be reported on the January 2, 2013, balance sheet if they are issued at 98.

b. Show how the bonds would be reported on the January 2, 2013, balance sheet if they are issued at 103.

M10-7 Recording Bonds Issued at Face Value

LO3

Waterbahn Waterslide Company issued 25,000, 10-year, 6 percent, $100 bonds on January 1, 2012, at face value. Interest is payable each December 31. Show the accounting equation effects and prepare journal entries for (*a*) the issuance of these bonds on January 1, 2012, and (*b*) the interest payment on December 31, 2012.

M10-8 Reporting a Contingent Liability

LO4

Buck's Coffee Shop is famous for its large servings of hot coffee. After a famous case involving McDonald's, the lawyer for Buck's warned management (during 2009) that it could be sued if someone were to spill hot coffee and be burned. "With the temperature of your coffee, I can guarantee that it's just a matter of time before you're sued for $1,000,000." Buck's owner felt that the likelihood was remote. Unfortunately, in 2010, the lawyer's prediction came true when a customer filed suit. After consulting with his attorney, the owner of Buck's felt that a loss was possible but not likely or probable. The case went to trial in 2011 and the jury awarded the customer $400,000 in damages, which the company immediately appealed. Accepting the fact that a loss was probable, Buck's owner believed however that a lower amount could be negotiated. During 2012, the customer and the company settled their dispute for $150,000. What is the proper reporting of this liability each year under ASPE? Would the reporting differ under IFRS?

M10-9 Computing the Quick Ratio and the Times Interest Earned Ratio

LO5

The balance sheet for Shaver Corporation reported the following: current assets $100,000; inventory $40,000; prepaids $10,000; current liabilities, $40,000; total shareholders' equity, $90,000; net income, $3,320; interest expense, $4,400; income before income taxes, $5,280. Compute Shaver's quick ratio and times interest earned ratio. Based on these ratios, does it appear Shaver will be able to meet its obligations to pay current liabilities and future interest obligations as they become payable?

M10-10 Analyzing the Impact of Transactions on the Quick Ratio

LO5

BSO, Inc., has liquid assets of $600,000 and current liabilities of $500,000, resulting in a quick ratio of 1.2. For each of the following transactions, determine whether the quick ratio will increase, decrease, or remain the same.

a. Purchased $20,000 of new inventory on credit.
b. Paid accounts payable in the amount of $50,000.
c. Recorded accrued salaries in the amount of $100,000.
d. Borrowed $250,000 from a local bank, to be repaid in 90 days.

EXERCISES

LO2

E10-1 Determining Financial Statement Effects of Transactions Involving Notes Payable

Zellers Inc.
Hudson's Bay Company

Many businesses borrow money during periods of increased business activity to finance inventory and accounts receivable. Each Christmas, Zellers, which is owned by the Hudson's Bay Company, builds up its inventory to meet the needs of Christmas shoppers. A large portion of Christmas sales are on credit. As a result, Zellers often collects cash from the sales several months after Christmas. Assume that on November 1, 2012, Zellers borrowed $6 million cash from Downtown Bank and signed a promissory note that matures in six months. The interest rate was 7.5 percent payable at maturity. The accounting period ends December 31.

Required:

1. Indicate the accounts, amounts, and effects (+ for increase, − for decrease, and NE for no effect) of the (a) issuance of the note on November 1, (b) impact of the adjusting entry on December 31, 2012, and (c) the payment of the note and interest on April 30, 2013, on the accounting equation. Use the following structure for your answer:

Date	Assets	=	Liabilities	+	Shareholders' Equity

2. If Zellers needs extra cash every Christmas season, should management borrow money on a long-term basis to avoid negotiating a new short-term loan each year? Explain your answer.

LO2

E10-2 Recording a Note Payable through Its Time to Maturity

Use the information in E10-1 to complete the following requirements.

Required:

1. Give the journal entry to record the note on November 1, 2012.
2. Give any adjusting entry required on December 31, 2012.
3. Give the journal entry to record payment of the note and interest on the maturity date, April 30, 2013, assuming that interest has not been recorded since December 31, 2012.

LO2

E10-3 Recording Payroll Costs

Check Figure:
[Req. 3]
EI payable for employer
= $1,050

Macier Company completed the salary and wage payroll for March 2012. The payroll provided the following details:

Salaries and wages earned	$230,000
Employee income taxes withheld	50,200
Canada Pension Plan	2,500
Employment Insurance	750

Required:

1. Considering both employee and employer payroll taxes, use the preceding information to calculate the total labour cost for the company.
   TIP: Employer CPP equals employee CPP. Employer EI equals 1.4 times employee EI.
2. Prepare the journal entry to record the payroll for March, including employee deductions (but excluding employer payroll taxes).
3. Prepare the journal entry to record the employer's CPP and EI contributions.

E10-4 Recording Payroll Costs with and without Withholdings
LO2

Assume that an employee of Rocco Rock Company earns $1,000 of gross wages during the current pay period, and is required to remit to the government $100 for income tax and $50 for CPP and EI. Consider the following two procedures for paying the employee:

Procedure 1 (Withholdings)	Procedure 2 (No Withholdings)
Rocco Rock Company pays the employee net wages of $850 and will remit income taxes and CPP/EI on behalf of the employee.	Rocco Rock Company pays the employee gross wages of $1,000 and the employee is responsible for remitting income taxes and CPP/EI himself.

Required:

1. Ignoring employer payroll taxes, under each procedure calculate (*a*) the total labour cost for the company, and (*b*) the amount of cash the employee will have after satisfying all responsibilities to the government.
2. Explain why procedure 1 (withholdings) is the approach required by the government.
3. Considering that employers are responsible for matching employees' CPP/EI contributions, explain why employers might also prefer procedure 1 over procedure 2.
4. Prepare the journal entries required by the employer under procedure 1, assuming that the employee is paid in cash, but the withholdings and matching employer CPP/EI contribution have not yet been paid. (Assume employer EI equals employee EI.)

E10-5 Determining the Impact of Current Liability Transactions, Including Analysis of the Quick Ratio
LO2, 5

Bryanger Company sells a wide range of inventories that are initially purchased on account. Occasionally, a short-term note payable is used to obtain cash for current use. The following transactions were selected from those occurring during 2012:

a. On January 10, 2012, purchased merchandise on credit for $18,000. The company uses a perpetual inventory system.
b. On March 1, 2012, borrowed $40,000 cash from City Bank and signed a promissory note with a face amount of $40,000, due at the end of six months, accruing interest at an annual rate of 8 percent, payable at maturity.

Required:

1. For each of the transactions, indicate the accounts, amounts, and effects (+ for increase, − for decrease, and NE for no effect) on the accounting equation. Use the following structure:

Date	Assets	=	Liabilities	+	Shareholders' Equity

2. What amount of cash is paid on the maturity date of the note?
3. Discuss the impact of each transaction on the quick ratio. (Assume Bryanger Company's quick ratio was 1.10 prior to each transaction.)

E10-6 Determining and Recording the Financial Statement Effects of Unearned Subscription Revenue
LO2

Reader's Digest Association is a publisher of magazines, books, and music collections. The following note is from its 2008 annual report:

Revenues
Sales of our magazine subscriptions are deferred (as unearned revenue) and recognized as revenues proportionately over the subscription period.

Assume that Reader's Digest (*a*) collected $394 million in 2011 for magazines that will be delivered later in 2011 and 2012, and (*b*) delivered $190 million worth of magazines on these subscriptions in 2011.

Required:

1. Using the information given, indicate the accounts, amounts, and accounting equation effects (+ for increase, − for decrease, and NE for no effect) of the transactions involving $394 million and $190 million.
2. Using the information given, prepare the journal entries that would be recorded in each year.

LO3 **E10-7 Preparing Journal Entries to Record Issuance of Bonds and Payment of Interest**

On January 1, 2012, Applied Tech Corporation (ATC) issued $600,000 in bonds that mature in 10 years. The bonds have a stated interest rate of 10 percent. When the bonds were issued, the market interest rate was 10 percent. The bonds pay interest once per year on December 31.

Required:

1. Determine the price at which the bonds were issued and the amount that ATC received at issuance.
2. Prepare the journal entry to record the bond issuance.
3. Prepare the journal entry to record the interest payment on December 31, 2012, assuming no interest has been accrued earlier in the year.

LO3 **E10-8 Preparing Journal Entries to Record Issuance of Bonds at Face Value, Payment of Interest, and Early Retirement**

On January 1, 2012, InnoSolutions, Inc., issued $200,000 in bonds at face value. The bonds have a stated interest rate of 6 percent. The bonds mature in 10 years and pay interest once per year on December 31.

Required:

Check Figure:
[Req. 3]
Loss on bond retirement
= $4,000

1. Prepare the journal entry to record the bond issuance.
2. Prepare the journal entry to record the interest payment on December 31, 2012. Assume no interest has been accrued earlier in the year.
3. Assume the bonds were retired immediately after the first interest payment at a quoted price of 102. Prepare the journal entry to record the early retirement of the bonds.

LO3, 5 **E10-9 Describing the Effects of a Premium Bond Issue and Interest Payment on the Financial Statements, Quick Ratio, and Times Interest Earned Ratio**

Grocery Company received $300,328 for $250,000, 11 percent bonds issued on January 1, 2011, at a market interest rate of 8 percent. The bonds stated that interest would be paid each December 31 and that they mature on December 31, 2020.

Required:

1. Describe how the bond issuance affects the 2011 balance sheet and income statement, specifically identifying the account names and direction of effects (ignore amounts). Also, describe its impact, if any, on the quick ratio and times interest earned ratio.
2. Without doing calculations, describe how the balance sheet and income statement are affected by the recording of interest on December 31, 2011. Also, describe the impact, if any, of the December 31 interest payment on the quick ratio and times interest earned ratio.

LO5 **E10-10 Calculating and Interpreting the Quick Ratio and Times Interest Earned Ratio**

Kraft Foods Inc.

According to one report, Kraft Foods Inc. sells enough Kool-Aid® mix to make 4,500 litres of the drink every minute during the summer and over 2.5 billion litres each year. At December 31, 2011, the company reported no short-term investments but did report the following amounts (in millions) in its financial statements:

	2011	2010
Cash and Cash Equivalents	$ 1,244	$ 567
Accounts Receivable, Net	4,704	5,197
Total Current Liabilities	11,044	17,086
Interest Expense	1,240	604
Income Tax Expense	728	1,002
Net Income	2,901	2,590

Required:

1. Compute the quick ratio and times interest earned ratio (to two decimal places) for 2011 and 2010.
2. Did Kraft appear to have increased or decreased its ability to pay current liabilities and future interest obligations as they became due? How can you explain the seemingly conflicting findings of your ratio analysis?

E10-11 (Supplement 10A) Recording the Effects of a Premium Bond Issue and First Interest Period (Straight-Line Amortization)

Refer to the information in E10-9 and assume that Grocery Company uses the straight-line method to amortize the bond premium.

Required:

1. Prepare the journal entry to record the bond issuance.
2. Prepare the journal entry to record the interest payment on December 31, 2011.

E10-12 (Supplement 10B) Recording the Effects of a Premium Bond Issue and First Interest Period (Effective-Interest Amortization)

Refer to the information in E10-9 and assume Grocery Company uses the effective-interest method to amortize the bond premium.

Required:

1. Prepare the journal entry to record the bond issuance.
2. Prepare the journal entry to record the interest payment on December 31, 2011.

Check Figure:
[Req. 2]
Debit "Premium on Bonds Payable" for $3,474

E10-13 (Supplement 10C) Recording the Effects of a Premium Bond Issue and First Interest Period (Simplified Effective-Interest Amortization)

Refer to the information in E10-9 and assume Grocery Company accounts for the bond using the short-cut approach shown in chapter Supplement 10C.

Required:

1. Prepare the journal entry to record the bond issuance.
2. Prepare the journal entry to record the interest payment on December 31, 2011.

E10-14 (Supplement 10A) Recording the Effects of a Discount Bond Issue and First Interest Payment and Preparing a Discount Amortization Schedule (Straight-Line Amortization)

On January 1, 2012, when the market interest rate was 9 percent, Selton Corporation completed a $200,000, 8 percent bond issue for $187,163. The bonds were dated January 1, 2012, pay interest each December 31, and mature in 10 years on December 31, 2021. Seton amortizes the bond discount using the straight-line method.

Required:

1. Prepare the journal entry to record the bond issuance.
2. Prepare the journal entry to record the interest payment on December 31, 2012.
3. Prepare a bond discount amortization schedule for these bonds. Round calculations to the nearest dollar.

E10-15 (Supplement 10B) Recording the Effects of a Discount Bond Issue and First Interest Payment and Preparing a Discount Amortization Schedule (Effective-Interest Amortization)

Refer to the information in E10-14 and assume Selton Corporation uses the effective-interest method to amortize the bond discount.

Required:

1. Prepare the journal entry to record the bond issuance.
2. Prepare the journal entry to record the interest payment on December 31, 2012.
3. Prepare a bond discount amortization schedule for these bonds. Round calculations to the nearest dollar.

E10-16 (Supplement 10C) Recording the Effects of a Discount Bond Issue and First Interest Payment and Preparing a Discount Amortization Schedule (Simplified Effective-Interest Amortization)

Refer to the information in E10-14 and assume Selton Corporation accounts for the bond using the simplified effective-interest method shown in Supplement 10C.

Required:

1. Prepare the journal entry to record the bond issuance.
2. Prepare the journal entry to record the interest payment on December 31, 2012.
3. Prepare a bond discount amortization schedule for these bonds. Round calculations to the nearest dollar.

COACHED PROBLEMS

LO2, 5

CP10-1 Determining Financial Effects of Transactions Affecting Current Liabilities with Evaluation of Effects on the Quick Ratio

EZ Curb

Assume that EZ Curb completed the following transactions during 2012. The annual accounting period ends December 31, 2012.

Jan. 8   Purchased merchandise on account at a cost of $14,000. (Assume a perpetual inventory system.)

     17   Paid for the January 8 purchase.

Apr. 1   Received $40,000 from National Bank after signing a 12-month, 6 percent, promissory note.

June 3   Purchased merchandise on account at a cost of $18,000.

July 5   Paid for the June 3 purchase.

Aug. 1   Rented out a small office in a building owned by EZ Curb and collected six months' rent in advance, amounting to $6,000. (Use an account called *Unearned Rent Revenue*.)

Dec. 20   Received a $100 deposit from a customer as a guarantee to return a large trailer "borrowed" for 30 days.
     TIP: Consider whether EZ Curb has an obligation to return the money when the trailer is returned.

Dec. 31   Determined that wages of $6,500 were earned but not yet paid on December 31 (ignore payroll taxes).

Dec. 31   Adjusted the accounts at year-end, relating to interest.

Dec. 31   Adjusted the accounts at year-end, relating to rent.

Required:

1. For each listed transaction and related adjusting entry, indicate the accounts, amounts, and effects (+ for increase, − for decrease, and NE for no effect) on the accounting equation, using the following format:

Date	Assets	=	Liabilities	+	Shareholders' Equity

2. For each transaction and related adjusting entry, state whether the quick ratio is increased, decreased, or there is no change. (Assume EZ Curb's quick ratio has always been greater than 1.0.)

LO2

CP10-2 Recording and Reporting Current Liabilities

Using data from CP10-1, complete the following requirements.

Required:

1. Prepare journal entries for each of the transactions.
2. Prepare any adjusting entries required on December 31, 2012.
3. Show how all of the liabilities arising from these items are reported on the balance sheet at December 31, 2012.

CP10-3 Comparing Bonds Issued at Par, Discount, and Premium

LO3

Sikes Corporation, whose annual accounting period ends on December 31, issued the following bonds:

> Date of bonds: January 1, 2012
> Maturity amount and date: $200,000 due in 10 years (December 31, 2021)
> Interest: 10 percent per year payable each December 31
> Date issued: January 1, 2012

Required:

1. Provide the following amounts to be reported on the January 1, 2012, financial statements immediately after the bonds are issued:

	Case A (issued at 100)	Case B (issued at 96)	Case C (issued at 102)
a. Bonds payable	$	$	$
b. Unamortized premium (or discount)			
c. Carrying value			

TIP: See Exhibit 10.5 for an illustration distinguishing Bonds Payable from their carrying value.

2. Assume that an acquaintance has written to you (an investment adviser) asking, "Why should I buy a bond at a premium when I can find one at a discount? Isn't that stupid? It's like paying list price for a car instead of negotiating a discount." Write a brief message in response to the question.

GROUP A PROBLEMS

Practise and learn online with Connect.

PA10-1 Determining Financial Effects of Transactions
Affecting Current Liabilities with Evaluation of Effects on the Quick Ratio

LO2, 5

Jack Hammer Company completed the following transactions during 2012. The annual accounting period ends December 31, 2012.

Apr. 30	Received $550,000 from Commerce Bank after signing a 12-month, 6 percent, promissory note.
June 6	Purchased merchandise on account at a cost of $75,000. (Assume a perpetual inventory system.)
July 15	Paid for the June 6 purchase.
Aug. 31	Signed a contract to provide security services to a small apartment complex and collected six months' fees in advance, amounting to $12,000. (Use an account called *Unearned Service Revenue*.)
Dec. 31	Determined salary and wages of $40,000 were earned but not yet paid as of December 31 (ignore payroll taxes).
Dec. 31	Adjusted the accounts at year-end, relating to interest.
Dec. 31	Adjusted the accounts at year-end, relating to security services.

Required:

1. For each listed transaction and related adjusting entry, indicate the accounts, amounts, and effects (+ for increase, − for decrease, and NE for no effect) on the accounting equation, using the following format:

Date	Assets	=	Liabilities	+	Shareholders' Equity

2. For each item, state whether the quick ratio is increased, decreased, or there is no change. (Assume Jack Hammer's quick ratio is greater than 1.0.)

Check Figure:
[Req. 2]
Aug. 31 transaction
decreases the quick ratio

PA10-2 Recording and Reporting Current Liabilities

LO2

Using data from PA10-1, complete the following requirements.

Required:

1. Prepare journal entries for each of the transactions.
2. Prepare all adjusting entries required on December 31, 2012.
3. Show how all of the liabilities arising from these items are reported on the balance sheet at December 31, 2012.

LO3 **PA10-3 Comparing Bonds Issued at Par, Discount, and Premium**

Net Work Corporation, whose annual accounting period ends on December 31, issued the following bonds:

> Date of bonds: January 1, 2012
> Maturity amount and date: $200,000 due in 10 years (December 31, 2021)
> Interest: 10 percent per year payable each December 31
> Date issued: January 1, 2012

Required:

Check Figure:
[Req. 1]
Case B has an unamortized discount of $6,000

1. Provide the following amounts to be reported on the January 1, 2012, financial statements immediately after the bonds were issued:

	Case A (issued at 100)	Case B (issued at 97)	Case C (issued at 101)
a. Bonds payable	$	$	$
b. Unamortized premium (or discount)			
c. Carrying value			

2. Assume that you are an investment adviser and a friend has written to you asking, "Why should I buy a bond at a premium when I can find one at a discount? Isn't that stupid? It's like paying list price for a car instead of negotiating a discount." Write a brief message in response to the question.

PA10-4 (Supplement 10A) Recording Bond Issue, Interest Payments (Straight-Line Amortization), and Early Bond Retirement

On January 1, 2011, Loop de Loop Raceway issued 600 bonds, each with a face value of $1,000, a stated interest rate of 5 percent paid annually on December 31, and a maturity date of December 31, 2013. On the issue date, the market interest rate was 6 percent, so the total proceeds from the bond issue were $583,950. Loop de Loop uses the straight-line bond amortization method.

Required:

1. Prepare a bond amortization schedule.
2. Give the journal entry to record the bond issue.
3. Give the journal entries to record the interest payments on December 31, 2011 and 2012.
4. Give the journal entry to record the interest and face value payment on December 31, 2013.
5. Assume the bonds are retired on January 1, 2013, at a price of 98. Give the journal entries to record the bond retirement.

PA10-5 (Supplement 10B) Recording Bond Issue, Interest Payments (Effective-Interest Amortization), and Early Bond Retirement

On January 1, 2011, Surreal Manufacturing issued 600 bonds, each with a face value of $1,000, a stated interest rate of 3 percent paid annually on December 31, and a maturity date of December 31, 2013. On the issue date, the market interest rate was 4 percent, so the total proceeds from the bond issue were $583,352. Surreal uses the effective-interest bond amortization method.

Required:

1. Prepare a bond amortization schedule.
2. Give the journal entry to record the bond issue.
3. Give the journal entries to record the interest payments on December 31, 2011 and 2012.

4. Give the journal entry to record the interest and face value payment on December 31, 2013.

5. Assume the bonds are retired on January 1, 2013, at a price of 101. Give the journal entry to record the bond retirement.

GROUP B PROBLEMS

PB10-1 Determining Financial Effects of Transactions Affecting Current Liabilities with Evaluation of Effects on the Quick Ratio

LO2, 5

TigerCom completed the following transactions during 2012. The annual accounting period ends December 31, 2012.

Jan.	3	Purchased merchandise on account at a cost of $24,000. (Assume a perpetual inventory system.)
	27	Paid for the January 3 purchase.
Apr.	1	Received $80,000 from Atlantic Bank after signing a 12-month, 5 percent, promissory note.
June	13	Purchased merchandise on account at a cost of $8,000.
July	25	Paid for the June 13 purchase.
Aug.	1	Rented out a small office in a building owned by TigerCom and collected eight months' rent in advance, amounting to $8,000. (Use an account called *Unearned Rent Revenue*.)
Dec.	31	Determined wages of $12,000 were earned but not yet paid on December 31 (ignore payroll taxes).
Dec.	31	Adjusted the accounts at year-end, relating to interest.
Dec.	31	Adjusted the accounts at year-end, relating to rent.

Required:

1. For each listed transaction and related adjusting entry, indicate the accounts, amounts, and effects (+ for increase, − for decrease, and NE for no effect) on the accounting equation, using the following format:

Date	Assets	=	Liabilities	+	Shareholders' Equity

2. For each item, state whether the quick ratio is increased, decreased, or there is no change. (Assume TigerCom's quick ratio is greater than 1.0.)

PB10-2 Recording and Reporting Current Liabilities

LO2

Using data from PB10-1, complete the following requirements.

Required:

1. Prepare journal entries for each of the transactions.

2. Prepare any adjusting entries required on December 31, 2012.

3. Show how all of the liabilities arising from these items are reported on the balance sheet at December 31, 2012.

Check Figure:
[Req. 3]
Total current liabilities
= $98,000

PB10-3 (Supplement 10A) Recording Bond Issue, Interest Payments (Straight-Line Amortization), and Early Bond Retirement

On January 1, 2011, Methodical Manufacturing issued 100 bonds, each with a face value of $1,000, a stated interest rate of 5 percent paid annually on December 31, and a maturity date of December 31, 2013. On the issue date, the market interest rate was 4.25 percent, so the total proceeds from the bond issue was $102,070. Methodical uses the straight-line bond amortization method.

Required:

1. Prepare a bond amortization schedule.

2. Give the journal entry to record the bond issue.

3. Give the journal entries to record the interest payments on December 31, 2011 and 2012.
4. Give the journal entry to record the interest and face value payment on December 31, 2013.
5. Assume the bonds are retired on January 1, 2013, at a price of 102. Give the journal entries to record the bond retirement.

PB10-4 (Supplement 10B) Recording Bond Issue, Interest Payments (Effective-Interest Amortization), and Early Bond Retirement

Refer to PB10-3. Assume Methodical uses the effective-interest bond amortization method.

Required:

1. Prepare a bond amortization schedule.
2. Give the journal entry to record the bond issue.
3. Give the journal entries to record the interest payments on December 31, 2011 and 2012.
4. Give the journal entry to record the interest and face value payment on December 31, 2013.
5. Assume the bonds are retired on January 1, 2013, at a price of 101. Give the journal entry to record the bond retirement.

PB10-5 (Supplement 10C) Recording Bond Issue, Interest Payments (Simplified Effective-Interest Amortization), and Early Bond Retirement

Assume the same facts as PB10-3, but now assume that Methodical uses the simplified effective-interest bond amortization method, as shown in Supplement 10C.

Required:

Check Figure:
[Req. 3]
Interest expense Dec. 31/12
= $4,310

1. Prepare a bond amortization schedule.
2. Give the journal entry to record the bond issue.
3. Give the journal entries to record the interest payments on December 31, 2011 and 2012.
4. Give the journal entry to record the interest and face value payment on December 31, 2013.
5. Assume the bonds are retired on January 1, 2013, at a price of 101. Give the journal entry to record the bond retirement.

SKILLS DEVELOPMENT CASES

LO5

Rona Inc.

S10-1 Finding Financial Information

Refer to the financial statements of Rona Inc. in Appendix A at the back of this book or download the annual report from the *Cases* section of Connect.

Required:

1. Calculate, to two decimal places, the company's quick ratio using amounts reported in its financial statements for the years ended December 27, 2009, and December 28, 2008. What do the changes in this ratio suggest about the company's ability to quickly pay its liabilities?
2. Calculate, to two decimal places, the company's times interest earned ratio for the year ended December 27, 2009. Does this ratio cause you any concern about the company's ability to meet future interest obligations as they become due?

LO5

Rona Inc.

S10-2 Comparing Financial Information

Refer to the financial statements of Rona Inc. in Appendix A and The Home Depot's in Appendix B at the back of this book or download the annual reports from the *Cases* section of Connect.

Required:

1. Calculate, to two decimal places, the companies' quick ratios using amounts reported in each of the financial statements for the 2009 fiscal year-end. What do the changes in this ratio suggest about the companies' ability to quickly pay their liabilities? Does it appear that Rona Inc. or The Home Depot is in a less secure position?
2. Calculate, to two decimal places, the companies' times interest earned ratios for the 2009 fiscal year end. Does it appear that Rona Inc. or The Home Depot will be better able to meet future interest obligations as they become payable?

S10-3 Internet-Based Team Research: Examining an Annual Report

As a team, select an industry to analyze. Using your Web browser, each team member should access the annual report for one publicly traded company in the industry, with each member selecting a different company. (See S1-3 in Chapter 1 for a description of possible resources for these tasks.)

Required:

1. On an individual basis, each team member should write a short report that incorporates the following:
   a. What are the most significant types of current liabilities owed by the company?
   b. Read the company's financial statement note regarding long-term debt and commitments and contingencies. Does the company have any significant amounts coming due in the next five years?
   c. Compute and analyze the quick ratio and times interest earned ratio.
2. Then, as a team, write a short report comparing and contrasting your companies using these attributes. Discuss any patterns across the companies that you as a team observe. Provide potential explanations for any differences discovered.

S10-4 Ethical Decision Making: A Real-Life Example

Many retired people invest a significant portion of their money in bonds of corporations because of their relatively low level of risk. During the 1980s, significant inflation caused some interest rates to rise to as high as 15 percent. Retired people who bought bonds that paid only 6 percent continued to earn at the lower rate. During the 1990s, inflation subsided and interest rates declined. Many corporations took advantage of the callability feature of these bonds and retired the bonds early. Many of these early retirements of high interest rate bonds were replaced with low interest rate bonds.

Required:

In your judgment, is it ethical for corporations to continue paying low interest rates when rates increase but to call bonds when rates decrease? Why or why not?

S10-5 Ethical Decision Making: A Mini-Case

Assume that you are a portfolio manager for a large insurance company. The majority of the money you manage is from retired schoolteachers who depend on the income you earn on their investments. You have invested a significant amount of money in the bonds of a large corporation and have just received news released by the company's president explaining that it is unable to meet its current interest obligations because of deteriorating business operations related to increased international competition. The president has a recovery plan that will take at least two years. During that time, the company will not be able to pay interest on the bonds and, she admits, if the plan does not work, bondholders will probably lose more than half of their money. As a creditor, you can force the company into immediate bankruptcy and probably get back at least 90 percent of the bondholders' money. You also know that your decision will cause at least 10,000 people to lose their jobs if the company ceases operations.

Required:

Given only these two options, what should you do? Consider who would be helped or harmed by the two options.

S10-6 Critical Thinking: Evaluating Effects on the Quick Ratio

Assume you work as an assistant to the chief financial officer of Fashions First, Inc. The CFO reminds you that the fiscal year-end is only two weeks away and that he is looking to you to ensure the company stays in compliance with its loan covenant to maintain a quick ratio of 1.25 or higher. A review of the general ledger indicates that cash and other liquid assets total $690,000 and current liabilities are $570,000. Your company has an excess of Cash ($300,000) and an equally large balance in Accounts Payable ($270,000), although none of its Accounts Payable are due until next month.

Required:

1. Determine whether the company is currently in compliance with its loan covenant.
2. Assuming the level of assets and liabilities remains unchanged until the last day of the fiscal year, evaluate whether Fashions First should pay down $90,000 of its Accounts Payable on the last day of the year, before the Accounts Payable become due.

S10-7 (Supplement 10A) Preparing a Bond Amortization Schedule (Straight-Line Amortization)

Assume the authors of a popular introductory accounting text have hired you to create spreadsheets that will calculate bond discount amortization schedules like those shown in this chapter. As usual, you e-mail your friend Owen for some guidance. Much to your disappointment, you receive an auto-reply message from Owen indicating that he's gone skiing in New Zealand. After a bit of panicking, you realize you can refer to Owen's previous e-mail messages for spreadsheet advice that will help you complete this task. From his advice for Chapter 9, you decide to create a data input section for the stated interest rate, market interest rate, face value, issue price, and years to maturity. The spreadsheet file also will have a separate amortization schedule worksheet that contains only formulas, references to the cells in the data input section, and references to other cells in the amortization schedule. All amounts will be rounded to the nearest dollar (using the Round function in Excel), which means the discount amortization in the final year might be off a few dollars (unless you use the IF function in Excel to eliminate any remaining discount in the final year of the bond's life, in the same way that Owen showed in Chapter 9 for declining-balance depreciation).

Required:

Prepare a worksheet that uses formulas to reproduce the straight-line bond discount amortization schedule shown in Supplement 10A. Display both the completed spreadsheet and a "formulas revealed" (Ctrl ~) version of it.

S10-8 (Supplement 10B) Preparing a Bond Amortization Schedule (Effective-Interest Amortization)

Refer to the information in S10-7 and prepare a worksheet that uses formulas to reproduce the effective-interest bond discount amortization schedule shown in Supplement 10B. Display both the completed spreadsheet and a "formulas revealed" (Ctrl ~) version of it.

S10-9 (Supplement 10C) Preparing a Bond Amortization Schedule (Simplified Effective-Interest Amortization)

Refer to the information in S10-7 and prepare a worksheet that uses formulas to reproduce the bond discount amortization schedule shown for simplified effective-interest amortization in chapter supplement 10C. Display both the completed spreadsheet and a "formulas revealed" (Ctrl ~) version of it.

CONTINUING CASE

Practise and learn online with Connect.

LO2   **CC10 Accounting for Debt Financing**

Nicole thinks that her business, Nicole's Getaway Spa (NGS), is doing really well and she is planning a large expansion. With such a large expansion, Nicole will need to finance some of it using debt. She signed a one-year note payable with the bank for $50,000 with a 6 percent interest rate. The note was issued October 1, 2012, interest is payable semiannually, and the end of Nicole's accounting period is December 31.

Required:

1. Prepare the journal entries required from the issuance of the note until its maturity on September 30, 2013, assuming that no entries are made other than at the end of the accounting period, when interest is payable and when the note reaches its maturity.
2. Is there any similarity between the way Notes Payable and Notes Receivable are accounted for? Explain.

Practise and learn online with Connect.

CHAPTER 11

Reporting and Interpreting Shareholders' Equity

FOCUS COMPANY:

Sun-Rype Products Ltd.

www.sunrype.ca

News about company shares, or stocks, is everywhere. You've probably read about them in *The Globe and Mail*, listened to news about them on MSNBC, or searched for information about them at Yahoo! Finance. Behind this fascination with shares is a dream that many people have: taking a small amount of money and turning it into a fortune. That's what Sun-Rype Products Ltd. has managed to do. BC Fruit Processors Ltd. was founded in 1946 and changed its name to Sun-Rype Products Ltd. in April 1959. The company went public in June 1998, issuing shares for $2.01 per share. As the company grew larger by acquiring and developing new products such as its popular and convenient fruit snacks, its earnings and share value began to grow. By 2001, the company's shares had doubled in value. And over this past decade alone, the share value has doubled again.

In this chapter, you will see how companies like Sun-Rype Products Ltd. account for various company share transactions, including issuances, splits, and dividends. Soon you'll understand many of the share terms used in the news.

THAT WAS
THEN

The last chapter focused on debt financing, as reported in the liabilities section of the balance sheet.

THIS IS
NOW

This chapter focuses on equity financing, as reported in the shareholders' equity section of the balance sheet.

ORGANIZATION OF THE CHAPTER

Understand the business	**S**tudy the accounting methods	**E**valuate the results	**R**eview the chapter
• Corporate ownership • Equity versus debt financing	• Common share transactions • Stock dividends and stock splits • Preferred shares • Retained earnings	• Earnings per share (EPS) • Return on equity (ROE) • Price/earnings (P/E) ratio	• Demonstration Cases • Chapter Summary • Key Terms • Homework Helper • Practice Material

Understand the Business

Learning Objective 1

Explain the role of shares (also called *stocks*) in financing a corporation.

CORPORATE OWNERSHIP

If you were to write down the names of 50 familiar businesses, probably all of them would be corporations. This is understandable because corporations account for a large percentage of the total sales reported by Canadian businesses.[1] Many Canadians own shares in corporations, either directly or indirectly through a mutual fund or pension program.

You probably recall from Chapter 1 that the act of creating a corporation is costly, so why is the corporate form so popular? One reason is that it limits the legal liability of its owners. Another reason is that corporations can raise large amounts of money because investors can easily participate in a corporation's ownership. This ease of participation is related to several factors.

- **Shares can be purchased in small amounts.** According to Yahoo! Finance, you could have become one of Sun-Rype's owners in 2011 by buying a share of the company for just $8.

- **Ownership interests are transferable.** The shares of public companies are regularly bought and sold on established markets such as the Toronto Stock Exchange (TSX). Sun-Rype's shares are traded on the TSX under the ticker symbol SR.TO.

- **Shareholders (or stockholders) are not liable for the corporation's debts.** Creditors have no legal claim on the personal assets of shareholders like they do on the personal assets belonging to owners of sole proprietorships and partnerships. So if you owned shares in the old Eaton's department store, which went bankrupt and was liquidated in 1999, you would have lost what you paid to buy the shares but, unless you personally guaranteed the company's debt, you wouldn't have had to chip in to help pay the hundreds of millions of dollars that the company owed.

The law recognizes a corporation as a separate legal entity. It may own assets, incur liabilities, expand and contract in size, sue others, be sued, and enter into contracts independently of its owners. A corporation exists separate and apart from its owners, which means it doesn't die when its owners die. Thomas Edison died in 1931, but the company he founded (General Electric) continues in existence today.

To protect everyone's rights, the creation and oversight of corporations are tightly regulated by law. Corporations are created by submitting an application to the government (provincial, territorial, or federal). Because laws vary across Canada, you might decide to create a corporation in a province or territory other than the one in which it operates. If the application to create a corporation is approved, the province or territory issues a charter, also called the *articles of incorporation*, which spells out information about the corporation such as its name, address, nature of business, and ownership structure. Federally incorporated companies are regulated by the Canada Business Corporations Act (CBCA), while provincially and territorially incorporated companies are regulated by the legislation of that corresponding province or territory.

The ownership structure of a corporation can vary from one company to the next. In the most basic form, a corporation must have one type of shares, appropriately called **common shares.** Owners of common shares usually enjoy a number of benefits:

1. **Voting rights.** For each share you own, you are allowed a set number of votes on major issues. Some classes of common shares can carry more votes than others, so watch for this if you care about voting on which accounting firm will be appointed as external auditors and who will serve on the board of directors. (In case you don't remember from Chapter 5, the board of directors is the group that appoints the corporation's officers and governs top management, as shown in Exhibit 11.1).

2. **Dividends.** Shareholders receive a share of the corporation's profits when these are distributed as dividends.

3. **Residual claim.** If the company ceases operations, shareholders share in any assets remaining after creditors have been paid.

4. **Preemptive rights.** Existing shareholders may be given the first chance to buy newly issued shares before they are offered to others.

YOU SHOULD KNOW

Common share: The basic voting share issued by a corporation to shareholders.

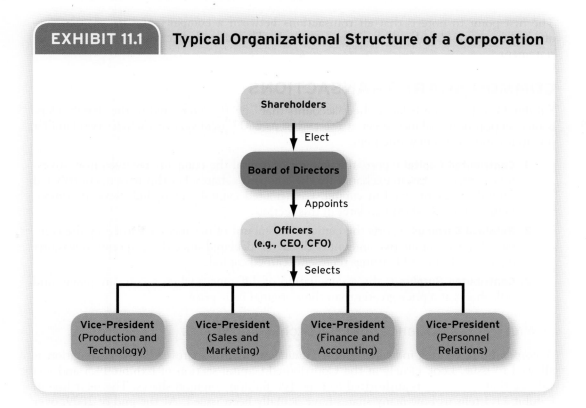

EXHIBIT 11.1 Typical Organizational Structure of a Corporation

EQUITY VERSUS DEBT FINANCING

Whenever a company needs a large amount of long-term financing, its executives have to decide whether to obtain it by issuing new shares to investors (called equity financing) or by borrowing money from lenders (debt financing). Each form of financing has certain advantages over the other, as listed in Exhibit 11.2. These factors play a big role in determining whether equity or debt financing is most appropriate for each particular corporation. One company, for example, might be primarily concerned about the impact of financing on income taxes and decide to rely on debt financing because its interest payments are tax-deductible. Another company might be so concerned about being able to pay its existing liabilities that it can't afford to take on additional debt. By using equity financing, which doesn't have to be repaid, the company could obtain the financing it needs. Ultimately, the decision to pursue additional equity or debt financing depends on the circumstances.

EXHIBIT 11.2	Advantages of Equity and Debt Financing
Advantages of Equity Financing	**Advantages of Debt Financing**
1. Equity does not have to be repaid. Debt must be repaid or refinanced.	1. Interest on debt is tax-deductible. Dividends on shares are not tax-deductible.
2. Dividends are optional. Interest must be paid on debt.	2. Debt does not change shareholder control. In contrast, a share issue gives new shareholders the right to vote and share in the earnings, diluting existing shareholders' control.

Study the Accounting Methods

The first point to note is that all transactions between a company and its shareholders affect the company's balance sheet accounts only. They do not affect the company's income statement.

COMMON SHARE TRANSACTIONS

Learning Objective 2

Explain and analyze common share transactions.

Exhibit 11.3 shows the balance sheet accounts that Sun-Rype reported in the shareholders' equity section of its balance sheet at the end of its 2009 fiscal year. It includes two familiar line items and a third new line item:

1. **Contributed Capital** reports the amount of capital the company received from investors' contributions, in exchange for the company's shares. For this reason, contributed capital represents paid-in capital. Contributed capital can include several components, which we'll explain later in this section.

2. **Retained Earnings** reports the cumulative amount of net income earned by the company less the cumulative amount of dividends declared since the corporation was first organized. Retained Earnings represents earned capital.

3. **Contributed Surplus** is the accumulation of differences when a company issues and sells shares at a price greater than their original issue price.

Authorization, Issuance, and Repurchase of Shares

A corporation's charter indicates the maximum number of shares that the corporation is allowed to issue. Look closely at the Contributed Capital section of Exhibit 11.3 and you will see that Sun-Rype is **authorized** to issue 100 million common shares. The next line in Exhibit 11.3 tells us how many shares have actually been issued. At the end of 2009, over 10 million common shares have been issued. **Issued shares** will be owned forever by one shareholder or another, unless the company has repurchased them.

The CBCA requires that, for the most part, repurchased shares be cancelled (retired). Only in certain jurisdictions in Canada and in limited circumstances can repurchased shares be held by a company, at which point they become known as **treasury shares.**

YOU SHOULD KNOW

Authorized shares: The maximum number of shares of a corporation that can be issued, as specified in the charter.

Issued shares: Shares that have been distributed by the corporation.

Treasury shares: Issued shares that have been reacquired by the company.

EXHIBIT 11.3   Explanation of Sun-Rype Products Ltd. Shareholders' Equity

SUN-RYPE PRODUCTS LTD.
Partial Balance Sheets
As of December 31,

(In thousands, except share amounts)	2009	2008	Explanation
SHAREHOLDERS' EQUITY			
Contributed Capital			
Common Shares, without par value	$17,756	$17,756	Basic voting shares
Authorized: 100,000,000 shares			Maximum number of shares
Issued: 10,827,600 shares			Number of shares distributed
Contributed Surplus	942	942	Amount in excess of par value
Total Contributed Capital	18,698	18,698	Total equity paid in by investors
Retained Earnings	17,047	10,280	Total equity earned by the company
Total Shareholders' Equity	$35,745	$28,978	

Treasury shares are used more often in the United States. During the time that treasury shares are held by a corporation, the shares do not carry voting, dividend, or other shareholder rights.

Shares that are owned by shareholders (not the corporation itself) are called **outstanding shares**. Because of the limited application of treasury shares in Canada, we felt it would be more beneficial to leave the detailed discussion and accounting application for treasury shares out of the text material. If you want to study this material further, it is available on Connect.

If Sun-Rype could report treasury shares in its shareholders' equity section of the balance sheet, it would show as a negative amount because it represents shares that are no longer outstanding with investors. From this information, you should be able to compute the number of shares still outstanding, which is important for financial analysts who need to express certain dollar amounts on a per share basis. Earnings per share (EPS)—a key financial ratio that we discuss later in this chapter—is expressed in terms of the number of outstanding shares owned by investors. Be sure you can map the number of shares reported in Exhibit 11.3 into relationships among the number of authorized, issued, outstanding, and treasury shares, as diagrammed in Exhibit 11.4.

YOU SHOULD KNOW

Outstanding shares: Shares that are currently held by shareholders (not the corporation itself).

EXHIBIT 11.4   **Authorized, Issued, Treasury, and Outstanding Shares**

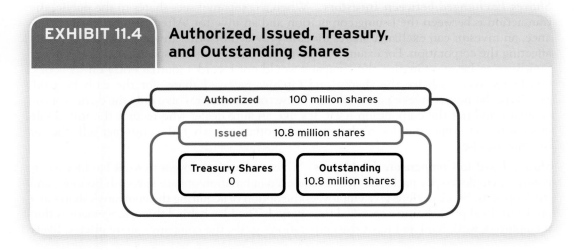

Par value (share): An insignificant value per share specified in the charter, which has no relationship to the market value of the share.

No-par value shares: Shares that have no specified legal value per share in the corporate charter.

COACH'S TIP

Don't confuse par value as it relates to shares with par value as it relates to bonds. They differ in meaning and how they are accounted for.

Share Authorization   Before a share can be issued, its specific rights and characteristics must be authorized and defined in the corporate charter. This authorization does not affect the accounting records, but it does establish certain characteristics that, later, will affect how shares are accounted for. One characteristic of importance is the share's **par value**. Oddly enough, *par value* has little meaning today—it is a legal concept and is not related in any way to the market value of a company's shares. The concept was originally introduced a long time ago to prevent shareholders from removing contributed capital of businesses that were about to go bankrupt. Stronger laws and regulations exist today to prevent this from happening, so par value no longer has a business use. In fact, the CBCA prohibits the use of par values, but they are still seen in some areas in Canada and are very common in the United States. So, instead, the CBCA allows the issuance of **no-par value shares**, which are similar to shares with par value except they do not have a specified legal value per share.

Share Issuance   A share issuance occurs when a corporation distributes its shares to existing or new shareholders, usually in exchange for cash. The very first issuance of a company's shares to the public is called an initial public offering, or IPO. This is what most people are referring to when they say a private company is going public. If a company has issued shares previously, additional issuances of new shares by the company are called seasoned new issues. Whether shares are issued as part of an IPO or as a seasoned new issue, a company accounts for it in the same way.

Most share issuances are cash transactions. To illustrate the accounting for a share issuance, assume that during the next fiscal year, Sun-Rype issues 100,000 no-par value shares at the $10 per share market price existing at the time of issuance. The accounting equation effects of this share issuance and the journal entry to record them would be

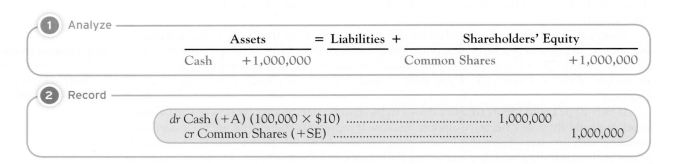

① Analyze

	Assets	= Liabilities +	Shareholders' Equity	
Cash	+1,000,000		Common Shares	+1,000,000

② Record

dr Cash (+A) (100,000 × $10) 1,000,000
    cr Common Shares (+SE) 1,000,000

COACH'S TIP

Remember the separate entity assumption in Chapter 1, which states that owners' transactions are recorded only if they directly involve the corporation.

Notice that the increase in Common Shares is the number of shares sold times the issue price per share. This is because the corporate charter did not specify a par value for the shares (no-par value shares), so the total proceeds from the share issuance will be entered into the Common Shares account.

Shares Exchanged between Investors   When a company issues shares to the public, the transaction is between the issuing corporation and an investor. After this initial share issuance, an investor can exchange shares for cash provided by other investors without directly affecting the corporation. For example, if investor Marita Gorski disposed of 1,000 shares of Sun-Rype to Jacques Grenier, the company would not record a journal entry on its books. Gorski received cash for the shares, and Grenier received shares for the cash he paid. Sun-Rype did not receive or pay anything. These transactions involve only the owners of the company and not the corporation itself. It's like an auto dealer who records the initial sale of a car to a customer but doesn't later record another sale when the customer sells the car to someone else.

Shares Used to Compensate Employees   To encourage employees to work hard for a corporation, employee pay packages often include a combination of base pay, cash bonuses, and stock options. Stock options give employees the option of acquiring the company's shares at a predetermined price during a specified time period. The idea behind this arrangement is that if employees work hard and meet the corporation's goals, the company's share price is likely to increase. If the share price increases, employees can exercise their option to acquire the company's shares at the lower predetermined price and then turn around and dispose of it at the higher market share price for a profit. If the share price declines, employees haven't lost anything. Accounting rules require that, at the time the company grants stock options, an expense must be reported for the estimated cost associated with stock options. The specific accounting procedures for this will be discussed in an intermediate accounting course.

SPOTLIGHT ON Ethics

At Whose Expense?

Some critics claim that stock options, which are intended to give the senior executives of a company the same goals as shareholders, often come at the expense of existing shareholders. When senior executives exercise their stock options to acquire new shares, existing shareholders lose voting power because their percentage of ownership in the company is diluted. Furthermore, critics contend that stock options create an incentive for senior executives to overstate financial results in an attempt to falsely increase the company's share price so they can exercise their options for huge personal gains.

Repurchase of Shares A corporation may want to repurchase its shares from existing shareholders for a variety of reasons, including (1) to distribute excess cash to shareholders, (2) to send a signal to investors that the company believes its own shares are worth acquiring, (3) to get back shares so that new shares can be issued as payment for purchases of other companies, (4) to get back shares so that new shares can be issued to employees as part of employee stock option plans, and (5) to create a demand for the company's shares, which may help to stabilize or increase the share price.

If a company repurchases its shares for reasons (2), (3), or (4), it will hold them in the company treasury for a period of time until they are reissued. Remember that in most situations and in most jurisdictions in Canada, the CBCA requires that repurchased shares to be cancelled. Therefore we will look only at cancelling the shares, while the scenario of holding them in treasury is covered on Connect.

Assume that during the next fiscal year, Sun-Rype repurchased 50,000 shares for $5 per share (50,000 shares × $5 = $250,000). Sun-Rype would first have to calculate the carrying (book) value of the outstanding shares at the time of this repurchase. Exhibit 11.3 shows that at its fiscal year-end on December 31, 2009, Sun-Rype had a total of 10,827,600 common shares outstanding for a total consideration of $17,756,000, or an average issue price of $1.64 per share. Sun-Rype therefore paid $5 per share to repurchase shares that had (on average) originally been issued for $1.64. One could say that Sun-Rype lost money on this repurchase of shares. However our accounting rules prohibit gains and losses on share transactions from going through the income statement, primarily to restrict companies from trading their own shares to manipulate earnings. Instead, these "losses" are debited directly to **Retained Earnings**, as shown below. Sun-Rype would have accounted for this transaction as follows:

YOU SHOULD KNOW

Retained Earnings:
Cumulative earnings of a company that are not distributed to the owners; profits from the current year and all prior years that are reinvested ("retained") in the business.

1 Analyze

	Assets	=	Liabilities	+	Shareholders' Equity	
Cash	−250,000	=			Common Shares (−SE)	−82,000
					Retained Earnings (−SE)	−168,000

2 Record

dr Common Shares (−SE) (50,000 × $1.64)	82,000	
dr Retained Earnings (−SE) [50,000 × ($5 − $1.64)]	168,000	
cr Cash (−A) (50,000 × $5)		250,000

If Sun-Rype had repurchased the shares for $1 instead of for $5, creating a "gain" instead of a "loss," the credit needed to balance the journal entry would have been made to a Contributed Capital account called **Contributed Surplus**, as follows:

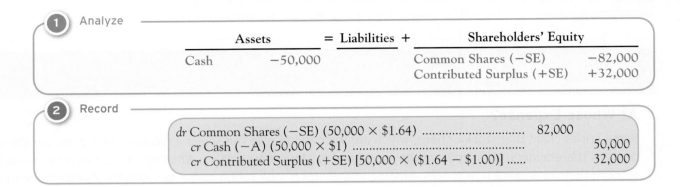

1 Analyze

	Assets	= Liabilities +	Shareholders' Equity	
Cash	−50,000		Common Shares (−SE)	−82,000
			Contributed Surplus (+SE)	+32,000

2 Record

dr Common Shares (−SE) (50,000 × $1.64)	82,000	
cr Cash (−A) (50,000 × $1)		50,000
cr Contributed Surplus (+SE) [50,000 × ($1.64 − $1.00)]		32,000

HOW'S IT GOING? Self-Study Practice

1. Assume that Oakley, Inc., issued 1,000 of its common shares, no-par value, for $20 per share. Show the accounting equation effects and journal entry for this transaction.

   1 Analyze

	Assets	= Liabilities +	Shareholders' Equity	
Cash	[ ]			+20,000

   2 Record

   dr [ ] [ ]

   cr [ ] [ ]

   cr [ ] [ ]

2. Assume that Oakley repurchased and cancelled 500 of its common shares in the stock market when they were selling for $25 per share. Show the journal entry to record this transaction.

   dr [ ] [ ]

   cr [ ] [ ]

After you have finished, check your answers with the solution in the margin.

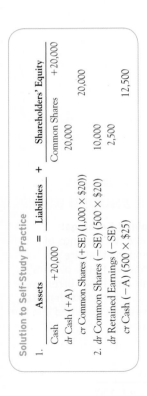

Solution to Self-Study Practice

1.	Assets	= Liabilities +	Shareholders' Equity	
Cash	+20,000		Common Shares	+20,000
dr Cash (+A)				20,000
cr Common Shares (+SE) (1,000 × $20))				20,000
2. dr Common Shares (−SE) (500 × $20)				10,000
dr Retained Earnings (−SE)				2,500
cr Cash (−A) (500 × $25)				12,500

Learning Objective 3

Explain and analyze cash dividends, stock dividends, and stock split transactions.

Dividends on Common Shares

Investors acquire common shares because they expect a return on their investment. This return can come in two forms: dividends and increases in share price. Some investors prefer to buy shares that pay little or no dividend (called a growth investment), because companies that reinvest the majority of their earnings tend to increase their future earnings potential, along with their share price. Dell Corporation, for example, has never paid a dividend, yet its share value has increased significantly over the years. Rather than wait for growth in share value, other investors, such as retired people who need a steady income, prefer to receive their return in the form of dividends. These people often seek shares that consistently pay dividends (called an income investment), such as Coca-Cola shares, which have paid cash dividends each year since 1920.

SPOTLIGHT ON Business Decisions

Dividend Cuts in Difficult Times

Under pressure to save cash during the global economic crisis, many big-name companies reversed or cut their policy to pay cash dividends in 2009. Although dividends are discretionary, companies are reluctant to cut them because doing so suggests the company is facing significant financial challenges. Huge percentage declines in 2009 dividends, as compared to prior years, were announced by

| General Electric | 67% | CBS Corp. | 81% |
| Motorola, Inc. | 75% | Black & Decker | 71% |

Consistent with this, if you look at the December 31, 2009, annual report for Sun-Rype Products Ltd., you will see that the company did not pay any dividends in 2009. This is in comparison to the $433,000 that the company paid out in 2008. However if you read further in the notes to the financial statements, you will see that Sun-Rype decided to use its cash flows to pay off $22 million of interest-bearing debt. So cutting dividends doesn't always indicate that a company is having financial difficulties.

A corporation does not have a legal obligation to pay dividends. It is a decision made by the board of directors, and it is made each time a dividend is to be paid. Once the board of directors formally declares a dividend, a liability is created. When Sun-Rype declares a dividend, it would send out a press release containing very important information, such as the press release shown below:

KELOWNA, BC, Feb. 28, 2012—Sun-Rype Products Ltd. (TSX: SRF) today announced that shareholders of record at the close of business on March 10, 2012, will be entitled to receive $0.05 per common share payable on March 15, 2012.

Notice that this press release contains three important dates: (1) the declaration date (February 28), (2) the date of record (March 10), and (3) the date of payment (March 15).

1. **Declaration Date–February 28.** The **declaration date** is the date on which the board of directors officially approves the dividend. As soon as the board makes the declaration, the company records an increase in its liabilities and a corresponding increase in the Dividends Declared account. Dividends Declared is a temporary account that summarizes dividends declared during the year and then is closed to Retained Earnings at year-end, causing a decrease in Retained Earnings. Remember, dividends are not expenses: they are distributions of a company's accumulated prior earnings, so they are reported on the statement of retained earnings (or the more general statement of shareholders' equity shown in Chapter 5). Dividends declared by a company are not reported on its income statement because they are not expenses. With approximately 10.8 million common shares outstanding (see Exhibit 11.4), Sun-Rype's $0.05 dividend per share equals $540,000 (10.8 million × $0.05 = $540,000). The accounting equation effects and journal entry to record them would be

YOU SHOULD KNOW

Declaration date: The date on which the board of directors officially approves a dividend, thereby creating a liability.

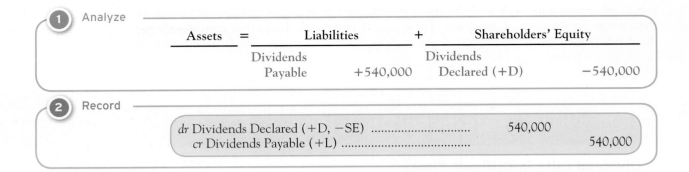

① Analyze

Assets	=	Liabilities	+	Shareholders' Equity
		Dividends Payable +540,000		Dividends Declared (+D) −540,000

② Record

dr Dividends Declared (+D, −SE) 540,000
   cr Dividends Payable (+L) 540,000

YOU SHOULD KNOW

Record date: The date on which the corporation prepares the list of current shareholders as shown on its records; dividends can be paid only to the shareholders who own shares on that date.

Payment date: The date on which a cash dividend is paid to the shareholders of record.

2. **Date of Record—March 10.** After a dividend is declared, the corporation needs some time to identify who will receive the dividend. The **record date** is the date on which the corporation finalizes its list of current shareholders. The dividend is payable only to those names listed on the record date. No journal entry is made on this date.

3. **Date of Payment—March 15.** The **payment date** is the date on which the cash is disbursed to pay the dividend liability. It follows the date of record, as described in the dividend announcement. Continuing our example above, when the dividend is paid and the liability satisfied on March 15, the accounting equation effects and journal entry are

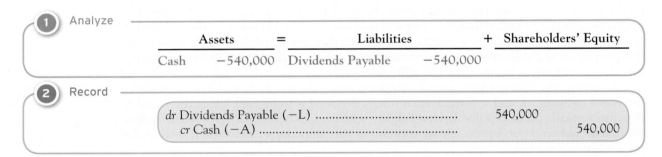

① Analyze

Assets	=	Liabilities	+	Shareholders' Equity
Cash −540,000		Dividends Payable −540,000		

② Record

dr Dividends Payable (−L) 540,000
   cr Cash (−A) 540,000

These three dates and the corresponding balance sheet effects are summarized in the timeline in Exhibit 11.5.

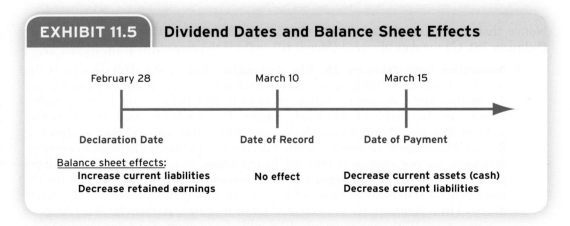

EXHIBIT 11.5   **Dividend Dates and Balance Sheet Effects**

The declaration of a cash dividend reduces shareholders' equity because Dividends Declared is closed into Retained Earnings at the end of each fiscal year. The payment of a cash dividend similarly reduces Cash (by the same amount). These two observations explain two key financial requirements that the board of directors must consider when declaring a cash dividend:

1. **Sufficient retained earnings.** The corporation must have accumulated a sufficient amount of Retained Earnings to cover the amount of the dividend. Incorporation laws often restrict cash dividends to the balance in Retained Earnings. A company may be further restricted by clauses in its loan agreements that require an even larger minimum balance in Retained Earnings. If the company were to violate such a loan covenant, a lender could require renegotiation of the loan and possibly demand its immediate repayment. Because restrictions on Retained Earnings can severely limit the ability to pay dividends, accounting rules require that companies disclose any restrictions in their financial statement notes.

2. **Sufficient cash.** The corporation must have sufficient cash to pay the dividend. Cash can be used in many ways, so the mere fact that Retained Earnings has a large credit balance does not mean that the company has sufficient cash to pay a dividend. Remember, retained earnings is not cash.

 HOW'S IT GOING? Self-Study Practice

Answer the following questions concerning dividends:

1. On which dividend date is a liability created?
2. A cash outflow occurs on which dividend date?
3. What are the two fundamental requirements for the payment of a dividend?

After you have finished, check your answers with the solution in the margin.

STOCK DIVIDENDS AND STOCK SPLITS

Stock Dividends

The term *dividend*, when used alone with no adjectives, implies a cash dividend. However, some dividends are not paid in cash but in additional shares. These dividends, called **stock dividends**, are distributed to a corporation's shareholders on a pro rata basis at no cost to the shareholder. The term *pro rata basis* means that each shareholder receives additional shares equal to the percentage of shares held. A shareholder who owns 10 percent of the outstanding shares would receive 10 percent of any additional shares issued as a stock dividend.

The value assigned to a stock dividend is the subject of much debate. In reality, a stock dividend by itself provides no economic value. All shareholders receive a pro rata distribution of shares, which means that each shareholder owns exactly the same proportion of the company after a stock dividend as he or she did before the dividend. If you get change for a dollar, you do not have more wealth because you hold four quarters instead of only one dollar. Similarly, if you own 10 percent of a company, you are not wealthier simply because the company declares a stock dividend and gives you (and all other shareholders) more shares of the company.

When a stock dividend is issued, the stock market reacts immediately with a proportional decline in the share price. Theoretically, if the share price was $60 before a stock dividend that doubles the number of shares outstanding, the price per share would fall to $30. Thus, an investor who owns 100 shares before the stock dividend would own 200 shares after the stock dividend, but the total share value before (100 × $60 = $6,000) would equal the value after (200 × $30 = $6,000). In reality, the fall in price is not exactly proportional to the number of new shares issued because the stock dividend makes the shares more attractive to investors who acquire shares in round lots (multiples of 100 shares). An investor with $10,000 might not buy shares selling for $150, for instance, because she cannot afford to buy 100 shares. However, she might buy the shares if the price was less than $100 as the result of a stock dividend. Thus, one of the main reasons for issuing a stock dividend is that it reduces the market price per share.

When a stock dividend occurs, the company must decrease Retained Earnings (to show that a dividend was declared) and increase Common Shares (to show that additional shares were issued). The CBCA requires that stock dividends be valued at the current market price of the shares. Let's assume that Sun-Rype issued a 2 percent stock dividend when the share price was $4 per share, and there were still 10.8 million common shares outstanding prior to the stock dividend. The company would account for this stock dividend by moving $864,000 (= 10.8 million × 2% × $4 share value) from Retained Earnings to Common Shares as follows:

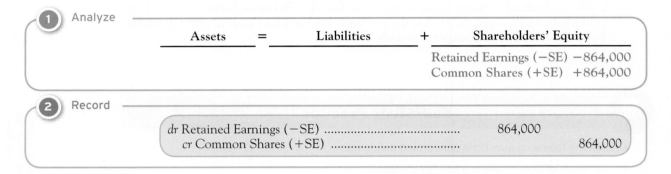

1 Analyze

Assets	=	Liabilities	+	Shareholders' Equity
				Retained Earnings (−SE) −864,000
				Common Shares (+SE) +864,000

2 Record

dr Retained Earnings (−SE) 864,000
    cr Common Shares (+SE)   864,000

Notice that the stock dividend does not change total shareholders' equity. It changes only the balances of some of the accounts that make up shareholders' equity.

Before we leave this section, we must caution you on a potential point of confusion. Some companies refer to 100 percent stock dividends as a "stock split effected as a stock dividend." Although they *say* stock split, they actually mean a stock dividend as described above. A true stock split is different, both in terms of how it is done and how it is accounted for, as we discuss in the following section.

Stock Splits

Stock splits are not dividends. While they are similar to a stock dividend, they are quite different in terms of how they occur and how they affect the shareholders' equity accounts. In a **stock split**, the total number of authorized shares is increased by a specified amount, such as 2-for-1. In this instance, each issued share is called in and two new shares are issued in its place. Cash is not affected when the company splits its shares, so the total resources of the company do not change. It's just like taking a four-slice pizza and cutting each slice into two smaller slices.

Typically, a stock split involves reducing the carrying value of all authorized shares, so that the total carrying value of the shares is unchanged. For instance, if a company with 1 million shares outstanding executes a 2-for-1 stock split, with a total issue price of $4,000,000, it reduces the per share book value of its shares and doubles the number of outstanding shares. The decrease in book value per share offsets the increase in the number of shares, so the financial position of the company is not affected and no journal entry is needed. By reading the following illustration from left to right, you can see these offsetting effects on the number of shares and book value per share.

Shareholders' Equity	Before a 2-for-1 Stock Split		After a 2-for-1 Stock Split	
Number of shares outstanding	1,000,000		2,000,000	
Book value per share	$ 4		$ 2	
Total book value outstanding	$ 4,000,000		$ 4,000,000	
Retained earnings	6,500,000		6,500,000	
Total shareholders' equity	$10,500,000		$10,500,000	

Exhibit 11.6 reviews the similarities and differences between a stock dividend and a stock split. Notice that although they have similar effects on the number of shares outstanding, they are accounted for differently.

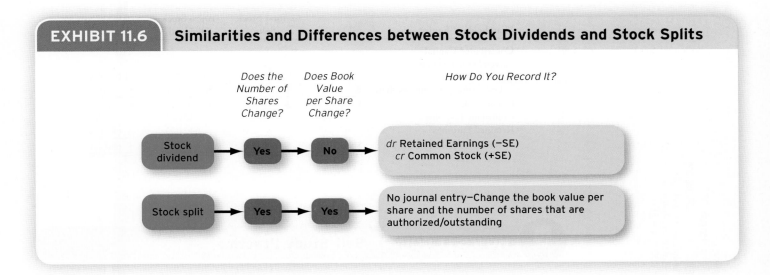

EXHIBIT 11.6   **Similarities and Differences between Stock Dividends and Stock Splits**

How does a company's board of directors choose between stock dividends and stock splits? The following Spotlight explains that accounting differences are a key factor in this decision.

SPOTLIGHT ON Business Decisions

Choosing Between Stock Dividends and Stock Splits

Both stock dividends and stock splits increase the number of shares outstanding and decrease the per share market price. A key difference between them is that a stock dividend causes a reduction in Retained Earnings, whereas a "true" stock split doesn't (see Exhibit 11.6).

By itself, this accounting difference might not mean much. Remember, though, that to declare a cash dividend, a company must maintain an adequate balance in Retained Earnings. If you're managing a company that you expect will struggle financially in the future, you'll prefer a stock split because it doesn't reduce Retained Earnings, so it doesn't reduce your ability to declare cash dividends in the future.

On the other hand, if you expect your company will be financially successful in the near future, you won't care that a stock dividend reduces Retained Earnings because future earnings will replenish that account to allow cash dividends to be declared. In fact, you'll probably *want* to declare a stock dividend to show how confident you are of your company's financial outlook. This reasoning suggests that **a company's board of directors may declare a stock dividend rather than a stock split to signal to financial statement users that the company expects significant future earnings** (which will replenish the reduction in Retained Earnings caused by the stock dividend).

Exhibit 11.7 shows the typical components of the shareholders' equity section of the balance sheet and highlights the amounts (in blue) that are changed by a 2-for-1 stock split, a 100% stock dividend, and an equivalent ($10,000) cash dividend. Notice that the cash dividend is the only distribution that affects total shareholders' equity because it is the only one that distributes the company's resources to shareholders.

EXHIBIT 11.7 **Comparison of Distributions to Shareholders**

| | | AFTER | | |
Shareholders' Equity	BEFORE	2-for-1 Stock Split	100% Stock Dividend	$10,000 Cash Dividend
Contributed Capital				
Number of common shares outstanding	1,000,000	2,000,000	2,000,000	1,000,000
Book value per common share	$ 0.01	$ 0.005	$ 0.01	$ 0.01
Common shares	$ 10,000	$ 10,000	$ 20,000	$ 10,000
Contributed Surplus	30,000	30,000	30,000	30,000
Retained Earnings	650,000	650,000	640,000	640,000
Total shareholders' equity	$ 690,000	$ 690,000	$ 690,000	$ 680,000

 HOW'S IT GOING? Self-Study Practice

Vandalay Industries wanted to reduce the market price of its shares, so it issued 10,000 new common shares in a 10 percent stock dividend when there were 100,000 shares outstanding and the market value was $30 per share.

1. Prepare the journal entry that Vandalay would use to record this transaction.

2. What journal entry would be required if the transaction instead involved a 2-for-1 stock split? Theoretically, what would be the new share price after the split?

After you have finished, check your answers with the solution in the margin.

Solution to Self-Study Practice

1. *dr* Retained Earnings (−SE) 300,000
   cr Common Stock (+SE) 300,000

2. No journal entry is required in the case of a stock split. Theoretically, the new price would be one-half of what it was before the 2-for-1 split ($30 × ½ = $15).

PREFERRED SHARES

In addition to common shares, some corporations issue **preferred shares** to a select group of investors. These special forms of shares differ from common shares, typically in the following ways:

1. **Preferred shares generally do not grant voting rights.** As a result, preferred shares do not appeal to investors who want some control over the operations of a company. However, they do appeal to existing common shareholders because the company can issue preferred shares to raise funds without reducing common shareholders' voting control.

2. **Dividends on preferred shares, if any, may be paid at a fixed rate,** specified as a dollar amount per share. For example, a "$0.60 preferred share" pays dividends each year of $0.60 per share. A fixed dividend can be attractive to certain investors, such as company founders or retirees, who seek a stable income from their investments.

3. **Preferred shares carry priority over common shares.** Preferred shareholders have higher priority than common shareholders if a corporation distributes assets to its owners through dividends or at liquidation. That is, any dividends the corporation declares must be paid to preferred shareholders before they can be paid to common shareholders. Also, if the corporation goes out of business, its assets will be sold and used to pay creditors and then preferred shareholders. Common shareholders are paid last from whatever assets remain after paying preferred shareholders.

Under IFRS, preferred shares are typically classified as shareholders' equity. However, if the issuing company is contractually obligated to pay dividends or redeem the shares at a future date, then preferred shares are classified as a liability. This classification can dramatically affect financial ratios that use total shareholders' equity (e.g., return on equity, discussed later in this chapter) or total liabilities (e.g., debt-to-assets ratio, discussed in Chapter 5).

Preferred Share Issuance

Just like a common share issuance, a preferred share issuance increases a company's cash and its shareholders' equity. To illustrate, assume that a company issued 10,000 preferred shares for $5 per share ($5 × 10,000 shares = $50,000 cash received). As shown below, the Preferred Shares account increases by its share price for each share issued ($5 × 10,000 = $50,000) and so does the amount of cash received:

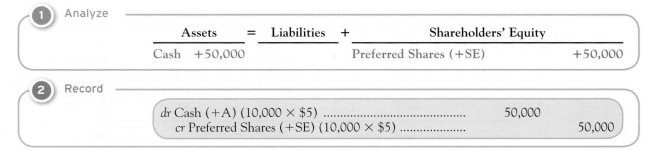

1 Analyze

Assets	=	Liabilities	+	Shareholders' Equity	
Cash +50,000				Preferred Shares (+SE)	+50,000

2 Record

dr Cash (+A) (10,000 × $5) 50,000
    cr Preferred Shares (+SE) (10,000 × $5) 50,000

Preferred Share Dividends

Because investors who acquire preferred shares give up voting rights that are available to investors in common shares, preferred shares offers dividend preferences. The two most common dividend preferences are called current and cumulative.

Current Dividend Preference A **current dividend preference** requires that preferred dividends be paid before any dividends are paid to holders of common shares. This preference is a feature of all preferred shares. After the current dividend preference has been met, and if no other preference exists, dividends may be paid to the common shareholders. To illustrate, consider the following example:

> **Flavoria Company**
>
> Preferred shares outstanding, 6%, book value $40,000; 2,000 shares
> Common shares outstanding, book value $50,000; 5,000 shares

Assume that the preferred shares carry only a current dividend preference and that the company declares dividends totalling $8,000 in 2011 and $10,000 in 2012. In each year, a fixed amount of the total dividends would first go to the preferred shareholders, and only the excess would go to the common shareholders.

Year	Total Dividends Declared	Dividends on 6% Preferred Stock*	Dividends on Common Stock[†]
2011	$ 8,000	$2,400	$5,600
2012	10,000	2,400	7,600

*Dividends on preferred shares = Total book value of shares ($40,000) × 6% dividend = $2,400
[†]Dividends on common shares = Total dividends declared − Dividends on preferred shares

YOU SHOULD KNOW

Current dividend preference: The feature of preferred shares that grants priority on preferred dividends over common dividends.

Had Flavoria Company not declared dividends in 2011, preferred shareholders would have had preference to $2,400 of dividends only in 2012. The current dividend preference does not carry over to later years unless the preferred shares are designated as cumulative, as discussed next.

YOU SHOULD KNOW

Cumulative dividend preference: Preferred share feature that requires current dividends not paid in full to accumulate for every year in which they are not paid. These cumulative unpaid amounts (called **dividends in arrears**) must be paid before any common dividends can be paid.

Cumulative Dividend Preference   A **cumulative dividend preference** states that if all or a part of the current dividend is not paid in full, the cumulative unpaid amount, known as **dividends in arrears**, must be paid before any future common dividends can be paid. Of course, if the preferred shares are noncumulative, dividends can never be in arrears; any preferred dividends that are not declared are permanently lost. Because preferred shareholders are unwilling to accept this unfavourable feature, preferred shares are usually cumulative.

To illustrate the cumulative preference, assume that Flavoria Company has the same amount of shares outstanding as in the last example. In this case, however, assume that dividends are in arrears for 2009 and 2010. The following table shows that, in 2011, dividends in arrears are satisfied first, followed by the current dividend preference, and the excess goes to common shareholders. In 2012, preferred dividends include only the current preference of that year because dividends in arrears were fulfilled in 2011.

Year	Total Dividends Declared	DIVIDENDS ON 6% PREFERRED SHARES		Dividends on Common Shares‡
		In Arrears*	Current†	
2011	$ 8,000	$4,800	$2,400	$ 800
2012	10,000	—	2,400	7,600

*Dividends in arrears preference = Book value of total shares ($40,000) × 6% dividend × 2 years = $4,800
†Current dividend preference = Book value of total shares ($40,000) × 6% dividend = $2,400
‡Dividends on common shares = Total dividends declared − Total dividends on preferred shares

Because dividends are not an actual liability until the board of directors declares them, dividends in arrears are not reported on the balance sheet. Instead, they are disclosed in the notes to the financial statements.

RETAINED EARNINGS

As its name suggests, Retained Earnings account represents the company's total earnings that have been retained in the business (rather than being distributed to shareholders). The balance in this account increases each year that the company reports net income on the income statement, and it decreases each year that the company reports a net loss (expenses greater than revenues) or declares cash or stock dividends to shareholders. Think of retained earnings as the amount of equity that the company itself has generated for shareholders (through profitable operations) but not yet distributed to them.

If a company ever accumulates more net losses than net income over its life, it will report a negative (debit) balance in the Retained Earnings account. This amount is (*a*) shown in parentheses in the shareholders' equity section of the balance sheet, (*b*) deducted when computing total shareholders' equity, and (*c*) typically called an Accumulated Deficit rather than Retained Earnings. Exhibit 11.8 provides an example of how this might look in the financial statements.

Evaluate the Results

Now that you know how dividends and other shareholders' equity transactions are accounted for inside a company, it's time to evaluate things from the outside. In this section, you will learn to use three ratios to evaluate how well a company appears to be using its capital to generate returns for the company and, ultimately, for its shareholders.

EXHIBIT 11.8

Reporting Negative Retained Earnings (Accumulated Deficit)

BOND DEVELOPMENTS INC.
Balance Sheet (Partial)
March 31, 2012
(in millions of dollars)

Shareholders' Equity:

Common Shares	$ 3
Contributed Surplus	3,143
Accumulated Deficit	(298)
Total Shareholders' Equity	$2,848

EARNINGS PER SHARE (EPS)

The most famous of all ratios, **earnings per share (EPS)**, reports how much profit is earned for each common share outstanding. The calculation of EPS can involve many details and intricacies, but in its basic form, it is computed by dividing "bottom line" net income by the average number of common shares outstanding. Most companies report EPS on the income statement immediately below Net Income or in the notes to the financial statements.[2]

You might be wondering why *earnings* per share is so popular when dividends and share prices ultimately determine the return to shareholders. The reason is that current earnings assist in predicting future dividends and share prices. If a company generates increased earnings in the current year, it will be able to pay higher dividends in future years if the company has adequate cash resources. In other words, current EPS influences expectations about future dividends, which investors factor into the current share price.

Another reason that EPS is so popular is that it allows you to easily compare results over time. For example, assume a company earned net income of $3.6 million in the third quarter of 2009, compared to $3.3 million for the same quarter in the previous year. It's hard to know whether the increase is good for shareholders because it's possible that the increase in net income was accompanied by an increase in the number of shares outstanding. By considering earnings on a per share basis, we adjust for the effect of additional shares issued, resulting in a clearer picture of what increases mean for each investor.

Learning Objective 5

Analyze the earnings per share (EPS), return on equity (ROE), and price/earnings (P/E) ratios.

 **COACH'S TIP**

Outstanding shares are issued shares minus treasury shares.

ACCOUNTING DECISION TOOLS

Name of Measure	Formula	What It Tells You
Earnings per share (EPS)	$$\frac{\text{Net Income}}{\text{Average Number of Common Shares Outstanding}}$$	• The amount of income generated for each common share owned by shareholders • A higher ratio means greater profitability
Return on equity (ROE)	$$\frac{\text{Net Income}}{\text{Average Shareholders' Equity}}$$	• The amount of income earned for each dollar of shareholders' equity • A higher ratio means shareholders are likely to enjoy greater returns
Price/earnings (P/E) ratio	$$\frac{\text{Current Share Price (per share)}}{\text{Earnings per Share (annual)}}$$	• How many times more than the current year's earnings investors are willing to pay for a company's common share • A higher number means investors anticipate an improvement in the company's future results

Exhibit 11.9 shows how to calculate EPS for Sun-Rype Products Ltd. We should caution you against comparing EPS across companies. The number of shares outstanding for one company can differ dramatically from the number outstanding for a different company, simply because one chooses to issue more shares than the other. Also, as you have seen in earlier chapters, net income can be affected by differences in how two companies cost inventory (Chapter 7), estimate bad debts (Chapter 8), amortize long-lived tangible assets (Chapter 9), and estimate losses from contingent liabilities (Chapter 10). So, while EPS is an effective and widely used measure for comparing a company with itself over time, it is not appropriate for comparing across companies.

| EXHIBIT 11.9 | Summary of EPS, ROE, and P/E Ratio Analyses |

SUN-RYPE

(In millions except share price)	2009	2008	2007
Net Income (loss)	$ 6,767	$(11,673)	$ 4,635
Average # shares	10,828	10,828	10,828
Shareholders' equity	$35,745	$ 28,978	$41,023
Price per share	$ 8.71	$ 5.79	$ 11.46

	2009	2008
$EPS = \dfrac{\text{Net income}}{\text{Avg. # shares}}$	$\dfrac{\$6,767}{10,828}$	$\dfrac{(\$11,673)}{10,828}$
	$= \$0.62$	$= \$(1.08)$

	2009	2008
$ROE = \dfrac{\text{Net income}}{\text{Average SE}}$	$\dfrac{\$6,767}{(\$35,745 + \$28,978)/2}$	$\dfrac{(\$11,673)}{(\$28,978 + \$41,023)/2}$
	$= 0.209$ or 20.9%	$= -0.334$ or -33.4%

	2009	2008
$P/E = \dfrac{\text{Share price}}{\text{EPS}}$	$\dfrac{\$8.71}{\$0.62}$	$\dfrac{\$5.79}{(\$1.08)}$
	$= 14.0$	$= -5.36$

RETURN ON EQUITY (ROE)

Like EPS, return on equity (ROE) reports a company's return to investors. However, rather than relate net income to the average *number* of shares outstanding, the return on equity (ROE) ratio relates net income to the average *dollars* of shareholder investment and earnings reinvested in the company.[3] Because ROE uses dollars contributed to and reinvested in the company, this ratio can be appropriately compared across companies.

The results reported in Exhibit 11.9 indicate that Sun-Rype's 2009 return to common shareholders was 20.9%, which is quite respectable. According to Yahoo! Finance, the average return on equity for the entire beverage industry was about 6.7 percent.

PRICE/EARNINGS (P/E) RATIO

While EPS and ROE are useful for evaluating a company's return to shareholders, they don't help you determine what a reasonable price would be for the company's shares. Sophisticated

COACH'S TIP

The denominator in the return on equity formula contains average shareholders' equity. Remember that this represents both contributed capital and retained earnings.

techniques to value a company are taught in advanced courses in finance, but for this course, let's focus on a simple tool. The price/earnings ratio is the most basic way to determine the value that investors place on a company's common shares. The P/E ratio, as most people call it, measures how many times more than current year's earnings investors are willing to pay for a company's shares. It is calculated as shown in Exhibit 11.9 by dividing a company's EPS for the year into the share price at the time its EPS is reported.

Generally, a relatively high P/E ratio means investors expect the company to improve in the future and increase its profits, so they have factored in the future earnings when determining the current share price. A relatively low P/E ratio typically means that they don't expect strong future performance. P/E ratios can vary significantly across industries, so you'll find them most meaningful when comparing a company over time with itself or with competitors in the same industry. Sun-Rype showed a P/E ratio in 2009 of 14.1, which exceeded the industry average (5.9). This suggests that investors were anticipating good things to come from Sun-Rype.

HOW'S IT GOING? Self-Study Practice

Sun-Rype reported shareholders' equity of $38,008 (thousands) at its 2006 fiscal year-end. Use this information, along with that in Exhibit 11.9, to calculate Sun-Rype's earnings per share (EPS), return on equity (ROE), and price/earnings (P/E) ratios for 2007.

2007 EPS:	2007 ROE:	2007 P/E:
☐ / ☐ = ☐	☐ / (☐ + ☐)/2 = ☐	☐ / ☐ = ☐

After you have finished, check your answers with the solution in the margin.

SPOTLIGHT ON IFRS and ASPE

Topic	ASPE	IFRS
Presentation of changes in Shareholders' Equity accounts	• Changes in retained earnings are presented in the "Statement of Retained Earnings." • Changes in capital accounts are disclosed in the notes to the financial statements.	• Changes in **all** equity accounts are presented in a separate statement called "Statement of Changes in Equity."

SUPPLEMENT 11A: Owners' Equity for Other Forms of Business

Owner's Equity for a Sole Proprietorship

A sole proprietorship is an unincorporated business owned by one person. Only two owner's equity accounts are needed: (1) a capital account for the proprietor (H. Simpson, Capital) and (2) a drawings (or withdrawal) account for the proprietor (H. Simpson, Drawings).

 **COACH'S TIP**

Because a sole proprietorship does not issue shares, its equity is called *owner's equity* rather than *shareholders' equity*. We use OE to designate an owner's equity account.

The capital account of a sole proprietorship serves two purposes: to record investments by the owner and to accumulate periodic income or loss. The drawings account is used to record the owner's withdrawals of cash or other assets from the business, similar to recording dividends declared by corporations. The drawings account is closed to the capital account at the end of each accounting period. So, after the drawings account is closed, the capital account reflects the cumulative total of all investments by the owner and all earnings of the business less all withdrawals from the entity by the owner.

In most respects, the accounting for a sole proprietorship is the same as for a corporation. Exhibit 11A.1 presents the recording of selected transactions of Homer's Dough Store and a statement of owner's equity, which replaces the statement of retained earnings.

Because a sole proprietorship does not pay income taxes, its financial statements do not report Income Tax Expense or Income Tax Payable. Instead, the net income of a sole proprietorship is taxed when it is included on the owner's personal income tax return. Likewise, the owner's salary is not recognized as an expense in a sole proprietorship because an employer/employee contractual relationship cannot exist with only one party involved. The owner's salary is therefore accounted for as a distribution of profits—a withdrawal—instead of salary expense, as it would be in a corporation.

Owner's Equity for a Partnership

A partnership is defined as "an association of two or more persons to carry on as co-owners of a business for profit." Small businesses and professionals such as accountants, doctors, and lawyers often use the partnership form of business.

A partnership is formed by two or more persons reaching mutual agreement about the terms of the relationship. The law does not require an application for a charter as in the case of a corporation. Instead, the agreement between the partners constitutes a partnership contract. This agreement should specify matters such as division of income, management responsibilities, transfer or sale of partnership interests, disposition of assets upon liquidation, and procedures to be followed in case of the death of a partner. If the partnership agreement does not specify these matters, the applicable provincial or territorial laws are binding.

In comparison to a corporation, the primary advantages of a partnership are (1) ease of formation, (2) complete control by the partners, and (3) lack of income taxes on the business itself. The primary disadvantage is the unlimited liability of each partner for the partnership's debts. If the partnership does not have sufficient assets to satisfy outstanding debt, creditors of the partnership can seize each partner's personal assets. In some cases, this can even result in one partner being held responsible for another partner's share of the partnership's debt.

As with a sole proprietorship, accounting for a partnership follows the same underlying principles as any other form of business organization, except for those entries that directly affect owners' equity. Accounting for partners' equity follows the same pattern as for a sole proprietorship, except that separate capital and drawings accounts must be established for each partner. Investments by each partner are credited to that partner's Capital account and withdrawals are debited to the respective Drawings account. The net income of a partnership is divided among the partners in accordance with the partnership agreement and credited to each account. The respective Drawings accounts are closed to the partner Capital accounts. After the closing process, each partner's Capital account reflects the cumulative total of all that partner's investments plus that partner's share of the partnership earnings less all of that partner's withdrawals.

Exhibit 11A.2 presents selected journal entries and partial financial statements for AB Partnership to illustrate the accounting for the distribution of income and partners' equity.

Another Business Form

In addition to sole proprietorships, partnerships, and corporations, another form of business exists in Canada. This form blends features of the "pure" organizational form described earlier in this chapter to create a hybrid business form such as a limited liability partnership (LLP).

Selected Entries during 2012

January 1, 2012

H. Simpson started a sole proprietorship by placing $150,000 cash in a bank account opened for the business. The accounting equation effects and journal entry follow:

Assets		=	Liabilities	+	Owner's Equity	
Cash	+150,000				H. Simpson, Capital	+150,000

dr Cash (+A) 150,000
  cr H. Simpson, Capital (+OE) 150,000

During 2012

Each month during the year, Simpson withdrew $1,000 cash from the business for personal living costs. Accordingly, each month the financial effects and required journal entry are:

Assets		=	Liabilities	+	Owner's Equity	
Cash	−1,000				H. Simpson, Drawings (+D)	−1,000

dr H. Simpson, Drawings (+D, −OE) 1,000
  cr Cash (−A) 1,000

Note: At December 31, 2012, after the last withdrawal, the drawings account reflected a debit balance of $12,000.

December 31, 2012

The usual journal entries for the year, including adjusting and closing entries for the revenue and expense accounts, resulted in revenue of $48,000 and expenses of $30,000. The net income of $18,000 was closed to the capital account as follows:

Assets	=	Liabilities	+	Owner's Equity	
				Revenues (−R)	−48,000
				Expenses (−E)	+30,000
				H. Simpson, Capital	+18,000

dr Individual Revenue Accounts (−R, −OE) 48,000
  cr Individual Expense Accounts (−E, +OE) 30,000
  cr H. Simpson, Capital (+OE) 18,000

December 31, 2012

The drawings account was closed as follows:

Assets	=	Liabilities	+	Owner's Equity	
				H. Simpson, Capital	−12,000
				H. Simpson, Drawings (−D)	+12,000

dr H. Simpson, Capital (−OE) 12,000
  cr H. Simpson, Drawings (−D, +OE) 12,000

HOMER'S DOUGH STORE
Statement of Owner's Equity
For the Year Ended December 31, 2012

H. Simpson, Capital, January 1, 2012	$ 0
Add: Capital contribution	150,000
Add: Net income for 2012	18,000
Total	168,000
Less: Withdrawals for 2012	(12,000)
H. Simpson, Capital, December 31, 2012	$156,000

The LLP in particular is an increasingly common form of business that combines legal characteristics of corporations (such as a separate legal identity and limited liability) with the tax treatment of partnerships (where tax is paid by the individual owners rather than by the

Selected Entries during 2012

January 1, 2012

A. Able and B. Baker organized AB Partnership on this date. Able contributed $60,000 cash and Baker contributed $40,000 cash to the partnership and they agreed to divide net income (and net loss) 60 percent and 40 percent, respectively. The financial effects of this investment on the business and the journal entry to record them are:

Assets	=	Liabilities	+	Partners' Equity	
Cash　　+100,000				A. Able, Capital	+60,000
				B. Baker, Capital	+40,000

dr Cash (+A) 100,000
　cr A. Able, Capital (+OE) .... 　　60,000
　cr B. Baker, Capital (+OE) .... 　　40,000

During 2012

The partners agreed that Able would withdraw $1,000 and Baker $650 per month in cash. Accordingly, each month the following financial effects were recorded with the journal entry that appears below:

Assets	=	Liabilities	+	Partners' Equity	
Cash　　−1,650				A. Able, Drawings (+D)	−1,000
				B. Baker, Drawings (+D)	−650

dr A. Able, Drawings (+D, −OE) 1,000
dr B. Baker, Drawings (+D, −OE) 650
　cr Cash (−A) .... 　　1,650

Note: At December 31, 2012, after the last withdrawals, the Drawings account for Able had a debit balance of $12,000 and the Drawings account for Baker had a debit balance of $7,800.

December 31, 2012

Assume that the normal closing entries for the revenue and expense accounts resulted in revenue of $78,000, expenses of $48,000, and net income of $30,000. The partnership agreement specified Able would receive 60 percent of net income ($18,000 = 60% × $30,000) and Baker would get 40 percent ($12,000 = 40% × $30,000). The financial effects and related closing entry follow:

Assets	=	Liabilities	+	Partners' Equity	
				Revenues (−R)	−78,000
				Expenses (−E)	+48,000
				A. Able, Capital	+18,000
				B. Baker, Capital	+12,000

dr Individual Revenue Accounts (−R, −OE) 78,000
　cr Individual Expense Accounts (−E, +OE) .... 　　48,000
　cr A. Able, Capital (+OE) (60% × $30,000) .... 　　18,000
　cr B. Baker, Capital (+OE) (40% × $30,000) .... 　　12,000

December 31, 2012

The financial effects of closing the drawings accounts and the related closing journal entry are:

Assets	=	Liabilities	+	Partners' Equity	
				A. Able, Capital	−12,000
				B. Baker, Capital	−7,800
				A. Able, Drawings (−D)	+12,000
				B. Baker, Drawings (−D)	+7,800

dr A. Able, Capital (−OE) 12,000
dr B. Baker, Capital (−OE) 7,800
　cr A. Able, Drawings (−D, +OE) .... 　　12,000
　cr B. Baker, Drawings (−D, +OE) .... 　　7,800

A separate statement of partners' capital, similar to a corporation's statement of shareholders' equity, is customarily prepared to supplement the balance sheet, as shown next:

AB PARTNERSHIP
Statement of Partners' Equity
For the Year Ended December 31, 2012

	A. Able	B. Baker	Total
Partners' equity, January 1, 2012	$ 0	$ 0	$ 0
Add: Additional contributions during the year	60,000	40,000	100,000
Add: Net income for the year	18,000	12,000	30,000
Totals	78,000	52,000	130,000
Less: Drawings during the year	(12,000)	(7,800)	(19,800)
Partners' equity, December 31, 2012	$66,000	$44,200	$110,200

business entity itself). Accounting for a limited liability partnership generally follows the methods shown earlier in this chapter.

The financial statements of an LLP follow the same format as those for a partnership, which differs from a corporation in the following ways: (1) the financial statements include an additional section entitled Distribution of Net Income; (2) the owners' equity section of the balance sheet is detailed for each owner; (3) the income statement does not report income tax expense because this form of business does not pay income tax (owners must report their share of the entity's profits on their individual tax returns); and (4) unless other contractual arrangements exist, amounts paid to the owners are not recorded as expenses but instead are accounted for as withdrawals of capital.

Review the Chapter

This section provides a chance to solidify your understanding of key points. It's worth your time to work through the following demonstration cases, scan the chapter summary, test your understanding of key terms, and then practise, practise, practise.

DEMONSTRATION CASE A: SHARE ISSUANCE AND REPURCHASES

This case focuses on selected transactions from the first year of operations of Zoogle Corporation, which became a public company on January 1, 2011, for the purpose of operating a lost-pet search business. The charter authorized the following shares:

> Common: 20,000 shares
> Preferred: $5, noncumulative, 5,000 shares

The following summarized transactions, selected from 2011, were completed on the dates indicated:

a. Jan. 1   Issued a total of 8,000 common shares for cash at $50 per share.

b. Feb. 1   Sold 2,000 preferred shares at $102 per share; cash collected in full.

c. July 1   Purchased 400 common shares that had been issued earlier. Zoogle Corporation paid the shareholder $54 per share and cancelled the shares.

d. Dec. 31   The board decided not to declare any dividends for the current year.

Required:

1. Give the appropriate journal entries, and show calculations for each transaction.
2. Prepare the shareholders' equity section of the balance sheet for Zoogle Corporation at December 31, 2011. Assume that Retained Earnings is $31,000 before these transactions are accounted for.

Suggested Solution

1. Journal entries:

a. Jan. 1, 2011	dr Cash (+A) ($50 × 8,000 shares)	400,000	
	cr Common Shares (+SE)		400,000
b. Feb. 1, 2011	dr Cash (+A) ($102 × 2,000 shares)	204,000	
	cr Preferred Shares (+SE)		204,000
c. July 1, 2011	dr Common Shares ($50 × 400) (−SE)	20,000	
	dr Retained Earnings [$400 × ($54 − $50)] (−SE).....	1,600	
	cr Cash (−A) ($54 × 400 shares)		21,600
d. Dec. 31, 2011	No journal entry is required.		

2. Shareholders' equity section of the balance sheet:

ZOOGLE CORPORATION
Partial Balance Sheet
At December 31, 2011

Shareholders' Equity		
Contributed Capital		
Preferred shares, $5, 5,000 authorized, 2,000 issued and outstanding shares	$204,000	
Common shares, authorized 20,000, issued 7,600 issued and outstanding shares	380,000	
Total Contributed Capital		$584,000
Retained Earnings		29,400
Total Shareholders' Equity		613,400

DEMONSTRATION CASE B: CASH AND STOCK DIVIDENDS

This case extends Demonstration Case A by focusing on dividend transactions occurring during Zoogle Corporation's second year. The following summarized transactions, selected from 2012, were completed on the dates indicated:

1. Nov. 1   To make the company's shares more affordable, the board declared a 100 percent stock dividend on the outstanding common shares. The share price at that time on the open market was $49.80.

2. Nov. 30   The stock dividend from Nov. 1 was issued on the common shares.

3. Dec. 1   The board declared a cash dividend on the preferred shares, payable on December 22, 2012, to shareholders of record as of December 15, 2012.

4. Dec. 31   The temporary Dividends Declared account was closed.

Required:

Give the appropriate journal entries, and show calculations for each transaction.

Suggested Solution

1. Nov. 1, 2012   *dr* Retained Earnings (−SE) 378,480

                 cr Common Shares Distributable (+SE)   378,480

                 [(7,600 common shares issued and outstanding) × $49.80]

Note: Because the stock dividend was only declared on November 1, the company would credit a Common Shares Distributable account, as the common shares have yet to be distributed. Then when the stock dividend is actually issued, the company would debit this same Common Shares Distributable account and credit the Common Shares account. This journal entry is shown next.

2. Nov. 30, 2012   *dr* Common Shares Distributable (−SE)................... 378,480

                 cr Common Shares (+SE).......................................   378,480

3. Dec. 1, 2012   *dr* Dividends Declared (+D, −SE) 10,000

                 cr Dividends Payable (+L)   10,000

                 (2,000 preferred shares × $5 dividend rate)...............

  Dec. 15, 2012   No journal entry is required.......................................

  Dec. 22, 2012   *dr* Dividends Payable (−L) 10,000

                 cr Cash (−A)   10,000

4. Dec. 31, 2012   *dr* Retained Earnings (−SE) 10,000

                 cr Dividends Declared (−D, +SE)   10,000

CHAPTER SUMMARY

Explain the role of shares (also called *stocks*) in financing a corporation. p. 460   **LO1**

- The law recognizes corporations as separate legal entities. Owners invest in a corporation and receive shares that can be bought from and sold to other investors. Shares provide a number of rights, including the rights to vote, to receive dividends, and to share in residual assets at liquidation.

Analyze and explain common share transactions. p. 462   **LO2**

- A number of key transactions involve common shares: (1) initial issuance of shares, (2) repurchase and cancellation of shares, (3) repurchase of shares into treasury, and (4) reissuance of treasury shares. The first two transactions are illustrated in this chapter, whereas the transactions dealing with treasury shares are in an online supplement that can be found on Connect. Note that these transactions have only balance sheet effects; corporations do not report income arising from gains or losses on transactions involving their own shares.

Explain and analyze cash dividends, stock dividends, and stock split transactions. p. 466   **LO3**

- Cash dividends reduce shareholders' equity (Retained Earnings) and create a liability (Dividends Payable) when they are declared by the board of directors (on the date of declaration). The liability is reduced when the dividends are paid (on the date of payment).

- Stock dividends are pro rata distributions of a company's shares to existing owners. The transaction typically is accounted for by transferring an amount out of Retained Earnings and into contributed capital accounts.

- A stock split also involves the distribution of additional shares to owners but no additional amount is transferred into the contributed capital accounts. Instead, the book value of the shares is reduced.

Describe the characteristics of preferred shares and analyze transactions affecting preferred shares. p. 472   **LO4**

- Preferred shares provide investors with certain advantages, including current dividend preferences and a preference on asset distributions in the event that the corporation is liquidated.

- If preferred shares carry cumulative dividend rights, any part of current dividends that are not paid (called *dividends in arrears*) must be paid in full before any additional dividends can be paid.

- The earnings per share (EPS) ratio is calculated by dividing net income by the average number of common shares outstanding during the year. This ratio makes it easy to compare a company's earnings over time but it does not allow reliable comparisons across companies because it does not adjust for likely differences in the number of shares that each company has outstanding.
- The return on equity (ROE) ratio relates earnings to each dollar contributed to and retained by the company. Because it is calculated using dollar amounts contributed to and retained by a company, it allows comparisons to be made across companies.
- The price/earnings (P/E) ratio relates the company's current share price to its most recent annual earnings per share, indicating the value that investors place on the company's shares.

ACCOUNTING DECISION TOOLS

Name of Measure	Formula	What It Tells You
Earnings per share (EPS)	$\dfrac{\text{Net Income}}{\text{Average Number of Common Shares Outstanding}}$	· The amount of income generated for each common share owned by shareholders · A higher ratio means greater profitability
Return on equity (ROE)	$\dfrac{\text{Net Income}}{\text{Average Shareholders' Equity}}$	· The amount earned for each dollar invested by shareholders · A higher ratio means shareholders are likely to enjoy greater returns
Price/earnings (P/E) ratio	$\dfrac{\text{Current Share Price}}{\text{Earnings per Share (annual)}}$	· How many times more than the current year's earnings investors are willing to pay for a company's common share · A higher number means investors anticipate an improvement in the company's future results

KEY TERMS

Authorized Shares p. 462
Common Share p. 461
Contributed Surplus p. 466
Cumulative Dividend Preference
p. 474
Current Dividend Preference p. 473
Declaration Date p. 467

Dividends in Arrears p. 474
Issued Shares p. 462
No-Par Value Shares p. 464
Outstanding Shares p. 463
Par Value p. 464
Payment Date p. 468
Preferred Shares p. 472

Record Date p. 468
Retained Earnings p. 465
Stock Dividend p. 469
Stock Split p. 470
Treasury Shares p. 462

See complete definitions in the glossary at the back of this text.

HOMEWORK HELPER

Alternative terms

- Shareholders are also called *stockholders*.

Helpful reminders

- Stock dividends are recorded at the current market price of the share.

Frequent mistakes

- Do not record a liability for dividends in arrears at the end of each year. They are recorded as a liability only when dividends are declared on the cumulative preferred shares.

Practice Material

QUESTIONS ($ Symbol indicates questions that require analysis from more than one perspective.)

1. Identify the primary advantages of the corporate form of business.

2. What are the relative advantages of equity versus debt financing?

3. Just prior to filing for bankruptcy protection in 2009, General Motors asked its bondholders to exchange their investment in GM's bonds for GM shares. The bondholders rejected this proposal. Why might GM have proposed this exchange? Why might the bondholders have rejected it? $

4. Explain each of the following terms: (a) authorized common shares, (b) issued common shares, and (c) outstanding common shares.

5. What are the differences between common shares and preferred shares?

6. What is the distinction between par value and no-par value shares?

7. What are the usual characteristics of preferred shares?

8. What are the two basic sources of shareholders' equity? Explain each.

9. What are treasury shares? Why do corporations acquire treasury shares?

10. What are the two financial requirements to support the declaration of a cash dividend? What are the effects of a cash dividend on assets and shareholders' equity?

11. What is the difference between cumulative and noncumulative preferred shares?

12. What is a stock dividend? How does a stock dividend differ from a cash dividend?

13. What are the primary reasons for issuing a stock dividend?

14. Your company has been very profitable and expects continued financial success. Its share price has reached a point where the company needs to make the cost of shares more affordable. Would you recommend a stock dividend or a stock split? Why? $

15. Identify and explain the three important dates related to dividends.

16. Why is the EPS number so popular? What are its limitations?

17. How do share repurchases affect the EPS and ROE ratios?

18. What is one interpretation of a high P/E ratio?

19. You work for a public company that has relied heavily on debt financing in the past and is now considering a preferred share issuance to reduce its debt-to-assets ratio. Debt-to-assets is one of the key ratios in your company's loan covenants. Should the preferred shares have a fixed annual dividend rate or a dividend that is determined yearly? In what way might this decision be affected by IFRS? $

Multiple-choice questions and corresponding answers can be found on Connect.

MINI-EXERCISES

M11-1 Analyzing and Recording the Issuance of Common Shares   LO2

To expand operations, Artagon Consulting issued 100,000 shares of previously unissued common shares with a par value of $1. The share price was $75 per share. Analyze the accounting equation effects and record the journal entry for the share issuance. Would your answer be different if the par value was $2 per share? If so, analyze the accounting equation effects and record the journal entry for the share issuance with a par value of $2.

M11-2 Analyzing and Recording the Issuance of No-Par Value Common Shares   LO2

Refer to M11-1. Assume the issued shares have no par value. Analyze the accounting equation effects and record the journal entry for the issuance of the no-par value shares at $75. Do the effects on total assets, total liabilities, and total shareholders' equity differ from those in M11-1?

M11-3 Determining the Effects of Share Issuance and Share Repurchase and Cancellation Transactions   LO2

TransUnited Limited issued 5,000 shares for $50 per share in the current year, and it issued 10,000 shares for $37 per share in the following year. The year after that, the company reacquired and cancelled 20,000 shares of its own shares for $45 per share. Determine the impact (increase, decrease, or no change) of each of these transactions on the following classifications:

1. Total assets.
2. Total liabilities.
3. Total shareholders' equity.
4. Net income.

M11-4 Recording Dividends

On April 15, 2012, the board of directors for AuctionPro declared a cash dividend of 40 cents per share payable to shareholders of record on May 20. The dividends will be paid on June 14. The company has 500,000 shares outstanding. Prepare any necessary journal entries for each date.

M11-5 Determining the Impact of a Stock Dividend

Stone Tools, Inc., announced a 100 percent stock dividend. Determine the impact (increase, decrease, no change) of this dividend on the following:
1. Total assets.
2. Total liabilities.
3. Common shares.
4. Total shareholders' equity.
5. Market value per share of common shares.

M11-6 Determining the Impact of a Stock Split

Complete the requirements of M11-5 assuming that the company announced a 2-for-1 stock split.

M11-7 Determining the Amount of a Preferred Dividend

Colliers Inc. has 100,000 shares of cumulative preferred shares outstanding. The preferred shares pay dividends in the amount of $2 per share but because of cash flow problems, the company did not pay any dividends last year. The board of directors plans to pay dividends in the amount of $1 million this year. What amount will go to preferred shareholders? How much will be available for dividends to common shareholders?

M11-8 Calculating and Interpreting Earnings per Share (EPS) and Return on Equity (ROE)

Academy Driving School reported the following in its financial statements:

	2012	2011
Number of common shares	11,500	11,500
Net income	$ 23,000	$ 18,000
Cash dividends paid on common shares	$ 3,000	$ 3,000
Total shareholders' equity	$240,000	$220,000

Calculate 2012 EPS and ROE. Another driving school in the same city reported a higher net income ($45,000) in 2012, yet its EPS and ROE ratios were lower than those for the Academy Driving School. Explain how this apparent inconsistency could occur.

M11-9 Determining the Impact of Transactions on Components of Earnings per Share (EPS) and Return on Equity (ROE)

Indicate the direction of effect (+ for increase, − for decrease, or NE for no effect) of each of the following transactions on the accounting equation in the table below. The first transaction is shown as an example.

	Assets	= Liabilities +	Shareholders' Equity
a. (Example) Purchased and cancelled 50 shares for $5,000. The original price paid for these shares was also $5,000 in total.	Cash −5,000		Common shares (+xSE) −5,000
b. Declared and paid a cash dividend of $600.			
c. Declared and issued a stock dividend valued at $10,000 on no-par preferred shares.			
d. Sold inventory for $80 cash, when it had cost $55.			
e. Issued common shares at par for $60,000 cash.			

M11-10 Inferring Financial Information Using the P/E Ratio   L05

In 2011, Rec Room Sports reported earnings per share of $8.50 when its share price was $212.50. In 2012, its earnings increased by 20 percent. If the P/E ratio remains constant, what is the price of the shares? Explain.

EXERCISES

Practise and learn online with Connect.

E11-1 Reporting Shareholders' Equity and Determining Dividend Policy   LO2, 3

Beamsley Corporation was organized in 2012 to operate a financial consulting business. The charter authorized 12,000 common shares, no par value. During the first year, the following selected transactions were completed:

a. Issued 6,000 shares of common shares for cash at $20 per share.
b. Issued 2,000 shares of common shares for cash at $23 per share.

Required:

1. Show the effects of each transaction on the accounting equation.
2. Give the journal entry required for each of these transactions.
3. Prepare the shareholders' equity section as it should be reported on the 2012 year-end balance sheet. At year-end, the accounts reflected a profit of $100.
4. Beamsley Corporation has $30,000 in the company's bank account. Should the company declare cash dividends at this time? Explain.

Check Figure:
[Req. 3]
Total shareholders' equity
= $166,100

E11-2 Preparing the Shareholders' Equity Section of the Balance Sheet   LO2, 4

Norwest Aviation received its charter during January 2012. The charter authorized the following shares:

> Preferred shares: 8 percent, no par value, authorized 20,000 shares.
> Common shares: no par value, authorized 50,000 shares.

During 2012, the following transactions occurred in the order given:

a. Issued a total of 40,000 common shares to the company's founders for $11 per share.
b. Issued 5,000 preferred shares at $18 per share.
c. Issued 3,000 common shares at $14 per share and 1,000 preferred shares at $28.
d. Net income for the first year was $48,000.

Required:

Prepare the shareholders' equity section of the balance sheet at December 31, 2012.

E11-3 Reporting the Shareholders' Equity Section of the Balance Sheet   LO2, 3, 4

Shelby Corporation was organized in January 2012 by ten shareholders to operate an air-conditioning sales and service business. The charter issued by the province authorized the following shares:

> Common shares, no par value, 200,000 shares.
> Preferred shares, no par value, 6 percent, 50,000 shares.

During January and February 2012, the following share transactions were completed:

a. Collected $40,000 cash from each of the ten organizers and issued 2,000 common shares to each of them.
b. Issued 15,000 preferred shares at $25 per share; collected in cash.

Net income for 2012 was $40,000; cash dividends declared and paid at year-end were $10,000.

Required:

Prepare the shareholders' equity section of the balance sheet at December 31, 2012.

E11-4 Determining the Effects of the Issuance of Common and Preferred Shares

RiteSide Limited was issued a charter on January 15, 2012, that authorized the following shares:

> Common shares, no par value, 100,000 shares, one vote per share.
> Preferred shares, 7 percent, no par value $10 per share, 5,000 shares, nonvoting.

During 2012, the following selected transactions were completed in the order given:

a. Issued 20,000 common shares at $18 cash per share.
b. Issued 3,000 preferred shares at $22 cash per share.
c. At the end of 2012, the accounts showed net income of $38,000.

Required:

1. Prepare the shareholders' equity section of the balance sheet at December 31, 2012.
2. Assume that you are a common shareholder. If RiteSide Limited needed additional capital, would you prefer to have it issue additional common shares or additional preferred shares? Explain.

E11-5 Recording and Reporting Shareholders' Equity Transactions

Ava School of Learning obtained a charter at the start of 2012 that authorized 50,000 shares of no-par common shares and 20,000 no-par preferred shares. During 2012, the following selected transactions occurred:

a. Collected $40 cash per share from four individuals and issued 5,000 common shares to each.
b. Issued 6,000 shares of common shares to an outside investor at $40 cash per share.
c. Issued 8,000 shares of preferred shares at $20 cash per share.

Check Figure:
[Req. 2]
Total shareholders' equity
= $1,236,000

Required:

1. Give the journal entries indicated for each of these transactions.
2. Prepare the shareholders' equity section of the balance sheet at December 31, 2012. At the end of 2012, the accounts reflected net income of $36,000. No dividends were declared.

E11-6 Finding Amounts Missing from the Shareholders' Equity Section

The shareholders' equity section on the December 31, 2012, balance sheet of Chemkast Corporation reported the following amounts:

Contributed Capital	
Preferred shares (par $20; authorized 10,000 shares, ? issued)	$104,000
Additional paid-in capital, preferred	14,300
Common shares (no-par; authorized 20,000 shares, issued and	
outstanding 8,000 shares)	600,000
Retained earnings	30,000

Assume that no shares of treasury shares have been sold in the past.

Required:

Complete the following statements and show your computations.

1. The number of preferred shares issued was _____.
2. The number of preferred shares outstanding was _____.
3. The average issue price of the preferred shares was $_____ per share.
4. The average issue price of the common shares was $_____ per share.
5. Total shareholders' equity is $_____.

E11-7 Recording Shareholders' Equity Transactions

The annual report for Malibu Beachwear reported the following transactions affecting shareholders' equity:

a. Repurchased and cancelled $3.5 million common shares.

b. Declared and paid cash dividends in the amount of $254.2 million.

c. Issued 100 percent common stock dividend involving 222.5 million additional shares with a total par value of $556.3 million.

Required:

1. Indicate the effect (increase, decrease, or no effect) of each of these transactions on total assets, liabilities, and shareholders' equity.

2. Prepare journal entries to record each of these transactions.

E11-8 Computing Dividends on Preferred Shares and Analyzing Differences

LO3, 4

The records of Hoffman Company reflected the following balances in the shareholders' equity accounts at December 31, 2011:

> Common shares, par $12 per share, 40,000 shares outstanding.
> Preferred shares, 8 percent, par $10 per share, 6,000 shares outstanding.
> Retained earnings, $220,000.

On January 1, 2012, the board of directors was considering the distribution of a $62,000 cash dividend. No dividends were paid during 2010 and 2011.

Required:

1. Determine the total and per share amounts that would be paid to the common shareholders and to the preferred shareholders under two independent assumptions:

    a. The preferred shares are noncumulative.

    b. The preferred shares are cumulative.

2. Briefly explain why the dividends per common share were less for the second assumption.

3. What factors would cause a more favourable dividend for the common shareholders?

Check Figure:
[Req. 1(a)]
Dividends paid to common shareholders = $57,200

E11-9 Recording the Payment of Dividends and Preparing a Statement of Retained Earnings

LO2, 3

The 2012 annual report for Sneer Corporation disclosed that the company declared and paid preferred dividends in the amount of $119.9 million in 2012. It also declared and paid dividends on common shares in the amount of $2 per share. During 2012, Sneer had 1,000,000,000 common shares authorized; 387,570,300 shares had been issued. The balance in Retained Earnings was $1,554 million on December 31, 2011, and 2012 Net Income was $858 million.

Required:

1. Prepare journal entries to record the declaration, and payment, of dividends on (*a*) preferred and (*b*) common shares.

2. Using the information given above, prepare a statement of retained earnings for the year ended December 31, 2012.

E11-10 Analyzing Stock Dividends

LO3

On December 31, 2011, the shareholders' equity section of the balance sheet of R & L Corporation reflected the following:

Common shares (par $10; authorized 60,000 shares, outstanding 25,000 shares)	$250,000
Additional paid-in capital	12,000
Retained earnings	75,000

On February 1, 2012, the board of directors declared a 12 percent stock dividend to be issued April 30, 2012. The market value of the shares on February 1, 2012, was $18 per share.

Required:

1. For comparative purposes, prepare the shareholders' equity section of the balance sheet (*a*) immediately before the stock dividend and (*b*) immediately after the stock dividend.

   TIP: Use two columns for the amounts in this requirement.

2. Explain the effects of this stock dividend on the assets, liabilities, and the components of shareholders' equity.

3. How would your answers to requirements 1 and 2 change if the stock dividend was 100 percent?

LO3 **E11-11 Accounting for Dividends during the Credit Crisis**

A press release contained the following announcement:

> *Castleton, Sask., April 30, 2012:* Ridgeton Corporation announced today that its Board of Directors declared a quarterly cash dividend of $0.12 per share of the Corporation's outstanding common shares, payable June 26, 2012, to shareholders of record at the close of business on June 12, 2012. This represents a reduction from the $0.42 quarterly dividend paid by the Corporation since 2010. Frederick Furter, chairman and chief executive officer, commented, "In today's uncertain and challenging economic environment, however, we believe it is important to preserve liquidity. By lowering the dividend to $0.12 per quarter, we will reduce cash outflows by $54 million in 2012. This action will strengthen our balance sheet, improve our credit metrics and provide greater financial flexibility."

At the time of the press release, Ridgeton had 150,000,000 shares authorized and 60 million outstanding. The par value for the company's shares is $0.50 per share.

Required:

1. Prepare journal entries as appropriate for each of the three dates mentioned above.
2. Explain how a dividend cut from $0.42 to $0.12 will strengthen the company's balance sheet.

LO3 **E11-12 Comparing Stock Dividends and Splits**

On July 1, 2012, Jones Limited had the following share structure:

Common shares, par $1; 200,000 authorized shares, 150,000 issued and outstanding	$150,000
Additional paid-in capital	88,000
Retained earnings	172,000

Required:

Complete the following table based on three independent cases involving share transactions:

Case 1: The board of directors declared and issued a 10 percent stock dividend when the share price was $8 per share.

Case 2: The board of directors declared and issued a 100 percent stock dividend when the share price was $8 per share.

Case 3: The board of directors voted a 2-for-1 stock split. The share price prior to the split was $8 per share.

Check Figure:
[Case 2]
Retained Earnings = $22,000

		Case 1	Case 2	Case 3
Items	Before Share Transactions	After 10% Stock Dividend	After 100% Stock Dividend	After Stock Split
Number of shares outstanding				
Par per share	$ 1	$	$	$
Common shares account	$	$	$	$
Additional paid-in capital	88,000			
Retained earnings	172,000			
Total shareholders' equity	$	$	$	$

E11-13 Analyzing Dividends in Arrears

Like many start-up companies, DomainCo struggled with cash flows as it developed new business opportunities. A student found a financial statement for DomainCo that stated that the increase in dividends in arrears on preferred shares this year was $264,000.

The student who read the note suggested that the DomainCo preferred share would be a good investment because of the large amount of dividend income that would be earned when the company started paying dividends again: "As the owner of the shares, I'll get dividends for the period I hold the shares plus some previous periods when I didn't even own the shares." Do you agree? Explain.

E11-14 Determining the Impact of Cash and Stock Dividends

Superior Corporation has the following shares outstanding:

> Preferred shares, 6 percent, par $15, outstanding shares, 8,000.
> Common shares, par $8, outstanding shares, 30,000.

On October 1, 2012, the board of directors declared dividends as follows:

> Preferred shares: Full cash preference amount, payable December 20, 2012.
> Common shares: 10 percent common stock dividend (i.e., one additional share for each 10 held), to be issued on December 20, 2012.

On December 20, 2012, the market prices were preferred shares, $40, and common shares, $32.

Required:

At each date indicated above, describe the overall effect of the cash and stock dividends on the assets, liabilities, and shareholders' equity of the company.

E11-15 Determining the Financial Statement Effects of Cash and Stock Dividends

Lynn Company has outstanding 60,000 common shares of $10 par value and 25,000 preferred shares of $20 par value (8 percent). On December 1, 2012, the board of directors voted an 8 percent cash dividend on the preferred shares and a 10 percent stock dividend on the common shares. At the date of declaration, the common share price was $35 and the preferred share price was $20 per share. The dividends are to be paid, or issued, on February 15, 2013. The annual accounting period ends December 31.

Required:

Explain the comparative effects of the two dividends on the assets, liabilities, and shareholders' equity (*a*) through December 31, 2012, (*b*) on February 15, 2013, and (*c*) in regard to the overall effects from December 1, 2012, through February 15, 2013. Use the following structure:

	Comparative Effects Explained	
Item	Cash Dividend on Preferred	Stock Dividend on Common
(a) Through December 31, 2012:		
Effect on Assets		
Effect on Liabilities		
Effect on Shareholders' Equity		

E11-16 Preparing a Statement of Retained Earnings and Partial Balance Sheet and Evaluating Dividend Policy

The following account balances were selected from the records of beverage maker Blake Corporation at December 31, 2012, after all adjusting entries were completed:

Common shares (par $15; authorized 100,000 shares, issued 35,000 shares)	$525,000
Additional paid-in capital	180,000
Dividends declared and paid in 2012	28,000
Retained earnings, January 1, 2012	76,000

Net income for the year was $48,000.

Required:

1. Prepare the statement of retained earnings for the year ended December 31, 2012, and the shareholders' equity section of the balance sheet at December 31, 2012.
2. Compute the ROE ratio, assuming total shareholders' equity was $629,000 on December 31, 2011. How does it compare to the ratios shown in Exhibit 11.9?

E11-17 Analyzing Share Repurchases and Stock Dividends

Winnebago is a familiar name on vehicles travelling Canadian highways. The company manufactures and sells large motor homes for vacation travel. These motor homes can be quickly recognized because of the company's "flying W" trademark. A July 2, 2007, press release contained the following information:

> Winnebago Industries, Inc., (NYSE: WGO) today announced a new $60 million shares repurchase authorization. Winnebago Industries has repurchased approximately 24.4 million shares of common shares for approximately $356.8 million since December 31, 1997.

Required:

1. Determine the impact of this share repurchase on the financial statements.
2. Why might the board have decided to repurchase the shares?
3. What impact will this purchase have on Winnebago's future dividend obligations?
4. Back on January 14, 2004, the company's board of directors declared a 2-for-1 stock split effected in the form of a 100 percent stock dividend distributed on March 5, 2004. Why would Winnebago choose a stock dividend rather than a stock split?
5. What impact would this stock dividend have had on Winnebago's financial statements? What impact would it have had on the EPS and ROE ratios?

LO2, 5

E11-18 Determining the Effect of a Share Repurchase on EPS and ROE

J. Bartley Pools Inc. reported the following in its financial statements for the quarter ended March 31, 2012.

	December 31, 2011	March 31, 2012
Common shares, $1 par, 50,000 shares outstanding	$ 50,000	$ 50,000
Additional paid-In capital	30,000	30,000
Retained earnings	20,000	20,000
Total shareholders' equity	$100,000	$100,000

During the quarter ended March 31, 2012, Bartley reported Net Income of $5,000 and declared and paid cash dividends totalling $5,000.

Required:

1. Calculate earnings per share (EPS) and return on equity (ROE) for the quarter ended March 31, 2012.
2. Assume that Bartley repurchases 10,000 of its common shares at a price of $2 per share on April 1, 2012. Also assume that during the quarter ended June 30, 2012, Bartley reported Net Income of $5,000 and declared and paid cash dividends totalling $5,000. Calculate earnings per share (EPS) and return on equity (ROE) for the quarter ended June 30, 2012.
3. Based on your calculations in requirements 1 and 2, what can you conclude about the impact of a share repurchase on EPS and ROE?

E11-19 (Supplement 11A) Comparing Shareholders' Equity Sections for Alternative Forms of Organization

Assume for each of the following independent cases that the annual accounting period ends on December 31, 2012, and that the total of all revenue accounts was $150,000 and the total of all expense accounts was $130,000.

Case A: Assume that the company is a *sole proprietorship* owned by Proprietor A. Prior to the closing entries, the Capital account reflected a credit balance of $50,000 and the Drawings account showed a balance of $8,000.

Case B: Assume that the company is a *partnership* owned by Partner A and Partner B. Prior to the closing entries, the owners' equity accounts reflected the following balances: A, Capital, $40,000; B, Capital, $38,000; A, Drawings, $5,000; and B, Drawings, $9,000. Profits and losses are divided equally.

Check Figure:
[Case B]
Total Partners' Equity
= $84,000

Case C: Assume that the company is a *corporation*. Prior to the closing entries, the shareholders' equity accounts showed the following: Capital Shares, par $10, authorized 30,000 shares, outstanding 15,000 shares; Additional Paid-In Capital, $5,000; Retained Earnings, $65,000.

Required:

1. Give all the closing entries required at December 31, 2012, for each of the separate cases.
2. Show how the equity section of the balance sheet would appear at December 31, 2012, for each case. Show computations.

COACHED PROBLEMS

CP11-1 Analyzing Accounting Equation Effects, Recording Journal Entries, and Preparing a Partial Balance Sheet Involving Share Issuance and repurchase Transactions

LO2

Worldwide Company obtained a charter from the province in January 2012 that authorized 200,000 no-par value common shares. During the first year, the company earned $38,200 and the following selected transactions occurred in the order given:

a. Issued 60,000 shares of the common shares at $12 cash per share.

b. Reacquired and cancelled 2,000 shares at $15 cash per share from shareholders.

c. Issued 1,000 common shares at $18 cash per share.

Required:

1. Indicate the effects of each transaction on the accounting equation.
2. Prepare journal entries to record each transaction.
3. Prepare the shareholders' equity section of the balance sheet at December 31, 2012.

> **TIP:** Because this is the first year of operations, Retained Earnings has a zero balance at the beginning of the year.
> **TIP:** Total Retained Earnings at December 31, 2012, equals $770,200.

CP11-2 Comparing Stock and Cash Dividends

LO2, 3, 4

Water Tower Company had the following shares outstanding and Retained Earnings at December 31, 2012:

Common shares (par $8; outstanding, 30,000 shares)	$240,000
Preferred shares, 7% (par $10; outstanding, 6,000 shares)	60,000
Retained earnings	280,000

On December 31, 2012, the board of directors is considering the distribution of a cash dividend to the common and preferred shareholders. No dividends were declared during 2010 or 2011. Three independent cases are assumed:

Case A The preferred shares are noncumulative; the total amount of 2012 dividends would be $30,000.

Case B The preferred shares are cumulative; the total amount of 2012 dividends would be $12,600. Dividends were not in arrears prior to 2010.

Case C Same as Case B, except the amount is $66,000.

Required:

1. Compute the amount of 2012 dividends, in total and per share, that would be payable to each class of shareholders for each case. Show computations.

TIP: Preferred shareholders with cumulative dividends are paid dividends for any prior years (in arrears) *and* for the current year before common shareholders are paid.

2. Complete the following schedule, which compares Case C to a 100 percent common stock dividend issued when the share price is $24.

	Amount of Dollar Increase (Decrease)	
Item	Case C (Cash Dividend)	Stock Dividend
Assets	$	$
Liabilities	$	$
Shareholders' Equity	$	$

LO5 **CP11-3 Computing and Interpreting Return on Equity (ROE) and Price/Earnings (P/E) Ratios**

Avery's Rentals, Inc., and Rent-A-Matic, Inc., are two publicly traded rental companies. They reported the following in their 2011 financial statements (in millions of dollars, except per share amounts and share prices):

	Avery's Rentals, Inc.		Rent-A-Matic, Inc.	
	2011	2010	2011	2010
Net income	$ 90.2	$ 80.3	$ 139.6	$ 76.3
Total shareholders' equity	761.5	673.4	1,079.2	947.1
Earnings per share	1.69	1.48	2.10	1.11
Share price when annual results reported	26.67	21.54	19.37	18.35

Required:

1. Compute the 2011 ROE for each company. Express ROE as a percentage rounded to one decimal place. Which company appears to generate greater returns on shareholders' equity in 2011?

   TIP: Remember that the bottom of the ROE ratio uses the *average* shareholders' equity.

2. Compute the 2011 P/E ratio for each company (rounded to one decimal place). Do investors appear to value one company more than the other? Explain.

GROUP A PROBLEMS

Practise and learn online with Connect.

LO2 **PA11-1 Analyzing Accounting Equation Effects, Recording Journal Entries, and Preparing a Partial Balance Sheet Involving Shares Issuance and Purchase Transactions**

Doulane Marine obtained a charter from the province in January 2012 that authorized 1,000,000 common shares. During the first year, the company earned $429,000 and the following selected transactions occurred in the order given:

a. Issued 700,000 common shares at $54 cash per share.
b. Reacquired and cancelled 25,000 shares at $50 cash per share.

Required:

1. Indicate the effects of each transaction on the accounting equation.
2. Prepare journal entries to record each transaction.
3. Prepare the shareholders' equity section of the balance sheet at December 31, 2012.

LO3 **PA11-2 Recording Cash Dividends**

Metro Chocolate Corp. produces chocolate bars and snacks under the brand names Blast and Soothe. A press release contained the following information:

March 5, 2012—Metro Chocolate Corp. today announced that its Board of Directors has declared a special "one-time" cash dividend of $1.00 per share on its one million outstanding common shares. The dividend will be paid on April 30 to shareholders of record at the close of business on March 26.

Required:

1. Prepare any journal entries that Metro Chocolate Corp. should make as a result of information in the press release. Assume that the company has 1.0 million shares outstanding on March 5, the par value is $0.01 per share, and the share price is $10 per share.

2. What two requirements would the board of directors have considered before making the dividend decisions?

PA11-3 Finding Missing Amounts

LO2, 3, 5

At December 31, 2012, the records of Kozmetsky Corporation provided the following selected and incomplete data:

> Common shares (no changes during 2012).
> Shares authorized, 5,000,000.
> Shares issued, ____?____ issue price $1 per share.
> Net income for 2012, $4,800,000.
> Common shares account $1,500,000.
> Dividends declared and paid during 2012, $2 per share.
> Retained earnings balance, January 1, 2012, $82,900,000.

Required:

1. Complete the following:
   Shares issued _____.
   Shares outstanding _____.
2. Earnings per share is $_____. Round your answer to two decimal places.
3. Total dividends paid on common shares during 2012 is $_____.

Check Figure:
[Req. 2]
EPS = $3.20

PA11-4 Comparing Stock and Cash Dividends

LO2, 3, 4

Ritz Company had the following shares outstanding and Retained Earnings at December 31, 2012:

Common shares (par $1; outstanding, 500,000 shares)	$500,000
Preferred shares, 8% (par $10; outstanding, 21,000 shares)	210,000
Retained earnings	900,000

On December 31, 2012, the board of directors is considering the distribution of a cash dividend to the common and preferred shareholders. No dividends were declared during 2010 or 2011. Three independent cases are assumed:

Case A: The preferred shares are noncumulative; the total amount of 2012 dividends would be $30,000.

Case B: The preferred shares are cumulative; the total amount of 2012 dividends would be $30,000. Dividends were not in arrears prior to 2010.

Case C: Same as Case B, except the amount is $75,000.

Required:

1. Compute the amount of dividends, in total and per share, payable to each class of shareholders for each case. Show computations. Round per share amounts to two decimal places.
2. Complete the following schedule, which compares case C to a 100 percent stock dividend on the outstanding common shares when the share price was $50.

Item	Amount of Dollar Increase (Decrease)	
	Case C (Cash Dividend)	Stock Dividend
Assets	$ ☐	$ ☐
Liabilities	$ ☐	$ ☐
Shareholders' Equity	$ ☐	$ ☐

LO5 **PA11-5 Computing and Interpreting Return on Equity (ROE) and Price/Earnings (P/E) Ratios**

Two magazine companies reported the following in their 2012 financial statements (in thousands of dollars, except per share amounts and share prices):

	Business Now		Fun and Games	
	2012	2011	2012	2011
Net income	$ 55,000	$ 54,302	$ 91,420	$172,173
Total shareholders' equity	587,186	512,814	894,302	934,098
Earnings per share	3.20	3.19	2.10	3.98
Share price when annual results reported	54.40	51.04	32.55	59.70

Required:

1. Compute the 2012 ROE for each company (express ROE as a percentage rounded to one decimal place). Which company appears to generate greater returns on shareholders' equity in 2012?
2. Compute the 2012 P/E ratio for each company. Do investors appear to value one company more than the other? Explain.
3. *Fun and Games* reacquired 32,804 (thousand) common shares in 2012 at $4 per share. Recalculate the company's ROE for 2012, assuming that this share repurchase did not occur. Does this new ROE change your interpretation of the ROE ratios calculated in requirement 1?

GROUP B PROBLEMS

LO2 **PB11-1 Analyzing Accounting Equation Effects, Recording Journal Entries, and Preparing a Partial Balance Sheet Involving Shares Issuance and Purchase Transactions**

Whyville Corporation obtained its charter from the province in January 2012, which authorized 500,000 common shares. During the first year, the company earned $58,000 and the following selected transactions occurred in the order given:

a. Issued 200,000 shares of the common shares at $23 cash per share.
b. Reacquired and cancelled 5,000 shares at $24 cash per share.

Required:

1. Indicate the effects of each transaction on the accounting equation.
2. Prepare journal entries to record each transaction.
3. Prepare the shareholders' equity section of the balance sheet at December 31, 2012.

LO3 **PB11-2 Recording Cash and Stock Dividends**

Yougi Corp., an animation studio, issued a press release that contained the following information:

April 1, 2012—Yougi Corp. today announced that its Board of Directors has declared a cash dividend of $0.50 per share on 605,000 outstanding preferred shares. The dividend will be paid on or before May 31, 2012, to preferred shareholders of record at the close of business on May 26, 2012. The Board of Directors also announced a 100 percent common stock dividend will occur on May 31, 2012, on its 1,900,000 outstanding $0.01 par common shares for shareholders of record on May 26, 2012.

Required:

1. Prepare any journal entries that Yougi Corp. should make as the result of information in the preceding report.

2. What two requirements would the board of directors have considered before making the dividend decision?

PB11-3 Finding Missing Amounts

LO2, 3, 5

At December 31, 2012, the records of Seafoam Enterprises provided the following selected and incomplete data:

> Common shares (no changes during 2012).
> Shares authorized, 10,000,000.
> Shares issued, _____?_____ issue price $10 per share.
> Net income for 2012, $2,400,000.
> Common shares account $750,000.
> Dividends declared and paid during 2012, $1 per share.
> Retained earnings balance, January 1, 2012, $36,400,000.

Required:

1. Complete the following:

   Shares issued _____.

   Shares outstanding _____.

2. Earnings per share is $_____. Round your answer to two decimal places.

3. Total dividends paid on common shares during 2012 is $_____.

PB11-4 Comparing Stock and Cash Dividends

LO2, 3, 4

Carlos Company had the following shares outstanding and Retained Earnings at December 31, 2012:

Common shares (par $1; outstanding, 490,000 shares)	$490,000
Preferred shares, 8% (par $10; outstanding, 19,000 shares)	190,000
Retained earnings	966,000

On December 31, 2012, the board of directors is considering the distribution of a cash dividend to the common and preferred shareholders. No dividends were declared during 2010 or 2011. Three independent cases are assumed:

Case A The preferred shares are noncumulative; the total amount of 2012 dividends would be $24,000.

Case B The preferred shares are cumulative; the total amount of 2012 dividends would be $24,000. Dividends were not in arrears prior to 2010.

Case C Same as Case B, except the amount is $67,000.

Required:

1. Compute the amount of 2012 dividends, in total and per share, payable to each class of shareholders for each case. Show computations. Round per share amounts to two decimal places.

2. Complete the following schedule, which compares Case C to a 100 percent stock dividend on the outstanding common shares when the share price was $45.

Check Figure:
[Case C, Req. 1]
Dividend paid to common shareholders = $21,400

	Amount of Dollar Increase (Decrease)	
Item	Case C (Cash Dividend)	Stock Dividend
Assets	$ ☐	$ ☐
Liabilities	$ ☐	$ ☐
Shareholders' Equity	$ ☐	$ ☐

LO5 · PB11-5 Computing and Interpreting Return on Equity (ROE)

Two music companies reported the following in their 2012 financial statements (in thousands of dollars, except per share amounts and share prices):

	Urban Youth		Sound Jonx	
	2012	2011	2012	2011
Net income	$ 27,500	$ 24,302	$ 41,500	$ 36,739
Total shareholders' equity	387,101	300,399	516,302	521,198
Earnings per share	1.10	1.00	0.95	0.85
Share price when annual results reported	20.35	18.50	16.15	14.45

Required:

Check Figure:
[Req. 1]
2012 ROE for Urban Youth
= 8.0%

1. Compute the 2012 ROE for each company (express ROE as a percentage rounded to one decimal place). Which company appears to generate greater returns on shareholders' equity in 2012?

2. Compute the 2012 P/E ratio for each company. Do investors appear to value one company more than the other? Explain.

3. Sound Jonx reacquired 5,000 (thousand) common shares in 2012 at $13 per share. Recalculate the company's ROE for 2012 assuming that this share repurchase did not occur. Does this new ROE change your interpretation of the ROE ratios calculated in requirement 1?

COMPREHENSIVE PROBLEM

LO2, 3 · C11-1 Financial Reporting of Bond Issuance and Common Share Issuance, Repurchase, and Cash Dividends (Chapters 10 and 11)

Americana Inc. reported the following shareholders' equity account balances on January 1, 2012.

Notes Payable (due 2015)	$10,000	Bonds Payable	$ 0
Common Shares, 1,000 issued	1,000	Retained Earnings	120,000

The company entered into the following transactions during 2012.

Jan.	15	Issued 5,000 common shares for $50,000 cash.
Feb.	15	Reacquired and cancelled 3,000 common shares for $33,000 cash.
Mar.	15	Issued 2,000 common shares for $24,000 cash.
Aug.	15	Issued 600 common shares for $4,600 cash.
Sept.	15	Declared (but did not yet pay) a $1 cash dividend on each outstanding common shares.
Oct.	1	Issued 100, 10-year, $1,000 bonds, at a quoted bond price of 101.

Required:

1. Analyze the effects of each transaction on total assets, liabilities, and shareholders' equity.
2. Prepare journal entries to record each transaction.
3. Prepare the noncurrent liabilities and shareholders' equity sections of the balance sheet at December 31, 2012. At the end of 2012, the accounts reflected net income of $20,000.

SKILLS DEVELOPMENT CASES

LO2, 3, 5 · S11-1 Finding Financial Information

Rona Inc.

Refer to the financial statements of Rona Inc. in Appendix A at the back of this book or download the annual report from the *Cases* section of Connect.

Required:

1. As of December 27, 2009, how many preferred shares were authorized? How many shares were issued? What does this suggest to you about the number of shares outstanding?

2. According to the Statement of Retained Earnings, what was the total dollar amount of cash dividends declared during the year ended December 27, 2009?

3. According to the income statement, how has Rona Inc.'s net earnings changed over the past year? Has the company's basic earnings per share changed over the past year? Are these patterns consistent?

S11-2 Comparing Financial Information

LO2, 3, 5
Rona Inc.

Refer to the financial statements of Rona Inc. in Appendix A and The Home Depot's in Appendix B at the back of this book or download the annual reports from the *Cases* section of Connect.

Required:

1. Did The Home Depot have more or fewer authorized common shares than Rona Inc. at the beginning of the fiscal year-end 2009?

2. From the Retained Earnings column in the statement of shareholders' equity, what total amount of cash dividends did The Home Depot declare during the year ended January 31, 2010? Compared to Rona Inc., is The Home Depot's policy on dividends better, worse, or just different?

3. How have The Home Depot's net earnings changed over the past three years? How has the company's basic earnings per share changed over the past three years?

S11-3 Internet-Based Team Research: Examining an Annual Report

LO3, 5

As a team, select an industry to analyze. Using your Web browser, each team member should access the annual report for one publicly traded company in the industry, with each member selecting a different company. (See S1-3 in Chapter 1 for a description of possible resources for these tasks.)

Required:

1. On an individual basis, each team member should write a short report that incorporates the following:
   a. What is the ownership structure for this company and how does this structure impact the reporting in the financial statements?
   b. Has the company declared cash or stock dividends during the past three years?
   c. What is the trend in the company's EPS over the past three years?
   d. Compute and analyze the return on equity ratio over the past two years.

2. Then, as a team, write a short report comparing and contrasting your companies using these attributes. Discuss any patterns across the companies that you as a team observe. Provide potential explanations for any differences discovered.

S11-4 Ethical Decision Making: A Real-Life Example

LO1, 2

Activision became a public company with an initial public offering of shares on June 9, 1983, at $12 per share. In June 2002, Activision issued 7.5 million additional shares to the public at approximately $33 per share in a seasoned new issue. In October 2002, when its shares were trading at about $22 per share, Activision executives announced that the company would spend up to $150 million to reacquire shares from investors. On January 8, 2003, *The Wall Street Journal* reported that several analysts were criticizing Activision's executives because the company had issued the shares to the public at a high price ($33) and then were offering to reacquire them at the going share market price, which was considerably lower than the issue price in 2002.

Required:

1. Do you think it was inappropriate for Activision to offer to reacquire the shares at a lower share price in October 2002?

2. Would your answer to question 1 be different if Activision had not issued additional shares in June 2002?

3. The above *Wall Street Journal* article also reported that, in December 2002, Activision executives had purchased, for their own personal investment portfolios, 530,000 shares in the company at the

then-current price of $13.32 per share. If you were an investor, how would you feel about executives buying shares in their own company?

4. Would your answer to question 3 be different if you also learned that the executives had disposed of nearly 2.5 million shares of Activision earlier in the year, when the price was at least $26.08 per share?

LO3   **S11-5 Ethical Decision Making: A Mini-Case**

You are the president of a very successful Internet company that has had a remarkably profitable year. You have determined that the company has more than $10 million in cash generated by operating activities not needed in the business. You are thinking about paying it out to shareholders as a special dividend. You discuss the idea with your vice-president, who reacts angrily to your suggestion:

> "Our share price has gone up by 200 percent in the last year alone. What more do we have to do for the owners? The people who really earned that money are the employees who have been working 12 hours a day, six or seven days a week to make the company successful. Most of them didn't even take vacations last year. I say we have to pay out bonuses and nothing extra for the shareholders."

As president, you know that you are hired by the board of directors, which is elected by the shareholders.

Required:

What is your responsibility to both groups? To which group would you give the $10 million? Why?

LO3   **S11-6 Critical Thinking: Making a Decision as an Investor**

You have retired after a long and successful career as a business executive and now spend a good portion of your time managing your retirement portfolio. You are considering three basic investment alternatives. You can invest in (1) corporate bonds paying 7 percent interest, (2) conservative shares that pay substantial dividends (typically 5 percent of the share price every year), and (3) growth-oriented technology shares that pay no dividends.

Required:

Analyze each of these alternatives and select one. Justify your selection.

LO1, 3   **S11-7 Charting Share Price Movement around Important Announcement Dates**

Using a Web search engine such as Google, find either an earnings or dividend announcement for two different companies. Using a source such as bigcharts.com, determine the closing share price for each company for each day during the five business days before and after the announcement. Using a separate worksheet for each company, prepare a line chart of its share price movement.

Required:

Examine the charts for each company. Does the share price appear to change as a consequence of the announcements? Explain why or why not.

CONTINUING CASE

Practise and learn online with Connect.

LO1, 2, 3, 4, 5   **CC11 Accounting for Equity Financing**

Nicole has been financing Nicole's Getaway Spa (NGS) using equity financing. Currently, NGS has authorized 100,000, $0.30 preferred shares and 200,000 common shares. Outstanding shares include 50,000 preferred shares and 40,000 common shares.

Recently the following transactions have taken place.

a. NGS repurchased and cancelled 1,000 common shares for $10 a share.

b. NGS issued 1,000 preferred shares for $12 a share.

c. On November 12, 2012, the board of directors declared a cash dividend on each outstanding preferred share.

d. The dividend was paid December 20, 2012.

Required:

1. Prepare the journal entries needed for each of the transactions.

2. If you were a common shareholder concerned about your voting rights, would you prefer Nicole to issue additional common shares or additional preferred shares? Why?

3. Describe the overall effect of each transaction on the assets, liabilities, and shareholders' equity of the company. (Use + for increase, − for decrease, and NE for no effect.)

4. How would each transaction affect the ROE ratio?

Endnotes

1. Supplement 11A near the end of this chapter discusses accounting for owners' equity in proprietorships, partnerships, and other business forms.

2. Although companies report their annual EPS numbers only at the end of their fiscal years, most analysts find it useful to update annual EPS as each quarter's results are reported. To do this, analysts will compute their own "trailing 12 months" (TTM) EPS measure by summing the most recent four quarters of EPS. This way, they can get a timely measure of year-long EPS without having to wait until the end of the fiscal year.

3. If a company has preferred shares outstanding, the ROE ratio can be adjusted to focus on the common shareholders' perspective. Simply deduct any preferred dividends from net income and exclude any preferred share accounts from the calculation of average shareholders' equity. This adjustment is not required in Sun-Rype's case because all its issued shares are common shares.

Practise and learn online with Connect.

CHAPTER 12

Reporting and Interpreting the Statement of Cash Flows

FOCUS COMPANY:
Under Armour, Inc.
www.underarmour.com

THAT WAS
THEN

In the previous chapters, you learned about the income statement, statement of retained earnings, and balance sheet.

THIS IS
NOW

This chapter focuses on the fourth main financial statement—the statement of cash flows.

Have you ever studied your bank statement to see how much money you bring in and pay out during a typical month? You don't have to be a financial genius to know that if you are spending more than you earn, your savings will quickly disappear and you will need to get a loan or some other source of financing to see you through.

Most businesses face the same issues you do. In 2007, for example, Under Armour, Inc.—famous for its frictionless sportswear—reported a net cash outflow from day-to-day operating activities. To ensure the company's long-term survival, managers had to stay on top of this change in the cash situation. Fortunately, the company had saved a great deal of cash in prior years. Managers were also able to negotiate some new loans to keep the business from running out of cash. By 2008, the company had turned things around and was again experiencing a positive net cash inflow from its operations.

Just like Under Armour's managers, investors and creditors also monitor the company's cash inflows and outflows. Investors want to know whether Under Armour is likely to pay dividends and creditors want to know whether Under Armour is likely to pay them the amounts they are owed. The statement of cash flows provides them with the information necessary for making such predictions. Similar to your personal bank statement, the statement of cash flows reports changes in a company's cash situation.

ORGANIZATION OF THE CHAPTER

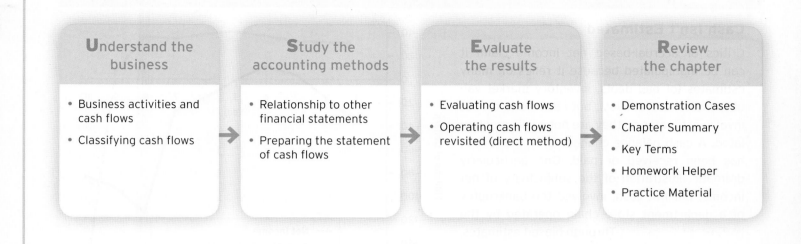

Understand the business	Study the accounting methods	Evaluate the results	Review the chapter
• Business activities and cash flows • Classifying cash flows	• Relationship to other financial statements • Preparing the statement of cash flows	• Evaluating cash flows • Operating cash flows revisited (direct method)	• Demonstration Cases • Chapter Summary • Key Terms • Homework Helper • Practice Material

Understand the Business

BUSINESS ACTIVITIES AND CASH FLOWS

To this point in the course, we've analyzed business activities to identify their financial effects on assets, liabilities, shareholders' equity, revenues, and expenses. We've emphasized that business activities have financial effects even when they don't involve cash. That's why accrual accounting exists. When accurately reported, accrual-based net income is the best measure of a company's profitability during the period.

Despite its importance, net income is not what companies use when they pay wages, dividends, or loans. These activities require cash, so financial statement users need information about the company's cash and changes in its cash. Neither the balance sheet nor the income statement provides this information. The balance sheet shows a company's cash balance at a point in time, but it doesn't explain the activities that caused changes in its cash. Cash may have been generated by the company's day-to-day operations, by the sale of the company's buildings, or by the negotiation of new loans. The income statement doesn't explain changes in cash because it focuses on just the operating results of the business, excluding cash that is received or paid when taking out or paying down loans, issuing or buying the company's own shares, and selling or investing in long-lived assets. Also, the timing of cash receipts and payments may differ from the accrual-based income statement, which reports revenues when they are earned and expenses when they are incurred. Under Armour, for example, reported a hefty amount of net income in each quarter of 2008, yet its related cash flows were negative in two of those four quarters. Such differences between net income and cash flows are the reason that the Accounting Standards for Private Enterprises (ASPE) and International Financial Reporting Standards (IFRS) require every company to report a statement of cash flows.

The statement of cash flows shows each major type of business activity that caused a company's cash to increase or decrease during the accounting period. For purposes of this statement, cash is defined to include cash and cash equivalents. As explained in Chapter 6, cash equivalents are short-term, highly liquid investments purchased within three months of maturity. They are considered equivalent to cash because they are both (1) readily convertible to known amounts of cash and (2) so close to maturity that their value is unlikely to change.

Learning Objective 1

Identify cash flows arising from operating, investing, and financing activities.

Cash Isn't Estimated

Critics of accrual-based net income claim it can be manipulated because it relies on many estimates (of bad debts, inventory market values, assets' useful lives), but cash flows do not involve estimates so they are not easily manipulated. A cash balance changes only when cash has been received or paid. One particularly dramatic illustration of the subjectivity of net income, but not cash, involved the bankruptcy of a department store chain operated by the W. T. Grant Company. Through biased estimates, the company reported net income for nine consecutive years but then shocked everyone when it declared bankruptcy and shut down the following year. At the time, a statement of cash flows wasn't required. Had it been required, the company would have reported negative operating cash flows in seven of the ten years.

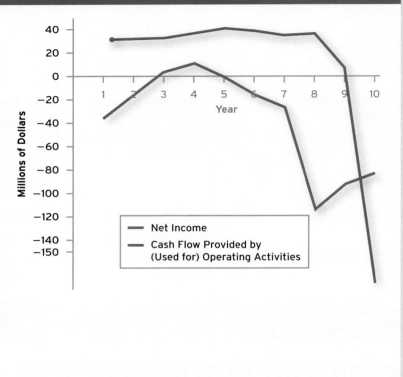

Source: James A. Largay, III, and Clyde P. Stickney, "Cash Flows, Ratio Analysis and the W. T. Grant Company Bankruptcy," *Financial Analysts Journal* 36:4, July/August 1980, pp. 51–54.

CLASSIFYING CASH FLOWS

The statement of cash flows requires that all cash inflows and outflows be classified as relating to the company's operating, investing, or financing activities. This classification of cash flows is useful because most companies experience different cash flow patterns as they develop and mature. Think back to Chapter 2 when Pizza Palace had just started. The first thing the owner needed to get his idea off the ground was **financing**, which he could then use to **invest** in assets that later would be needed to **operate** his business. At this early stage, financing and investing cash flows were crucial for Pizza Palace. For an established business, like Activision in Chapter 5, operating activities often are the focus. Financial statement users are interested in a company's ability to generate operating cash flows that will allow it to continue investing in additional assets and repay the financing it originally obtained. Creditors and investors will tolerate poor operating cash flows for only so long before they stop lending to or investing in the company. For any company to survive in the long run, the amount of cash generated through daily operating activities has to exceed the amount spent on them.

A condensed version of Under Armour's statement of cash flows is presented in Exhibit 12.1. Don't worry about the details in the three cash flow categories yet. For now, focus on the categories' totals. Notice that each category can result in net cash inflows (represented by a positive number) or net cash outflows (represented by a negative number by using brackets). The sum of these three categories ($90 − $30 + $25 = $85) represents the overall change in cash on the balance sheet between the beginning and end of the period ($85 + $102 = $187).

Under Armour's 2009 cash flows in Exhibit 12.1 suggest the company is financially healthy. The company generated $90 million cash from its day-to-day operations. This money

EXHIBIT 12.1   Under Armour's Condensed Statement of Cash Flows

UNDER ARMOUR, INC. Statement of Cash Flows For the Year Ended December 31, 2009		Explanations
(In millions)		
Cash Flows from Operating Activities		Cash flows related to day-to-day activities
Net income	$ 47	Assume net income (NI) generates cash inflow
Amortization	23	Amortization decreased NI but didn't decrease cash
Changes in current assets and current liabilities	20	Differences in the timing of net income and cash flows
Net cash provided by operating activities	90	Indicates overall cash impact of operating activities
Cash Flows Used in Investing Activities		Cash flows related to long-term assets
Purchase of equipment	(23)	Cash was used to purchase equipment
Purchase of intangible and other assets	(7)	Cash was used to purchase intangibles
Net cash used in investing activities	(30)	Indicates overall cash impact of investing activities
Cash Flows from Financing Activities		Cash flows from transactions with lenders, investors
Additional borrowings of long-term debt	24	Cash received from borrowing
Payments on long-term debt	(22)	Cash used to repay amounts previously borrowed
Proceeds from share issuance	23	Cash received from issuing shares
Net cash provided by financing activities	25	Indicates overall cash impact of financing activities
Net Change in Cash and Cash Equivalents	85	$90 + $(30) + $25 = $85
Cash and cash equivalents, beginning of year	102	Cash balance at beginning of the period
Cash and cash equivalents, end of year	$187	Cash balance at end of the period (on balance sheet)

allowed Under Armour to invest $30 million in additional long-term assets and, combined with $25 million of net cash inflow from financing activities, build its cash balance at the end of the year. To learn the specific causes of these cash flows, you would consider the details of each category, as we will do now.

Operating Activities

Cash flows from operating activities (or cash flows from operations) are the cash inflows and outflows related directly to the revenues and expenses reported on the income statement. Operating activities involve day-to-day business activities with customers, suppliers, employees, landlords, and others. Typical cash flows from operating activities include

Inflows	Outflows
Cash provided by	*Cash used for*
Collecting from customers	Purchasing services (electricity, etc.) and goods for resale
Receiving dividends	Paying salaries and wages
Receiving interest	Paying income taxes
	Paying interest

The difference between these cash inflows and outflows is reported on the statement of cash flows as a subtotal, Net Cash Provided by (Used for) Operating Activities.

Investing Activities

Cash flows from investing activities are the cash inflows and outflows related to the purchase and disposal of investments and long-lived assets. Typical cash flows from investing activities include the following:

Inflows	Outflows
Cash provided by	**Cash used for**
Sale or disposal of property, plant, and equipment	Purchase of property, plant, and equipment
Sale or maturity of investments in securities	Purchase of investments in securities

The difference between these cash inflows and outflows is reported on the statement of cash flows as a subtotal, Net Cash Provided by (Used in) Investing Activities.

Financing Activities

Cash flows from financing activities include exchanges of cash with shareholders and cash exchanges with lenders (for principal on loans). Common cash flows from financing activities include

Inflows	Outflows
Cash provided by	**Cash used for**
Borrowing from lenders through formal debt contracts	Repaying principal to lenders
Issuing shares to owners	Repurchasing shares from owners
	Paying cash dividends to owners

The difference between these cash inflows and outflows is reported on the statement of cash flows as a subtotal, Net Cash Provided by (Used in) Financing Activities.

One way to classify cash flows into operating, investing, and financing categories is to think about the balance sheet accounts to which the cash flows relate. Although exceptions exist, a general rule is that operating cash flows cause changes in current assets and current liabilities, investing cash flows affect noncurrent assets, and financing cash flows affect noncurrent liabilities or shareholders' equity accounts.[1] Exhibit 12.2 shows how this general rule relates the three sections of the statement of cash flows (SCF) to each of the main sections of a classified balance sheet.

EXHIBIT 12.2 **Relationships between Classified Balance Sheet and Statement of Cash Flows (SCF) Categories**

SCF Categories	Classified Balance Sheet Categories	
Operating	Current assets	Current liabilities
Investing	Noncurrent assets	Noncurrent liabilities
Financing		Shareholders' equity

💡 HOW'S IT GOING? Self-Study Practice

Brunswick Corporation produces the Life Fitness line of gym equipment. A listing of some of its cash flows follows. Indicate whether each item is disclosed in the operating activities (O), investing activities (I), or financing activities (F) section of the statement of cash flows.

☐ *a.* Shares issued to shareholders.

☐ *b.* Collections from customers.

☐ *c.* Interest paid on debt.

☐ *d.* Purchase of plant and equipment.

☐ *e.* Purchase of investment securities.

☐ *f.* Cash dividends paid.

After you have finished, check your answers with the solution in the margin.

YOU SHOULD KNOW

Cash flows from financing activities: Cash inflows and outflows related to financing sources external to the company (owners and lenders).

Solution to Self-Study Practice

a. F, *b.* O, *c.* O, *d.* I, *e.* I, *f.* F

Classification Choices under IFRS

To create consistency across companies, ASPE restricts interest and dividend classifications to a single category. IFRS, on the other hand, allows managers to choose between categories, as follows.

	COMPANY PAYS		COMPANY RECEIVES	
	Dividends	Interest	Dividends	Interest
ASPE	F	O	O	O
IFRS	O, F	O, F	O, I	O, I

ASPE classifies dividends paid as financing because they are transactions with shareholders. IFRS allows dividends paid to be classified as operating to assist users in determining the company's ability to pay dividends out of operating cash flows. ASPE requires the other three items to be classified as operating because they enter into the determination of net income. IFRS allows interest paid to be classified as financing because it is a cost of obtaining financial resources. IFRS allows interest and dividends received to be classified as investing because they are returns on investments.

Study the Accounting Methods

RELATIONSHIP TO OTHER FINANCIAL STATEMENTS

The statement of cash flows is intended to provide a cash-based view of a company's business activities during the accounting period. It uses the same transactions that have been reported in the income statement and balance sheet but converts them from the accrual basis to a cash basis. This conversion involves analyzing the income statement and the changes in balance sheet accounts, and relating these changes to the three cash flow categories. To prepare a statement of cash flows, you need the following:

1. **Comparative balance sheets,** showing beginning and ending balances, used in calculating the cash flows from all activities (operating, investing, and financing).

2. **A complete income statement,** used primarily in calculating cash flows from operating activities.

3. **Additional data** concerning selected accounts that increase and decrease as a result of investing and/or financing activities.

The approach to preparing the cash flow statement focuses on changes in the balance sheet accounts. It relies on a simple rearrangement of the balance sheet equation:

Assets = Liabilities + Shareholders' Equity

First, assets can be split into cash and all other assets, which we'll call noncash assets:

Cash + Noncash Assets = Liabilities + Shareholders' Equity

If we move the noncash assets to the right side of the equation, we get

$$\text{Cash} = \text{Liabilities} + \text{Shareholders' Equity} - \text{Noncash Assets}$$

Given this relationship, the changes in cash between the beginning and end of the period must equal the changes in the amounts on the right side of the equation between the beginning and end of the period:

$$\text{Change in Cash} = \text{Change in (Liabilities} + \text{Shareholders' Equity} - \text{Noncash Assets)}$$

This equation says that changes in cash must be accompanied by and can be accounted for by the changes in liabilities, shareholders' equity, and noncash assets.

PREPARING THE STATEMENT OF CASH FLOWS

Based on the idea that the change in cash equals the sum of the changes in all other balance sheet accounts, we use the following steps to prepare the statement of cash flows:

1. **Determine the change in each balance sheet account.** From this year's ending balance, subtract this year's beginning balance (i.e., last year's ending balance).

2. **Identify the cash flow category or categories to which each account relates.** Use Exhibit 12.2 as a guide, but be aware that some accounts may include two categories of cash flows. Retained Earnings, for example, can include both financing cash flows (paying dividends) and operating cash flows (generating net income). Similarly, Accumulated Amortization can be affected by operating activities (amortization for using equipment in daily operations) as well as investing activities (disposing of equipment).

3. **Create schedules that summarize operating, investing, and financing cash flows.**

We will follow these three steps to prepare a statement of cash flows for Under Armour for the year ended December 31, 2009. Step 1 requires that we subtract each account's beginning balance from its ending balance, as we have done in the right side of Exhibit 12.3. Next, for step 2, we indicated whether each account's cash flows relate to operating (O), investing (I), and/or financing (F) activities. Notice that Cash is not classified as O, I, or F, because Cash is not reported in these three sections but instead appears at the bottom of the statement of cash flows, as shown earlier in Exhibit 12.1. Step 3 in preparing a statement of cash flows is explained in the following sections.

Direct and Indirect Reporting of Operating Cash Flows

Two alternative methods may be used when presenting the operating activities section of the statement of cash flows:

1. The **direct method** reports the total cash inflow or outflow from each main type of transaction (that is, transactions with customers, suppliers, employees, etc.). The difference between these cash inflows and outflows equals the Net Cash Provided by (Used in) Operating Activities.

2. The **indirect method** starts with net income from the income statement and adjusts it by eliminating the effects of items that do not involve cash (for example, amortization) and including items that do have cash effects. Adjusting net income for these items yields the amount of Net Cash Provided by (Used in) Operating Activities.

Direct Method		Indirect Method	
Cash collected from customers	$ 858		
Cash paid to suppliers of inventory	(413)		
Cash paid to employees and suppliers of services	(317)	Net income	$47
Cash paid for interest	(2)	Amortization	23
Cash paid for income tax	(36)	Changes in current assets and current liabilities	20
Net cash provided by (used in) operating activities	$ 90	Net cash provided by (used in) operating activities	$90

EXHIBIT 12.3 | **Information for Preparing a Statement of Cash Flows**

UNDER ARMOUR, INC.
Balance Sheet*

(In millions)	December 31, 2009	December 31, 2008	Step ① Change	Step ② Related Cash Flow Section
Assets				
Current Assets:				
Cash and Cash Equivalents	$187	$102	+85	Cash
Accounts Receivable	79	81	−2	O
Inventories	149	182	−33	O
Prepaid Expenses	33	31	+2	O
Total Current Assets	448	396		
Equipment	143	120	+23	I
Less: Accumulated Amortization	(70)	(47)	−23	O (no I; see note 2 below)
Intangible and Other Assets	25	18	+7	I
Total Assets	$546	$487		
Liabilities and Shareholders' Equity				
Current Liabilities:				
Accounts Payable	$ 69	$ 72	−3	O
Accrued Liabilities	51	61	−10	O
Total Current Liabilities	120	133		
Long-Term Debt	25	23	+2	F
Total Liabilities	145	156		
Shareholders' Equity:				
Contributed Capital	198	175	+23	F
Retained Earnings	203	156	+47	O (no F; see note 1 below)
Total Shareholders' Equity	401	331		
Total Liabilities and Shareholders' Equity	$546	$487		

UNDER ARMOUR, INC.
Income Statement*
For the Year Ended December 31, 2009

(In millions)	
Net Sales	$856
Cost of Goods Sold	443
Gross Profit	413
Operating Expenses:	
Selling, General, and Administrative Expenses	305
Amortization Expense	23
Total Operating Expenses	328
Income from Operations	85
Interest Expense	2
Net Income before Income Tax Expense	83
Income Tax Expense	36
Net Income	$ 47

Additional data

1. No dividends were declared or paid.
2. No disposals or impairments of equipment or intangibles occurred.
3. Equipment costing $23 million and intangibles costing $7 million were purchased with cash.
4. Long-term debt of $22 million was repaid and $24 million in new loans was issued.
5. Shares issued for $23 million.

*Certain balances have been adjusted to simplify the presentation.

The point to remember about the direct and indirect methods is that they are simply different ways to arrive at the same number. Net cash flows provided by (used in) operating activities are always the same under the direct and indirect methods. Also, the choice between the two methods affects only the operating activities section of the statement of cash flows, not the investing and financing sections.

SPOTLIGHT ON THE WORLD

Direct vs. Indirect Method Presentation

ASPE and IFRS currently allow companies to use either the direct or indirect method. The Financial Accounting Standards Board (FASB) and the International Accounting Standards Board (IASB) recently proposed removing this choice and allowing only the direct method because the direct method is more detailed and shows the operating cash receipts and cash payments. This is consistent with the objective of a cash flow statement. However, providing more details for the financial statement users means more time and costs for everyone involved. Conversely, the indirect method is less time-consuming and it is less costly to accumulate and present the information. If adopted, this proposal would significantly change the way companies report their statement of cash flows. Currently, about 99 percent of large Canadian companies, including Bombardier, use the indirect method.

Learning Objective 2

Report cash flows from operating activities, using the indirect method.

We focus on the indirect method in the following section because it is currently the most commonly used method in Canada. The direct method, which may be required by ASPE and IFRS in the future, is presented in the last section of this chapter.

Determining Operating Cash Flows Using the Indirect Method

When using the indirect method, the schedule of operating activities has the following format. We explain each of these items below and then, on pages 511–514, we demonstrate how to use Under Armour's information in Exhibit 12.3 to create such a schedule.

Net income
Items included in net income that do not involve cash
    + Amortization
    + Losses on disposal of long-term assets or retirement of long-term debt
    − Gains on disposal of long-term assets or retirement of long-term debt
Changes in current assets and current liabilities
    + Decreases in current assets
    − Increases in current assets
    − Decreases in current liabilities
    + Increases in current liabilities
Net cash flow provided by (used in) operating activities

Net income. When preparing a schedule to determine operating cash flows using the indirect method, start with net income as reported on the last line of the company's income statement. By starting with net income, it's as if we are assuming all revenues resulted in cash inflows and all expenses resulted in cash outflows. But we know this is not true, however, so we adjust net income to eliminate items that are included in net income but do not involve cash and to include items that were excluded from net income but do involve cash.

+Amortization. When initially recording amortization in the accounting system, we increase Amortization Expense (with a debit) and increase Accumulated Amortization (with a credit). Notice that amortization does not involve cash. To eliminate the effect of having deducted Amortization Expense in the income statement, we add it back in the statement of cash flows.

+ Losses on disposal of long-term assets and retirement of long-term debt.

− Gains on disposal of long-term assets and retirement of long-term debt. When long-term assets are disposed of and when long-term debt has been retired early, a corresponding loss or gain can result from these transactions. The amount of the loss is reported on the income statement and reduces the amount of net income the company would have otherwise reported. The amount of the gain is also reported on the income statement and increases the amount of net income the company would have otherwise reported. However, this loss or gain amount is not usually the same as the cash flow that resulted from the transaction. The actual cash flow is the cash proceeds received on the disposal of the long-term asset or the cash payment paid to retire the long-term debt. Therefore we need to eliminate the effect of having incurred the loss or gain by adding back the loss or subtracting the gain in the statement of cash flows. Then we can properly deal with the cash proceeds received on the disposal of the long-term asset in the investing section of the cash flow statement, and the cash payment to retire the long-term debt is dealt with in the financing section of the cash flow statement. Supplement 12A later in this chapter explains in more detail how these transactions affect the statement of cash flows.

+ Decreases in current assets. Adding decreases in current assets serves two purposes. First, it eliminates the effects of some transactions that decreased net income but did not affect cash in the current period. For example, when Supplies are used, net income decreases but cash is not affected. To eliminate these noncash effects from our cash flow computations, we must add back decreases in Supplies and other current assets. Second, adding decreases in current assets allows us to include the cash effects of other transactions that did not affect net income in the current period but did increase cash. For example, Cash increases when Accounts Receivable are collected. These cash inflows are captured by adding the amount by which this current asset had decreased.

− Increases in current assets. Subtracting increases in current assets similarly serves two purposes. First, it eliminates the effects of transactions that increased net income but did not affect cash in the current period. For example, net income increases when a company provides services on account, but cash is not affected. We eliminate these noncash effects by subtracting increases in current assets. Second, subtracting increases in current assets allows us to include the cash effects of other transactions that did not affect net income in the current period but did decrease cash. For example, Cash decreases when a company prepays its insurance or rent, but net income isn't affected until these assets are used up. The cash outflows can be captured by subtracting the increase in these current assets.

− Decreases in current liabilities. Subtracting decreases in current liabilities serves two purposes. First, it eliminates the effects of transactions that increased net income but did not affect cash. For example, a company decreases Unearned Revenue and increases net income in the current period when it fulfills its prior obligations to provide services, but cash is not affected. To eliminate these noncash effects, we subtract decreases in current liabilities. Second, subtracting decreases in current liabilities allows us to include the cash effects of other transactions that did not affect net income in the current period but did decrease cash. For example, Cash decreases when a company pays wages that were incurred and expensed in a previous period. These cash outflows are captured by subtracting decreases in current liabilities.

+ Increases in current liabilities. Adding increases in current liabilities serves two purposes. First, it eliminates the effects of transactions that decreased net income but did not affect cash. For example, when interest is accrued, a company decreases net income but its cash is not affected. To eliminate these noncash effects, we add back increases in current liabilities. Second, adding increases in current liabilities allows us to include the cash effects of other transactions that did not affect net income in the current period but did increase cash. For example, Cash and Unearned Revenue increase when the company receives cash in advance of providing services. Adding the increase in current liabilities captures these cash inflows.

Under Armour's Operating Cash Flows—Indirect Method

The preceding approach to preparing an operating cash flow schedule can be applied to Under Armour's information in Exhibit 12.3. By taking the amount of the change in each account marked by an O in Exhibit 12.3, we have prepared an operating cash flow schedule for Under Armour in Exhibit 12.4. Understanding the causes of increases or decreases in each current asset and current liability is the key to understanding the logic behind the items in the schedule. Take your time reading the following explanations and make sure you understand the reasons for each item.

EXHIBIT 12.4 | **Under Armour's Schedule of Operating Cash Flows**

Item	Amount (in millions)	Explanation
Net income	$47	Starting point, from the income statement
Items included in net income that do not involve cash		
+ Amortization	23	Amortization is a noncash expense
Changes in current assets and current liabilities		
+ Decrease in Accounts Receivable	2	Cash collections greater than sales on account
+ Decrease in Inventories	33	Cost of goods sold greater than purchases
− Increase in Prepaid Expenses	(2)	Prepayments greater than related expenses
− Decrease in Accounts Payable	(3)	Payments to suppliers greater than purchases
− Decrease in Accrued Liabilities	(10)	Cash payments greater than accrued expenses
Net cash flow provided by (used in) operating activities	$90	Overall increase in cash from operations

---

COACH'S TIP

The amortization add-back is not intended to suggest that amortization creates an increase in cash. Rather, it just shows that amortization does not cause a decrease in cash. This is a subtle, but very important, difference in interpretation.

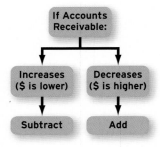

Net Income + Amortization   Net income and amortization are always the first two lines to appear in a statement of cash flows prepared using the indirect method. They begin the process of converting net income to operating cash flows. They also begin the process of explaining the change in Cash by accounting for changes in the other balance sheet accounts. In the case of Under Armour, the $47 million of net income fully accounts for the change in Retained Earnings (the company had no dividends). Similarly, the $23 million of amortization accounts for the change in Accumulated Amortization (the company had no disposals).[2]

Decrease in Accounts Receivable   Accounts Receivable increases when sales are made on account and it decreases when cash is collected from customers. An overall decrease in this account, then, implies that cash collections were greater than sales on account. To convert from the lower sales number that is included in net income to the higher cash collected from customers, we add the difference ($2 million).

   Another way to remember whether to add or subtract the difference is to think about whether the overall change in the account balance is explained by a debit or credit. If the change in the account is explained by a debit, the adjustment in the cash flow schedule is reported like a corresponding credit to cash (subtracted). In Under Armour's case, the decrease in Accounts Receivable is explained by a credit, so the adjustment in the cash flow schedule is reported like a debit to cash (an increase), as follows:

Accounts Receivable (A)	
Beg. bal.	Collections of cash
Sales on account	from customers
End. bal.	

Accounts Receivable (A)			
Beg. bal.	81		
		2	Decrease
End. bal.	79		

CASH FLOWS FROM OPERATING ACTIVITIES	
Net income	47
+ Accounts receivable decrease	2
. . .	. . .
Net cash inflow	—

Decrease in Inventory   The income statement reports the cost of merchandise sold during the period, but cash flow from operating activities must report cash purchases of inventory. As shown in the T-account in the margin on the next page, purchases of goods increase the balance in inventory, and recording merchandise sold decreases the balance in inventory.

Inventories (A)			Inventories (A)		
Beg. bal.			Beg. bal.	182	
Purchases	Cost of goods sold				33 Decrease
End. bal.			End. bal.	149	

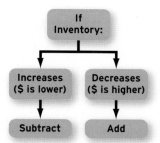

Under Armour's $33 million inventory decrease means that the amount of cost of goods sold is more than the purchases. The decrease (the extra sales) must be added to net income to convert to cash flow from operating activities in Exhibit 12.4. (An increase would be subtracted.)

Increase in Prepaid Expenses The income statement reports expenses of the period, but cash flow from operating activities must reflect the cash payments. Cash prepayments increase the balance in prepaid expenses, and recording of expenses decreases the balance in prepaid expenses.

Prepaid Expenses (A)			Prepaid Expenses (A)		
Beg. bal.			Beg. bal.	31	
Cash prepayments	Used-up / expensed		Increase	2	
End. bal.			End. bal.	33	

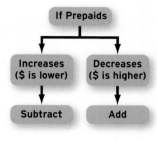

Under Armour's $2 million increase in Prepaid Expenses means that cash prepayments this period were more than expenses. These extra cash prepayments must be subtracted in Exhibit 12.4. (A decrease would be added.)

Decrease in Accounts Payable Cash flow from operations must reflect cash purchases, but not all purchases are for cash. Purchases on account increase Accounts Payable and cash paid to suppliers decreases Accounts Payable.

Accounts Payable (L)			Accounts Payable (L)		
	Beg. bal.			Beg. bal.	72
Cash payments	Purchases on account		Decrease 3		
	End. bal.			End. bal.	69

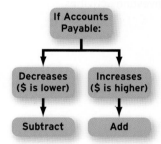

Accounts Payable decreased by $3 million, which means that cash payments to suppliers were larger than purchases on account. This decrease in Accounts Payable (cash payments are more than purchases) must be subtracted in Exhibit 12.4. (An increase would be added.)

Increase in Accrued Liabilities The income statement reports all accrued expenses, but the cash flow statement must reflect only the actual payments for expenses. Recording accrued expenses increases the balance in Accrued Liabilities and cash payments for the expenses decreases Accrued Liabilities.

Accrued Liabilities (L)			Accrued Liabilities (L)		
	Beg. bal.			Beg. bal.	61
Cash payments	Accrued expenses		Decrease 10		
	End. bal.			End. bal.	51

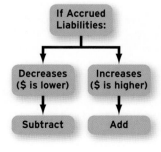

Under Armour's Accrued Liabilities decreased by $10 million, which indicates that more expenses were paid than accrued. Consequently, this difference (representing more cash paid) must be subtracted back in Exhibit 12.4. (An increase would be added.)

By scanning Exhibit 12.3 on page 509, you can see that you have now considered the changes in all balance sheet accounts that relate to operating activities (marked by the letter O). The last step in determining the net cash flow provided by (used in) operating activities is to calculate a total. As shown in Exhibit 12.4, the combined effects of all operating cash flows are a net inflow of $90 million.

Now that you have seen how to compute operating cash flows using the indirect method, take a moment to complete the following Self-Study Practice.

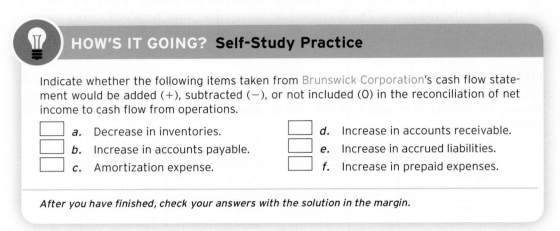

💡 HOW'S IT GOING? Self-Study Practice

Indicate whether the following items taken from Brunswick Corporation's cash flow statement would be added (+), subtracted (−), or not included (O) in the reconciliation of net income to cash flow from operations.

☐ **a.** Decrease in inventories.   ☐ **d.** Increase in accounts receivable.

☐ **b.** Increase in accounts payable.   ☐ **e.** Increase in accrued liabilities.

☐ **c.** Amortization expense.   ☐ **f.** Increase in prepaid expenses.

After you have finished, check your answers with the solution in the margin.

Solution to Self-Study Practice

a. +, *b.* +, *c.* +, *d.* −, *e.* +, *f.* −

Learning Objective 3

Report cash flows from investing activities.

Under Armour's Investing Cash Flow Calculations

To prepare the investing section of the statement of cash flows, you must analyze accounts related to long-lived tangible and intangible assets.[3] Unlike the analysis of operating activities, where you were concerned only with the *net* change in selected balance sheet accounts, an analysis of investing (and financing) activities requires that you identify and separately report the causes of *both* increases and decreases in account balances. The following relationships are the ones that you will encounter most frequently:

Related Balance Sheet Accounts	Investing Activity	Cash Flow Effect
Property, Plant, and Equipment	Purchase of property, plant, and equipment for cash	Outflow
	Sale of property, plant, and equipment for cash	Inflow
Intangible Assets	Purchase of intangible assets	Outflow
	Sale of intangible assets	Inflow

Under Armour's balance sheet (Exhibit 12.3) shows two investing assets (noted with an I) that changed during the year: Equipment and Intangible and Other Assets.

Equipment To determine the cause of the change in the Equipment account, accountants would examine the detailed accounting records for equipment. Purchases of equipment increase the account, and disposals of equipment decrease it. The additional data in Exhibit 12.3 indicates that Under Armour purchased equipment for $23 million cash. This purchase is a cash outflow, which we subtract in the schedule of investing activities in Exhibit 12.5. In our example, this purchase fully accounts for the change in the Equipment balance, as shown in the Equipment T-account. Thus, we can assume that Under Armour

Equipment (A)			
Beg. bal.	120		
Purchases	23	Disposals	0
End. bal.	143		

EXHIBIT 12.5   Under Armour's Schedule of Investing Cash Flows

Item	Amount (in millions)	Explanation
Purchase of equipment	$(23)	Payment of cash for equipment
Purchase of intangible and other assets	(7)	Payment of cash for intangibles
Net cash provided by (used in) investing activities	(30)	Subtotal for the statement of cash flows

did not dispose of any equipment during the year. Supplement 12A explains how disposals of property, plant, and equipment affect the statement of cash flows.

Intangible and Other Assets   A similar approach is used to determine cash flows associated with intangible assets. Analysis of Under Armour's detailed records indicates that the company did not have any reductions in its intangible assets as a result of disposals, impairments, or amortization during the year. However, Under Armour did purchase intangible assets for $7 million cash, as noted in the additional data in Exhibit 12.3. This cash outflow is subtracted in the schedule of investing activities in Exhibit 12.5.

Under Armour's Financing Cash Flow Calculations

This section of the cash flow statement includes changes in liabilities owed to owners (Dividends Payable) and financial institutions (Notes Payable and other types of debt), as well as changes in shareholders' equity accounts. Interest is considered an operating activity so it is excluded from financing cash flows. The following relationships are the ones that you will encounter most often:

Learning Objective 4

Report cash flows from financing activities.

Related Balance Sheet Accounts	Financing Activity	Cash Flow Effect
Notes Payable	Borrowing cash from bank or other financial institutions	Inflow
	Repayment of loan principal	Outflow
Bonds Payable	Issuance of bonds for cash	Inflow
	Repayment of bond face value	Outflow
Contributed Capital	Issuance of shares for cash	Inflow
	Repurchase of shares with cash	Outflow
Retained Earnings	Payment of cash dividends	Outflow

COACH'S TIP

Dividends paid are financing cash flows. Dividends received, however, are operating cash flows.

To compute cash flows from financing activities, you should review changes in all debt and shareholders' equity accounts. Increases and decreases must be identified and reported separately. Under Armour's balance sheet in Exhibit 12.3 indicates that Long-Term Debt and Contributed Capital changed during the period as a result of financing cash flows (noted with an F).

Long-Term Debt   The additional data in Exhibit 12.3 indicates that Long-Term Debt was affected by both cash inflows and outflows, as shown in the T-account below.

Long-term Debt (L)			
		Beg. bal.	23
Repayments	22	Borrowings	24
		End. bal.	25

These cash flows are reported separately in the schedule of financing activities shown in Exhibit 12.6.

Contributed Capital Under Armour did not repurchase shares during the year, but it did issue shares for $23 million cash. This share issuance fully accounts for the change in Contributed Capital, as shown in the following T-account. This cash inflow is listed in the schedule of financing activities in Exhibit 12.6.

Contributed Capital (SE)		
	Beg. bal.	175
	Shares issued	23
	End. bal.	<u>198</u>

Retained Earnings Net income increases Retained Earnings and any dividends declared decrease Retained Earnings. Net income has already been accounted for as an operating cash flow. In Under Armour's case, no dividends were declared or paid in 2009 (see the additional data in Exhibit 12.3). As shown in the following T-account, dividends would have decreased Retained Earnings if they had been declared; their payment would have been reported as a cash outflow in the financing section of the statement of cash flows.

Retained Earnings (SE)			
Dividends	0	Beg. bal.	156
		Net income	47
		End. bal.	<u>203</u>

EXHIBIT 12.6 **Under Armour's Schedule of Financing Cash Flows**

Item	Amount (in millions)	Explanation
Additional borrowings of long-term debt	$24	Cash received when new loan obtained
Payments on long-term debt	(22)	Cash paid on loan principal
Proceeds from share issuance	23	Cash received from shareholders for new shares
Net cash provided by financing activities	<u>25</u>	Subtotal for the statement of cash flows

---

COACH'S TIP

If you have difficulty remembering the order in which to report operating (O), investing (I), and financing (F) cash flows, say to yourself, "O, IF only I could remember!"

Under Armour's Statement of Cash Flows

Now that you have determined the cash flows for the three main types of business activities in Exhibits 12.4, 12.5, and 12.6, you can prepare the statement of cash flows in a proper format. Exhibit 12.7 shows the statement of cash flows for Under Armour using the indirect method. Notice that the net increase (decrease) subtotal combines cash flows from operating, investing, and financing activities to produce an overall net change in cash. This net change is added to the beginning cash balance to arrive at the ending cash balance, which is the same cash balance as reported on the balance sheet.

EXHIBIT 12.7

Under Armour's Statement of Cash Flows (Indirect Method)

UNDER ARMOUR, INC.
Statement of Cash Flows*
For the Year Ended December 31, 2009

(In millions)

Cash Flows from Operating Activities	
Net income	$ 47
Adjustments to reconcile net income to net cash provided by operating activities:	
Amortization	23
Changes in current assets and current liabilities	
Accounts Receivable	2
Inventories	33
Prepaid Expenses	(2)
Accounts Payable	(3)
Accrued Liabilities	(10)
Net cash provided by (used in) operating activities	90
Cash Flows from Investing Activities	
Purchase of equipment	(23)
Purchase of intangible and other assets	(7)
Net cash provided by (used in) investing activities	(30)
Cash Flows from Financing Activities	
Additional borrowings of long-term debt	24
Payments on long-term debt	(22)
Proceeds from share issuance	23
Net cash provided by (used in) financing activities	25
Net increase (decrease) in cash and cash equivalents	85
Cash and cash equivalents at beginning of period	102
Cash and cash equivalents at end of period	$187
Supplemental Disclosures	
Cash paid for interest	$ 2
Cash paid for income tax	36

> **COACH'S TIP**
>
> When doing homework problems, assume that all changes in noncurrent account balances are caused by cash transactions (unless the problem also describes changes caused by noncash investing and financing activities).

*Certain amounts have been adjusted to simplify the presentation.

Supplemental Disclosures   In addition to their cash flows, all companies are required to report material investing and financing transactions that did not have cash flow effects (called noncash investing and financing activities). For example, the purchase of a $10,000 piece of equipment with a $10,000 note payable to the supplier does not cause either an inflow or an outflow of cash. As a result, these activities are not listed in the three main sections of the statement of cash flows. This important information is normally presented for users in a supplementary schedule to the statement of cash flows or in the financial statement notes. Supplementary information must also disclose (for companies using the indirect method) the amount of cash paid for interest and for income taxes. An example of this disclosure is shown at the bottom of Exhibit 12.7.

Learning Objective 5

Interpret cash flows from operating, investing, and financing activities.

Unlike the income statement, which summarizes its detailed information in one number (net income), the statement of cash flows does not provide a summary measure of cash flow performance. Instead, it must be evaluated in terms of the cash flow pattern suggested by the subtotals of each of the three main sections. As we discussed at the beginning of this chapter, expect different patterns of cash flows from operating, investing, and financing activities, depending on how well established a company is. An established, healthy company will show positive cash flows from operations, which are sufficiently large to pay for replacing existing property, plant, and equipment and to pay dividends to shareholders. Any additional cash (called free cash flow) can (*a*) be used to expand the business through additional investing activities, (*b*) be used for other financing activities, or (*c*) simply build up the company's cash balance. After considering where the company stands in relation to this big picture, you should then look at the details within each of the three sections.

EVALUATING CASH FLOWS

The operating activities section indicates how well a company is able to generate cash internally through its operations and management of current assets and current liabilities. Most analysts believe this is the most important section of the statement because, in the long run, operations are the only continuing source of cash. Investors will not invest in a company if they do not believe that cash generated from operations will be available to pay dividends or expand the company. Similarly, creditors will not lend money or extend credit if they believe that cash generated from operations will be insufficient to repay them.

When evaluating the operating activities section of the statement of cash flows, consider the absolute amount of cash flow (is it positive or negative?), keeping in mind that operating cash flows have to be positive over the long run for a company to be successful. Also, look at the relationship between operating cash flows and net income, using a ratio called the *quality of income ratio*.

ACCOUNTING DECISION TOOLS

Name of Measure	Formula	What It Tells You
Quality of income ratio	$\dfrac{\text{Net Cash Flow from Operating Activities}}{\text{Net Income}}$	• Whether operating cash flows and net income are in sync • A ratio near 1.0 means operating cash flows and net income are in sync

The quality of income ratio measures the portion of income that was generated in cash. All other things equal, a quality of income ratio near 1.0 indicates a high likelihood that revenues are realized in cash and that expenses are associated with cash outflows. This ratio is most useful when compared to industry competitors or to prior periods. Any major deviations (say below 0.5 or above 1.5) should be investigated. In some cases, a deviation may be nothing to worry about, but in others, it could be the first sign of big problems to come. Four potential causes of deviations to consider include

1. **Seasonality.** As in Under Armour's case, seasonal variations in sales and inventory levels can cause the ratio to fluctuate from one quarter to the next. Usually, this isn't a cause for alarm.

2. **The corporate life cycle (growth in sales).** New companies often experience rapid sales growth. When sales are increasing, accounts receivable and inventory normally increase faster than the cash flows being collected from sales. This often reduces operating cash flows below net income, which, in turn, reduces the ratio. This isn't a big

deal, provided that the company can obtain cash from financing activities until operating activities begin to generate more positive cash flows.

3. **Changes in revenue and expense recognition.** Most cases of fraudulent financial reporting involve aggressive revenue recognition (recording revenues before they are earned) or delayed expense recognition (failing to report expenses when they are incurred). Both of these tactics cause net income to increase in the current period, making it seem as though the company has improved its performance. Neither of these tactics, though, affects cash flows from operating activities. As a result, if revenue and expense recognition policies are changed to boost net income, the quality of income ratio will drop, providing one of the first clues that the financial statements might contain errors or fraud.

4. **Changes in working capital management.** Working capital is a measure of the amount by which current assets exceed current liabilities. If a company's current assets (such as accounts receivable and inventories) are allowed to grow out of control, its operating cash flows and quality of income ratio will decrease. More efficient management will have the opposite effect. To investigate this potential cause more closely, use the inventory and accounts receivable turnover ratios covered in Chapters 7 and 8.

SPOTLIGHT ON Business Decisions

Quality of Income Deteriorates Prior to Bankruptcy

Lehman Brothers Holdings Inc. was one of the largest and most profitable financial services companies in the world. But cash flow and working capital management problems contributed to the company's bankruptcy only a month before the stock market crash of 2008. The following comparison of Lehman's net income and net operating cash flows reveals the company's problems:

(In billions)	2006	2007	2008
Net income	$ 3.3	$ 4.0	$ 4.2
Net cash provided by (used in) operating activities	(12.2)	(36.4)	(45.6)

Another key issue that analysts assess using the statement of cash flows is a company's ability to generate enough cash internally to purchase new long-term assets. The capital acquisitions ratio is commonly used to determine the extent to which purchases of property, plant, and equipment (PPE) were financed from operating activities (without the need for outside debt or equity financing or the sale of investments or other long-term assets). A ratio greater than 1.0 indicates that, all else equal, outside financing was not needed to replace equipment in the current period. Assuming this continues in the future, the higher a company's capital acquisitions ratio, the less likely that external financing will be needed to fund future expansion.

ACCOUNTING DECISION TOOLS

Name of Measure	Formula	What It Tells You
Capital acquisitions ratio	$\dfrac{\text{Net Cash from Operations}}{\text{Cash Paid for PPE}}$	• Whether operating cash flows are sufficient to pay for PPE purchases • A higher ratio means less need for external financing

The cash paid for property, plant, and equipment (used in the bottom part of the ratio) is reported in the investing activities section of the statement of cash flows. These expenditures can vary greatly from year to year, so the ratio typically is calculated as an average over a longer period, for instance, three years. When calculating the ratio, enter these expenditures as positive amounts (without brackets).

In Exhibit 12.8, we present the three-year average capital acquisitions ratio for Under Armour. The ratio shows that, over the three years, Under Armour was able to pay for its purchases of property, plant, and equipment with cash generated from operating activities and did not require outside financing.

EXHIBIT 12.8 **Capital Acquisitions Ratio Computation**

(In millions)	Relevant Information				Average 2007–09 Ratio Calculation
	2009	2008	2007	Average	$\frac{\$48}{31} = 1.5$
Net operating cash	$90	$79	$(25)	$48	
Cash for PPE	23	36	34	31	

HOW'S IT GOING? Self-Study Practice

The relevant cash flows for NIKE, Inc., are shown below. Calculate the capital acquisitions ratio for NIKE and compare it to Under Armour's ratio in Exhibit 12.8.

(In billions)	2009	2008	2007	Average	Ratio
Cash flow from operating activities	$1.7	$1.9	$1.9	$⬚	⬚
Purchases of property, plant, and equipment	0.5	0.4	0.3	0.4	

After you have finished, check your answers with the solution in the margin.

Solution to Self-Study Practice

$1.8 ÷ $0.4 = 4.5 or 450%
NIKE's operations generated four and a half times more cash than was spent on property, plant, and equipment. This suggests that NIKE has more free cash flow than Under Armour to use for other purposes, such as paying dividends and repaying loans.

Because equipment needs differ dramatically across industries (for example, consider Under Armour versus Google), a particular company's ratio should be compared only with its prior years' figures or with other companies in the same industry. Also, while a high ratio can indicate strong cash flows, it also might suggest a failure to update plant and equipment, which can limit a company's ability to compete in the future. The main point is that you have to interpret the ratio in relation to the company's other activities and business strategy.

OPERATING CASH FLOWS REVISITED (DIRECT METHOD)

Learning Objective 6

Report and interpret cash flows from operating activities, using the direct method.

Earlier in this chapter, we discussed the indirect method of presenting a company's statement of cash flows. This method computes operating cash flows indirectly, by adding and subtracting items from Net Income. Because these items, by themselves, don't mean a lot, analyses of operating cash flows are limited to using just the overall Net Cash Provided by (Used for) Operating Activities. In contrast, the direct method of presentation provides more detailed information on each input into overall operating cash flows, which allows analysts to conduct more detailed analyses.

Exhibit 12.9 presents Under Armour's statement of cash flows using the direct method. Because this method lists each operating cash flow component, it allows more detailed analyses of operating cash flows. For example, the direct method would allow Under Armour's managers to determine that a 10 percent increase in product costs in 2009 would have required an additional cash outflow to inventory suppliers of $41.3 million (= 10% × $413 million). To cover these additional cash outflows, Under Armour could raise prices by 4.9 percent, which would generate a $42 million (= 4.9% × $858 million) cash inflow from customer collections.

EXHIBIT 12.9 | **Under Armour's Statement of Cash Flows (Direct Method)**

UNDER ARMOUR, INC. Statement of Cash Flows For the Year Ended December 31, 2009		Explanation
(In millions)		
Cash Flows from Operating Activities		Cash flows related to day-to-day activities
Cash collected from customers	$858	Cash collected on account and from any cash sales
Cash paid to suppliers of inventory	(413)	Cash paid in the current period to acquire inventory
Cash paid to employees and suppliers of services	(317)	Cash paid for salaries, wages, utilities, rent, etc.
Cash paid for interest	(2)	Separate reporting of these items fulfills the role of
Cash paid for income tax	(36)	the supplemental disclosures in Exhibit 12.7
Net cash provided by (used in) operating activities	90	Indicates overall cash impact of operating activities
Cash Flows from Investing Activities		Cash flows related to long-term assets
Purchase of equipment	(23)	Cash was used to purchase equipment
Purchase of intangible and other assets	(7)	Cash was used to purchase intangibles
Net cash provided by (used in) investing activities	(30)	Indicates overall cash impact of investing activities
Cash Flows from Financing Activities		Cash flows from transactions with lenders, investors
Proceeds from long-term debt	24	Cash received from borrowing
Payments on long-term debt	(22)	Cash used to repay amounts previously borrowed
Proceeds from share issuances	23	Cash received from issuing shares
Net cash provided by (used in) financing activities	25	Indicates overall cash impact of financing activities
Net Change in Cash and Cash Equivalents	85	$90 + $(30) + $25 = $85
Cash and cash equivalents, beginning of year	102	Cash balance at beginning of the period
Cash and cash equivalents, end of year	$187	Cash balance at end of the period (on balance sheet)

The direct method also provides financial statement users with more information to identify potential relationships between cash inflows and outflows. An increase in some activities, such as sales, generally leads to an increase in cash inflows from customers and cash outflows to inventory suppliers. However, an increase in sales activity only loosely affects other cash outflows, such as interest paid on loans. Knowing the detailed components of operating cash flows allows analysts to more reliably predict a company's future cash flows.[4]

In the remainder of this section, we describe how to prepare the statement of cash flows using the direct method. We focus on preparing just the operating activities section. For instructions on preparing the investing and financing activities sections, which are identical under both the direct and indirect methods, see pages 514–516.

Reporting Operating Cash Flows with the Direct Method

The direct method presents a summary of all operating transactions that result in either a debit or a credit to cash. It is prepared by adjusting each revenue and expense on the income statement from the accrual basis to the cash basis. We will complete this process for all of the revenues and expenses reported in the Under Armour income statement in Exhibit 12.3 to show the calculations underlying the operating cash flows in Exhibit 12.9. Notice that with the direct method, we work directly with each revenue and expense listed on the income statement and ignore any totals or subtotals (such as net income).

Converting Sales Revenues to Cash Inflows

When sales are recorded, Accounts Receivable increases, and when cash is collected, Accounts Receivable decreases. This means that if Accounts Receivable decreases by $2 million, then cash collections were $2 million more than sales on account. To convert sales revenue to the cash collected, we need to add $2 million to Sales Revenue. The following flow chart shows this visually:

Using information from Under Armour's income statement and balance sheet presented in Exhibit 12.3, we compute cash collected from customers as follows:

Accounts Receivable (A)			
Beg. bal.	81		
		Decrease	2
End. bal.	79		

Net Sales	$856
+ Decrease in Accounts Receivable	2
Cash collected from customers	$858

Converting Cost of Goods Sold to Cash Paid to Suppliers

Cost of Goods Sold represents the cost of merchandise sold during the accounting period, which may be more or less than the amount of cash paid to suppliers during the period. In Under Armour's case, Inventory decreased during the year, implying the company sold more merchandise than it bought. If the company paid cash to suppliers of inventory, it would have paid less cash to suppliers than the amount of Cost of Goods Sold. So, the decrease in Inventory must be subtracted from Cost of Goods Sold to compute cash paid to suppliers.

Typically, companies buy inventory on account from suppliers (as indicated by an Accounts Payable balance on the balance sheet). Consequently, we need to consider more than just the change in Inventory to convert Cost of Goods Sold to cash paid to suppliers. The credit purchases and payments that are recorded in Accounts Payable must also be considered. Credit purchases increase Accounts Payable, and cash payments decrease it. The overall decrease in Accounts Payable reported by Under Armour in Exhibit 12.3 indicates that cash payments were more than credit purchases, so the difference must be added in the computation of total cash payments to suppliers.

In summary, to fully convert Cost of Goods Sold to a cash basis, you must consider changes in both Inventory and Accounts Payable as follows:

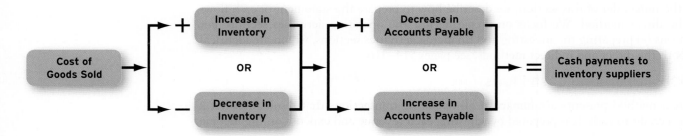

Using information from Exhibit 12.3, we compute cash paid to suppliers as follows:

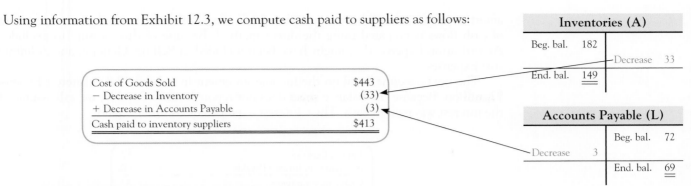

Cost of Goods Sold	$443
− Decrease in Inventory	(33)
+ Decrease in Accounts Payable	(3)
Cash paid to inventory suppliers	$413

Inventories (A)

Beg. bal.	182		
		Decrease	33
End. bal.	149		

Accounts Payable (L)

		Beg. bal.	72
Decrease	3		
		End. bal.	69

Converting Operating Expenses to a Cash Outflow   The total amount of an expense on the income statement may differ from the cash outflow associated with that activity. Some amounts, like prepaid rent, are paid before they are recognized as expenses. When prepayments are made, the balance in the asset Prepaid Expenses increases. When expenses are recorded, Prepaid Expenses decreases. When we see Under Armour's prepaids increase by $2 million during the year, it means the company paid more cash than it recorded as operating expenses. This amount must be added in computing cash paid to service suppliers for operating expenses.

Some other expenses, like wages, are paid for after they are incurred. In this case, when expenses are recorded, the balance in Accrued Liabilities increases. When payments are made, Accrued Liabilities decreases. When Under Armour's Accrued Liabilities decreased by $10 million, it means the company paid more cash than it recorded as operating expenses. This amount must be added when computing cash paid to employees and service suppliers for operating expenses.

Generally, operating expenses such as Selling, General, and Administrative Expenses can be converted from the accrual basis to the cash basis in the following manner:

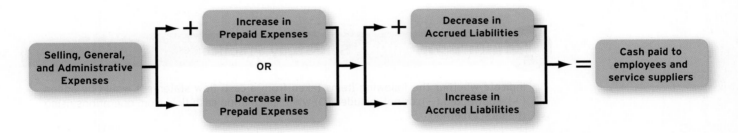

Using information from Exhibit 12.3, we can compute the total cash paid as follows:

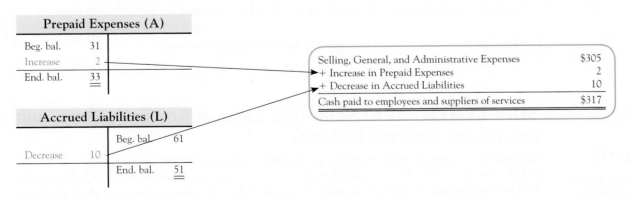

Prepaid Expenses (A)

Beg. bal.	31
Increase	2
End. bal.	33

Accrued Liabilities (L)

		Beg. bal.	61
Decrease	10		
		End. bal.	51

Selling, General, and Administrative Expenses	$305
+ Increase in Prepaid Expenses	2
+ Decrease in Accrued Liabilities	10
Cash paid to employees and suppliers of services	$317

You don't have to convert Amortization Expense on the income statement to the cash basis for the statement of cash flows because amortization doesn't involve cash. It merely reports previously incurred costs as an expense in the current period. Noncash expenses like amortization (or, similarly, revenues that don't affect cash) are omitted when the statement of cash flows is prepared using the direct method. Because of this, be sure to exclude any Amortization Expense that might have been included in Selling, General, and Administrative Expenses.

The next account listed on the income statement in Exhibit 12.3 is Interest Expense of $2 million. Because the balance sheet does not report Interest Payable, we will assume all of the interest was paid in cash. Thus, interest expense equals interest paid.

Interest Expense	$2
No change in Interest Payable	0
Cash paid for interest	$2

The same logic can be applied to income taxes. Under Armour presents Income Tax Expense of $36 million. Exhibit 12.3 does not report an Income Tax Payable balance, so we assume income tax paid is equal to income tax expense.

Income Tax Expense	$36
No change in Income Tax Payable	0
Cash paid for income tax	$36

You have now seen in this section how to determine each amount reported in the operating activities section of a statement of cash flows prepared using the direct method. For a quick check on your understanding of this material, complete the following Self-Study Practice.

HOW'S IT GOING? Self-Study Practice

Indicate whether the following items taken from a cash flow statement would be added (+), subtracted (−), or not included (0) when calculating cash flow from operations using the direct method.

a. Cash paid to suppliers.

b. Payment of dividends to shareholders.

c. Cash collections from customers.

d. Purchase of plant and equipment for cash.

e. Payments of interest to lenders.

f. Payment of taxes to the government.

After you have finished, check your answers with the solution in the margin.

Solution to Self-Study Practice

a. −, b. 0, c. +, d. 0, e. −, f. −

SUPPLEMENT 12A: Reporting Sales of Property, Plant, and Equipment (Indirect Method)

COACH'S TIP

If you're a little rusty on the journal entry to record this disposal, it would be worth your time to review the material on pages 381 and 382 of Chapter 9.

Whenever a company sells property, plant, and equipment (PPE), it records three things: (1) decreases in the PPE accounts for the assets sold, (2) an increase in the Cash account for the cash received on disposal, and (3) a gain if the cash received is more than the book value of the assets sold (or a loss if the cash received is less than the book value of the assets sold). The only part of this transaction that qualifies for the statement of cash flows is the cash received on disposal. This cash inflow is classified as an investing activity, just like the original equipment purchase.

Okay, that seems straightforward, so why do we have a separate chapter supplement for this kind of transaction? Well, there is one complicating factor. Gains and losses on disposal are included in the computation of net income, which is the starting point for the operating activities section when prepared using the indirect method. So, just as we had to add back the amortization subtracted on the income statement, we also have to add back losses reported on disposals of PPE. As the following example shows, the flip side is true for gains on disposal (they are subtracted).

To illustrate, assume that Under Armour sold a piece of its manufacturing equipment for $7 million. The equipment originally cost $15 million and had $10 million of accumulated amortization at the time of disposal. The disposal would have been analyzed and recorded as follows (in millions):

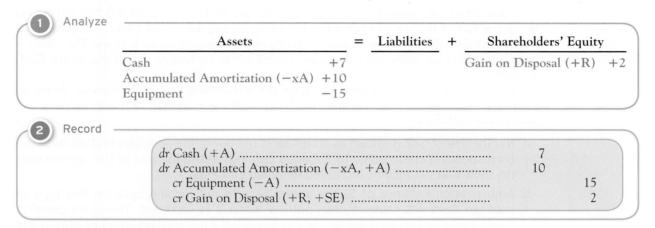

The $7 million inflow of cash would be reported as an investing activity. The $10 million and $15 million are taken into account when considering changes in the Accumulated Amortization and Equipment account balances. Lastly, the $2 million Gain on Disposal was included in net income, so we must remove (subtract) it in the operating activities section of the statement. Thus, the disposal would affect two parts of the statement of cash flows:

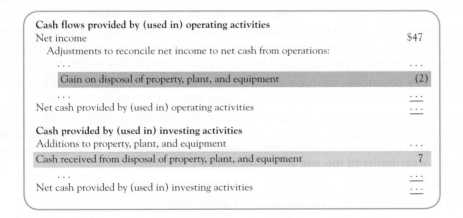

SUPPLEMENT 12B: Spreadsheet Approach (Indirect Method)

As situations become more complex, the analytical approach that we used to prepare the statement of cash flows for Under Armour becomes cumbersome and inefficient. In actual practice, many companies use a spreadsheet approach to prepare the statement of cash flows. The spreadsheet is based on the same logic that we used in the main body of the chapter. The spreadsheet's primary advantage is that it offers a more systematic way to keep track of information. You may find it useful even in simple situations.

COACH'S TIP

Think of the statement of cash flows (in the bottom half of the spreadsheet) as a big Cash T-account.

Exhibit 12B.1 shows the Under Armour spreadsheet, which we created as follows:

1. Make four columns to record dollar amounts. The first column is for the beginning balances for items reported on the balance sheet, the next two columns reflect debit and credit changes to those balances, and the final column contains the ending balances for the balance sheet accounts.

2. Enter each account name from the balance sheet in the far left of the top half of the spreadsheet.

3. As you analyze changes in each balance sheet account, enter the explanation of each item to be reported on the statement of cash flows in the far left of the bottom half of the spreadsheet.

Changes in the various balance sheet accounts are analyzed in terms of debits and credits in the top half of the spreadsheet, with the corresponding debits and credits being recorded in the bottom half of the spreadsheet in terms of their impact on cash flows. The changes in balance sheet accounts other than cash contribute to explaining the change in the Cash account.

Let's go through each of the entries on the spreadsheet for Under Armour shown in Exhibit 12B.1, starting with the first one shown in the bottom half of the spreadsheet (all amounts in millions).

a. Net income of $47 is shown as an inflow in the operating activities section, with the corresponding credit going to Retained Earnings in the top half of the spreadsheet (to show that net income increased Retained Earnings).

b. Amortization Expense of $23 is added back to net income because this type of expense does not cause a cash outflow when it is recorded. The corresponding credit explains the increase in the Accumulated Amortization account during the period.

c. The decrease in Accounts Receivable means that cash collections from customers were more than sales on account. Net income includes the sales number, so to adjust up to the actual cash collected, we add the extra amount. This appears in our spreadsheet as if it is a debit to Cash and a corresponding credit to Accounts Receivable.

d. This entry reconciles the purchases of Inventory with Cost of Goods Sold. It is added to net income because more inventory was sold than purchased.

e. This entry reconciles the prepayment of expenses with their expiration. It is subtracted from net income because cash payments for new prepayments are more than the amounts that were reported as expenses when they expired.

f. This entry reconciles cash paid to suppliers with purchases on account. It is subtracted because more was paid in cash than was purchased on account.

g. This entry reconciles the accrual of liabilities for operating expenses with payments for these expenses. The decrease in Accrued Liabilities is subtracted because the cash paid for accrued liabilities was more than the expenses accrued. The credit to Cash corresponds to the net debit to Accrued Liabilities.

h. This entry records the cash purchases of new equipment.

i. This entry records the cash purchase of intangibles.

j. This entry records cash provided by borrowing additional long-term debt.

k. This entry records cash used to repay long-term debt.

l. This entry records the cash received from issuing shares.

m. This entry shows that the change in cash (in the top part of the spreadsheet) is accounted for by the net cash flows listed in the bottom part of the spreadsheet.

Check to see that Debits = Credits in your spreadsheet, because if they don't, you've missed something along the way. The bottom part of the spreadsheet can be used to prepare the formal statement of cash flows shown in Exhibit 12.7.

UNDER ARMOUR, INC.
Statement of Cash Flow Spreadsheet
For the Year Ended December 31, 2009

		Analysis of Changes		
(in millions)	Beginning Balances, December 31, 2008	Debit	Credit	Ending Balances, December 31, 2009
Items from Balance Sheet				
Cash and Cash Equivalents (A)	102	(m) 85		187
Accounts Receivable (A)	81		(c) 2	79
Inventories (A)	182		(d) 33	149
Prepaid Expenses (A)	31	(e) 2		33
Equipment (A)	120	(h) 23		143
Accumulated Amortization (xA)	47		(b) 23	70
Intangible and Other Assets (A)	18	(i) 7		25
Accounts Payable (L)	72	(f) 3		69
Accrued Liabilities (L)	61	(g) 10		51
Long-Term Debt (L)	23	(k) 22	(j) 24	25
Contributed Capital (SE)	175		(l) 23	198
Retained Earnings (SE)	156		(a) 47	203

	Cash		
	Inflows	Outflows	Subtotals
Statement of Cash Flows			
Cash flows from operating activities:			
Net income	(a) 47		
Adjustments to reconcile net income to cash provided by operating activities:			
Amortization	(b) 23		
Changes in current assets and current liabilities			
Accounts Receivable	(c) 2		
Inventories	(d) 33		
Prepaid Expenses		(e) 2	
Accounts Payable		(f) 3	
Accrued Liabilities		(g) 10	
			90
Cash flows from investing activities:			
Purchase of equipment		(h) 23	
Purchase of intangible and other assets		(i) 7	
			(30)
Cash flows from financing activities:			
Additional borrowings of long-term debt	(j) 24		
Payments of long-term debt		(k) 22	
Proceeds from share issuance	(l) 23		
			25
Net increase in Cash and Cash Equivalents		(m) 85	
	152	152	85

Topic	ASPE	IFRS
Classification of interest and dividends		
• Dividends paid	• Dividends paid that are charged directly to retained earnings are presented as a financing cash flow.	• Dividends paid can be presented as either an operating or a financing cash flow.
• Interest paid	• Interest paid that is recognized in net income is presented as an operating cash flow.	• Interest paid can be presented as either an operating or a financing cash flow.
• Dividends received	• Dividends received are classified as an operating cash flow.	• Dividends received can be presented as either an operating or an investing cash flow.
• Interest received	• Interest received is classified as an operating cash flow.	• Interest received can be presented as either an operating or an investing cash flow.
Disclosures		
• Income taxes	• Income taxes paid are not required to be disclosed on the statement of cash flows.	• Income taxes paid are required to be disclosed on the statement of cash flows.
• Restrictions on cash and cash equivalents	• The amounts of cash and cash equivalents that are restricted for a particular use are required to be disclosed on the statement of cash flows.	• The amounts of cash and cash equivalents that are restricted for a particular use are required to be disclosed on the statement of cash flows, along with an explanation of the restrictions.

Review the Chapter

This section provides a chance to solidify your understanding of key points. It's worth your time to work through the following demonstration cases, scan the chapter summary, test your understanding of key-terms, and then practise, practise, practise.

DEMONSTRATION CASE A: INDIRECT METHOD

During one quarter (ended March 31), Brunswick Corporation reported net income of $3,800 (all numbers in thousands). The balance in cash and cash equivalents at the beginning of the quarter (on January 1) was $351,400; at the end of the quarter (on March 31), it was $280,000. The company also reported the following activities:

a. Borrowed $2,200 of debt.

b. Accounts receivable increased by $40,300.

c. Paid $31,800 in cash for purchase of property, plant, and equipment.

d. Recorded amortization of $35,600.

e. Salaries payable increased by $10,210.

f. Other accrued liabilities decreased by $35,000.

g. Prepaid expenses decreased by $14,500.

h. Inventories increased by $20,810.

i. Accounts payable decreased by $10,200.

j. Issued shares to employees for $400 in cash.

Required:

Based on this information, prepare the cash flow statement using the indirect method. Evaluate the cash flows reported in the statement.

Suggested Solution

BRUNSWICK CORPORATION   **≋BRUNSWICK**
Statement of Cash Flows
For the Quarter Ended March 31

(In thousands)

Cash Flows from Operating Activities	
Net income	$ 3,800
Adjustments	
Amortization	35,600
Change in Accounts Receivable	(40,300)
Change in Inventories	(20,810)
Change in Prepaid Expenses	14,500
Change in Accounts Payable	(10,200)
Change in Salaries Payable	10,210
Change in Other Accrued Liabilities	(35,000)
Net cash provided by (used in) operating activities	(42,200)
Cash Flows from Investing Activities	
Additions to property, plant, and equipment	(31,800)
Net cash provided by (used in) investing activities	(31,800)
Cash Flows from Financing Activities	
Proceeds from debt borrowings	2,200
Proceeds from issuance of share to employees	400
Net cash provided by (used in) financing activities	2,600
Increase (decrease) in Cash and Cash Equivalents	(71,400)
Cash and Cash Equivalents, January 1	351,400
Cash and Cash Equivalents, March 31	$280,000

Despite reporting profits this quarter, the company has negative cash flows from operations. This is caused primarily by buildups of accounts receivable and inventories, with no corresponding reduction in spending for accounts payable and other accrued liabilities. This is potentially troublesome because it suggests the company may be encountering difficulties in selling its products and collecting on past sales. In addition to the drain on cash for operating activities, the company also spent over $30 million for additional property, plant, and equipment. Financing activities had relatively little effect on cash flows during the period. The company entered this quarter with lots of cash (over $350 million) and, despite the shortfall in cash flow, still has lots remaining to finance future activities.

DEMONSTRATION CASE B: DIRECT METHOD

During one quarter (ended March 29), Cybex International reported that its cash and cash equivalents had increased from $216 on December 31 to $469 on March 29 (all amounts in thousands). The company also indicated the following:

a. Paid $13,229 to suppliers for inventory purchases.

b. Borrowed $2,400 from one of the company's main shareholders.

_c._ Paid $554 in cash for purchase of property, plant, and equipment.

_d._ Reported sales on account of $20,608. The company reported Accounts Receivable of $13,628 at the beginning of the quarter and $12,386 at the end of the quarter.

_e._ Paid operating expenses to employees and suppliers of services totalling $6,188.

_f._ Cash payments for interest totalled $1,060.

_g._ Made payments of $2,625 for principal owed on long-term debt.

_h._ Paid $284 cash for other financing activities.

_i._ Paid $57 cash for income taxes.

Required:

Based on this information, prepare the cash flow statement using the direct method. Evaluate the cash flows reported in the statement.

Suggested Solution

CYBEX INTERNATIONAL **Statement of Cash Flows** **For the Quarter Ended March 29**	
(In thousands)	
Cash Flows from Operating Activities	
Cash collected from customers ($13,628 + $20,608 − $12,386)	$21,850
Cash paid to suppliers of inventory	(13,229)
Cash paid to employees and suppliers of services	(6,188)
Cash paid for interest	(1,060)
Cash paid for income taxes	(57)
Net cash flow provided by operating activities	1,316
Cash Flows from Investing Activities	
Additions to property, plant, and equipment	(554)
Net cash flow provided by (used in) investing activities	(554)
Cash Flows from Financing Activities	
Proceeds from borrowing from a related party (shareholder)	2,400
Repayment of long-term debt principal	(2,625)
Payments for other financing activities	(284)
Net cash flow provided by (used in) financing activities	(509)
Increase (decrease) in Cash and Cash Equivalents	253
Cash and Cash Equivalents, December 31	216
Cash and Cash Equivalents, March 29	$ 469

Cybex reported a net inflow of $1,316 cash from operating activities during the quarter. These cash flows were more than enough to pay for the property, plant, and equipment purchased this quarter, as indicated by its capital acquisitions ratio of 2.38 ($1,316 ÷ $554). Some of the extra cash from operations that was not used to purchase property, plant, and equipment (also called _free cash flow_) could be used to pay down debt or to increase the company's cash balance. The financing activities section suggests that the company paid down a significant amount of long-term debt ($2,625), in part by borrowing funds from a related party ($2,400). Borrowing from a related party (particularly a major shareholder) is unusual, which would prompt analysts to investigate further. The company's quarterly report explains that its lenders had demanded immediate repayment of their loans because the company had violated its debt covenants. A major shareholder loaned money to the company so that it could make this repayment.

CHAPTER SUMMARY

LO1 **Identify cash flows arising from operating, investing, and financing activities.** p. 503

- The statement has three main sections: Cash flows from operating activities, which are related to earning income from normal operations; Cash flows from investing activities, which are related to the acquisition and sale of productive assets; and Cash flows from financing activities, which are related to external financing of the enterprise.

- The net cash inflow or outflow for the period is the same amount as the increase or decrease in cash and cash equivalents for the period on the balance sheet. Cash equivalents are highly liquid investments purchased within three months of maturity.

Report cash flows from operating activities, using the indirect method. p. 510   **LO2**

- The indirect method for reporting cash flows from operating activities reports a conversion of net income to net cash flow from operating activities.
- The conversion involves additions and subtractions for (1) noncash expenses (such as amortization expense) and revenues that do not affect current assets or current liabilities, and (2) changes in each of the individual current assets (other than cash) and current liabilities (other than debt to financial institutions, which relates to financing).

Report cash flows from investing activities. p. 514   **LO3**

- Investing activities reported on the cash flow statement include cash payments to acquire fixed assets and investments and cash proceeds from the sale of fixed assets and investments.

Report cash flows from financing activities. p. 515   **LO4**

- Cash inflows from financing activities include cash proceeds from issuance of debt and common shares. Cash outflows include cash principal payments on debt, cash paid for the repurchase of the company's shares, and cash dividend payments. Cash payments associated with interest are a cash flow from operating activities.

Interpret cash flows from operating, investing, and financing activities. p. 518   **LO5**

- A healthy company will generate positive cash flows from operations, some of which will be used to pay for purchases of property, plant, and equipment. Any additional cash (called *free cash flow*) can be used to further expand the business, pay down some of the company's debt, or simply build up the cash balance. A company is in trouble if it is unable to generate positive cash flows from operations in the long run because eventually creditors will stop lending to the company and shareholders will stop investing in it.
- Two common ratios for assessing cash flows are the quality of income ratio and the capital acquisitions ratio.

Report and interpret cash flows from operating activities, using the direct method. p. 520   **LO6**

- The direct method for reporting cash flows from operating activities accumulates all of the operating transactions that result in either a debit or a credit to cash into categories. The most common inflows are cash received from customers and dividends and interest on investments. The most common outflows are cash paid for purchase of services and goods for resale, salaries and wages, income taxes, and interest on liabilities. It is prepared by adjusting each item on the income statement from an accrual basis to a cash basis.

ACCOUNTING DECISION TOOLS

Name of Measure	Formula	What It Tells You
Quality of income ratio	$$\dfrac{\text{Net Cash Flow from Operating Activities}}{\text{Net Income}}$$	• Whether operating cash flows and net income are in sync • A ratio near 1.0 means operating cash flows and net income are in sync
Capital acquisitions ratio	$$\dfrac{\text{Net Cash Flow from Operating Activities}}{\text{Cash Paid for PPE}}$$	• Whether operating cash flows are sufficient to pay for PPE purchases • A higher ratio means less need for external financing

KEY TERMS

See complete definitions in the glossary in the back of this text.

HOMEWORK HELPER

Helpful reminders

- Although some exceptions exist, operating activities typically affect current assets and current liabilities; investing activities typically affect noncurrent assets; and financing activities typically affect noncurrent liabilities and shareholders' equity accounts.
- The typical additions and subtractions that are required when using the indirect method to reconcile net income with cash flow from operating activities are as follows:

COACH'S TIP

Notice in this table that, to reconcile net income to cash flows from operations, you
- Add the change when the current asset decreases or current liability increases.
- Subtract the change when the current asset increases or current liability decreases.

Item	Additions and Subtractions to Reconcile Net Income to Cash Flow From Operating Activities*	
	When Item Increases	When Item Decreases
Amortization	+	n/a
Accounts Receivable	−	+
Inventory	−	+
Prepaid Expenses	−	+
Accounts Payable	+	−
Accrued Liabilities	+	−

*This summary excludes additions and subtractions for losses and gains arising on disposal of certain assets, which are discussed in Supplement 12A.

- The following adjustments are commonly made to convert income statement items to the related operating cash flow amounts for the direct method:

Income Statement Account	+/− Change in Balance Sheet Account(s)	= Operating Cash Flow
Sales Revenue	+ Decrease in Accounts Receivable (A) − Increase in Accounts Receivable (A)	= Cash collected from customers
Cost of Goods Sold	+ Increase in Inventory (A) − Decrease in Inventory (A) − Increase in Accounts Payable (L) + Decrease in Accounts Payable (L)	= Cash paid to suppliers of inventory
Other Expenses	+ Increase in Prepaid Expenses (A) − Decrease in Prepaid Expenses (A) − Increase in Accrued Expenses (L) + Decrease in Accrued Expenses (L)	= Cash paid to employees and suppliers of services (e.g., wages, rent, utilities)
Interest Expense	− Increase in Interest Payable (L) + Decrease in Interest Payable (L)	= Cash paid for interest
Income Tax Expense	− Increase in Income Taxes Payable (Deferred Taxes) (L) + Decrease in Income Taxes Payable (Deferred Taxes) (L)	= Cash paid for income tax

Frequent mistakes

- Do not merely report the net change in all balance sheet accounts. Some accounts (typically those affected by investing and financing activities) include both inflows and outflows of cash, which must be reported separately.

Practice Material

QUESTIONS (⑤ Symbol indicates questions that require analysis from more than one perspective.)

1. Compare the purposes of the income statement, the balance sheet, and the statement of cash flows.

2. What information does the statement of cash flows report that is not reported on the other required financial statements?

3. What are cash equivalents? How are they reported on the statement of cash flows?

4. What are the major categories of business activities reported on the statement of cash flows? Define each of these activities.

5. What are the typical cash inflows from operating activities? What are the typical cash outflows from operating activities?

6. Describe the types of items used to compute cash flows from operating activities under the two alternative methods of reporting.

7. Under the indirect method, amortization expense is added to net income to report cash flows from operating activities. Does amortization cause an inflow of cash?

8. Explain why cash outflows during the period for purchases and salaries are not specifically reported on a statement of cash flows prepared using the indirect method.

9. Explain why a $50,000 increase in inventory during the year must be included in computing cash flows from operating activities under both the direct and indirect methods.

10. Loan covenants require that E-Gadget Corporation (EGC) generate $200,000 cash from operating activities each year. Without intervention during the last month of the current

year, EGC will generate only $180,000 cash from operations. What are the pros and cons of each of the following possible interventions: (a) pressuring customers to pay overdue accounts, (b) delaying payment of amounts owing to suppliers, and (c) purchasing additional equipment to increase amortization? ⑤

11. As a junior analyst, you are evaluating the financial performance of Digil Corporation. Impressed by this year's growth in sales (20 percent increase), receivables (40 percent increase), and inventories (50 percent increase), you plan to report a favourable evaluation of the company. Your supervisor cautions you that those increases may signal difficulties rather than successes. When you ask what she means, she just says you should look at the company's statement of cash flows. What do you think you will find there? What are the cash flow effects when a company's receivables and inventories increase faster than its sales? ⑤

12. What are the typical cash inflows from investing activities? What are the typical cash outflows from investing activities?

13. What are the typical cash inflows from financing activities? What are the typical cash outflows from financing activities?

14. What are noncash investing and financing activities? Give one example. How are noncash investing and financing activities reported on the statement of cash flows?

15. (Supplement 12A) How is the sale of equipment reported on the statement of cash flows using the indirect method?

Multiple-choice questions and corresponding answers can be found on Connect.

MINI-EXERCISES

M12-1 Computing Cash Flows from Operating Activities (Indirect Method)

LO2

For each of the following independent cases, compute cash flows from operating activities. Assume the list below includes all balance sheet accounts related to operating activities.

	Case A	Case B	Case C
Net income	$200,000	$ 20,000	$360,000
Amortization expense	40,000	150,000	80,000
Accounts receivable increase (decrease)	100,000	(200,000)	(20,000)
Inventory increase (decrease)	(50,000)	(100,000)	50,000
Accounts payable increase (decrease)	(110,000)	120,000	70,000
Accrued liabilities increase (decrease)	60,000	(220,000)	(80,000)

M12-2 Computing Cash Flows from Operating Activities (Indirect Method)

LO2

For the following two independent cases, show the cash flows from the operating activities section of the 2011 statement of cash flows using the indirect method.

	Case A		Case B	
	2011	2010	2011	2010
Sales Revenue	$10,000	$9,000	$21,000	$18,000
Cost of Goods Sold	6,000	5,500	12,000	11,000
Gross Profit	4,000	3,500	9,000	7,000
Amortization Expense	1,000	1,000	2,000	1,500
Salaries Expense	2,500	2,000	5,000	5,000
Net Income	500	500	2,000	500
Accounts Receivable	300	400	750	600
Inventories	600	500	790	800
Accounts Payable	800	700	800	850
Salaries Payable	1,000	1,200	200	250

LO3 **M12-3 Computing Cash Flows from Investing Activities**

Based on the following information, compute cash flows from investing activities under ASPE.

Cash collections from customers	$800	Sale of investments	300
Purchase of used equipment	350	Dividends received	100
Amortization expense	200	Interest received	200

LO4 **M12-4 Computing Cash Flows from Financing Activities**

Based on the following information, compute cash flows from financing activities under ASPE.

Purchase of investments	$ 250
Dividends paid	800
Interest paid	400
Additional borrowing from bank	2,000

LO1, 3, 4 **M12-5 Computing Cash Flows Under IFRS**

Refer to M12-3 and M12-4. Calculate the maximum investing and financing cash inflows that could be reported under IFRS.

LO5 **M12-6 Interpreting Cash Flows from Operating, Investing, and Financing Activities**

Quantum Dots, Inc., is a nanotechnology company that manufactures "quantum dots," which are tiny pieces of silicon consisting of 100 or more molecules. Quantum dots can be used to illuminate very small objects, enabling scientists to see the blood vessels beneath a mouse's skin ripple with each heartbeat, at the rate of 100 times per second. Evaluate this research-intensive company's cash flows, assuming the following was reported in its statement of cash flows.

	Current Year	Previous Year
Cash Flows from Operating Activities		
Net cash provided by (used for) operating activities	$ (50,790)	$ (46,730)
Cash Flows from Investing Activities		
Purchases of research equipment	(250,770)	(480,145)
Proceeds from selling all short-term investments	35,000	0
Net cash provided by (used for) investing activities	(215,770)	(480,145)
Cash Flows from Financing Activities		
Additional long-term debt borrowed	100,000	200,000
Proceeds from shares issuance	140,000	200,000
Cash dividends paid	0	(10,000)
Net cash provided by (used for) financing activities	240,000	390,000
Net increase (decrease) in cash	(26,560)	(136,875)
Cash at beginning of period	29,025	165,900
Cash at end of period	$ 2,465	$ 29,025

M12-7 Calculating and Interpreting the Capital Acquisitions Ratio

LO5

Capital Corporation reported the following information in its statement of cash flows:

	2009	2010	2011
Net cash flow from operating activities	$35,000	$32,000	$23,000
Purchases of property, plant, and equipment	31,818	22,857	20,325

Calculate, to one decimal place, the average capital acquisitions ratio for the period covering 2009–2011 and the capital acquisitions ratio for *each* year during the period. What does this analysis tell you about the company's need for using external financing to replace property, plant, and equipment?

M12-8 Calculating and Interpreting the Quality of Income Ratio

LO5

Dan's Products reported net income of $80,000, amortization expense of $2,000, and cash flow from operations of $60,000. Compute the quality of income ratio. What does the ratio tell you about the company's accrual of revenues and/or deferral of expenses?

M12-9 Computing Cash Flows from Operating Activities (Direct Method)

LO6

For each of the following independent cases, compute cash flows from operating activities using the direct method. Assume the list below includes all items relevant to operating activities.

	Case A	Case B	Case C
Sales revenue	$70,000	$55,000	$95,000
Cost of goods sold	35,000	32,000	65,000
Amortization expense	10,000	2,000	10,000
Other operating expenses	5,000	13,000	8,000
Net income	20,000	8,000	12,000
Accounts receivable increase (decrease)	(1,000)	4,000	3,000
Inventory increase (decrease)	2,000	0	(4,000)
Accounts payable increase (decrease)	0	3,000	(2,000)
Accrued liabilities increase (decrease)	1,000	(2,000)	1,000

M12-10 Computing Cash Flows from Operating Activities (Direct Method)

LO6

Refer to the two cases presented in M12-2, and show the cash flow from the operating activities section of the 2011 statement of cash flows, using the direct method.

EXERCISES

E12-1 Understanding the Computation of Cash Flows from Operating Activities (Indirect Method)

Practise and learn online with Connect.

LO2

Suppose your company sells services of $150 in exchange for $100 cash and $50 on account. Amortization of $40 also is recorded.

Required:

1. Show the journal entries to record these transactions.
2. Calculate the amount that should be reported as net cash flow from operating activities.
3. Calculate the amount that should be reported as net income.
4. Show how the indirect method would convert net income (requirement 3) to net cash flow from operating activities (requirement 2).
5. What general rule about converting net income to operating cash flows is revealed by your answer to requirement 4?

E12-2 Understanding the Computation of Cash Flows from Operating Activities (Indirect Method)

LO2

Suppose your company sells goods for $300, of which $200 is received in cash and $100 is on account. The goods cost your company $125 in a previous period. Your company also recorded wages of $70, of which only $30 has been paid in cash.

Required:

1. Show the journal entries to record these transactions.
2. Calculate the amount that should be reported as net cash flow from operating activities.
3. Calculate the amount that should be reported as net income.
4. Show how the indirect method would convert net income (requirement 3) to net cash flow from operating activities (requirement 2).
5. What general rule about converting net income to operating cash flows is revealed by your answer to requirement 4?

LO2, 5 **E12-3 Preparing and Evaluating a Simple Statement of Cash Flows (Indirect Method)**

Suppose your company's income statement reports $105 of net income, and its comparative balance sheet indicates the following.

	Beginning	Ending
Cash	$ 35	$205
Accounts Receivable	75	175
Inventory	260	135
Total	$370	$515
Wages Payable	$ 10	$ 50
Retained Earnings	360	465
Total	$370	$515

Required:

1. Prepare the operating activities section of the statement of cash flows, using the indirect method.
2. Identify the most significant cause of the difference between the company's net income and net cash flow from operating activities.

LO1, 2, 5 **E12-4 Preparing and Evaluating a Simple Statement of Cash Flows (Indirect Method)**

Suppose the income statement for Goggle Company reports $70 of net income, after deducting amortization of $35. The company bought equipment costing $60 and obtained a long-term bank loan for $60. The company's comparative balance sheet, at December 31, indicates the following.

	2010	2011	Change
Cash	$ 35	$205	
Accounts Receivable	75	175	
Inventory	260	135	
Equipment	500	560	
Accumulated Amortization	(45)	(80)	
Total	$825	$995	
Wages Payable	$ 10	$ 50	
Long-Term Debt	445	505	
Contributed Capital	10	10	
Retained Earnings	360	430	
Total	$825	$995	

Required:

1. Calculate the change in each balance sheet account, and indicate whether each account relates to operating, investing, and/or financing activities.
2. Prepare a statement of cash flows using the indirect method.
3. In one sentence, explain why an increase in accounts receivable is subtracted.
4. In one sentence, explain why a decrease in inventory is added.
5. In one sentence, explain why an increase in wages payable is added.
6. Are the cash flows typical of a start-up, healthy, or troubled company? Explain.

E12-5 Reporting Cash Flows from Operating Activities (Indirect Method) LO2

The following information pertains to Guy's Gear Company:

Sales		$80,000
Expenses:		
Cost of Goods Sold	$50,000	
Amortization Expense	6,000	
Salaries Expense	12,000	68,000
Net Income		$12,000
Accounts Receivable decrease	$ 5,000	
Merchandise Inventory increase	8,000	
Salaries Payable increase	500	

Required:

Present the operating activities section of the statement of cash flows for Guy's Gear Company using the indirect method.

E12-6 Reporting and Interpreting Cash Flows from Operating Activities from an LO2, 5
Analyst's Perspective (Indirect Method)

New Vision Company completed its income statement and balance sheet for 2011 and provided the following information:

Service Revenue		$66,000
Expenses:		
Salaries	$42,000	
Amortization	7,300	
Utilities	7,000	
Other	1,700	58,000
Net Income		$ 8,000
Decrease in Accounts Receivable	$12,000	
Bought a small service machine	5,000	
Increase in Salaries Payable	9,000	
Decrease in Other Accrued Liabilities	4,000	

Required:

1. Present the operating activities section of the statement of cash flows for New Vision Company using the indirect method.
2. Of the potential causes of differences between cash flow from operations and net income, which are the most important to financial analysts?

E12-7 Reporting and Interpreting Cash Flows from Operating Activities from an LO2, 5
Analyst's Perspective (Indirect Method)

Pizza International Inc. operates 700 family restaurants around the world. The company's annual report contained the following information (in thousands):

Operating Activities			
Net loss	$(9,482)	Decrease in accounts payable	$ 2,282
Amortization	33,305	Decrease in accrued liabilities	719
Increase in receivables	170	Increase in income taxes payable	1,861
Decrease in inventories	643	Reduction of long-term debt	12,691
Increase in prepaid expenses	664	Additions to equipment	29,073

Required:

1. Based on this information, compute cash flow from operating activities using the indirect method.
2. What were the major reasons that Pizza International was able to report positive cash flow from operations despite having a net loss?
3. Of the potential causes of differences between cash flow from operations and net income, which are the most important to financial analysts?

E12-8 Preparing and Evaluating a Statement of Cash Flows (Indirect Method) from Comparative Balance Sheets and Income Statements

Consultex Company was founded in 2009 as a small financial consulting business. The company had done reasonably well in 2009–2011, but noticed that its cash was beginning to dwindle early in 2012. In January 2012, Consultex had paid $16,000 to purchase land and repaid $2,000 principal on an existing promissory note. In March 2012, the company paid $2,000 cash in dividends and $1,000 to repurchase Consultex shares that had previously been issued for $1,000. To improve its cash position, Consultex borrowed $5,000 by signing a new promissory note in May 2012 and also issued shares to a new private investor for $12,000 cash. Comparative balance sheets and income statements for the most recent fiscal year are presented below.

CONSULTEX COMPANY
Balance Sheet
October 31

	2012	2011
Assets		
Cash	$11,000	$14,000
Accounts Receivable	14,000	12,000
Prepaid Rent	2,000	3,000
Land	26,000	10,000
Total Assets	$53,000	$39,000
Liabilities and Shareholders' Equity		
Wages Payable	$ 2,000	$ 3,000
Income Taxes Payable	1,000	1,000
Notes Payable (long-term)	15,000	12,000
Contributed Capital	20,000	9,000
Retained Earnings	15,000	14,000
Total Liabilities and Shareholders' Equity	$53,000	$39,000

CONSULTEX COMPANY
Income Statement
For the Year Ended October 31

	2012	2011
Sales Revenue	$158,000	$161,000
Wages Expense	98,000	97,000
Rent Expense	36,000	30,000
Other Operating Expenses	19,700	20,000
Income before Income Tax Expense	4,300	14,000
Income Tax Expense	1,300	4,200
Net Income	$ 3,000	$ 9,800

Check Figure:
[Req. 1]
Cash provided by financing activities = $12,000

Required:

1. Prepare a properly formatted statement of cash flows for Consultex for the year ended October 31, 2012 (using the indirect method).

2. What one thing can Consultex reasonably change in 2013 to avoid depleting its cash?

E12-9 Analyzing Cash Flows from Operating Activities (Indirect Method) and Calculating and Interpreting the Quality of Income Ratio

Assume the 2011 annual report for PepsiCo contained the following information for the period (in millions):

Net income	$5,142	Increase in prepaid expense	$ 68
Cash dividends paid	2,541	Increase in accounts payable	718
Amortization	1,543	Decrease in taxes payable	180
Increase in accounts receivable	549	Increase in other liabilities related to operations	738
Increase in inventory	345		

Required:

1. Compute cash flows from operating activities for PepsiCo using the indirect method.
2. Compute the quality of income ratio to one decimal place.
3. What was the main reason that PepsiCo's quality of income ratio did not equal 1.0?

E12-10 Calculating and Understanding Operating Cash Flows Relating to Inventory Purchases (Indirect Method)   LO2

The following information was reported by three companies. When completing the requirements, assume that any and all purchases on account are for inventory.

	Azure Corporation	Best Bikes	Charlotte's Cycles
Cost of goods sold	$175	$175	$350
Inventory purchases from suppliers made using cash	200	0	200
Inventory purchases from suppliers made on account	0	200	200
Cash payments to suppliers on account	0	160	160
Beginning inventory	100	100	200
Ending inventory	125	125	250
Beginning accounts payable	0	80	80
Ending accounts payable	0	120	120

Required:

1. What amount did each company deduct on the income statement related to inventory?
2. What total amount did each company pay out in cash during the period related to inventory purchased with cash and on account?
3. By what amount do your answers in 1 and 2 differ for each company?
4. By what amount did each company's inventory increase (decrease)? By what amount did each company's accounts payable increase (decrease)?
5. Using the indirect method of presentation, what amount(s) must each company add (deduct) from net income to convert from accrual to cash basis?
6. Describe any similarities between your answers to requirements 3 and 5. Are these answers the same? Why or why not?

E12-11 Reporting Cash Flows from Investing and Financing Activities   LO3, 4

Rowen Furniture Corporation reported the following activities in a recent quarter:

Net income	$ 4,135	Payments to reduce long-term debt	$ 46
Purchase of property, plant, and equipment	871	Sale of investments	134
Borrowings under line of credit (bank)	1,417	Cash proceeds from sale of property and equipment	6,594
Proceeds from issuance of shares	11	Cash dividends paid	277
Cash received from customers	29,164	Interest paid	90

Required:

Based on this information, present the cash flows from investing and financing activities sections of the cash flow statement, using ASPE.

E12-12 Reporting and Interpreting Cash Flows from Investing and Financing Activities with Discussion of Management Strategy

Payton Place Industries, Inc., is a manufacturer of steel products for customers such as House Depot and Private Motors. In the year ended December 31, 2011, it reported the following activities:

Net income	$24,068	Proceeds from sale of property, plant, and equipment	28,669
Purchase of property, plant, and equipment	21,595	Decrease in accounts receivable	12,273
Payments on notes payable (bank)	184,937	Proceeds from notes payable (bank)	53,439
Net proceeds from share issuance	250	Payment of dividends	5,985
Amortization	33,907	Other financing cash outflows	1,694

Required:

1. Based on this information, present the cash flows from the investing and financing activities sections of the cash flow statement.
2. Referring to your response to requirement 1, comment on whether you think Payton's cash flows are typical of a healthy or a struggling company.

LO5   **E12-13 Analyzing and Interpreting the Capital Acquisitions Ratio**

Sportsnet Enterprises reported the following data for the three most recent years:

	(In thousands)		
	2011	2010	2009
Cash flows from operating activities	$ 801	$1,480	$619
Cash flows from investing activities	(1,504)	(1,415)	(662)
Cash flows from financing activities	42,960	775	360

Check Figure:
[Req. 1]
Capital acquisitions
ratio = 0.81

Required:

1. Assuming that all investing activities involved acquisition of new plant and equipment, compute the capital acquisitions ratio for the three-year period in total.
2. During the three-year period, what portion of Sportsnet's investing activities was financed from cash flows from operating activities? What portion was financed from external sources or pre-existing cash balances during the three-year period?
3. What are two plausible explanations for the dramatic increase in cash flow from financing activities during the period?

LO5   **E12-14 Calculating and Interpreting the Capital Acquisitions Ratio**

Walt Disney Company   Assume that the Walt Disney Company reported the following in its 2011 annual report (in millions).

	2011	2010	2009
Net income	$4,427	$4,687	$3,374
Net cash provided by operating activities	5,446	5,398	5,960
Purchase of parks, resorts, and other property	(1,578)	(1,566)	(1,292)

Required:

1. Calculate, to two decimal places, the average capital acquisitions ratio for the period covering 2009–2011.
2. Interpret the results of your calculations in requirement 1. What do they suggest about the company's need for external financing to acquire property and equipment?

LO5   **E12-15 Calculating and Interpreting the Quality of Income Ratio**

Walt Disney Company   Refer to the information about the Walt Disney Company in E12-14.

Required:

1. Calculate, to one decimal place, the quality of income ratio for each year.

2. Interpret the results of your calculations in requirement 1. Given what you know about the Walt Disney Company from your own personal observations, provide one reason that could explain the sizable difference between net income and net cash provided by operating activities.

E12-16 Comparing the Direct and Indirect Methods

LO2, 6

To compare statement of cash flows reporting under the direct and indirect methods, enter check marks to indicate which line items are reported on the statement of cash flows with each method.

Cash Flows (and Related Changes)	Statement of Cash Flows Method	
	Direct	Indirect
1. Net income		
2. Receipts from customers		
3. Accounts receivable increase or decrease		
4. Payments to suppliers		
5. Inventory increase or decrease		
6. Accounts payable increase or decrease		
7. Payments to employees		
8. Wages payable, increase or decrease		
9. Amortization expense		
10. Cash flows from operating activities		
11. Cash flows from investing activities		
12. Cash flows from financing activities		
13. Net increase or decrease in cash during the period		

E12-17 Reporting and Interpreting Cash Flows from Operating Activities from an Analyst's Perspective (Direct Method)

LO5, 6

Refer to the information for New Vision Company in E12-6.

Required:

1. Present the operating activities section of the statement of cash flows for New Vision Company using the direct method. Assume that Other Accrued Liabilities relate to Other Expenses on the income statement.

2. Of the potential causes of differences between cash flow from operations and net income, which are the most important to financial analysts?

E12-18 Reporting and Interpreting Cash Flows from Operating Activities from an Analyst's Perspective (Direct Method)

LO5, 6

Refer back to the information given for E12-7, plus the following summarized income statement for Pizza International Inc. (in millions):

Revenues	$136,500
Cost of Sales	45,500
Gross Profit	91,000
Salary Expense	56,835
Amortization	33,305
Other Expenses	7,781
Net Loss before Income Tax Expense	(6,921)
Income Tax Expense	2,561
Net Loss	$ (9,482)

Required:

1. Based on this information, compute cash flow from operating activities using the direct method. Assume that Prepaid Expenses and Accrued Liabilities relate to other expenses.

Check Figure:
[Req. 1]
Net cash flow from operating activities = $22,492

2. What were the major reasons that Pizza International was able to report positive cash flow from operations despite having a net loss?

3. Of the potential causes of differences between cash flow from operations and net income, which are the most important to financial analysts?

E12-19 (Supplement 12A) Determining Cash Flows from the Sale of Property

During fiscal 2011, M&Q Entertainment sold its Ferentio assets for $20,360,000 cash and recorded a gain on disposal of $18,360,000, which was included in the company's net income of $43,445,000.

Required:

1. Show how the disposal would be reported on the statement of cash flows, using the following format (which assumes the indirect method):

> (In thousands)
> _____
>
> Cash flows from operating activities
> Net income $43,445
> Gain on sale of property
> Cash flows from investing activities
> Proceeds from disposition of property

2. Compute the book value of the Ferentio assets that were sold.

E12-20 (Supplement 12B) Preparing a Statement of Cash Flows, Indirect Method: Complete Spreadsheet

To prepare a statement of cash flows for Golf Champion Store, you examined the company's accounts, noting the following:

> Purchased equipment, $20,000, and issued a promissory note in full payment.
> Purchased a long-term investment for cash, $15,000.
> Paid cash dividend, $12,000.
> Sold equipment for $6,000 cash (cost, $21,000, accumulated amortization, $15,000).
> Issued no-par shares, 500 shares at $12 per share cash.
> Net income was $20,200.
> Amortization expense was $3,000.

You also created the following spreadsheet to use when preparing the statement of cash flows.

	Beginning Balances, December 31, 2011	Analysis of Changes Debit	Analysis of Changes Credit	Ending Balances, December 31, 2012
Balance Sheet Items				
Cash	$ 20,500			$ 19,200
Accounts Receivable	22,000			22,000
Merchandise Inventory	68,000			75,000
Investments	0			15,000
Equipment	114,500			113,500
Accumulated Amortization	32,000			20,000
Accounts Payable	17,000			14,000
Wages Payable	2,500			1,500
Income Taxes Payable	3,000			4,500
Notes Payable	54,000			74,000
Contributed Capital	100,000			106,000
Retained Earnings	16,500			24,700
		Inflows	Outflows	
Statement of Cash Flows				
Cash flows from operating activities				
Cash flows from investing activities				
Cash flows from financing activities				
Net increase (decrease) in cash				
Totals				

Required:

1. Complete the spreadsheet.
2. Prepare the 2012 statement of cash flows using the indirect method.

CP12-1 Preparing a Statement of Cash Flows (Indirect Method)

LO2, 3, 4, 5

Hunter Company is developing its annual financial statements at December 31, 2012. The statements are complete except for the statement of cash flows. The completed comparative balance sheets and income statement are summarized below:

	2012	2011
Balance Sheet at December 31		
Cash	$ 44,000	$ 18,000
Accounts Receivable	27,000	29,000
Merchandise Inventory	30,000	36,000
Property and Equipment	111,000	102,000
Less: Accumulated Amortization	(36,000)	(30,000)
	$176,000	$155,000
Accounts Payable	$ 25,000	$ 22,000
Wages Payable	800	1,000
Note Payable, Long-Term	38,000	48,000
Contributed Capital	80,000	60,000
Retained Earnings	32,000	24,000
	$176,000	$155,000
Income Statement for 2012		
Sales	$100,000	
Cost of Goods Sold	61,000	
Other Expenses	27,000	
Net Income	$ 12,000	

Additional Data:

a. Bought equipment for cash, $9,000.
b. Paid $10,000 on the long-term note payable.
c. Issued new shares for $20,000 cash.
d. Declared and paid a $3,800 cash dividend.
e. Other expenses included amortization, $6,000; wages, $10,000; taxes, $3,000; other, $8,000.
f. Accounts Payable includes only inventory purchases made on credit. Because there are no liability accounts relating to taxes or other expenses, assume that these expenses were fully paid in cash.

Required:

1. Prepare the statement of cash flows for the year ended December 31, 2012, using the indirect method.

   TIP: Net cash flows provided by operating activities equal $28,800.
   TIP: Net cash used in investing activities equals $9,000.
   TIP: Net cash provided by financing activities equals $6,200

2. Use the statement of cash flows to evaluate Hunter's cash flows.

   TIP: The demonstration cases provide good examples of information to consider when evaluating cash flows.

CP12-2 Preparing and Interpreting a Statement of Cash Flows (Indirect Method)

LO2, 3, 4, 5

Soft Touch Company was started several years ago by two golf instructors. The company's comparative balance sheets and income statement follow, along with additional information.

	2012	2011
Balance Sheet at December 31		
Cash	$12,000	$ 8,000
Accounts Receivable	2,000	3,500
Equipment	11,000	10,000
Less: Accumulated Amortization	(3,000)	(2,500)
	$22,000	$19,000
Accounts Payable	$ 1,000	$ 2,000
Wages Payable	1,000	1,500
Long-Term Bank Loan Payable	3,000	1,000
Contributed Capital	10,000	10,000
Retained Earnings	7,000	4,500
	$22,000	$19,000
Income Statement for 2012		
Lessons Revenue	$75,000	
Wages Expense	70,000	
Amortization Expense	500	
Income Tax Expense	2,000	
Net Income	$ 2,500	

Additional Data:

a. Bought new golf clubs using cash, $1,000.

b. Borrowed $2,000 cash from the bank during the year.

c. Accounts Payable includes only purchases of services made on credit for operating purposes. Because there are no liability accounts relating to income tax, assume that this expense was fully paid in cash.

Required:

1. Prepare the statement of cash flows for the year ended December 31, 2012, using the indirect method.

    TIP: Net cash flows provided by operating activities equal $3,000.
    TIP: Net cash used in investing activities equals $1,000.
    TIP: Net cash provided by financing activities equals $2,000

2. Use the statement of cash flows to evaluate the company's cash flows.

    TIP: The demonstration cases provide good examples of information to consider when evaluating cash flows.

LO3, 4, 5, 6   **CP12-3 Preparing and Interpreting a Statement of Cash Flows (Direct Method)**

Refer to CP12-2.

Required:

Complete requirements 1 and 2 using the direct method.

    TIP: Remember to exclude amortization expense when converting to the cash basis.
    TIP: Net cash flows provided by (used in) operating, investing and financing activities are the same as in CP12-2.

GROUP A PROBLEMS

LO2   **PA12-1 Computing Cash Flows from Operating Activities (Indirect Method)**

The income statement and selected balance sheet information for Direct Products Company for the year ended December 31, 2012, follow.

Income Statement	
Sales Revenue	$48,600
Expenses:	
Cost of Goods Sold	21,000
Amortization Expense	2,000
Salaries Expense	9,000
Rent Expense	4,500
Insurance Expense	1,900
Interest Expense	1,800
Utilities Expense	1,400
Net Income	$ 7,000

Selected Balance Sheet Accounts	2012	2011
Accounts Receivable	$560	$580
Merchandise Inventory	990	770
Accounts Payable	440	460
Prepaid Rent	25	20
Prepaid Insurance	25	28
Salaries Payable	100	70
Utilities Payable	20	15

Required:

Prepare the cash flows from operating activities section of the 2012 statement of cash flows using the indirect method.

Check Figure:
Net cash flow from operating activities = $8,813

PA12-2 Preparing a Statement of Cash Flows (Indirect Method)

XS Supply Company is developing its annual financial statements at December 31, 2012. The statements are complete except for the statement of cash flows. The completed comparative balance sheets and income statement are summarized:

LO2, 3, 4, 5

	2012	2011
Balance Sheet at December 31		
Cash	$ 34,000	$ 29,000
Accounts Receivable	35,000	28,000
Merchandise Inventory	41,000	38,000
Property and Equipment	121,000	100,000
Less: Accumulated Amortization	(30,000)	(25,000)
	$201,000	$170,000
Accounts Payable	$ 36,000	$ 27,000
Wages Payable	1,200	1,400
Note Payable, Long-Term	38,000	44,000
Contributed Capital	88,600	72,600
Retained Earnings	37,200	25,000
	$201,000	$170,000
Income Statement for 2012		
Sales	$120,000	
Cost of Goods Sold	70,000	
Other Expenses	37,800	
Net Income	$ 12,200	

Additional Data:

a. Bought equipment for cash, $21,000.
b. Paid $6,000 on the long-term note payable.
c. Issued new shares for $16,000 cash.
d. No dividends were declared or paid.
e. Other expenses included amortization, $5,000; wages, $20,000; taxes, $6,000; other, $6,800.
f. Accounts Payable includes only inventory purchases made on credit. Because there are no liability accounts relating to taxes or other expenses, assume that these expenses were fully paid in cash.

Required:

1. Prepare the statement of cash flows for the year ended December 31, 2012, using the indirect method.
2. Evaluate the statement of cash flows.

PA12-3 Preparing and Interpreting a Statement of Cash Flows (Indirect Method)

Heads Up Company was started several years ago by two hockey instructors. The company's comparative balance sheets and income statement follow, along with additional information.

	2012	2011
Balance Sheet at December 31		
Cash	$ 6,000	$4,000
Accounts Receivable	1,000	1,750
Equipment	5,500	5,000
Less: Accumulated Amortization	(1,500)	(1,250)
	$11,000	$9,500
Accounts Payable	$ 500	$1,000
Wages Payable	500	750
Long-Term Bank Loan Payable	1,500	500
Contributed Capital	5,000	5,000
Retained Earnings	3,500	2,250
	$11,000	$9,500
Income Statement for 2012		
Lessons Revenue	$37,500	
Wages Expense	35,000	
Amortization Expense	250	
Income Tax Expense	1,000	
Net Income	$ 1,250	

Additional Data:

a. Bought new hockey equipment for cash, $500.
b. Borrowed $1,000 cash from the bank during the year.
c. Accounts Payable includes only purchases of services made on credit for operating purposes. Because there are no liability accounts relating to income tax, assume that this expense was fully paid in cash.

Required:

1. Prepare the statement of cash flows for the year ended December 31, 2012, using the indirect method.
2. Use the statement of cash flows to evaluate the company's cash flows.

LO6 **PA12-4 Computing Cash Flows from Operating Activities (Direct Method)**

Refer to the information in PA12-1.

Check Figure:
Cash payments to suppliers = $(21,240)

Required:

Prepare the cash flows from operating activities section of the 2012 statement of cash flows using the direct method.

LO3, 4, 5, 6 **PA12-5 Preparing and Interpreting a Statement of Cash Flows (Direct Method)**

Refer to PA12-3.

Required:

Complete requirements 1 and 2 using the direct method.

GROUP B PROBLEMS

LO2 **PB12-1 Computing Cash Flows from Operating Activities (Indirect Method)**

The income statement and selected balance sheet information for Calendars Incorporated for the year ended December 31, 2012, is presented below.

Income Statement	
Sales Revenue	$78,000
Expenses:	
Cost of Goods Sold	36,000
Amortization Expense	16,000
Salaries Expense	10,000
Rent Expense	2,500
Insurance Expense	1,300
Interest Expense	1,200
Utilities Expense	1,000
Net Income	$10,000

Selected Balance Sheet Accounts	2012	2011
Merchandise Inventory	$ 430	$ 490
Accounts Receivable	1,800	1,500
Accounts Payable	1,200	1,300
Salaries Payable	450	300
Utilities Payable	100	0
Prepaid Rent	50	100
Prepaid Insurance	70	90

Required:

Prepare the cash flows from operating activities section of the 2012 statement of cash flows using the indirect method.

PB12-2 **Preparing a Statement of Cash Flows (Indirect Method)**   LO2, 3, 4, 5

Audio City Inc. is developing its annual financial statements at December 31, 2012. The statements are complete except for the statement of cash flows. The completed comparative balance sheets and income statement are summarized below:

	2012	2011
Balance Sheet at December 31		
Cash	$ 63,000	$ 65,000
Accounts Receivable	15,000	20,000
Merchandise Inventory	22,000	20,000
Property and Equipment	210,000	150,000
Less: Accumulated Amortization	(60,000)	(45,000)
	$250,000	$210,000
Accounts Payable	$ 8,000	$ 19,000
Wages Payable	2,000	1,000
Note Payable, Long-Term	60,000	75,000
Contributed Capital	100,000	70,000
Retained Earnings	80,000	45,000
	$250,000	$210,000
Income Statement for 2012		
Sales	$190,000	
Cost of Goods Sold	90,000	
Other Expenses	60,000	
Net Income	$ 40,000	

Additional Data:

a. Bought equipment for cash, $60,000.

b. Paid $15,000 on the long-term note payable.

c. Issued new shares for $30,000 cash.

d. Dividends of $5,000 were paid in cash.

e. Other expenses included amortization, $15,000; wages, $20,000; taxes, $25,000.

f. Accounts Payable includes only inventory purchases made on credit. Because a liability relating to taxes does not exist, assume that the taxes were fully paid in cash.

Required:

1. Prepare the statement of cash flows for the year ended December 31, 2012, using the indirect method.

2. Evaluate the statement of cash flows.

Check Figure:
[Req. 1]
Net decrease in cash during
the year = $(2,000)

PB12-3 Preparing and Interpreting a Statement of Cash Flows (Indirect Method)

Buddies' Dive In Company was started several years ago by two diving instructors. The company's comparative balance sheets and income statement are presented below, followed by additional information.

	2012	2011
Balance Sheet at December 31		
Cash	$ 3,200	$4,000
Accounts Receivable	1,000	500
Prepaid Expenses	100	50
	$ 4,300	$4,550
Wages Payable	$ 350	$1,100
Contributed Capital	1,200	1,000
Retained Earnings	2,750	2,450
	$ 4,300	$4,550
Income Statement for 2012		
Lessons Revenue	$33,950	
Wages Expense	30,000	
Other Operating Expenses	3,650	
Net Income	$ 300	

Additional Data:

a. Prepaid Expenses relate to rent paid in advance.
b. Other Operating Expenses were paid in cash.
c. An owner contributed capital by paying $200 cash in exchange for company shares.

Required:

1. Prepare the statement of cash flows for the year ended December 31, 2012, using the indirect method.
2. Use the statement of cash flows to evaluate the company's cash flows.

LO6 **PB12-4 Computing Cash Flows from Operating Activities (Direct Method)**

Refer to the information in PB12-1.

Required:

Prepare the cash flows from the operating activities section of the 2012 statement of cash flows using the direct method.

LO3, 4, 5, 6 **PB12-5 Preparing and Interpreting a Statement of Cash Flows (Direct Method)**

Check Figure:
[Req. 1]
Net decrease in cash during the year = $(800)

Refer to PB12-3.

Required:

Complete requirements 1 and 2 using the direct method.

SKILLS DEVELOPMENT CASES

LO1, 5

Rona Inc.

S12-1 Finding Financial Information

Refer to the financial statements of Rona Inc. in Appendix A at the back of this book or download the annual report from the *Cases* section of Connect.

Required:

1. Which of the two basic reporting approaches for the cash flows from operating activities did Rona Inc. use?
2. What amount of tax payments did Rona make during the year ended December 27, 2009? Where did you find this information?
3. In the 2009 fiscal year, Rona generated $223 million from operating activities. Where did Rona spend this money? List the two largest cash outflows.

S12-2 Comparing Financial Information

Refer to the financial statements of Rona Inc. in Appendix A and The Home Depot in Appendix B at the back of this book or download the annual reports from the *Cases* section of Connect.

Required:

1. Which of the two basic reporting approaches for the cash flows from operating activities did The Home Depot use? Is this the same as what Rona Inc. used?
2. What amount of cash did The Home Depot receive from disposing of property and equipment during the year ended January 31, 2010?
3. In the 2009–10 fiscal year, The Home Depot generated $5,125 million from operating activities. Where did The Home Depot spend this money? List the two largest cash outflows reported in the investing or financing activities sections. Do The Home Depot's uses differ significantly from those of Rona?

S12-3 Internet-Based Team Research: Examining an Annual Report

As a team, select an industry to analyze. Using your Web browser, each team member should access the annual report for one publicly traded company in the industry, with each member selecting a different company. (See S1-3 in Chapter 1 for a description of possible resources for these tasks.)

Required:

1. On an individual basis, each team member should write a short report that incorporates the following:
   a. Has the company generated positive or negative operating cash flows during the past three years?
   b. Has the company been expanding over that period? If so, what appears to have been the source of financing for this expansion (operating cash flow, additional borrowing, issuance of shares)?
   c. Compute and analyze the capital acquisitions ratio averaged over the past three years.
   d. Compute and analyze the quality of income ratio in each of the past three years.
2. Then, as a team, write a short report comparing and contrasting your companies using these attributes. Discuss any patterns across the companies that you as a team observe. Provide potential explanations for any differences discovered.

S12-4 Ethical Decision Making: A Real-Life Example

In a press release on February 19, 2004, the U.S. Securities and Exchange Commission described a number of fraudulent transactions that Enron executives concocted in an effort to meet the company's financial targets. One particularly well-known scheme is called the "Nigerian barge" transaction. According to court documents, Enron arranged to sell three electricity-generating power barges moored off the coast of Nigeria. The "buyer" was the investment banking firm of Merrill Lynch. Although Enron reported this transaction as a sale in its income statement, it turns out that this was no ordinary sale. Merrill Lynch didn't really want the barges and had agreed to buy them only because Enron guaranteed, in a secret side deal, that it would arrange for the barges to be bought back from Merrill Lynch within six months of the initial transaction. In addition, Enron promised to pay Merrill Lynch a hefty fee for doing the deal. In an interview on National Public Radio on August 17, 2002, Michigan Senator Carl Levin declared, the "case of the Nigerian barge transaction was, by any definition, a loan."

Required:

1. Discuss whether the Nigerian barge transaction should have been considered a loan rather than a sale. As part of your discussion, consider the following questions. Doesn't the Merrill Lynch payment to Enron at the time of the initial transaction automatically make it a sale, not a loan? What aspects of the transaction are similar to a loan? Which aspects suggest revenue has not been earned by Enron?
2. The income statement effect of recording the transaction as a sale rather than as a loan is fairly clear: Enron was able to boost its revenues and net income. What is somewhat less obvious, but nearly as important, are the effects on the statement of cash flows. Describe how including the

transaction with sales of other Enron products, rather than as a loan, would change the statement of cash flows.

3. How would the difference in the statement of cash flows (described in your response to requirement 2) affect financial statement users?

LO1, 5 ### S12-5 Ethical Decision Making: A Mini-Case

Assume that you serve on the board of a local golf and country club. In preparation for renegotiating the club's bank loans, the president indicates that the club needs to increase its operating cash flows before the end of the current year. The club's treasurer reassures the president and other board members that he knows a couple of ways to boost the club's operating cash flows. First, he says, the club can sell some of its accounts receivable to a collections company that is willing to pay the club $97,000 up front for the right to collect $100,000 of the overdue accounts. That will immediately boost operating cash flows. Second, he indicates that the club paid about $200,000 last month to relocate the 18th fairway and green closer to the clubhouse. The treasurer indicates that although these costs have been reported as expenses in the club's own monthly financial statements, he feels an argument can be made for reporting them as part of land and land improvements (a long-lived asset) in the year-end financial statements that would be provided to the bank. He explains that, by recording these payments as an addition to a long-lived asset, they will not be shown as a reduction in operating cash flows.

Required:

1. Does the sale of accounts receivable to generate immediate cash harm or mislead anyone? Would you consider it an ethical business activity?
2. What category in the statement of cash flows is used when reporting cash spent on long-lived assets, such as land improvements? What category is used when cash is spent on expenses, such as costs for regular upkeep of the grounds?
3. What facts are relevant to deciding whether the costs of the 18th hole relocation should be reported as an asset or as an expense? Is it appropriate to make this decision based on the impact it could have on operating cash flows?
4. As a member of the board, how would you ensure that an ethical decision is made?

LO2 ### S12-6 Critical Thinking: Interpreting Adjustments Reported on the Statement of Cash Flows from a Management Perspective (Indirect Method)

QuickServe, a chain of convenience stores, was experiencing some serious cash flow difficulties because of rapid growth. The company did not generate sufficient cash from operating activities to finance its new stores, and creditors were not willing to lend money because the company had not produced any income for the previous three years. The new controller for QuickServe proposed a reduction in the estimated life of store equipment to increase amortization expense; thus, "we can improve cash flows from operating activities because amortization expense is added back on the statement of cash flows." Other executives were not sure that this was a good idea because the increase in amortization would make it more difficult to report positive earnings: "Without income, the bank will never lend us money."

Required:

What action would you recommend for QuickServe? Why?

LO2 ### S12-7 Using a Spreadsheet that Calculates Cash Flows from Operating Activities (Indirect Method)

You've recently been hired by B2B Consultants to provide financial advisory services to small-business managers. B2B's clients often need advice on how to improve their operating cash flows and, given your accounting background, you're frequently called on to show them how operating cash flows would change if they were to speed up their sales of inventory and their collections of accounts receivable or delay their payment of accounts payable. Each time you're asked to show the effects of these business decisions on the cash flows from operating activities, you get the uneasy feeling that you might inadvertently miscalculate their effects. To deal with this once and for all, you e-mail your friend Owen and ask him to prepare a template that automatically calculates the net operating cash flows from a simple comparative balance sheet. You received his reply today.

Hey pal. I like your idea of working smarter, not harder. Too bad it involved me doing the thinking. Anyhow, I've created a spreadsheet file that contains four worksheets. The first two tabs (labelled BS and IS) are the input sheets where you would enter the numbers from each client's comparative balance sheets and income statement. Your clients are small, so this template allows for only the usual accounts. Also, I've assumed that amortization is the only reason for a change in accumulated amortization. If your clients' business activities differ from these, you'll need to contact me for more complex templates. The third worksheet calculates the operating cash flows using the indirect method and the fourth does this calculation using the direct method. I'll attach the screenshots of each of the worksheets so you can create your own. To answer "what if" questions, all you'll need to do is change selected amounts in the balance sheet and income statement.

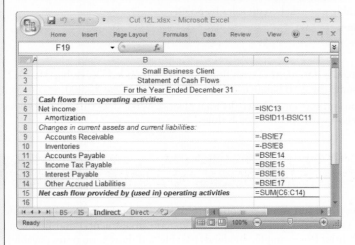

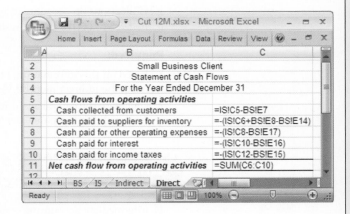

Required:

Copy the account balances from the worksheets for the balance sheet and income statement into a spreadsheet file. Enter formulas into the balance sheet worksheet to compute the change in each account balance, and then enter the formulas for the statement of cash flows (indirect method only) into a third worksheet. From this third worksheet, report the net cash flow provided by (used in) operating activities.

S12-8 Using a Spreadsheet That Calculates Cash Flows from Operating Activities (Direct Method)   LO6

Refer to the information presented in S12-7.

Required:

Complete the same requirements, except use the direct method only.

L05 **S12-9 Using a Spreadsheet to Answer "What If" Management Decisions (Indirect or Direct Method)**

Change the amounts for selected balance sheet accounts in the spreadsheets created for either S12-7 or S12-8 to calculate the net cash flows from operating activities if, just before the current year-end, the company's management took the actions listed in the following requirements. Consider each question independently, unless indicated otherwise.

Required:

1. What if the company collected $10,000 of the accounts receivable?
2. What if the company had paid down its interest payable by an extra $2,000?
3. What if the company waited an additional month before paying $6,000 of its accounts payable?
4. What if the company had reported $5,000 more amortization expense?
5. What if all four of the above events had taken place at the same time?

CONTINUING CASE

Practise and learn online with Connect.

L02, 3, 4, 5 **CC12 Accounting for Cash Flows**

During a recent year (ended December 31, 2012), Nicole's Getaway Spa (NGS) reported net income of $2,300. The company reported the following activities:

a. Increase in inventories of $400.
b. Amortization of $3,000.
c. Increase of $2,170 in prepaid expenses.
d. Payments of $4,600 on long-term debt.
e. Purchased new spa equipment for $7,582.
f. Payments on accounts payable exceeded purchases by $320.
g. Collections on accounts receivable exceeded credit sales by $859.
h. Issued $10,000 of common shares.

Required:

1. Based on this information, prepare a statement of cash flows for the year ended December 31, 2012, using the indirect method. Assume the cash balance at December 31, 2011, was $7,000.
2. Calculate the capital acquisitions ratio (round to two decimal places). What does this tell you about NGS's ability to finance expansion with operating cash flows?

Endnotes

1. Intermediate accounting courses discuss in detail exceptions to this general rule. Exceptions include investing activities that affect current assets (for example, short-term investments) and financing activities that affect current liabilities (for example, dividends payable and short-term notes payable).
2. Impairment losses (discussed in Chapter 9) are handled in exactly the same way as amortization. Gains and losses on fixed asset disposals also are dealt with in a similar manner and are discussed in this chapter's Supplement 12A.
3. Investing activities also affect other assets described in Appendix E (investments in other companies). Although not shown here, the cash flows for investments are similar to those shown in this section for equipment and intangible assets.
4. Steven F. Orpurt and Yoonseok Zang, "Do Direct Cash Flow Disclosures Help Predict Future Operating Cash Flows and Earnings?" *The Accounting Review* 84:3, May 2009, pp. 893–936.

Practise and learn online with Connect.

CHAPTER 13

Measuring and Evaluating Financial Performance

YOUR LEARNING OBJECTIVES

Understand the business

LO1 Describe the purposes and uses of horizontal, vertical, and ratio analyses.

Study the accounting methods

LO2 Use horizontal (trend) analyses to recognize financial changes that unfold over time.

LO3 Use vertical (common-size) analyses to understand important relationships within financial statements.

LO4 Calculate financial ratios to assess profitability, liquidity, and solvency.

Evaluate the results

LO5 Interpret the results of financial analyses.

LO6 Describe how analyses depend on key accounting decisions and concepts.

Review the chapter

Chapter Summary, page 573
Additional resources on Connect

FOCUS COMPANY:
The Home Depot, Inc.
www.homedepot.ca

Measuring and evaluating financial performance is like judging gymnastics or figure skating at the Olympics. You have to know three things: (1) the general categories to evaluate for each event, (2) the particular elements to consider within each category, and (3) how to measure performance for each element. On the financial side, analysts follow the same process. They evaluate general categories such as profitability, liquidity, and solvency, which are separated into particular elements such as gross profit margin and net profit margin. For each of these elements, analysts measure performance by computing various percentages and ratios, which themselves are based on information reported in the financial statements.

In this chapter, we focus on The Home Depot, the largest home improvement specialty retailer in the world. The Home Depot currently operates in 10 Canadian provinces, 50 U.S. states, the District of Columbia, Puerto Rico, the U.S. Virgin Islands, Mexico, and China. The company has 179 stores in Canada and employs over 27,000 people in Canada alone. Yet the company's continued success still requires innovations to increase sales in existing markets and to successfully enter new markets. At the same time, The Home Depot must control costs while maintaining a high level of customer service in its stores. Finally, The Home Depot's management must anticipate the actions of its rivals, such as Rona and Lowe's, and deal with changes in overall demand for building products over which it has no control.

How do managers, analysts, investors, and creditors assess The Home Depot's success in meeting these challenges? This is the purpose of financial statement analysis. Our discussion begins with an explanation of how to analyze financial statements to understand the financial results of a company's business activities. We conclude the chapter with a review of the key accounting decisions that analysts consider when evaluating financial statements.

THAT WAS
THEN

In the previous chapters, you learned how to report and interpret the financial effects of various business activities.

THIS IS
NOW

This chapter synthesizes previous chapters by evaluating the financial statements and accounting decisions of a publicly traded company.

ORGANIZATION OF THE CHAPTER

Understand the business	**S**tudy the accounting methods	**E**valuate the results	**R**eview the chapter
• Horizontal, vertical, and ratio analyses	• Horizontal (trend) computations • Vertical (common-size) computations • Ratio computations	• Interpreting horizontal and vertical analyses • Interpreting ratio analyses • Underlying accounting decisions and concepts	• Demonstration Case • Chapter Summary • Key Terms • Homework Helper • Practice Material

Understand the Business

Learning Objective 1

Describe the purposes and uses of horizontal, vertical, and ratio analyses.

As you first learned in Chapter 1, the goal of accounting is to provide information that allows decision makers to understand and evaluate the results of business activities. Throughout the course, you have learned how financial statements are used in a variety of decisions. Creditors use financial statements to assess compliance with loan covenants. Managers analyze financial statements to evaluate past financial performance and make future decisions. And, of course, analysts use financial statements to generate advice for investors and others. You have learned that no single number fully captures the results of all business activities nor does it predict a company's success or failure. Instead, to understand and evaluate the results of business activities, you need to look at a business from many different angles. An understanding of whether a business is successful will emerge only after you have learned to combine all of your evaluations into a complete picture or story that depicts the company's performance. Our goal for this chapter is to demonstrate how you can do this, relying on horizontal, vertical, and ratio analyses to develop the "story" of how well a company has performed.

HORIZONTAL, VERTICAL, AND RATIO ANALYSES

Most good stories have a plot, which the reader comes to understand as it unfolds over time or as one event relates to another. This is the same way that financial analyses work. Horizontal (trend) analyses are conducted to help financial statement users recognize important financial changes that unfold over time. Horizontal analyses compare individual financial statement line items horizontally (from one period to the next), with the general goal of identifying significant sustained changes (trends). These changes are typically described in terms of dollar amounts and year-over-year percentages. For example, trend analyses could be used to determine the dollar amount and percentage by which Cost of Goods Sold increased this year, relative to prior years. Vertical analyses focus on important relationships between items on the same financial statement. These items are compared vertically (one account balance versus another) and are typically expressed as percentages to reveal the relative contributions made by each financial statement item. For example, vertical analyses could show that operating expenses consume one-quarter of a company's net sales revenue. Ratio analyses are conducted to understand relationships among various items reported in one or more of the financial statements. Ratio analyses allow you to evaluate how well a company has performed given the level of other company resources. For example, while vertical analyses can show that Cost of Goods Sold consumes 65 percent of Net Sales and horizontal analyses can show that this percentage has increased over time, ratio analyses can relate these amounts to inventory levels to evaluate inventory management decisions.

Before we show you how to calculate horizontal, vertical, and ratio analyses (in the next section), we must emphasize that no analysis is complete unless it leads to an interpretation that helps financial statement users understand and evaluate a company's financial results. Without interpretation, these computations can appear as nothing more than a list of disconnected numbers.

Study the Accounting Methods

HORIZONTAL (TREND) COMPUTATIONS

Horizontal (trend) analyses help financial statement users to recognize financial changes that unfold over time. This approach compares individual financial statement items from year to year with the general goal of identifying significant sustained changes or trends. For example, trend analysis can be used to determine the dollar and percentage changes in the cost of goods sold this year relative to prior years. Because this type of analysis compares the results on each line of the financial statements across several years, trend analysis is also known as *horizontal analysis*. Because it compares results over a series of periods, it is sometimes called *time-series analysis*.

Regardless of the name, trend analyses are usually calculated in terms of year-to-year dollar and percentage changes. A year-to-year percentage change expresses the current year's dollar change as a percentage of the prior year's total by using the following calculation:

> $$\frac{\text{Year-to-Year}}{\text{Change (\%)}} = \frac{\text{Change This Year}}{\text{Prior Year's Total}} \times 100 = \frac{(\text{Current Year's Total} - \text{Prior Year's Total})}{\text{Prior Year's Total}} \times 100$$

To demonstrate how to calculate a trend, we analyze The Home Depot's financial statements. Summaries of The Home Depot's balance sheets and income statements from two recent years appear in Exhibits 13.1 and 13.2. Dollar and percentage changes from fiscal year 2008 to 2009[1] are shown to the right of the balance sheet and income statement. The dollar changes were calculated by subtracting the fiscal 2008 balances from the fiscal 2009 balances. The percentage changes were calculated by dividing those differences by the fiscal 2009 balances. For example, according to Exhibit 13.1, Cash and Cash Equivalents increased by $902 (= $1,421 − $519) in fiscal 2009 relative to fiscal 2008 (all numbers in millions). That dollar amount represented an increase of 173.8% [= ($902 ÷ $519) × 100].

In a later section, we will explain and evaluate the underlying causes of significant changes in account balances. But before we leave this topic, we must note that not all large percentage changes will be significant. For example, the 44 percent decrease in Other Assets is the largest percentage change on the balance sheet (Exhibit 13.1) with the exception of Cash and Cash Equivalents. However the dollar amount is relatively small when compared to other changes, such as the $1,113 decrease in Long-Term Liabilities. To avoid focusing on unimportant changes, use the percentage changes to identify potentially significant changes but then check the dollar change to make sure that it too is significant.

Learning Objective 2

Use horizontal (trend) analyses to recognize financial changes that unfold over time.

YOU SHOULD KNOW

Horizontal (trend) analyses: Comparing results across time, often expressing changes in account balances as a percentage of prior year balances.

THE HOME DEPOT
Balance Sheets
(In millions)

	January 30, 2010 (Fiscal 2009)	February 1, 2009 (Fiscal 2008)	Increase (Decrease) Amount	Percentage*
Assets				
Current Assets				
Cash and Cash Equivalents	$ 1,421	$ 519	$ 902	173.8%
Short-Term Investments	6	6	—	0.0
Accounts Receivable, Net	964	972	(8)	(0.8)
Inventories	10,188	10,673	(485)	(4.5)
Other Current Assets	1,321	1,192	129	10.8
Total Current Assets	13,900	13,362	538	4.0
Property and Equipment, Net	25,550	26,234	(684)	(2.6)
Notes Receivable	33	36	(3)	(8.3)
Goodwill	1,171	1,134	37	3.3
Other Assets	223	398	(175)	(44.0)
Total Assets	$40,877	$41,164	$ (287)	(0.7)
Liabilities and Shareholders' Equity				
Current Liabilities	$10,363	$11,153	$ (790)	(7.1)
Long-Term Liabilities	11,121	12,234	(1,113)	(9.1)
Total Liabilities	21,484	23,387	(1,903)	(8.1)
Shareholders' Equity	19,393	17,777	1,616	9.1
Total Liabilities and Shareholders' Equity	$40,877	$41,164	$ (287)	(0.7)

*Amount of Increase (Decrease) ÷ Fiscal 2008 × 100

THE HOME DEPOT
Income Statements
(In millions)

Year Ended:	January 30, 2010 (Fiscal 2009)	February 1, 2009 (Fiscal 2008)	Increase (Decrease) Amount	Percentage*
Net Sales Revenue	$66,176	$71,288	$(5,112)	(7.2)%
Cost of Sales	43,764	47,298	(3,534)	(7.5)
Gross Profit	22,412	23,990	(1,578)	(6.6)
Operating and Other Expenses	17,609	19,631	(2,022)	(10.3)
Interest and Other Expense	821	769	52	6.8
Income Tax Expense	1,362	1,278	84	6.6
Net Income from Continuing Operations	2,620	2,312	308	13.3
Earnings (loss) from Discontinued Operations	41	(52)	93	178.9
Net Income	$ 2,661	$ 2,260	$ 401	17.7
Basic Earnings per Share	$ 1.58	$ 1.34	$ 0.24	17.9

*Amount of Increase (Decrease) ÷ Fiscal 2008 × 100

VERTICAL (COMMON-SIZE) COMPUTATIONS

A second type of analysis, **vertical (common-size) analysis,** focuses on important relationships within a financial statement. When a company is growing or shrinking overall, it is difficult to tell from the dollar amounts whether the proportions within each statement category are changing. Common-size financial statements provide this information by expressing each financial statement amount as a percentage of another amount on that statement. The usefulness of common-size statements is illustrated in Exhibits 13.3 and 13.4 by showing The Home Depot's balance sheet and income statements presented in the common-size format.

In a common-size balance sheet, each asset appears as a percentage of total assets, and each liability or shareholders' equity item appears as a percentage of total liabilities and shareholders' equity. For example, in Exhibit 13.3, which presents The Home Depot's common-size balance sheets, Cash and Cash Equivalents was 3.5 percent of total assets [= ($1,421 ÷ $40,877) × 100] at the end of fiscal 2009.

EXHIBIT 13.3 | **Vertical (Common-Size) Analysis of The Home Depot's Summarized Balance Sheets**

THE HOME DEPOT Balance Sheets (In millions)	Fiscal 2009		Fiscal 2008	
	Amount	Percentage	Amount	Percentage
Assets				
Current Assets				
Cash and Cash Equivalents	$ 1,421	3.5%	$ 519	1.3%
Short-Term Investments	6	0.00	6	0.00
Accounts Receivable, Net	964	2.4	972	2.4
Inventories	10,188	24.9	10,673	25.9
Other Current Assets	1,321	3.2	1,192	2.9
Property and Equipment, Net	25,550	62.5	26,234	63.7
Notes Receivable	33	0.1	36	0.1
Goodwill	1,171	2.9	1,134	2.8
Other Assets	223	0.6	398	1.0
Total Assets	$40,877	100.0%	$41,164	100.0%*
Liabilities and Shareholders' Equity				
Current Liabilities	$10,363	25.4%	$11,153	27.1%
Long-Term Liabilities	11,121	27.2	12,234	29.7
Shareholders' Equity	19,393	47.4	17,777	43.2
Total Liabilities and Shareholders' Equity	$40,877	100.0%	$41,164	100.0%

*Numbers might not add due to rounding.

The common-size income statement reports each income statement item as a percentage of sales. For example, in Exhibit 13.4, which presents common-size income statements for The Home Depot for fiscal 2009 and 2008, cost of sales was equal to 66.1 percent of net sales revenue in 2009 [= ($43,764 ÷ $66,176) × 100].

RATIO COMPUTATIONS

Ratio analyses help financial statement users to understand relationships among various items reported in the financial statements. These analyses compare the amounts for one or more line items to the amounts for other line items in the same year. Ratio analyses are useful because they consider differences in the size of the amounts being compared, similar to common-size statements. In fact, some of the most popular ratios, such as net profit margin

THE HOME DEPOT
Income Statements
(In millions)

	Fiscal 2009		Fiscal 2008	
	Amount	Percentage	Amount	Percentage
Net Sales Revenue	$66,176	100.0%	$71,288	100.0%
Cost of Sales	43,764	66.1	47,298	66.3
Gross Profit	22,412	33.9	23,990	33.7
Operating and Other Expenses	17,609	26.6	19,631	27.5
Interest and Other Expenses	821	1.2	769	1.1
Income Tax Expense	1,362	2.1	1,278	1.8
Net Income from Continuing Operations	2,620	4.0	2,312	3.3
Earnings (loss) from Discontinued Operations	41	0.1	(52)	0.1
Net Income	$ 2,661	4.0%*	$ 2,260	3.2%

*Numbers might not add due to rounding.

and the debt-to-assets ratio, are taken directly from the common-size statements. Ratios allow users to evaluate how well a company has performed given the level of its other resources.

Most analysts classify ratios into three categories:

1. **Profitability** ratios, which relate to the company's performance in the current period—in particular, the company's ability to generate income.

2. **Liquidity** ratios, which relate to the company's short-term survival—in particular, the company's ability to use current assets to repay liabilities as they become due.

3. **Solvency** ratios, which relate to the company's long-run survival—in particular, the company's ability to repay lenders when debt matures and to make the required interest payments prior to the date of maturity.

Exhibit 13.5 organizes the ratios introduced in previous chapters according to these three categories, and demonstrates their calculations for fiscal 2009 using data from Exhibits 13.1 and 13.2.

 HOW'S IT GOING? Self-Study Practice

Let's assume for the year ended February 1, 2010, that Rona reported net income of $2.2 billion on sales of $71.3 billion. If the company's cost of sales that year was $47.3 billion, what was the company's gross profit percentage and net profit margin? If sales were $77.3 billion in the prior year, what was the year-over-year percentage decrease in the most recent year?

$$\text{Gross Profit Percentage} = \frac{(\$\boxed{} - \$\boxed{}) \text{ billion}}{\$71.3 \text{ billion}} \times 100 = \boxed{}$$

$$\text{Net Profit Margin} = \frac{\$2.2 \text{ billion}}{\boxed{}} \times 100 = \boxed{}$$

$$\text{Sales Decrease (Percentage)} = \frac{(\$\boxed{} - \$\boxed{}) \text{ billion}}{\$\boxed{} \text{ billion}} \times 100 = \boxed{}$$

After you have finished, check your answers with the solution in the margin.

Solution to Self-Study Practice

Gross Profit Percentage = ($71.3 − $47.3)/$71.3 × 100
= 33.7%

Net Profit Margin = $2.2/$71.3 × 100 = 3.1%

Sales Decrease (Percentage) = ($71.3 − $77.3)/$77.3 × 100
= −7.8%

EXHIBIT 13.5 | **Common Ratios Used in Financial Statement Analysis**

Profitability Ratios

THE HOME DEPOT
Fiscal 2009

(1) Net Profit Margin $= \dfrac{\text{Net Income}}{\text{Net Sales Revenue}} \times 100$
(Ch. 5, p. 211)

$\dfrac{\$2,661}{\$66,176} \times 100 = 4.0\%$

(2) Gross Profit Percentage $= \dfrac{\text{Net Sales Revenue} - \text{Cost of Goods Sold}}{\text{Net Sales Revenue}} \times 100$
(Ch. 6, p. 256)

$\dfrac{\$66,176 - \$43,764}{\$66,176} \times 100 = 33.9\%$

(3) Asset Turnover $= \dfrac{\text{Net Sales Revenue}}{\text{Average Total Assets}}$
(Ch. 5, p. 211)

$\dfrac{\$66,176}{(\$40,877 + \$41,164)/2} = 1.61$

(4) Fixed Asset Turnover $= \dfrac{\text{Net Sales Revenue}}{\text{Average Net Fixed Assets}}$
(Ch. 9, p. 385)

$\dfrac{\$66,176}{(\$25,550 + \$26,234)/2} = 2.56$

(5) Return on Equity (ROE) $= \dfrac{\text{Net Income}}{\text{Average Shareholders' Equity}} \times 100$
(Ch. 11, p. 484)

$\dfrac{\$2,661}{(\$19,393 \times \$17,777)/2} \times 100 = 14.3\%$

(6) Earnings per Share (EPS) $= \dfrac{\text{Net Income*}}{\text{Average Number of Common Shares Outstanding}}$
(Ch. 11, p. 484)

$\dfrac{\$2,661}{1,683} = \$1.58$

(7) Quality of Income $= \dfrac{\text{Net Cash from Operations}}{\text{Net Income}}$
(Ch. 12, p. 518)

$\dfrac{\$5,125}{\$2,661} = 1.93$

(8) Price/Earnings Ratio $= \dfrac{\text{Share Price}}{\text{EPS}}$
(Ch. 11, p. 484)

$\dfrac{\$27.30}{\$1.58} = 17.3$

Liquidity Ratios

(9) Receivables Turnover $= \dfrac{\text{Net Sales Revenue}}{\text{Average Net Receivables}}$
(Ch. 8, p. 341)

$\dfrac{\$66,176}{(\$964 + \$972)/2} = 68.4$

Days to Collect $= \dfrac{365}{\text{Receivables Turnover Ratio}}$
(Ch. 8, p. 341)

$\dfrac{365}{68.4} = 5.3$

(10) Inventory Turnover $= \dfrac{\text{Cost of Goods Sold}}{\text{Average Inventory}}$
(Ch. 7, p. 298)

$\dfrac{\$43,764}{(\$10,188 + \$10,673)/2} = 4.2$

Days to Sell $= \dfrac{365}{\text{Inventory Turnover Ratio}}$
(Ch. 7, p. 298)

$\dfrac{365}{4.2} = 86.9$

(11) Current Ratio $= \dfrac{\text{Current Assets}}{\text{Current Liabilities}}$
(Ch. 2, p. 61)

$\dfrac{\$13,900}{\$10,363} = 1.34$

(12) Quick Ratio $= \dfrac{\text{Cash} + \text{Short-Term Investments} + \text{Accounts Receivable, Net}}{\text{Current Liabilities}}$
(Ch. 10, p. 445)

$\dfrac{\$1,421 + \$6 + \$964}{\$10,363} = 0.23$

Solvency Ratios

(13) Debt to Assets $= \dfrac{\text{Total Liabilities}}{\text{Total Assets}}$
(Ch. 5, p. 211)

$\dfrac{\$21,484}{\$40,877} = 0.53$

(14) Times Interest Earned $= \dfrac{\text{Net Income} + \text{Interest Expense} + \text{Income Tax Expense}}{\text{Interest Expense}}$
(Ch. 10, p. 445)

$\dfrac{\$2,661 + \$821 + \$1,362}{\$821} = 5.9$

(15) Capital Acquisitions Ratio $= \dfrac{\text{Net Cash from Operations}}{\text{Cash Paid for PPE}}$
(Ch. 12, p. 519)

$\dfrac{\$5,125}{\$976} = 5.25$

*If a company has preferred shares outstanding, preferred dividends are subtracted from net income in the numerator to assess the earnings for each common share.

INTERPRETING HORIZONTAL AND VERTICAL ANALYSES

As noted in the previous section, financial statement analyses are not complete unless they lead to interpretations that help users understand and evaluate a company's financial results. When interpreting analyses, your goals should be to understand what each analysis is telling you and then combine your findings into a coherent "story" that explains the results of the company's business activities. We demonstrate how to do this, beginning with interpretations of each set of analyses shown in Exhibits 13.1–13.5 and later concluding with an overall summary of The Home Depot's results.

Trends Revealed in Horizontal Analyses

Learning Objective 5

Interpret the results of financial analyses.

Horizontal (trend) analysis of The Home Depot's balance sheet in Exhibit 13.1 shows that the company did not significantly grow or decline in fiscal 2009. Overall, total assets decreased only approximately 0.7 percent. The Home Depot explains the activities of the company in its Management's Discussion and Analysis (MD&A) section of the 2009 annual report. In fiscal 2009, The Home Depot made significant progress on its merchandising tools, which helped the company better manage markdown and clearance activity and control inventory better overall. This also allowed the company to reduce its inventory while improving its in-stock rate. Having better control of inventory allows The Home Depot to spend its cash in other areas, such as reducing Long-Term Debt by just over $1 billion.

Horizontal analysis of The Home Depot's income statement in Exhibit 13.2 indicates that the company faced a challenging economic environment in fiscal 2009, similar to that of 2008. Net Sales Revenue fell by 7 percent, which The Home Depot's MD&A explains was a result of the slowdown in the global economy and weaknesses in the United States residential construction, housing, and home improvement markets. At the same time, The Home Depot rolled out some new programs in fiscal 2009 that have brought beneficial simplification and focus to the business. We can see the benefits of these programs by a decrease in operating and other expenses of 10.3 percent. The overall impact on The Home Depot was an increase in Net Income of $401 million (17.7 percent).

In summary, the story revealed by the trend analysis is that despite the troubling economy in 2009, The Home Depot was able to implement programs and ideas to help streamline and better organize the company. This in turn allowed it to cut expenses, which offset the decrease in Net Sales Revenue.

Relationships Noted in Vertical Analyses

Vertical (common-size) analysis of The Home Depot's balance sheet in Exhibit 13.3 highlights key elements of the company. Its most significant assets have always been Inventories and Property and Equipment, but with the increases in inventory control mentioned earlier, inventory decreased and represented 24.9 percent of The Home Depot's total assets. Knowing that the economy hadn't completely recovered from 2008, according to The Home Depot's MD&A, the company decided to spend approximately $881 million less on property and equipment purchases. As noted in the horizontal analysis, the company's financing strategy was to reduce long-term debt, which it did by over $1 billion. This contributed to a shift in 2009 from debt to equity. Compared to fiscal 2008, when debt financing was 57 percent and equity was only 43 percent, the payment of Long-Term Debt allowed the debt financing to then represent only 53 percent. Equity financing therefore increased to 47 percent.

Vertical analysis of The Home Depot's income statement in Exhibit 13.4 indicates that Cost of Sales and Operating Expenses are the most important determinants of the company's profitability. Cost of Sales consumed 66.1 percent of Sales in 2009 and Operating Expenses consumed an additional 26.6 percent. Much of the increase in the company's Net Income (from 3.2 percent of Sales in 2008 to 4.0 in 2009) is explained by these two categories of expenses, as suggested by the horizontal analyses.

These findings from the vertical analyses serve to underscore findings from the horizontal analyses. The emerging story is that The Home Depot's success depends on its ability to streamline processes and benefit from the savings to offset the reduction in sales due to the weak economy that still existed in 2009.

INTERPRETING RATIO ANALYSES

As shown throughout other chapters in this book, benchmarks help when interpreting a company's ratios. These benchmarks can include the company's prior year results, as well as the results of close competitors or the average for the industry. In a competitive economy, companies strive to outperform one another, so comparisons against other companies can provide clues about who is likely to survive and thrive in the long run.

In the following analyses, we compare The Home Depot's financial ratios to the prior year and in some cases to those for Rona Inc. and the home improvement industry as a whole. (Rona's and The Home Depot's annual reports for fiscal 2009 are provided in Appendix A and Appendix B, respectively, at the back of this book or can be downloaded from the *Cases* section of Connect.)

Profitability Ratios

The analyses in this section focus on the level of profits The Home Depot generated during the period. We will analyze ratios (1) through (8) from Exhibit 13.5. The first two profitability ratios come right from the common-size income statement in Exhibit 13.4.

(1) Net Profit Margin Net profit margin represents the percentage of sales revenues that ultimately make it into net income, after deducting expenses. Using the equation in Exhibit 13.5, the calculation of The Home Depot's net profit margin for each of the two years yields

Fiscal Year		2009	2008
$\text{Net Profit Margin} = \dfrac{\text{Net Income}}{\text{Net Sales Revenue}} \times 100$		4.0%	3.2%

As discussed in the previous sections, although The Home Depot was faced with a challenging economic environment in 2009, it was able to cut costs enough to increase net income more than the decline of Net Sales Revenue. This allowed for the net profit margin to increase in 2009 over 2008 despite the weaker sales level

(2) Gross Profit Percentage Our earlier analysis indicated that The Home Depot's gross profit from 2008 to 2009 decreased in terms of total dollars, but it did not indicate whether that decrease was caused by less total sales or less profit per sale. The gross profit percentage is particularly helpful in this kind of analysis because it indicates how much profit was made, on average, on each dollar of sales after deducting the cost of goods sold. The Home Depot's gross profit percentage for 2008 and 2009 was

Fiscal Year		2009	2008
$\text{Gross Profit Percentage} = \dfrac{\text{Net Sales Revenue} - \text{Cost of Goods Sold}}{\text{Net Sales Revenue}} \times 100 =$		33.9%	33.7%

This analysis shows that in 2009, after deducting the cost of merchandise sold, 33.9 cents of each sales dollar were left to cover other costs, such as employee wages, advertising, and utilities, and to provide profits to the shareholders. The slight increase in the gross profit percentage from 2008 to 2009 (33.7% − 33.9%) means that The Home Depot made 0.002¢ more gross profit on each dollar of sales in 2009 than in 2008. There are two potential explanations for this slight increase: (1) The Home Depot charged higher selling prices without experiencing a corresponding increase in the cost of merchandise and (2) The Home Depot obtained merchandise at a lower unit cost. The MD&A section of The Home Depot's annual report explained that the increase in inventory control and inventory costs would ultimately help reduce the cost of the merchandise itself as the inventory is being better managed.

(3) Asset Turnover   The asset turnover ratio indicates the amount of sales revenue generated for each dollar invested in assets during the period. The Home Depot's ratios for the two years were

	2009	2008
$\text{Asset Turnover} = \dfrac{\text{Net Sales Revenue}}{\text{Average Total Assets}} =$	1.61	1.67

The asset turnover ratio suggests that The Home Depot's assets did not generate sales as efficiently in 2009 as in the previous year. To understand why, it is helpful to focus on the key assets used to generate sales. For a retailer such as The Home Depot, the key asset is store properties, which we can compare to sales using the fixed asset turnover ratio, discussed next.

(4) Fixed Asset Turnover   The fixed asset turnover ratio indicates how much revenue the company generates in sales for each dollar invested in fixed assets, such as store buildings and the property they sit on. The Home Depot's fixed asset turnover ratios for the two years were

	2009	2008
$\text{Fixed Asset Turnover} = \dfrac{\text{Net Sales Revenue}}{\text{Average Net Fixed Assets}} =$	2.56	2.65

This analysis shows that The Home Depot had $2.56 of sales in 2009 for each dollar invested in fixed assets. Although the decline from 2008 was not good, it is understandable because 2009 was a difficult year for retailers, as consumers struggled to keep their jobs and pay their mortgages, let alone work on major home improvement projects. The Home Depot's 2009 fixed asset turnover also suffered because the company's Net Sales Revenue dropped during the year. Still, The Home Depot's fixed asset turnover ratio was low compared to that of its main competitor, Rona, whose fixed asset turnover ratio was 5.53 in 2009. In terms of using fixed assets to generate sales revenue, Rona had a competitive advantage over The Home Depot in 2009. In other words, The Home Depot was operating less efficiently than its major competitor.

(5) Return on Equity (ROE)   The return on equity ratio compares the amount of net income to average shareholders' equity. Like the interest rate on your bank account, ROE reports the net amount earned during the period as a percentage of each dollar contributed by shareholders and retained in the business. The Home Depot's ROE ratios for 2008 and 2009 were

	2009	2008
$\text{Return on Equity (ROE)} = \dfrac{\text{Net Income}}{\text{Average Shareholders' Equity}} \times 100 =$	14.3%	12.7%

The Home Depot's ROE increase from 12.7 to 14.3 percent was inevitable, given our previous analyses. Specifically, horizontal analysis indicated that the company had increased its shareholders' equity to finance debt repayment. But with the weakened North American economy, sales decreased in 2009, and each dollar of sales generated less profit, as indicated by the net profit margin. Taken together, these results imply that net income as a percentage of average shareholders' equity was sure to fall in 2009. But it didn't. Instead it increased.

This is due to the fact that although profit on each sale decreased in 2009 from 2008, The Home Depot was able to cut Operating Expenses enough to still increase Net Income. This increased the average shareholders' equity, which in turn increased the ROE.

(6) Earnings per Share (EPS)   Earnings per Share indicates the amount of earnings generated for each common share outstanding. Consistent with the increase in ROE, the EPS ratio increased from $1.34 in 2008 to $1.58 in 2009, as shown below. This represents an increase of $0.24 per share ($1.58 − $1.34).

Fiscal Year		2009	2008
Earnings per Share (EPS) $= \dfrac{\text{Net Income}}{\text{Average Number of Common Shares Outstanding}}$		$1.58	$1.34

(7) Quality of Income   The quality of income ratio relates operating cash flows (from the statement of cash flows) to net income, as follows:

Fiscal Year		2009	2008
Quality of Income $= \dfrac{\text{Net Cash from Operations}}{\text{Net Income}}$		1.92	2.45

The ratio of 1.92 in 2009 indicates that The Home Depot generated $1.92 of operating cash flow for every dollar of net income. Because this ratio is much greater than 1.0, it is interpreted as "high quality," meaning that operations are producing even more positive results (cash flows from operating activities) than is suggested by the net income number. Most cash-based businesses, like home improvement stores, have high quality of income ratios because their sales are collected in cash immediately, and they report substantial noncash expenses like amortization. Consistent with this expectation, we see a high quality of income ratio for Rona (2.05) for fiscal 2009.

(8) Price/Earnings (P/E) Ratio   The P/E ratio relates the company's share price to its EPS, as follows:

Fiscal Year		2009	2008
Price/Earnings Ratio $= \dfrac{\text{Share Price}}{\text{EPS}}$		17.3	16.8

Using the going price for The Home Depot's shares when its 2009 and 2008 earnings were announced, the P/E ratio increased slightly in 2009 at 17.3 versus 16.8 in 2008. This means investors were willing to pay 17.3 times earnings to buy a share of The Home Depot's shares. Rona's P/E ratio at that time was around 14.0, suggesting that investors were less willing to buy shares in Rona than in The Home Depot.

Let's pause to summarize what we've learned so far. In fiscal 2009, The Home Depot continued to deal with the economic crisis where consumers were faced with rising interest and fuel costs and swelling unemployment rates, so they cut back on unnecessary spending such as major home improvement projects. To combat the fall in demand for its products and services, The Home Depot streamlined processes and improved inventory control at the individual store level. This allowed the company's net income to increase by 26.5 percent, or $0.24 per share. Investors seemed to be happy with the results and the progress made in 2009, because they were more willing to buy The Home Depot's shares in 2009 than they were in 2008 (at a price of 17.3 times earnings in 2009). The bottom line is that The Home Depot fared reasonably well during the continuation of the economic crisis in 2009.

Liquidity Ratios

The analyses in this section focus on a company's ability to survive in the short term by converting assets to cash that can be used to pay current liabilities as they come due. We interpret ratios (9) through (12) from Exhibit 13.5.

(9) Receivables Turnover Most home improvement retailers have low levels of accounts receivable relative to sales revenue because they collect the majority of their sales immediately in cash. Although the formula calls for net credit sales in the top of the ratio, companies rarely report their credit sales and cash sales separately. Consequently, financial statement users typically use total net sales revenue in the formula, which results in a receivables turnover ratio that is not terribly meaningful for businesses that make few sales on account. The formula is presented in Exhibit 13.5 simply to remind you of how it's calculated.

(10) Inventory Turnover The inventory turnover ratio indicates how frequently inventory is bought and sold during the year. The measure "days to sell" converts the inventory turnover ratio into the average number of days needed to sell each purchase of inventory.

Fiscal Year	2009	2008
$\text{Inventory Turnover} = \dfrac{\text{Cost of Goods Sold}}{\text{Average Inventory}}$	4.2	4.2
$\text{Days to Sell} = \dfrac{365}{\text{Inventory Turnover Ratio}}$	86.9	86.9

Although the weaker economy still existed in 2009, the inventory controls that The Home Depot implemented allowed it to maintain its inventory turnover at 4.2 times a year. On average, its inventory took 86.9 days to sell. These results are encouraging because almost every retailer's success depends on its ability to offer customers the right product when they need it at a price that beats the competition. Although most retailers experienced a decline in inventory turnover in 2009, The Home Depot's increase was very encouraging. The Home Depot enjoys a faster inventory turnover than other competitors because it carries fewer big-ticket items.

Turnover ratios vary significantly from one industry to the next. Companies in the food industry (restaurants and grocery stores) have high inventory turnover ratios because their inventory is subject to spoilage. Companies that sell expensive merchandise (automobiles and high-fashion clothes) have much slower turnover because sales of those items are infrequent, but these companies must carry lots of inventory so that customers have a wide selection to choose from when they do buy.

(11) Current Ratio The current ratio compares current assets to current liabilities, as follows:

Fiscal Year	2009	2008
$\text{Current Ratio} = \dfrac{\text{Current Assets}}{\text{Current Liabilities}}$	1.34	1.20

The current ratio measures the company's ability to pay its current liabilities. The Home Depot's ratio decreased from 2008 to 2009, given that a larger amount of Cash and Cash Equivalents was on hand at the end of 2009. Also with repaying some of the Long-Term Debt in 2009, the amount of the remaining Long-Term Debt to be paid in the current year (therefore a current liability) decreases as well. In this industry, a current ratio greater than 1.0 is deemed acceptable. Most analysts would judge The Home Depot's ratio to be very strong, especially considering the company's ability to generate cash.

(12) Quick Ratio The quick ratio compares the sum of cash, short-term investments, and accounts receivable to current liabilities as follows:

Fiscal Year	2009	2008
Quick Ratio = $\dfrac{\text{Cash} + \text{Short-Term Investments} + \text{Accounts Receivable, Net}}{\text{Current Liabilities}}$	0.23	0.13

The quick ratio is a much more stringent test of short-term liquidity than is the current ratio. The Home Depot's quick ratio increased in 2009, just as its current ratio did. The low quick ratio shown here is typical for industries where most customers buy with cash or credit card. These forms of payment result in very low levels of accounts receivable and the cash received from sales is often used immediately in other business activities. In industries where credit sales are common, the quick ratio may be much higher. For example, the average quick ratio in 2009 for the homebuilding industry was 0.66.

Solvency Ratios

The analyses in this section focus on The Home Depot's ability to survive over the long term—that is, its ability to repay debt when it matures, pay interest until that time, and finance the replacement and/or expansion of long-term assets. We interpret ratios (13) through (15) from Exhibit 13.5.

(13) Debt to Assets The debt-to-assets ratio indicates the proportion of total assets that creditors finance. Remember that creditors must be paid regardless of how difficult a year the company may have had. The higher this ratio, the riskier is the company's financing strategy. The Home Depot's ratio for the two years was

	2009	2008
Debt to Assets = $\dfrac{\text{Total Liabilities}}{\text{Total Assets}}$ =	0.53	0.57

The Home Depot's ratio of 0.53 in 2009 indicates that creditors contributed 53 percent of the company's financing, implying that shareholders' equity was the company's main source of financing at 47 percent (100 percent − 53 percent). The debt-to-assets ratio decreased slightly from 2008 to 2009, suggesting that The Home Depot relied less on creditors and more on shareholders when financing its acquisition of assets.

(14) Times Interest Earned The times interest earned ratio indicates how many times the company's interest expense was covered by its operating results. This ratio is calculated using accrual-based interest expense and net income before interest and income taxes, as follows:

	2009	2008
Times Interest Earned = $\dfrac{\text{Net Income} + \text{Interest Expense} + \text{Income Tax Expense}}{\text{Interest Expense}}$	5.9	5.6

A times interest earned ratio above 1.0 indicates that net income (before the costs of financing and taxes) is sufficient to cover the company's interest expense. The Home Depot's ratio of 5.9 indicates the company was generating more than enough profit to cover its interest expense.

COACH'S TIP

Instead of the debt-to-assets ratio, analysts might use a debt-to-equity ratio, which gives the same basic information as debt-to-assets. Debt-to-equity typically is calculated as Total Liabilities ÷ Total Shareholders' Equity. As with debt-to-assets, the higher the debt-to-equity ratio, the more the company relies on debt (rather than equity) financing.

COACH'S TIP

If the company reports a net loss rather than net income, include the loss as a negative number in the formula. A negative ratio indicates that the operating results (before the costs of financing and taxes) are insufficient to cover interest costs.

(15) Capital Acquisitions Ratio The capital acquisitions ratio compares cash flows from operations with cash paid for property and equipment. The ratio for the two years follows:

Fiscal Year		2009	2008
Capital Acquisitions = $\dfrac{\text{Net Cash from Operations}}{\text{Cash Paid for PPE}}$		5.25	2.93

The 5.25 capital acquisitions ratio in 2009 indicates that The Home Depot was able to pay for all its purchases of property, plant, and equipment using cash generated from operating activities.

In sum, these solvency ratios suggest that The Home Depot was financially well-positioned, even though the economy sputtered. In fiscal 2009, the company reduced its reliance on debt and was able to comfortably cover the interest expense incurred on that debt. Further, the company was able to purchase additional property, plant, and equipment without taking on more debt because its cash flow from operating activities exceeded the cost of its new property and equipment.

HOW'S IT GOING? Self-Study Practice

Show the computations for the following two ratios for The Home Depot for fiscal 2008. Use the information in Exhibits 13.1 and 13.2.

a. Times interest earned ratio

b. Current ratio

After you have finished, check your answers with the solution in the margin.

UNDERLYING ACCOUNTING DECISIONS AND CONCEPTS

Accounting Decisions

Learning Objective 6

Describe how analyses depend on key accounting decisions and concepts.

In the analyses just presented, we compared The Home Depot's results with those of Rona Inc. When appropriate, we discussed how differences in the two companies' strategies (for example, relying on debt versus equity financing) and business operations (for example, carrying big-ticket versus less expensive items) affected their financial ratios. We should also consider whether differences between the two companies' financial ratios might be caused by differences in their accounting decisions.

Information about a company's accounting decisions is presented in a note to the financial statements. Exhibit 13.6 shows the policies that three home improvement retailers follow

EXHIBIT 13.6	Comparison of Accounting Methods		

	The Home Depot	Rona	Lowe's
Inventory	FIFO	Weighted Average Cost	FIFO
Amortization	Straight-line Buildings: 5–45 yrs Equipment: 3–20 yrs	Straight-line Buildings: 25 yrs Equipment: 3–10 yrs	Straight-line Buildings: 10–40 yrs Equipment: 3–15 yrs

in accounting for inventory and amortization—two line items that can have a noticeable impact on a retailer's results. Take a moment to study the exhibit.

As you can see, the three companies follow similar but not identical policies. The Home Depot and Lowe's use the FIFO method of accounting for inventory and cost of goods sold; Rona Inc. uses the weighted average method. Although these two methods result in different numbers, the overall impact on the companies' financial ratios should be minor because inventory costs did not rise rapidly in 2009.

All three companies calculate amortization using the straight-line method, with a similar range of estimated useful lives for buildings and equipment. Because buildings and equipment make up such a large portion of each company's assets, these similarities go a long way toward making their financial results comparable. In conclusion, although the companies' accounting policies have some differences, these policies are unlikely to have a major impact on our comparisons.

SPOTLIGHT ON THE WORLD

Caution Required When Comparing Financial Statements

Rona Inc. dominates the Canadian home improvement industry, as does The Home Depot in the United States. Kingfisher plc is Europe's largest home improvement retailer, with market-leading positions in the United Kingdom, France, Poland, Turkey, and China. Comparing annual report financial statements for Kingfisher (Appendix C) and The Home Depot (Appendix B) for the 2009 fiscal year, Kingfisher's gross profit percentage of 36.2 percent appears to be better than The Home Depot's 33.9 percent, despite Kingfisher's 3 percent cost of sales increase. Direct comparisons however should be made with caution, as companies may be using different standards for financial reporting purposes. In this case, for example, Kingfisher follows IFRS, while The Home Depot uses U.S. GAAP. Rona annual report statements have also been provided at the back of this book (in Appendix A), so, you can compare Kingfisher's use of IFRS to Rona's use of Canadian GAAP and The Home Depot's use of U.S. GAAP.

Accounting Concepts

Before wrapping up this chapter, it's worth revisiting the accounting concepts that were introduced in previous chapters. At this stage of the course, you should have developed a fairly good understanding of the rules of accounting and be better able to appreciate why accounting relies on these particular concepts. Exhibit 13.7 presents the conceptual framework for financial accounting and reporting that was first introduced in Chapter 1. The concepts that you have already learned about in prior chapters are highlighted in red in Exhibit 13.7.

EXHIBIT 13.7 | Conceptual Framework for Financial Accounting and Reporting

Objective of External Financial Reporting
To provide useful financial information to external users for decision making (Ch.1)
- It must be relevant and a faithful representation of the business
- It is more useful if it is comparable, verifiable, timely, and understandable

Elements to Be Measured and Reported
- Assets, Liabilities, Shareholders' Equity, Revenues, Expenses (Ch.1)

Concepts for Measuring and Reporting Information
- **Assumptions:** Unit of Measure (Ch.1), Separate Entity (Ch.1), Going Concern, Time Period (Ch.3)
- **Principles:** Cost (Ch.2), Revenue Recognition (Ch.3), Matching (Ch.3), Full Disclosure
- **Exceptions:** Cost–Benefit, Materiality (Ch.5), Industry Practices

As shown in Exhibit 13.7, the primary objective of financial accounting and reporting is to provide useful financial information for people external to a company to use in making decisions about the company. To be useful, this information must be relevant and faithfully represent the underlying business.

As Exhibit 13.7 indicates, only four accounting concepts have not been introduced in previous chapters, so we will explain them here. The **going-concern** (also called *continuity*) **assumption** quietly underlies accounting rules. It is the belief that any business will be capable of continuing its operations long enough to realize its recorded assets and meet its obligations in the normal course of business. If a company runs into severe financial difficulty (such as bankruptcy), this assumption may no longer be appropriate, leading to what is called a *going-concern problem*. If a company encounters a going-concern problem, it may need to adjust the amount and classification of items in its financial statements, which would be explained in the financial statement notes and to which the auditor's report would draw attention. Some of the factors that commonly contribute to going-concern problems are listed in Exhibit 13.8. Notice that some of the analyses presented earlier in this chapter are key inputs into determining whether a company has a going-concern problem.

YOU SHOULD KNOW

Going-concern assumption: A business is assumed to be capable of continuing its operations long enough to meet its obligations.

EXHIBIT 13.8	Factors Contributing to Going-Concern Problems

Revealed by Financial Analyses	Revealed by Other Analyses
• Declining sales	• Overdependence on one customer
• Declining gross profit	• Insufficient product innovation/quality
• Significant one-time expenses	• Significant barriers to expansion
• Fluctuating net income	• Loss of key personnel without replacement
• Insufficient current assets	• Inability to negotiate favourable purchases
• Excessive reliance on debt financing	• Inadequate maintenance of long-lived assets
• Adverse financial commitments	• Loss of a key patent

YOU SHOULD KNOW

Full disclosure principle: Financial statements should present information needed to understand the financial results of the company's business activities.

Industry practices constraint: Companies in certain industries may follow accounting rules peculiar to that industry.

Cost-benefit constraint: Companies should follow accounting rules to the extent that the benefits outweigh the costs of doing so.

One of the principles of accounting that was not previously explained is full disclosure. Simply put, according to the **full disclosure principle,** financial reports should present all information that is needed to properly interpret the results of the company's business activities. This doesn't mean that every single transaction needs to be explained in detail, but rather that adequate information needs to be presented to allow financial statement users to fairly interpret reports about the company's income, financial position, and cash flows.

Despite the best efforts to make accounting rules applicable in as many situations as possible, there are limits on how broadly they can be applied. These limits, or constraints, are listed in Exhibit 13.7. Two constraints not introduced in previous chapters relate to industry practices and cost–benefit trade-offs. The **industry practices constraint** is that companies in some industries, such as financial services and oil, gas, and agricultural production, have such unique circumstances that they need to use accounting rules that differ somewhat from what companies in most other industries use. The **cost–benefit constraint** recognizes that it is costly for companies to gather all the financial information that could possibly be reported. Accounting rules need to be implemented only to the extent that the informational benefits outweigh the costs of doing so.

Before we finish the discussion of this topic, take a moment to complete the following Self-Study Practice. It'll give you a good idea of whether you need a detailed review of the concepts introduced in earlier chapters or whether you're ready to move on to review and practise key aspects of this chapter.

HOW'S IT GOING? Self-Study Practice

Match each statement below to the assumption, principle, or constraint to which it most closely relates.

1. Everything comes down to dollars and cents.
2. That's not our issue. It's for somebody else to report.
3. Don't sweat it. It's not big enough to worry about.
4. We'll make an exception, but only because you're special.
5. If it relates to this period, you'd better report it.
6. I've told you everything you could possibly want to know.
7. At that rate, you may not survive past the end of the year.
8. I know it's a long time, but let's look at it in stages.
9. You can reach a point where it's just not worth all the trouble.

(a) Separate entity
(b) Matching
(c) Going concern
(d) Unit of measure
(e) Time period
(f) Cost-benefit
(g) Materiality
(h) Industry practices
(i) Full disclosure

After you have finished, check your answers with the solution in the margin.

You have now seen enough to interpret most basic financial statements. When analyzing real-world financial statements, you will probably encounter nonrecurring or other special items reported in the income statement. These items are discussed in the following Supplement 13A.

SUPPLEMENT 13A: Nonrecurring and Other Special Items

Nonrecurring Items

Until 2005, three different types of nonrecurring items were reported in income statements: discontinued operations, extraordinary items, and the cumulative effects of changes in accounting methods. Recently, however, new accounting standards have nearly eliminated income statement reporting of extraordinary items and the cumulative effects of changes in accounting methods. In fact, the definition of extraordinary has become so restricted that few events—not even the losses that arose from Hurricane Katrina—qualify as extraordinary. The cumulative effects of changes in accounting methods are reported as adjustments to Retained Earnings rather than as part of the income statement in the period when the change is made. (The technical procedures used to make these adjustments are discussed in intermediate accounting courses.) That leaves only one remaining nonrecurring item—discontinued operations.

Discontinued operations result from abandoning or selling a major business component. Because an abandoned or sold business unit will not affect financial results in future years, its results for the current year are reported on a separate line of the income statement following Income Tax Expense. This discontinued operations line includes any gain or loss on disposal of the discontinued operation as well as any operating income generated before its disposal. Because this appears below the Income Tax Expense line, any related tax effects are netted against (included with) the gains or losses on discontinued operations. Exhibit 13A.1 shows how The Home Depot reported discontinued operations one year.

YOU SHOULD KNOW

Discontinued operations: Result from the disposal of a major component of the business and are reported net of income tax effects.

THE HOME DEPOT, INC.
Condensed Income Statements
For the Year Ended January 31, 2010
(in millions)

Net Sales	$66,176
Cost of Sales	43,764
Gross Profit	22,412
Selling, General, and Administrative Expenses	15,902
Amortization Expense	1,707
Income from Operations	4,803
Interest and Other Expenses, Net	821
Income from Continuing Operations before Income Tax Expense	3,982
Income Tax Expense	1,362
Net Income from Continuing Operations	2,620
Income from Discontinued Operations, Net of Tax	41
Net Income	$ 2,661

Other Special Items: ASPE vs. IFRS

In some cases, companies include additional items on their income statements after the net income line. These items may be added to or subtracted from net income to arrive at the amount of comprehensive income. These companies would be using IFRS because ASPE does not use comprehensive income. As you can learn in detail in intermediate financial accounting courses, these items represent gains or losses relating to changes in the value of certain balance sheet accounts. While most gains and losses are included in the computation of net income, some (relating to changes in foreign currency exchange rates and the value of certain investments, for example) are excluded from net income and included only in comprehensive income. The main reason for excluding these gains and losses from net income is that the changes in value that created them may well disappear before they are ever realized (when the company sells the related assets or liabilities). For this reason, most analysts will take a moment to consider the size of these special items in relation to net income. If the amount is not large, they will exclude the items in calculating profitability ratios.

SUPPLEMENT 13B: Reviewing and Contrasting ASPE and IFRS

In this supplement, we review and contrast ASPE and IFRS as they relate to topics raised in earlier chapters of this text. We begin with a theoretical discussion of similarities and differences between ASPE and IFRSP that potentially affect the accounting rules for specific topics. We then follow with a summary of specific topic discussions.

Overview

Generally speaking, ASPE and IFRS are similar in that both aim to guide businesses in reporting financial information that is relevant and that faithfully represents the underlying activities of businesses. At a basic level, these accounting rules describe (1) when an item should be recognized in the accounting system, (2) how that item should be classified (e.g., asset or expense, revenue or liability), and (3) the amount at which each item should be measured.

Although some exceptions exist, both ASPE and IFRS require that items be recorded only after an exchange between the company and another party. Initially, these items are recorded at the value they enter the company (called the *entry price* or *historical cost*). Later, this value may be revised (upward or downward) as a result of events or changes in circumstances. The new value may be (1) the entry price adjusted for items such as interest or amortization, (2) a current market price, or (3) another computed amount (such as the *fair value* or *exit price* that the company would receive or pay in the future for that item).

Many differences between ASPE and IFRS that we have noted in this book relate to cases where IFRS requires or allows companies to report items using values that differ from those required or allowed by ASPE. For example, in Chapter 7, we noted that IFRS allows (and ASPE prohibits) the reversal of write-downs in inventory value. Similarly, in Chapter 9, we noted that IFRS allows companies to report fixed assets at fair values. Intermediate accounting courses will expand on these situations and add others. For now, though, just focus on gaining a general awareness of the ways in which accounting rules may differ. Refer to the following Spotlight on IFRS and ASPE, which gives a quick review of the specific cases introduced in previous chapters.

SPOTLIGHT ON IFRS and ASPE

Specific Topics Introduced in Earlier Chapters

Chapter 1
- **Page 19**. Discusses financial reporting standards in Canada and the basic differences between ASPE and IFRS.

Chapter 2
- **Page 63**. Discusses differences in level of detail in ASPE versus IFRS materials, and the increased role for transaction analysis skills and judgment in accounting.

Chapter 5
- **Pages 206–208**. Outlines financial statement presentation differences, including financial statement titles, ordering of accounts, and grouping of items. Illustrates a European company's statement of financial position and presents a glimpse into future possible directions for financial statement formatting.

Chapter 7
- **Page 293**. Explains that IFRS prohibits LIFO.
- **Page 300**. Discusses how IFRS allows (and ASPE prohibits) reversals of write-downs when inventory recovers in value.

Chapter 9
- **Page 371**. Discusses IFRS's accounting for component costs.
- **Page 384**. Discusses IFRS's accounting for R&D and revaluation at fair value.

Chapter 10
- **Page 420**. Discusses IFRS's current classification of long-term debt involving violated loan covenants.
- **Page 429**. Discusses IFRS's threshold for accruing contingent liabilities.

Chapter 11
- **Page 473**. Discusses classification of some preferred shares as a liability.

Chapter 12
- **Page 507**. Illustrates differences in classification of dividends and interest received and paid, under IFRS and ASPE.

Chapter 13
- **Page 567**. Discusses the potential impact of accounting differences on ratio analyses.

This section provides a chance to solidify your understanding of key points. It's worth your time to work through the following demonstration case, scan the chapter summary, test your understanding of key-terms, and then practise, practise, practise.

DEMONSTRATION CASE

The following information was taken from Avericana Company's fiscal 2012 annual report.

(In millions of dollars)	Year Ended January 28, 2012 (Fiscal 2011)	
Net Sales Revenue	$90,837	
Cost of Goods Sold	61,054	
Net Income	5,761	
	January 28, 2012 (Fiscal 2011)	January 29, 2011 (Fiscal 2010)
Inventory	$12,822	$11,401
Current Assets	18,000	15,269
Property and Equipment, Net	26,605	24,901
Total Assets	52,263	44,405
Current Liabilities	12,931	12,706
Total Liabilities	27,233	17,496

Required:

1. Compute the following ratios for Avericana for the year ended January 28, 2012.
   Fixed Asset Turnover
   Return on Equity
   Days to Sell
   Current Ratio
   Debt to Assets

2. Interpret the meaning of the ratios you calculated in requirement 1.

Suggested Solution

1. Calculating ratios:

Fixed Asset Turnover = Net Sales Revenue/Average Net Fixed Assets
   = $90,837 ÷ [($26,605 + $24,901) ÷ 2]
   = 3.53

Return on Equity = Net Income/Average Shareholders' Equity
   = $5,761 ÷ [($25,030 + $26,909) ÷ 2]
   = 0.2218, or 22.2%

Days to Sell = 365 ÷ Inventory Turnover Ratio
   = 365 ÷ (Cost of Goods Sold/Average Inventory)
   = 365 ÷ [$61,054 ÷ [($12,822 + $11,401) ÷ 2]]
   = 72

Current Ratio = Current Assets/Current Liabilities
   = $18,000 ÷ $12,931
   = 1.39

Debt to Assets = Total Liabilities/Total Assets
   = $27,233 ÷ $52,263
   = 0.52

2. Interpreting ratios

- The fixed asset turnover ratio of 3.53 means that, on average, Avericana generated $3.53 of sales for each dollar of fixed assets.

- The return on equity of 22.2 percent means that Avericana's net income for the year was 22.2 percent of the amount investors contributed to and left in the company.

- The days to sell ratio of 72 means that, on average, 72 days elapsed between the time Avericana acquired the inventory and the time the company sold it.

- The current ratio of 1.39 means that at year-end, Avericana had $1.39 of current assets for each dollar of current liabilities.

- The debt-to-assets ratio of 0.52 means that Avericana relied on short-term and long-term debt to finance 52 percent of its assets, implying that shareholders' equity financed 48 percent ($=100 - 52$) of its total assets.

CHAPTER SUMMARY

Describe the purposes and uses of horizontal, vertical, and ratio analyses. p. 554   LO1

- Horizontal analyses (also called *trend analyses*) compare financial statement items to comparable amounts in prior periods with the goal of identifying sustained changes or trends.

- Vertical analyses create common-size financial statements that express each line of the income statement (or balance sheet) as a percentage of total sales (or total assets).

- Ratio analyses compare one or more financial statement items to an amount for other items for the same year. Ratios take into account differences in the size of amounts to allow for evaluations of performance given existing levels of other company resources.

Use horizontal (trend) analyses to recognize financial changes that unfold over time. p. 555   LO2

- Trend analyses involve computing the dollar amount by which each account changes from one period to the next and expressing that change as a percentage of the balance for the prior period.

Use vertical (common-size) analyses to understand important relationships within financial statements. p. 557   LO3

- Vertical (common-size) analyses indicate the proportions within each financial statement category.

Calculate financial ratios to assess profitability, liquidity, and solvency. p. 557   LO4

- Financial ratios are commonly classified with relation to profitability, liquidity, or solvency. Exhibit 13.5 lists common ratios in these three categories and shows how to compute them.

- Profitability ratios focus on measuring the adequacy of a company's income by comparing it to other items reported on the financial statements.

- Liquidity ratios measure a company's ability to meet its current debt obligations.

- Solvency ratios measure a company's ability to meet its long-term debt obligations.

Interpret the results of financial analyses. p. 560   LO5

- Financial analyses are not complete unless they lead to an interpretation that helps financial statement users understand and evaluate a company's financial results.

- An understanding of whether a business is successful emerges only after you have learned to combine analyses into a complete picture or story that depicts the company's performance.

- To assist in developing this picture or story, most analysts use benchmarks for comparison, such as the company's performance in prior years or competitors' performance in the current year.

Describe how analyses depend on key accounting decisions and concepts. p. 566   LO6

- Before comparing across companies or time periods, users should determine the extent to which differences in accounting decisions (e.g., methods used to account for inventory, amortization, contingent liabilities, etc.) might reduce comparability or consistency of the financial information being compared.

- Many accounting concepts were presented throughout earlier chapters, all of which aim to make accounting information more useful for creditors and investors. Four new concepts were explained in this chapter:

1. Going-concern (continuity) assumption—A business is assumed to continue to operate into the foreseeable future.
2. Full disclosure principle—A company's financial statements should provide all information that is important to users' decisions.
3. Industry practices constraint—General purpose accounting rules may not apply equally to all industries, recognizing that some industries may use industry-specific measurements and reporting practices.
4. Cost–benefit constraint—Accounting rules should be followed to the extent that the benefits to users outweigh the costs of providing the required information.

ACCOUNTING DECISION TOOLS

See Exhibit 13.5 on page 559 for a summary

KEY TERMS

Cost–Benefit Constraint p. 568
Discontinued Operations p. 569
Full Disclosure Principle p. 568
Going-Concern Assumption p. 568

Horizontal (Trend) Analyses p. 555
Industry Practices Constraint p. 568
Liquidity p. 558
Profitability p. 558

Solvency p. 558
Vertical (Common-Size) Analyses p. 557

See complete definitions in the glossary in the back of this text.

HOMEWORK HELPER

Helpful reminders

- Ratios that include both income statement and balance sheet accounts require you to calculate an average for the balance sheet accounts rather than just use the end-of-period balance. An average ensures that the balance sheet data cover the same period as the income statement data.
- To calculate averages for the current and prior years, you will need three years of balance sheet data. (The statement of shareholders' equity reports three years of shareholders' equity data. To calculate averages for other balance sheet accounts, you will need comparative balance sheets from at least two annual reports.)
- The pronoun for referring to a specific company is "it," not "they" and "its," not "their."

Frequent mistakes

- In calculating year-over-year percentages, divide the change in the account balance by its balance from the prior year, not the current year.

Practice Material

QUESTIONS (⑤ Symbol indicates questions that require analysis from more than one perspective.)

1. What is the general goal of trend analysis?
2. How is a year-over-year percentage calculated?
3. What is ratio analysis? Why is it useful?
4. What benchmarks are commonly used for interpreting ratios?

5. In what three categories of performance are most financial ratios reported? To what in particular do each of these categories relate?
6. Why are some analyses called *horizontal* and others called *vertical?*

7. Slow Cellar's current ratio increased from 1.2 to 1.5. What is one favourable interpretation of this change? What is one unfavourable interpretation of this change? Ⓢ

8. From 2011 to 2012, Colossal Company's current ratio increased and its quick ratio decreased. What does this imply about the level of inventory and prepaids? Ⓢ

9. From 2011 to 2012, Mechanic International reported that its Net Sales increased from $300,000 to $400,000, and its Gross Profit increased from $90,000 to $130,000. Was the Gross Profit increase caused by (a) an increase in sales volume only, (b) an increase in gross profit per sale only, or (c) a combination of both? Explain your answer. Ⓢ

10. Explain whether the following situations, taken independently, would be favourable or unfavourable: (a) increase in gross profit percentage, (b) decrease in inventory turnover ratio, (c) increase in earnings per share, (d) decrease in days to collect, (e) increase in net profit margin, and (f) decrease in quick ratio.

11. What are the two essential characteristics of useful financial information? What other characteristics enhance the usefulness of financial information?

12. What is the primary objective of financial reporting?

13. What is the full disclosure principle?

14. What is the going-concern assumption? What is a going-concern problem? What factors can contribute to such a problem?

15. How do industry practices and cost–benefit constraints impact financial reporting?

16. TechCo is a U.S. company that uses the LIFO inventory method. You plan to compare its ratios to Euroten, but you are concerned because Euroten uses IFRS. What accounting policy difference is certain to exist between the two companies? Of the ratios in Exhibit 13.5, name five that will be affected by this difference. Ⓢ

17. (Supplement 13A) Name the most commonly reported non-recurring item, and explain where and how it is reported on the income statement.

Multiple-choice questions and corresponding answers can be found on Connect.

MINI-EXERCISES

M13-1 Calculations for Horizontal Analyses
LO2

Using the following income statements, perform the calculations needed for horizontal analyses. Round percentages to one decimal place.

LOCKEY FENCING CORPORATION
Income Statements
For the Years Ended December 31

	2012	2011
Net Sales	$100,000	$75,000
Cost of Goods Sold	58,000	45,000
Gross Profit	42,000	30,000
Selling, General, and Administrative Expenses	9,000	4,500
Income from Operations	33,000	25,500
Interest Expense	3,000	3,750
Income before Income Tax	30,000	21,750
Income Tax Expense	9,000	6,525
Net Income	$ 21,000	$15,225

M13-2 Calculations for Vertical Analyses
LO3

Refer to M13-1. Perform the calculations needed for vertical analyses. Round percentages to one decimal place.

M13-3 Interpreting Horizontal Analyses
LO5

Refer to the calculations from M13-1. What are the two most significant year-over-year changes in terms of dollars and in terms of percentages? Give one potential cause of each of these changes.

M13-4 Inferring Financial Information Using Gross Profit Percentage
LO4

Your campus computer store reported Sales Revenue of $168,000. The company's gross profit percentage was 60.0 percent. What amount of Cost of Goods Sold did the company report?

LO2, 3, 4 **M13-5 Inferring Financial Information Using Gross Profit Percentage and Year-over-Year Comparisons**

A consumer products company reported a 25 percent increase in sales from 2011 to 2012. Sales in 2011 were $200,000. In 2012, the company reported Cost of Goods Sold in the amount of $150,000. What was the gross profit percentage in 2012? Round to one decimal place.

LO4 **M13-6 Computing the Return on Equity Ratio**

Given the following data, compute the 2012 return on equity ratio (expressed as a percentage with one decimal place).

	2012	2011
Net Income	$ 1,850,000	$ 1,600,000
Shareholders' Equity	10,000,000	13,125,000
Total Assets	24,000,000	26,000,000
Interest Expense	400,000	300,000

LO4, 5 **M13-7 Analyzing the Inventory Turnover Ratio**

A manufacturer reported an inventory turnover ratio of 8.6 during 2011. During 2012, management introduced a new inventory control system that was expected to reduce average inventory levels by 25 percent without affecting sales volume. Given these circumstances, would you expect the inventory turnover ratio to increase or decrease during 2012? Explain.

LO4 **M13-8 Inferring Financial Information Using the Current Ratio**

Mystic Laboratories reported total assets of $11,200,000 and noncurrent assets of $1,480,000. The company also reported a current ratio of 1.5. What amount of current liabilities did the company report?

LO4 **M13-9 Inferring Financial Information Using the P/E Ratio**

In 2011, Big W Company reported earnings per share of $2.50 when its shares were selling for $50.00. If its 2012 earnings increase by 10 percent and the P/E ratio remains constant, what will be the price of its shares?

LO4, 5 **M13-10 Identifying Relevant Ratios**

Identify the ratio that is relevant to answering each of the following questions.

a. How much net income does the company earn from each dollar of sales?
b. Is the company financed primarily by debt or equity?
c. How many dollars of sales were generated for each dollar invested in fixed assets?
d. How many days, on average, does it take the company to collect on credit sales made to customers?
e. How much net income does the company earn for each dollar that owners have invested in it?
f. Does the company's net income convert into more or less cash flow from operating activities?
g. Does the company have sufficient assets to convert into cash for paying liabilities as they come due in the upcoming year?

EXERCISES

Mc Graw Hill **connect**™
Practise and learn online with Connect.

LO2, 3, 5 **E13-1 Preparing and Interpreting a Schedule for Horizontal and Vertical Analyses**

Suncor Energy Inc.

The average price of a litre of gas in 2011 jumped $0.17 (16 percent) from $1.04 in 2010 to $1.21 in 2011. Let's see whether these changes are reflected in the income statement of Suncor Energy Inc. for the year ended December 31, 2011 (amounts in billions).

	2011	2010
Total Revenues	$273	$221
Costs of Crude Oil and Products	171	133
Other Operating Costs	59	56
Income before Income Tax Expense	43	32
Income Tax Expense	19	13
Net Income	$ 24	$ 19

Required:

1. Conduct a horizontal analysis by calculating the year-over-year changes in each line item, expressed in dollars and in percentages (rounded to one decimal place). How did the change in gas prices compare to the changes in Suncor's total revenues and costs of crude oil and products?

2. Conduct a vertical analysis by expressing each line as a percentage of total revenues (round to one decimal place). Excluding income tax and other operating costs, did Suncor earn more profit per dollar of revenue in 2011 compared to 2010?

E13-2 Computing and Interpreting Profitability Ratios

Use the information for Suncor Energy Inc. in E13-1 to complete the following requirements.

LO4, 5

Suncor Energy Inc.

Required:

1. Compute the gross profit percentage for each year (one decimal place). Assuming that the change for 2010 to 2011 is the beginning of a sustained trend, is Suncor likely to earn more or less gross profit from each dollar of sales in 2012?

2. Compute the net profit margin for each year (expressed as a percentage with one decimal place). Given your calculations here and in requirement 1, explain whether Suncor did a better or worse job of controlling expenses other than the costs of crude oil and products in 2011 relative to 2010.

3. Assume Suncor reported average net fixed assets of $85 billion in 2011 and $74 billion in 2010. Compute the fixed asset turnover ratios for both years (round to two decimal places). Did the company better utilize its investment in fixed assets to generate revenues in 2011 or 2010?

4. Assume Suncor reported average shareholders' equity of $82 billion in 2011 and $73 billion in 2010. Compute the return on equity ratios for both years (expressed as a percentage with one decimal place). Did the company generate greater returns for shareholders in 2011 or 2010?

Check Figure:
[Req. 3]
2011 Fixed Asset
Turnover = $3.21

E13-3 Preparing and Interpreting a Schedule for Horizontal and Vertical Analyses

LO2, 3, 5

Assume the average cost of computer equipment fell 20.9 percent between 2010 and 2011. Let's see whether these changes are reflected in the income statement of Computer Tycoon Inc. for the year ended December 31, 2011.

	2011	2010
Sales Revenues	$98,913	$121,761
Cost of Goods Sold	59,249	71,583
Gross Profit	39,664	50,178
Selling, General, and Administrative Expenses	36,943	36,934
Interest Expense	565	474
Income before Income Tax Expense	2,156	12,770
Income Tax Expense	1,024	5,540
Net Income	$ 1,132	$ 7,230

Required:

1. Conduct a horizontal analysis by calculating the year-over-year changes in each line item, expressed in dollars and in percentages (rounded to one decimal place). How did the change in computer prices compare to the changes in Computer Tycoon's sales revenues?

2. Conduct a vertical analysis by expressing each line as a percentage of total revenues (round to one decimal place). Excluding income tax, interest, and selling, general, and administrative expenses, did Computer Tycoon earn more profit per dollar of sales in 2011 compared to 2010?

E13-4 Computing Profitability Ratios

LO4, 5

Use the information in E13-3 to complete the following requirements.

Required:

1. Compute the gross profit percentage for each year (one decimal place). Assuming that the change for 2010 to 2011 is the beginning of a sustained trend, is Computer Tycoon likely to earn more or less gross profit from each dollar of sales in 2012?

2. Compute the net profit margin for each year (expressed as a percentage with one decimal place). Given your calculations here and in requirement 1, explain whether Computer Tycoon did a better or worse job of controlling operating expenses in 2011 relative to 2010.

3. Computer Tycoon reported average net fixed assets of $54,200 in 2011 and $45,100 in 2010. Compute the fixed asset turnover ratios for both years (round to two decimal places). Did the company better utilize its investment in fixed assets to generate revenues in 2011 or 2010?

4. Computer Tycoon reported average shareholders' equity of $54,000 in 2011 and $40,800 in 2010. Compute the return on equity ratios for both years (expressed as a percentage with one decimal place). Did the company generate greater returns for shareholders in 2011 than in 2010?

Check Figure:
[Req. 4]
2011 Return on Equity = 2.1%

LO4, 5 **E13-5 Computing a Commonly Used Solvency Ratio**

Use the information in E13-3 to complete the following requirement.

Required:

Compute the times interest earned ratios for 2011 and 2010. In your opinion, does Computer Tycoon generate sufficient net income (before taxes and interest) to cover the cost of debt financing?

LO4 **E13-6 Matching Each Ratio with Its Computational Formula**

Match each ratio or percentage with its formula by entering the appropriate letter for each numbered item.

Ratios or Percentages	Formula
_____ 1. Current ratio	A. Net income ÷ Net sales revenue
_____ 2. Net profit margin	B. (Net sales revenue − Cost of goods sold) ÷ Net sales revenue
_____ 3. Inventory turnover ratio	C. Current assets ÷ Current liabilities
_____ 4. Gross profit percentage	D. Cost of goods sold ÷ Average inventory
_____ 5. Fixed asset turnover	E. Net credit sales revenue ÷ Average net receivables
_____ 6. Capital acquisitions ratio	F. Net cash flows from operating activities ÷ Net income
_____ 7. Return on equity	G. Net income ÷ Average number of common shares outstanding
_____ 8. Times interest earned	H. Total liabilities ÷ Total assets
_____ 9. Debt-to-assets ratio	I. (Net income + Interest expense + Income tax expense) ÷ Interest expense
_____ 10. Price/earnings ratio	J. Net cash flows from operating activities ÷ Cash paid for property, plant, and equipment
_____ 11. Receivables turnover ratio	K. Current market price per share ÷ Earnings per share
_____ 12. Earnings per share	L. Net income ÷ Average total shareholders' equity
_____ 13. Quality of income ratio	M. Net sales revenue ÷ Average net fixed assets

LO4, 5 **E13-7 Computing and Interpreting Selected Liquidity Ratios**

Double West Suppliers (DWS) reported sales for the year of $300,000, all on credit. The average gross profit percentage was 40 percent on sales. Account balances follow:

	Beginning	Ending
Accounts receivable (net)	$45,000	$55,000
Inventory	60,000	40,000

Required:

Check Figure:
[Req. 2]
Average days to sell =
101.4 days

1. Compute the turnover ratios for accounts receivable and inventory (round to one decimal place).

2. By dividing 365 by your ratios from requirement 1, calculate the average days to collect receivables and the average days to sell inventory (round to one decimal place).

3. Explain what each of these ratios and measures mean for DWS.

E13-8 Computing and Interpreting Liquidity Ratios

LO4, 5

Assume that for the 2011 fiscal year, AstroCo reported sales revenue of $2.8 billion and cost of goods sold of $1.6 billion.

Fiscal Year	2011	2010
Balance Sheet (amounts in millions)		
Cash	$ 70	$ 35
Accounts Receivable, less allowance of $15 and $15	430	410
Inventories	240	230
Prepaid Expenses	10	15
Other Current Assets	410	345
Accounts Payable	95	65
Wages Payable	50	60
Income Tax Payable	10	70
Other Current Liabilities	210	205

Required:

Assuming that all sales are on credit, compute the current ratio (two decimal places), inventory turnover ratio (one decimal place), and accounts receivable turnover ratio (one decimal place) for 2011. Explain what each ratio means for AstroCo.

E13-9 Computing the Accounts Receivable and Inventory Turnover Ratios

LO4, 5

Procter & Gamble is a multinational corporation that manufactures and markets many products that you use every day. In 2011, assume that sales for the company were $83,503 (all amounts in millions) and that all sales were on credit. The average gross profit percentage was 51.3 percent. Account balances follow:

P&G

	Beginning	Ending
Accounts receivable (net)	$6,761	$6,629
Inventory	8,416	6,819

Required:

1. Rounded to one decimal place, compute the turnover ratios for accounts receivable and inventory.
2. By dividing 365 by your ratios from requirement 1, calculate the average days to collect receivables and the average days to sell inventory.
3. Interpret what these ratios and measures mean for P&G.

E13-10 Inferring Financial Information from Profitability and Liquidity Ratios

LO4, 5

Loonie Corporation stores feature quality merchandise at low prices to meet the needs of middle-, low-, and fixed-income families. For the year ended January 30, 2012, the company reported average inventories of $1,352 (in millions) and an inventory turnover of 5.47. Average total fixed assets were $1,272 (million), and the fixed asset turnover ratio was 8.22.

Required:

1. Calculate Loonie's gross profit percentage (expressed as a percentage with one decimal place). What does this imply about the amount of gross profit made from each dollar of sales?

   TIP: Work backward from the fixed asset turnover and inventory turnover ratios to compute the amounts needed for the gross profit percentage.

2. Is this an improvement from the gross profit percentage of 28.2 percent earned during the previous year?

Check Figure:
[Req. 1]
Net sales = $10,455,840,000

E13-11 Analyzing the Impact of Selected Transactions on the Current Ratio

LO4

In its most recent annual report, Laurentian Beverages reported current assets of $54,000 and a current ratio of 1.80. Assume that the following transactions were completed: (1) purchased merchandise for $6,000 on account, and (2) purchased a delivery truck for $10,000, paying $1,000 cash and signing a two-year promissory note for the balance.

Required:

Compute the updated current ratio, rounded to two decimal places, after each transaction.

LO4, 5   **E13-12 Analyzing the Impact of Selected Transactions on the Current Ratio**

In its most recent annual report, Sunrise Corp. reported current assets of $1,090,000 and current liabilities of $602,000.

Required:

Determine for each of the following transactions whether the Sunrise's current ratio, and each of its two components, will increase, decrease, or have no change: (1) sold long-term assets for cash, (2) accrued severance pay for terminated employees, (3) wrote down the carrying value of certain inventory items that were deemed to be obsolete, and (4) acquired new inventory by signing an 18-month promissory note (the supplier was not willing to provide normal credit terms).

LO4, 5   **E13-13 Analyzing the Impact of Selected Transactions on the Current Ratio**

SportChek

SportChek is Canada's largest retailer of sporting goods and sports apparel and footwear, with over 130 stores across Canada. Assume one of the SportChek stores reported current assets of $88,000 and its current ratio was 1.75. Assume that the following transactions were completed: (1) paid $6,000 on accounts payable, (2) purchased a delivery truck for $10,000 cash, (3) wrote off a bad account receivable for $2,000, and (4) paid previously declared dividends in the amount of $25,000.

Required:

Compute the updated current ratio, rounded to two decimal places, after each transaction.

LO4, 5   **E13-14 Analyzing the Impact of Selected Transactions on the Current Ratio**

A company has current assets that total $500,000 and a current ratio of 2.00, and uses the perpetual inventory method. Assume that the following transactions are completed: (1) sold $12,000 in merchandise on short-term credit for $15,000, (2) declared but did not pay dividends of $50,000, (3) paid prepaid rent in the amount of $12,000, (4) paid previously declared dividends in the amount of $50,000, (5) collected an account receivable in the amount of $12,000, and (6) reclassified $40,000 of long-term debt as a current liability.

Required:

Compute the updated current ratio, rounded to two decimal places, after each transaction.

LO6   **E13-15 Analyzing the Impact of Alternative Inventory Methods on Selected Ratios**

Company A uses the FIFO method to cost inventory, and Company B uses the LIFO method. The two companies are exactly alike except for the difference in inventory costing methods. Costs of inventory items for both companies have been falling steadily in recent years, and each company has increased its inventory each year. Ignore income tax effects.

Required:

Identify which company will report the higher amount for each of the following ratios. If it is not possible to identify which will report the higher amount, explain why.
1. Current ratio.
2. Debt-to-assets ratio.
3. Earnings per share.

COACHED PROBLEMS

LO2, 5   **CP13-1 Analyzing Comparative Financial Statements Using Horizontal Analyses**

The comparative financial statements prepared at December 31, 2012, for Golden Corporation showed the following summarized data:

	2012	2011	Increase (Decrease) 2012 over 2011 Amount	Percentage
Income Statement				
Sales revenue	$180,000	$165,000		
Cost of goods sold	110,000	100,000		
Gross profit	70,000	65,000		
Operating expenses	53,300	50,400		
Interest expense	2,700	2,600		
Income before income taxes	14,000	12,000		
Income tax expense	4,000	3,000		
Net income	$ 10,000	$ 9,000		
Balance Sheet				
Cash	$ 4,000	$ 8,000		
Accounts receivable (net)	19,000	23,000		
Inventory	40,000	35,000		
Property and equipment (net)	45,000	38,000		
	$108,000	$104,000		
Current liabilities (no interest)	$ 16,000	$ 19,000		
Long-term liabilities (6% interest)	45,000	45,000		
Common shares (par $5)	30,000	30,000		
Additional paid-in capital	5,000	5,000		
Retained earnings	12,000	5,000		
	$108,000	$104,000		

Required:

1. Complete the two final columns shown beside each item in Golden Corporation's comparative financial statements. Round the percentages to one decimal place.

   TIP: Calculate the increase (decrease) by subtracting 2011 from 2012. Calculate the percentage by dividing the amount of increase (decrease) by the 2011 balance.

2. Does anything significant jump out at you from the horizontal (trend) analyses?

CP13-2 Analyzing Comparative Financial Statements Using Selected Ratios   LO4, 5

Use the data given in CP13-1 for Golden Corporation.

Required:

1. Compute the gross profit percentage for 2012 and 2011. Round the percentages to one decimal place. Is the trend going in the right direction?

2. Compute the net profit margin for 2012 and 2011. Round the percentages to one decimal place. Is the trend going in the right direction?

3. Compute the earnings per share for 2012 and 2011. Does the trend look good or bad? Explain.

   TIP: To calculate EPS, use the balance in Common Shares to determine the number of shares outstanding. Common Shares equals the par value per share times the number of shares.

4. Shareholders' equity totalled $30,000 at the end of 2010. Compute the return on equity (ROE) ratios for 2011 and 2012. Express the ROE as percentages rounded to one decimal place. Is the trend going in the right direction?

5. Net property and equipment totalled $35,000 at the end of 2010. Compute the fixed asset turnover ratios for 2012 and 2011. Round the ratios to two decimal places. Is the trend going in the right direction?

6. Compute the debt-to-assets ratios for 2012 and 2011. Round the ratios to two decimal places. Is debt providing financing for a larger or smaller proportion of the company's asset growth? Explain.

7. Compute the times interest earned ratios for 2012 and 2011. Round the ratios to one decimal place. Do they look good or bad? Explain.

8. After Golden released its 2012 financial statements, the company's shares were trading at $30. After the release of its 2011 financial statements, the company's share price was $21 per share. Compute the P/E ratios for both years, rounded to one decimal place. Does it appear that investors have become more (or less) optimistic about Golden's future success?

LO4, 5, 6   **CP13-3 Using Ratios to Compare Alternative Investment Opportunities**

The 2012 financial statements for the Armstrong and Blair companies are summarized here:

	Armstrong Company	Blair Company
Balance Sheet		
Cash	$ 35,000	$ 22,000
Accounts Receivable, Net	40,000	30,000
Inventory	100,000	40,000
Property and Equipment, Net	180,000	300,000
Other Assets	45,000	408,000
Total Assets	$400,000	$800,000
Current Liabilities	$100,000	$ 50,000
Long-Term Debt	60,000	370,000
Total Liabilities	160,000	420,000
Common Share (par $10)	150,000	200,000
Additional Paid-In Capital	30,000	110,000
Retained Earnings	60,000	70,000
Total Liabilities and Shareholders' Equity	$400,000	$800,000
Income Statement		
Sales Revenue (1/3 on credit)	$450,000	$810,000
Cost of Goods Sold	(245,000)	(405,000)
Expenses (including interest and income tax)	(160,000)	(315,000)
Net Income	$ 45,000	$ 90,000
Selected Data from 2011 Statements		
Accounts Receivable, Net	$ 20,000	$ 38,000
Inventory	92,000	45,000
Property and Equipment, Net	180,000	300,000
Long-Term Debt	60,000	70,000
Total Shareholders' Equity	231,000	440,000
Other Data		
Estimated value of each share at end of 2012	$ 18	$ 27

The companies are in the same line of business and are direct competitors in a large metropolitan area. Both have been in business approximately 10 years, and each has had steady growth. One-third of both companies' sales are on credit. Despite these similarities, the management of each has a different viewpoint in many respects. Blair is more conservative, and as its president said, "We avoid what we consider to be undue risk." Both companies use straight-line amortization, but Blair estimates slightly shorter useful lives than Armstrong does. No shares were issued in 2012, and neither company is publicly held. Blair Company has an annual audit by a CA but Armstrong Company does not.

Required:

1. Calculate the ratios in Exhibit 13.5 for which sufficient information is available. Round all calculations to two decimal places.

    TIP: To calculate EPS, use the balance in Common Shares to determine the number of shares outstanding. Common Shares equals the par value per share times the number of shares.

2. A client of yours has decided to buy shares in one of the two companies. Based on the data given, prepare a comparative written evaluation of the ratio analyses (and any other available information) and conclude with your recommended choice.

    TIP: Comment on how accounting differences affect your evaluations, if at all.

PA13-1 Analyzing Financial Statements Using Horizontal Analyses

LO2, 5

The comparative financial statements prepared at December 31, 2012, for Pinnacle Plus showed the following summarized data:

| | 2012 | 2011 | Increase (Decrease) 2012 over 2011 | |
			Amount	Percentage
Income Statement				
Sales Revenue*	$110,000	$ 99,000		
Cost of Goods Sold	52,000	48,000		
Gross Profit	58,000	51,000		
Operating Expenses	36,000	33,000		
Interest Expense	4,000	4,000		
Income before Income Tax Expense	18,000	14,000		
Income Tax Expense (30%)	5,400	4,200		
Net Income	$ 12,600	$ 9,800		
Balance Sheet				
Cash	$ 49,500	$ 18,000		
Accounts Receivable, Net	37,000	32,000		
Inventory	25,000	38,000		
Property and Equipment, Net	95,000	105,000		
Total Assets	$206,500	$193,000		
Accounts Payable	$ 42,000	$ 35,000		
Income Tax Payable	1,000	500		
Note Payable, Long-Term	40,000	40,000		
Total Liabilities	83,000	75,500		
Common Shares (par $10)	90,000	90,000		
Retained Earnings[†]	33,500	27,500		
Total Liabilities and Shareholders' Equity	$206,500	$193,000		

*One-half of all sales are on credit.

[†]During 2012, cash dividends amounting to $6,600 were declared and paid.

Required:

1. Complete the two final columns shown beside each item in Pinnacle's comparative financial statements. Round the percentages to one decimal place.
2. Does anything significant jump out at you from the horizontal analyses?

PA13-2 Analyzing Comparative Financial Statements Using Selected Ratios

LO4, 5

Use the data given in PA13-1 for Pinnacle Plus.

Required:

1. Compute the gross profit percentage in 2012 and 2011. Round the percentages to one decimal place. Is the trend going in the right direction?
2. Compute the net profit margin for 2012 and 2011. Round the percentages to one decimal place. Is the trend going in the right direction?
3. Compute the earnings per share for 2012 and 2011. Does the trend look good or bad? Explain.
4. Shareholders' equity totalled $100,000 at the end of 2010. Compute the return on equity (ROE) ratios for 2012 and 2011. Express the ROE as percentages rounded to one decimal place. Is the trend going in the right direction?
5. Net property and equipment totalled $110,000 at the end of 2010. Compute the fixed asset turnover ratios for 2012 and 2011. Round the ratios to two decimal places. Is the trend going in the right direction?
6. Compute the debt-to-assets ratios for 2012 and 2011. Round the ratios to two decimal places. Is debt providing financing for a larger or smaller proportion of the company's asset growth? Explain.

Check Figure:
[Req. 3]
2012 Earnings per
Share = $1.40

7. Compute the times interest earned ratios for 2012 and 20112. Round the ratios to one decimal place. Do they look good or bad? Explain.

8. After Pinnacle Plus released its 2012 financial statements, the company's shares were trading at $18. After the release of its 2011 financial statements, the company's share price was $15 per share. Compute the P/E ratios for both years, rounded to one decimal place. Does it appear that investors have become more (or less) optimistic about Pinnacle's future success?

LO3, 5 **PA13-3 Vertical Analysis of a Balance Sheet**

A condensed balance sheet for Simultech Corporation and a partially completed vertical analysis are presented below.

SIMULTECH CORPORATION
Balance Sheet (summarized)
January 31, 2012
(In millions of dollars)

Cash and Short-Term Investments	$ 433	29%	Current Liabilities	$ 409	27%
Accounts Receivable	294	19	Long-Term Liabilities	495	33
Inventories	206	14	Total Liabilities	904	*b*
Other Current Assets	109	*a*	Contributed Capital	118	*c*
Property and Equipment	27	2	Retained Earnings	492	30
Other Assets	445	29	Total Shareholders' Equity	610	*d*
Total Assets	$1,514	100%	Total Liabilities &Shareholders' Equity	$1,514	100%

Required:

1. Complete the vertical analysis by computing each line item (*a*)–(*d*) as a percentage of total assets. Round to the nearest whole percentage.

2. What percentages of Simultech's assets relate to inventories versus property and equipment? What does this tell you about the relative significance of these two assets to Simultech's business?

3. What percentage of Simultech's assets is financed by total shareholder's equity? By total liabilities?

LO3, 5 **PA13-4 Vertical Analysis of an Income Statement**

A condensed income statement for Simultech Corporation and a partially completed vertical analysis are presented below.

SIMULTECH CORPORATION
Income Statement (summarized)
(In millions of dollars)

	For the Years Ended			
	January 31, 2012		January 31, 2011	
Sales Revenues	$2,062	100%	$2,200	100%
Cost of Goods Sold	1,637	79	1,721	*d*
Selling, General, and Administrative Expenses	333	*a*	346	16
Other Operating Expenses	53	3	12	1
Interest Expense	22	*b*	26	1
Income before Income Tax Expense	17	1	95	*e*
Income Tax Expense	6	0	33	1
Net Income	$ 11	*c*%	$ 62	*f*%

Required:

1. Complete the vertical analysis by computing each line item (a)–(f) as a percentage of sales revenues. Round to the nearest whole percentage.

2. Does Simultech's Cost of Goods Sold for the year ended January 31, 2012, as a percentage of revenues, represent better or worse performance as compared to that for the year ended January 31, 2011?

3. Do the percentages for (c) and (f) that you calculated in 1 indicate whether Simultech's net profit margin has changed over the two years?

PA13-5 Using Ratios to Compare Loan Requests from Two Companies   LO4, 5, 6

The 2012 financial statements for Royale and Cavalier companies are summarized here:

	Royale Company	Cavalier Company
Balance Sheet		
Cash	$ 25,000	$ 45,000
Accounts Receivable, Net	55,000	5,000
Inventory	110,000	25,000
Property and Equipment, Net	550,000	160,000
Other Assets	140,000	57,000
Total Assets	$880,000	$292,000
Current Liabilities	$120,000	$ 15,000
Long-Term Debt	190,000	55,000
Capital Shares (par $20)	480,000	210,000
Additional Paid-In Capital	50,000	4,000
Retained Earnings	40,000	8,000
Total Liabilities and Shareholders' Equity	$880,000	$292,000
Income Statement		
Sales Revenue	$800,000	$280,000
Cost of Goods Sold	(480,000)	(150,000)
Expenses (including interest and income tax)	(240,000)	(95,000)
Net Income	$ 80,000	$ 35,000
Selected Data from 2011 Statements		
Accounts Receivable, Net	$ 47,000	$ 11,000
Long-Term Debt	190,000	55,000
Property and Equipment, Net	550,000	160,000
Inventory	95,000	38,000
Total Shareholders' Equity	570,000	202,000
Other Data		
Per share price at end of 2012	$ 14.00	$ 11.00

These two companies are in the same business and the same province but in different cities. One-half of Royale's sales and one-quarter of Cavalier's sales are on credit. Each company has been in operation for about 10 years. Both companies received an unqualified audit opinion on the financial statements. Royale Company wants to borrow $75,000 cash, and Cavalier Company is asking for $30,000. The loans will be for a two-year period. Both companies estimate bad debts based on an aging analysis, but Cavalier has estimated slightly higher uncollectable rates than Royale. Neither company issued shares in 2012.

Required:

1. Calculate the ratios in Exhibit 13.5 for which sufficient information is available. Round all calculations to two decimal places.

2. Assume that you work in the loan department of a local bank. You have been asked to analyze the situation and recommend which loan is preferable. Based on the data given, your analysis prepared in requirement 1, and any other information (e.g., accounting policies and decisions), give your choice and the supporting explanation.

PB13-1 Analyzing Financial Statements Using Horizontal and Ratio Analyses

The comparative financial statements prepared at December 31, 2012, for Tiger Audio showed the following summarized data:

	2012	2011	Increase (Decrease) 2012 over 2011 Amount	Percentage
Income Statement				
Sales Revenue	$222,000	$185,000		
Cost of Goods Sold	127,650	111,000		
Gross Profit	94,350	74,000		
Operating Expenses	39,600	33,730		
Interest Expense	4,000	3,270		
Income before Income Tax Expense	50,750	37,000		
Income Tax Expense (30%)	15,225	11,100		
Net Income	$ 35,525	$ 25,900		
Balance Sheet				
Cash	$ 40,000	$ 38,000		
Accounts Receivable, Net	18,500	16,000		
Inventory	25,000	22,000		
Property and Equipment, Net	127,000	119,000		
Total Assets	$210,500	$195,000		
Accounts Payable	$ 27,000	$ 25,000		
Income Tax Payable	3,000	2,800		
Note Payable, Long-Term	75,500	92,200		
Total Liabilities	105,500	120,000		
Capital Shares (par $1)	25,000	25,000		
Retained Earnings	80,000	50,000		
Total Liabilities and Shareholders' Equity	$210,500	$195,000		

Required:

1. Complete the two final columns shown beside each item in Tiger Audio's comparative financial statements. Round the percentages to one decimal place.
2. Does anything significant jump out at you from the year-over-year analyses?

PB13-2 Analyzing Comparative Financial Statements Using Selected Ratios

Use the data given in PB13-1 for Tiger Audio.

Required:

Check Figure:
[Req. 4]
2012 Return on
Equity = 39.5%

1. Compute the gross profit percentage in 2012 and 2011. Is the trend going in the right direction?
2. Compute the net profit margin for 2012 and 2011. Is the trend going in the right direction?
3. Compute the earnings per share for 2012 and 2011. Does the trend look good or bad? Explain.
4. Shareholders' equity totalled $65,000 at the end of 2010. Compute the return on equity ratios for 2012 and 2011. Is the trend going in the right direction?
5. Net property and equipment totalled $115,000 at the end of 2010. Compute the fixed asset turnover ratios for 2012 and 2011. Is the trend going in the right direction?
6. Compute the debt-to-assets ratios for 2012 and 2011. Is debt providing financing for a larger or smaller proportion of the company's asset growth? Explain.
7. Compute the times interest earned ratios for 2012 and 2011. Do they look good or bad? Explain.
8. After Tiger released its 2012 financial statements, the company's shares were trading at $17. After the release of its 2011 financial statements, the company's share price was $12 per share. Compute the P/E ratios for both years. Does it appear that investors have become more or less optimistic about Tiger's future success?

PB13-3 Interpreting Profitability, Liquidity, Solvency, and P/E Ratios

LO4, 5

Mattel and Hasbro are the two largest manufacturers of games and toys in the world. Mattel sells some $9 billion of products each year, while annual sales of Hasbro products exceed $4 billion. Compare the two companies as a potential investment based on the following assumed ratios:

Ratio	Mattel	Hasbro
Gross profit percentage	45.5%	57.7%
Net profit margin	6.5%	7.3%
Return on equity	17.1%	21.8%
EPS	$ 1.05	$ 2.18
Receivables turnover ratio	8.9	10.5
Inventory turnover ratio	6.2	5.7
Current ratio	2.38	2.54
Debt to assets	0.31	0.35
P/E ratio	15.9	13.8

Required:

1. Which company appears more profitable? Describe the ratio(s) that you used to reach this decision.
2. Which company appears more liquid? Describe the ratio(s) that you used to reach this decision.
3. Which company appears more solvent? Describe the ratio(s) that you used to reach this decision.
4. Are the conclusions from your analyses in requirements 1–3 consistent with the value of the two companies, as suggested by their P/E ratios? If not, offer one explanation for any apparent inconsistency.

PB13-4 Using Ratios to Compare Loan Requests from Two Companies

LO4, 5, 6

The 2012 financial statements for Thor and Gunnar Companies are summarized here:

	Thor Company	Gunnar Company
Balance Sheet		
Cash	$ 35,000	$ 54,000
Accounts Receivable, Net	77,000	6,000
Inventory	154,000	30,000
Property and Equipment, Net	770,000	192,000
Other Assets	196,000	68,400
Total Assets	$1,232,000	$350,400
Current Liabilities	$ 168,000	$ 18,000
Long-Term Debt (12% interest rate)	266,000	66,000
Capital Shares (par $20)	672,000	252,000
Additional Paid-In Capital	70,000	4,800
Retained Earnings	56,000	9,600
Total Liabilities and Shareholders' Equity	$1,232,000	$350,400
Income Statement		
Sales Revenue	$1,120,000	$336,000
Cost of Goods Sold	(672,000)	(180,000)
Expenses (including interest and income tax)	(336,000)	(114,000)
Net Income	$ 112,000	$ 42,000
Selected Data from 2011 Statements		
Accounts Receivable, Net	$ 65,800	$ 13,200
Inventory	133,000	45,600
Property and Equipment, Net	770,000	192,000
Long-Term Debt (12% interest rate)	266,000	66,000
Total Shareholders' Equity	798,000	266,400
Other Data		
Per share price at end of 2012	$ 13.20	$ 19.60

These two companies are in the same business and in the same province but in different cities. One-half of Thor's sales and one-quarter of Gunnar's sales are on credit. Each company has been in operation for about 10 years. Both companies received an unqualified audit opinion on the financial statements. Thor Company wants to borrow $105,000, and Gunnar Company is asking for $36,000. The loans will be for a two-year period. Neither company issued shares in 2012.

Required:

1. Calculate the ratios in Exhibit 13.5 for which sufficient information is available. Round all calculations to two decimal places.

2. Assume that you work in the loan department of a local bank. You have been asked to analyze the situation and recommend which loan is preferable. Based on the data given, your analysis prepared in requirement 1, and any other information, give your choice and the supporting explanation.

LO5   **PB13-5 Analyzing an Investment by Comparing Selected Ratios**

You have the opportunity to invest $10,000 in one of two companies from a single industry. The only information you have is shown here. The word *high* refers to the top third of the industry; *average* is the middle third; *low* is the bottom third.

Ratio	Company A	Company B
EPS	High	High
Return on equity	High	Average
Debt to assets	High	Low
Current	Low	Average
Price/earnings	Low	High

Required:

Which company would you select? Write a brief explanation for your choice.

SKILLS DEVELOPMENT CASES

LO4   **S13-1 Computing Ratios**

Rona Inc.

To benchmark The Home Depot's financial results, we reported the following ratios for Rona Inc. fiscal year ended December 27, 2009: fixed asset turnover (5.53), return on equity (8.5%), quality of income (2.05), days to sell (80), and debt to assets (0.35). Show that you can compute these ratios using the financial statements of Rona Inc. in Appendix A at the back of this book or download the annual report from the *Cases* section of Connect.

LO5   **S13-2 Evaluating Financial Information**

The Lumber Yard Ltd. competes with Hardesty Inc. in product lines such as hardwood flooring, noise-reducing underlay, and mouldings. The two companies reported the following financial results in fiscal 2011:

	The Lumber Yard Ltd.	Hardesty Inc.
Gross profit percentage	35.0%	34.2%
Net profit margin	4.7%	4.6%
Return on equity	21.1%	12.9%
Earnings per share	$ 0.83	$ 1.51

Required:

1. Explain how The Lumber Yard Ltd. could have a substantially higher gross profit percentage than Hardesty Inc. but a nearly identical net profit margin. What does this suggest about the relative ability of the two companies to control operating expenses?

2. Explain how The Lumber Yard Ltd. could have a higher return on equity but lower earnings per share. What does this suggest about the companies' relative number of outstanding shares? What other explanations could account for this seemingly contradictory pattern?

S13-3 Internet-Based Team Research: Examining an Annual Report

LO1, 2, 3, 4, 5, 6

As a team, select an industry to analyze. Using your Web browser, each team member should access the annual report for one publicly traded company in the industry, with each member selecting a different company. (See S1-3 in Chapter 1 for a description of possible resources for these tasks.)

Required:

1. On an individual basis, each team member should write a short report that incorporates horizontal and vertical analyses and as many of the ratios from the chapter as are applicable given the nature of the selected company.
2. Then, as a team, write a short report comparing and contrasting your companies using these attributes. Discuss any patterns across the companies that you as a team observe. Provide potential explanations for any differences discovered. Consider the impact of differences in accounting policies.

S13-4 Ethical Decision Making: A Real-Life Example

LO6

Weiss Ratings

One study done by Weiss Ratings focused on auditors' ability to predict bankruptcy. The study criticized auditors for failing to identify and report going-concern problems for audit clients that later went bankrupt. Based on a sample of 45 bankrupt companies, the Weiss study concluded that if auditors had noted unusual levels for just two of seven typical financial ratios, they would have identified 89 percent of the sample companies that later went bankrupt. A follow-up to the Weiss study found that if the criteria in the Weiss study had been applied to a larger sample of nonbankrupt companies, 46.9 percent of non-bankrupt companies would have been predicted to go bankrupt.[2] In other words, the Weiss criteria would have incorrectly predicted bankruptcy for nearly half of the companies in the follow-up study and would have led the auditors to report that these clients had substantial going-concern problems when, in fact, they did not. Discuss the negative consequences that arise when auditors fail to identify and report going-concern problems. Who is harmed by these failures? Discuss the negative consequences that arise when auditors incorrectly report going-concern problems when they do not exist. Who is harmed by these errors? In your opinion, which of the potential consequences is worse?

S13-5 Ethical Decision Making: A Mini-Case

LO4, 5

Capital Investments Corporation (CIC) requested a sizable loan from First Canadian Bank to acquire a large piece of land for future expansion. CIC reported current assets of $1,900,000 (including $430,000 in cash) and current liabilities of $1,075,000. First Canadian denied the loan request for a number of reasons, including the fact that the current ratio was below 2:1. When CIC was informed of the loan denial, the controller of the company immediately paid $420,000 that was owed to several trade creditors. The controller then asked First Canadian to reconsider the loan application. Based on these abbreviated facts, would you recommend that First Canadian approve the loan request? Why? Are the controller's actions ethical?

S13-6 Critical Thinking: Analyzing the Impact of Alternative Amortization Methods on Ratio Analysis

LO4, 5, 6

Speedy Company uses the double-declining-balance method to depreciate its property, plant, and equipment, and Turtle Company uses the straight-line method. The two companies are exactly alike except for the difference in amortization methods.

Required:

1. Identify the financial ratios discussed in this chapter that are likely to be affected by the difference in amortization methods.
2. Which company will report the higher amount for each ratio that you have identified in response to requirement 1? If you cannot be certain, explain why.

S13-7 Using a Spreadsheet to Calculate Financial Statement Ratios

LO2, 3

Enter the account names and dollar amounts from the comparative balance sheets in Exhibit 13.1 into a worksheet in a spreadsheet file. Create a second copy of the worksheet in the same spreadsheet file.

Required:

1. To the right of the comparative numbers in the first worksheet, enter the necessary formulas to compute the amount and percent change as shown in Exhibit 13.1.
2. To the right of each column in the second worksheet, enter the necessary formulas to create common-size statements similar to those shown in Exhibit 13.3.

L04, 5 **CC13 Evaluating Profitability, Liquidity, and Solvency**

Looking back over the past few years, it is clear that Nicole Mackisey has accomplished a lot running her business, Nicole's Getaway Spa (NGS). Nicole is curious about her company's performance as she compares its financial statements.

	2012	2011	2010
Balance Sheet			
Cash	$ 6,700	$ 4,200	$ 3,800
Accounts Receivable, Net	2,000	2,500	1,800
Inventory	1,200	3,000	1,600
Prepaid Expenses	750	1,050	200
Other Current Assets	300	350	200
Total Current Assets	10,950	11,100	7,600
Property and Equipment	64,000	79,000	27,000
Total Assets	$74,950	$90,100	$34,600
Current Liabilities	$ 8,000	$ 8,000	$ 9,000
Long-Term Liabilities	35,000	50,000	14,000
Total Liabilities	43,000	58,000	23,000
Contributed Capital	25,000	30,000	10,900
Retained Earnings	6,950	2,100	700
Total Shareholders' Equity	31,950	32,100	11,600
Total Liabilities and Shareholders' Equity	$74,950	$90,100	$34,600
Income Statement			
Sales Revenue	$80,000	$56,000	$44,000
Cost of Goods Sold	65,000	48,000	35,000
Gross Profit	15,000	8,000	9,000
Operating Expenses	4,000	2,000	7,000
Income from Operations	11,000	6,000	2,000
Interest Expense	1,000	3,100	800
Income before Income Tax Expense	10,000	2,900	1,200
Income Tax Expense	3,050	800	500
Net Income	$ 6,950	$ 2,100	$ 700

• Net Cash Flows from Operating Activities:
  2012: $3,000; 2011: $2,500; and 2010: $2,300

Required:

1. Was NGS more profitable in 2011 or 2012? Use the gross profit percentage, quality of income ratio, return on equity, and asset turnover ratio to help in making a decision (round each ratio to two decimal places).

2. Was NGS more liquid in 2011 or 2012? Use the current ratio and quick ratio to help in making a decision (round each ratio to two decimal places).

3. Was NGS more solvent in 2011 or 2012? Use the debt-to-assets ratio and times interest earned ratio to help in making a decision (round each ratio to two decimal places).

Endnotes

1. Like many retail companies, The Home Depot's fiscal year-end is at the end of January.

2. Michael D. Akers, Meredith A. Maher, and Don E. Giacomino, "Going-Concern Opinions: Broadening the Expectations Gap," *CPA Journal*, October 2003. Retrieved June 12, 2009, from www.nysscpa.org/cpajournal/2003/1003/features/f103803.htm.

Excerpts from the Fiscal 2009 Annual Report of Rona Inc.

Note: The materials in this appendix have been selected from the full annual report of Rona Inc. for fiscal year 2009, which ended December 27, 2009. The complete annual report is available on Connect or from Rona's Web site at www.rona.ca.

MANAGEMENT'S REPORT ON THE CONSOLIDATED FINANCIAL STATEMENTS

Management is fully accountable for the consolidated financial statements of RONA inc. as well as the financial information contained in this Annual Report. This responsibility is based on a judicious choice of appropriate accounting principles and methods, the application of which requires making estimates and informed judgments. It also includes ensuring that the financial information in the annual report is consistent with the consolidated financial statements. These consolidated financial statements were prepared in accordance with Canadian generally accepted accounting principles and were approved by the Board of Directors.

RONA inc. maintains accounting and control systems which, in the opinion of management, provide reasonable assurance regarding the accuracy, relevance and reliability of financial information and the well-ordered and efficient management of the Company's business activities.

The Board of Directors fulfills its duty in respect of the consolidated financial statements contained in this Annual Report principally through its Audit Committee. This Committee is comprised solely of outside directors and is responsible for making recommendations for the nomination of external auditors. Moreover, this Committee, which holds periodic meetings with members of management and internal and external auditors, has reviewed the consolidated financial statements of RONA inc. and recommended their approval to the Board of Directors. The internal and external auditors have access to the Committee without management.

The attached consolidated financial statements have been audited by the firm Raymond Chabot Grant Thornton LLP, Chartered Accountants, and their report indicates the scope of their audit and their opinion on the consolidated financial statements.

Robert Dutton
President and Chief Executive Officer

Claude Guévin CA
Executive Vice President and Chief Financial Officer

Boucherville, February 9, 2010

AUDITORS' REPORT TO THE SHAREHOLDERS OF RONA INC.

We have audited the consolidated balance sheets of RONA inc. as at December 27, 2009 and December 28, 2008 and the consolidated statements of earnings, retained earnings, contributed surplus and cash flows for the years then ended. These financial statements are the responsibility of the Company's management. Our responsibility is to express an opinion on these financial statements based on our audits.

We conducted our audits in accordance with Canadian generally accepted auditing standards. Those standards require that we plan and perform an audit to obtain reasonable assurance whether the financial statements are free of material misstatements. An audit includes examining, on a test basis, evidence supporting the amounts and disclosures in the financial statements. An audit also includes assessing the accounting principles used and significant estimates made by management, as well as evaluating the overall financial statement presentation.

In our opinion, these consolidated financial statements present fairly, in all material respects, the financial position of the Company as at December 27, 2009 and December 28, 2008 and the results of its operations and its cash flows for the years then ended in accordance with Canadian generally accepted accounting principles.

Raymond Chabot Grant Thornton LLP [1]

Montréal, February 9, 2010

_____

[1] Chartered accountant auditor permit no. 9737

A.2

CONSOLIDATED EARNINGS

Years ended December 27, 2009 and December 28, 2008
(In thousands of dollars, except earnings per share)

	2009	2008 (Restated – Note 2)
Sales	$ 4,677,359	$ 4,891,122
Earnings before the following items (Note 6)	332,994	364,729
Interest on long-term debt	20,951	28,106
Interest on bank loans	2,586	2,134
Depreciation and amortization (Notes 12,14,15)	103,160	100,958
	126,697	131,198
Earnings before income taxes and non-controlling interest	206,297	233,531
Income taxes (Note 7)	62,714	71,928
Earnings before non-controlling interest	143,583	161,603
Non-controlling interest	5,331	5,152
Net earnings and comprehensive income	$ 138,252	$ 156,451
Net earnings per share (Note 27)		
Basic	$ 1.12	$ 1.35
Diluted	$ 1.11	$ 1.34

The accompanying notes are an integral part of the consolidated financial statements.

CONSOLIDATED RETAINED EARNINGS
CONSOLIDATED CONTRIBUTED SURPLUS

Years ended December 27, 2009 and December 28, 2008
(In thousands of dollars)

	2009	2008 (Restated – Note 2)
Consolidated Retained Earnings		
Balance, beginning of year, as previously reported	$ 1,053,166	$ 892,967
Change in accounting policy – Goodwill and intangible assets (Note 2)	(24,290)	(20,542)
Restated balance, beginning of year	1,028,876	872,425
Net earnings	138,252	156,451
	1,167,128	1,028,876
Expenses relating to the issue of common shares, net of income tax recovery of $2,042	5,320	–
Balance, end of year	$ 1,161,808	$ 1,028,876
Consolidated Contributed Surplus		
Balance, beginning of year	$ 12,563	$ 11,045
Compensation cost relating to stock option plans	946	1,518
Exercise of stock options	(34)	–
Balance, end of year	$ 13,475	$ 12,563

The accompanying notes are an integral part of the consolidated financial statements.

CONSOLIDATED CASH FLOWS

Years ended December 27, 2009 and December 28, 2008
(In thousands of dollars)

	2009	2008 (Restated– Note 2)
Operating activities		
Net earnings	$ 138,252	$ 156,451
Non-cash items		
Depreciation and amortization	103,160	100,958
Derivative financial instruments	(1,116)	1,192
Future income taxes	9,225	(2,917)
Net gain on disposal of assets	(2,358)	(2,796)
Impairment charge on fixed assets held for sale	2,050	–
Compensation cost relating to stock option plans	946	1,518
Compensation cost relating to share unit plans	2,557	1,091
Non-controlling interest	5,331	5,152
Other items	1,975	3,465
	260,022	264,114
Changes in working capital items (Note 8)	22,752	83,373
Cash flows from operating activities	282,774	347,487
Investing activities		
Business acquisitions (Note 9)	(3,734)	(4,824)
Advances to joint ventures and other advances	5	8,139
Other investments	(3,995)	(3,155)
Fixed assets	(115,713)	(161,869)
Intangible assets	(46,186)	(34,276)
Other assets	(4,837)	(10,565)
Disposal of fixed assets	6,291	11,686
Disposal of investments	2,422	10,618
Cash flows from investing activities	(165,747)	(184,246)
Financing activities		
Bank loans and revolving credit	(43,046)	(131,518)
Other long-term debt	646	8,560
Repayment of other long-term debt and redemption of preferred shares	(15,819)	(33,946)
Issue of common shares	176,936	5,592
Cash dividends paid by a subsidiary to non-controlling interest	(1,470)	(2,450)
Expenses relating to the issue of common shares	(7,362)	–
Cash flows from financing activities	109,885	(153,762)
Net increase in cash	226,912	9,479
Cash, beginning of year	12,345	2,866
Cash, end of year	$ 239,257	$ 12,345
Supplementary information		
Interest paid	$ 25,493	$ 33,165
Income taxes paid	$ 49,450	$ 75,508

The accompanying notes are an integral part of the consolidated financial statements.

A.4

CONSOLIDATED BALANCE SHEETS
December 27, 2009 and December 28, 2008
(In thousands of dollars)

	2009	2008 (Restated – Note 2)
Assets		
Current assets		
Cash	$ 239,257	$ 12,345
Accounts receivable (Note 10)	250,845	234,027
Income taxes receivable	2,436	6,475
Inventory (Note 5)	726,262	763,239
Prepaid expenses	18,114	11,202
Derivative financial instruments (Note 23)	801	1,089
Future income taxes (Note 7)	15,914	19,274
	1,253,629	1,047,651
Investments (Note 11)	11,978	10,186
Fixed assets (Note 12)	868,359	822,375
Fixed assets held for sale (Note 13)	13,242	34,870
Goodwill	455,572	454,889
Intangible assets (Note 14)	89,828	57,056
Other assets (Note 15)	29,682	27,210
Future income taxes (Note 7)	27,593	24,681
	$ 2,749,883	$ 2,478,918
Liabilities		
Current liabilities		
Bank loans (Note 16)	$ 5,211	$ 8,468
Accounts payable and accrued liabilities	427,817	422,318
Derivative financial instruments (Note 23)	776	2,180
Future income taxes (Note 7)	4,900	4,461
Instalments on long-term debt (Note 17)	9,996	15,696
	448,700	453,123
Long-term debt (Note 17)	430,524	478,475
Other long-term liabilities (Note 18)	31,317	28,571
Future income taxes (Note 7)	27,542	21,304
Non-controlling interest	32,761	29,220
	970,844	1,010,693
Shareholders' equity		
Capital stock (Note 20)	603,756	426,786
Retained earnings	1,161,808	1,028,876
Contributed surplus	13,475	12,563
	1,779,039	1,468,225
	$ 2,749,883	$ 2,478,918

The accompanying notes are an integral part of the consolidated financial statements.

On behalf of the Board,

J. Spencer Lanthier
Chairman of the Audit Committee

Jean Gaulin
Chairman of the Board of Directors

NOTES TO CONSOLIDATED FINANCIAL STATEMENTS

December 27, 2009 and December 28, 2008
(In thousands of dollars, except amounts per share)

1. Governing statutes and nature of operations

The Company, incorporated under Part IA of the Companies Act (Quebec), is a distributor and a retailer of hardware, home improvement and gardening products in Canada.

2. Changes in accounting policies

Goodwill and intangible assets

At the beginning of 2009, the Company, in accordance with transitional provisions, retroactively adopted Section 3064 of the Canadian Institute of Chartered Accountants' (CICA) Handbook, *Goodwill and intangible assets,* which replaces Section 3062 of the same title. The section establishes standards for the recognition, measurement, presentation and disclosure of goodwill and intangible assets, including internally generated intangible assets. Pre-opening expenses for stores

and distribution centres (previously included in other assets), advertising costs, including those related to store openings and costs incurred for Olympic and Paralympic sponsorship (previously included in prepaid expenses) no longer meet the capitalization criteria of the new section. The balances in these asset accounts as at December 31, 2007– that is, at the beginning of first quarter 2008 – were restated and included in retained earnings and the results of operations of 2008 were also restated. In addition, certain amounts previously included in fixed assets were reclassified to intangible assets as a result of this change in accounting policy.

The impact of the recommendations of the new section on the consolidated financial statements is as follows:

	December 28, 2008		
	Previously reported	Adjustments	Restated
Consolidated Earnings			
Earnings before the following items	$ 377,101	$ (12,372)	$ 364,729
Depreciation and amortization	108,091	(7,133)	100,958
Income taxes	73,541	(1,613)	71,928
Non-controlling interest	5,030	122	5,152
Net earnings and comprehensive income	160,199	(3,748)	156,451
Net earnings per share – basic	1.39	(0.04)	1.35
Net earnings per share – diluted	1.37	(0.03)	1.34
Consolidated Cash Flows			
Net earnings	$ 160,199	$ (3,748)	$ 156,451
Depreciation and amortization	108,091	(7,133)	100,958
Future income taxes	(1,733)	(1,184)	(2,917)
Non-controlling interest	5,030	122	5,152
Changes in working capital items	75,336	9,128	84,464
Fixed assets	(196,145)	34,276	(161,869)
Intangible assets	–	(34,276)	(34,276)
Other assets	(13,380)	2,815	(10,565)
Consolidated Balance Sheets			
Assets			
Income taxes receivable	$ 6,046	$ 429	$ 6,475
Prepaid expenses	33,104	(21,902)	11,202
Future income taxes – current	13,800	5,474	19,274
Fixed assets	875,634	(53,259)	822,375
Intangible assets	3,797	53,259	57,056
Other assets	38,466	(11,256)	27,210
Liabilities			
Future income taxes – current	4,854	(393)	4,461
Future income taxes – long-term	23,998	(2,694)	21,304
Non-controlling interest	29,098	122	29,220
Retained earnings – beginning of year	892,967	(20,542)	872,425

A.6

CONSOLIDATED FINANCIAL STATEMENTS

2. Changes in accounting policies (continued)

Credit risk and the fair value of financial assets and financial liabilities

In January 2009, the Emerging Issues Committee of the CICA issued EIC–173, *Credit risk and the fair value of financial assets and financial liabilities,* which provides guidance on how to measure financial assets and liabilities, taking into account the company's own credit risk and the counterparty credit risk in determining the fair value of financial assets and financial liabilities including financial derivatives. The adoption of these recommendations had no material impact on the results, financial position and cash flows of the Company.

Financial instruments – disclosures

In June 2009, the CICA issued revisions release no. 54, which includes several amendments to Section 3862, *Financial instruments – disclosures.* This Section has been amended to include additional disclosure requirements about fair value measurements of financial instruments and to enhance liquidity risk disclosures. The amendments apply to annual financial statements relating to fiscal years ending after September 30, 2009. The Company adopted the amendments to Section 3862 in the fourth quarter and this had no impact on the Company's results, financial position or cash flows.

3. Effect of new accounting standards not yet implemented

Business combinations

In January 2009, the CICA issued Section 1582, *Business combinations,* which replaces Section 1581 of the same title. This section applies prospectively to business combinations for which the date of acquisition is in fiscal years beginning on or after January 1, 2011. The section establishes standards for accounting for a business combination.

Consolidated financial statements and non-controlling interests

In January 2009, the CICA issued Section 1601, *Consolidated financial statements,* and Section 1602, *Non-controlling interests,* which together replace Section 1600, *Consolidated financial statements.* These sections apply to interim and annual consolidated financial statements for fiscal years beginning on or after January 1, 2011. They establish standards for the preparation of consolidated financial statements and accounting for a non-controlling interest in a subsidiary in the consolidated financial statements subsequent to a business combination.

International financial reporting standards (IFRS)

In February 2008, the Accounting Standards Board of Canada announced that Canadian GAAP for publicly accountable enterprises will be replaced by IFRS for financial statements relating to fiscal years beginning on or after January 1, 2011. When converting from Canadian GAAP to IFRS, the Company will prepare both current and comparative information using IFRS. The Company expects this transition to have an impact on its accounting policies, financial reporting and information systems.

The Company is currently evaluating the impact of these new standards on its consolidated financial statements.

4. Summary of significant accounting policies

Accounting estimates

The preparation of financial statements in accordance with Canadian generally accepted accounting principles requires management to make estimates and assumptions that affect the amounts recorded in the financial statements and notes to financial statements. Significant estimates in these consolidated financial statements relate to the valuation of accounts receivable, inventory, long-term assets, goodwill, store closing costs, income taxes as well as certain economic and actuarial assumptions used in determining the cost of pension plans and accrued benefit obligations. These estimates are based on management's best knowledge of current events and actions that the Company may undertake in the future. Actual results may differ from those estimates.

Principles of consolidation

These financial statements include the accounts of the Company and its subsidiaries. Moreover, the Company includes its share in the assets, liabilities and earnings of joint ventures in which the Company has an interest. This share is accounted for using the proportionate consolidation method.

Revenue recognition

The Company recognizes revenue at the time of sale in stores or upon delivery of the merchandise, when the sale is accepted by the customer and when collection is reasonably assured. Interest relating to receivables and loans and advances is recorded monthly in accordance with contractual provisions.

Inventory valuation

Inventory is valued at the lower of cost and net realizable value. Cost is determined using the weighted average cost method.

Vendor rebates

The Company records cash consideration received from vendors as a reduction in the price of vendors' products and reflects it as a reduction to cost of goods sold and related inventory when recognized in the consolidated statements of earnings and consolidated balance sheets. Certain exceptions apply where the cash consideration received is either a reimbursement of incremental selling costs incurred by the reseller or a payment for goods or services delivered to the vendor, in which case the rebate is reflected as a reduction of operating expenses.

The Company recognizes these rebates when receipt is more likely than not and the amounts can be reasonably estimated.

Customer rebates

The Company records cash consideration paid to customers as a reduction in the selling price of the product and classifies it as a reduction to sales in the consolidated statement of earnings.

Fixed assets

Fixed assets are recorded at cost including capitalized interest, if applicable. Depreciation commences when the assets are put into use and is recognized using the straight-line method and the following annual rates in order to depreciate the cost of these assets over their estimated useful lives.

	Rates
Parking lots	8% and 12.5%
Buildings	4%
Leasehold improvements	5% to 33%
Furniture and equipment	10% to 30%
Computer hardware	10% to 33%

Impairment of long-term assets

Fixed assets are tested for recoverability when events or changes in circumstances indicate that their carrying amount may not be recoverable. The carrying amount of a long-term asset is not recoverable when it exceeds the sum of the undiscounted cash flows expected from its use and eventual disposal. In such a case, an impairment loss must be recognized and is equivalent to the excess of the carrying amount of the long-term asset over its fair value.

Intangible assets

Software and trademarks with definite lives are recorded at cost. Trademarks are amortized on a straight-line basis over periods ranging from five to seven years and software is amortized on a straight-line basis over periods ranging from four to ten years. The amortization method and estimate of useful life are reviewed annually.

Trademarks with indefinite lives are tested for impairment annually or more frequently if events or changes in circumstances indicate that the carrying amount may not be recoverable. An impairment loss is recognized when the carrying amount of the asset exceeds its fair value.

4. Summary of significant accounting policies (continued)

Goodwill
Goodwill is the excess of the cost of acquired enterprises over the net of the amounts assigned to assets acquired and liabilities assumed. Goodwill is not amortized and is tested for impairment annually or more frequently if events or changes in circumstances indicate that it is impaired. The impairment test consists of a comparison of the fair value of the Company's reporting units with their carrying amount. When the carrying amount of a reporting unit exceeds the fair value, the Company compares the fair value of goodwill related to the reporting unit to its carrying value and recognizes an impairment loss equal to the excess. The fair value of a reporting unit is calculated based on evaluations of discounted cash flows.

Other assets
Financing costs relate to credit facilities and are amortized on a straight-line basis over the financing term over a period of six years.

Costs related to sale and leaseback agreements are amortized over the lease term according to the straight-line method.

Dealer recruitment costs are amortized on a straight-line basis over a period of five years.

Income taxes
The Company uses the liability method of accounting for income taxes. Under this method, future income tax assets and liabilities are determined according to differences between the carrying amounts and tax bases of assets and liabilities. They are measured by applying enacted or substantively enacted tax rates and laws at the date of the financial statements for the years in which the temporary differences are expected to reverse.

Other long-term liabilities
Other long-term liabilities consist of a deferred gain on a sale and leaseback transaction and deferred lease obligations. They are amortized using the straight-line method over the terms of the leases.

Deferred lease obligations result from the recognition, by the Company, of the rental expense on a straight-line basis over the lease term when leases contain a predetermined fixed escalation of the minimum rent.

Stock option plans
The Company accounts for options issued according to the fair value based method. Compensation cost is measured at the grant date and is recognized over the applicable stock option vesting period. Any consideration received from employees when options are exercised or stock is purchased is credited to share capital as well as the related compensation cost recorded as contributed surplus.

Share unit plan for officers
The Company offers a restricted share unit plan (RSU) to officers and key employees of the Company and its subsidiaries. The RSUs are vested over a maximum term of three years based on performance targets. The RSUs are recognized as a compensation expense on a straight-line basis over the vesting period based on the forecasted attainment of targets. The RSUs are revalued at fair market value at the end of each reporting period until the vesting date using the market price of the Company's common shares. Fair market value changes are accounted for as compensation expense with a corresponding charge to accounts payable and accrued liabilities.

Share unit plan for directors
Members of the Company's Board of Directors, who are not Company's management, may elect to receive all or a portion of their annual fees in the form of deferred share units (DSUs). The DSU compensation liability is accounted for based on the number of units outstanding and the average market value of the Company's common shares. Fair market value changes are accounted for as compensation expense with a corresponding charge to accounts payable and accrued liabilities.

Foreign currency translation
Monetary items on the balance sheet are translated at the exchange rates in effect at year end, while non-monetary items are translated at the historical rates of exchange. Revenues and expenses are translated at the rates of exchange in effect on the transaction date or at the average exchange rates for the period. Gains or losses resulting from the translation are included in earnings for the year.

Financial instruments
Financial assets and liabilities are initially measured at fair value and their subsequent measurement depends on their classification as described below:

- Cash is classified as a "financial asset held for trading" and is measured at fair value. All changes in fair value are recognized in earnings;

- Accounts receivable and long-term loans and advances (included in investments) are classified as "loans and receivables" and are recognized at cost which, at initial measurement, corresponds to fair value. Subsequent revaluations of accounts receivable are recorded at amortized cost which generally corresponds to initial measurement less any allowance for doubtful accounts. Subsequent revaluations of long-term loans and advances are recognized at amortized cost using the effective interest method;

- Bank loans, accounts payable and accrued liabilities and the revolving credit are classified as "other financial liabilities". They are initially measured at fair value and subsequent revaluations are recognized at amortized cost using the effective interest method;

- Long-term debt is classified as "other financial liabilities". With the exception of the revolving credit, long-term debt is measured at amortized cost, which corresponds to the initially recognized amount plus accumulated amortization of financing costs. The initially recognized amount corresponds to the principal amount of the debt less applicable financing costs;

- The Company uses derivative financial instruments to manage foreign exchange risk. The Company does not use derivative financial instruments for speculative or trading purposes. The derivatives are classified as "assets or liabilities held for trading" and are measured at fair value;

- Transaction costs related to other financial liabilities are recorded as a reduction in the carrying amount of the related financial liability;

- The Company records as a separate asset or liability only those derivatives embedded in hybrid financial instruments issued, acquired or substantially modified by the Company as of December 29, 2002 when these hybrid instruments are not recorded as held for trading and remained outstanding at January 1, 2007. Embedded derivatives that are not closely related to the host contracts must be separated from the host contract, classified as a financial instrument held for trading and measured at fair value with changes in fair value recognized in earnings. The Company has not identified any embedded derivatives to be separated other than derivatives embedded in purchase contracts concluded in a foreign country and settled in a foreign currency that is not the conventional currency of either of the two principal parties to the contract. Although the payments are made in a foreign currency that is routinely used in the economic environment where the transaction occurred, the Company has decided to separate the embedded derivatives.

A.8

4. Summary of significant accounting policies (continued)

Employee future benefits

The Company accrues its obligations under employee benefit plans and the related costs, net of plan assets.

The Company has adopted the following accounting policies for the defined benefit plans:

- The actuarial determination of the accrued benefit obligations for pension uses the projected benefit method prorated on service and management's best estimate of expected plan investment performance, salary escalation and retirement ages of employees;
- For the purpose of calculating the expected return on plan assets, those assets are valued at fair value;
- Past service costs from plan amendments are deferred and amortized on a straight-line basis over the average remaining service period of employees active at the date of amendments;
- Actuarial gains (losses) arise from the difference between actual long-term rate of return on plan assets for a period and the expected long-term rate of return on plan assets for that period or from changes in actuarial assumptions used to determine the accrued benefit obligations. The excess of the net actuarial gain (loss) over 10% of the greater of the benefit obligations and the fair value of plan assets is amortized over the average remaining service period of the active employees. The average remaining service period of the active employees covered by the pension plans is 12 years (12 years as at December 28, 2008);
- The transitional obligation is amortized on a straight-line basis over a period of 10 years, which is the average remaining service period of employees expected to receive benefits under the benefit plan in 2000.

For defined contribution plans, the pension expense recorded in earnings is the amount of contributions the Company is required to pay for services rendered by employees.

Earnings per share and information pertaining to number of shares

Earnings per share are calculated by dividing net earnings available for common shareholders by the weighted average number of common shares outstanding during the year. Diluted earnings per share are calculated taking into account the dilution that would occur if the securities or other agreements for the issuance of common shares were exercised or converted into common shares at the later of the beginning of the period or the issuance date. The treasury stock method is used to determine the dilutive effect of the stock options. This method assumes that proceeds of the stock options during the year are used to redeem common shares at their average price during the period.

Fiscal year

The Company's fiscal year ends on the last Sunday of December. The fiscal years ended December 27, 2009 and December 28, 2008 include 52 weeks of operations.

Comparative figures

Certain comparative figures have been reclassified to conform to the presentation adopted in the current year.

5. Inventory

For the year ended December 27, 2009, an amount of $3,397,928 of inventory was expensed in the consolidated results ($3,571,962 as at December 28, 2008). This amount includes an inventory write-down charge of $35,986 ($46,752 as at December 28, 2008).

6. Store closing costs

Exit and disposal costs and write-down of assets

In April 2008, management approved a detailed plan to close four of its stores included in the corporate and franchised stores segment. Three of these stores were closed in 2008 and one was closed in the second quarter of 2009. During the year ended December 27, 2009, the Company recognized the following costs:

	2009	2008
Lease obligations	$ 14,355	$ 4,231
Inventory write-down	525	2,214
Termination benefits	–	277
Total recorded in earnings before the following items	14,880	6,722
Fixed assets write-down	–	2,857
Total costs	$ 14,880	$ 9,579

The liability for exit and disposal costs and write-down of assets, included in accounts payable and accrued liabilities, is as follows:

	2009	2008
Balance, beginning of year	$ 3,575	$ –
Costs recognized:		
Lease obligations	14,355	4,231
Termination benefits	–	277
Less: cash payments	(3,590)	(933)
Balance, end of year	$ 14,340	$ 3,575

Other closing costs

During the year ended December 27, 2009, in addition to the exit and disposal costs and write-down of assets, the Company recorded operating costs, including interest and depreciation, for the liquidation of the assets of these stores in the amount of $1,230 ($5,202 as at December 28, 2008).

7. Income taxes

	2009	2008
Current	$ 53,489	$ 74,845
Future	9,225	(2,917)
	$ 62,714	$ 71,928

Future income taxes arise mainly from the changes in temporary differences.

APPENDIX B

Excerpts from the Fiscal 2009 Annual Report of The Home Depot, Inc.

Note: The materials in this appendix have been selected from the full annual report of The Home Depot, Inc., for fiscal year 2009, which ended January 31, 2010. The complete annual report is available on Connect or from The Home Depot's Web site at www.homedepot.com.

Item 8.   Financial Statements and Supplementary Data.

Management's Responsibility for Financial Statements

The financial statements presented in this Annual Report have been prepared with integrity and objectivity and are the responsibility of the management of The Home Depot, Inc. These financial statements have been prepared in conformity with U.S. generally accepted accounting principles and properly reflect certain estimates and judgments based upon the best available information.

The financial statements of the Company have been audited by KPMG LLP, an independent registered public accounting firm. Their accompanying report is based upon an audit conducted in accordance with the standards of the Public Company Accounting Oversight Board (United States).

The Audit Committee of the Board of Directors, consisting solely of independent directors, meets five times a year with the independent registered public accounting firm, the internal auditors and representatives of management to discuss auditing and financial reporting matters. In addition, a telephonic meeting is held prior to each quarterly earnings release. The Audit Committee retains the independent registered public accounting firm and regularly reviews the internal accounting controls, the activities of the independent registered public accounting firm and internal auditors and the financial condition of the Company. Both the Company's independent registered public accounting firm and the internal auditors have free access to the Audit Committee.

Management's Report on Internal Control over Financial Reporting

Our management is responsible for establishing and maintaining adequate internal control over financial reporting, as such term is defined in Rule 13a-15(f) promulgated under the Securities Exchange Act of 1934, as amended (the "Exchange Act"). Under the supervision and with the participation of our management, including our Chief Executive Officer and Chief Financial Officer, we conducted an evaluation of the effectiveness of our internal control over financial reporting as of January 31, 2010 based on the framework in *Internal Control – Integrated Framework* issued by the Committee of Sponsoring Organizations of the Treadway Commission (COSO). Based on our evaluation, our management concluded that our internal control over financial reporting was effective as of January 31, 2010 in providing reasonable assurance regarding the reliability of financial reporting and the preparation of financial statements for external purposes in accordance with U.S. generally accepted accounting principles. The effectiveness of our internal control over financial reporting as of January 31, 2010 has been audited by KPMG LLP, an independent registered public accounting firm, as stated in their report which is included on page 30 in this Form 10-K.

/s/   FRANCIS S. BLAKE
Francis S. Blake
Chairman &
Chief Executive Officer

/s/   CAROL B. TOMÉ
Carol B. Tomé
Chief Financial Officer &
Executive Vice President – Corporate Services

Report of Independent Registered Public Accounting Firm

The Board of Directors and Stockholders
The Home Depot, Inc.:

We have audited the accompanying Consolidated Balance Sheets of The Home Depot, Inc. and subsidiaries as of January 31, 2010 and February 1, 2009, and the related Consolidated Statements of Earnings, Stockholders' Equity and Comprehensive Income, and Cash Flows for each of the fiscal years in the three-year period ended January 31, 2010. These Consolidated Financial Statements are the responsibility of the Company's management. Our responsibility is to express an opinion on these Consolidated Financial Statements based on our audits.

We conducted our audits in accordance with the standards of the Public Company Accounting Oversight Board (United States). Those standards require that we plan and perform the audit to obtain reasonable assurance about whether the financial statements are free of material misstatement. An audit includes examining, on a test basis, evidence supporting the amounts and disclosures in the financial statements. An audit also includes assessing the accounting principles used and significant estimates made by management, as well as evaluating the overall financial statement presentation. We believe that our audits provide a reasonable basis for our opinion.

In our opinion, the Consolidated Financial Statements referred to above present fairly, in all material respects, the financial position of The Home Depot, Inc. and subsidiaries as of January 31, 2010 and February 1, 2009, and the results of their operations and their cash flows for each of the fiscal years in the three-year period ended January 31, 2010, in conformity with U.S. generally accepted accounting principles.

We also have audited, in accordance with the standards of the Public Company Accounting Oversight Board (United States), The Home Depot, Inc.'s internal control over financial reporting as of January 31, 2010, based on criteria established in *Internal Control – Integrated Framework* issued by the Committee of Sponsoring Organizations of the Treadway Commission (COSO), and our report dated March 25, 2010 expressed an unqualified opinion on the effectiveness of the Company's internal control over financial reporting.

/s/ KPMG LLP

Atlanta, Georgia
March 25, 2010

THE HOME DEPOT, INC. AND SUBSIDIARIES
CONSOLIDATED STATEMENTS OF EARNINGS

	Fiscal Year Ended[1]		
amounts in millions, except per share data	January 31, 2010	February 1, 2009	February 3, 2008
NET SALES	$66,176	$71,288	$77,349
Cost of Sales	43,764	47,298	51,352
GROSS PROFIT	22,412	23,990	25,997
Operating Expenses:			
Selling, General and Administrative	15,902	17,846	17,053
Depreciation and Amortization	1,707	1,785	1,702
Total Operating Expenses	17,609	19,631	18,755
OPERATING INCOME	4,803	4,359	7,242
Interest and Other (Income) Expense:			
Interest and Investment Income	(18)	(18)	(74)
Interest Expense	676	624	696
Other	163	163	—
Interest and Other, net	821	769	622
EARNINGS FROM CONTINUING OPERATIONS BEFORE PROVISION FOR INCOME TAXES	3,982	3,590	6,620
Provision for Income Taxes	1,362	1,278	2,410
EARNINGS FROM CONTINUING OPERATIONS	2,620	2,312	4,210
EARNINGS (LOSS) FROM DISCONTINUED OPERATIONS, NET OF TAX	41	(52)	185
NET EARNINGS	$ 2,661	$ 2,260	$ 4,395
Weighted Average Common Shares	1,683	1,682	1,849
BASIC EARNINGS PER SHARE FROM CONTINUING OPERATIONS	$ 1.56	$ 1.37	$ 2.28
BASIC EARNINGS (LOSS) PER SHARE FROM DISCONTINUED OPERATIONS	$ 0.02	$ (0.03)	$ 0.10
BASIC EARNINGS PER SHARE	$ 1.58	$ 1.34	$ 2.38
Diluted Weighted Average Common Shares	1,692	1,686	1,856
DILUTED EARNINGS PER SHARE FROM CONTINUING OPERATIONS	$ 1.55	$ 1.37	$ 2.27
DILUTED EARNINGS (LOSS) PER SHARE FROM DISCONTINUED OPERATIONS	$ 0.02	$ (0.03)	$ 0.10
DILUTED EARNINGS PER SHARE	$ 1.57	$ 1.34	$ 2.37

(1)Fiscal years ended January 31, 2010 and February 1, 2009 include 52 weeks. Fiscal year ended February 3, 2008 includes 53 weeks.

See accompanying Notes to Consolidated Financial Statements.

THE HOME DEPOT, INC. AND SUBSIDIARIES
CONSOLIDATED BALANCE SHEETS

amounts in millions, except share and per share data	January 31, 2010	February 1, 2009
ASSETS		
Current Assets:		
Cash and Cash Equivalents	$ 1,421	$ 519
Short-Term Investments	6	6
Receivables, net	964	972
Merchandise Inventories	10,188	10,673
Other Current Assets	1,321	1,192
Total Current Assets	13,900	13,362
Property and Equipment, at cost:		
Land	8,451	8,301
Buildings	17,391	16,961
Furniture, Fixtures and Equipment	9,091	8,741
Leasehold Improvements	1,383	1,359
Construction in Progress	525	625
Capital Leases	504	490
	37,345	36,477
Less Accumulated Depreciation and Amortization	11,795	10,243
Net Property and Equipment	25,550	26,234
Notes Receivable	33	36
Goodwill	1,171	1,134
Other Assets	223	398
Total Assets	$ 40,877	$ 41,164
LIABILITIES AND STOCKHOLDERS' EQUITY		
Current Liabilities:		
Accounts Payable	$ 4,863	$ 4,822
Accrued Salaries and Related Expenses	1,263	1,129
Sales Taxes Payable	362	337
Deferred Revenue	1,158	1,165
Income Taxes Payable	108	289
Current Installments of Long-Term Debt	1,020	1,767
Other Accrued Expenses	1,589	1,644
Total Current Liabilities	10,363	11,153
Long-Term Debt, excluding current installments	8,662	9,667
Other Long-Term Liabilities	2,140	2,198
Deferred Income Taxes	319	369
Total Liabilities	21,484	23,387
STOCKHOLDERS' EQUITY		
Common Stock, par value $0.05; authorized: 10 billion shares; issued: 1.716 billion shares at January 31, 2010 and 1.707 billion shares at February 1, 2009; outstanding: 1.698 billion shares at January 31, 2010 and 1.696 billion shares at February 1, 2009	86	85
Paid-In Capital	6,304	6,048
Retained Earnings	13,226	12,093
Accumulated Other Comprehensive Income (Loss)	362	(77)
Treasury Stock, at cost, 18 million shares at January 31, 2010 and 11 million shares at February 1, 2009	(585)	(372)
Total Stockholders' Equity	19,393	17,777
Total Liabilities and Stockholders' Equity	$40,877	$ 41,164

See accompanying Notes to Consolidated Financial Statements.

THE HOME DEPOT, INC. AND SUBSIDIARIES

CONSOLIDATED STATEMENTS OF STOCKHOLDERS' EQUITY AND COMPREHENSIVE INCOME

amounts in millions, except per share data	Common Stock Shares	Common Stock Amount	Paid-In Capital	Retained Earnings	Accumulated Other Comprehensive Income (Loss)	Treasury Stock Shares	Treasury Stock Amount	Stockholders' Equity	Total Comprehensive Income
BALANCE, JANUARY 28, 2007	**2,421**	**$ 121**	**$ 7,930**	**$33,052**	**$310**	**(451)**	**$(16,383)**	**$ 25,030**	
Cumulative Effect of the Adoption of FIN 48	—	—	—	(111)	—	—	—	(111)	
Net Earnings	—	—	—	4,395	—	—	—	4,395	$4,395
Shares Issued Under Employee Stock Plans	12	1	239	—	—	—	—	240	
Tax Effect of Sale of Option Shares by Employees	—	—	4	—	—	—	—	4	
Translation Adjustments	—	—	—	—	455	—	—	455	455
Cash Flow Hedges, net of tax	—	—	—	—	(10)	—	—	(10)	(10)
Stock Options, Awards and Amortization of Restricted Stock	—	—	206	—	—	—	—	206	
Repurchase of Common Stock	—	—	—	—	—	(292)	(10,815)	(10,815)	
Retirement of Treasury Stock	(735)	(37)	(2,608)	(24,239)	—	735	26,884	—	
Cash Dividends ($0.90 per share)	—	—	—	(1,709)	—	—	—	(1,709)	
Other	—	—	29	—	—	—	—	29	
Comprehensive Income									$4,840
BALANCE, FEBRUARY 3, 2008	**1,698**	**$ 85**	**$ 5,800**	**$11,388**	**$755**	**(8)**	**$ (314)**	**$ 17,714**	
Net Earnings	—	—	—	2,260	—	—	—	2,260	$2,260
Shares Issued Under Employee Stock Plans	9	—	68	—	—	—	—	68	
Tax Effect of Sale of Option Shares by Employees	—	—	7	—	—	—	—	7	
Translation Adjustments	—	—	—	—	(831)	—	—	(831)	(831)
Cash Flow Hedges, net of tax	—	—	—	—	(1)	—	—	(1)	(1)
Stock Options, Awards and Amortization of Restricted Stock	—	—	176	—	—	—	—	176	
Repurchase of Common Stock	—	—	—	—	—	(3)	(70)	(70)	
Cash Dividends ($0.90 per share)	—	—	—	(1,521)	—	—	—	(1,521)	
Other	—	—	(3)	(34)	—	—	12	(25)	
Comprehensive Income									$1,428
BALANCE, FEBRUARY 1, 2009	**1,707**	**$ 85**	**$ 6,048**	**$12,093**	**$ (77)**	**(11)**	**$ (372)**	**$ 17,777**	
Net Earnings	—	—	—	2,661	—	—	—	2,661	$2,661
Shares Issued Under Employee Stock Plans	9	1	57	—	—	—	—	58	
Tax Effect of Sale of Option Shares by Employees	—	—	(2)	—	—	—	—	(2)	
Translation Adjustments	—	—	—	—	426	—	—	426	426
Cash Flow Hedges, net of tax	—	—	—	—	11	—	—	11	11
Stock Options, Awards and Amortization of Restricted Stock	—	—	201	—	—	—	—	201	
Repurchase of Common Stock	—	—	—	—	—	(7)	(213)	(213)	
Cash Dividends ($0.90 per share)	—	—	—	(1,525)	—	—	—	(1,525)	
Other	—	—	—	(3)	2	—	—	(1)	2
Comprehensive Income									$3,100
BALANCE, JANUARY 31, 2010	**1,716**	**$ 86**	**$ 6,304**	**$13,226**	**$ 362**	**(18)**	**$ (585)**	**$ 19,393**	

See accompanying Notes to Consolidated Financial Statements.

THE HOME DEPOT, INC. AND SUBSIDIARIES

CONSOLIDATED STATEMENTS OF CASH FLOWS

amounts in millions	Fiscal Year Ended[1]		
	January 31, 2010	February 1, 2009	February 3, 2008
CASH FLOWS FROM OPERATING ACTIVITIES:			
Net Earnings	$ 2,661	$ 2,260	$ 4,395
Reconciliation of Net Earnings to Net Cash Provided by Operating Activities:			
Depreciation and Amortization	1,806	1,902	1,906
Impairment Related to Rationalization Charges	—	580	—
Impairment of Investment	163	163	—
Stock-Based Compensation Expense	201	176	207
Changes in Assets and Liabilities, net of the effects of acquisitions and disposition:			
(Increase) Decrease in Receivables, net	(23)	121	116
Decrease (Increase) in Merchandise Inventories	625	743	(491)
Decrease (Increase) in Other Current Assets	4	(7)	109
Increase (Decrease) in Accounts Payable and Accrued Expenses	59	(646)	(465)
Decrease in Deferred Revenue	(21)	(292)	(159)
(Decrease) Increase in Income Taxes Payable	(174)	262	—
Decrease in Deferred Income Taxes	(227)	(282)	(348)
(Decrease) Increase in Other Long-Term Liabilities	(19)	306	186
Other	70	242	271
Net Cash Provided by Operating Activities	5,125	5,528	5,727
CASH FLOWS FROM INVESTING ACTIVITIES:			
Capital Expenditures, net of $10, $37 and $19 of non-cash capital expenditures in fiscal 2009, 2008 and 2007, respectively	(966)	(1,847)	(3,558)
Proceeds from Sale of Business, net	—	—	8,337
Payments for Businesses Acquired, net	—	—	(13)
Proceeds from Sales of Property and Equipment	178	147	318
Purchases of Investments	—	(168)	(11,225)
Proceeds from Sales and Maturities of Investments	33	139	10,899
Net Cash (Used in) Provided by Investing Activities	(755)	(1,729)	4,758
CASH FLOWS FROM FINANCING ACTIVITIES:			
(Repayments of) Proceeds from Short-Term Borrowings, net	—	(1,732)	1,734
Repayments of Long-Term Debt	(1,774)	(313)	(20)
Repurchases of Common Stock	(213)	(70)	(10,815)
Proceeds from Sales of Common Stock	73	84	276
Cash Dividends Paid to Stockholders	(1,525)	(1,521)	(1,709)
Other Financing Activities	(64)	(128)	(105)
Net Cash Used in Financing Activities	(3,503)	(3,680)	(10,639)
Increase (Decrease) in Cash and Cash Equivalents	867	119	(154)
Effect of Exchange Rate Changes on Cash and Cash Equivalents	35	(45)	(1)
Cash and Cash Equivalents at Beginning of Year	519	445	600
Cash and Cash Equivalents at End of Year	$ 1,421	$ 519	$ 445
SUPPLEMENTAL DISCLOSURE OF CASH PAYMENTS MADE FOR:			
Interest, net of interest capitalized	$ 664	$ 622	$ 672
Income Taxes	$ 2,082	$ 1,265	$ 2,524

(1)Fiscal years ended January 31, 2010 and February 1, 2009 include 52 weeks. Fiscal year ended February 3, 2008 includes 53 weeks.

See accompanying Notes to Consolidated Financial Statements.

NOTES TO CONSOLIDATED FINANCIAL STATEMENTS

1. SUMMARY OF SIGNIFICANT ACCOUNTING POLICIES

Business, Consolidation and Presentation

The Home Depot, Inc. and its subsidiaries (the "Company") operate The Home Depot stores, which are full-service, warehouse-style stores averaging approximately 105,000 square feet in size. The stores stock approximately 30,000 to 40,000 different kinds of building materials, home improvement supplies and lawn and garden products that are sold to do-it-yourself customers, do-it-for-me customers and professional customers. At the end of fiscal 2009, the Company was operating 2,244 stores, which included 1,976 The Home Depot stores in the United States, including the Commonwealth of Puerto Rico and the territories of the U.S. Virgin Islands and Guam ("U.S."), 179 The Home Depot stores in Canada, 79 The Home Depot stores in Mexico and 10 The Home Depot stores in China. The Consolidated Financial Statements include the accounts of the Company and its wholly-owned subsidiaries. All significant intercompany transactions have been eliminated in consolidation.

Fiscal Year

The Company's fiscal year is a 52- or 53-week period ending on the Sunday nearest to January 31. Fiscal years ended January 31, 2010 ("fiscal 2009") and February 1, 2009 ("fiscal 2008") include 52 weeks. The fiscal year ended February 3, 2008 ("fiscal 2007") includes 53 weeks.

Use of Estimates

Management of the Company has made a number of estimates and assumptions relating to the reporting of assets and liabilities, the disclosure of contingent assets and liabilities, and reported amounts of revenues and expenses in preparing these financial statements in conformity with U.S. generally accepted accounting principles. Actual results could differ from these estimates.

Fair Value of Financial Instruments

The carrying amounts of Cash and Cash Equivalents, Receivables and Accounts Payable approximate fair value due to the short-term maturities of these financial instruments. The fair value of the Company's investments is discussed under the caption "Short-Term Investments" in this Note 1. The fair value of the Company's Long-Term Debt is discussed in Note 11.

Cash Equivalents

The Company considers all highly liquid investments purchased with original maturities of three months or less to be cash equivalents. The Company's Cash Equivalents are carried at fair market value and consist primarily of high-grade commercial paper, money market funds and U.S. government agency securities.

Short-Term Investments

Short-Term Investments are recorded at fair value based on current market rates and are classified as available-for-sale.

Accounts Receivable

The Company has an agreement with a third-party service provider who directly extends credit to customers, manages the Company's private label credit card program and owns the related receivables. We evaluated the third-party entities holding the receivables under the program and concluded that they should not be consolidated by the Company. The agreement with the third-party service provider expires in 2018, with the Company having the option, but no obligation, to purchase the receivables at the end of the agreement. The deferred interest charges incurred by the Company for its deferred financing programs offered to its customers are included in Cost of Sales. The interchange fees charged to the Company for the customers' use of the cards and the profit sharing with the third-party administrator are included in Selling, General and Administrative expenses ("SG&A"). The sum of the three is referred to by the Company as "the cost of credit" of the private label credit card program.

In addition, certain subsidiaries of the Company extend credit directly to customers in the ordinary course of business. The receivables due from customers were $38 million and $37 million as of January 31, 2010 and February 1, 2009, respectively. The Company's valuation reserve related to accounts receivable was not material to the Consolidated Financial Statements of the Company as of the end of fiscal 2009 or 2008.

Merchandise Inventories

The majority of the Company's Merchandise Inventories are stated at the lower of cost (first-in, first-out) or market, as determined by the retail inventory method. As the inventory retail value is adjusted regularly to reflect market conditions, the inventory valued using the retail method approximates the lower of cost or market. Certain subsidiaries, including retail operations in Canada, Mexico and China, and distribution centers, record Merchandise Inventories at the lower of cost or market, as determined by a cost method. These Merchandise Inventories represent approximately 18% of the total Merchandise Inventories balance. The Company evaluates the inventory valued using a cost method at the end of each quarter to ensure that it is carried at the lower of cost or market. The valuation allowance for Merchandise Inventories valued under a cost method was not material to the Consolidated Financial Statements of the Company as of the end of fiscal 2009 or 2008.

Independent physical inventory counts or cycle counts are taken on a regular basis in each store and distribution center to ensure that amounts reflected in the accompanying Consolidated Financial Statements for Merchandise Inventories are properly stated. During the period between physical inventory counts in stores, the Company accrues for estimated losses related to shrink on a store-by-store basis based on historical shrink results and current trends in the business. Shrink (or in the case of excess inventory, "swell") is the difference between the recorded amount of inventory and the physical inventory. Shrink may occur due to theft, loss, inaccurate records for the receipt of inventory or deterioration of goods, among other things.

Income Taxes

The Company provides for federal, state and foreign income taxes currently payable, as well as for those deferred due to timing differences between reporting income and expenses for financial statement purposes versus tax purposes. Deferred tax assets and liabilities are recognized for the future tax consequences attributable to temporary differences between the financial statement carrying amounts of existing assets and liabilities and their respective tax bases. Deferred tax assets and liabilities are measured using enacted income tax rates expected to apply to taxable income in the years in which those temporary differences are expected to be recovered or settled. The effect of a change in income tax rates is recognized as income or expense in the period that includes the enactment date.

The Company and its eligible subsidiaries file a consolidated U.S. federal income tax return. Non-U.S. subsidiaries and certain U.S. subsidiaries, which are consolidated for financial reporting purposes, are not eligible to be included in the Company's consolidated U.S. federal income tax return. Separate provisions for income taxes have been determined for these entities. The Company intends to reinvest substantially all of the unremitted earnings of its non-U.S. subsidiaries and postpone their remittance indefinitely. Accordingly, no provision for U.S. income taxes for these non-U.S. subsidiaries was recorded in the accompanying Consolidated Statements of Earnings.

Depreciation and Amortization

The Company's Buildings, Furniture, Fixtures and Equipment are recorded at cost and depreciated using the straight-line method over the estimated useful lives of the assets. Leasehold Improvements are amortized using the straight-line method over the original term of the lease or the useful life of the improvement, whichever is shorter. The Company's Property and Equipment is depreciated using the following estimated useful lives:

	Life
Buildings	5 – 45 years
Furniture, Fixtures and Equipment	3 – 20 years
Leasehold Improvements	5 – 45 years

Capitalized Software Costs

The Company capitalizes certain costs related to the acquisition and development of software and amortizes these costs using the straight-line method over the estimated useful life of the software, which is three to six years. These costs are included in Furniture, Fixtures and Equipment in the accompanying Consolidated Balance Sheets. Certain development costs not meeting the criteria for capitalization are expensed as incurred.

Revenues

The Company recognizes revenue, net of estimated returns and sales tax, at the time the customer takes possession of merchandise or receives services. The liability for sales returns is estimated based on historical return levels. When the Company receives payment from customers before the customer has taken possession of the merchandise or the service has been performed, the amount received is recorded as Deferred Revenue in the accompanying Consolidated Balance Sheets until the sale or service is complete. The Company also records Deferred Revenue for the sale of gift cards and recognizes this revenue upon the redemption of gift cards in Net Sales. Gift card breakage income is recognized based upon historical redemption patterns and represents the balance of gift cards for which the Company believes the likelihood of redemption by the customer is remote. During fiscal 2009, 2008 and 2007, the Company recognized $40 million, $37 million and $36 million, respectively, of gift card breakage income. This income is recorded as other income and is included in the accompanying Consolidated Statements of Earnings as a reduction in SG&A.

Services Revenue

Net Sales include services revenue generated through a variety of installation, home maintenance and professional service programs. In these programs, the customer selects and purchases material for a project and the Company provides or arranges professional installation. These programs are offered through the Company's stores. Under certain programs, when the Company provides or arranges the installation of a project and the subcontractor provides material as part of the installation, both the material and labor are included in services revenue. The Company recognizes this revenue when the service for the customer is complete.

All payments received prior to the completion of services are recorded in Deferred Revenue in the accompanying Consolidated Balance Sheets. Services revenue was $2.6 billion, $3.1 billion and $3.5 billion for fiscal 2009, 2008 and 2007, respectively.

Self-Insurance

The Company is self-insured for certain losses related to general liability, product liability, automobile, workers' compensation and medical claims. The expected ultimate cost for claims incurred as of the balance sheet date is not discounted and is recognized as a liability. The expected ultimate cost of claims is estimated based upon analysis of historical data and actuarial estimates.

Prepaid Advertising

Television and radio advertising production costs, along with media placement costs, are expensed when the advertisement first appears. Amounts included in Other Current Assets in the accompanying Consolidated Balance Sheets relating to prepayments of production costs for print and broadcast advertising as well as sponsorship promotions were not material at the end of fiscal 2009 and 2008.

Vendor Allowances

Vendor allowances primarily consist of volume rebates that are earned as a result of attaining certain purchase levels and advertising co-op allowances for the promotion of vendors' products that are typically based on guaranteed minimum amounts with additional amounts being earned for attaining certain purchase levels. These vendor allowances are accrued as earned, with those allowances received as a result of attaining certain purchase levels accrued over the incentive period based on estimates of purchases.

Volume rebates and certain advertising co-op allowances earned are initially recorded as a reduction in Merchandise Inventories and a subsequent reduction in Cost of Sales when the related product is sold. Certain advertising co-op allowances that are reimbursements of specific, incremental and identifiable costs incurred to promote vendors' products are recorded as an offset against advertising expense. In fiscal 2009, 2008 and 2007, gross advertising expense was $897 million, $1.0 billion and $1.2 billion, respectively, and is included in SG&A. Specific, incremental and identifiable advertising co-op allowances were $105 million, $107 million and $120 million for fiscal 2009, 2008 and 2007, respectively, and were recorded as an offset to advertising expense in SG&A.

Cost of Sales

Cost of Sales includes the actual cost of merchandise sold and services performed, the cost of transportation of merchandise from vendors to the Company's stores, locations or customers, the operating cost of the Company's sourcing and distribution network and the cost of deferred interest programs offered through the Company's private label credit card program.

The cost of handling and shipping merchandise from the Company's stores, locations or distribution centers to the customer is classified as SG&A. The cost of shipping and handling, including internal costs and payments to third parties, classified as SG&A was $426 million, $501 million and $571 million in fiscal 2009, 2008 and 2007, respectively.

Impairment of Long-Lived Assets

The Company evaluates its long-lived assets each quarter for indicators of potential impairment. Indicators of impairment include current period losses combined with a history of losses, management's decision to relocate or close a store or other location before the end of its previously estimated useful life, or when changes in other circumstances indicate the carrying amount of an asset may not be recoverable. The evaluation for long-lived assets is performed at the lowest level of identifiable cash flows, which is generally the individual store level.

The assets of a store with indicators of impairment are evaluated by comparing its undiscounted cash flows with its carrying value. The estimate of cash flows includes management's assumptions of cash inflows and outflows directly resulting from the use of those assets in operations, including gross margin on Net Sales, payroll and related items, occupancy costs, insurance allocations and other costs to operate a store. If the carrying value is greater than the undiscounted cash flows, an impairment loss is recognized for the difference between the carrying value and the estimated fair market value. Impairment losses are recorded as a component of SG&A in the accompanying Consolidated Statements of Earnings. When a leased location closes, the Company also recognizes in SG&A the net present value of future lease obligations less estimated sublease income.

As part of its Rationalization Charges, the Company recorded no asset impairment and $84 million of lease obligation costs in fiscal 2009 compared to $580 million of asset impairments and $252 million of lease obligation costs in fiscal 2008. See Note 2 for more details on the Rationalization Charges. The Company also recorded impairments on other closings and relocations in the ordinary course of business, which were not material to the Consolidated Financial Statements in fiscal 2009, 2008 and 2007.

Goodwill and Other Intangible Assets

Goodwill represents the excess of purchase price over the fair value of net assets acquired. The Company does not amortize goodwill, but does assess the recoverability of goodwill in the third quarter of each fiscal year, or more often if indicators warrant, by determining whether the fair value of each reporting unit supports its carrying value. The fair values of the Company's identified reporting units were estimated using the present value of expected future discounted cash flows.

The Company amortizes the cost of other intangible assets over their estimated useful lives, which range from 1 to 20 years, unless such lives are deemed indefinite. Intangible assets with indefinite lives are tested in the third quarter of each fiscal year for impairment, or more often if indicators warrant. The Company recorded no impairment charges for goodwill or other intangible assets for fiscal 2009, 2008 or 2007.

Stock-Based Compensation

The per share weighted average fair value of stock options granted during fiscal 2009, 2008 and 2007 was $6.61, $6.46 and $9.45, respectively. The fair value of these options was determined at the date of grant using the Black- Scholes option-pricing model with the following assumptions:

	Fiscal Year Ended		
	January 31, 2010	February 1, 2009	February 3, 2008
Risk-free interest rate	2.3%	2.9%	4.4%
Assumed volatility	41.5%	33.8%	25.5%
Assumed dividend yield	3.9%	3.5%	2.4%
Assumed lives of option	6 years	6 years	6 years

Derivatives

The Company uses derivative financial instruments from time to time in the management of its interest rate exposure on long-term debt and its exposure on foreign currency fluctuations. The Company accounts for its derivative financial instruments in accordance with the Financial Accounting Standards Board Accounting Standards Codification ("FASB ASC") 815-10. The fair value of the Company's derivative financial instruments is discussed in Note 5.

Comprehensive Income

Comprehensive Income includes Net Earnings adjusted for certain revenues, expenses, gains and losses that are excluded from Net Earnings under U.S. generally accepted accounting principles. Adjustments to Net Earnings and Accumulated Other Comprehensive Income consist primarily of foreign currency translation adjustments.

Foreign Currency Translation

Assets and Liabilities denominated in a foreign currency are translated into U.S. dollars at the current rate of exchange on the last day of the reporting period. Revenues and expenses are generally translated using average exchange rates for the period and equity transactions are translated using the actual rate on the day of the transaction.

Segment Information

The Company operates within a single reportable segment primarily within North America. Net Sales for the Company outside of the U.S. were $7.0 billion for fiscal 2009 and were $7.4 billion for fiscal 2008 and 2007. Long-lived assets outside of the U.S. totaled $3.0 billion and $2.8 billion as of January 31, 2010 and February 1, 2009, respectively.

2.   RATIONALIZATION CHARGES

In fiscal 2008, the Company reduced its square footage growth plans to improve free cash flow, provide stronger returns for the Company and invest in its existing stores to continue improving the customer experience. As a result of this store rationalization plan, the Company determined that it would no longer pursue the opening of approximately 50 U.S. stores that had been in its new store pipeline. The Company expects to dispose of or sublet these pipeline locations over varying periods. The Company also closed 15 underperforming U.S. stores in the second quarter of fiscal 2008, and the Company expects to dispose of or sublet those locations over varying periods.

Also in fiscal 2008, the Company announced that it would exit its EXPO, THD Design Center, Yardbirds and HD Bath businesses (the "Exited Businesses") in order to focus on its core The Home Depot stores. The Company closed the Exited Businesses in the first quarter of fiscal 2009 and expects to dispose of or sublet those locations over varying periods. These steps impacted approximately 5,000 associates in those locations, their support functions and their distribution centers.

Finally, in January 2009 the Company restructured its support functions to better align the Company's cost structure. These actions impacted approximately 2,000 associates.

The Company recognized $146 million and $951 million in total pretax charges for fiscal 2009 and 2008, respectively, related to these actions (collectively, the "Rationalization Charges"). The significant components of the total expected charges and charges incurred to date are as follows (amounts in millions):

	Total Expected Charges	Fiscal 2008 Charges	Fiscal 2009 Charges	Estimated Remaining Charges
Asset impairments	$ 580	$580	$ —	$ —
Lease obligation costs, net	336	252	84	—
Severance	86	78	8	—
Other	95	41	54	—
Total	$1,097	$951	$146	$ —

Inventory markdown costs reflected in Other are included in Cost of Sales in the accompanying Consolidated Statements of Earnings, and costs related to asset impairments, lease obligations, severance and other miscellaneous costs are included in SG&A expenses. Asset impairment charges, including contractual costs to complete certain assets, were determined based on fair market value using market data for each individual property. Lease obligation costs represent the present value of contractually obligated rental payments offset by estimated sublet income, including estimates of the time required to sublease the locations. The payments related to the leased locations therefore are not generally incremental uses of cash.

Activity related to Rationalization Charges for fiscal 2009 and 2008 was as follows (amounts in millions):

	Fiscal 2008 Charges	Cash Uses	Non-cash Uses	Accrued Balance February 1, 2009	Fiscal 2009 Charges	Cash Uses	Non-cash Uses	Accrued Balance January 31, 2010
Asset impairments	$580	$—	$542	$ 38	$ —	$ —	$15	$ 23
Lease obligation costs, net	252	39	—	213	84	106	—	191
Severance	78	6	—	72	8	80	—	—
Other	41	18	3	20	54	71	3	—
Total	$951	$63	$545	$343	$146	$257	$18	$214

3. CHANGE IN ACCOUNTING PRINCIPLE

During fiscal 2008, the Company implemented a new enterprise resource planning ("ERP") system, including a new inventory system, for its retail operations in Canada. Along with this implementation, the Company changed its method of accounting for Merchandise Inventories for its retail operations in Canada from the lower of cost (first-in, first-out) or market, as determined by the retail inventory method, to the lower of cost or market using a weighted-average cost method. As of the end of fiscal 2008, the implementation of the new inventory system and related conversion to the weighted-average cost method for Canadian retail operations was complete.

The new ERP system allows the Company to utilize the weighted-average cost method, which the Company believes will result in greater precision in the costing of inventories and a better matching of cost of sales with revenue generated. The effect of the change on the Merchandise Inventories and Retained Earnings balances was not material. Prior to the inventory system conversion, the Company could not determine the impact of the change to the weighted-average cost method, and therefore, could not retroactively apply the change to periods prior to fiscal 2008.

4. DISPOSITION AND ACQUISITIONS

On August 30, 2007, the Company closed the sale of HD Supply. The Company received $8.3 billion of net proceeds for the sale of HD Supply and recognized a $4 million loss, net of tax, in fiscal 2007. Settlement of working capital matters arising from the sale of HD Supply resulted in earnings from discontinued operations of $41 million, net of tax, in fiscal 2009 and a loss from discontinued operations of $52 million, net of tax, in fiscal 2008.

In connection with the sale, the Company purchased a 12.5% equity interest in the newly formed HD Supply for $325 million. In fiscal 2008, the Company determined its 12.5% equity interest in HD Supply was impaired and recorded a $163 million charge to write-down the investment. In fiscal 2009, the Company determined its equity interest in HD Supply was further impaired and recorded an additional charge of $163 million to write-down the remaining investment. These charges are included in Interest and Other, net, in the accompanying Consolidated Statements of Earnings.

Also in connection with the sale, the Company guaranteed a $1.0 billion senior secured amortizing term loan ("guaranteed loan") of HD Supply. The fair value of the guarantee, which was determined to be approximately $16 million, is recorded as a liability of the Company and included in Other Long-Term Liabilities. The Company is responsible for up to $1.0 billion and any unpaid interest in the event of non payment by HD Supply. The guaranteed loan is collateralized by certain assets of HD Supply. The original expiration date of the guarantee was August 30, 2012. On March 19, 2010, the Company amended the expiration date and extended it to April 1, 2014.

In accordance with FASB ASC 360-10, the Company reclassified the results of HD Supply as discontinued operations in its Consolidated Statements of Earnings for all periods presented.

The following table presents Net Sales and Earnings of HD Supply through August 30, 2007 and the gains and losses on disposition which have been classified as discontinued operations in the Consolidated Statements of Earnings for fiscal 2009, 2008 and 2007 (amounts in millions):

	Fiscal Year Ended		
	January 31, 2010	February 1, 2009	February 3, 2008
Net Sales	$—	$ —	$7,391
Earnings Before Provision for Income Taxes	$—	$ —	$ 291
Provision for Income Taxes	—	—	(102)
Gain (Loss) from Discontinued Operations, net	41	(52)	(4)
Earnings (Loss) from Discontinued Operations, net of tax	$41	$(52)	$ 185

APPENDIX C

Excerpts from the Fiscal 2009/10 Annual Report of Kingfisher plc

Note: The materials in this appendix have been selected from the full annual report of Kingfisher plc for fiscal year 2009/10, which ended January 30, 2010. The complete annual report is available on Connect or from Kingfisher's Web site at www.kingfisher.co.uk.

Independent auditors' report to the members of Kingfisher plc

We have audited the Group financial statements of Kingfisher plc for the year ended 30 January 2010 which comprise the Consolidated income statement, Consolidated statement of comprehensive income, Consolidated statement of changes in equity, Consolidated balance sheet, Consolidated cash flow statement and the related notes 1 to 37. The financial reporting framework that has been applied in their preparation is applicable law and International Financial Reporting Standards (IFRSs) as adopted by the European Union.

This report is made solely to the Company's members, as a body, in accordance with Chapter 3 of Part 16 of the Companies Act 2006. Our audit work has been undertaken so that we might state to the Company's members those matters we are required to state to them in an auditors' report and for no other purpose. To the fullest extent permitted by law, we do not accept or assume responsibility to anyone other than the Company and the Company's members as a body, for our audit work, for this report, or for the opinions we have formed.

Respective responsibilities of directors and auditors

As explained more fully in the Directors' statement of responsibility, the directors are responsible for the preparation of the Group financial statements and for being satisfied that they give a true and fair view. Our responsibility is to audit the Group financial statements in accordance with applicable law and International Standards on Auditing (UK and Ireland). Those standards require us to comply with the Auditing Practices Board's (APB's) Ethical Standards for Auditors.

Scope of the audit of the financial statements

An audit involves obtaining evidence about the amounts and disclosures in the financial statements sufficient to give reasonable assurance that the financial statements are free from material misstatement, whether caused by fraud or error. This includes an assessment of: whether the accounting policies are appropriate to the Group's circumstances and have been consistently applied and adequately disclosed; the reasonableness of significant accounting estimates made by the directors; and the overall presentation of the financial statements.

Opinion on financial statements

In our opinion the Group financial statements:
– give a true and fair view of the state of the Group's affairs as at 30 January 2010 and of its profit for the year then ended;
– have been properly prepared in accordance with IFRSs as adopted by the European Union; and
– have been prepared in accordance with the requirements of the Companies Act 2006 and Article 4 of the IAS Regulation.

Opinion on other matter prescribed by the Companies Act 2006

In our opinion:
– the part of the Directors' remuneration report to be audited has been properly prepared in accordance with the Companies Act 2006; and
– the information given in the Directors' report for the financial year for which the financial statements are prepared is consistent with the Group financial statements.

Matters on which we are required to report by exception

We have nothing to report in respect of the following:

Under the Companies Act 2006 we are required to report to you if, in our opinion:
– certain disclosures of directors' remuneration specified by law are not made; or
– we have not received all the information and explanations we require for our audit.

Under the Listing Rules we are required to review:
– the directors' statement contained within the Directors' statement of responsibility in relation to going concern; and
– the part of the Corporate governance statement relating to the Company's compliance with the nine provisions of the June 2008 Combined Code specified for our review.

Other matter

We have reported separately on the Parent Company financial statements of Kingfisher plc for the year ended 30 January 2010.

Panos Kakoullis (Senior Statutory Auditor)
for and on behalf of Deloitte LLP
Chartered Accountants and Statutory Auditors
London, United Kingdom
24 March 2010

Consolidated income statement

Year ended 30 January 2010

£ millions	Notes	2009/10 Before exceptional items	Exceptional items (note 5)	Total	2008/09 Before exceptional items	Exceptional items (note 5)	Total
Sales	4	**10,503**	**–**	**10,503**	10,026	–	10,026
Cost of sales		**(6,706)**	**–**	**(6,706)**	(6,504)	(21)	(6,525)
Gross profit		**3,797**	**–**	**3,797**	3,522	(21)	3,501
Selling and distribution expenses		**(2,712)**	**–**	**(2,712)**	(2,624)	(105)	(2,729)
Administrative expenses		**(536)**	**–**	**(536)**	(496)	(124)	(620)
Other income		**31**	**17**	**48**	22	13	35
Share of post-tax results of joint ventures and associates	17	**26**	**–**	**26**	22	(36)	(14)
Operating profit		**606**	**17**	**623**	446	(273)	173
Analysed as:							
Retail profit	4	**664**	**17**	**681**	503	(113)	390
Impairment of goodwill and investment in associate		**–**	**–**	**–**	–	(160)	(160)
Central costs		**(41)**	**–**	**(41)**	(41)	–	(41)
Share of interest and tax of joint ventures and associates		**(17)**	**–**	**(17)**	(16)	–	(16)
Finance costs		**(76)**	**–**	**(76)**	(119)	–	(119)
Finance income		**19**	**–**	**19**	36	–	36
Net finance costs	6	**(57)**	**–**	**(57)**	(83)	–	(83)
Profit before taxation	7	**549**	**17**	**566**	363	(273)	90
Income tax expense	9	**(174)**	**(7)**	**(181)**	(95)	7	(88)
Profit from continuing operations		**375**	**10**	**385**	268	(266)	2
Profit from discontinued operations	34	**–**	**–**	**–**	26	178	204
Profit for the year		**375**	**10**	**385**	294	(88)	206

Attributable to:							
Equity shareholders of the Company				**388**			209
Minority interests				**(3)**			(3)
				385			206

Earnings per share	10				
Continuing operations:					
Basic				**16.5p**	0.2p
Diluted				**16.4p**	0.2p
Adjusted basic				**16.4p**	11.0p
Adjusted diluted				**16.3p**	11.0p
Total operations:					
Basic				**16.5p**	8.9p
Diluted				**16.4p**	8.9p

The proposed final dividend for the year ended 30 January 2010, subject to approval by shareholders at the Annual General Meeting, is 3.575p per share.

C.3

Consolidated statement of comprehensive income

Year ended 30 January 2010

£ millions	Notes	2009/10	2008/09
Profit for the year		**385**	206
Actuarial losses on post employment benefits	27	**(165)**	(191)
Currency translation differences			
Group		**15**	159
Joint ventures and associates		**(6)**	32
Gains transferred to income statement		**–**	(80)
Cash flow hedges			
Fair value (losses)/gains		**(13)**	33
Gains transferred to inventories		**(5)**	(10)
Tax on other comprehensive income		**55**	35
Other comprehensive income for the year		**(119)**	(22)
Total comprehensive income for the year		**266**	184
Attributable to:			
Equity shareholders of the Company		**271**	180
Minority interests		**(5)**	4
		266	184

Consolidated statement of changes in equity

Year ended 30 January 2010

£ millions	Notes	Share capital	Share premium	Own shares held	Retained earnings	Other reserves (note 29)	Total	Minority interests	Total equity
						Attributable to equity shareholders of the Company			
At 1 February 2009		**371**	**2,188**	**(57)**	**1,768**	**513**	**4,783**	**15**	**4,798**
Profit for the year		–	–	–	**388**	–	**388**	**(3)**	**385**
Actuarial losses on post employment benefits	27	–	–	–	(165)	–	(165)	–	(165)
Currency translation differences									
Group		–	–	–	–	17	17	(2)	15
Joint ventures and associates		–	–	–	–	(6)	(6)	–	(6)
Cash flow hedges									
Fair value losses		–	–	–	–	(13)	(13)	–	(13)
Gains transferred to inventories		–	–	–	–	(5)	(5)	–	(5)
Tax on other comprehensive income		–	–	–	45	10	55	–	55
Other comprehensive income for the year		**–**	**–**	**–**	**(120)**	**3**	**(117)**	**(2)**	**(119)**
Total comprehensive income for the year		–	–	–	268	3	271	(5)	266
Share-based compensation		–	–	–	20	–	20	–	20
Shares issued under share schemes		–	3	–	–	–	3	–	3
Own shares purchased		–	–	(7)	–	–	(7)	–	(7)
Own shares disposed		–	–	10	(10)	–	–	–	–
Dividends		–	–	–	(125)	–	(125)	–	(125)
At 30 January 2010		**371**	**2,191**	**(54)**	**1,921**	**516**	**4,945**	**10**	**4,955**
At 3 February 2008		371	2,188	(66)	1,815	405	4,713	11	4,724
Profit for the year		–	–	–	209	–	209	(3)	206
Actuarial losses on post employment benefits	27	–	–	–	(191)	–	(191)	–	(191)
Currency translation differences									
Group		–	–	–	–	152	152	7	159
Joint ventures and associates		–	–	–	–	32	32	–	32
Gains transferred to income statement		–	–	–	–	(80)	(80)	–	(80)
Cash flow hedges									
Fair value gains		–	–	–	–	33	33	–	33
Gains transferred to inventories		–	–	–	–	(10)	(10)	–	(10)
Tax on other comprehensive income		–	–	–	54	(19)	35	–	35
Other comprehensive income for the year		–	–	–	(137)	108	(29)	7	(22)
Total comprehensive income for the year		–	–	–	72	108	180	4	184
Share-based compensation		–	–	–	15	–	15	–	15
Own shares disposed		–	–	9	(9)	–	–	–	–
Dividends		–	–	–	(125)	–	(125)	(1)	(126)
Capital injections from minority interests		–	–	–	–	–	–	1	1
At 31 January 2009		371	2,188	(57)	1,768	513	4,783	15	4,798

Consolidated balance sheet
At 30 January 2010

£ millions	Notes	2009/10	2008/09
Non-current assets			
Goodwill	12	**2,395**	2,396
Other intangible assets	13	**70**	73
Property, plant and equipment	14	**3,612**	3,699
Investment property	15	**24**	24
Investments in joint ventures and associates	17	**234**	219
Deferred tax assets	25	**27**	26
Derivatives	23	**81**	180
Other receivables	19	**22**	17
		6,465	6,634
Current assets			
Inventories	18	**1,545**	1,792
Trade and other receivables	19	**494**	508
Derivatives	23	**24**	107
Current tax assets		**58**	33
Cash and cash equivalents	20	**1,260**	1,157
		3,381	3,597
Total assets		**9,846**	10,231
Current liabilities			
Trade and other payables	21	**(2,374)**	(2,362)
Borrowings	22	**(647)**	(389)
Derivatives	23	**(25)**	(38)
Current tax liabilities		**(348)**	(206)
Provisions	26	**(36)**	(69)
		(3,430)	(3,064)
Non-current liabilities			
Other payables	21	**(74)**	(33)
Borrowings	22	**(883)**	(1,907)
Derivatives	23	**(47)**	(76)
Deferred tax liabilities	25	**(197)**	(226)
Provisions	26	**(62)**	(53)
Post employment benefits	27	**(198)**	(74)
		(1,461)	(2,369)
Total liabilities		**(4,891)**	(5,433)
Net assets	4	**4,955**	4,798
Equity			
Share capital	28	**371**	371
Share premium		**2,191**	2,188
Own shares held		**(54)**	(57)
Retained earnings		**1,921**	1,768
Other reserves	29	**516**	513
Total attributable to equity shareholders of the Company		**4,945**	4,783
Minority interests		**10**	15
Total equity		**4,955**	4,798

The financial statements were approved by the Board of Directors on 24 March 2010 and signed on its behalf by:

Ian Cheshire
Group Chief Executive

Kevin O'Byrne
Group Finance Director

Consolidated cash flow statement

Year ended 30 January 2010

£ millions	Notes	2009/10	2008/09
Operating activities			
Cash generated by operations	31	**1,130**	867
Income tax paid		**(151)**	(77)
French tax receipt	9	**148**	–
Net cash flows from operating activities		**1,127**	790
Investing activities			
Purchase of minority interests		**–**	(7)
Purchase of property, plant and equipment, investment property and intangible assets	4	**(256)**	(390)
Disposal of property, plant and equipment, investment property and intangible assets		**59**	62
Disposal of other investments		**–**	12
Dividends received from joint ventures and associates		**5**	3
Net cash flows from investing activities		**(192)**	(320)
Financing activities			
Interest paid		**(72)**	(111)
Interest element of finance lease rental payments		**(5)**	(5)
Interest received		**14**	22
Repayment of bank loans		**(130)**	(37)
Repayment of Medium Term Notes and other fixed term debt		**(500)**	–
Receipt/(payment) on financing derivatives		**78**	(5)
Capital element of finance lease rental payments		**(14)**	(12)
Issue of share capital to minority interests		**–**	1
Purchase of own shares		**(7)**	–
Dividends paid to equity shareholders of the Company		**(125)**	(125)
Dividends paid to minority interests		**–**	(1)
Net cash flows from financing activities		**(761)**	(273)
Net increase in cash and cash equivalents and bank overdrafts from continuing operations		**174**	197
Net cash flows from operating activities		**–**	23
Net cash flows from investing activities		**–**	522
Net cash flows from financing activities		**–**	1
Net increase in cash and cash equivalents and bank overdrafts from discontinued operations	34	**–**	546
Net increase in cash and cash equivalents and bank overdrafts		**174**	743
Cash and cash equivalents and bank overdrafts at beginning of year		**994**	195
Exchange differences		**(33)**	56
Cash and cash equivalents and bank overdrafts at end of year	32	**1,135**	994

Notes to the consolidated financial statements

1 General information

Kingfisher plc ('the Company'), its subsidiaries, joint ventures and associates (together 'the Group') supply home improvement products and services through a network of retail stores and other channels, located mainly in the United Kingdom, continental Europe and China.

Kingfisher plc is a Company incorporated in the United Kingdom. The nature of the Group's operations and its principal activities are set out in the Business review on pages 1 to 28.

The address of its registered office is 3 Sheldon Square, Paddington, London W2 6PX.

The Company is listed on the London Stock Exchange.

These consolidated financial statements have been approved for issue by the Board of Directors on 24 March 2010.

2 Principal accounting policies

The principal accounting policies applied in the preparation of these consolidated financial statements are set out below. These policies have been consistently applied to the years presented, unless otherwise stated.

a. Basis of preparation

The consolidated financial statements of the Company, its subsidiaries, joint ventures and associates are made up to the nearest Saturday to 31 January each year, except as disclosed in note 17 and in note 4 of the Company's separate financial statements. The current financial year is the 52 weeks ended 30 January 2010 ('the year'). The comparative financial year is the 52 weeks ended 31 January 2009 ('the prior year').

The directors of Kingfisher plc, having made appropriate enquiries, consider that adequate resources exist for the Group to continue in operational existence for the foreseeable future and that, therefore, it is appropriate to adopt the going concern basis in preparing the consolidated financial statements for the year ended 30 January 2010. Refer to the Directors' statement of responsibility on page 34.

The consolidated financial statements have been prepared in accordance with International Financial Reporting Standards ('IFRS') as adopted by the European Union, IFRIC interpretations and those parts of the Companies Act 2006 applicable to companies reporting under IFRS.

The following new standards and amendments, which are mandatory for the first time for the financial year beginning 1 February 2009, are relevant for the Group:

IAS 1 (revised)	Presentation of financial statements	Requires non-owner changes in equity to be shown in either one performance statement (the statement of comprehensive income) or two statements (the income statement and statement of comprehensive income). The Group has elected to present two statements. Owner changes in equity are required to be shown in a statement of changes in equity.
IAS 38 (amendment)	Intangible assets – Catalogue costs	Expenses incurred in printing mail order catalogues are recognised once the catalogues are printed and not when they are distributed to customers. The impact of this on the results presented has not been significant.
IFRS 2 (amendment)	Share-based payments – Vesting conditions and cancellations	Clarifies that vesting conditions are service conditions and performance conditions only. Other features that are not vesting conditions are required to be included in the grant date fair value. The impact of this on the results presented has not been significant.
IFRS 7 (amendment)	Improving disclosures about financial instruments	The amendments to IFRS 7 introduce a three level hierarchy for fair value measurement disclosures and require entities to provide additional disclosures about the relative reliability of fair value measurements. In addition, the amendments clarify the existing requirements for the disclosure of liquidity risk. These requirements have been incorporated into the relevant financial instrument disclosures.
IFRS 8	Operating segments	IFRS 8 replaces IAS 14, 'Segment reporting'. It requires a 'management approach' under which segment information is presented on the same basis as that used for internal reporting purposes. This has resulted in Ireland moving from 'Other International' to 'UK & Ireland' (previously 'UK') and the presentation of new segmental assets and other information. Refer to note 4 for further information.

The following new standard and interpretation, which are mandatory for the first time for the financial year beginning 1 February 2009, are relevant but were already applied by the Group:
- IAS 23, 'Borrowing costs (revised)'; and
- IFRIC 13, 'Customer loyalty programmes'.

The following amendments to standards and interpretation, which are mandatory for the first time for the financial year beginning 1 February 2009, are either not currently relevant or material for the Group:
- IAS 39 (amendment), 'Financial instruments: Recognition and measurement';
- IAS 39 and IFRS 7 (amendment), 'Reclassification of financial assets'; and
- IFRIC 16, 'Hedges of a net investment in a foreign operation'.

At the date of authorisation of these financial statements, the following new standard and amendments, which are expected to be relevant to the Group's results, were issued but not yet effective:

IAS 27 (amendment)	Consolidated and separate financial statements - Non-controlling interests (effective from 1 July 2009)	Requires the effects of all transactions with non-controlling (minority) interests to be recorded in equity if there is no change in control. They will no longer result in goodwill or gains and losses. The amended standard also specifies the accounting when control is lost. Any remaining interest in the entity is remeasured to fair value and a gain or loss is recognised in profit or loss. This will be applied in the Group's 2010/11 financial statements.
IFRS 3 (amendment)	Business combinations (effective from 1 July 2009)	Harmonises business combination accounting with US GAAP. The amended standard will continue to apply the acquisitions method to business combinations, but with certain significant changes. All payments to purchase a business will be recorded at fair value at the acquisition date, with some contingent payments subsequently remeasured at fair value through income. Goodwill and non-controlling (minority) interests may be calculated on a gross or net basis. All transaction costs will be expensed. This will be applied in the Group's 2010/11 financial statements.
IFRS 9	Financial instruments (effective from 1 January 2013)	Introduces new requirements for classifying and measuring financial assets. This includes the removal of available-for-sale financial assets and held-to-maturity investments, and the introduction of a new category of financial assets at fair value through other comprehensive income. This is still subject to endorsement by the European Union, but is currently expected to be applied in the Group's 2013/14 financial statements.

The consolidated financial statements have been prepared under the historical cost convention, as modified by the use of valuations for certain financial instruments, share-based payments and post employment benefits. A summary of the Group's principal accounting policies is set out below.

The preparation of financial statements in conformity with IFRS requires the use of certain accounting estimates and assumptions. It also requires management to exercise its judgement in the process of applying the Group's accounting policies. The areas involving critical accounting estimates and judgements, which are significant to the consolidated financial statements, are disclosed in note 3.

Use of non-GAAP measures
Kingfisher believes that retail profit, adjusted pre-tax profit, effective tax rate, adjusted post-tax profit and adjusted earnings per share provide additional useful information on underlying trends to shareholders. These and other non-GAAP measures such as net debt are used by Kingfisher for internal performance analysis and incentive compensation arrangements for employees. The terms 'retail profit', 'exceptional items', 'adjusted', 'effective tax rate' and 'net debt' are not defined terms under IFRS and may therefore not be comparable with similarly titled measures reported by other companies. They are not intended to be a substitute for, or superior to, GAAP measures.

Retail profit is defined as continuing operating profit before central costs (principally the costs of the Group's head office), exceptional items, amortisation of acquisition intangibles and the Group's share of interest and tax of joint ventures and associates.

The separate reporting of non-recurring exceptional items, which are presented as exceptional within their relevant income statement category, helps provide an indication of the Group's underlying business performance. The principal items which are included as exceptional items are:
- non trading items included in operating profit such as profits and losses on the disposal, closure or impairment of subsidiaries, joint ventures, associates and investments which do not form part of the Group's trading activities;
- profits and losses on the disposal of properties; and
- the costs of significant restructuring and incremental acquisition integration costs.

The term 'adjusted' refers to the relevant measure being reported for continuing operations excluding exceptional items, financing fair value remeasurements, amortisation of acquisition intangibles, related tax items and prior year tax items. Financing fair value remeasurements represent changes in the fair value of financing derivatives, excluding interest accruals, offset by fair value adjustments to the carrying amount of borrowings and other hedged items under fair value hedge relationships. Financing derivatives are those that relate to underlying items of a financing nature.

The effective tax rate represents the effective income tax expense as a percentage of continuing profit before taxation excluding exceptional items. Effective income tax expense is the continuing income tax expense excluding tax on exceptional items and tax adjustments in respect of prior years and changes in tax rates.

Net debt comprises borrowings and financing derivatives (excluding accrued interest), less cash and cash equivalents and current other investments.

b. Basis of consolidation
The consolidated financial statements incorporate the financial statements of the Company, its subsidiaries, joint ventures and associates.

(i) Subsidiaries
Subsidiary undertakings are all entities over which the Group has the power to govern the financial and operating policies, generally accompanying a shareholding of more than one half of the voting rights. Subsidiary undertakings acquired during the period are recorded under the acquisition method of accounting and their results included from the date of acquisition. The results of subsidiaries which have been disposed of during the period are included up to the effective date of disposal.

The acquisition method of accounting is used to account for the acquisition of subsidiaries by the Group. The cost of an acquisition is measured as the fair value of the assets given, equity instruments issued and liabilities incurred or assumed at the date of exchange, plus costs directly attributable to the acquisition. Identifiable assets acquired and liabilities and contingent liabilities assumed in a business combination are measured initially at their fair values at the acquisition date, irrespective of the extent of any minority interest. The excess of the cost of acquisition over the fair value of the Group's share

2 Principal accounting policies continued

of the identifiable net assets acquired is recorded as goodwill. If the cost of acquisition is less than the fair value of the net assets of the subsidiary acquired, the difference is recognised directly in the income statement.

Intercompany transactions, balances and unrealised gains on transactions between Group companies are eliminated. Unrealised losses are also eliminated unless the transaction provides evidence of an impairment of the asset transferred. Accounting policies of acquired subsidiaries have been changed where necessary to ensure consistency with the policies adopted by the Group.

(ii) Joint ventures and associates

Joint ventures are entities over which the Group has joint control, with a third party, to govern the financial and operating activities of that entity. The equity method is used to account for the Group's investments in joint ventures.

Associates are entities over which the Group has the ability to exercise significant influence but not control, generally accompanying a shareholding of between 20% and 50% of the voting rights. The equity method is used to account for the Group's investments in associates.

Under the equity method investments are initially recognised at cost. The Group's investments in joint ventures and associates include goodwill (net of any accumulated impairment losses) identified on acquisition.

The Group's share of post-acquisition profits or losses is recognised in the income statement within operating profit, and its share of post-acquisition movements in reserves is recognised in reserves. The cumulative post-acquisition movements are adjusted against the carrying amount of the investment. When the Group's share of losses equals or exceeds its interest, including any other long term receivables, the Group does not recognise any further losses, unless it has incurred obligations or made payments on behalf of the joint venture or associate.

Unrealised gains on transactions between the Group and its joint ventures and associates are eliminated to the extent of the Group's interest. Unrealised losses are also eliminated unless the transaction provides evidence of an impairment of the asset transferred. Accounting policies of joint ventures and associates have been changed where necessary to ensure consistency with the policies adopted by the Group.

c. Foreign currencies

(i) Presentation and functional currencies

The consolidated financial statements are presented in Sterling, which is the Group's presentation currency. Items included in the financial statements of each of the Group's entities are measured using the currency of the primary economic environment in which the entity operates (i.e. its functional currency).

(ii) Transactions and balances

Transactions denominated in foreign currencies are translated into the functional currency at the exchange rates prevailing on the date of the transaction or, for practical reasons, at average monthly rates where exchange rates do not fluctuate significantly.

Monetary assets and liabilities denominated in foreign currencies are translated into Sterling at the rates of exchange at the balance sheet date. Exchange differences on monetary items are taken to the income statement. Exceptions to this are where the monetary items form part of the net investment in a foreign operation or are designated and effective net investment or cash flow hedges. Such exchange differences are initially deferred in equity.

(iii) Group companies

The balance sheets of overseas subsidiary undertakings are expressed in Sterling at the rates of exchange at the balance sheet date. Profits and losses of overseas subsidiary undertakings are expressed in Sterling at average exchange rates for the period. Exchange differences arising on the retranslation of foreign operations are recognised in a separate component of equity.

On consolidation, exchange differences arising from the retranslation of the net investment in foreign entities, and of borrowings and other currency instruments designated as hedges of such investments, are taken to equity. When a foreign operation is sold, such exchange differences are recognised in the income statement as part of the gain or loss on disposal.

Goodwill and fair value adjustments arising on the acquisition of a foreign entity are treated as assets and liabilities of the foreign entity and translated at the rates of exchange at the balance sheet date.

Principal rates of exchange:

	2009/10		2008/09	
	Average rate	Year end rate	Average rate	Year end rate
Euro/£	**1.13**	**1.15**	1.24	1.12
US Dollar/£	**1.58**	**1.61**	1.81	1.44
Polish Zloty/£	**4.86**	**4.69**	4.39	5.02
Chinese Renminbi/£	**10.79**	**11.01**	12.51	9.86

d. Revenue recognition

Sales represent the supply of home improvement products and services. Sales exclude transactions made between companies within the Group, Value Added Tax, other sales-related taxes and are net of returns, trade and staff discounts.

Sales of in-store products are generally recognised at the point of cash receipt. Where award credits such as vouchers or loyalty points are provided as part of the sales transaction, the amount allocated to the credits is deferred and recognised when the credits are redeemed and the Group fulfils its obligations to supply the awards.

Sales are also recognised when the product has been delivered or, for installation income, when the service has been performed. Sales from delivered products and services represent only a small component of the Group's sales as the majority relates to in-store purchases of product.

Other income is generally composed primarily of external rental income and profits and losses on disposal of assets. Rental income from operating leases is recognised on a straight line basis over the term of the relevant lease. Initial direct costs incurred in negotiating and arranging an operating lease are added to the carrying amount of the leased asset and recognised on a straight line basis over the lease term.

e. Rebates

Rebates received from suppliers mainly comprise volume related rebates on the purchase of inventories.

Volume related rebates are recognised based on actual purchases in the period as a proportion of total purchases forecast over the rebate period where it is probable the rebates will be received and the amounts can be estimated reliably.

Rebates relating to inventories purchased but still held at the balance sheet date are deducted from the carrying value so that the cost of inventories is recorded net of applicable rebates. Such rebates are credited to the income statement when the goods are sold.

f. Dividends

Interim dividends are recognised when they are paid to the Company's shareholders. Final dividends are recognised when they are approved by the Company's shareholders.

g. Intangible assets

(i) Goodwill

Goodwill is carried at cost less accumulated impairment losses. Goodwill is not amortised and is tested annually for impairment by assessing the recoverable amount of each cash generating unit or groups of cash generating units to which the goodwill relates. The recoverable amount is assessed by reference to the net present value of expected future pre-tax cash flows ('value-in-use') or fair value less costs to sell if higher. The discount rate applied is based upon the Group's weighted average cost of capital with appropriate adjustments for the risks associated with the relevant cash generating unit or groups of cash generating units. When the recoverable amount of the goodwill is less than its carrying amount, an impairment loss is recognised immediately in the income statement which cannot subsequently be reversed. Gains and losses on the disposal of an entity include the carrying amount of goodwill relating to the entity sold.

(ii) Computer software

Acquired computer software licences are capitalised on the basis of the costs incurred to acquire and bring to use the specific software. These costs are amortised over their estimated useful lives of two to five years.

Costs that are directly associated with the production of identifiable and unique software products controlled by the Group, which are expected to generate economic benefits exceeding costs beyond one year, are recognised as intangible assets. Direct costs include software development, employee and consultancy costs and an appropriate portion of relevant overheads. Costs associated with identifying, sourcing, evaluating or maintaining computer software are recognised as an expense as incurred.

h. Property, plant and equipment

(i) Cost

Property, plant and equipment held for use in the business are carried at cost less accumulated depreciation and any provisions for impairment.

(ii) Depreciation

Depreciation is provided to reflect a straight line reduction from cost to estimated residual value over the estimated useful life of the asset as follows:

Freehold land	– not depreciated
Freehold and long leasehold buildings	– over remaining useful life down to residual value
Short leasehold land and buildings	– over remaining period of the lease
Fixtures and fittings	– between 4 and 20 years
Computers and electronic equipment	– between 2 and 5 years
Motor cars	– 4 years
Commercial vehicles	– between 3 and 10 years

Long leaseholds are defined as those having remaining lease terms of more than 50 years. Asset lives and residual values are reviewed at each balance sheet date.

(iii) Impairment

Property, plant and equipment are reviewed for impairment if events or changes in circumstances indicate that the carrying amount may not be recoverable. When a review for impairment is conducted, the recoverable amount is assessed by reference to the net present value of expected future pre-tax cash flows ('value-in-use') of the relevant cash generating unit or fair value less costs to sell if higher. The discount rate applied is based upon the Group's weighted average cost of capital with appropriate adjustments for the risks associated with the relevant cash generating unit. Any impairment in value is charged to the income statement in the period in which it occurs.

(iv) Disposal

The gain or loss arising on the disposal or retirement of an asset is determined as the difference between the sales proceeds and the carrying amount of the asset and is recognised in the income statement. Sales of land and buildings are accounted for when there is an unconditional exchange of contracts.

(v) Subsequent costs

Subsequent costs are included in the related asset's carrying amount or recognised as a separate asset, as appropriate, only when it is probable that future economic benefits associated with the item will flow to the Group and the cost of the item can be measured reliably. All other repairs and maintenance are charged to the income statement in the period in which they are incurred.

i. Leased assets

Where assets are financed by leasing agreements which give rights approximating to ownership, the assets are treated as if they had been purchased outright. The amount capitalised is the lower of the fair value or the present value of the minimum lease payments during the lease term at the inception of the lease. The assets are depreciated over the shorter of the lease term or their useful life. Obligations relating to finance leases, net of finance charges in respect of future periods, are included, as appropriate, under borrowings due within or after one year. The finance charge element of rentals is charged to finance costs in the income statement over the lease term.

All other leases are operating leases and the rental payments are generally charged to the income statement in the period to which the payments relate, except for those leases which incorporate fixed minimum rental uplift clauses. Leases which contain fixed minimum rental uplifts are charged to the income statement on a straight line basis over the lease term.

Where a lease is taken out for land and buildings combined, the buildings element of the lease may be capitalised as a finance lease if it meets the criteria for a finance lease, but the land element will in most cases be classified as an operating lease. If the contracted lease payments are not split between land and buildings in the lease contract, the split is made based on the market values of the land and buildings at the inception of the lease.

Incentives received or paid to enter into lease agreements are released to the income statement on a straight line basis over the lease term.

j. Investment property

Investment property is property held by the Group to earn rental income or for capital appreciation. The Group's investment properties are carried at cost less depreciation and provision for impairment.

k. Capitalisation of borrowing costs

Interest on borrowings to finance the construction of properties held as non-current assets is capitalised from the date work starts on the property to the date when substantially all the activities which are necessary to get the property ready for use are complete. Where construction is completed in parts, each part is considered separately when capitalising interest. Interest is capitalised before any allowance for tax relief.

l. Inventories

Inventories are carried at the lower of cost and net realisable value, on a weighted average cost basis.

Cost includes appropriate attributable overheads and direct expenditure incurred in the normal course of business in bringing goods to their present location and condition. Costs of inventories include the transfer from equity of any gains or losses on qualifying cash flow hedges relating to purchases.

Net realisable value represents the estimated selling price in the ordinary course of the business less the estimated costs necessary to make the sale. Write downs to net realisable value are made for slow moving, damaged or obsolete items and other events or conditions resulting in expected selling prices being lower than cost. The carrying value of inventories reflects known and expected losses of product in the ordinary course of business.

m. Employee benefits

(i) Post employment benefits

The Group operates various defined benefit and defined contribution pension schemes for its employees, some of which are required by local legislation. A defined benefit scheme is a pension scheme which defines an amount of pension benefit which an employee will receive on retirement. A defined contribution scheme is a pension scheme under which the Group usually pays fixed contributions into a separate entity. In all cases other than some of the legally required schemes, a separate fund is being accumulated to meet the accruing liabilities. The assets of each of these funds are either held under trusts or managed by insurance companies and are entirely separate from the Group's assets.

2 Principal accounting policies continued

The asset or liability recognised in the balance sheet in respect of defined benefit pension schemes is the fair value of scheme assets less the present value of the defined benefit obligation at the balance sheet date, together with an adjustment for any past service costs not yet recognised. The defined benefit obligation is calculated annually by independent actuaries using the projected unit credit method. The present value of the defined benefit obligation is determined by discounting the estimated future cash outflows using interest rates of high quality corporate bonds which are denominated in the currency in which the benefits will be paid and which have terms to maturity approximating to the terms of the related pension liability.

Actuarial gains and losses arising from experience adjustments and changes in actuarial assumptions are credited or charged to the statement of comprehensive income as they arise.

Past service costs are recognised immediately in the income statement, unless the changes to the pension scheme are conditional on the employees remaining in service for a specified period of time (the vesting period). In this case, the past service costs are amortised on a straight line basis over the vesting period.

For defined contribution schemes, the Group pays contributions to privately administered pension schemes on a contractual basis. The Group has no further payment obligations once the contributions have been paid. The contributions are recognised as an employee benefit expense when they are due.

(ii) Share-based compensation
The Group operates several equity-settled, share-based compensation schemes. The fair value of the employee services received in exchange for the grant of options or deferred shares is recognised as an expense and is calculated using Black-Scholes and stochastic models. The total amount to be expensed over the vesting period is determined by reference to the fair value of the options or deferred shares granted, excluding the impact of any non-market vesting conditions. The value of the charge is adjusted to reflect expected and actual levels of options vesting due to non-market vesting conditions.

n. Taxation
The income tax expense represents the sum of the tax currently payable and deferred tax.

The tax currently payable is based on taxable profit for the year. Taxable profit differs from profit before taxation as reported in the income statement because it excludes items of income or expense which are taxable or deductible in other years or which are never taxable or deductible.

Deferred tax is the tax expected to be payable or recoverable on differences between the carrying amounts of assets and liabilities in the financial statements and the corresponding tax bases used in the computation of taxable profit and is accounted for using the balance sheet liability method.

Deferred tax liabilities are generally recognised for all taxable temporary differences. Deferred tax assets are recognised to the extent that it is probable that taxable profits will be available against which deductible temporary differences or unused tax losses can be utilised. Deferred tax liabilities are not recognised if the temporary difference arises from the initial recognition of goodwill in a business combination. Deferred tax assets and liabilities are not recognised if the temporary difference arises from the initial recognition (other than in a business combination) of other assets and liabilities in a transaction which affects neither the taxable profit nor the accounting profit. Deferred tax liabilities are recognised for taxable temporary differences arising on investments in subsidiaries, joint ventures and associates, except where the Group is able to control the reversal of the temporary difference and it is probable that the temporary difference will not reverse in the foreseeable future.

The carrying amount of deferred tax assets is reviewed at each balance sheet date and reduced to the extent that it is no longer probable that sufficient taxable profits will be available to allow all or part of the asset to be recovered.

Current and deferred tax are calculated using tax rates which have been enacted or substantively enacted by the balance sheet date and are expected to apply in the period when the liability is settled or the asset is realised.

Current and deferred tax are charged or credited to the income statement, except when it relates to items charged or credited directly to equity, in which case the current or deferred tax is also recognised directly in equity.

Current and deferred tax assets and liabilities are offset against each other when they relate to income taxes levied by the same tax jurisdiction and when the Group intends to settle its current tax assets and liabilities on a net basis.

o. Provisions
Provisions are recognised when the Group has a present legal or constructive obligation as a result of past events, it is more likely than not that an outflow of resources will be required to settle the obligation and the amount can be reliably estimated. Provisions are not recognised for future operating losses.

If the effect of the time value of money is material, provisions are determined by discounting the expected future cash flows at a pre-tax rate which reflects current market assessments of the time value of money and, where appropriate, the risks specific to the liability.

p. Financial instruments
Financial assets and financial liabilities are recognised on the Group's balance sheet when the Group becomes a party to the contractual provisions of the instrument. Financial assets are derecognised when the contractual rights to the cash flows from the financial asset expire or the Group has substantially transferred the risks and rewards of ownership. Financial liabilities (or a part of a financial liability) are derecognised when the obligation specified in the contract is discharged or cancelled or expires.

(i) Cash and cash equivalents
Cash and cash equivalents include cash in hand, deposits held on call with banks and other short term highly liquid investments with original maturities of three months or less.

(ii) Borrowings
Interest bearing borrowings are recorded at the proceeds received, net of direct issue costs and subsequently measured at amortised cost. Where borrowings are in designated and effective fair value hedge relationships, adjustments are made to their carrying amounts to reflect the hedged risks. Finance charges, including premiums payable on settlement or redemption and direct issue costs, are amortised to the income statement using the effective interest method.

(iii) Other investments
Other investments include bank deposits, government bonds and other short term investments with an original maturity of more than three months.

(iv) Trade receivables
Trade receivables are initially recognised at fair value and are subsequently measured at amortised cost less any provision for bad and doubtful debts.

(v) Trade payables
Trade payables are initially recognised at fair value and are subsequently measured at amortised cost.

(vi) Derivatives and hedge accounting

Where hedge accounting is not applied, or to the extent to which it is not effective, changes in the fair value of derivatives are recognised in the income statement as they arise. Changes in the fair value of derivatives transacted as hedges of operating items and financing items are recognised in operating profit and net finance costs respectively.

Derivatives are initially recorded at fair value on the date a derivative contract is entered into and are subsequently carried at fair value. The accounting treatment of derivatives and other financial instruments classified as hedges depends on their designation, which occurs at the start of the hedge relationship. The Group designates certain financial instruments as:
– a hedge of the fair value of an asset or liability or unrecognised firm commitment ('fair value hedge');
– a hedge of a highly probable forecast transaction or firm commitment ('cash flow hedge'); or
– a hedge of a net investment in a foreign operation ('net investment hedge').

Fair value hedges

For an effective hedge of an exposure to changes in fair value, the hedged item is adjusted for changes in fair value attributable to the risk being hedged with the corresponding entry being recorded in the income statement. Gains or losses from remeasuring the corresponding hedging instrument are recognised in the same line of the income statement.

Cash flow hedges

Changes in the effective portion of the fair value of derivatives that are designated as hedges of future cash flows are recognised directly in equity, and the ineffective portion is recognised immediately in the income statement where relevant. If the cash flow hedge of a firm commitment or forecast transaction results in the recognition of a non-financial asset or liability, then, at the time it is recognised, the associated gains or losses on the derivative that had previously been recognised in equity are included in the initial measurement of the non-financial asset or liability. For hedges that result in the recognition of a financial asset or liability, amounts deferred in equity are recognised in the income statement in the same period in which the hedged item affects net profit or loss.

Net investment hedges

Where the Group hedges net investments in foreign operations through foreign currency borrowings, the gains or losses on the retranslation of the borrowings are recognised in equity. If the Group uses derivatives as the hedging instrument, the effective portion of the hedge is recognised in equity, with any ineffective portion being recognised in the income statement. Gains and losses accumulated in equity are recycled through the income statement on disposal of the foreign operation.

In order to qualify for hedge accounting, the Group documents in advance the relationship between the item being hedged and the hedging instrument. The Group also documents and demonstrates an assessment of the relationship between the hedged item and the hedging instrument, which shows that the hedge has been and will be highly effective on an ongoing basis. The effectiveness testing is re-performed at each period end to ensure that the hedge remains highly effective.

Hedge accounting is discontinued when the hedging instrument expires or is sold, terminated or exercised, or no longer qualifies for hedge accounting. At that time, any cumulative gain or loss on the hedging instrument recognised in equity is retained in equity until the highly probable forecast transaction occurs. If a hedged transaction is no longer expected to occur, the net cumulative gain or loss recognised in equity is transferred to the income statement.

Derivatives embedded in other financial instruments or other host contracts are treated as separate derivatives when their risks and characteristics are not closely related to those of host contracts, and the host contracts are not carried at fair value with unrealised gains or losses reported in the income statement.

3 Critical accounting estimates and judgements

The preparation of consolidated financial statements under IFRS requires the Group to make estimates and assumptions that affect the application of policies and reported amounts. Estimates and judgements are continually evaluated and are based on historical experience and other factors including expectations of future events that are believed to be reasonable under the circumstances. Actual results may differ from these estimates. The estimates and assumptions which have a significant risk of causing a material adjustment to the carrying amount of assets and liabilities within the next financial year are discussed below.

Impairment of goodwill and other assets

As required, the Group applies procedures to ensure that its assets are carried at no more than their recoverable amount. The procedures, by their nature, require estimates and assumptions to be made. The most significant are set out below.

The Group is required, on at least an annual basis, to test whether goodwill has suffered any impairment. As part of this testing the recoverable amounts of cash generating units have been determined based on value-in-use calculations. The use of this method requires the estimation of future cash flows expected to arise from the continuing operation of the cash generating unit and the choice of a suitable discount rate in order to calculate the present value of the forecast cash flows. Actual outcomes could vary significantly from these estimates. Further information on the impairment tests undertaken, including the key assumptions, is given in note 12.

Property, plant and equipment are reviewed for impairment if events or changes in circumstances indicate that the carrying amount may not be recoverable. When a review for impairment is conducted, the recoverable amount of an asset or a cash generating unit is determined based on value-in-use calculations prepared on the basis of management's assumptions and estimates.

At each reporting date the Group is required to assess whether there is objective evidence that its investments in associates and joint ventures may be impaired. This requires estimates of the investments' recoverable amounts, including present values of the Group's share of future cash flows.

Inventories

As inventories are carried at the lower of cost and net realisable value this requires the estimation of the eventual sales price of goods to customers in the future. A high degree of judgement is applied when estimating the impact on the carrying value of inventories of factors such as slow moving items, shrinkage, damage and obsolescence. The quantity, age and condition of inventories are regularly measured and assessed as part of range reviews and inventory counts undertaken throughout the year and across the Group. Refer to note 18 for further information.

Income taxes

The Group is subject to income taxes in numerous jurisdictions. Significant judgement is required in determining the provision for income taxes in each territory. There are many transactions and calculations for which the ultimate tax determination is uncertain during the ordinary course of business. The Group recognises liabilities for anticipated tax audit issues based on estimates of whether additional taxes will be due. Where the final outcome of these matters is different from the amounts which were initially recorded, such differences will impact the income tax and deferred tax provisions in the period in which such determination is made. Refer to notes 9 and 25 for further information.

Present and Future Value Concepts

The concepts of present value (PV) and future value (FV) are based on the time value of money. The **time value of money** is the idea that, quite simply, money received today is worth more than money to be received one year from today (or at any other future date), because it can be used to earn interest. If you invest $1,000 today at 10 percent, you will have $1,100 in one year. So $1,000 in one year is worth less than $1,000 today because you lose the opportunity to earn interest on that $1,000.

In some business situations, you will know the dollar amount of a cash flow that will occur in the future and will need to determine its value now. This type of situation is known as a **present value** problem. The opposite situation occurs when you know the dollar amount of a cash flow that occurs today and need to determine its value at some point in the future. These situations are called **future value** problems. As mentioned previously, the value of money changes over time because money can earn interest. The following table illustrates the basic difference between present value and future value problems:

	Now	Future
Present value	?	$1,000
Future value	$1,000	?

Present and future value problems may involve two types of cash flow: a single payment or an annuity (which is the fancy word for a series of equal cash payments). Combining two types of time value of money problems with two types of cash flows yields four different situations:

1. Future value of a single payment
2. Present value of a single payment
3. Future value of an annuity
4. Present value of an annuity

Most inexpensive hand-held calculators and any spreadsheet program can perform the detailed mathematical computations required to solve future value and present value problems. In later courses and in all business situations, you will probably use a calculator or computer to solve these problems. At this stage, we encourage you to solve problems using Tables D.1 through D.4 near the end of this appendix. We believe that using the tables will give you a better understanding of how and why present and future value concepts apply to business problems. The tables give the value of a $1 cash flow (single payment or annuity) for different periods (*n*) and at different interest rates (*i*). If a problem involves payments other than $1, multiply the value from the table by the amount of the payment.[1] Just before the tables near the end of this appendix, we explain how to use Excel to compute present values.

YOU SHOULD KNOW

Time value of money: The idea that money received today is worth more than the same amount received in the future because money received today can be invested to earn interest over time.

Present value: The current value of an amount to be received in the future; it is calculated by discounting a future amount for compound interest.

Future value: The sum to which an amount will increase as the result of compound interest.

FUTURE VALUE OF A SINGLE AMOUNT

In problems involving the future value of a single amount, you will be asked to calculate how much money you will have in the future as the result of investing a certain amount in the present. If you were to receive a gift of $10,000, for instance, you might decide to put it into a savings account and use the money as a down payment on a home after you graduate. The future value computation would tell you how much money will be available when you graduate.

To solve a future value problem, you need to know three items:

1. Amount to be invested.
2. Interest rate (i) the amount will earn.
3. Number of periods (n) in which the amount will earn interest.

The future value concept is based on compound interest, which simply means that interest is calculated on top of interest. Thus, the amount of interest for each period is calculated using the principal plus any interest not paid out in prior periods. Graphically, the calculation of the future value of $1 for three periods at an interest rate of 10 percent can be represented as follows:

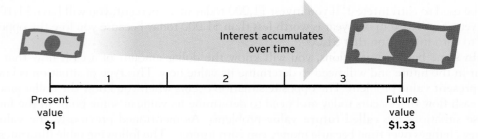

Assume that on January 1, 2012, you deposit $1,000 in a savings account at 10 percent annual interest, compounded annually. At the end of three years, the $1,000 will have increased to $1,331 as follows:

Year	Amount at Start of Year	+	Interest During the Year	=	Amount at End of Year
1	$1,000	+	$1,000 × 10% = $100	=	$1,100
2	1,100	+	1,100 × 10% = 110	=	1,210
3	1,210	+	1,210 × 10% = 121	=	1,331

We can avoid the detailed arithmetic by referring to Table D.1, Future Value of $1, on page D.13. For $i = 10\%$, $n = 3$, we find the value 1.3310. We then compute the balance at the end of year 3 as follows:

From Table D.1, Interest rate = 10% $n = 3$

$$\$1{,}000 \times 1.3310 = \$1{,}331$$

Note that the increase of $331 is due to the time value of money. It is interest revenue to the owner of the savings account and interest expense to the bank.

PRESENT VALUE OF A SINGLE AMOUNT

The present value of a single amount is the worth to you today of receiving that amount some time in the future. For instance, you might be offered an opportunity to invest in a financial instrument that would pay you $1,000 in three years. Before you decided whether to invest, you would want to determine the present value of the instrument.

To compute the present value of an amount to be received in the future, we must discount (a procedure that is the opposite of compounding) at i interest rate for n periods. In discounting, the interest is subtracted rather than added, as it is in compounding. Graphically, the present value of $1 due at the end of the third period with an interest rate of 10 percent can be represented as follows:

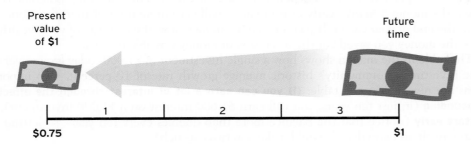

Present
value
of $1

Future
time

1   2   3

$0.75 $1

Assume that today is January 1, 2012, and you have the opportunity to receive $1,000 cash on December 31, 2014. At an interest rate of 10 percent per year, how much is the $1,000 payment worth to you on January 1, 2012? You could discount the amount year by year,[2] but it is easier to use Table D.2, Present Value of $1, on page D.14. For $i = 10\%$, $n = 3$, we find that the present value of $1 is 0.7513. The present value of $1,000 to be received at the end of three years can be computed as follows:

$$\$1,000 \times 0.7513 = \$751.30$$

From Table D.2,
Interest rate = 10%
$n = 3$

It's important to learn not only how to compute a present value but also to understand what it means. The $751.30 is the amount you would pay now to have the right to receive $1,000 at the end of three years, assuming an interest rate of 10 percent. Conceptually, you should be indifferent between having $751.30 today and receiving $1,000 in three years. If you had $751.30 today but wanted $1,000 in three years, you would deposit the money in a savings account that pays 10 percent interest and it would grow to $1,000 in three years. Alternatively, if you had a contract that promised you $1,000 in three years, you could sell it to an investor for $751.30 in cash today because it would permit the investor to earn the difference in interest.

What if you could earn only 6 percent during the three-year period from January 1, 2012, to December 31, 2014? What would be the present value on January 1, 2012, of receiving $1,000 on December 31, 2014? To answer this we would take the same approach, using Table D.2, except that the interest rate would change to $i = 6\%$. Referring to Table D.2, we see the present value factor for $i = 6\%$, $n = 3$, is 0.8396. Thus, the present value of $1,000 to be received at the end of three years, assuming a 6 percent interest rate, would be computed as $1,000 $\times$ 0.8396 = $839.60. Notice that when we assume a 6 percent interest rate the present value is greater than when we assumed a 10 percent interest rate. The reason for this difference is that, to reach $1,000 three years from now, you'd need to deposit more money in a savings account now if it earns 6 percent interest than if it earns 10 percent interest.

HOW'S IT GOING? Self-Study Practice

1. If the interest rate in a present value problem increases from 8 percent to 10 percent, will the present value increase or decrease?
2. What is the present value of $10,000 to be received 10 years from now if the interest rate is 5 percent, compounded annually?
3. If $10,000 is deposited now in a savings account that earns 5 percent interest compounded annually, how much will it be worth 10 years from now?

After you have finished, check your answers with the solution in the margin.

The Power of Compounding

Compound interest is a remarkably powerful economic force. In fact, the ability to earn interest on interest is the key to building economic wealth. If you save $1,000 per year for the first ten years of your career, you will have more money when you retire than you would if you had saved $15,000 per year for the last ten years of your career. This surprising outcome occurs because the money you save early in your career will earn more interest than the money you save at the end of your career. If you start saving money now, the majority of your wealth will not be the money you saved but the interest your money was able to earn.

The table in the margin shows how a single investment of $1,000 today grows over time at the investment community's historic average growth rate of 10 percent. Two important lessons are revealed in the table: **(1) you can earn a lot of interest through the effects of compounding** (in just ten years, you will earn $1,600 interest on a $1,000 investment), and **(2) start early** (notice that the balance more than doubles every ten years, so letting your investment sit an extra decade could make you twice as rich).

Period	Value
Now	$ 1,000
10 years	$ 2,600
20 years	$ 6,700
30 years	$ 17,400
40 years	$ 45,300
50 years	$117,400
60 years	$304,500
70 years	$789,700

Computing Future and Present Values of an Annuity

Instead of a single payment, many business problems involve multiple cash payments over a number of periods. An **annuity** is a series of consecutive payments characterized by

1. An equal dollar amount each interest period.
2. Interest periods of equal length (year, half a year, quarter, or month).
3. An equal interest rate each interest period.

Examples of annuities include monthly payments on a car or house, yearly contributions to a savings account, and monthly pension benefits.

FUTURE VALUE OF AN ANNUITY

If you are saving money for some purpose, such as a new car or a trip to Europe, you might decide to deposit a fixed amount of money in a savings account each month. The future value of an annuity computation will tell you how much money will be in your savings account at some point in the future.

The future value of an annuity includes compound interest on each payment from the date of payment to the end of the term of the annuity. Each new payment accumulates less interest than prior payments, only because the number of periods remaining in which to accumulate interest decreases. The future value of an annuity of $1 for three periods at 10 percent may be represented graphically as

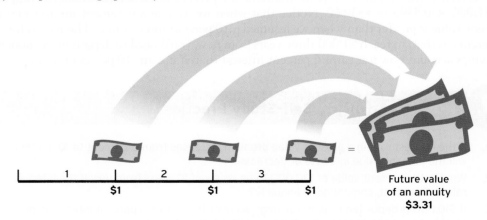

Assume that each year for three years, you deposit $1,000 cash in a savings account at 10 percent interest per year. You make the first $1,000 deposit on December 31, 2012, the second one on December 31, 2013, and the third and last one on December 31, 2014. The first $1,000 deposit earns compound interest for two years (for total principal and interest of $1,210); the second deposit earns interest for one year (for total principal and interest of $1,100). The third deposit earns no interest because it was made on the day that the balance is computed. So, the total amount in the savings account at the end of three years is $3,310 ($1,210 + $1,100 + $1,000).

To calculate the future value of this annuity, we could compute the interest on each deposit, similar to what's described above. However, a faster way is to refer to Table D.3, Future Value of Annuity of $1, on page D.15. For $i = 10\%$, $n = 3$, we find the value 3.3100. The future value of your three deposits of $1,000 each can be computed as follows:

> From Table D.3,
> Interest rate = 10%
> $n = 3$

$$\$1,000 \times 3.3100 = \$3,310$$

PRESENT VALUE OF AN ANNUITY

The present value of an annuity is the value now of a series of equal amounts to be received (or paid out) for some specified number of periods in the future. It is computed by discounting each of the equal periodic amounts. A good example of this type of problem is a retirement program that offers employees a monthly income after retirement. The present value of an annuity of $1 for three periods at 10 percent can be represented graphically as

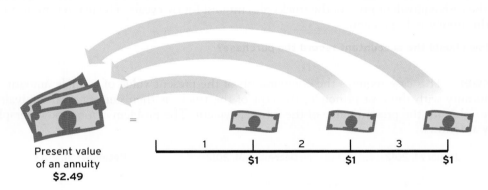

Present value
of an annuity
$2.49

Assume you are to receive $1,000 cash on each December 31, 2012, 2013, and 2014. How much would the sum of these three $1,000 future amounts be worth on January 1, 2012, assuming an interest rate of 10 percent per year? One way to determine this is to use Table D.2 to calculate the present value of each single amount as follows:

		FACTOR FROM TABLE D.2		
Year	Amount	i = 10%		Present Value
1	$1,000	×	0.9091 ($n = 1$)	=	$ 909.10
2	$1,000	×	0.8264 ($n = 2$)	=	826.40
3	$1,000	×	0.7513 ($n = 3$)	=	751.30
			Total present value	=	$2,486.80

Alternatively, we can compute the present value of this annuity more easily by using Table D.4, Present Value of Annuity of $1 (on page D.16), as follows:

> From Table D.4,
> Interest rate = 10%
> $n = 3$

$$\$1,000 \times 2.4869 = \$2,487 \text{ (rounded)}$$

INTEREST RATES AND INTEREST PERIODS

The preceding illustrations assumed annual periods for compounding and discounting. Although interest rates are almost always quoted on an annual basis, many compounding periods encountered in business are less than one year. When interest periods are less than a year, the values of *n* and *i* must be restated to be consistent with the length of the interest compounding period.

To illustrate, 12 percent interest compounded annually for five years requires the use of $n = 5$ and $i = 12\%$. If compounding is quarterly, however, there will be four interest periods per year (20 interest periods in five years), and the quarterly interest rate is one quarter of the annual rate (3 percent per quarter). Therefore, 12 percent interest compounded quarterly for five years requires use of $n = 20$ and $i = 3\%$.

Accounting Applications of Present Values

Many business transactions require the use of future and present value concepts. In finance classes, you will see how to apply future value concepts. In this section, we apply present value concepts to three common accounting cases.

Case A—Present Value of a Single Amount

On January 1, 2012, assume that General Mills bought some new delivery trucks. The company signed a note and agreed to pay $200,000 on December 31, 2013, an amount representing the cash equivalent price of the trucks plus interest for two years. The market interest rate for this note was 12 percent.

1. How should the accountant record the purchase?

Answer This case requires the computation of the present value of a single amount. In conformity with the cost principle, the cost of the trucks is their current cash equivalent price, which is the present value of the future payment. The problem can be shown graphically as follows:

January 1, 2012   December 31, 2012   December 31, 2013

? $200,000

The present value of the $200,000 is computed as follows:

From Table D.2,
Interest rate = 12%
n = 2

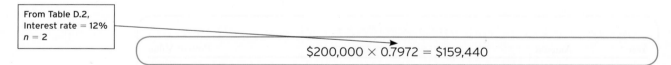

$200,000 × 0.7972 = $159,440

This transaction has the following financial effects, and would be recorded with the journal entry shown below.

Assets		=	Liabilities		+	Shareholders' Equity
Delivery Trucks	+159,440		Note Payable	+159,440		

dr Delivery Trucks (+A)	159,440	
cr Note Payable (+L)		159,440

2. How should the effects of interest be reported at the end of 2012 and 2013?

Answer Interest expense would be calculated, reported, and recorded as follows:

December 31, 2012

Interest = Principal × Rate × Time
= $159,440 × 12% × 12/12 = $19,132 (rounded)

Assets	=	Liabilities		+	Shareholders' Equity	
		Note Payable	+19,132		Interest Expense (+E)	−19,132

dr Interest Expense (+E, −SE) 19,132
  cr Note Payable (+L) 19,132

> **COACH'S TIP**
>
> The interest is recorded in the Note Payable account because it would be paid as part of the note at maturity. Alternatively, the interest could be recorded in an Interest Payable account separate from the Note Payable.

December 31, 2013

Interest = Principal × Rate × Time
= ($159,440 × $19,132) × 12% × 12/12 = $21,428 (rounded)

Assets	=	Liabilities		+	Shareholders' Equity	
		Note Payable	+21,428		Interest Expense (+E)	−21,428

dr Interest Expense (+E, −SE 21,428
  cr Note Payable (+L) 21,428

3. What is the effect of the $200,000 debt payment made on December 31, 2013?

Answer   At this date, the amount to be paid is the balance in Note Payable, after it has been updated for interest pertaining to 2013, as shown in the T-account in the margin. Notice that, just prior to its repayment, the balance for the note on December 31, 2013, is the same as the maturity amount on the due date.

The debt payment has the following financial effects, and would be recorded with the journal entry shown below.

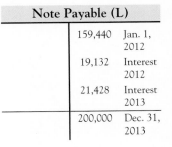

	Note Payable (L)	
	159,440	Jan. 1, 2012
	19,132	Interest 2012
	21,428	Interest 2013
200,000		Dec. 31, 2013

Assets		=	Liabilities		+	Shareholders' Equity
Cash	−200,000		Note Payable	−200,000		

dr Note Payable (−L) 200,000
  cr Cash (−A) 200,000

Case B—Present Value of an Annuity

On January 1, 2012, assume that General Mills bought new milling equipment. The company elected to finance the purchase with a note payable to be paid off in three years in annual instalments of $163,686. Each instalment includes principal plus interest on the unpaid balance at 11 percent per year. The annual instalments are due on December 31, 2012, 2013, and 2014. This problem can be shown graphically as follows:

January 1, 2012	December 31, 2012	December 31, 2013	December 31, 2014
?	$163,686	$163,686	$163,686

1. What is the amount of the note?

Answer   The note is the present value of each instalment payment, $i = 11\%$ and $n = 3$. This is an annuity because the note repayment is made in three equal instalments. The amount of the note is computed as follows:

From Table D.4,
Interest rate = 11%
$n = 3$

$$\$163{,}686 \times 2.4437 = \$400{,}000$$

The acquisition on January 1, 2012, would be accounted for as follows:

Assets		=	Liabilities		+ Shareholders' Equity
Milling Equipment	+400,000		Note Payable	+400,000	

dr Milling Equipment (+A) 400,000
    cr Note Payable (+L)   400,000

2. How should the payments made at the end of each year be accounted for?

Answer:

December 31, 2012
Each payment includes both interest and principal. The interest part of the first payment is calculated as

$$\text{Interest} = \text{Principal} \times \text{Rate} \times \text{Time}$$
$$= \$400{,}000 \times 11\% \times 12/12 = \$44{,}000$$

Now that we know the interest component, the principal portion of the first payment of $163,686 can be calculated ($163,686 − $44,000 = $119,686). Thus, the first payment on December 31, 2012, would be accounted for as

Assets		=	Liabilities		+	Shareholders' Equity	
Cash	−163,686		Note Payable	−119,686		Interest Expense (+E)	−44,000

dr Interest Expense (+E, −SE) 44,000
dr Note Payable (−L) ($163,686 − $44,000) 119,686
    cr Cash (−A)   163,686

December 31, 2013
The interest portion of the second and third payments would be calculated in the same way, although notice that the principal balance in the Note Payable account changes after each payment.

$$\text{Interest} = \text{Principal} \times \text{Rate} \times \text{Time}$$
$$= [(\$400{,}000 - \$119{,}686) \times 11\% \times 12/12] = \$30{,}835$$
$$\text{Principal} = \text{Payment} - \text{Interest}$$
$$= \$163{,}686 - \$30{,}835 = \$132{,}851$$

Assets	=	Liabilities	+	Shareholders' Equity	
Cash −163,686		Note Payable −132,851		Interest Expense (+E)	−30,835

```
dr Interest Expense (+E, −SE) .....................................................  30,835
dr Note Payable (−L) ..................................................................  132,851
   cr Cash (−A) ..........................................................................            163,686
```

December 31, 2014

```
        Interest = Principal × Rate × Time
                 = [($400,000 − $119,686 − $132,851) × 11% × 12/12]
                 = $16,223 (adjusted to accommodate rounding)
       Principal = Payment − Interest
                 = $163,686 − $16,223 = $147,463
```

	Note Payable (L)	
		400,000 Jan. 1, 2012
Dec. 31, 2012 119,686		
Dec. 31, 2013 132,851		
Dec. 31, 2014 147,463		
		0 Dec. 31, 2014

Assets	=	Liabilities	+	Shareholders' Equity	
Cash −163,686		Note Payable −147,463		Interest Expense (+E)	−16,223

```
dr Interest Expense (+E, −SE) .....................................................  16,223
dr Note Payable (−L) ..................................................................  147,463
   cr Cash (−A) ..........................................................................            163,686
```

Case C—Present Value of a Single Amount and an Annuity

On January 1, 2012, assume that General Mills issued 100 four-year $1,000 bonds. The bonds pay interest annually at a rate of 6 percent of face value. What total amount would investors be willing to pay for the bonds if they require an annual return of (*a*) 4 percent, (*b*) 6 percent, or (*c*) 8 percent?

Answer This case requires the computation of the present value of a single amount (the $100,000 face value paid at maturity) plus the present value of an annuity (the annual interest payments of $6,000). The problem can be shown graphically as follows:

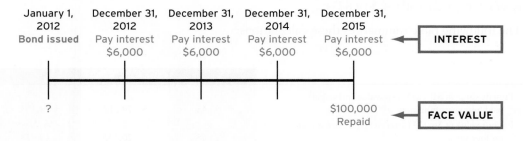

> **COACH'S TIP**
>
> Each interest payment of $6,000 is calculated as $100,000 × 6% × 12/12.

(a) 4 Percent Market Interest Rate

The present value of the $100,000 face value is computed as follows:

> From Table D.2, Interest rate = 4%
> *n* = 4

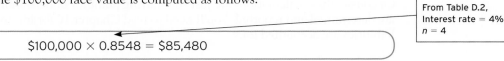

$100,000 × 0.8548 = $85,480

The present value of the $6,000 annuity is computed as follows:

From Table D.4,
Interest rate = 4%
n = 4

$$\$6,000 \times 3.6299 = \$21,780*$$

*Adjusted to accommodate rounding in the present value factor.

The present value of the total bond payments, computed using the discount rate of 4 percent, is $107,260 (= $85,480 + $21,780).

(b) 6 Percent Market Interest Rate

The present value of the $100,000 face value is computed as follows:

From Table D.2,
Interest rate = 6%
n = 4

$$\$100,000 \times 0.7921 = \$79,210$$

The present value of the $6,000 annuity is computed as follows:

From Table D.4,
Interest rate = 6%
n = 4

$$\$6,000 \times 3.4651 = \$20,790*$$

*Adjusted to accommodate rounding in the present value factor.

The present value of the total bond payments, computed using the discount rate of 6 percent, is $100,000 (= $79,210 + $20,790).

(c) 8 Percent Market Interest Rate

The present value of the $100,000 face value is computed as follows:

From Table D.2,
Interest rate = 8%
n = 4

$$\$100,000 \times 0.7350 = \$73,503*$$

*Adjusted to accommodate rounding in the present value factor.

The present value of the $6,000 annuity is computed as follows:

From Table D.4,
Interest rate = 8%
n = 4

$$\$6,000 \times 3.3121 = \$19,873$$

COACH'S TIP

The present values in (a), (b), and (c) demonstrate the calculation of the bond issue prices used in Chapter 10.

The present value of the total bond payments, computed using the discount rate of 8 percent, is $93,376 (= $73,503 + $19,873).

The following table summarizes these calculations:

	MARKET INTEREST RATES		
	4%	6%	8%
Present value of $100,000 face value (principal) paid four years from now	$ 85,480	$ 79,210	$ 73,503
Present value of $6,000 (interest) paid once a year for four years	21,780	20,790	19,873
Bond price	**$107,260**	**$100,000**	**$93,376**

Of course, these calculations are just the starting point for understanding how bond liabilities are determined and reported. You'll need to read Chapter 10 for information about how bond liabilities are accounted for.

PRESENT VALUE COMPUTATIONS USING EXCEL

While the present value tables are useful for educational purposes, most present value problems in business are solved with calculators or Excel spreadsheets. Because of the widespread availability of Excel, we will show you how to solve present value problems using Excel. Slightly different versions of Excel are available. The illustrations in this text are based on Microsoft Office 2007.

Present Value of a Single Payment

The calculation of a present value amount is based on a fairly simple mathematical formula:

$$PV = \text{Payment}/(1+i)^n$$

In this formula, *payment* is the cash payment made at some point in the future, i is the interest rate each period, and n is the number of periods in the problem. We could use this formula to solve all problems involving the present value of a single payment. It is, of course, easier to use a present value table (like the one in this appendix) which is derived by solving the present value formula for various interest rates and numbers of periods. Unfortunately, a table that included all interest rates and numbers of periods actually encountered in business would be too large to work with. As a result, most accountants and analysts use Excel to compute a present value.

To compute the present value of a single payment in Excel, you enter the present value formula in a cell, using the format required by Excel. You should select a cell and enter the following formula:

$$= \text{Payment}/(1+i)\char`\^n$$

To illustrate, if you want to solve for the present value of a $100,000 payment to be made in five years with an interest rate of 10 percent, you would enter the following in the function field:

$$= 100,000/(1.10)\char`\^5$$

Based on this entry, Excel would compute the present value of $62,092.13. This answer is slightly different from the answer you would have if you used the present value tables at the end of this appendix. The tables are rounded based on four digits. Excel does not round and, therefore, provides a more accurate computation.

Present Value of an Annuity

The formula for computing the present value of an annuity is a little more complicated than that for computing the present value of a single payment. As a result, Excel has been programmed to include the formula so that you do not have to enter it yourself.

To compute the present value of an annuity in Excel, select a cell, click on the Formulas tab, and then click on the function button (fx). The following dropdown box will appear:

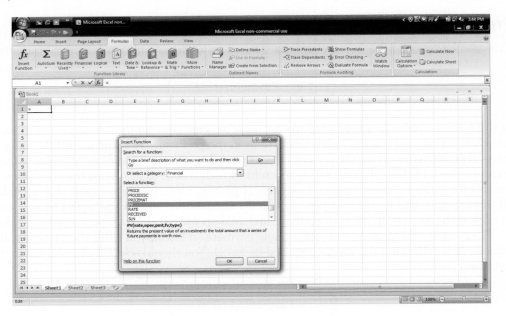

In the "Select a Category" window, pick "Financial" and then scroll down to "Select a Function" and click on "PV." Then, click on "OK" and a new dropdown box will appear:

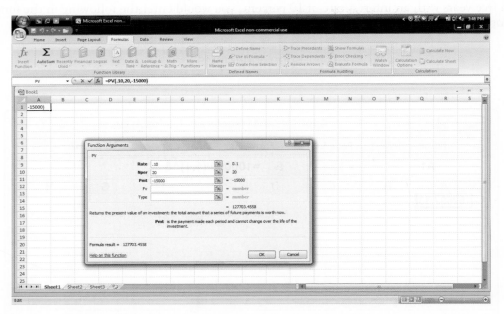

In this box, enter the interest rate, 10 percent in this example, beside Rate. Notice that the rate must be entered as a decimal (i.e., .10). Enter the number of periods (20) beside Nper. Excel has an unusual convention associated with the payment. It must be entered as a negative amount (−15000) beside Pmt. Do not include a comma or brackets with the amount you enter. When you click on "OK," Excel will enter the present value in the cell you selected. In this example, the value determined by Excel is $127,703.46.

TABLE D.1 | Future Value of $1

Periods	2%	3%	3.75%	4%	4.25%	5%	6%	7%	8%
0	1.	1.	1.	1.	1.	1.	1.	1.	1.
1	1.02	1.03	1.0375	1.04	1.0425	1.05	1.06	1.07	1.08
2	1.0404	1.0609	1.0764	1.0816	1.0868	1.1025	1.1236	1.1449	1.1664
3	1.0612	1.0927	1.1168	1.1249	1.1330	1.1576	1.1910	1.2250	1.2597
4	1.0824	1.1255	1.1587	1.1699	1.1811	1.2155	1.2625	1.3108	1.3605
5	1.1041	1.1593	1.2021	1.2167	1.2313	1.2763	1.3382	1.4026	1.4693
6	1.1262	1.1941	1.2472	1.2653	1.2837	1.3401	1.4185	1.5007	1.5869
7	1.1487	1.2299	1.2939	1.3159	1.3382	1.4071	1.5036	1.6058	1.7138
8	1.1717	1.2668	1.3425	1.3686	1.3951	1.4775	1.5938	1.7182	1.8509
9	1.1951	1.3048	1.3928	1.4233	1.4544	1.5513	1.6895	1.8385	1.9990
10	1.2190	1.3439	1.4450	1.4802	1.5162	1.6289	1.7908	1.9672	2.1589
20	1.4859	1.8061	2.0882	2.1911	2.2989	2.6533	3.2071	3.8697	4.6610

Periods	9%	10%	11%	12%	13%	14%	15%	20%	25%
0	1.	1.	1.	1.	1.	1.	1.	1.	1.
1	1.09	1.10	1.11	1.12	1.13	1.14	1.15	1.20	1.25
2	1.1881	1.2100	1.2321	1.2544	1.2769	1.2996	1.3225	1.4400	1.5625
3	1.2950	1.3310	1.3676	1.4049	1.4429	1.4815	1.5209	1.7280	1.9531
4	1.4116	1.4641	1.5181	1.5735	1.6305	1.6890	1.7490	2.0736	2.4414
5	1.5386	1.6105	1.6851	1.7623	1.8424	1.9254	2.0114	2.4883	3.0518
6	1.6771	1.7716	1.8704	1.9738	2.0820	2.1950	2.3131	2.9860	3.8147
7	1.8280	1.9487	2.0762	2.2107	2.3526	2.5023	2.6600	3.5832	4.7684
8	1.9926	2.1436	2.3045	2.4760	2.6584	2.8526	3.0590	4.2998	5.9605
9	2.1719	2.3579	2.5580	2.7731	3.0040	3.2519	3.5179	5.1598	7.4506
10	2.3674	2.5937	2.8394	3.1058	3.3946	3.7072	4.0456	6.1917	9.3132
20	5.6044	6.7275	8.0623	9.6463	11.5231	13.7435	16.3665	38.3376	86.7362

Periods	2%	3%	3.75%	4%	4.25%	5%	6%	7%	8%
1	0.9804	0.9709	0.9639	0.9615	0.9592	0.9524	0.9434	0.9346	0.9259
2	0.9612	0.9426	0.9290	0.9246	0.9201	0.9070	0.8900	0.8734	0.8573
3	0.9423	0.9151	0.8954	0.8890	0.8826	0.8638	0.8396	0.8163	0.7938
4	0.9238	0.8885	0.8631	0.8548	0.8466	0.8227	0.7921	0.7629	0.7350
5	0.9057	0.8626	0.8319	0.8219	0.8121	0.7835	0.7473	0.7130	0.6806
6	0.8880	0.8375	0.8018	0.7903	0.7790	0.7462	0.7050	0.6663	0.6302
7	0.8706	0.8131	0.7728	0.7599	0.7473	0.7107	0.6651	0.6227	0.5835
8	0.8535	0.7894	0.7449	0.7307	0.7168	0.6768	0.6274	0.5820	0.5403
9	0.8368	0.7664	0.7180	0.7026	0.6876	0.6446	0.5919	0.5439	0.5002
10	0.8203	0.7441	0.6920	0.6756	0.6595	0.6139	0.5584	0.5083	0.4632
20	0.6730	0.5537	0.4789	0.4564	0.4350	0.3769	0.3118	0.2584	0.2145

Periods	9%	10%	11%	12%	13%	14%	15%	20%	25%
1	0.9174	0.9091	0.9009	0.8929	0.8850	0.8772	0.8696	0.8333	0.8000
2	0.8417	0.8264	0.8116	0.7972	0.7831	0.7695	0.7561	0.6944	0.6400
3	0.7722	0.7513	0.7312	0.7118	0.6931	0.6750	0.6575	0.5787	0.5120
4	0.7084	0.6830	0.6587	0.6355	0.6133	0.5921	0.5718	0.4823	0.4096
5	0.6499	0.6209	0.5935	0.5674	0.5428	0.5194	0.4972	0.4019	0.3277
6	0.5963	0.5645	0.5346	0.5066	0.4803	0.4556	0.4323	0.3349	0.2621
7	0.5470	0.5132	0.4817	0.4523	0.4251	0.3996	0.3759	0.2791	0.2097
8	0.5019	0.4665	0.4339	0.4039	0.3762	0.3506	0.3269	0.2326	0.1678
9	0.4604	0.4241	0.3909	0.3606	0.3329	0.3075	0.2843	0.1938	0.1342
10	0.4224	0.3855	0.3522	0.3220	0.2946	0.2697	0.2472	0.1615	0.1074
20	0.1784	0.1486	0.1240	0.1037	0.0868	0.0728	0.0611	0.0261	0.0115

TABLE D.3   Future Value of Annuity of $1

Periods*	2%	3%	3.75%	4%	4.25%	5%	6%	7%	8%
1	1.	1.	1.	1.	1.	1.	1.	1.	1.
2	2.02	2.03	2.0375	2.04	2.0425	2.05	2.06	2.07	2.08
3	3.0604	3.0909	3.1139	3.1216	3.1293	3.1525	3.1836	3.2149	3.2464
4	4.1216	4.1836	4.2307	4.2465	4.2623	4.3101	4.3746	4.4399	4.5061
5	5.2040	5.3091	5.3893	5.4163	5.4434	5.5256	5.6371	5.7507	5.8666
6	6.3081	6.4684	6.5914	6.6330	6.6748	6.8019	6.9753	7.1533	7.3359
7	7.4343	7.6625	7.8386	7.8983	7.9585	8.1420	8.3938	8.6540	8.9228
8	8.5830	8.8923	9.1326	9.2142	9.2967	9.5491	9.8975	10.2598	10.6366
9	9.7546	10.1591	10.4750	10.5828	10.6918	11.0266	11.4913	11.9780	12.4876
10	10.9497	11.4639	11.8678	12.0061	12.1462	12.5779	13.1808	13.8164	14.4866
20	24.2974	26.8704	29.0174	29.7781	30.5625	33.0660	36.7856	40.9955	45.7620

Periods*	9%	10%	11%	12%	13%	14%	15%	20%	25%
1	1.	1.	1.	1.	1.	1.	1.	1.	1.
2	2.09	2.10	2.11	2.12	2.13	2.14	2.15	2.20	2.25
3	3.2781	3.3100	3.3421	3.3744	3.4069	3.4396	3.4725	3.6400	3.8125
4	4.5731	4.6410	4.7097	4.7793	4.8498	4.9211	4.9934	5.3680	5.7656
5	5.9847	6.1051	6.2278	6.3528	6.4803	6.6101	6.7424	7.4416	8.2070
6	7.5233	7.7156	7.9129	8.1152	8.3227	8.5355	8.7537	9.9299	11.2588
7	9.2004	9.4872	9.7833	10.0890	10.4047	10.7305	11.0668	12.9159	15.0735
8	11.0285	11.4359	11.8594	12.2997	12.7573	13.2328	13.7268	16.4991	19.8419
9	13.0210	13.5975	14.1640	14.7757	15.4157	16.0853	16.7858	20.7989	25.8023
10	15.1929	15.9374	16.7220	17.5487	18.4197	19.3373	20.3037	25.9587	33.2529
20	51.1601	57.2750	64.2028	72.0524	80.9468	91.0249	102.4436	186.6880	342.9447

*There is one payment each period.

Periods*	2%	3%	3.75%	4%	4.25%	5%	6%	7%	8%
1	0.9804	0.9709	0.9639	0.9615	0.9592	0.9524	0.9434	0.9346	0.9259
2	1.9416	1.9135	1.8929	1.8861	1.8794	1.8594	1.8334	1.8080	1.7833
3	2.8839	2.8286	2.7883	2.7751	2.7620	2.7232	2.6730	2.6243	2.5771
4	3.8077	3.7171	3.6514	3.6299	3.6086	3.5460	3.4651	3.3872	3.3121
5	4.7135	4.5797	4.4833	4.4518	4.4207	4.3295	4.2124	4.1002	3.9927
6	5.6014	5.4172	5.2851	5.2421	5.1997	5.0757	4.9173	4.7665	4.6229
7	6.4720	6.2303	6.0579	6.0021	5.9470	5.7864	5.5824	5.3893	5.2064
8	7.3255	7.0197	6.8028	6.7327	6.6638	6.4632	6.2098	5.9713	5.7466
9	8.1622	7.7861	7.5208	7.4353	7.3513	7.1078	6.8017	6.5152	6.2469
10	8.9826	8.5302	8.2128	8.1109	8.0109	7.7217	7.3601	7.0236	6.7101
20	16.3514	14.8775	13.8962	13.5903	13.2944	12.4622	11.4699	10.5940	9.8181

Periods*	9%	10%	11%	12%	13%	14%	15%	20%	25%
1	0.9174	0.9091	0.9009	0.8929	0.8550	0.8772	0.8696	0.8333	0.8000
2	1.7591	1.7355	1.7125	1.6901	1.6681	1.6467	1.6257	1.5278	1.4400
3	2.5313	2.4869	2.4437	2.4018	2.3612	2.3216	2.2832	2.1065	1.9520
4	3.2397	3.1699	3.1024	3.0373	2.9745	2.9137	2.8550	2.5887	2.3616
5	3.8897	3.7908	3.6959	3.6048	3.5172	3.4331	3.3522	2.9906	2.6893
6	4.4859	4.3553	4.2305	4.1114	3.9975	3.8887	3.7845	3.3255	2.9514
7	5.0330	4.8684	4.7122	4.5638	4.4226	4.2883	4.1604	3.6046	3.1611
8	5.5348	5.3349	5.1461	4.9676	4.7988	4.6389	4.4873	3.8372	3.3289
9	5.9952	5.7590	5.5370	5.3282	5.1317	4.9464	4.7716	4.0310	3.4631
10	6.4177	6.1446	5.8892	5.6502	5.4262	5.2161	5.0188	4.1925	3.5705
20	9.1285	8.5136	7.9633	7.4694	7.0248	6.6231	6.2593	4.8696	3.9539

*There is one payment each period.

KEY TERMS

Annuity p. D.4

Future Value p. D.1

Present Value p. D.1

Time Value of Money p. D.1

See complete definitions in the glossary in the back of this text.

Practice Material

QUESTIONS

1. Explain the concept of the time value of money.
2. Explain the basic difference between future value and present value.
3. If you deposited $10,000 in a savings account that earns 2 percent, how much would you have at the end of 10 years? Use a convenient format to display your computations.
4. If you hold a valid contract that will pay you $8,000 cash 10 years from now and the going rate of interest is 10 percent, what is its present value? Use a convenient format to display your computations.
5. What is an annuity?
6. Use Tables D.1 through D.4 to complete the following schedule:

	Table Values		
	$i = 5\%$, $n = 4$	$i = 10\%$, $n = 7$	$i = 14\%$, $n = 10$
FV of $1			
PV of $1			
FV of annuity of $1			
PV of annuity of $1			

7. If you deposit $1,000 at the end of each period for 10 interest periods and you earn 8 percent interest, how much would you have at the end of period 10?

Multiple-choice questions and corresponding answers can be found on Connect.

MINI-EXERCISES

MD-1 Computing the Present Value of a Single Payment

What is the present value of $500,000 to be paid in 10 years, with an interest rate of 8 percent?

MD-2 Computing the Present Value of an Annuity

What is the present value of 10 equal payments of $15,000, with an interest rate of 10 percent?

MD-3 Computing the Present Value of a Complex Contract

As a result of a slowdown in operations, Mercantile Stores is offering to employees who have been terminated a severance package of $100,000 cash; another $100,000 to be paid in one year; and an annuity of $30,000 to be paid each year for 20 years. What is the present value of the package, assuming an interest rate of 8 percent?

MD-4 Computing the Future Value of an Annuity

You plan to retire in 20 years. Calculate whether it is better for you to save $25,000 a year for the last 10 years before retirement or $15,000 for each of the 20 years. Assume you are able to earn 10 percent interest on your investments.

EXERCISES

ED-1 Computing Growth in a Savings Account: A Single Amount

On January 1, 2012, you deposited $6,000 in a savings account. The account will earn 10 percent annual compound interest, which will be added to the fund balance at the end of each year.

Required (round to the nearest dollar):

1. What will be the balance in the savings account at the end of 10 years?
2. What will the interest be for the 10 years?
3. How much interest revenue did the fund earn in 2012? How much will it earn in 2013?

ED-2 Computing Deposit Required and Accounting for a Single-Sum Savings Account

On January 1, 2012, Alan King decided to transfer an amount from his chequing account into a savings account that later will provide $80,000 to send his son to university (four years from now). The savings account will earn 8 percent, which will be added to the fund each year-end.

Required (show computations and round to the nearest dollar):

1. How much must Alan deposit on January 1, 2012?
2. Give the journal entry that Alan should make on January 1, 2012, to record the transfer.
3. What will the interest be for the four years?
4. Give the journal entry that Alan should make on (a) December 31, 2012, and (b) December 31, 2013.

ED-3 Recording Growth in a Savings Account with Equal Periodic Payments

On each December 31, you plan to transfer $2,000 from your chequing account into a savings account. The savings account will earn 9 percent annual interest, which will be added to the savings account balance at each year-end. The first deposit will be made December 31, 2012 (at the end of the period).

Required (show computations and round to the nearest dollar):

1. Give the required journal entry on December 31, 2012.
2. What will be the balance in the savings account at the end of the 10th year (i.e., 10 deposits)?
3. What will be the total amount of interest earned on the 10 deposits?
4. How much interest revenue will the fund earn in 2013? 2014?
5. Give all journal entries that will be required at the end of 2013 and 2014.

ED-4 Computing Growth for a Savings Fund with Periodic Deposits

On January 1, 2012, you plan to take a trip around the world when you graduate four years from now. Your grandmother wants to deposit sufficient funds for this trip into a savings account for you. On the basis of a budget, you estimate that the trip currently would cost $15,000. Being the generous and sweet lady she is, your grandmother decided to deposit $3,500 into the fund at the end of each of the next four years, starting on December 31, 2012. The savings account will earn 6 percent annual interest, which will be added to the savings account at each year-end.

Required (show computations and round to the nearest dollar):

1. How much money will you have for the trip at the end of year 4 (i.e., after four deposits)?
2. What will be the total amount of interest earned over the four years?
3. How much interest revenue will the fund earn in 2012, 2013, 2014, and 2015?

ED-5 Computing Value of an Asset Based on Present Value

You have the chance to purchase an oil well. Your best estimate is that the oil well's net royalty income will average $25,000 per year for five years. There will be no residual value at that time. Assume that the cash inflow occurs at each year-end and that, considering the uncertainty in your estimates, you expect to earn 15 percent per year on the investment. What should you be willing to pay for this investment right now?

COACHED PROBLEM

CPD-1 Comparing Options Using Present Value Concepts

After hearing a knock at your front door, you are surprised to see the Prize Patrol from a large, well-known magazine subscription company. It has arrived with the good news that you are the winner of

$20 million. You discover that you have three options: (1) you can receive $1 million per year for the next 20 years, (2) you can have $8 million today, or (3) you can have $2 million today and receive $700,000 for each of the next 20 years. Your financial adviser tells you that it is reasonable to expect to earn 10 percent on investments. Which option do you prefer? What factors influence your decision?

> **TIP:** All three scenarios require you to determine today's value of the various payment options. These are present value problems.

GROUP A PROBLEM

PAD-1 Comparing Options Using Present Value Concepts

You are the successful senior vice-president of a large bank, and you are preparing for retirement. After visiting the Human Resources office, you found that you have several retirement options: (1) you can receive an immediate cash payment of $1 million, (2) you can receive $60,000 per year for life (your remaining life expectancy is 20 years), or (3) you can receive $50,000 per year for 10 years and then $70,000 per year for life (this option is intended to give you some protection against inflation). You have determined that you can earn 8 percent on your investments. Which option do you prefer and why?

GROUP B PROBLEM

PBD-1 Comparing Options Using Present Value Concepts

After incurring a serious injury caused by a manufacturing defect, your friend has sued the manufacturer for damages. Your friend received three offers from the manufacturer to settle the lawsuit: (1) receive an immediate cash payment of $100,000, (2) receive $6,000 per year for life (your friend's remaining life expectancy is 20 years), or (3) receive $5,000 per year for 10 years and then $7,000 per year for life (this option is intended to compensate your friend for increased aggravation of the injury over time). Your friend can earn 8 percent interest and has asked you for advice. Which option would you recommend and why?

Endnotes

1. Present value and future value problems involve cash flows. The basic concepts are the same for cash inflows (receipts) and cash outflows (payments). No fundamental differences exist between present value and future value calculations for cash payments versus cash receipts.
2. The detailed discounting is as follows:

Periods	Interest for the Year	Present Value*
1	$1,000 − ($1,000 × 1/1.10) = $90.91	$1,000 − $90.91 = $909.09
2	$909.09 − ($909.09 × 1/1.10) = $82.65	$909.09 − $82.65 = $826.44
3	$826.44 − ($826.44 × 1/1.10) = $75.14†	$826.44 − $75.14 = $751.30

*Verifiable in Table D.2.

†Adjusted for rounding

Practise and learn online with Connect.

Reporting and Interpreting Investments in Other Corporations

The full version of Appendix E is available on Connect.

Appendix Introduction

Along with financial hardship, the 2008 stock market crash generated a great deal of criticism of the accounting rules applied to investments in other corporations. As you will read in Appendix E (available on Connect), these rules use fair values when accounting for certain types of investments. Critics complained that use of fair values ("mark-to-market accounting") had forced companies to report losses simply because the economic crisis had caused reductions in their investment values. Critics argued that these losses did not accurately reflect reality and that each reported loss caused further reductions in investment value, like the downward spiral of a toilet flush. Supporters of the accounting rules countered that the accounting rules did not cause the economic crisis. Rather, the accounting rules merely exposed the underlying economic problems that existed.

To read about the following topics, download Appendix E from Connect.

An Overview

- Reasons companies invest
- Identifying investment types and accounting methods

Accounting for Passive Investments

- Debt investments held to maturity: amortized cost method
- Passive investments: cost or FV-NI method

Accounting for Influential Investments

- Investments for significant influence: equity method
- Investments with controlling interests: consolidated statements

Reporting and Interpreting Investments in Other Corporations

The full version of Appendix E is available on Connect.

A

Accounting A system of analyzing, recording, and summarizing the results of a business's activities and then reporting the results to decision makers. (3)

Accounting Standards for Private Enterprises (ASPE) Standards that address issues that are more relevant in a private enterprise environment and therefore can be used by private enterprises only. (16)

Accounts Accumulate and report the effects of each different business activity. (8)

Accounting Period The time period covered by the financial statements.

Accounting Process The process used by businesses to analyze, record, and summarize transactions and adjustments, prepare financial statements, and prepare the records for the next cycle.

Accounts Payable Amounts owed by the business to suppliers for past transactions.

Accounts Receivable (Trade Receivables, Receivables) Amounts owed to a business by its customers. (330)

Accrual Basis Accounting Reports revenues when they are earned and expenses when they are incurred, regardless of the timing of cash receipts or payments; required under GAAP. (94)

Accrued Expenses See *Accrued Liabilities*. (415)

Accrued Liabilities Liabilities for expenses that have been incurred but not yet billed or paid at the end of the accounting period. (415)

Acquisition Cost Cash equivalent amount paid or to be paid for an asset.

Adjusted Trial Balance A list of all accounts and their adjusted balances to check on the equality of recorded debits and credits. (152)

Adjusting Journal Entries (AJEs) Record the effects of each period's adjustments in a debits-equal-credits format. (141)

Adjustments Entries made at the end of every accounting period to report revenues and expenses in the proper period and assets and liabilities at appropriate amounts. (139)

Aging of Accounts Receivable Method (also called the *balance sheet approach*) Estimates uncollectable accounts based on the age of each account receivable. (333)

Allowance for Doubtful Accounts (Allowance for Bad Debts, Allowance for Uncollectable Accounts, Reserve for Bad Debts) Contra-asset account containing the estimated dollar value of uncollectable accounts receivable.

Allowance Method An accounting method that reduces accounts receivable (as well as net income) for an estimate of uncollectable accounts (bad debts). (330)

Amortizable cost The portion of the asset's cost that will be used up during its life. It is calculated as asset cost minus residual value, and it is allocated to Amortization Expense throughout the asset's life. (375)

Amortization (also called *depreciation*) The process of allocating the cost of buildings, vehicles, and equipment over their productive lives, using a systematic and rational method. (146)

Annuity A series of periodic cash receipts or payments that are equal in amount each interest period. (Appendix D)

Assets Resources presently owned by a business that generate future economic benefits. (42)

Asset Turnover Ratio Indicates how well assets are being used to generate revenues by dividing total assets into total revenue. (212)

Audit An examination of a company's financial statements (and management's report on internal control effectiveness) with the goal of detecting misstatements.

Audit Report Describes the auditors' opinion of the fairness of the financial statement presentations and management's assessment of internal control effectiveness.

Authorized Shares The maximum number of shares of a corporation that can be issued, as specified in the charter. (462)

Average Cost Method See *Weighted Average Cost*. (290)

B

Bad Debt Expense (Doubtful Accounts Expenses, Uncollectable Accounts Expense, Provision for Uncollectable Accounts) Reports the estimated amount of this period's credit sales that customers will fail to pay. (331)

Balance When used as a noun, balance is the dollar amount recorded in an account; when used as a verb, balance is the act of ensuring total assets equal total liabilities plus shareholders' equity.

Balance Sheet Reports the amount of assets, liabilities, and shareholders' equity of an accounting entity at a point in time. (9)

Bank Reconciliation An internal report prepared to verify the accuracy of both the bank statement and the cash accounts of a business or individual. (244)

Bank Statement Monthly report from a bank that shows deposits recorded, checks cleared, other debits and credits, and a running bank balance.

Basic Accounting Equation (Balance Sheet Equation) Assets = Liabilities + Shareholders' Equity. (6)

Board of Directors A group of people elected by the shareholders of a company to oversee the decisions made by officers and managers of the company.

Bond Certificate The bond document that each bondholder receives.

Bond Discount The difference between issue price and face value when a bond is sold for less than face value.

Bond Premium The difference between issue price and face value when a bond is sold for more than face value.

Bond Principal The amount (1) payable at the maturity of the bond and (2) on which the periodic cash interest payments are computed.

Book (*or* Carrying) Value The acquisition cost of an asset less accumulated amortization; also called *carrying value*. (374)

C

Callable Bonds Bonds that may be called for early repayment at the option of the company that issued the bond.

Canadian Auditing Standards (CAS) Provide auditors with up-to-date tools and required procedures in order to carry out high-quality financial statement audits in today's complex business environment. (17)

Capital Cost Allowance The amortization process required by the Canada Revenue Agency for calculating taxable income and income taxes. (379)

Capitalize To record a cost as an asset rather than an expense. (369)

Carrying Value The amount an asset or liability is reported at ("carried at") in the financial statements. It is also known as *net book value* or simply *book value*. (146)

Cash Money or any instrument that banks will accept for deposit and immediate credit to the company's account. (249)

Cash Basis Accounting Reports revenues when cash is received and expenses when cash is paid; not allowed under GAAP. (93)

Cash Equivalents Short-term, highly liquid investments purchased within three months of maturity. (249)

Cash Flows from Financing Activities Cash inflows and outflows related to financing sources external to the company (owners and lenders). (506)

Cash Flows from Investing Activities Cash inflows and outflows related to the sale or purchase of investments and long-lived assets. (505)

Cash Flows from Operating Activities (*or* Cash Flows from Operations) Cash inflows and outflows related to components of net income. (505)

Chart of Accounts A summary of all account names (and corresponding account numbers) used to record financial results in the accounting system. (45)

Classified Balance Sheet Shows a subtotal for current assets and current liabilities. (59)

Closing Journal Entries Made at the end of the accounting period to transfer balances in temporary accounts to Retained Earnings and to establish a zero balance in each of the temporary accounts.

Common Share The basic voting share issued by a corporation to shareholders. (461)

Comparable Information Information that can be compared across businesses because similar accounting methods have been applied.

Comparative Financial Statements Report numbers for two or more time periods. (201)

Conservatism Using the least optimistic measures when uncertainty exists about the value of an asset or liability. (61)

Consistent Information Information that can be compared over time because similar accounting methods have been applied.

Consolidated Financial Statements The financial statements of parent and subsidiary companies combined into a single set of financial statements. (Appendix E)

Contingent Liabilities Potential liabilities that have arisen as a result of a past transaction or event; their ultimate outcome will not be known until a future event occurs or fails to occur. (429)

Contra-Account An account that is an offset to, or reduction of, another account. (146)

Contract Rate See *Stated Interest Rate*. (461)

Contributed Capital The result of owners providing to the business cash (and sometimes other assets).

Convertible Bonds Bonds that may be converted to other securities of the issuer (usually common share).

Copyright A form of protection provided to the original authors of literary, musical, artistic, dramatic, and other works of authorship. (382)

Corporation A business organized as a legal entity separate and distinct from its owners.

Cost The amount of resources that a company sacrifices to obtain goods or services; often said to be incurred when the company pays cash or uses credit to acquire the item.

Cost-Benefit Constraint Companies should follow accounting rules to the extent that the benefits outweigh the costs of doing so. (568)

Cost of Goods Sold (CGS) Equation BI + P − EI = CGS; beginning inventory plus purchases minus ending inventory. (288)

Cost Principle Assets and liabilities should initially be recorded at their original cost to the company. (43)

Coupon Rate See *Stated Interest Rate*. (461)

Credit The right side of an account, or the act of entering an amount into the right side of an account. (52)

Creditor Any business or individual to whom the company owes money.

Cross-Sectional Analysis Compares the results of one company with those of others in the same section of the industry. (209)

Cumulative Dividend Preference Preferred share feature that requires current dividends not paid in full to accumulate for every year in which they are not paid. These cumulative unpaid amounts (called *dividends in arrears*) must be paid before any common dividends can be paid.(474)

Current Assets To be used up or converted into cash within 12 months of the balance sheet date. (59)

Current Dividend Preference The feature of preferred shares that grants priority on preferred dividends over common dividends. (473)

Current Liabilities Debts and obligations that will be paid, settled, or fulfilled within 12 months of the balance sheet date. (59)

Current Ratio Ratio of current assets to current liabilities, used to evaluate liquidity.

D

Days to Collect A measure of the average number of days from the time a sale is made on account to the time it is collected. (341)

Days to Sell A measure of the average number of days from the time inventory is bought to the time it is sold. (298)

Debit The left side of an account, or the act of entering an amount into the left side of an account. (52)

Debt Covenants See *Loan Covenants*. (209)

Debt-to-Assets Ratio Indicates financing risk by computing the proportion of total assets financed by debt. (211)

Declaration Date The date on which the board of directors officially approves a dividend, thereby creating a liability. (467)

Declining-Balance Amortization Method Assigns more amortization to early years of an asset's life and less amortization to later years. (377)

Deferred Expenses Previously acquired assets that need to be adjusted at the end of the accounting period to reflect the amount of expense incurred in using the asset to generate revenue.

Deferred Revenues Previously recorded liabilities that need to be adjusted at the end of the period to reflect the amount of revenue earned.

Depletion The process of allocating a natural resource's cost over the period of its extraction or harvesting. (388)

Depreciable Cost The portion of the asset's cost that will be used up during its life. It is calculated as asset cost minus residual value, and it is allocated to depreciation expense throughout the asset's life. (409)

Depreciation Process of allocating the cost of buildings and equipment over their productive lives using a systematic and rational method of allocation. (374)

Direct Method Reports the components of cash flows from operating activities as gross receipts and gross payments. (508)

Direct Write-Off Method A non-GAAP alternative to the allowance method of accounting for uncollectable accounts. (343)

Discontinued Operations Result from the disposal of a major component of the business and are reported net of income tax effects. (569)

Discount The amount by which a bond's issue price is less than its face value. (423)

Discount Rate The interest rate used to compute present values.

Dividends Payments a company periodically makes to its shareholders as a return on their investment.

Dividends in Arrears Dividends from prior years on cumulative preferred shares that have not been paid in full. (474)

E

Earnings Forecasts Predictions of earnings for future accounting periods.

Earned To have done what is necessary to obtain the right to receive payment.

EBITDA Abbreviation for "earnings before interest, taxes, depreciation, and amortization," which is a measure of operating performance that some managers and analysts use in place of net income. (387)

Effective-Interest Method of Amortization Allocates the amount of bond premium or discount over each period of a bond's life in amounts corresponding to the bond's carrying value. (433)

Effective Interest Rate Another name for the market rate of interest on a bond.

Electronic Funds Transfer Funds transferred into or out of your account.

Estimated Useful Life Expected service life of a long-lived asset to the present owner.

Expenditures Outflows of cash for any purpose.

Expenses Costs of business necessary to earn revenues. (91)

Extraordinary Items Gains and losses that are both unusual in nature and infrequent in occurrence.

Extraordinary Repairs Expenditures that increase a tangible asset's economic usefulness in the future and are recorded as increases in asset accounts, not as expenses. (373)

F

Face Value The amount payable on a bond's maturity date. (422)

Factoring An arrangement where receivables are sold to another company (called a *factor*) for immediate cash (minus a factoring fee). (343)

Financial Statements Accounting reports that summarize the financial results of business and financing activities. (5)

Financial Statement Users People who base their decisions, in part, on information reported in a company's financial statements.

Financing Activities Related to exchanging money with lenders or owners.

Finished Goods Inventory Manufactured goods that are completed and ready for sale.

First-In, First-Out (FIFO) Method Assumes that the costs of the first goods purchased (first in) are the costs of the first goods sold (first out). (290)

Fiscal Any matters relating to money; typically used to describe a specified period of time used for financial reporting.

Fixed Assets Tangible assets that are fixed in place, such as land, buildings, and production equipment.

FOB Destination A term of sale indicating that goods are owned by the seller until they are delivered to the customer. (251)

FOB Shipping Point A term of sale indicating that goods are owned by the customer the moment they leave the seller's premises. (251)

Franchise A contractual right to sell certain products or services, use certain trademarks, or perform activities in a certain geographical region. (383)

Full Disclosure Principle Financial statements should present information needed to understand the financial results of the company's business activities. (568)

Future Value The sum to which an amount will increase as the result of compound interest. (Appendix D)

G

Generally Accepted Accounting Principles (GAAP) Rules of accounting approved by the Canadian Institute of Chartered Accountants for use in Canada.(15)

Going-Concern Assumption A business is assumed to be capable of

continuing its operations long enough to meet its obligations. (568)

Goods Available for Sale The sum of beginning inventory and purchases for the period. (288)

Goodwill The premium a company pays to obtain the favourable reputation associated with another company. (383)

Gross Profit (*or* Gross Margin) Net sales minus cost of goods sold. It is a subtotal, not an account. (255)

Gross Profit Percentage A ratio indicating the percentage of profit earned on each dollar of sales, after considering the cost of products sold. (256)

H

Historical Cost Principle See *Cost Principle*. (47)

Horizontal (trend) analyses Comparing results across time, often expressing changes in account balances as a percentage of prior year balances. (555)

I

Impairment Occurs when the cash to be generated by an asset is estimated to be less than the carrying value of that asset. (380)

Imprest System A process that controls the amount paid to others by limiting the total amount of money available for making payments to others. (244)

Income from Operations (Operating Income) Equals net sales less cost of goods sold and other operating expenses.

Income Statement Reports the amount of revenues less expenses for a period of time. (8)

Incur To make oneself subject to; typically refers to expenses, which are incurred by using up the economic benefits of assets or becoming obligated for liabilities, resulting in a decrease in the company's resources in the current period.

Indirect Method Presents the operating activities section of the cash flow statement by adjusting net income to compute cash flows from operating activities. (508)

Industry Practices Constraint Companies in certain industries may follow accounting rules peculiar to that industry. (568)

Intangible Assets Assets that have special rights but not physical substance.

Interest Formula $I = P \times R \times T$, where I = interest calculated; P = principal; R = annual interest rate; and T = time period covered in the interest calculation (number of months out of 12). (337)

Internal Controls Methods to protect against theft of assets, enhance the reliability of accounting information, promote efficient and effective operations, and ensure compliance with applicable laws and regulations. (236)

International Financial Reporting Standards (IFRS) Rules of accounting created by the International Accounting Standards Board (IASB) for international use. (15)

Inventory Tangible property held for sale in the normal course of business or used in producing goods or services for sale.

Inventory Turnover The process of buying and selling inventory. (298)

Investing Activities Involve buying or selling long-lived items such as land, buildings, and equipment.

Issue Price The amount of money that a lender pays (and the company receives) when a bond is issued. (423)

Issued Shares Shares that have been distributed by the corporation. (462)

J

Journal Used to record the effects of each day's transactions; organized by date. (51)

Journal Entries Indicate the effects of each day's transactions in a debits-equal-credits format. (52)

Journalize The process of noting a transaction in the journal in the debits-equal-credits journal entry format.

L

Last-In, First-Out (LIFO) Assumes that the most recently purchased units (the last in) are sold first. (300)

Ledger Used to summarize the effects of journal entries on each account; organized by account. (51)

Lender A creditor that has loaned money to the company.

Liabilities Amounts presently owed by a business. (42)

Licensing Right The limited permission to use property according to specific terms and conditions set out in a contract. (430)

Line Item An account name or title reported in the body of a financial statement; can represent a single account or the total of several accounts.

Line of Credit A prearranged agreement that allows a company to borrow any amount of money at any time, up to a prearranged limit. (430)

Liquidity The extent to which a company is able to pay its currently maturing obligations. (558)

Loan Covenants Terms of a loan agreement that, if broken, entitle the lender to renegotiate loan terms or to force repayment. (196)

Long-Lived Assets Resources owned by a business that enable it to produce the goods or services that are sold to customers. (368)

Long-Term Assets Resources that will be used up or turned into cash more than 12 months after the balance sheet date.

Long-Term Liabilities All of the entity's obligations that are not classified as current liabilities.

Lower of Cost and Net Realizable Value (LC&NRV) A valuation rule that requires Inventory to be written down when its net realizable value or current replacement cost falls below its original historical cost. (294)

M

Manufacturing Company Sells goods that it has made itself. (236)

Market Interest Rate The rate of interest that investors demand from a bond. (425)

Matching Principle The requirement under accrual basis accounting to record expenses in the same period as the revenues they generate, not necessarily the period in which cash is paid for them. (96)

Materiality A misstatement large enough to influence the decisions of financial statement users. (204)

Maturity Date The date on which a bond is due to be paid in full. (422)

Merchandise Inventory Goods held for resale in the ordinary course of business.

Merchandising Company Sells goods that have been obtained from a supplier. (236)

Multistep Income Statement Presents important subtotals, such as gross profit, to help distinguish core operating results from other, less significant items that affect net income. (255)

N

Net To combine by subtracting one or more amounts from another.

Net Assets The shorthand term used to refer to assets minus liabilities. (383)

Net Book Value (Book Value, Carrying Value) The amount at which an asset or liability is reported after deducting any contra-accounts.

Net Income The excess of revenues over expenses. (92)

Net Income before Income Taxes Revenues and gains minus losses and all expenses except income tax expense.

Net Profit Margin Ratio Indicates how well expenses are controlled, by dividing net income by revenue. (212)

Net Sales Total sales revenue minus Sales Returns and Allowances and Sales Discounts.

Noncash Investing and Financing Activities Transactions that do not have direct cash flow effects; reported as a supplement to the statement of cash flows in narrative or schedule form.

Noncurrent (or Long-Term) Assets and liabilities that do not meet the definition of *current*. (59)

No-Par Value Shares Shares that have no specified legal value per share in the corporate charter. (464)

Notes (Footnotes) Provide supplemental information about the financial condition of a company, without which the financial statements cannot be fully understood.

Notes Receivable A promise that requires another party to pay the business according to a written agreement. (330)

NSF (Not Sufficient Funds) Cheques Another name for bounced cheques. They occur when the cheque writer does not have sufficient funds to cover the amount of the cheque. (246)

O

Obsolescence The process of becoming out of date or falling into disuse.

Operating Activities The day-to-day events involved in running a business.

Operating Cycle (Cash-to-Cash Cycle) The time and activities needed for a company to sell goods and services to customers, collect cash from customers, and pay cash to suppliers.

Ordinary Repairs and Maintenance Expenditures for routine operating upkeep of long-lived assets that are recorded as expenses. (373)

Outstanding Shares Shares that are currently held by shareholders (not the corporation itself). (463)

P

Parent Company The entity that gains a controlling influence over another company (a subsidiary). (Appendix E)

Partnerships Business organizations owned by two or more people. Each partner often is personally liable for debts that the partnership cannot pay.

Par Value For shares, an insignificant value per share specified in the charter, which has no relationship to the market value of the share. (464)

Passive investments Investments that are purchased with excess funds with the intent of earning a return. (Appendix E)

Patent A right to exclude others from making, using, selling, or importing an invention. (382)

Payment Date The date on which a cash dividend is paid to the shareholders of record. (468)

Percentage of Credit Sales Method (also called the *income statement approach*) Estimates bad debts based on the historical percentage of sales that lead to bad debt losses. (333)

Periodic Inventory System Inventory records are updated "periodically," at the end of the accounting period; the inventory must be physically counted. (250)

Permanent Accounts Track financial results from year to year by carrying their ending balances into the next year. (156)

Perpetual Inventory System Inventory records are updated "perpetually," every time inventory is bought, sold, or returned. (250)

Post-Closing Trial Balance An internal report prepared as the last step in the accounting cycle to check that debits equal credits and all temporary accounts have been closed. (158)

Posting The process of transferring details of journal entries into the corresponding ledger accounts. (53)

Preferred Shares Shares that have specified rights over common shares. (472)

Premium The amount by which a bond's issue price exceeds its face value. (423)

Prepaid Expenses A general account name used to describe payments made in advance of receiving future services; typically includes prepaid rent, prepaid insurance, and other specific types of prepayments.

Present Value The current value of an amount to be received in the future; it is calculated by discounting a future amount for compound interest. (Appendix D)

Press Release A written public news announcement normally distributed to major news services.

Private Enterprises Do not have publicly traded shares in an open market nor do they hold assets in a fiduciary capacity for someone else. Have the option to use IFRS or ASPE. (16)

Profit An alternative term for *net income*.

Profitability The extent to which a company generates income. (558)

Publicly accountable profit-oriented enterprises Have shares traded in a public market or hold assets in a fiduciary capacity for someone else and are required to use IFRS. (15)

Purchase Discount A cash discount received for prompt payment of a purchase on account. (297)

Purchase Returns and Allowances A reduction in the cost of inventory purchases associated with unsatisfactory goods. (296)

Q

Qualified Audit Opinion Indicates that either the financial statements do not follow GAAP or the auditors were not able to complete the tests needed to determine whether the financial statements follow GAAP. (204)

Quick Ratio The ratio of liquid assets to current liabilities. Liquid assets include cash and cash equiva-

lents, short-term investments, and accounts receivable (net of doubtful accounts). (430)

R

Ratio (Percentage) Analysis An analytical tool that measures the proportional relationship between two financial statement amounts.

Raw Materials Inventory Items acquired for the purpose of processing into finished goods.

Receivables Turnover The process of selling and collecting on an account. The receivables turnover ratio determines the average number of times this process occurs during the period. (34)

Record Date The date on which the corporation prepares the list of current shareholders as shown on its records; dividends can be paid only to the shareholders who own shares on that date. (468)

Relevant Information Information that can influence a decision. It is timely and has predictive and/or feedback value.

Reliable Information Information that is accurate, unbiased, and verifiable.

Research and Development Expenses Expenditures that may someday lead to patents, copyrights, or other intangible assets; the uncertainty about their future benefits requires that they be expensed. (383)

Residual (*or* Salvage) Value The estimated amount to be recovered at the end of the company's estimated useful life of an asset. (375)

Retained Earnings Cumulative earnings of a company that are not distributed to the owners; profits from the current year and all prior years that are reinvested ("retained") in the business.

Revenue Principle The requirement under accrual basis accounting to record revenues when they are earned, not necessarily when cash is received for them. (94)

Revenue Recognition Policy An accounting policy that describes when a company reports revenue from providing services or goods to customers.

Revenues Amounts earned by selling goods or services to customers. (91)

S

Sales Discount A sales price reduction given to customers for prompt payment of their account balance. (253)

Sales Returns and Allowances Refunds and price reductions given to customers after goods have been sold and found unsatisfactory. (252)

Salvage Value See *Residual Value*.

Sarbanes-Oxley Act (SOX) Created by the U.S. Congress after the fall of Enron due to accounting fraud. Includes regulations on many topics, including internal control systems and certification of executives. (18)

Securities and Exchange Commission (SEC) The U.S. government agency that determines the financial statements that public companies must provide to shareholders and the rules that they must use in producing those statements.

Segregation of Duties An internal control designed into the accounting system to prevent an employee from making a mistake or committing a dishonest act as part of one assigned duty, and then also covering it up through another assigned duty. (238)

Separate Entity Assumption The financial reports of a business are assumed to include the results of only that business's activities. (6)

Service Company Sells services rather than physical goods. (236)

Shareholders' Equity (or Owners' Equity or Stockholders' Equity) The amount invested and reinvested in a company by its shareholders. (42)

Single-Step Income Statement Reports net income by subtracting a single group of expenses from a single group of revenues. (201)

Sole Proprietorship A business organization owned by one person who is liable for debts that the business cannot pay.

Solvency The ability to survive long enough to repay lenders when debt matures. (558)

Specific Identification The inventory costing method that identifies the cost of the specific item that was sold. (289)

Stated Interest Rate The rate stated on the face of the bond, which is used to compute interest payments. (422)

Statement of Cash Flows Reports the operating, investing, and financing activities that caused increases and decreases in cash during the period. (11)

Statement of Retained Earnings Reports the way that net income and the distribution of dividends affected the financial position of the company during the period. (9)

Stock Dividend Additional shares of a corporation distributed to shareholders in the form of a dividend. (469)

Stock Split An increase in the total number of authorized shares by a specified ratio; does not affect retained earnings. (470)

Straight-Line Amortization Method 1) For tangible and intangible assets, the systematic and rational allocation of the cost of the asset in equal periodic amounts over its useful life. (376) (2) For bonds payable, evenly allocates the amount of bond premium or discount over each period of a bond's life to adjust interest expense for differences between its stated interest rate and market interest rate. (431)

Subsidiary Company A business that is controlled by another company (the parent). (Appendix E)

T

T-Account A simplified version of a ledger account used for summarizing the effects of journal entries. (53)

Tangible Assets Assets that have physical substance.

Temporary Accounts Track financial results for a limited period of time by having their balances zeroed out at the end of each accounting year. (156)

Tests of Liquidity Ratios that measure a company's ability to meet its currently maturing obligations.

Tests of Profitability Ratios that compare income with one or more primary activities.

Tests of Solvency Ratios that measure a company's ability to meet its long-term obligations.

Ticker Symbol The one- to four-letter abbreviation used to identify a company on a public securities exchange.

Time Period Assumption The long life of a company is divided into shorter periods, such as months, quarters, and years. (92)

Time-Series Analysis Compares a company's results for one period to its own results over a series of time periods. (209)

Times Interest Earned Ratio Divides net income before interest and taxes by interest expense to determine the extent to which earnings before taxes and financing costs are sufficient to cover interest incurred on debt. (431)

Time Value of Money The idea that money received today is worth more than the same amount received in the future because money received today can be invested to earn interest over time. (Appendix D)

Trademark A special name, image, or slogan identified with a product or company. (382)

Transaction An event or activity that has a direct and measurable financial effect on the assets, liabilities, or shareholders' equity of a business. (44)

Transaction Analysis The process of studying a transaction to determine its economic effect on the business in terms of the accounting equation.

Treasury Shares Issued shares that have been reacquired by the company. (462)

Trial Balance An internal report that lists all accounts and their balances to check on the equality of total recorded debits and total recorded credits. (104)

U

Unearned Revenue A liability representing a company's obligation to provide goods or services to customers in the future. (95)

Unit of Measure Assumption Results of business activities should be reported in an appropriate monetary unit, which in Canada is the Canadian dollar. (8)

Units-of-Production Amortization Method Allocates the cost of an asset over its useful life based on the relationship of its periodic output to its total estimated output. (376)

Unqualified Audit Opinion Indicates that the financial statements are presented in accordance with GAAP. (204)

Useful Life The expected service life of an asset to the present owner. (375)

V

Vertical (common-size) analyses Expressing each financial statement amount as a percentage of another amount on the same financial statement. (557)

Voucher System A process for approving and documenting all purchases and payments on account. (243)

W

Weighted Average Cost An inventory costing assumption that uses the weighted average unit cost of the goods available for sale for both cost of goods sold and ending inventory. (290)

Work in Process Inventory Goods in the process of being manufactured.

Write-Off The act of removing an uncollectable account and its corresponding allowance from the accounting records. (332)

Y

Yield See *Market Interest Rate*. (425)

Chapter 1

p. 1 © Funkyfood London - Paul Williams / Alamy
p. 2 (both) © The McGraw-Hill Companies, Inc./Brian Moeskau, photographer

Chapter 2

p. 41 Dick Luria/Photodisc/Getty Images
p. 43 Money bundle: © McGraw-Hill Ryerson; Pizza oven: © Courtesy of Toastmaster; Cheque: © David A. letz/ Editorial Image, LLC; Pizza pan: © Jamie / Duplass/Almay; Invoice © Studio 101/Almay
p. 46 Money bundle: © McGraw-Hill Ryerson; Restaurant booths: © Creatrixcordis/iStock
p. 49 Pizza pan: © Studio 101/Almay; Shoe sole presses: © Corbis Premium RF/Alamy
p. 60 Courtesy of Yum! Brands, Inc.

Chapter 3

p. 89 © Ted Pink /Almay
p. 93 AP Photo/Douglas C. Pzac

Chapter 4

p. 138 © Yellow Dog Productions/Taxi/ Getty
p. 142 © Bernd Euler/VISUM/The Image Works

Chapter 5

p. 194 Reprinted by permission of Activision, www.activision.com
p. 205 ©Thomas Lohnes / AFP / Getty

Chapter 6

p. 235 (photo) © bgwalker/iStockPhoto; (logo) Walmart logo courtesy of Walmart Stores, Inc.
p. 238 Money image: © Royalty-Free/ Corbis; Bank cheque: © Jill Battaglia/ iStock Photo
p. 241 Cash register: © C Squared Studios/Getty Images; Vault: © PhotoDisc/Getty Images
p. 252 Walmart photo: © Justin Sullivan/Getty.

Chapter 7

p. 285 © Tim Boyle/Getty
p. 287 ae.com

Chapter 8

p. 328 © Najlah Feanny/Corbis

Chapter 9

p. 367 Photo courtesy of Paramount Canada's Wonderland
p. 370 (left and centre): Courtesy of Cedar Point; (right): © Jupiterimages/ Thinkstock/ Getty
p. 373 Ingram Publishing

Chapter 10

p. 412 Dick Hemingway

Chapter 11

p. 459 (photo): Dick Hemingway; Courtesy of Sun-Rype Ltd.

Chapter 12

p. 502 Courtesy of Under Armour, Inc.

Chapter 13

p. 553 Indu Arora

Appendix A Reprinted by permission of Rona Inc.

Appendix B Reprinted by permission of The Home Depot

Appendix C Reprinted by permission of Kingfisher plc

T

T2, 417
T-accounts, 53-56, 99-107
  in account balances, 53
  in adjustments, 144, 145, 146, 147, 148, 149, 150, 151, 152, 153
Tangible assets, 368, 369-382
  acquisition of, 369-373
  ASPE *vs.* IFRS, 384
  asset impairment losses, 380
  defined, 368
  disposal of, 381-382, 386-387
  use of, 373-380
Tax
  accrued income tax, 417
  amortization, 379
  income tax expense, 149-150, 293, 524
  income tax payable, 150
  inventory costing methods, 293
  payroll taxes, 416-417
  sales tax payable, 420-421
Temporary accounts, 156-159
Time lags, 246, 247-248
Time period assumption, 92, 93
Time-series analysis, 209
Times interest earned ratio, 431, 565
Time value of money, D.1
Trademark, 383, 384
Transaction analysis, 44-51
  accrual basis accounting, 99-104
  ASPE vs. IFRS balance sheet, 63
  bank loan, 47
  business activities, 45-49
  contributed capital, 46
  debit/credit framework, 51-58
  demonstration case, 63-66
  external exchange, 44
  internal exchange, 44
  journal entries, 52-53
  measurable exchanges, 61
  notes payable, 47
  recording and summarizing transactions, 50-51
Transportation cost, 296
Trial balance
  adjusted, 152-153
  post-closing, 158-159
  unadjusted, 104-106

U

Unadjusted trial balance, 104-106
Uncollectable notes, 340
Unearned revenue, 95, 99, 107, 147, 421-422
Unit of measure assumption, 8
Units-of-production amortization method, 376
Unlimited life, 384
Unqualified audit opinion, 204, 205
"Useful" financial information, 16
Useful life, 375, 387

V

Vertical (common-size) analysis
  computations, 557
  interpretation, 560-561
Voting rights, 461
Voucher system, 243

W

Weighted average method, 290, 291-292, 303
Work in process inventory, 286
Write-downs, 294-295, 300
Write-off, 332

Y

Year-end closing, 156
Year-to-year change, 555

Ratios Used For Financial Analyses

Ratio	Basic Computation	Chapter
Tests of Profitability		
a. Asset turnover	$$\frac{\text{Net sales revenue}}{\text{Average total assets}}$$	5
b. Fixed asset turnover	$$\frac{\text{Net sales revenue}}{\text{Average net fixed assets}}$$	9
c. Net profit margin	$$\frac{\text{Net income}}{\text{Net sales revenue}}$$	5
d. Gross profit percentage	$$\frac{\text{Net sales revenue} - \text{Cost of goods sold}}{\text{Net sales revenue}} \times 100$$	6
e. Return on equity	$$\frac{\text{Net income}}{\text{Average shareholders' equity}}$$	11
f. Earnings per share	$$\frac{\text{Net income}}{\text{Average number of common shares outstanding}}$$	11
g. Quality of income	$$\frac{\text{Net cash flows from operating activities}}{\text{Net income}}$$	12
h. Price/earnings (P/E) ratio	$$\frac{\text{Current share price (per share)}}{\text{Earnings per share (annual)}}$$	11
Tests of Liquidity		
i. Receivables turnover (and days to collect)	$$\frac{\text{Net credit sales revenue}}{\text{Average net receivables}}$$	8
j. Inventory turnover (and days to sell)	$$\frac{\text{Cost of goods sold}}{\text{Average inventory}}$$	7
k. Current ratio	$$\frac{\text{Current assets}}{\text{Current liabilities}}$$	2
l. Quick ratio	$$\frac{\text{Cash} + \text{Short-term investments} + \text{Accounts receivable}}{\text{Current liabilities}}$$	10
Tests of Solvency		
m. Debt-to-assets	$$\frac{\text{Total liabilities}}{\text{Total assets}}$$	5
n. Times interest earned	$$\frac{\text{Net income} + \text{Interest expense} + \text{Income tax expense}}{\text{Interest expense}}$$	10
o. Capital acquisitions	$$\frac{\text{Net cash flows from operating activities}}{\text{Cash paid for property, plant, and equipment}}$$	12

Conceptual Framework for Financial Accounting and Reporting Using ASPE

PRIMARY OBJECTIVE OF EXTERNAL FINANCIAL REPORTING

To provide useful financial information to external users (particularly investors and creditors) for decision making (assessing future cash flows) [Ch. 5]

ELEMENTS OF FINANCIAL STATEMENTS

Asset—economic resource with probable future benefits [Ch. 2]

Liability—probable future sacrifices of economic resources [Ch. 2]

Shareholders' Equity—financing provided by owners and operations (residual interest to owners) [Ch. 2]

Revenue—increase in assets or settlement of liabilities from ongoing operations [Ch. 3]

Expense—decrease in assets or increase in liabilities from ongoing operations [Ch. 3]

Gain—increase in assets or settlement of liabilities from peripheral activities [Ch. 3]

Loss—decrease in assets or increase in liabilities from peripheral activities [Ch. 3]

QUALITATIVE CHARACTERISTICS OF USEFUL FINANCIAL INFORMATION

To be useful, information should possess:

Relevance—be capable of making a difference in decisions [Ch. 5]
  -feedback value (assess prior expectations)
  -predictive value (extrapolate into the future)
  -timeliness (available to help with decisions)

Reliability—can be relied on [Ch. 5]
  -representational faithfulness (represents reality)
  -verifiability (can be verified independently)
  -neutrality (unbiased)

Comparability and consistency—information should be comparable across companies and consistent over time [Ch. 5]

Understandability—information should be understandable by readers if they have a reasonable grasp of business, economics, and accounting and they study the information with diligence [Ch. 13]

ASSUMPTIONS

Separate entity—activities of the business are separate from activities of the owners [Ch. 1]

Unit of measure—accounting measurements are in the national monetary unit [Ch. 2]

Time period—the long life of a company can be reported over a series of shorter time periods [Ch. 3]

Going concern (continuity)—entity will not go out of business in the near future [Ch. 13]

PRINCIPLES

Historical cost—cash equivalent price on the transaction date is used initially to measure elements [Ch. 2]

Revenue recognition—record revenue when earned, measurable, and realizable [Ch. 3]

Matching—record expenses in the same period as the revenues they help to generate [Ch. 3]

Full disclosure—provide all information sufficiently important to influence a decision [Ch. 13]

CONSTRAINTS

Conservatism—exercise care not to overstate assets and revenues or understate liabilities and expenses [Ch. 2]

Materiality—relatively small amounts not likely to influence decisions are to be recorded in the most cost-beneficial way [Ch. 5]

Cost–benefit—benefits to users should outweigh costs of providing information [Ch. 13]